COMPENDIUM 2002

OF SELECTED PUBLICATIONS

THE AMERICAN COLLEGE OF
OBSTETRICIANS AND GYNECOLOGISTS
WOMEN'S HEALTH CARE PHYSICIANS

The *2002 Compendium of Selected Publications* contains current clinical practice documents published by the American College of Obstetricians and Gynecologists (ACOG) as of December 31, 2001. The information in these documents should not be viewed as establishing standards or dictating rigid rules. The guidelines are general and intended to be adapted to many different situations, taking into account the needs and resources particular to the locality, the institution, or the type of practice. Variations and innovations that improve the quality of patient care are to be encouraged rather than restricted. The purpose of these guidelines will be well served if they provide a firm basis on which local norms may be built.

The American College of Obstetricians and Gynecologists
409 12th Street, SW
PO Box 96920
Washington, DC 20090-6920

ISBN: 0-915473-78-X   12345/65432

Publications may be ordered through the ACOG Distribution Center by calling toll free 800-762-2264. To receive order forms via facsimile, call (732) 885-6364 and follow the audio instructions. Publications also may be ordered from the ACOG web site at www.acog.org.

Contents

Foreword

The *2002 Compendium of Selected Publications* is a compilation of selected ACOG clinical practice guidelines in effect as of December 31, 2001. In this single, fully indexed volume, it is possible to refer to virtually any topic in obstetrics and gynecology that ACOG has addressed. This resource is invaluable for reference or referral to key areas in the specialty throughout the year.

The Compendium includes documents from ACOG series. These series are developed by committees of experts and reviewed by leaders in the specialty and the College. Each document is reviewed periodically and either reaffirmed, replaced, or withdrawn to ensure its continued appropriateness to practice. The contribution of the many groups and individuals who participated in the process is gratefully acknowledged.

Each section of the Compendium is devoted to a particular series, and includes those documents considered current at the time of publication:

■ Committee Opinions: Brief focused documents that address clinical issues of an urgent or emergent nature or nonclinical topics such as policy, economics, and social issues that relate to obstetrics and gynecology. They are consensus statements that may or may not be based on scientific evidence.

■ Educational Bulletins: Treatises on specific topics designed to update practicing obstetrician–gynecologists with concise, clinically oriented reviews. Information in these bulletins is supported by satisfactory documentation.

■ Practice Bulletins: Evidence-based guidelines developed to indicate a preferred method of diagnosis and management of a condition. The evidence is graded, and peer-reviewed research determines the recommendations in the document.

■ Practice Patterns: Precursor to the Practice Bulletin series, this series launched ACOG's effort to develop evidence-based practice guidelines.

■ Policy Statements: Position papers on key issues approved by the Executive Board.

Preceding each section is a complete alphabetical listing of current documents in the series. Those published within the year are indicated with an asterisk. Also provided are lists of titles of all series, grouped by committee or category in order of publication. These lists also include withdrawn titles.

As the practice of medicine evolves, so too do ACOG documents. As a part of the continuing process of review and revision, many documents initially published as a separate installment of a series evolve to become a part of a broader effort to educate and inform our Fellows. At one end of the spectrum may be a Committee Opinion that focuses on a highly specialized area of practice, whereas the other end of the spectrum may be represented by one of ACOG's comprehensive volumes on practice guidelines such as *Guidelines for Perinatal Care* or *Guidelines for Women's Health Care*. These books carry equal weight as practice guidelines and should be considered adjuncts to the documents in the series. To help make the information more manageable, many individual documents will be consolidated in new separate volumes on *Ethics in Obstetrics and Gynecology, Genetics, Adolescent Health,* and *Special Issues in Women's Health*. These books, the contents of which is listed on the following page, will be published in 2002 and distributed to all Fellows.

As new documents are released throughout the year, which may replace existing documents in the Compendium, they will be included in the ACOG publications section of ACOG's official journal *Obstetrics & Gynecology*. Single copies can be obtained from the Resource Center (202-863-2518) and the series are available for sale as complete sets or subscriptions (call 800-762-2264 to order). These documents also are available to members on our web site: www.acog.org. To verify the status of documents, contact the Resource Center or check our web site.

We are making every effort to provide health professionals with current, quality information on the practice of obstetrics and gynecology. The *2002 Compendium of Selected Publications* represents still another way to disseminate material designed to promote women's health.

—Ralph W. Hale, MD, Executive Vice President

The Scope of Practice of Obstetrics and Gynecology

ACOG OPERATIONAL MISSION STATEMENT

The American College of Obstetricians and Gynecologists (ACOG) is a membership organization of obstetrician–gynecologists dedicated to the advancement of women's health through education, advocacy, practice and research.

VISION STATEMENT

Obstetrics and gynecology is a discipline dedicated to the broad, integrated medical and surgical care of women's health throughout their lifespan. The combined discipline of obstetrics and gynecology requires extensive study and understanding of reproductive physiology, including the physiologic, social, cultural, environmental, and genetic factors that influence disease in women. This study and understanding of the reproductive physiology of women gives obstetricians and gynecologists a unique perspective in addressing gender-specific health care issues.

Primary and preventive counseling and education are essential and integral parts of the practice of an obstetrician–gynecologist as they advance the individual and community-based health of women of all ages.

Obstetricians and gynecologists may choose a wide or more focused scope of practice from primary ambulatory health to concentration in a particular area of specialization.

Approved by the Executive Board
May 25, 2000

Code *of* Professional Ethics

of the American College of Obstetricians and Gynecologists

Obstetrician–gynecologists, as members of the medical profession, have ethical responsibilities not only to patients, but also to society, to other health professionals, and to themselves. The following ethical foundations for professional activities in the field of obstetrics and gynecology are the supporting structures for the Code of Conduct. The Code implements many of these foundations in the form of rules of ethical conduct. Certain documents of the American College of Obstetricians and Gynecologists, including Committee Opinions and *Ethics in Obstetrics and Gynecology,* also provide additional ethical rules. Selections relevant to specific points are set forth in the Code of Conduct, and those particular documents are incorporated into the Code by reference. Noncompliance with the Code, including referenced documents, may affect an individual's initial or continuing Fellowship in the American College of Obstetricians and Gynecologists. These documents may be revised or replaced periodically, and Fellows should be knowledgeable about current information.

Ethical Foundations

I.   The patient–physician relationship: The welfare of the patient *(beneficence)* is central to all considerations in the patient–physician relationship. Included in this relationship is the obligation of physicians to respect the rights of patients, colleagues, and other health professionals. The respect for the right of individual patients to make their own choices about their health care *(autonomy)* is fundamental. The principle of justice requires strict avoidance of discrimination on the basis of race, color, religion, national origin, or any other basis that would constitute illegal discrimination *(justice).*

II.   Physician conduct and practice: The obstetrician–gynecologist should deal honestly with patients and colleagues *(veracity).* This includes not misrepresenting himself or herself through any form of communication in an untruthful, misleading, or deceptive manner. Furthermore, maintenance of medical competence through study, application, and enhancement of medical knowledge and skills is an obligation of practicing physicians. Any behavior that diminishes a physician's capability to practice, such as substance abuse, must be immediately addressed and rehabilitative services instituted. The physician should modify his or her practice until the diminished capacity has been restored to an acceptable standard to avoid harm to patients *(nonmaleficence)*. All physicians are obligated to respond to evidence of questionable conduct or unethical behavior by other physicians through appropriate procedures established by the relevant organization.

III. Avoiding conflicts of interest: Potential conflicts of interest are inherent in the practice of medicine. Physicians are expected to recognize such situations and deal with them through public disclosure. Conflicts of interest should be resolved in accordance with the best interest of the patient, respecting a woman's autonomy to make health care decisions. The physician should be an advocate for the patient through public disclosure of conflicts of interest raised by health payor policies (managed care or others) or hospital policies.

IV. Professional relations: The obstetrician–gynecologist should respect and cooperate with other physicians, nurses, and other health care professionals.

V.   Societal responsibilities: The obstetrician–gynecologist has a continuing responsibility to society as a whole and should support and participate in activities that enhance the community. As a member of society, the obstetrician–gynecologist must respect the laws of that society. As professionals and members of medical societies, physicians are required to uphold the dignity and honor of the profession.

Code of Conduct

I.   Patient–Physician Relationship

1. The patient–physician relationship is the central focus of all ethical concerns, and the welfare of the patient should form the basis of all medical judgments.

2. The obstetrician–gynecologist should serve as the patient's advocate and exercise all reasonable means to ensure that the most appropriate care is provided to the patient.

3. The patient–physician relationship has an ethical basis and is built on confidentiality, trust, and honesty. If no patient–physician relationship exists, a physician may refuse to provide care, except in emergencies. Both the patient and the obstetrician–gynecologist are free to establish or discontinue the patient–physician relationship. The obstetrician–gynecologist must adhere to all applicable legal or contractual constraints in dissolving the patient–physician relationship.

4. Sexual misconduct on the part of the obstetrician–gynecologist is an abuse of professional power and a violation of patient trust. Sexual contact or a romantic relationship between a physician and a current patient is always unethical (1).

5. The obstetrician–gynecologist has an obligation to obtain the informed consent of each patient (2). In obtaining informed consent for any course of medical or sur-

gical treatment, the obstetrician–gynecologist should present to the patient, or to the person legally responsible for the patient, in understandable terms, pertinent medical facts and recommendations consistent with good medical practice. Such information should include alternate modes of treatment and the objectives, risks, benefits, possible complications, and anticipated results of such treatment.

6. It is unethical to prescribe, provide, or seek compensation for therapies that are of no benefit to the patient.

7. The obstetrician–gynecologist should respect the rights of patients, colleagues, and others and safeguard patient information and confidences within the limits of the law. If during the process of providing information for consent it is known that results of a particular test or other information must be given to governmental authorities or other third parties, that should be explained to the patient (3).

8. The obstetrician–gynecologist should not discriminate against patients based on race, color, national origin, religion, or on any other basis that would constitute illegal discrimination.

II. Physician Conduct and Practice

1. The obstetrician–gynecologist should recognize the boundaries of his or her particular competencies and expertise, and provide only those services and use only those techniques for which he or she is qualified by education, training, or experience.

2. The obstetrician–gynecologist should participate in continuing medical education activities to maintain current scientific and professional knowledge relevant to the medical services he or she renders. The obstetrician–gynecologist should provide medical care involving new therapies or techniques only after undertaking appropriate training and study.

3. In emerging areas of medical treatment where recognized medical guidelines do not exist, the obstetrician–gynecologist should exercise careful judgment and take appropriate precautions to protect patient welfare.

4. The obstetrician–gynecologist should not publicize or represent himself or herself in any untruthful, misleading, or deceptive manner to patients, colleagues, other health care professionals, or the public.

5. The obstetrician–gynecologist who has reason to believe that he or she is infected with the human immunodeficiency virus or other serious infectious agents that might be communicated to patients should voluntarily be tested for the protection of his or her patients. In making decisions about patient-care activities, a physician infected with such an agent should adhere to the fundamental professional obligation to avoid harm to patients (4).

6. The obstetrician–gynecologist should not practice medicine while impaired by alcohol, drugs, or physical or mental disability. The obstetrician–gynecologist who experiences substance abuse problems or who is physically or emotionally impaired should seek appropriate assistance to address these problems and limit his or her practice until the impairment no longer affects the quality of patient care.

III. Conflicts of Interest

1. Potential conflicts of interest are inherent in the practice of medicine. Conflicts of interest should be resolved in accordance with the best interest of the patient, respecting a woman's autonomy to make health care decisions. If there is concern about a possibly significant conflict of interest, the physician should disclose his or her concerns to the patient. If a conflict of interest cannot be resolved, the obstetrician–gynecologist should take steps to withdraw from the care of the patient. If conflicts of interest are unresolved, the physician should seek consultation with colleagues or an institutional ethics committee.

2. Commercial promotions of medical products and services may generate bias unrelated to product merit, creating, or appearing to create, inappropriate undue influence. The obstetrician–gynecologist should be aware of this potential conflict of interest and offer medical advice that is as accurate, balanced, complete, and devoid of bias as possible (5, 6).

3. The obstetrician–gynecologist should prescribe drugs, devices, and other treatments based solely upon medical considerations and patient needs, regardless of any direct or indirect interests in or benefit from a pharmaceutical firm or other supplier.

4. When the obstetrician–gynecologist receives anything of substantial value, including royalties, from companies in the health care industry, such as a manufacturer of pharmaceuticals and medical devices, this fact should be disclosed to patients and colleagues when material.

5. Financial and administrative constraints imposed by managed care may create disincentives to treatment otherwise recommended by the obstetrician–gynecologist as in the patient's best interest. Any pertinent constraints should be disclosed to the patient (7).

IV. Professional Relations

1. The obstetrician–gynecologist's relationships with other physicians, nurses, and health care professionals should reflect fairness, honesty, and integrity, sharing a mutual respect and concern for the patient.

2. The obstetrician–gynecologist should consult, refer, or cooperate with other physicians, health care professionals, and institutions to the extent necessary to serve the best interests of their patients.

3. The obstetrician–gynecologist should respect all laws, uphold the dignity and honor of the profession, and accept the profession's self-imposed discipline. The professional competence and conduct of obstetrician–gynecologists are best examined by professional associations, hospital peer-review committees, and state medical and/ or licensing boards. These groups deserve the full participation and cooperation of the obstetrician–gynecologist.

4. The obstetrician–gynecologist should strive to address through the appropriate procedures the status of those physicians who demonstrate questionable competence, impairment, or unethical or illegal behavior. In addition, the obstetrician–gynecologist should cooperate with appropriate authorities to prevent the continuation of such behavior.

V. Societal Responsibilities

1. The obstetrician–gynecologist should support and participate in those health care programs, practices, and activities that contribute positively, in a meaningful and cost-effective way, to the welfare of individual patients, the health care system, or the public good.

2. Obstetrician–gynecologists who provide expert medical testimony in courts of law recognize their duty to testify truthfully. The obstetrician–gynecologist should not testify concerning matters about which he or she is not knowledgeable (8). The obstetrician–gynecologist should be prepared to have testimony, given in any judicial proceeding, subjected to peer review by an institution or professional organization to which he or she belongs. It is unethical for a physician to accept compensation that is contingent on the outcome of litigation.

References

1. American College of Obstetricians and Gynecologists. Sexual misconduct in the practice of obstetrics and gynecology: ethical considerations. In: Ethics in obstetrics and gynecology. Washington, DC: ACOG, 2002:89–91

2. American College of Obstetricians and Gynecologists. Ethical dimensions of informed consent. In: Ethics in obstetrics and gynecology. Washington, DC: ACOG, 2002:19–27

3. American College of Obstetricians and Gynecologists. Ethical guidance for patient testing. In: Ethics in obstetrics and gynecology. Washington, DC: ACOG, 2002:32–34

4. American College of Obstetricians and Gynecologists. Human immunodeficiency virus: ethical guidelines for obstetricians and gynecologists. In: Ethics in obstetrics and gynecology. Washington, DC: ACOG, 2002:43–47

5. American College of Obstetricians and Gynecologists. Guidelines for relationships with industry. In: Ethics in obstetrics and gynecology. Washington, DC: ACOG, 2002:40–42

6. American College of Obstetricians and Gynecologists. Commercial enterprises in medical practice: selling and promoting products. In: Ethics in obstetrics and gynecology. Washington, DC: ACOG, 2002:7–9

7. American College of Obstetricians and Gynecologists. Physician responsibility under managed care: patient advocacy in a changing health care environment. In: Ethics in obstetrics and gynecology. Washington, DC: ACOG, 2002:64–68

8. American College of Obstetricians and Gynecologists. Ethical issues related to expert testimony by obstetricians and gynecologists. In: Ethics in obstetrics and gynecology. Washington, DC: ACOG, 2002:38–39

2002 COMPENDIUM
OF SELECTED PUBLICATIONS

Committee Opinions

*Published in 2001

Committee Opinions

*Published in 2001

ACOG

Committee on
Obstetric Practice

Committee Opinion

Number 264, December 2001

Air Travel During Pregnancy

ABSTRACT: *In the absence of obstetric or medical complications, pregnant women can observe the same general precautions for air travel as the general population and can fly safely up to 36 weeks of gestation. In-craft environmental conditions such as low cabin humidity and changes in cabin pressure, coupled with the physiologic changes of pregnancy, do result in maternal adaptations, which could have transient effects on the fetus. Pregnant air travelers with medical problems that may be exacerbated by a hypoxic environment, but who must travel by air, should be prescribed supplemental oxygen during air travel. Pregnant women at significant risk for premature labor or with placental abnormalities should avoid air travel. Because air turbulence cannot be predicted and the risk for trauma is significant, pregnant women should be instructed to continuously use their seat belts while seated, as should all air travelers. Pregnant air travelers may take precautions to ease in-flight discomfort, and although no hard evidence exists, preventive measures can be employed to minimize risks.*

Air travel during pregnancy is safe for most women and most U.S. airlines allow pregnant women to fly up to 36 weeks of gestation. For specific airline requirements, the patient should check with the specific carrier because documentation of gestational age may be required. For international airlines the cutoff is 35 weeks of gestation.

In the absence of complications, pregnant women can observe the same general precautions while traveling as the general population. Travel is not recommended at any time during pregnancy for women who have either medical or obstetric complications for which likely emergencies cannot be predicted. Such complications may include increased risks for, or evidence of, preterm delivery, pregnancy induced hypertension, poorly controlled type 1 or type 2 diabetes, or sickle cell disease or trait, which may be exacerbated by high altitude. Pregnant women should be informed that the most common obstetric emergencies occur in the first and third trimesters.

Some unconfirmed reports indicate that flight attendants experience twice the incidence (relative risk=1.9) of first trimester spontaneous abortions as other women, but not other employed women. There is no evidence of an increased risk of spontaneous abortion among other air travelers (1). Most airlines restrict the working air travel of flight attendants after 20 weeks of gestation. Airlines also restrict commercial airline pilots from flying once pregnancy is diagnosed.

Requests for authorization to make photocopies should be directed to:

Copyright Clearance Center
222 Rosewood Drive
Danvers, MA 01923
(978) 750-8400

ISSN 1074-861X

The American College of Obstetricians and Gynecologists
409 12th Street, SW
PO Box 96920
Washington, DC 20090-6920

12345/54321

Air travel during pregnancy. ACOG Committee Opinion No. 264. American College of Obstetricians and Gynecologists. Obstet Gynecol 2001;98:1187–1188

3

In-craft environmental conditions such as changes in cabin pressure and low humidity, coupled with the physiologic changes of pregnancy, do result in maternal adaptations, which could have transient effects on the fetus. A significant environmental change is the reduction of cabin humidity to less than 25%, which causes hemoconcentration and increases the risk for venous thrombosis and potentially the risk for premature labor.

On long commercial flights traveling at 39,000–41,000 feet, cabin pressure is maintained at the equivalent of an altitude pressure of 8,000 feet. While at 32,000 feet the cabin pressure is set at the equivalent of 6,000 feet. The conditions at a cabin pressure of 8000 feet will create a more hypoxic environment than those at 6000 feet. Acute ascent to 6,000 feet does not elicit ominous fetal responses, but it does produce transient maternal cardiopulmonary adaptations. Among these adaptations are increased heart rate, increased blood pressure, and a significant decrease in aerobic capacity (2, 3). In pregnancy there is limited aerobic capacity. At 6,000 feet the oxygen consumption in pregnant women is 13% (L/min) lower than at sea level (3), in comparison with non-pregnant women for whom the decrease is only 3% lower (4). These changes are associated with a reduction in partial oxygen pressure, which should not affect normal pregnant women, but it could affect those with a compromised cardiovascular system. Therefore, pregnant air travelers with medical problems that may be exacerbated by a hypoxic environment, but who must travel by air, should be prescribed supplemental oxygen during air travel. Pregnant women at significant risk for premature labor or with placental abnormalities should avoid air travel.

Several precautions may ease discomfort for pregnant air travelers. For example, gas-producing foods or drinks should be avoided before scheduled flights since entrapped gases expand at altitude (5). Preventive antiemetic medication should be considered for women with increased nausea.

The risks associated with long hours of air travel immobilization and low cabin humidity, such as lower extremity edema and venous thrombotic events, have recently been the focus of attention for all air travelers. There are no published reports of such events in pregnancy; however, concerns regarding the relationship of venous stasis to in-flight thromboembolism have been raised. Despite the lack of tangible evidence, certain preventive measures can be employed to minimize these risks, ie, support stockings and periodic movement of the lower extremities. Because air turbulence cannot be predicted and the risk for trauma is significant, pregnant women should be instructed to continuously use their seatbelts while seated, as should all air travelers. The seatbelt should be belted low on the hipbones, between the protuberant abdomen and pelvis.

Available information suggests that noise vibration and cosmic radiation present a negligible risk for the pregnant air traveler (6, 7). In the absence of a reasonable expectation for obstetric or medical complications, air travel is safe for pregnant women up to 36 weeks of gestation.

References

1. Daniell WE, Vaughan TL, Millies BA. Pregnancy outcomes among female flight attendants. Aviat Space Environ Med;1990;61:840–884
2. Huch R, Baumann H, Fallenstein F, Schneider KT, Holdener F, Huch A. Physiologic changes in pregnant women and their fetuses during jet air travel. Am J Obstet Gynecol 1986;154:996–1000
3. Artal R, Fortunato V, Welton A, Constantino N, Khodiguian N, Villalobos L, et al. A comparison of cardiopulmonary adaptations to exercise in pregnancy at sea level and altitude. Am J Obstet Gynecol 1995;172:1170–1178; discussion 1178–1180
4. Brooks GA, Fahey TD, White TP, Baldwin KM. Exercise, atmospheric pressure, air pollution, and travel. In: Exercise physiology: human bioenergetics and its applications. 3rd ed. Mountain View, California: Mayfield Publishing Company, 2000:504–436
5. Bia FJ. Medical considerations for the pregnant traveler. Infect Dis Clin N Am 1992;6:371–388
6. Morrell S, Taylor R, Lyle D. A review of health effects of aircraft noise. Aust N Z J Public Health 1997;21:221–236
7. Friedberg W, Faulkner DN, Snyder L, Darden EB Jr, O'Brien K. Galactic cosmic radiation exposure and associated health risks for air carrier crewmembers. Aviat Space Environ Med 1989;60:1104–1108

ACOG

Committee on
Gynecologic Practice

Committee Opinion

Number 244, November 2000

Androgen Treatment of Decreased Libido

Sexual dysfunction is a complex disorder with multiple etiologies, of which psychosocial elements, chronic illness, and alcohol and other substance abuse have been implicated. Often, a specific cause cannot be defined. The prevalence of sexual dysfunction appears to increase with age. In the United States, the National Health and Social Life Survey of 1,749 women revealed that 43% experienced sexual dysfunction (1). Androgens have been proposed for some women as treatment of certain types of sexual dysfunction.

Loss of sexual drive or libido is one manifestation of sexual dysfunction. Libido appears to be influenced by both androgens and estrogens. Androgens do consistently increase libido at superphysiologic levels, but physiologic androgen replacement therapy has not been shown to consistently affect libido (2). Formulations currently available in the United States generally achieve superphysiologic serum levels at least two times the premenopausal range of values.

A relationship between libido and hormonal changes, particularly those associated with menopause, has been suspected for many years as a result of declining ovarian function. After menopause, total estrogen production decreases by approximately 80% and androgen production declines by about 50%. Of the latter, androstenedione, the primary ovarian androgen, and dehydroepiandrosterone sulfate, the principal adrenal androgen, demonstrate the greatest decline, decreasing 75% and 50%, respectively. Ovarian testosterone production is near normal during the first 5 years after menopause but declines thereafter. There is a proportionately greater reduction of circulating unbound testosterone, despite sex hormone-binding globulin decreases, which are the result of diminished estrogen production.

Available oral testosterone preparations include methyltestosterone with or without esterified estrogens, fluoxymesterone, and testosterone undecanoate. Testosterone can be administered intramuscularly as well as topically, with transdermal patches or gel. Reported side effects include hoarseness, acne, increased facial hair, clitoromegaly, hepatotoxicity, alopecia, and undesirable lipoprotein alterations. The doses in the transdermal patch are formulated specifically for male hormone replacement. Implantable testosterone pellets are available in other countries.

The American College of Obstetricians and Gynecologists
409 12th Street, SW
PO Box 96920
Washington, DC 20090-6920

12345/43210

Dehydroepiandrosterone (DHEA) also has been used for androgen replacement therapy. Benefits ascribed to DHEA include increased bone mineral density, estrogenic stimulation of vaginal cytology, and enhancement of the immune system. However, a prospective, randomized controlled trial of symptomatic, perimenopausal women who received 50 mg of DHEA supplementation for 3 months did not describe improvement in libido, mood, dysphoria, cognition, or well-being (3). Potential adverse effects of DHEA at higher doses include effects on lipoprotein levels, cortisol, glucose tolerance, and central obesity. Some DHEA products, such as those derived from the Mexican wild yam, may have virilizing effects and may be hepatotoxic. Doses should not exceed 50 mg, and even at this dose a 10% reduction in high-density lipoprotein cholesterol has been observed after 3 months of therapy (3). In addition, because the manufacture of DHEA and other supplements is not standardized, there can be uncertainty as to the identity of the active ingredient and the amount of its dose.

Diminished libido also has been treated with sildenafil citrate, and anecdotal experiences have been described. However, there have been no reported controlled trials or other studies documenting its efficacy.

Although androgen therapy has been prescribed for sexual dysfunction for many years, data regarding its safety and efficacy are incomplete and physiologic androgen replacement therapy has not been shown to consistently affect the libido. Measurement of free or total testosterone levels for diagnosis or monitoring is not clinically useful. Patients most likely to benefit from androgen therapy are young women who have undergone oophorectomy (4). Although it is possible that other women experiencing decreased libido may benefit from a trial of androgen therapy, the lack of definitive data should lead to a cautious approach. In general, lower doses of oral preparations are preferred. Appropriate monitoring for side effects, including lipoprotein alteration, should be undertaken.

References

1. Berman JR, Berman L, Goldstein I. Female sexual dysfunction: incidence, pathophysiology, evaluation, and treatment options. Urology 1999;54:385–391
2. Casson PR, Carson SA, Buster JE. Testosterone delivery systems for women: present status and future promise. Semin Reprod Endocrinol 1998;16:153–159
3. Barnhart KT, Freeman E, Grisso JA, Rader DJ, Sammel M, Kapoor S, et al. The effect of dehydroepiandrosterone supplementation to symptomatic perimenopausal women on serum endocrine profiles, lipid parameters, and health-related quality of life. J Clin Endocrinol Metab 1999;84:3896–3902
4. Sherwin BB, Gelfand MM. Differential symptom response to parenteral estrogen and/or androgen administration in the surgical menopause. Am J Obstet Gynecol 1985;151:153–160

ACOG

Committee on
Obstetric Practice

Committee Opinion

Number 210, October 1998   *(Replaces #147, December 1994)*

Antenatal Corticosteroid Therapy for Fetal Maturation

For the past two decades, approximately 10% of all births in the United States have been preterm. Preterm birth results in approximately three fourths of all neonatal deaths not associated with congenital malformations. Moreover, neonatal morbidity is high among surviving infants born preterm, and complications such as respiratory distress syndrome (RDS), intraventricular hemorrhage, and necrotizing enterocolitis are common.

Antenatal corticosteroid therapy has been used for more than two decades in an attempt to reduce the frequency of neonatal complications, especially RDS. The beneficial effect of corticosteroids on fetal lung maturation was reported first in 1972. The type and dosage of corticosteroids, the optimal timing of treatment, and the gestational ages at which steroids are beneficial varied in early reports.

Data now have accumulated that document the benefit of corticosteroid therapy for reducing the frequency not only of RDS, but also of intraventricular hemorrhage and neonatal mortality. With regard to the type of steroids, both dexamethasone and betamethasone appear to be appropriate. These agents are virtually identical in structure and biologic activity, have a long half-life (up to 72 hours), and cross the placenta in biologically active forms. Moreover, they have little or no mineralocorticoid activity.

With regard to safety, there is no convincing scientific evidence that antenatal corticosteroid therapy increases the risk of neonatal infection or adrenal suppression. Follow-up studies of children up to 12 years of age indicate there is no apparent risk of adverse neurodevelopmental outcome associated with antenatal corticosteroids. The maternal risk of infection when corticosteroids are given to women with preterm premature rupture of membranes seems small and is outweighed by the benefit.

In 1994, the National Institute of Child Health and Human Development and the Office of Medical Applications of Research of the National Institutes of Health (NIH) convened a consensus conference sponsored by the National Heart, Lung, and Blood Institute and the National Institute of Nursing on the effects of corticosteroids for fetal maturation. It is clear that antenatal corticosteroids decrease the incidence of RDS in infants born at 29–34 weeks of gestation. Although antenatal corticosteroids do not necessarily decrease the incidence of RDS in infants born at 24–28 weeks of gestation, they reduce its severity. More importantly, antenatal corticosteroids clearly reduce mortality and the incidence of intraventricular hemorrhage in infants born at 24–28 weeks of gestation.

The American College of Obstetricians and Gynecologists

409 12th Street, SW
PO Box 96920
Washington, DC 20090-6920

12345/21098

The NIH consensus panel made several recommendations for the use of antenatal corticosteroids (see box). The panel also identified several areas in which further research is needed. This includes the appropriate repeat doses and the short- and long-term benefits and risks of repeat administration of antenatal corticosteroids 7 days after the initial course.

The Committee on Obstetric Practice supports the conclusions of the NIH consensus conference. The decision to administer corticosteroids may be based either on clinical circumstances likely to result in spontaneous preterm delivery within 7 days or complications likely to lead to a decision to perform preterm delivery within 7 days. Because of the possible adverse fetal effects and possible effects on maternal immune status of repeated, weekly courses of steroids, it seems reasonable to adopt a rescue approach to therapy in the treatment of preterm labor rather than a routine readministration regimen. Following the initial course of corticosteroids, repeated doses should be given only on an as-needed basis (ie, if the woman is retreated for threatened preterm birth).

National Institutes of Health Consensus Panel Recommendations

- The benefits of antenatal administration of corticosteroids to fetuses at risk of preterm delivery vastly outweigh the risks. These benefits include not only a reduction in the risk of RDS but also a substantial decrease in mortality and intraventricular hemorrhage.

- All women between 24 and 34 weeks of pregnancy at risk for preterm delivery are candidates for antenatal corticosteroid therapy.

- Fetal race, gender, and availability of surfactant therapy should not influence the decision to use antenatal corticosteroid therapy.

- A patient eligible for therapy with tocolytic agents also should be eligible for treatment with antenatal corticosteroids when she requires repetitive intravenous tocolytics.

- Treatment should consist of either two doses of 12 mg of betamethasone, intramuscularly, given 24 hours apart or four doses of 6 mg of dexamethasone, intramuscularly, given 12 hours apart. Optimal benefits begin 24 hours after initiation of therapy and last 7 days.

- Because treatment for less than 24 hours still can result in significant reductions in neonatal mortality, antenatal corticosteroids should be given unless immediate delivery is anticipated.

- Antenatal corticosteroid use is recommended in women with preterm premature rupture of membranes at less than 30–32 weeks of gestation in the absence of clinical chorioamnionitis because of the high risk of intraventricular hemorrhage at these early gestational ages.

- In women with complicated pregnancies for whom delivery before 34 weeks of gestation is likely, antenatal corticosteroid use is recommended unless there is evidence that corticosteroids will have an adverse effect on the mother or delivery is imminent.

Adapted from Effect of antenatal steroids for fetal maturation on perinatal outcomes. NIH Consens Statement 1994 Feb 28–Mar 2; 12(2):1–24

Bibliography

Crowley P. Corticosteroids after preterm premature rupture of membranes. Obstet Gynecol Clin North Am 1992;19:317–326

Crowley P, Chalmers I, Keirse MJ. The effects of corticosteroid administration before preterm delivery: an overview of the evidence from controlled trials. Br J Obstet Gynaecol 1990; 97:11–25

Effects of antenatal dexamethasone administration in the infant; long-term follow-up. J Pediatr 1984;104:259–267

Effect of antenatal dexamethasone administration on the prevention of respiratory distress syndrome. Am J Obstet Gynecol 1981;141:276–287

Effect of antenatal steroids for fetal maturation on perinatal outcomes. NIH Consens Statement 1994 Feb 28–Mar 2;12(2): 1–24

Gamsu HR, Mullinger BM, Donnai P, Dash CH. Antenatal administration of betamethasone to prevent respiratory distress syndrome in premature infants: report of a UK multicentre trial. Br J Obstet Gynaecol 1989;96:401–410

Garite TJ, Freeman RK, Linzey EM, Braly PS, Dorchester WL. Prospective randomized study of corticosteroids in the management of premature rupture of the membranes and the premature gestation. Am J Obstet Gynecol 1981;141:508–515

Garite TJ, Rumney PJ, Briggs GG, Harding JA, Nageotte MP, Towers CV, et al. A randomized, placebo-controlled trial of betamethasone for the prevention of respiratory distress syndrome at 24 to 28 weeks' gestation. Am J Obstet Gynecol 1992;166:646–651

Liggins GC, Howie RN. A controlled trial of antepartum glucocorticoid treatment for prevention of the respiratory distress syndrome in premature infants. Pediatrics 1972;50:515–525

Ohlsson A. Treatments of preterm premature rupture of the membranes: a meta-analysis. Am J Obstet Gynecol 1989;160: 890–906

Schmand B, Neuvel J, Smolders-de Haas H, Hoeks J, Treffers PE, Koppe JG. Psychological development of children who were treated antenatally with corticosteroids to prevent respiratory distress syndrome. Pediatrics 1990;86:58–64

Teramo K, Hallman M, Raivio KO. Maternal glucocorticoid in unplanned premature labor. Controlled study of the effects of betamethasone phosphate on the phospholipids of the gastric aspirate and on the adrenal cortical function of the newborn infant. Pediatr Res 1980;14:326–329

ACOG

Committee on
Obstetric Practice

Committee Opinion

Number 260, October 2001

Circumcision

ABSTRACT: The American College of Obstetricians and Gynecologists supports the current position of the American Academy of Pediatrics that finds the existing evidence insufficient to recommend routine neonatal circumcision. Given this circumstance, parents should be given accurate and impartial information to help them make an informed decision. There is ample evidence that newborns circumcised without analgesia experience pain and stress. If circumcision is performed, analgesia should be provided.

Some studies have shown potential medical benefits to newborn male circumcision; however, these benefits are modest. The exact incidence of complications after circumcision is not known, but data indicate that the rate is low, and the most common complications are local infection and bleeding. The current position of the American Academy of Pediatrics is that the existing evidence is insufficient to recommend routine neonatal circumcision. The American College of Obstetricians and Gynecologists Committee on Obstetric Practice supports this position. Given this circumstance, parents should be given accurate and impartial information to help them make an informed decision. It is reasonable for parents to take cultural, religious, and ethnic traditions, as well as medical factors, into consideration when making this decision. Circumcision of newborns should be performed only on healthy and stable infants.

There is ample evidence that newborns circumcised without analgesia experience pain and stress. Analgesia has been found to be safe and effective in reducing the pain associated with circumcision. Therefore, if circumcision is performed, analgesia should be provided. Swaddling, sucrose by mouth, and acetaminophen administration may reduce the stress response but are not sufficient for the operative pain and cannot be recommended as the sole method of analgesia. EMLA cream, dorsal penile nerve block, and subcutaneous ring block are all reasonable options, although the subcutaneous ring block may provide the most effective analgesia.

ISSN 1074-861X

The American College of Obstetricians and Gynecologists
409 12th Street, SW
PO Box 96920
Washington, DC 20090-6920

12345/54321

Circumcision. ACOG Committee Opinion No. 260. American College of Obstetricians and Gynecologists. Obstet Gynecol 2001;98:707-708

References

1. Circumcision policy statement. Task Force on Circumcision. American Academy of Pediatrics. Pediatrics 1999;103:686–693
2. Prevention and management of pain and stress in the neonate. American Academy of Pediatrics. Committee on Fetus and Newborn. Committee on Drugs. Section on Anesthesiology. Section on Surgery. Canadian Paediatric Society. Fetus and Newborn Committee. Pediatrics 2000;105:454–461

ACOG

Committee on
Coding and
Nomenclature

Committee Opinion

Number 249, January 2001

Coding Responsibility

Physicians are responsible for accurately coding the services they provide to their patients. Likewise, insurers are obligated to process all legitimate insurance claims for covered services accurately and in a timely manner. It is inappropriate for physicians to code or for insurers to process claims incorrectly in order to enhance or reduce reimbursement. When either party engages in such a practice intentionally and repetitively, it should be considered dishonest and may be subject to civil and criminal penalties.

ISSN 1074-861X

The American College of Obstetricians and Gynecologists
409 12th Street, SW
PO Box 96920
Washington, DC 20090-6920

12345/54321

ACOG

Committee on
Primary Care

Committee Opinion

Number 227, November 1999

Complementary and Alternative Medicine

In 1990, 34% of adults in the United States used complementary and alternative medicine (CAM). In 1997, 42% of adults in the United States and Canada used CAM, and the use by women was 49%. This trend of increased CAM use will continue as it is reinforced and supported by continuing media attention; intense commercial efforts by providers of CAM products and services, including proprietary pharmaceutical companies; third-party reimbursement for some CAM practices and products; and the increasing over-the-counter access to CAM products in drugstores and supermarkets. The purpose of this Committee Opinion is to provide an overview of CAM, to recommend that physicians ask patients about their use of CAM, and to provide sources of additional information about the subject.

The physician, in the role of patient advocate, has an ethical responsibility to promote and protect the patient's well-being. This function includes the ability to engage in a dialogue that honors the patient's values and promotes shared decision making. Inquiring about the patient's motivation for and use of CAM and providing information on safety and effectiveness can be integral to this role.

Complementary and alternative medicine can be defined as those systems, practices, interventions, modalities, professions, therapies, applications, theories, or claims that are currently not an integral part of the dominant or conventional medical system (known as allopathy in North America). Importantly, over time some of the individual modalities do overlap with or become integrated into Western medicine. The spectrum of CAM encompasses over 350 different techniques and treatments. These can be classified into at least seven major categories:

1. *Mind–body interventions* include yoga, relaxation response techniques, meditation, t'ai chi, hypnotherapy, spirituality, support groups, and biofeedback.
2. *Alternative systems of medical practice* are exemplified by Traditional Chinese Medicine. Other systems in this category include homeopathy, ayurveda, naturopathy, chiropractic, Native-American medicine, and the various forms of acupuncture.

The Committee wishes to thank Ronald A. Chez, MD, for his assistance in the development of this opinion. This document reflects emerging clinical and scientific advances as of the date issued and is subject to change. The information should not be construed as dictating an exclusive course of treatment or procedure to be followed.

The American College of Obstetricians and Gynecologists
409 12th Street, SW
PO Box 96920
Washington, DC 20090-6920

12345/32109

3. *Pharmacologic and biologic* treatments, a diverse and large category, includes folk medicine, medicinal plants, processed blood products, and autogenous vaccines.

4. *Herbal medicine,* another large category, is the use of botanicals with pharmacologic activity. A number of these substances have formed the basis of the Western pharmacopeia. Currently, the public's attention is focused on St. John's wort for depressive disorders, echinacea for upper respiratory infections, valerian for sleep disorders, garlic for hypercholesterolemia, and ginkgo biloba for circulatory disorders.

5. *Diet and nutrition* encompass the use of vitamins, minerals, and nutritional supplements in general, and cancer and cardiovascular disease diets in particular. Treatments include megadosing, elimination of or excessive intake of certain foods, vegetarian and macrobiotic diets, and diets associated with various physicians.

6. *Manual healing methods* include massage, chiropractic and osteopathic manipulation, and biofield therapeutics (eg, Reiki, polarity, reflexology, and therapeutic touch).

7. *Bioelectromagnetic applications* include the use of magnets for musculoskeletal and neurologic pain; low-frequency thermal waves in diathermy; nonionizing, nonthermal applications such as pulsed electromagnetic waves as now used in the treatment of bone fractures; and transcutaneous electrical nerve stimulation for pain relief.

Most patients who use CAM are self-referred and do not tell their physicians they are doing so. Thus, their medical record is incomplete, and the possibility of medical risk cannot be addressed. Patients can be asked questions similar to "Have you used or have you been considering other kinds of treatment or medications for relief of your symptoms or to maintain wellness?" Follow-up questions to a positive answer can include asking when she decided to use CAM, what results she was expecting, how she chose the method, and how it has worked for her. This information can then be documented in the patient's medical record.

Safety is the critical issue when a patient asks about the merit of using a CAM product or intervention. The potential can exist for both direct and indirect risks. These risks can include patient delay in or avoidance of seeking appropriate conventional treatment, a misdiagnosis, toxic reactions from ingested substances, and interference with the mechanism of action of a prescribed drug or treatment.

Over-the-counter herbal preparations and dietary supplements, such as those marketed to relieve menopausal symptoms, may be of particular concern to the obstetrician–gynecologist. As defined in the 1994 Dietary Supplement and Health Education Act passed by Congress and as opposed to prescription items, these products are not subject to standardized manufacture, supporting clinical data, or approval or supervision by the U.S. Food and Drug Administration. Thus, there can be uncertainty as to the identity of the active ingredient and the amount of its dose. Also, the chemical composition may vary from manufacturer to manufacturer and by lot number, and there may be adulteration without this being identified on the label. Some of these problems will be addressed with the new federal regulation requiring that dietary supplement ingredients are labeled in a manner analogous to food labels, increased legislated U.S. Food and Drug Administration authority for these products, and increased attention by the Federal Trade Commission to advertised claims.

Concerns about safety can be tempered for some CAM modalities. For instance, it is unlikely that homeopathic preparations, acupuncture, biofeedback, or prayer will be associated with direct adverse side effects. In contrast, intravenous hydrogen peroxide, chelation therapy, and megadosing of supplements can be toxic and dangerous. Accordingly, when informed that the patient is using CAM, her clinician can advise if there is supporting published research, warn about real or potential dangers, ascertain if it can be continued in conjunction with conventional treatment, and monitor for positive and negative effects over time.

Some patients will request a referral to a local alternative care provider. Any such referral should be made only to a state-licensed provider and at an arm's length relationship. All states license chiropractors, but not all license other CAM providers, such as naturopaths, acupuncturists, or massage therapists. Physicians should be aware of possible liability consequences of such referrals. If the referral itself is negligent because it is inconsistent with reasonable practice, the referring physician may be exposed to liability if the patient is injured by the subsequent treatment. Also, liability may arise if the referring physician supervises the CAM care, jointly treats the patient, or knows or should have known that the CAM provider is incompetent.

It can be anticipated that patients will continue to use CAM with or without physician referral. Accompanying this use is the public's expectation that health insurance plans will reimburse for CAM treatment. A growing number of third-party payers have responded by doing so under a variety of clinical guidelines. This willingness can result in conflict between physicians and CAM providers if important operational issues are not addressed. These issues include the creation of protocols and plans of care for specific diagnoses, procedures for monitoring and follow-up with finite clinical endpoints, evidence for safety and effectiveness, and identified criteria for referral to conventional care.

Each physician can determine to what extent he or she wishes to learn more about various aspects of CAM. There are a number of ways to obtain information. Clinical studies in peer-reviewed, conventional medical journals now appear on a regular basis. In addition to continuing medical education courses, there are peer-reviewed medical journals, textbooks, and newsletters devoted to the subject. Computer databases and webpages specifically oriented to CAM now are accessible by both physicians and patients.

In the coming years, it is probable that there will be a blending of conventional medicine with various CAM therapies as evidence-based research data support clinical decision making in patient care. This comprehensive approach may become known as integrated medical care.

Bibliography

Blumenthal M, ed. The complete German Commission E Monographs. Therapeutic guide to herbal medicines. Austin, TX: American Botanical Council, 1998

Chez RA, Jonas WB, Eisenberg D. The physician and complementary and alternative medicine. In: Jonas WB, Levin JS, eds. Essentials of Complementary and Alternative Medicine. Philadelphia: Lippincott Williams & Wilkins, 1999:31–45

Jonas WB, Levin JS, eds. Essentials of complementary and alternative medicine. Philadelphia: Lippincott Williams and Wilkins, 1999

National Institutes of Health. Alternative medicine: expanding medical horizons: a report to the National Institutes of Health on alternative medical systems and practices in the United States. National Institutes of Health, Workshop on Alternative Medicine, 1995; NIH publication no. 94-066

Newall CA, Anderson LA, Phillipson JD. Herbal medicines, a guide for health-care professionals. London: Pharmaceutical Press, 1996

PDR for Herbal Medicines. Montvale, NJ: Medical Economics Co., 1998

Segen JC. Dictionary of alternative medicine. Stamford, Connecticut: Appleton & Lange, 1998

Resources

Newsletters

Complementary Medicine for the Physician, W.B. Saunders Periodicals Customer Service, 6277 Sea Harbor Drive, Orlando, FL 32887-4800, (800) 654-2452

Alternative Therapies in Women's Health, American Health Consultants, PO Box 740056, Atlanta, GA 30374, (800) 688-2421

Alternative Medicine Alert, American Health Consultants, PO Box 740056, Atlanta, GA 30374, (800) 688-2421

HerbalGram, American Botanical Council, PO Box 144345, Austin, TX 78714-4345, (800) 373-7105

Web Sites

The National Library of Medicine
(http://www.ncbi.nlm.nih.gov/PubMed/)

The National Center for Complementary and Alternative Medicine (http://nccam.nih.gov/)

The NIH Office of Dietary Supplements
(http://odp.od.nih.gov/ods/)

The Richard and Hinda Rosenthal Center for Complementary & Alternative Medicine
(http://cpmcnet.columbia.edu/dept/rosenthal/)

The American Botanical Council (http://www.herbalgram.org/)

HealthWorld Online (http://www.healthy.net/)

Quackwatch (www.quackwatch.com)

ACOG

Committee on
Gynecologic Practice

Committee Opinion

Number 242, October 2000

This document reflects emerging clinical and scientific advances as of the date issued and is subject to change. The information should not be construed as dictating an exclusive course of treatment or procedure to be followed.

ISSN 1074-861X

The American College of Obstetricians and Gynecologists
409 12th Street, SW
PO Box 96920
Washington, DC 20090-6920

12345/43210

Concurrent Chemoradiation in the Treatment of Cervical Cancer

Recently, data from several large randomized clinical trials have been published supporting the use of concurrent platinum-based chemotherapy in women who require radiation therapy for treatment of cervical cancer. The results of these well-designed studies are consistent and suggest improved local control and overall survival when cisplatin-based chemotherapy is added for women who will receive radiation therapy as either front-line or salvage therapy for cervical cancer. The risk of death from cervical cancer was reduced by 30–50% in women treated with concurrent chemoradiation. The addition of chemotherapy to radiation therapy appears to benefit women with locally advanced cervical cancer who were treated with primary radiation therapy, as well as those with early-stage disease and poor histologic prognostic factors who were treated with postoperative adjunctive radiation therapy. Toxicity was observed in association with this combination therapy but was manageable.

Based on these data, the National Cancer Institute issued a rare clinical announcement suggesting that "strong consideration should be given to the incorporation of concurrent cisplatin-based chemotherapy with radiation therapy in women who require radiation therapy for treatment of cervical cancer." The Committee on Gynecologic Practice supports this recommendation of the National Cancer Institute.

Bibliography

Keys HM, Bundy BN, Stehman FB, Muderspach LI, Chafe WE, Suggs CL 3rd, et al. Cisplatin, radiation, and adjuvant hysterectomy compared with radiation and adjuvant hysterectomy for bulky stage IB cervical carcinoma. N Engl J Med 1999;340:1154–1161 [published erratum appears in N Engl J Med 1999;341:708]

Morris M, Eifel PJ, Lu J, Grigsby PW, Levenback C, Stevens RE, et al. Pelvic radiation with concurrent chemotherapy compared with pelvic and para-aortic radiation for high-risk cervical cancer. N Engl J Med 1999;340:1137–1143

National Cancer Institute. Clinical announcement: concurrent chemoradiation for cervical cancer. February, 1999. Available at: <http://cancertrials.nci.nih.gov/types/cervical/announcement/text.html>. Retrieved June 16, 2000

Peters WA 3rd, Liu PY, Barrett RJ 2nd, Gordon W Jr, Stock RJ, Berek JS, et al. Concurrent chemotherapy and pelvic radiation therapy compared with pelvic radiation therapy alone as adjuvant therapy after radical surgery in high-risk early-stage cancer of the cervix. J Clin Oncol 2000;18:1606–1613

Rose PG, Bundy BN, Watkins EB, Thigpen JT, Deppe G, Maiman MA, et al. Concurrent cisplatin-based radiotherapy and chemotherapy for locally advanced cervical cancer. N Engl J Med 1999;340:1144–1153 [published erratum appears in N Engl J Med 1999;341:708]

Whitney CW, Sause W, Bundy BN, Malfetano JH, Hannigan EV, Fowler WC Jr, et al. Randomized comparison of fluorouracil plus cisplatin versus hydroxyurea as an adjunct to radiation therapy in stage IIB-IVA carcinoma of the cervix with negative para-aortic lymph nodes: a Gynecologic Oncology Group and Southwest Oncology Group study. J Clin Oncol 1999;17: 1339–1348

ACOG

Committee on
Professional Liability

Requests for authorization to make photocopies should be directed to:

Copyright Clearance Center
222 Rosewood Drive
Danvers, MA 01923
(978) 750-8400

ISSN 1074-861X

The American College of Obstetricians and Gynecologists
409 12th Street, SW
PO Box 96920
Washington, DC 20090-6920

12345/43210

Committee Opinion

Number 236, June 2000 *(Replaces No. 150, December 1994)*

Coping with the Stress of Malpractice Litigation

The American College of Obstetricians and Gynecologists (ACOG) has long been concerned about the psychologic and emotional impact of medical malpractice litigation on physicians, especially because 76.5% of ACOG Fellows have been sued at least once. As studies have shown, defendant physicians may experience a wide range of distressing emotions and increased stress, which can disrupt their personal lives and the lives of their families, their relationships with patients, and their medical practices. Because a medical liability case in obstetrics and gynecology takes an average of 4.2 years to resolve, this stressful period can seem interminable for all involved.

Physicians often are told by claims adjusters and defense attorneys that they should not speak to anyone regarding any aspect of the malpractice case. Nevertheless, physicians often need to express emotional responses to being sued. Literal adherence to the advice to "speak to no one" can result in isolation, increased stress, and dysfunctional behavior. Such behavior may jeopardize family relationships and may also affect the physician's ability to function professionally and to represent himself or herself appropriately and effectively during a trial. Therefore, the physician is encouraged to inform family members of the lawsuit, the allegations, the potential for publicity, and any expected testimony while maintaining confidentiality. Children should be told about the lawsuit and their questions honestly answered, commensurate with their age and ability to process the information. Open communication with family members will assist in reducing emotional isolation and self-blame.

Certainly, legal and clinical aspects of a case must be kept confidential. An exception to this rule, however, might be in the context of professional counseling. Any clinical aspects of a malpractice case that are discussed in counseling should be disclosed within the confines of a formal counselor–patient relationship to ensure the confidentiality privilege. Confidentiality may be lost if third parties are present.

Obstetrician–gynecologists should recognize that being a defendant in a medical liability lawsuit can be one of life's most stressful experiences. Although negative emotions in response to a lawsuit are normal, physicians may need help from professionals or peers to cope with this stress. State or local medical societies and medical liability insurance carriers often sponsor support groups for defendant physicians and their families. In the absence of such services, individual professional counseling can be of great benefit.

Bibliography

Bark P, Vincent C, Olivieri L, Jones A. Impact of litigation on senior clinicians: implications for risk management. Qual Health Care 1997;6:7–13

Charles, SC. How to handle the stress of litigation. Clin Plast Surg 1999;26:69–77

Charles, SC. The doctor–patient relationship and medical malpractice litigation. Bull Menninger Clin 1993;57:195–207

Charles, SC. Psychological reactions to medical malpractice suits and the development of support groups as a response. Instr Course Lect 1988;37:289–292

Frisch PR, Charles SC, Gibbons RP, Hedeker D. Role of previous claims and specialty on the effectiveness of risk management education for office-based physicians. West J Med 1995; 163:346–350

Martin CA, Wilson JF, Fiebelman ND 3d, Gurley DN, Miller TW. Physicians' psychologic reactions to malpractice litigation. South Med J 1991;84:1300–1304

Pyskoty CE, Byrne TE, Charles SC, Frankel KJ. Malpractice litigation as a factor in choosing a medical specialty. West J Med 1990;152:309–312

ACOG

Committee on
Obstetric Practice

Committee Opinion

Number 258, September 2001

Fetal Pulse Oximetry

ABSTRACT: The U.S. Food and Drug Administration recently approved the marketing of the Nellcor N-400 Fetal Oxygen Saturation Monitoring System, a fetal pulse oximeter. The American College of Obstetricians and Gynecologists Committee on Obstetric Practice cannot endorse the adoption of this device in clinical practice at this time because of concerns that its introduction could further escalate the cost of medical care without necessarily improving clinical outcome. The committee recommends that prospective randomized clinical trials be conducted to evaluate the clinical use of this new technology in conjunction with fetal well-being assessment.

Electronic fetal heart rate (FHR) monitoring is used routinely in labor to screen for fetal well-being. The diagnostic value of FHR monitoring is limited. When the FHR tracing is reassuring, it has a predictive value of 99% for fetal well-being, while an abnormal FHR tracing has a positive predictive value of only 50% for fetal compromise. Over the past three decades, the national cesarean delivery rate has increased significantly, in part, as a result of this technology intended to reduce perinatal morbidity and mortality and to prevent long-term neurologic damage. To further refine assessment of fetal well-being in labor, several diagnostic and intervention techniques have been introduced (eg, fetal scalp pH sampling, fetal scalp stimulation, and fetal acoustic stimulation). None of these methods have been universally or routinely adopted by clinicians.

The U.S. Food and Drug Administration (FDA) recently approved the marketing of the Nellcor N-400 Fetal Oxygen Saturation Monitoring System, a fetal pulse oximeter. The device's primary proposed use is as an adjunct to FHR monitoring to continuously monitor fetal intrapartum oxygen saturation in a singleton vertex fetus with a gestational age equal to or greater than 36 weeks in the presence of a nonreassuring heart rate pattern after fetal membranes have ruptured.

It is essential to recognize that the FDA primarily evaluates a device's safety and ability to accurately measure or quantify a certain physiologic function. It appears from the data supplied to the FDA by the company that this device, under certain conditions, can assess fetal oxygenation safely and effectively. The FDA had no additional outcome data available.

In a company-sponsored study, it has been reported that when the Nellcor N-400 Fetal Oxygen Saturation Monitoring System is used in conjunction

ISSN 1074-861X

The American College of Obstetricians and Gynecologists
409 12th Street, SW
PO Box 96920
Washington, DC 20090-6920

12345/54321

Fetal pulse oximetry. ACOG Committee Opinion No. 258. American College of Obstetricians and Gynecologists. Obstet Gynecol 2001;98:523-524

with FHR monitoring (under specific conditions), there was a reduction in cesarean delivery rates for nonreassuring FHR tracings, but there was no difference in the overall cesarean delivery rates as a result of an increase in cesarean delivery for dystocia (1). Several environmental factors and physiologic events (eg, fetal scalp congestion, color and thickness of fetal hair, skin thickness, vernix caseosa, site of application, fetal presentation, uterine activity, movement artifacts) can affect the accuracy of the fetal pulse oximetry readings. Reliable readings can be obtained approximately 60–70% of the time.

The American College of Obstetricians and Gynecologists Committee on Obstetric Practice currently cannot endorse the adoption of this device in clinical practice. The committee is particularly concerned that the introduction of this technology to clinical practice could further escalate the cost of medical care without necessarily improving clinical outcome. The committee recommends that prospective randomized clinical trials be conducted to evaluate the clinical use of this new technology in conjunction with fetal well-being assessment. Given that this technology is new, attention should be paid to any adverse outcomes, including falsely reassuring fetal pulse oximetry data. Moreover, such untoward events should be reported to FDA MedWatch, the FDA Medical Products Reporting Program.

Reference

1. Garite TJ, Dildy GA, McNamara H, Nageotte MP, Boehm FH, Dellinger EH. A multicenter controlled trial of fetal pulse oximetry in the intrapartum management of nonreassuring fetal heart rate patterns. Am J Obstet Gynecol 2000;183:1049–1058

ACOG

Committee on
Obstetric Practice

Committee Opinion

Number 252, March 2001

The American College of Obstetricians and Gynecologists
409 12th Street, SW
PO Box 96920
Washington, DC 20090-6920

12345/54321

Fetal Surgery for Open Neural Tube Defects

Open neural tube defects occur in 1.5 to 2.0 births per 1,000 in the United States (1). Meningomyelocele is the most common congenital anomaly of the central nervous system and often results in diminished motor function, incontinence, and developmental delay (2, 3). Reports of small, uncontrolled case studies of in utero surgical correction of neural tube defects have documented a mean gestational age at delivery of 33 weeks following these procedures (2, 4). Several short-term measures of neurologic outcome were reported improved compared with historic controls (2). Long-term improvement in overall neurologic outcome has yet to be demonstrated (2, 4–10). However, these approaches, whether involving open (hysterotomy) or endoscopic surgery, may result in serious fetal and maternal complications (6, 11–13). Fetal surgical repair of meningomyelocele exposes the mother to the risks of anesthesia, hemorrhage, chorioamnionitis and sepsis, thrombosis, tocolytic-induced pulmonary edema, and uterine rupture. In addition, preterm labor, preterm premature rupture of membranes, and oligohydramnios may occur in up to 50% of patients (2). Evolving surgical techniques and tocolytic therapy have modestly improved outcome, but the risk of preterm birth is considerable.

Because of concerns about safety and unproven benefits, fetal surgery for the correction of open neural tube defects should be considered investigational. This surgery should only be conducted in a collaborative research setting in highly specialized centers. Any studies should be performed under strict institutional review board supervision and with the informed consent of the patients. Such informed consent should appropriately address the maternal, fetal, and future reproductive risks of the proposed surgery as well as its potential benefits. A multicenter, randomized, controlled trial of sufficient power to evaluate maternal and fetal risks, and short- and long-term neurological outcomes in the children should be conducted prior to acceptance of this procedure. Finally, in view of the unproven short- and long-term benefits of such procedures to the affected infant and child, every reasonable effort should be made to maximize maternal safety.

References

1. Shurtleff DB, Lemire RJ. Epidemiology, etiologic factors, and prenatal diagnosis of open spinal dysraphism. Neurosurg Clin N Am 1995;6:183–193

2. Bruner JP, Tulipan N, Paschall RL, Boehm FH, Walsh WF, Silva SR, et al. Fetal surgery for myelomeningocele and the incidence of shunt-dependent hydrocephalus. JAMA 1999;282:1819–1825

3. Shurtleff DB, Luthy DA, Benedetti TJ, Hickok DE, Stuntz T, Kropp RJ. The outcome of pregnancies diagnosed as having a fetus with meningomyelocele. Z Kinderchir 1987;42 Suppl 1:50–52

4. Sutton LN, Adzick NS, Bilaniuk LT, Johnson MP, Crombleholme TM, Flake AW. Improvement in hindbrain herniation demonstrated by serial fetal magnetic resonance imaging following fetal surgery for myelomeningocele. JAMA 1999;282:1826–1831

5. Brunelli G, Brunelli F. Experimental foetal microsurgery as related to myelomeningocele. Microsurgery 1984;5:24–29

6. Bruner JP, Richards WO, Tulipan NB, Arney TL. Endoscopic coverage of fetal myelomeningocele in utero. Am J Obstet Gynecol 1999;180:153–158

7. Bruner JP, Tulipan NE, Richards WO. Endoscopic coverage of fetal open myelomeningocele in utero [letter]. Am J Obstet Gynecol 1997;176:256–257

8. Meuli M, Meuli-Simmen C, Hutchins GM, Seller MJ, Harrison MR, Adzick NS. The spinal cord lesion in human fetuses with myelomeningocele: implications for fetal surgery. J Pediatr Surg 1997;32:448–452

9. Meuli M, Meuli-Simmen C, Yingling CD, Hutchins GM, Timmel GB, Harrison MR, et al. In utero repair of experimental myelomeningocele saves neurological function at birth. J Pediatr Surg 1996;31:397–402

10. Meuli-Simmen C, Meuli M, Hutchins GM, Harrison MR, Buncke HJ, Sullivan KM, et al. Fetal reconstructive surgery: experimental use of the latissimus dorsi flap to correct myelomeningocele in utero. Plast Reconstr Surg 1995;96:1007–1011

11. Olutoye OO, Adzick NS. Fetal surgery for myelomeningocele. Semin Perinatol 1999;23:462–473

12. Tulipan N, Hernanz-Schulman M, Lowe LH, Bruner JP. Intrauterine myelomeningocele repair reverses preexisting hindbrain herniation. Pediatr Neurosurg 1999;31:137–142

13. Simpson JL. Fetal surgery for myelomeningocele: promise, progress, and problems [editorial]. JAMA 1999;282:1873–1874

ACOG Committee Opinion

Committee on
Obstetric Practice

Number 158, September 1995

Guidelines for Diagnostic Imaging During Pregnancy

Various imaging modalities are available for diagnosis during pregnancy. These include X-ray, ultrasonography, magnetic resonance imaging (MRI), and nuclear medicine studies. Of these, diagnostic X-ray is the most frequent cause of anxiety for both obstetrician and patient. Much of this anxiety is secondary to a general belief that any radiation exposure is harmful and will result in an anomalous fetus. This anxiety could lead to inappropriate therapeutic abortion and litigation. In fact, most diagnostic radiologic procedures are associated with little, if any, known significant fetal risks. Moreover, according to the American College of Radiology, no single diagnostic X-ray procedure results in radiation exposure to a degree that would threaten the well-being of the developing preembryo, embryo, and fetus. Thus, exposure to X-ray during pregnancy is not an indication for therapeutic abortion (1, 2).

Some women are exposed to X-rays before the diagnosis of pregnancy. Occasionally, X-ray procedures will be indicated during pregnancy for significant medical problems or trauma. To enable physicians to counsel patients appropriately, the following information is provided about the potential risks and measures that can reduce diagnostic X-ray exposure.

X-Ray Exposure

Ionizing radiation can result in the following three harmful effects: 1) cell death and teratogenic effects, 2) carcinogenesis, and 3) genetic effects or mutations in germ cells (1, 2). There is little or no information to estimate either the frequency or magnitude of adverse genetic effects on future generations.

Units traditionally used to measure the effects of X-ray include the rad and roentgen equivalent man (rem). Modern units include the gray (Gy) and sievert (Sv). The definitions of these are summarized in Table 1.

The estimated fetal exposure from some common radiologic procedures is summarized in Table 2 (3–13). A plain X-ray generally exposes the fetus to very small amounts of radiation. Commonly during pregnancy, the uterus is shielded for nonpelvic procedures. Most fluoroscopic examinations result in fetal exposure of millirads except barium enema or small bowel series. Although computed tomography pelvimetry can result in fetal exposures as high as 1.5 rad, exposure can be reduced to approximately 250 mrad (includ-

The American College of Obstetricians and Gynecologists

409 12th Street, SW,
Washington, DC 20024-2188

12345/98765

Table 1. Commonly Used Measures of Radiation

Measure	Definition	Unit	Unit
Exposure	Number of ions produced by X-rays per kilogram of air	Roentgen (R)	Roentgen (R)
Dose	Amount of energy deposited per kilogram of tissue	Rad (rad)*	Gray (Gy) 1 Gy = 100 rad
Relative effective dose	Amount of energy deposited per kilogram of tissue normalized for biological effectiveness	Roentgen equivalent man (rem)*	Sievert (Sv) 1 Sv = 100 rem

* For diagnostic X-rays, 1 rad = 1 rem.

Cunningham FG, MacDonald PC, Gant NF, Leveno KJ, Gilstrap LC III. Imaging modalities during pregnancy. In: Williams obstetrics. 19th ed. Norwalk, Connecticut: Appleton & Lange, 1993:982

Table 2. Estimated Fetal Exposure From Some Common Radiologic Procedures

Procedure	Fetal Exposure
Chest X-ray (2 views)	0.02–0.07 mrad
Abdominal film (single view)	100 mrad
Intravenous pyelography	≥1 rad*
Hip film (single view)	200 mrad
Mammography	7–20 mrad
Barium enema or small bowel series	2–4 rad
CT† scan of head or chest	<1 rad
CT scan of abdomen and lumbar spine	3.5 rad
CT pelvimetry	250 mrad

* Exposure depends on the number of films.

† CT indicates computed tomography.

ing fetal gonad exposure) by using a low-exposure technique (13).

Cell Death and Teratogenic Effects

Data from animals suggest that exposure to high-dose ionizing radiation (ie, much greater than that used in diagnostic procedures) before implantation will most likely be lethal to the embryo (1). In other words, cell death is most likely an "all or none" phenomenon in early embryonic development.

A myriad of teratogenic effects has developed in animals exposed to large doses of radiation (ie, 100–200 rad). However, in humans, growth restriction, microcephaly, and mental retardation are the most common adverse effects from high-dose radiation (2, 3, 14). Based on data from atomic bomb survivors, it appears that the risk of central nervous system effects is greatest with exposure at 8–15 weeks of gestation, with no proven risk at less than 8 weeks of gestation or at greater than 25 weeks of gestation (2, 15). Thus, at 8–15 weeks of gestation, the fetus is at greatest risk for radiation-induced mental retardation, and the risk appears to be a "nonthreshold linear function of dose" at doses of at least 20 rad (2, 3, 15, 16). For example, the risk of severe mental retardation in fetuses exposed to ionizing radiation is approximately 40% at 100 rad of exposure and as high as 60% at 150 rad of exposure (2, 15). It has been suggested that a threshold for this adverse effect may exist in the range of 20–40 rad (14, 15). Fortunately, even multiple diagnostic X-ray procedures rarely result in ionizing radiation exposure to this degree. In summary, fetal risks of anomalies, growth restriction, or abortions are not increased with radiation exposure of less than 5 rad, a level above the range of exposure for diagnostic procedures (1).

Carcinogenesis

The risk of carcinogenesis as a result of in utero exposure to ionizing radiation is unclear but is probably very small. It has been estimated that 1 in 2,000 children exposed to ionizing radiation in utero will develop childhood leukemia. This is increased from a background rate of approximately 1 in 3,000 (17). If elective abortion were chosen in every instance of fetal exposure to radiation, 1,999 exposed, normal fetuses would be aborted for each case of leukemia prevented (1, 4). It has been estimated that the risk of radiation-induced carcinogenesis may indeed be higher in children compared with adults but that such risks are not likely to exceed 1 in 1,000 children per rad (5). Thus, abortion should not be recommended solely on the basis of exposure to diagnostic radiation.

Ultrasonography

Ultrasonography uses sound waves and is not a form of ionizing radiation. There have been no reports of documented adverse fetal effects for diagnostic ultrasound procedures, including duplex Doppler imaging. Energy exposure from ultrasonography has been arbitrarily limited to 94mW/cm² by the U.S. Food and Drug Administration. There are no contraindications to ultrasound procedures during pregnancy, and this modality has largely replaced X-ray as the primary method of fetal imaging during pregnancy.

Magnetic Resonance Imaging

With MRI, magnets that alter the energy state of hydrogen protons are used instead of ionizing radiation (18). This technique could prove especially useful for diagnosis and evaluation of fetal central nervous system anomalies and growth restriction. Although there have been no documented adverse fetal effects reported, the National Radiological Protection Board arbitrarily advises against its use in the first trimester (19). However, MRI has been proven useful for evaluation of maternal pelvic masses and for evaluation of fetal growth restriction (20).

Nuclear Medicine

Nuclear studies such as pulmonary ventilation–perfusion, thyroid, bone, and renal scans are performed by "tagging" a chemical agent with a radioisotope. The fetal exposure depends on the physical and biochemical properties of the radioisotope (3).

Technetium Tc 99m is one of the most commonly used isotopes and is used for brain, bone, renal, and cardiovascular scans. In general, these latter procedures result in a uterus, embryo, or fetal exposure of less than 0.5 rad (3, 5).

One of the more common nuclear medicine studies performed during pregnancy is the ventilation–perfusion scan for suspected pulmonary embolism. Macroaggregated albumin labeled with 99mTc is used for the perfusion portion, and inhaled xenon gas (^{127}Xe or ^{133}Xe) is used for the ventilation portion. The amount of radiation to which the fetus is exposed is extremely small (approximately 50 mrad) (21).

Radioactive iodine readily crosses the placenta and can adversely affect the fetal thyroid, especially if used after 10–12 weeks of gestational age. Radioactive isotopes of iodine used for treatment of hyperthyroidism are contraindicated during pregnancy, and such therapy should be delayed until after delivery. If a diagnostic scan of the thyroid is essential, ^{123}I or 99mTc should be used in place of ^{131}I (21).

Guidelines

The following guidelines for X-ray examination or exposure during pregnancy are suggested:

1. Women should be counseled that X-ray exposure from a single diagnostic procedure does not result in harmful fetal effects. Specifically, exposure to less than 5 rad has not been associated with an increase in fetal anomalies or pregnancy loss.

2. Concern about possible effects of high-dose ionizing radiation exposure should not prevent medically indicated diagnostic X-ray procedures from being performed on the mother. During pregnancy, other imaging procedures not associated with ionizing radiation (eg, ultrasonography, MRI) should be considered instead of X-rays when possible.

3. Ultrasonography and MRI are not associated with known adverse fetal effects. However, until more information is available, MRI is not recommended for use in the first trimester.

4. Consultation with a radiologist may be helpful in calculating estimated fetal dose when multiple diagnostic X-rays are performed on a pregnant patient.

5. The use of radioactive isotopes of iodine is contraindicated for therapeutic use during pregnancy.

References

1. Brent RL. The effect of embryonic and fetal exposure to x-ray, microwaves, and ultrasound: counseling the pregnant and nonpregnant patient about these risks. Semin Oncol 1989;16:347–368

2. Hall EJ. Scientific view of low-level radiation risks. Radiographics 1991;11:509–518

3. Twickler DM, Clarke G, Cunningham FG. Diagnostic imaging in pregnancy. Supplement. Williams obstetrics. 18th ed. Norwalk, Connecticut: Appleton & Lange, June/July 1992:1–15

4. Early diagnosis of pregnancy. An invitational symposium. Comment on editorial. J Reprod Med 1974;12:6

5. Mettler FA, Guiberteau MJ. Essentials of nuclear medicine imaging. Philadelphia: WB Saunders, 1991:320–321

6. Rosenstein M. Handbook of selected organ doses for projections common in diagnostic radiology. Rockville, Maryland: Department of Health and Human Services, Food and Drug Administration, 1988; DHHS publication no. (FDA):89-8031

7. Laws PW, Rosenstein M. A somatic dose index for diagnostic radiology. Health Phys 1978;35:629–642

8. Conway BJ. Nationwide evaluation of x-ray trends: tabulation and graphical summary of surveys 1984 through 1987. Frankfort, Kentucky: Conference of Radiation Control Program Directors, Inc, 1989

9. National Council on Radiation Protection and Measurements. Exposure of the U.S. population from diagnostic medical radiation. Bethesda, Maryland: NCRPM, 1989. 26; report no. 100

10. Bednarek DR, Rudin S, Wong R, Andres ML. Reduction of fluoroscopic exposure for the air-contrast barium enema. Br J Radiol 1983;56:823–828

11. Shope TB, Gagne RM, Johnson GC. A method for describing the doses delivered by transmission x-ray computed tomography. Med Phys 1981;8:488–495

12. Ragozzino MW, Breckle R, Hill LM, Gray JE. Average fetal depth in utero: data for estimation of fetal absorbed radiation dose. Radiology 1986;158:513–515

13. Moore MM, Shearer DR. Fetal dose estimates for CT pelvimetry. Radiology 1989;171:265–267

14. Otake M, Yoshimaru H, Schull WJ. Severe mental retardation among the prenatally exposed survivors of the atomic bombing of Hiroshima and Nagasaki: a comparison of the old and new dosimetry systems. Hiroshima, Japan: Radiation Effects Research Foundation, 1987; Radiation Effects Research Foundation technical report no. 16-87

15. Committee on Biological Effects of Ionizing Radiation, Board on Radiation Effects Research Commission on Life Sciences, National Research Council. Health effects of exposure to low levels of ionizing radiation: BEIR V. Washington, DC: National Academy Press, 1990:352–370

16. Schull WJ, Otake M. Neurological deficit among the survivors exposed to the atomic bombing of Hiroshima and Nagasaki: a reassessment and new directions. In: Kriegel H, Schmahl W, Gerber GB, Stive FE, eds. Radiation risks to the developing nervous system. New York: Gustave Fischer Verlag, 1986:399–419

17. Miller RW. Epidemiological conclusions from radiation toxicity studies. In: Fry RJM, Grahn D, Griem ML, Rust JH, eds. Late effects of radiation. London: Taylor & Francis, 1970

18. Curry TS III, Dowdey JE, Murry RC Jr, eds. Christensen's physics of diagnostic radiology. 4th ed. Philadelphia: Lea & Febiger, 1990:1, 470

19. Garden AS, Griffiths RD, Weindling AM, Martin PA. Fast-scan magnetic resonance imaging in fetal visualization. Am J Obstet Gynecol 1991;164:1190–1196

20. Cunningham FG, MacDonald PC, Gant NF, Leveno KJ, Gilstrap LC III. Imaging modalities during pregnancy. In: Williams obstetrics. 19th ed. Norwalk, Connecticut: Appleton & Lange, 1993:981–989

21. Ginsberg JS, Hirsh J, Rainbow AJ, Coates G. Risks to the fetus of radiologic procedures used in the diagnosis of maternal venous thromboembolic disease. Thromb Haemost 1989;61:189–196

ACOG

Committee on
Gynecologic Practice

Committee Opinion

Number 203, July 1998   *(Replaces #199, February 1998)*

Hepatitis Virus Infections in Obstetrician–Gynecologists

The current epidemic of human immunodeficiency virus (HIV) infection has escalated concerns about transmission from infected patients to health care workers. The concerns about HIV have increased attention to hepatitis B virus (HBV). It appears that surgeons who follow recommended infection-control procedures are at little risk of acquiring HIV while caring for HIV-infected patients (1, 2). In contrast, surgeons can readily acquire HBV from infected patients (1, 3).

The College routinely has recommended hepatitis B vaccination for obstetrician–gynecologists who are exposed to blood or blood products. Postvaccination testing for antibodies, which is recommended by the Centers for Disease Control and Prevention, can validate immunization (4). Individuals who are antibody negative after immunization should be tested for hepatitis B surface antigen to identify carriers as a result of previous HBV infection (5). The Committee on Gynecologic Practice supports the recommendation that surgeons who perform invasive procedures and who do not have evidence of immunity to HBV should know their hepatitis B surface antigen status and, if it is positive, also should know their hepatitis B e antigen status (6, 7).

The risk of acquiring hepatitis C virus (HCV) infection appears to be lower than the risk of acquiring HBV and higher than the risk of acquiring HIV (2, 3). Nonetheless, HCV is the most common cause of chronic viral hepatitis, and even chronic HCV infection symptoms typically are silent or minimal (8). Thus, surgeons who perform exposure-prone procedures should consider being tested for anti-HCV antibody and, if positive, should confirm seropositive status by documenting HCV RNA in the serum with reverse transcription polymerase chain reaction testing (8–10). Institutional and local health department rules usually are available to guide health care workers who test positive for bloodborne viruses.

References

1. Henderson DK. Human immunodeficiency virus infection in patients and providers. In: Wenzel RP, ed. Prevention and control of nosocomial infections. 2nd ed. Baltimore: Williams and Wilkins, 1993:42–47
2. Gerberding JL. Management of occupational exposures to blood-borne viruses. N Engl J Med 1995;332:444–451

3. Shapiro CN. Occupational risk of infection with hepatitis B and hepatitis C virus. Surg Clin N Am 1995;75:1047–1056
4. Centers for Disease Control and Prevention. Protection against viral hepatitis: recommendations of the Immunization Practices Advisory Committee. MMWR 1990;39 (RR-2):13
5. Rhodes RS. Hepatitis B virus, surgeons, and surgery. Bull Am Coll Surg 1995;80(6):32–42
6. Centers for Disease Control and Prevention. Recommendations for preventing transmission of human immunodeficiency virus and hepatitis B virus to patients du27 ring exposure-prone invasive procedures. MMWR 1991;40 (RR-8):1–9
7. American College of Surgeons. Statement on the surgeon and hepatitis B infection. Bull Am Coll Surg 1995;80(5):33–35
8. Sharara AI, Hunt CM, Hamilton JD. Update: hepatitis C. Ann Intern Med 1996;125:658–668
9. Centers for Disease Control and Prevention. Recommendations for follow-up of health-care workers after occupational exposure to hepatitis C virus. MMWR 1997;46:603–606
10. Dore GJ, Kaldor JM, McCaughan GW. Systematic review of role of polymerase chain reaction in defining infectiousness among people infected with hepatitis C virus. BMJ 1997;315:333–337

ACOG

Committee on
Gynecologic Practice

Committee Opinion

Number 235, May 2000   *(Replaces No. 126, August 1993)*

Hormone Replacement Therapy in Women Treated for Endometrial Cancer

Hormone replacement therapy (HRT), which provides estrogen with or without a progestin, usually is initiated in estrogen-deficient women in an attempt to ameliorate menopausal symptoms and to provide long-term health benefits, such as reduced risk of osteoporosis, potential decreased risk of heart disease, and potential improvement of cognitive function. In women who have been treated previously for endometrial carcinoma, these benefits must be weighed against the risk of stimulating tumor growth and recurrence. Recently, numerous different HRT modalities and delivery systems have become available, including transdermal and intravaginal preparations, plant-based estrogens and progestins, as well as selective estrogen receptor modulators (SERMs), all of which are marketed as providing these short- and long-term benefits while minimizing adverse side effects and outcomes. Although retrospective studies have pointed to an absence of adverse outcomes, currently no conclusive data are available to support specific recommendations regarding the use of HRT in women previously treated for endometrial carcinoma.

In the absence of HRT, the following outcomes may be expected in women treated for endometrial cancer:

- A well-differentiated neoplasm of endometrioid cell type with superficial invasion would render an approximate 5% risk of recurrent disease.
- A moderately differentiated neoplasm of endometrioid cell type with up to one half myometrial invasion would render a 10–15% risk of recurrent disease. The risk may be as high as 50% for nonendometrioid-type tumors and serous papillary tumors.
- A poorly differentiated neoplasm, regardless of cell type, with invasion of over one half of the myometrium would render a 40–50% risk of recurrent disease.

The effect of HRT on the recurrence risk of endometrial cancer is unknown. In the absence of well-designed studies, the selection of appropriate candidates for estrogen treatment should be based on prognostic indicators, including depth of invasion, degree of differentiation, and cell type.

These predictors can assist the physician in describing the risks of recurrent tumors to the patient and can assist the patient in determining the amount of risk she is willing to assume. The decision to prescribe HRT for a patient with a history of endometrial cancer should be based on the patient's perceived benefits and risks after careful counseling. The need for progestational agents in addition to estrogen is unknown at present, although progesterone supplementation after endometrial cancer therapy does not affect recurrence rate.

The introduction of SERMs may extend the options available to estrogen-deficient women. Although recent studies are encouraging, there is no information regarding the efficacy and safety of these drugs in preventing endometrial cancer or for long-term use. Raloxifene, a nonsteroidal benzothiophene approved by the U.S. Food and Drug Administration for osteoporosis prevention, has been demonstrated to exert an antiresorptive effect on bone similar to, but less effective than, that of conjugated estrogen (1). Raloxifene does not stimulate breast or endometrial tissue in postmenopausal women (2). When compared with combination estrogen and progestin, raloxifene demonstrates similar but less extensive effects on serum lipids (3). Raloxifene does not alleviate vasomotor symptoms and may be associated with symptoms of vaginal atrophy.

Because the metabolic changes of estrogen deficiency are significant, estrogen-deficient women should be given complete information, including counseling about alternative therapies, to enable them to make an informed decision. For some women, the sense of well-being afforded by the successful treatment of menopausal symptoms, the reduction of the risk of osteoporosis, and the potential provision of cardiovascular protection may outweigh the risk of stimulating tumor growth.

In summary, the area of HRT in estrogen-deficient women continues to expand at a rapid pace as newer products promise increasing benefits while minimizing adverse outcomes. Although new research appears promising, there is a clear paucity of data upon which to base specific recommendations, particularly in women who have previously been treated for endometrial carcinoma. At this time, the decision to use HRT in these women should be individualized on the basis of potential benefit and risk to the patient.

References

1. Heaney RP, Draper MW. Raloxifene and estrogen: comparative bone-remodeling kinetics. J Clin Endocrinol Metab 1997;82:3425–3429
2. Delmas PD, Bjarnason NH, Mitlak BH, Ravoux AC, Shah AS, Huster WJ, et al. Effects of raloxifene on bone mineral density, serum cholesterol concentrations, and uterine endometrium in postmenopausal women. N Engl J Med 1997;337:1641–1647
3. Walsh BW, Kuller LH, Wild RA, Paul S, Farmer M, Lawrence JB, et al. Effects of raloxifene on serum lipids and coagulation factors in healthy postmenopausal women. JAMA 1998;279:1445–1451

ACOG Committee Opinion

Committee on Gynecologic Practice

Number 226, November 1999 (Replaces #135, April 1994)

Hormone Replacement Therapy in Women with Previously Treated Breast Cancer

The use of hormone replacement therapy (estrogen with or without a progestin [HRT]) in women previously treated for breast cancer continues to be controversial. Unfortunately, reliable experimental data that would permit a definitive statement on this issue are lacking. In light of strong evidence suggesting the clinical benefits of HRT in postmenopausal women, this subject warrants review. The purpose of this Committee Opinion is to review the available evidence and its limitations and to provide recommendations for the use of HRT in women with previously treated breast cancer.

In general, recent thinking has been that the risk of recurrent disease in women previously treated for breast cancer precluded consideration of HRT. This conclusion is based on the results of both laboratory and clinical studies. Estrogen has been shown in vitro to stimulate growth of normal and malignant breast cells in tissue culture (1). This finding, together with the natural history of breast cancer, including risk factors, has led to the opinion that estrogen administration, including use of low-dose formulations, may promote breast cancer in women with active disease. In addition, the results of some early epidemiologic studies have been interpreted as evidence that HRT increases the risk of breast cancer in postmenopausal women (2–5). Finally, because an increased risk of breast cancer is associated with early menarche, late menopause, late onset of first pregnancy, and increased circulating free estrogen levels in obese women, it has been a common belief that less total endogenous estrogen exposure over a lifetime may reduce the incidence of disease. Therefore, the concern about estrogen use in women with a prior diagnosis of breast cancer has been that residual cancer may be reactivated, and mammary cells that have undergone malignant transformation may be stimulated to grow.

Hormone Replacement Therapy and Risk of Breast Cancer Development in the General Population

There is no consensus on the association of HRT with the risk of breast cancer in postmenopausal women. More than 50 epidemiologic studies have failed to demonstrate consistently or conclusively a detrimental impact of replacement estrogen use on the incidence of breast cancer.

Efforts to analyze critically the data by carefully selecting the most acceptable studies and subjecting them to meta-analysis have not clarified the situation. Overall, these studies failed to show an increased risk of postmenopausal women developing breast cancer associated with hormone replacement (6–11).

Several studies showing an increased observed risk involved both premenopausal and postmenopausal women or women using synthetic estrogen. Risk of long-term use (>15 years) cannot be calculated without extrapolation. Current users had a small increased risk that could reflect either a real increase in risk because of a promoter mechanism or an increase in detection of cases (detection bias) because of participation in a study (6–11).

In addition, data suggest the following:

- The use of progestin in combination with estrogen does not protect the user from increased breast cancer risk (10–12).
- A positive family history of breast cancer does not pose an increased risk for development of cancer in HRT users (6, 11).
- A history of benign breast disease does not increase the risk of development of breast cancer in HRT users (8, 11).

These data suggest that the question remains unanswered as to whether the risk of breast cancer is increased in postmenopausal women taking estrogen at recommended replacement doses. Lack of studies of adequate design, patient numbers, and duration of HRT preclude total reassurance that HRT is safe in these women. The ongoing Women's Health Initiative may resolve some of these issues. Quality-of-life issues and possible reduced morbidity and mortality from coronary artery disease and hip fractures must be factored in when counseling women for overall health benefits versus risks of HRT (13).

One study involved a hypothetical analysis of 10,000 50-year-old women using HRT for 25 years, with health outcomes extrapolated to age 75 (14). In this group, 574 deaths would be prevented, and women using estrogen would gain 3,951 quality-adjusted life years compared with women not using estrogen.

Pregnancy and Breast Cancer

Several studies have been performed to examine morbidity and mortality in pregnant women who develop carcinoma of the breast. Overall, the results do not indicate a reduced survival rate in these individuals despite usually greater nodal involvement (15–18).

Compared with individuals who did not become pregnant, women treated for breast cancer who experience subsequent pregnancy have not been shown to consistently demonstrate either an increased or a decreased risk of recurrence (19–22).

Hormone Replacement Therapy and Risk of Breast Cancer Recurrence

Individuals with prior breast cancer are at increased risk for a second primary breast cancer, and those women with the best prognosis (stage I, small tumors with negative nodes) still have a 30% chance of recurrence in 10 years (23–26). Whether continued exposure to endogenous estrogens is instrumental in this process is unclear. There are no data that support an increased risk of breast cancer recurrence or reduction in survival rate after administration or reinstitution of HRT. Several authors have recently evaluated small groups of selected women using estrogen after being treated for breast cancer (27–30). Although the numbers studied are small, the patients usually are low risk, and the follow-up intervals are short, none of these reports showed evidence of progression or recurrence of disease and one showed fewer tumor recurrences in the HRT group. In addition, the relief of symptoms of estrogen deficiency and the possible reduced risks of osteoporosis and coronary artery disease support consideration of estrogen therapy (31). Patients included in studies are generally those who are otherwise well and may represent predominantly earlier stages of disease. Further studies involving a longer period of observation are necessary to interpret these findings adequately.

Consistent with a possible role for estrogen in recurrent breast cancer is the clinical observation that the selective estrogen receptor modulator (SERM) tamoxifen has a distinctly antiestrogenic profile in regard to its effect on the breast and reduces the rate of breast cancer recurrence (23–26). Tamoxifen now is used frequently as adjunctive therapy in the treatment of breast cancer, particularly in women whose disease is lymph-node negative, hormone-receptor positive (32). The consideration of tamoxifen with estrogen also is being explored (33). The National Surgical Adjuvant Breast and Bowel Project data showed no additional benefit of administration of tamoxifen beyond 5 years in adjunctive treatment of early breast cancer (34).

As a SERM, tamoxifen has estrogenic effects as well. These may one day lead to its use as an alternative to HRT. However, the effects of tamoxifen on preservation of bone density and coronary artery disease must be studied carefully (35). Levels of total cholesterol and low-density lipoprotein cholesterol in serum are lower in women treated with tamoxifen compared with those who are not treated, creating a similar lipid profile to that of postmenopausal women receiving HRT (36, 37). Levels of high-density lipoprotein cholesterol in women using tamoxifen may remain within the pretreatment range or decrease slightly with increased duration of use (36, 37). In addition, it has been reported that tamoxifen may be associated with a reduced calcium loss from bone and a possible reduced incidence of heart disease, although these findings have not been substantiated fully (35–37). The effects of tamoxifen versus estrogen on quality-of-life issues such as effect on genital tissues, dyspareunia, and hot flashes must be considered as well.

Somewhat worrisome is an apparent associated increase in the incidence of abnormal endometrial findings, including malignancy, in tamoxifen-treated patients (38). Although this phenomenon may be dose related or may have resulted from a preexisting endometrial abnormality, there are other features of tamoxifen therapy that point to an estrogen agonistic effect.

More recently, the SERM raloxifene, which is chemically related to tamoxifen, has been developed (39). Although its role in the treatment of breast cancer is unknown, it has offered an alternative to estrogen therapy. Its benefits are preservation of bone density and prevention of osteoporosis. It also appears to be an estrogen antagonist in the endo-metrium as well as in the breast (40). Its influence on lipid profile includes a slight lowering of cholesterol and low-density lipoprotein cholesterol (41). The effect of raloxifene on the central nervous system is unknown, but increased hot flashes are a documented side effect. Venous thromboembolic disease is a contradiction to its use.

Steroid Contraceptives and Breast Cancer Development

Steroid contraceptives theoretically may increase the risk of development or recurrence of breast cancer. Recent reviews of combination preparations with lower estrogen dosage (≤ 35 mcg of ethinyl estradiol) showed no evidence of a worse prognosis in a small number of women using oral contraceptive pills in the year preceding breast cancer diagnosis. Also, tumors seen in oral contraceptive users were better differentiated (42). The World Health Organization Collaborative Study of Neoplasia and Steroid Contraceptives suggested that contraceptive doses of

progestins taken long term did not appear to increase the risk of breast cancer (43).

Research Limitations

Although many studies have looked at the risks of development or recurrence of breast cancer in association with HRT, steroid contraceptive use, and pregnancy, accurate interpretation of the data remains difficult.

Study parameters, such as design, medication types or dosages, patient age, or length of medication use, may vary in research in general, although such variations have been a particular problem when evaluating evidence for the role of HRT in development or recurrence of breast cancer. Similarly, numbers of study subjects and length of follow-up differ widely. The number of variables makes confounding factors possible. In addition, comparing qualitative outcomes, such as relief of menopausal symptoms and other quality-of-life issues, with numerical values (quantitative statistics) is controversial.

Interpretation of the results of studies in this review is difficult because relative risks reported are usually between 1.0 and 2.0. Such low levels of relative risk may be due to slight actual increased risk or to confounding factors or study biases.

Conclusions

There are no conclusive data to indicate an increased risk of recurrent breast cancer in postmenopausal women receiving HRT. No woman can be guaranteed protection from recurrence. Late manifestations of recurrent disease and an apparent predisposition to recurrence shown by selected subgroups of women cannot be ignored. However, the benefits of HRT are well recognized and contribute to the quality and length of life in postmenopausal women.

The following recommendations are made for postmenopausal women with previously treated breast cancer:

- The use of HRT may be considered.
- Because there are no specific data regarding particular stages or histologic types of breast cancer in which HRT may have a greater or lesser effect on breast cancer progression, caution must be exercised in all instances.
- Hormone replacement therapy should always be used in a treatment plan that includes dietary control, exercise, and, when appropriate, weight reduction and behavior modification, such as cessation of smoking and reduction of alcohol intake.

- Women with breast cancer who use HRT must continue to be monitored for recurrent disease, and, if malignancy recurs further, the use of HRT must be reevaluated.
- When the clinician explains the benefits of HRT use to the patient, this must be accompanied by a thorough explanation of the extent of current knowledge that, by necessity, will entail consultation with the patient's oncologist.

The uncertainty of this dilemma supports the need for extensive randomized, prospective trials in order to provide women with a rational and reasonable basis for therapeutic alternatives.

References

1. Thomas DB, Persing JP, Hutchinson WB. Exogenous estrogens and other risk factors for breast cancer in women with benign breast disease. J Natl Cancer Inst 1982;69:1017–1025
2. Brinton LA, Hoover RN, Szklo M, Fraumeni JF Jr. Menopausal estrogen use and risk of breast cancer. Cancer 1981;47:2517–2522
3. Hoover R, Gray LA Sr, Cole P, MacMahon B. Menopausal estrogens and breast cancer. N Engl J Med 1976;295:401–405
4. Ross RK, Paganini-Hill A, Gerkins VR, Mack TM, Pfeffer R, Arthur M, et al. A case-control study of menopausal estrogen therapy and breast cancer. JAMA 1980;243:1635–1639
5. Hoover R, Glass A, Finkle WD, Azevedo D, Milne K. Conjugated estrogens and breast cancer risk in women. J Natl Cancer Inst 1981;67:815–820
6. Armstrong BK. Oestrogen therapy after the menopause—boon or bane? Med J Aust 1988;148:213–214
7. Henrich JB. The postmenopausal estrogen/breast cancer controversy. JAMA 1992;268:1900–1902
8. Dupont WD, Page DL. Menopausal estrogen replacement therapy and breast cancer. Arch Intern Med 1991;151:67–72
9. Steinberg KK, Thacker SB, Smith SJ, Stroup DF, Zack MM, Flanders WD, et al. A meta-analysis of the effect of estrogen replacement therapy on the risk of breast cancer. JAMA 1991;265:1985–1990
10. Sillero-Arenas M, Delgado-Rodriguez M, Rodrigues-Canteras R, Bueno-Cavanillas A, Galvez-Vargas R. Menopausal hormone replacement therapy and breast cancer: a meta-analysis. Obstet Gynecol 1992;79:286–294
11. Colditz GA, Egan KM, Stampfer MJ. Hormone replacement therapy and risk of breast cancer: results from epidemiologic studies. Am J Obstet Gynecol 1993;168:1473–1480
12. Wren BG, Eden JA. Do progestogens reduce the risk of breast cancer? A review of the evidence. Menopause 1996;3:4–12
13. Col NF, Eckman MH, Karas RH, Pauker SG, Goldberg RJ, Ross EM, et al. Patient-specific decisions about hormone replacement therapy in postmenopausal women. JAMA 1997;277:1140–1147
14. Gorsky RD, Koplan JP, Peterson HB, Thacker SB. Relative risks and benefits of long-term estrogen replacement therapy: a decision analysis. Obstet Gynecol 1994; 83:161–166
15. Ribeiro G, Jones DA, Jones M. Carcinoma of the breast associated with pregnancy. Br J Surg 1986;73:607–609
16. Donegan WL. Breast cancer and pregnancy. Obstet Gynecol 1977;50:244–252
17. White TT, White WC. Breast cancer and pregnancy; report of 49 cases followed 5 years. Ann Surg 1956;144:384–393
18. King RM, Welch JS, Martin JK Jr, Coulam CB. Carcinoma of the breast associated with pregnancy. Surg Gynecol Obstet 1985;160:228–232
19. Cooper DR, Butterfield J. Pregnancy subsequent to mastectomy for cancer of the breast. Ann Surg 1970;171: 429–433
20. Rissanen PM. Pregnancy following treatment of mammary carcinoma. Acta Radiol Ther Phys Biol 1969;8:415– 422
21. Lambe M, Hsieh C, Trichopoulos D, Ekbom A, Pavia M, Adami HO. Transient increase in the risk of breast cancer after giving birth. N Engl J Med 1994:331:5–9
22. Guinee VF, Olsson H, Moller T, Hess KR, Taylor SH, Fahey T, et al. Effect of pregnancy on prognosis for young women with breast cancer. Lancet 1994:343:1587–1589
23. Systemic treatment of early breast cancer by hormonal, cytotoxic, or immune therapy. 133 randomised trials involving 31,000 recurrences and 24,000 deaths among 75,000 women. Early Breast Cancer Trialists' Collaborative Group. Lancet 1992;339:1–15
24. Systemic treatment of early breast cancer by hormonal, cytotoxic, or immune therapy. 133 randomised trials involving 31,000 recurrences and 24,000 deaths among 75,000 women. Early Breast Cancer Trialists' Collaborative Group. Lancet 1992;339:71–85
25. Forbes JF. The control of breast cancer: the role of tamoxifen. Semin Oncol 1997;24(Suppl 1):S1-5–S1-19
26. Powles TJ. Efficacy of tamoxifen as therapy of breast cancer. Semin Oncol 1997;24(Suppl 1):S1-48–S1-54
27. DiSaia PJ, Odicino F, Grosen EA, Cowan B, Pecorelli S, Wile AG. Hormone replacement therapy in breast cancer. Lancet 1993;342:1232
28. Powles TJ, Hickish T, Casey S, O'Brien M. Hormone replacement after breast cancer. Lancet 1993;342:60–61
29. Wile AG, Opfell RW, Margileth DA. Hormone replacement therapy in previously treated breast cancer patients. Am J Surg 1993;165:372–375
30. Dhodapkar MV, Ingle JN, Ahmann DL. Estrogen replacement therapy withdrawal and regression of metastatic breast cancer. Cancer 1995;75:43–46
31. Roy JA, Sawka CA, Pritchard KI. Hormone replacement therapy in women with breast cancer. Do the risks outweigh the benefits? J Clin Oncol 1996;14:997–1006
32. Fisher B, Costantino J, Redmond C, Poisson R, Bowman D, Couture J, et al. A randomized clinical trial evaluating tamoxifen in the treatment of patients with node-negative breast cancer who have estrogen-receptor-positive tumors. N Engl J Med 1989;320:479–484
33. Powles TJ. Tamoxifen and oestrogen replacement. Lancet 1990;336:48
34. Fisher B, Costantino JP, Redmond CK, Fisher ER, Wickerham DL, Cronin WM. Endometrial cancer in tamoxifen-treated breast cancer patients: findings from the National Surgical Adjuvant Breast and Bowel Project (NSABP) B-14. J Natl Cancer Inst 1994:86:527–537
35. Love RR, Mazess RB, Barden HS, Epstein S, Newcomb PA, Jordan VC, et al. Effects of tamoxifen on bone mineral

density in postmenopausal women with breast cancer. N Engl J Med 1992;326:852–856

36. Love RR, Surawicz TS, Williams EC. Antithrombin III level, fibrinogen level, and platelet count changes with adjuvant tamoxifen therapy. Arch Intern Med 1992;152: 317–320

37. Love RR, Wiebe DA, Newcombe PA, Cameron L, Leventhal H, Jordan VC, et al. Effects of tamoxifen on cardiovascular risk factors in postmenopausal women. Ann Intern Med 1991;115:860–864

38. Kedar RP, Bourne TH, Powles TJ, Collins WP, Ashley SE, Cosgrove DO, et al. Effects of tamoxifen on uterus and ovaries of postmenopausal women in a randomised breast cancer prevention trial. Lancet 1994;343:1318–1321

39. Mitlak BH, Cohen FJ. In search of optimal long-term female hormone replacement: the potential of selective estrogen receptor modulators. Horm Res 1997;48: 155–163

40. Delmas PD, Bjarnason NH, Mitlak BH, Ravoux AC, Shah AS, Huster WJ, et al. Effects of raloxifene on bone mineral density, serum cholesterol concentrations, and uterine endometrium in postmenopausal women. N Engl J Med 1997;337:1641–1647

41. Walsh BW, Kuller LH, Wild RA, Paul S, Farmer M, Lawrence JB, et al. Effects of raloxifene on serum lipids and coagulation factors in healthy postmenopausal women. JAMA 1998;279:1445–1451

42. Breast cancer and hormonal contraceptives: collaborative reanalysis of individual data on 53,297 women with breast cancer and 100,239 women without breast cancer from 54 epidemiological studies. Collaborative Group on Hormonal Factors in Breast Cancer. Lancet 1996;347:1713–1727

43. Breast cancer and depot-medroxyprogesterone acetate: a multinational study. WHO Collaborative Study of Neoplasia and Steroid Contraceptives. Lancet 1991;338:833–838

ACOG

Committee on
Coding and
Nomenclature

Committee Opinion

Number 250, January 2001

Inappropriate Reimbursement Practices by Third-Party Payers

The American College of Obstetricians and Gynecologists (ACOG) Committee on Coding and Nomenclature believes that physicians must code accurately the services they provide and the diagnoses that justify those services for purposes of appropriate payment. This requirement is consistent with the rules established by the American Medical Association (AMA) Current Procedural Terminology Editorial Panel and published as the *Current Procedural Terminology* (CPT) and with those established by the International Classification of Diseases, Ninth Revision, Clinical Modification (ICD-9-CM), which are published in the American Hospital Association's *ICD-9-CM Coding Clinic*. In fairness, payers should be equally obligated to pay physicians based on the CPT standards and accept for processing all ICD-9-CM codes recorded on the claim. Currently, no such obligation for payers exists.

Inappropriate Billing Denials

Five frequently encountered billing situations account for most payers' inappropriate first-time total or partial denials of correctly coded services. Each of these situations can inappropriately deny payment to physicians for medically indicated and correctly coded services because of payers' payment policies.

1. Inappropriately bundling correctly coded multiple surgical procedures—Current Procedural Terminology clearly describes surgical procedures that may be performed to treat various conditions. Each CPT code describes a specific procedure that was valued under the Resource Based Relative Value Scale (RBRVS) on the basis of a description of the work it entails. Many patients, especially those with complex clinical situations, need more than one surgical procedure to be performed at an operative session. For instance, a patient may require a vaginal hysterectomy because of severe irregular bleeding, but also might require repair of a symptomatic cystocele and rectocele. Because no single CPT code describes this combination of procedures, the physician should apply multiple CPT codes with appropriate modifiers to the secondary procedures as mandated by

Requests for authorization to make photocopies should be directed to:

Copyright Clearance Center
222 Rosewood Drive
Danvers, MA 01923
(978) 750-8400

ISSN 1074-861X

The American College of Obstetricians and Gynecologists
409 12th Street, SW
PO Box 96920
Washington, DC 20090-6920

12345/54321

CPT rules. Furthermore, the physician should expect reimbursement for all of the provided services defined by the CPT codes.

Despite the accuracy of the above statement regarding reimbursement for multiple procedures, payers often cite the efforts of Medicare to reduce payments for inappropriately unbundled CPT codes by physicians as justification for denial of physician claims for appropriately coded services. Indeed, the Health Care Financing Administration has established the Correct Coding Initiative (CCI), a process for bundling together many services that should not be paid separately. The process continues to undergo refinement with input from the AMA and medical specialty societies.

Unfortunately, some commercial software products that do not adhere to either CPT or CCI guidelines are being used by third-party payers to identify CPT codes for services that will not be reimbursed when coded together. For example, some of these products incorrectly bundle anterior and posterior colporrhaphy with enterocele repair into the code for vaginal hysterectomy, presumably because all of these procedures are performed through a vaginal approach. The AMA Correct Coding and Policy Committee, with input from ACOG staff, has identified many instances of inappropriate denial of reimbursement with some of these commercial bundling products. Physicians should appeal such denials (see the box) and cite the content of this document in requesting appropriate payment for these services.

2. *Ignoring modifiers that explain qualifying circumstances*—Current Procedural Terminology modifiers provide a coding shorthand that helps explain situations for which either increased or reduced payment is justified. There is, at present, no insurance industry standard for recognizing modifiers.

The American College of Obstetricians and Gynecologists believes that third-party payers should follow existing CPT guidelines and coding options, including recognition of all CPT modifiers, to ensure that all circumstances concerning the service performed are recognized. Payers who ignore correctly applied CPT modifiers inappropriately underreimburse physicians for the services provided.

3. *Denying payment for diagnostic and therapeutic procedures performed on the same day of service*—In certain clinical situations, a diagnostic surgical procedure is performed to determine

---

Seven Steps for Appealing Denied Claims

Take these steps when appealing inappropriate reimbursement practices by third-party payers:

1. Keep in mind that this is a negotiation process that will succeed only if the insurer is convinced that a charge is fair for the patient and the physician. It is important to use accepted coding standards when attempting to show that an insurer's policy is wrong. Polite but direct communication is more likely to achieve desired results than confrontation.

2. Have your staff contact the claims department of the insurer and discuss the reason for denial with the claims processor. These discussions should be based on clinical facts that rely on the Current Procedural Terminology (CPT) code definition of the service and the standard of care implied by the CPT code as it was valued under the Medicare Resource Based Relative Value Scale (RBRVS) system. Document all communication with the insurer (date, person from office making the call, person spoken with, results).

3. If staff is unsuccessful, contact the medical director of the payer yourself. Maintain open lines of communication with the medical director to discuss inappropriate payment policies and accepted coding standards.

4. Involve the state medical society in disputes with insurers. Many state societies will become very involved when patterns of abuse emerge.

5. Contact the American College of Obstetricians and Gynecologists (ACOG) for assistance in dealing with inappropriately denied medically indicated services that are covered by the patient's insurance policy and clearly were correctly reported. Contact ACOG's Department of Health Economics by fax or mail after downloading a complaint form from ACOG's web site (www.acog.org), or call (202) 863-2447 for assistance.

6. Send a copy of any correspondence between the practice and the payer dealing with unresolved problems to the insurance commissioner or equivalent regulatory authority in your state.

7. Involve your patient when inappropriate billing problems cannot be resolved in other ways. Physicians are not responsible for the insurance plan selected by the patient. Many third-party payers will revise their payment policies when they receive a complaint from the patient or patient's employer or union.

whether a therapeutic surgical procedure is required. When this occurs, it often is appropriate for the two procedures to be done at one time rather than at two distinct times. For example, if a diagnostic laparoscopy for a suspected benign condition reveals cancer, the physician may decide to perform a laparotomy to remove the cancer at the same operative session. In such a situation, many payers deny payment for the diagnostic laparoscopy even though performance of both the diagnostic and therapeutic procedures at the same time is medically indicated and requires additional physician work above that of the therapeutic procedure alone. In accordance with CPT guidelines, both procedures should be coded and the physician should be paid for both when the procedures have been documented appropriately and coded correctly. In the example, proper coding for the diagnostic service in addition to a therapeutic procedure would at the present time require the use of modifier –59 to identify the diagnostic procedure as distinct. In addition, however, the diagnostic procedure must be justified with a specific ICD-9-CM diagnostic code, which may or may not be the same as the ICD-9-CM code for the therapeutic procedure.

The practice by payers of bundling diagnostic and therapeutic procedures to reduce physicians' payment is inappropriate. Physicians have a legal obligation to code correctly. Insurers are equally obligated not to alter coding by physicians that is in accordance with approved CPT guidelines.

4. *Precertifying consultations at a predetermined level*—Some payers require precertification of a consultation and typically authorize a predetermined level of service based on the diagnostic information provided by the physician who requested the consultation. By contrast, the CPT guidelines state that the correct level of consultation is determined by the extent of the history, physical examination, and complexity of the medical decision-making process for each patient. This definition of services was used by Medicare under RBRVS to assign the relative value for physician consultation. Each patient who requires a consultation does so with a medical history typically including co-morbidities that can dramatically alter the physician work required to provide this service. Often such co-morbidities will necessitate a more thorough history and physical examination and involve more complex medical decision making than required in their absence. For example, a

request for a consultation to assess fetal well-being in an otherwise healthy patient who has had an uneventful pregnancy will not resemble a consultation for this same problem when the patient has preexisting complications of pregnancy, such as cardiac disease, uncontrolled diabetes mellitus, or a history of poor obstetric outcomes.

Because it is not possible to determine prospectively the level of service that will be required to evaluate and recommend treatment based on the uniqueness of each patient's problems, payers should precertify for an unspecified level of consultation that is paid at the appropriate level once the service has been provided.

5. *Denying diagnostic tests or studies performed at the same encounter as a distinct evaluation and management service*—The CPT manual states:

> The actual performance and/or interpretation of diagnostic tests/studies ordered during a patient encounter are not included in the levels of [evaluation and management (E/M)] services. Physician performance of diagnostic tests/studies for which specific CPT codes are available may be reported separately, in addition to the appropriate E/M code.

With this statement, CPT has clarified that diagnostic tests and studies, including colposcopies, biopsies, diagnostic ultrasound examinations, and cystometrics, are ordered on the basis of clinical criteria for each patient and not as a routine service. This definition means that tests performed at the time of an outpatient or other E/M encounter are not to be paid as part of the E/M service, but rather are to be paid separately. The E/M codes in CPT were valued under the Medicare RBRVS fee schedule on the basis of the CPT guidelines; these values do not include any diagnostic tests or studies.

The payer may deny reimbursement of diagnostic tests or studies at the time of an E/M encounter because the payer's payment policies might have been formulated with a lack of understanding of CPT coding standards that separate physician work included with the E/M service from the diagnostic test or study. This lack of understanding may lead the payer to inappropriately include all services provided to the patient at the E/M encounter as part of that service. The payer also may deny payment because the physician failed to add a modifier –25 to the billed E/M code to bypass the payer's established coding edits to ensure appropriate payment for both services.

Possible Remedies

The physician should ensure that his or her billing staff are knowledgeable about:

- What is normally included and what is excluded from the service being billed (This information is provided in the most current edition of ACOG's *OB-GYN Coding Manual: Components of Correct Procedural Coding.**)
- How to link each service billed with one or more specific ICD-9-CM diagnostic codes that specifically justifies the reason for the service (This information is available in the most current edition of ACOG's *ICD-9-CM: Diagnostic Coding in Obstetrics and Gynecology.**)

---

* These resources are available from the American College of Obstetricians and Gynecologists.

- The correct application of CPT modifiers, when indicated (This information may be found in the appendixes of the current AMA CPT manual and in the current edition of ACOG's *CPT Coding in Obstetrics and Gynecology.**)
- Billing rules established by individual payers

The billing office should communicate clearly the indication for performing all coded services on the same date of service by reporting the most specific ICD-9-CM diagnostic codes. In some encounters, the justification for all services rendered may be documented by a single ICD-9-CM code. When a patient has multiple complaints or problems, multiple ICD-9-CM codes should be used.

Committee Opinion

Number 197, February 1998   (*Replaces #137, April 1994*)

Inappropriate Use of the Terms Fetal Distress and Birth Asphyxia

The Committee on Obstetric Practice is concerned about the continued use of the terms *fetal distress* as an antepartum or intrapartum diagnosis and *birth asphyxia* as a neonatal diagnosis. The Committee reaffirms that the term *fetal distress* is imprecise and nonspecific. The term has a low positive predictive value even in high-risk populations and is often associated with an infant who is in good condition at birth as determined by the Apgar score or umbilical cord blood gas analysis or both. The communication between clinicians caring for the woman and those caring for her neonate is best served by replacing the term *fetal distress* with *nonreassuring fetal status,* followed by a further description of findings (eg, repetitive variable decelerations, fetal bradycardia, and biophysical profile score of 2). Whereas *fetal distress* implies an ill fetus, *nonreassuring fetal status* describes the clinician's interpretation of data regarding fetal status (ie, the clinician is not reassured by the findings). This acknowledges the imprecision inherent in the interpre-tation of the data. Accordingly, the term *nonreassuring fetal status* is consistent with the delivery of a vigorous infant, and a good outcome does not have to be justified.

Because of the limitations of the term *fetal distress,* its use may result in inappropriate actions, such as an unnecessarily urgent delivery under general anesthesia. Fetal heart rate patterns or auscultatory findings should be considered when the degree of urgency, mode of delivery, and type of anesthesia to be given are determined. Performing a cesarean delivery for a nonreassuring fetal heart rate pattern does not necessarily preclude the use of regional anesthesia.

Effective October 1, 1998, all inclusion terms except *metabolic acidemia* will be removed from the current International Classification of Diseases (ICD) code for fetal distress. All other terms will be indexed to a new code to indicate an abnormality of the heart rate or rhythm, or they will be referenced to other more appropriate codes. A similar revision will be made to the perinatal ICD codes used by pediatricians. These changes have been made because of the waning use of *fetal distress* in clinical practice.

The term *asphyxia* should be reserved for the clinical context of damaging acidemia, hypoxia, and metabolic acidosis. The Committee strongly sup-

Copyright © February 1998
ISSN 1074-861X

The American College of Obstetricians and Gynecologists
409 12th Street, SW
PO Box 96920
Washington, DC 20090-6920

12345/21098

ports the concept that a neonate who has had hypoxia proximate to delivery severe enough to result in hypoxic encephalopathy will show other signs of hypoxic damage, including all of the following:

- Profound metabolic or mixed acidemia (pH <7.00) on an umbilical cord arterial blood sample, if obtained

- Persistent Apgar score of 0–3 for longer than 5 minutes

- Evidence of neonatal neurologic sequelae (eg, seizures, coma, hypotonia, and one or more of the following: cardiovascular, gastrointestinal, hematologic, pulmonary, or renal system dysfunction)

ACOG Committee Opinion

Number 164, December 1995

Incidental Appendectomy

Incidental appendectomy is defined as the surgical removal of the appendix at the time of a procedure unrelated to appendiceal pathology. Routine performance of incidental appendectomy has been controversial for almost 100 years. In the past, concern focused primarily on the procedure's safety. Numerous studies attest to the safety of the procedure at the time of laparotomy, with the possible exception of an increased risk of postoperative wound infections in patients older than 65. Safety has been less well documented when the procedure is done laparoscopically.

More recently, the debate has focused on the cost–benefit issue, especially in persons at low risk for appendicitis. Throughout this century, the incidence of appendicitis and its associated morbidity and mortality have fallen precipitously. Based on the work of Addiss et al (1), the preventive value of incidental appendectomy for women was studied. With the exception of the very youngest age groups, it is clear that the preventive value of incidental appendectomy is relatively low.

Conversely, very little objective analytical data exist comparing costs. In 1987, Sugimoto and Edwards conducted a cost analysis of incidental appendectomy (2). The cost savings associated with prevented cases was well below the cost of incidental appendectomy. The authors therefore concluded that the morbidity and mortality associated with appendicitis was not significant when compared with the cost of incidental appendectomies aimed at prevention.

Although incidental appendectomy, performed by either laparotomy or laparoscopy, may only be routinely indicated in certain select groups of patients, the benefits of eliminating future emergency appendectomy and simplifying the differential diagnosis of pelvic pain may outweigh any risk or cost concerns (3–7). These subgroups include women 10–30 years of age (high-incidence group), women undergoing exploratory surgery for unexplained pelvic or right lower quadrant pain, or women in whom endometriosis is found. Other subgroups include women in whom abdominal radiation is anticipated, the mentally handicapped or those unable to provide a clear history, and women undergoing extensive surgery in whom major adhesions are anticipated postoperatively or there are other relative contraindications to abdominal surgery in the future. Patients with fixation of the appendix to the ovary or tube and patients with appendiceal calculus or fecalith should be considered for appendectomy as a definite prophylactic measure.

Nonemergent appendectomy is contraindicated in certain patients. These include those with known Crohn disease, an inaccessible appendix, a history of prior abdominal radiation treatment, or presence of vascular grafts or material in the abdomen and those whose medical condition is unstable at the time.

In conclusion, incidental appendectomy appears to be associated with slight if any increased risk to patients in otherwise good condition. However, except for a select group of patients, the benefit of this procedure to the patient may also be slight.

References

1. Addiss DG, Shaffer N, Fowler BS, Tauxe RV. The epidemiology of appendicitis and appendectomy in the United States. Am J Epidemiol 1990;132:910–925

2. Sugimoto T, Edwards D. Incidence and costs of incidental appendectomy as a preventive measure. Am J Public Health 1987;77:471–475

3. Grimes DA. Frontiers of operative laparoscopy: a review and critique of the evidence. Am J Obstet Gynecol 1992; 166:1062–1071

4. Luckmann R. Incidence and case fatality rates for acute appendicitis in California. A population-based study of the effects of age. Am J Epidemiol 1989;129:905–918

5. Nezhat C, Nezhat F. Incidental appendectomy during videolaseroscopy. Am J Obstet Gynecol 1991;165:559–564

6. Pelosi MA, Villalona E. Laparoscopic hysterectomy, appendectomy, and cholecystectomy. N J Med 1993;90: 207–212

7. Warren JL, Penberthy LT, Addiss DG, McBean AM. Appendectomy incidental to cholecystectomy among elderly Medicare beneficiaries. Surg Gynecol Obstet 1993; 177:288–294

ACOG

Committee on
Obstetric Practice

Committee Opinion

Number 228, November 1999

Induction of Labor with Misoprostol

Induction of labor is a common obstetric intervention in the United States, occurring in up to 15% of all pregnancies. The American College of Obstetricians and Gynecologists supports induction of labor as a worthwhile therapeutic option when the benefits of expeditious delivery outweigh the risks of continuing the pregnancy (1). Prostaglandin E_2 (PGE_2), applied locally to the cervix or vagina, has been widely studied as an induction agent, and has been found to be safe and effective (2, 3). Two such agents have been approved by the U.S. Food and Drug Administration for this purpose and are commercially available as dinoprostone preparations. Recent studies have explored the effectiveness and safety of misoprostol for induction of labor. This prostaglandin E_1 analogue is less expensive, more stable, and easier to store than dinoprostone preparations. However, misoprostol currently is approved by the U.S. Food and Drug Administration for the treatment of peptic ulcer disease and not for induction of labor. Moreover, the manufacturer does not plan to pursue approval for this indication (4).

At least 19 prospective, randomized clinical trials involving more than 1,900 patients receiving doses of misoprostol ranging from 25 mcg to 200 mcg in a variety of dosage schedules have been performed. Most researchers have administered misoprostol in tablet form into the posterior fornix of the vagina, but it also has been mixed into a hydroxymethylcellulose gel or applied intracervically.

In general, misoprostol has been found to be an effective agent for the induction of labor. When compared with placebo, misoprostol use decreased oxytocin requirements and achieved higher rates of vaginal delivery within 24 hours of induction. Misoprostol also compared favorably with intracervical and intravaginal PGE_2 preparations; many studies demonstrated shorter times to delivery and reduced oxytocin requirements after misoprostol administration (5). Some studies suggest that misoprostol may reduce the rate of cesarean delivery, but further randomized clinical trials using the 25 mcg dose are required to confirm this observation (5). There have been reports of uterine rupture following misoprostol use for cervical ripening in patients with prior uterine surgery. Thus, until reassuring studies are available, misoprostol is not recommended for cervical ripening in patients who have had prior cesarean delivery or major uterine surgery (6).

When given in doses of 50 mcg or more, misoprostol use has been associated with an increased rate of uterine tachysystole (six or more uterine con-

ISSN 1074-861X

The American College of Obstetricians and Gynecologists
409 12th Street, SW
PO Box 96920
Washington, DC 20090-6920

12345/32109

tractions in 10 minutes in consecutive 10-minute intervals) compared with either placebo or PGE_2 preparations. In two studies in which 50 mcg of misoprostol was administered intravaginally every 4 hours, researchers found increased rates of meconium passage (7) and cesarean delivery due to uterine hyperstimulation syndrome (8) when compared with dinoprostone. However, an increase in neonatal morbidity after misoprostol administration has not been documented. In trials where 25 mcg of misoprostol was administered intravaginally as frequently as every 3 hours, there did not appear to be an increase in uterine tachysystole, hyperstimulation, or meconium passage when compared with PGE_2 (9, 10). Moreover, this dosing regimen appeared to be at least as effective in inducing labor as the PGE_2 preparations.

Currently, misoprostol is available in 100 mcg and 200 mcg tablets, and the 100 mcg tablet is not scored. If misoprostol is used for cervical ripening and induction, one quarter of a 100 mcg tablet (ie, approximately 25 mcg) should be considered for the initial dose.

Given the current evidence, intravaginal misoprostol tablets appear to be effective in inducing labor in pregnant women who have unfavorable cervices. The use of higher doses (50 mcg every 6 hours) may be appropriate in some situations, although increasing the dose appears to be associated most closely with uterine tachysystole and possibly with uterine hyperstimulation and meconium staining of amniotic fluid. Further prospective trials are required to define an optimal dosing regimen for misoprostol. However, misoprostol is not recommended for patients with prior uterine surgery (11). Patients undergoing such therapy should receive fetal heart rate and uterine activity monitoring in a hospital setting until further studies evaluate and confirm the safety of outpatient therapy.

References

1. American College of Obstetricians and Gynecologists. Induction of labor. ACOG Practice Bulletin. Washington, DC: ACOG, 1999
2. Brindley BA, Sokol RJ. Induction and augmentation of labor: basis and methods for current practice. Obstet Gynecol Surv 1988;43:730–743
3. Rayburn WF. Prostaglandin E_2 gel for cervical ripening and induction of labor: a critical analysis. Am J Obstet Gynecol 1989;160:529–534
4. Bauer TA, Brown D, Chai LK. Vaginal misoprostol for term labor induction. Ann Pharmacother 1997;31:1391–1393
5. Sanchez-Ramos L, Kaunitz AM, Wears RL, Delke I, Gaudier FL. Misoprostol for cervical ripening and labor induction: a meta-analysis. Obstet Gynecol 1997;89:633–642
6. Hofmeyr GJ. Vaginal misoprostol for cervical ripening and labour induction in late pregnancy. The Cochrane Library 1999; Issue 2:1–18 (Meta-analysis)
7. Wing DA, Jones MM, Rahall A, Goodwin TM, Paul RH. A comparison of misoprostol and prostaglandin E_2 gel for preinduction cervical ripening and labor induction. Am J Obstet Gynecol 1995;172:1804–1810
8. Buser D, Mora G, Arias F. A randomized comparison between misoprostol and dinoprostone for cervical ripening and labor induction in patients with unfavorable cervices. Obstet Gynecol 1997;89:581–585
9. Wing DA, Paul RH. A comparison of different dosing regimens of vaginally administered misoprostol for preinduction cervical ripening and labor induction. Am J Obstet Gynecol 1996;175:158–164
10. Wing DA, Ortiz-Omphroy G, Paul RH. A comparison of intermittent vaginal administration of misoprostol with continuous dinoprostone for cervical ripening and labor induction. Am J Obstet Gynecol 1997;177:612–618
11. Wing DA, Lovett K, Paul RH. Disruption of prior uterine incision following misoprostol for labor induction in women with previous cesarean section. Obstet Gynecol 1998;91:828–830

ACOG

Committee on
Professional Liability

Committee Opinion

Number 237, June 2000   *(Replaces No. 166, December 1995)*

Informed Refusal

Informed refusal is a relatively recent concept of law regarding patient–physician relations, and it has developed in conjunction with the law of informed consent. Almost universally, informed-consent laws have been liberalized in recent years from the relatively paternalistic "professional or reasonable physician" standard to the "materiality or patient viewpoint" standard. In the professional or reasonable physician standard, a physician must disclose to a patient the risks and benefits that are customarily disclosed by the medical community for that treatment, test, or procedure. In the materiality or patient viewpoint standard, a physician must disclose to the patient the risks and benefits that a reasonable person in the patient's position would want to know in order to make an informed decision. As the perspective for evaluating the level of disclosure of risks and benefits in informed consent has changed, it has become clear that patients are entitled to participate with their physicians in a process of shared decision making with regard to medical procedures, tests, or treatments (1).

Once a patient has been informed of the material risks and benefits involved with a treatment, test, or procedure, that patient has the right to exercise full autonomy in deciding whether to undergo the treatment, test, or procedure or whether to make a choice among a variety of treatments, tests, or procedures. In the exercise of that autonomy, the informed patient also has the right to refuse to undergo any of these treatments, tests, or procedures. This election by the patient to forgo a treatment, test, or procedure that has been offered or recommended by the physician constitutes informed refusal.

Documentation always has been an important component of informed consent. Performing an operative procedure on a patient without the patient's permission can constitute "battery" under common law. In most circumstances this is a criminal act, and documentation of the patient's consent is protection against liability. In many instances, the documentation is an informed-consent form signed by the patient, but in some situations a notation in the patient's medical record is sufficient and appropriate.

Documentation rarely has been an important component of informed refusal in the past but has become more important in the present health care environment. Managed care and increased patient autonomy are two factors that warrant a reexamination of the need for documentation of informed refusal. The widespread implementation of managed care and utilization review has created a conflict between cost containment and medical necessity.

It is not uncommon for a physician to recommend a treatment, test, or procedure to a patient that will not be paid for by a third-party insurance carrier, in whole or in part. Legal precedents have established that an attending physician should act as a patient advocate in such coverage disputes and attempt to convince the managed care organization that coverage is warranted. In spite of that obligation, however, there will be many situations in which physician advocacy will not prevail and coverage will be denied. In such circumstances, a physician should discuss with the patient whether she wishes to pay for the treatment, test, or procedure personally or seek alternative funding. If the patient then refuses to undergo the treatment, test, or procedure for economic reasons, the physician should document that informed refusal in the patient's medical record. In some situations the physician might want to obtain a written statement from the patient, acknowledging that the risk of refusal was fully explained.

The increased respect accorded individual patient autonomy in medical decision making has given rise to other circumstances when documentation of an informed refusal is appropriate. In spite of a physician's medical advice or recommendation, a patient who is informed of the material risks and benefits of a particular treatment, test, or procedure may elect to forgo all or some of these or may decline a procedure or test that might be recommended or become necessary during treatment. Such a refusal may be based on religious beliefs, personal preference, or comfort.

Whenever a patient refuses a treatment, test, or procedure, a physician should document the informed refusal in the patient's medical record and include the following information:

- The patient's refusal to consent to a treatment, test, or procedure
- The reasons stated by the patient for refusal
- Documentation that the need for the treatment, test, or procedure has been explained
- A statement that the consequences of the refusal, including possible jeopardy to health or life, have been described to the patient

Reference

1. American College of Obstetricians and Gynecologists. Ethical dimensions of informed consent. ACOG Committee Opinion 108. Washington, DC: ACOG, 1992

ACOG

Committee on
Gynecologic Practice

Committee Opinion

Number 191, October 1997   (*Replaces #134, March 1994*)

Length of Hospital Stay for Gynecologic Procedures

The American College of Obstetricians and Gynecologists is concerned about the compromise in quality of care that can occur as a result of the "cost-saving" measure of reducing length of hospital stay. Length-of-stay normative data record the average stay in hospital days for a given gynecologic procedure and reflect generally recognized practice across geographic areas. These data have changed radically in the past several years and are continuing to change.

Length-of-stay determinants are based upon a range of individual factors, such as concurrent disease process, severity of illness, intensity of care required, and therapeutic approach. Although standard protocols or predetermined number of days for length of stay can offer general guidance, individual patient characteristics, physician judgment, and physician–patient consultation always should determine length of stay in individual cases.

After gynecologic surgery, a patient's readiness for release from the hospital should be based on positive discharge criteria. These criteria generally include (but are not limited to)

- Stable vital signs
- No evidence of untreated infections
- Adequate oral intake
- Satisfactory bowel and urinary tract function

Before discharge, instructions regarding diet, medications, wound and drainage device care, activity, and follow-up should be communicated to the patient or her caregivers. The patient or her caregivers should understand the instructions and be able to provide ongoing care and monitor recovery as needed.

The American College of Obstetricians and Gynecologists

409 12th Street, SW
PO Box 96920
Washington, DC 20090-6920

12345/10987

ACOG

Committee on
Gynecologic Practice

Committee Opinion

Number 245, December 2000

Mifepristone for Medical Pregnancy Termination

Mifepristone (RU-486), an antiprogestin, has been approved by the U.S. Food and Drug Administration (FDA) for use in combination with the prostaglandin misoprostol as a medical method for terminating intrauterine pregnancy up to 49 days from the first day of the last menstrual period.

This method has been well-tested and extensively used. Since 1988, almost 500,000 women in 20 countries have used mifepristone in combination with one of several prostaglandins to terminate intrauterine pregnancies (1). This method is very effective: studies indicate one dose of mifepristone, when combined with one dose of misoprostol 2 days later, is 92–99% successful in terminating intrauterine pregnancies up to 49 days from the first day of the last menstrual period (2). Accurate dating of gestational age is essential to reduce complications and increase efficacy. Failures include an ongoing pregnancy rate of 1% or less and a rate of incomplete abortion requiring surgical intervention of 5% or less (2).

This regimen appears to be as safe as surgical abortion performed under the safest conditions (3). It is usually well-tolerated and has been reported to be acceptable by the majority of women using it (1). Vaginal bleeding, a natural consequence of the abortion process, occurs in all women using mifepristone. Other common effects include abdominal pain, nausea, vomiting, and diarrhea. Hospitalization, surgical intervention, and intravenous-fluid administration for these effects are rarely needed, but 24-hour availability of a clinician is required for assessment of potential complications. Careful clinical follow-up is necessary to ensure that termination is complete. Because of potential teratogenicity with this regimen, patients should be counseled appropriately.

Contraindications include chronic adrenal failure, severe asthma, long-term glucocorticoid therapy, an intrauterine device (IUD) in place, inherited porphyrias, and a history of allergy to mifepristone, misoprostol, or other prostaglandin. Mifepristone should be used cautiously in women with complicated diabetes mellitus, severe anemia, and hemorrhagic disorders, and in those receiving anticoagulant treatment (4). Mifepristone is ineffective in the termination of ectopic pregnancies and is less effective in the termination of intrauterine pregnancies after 49 days from the first day of the last menstrual period.

The FDA has approved mifepristone for distribution to physicians only. Under terms of the approval, the protocol requires three office visits, and the drug may be administered only in a clinic, medical office, or hospital, by or under the supervision of a physician who meets the following qualifications. Physicians must be able to:

- Assess the gestational age of an embryo and diagnose ectopic pregnancies
- Provide surgical intervention in cases of incomplete abortion or severe bleeding, or have made plans to provide such care through others
- Assure patient access to medical facilities equipped to provide blood transfusions and resuscitation, if necessary

Physicians will indicate that they meet these qualifications by signing and returning a prescriber's agreement to the distributor. The physician also is required to have patients read a medication guide and sign a patient agreement provided by the distributor. Physicians must notify the distributor of any ongoing pregnancy and report any hospitalization, transfusion, or other serious events.

Additional information regarding mifepristone is available on the FDA web site at <www.fda.gov/cder> or by contacting the FDA at <druginfo@cder.fda.gov> or (301) 827-4570. The distributor of mifepristone also provides a web site at <www.earlyoptionpill.com> and can be contacted by phone toll free at 877-432-7596.

In conclusion, approval of mifepristone for use in combination with misoprostol provides women with an effective and safe alternative to surgical abortion for very early intrauterine pregnancy termination.

References

1. Virgo KS, Carr TR, Hile A, Virgo JM, Sullivan GM, Kaikati JG. Medical versus surgical abortion: a survey of knowledge and attitudes among abortion clinic patients. Womens Health Issues 1999;9:143–154
2. Spitz IM, Bardin CW, Benton L, Robbins A. Early pregnancy termination with mifepristone and misoprostol in the United States. N Engl J Med 1998;338:1241–1247
3. Spitz IM, Bardin CW. Mifepristone (RU 486)—a modulator of progestin and glucocorticoid action. N Engl J Med 1993:329:404–412
4. Christin-Maitre S, Bouchard P, Spitz IM. Medical termination of pregnancy. N Engl J Med 2000;342:946–956

ACOG

Committee on
Obstetric Practice

Committee Opinion

Number 265, December 2001

Mode of Term Singleton Breech Delivery

ABSTRACT: Recently, researchers conducted a large, international multicenter randomized clinical trial comparing a policy of planned cesarean birth to planned vaginal birth. Given the results of this exceptionally large and well-controlled clinical trial, the American College of Obstetricians and Gynecologists Committee on Obstetric Practice recommends that obstetricians continue their efforts to reduce breech presentations in singleton gestations through the application of external cephalic version whenever possible. As a result of the findings of the study, planned vaginal delivery of a singleton term breech may no longer be appropriate. In those instances in which breech vaginal deliveries are pursued, great caution should be exercised. Patients with persistent breech presentation at term in a singleton gestation should undergo a planned cesarean delivery. A planned cesarean delivery does not apply to patients presenting with advanced labor and likely to have an imminent delivery of a fetus in a breech presentation or to patients whose second twin is in a nonvertex presentation.

During the past decade there has been an increasing trend in the United States to deliver term singleton fetuses in a breech presentation by cesarean delivery. In 1999, the rate of cesarean delivery for mothers in labor with breech presentation was 84.5 (1). The number of practitioners with the skills and experience to perform vaginal breech delivery has decreased. In academic medical centers where faculty support for teaching vaginal breech delivery to residents remains high, there may be insufficient numbers of vaginal breech deliveries to adequately teach this procedure (2).

Recently, researchers conducted a large, international multicenter randomized clinical trial comparing a policy of planned cesarean birth with planned vaginal birth (3). These investigators noted that perinatal mortality, neonatal mortality, and serious neonatal morbidity were significantly lower among the planned cesarean group compared with planned vaginal birth group (17/1039 [1.6%] versus 52/1039 [5.0%]) while there was no difference in maternal morbidity or mortality observed between the groups (3). The benefits of planned cesarean delivery remained after correcting for numerous potential confounding factors, including birth weight, gestational age at delivery, and maternal parity, as well as the potential effect modifier of the experience of the physician. Most concerning was their finding that the reduction

Mode of term singleton breech delivery. Committee Opinion No. 265. American College of Obstetricians and Gynecologists. Obstet Gynecol 2001;98:1189–1190

in risk attributable to planned cesarean delivery was greatest among centers in industrialized nations with low overall perinatal mortality rates (0.4% versus 5.7%). Among such settings, typical of current practice in the United States, a policy of planned cesarean birth for breech presentation would result in seven cesarean births to avoid one infant death or serious morbidity. These data are consistent with previously reported increases in poor obstetric outcomes in vaginal breech deliveries (4).

Given the results of this exceptionally large and well-controlled clinical trial, the American College of Obstetricians and Gynecologists Committee on Obstetric Practice recommends that obstetricians continue their efforts to reduce breech presentations in singleton gestations through the application of external cephalic version whenever possible. The success rate for versions ranges from 35% to 86% in the literature with an average of 58% (5,6). As a result of the findings of the study, planned vaginal delivery of a singleton term breech may no longer be appropriate. In those instances in which breech vaginal deliveries are pursued, great caution should be exercised. Patients with a persistent breech presentation at term in a singleton gestation should undergo a planned cesarean delivery. If the patient refuses a planned cesarean delivery, informed consent should be obtained and should be documented. A planned cesarean delivery does not apply to patients presenting with advanced labor and likely to have an imminent delivery of a fetus in a breech presentation or to patients whose second twin is in a nonvertex presentation.

References

1. Ventura SJ, Martin JA, Curtin SC, Menacker F, Hamilton BE. Births: final data for 1999. Natl Vital Stat Rep 2001;49(1):1–100
2. Lavin JP Jr, Eaton J, Hopkins M. Teaching vaginal breech delivery and external cephalic version. A survey of faculty attitudes. J Reprod Med 2000;45:808–812
3. Hannah ME, Hannah WJ, Hewson SA, Hodnett ED, Saigal S, Willan AR. Planned caesarean section versus planned vaginal birth for breech presentation at term: a randomised multicentre trial. Term Breech Trial Collaborative Group. Lancet 2000;356:1375–1383
4. Gifford DS, Morton SC, Fiske M, Kahn K. A meta-analysis of infant outcomes after breech delivery. Obstet Gynecol 1995;85:1047–1054
5. Van Veelen AJ, Van Cappellen AW, Flu PK, Straub MJ, Wallenburg HC. Effect of external cephalic version in late pregnancy on presentation at delivery: a randomized controlled trial. Br J Obstet Gynaecol 1989;96:916–921
6. Mahomed K, Seeras R, Coulson R. External cephalic version at term. A randomized controlled trial using tocolysis. Br J Obstet Gynaecol 1991:98:8–13

Recommended Reading

Cheng M, Hannah M. Breech delivery at term: a critical review of the literature. Obstet Gynecol 1993;82:605–618

The Canadian consensus on breech management at term. SOGC Policy Statement. Society of Obstetricians and Gynaecologists of Canada. J SOGC 1994;16:1839–1848

Committee on
Obstetric Practice

Committee Opinion

Number 180, November 1996

New Ultrasound Output Display Standard

Ultrasonography is the most commonly used method of imaging in pregnancy. The potential for bioeffects of ultrasonography can be estimated by measuring the acoustic output. No independently confirmed adverse effects on the fetus resulting from prenatal diagnostic ultrasound exposure have been reported to date. Nevertheless, obstetricians who perform ultrasonography should be familiar with current safety standards of the equipment with regard to acoustic output. Recently, the U.S. Food and Drug Administration, together with the American Institute of Ultrasound in Medicine, the American College of Obstetricians and Gynecologists, the National Electrical Manufacturers Association, and several other organizations, has developed standards for the display directly on the ultrasound screen of meaningful information about the acoustic output of ultrasound equipment. It is important for obstetricians who use ultrasonography to be familiar with this new standard and to ensure that recommended limits of acoustic output are not exceeded.

The two measurements of acoustic output that may be displayed are the thermal index (TI) and the mechanical index (MI). They are defined as follows:

- TI—A calculated estimate of temperature rise due to ultrasound absorption
- MI—A relative measure of the compressive and decompressive mechanical effects of ultrasound pulses

For applicable devices, at least one of the two measurements must be displayed on the screen at all times. Some equipment will display both. If only one is shown, it will be the MI for imaging and the TI for Doppler studies.

Thermal Index

If the value of the TI is below 1.0, temperature changes are not a concern. Values higher than 1.0, however, could result in significant temperature changes, even with only a few minutes of exposure.

Change in tissue temperature is affected by many factors, including the type of tissue being insonated, the duration and area of exposure, and the blood flow to the area. Measurable temperature changes in insonated tissues are possible, particularly at soft tissue–bone interfaces. Significant thermal effects of imaging ultrasonography are highly unlikely not only because of the relatively large area insonated but also because much more time of the duty cycle of the machine is spent receiving returning echoes than creating pulses of energy. On the other hand, pulsed Doppler ultrasonography uses long energy pulses that are highly focused on a small area of tissue and could result in greater thermal change.

Some equipment may allow the user to display various subsets of the TI. Currently available subsets are TIS (TI, soft tissue; appropriate for first-trimester fetal examinations), TIB (TI, bone; appropriate for second- and third-trimester fetal examinations), or TIC (TI, cranial; used only for transcranial Doppler).

Mechanical Index

The MI is calculated as the peak rarefactional pressure of the ultrasound pulse divided by the square root of the transducer center frequency. An MI value below 1 is not of concern regarding potential bioeffects on the fetus.

The potential mechanical bioeffect of most concern is cavitation, or the formation of microbubbles in tissue due to cyclic compressive and decompressive effects of the sound wave emitted by the transducer. The amount of energy reaching the fetus depends on the thickness of intervening tissues and the attenuation of energy within the tissues. The latter relates to how much energy is absorbed versus how much is scattered in different directions.

Acoustic Output Regulations

In the past, the Food and Drug Administration limited acoustic output for the fetal application to 94 mW/cm^2 spatial peak temporal average. Manufacturers of ultrasound equipment are only required to limit the power outputs of their machines to 720 mW/cm^2 spatial peak temporal average and to display the TI or MI if these indices can exceed 1. Ultrasound machines in which TI or MI cannot exceed 1 are not required to display these indices.

Appropriate Use of Fetal Ultrasonography

Many ultrasound machines are designed for multiple uses and can have power outputs above the limits placed by the Food and Drug Administration. Even "fetal presets" may exceed these limits in some configurations, including color Doppler or power Doppler mode. Thus, obstetricians could be using equipment with acoustic outputs that are set at levels above those that are considered acceptable for fetal exposure.

The appropriate use of fetal ultrasonography includes performing examinations only when there is diagnostic information to be obtained. Attention should be directed to the acoustic output and the length of the examination. The display of TI or MI or both provides information about the actual acoustic output of the instrument being operated. Awareness of the TI or MI by the sonologist can be used to minimize fetal exposure to acoustic output, while obtaining the needed diagnostic information. In general, the lowest possible output settings that will allow obtaining adequate imaging should be used. This is known as the ALARA (as low as reasonably achievable) principle. Other controls, such as the gain, which amplifies returning echoes, can be adjusted to enhance the images obtained without increasing the acoustic output. Use of the TI and MI allows the sonologist to implement the ALARA principle more effectively than has been possible previously.

Bibliography

American Institute of Ultrasound in Medicine. Bioeffects and safety of diagnostic ultrasound. Laurel, Maryland: AIUM, 1993

American Institute of Ultrasound in Medicine. Medical ultrasound safety. Laurel, Maryland: AIUM, 1994

American Institute of Ultrasound in Medicine. Standard for real-time display of thermal and mechanical acoustic output indices on diagnostic ultrasound equipment. Laurel, Maryland: AIUM, 1992

ACOG

Committee on
Gynecologic Practice

Committee Opinion

Number 253, March 2001

*(Replaces Statement of Policy on
Liposuction, January 1988)*

Nongynecologic Procedures

Cosmetic procedures (such as laser hair removal, body piercing, tattoo removal, and liposuction) are not considered gynecologic procedures and, therefore, generally are not taught in approved obstetric and gynecologic residencies. Because these are not considered gynecologic procedures, it is inappropriate for the College to establish guidelines for training. As with other surgical procedures, credentialing for cosmetic procedures should be based on education, training, experience, and demonstrated competence.

ISSN 1074-861X

The American College of Obstetricians and Gynecologists
409 12th Street, SW
PO Box 96920
Washington, DC 20090-6920

12345/54321

ACOG
Committee on Obstetric Practice

American Society of Anesthesiologists
Committee on Obstetric Anesthesia

The American College of Obstetricians and Gynecologists
409 12th Street, SW
PO Box 96920
Washington, DC 20090-6920

12345/54321

Committee Opinion

Number 256, May 2001

Optimal Goals for Anesthesia Care in Obstetrics

This joint statement from the American Society of Anesthesiologists (ASA) and the American College of Obstetricians and Gynecologists (ACOG) has been designed to address issues of concern to both specialties. Good obstetric care requires the availability of qualified personnel and equipment to administer general or regional anesthesia both electively and emergently. The extent and degree to which anesthesia services are available varies widely among hospitals. However, for any hospital providing obstetric care, certain optimal anesthesia goals should be sought. These include:

I. Availability of a licensed practitioner who is credentialed to administer an appropriate anesthetic whenever necessary

   For many women, regional anesthesia (epidural, spinal, or combined spinal epidural) will be the most appropriate anesthetic.

II. Availability of a licensed practitioner who is credentialed to maintain support of vital functions in any obstetric emergency

III. Availability of anesthesia and surgical personnel to permit the start of a cesarean delivery within 30 minutes of the decision to perform the procedure; in cases of vaginal birth after cesarean delivery (VBAC), appropriate facilities and personnel, including obstetric anesthesia, nursing personnel, and a physician capable of monitoring labor and performing cesarean delivery, immediately available during active labor to perform an emergency cesarean delivery (1)

   The definition of immediately available personnel and facilities remains a local decision based on each institution's available resources and geographic location.

IV. Appointment of a qualified anesthesiologist to be responsible for all anesthetics administered

   There are many obstetric units where obstetricians or obstetrician-supervised nurse anesthetists administer anesthetics. The administration of general or regional anesthesia requires both medical judgment and technical skills. Thus, a physician with privileges in anesthesiology should be readily available.

Persons administering or supervising obstetric anesthesia should be qualified to manage the infrequent but occasionally life-threatening complications of major regional anesthesia such as respiratory and cardiovascular failure, toxic local anesthetic convulsions, or vomiting and aspiration. Mastering and retaining the skills and knowledge necessary to manage these complications require adequate training and frequent application.

To ensure the safest and most effective anesthesia for obstetric patients, the director of anesthesia services, with the approval of the medical staff, should develop and enforce written policies regarding provision of obstetric anesthesia. These include:

I. Availability of a qualified physician with obstetric privileges to perform operative vaginal or cesarean delivery during administration of anesthesia

Regional and/or general anesthesia should not be administered until the patient has been examined and the fetal status and progress of labor evaluated by a qualified individual. A physician with obstetric privileges who has knowledge of the maternal and fetal status and the progress of labor, and who approves the initiation of labor anesthesia should be readily available to deal with any obstetric complications that may arise.

II. Availability of equipment, facilities, and support personnel equal to that provided in the surgical suite

This should include the availability of a properly equipped and staffed recovery room capable of receiving and caring for all patients recovering from major regional or general anesthesia. Birthing facilities, when used for analgesia or anesthesia, must be appropriately equipped to provide safe anesthetic care during labor and delivery or postanesthesia recovery care.

III. Personnel other than the surgical team should be immediately available to assume responsibility for resuscitation of the depressed newborn

The surgeon and anesthesiologist are responsible for the mother and may not be able to leave her to care for the newborn even when a regional anesthetic is functioning adequately. Individuals qualified to perform neonatal resuscitation should demonstrate:

A. Proficiency in rapid and accurate evaluation of the newborn condition, including Apgar scoring

B. Knowledge of the pathogenesis of a depressed newborn (acidosis, drugs, hypovolemia, trauma, anomalies, and infection), as well as specific indications for resuscitation

C. Proficiency in newborn airway management, laryngoscopy, endotracheal intubations, suctioning of airways, artificial ventilation, cardiac massage, and maintenance of thermal stability

In larger maternity units and those functioning as high-risk centers, 24-hour in-house anesthesia, obstetric and neonatal specialists are usually necessary. Preferably, the obstetric anesthesia services should be directed by an anesthesiologist with special training or experience in obstetric anesthesia. These units will also frequently require the availability of more sophisticated monitoring equipment and specially trained nursing personnel.

A survey jointly sponsored by the ASA and ACOG found that many hospitals in the United States have not yet achieved the goals mentioned previously. Deficiencies were most evident in smaller delivery units. Some small delivery units are necessary because of geographic considerations. Currently, approximately 50% of hospitals providing obstetric care have fewer than 500 deliveries per year. Providing comprehensive care for obstetric patients in these small units is extremely inefficient, not cost-effective and frequently impossible. Thus, the following recommendations are made:

1. Whenever possible, small units should consolidate.

2. When geographic factors require the existence of smaller units, these units should be part of a well-established regional perinatal system.

The availability of the appropriate personnel to assist in the management of a variety of obstetric problems is a necessary feature of good obstetric care. The presence of a pediatrician or other trained physician at a high-risk cesarean delivery to care for the newborn or the availability of an anesthesiologist during active labor and delivery when VBAC is attempted and at a breech or twin delivery are examples. Frequently, these professionals spend a considerable amount of time standing by for the possibility that their services may be needed emergently but may ultimately not be required to perform the tasks for which they are present. Reasonable compensation for these standby services is justifiable and necessary.

A variety of other mechanisms have been suggested to increase the availability and quality of anesthesia services in obstetrics. Improved hospital design, to place labor and delivery suites closer to the operating rooms, would allow for more efficient supervision of nurse anesthetists. Anesthesia equipment in the labor and delivery area must be comparable to that in the operating room.

Finally, good interpersonal relations between obstetricians and anesthesiologists are important. Joint meetings between the two departments should be encouraged. Anesthesiologists should recognize the special needs and concerns of the obstetrician and obstetricians should recognize the anesthesiologist as a consultant in the management of pain and life-support measures. Both should recognize the need to provide high quality care for all patients.

Reference

1. American College of Obstetricians and Gynecologists. Vaginal birth after previous cesarean delivery. ACOG Practice Bulletin 5. Washington, DC: ACOG, 1999

Bibliography

Committee on Perinatal Health. Toward improving the outcome of pregnancy: the 90s and beyond. White Plains, New York: March of Dimes Birth Defects Foundation, 1993

ACOG
Committee on
Obstetric Practice

American Society of
Anesthesiologists
Committee on
Obstetric Anesthesia

This document reflects emerging clinical and scientific advances as of the date issued and is subject to change. The information should not be construed as dictating an exclusive course of treatment or procedure to be followed.

ISSN 1074-861X

The American College of
Obstetricians and Gynecologists
409 12th Street, SW
PO Box 96920
Washington, DC 20090-6920

12345/43210

Committee Opinion

Number 231, February 2000   *(Replaces #118, January 1993)*

Pain Relief During Labor

Labor results in severe pain for many women. There is no other circumstance where it is considered acceptable for a person to experience untreated severe pain, amenable to safe intervention, while under a physician's care. In the absence of a medical contraindication, maternal request is a sufficient medical indication for pain relief during labor. Pain management should be provided whenever medically indicated.

Nonetheless, the American Society of Anesthesiologists (ASA) and the American College of Obstetricians and Gynecologists (ACOG) have received reports that some third-party payers have denied reimbursement for regional analgesia and anesthesia during labor unless a physician has documented the presence of a "medical indication" for regional analgesia and anesthesia. Of the various pharmacologic methods used for pain relief during labor and delivery, regional analgesia techniques—epidural, spinal, and combined spinal epidural—are the most flexible, effective, and least depressing to the central nervous system, allowing for an alert participating mother and an alert neonate. It is the position of ACOG and ASA that third-party payers who provide reimbursement for obstetric services should not deny reimbursement for regional analgesia and anesthesia because of an absence of other "medical indications."

ACOG Committee Opinion

Committee on
Gynecologic Practice

Number 243, November 2000

Performance and Interpretation of Imaging Studies by Obstetrician–Gynecologists

Obstetrician–gynecologists are experienced in diagnostic imaging methods and receive privileges to perform and interpret imaging studies on the basis of their training, experience, and demonstrated current competence. Obstetrician–gynecologists can perform the immediate and timely interpretation of imaging studies, correlate these studies with clinical findings, counsel the patient, and assume the responsibility for determining the treatment of the patient.

Education and Training

By virtue of their education and experience, obstetrician–gynecologists are qualified to perform the imaging studies that are a necessary and integral part of obstetric–gynecologic care. Training in diagnostic imaging is a part of obstetric–gynecologic residencies, and questions related to this field are a part of the certifying examinations of the American Board of Obstetrics and Gynecology. For example, the performance and interpretation of ultrasound images are required components of obstetric and gynecologic residency training and are monitored by the Residency Review Committee for Obstetrics and Gynecology. In addition to interpreting images in descriptive terms, obstetrician–gynecologists add functional, anatomical, and clinical assessments, resulting in patient-specific information. It is the obstetric–gynecologic interpretation of the images, in concert with the history and physical examination, that determines the course of treatment and carries with it the responsibility for patient care. A written report, signed by the interpreting physician, should be considered an integral part of the performance and interpretation of an imaging study.

Timeliness

For optimal patient care, imaging studies should be performed and interpreted in a timely manner. Many obstetric–gynecologic imaging procedures are performed when the patient is in the obstetrician–gynecologist's office or in

The American College of Obstetricians and Gynecologists
409 12th Street, SW
PO Box 96920
Washington, DC 20090-6920

12345/43210

the labor and delivery suite so that judgments can be made, without delay, at the time of clinical decision making.

Appropriate management of certain obstetric–gynecologic emergencies, such as suspected ectopic pregnancy, requires timely performance and interpretation of imaging studies. In many cases, the obstetrician–gynecologist is the most appropriate physician to provide these services.

Conclusion

The responsibility for obstetric–gynecologic patient care rests with the treating obstetrician–gynecologist and may include the immediate performance and interpretation of diagnostic imaging studies. Obstetrician–gynecologists are qualified to perform and interpret obstetric–gynecologic imaging studies. The American College of Obstetricians and Gynecologists believes that obstetrician–gynecologists are entitled to adequate compensation for the cost and work involved in providing these services. Any policy that prohibits obstetrician–gynecologists from performing and interpreting imaging studies of which they are competent interferes with the patient's access to optimal care. Such a policy is likely to ultimately increase the cost of providing such services and substantially increases the risk of less than optimal outcomes in those patients requiring timely management of obstetric–gynecologic emergencies.

ACOG

Committee on
Obstetric Practice

American Academy
of Pediatrics
Committee on
Fetus and Newborn

Copyright © November 1995
by AAP/ACOG
ISSN 1074-861X

The American College of Obstetricians and Gynecologists
409 12th Street, SW
Washington, DC 20024-2188

12345/98765

Committee Opinion

Number 163, November 1995

Perinatal Care at the Threshold of Viability

The survival rate for infants born prematurely has changed over the last two decades and is likely to change in the future. Currently, the birth of an infant at or before 25 weeks of gestation or weighing less than 750 g presents a variety of complex medical, social, and ethical decisions. Although the prevalence of such births is low, the impact on the infants, their families, the health care system, and society is profound.

The survival of infants born from 23 to 25 weeks of gestation increases with each additional week of gestation. However, the overall neonatal survival rate for infants born during this early gestational period remains less than 40% (1, 2). Of those who survive, about 40% have moderate or serious disabilities, and many have neurobehavioral dysfunction and poor school performance (3, 4). Many require prolonged intensive care and long-term care (2). The commitment for all aspects of care may be extensive, multidisciplinary, lifelong, and costly. Because the families bear the emotional and financial consequences of the birth of an extremely low birth weight infant, it is essential to inform the prospective parents regarding the expectations for infant outcome and the risks and benefits of various approaches to care.

Counseling Regarding Potential Fetal Outcomes

Most parents are unfamiliar with the complexities of care required for an extremely premature infant, both in the intensive care unit and after discharge from the hospital. Therefore, it is often necessary to provide the information in small segments at frequent intervals to allow the parents to comprehend the messages. The family can benefit from a clear explanation of the various supportive procedures that will likely be necessary in the infant's first days of life. Family members should also be provided with an overview of the potential complications of prolonged intensive care. Finally, they should be informed of the range of survival rates and of the rates of long-term disabilities that can be expected. In compiling such information, practitioners should consider data reported in the current literature as well as outcomes based on local experience; they should allow for some error in the best estimate of gestational age and fetal weight.

Neonatal survival rates experienced over the last decade in different neonatal units are provided in Table 1. These rates do not represent ultimate survival rates, as deaths may occur in the postneonatal period. The prevalence

Table 1. Neonatal Survival by Gestational Age and Birth Weight

	Mean (%) Survival Rates (Range) Reported for*	
Factor	1987–1988	1989–1990
Age (wk)		
23	23 (0–33)	15 (0–29)
24	34 (10–57)	54 (27–100)
25	54 (30–72)	59 (47–74)
Weight (g)		
501–600	21 (0–44)	20 (0–33)
601–700	33 (9–50)	41 (25–56)
701–800	53 (31–73)	65 (38–83)

* Rates were reported by the National Institute of Child Health and Human Development neonatal centers.

Data from Hack M, Horbar JD, Malloy MH, Tyson JE, Wright E, Wright L. Very low birth weight outcomes of the National Institute of Child Health and Human Development Neonatal Network. Pediatrics 1991;87:587–597 and Hack M, Wright LL, Shankaran S, Tyson JE, Horbar JD, Bauer CR, et al. Very-low-birth-weight outcomes of the National Institute of Child Health and Human Development Neonatal Network, November 1989 to October 1990. Am J Obstet Gynecol 1995;172:457–464

of a number of morbidities common to these extremely premature infants is shown in Table 2.

It is difficult to counsel parents regarding long-term disabilities because outcomes are only now being reported for neonates born since the use of surfactant became common and who have survived to school age. Recent experience suggests that almost half of the surviving children who weigh less than 750 g at birth experience moderate or severe disability, including blindness and cerebral palsy, and require special education. Many infants have more than one disability. Families should be counseled that, despite the high rate of overall disability, many of these children are educable and can function within their family unit.

The estimation of gestational age before premature delivery forms the main basis for subsequent decision making. Clinical assessment to determine gestational age is usually appropriate for the woman with regular menstrual cycles and a known last menstrual period that was confirmed by an early examination. Fetal measurements derived through the use of ultrasonography at the time of anticipated delivery should not be used to alter estimated gestational age unless there is a discrepancy of 2 weeks or more between the age derived by menstrual dating and the age derived sonographically or the woman is uncertain about the date of her last menstrual period. Ultrasonography may provide useful information regarding the presence or absence of fetal malforma-

tions that may alter the prognosis. The accuracy of sonographic measurements and the ability to ascertain malformations, however, may be reduced in the presence of oligohydramnios, such as occurs with ruptured membranes.

Even in ideal circumstances, the 95% confidence limits for a formula-based estimate of fetal weight are ±15% to 20% (5). Thus, an infant estimated to weigh 600 g may have an actual birth weight of less than 500 g or more than 700 g. Even relatively small discrepancies of 1 or 2 weeks in gestational age or 100–200 g in birth weight may have major implications for survival and long-term morbidity. This underscores the importance of counseling about the range of possible outcomes. Furthermore, multiple gestation increases the difficulty of accurate gestational age assessment, and the prognosis for one infant ultimately may differ from that of the other(s).

Ideally, the obstetric and neonatal physicians, primary care physicians, and neonatal nurses should confer before recommendations are made to the parents. The range of possible outcomes and management options can then be outlined for the patient and her family. If maternal transport may be needed, the obstetrician should be knowledgable about the available regional resources and be prepared to provide basic information to the parents if the specific clinical circumstances warrant. More detailed counseling can then be accomplished at the receiving unit. Additional medical opinions and input from other

Table 2. Serious Morbidities in Infants With Birth Weight <750 g Experienced by the NICHD Neonatal Centers, 1989–1990*

Condition	Frequency (%)	Range (%)
Respiratory distress syndrome	86	80–100
Ventilator support at 28 days†	72	23–100
Chronic lung disease‡	35	8–82
Necrotizing enterocolitis	9	2–19
Septicemia	34	13–50
Grade III intraventricular hemorrhage	13	5–20
Grade IV intraventricular hemorrhage	17	0–24
Seizures	10	2–14
Periventricular leukomalacia	11	7–20

* NICHD indicates the National Institute of Child Health and Human Development.

† Data are for infants alive at 28 days.

‡ Data are for survivors.

Data from Hack M, Wright LL, Shankaran S, Tyson JE, Horbar JD, Bauer CR, et al. Very-low-birth-weight outcomes of the National Institute of Child Health and Human Development Neonatal Network, November 1989 to October 1990. Am J Obstet Gynecol 1995;172:457–464

important sources such as clergy, social workers, and the institution's bioethics committee may be offered to the parents. Counseling should be sensitive to cultural and ethnic diversity, and a skilled translator should be available for parents whose primary language differs from the language of the care providers. It should be emphasized that the prognosis for the newborn may change after birth since a more accurate assessment of the newborn's gestational age and condition may be made at that time.

Counseling Regarding the Risks and Benefits of Management Options

Obstetric Management

Decisions regarding obstetric management must be made by the parents and their physicians if the neonate's prognosis is uncertain; the decisions must be documented in the obstetric records. Some decisions, such as the choice of cesarean birth, can result in increased risk of morbidity to the woman.

Few studies have been done to evaluate the influence of obstetric management on the outcome of infants at the threshold of viability. Furthermore, literature on this subject is largely retrospective and often lacks sufficient data regarding potential confounding variables. Despite these limitations, study results have consistently failed to document benefits of cesarean delivery for extremely premature infants (6–10). It has even been difficult to document improved outcome with cesarean birth for infants in the breech position who are extremely premature (7, 8). Furthermore, injuries to the infant can occur during a difficult cesarean birth.

Physicians should avoid characterizing managements of uncertain benefit as "doing everything possible." Rather, they should hold discussions with the family regarding available data and provide an explanation of the risks incurred by management options, including route of delivery. In the case of cesarean delivery, risks to the woman include not only those incurred during the perioperative period but also long-term implications for childbearing since a vertical uterine incision is often used. A vertical uterine incision at these gestational ages may extend into the upper segment and would preclude the option of vaginal birth in future pregnancy. Counseling regarding management decisions such as whether to effect maternal transport should include a discussion of the potential disadvantages of separating the mother from supportive family members and familiar caregivers when benefit for the mother or baby is uncertain.

Parents should be encouraged to actively participate in discussion regarding maternal transport and other management decisions. Counseling about management options and potential outcome allows the family to more easily choose a course of action that is both medically appropriate and consistent with their own personal values and goals. Whenever possible, a nondirective approach needs to be used; in some circumstances, however, directive counseling may be appropriate (11). Counseling may result in the family choosing a noninterventive approach to delivery and management. Because the benefits of different types of obstetric management have not been delineated, families should be supported in such decisions.

Neonatal Management

Ethical decisions regarding the extent of resuscitative efforts and subsequent support of the neonate are complex (12–14). Parents should understand that decisions about neonatal management made before delivery may be altered depending on the condition of the neonate at birth, the postnatal gestational age assessment, and the infant's response to resuscitative and stabilization measures. Recommendations regarding the extent of continuing support depend on frequent reevaluations of the infant's condition and prognosis.

When a decision is made not to resuscitate the infant or to discontinue resuscitation, the family should be treated with dignity and compassion. This should include the acknowledgment of the birth of the infant. Humane and compassionate care must be provided to the infant, including careful handling, maintaining a neutral thermal environment, and gentle monitoring of vital signs.

When medical support is discontinued or death is inevitable, time should be allowed for the parents and other family members to hold, touch, and interact with the infant if they desire to do so, both before and after the infant has died. Naming the infant and obtaining a photograph may be important to the parents, and a crib card and name band should be provided. Birth weight and other measurements should be provided to the family as well. Clergy and other family and friends should be allowed access to the infant in a setting that maintains the dignity of both the family and infant.

Support should be provided to the family by physicians, nurses, and other staff beyond the time of the infant's death. Perinatal loss support groups, intermittent contact by phone, and a later conference with the family to review the medical events surrounding the infant's death and to evaluate the grieving response of the parents may be considered.

Summary

The survival rate for infants at the threshold of viability has been improving. However, there are insufficient data regarding the cost(s) of initial and ongoing care of these infants and the long-term outcome of survivors. Furthermore, there has been little study of the impact of obstetric management on the survival rates of extremely low birth weight infants and on long-term morbidities. Continued research on these issues is imperative, and physicians need to remain informed of changing statistics.

References

1. Hack M, Horbar JD, Malloy MH, Tyson JE, Wright E, Wright L. Very low birth weight outcomes of the National Institute of Child Health and Human Development Neonatal Network. Pediatrics 1991;87:587–597
2. Hack M, Wright LL, Shankaran S, Tyson JE, Horbar JD, Bauer CR, et al. Very-low-birth-weight outcomes of the National Institute of Child Health and Human Development Neonatal Network, November 1989 to October 1990. Am J Obstet Gynecol 1995;172:457–464
3. Ehrenhaft PM, Wagner JL, Herdman RC. Changing prognosis for very low birth weight infants. Obstet Gynecol 1989;74:528–535
4. Hack M, Taylor HG, Klein N, Eiben R, Schatschneider C, Mercuri-Minich N. School-age outcomes in children with birth weights under 750 g. N Engl J Med 1994;331:753–759
5. Hadlock FP, Harrist RB, Sharman RS, Deter RL, Park SK. Estimation of fetal weight with the use of head, body, and femur measurements—a prospective study. Am J Obstet Gynecol 1985;151:333–337
6. Hack M, Fanaroff AA. Outcomes of extremely-low-birth-weight infants between 1982 and 1988. N Engl J Med 1989;321:1642–1647
7. Malloy MH, Rhoads GG, Schramm W, Land G. Increasing cesarean section rates in very low-birth weight infants. Effect on outcome. JAMA 1989;262:1475–1478
8. Malloy MH, Onstad L, Wright E. The effect of cesarean delivery on birth outcome in very low birth weight infants. National Institute of Child Health and Human Development Neonatal Research Network. Obstet Gynecol 1991;77:498-503
9. Worthington D, Davis LE, Grausz JP, Sobocinski K. Factors influencing survival and morbidity with very low birth weight delivery. Obstet Gynecol 1983;62:550–555
10. Kitchen W, Ford GW, Doyle LW, Rickards AL, Lissenden JV, Pepperell RJ, et al. Cesarean section or vaginal delivery at 24 to 28 weeks' gestation: comparison of survival and neonatal and two-year morbidity. Obstet Gynecol 1985;66:149–157
11. American College of Obstetricians and Gynecologists. Ethical decision-making in obstetrics and gynecology. ACOG Technical Bulletin 136. Washington, DC: ACOG, 1989
12. Rhoden NK. Treating Baby Doe: the ethics of uncertainty. Hastings Cent Rep 1986;16(4):34–42
13. Lantos JD, Meadow W, Miles SH, Ekwo E, Paton J, Hageman JR, et al. Providing and forgoing resuscitative therapy for babies of very low birth weight. J Clin Ethics 1992;3:283–287
14. Allen MC, Donohue PK, Dusman AE. The limit of viability—neonatal outcome of infants born at 22 to 25 weeks' gestation. N Engl J Med 1993;329:1597–1601

acog committee opinion

Committee on Obstetrics: Maternal and Fetal Medicine

Number 125—July 1993
(Replaces #102, December 1991)

Placental Pathology

Recently, there has been heightened interest in clinical–pathologic correlation between placental abnormalities and adverse pregnancy outcome. When a skilled and systematic examination of the umbilical cord, membranes, and placenta is performed on properly prepared specimens, insight into antepartum pathophysiology may be gained under certain circumstances.

In most of these instances, such as chorioamnionitis, the diagnosis already will have been made on clinical grounds, with the placental examination providing confirmation. In other cases of poor outcome, a disorder that was not suspected clinically may be revealed by placental pathology. Examples of pathologic findings and the disorders they suggest include the microabscesses of listeriosis and amnion nodosum suggesting long-standing oligohydramnios. The underlying pathophysiology of these lesions has been confirmed by laboratory testing or consistent and specific clinical associations.

The significance of other findings, such as villous edema, hemorrhagic endovasculitis, and chronic villitis, has not been as well delineated. These lesions, among others, have been variously reported to correlate with poor short-term and long-term neonatal outcome. The paucity of properly designed studies of adequate size with appropriate outcome parameters has prevented universal agreement as to positive predictive values, underlying pathophysiology, or even the consistency of clinical correlations with these findings. Furthermore, the distribution of pathologists with the expertise to interpret more subtle placental findings is uneven from region to region. Although a protocol for obtaining routine placental pathologic examination under certain obstetric and neonatal conditions has been recommended (1), there are few data to support the clinical utility of this approach.

In addition to the issue of positive and negative predictive values of the spectrum of placental findings, there are practical concerns regarding examination of the placenta. In some instances, a neonatal problem may not be ascertained until days or weeks after birth, when the placenta is no longer available. Different approaches have been recommended to address this problem, including routinely examining all placentas, securing a small section from each placenta in a fixed state for an indefinite period, and saving all placentas unfixed at 4°C for 1 week before discarding. However, routine determinations of placental pathology are not feasible on either a cost or manpower basis, and a small portion of placenta obtained at random would be unlikely to provide useful information. The practice of saving all placentas for 1 week after delivery would permit ascertaining most neonatal problems in which pathologic examination of the placenta may be appropriate, but the effectiveness of this approach has not been proven.

In conclusion, an examination of the umbilical cord, membranes, and placenta may assist the obstetric care provider in clinical–pathologic correlation when there is an adverse perinatal outcome. However, the scientific basis for clinical correlation with placental pathology is still evolving, and the benefit of securing specimens on a routine basis is as yet unproven. Continued research and education in this field should be encouraged. Research should be designed with the goal of defining clinical indications for placental examination. In contrast, pathologic examination of the stillborn fetus and placenta is always potentially informative. Obstetric providers should be persistent in seeking consent from parents for autopsy examinations.

REFERENCE

1. College of American Pathologists Conference XIX. The examination of the placenta: patient care and risk management. Arch Pathol Lab Med 1991;115: 641–732

The American College of Obstetricians and Gynecologists
409 12th Street, SW • Washington, DC 20024-2188

12345/76543

Committee on Obstetric Practice

Committee Opinion

Number 173, June 1996

Prevention of Early-Onset Group B Streptococcal Disease in Newborns

During the past two decades, group B streptococci (GBS), or *Streptococcus agalactiae*, has emerged as an important cause of perinatal morbidity and mortality. The gram-positive organism can colonize the lower gastrointestinal tract, and secondary spread to the genitourinary tract is common. Between 10 to 30% of pregnant women are colonized with GBS in the vaginal or rectal areas (1–4). The organism may cause urinary tract infection, amnionitis, endometritis, and wound infection in women who are pregnant or recently delivered. Recently, a multistate active surveillance system in a population of 10 million persons found that 6% of early-onset GBS infections resulted in death (5). Morbidity due to overwhelming sepsis and to neurologic sequelae of meningitis is also clinically important but more difficult to estimate.

Vertical transmission of GBS during labor or delivery may result in invasive infection in the newborn during the first week of life. This is known as early-onset GBS infection and constitutes approximately 80% of GBS disease in the newborn. Late-onset GBS disease in the newborn may be the result of vertical transmission or of nosocomial or community-acquired infection. Invasive GBS disease in the newborn is characterized primarily by sepsis, pneumonia, or meningitis. Annually, approximately 7,600 episodes of GBS sepsis occur in newborns (a rate of 1.8/1,000 live births) in the United States and result in about 310 deaths among infants less than 90 days of age, a case–fatality rate of 5–20% (5–7).

Factors Associated with Early-Onset Disease

A number of obstetric factors have been associated with an increased likelihood of early-onset GBS disease in the newborn (8). These include prenatal cultures colonized with GBS, premature deliveries, prolonged rupture of membranes, or intrapartum fever. The incidence of GBS disease is also higher among infants born to African–American mothers (5, 9) and to mothers less than 20 years of age (9–10). Also more likely to be infected are neonates born to mothers with a history of birth of an infant with GBS disease (11–13), heavy colonization such as that seen with GBS bacteriuria (14–18), and low levels of anti-GBS capsular antibody (19). An apparent increased risk in twins may be attributable to the increased frequency of prematurity and of low birth weight with multiple gestations (20–21).

The American College of Obstetricians and Gynecologists

409 12th Street, SW
PO Box 96920
Washington, DC 20090-6920

12345/09876

Ideally, GBS disease would be prevented by active immunization of the mother and newborn. As yet, vaccines have not been developed for clinical use. Therefore, the primary strategy for preventing GBS disease is chemoprophylaxis using antibiotics. Several strategies have been recommended for the prevention of early-onset GBS, including intrapartum chemoprophylaxis that is based on risk factors such as GBS carriers identified by culture during pregnancy and certain intrapartum complications.

Several studies of colonized women who were treated during the third trimester found that a wide range of patients (20–70%) remained colonized at term (22–24). In one study of 20 colonized women treated in the third trimester, however, none of the 19 who were reexamined at term by culture remained colonized (25). Similarly, immediate postnatal treatment with antibiotics has not been shown to be effective in reducing overall mortality from infection (26–28). In one study, this finding was related partly to higher mortality resulting from penicillin-resistant pathogens (27). Because GBS infection may be acquired in utero, the administration of antimicrobial agents to the newborn, while important in the treatment of infection, will not always prevent early-onset GBS disease.

Intrapartum administration of antibiotics to the mother (during labor or after rupture of the membranes, but before delivery) has been demonstrated to reduce early-onset neonatal GBS disease. Several investigators have found that antibiotics administered intrapartum to all women determined to be colonized by prenatal cultures has reduced the incidence of early-onset disease (29–32). Others have found a benefit of selective administration of intrapartum antibiotics to colonized women on the basis of the development of other intrapartum risk factors such as premature labor, prolonged rupture of membranes, and intrapartum fever (33–34). Studies focused specifically on prophylactic treatment on the basis of prolonged rupture of membranes (35) and heavy genital colonization (36–37) have also been reported. A recent metaanalysis of seven trials studied groups of women, all of whom were carriers or were carriers with additional obstetric risk factors (38). They estimated a 30-fold reduction in early-onset GBS disease with the administration of intrapartum chemoprophylaxis.

Appropriate culture technique requires obtaining a swab from the lower vagina (introitus) and perianal area and using selective broth media. Obtaining the culture does not require visualization of the cervix with a speculum. Use of prenatal cultures remote from term to identify women who are colonized with GBS at delivery is controversial. Many of the afore-mentioned studies primarily have used cultures taken early in the third trimester. In one study, 7.4% of women who had negative cultures at 26–28 weeks of gestation were found to carry GBS at delivery, and a single positive culture during pregnancy had a 67% predictive value at delivery (4). The estimated sensitivity and specificity were 70.0% and 90.4%, respectively. Among 26 women who delivered within 5 weeks after a culture was obtained, there were no false-positive or false-negative culture results (4). In another study of 16 infants who developed early-onset GBS disease, 14 (88%) were born to mothers who had positive prenatal cultures (34). Larger studies evaluating the sensitivity, specificity, and predictive value of a positive culture close to delivery are urgently needed.

Strategies for Antibiotic Prophylaxis

Different strategies for selecting women to receive intrapartum antibiotic prophylaxis of early-onset GBS disease in newborns have been proposed. Boyer and Gotoff, on the basis of findings of their own studies, recommend 26–28-week cultures followed by intrapartum antibiotic prophylaxis for those women identified as GBS carriers who subsequently had rupture of membranes greater than 12 hours, onset of labor or rupture of membranes at less than 37 weeks of gestation, or intrapartum fever (39). They estimate that this strategy will result in intrapartum treatment of approximately 3.4% of women and prevent one half of early-onset GBS disease in newborns. These figures will vary, depending on differences in populations for whom care is being provided. In 1992, this approach was endorsed in a statement issued by the American Academy of Pediatrics (40). The statement extended intrapartum risk factors to include multiple gestation in a GBS carrier and previous birth of an infant with GBS disease.

In contrast, the American College of Obstetricians and Gynecologists (ACOG) has supported use of intrapartum antibiotic prophylaxis based on the clinical risk factors of preterm labor (less than 37 weeks), preterm premature rupture of membranes (preterm PROM) (less than 37 weeks), rupture of membranes greater than 18 hours, previous birth of a child with GBS disease, or maternal fever during labor (greater than or equal to 38°C or 100.4°F). The ACOG criterion of greater than 18 hours of rupture of membranes was selected on the basis of an observational study by Boyer et al demonstrating a statistically significant increase in attack rate of GBS with rupture of membranes more than 18 hours (4). The strategy supported by ACOG did not incorporate the use of cultures because of several concerns. These included the potential acquisition of GBS following a negative culture in patients who might later develop an intrapartum risk factor and concern about the predictive value of positive cultures remote from term.

Rouse et al reported a decision analysis of 19 different strategies for the prevention of early-onset neonatal GBS sepsis (41). In the absence of randomized clinical trials, this type of analysis allows consideration of which strategies may be reasonable for clinical use and further study. The difference in approaches for the prevention of early-onset GBS disease has caused considerable controversy and confusion among providers of obstetric care as to the most appropriate strategy to use in clinical practice (42–43). This confusion has occurred because the ideal strategy for prevention of early-onset GBS in clinical practice has not been scientifically determined. No clinical trials comparing these different strategies have been conducted. To compare the efficacy of the strategies using antepartum culture and selective intrapartum prophylaxis with intrapartum prophylaxis based on clinical risk factors alone, estimates are that at least 100,000 pregnant women would need to be studied in each arm of a randomized prospective trial (44). It is, therefore, unlikely that a study will resolve the controversy. However, either of these two strategies is expected to reduce the occurrence of early-onset GBS disease significantly. Nevertheless, it should be noted that neither will prevent all early-onset GBS disease.

Recently, the Centers for Disease Control and Prevention (CDC) issued recommendations for the active prevention of GBS (43). The ACOG Committee on Obstetric Practice concurs with those recommendations. The recommendations relevant to maternal care are listed in the appendix. Important differences from previous recommendations include the following:

- The use of *either* a strategy based on late prenatal culture (35–37 weeks) as the primary risk determinant *or* a strategy based solely on clinical risk factors
- The offer, when the culture-based strategy is used, of intrapartum antibiotic prophylaxis to all women who have a positive culture, irrespective of intrapartum risk factors
- The use of penicillin as an alternative to ampicillin for prophylaxis

In addition, CDC provides a sample empiric-care algorithm for management of newborns born to mothers who received intrapartum antimicrobial prophylaxis for GBS disease (not included in the appendix).

Commentary

The Committee supports the recommendation that obstetric providers adopt a strategy for the prevention of early-onset GBS disease in the newborn. This strategy should be based on intrapartum administration of antibiotic agents to patients at increased risk of delivering an infant who develops GBS disease. Risk may be based solely on clinical risk factors or late prenatal cultures for GBS. The Committee concurs with the specific drugs, dosage, and routes of administration recommended by CDC (see appendix). Patients should be informed of the GBS prevention strategy used. This may be accomplished by providing patient information materials such as the patient information pamphlet produced by ACOG.

If the strategy adopted by the provider is based solely on clinical risk factors, some patients may request that GBS cultures be done. Such requests from informed patients should be honored by obtaining culture at 35–37 weeks of gestation as recommended by CDC (45). Cultures taken remote from term, particularly during early pregnancy, may have less predictive value for carrier status at delivery and are *not* recommended, nor is antepartum treatment for GBS carriers.

Irrespective of the strategy adopted by the obstetric provider, all women who have had a previous infant with GBS disease or who have had GBS bacteriuria during the current pregnancy should be offered intrapartum chemoprophylaxis.

Neither the strategy using late prenatal culture (35–37 weeks of gestation) as the primary indicator of risk nor the strategy based on intrapartum risk factors alone has been evaluated extensively in clinical practice or compared by randomized controlled trials. Approximately 4% of neonates born to women who are carriers and who have intrapartum clinical risk factors are expected to have GBS disease. By comparison, 0.5% (1 in 200) of neonates born to women who are carriers but have no other risk factors are expected to have GBS disease. When a strategy is used that incorporates late prenatal cultures and offers of intrapartum chemoprophylaxis to women who are carriers but have no other risk factors, most of these women can be expected to accept intrapartum treatment. Using a number of assumptions, Rouse and colleagues have estimated that this strategy will result in intrapartum treatment of 26.7% of women and prevent 86% of early-onset GBS in the newborn (41). Similarly, using a number of assumptions, a strategy based solely on intrapartum risk factors could result in intrapartum treatment of 18.3% of women and prevent 68.8% of early-onset GBS in the newborn (41).

Because these are estimates, they will need further validation and comparison in clinical practice.

The Committee is concerned that with implementation of these strategies, the widespread use of intrapartum prophylaxis (eg, up to 18.3% or 26.7% of women) will lead to emergence of resistant pathogens. Also, the benefit of GBS prevention must be weighed against the risk to the mother and the fetus of maternal allergic reactions during labor. Although the risk of fatal anaphylaxis has been estimated at 1 per 100,000, the risk of less severe anaphylactic or allergic reactions to the laboring mother and fetus are important (46–47). The Committee agrees with CDC that local responsible health agencies should establish surveillance systems to monitor the incidence of early-onset neonatal GBS disease, the emergence of infection in mothers and newborns that is caused by resistant organisms, and other complications of widespread maternal antibiotic administration such as severe allergic reactions.

Comparative scientific evidence is insufficient for the Committee to determine criteria for the provider or obstetric service to use in selecting one of the two recommended strategies. In considering which strategy to adopt, practitioners and obstetric services may wish to consider a number of factors that may affect the implementation or effectiveness of one strategy or the other in their patient population. These may include, but not be limited to, GBS carrier rates in the population served, the frequency of obstetric complications that are associated with an increased risk of early-onset GBS disease in the newborn (eg, prematurity, preterm PROM, and fever in labor), and practical considerations regarding implementation. Information system technology now available theoretically could significantly enhance access to culture results. The potential benefits of information technology, however, have not yet been fully realized in actual clinical practice. Lack of prompt availability of culture results may render use of late prenatal cultures impractical in some settings.

Irrespective of the strategy adopted, the Committee believes that if the results of late prenatal cultures are not available, intrapartum prophylaxis should be offered only on the basis of the presence of intrapartum risk factors for early-onset GBS disease. This is consistent with CDC recommendations.

The Committee lacks sufficient evidence for recommending a course of management, specifically predelivery antibiotic prophylaxis for prevention of early onset GBS disease in newborns, for women with positive GBS culture results who have elective cesarean delivery with intact membranes. Evidence is also insufficient to recommend a single course of management when a woman has preterm PROM at less than 37 weeks of gestation. Culture for GBS should be obtained in all women with preterm PROM. Following culture, antibiotic prophylaxis may be withheld. Antibiotics should be started if positive culture results are obtained or if labor begins before culture results are available. An acceptable alternative approach is to initiate prophylactic antibiotics until culture results are available. Treatment can be discontinued if the culture is negative for GBS. The appropriate duration of treatment for patients who have preterm PROM and positive GBS cultures has not been determined.

References

1. Anthony BF, Okada DM, Hobel CJ. Epidemiology of group B streptococcus: longitudinal observations during pregnancy. J Infect Dis 1978;137:524–530
2. Regan JA, Klebanoff MA, Nugent RP. The epidemiology of group B streptococcal colonization in pregnancy. Vaginal Infections and Prematurity Study Group. Obstet Gynecol 1991;77:604–610
3. Dillon HC Jr, Gray E, Pass MA, Gray BM. Anorectal and vaginal carriage of group B streptococci during pregnancy. J Infect Dis 1982;145:794–799
4. Boyer KM, Gadzala CA, Kelly PD, Burd LI, Gotoff SP. Selective intrapartum chemoprophylaxis of neonatal group B streptococcal early-onset disease. II. Predictive value of prenatal cultures. J Infect Dis 1983;148:802–809
5. Zangwill KM, Schuchat A, Wenger JD. Group B streptococcal disease in the United States, 1990: report from a multistate active surveillance system. MMWR 41(6): 25–32
6. Baker CJ, Edwards MS. Group B streptococcal infections. In: Remington JS, Klein JO, eds. Infectious diseases of the fetus and newborn infant. 4th ed. Philadelphia: WB Saunders, 1995:980–1054
7. Weisman LE, Stoll BJ, Cruess DF, Hall RT, Merenstein GB, Hemming VG. Early-onset group B streptococcal sepsis: a current assessment. J Pediatr 1992;121:428–433
8. Boyer KM, Gotoff SP. Strategies for chemoprophylaxis of GBS early-onset infections. Antibiot Chemother 1985;35: 267–280
9. Schuchat A, Oxtoby M, Cochi S, Sikes RK, Hightower A, Plikaytis B, et al. Population-based risk factors for neonatal group B streptococcal disease: results of a cohort study in metropolitan Atlanta. J Infect Dis 1990;162:672–677
10. Schuchat A, Deaver-Robinson K, Plikaytis BD, Zangwill KM, Mohle-Boetani J, Wenger JD. Multistate case-control study of maternal risk factors for neonatal group B streptococcal disease. The Active Surveillance Group. Pediatr Infect Dis J 1994;13:623–629
11. Carstensen H, Christensen KK, Grennert L, Persson K, Polberger S. Early-onset neonatal group B streptococcal septicaemia in siblings. J Infect 1988;17:201–204
12. Faxelius G, Bremme K, Kvist-Christensen K, Christensen P, Ringertz S. Neonatal septicemia due to group B streptococcal–perinatal risk factors and outcome of subsequent pregnancies. J Perinat Med 1988;16:423–430
13. Christensen KK, Dahlander K, Linden V, Svenningsen N, Christensen P. Obstetrical care in future pregnancies after

fetal loss in group B streptococcal septicemia. A prevention program based on bacteriological and immunological follow-up. Eur J Obstet Gynecol Reprod Biol 1981;12:143–150

14. Pass MA, Gray BM, Khare S, Dillon HC Jr. Prospective studies of group B streptococcal infections in infants. J Pediatr 1979;95:437–443

15. Wood EG, Dillon HC Jr. A prospective study of group B streptococcal bacteriuria in pregnancy. Am J Obstet Gynecol 1981;140:515–520

16. Moller M, Thomsen AC, Borch K, Dinesen K, Zdravkovic M. Rupture of fetal membranes and premature delivery associated with group B streptococci in urine of pregnant women. Lancet 1984;2(8394):69–70

17. Liston TE, Harris RE, Foshee S, Null DM Jr. Relationship of neonatal pneumonia to maternal urinary and neonatal isolates of group B streptococci. South Med J 1979;72:1410–1412

18. Persson K, Christensen KK, Christensen P, Forsgren A, Jorgensen C, Persson PH. Asymptomatic bacteriuria during pregnancy with special reference to group B streptococci. Scand J Infect Dis 1985;17:195–199

19. Baker CJ, Kasper DL. Correlation of maternal antibody deficiency with susceptibility to neonatal group B streptococcal infection. N Engl J Med 1976;294:753–756

20. Pass MA, Khare S, Dillon HC Jr. Twin pregnancies: incidence of group B streptococcal colonization and disease. J Pediatr 1980;97:635–637

21. Edwards MS, Jackson CV, Baker CJ. Increased risk of group B streptococcal disease in twins. JAMA 1981;245:2044–2046

22. Hall RT, Barnes W, Krishnan L, Harris DJ, Rhodes PG, Fayez J. Antibiotic treatment of parturient women colonized with group B streptococci. Am J Obstet Gynecol 1976;124:630–634

23. Gardner SE, Yow MD, Leeds LJ, Thompson PK, Mason EO Jr, Clark DJ. Failure of penicillin to eradicate group B streptococcal colonization in the pregnant woman. A couple study. Am J Obstet Gynecol 1979;135:1062–1065

24. Lewin EB, Amstey MS. Natural history of group B streptococcus colonization and its therapy during pregnancy. Am J Obstet Gynecol 1981;139:512–515

25. Merenstein GB, Todd WA, Brown G, Yost CC, Luzier T. Group B beta-hemolytic streptococcus: randomized controlled treatment study at term. Obstet Gynecol 1980;55:315–318

26. Pyati SP, Pildes RS, Jacobs NM, Ramamurthy RS, Heh TF, Raval DS, et al. Penicillin in infants weighing two kilograms or less with early-onset group B streptococcal disease. N Engl J Med 1983;308:1383–1389

27. Siegel JD, McCracken GH Jr, Threlkeld N, Milvenan B, Rosenfeld CR. Single dose penicillin prophylaxis against neonatal group B streptococcal infections. A controlled trial in 18,738 newborn infants. N Engl J Med 1980;303:769–775

28. Siegel JD, McCracken GH Jr, Threlkeld N, DePasse BM, Rosenfeld CR. Single-dose penicillin prophylaxis of neonatal group B streptococcal disease. Lancet 1982;1(8287):1426–1430

29. Matorras R, Garcia-Perea A, Omenaca F, Diez-Enciso M, Madero R, Usandizaga JA. Intrapartum chemoprophylaxis of early-onset group B streptococcal disease. Eur J Obstet Gynecol Reprod Biol 1991;40:57–62

30. Lim DV, Morales WJ, Walsh AF, Kazanis D. Reduction of morbidity and mortality rates for neonatal group B streptococcal disease through early diagnosis and chemoprophylaxis. J Clin Microbiol 1986;23:489–492

31. Allardice JG, Baskett TF, Seshia MM, Bowman N, Malazdrowicz R. Perinatal group B streptococcal colonization and infection. Am J Obstet Gynecol 1982;142:617–620

32. Garland SM, Fliegner JR. Group B streptococcus (GBS) and neonatal infections: the case for intrapartum chemoprophylaxis. Aust N Z J Obstet Gynaecol 1991;31:119–122

33. Boyer KM, Gadzala CA, Burd LI, Fisher DE, Paton JB, Gotoff SP. Selective intrapartum chemoprophylaxis of neonatal group B streptococcal early-onset disease. I. Epidemiologic rationale. J Infect Dis 1983;148:795–801

34. Boyer KM, Gotoff SP. Antimicrobial prophylaxis of neonatal group B streptococcal sepsis. Clin Perinatol 1988;15:831–850

35. Morales WJ, Lim D. Reduction of group B streptococcal maternal and neonatal infections in preterm pregnancies with premature rupture of membranes through a rapid identification test. Am J Obstet Gynecol 1987;157:13–16

36. Morales WJ, Lim DV, Walsh AF. Prevention of neonatal group B streptococcal sepsis by the use of a rapid screening test and selective intrapartum chemoprophylaxis. Am J Obstet Gynecol 1986;155:979–983

37. Tuppurainen N, Hallman M. Prevention of neonatal group B streptococcal disease: intrapartum detection and chemoprophylaxis of heavily colonized parturients. Obstet Gynecol 1989;73:583–587

38. Allen UD, Navas L, King SM. Effectiveness of intrapartum penicillin prophylaxis in preventing early-onset group B streptococcal infection: results of a meta-analysis. Can Med Assoc J 1993;149:1659–1665

39. Boyer KM, Gotoff SP. Prevention of early-onset neonatal group B streptococcal disease with selective intrapartum chemoprophylaxis. N Engl J Med 1986;314:1665–1669

40. American Academy of Pediatrics Committee on Infectious Diseases and Committee on Fetus and Newborn. Guidelines for prevention of group B streptococcal (GBS) infection by chemoprophylaxis. Pediatrics 1992;90:775–778

41. Rouse DJ, Goldenberg RL, Cliver SP, Cutter GR, Mennemeyer ST, Fargason CA Jr. Strategies for the prevention of early-onset neonatal group B streptococcal sepsis: a decision analysis. Obstet Gynecol 1994;83:483–494

42. Towers CV. Group B streptococcus: the US controversy. Lancet 1995;346:197–199

43. Centers for Disease Control and Prevention. Prevention of perinatal group B streptococcal disease: a public health perspective. MMWR 1996;45(RR-7):1–24

44. Landon MB, Harger J, McNellis D, Mercer B, Thom EA. Prevention of neonatal group B streptococcal infection. Obstet Gynecol 1994;84:460–462

45. American College of Obstetricians and Gynecologists. Ethical guidance for patient testing. ACOG Committee Opinion 159. Washington DC: ACOG, 1995

46. Schwartz B, Schuchat A, Oxtoby MJ, Cochi SL, Hightower A, Broome CV. Invasive group B streptococcal disease in adults. A population-based study in metropolitan Atlanta. JAMA 1991;266:1112–1114

47. Gilman AG, Rall TW, Nies AS, Taylor P. Goodman and Gilman's the pharmacological basis of therapeutics. 8th ed. New York: Pergamon Press, 1990

Appendix

CDC Recommendations for GBS Prophylaxis*

1. Obstetric care practitioners, in conjunction with supporting laboratories and labor and delivery facilities, should adopt a strategy for the prevention of early-onset GBS disease in neonates. Patients should be informed regarding the GBS prevention strategy available to them. Individual patient requests regarding GBS cultures should be honored. Insurance coverage for obstetrical care should include payment for GBS cultures.

2. Regardless of the preventive strategy used, women should be managed as follows:

   a) Treat women found to have symptomatic or asymptomatic GBS bacteriuria during pregnancy at the time of diagnosis. Because such women are usually heavily colonized with GBS, they should receive intrapartum chemoprophylaxis.

   b) Give intrapartum chemoprophylaxis to women with a history of previously giving birth to an infant with GBS disease; prenatal screening is not necessary.

3. Until further data become available to define the most effective prevention strategy, the following strategies are appropriate:

   a) Screen all pregnant women at 35–37 weeks gestation for anogenital GBS colonization (Fig. 1). Patients should be informed of screening results and of potential benefits and risks of intrapartum chemoprophylaxis for GBS carriers. Information systems should be developed and monitored to assure that prenatal culture results are available at the time and place of delivery. Offer intrapartum chemoprophylaxis to all pregnant women identified as GBS carriers by culture at 35–37 weeks.

      i) If the result of GBS cultures is not known at the time of labor, intrapartum chemoprophylaxis should be administered if one of the following is present: gestation < 37 weeks, duration of membrane rupture ≥ 18 hours, or temperature ≥ 38°C (100.4°F).

      ii) Use culture techniques that maximize the likelihood of GBS recovery. Since lower vaginal and rectal cultures are recommended, cultures should not be collected by speculum examination. The optimal method for GBS screening is collection of a single standard culture swab or two separate swabs of the distal vagina and anorectum. Swabs may be placed in a transport medium (eg, Amies) if the microbiology laboratory is offsite. The sample should be identified for the laboratory as specifically for GBS culture. Specimens should be inoculated into selective broth medium (either SBM broth or Lim broth), followed by overnight incubation and then subculture onto solid blood agar medium. In this screening culture, there is no need for the laboratory to culture for other organisms.

      iii) Laboratories should report results to the anticipated site of delivery as well as to the health care provider who ordered the test. Ideally, laboratories that perform GBS cultures will assure clinicians 24-hour, 7-day-a-week access to culture results.

      iv) Oral antimicrobial agents should not be used to treat women who are found to be colonized with GBS during prenatal screening. Such treatment is not effective in eliminating carriage or preventing neonatal disease.

   b) A chemoprophylaxis strategy based only on the presence of intrapartum risk factors (eg, gestation < 37 weeks, duration of membrane rupture ≥ 18 hours, or temperature ≥ 38°C) is an acceptable alternative (Fig. 2).

4. For intrapartum chemoprophylaxis, use intravenous penicillin G (5 million units initially and then 2.5 million units every 4 hours) until delivery. Intravenous ampicillin (2 g initially and then 1 g every 4 hours until delivery) is an acceptable alternative to penicillin G, but penicillin G is preferred since it has a narrow spectrum and is therefore less likely to select for antibiotic-resistant organisms. Clindamycin or erythromycin may be

---

* Centers for Disease Control and Prevention. Prevention of perinatal group B streptococcal disease: a public health perspective. MMWR 1996;45(RR-7):1–24

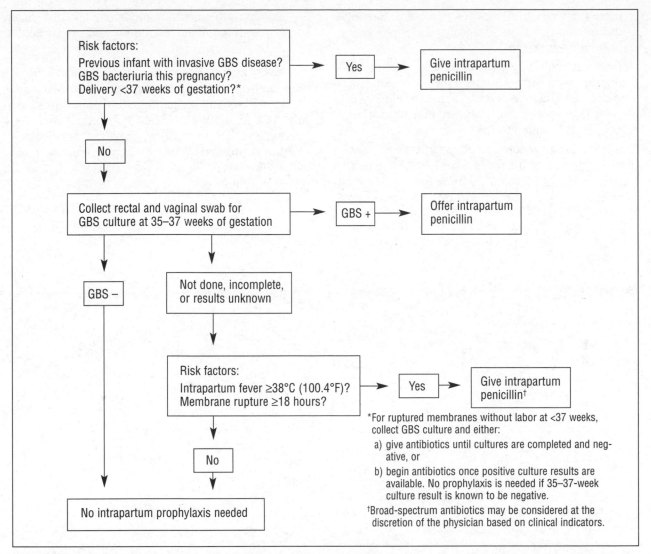

Fig. 1. Prevention strategy for early-onset group B streptococci (GBS) disease using prenatal screening at 35–37 weeks. (Centers for Disease Control and Prevention. Prevention of perinatal group B streptococcal disease: a public health perspective. MMWR 1996;45[RR-7]:1–24)

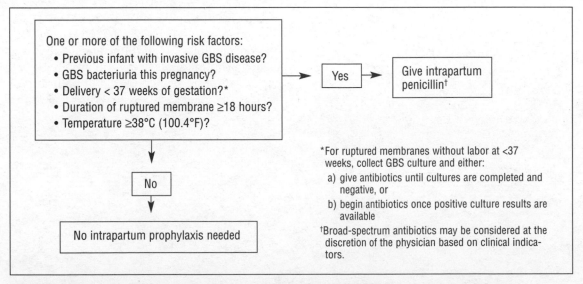

Fig. 2. Prevention strategy for early-onset group B streptococci (GBS) disease using risk factors. (Centers for Disease Control and Prevention. Prevention of perinatal group B streptococcal disease: a public health perspective. MMWR 1996;45[RR-7]:1–24)

used for women allergic to penicillin, although the efficacy of these drugs for GBS prevention has not be assessed.

(Women with a clinical diagnosis of chorioamnionitis who are receiving other treatment regimens that include agents active against GBS, such as ampicillin or clindamycin, do not need penicillin G added to the regimen)....

6. Local health agencies, in conjunction with appropriate groups of hospitals, should consider establishing surveillance to monitor the incidence of neonatal GBS disease, occurrence of adverse reactions to chemoprophylaxis, and the emergence of perinatal infections due to penicillin-resistant organisms.

Investigations designed to evaluate and compare these and other strategies are urgently needed. Such studies will require the participation of multiple institutions and should evaluate outcomes, including perinatal GBS infections, adverse reactions to chemoprophylaxis, and perinatal infections due to penicillin-resistant organisms. Characterization of protocol failures is also important.

ACOG Committee Opinion

Committee on
Gynecologic Practice

Number 246, December 2000   *(Replaces No. 229, December 1999)*

Primary and Preventive Care: Periodic Assessments

The following charts are updated versions of those previously published by the American College of Obstetricians and Gynecologists (ACOG) in *Guidelines for Women's Health Care* (1996); Primary Care Review No. 1, "Primary and Preventive Care" (1997); and Committee Opinion No. 229. This version replaces those previous versions. The policies and recommendations of ACOG committees regarding specific aspects of the health care of women have been incorporated; they may differ from the recommendations of other groups. Except as noted, these recommendations are for nonpregnant women.

Periodic assessments provide an excellent opportunity to counsel patients about preventive care. These assessments, yearly or as appropriate (unless otherwise noted), should include screening, evaluation, and counseling based on age and risk factors. Personal behavioral characteristics are important aspects of a woman's health. Positive behaviors, such as exercise, should be reinforced. The following guidelines indicate routine assessments for women based on age groups and risk factors (Table 1) and list leading causes of death and morbidity for each age group identified by various sources (see box). It is recognized that variations may be required to adjust to the needs of a specific individual. For example, certain risk factors may influence additional assessments and interventions. Physicians should be alert to high-risk factors (indicated by an asterisk and further elucidated in Table 1). During evaluation, the patient should be made aware of high-risk conditions that require targeted screening or treatment.

The material in these charts is based heavily on evidence of effectiveness and cost-effectiveness. It should be recognized, however, that making these determinations is both complex and inexact in the present environment. Nonetheless, the progress that has been made is encouraging, and the goal is desirable and of great importance. Although there will be differences of opinion regarding some specific recommendations, the major benefit to be derived should not be lost in debating those issues.

ISSN 1074-861X

The American College of Obstetricians and Gynecologists
409 12th Street, SW
PO Box 96920
Washington, DC 20090-6920

12345/43210

Periodic Assessment
Ages 13–18 Years

Screening

History

Reason for visit

Health status: medical, surgical, family

Dietary/nutrition assessment

Physical activity

Use of complementary and alternative medicine

Tobacco, alcohol, other drug use

Abuse/neglect

Sexual practices

Physical Examination

Height

Weight

Blood pressure

Secondary sexual characteristics (Tanner staging)

Pelvic examination (yearly when sexually active or beginning at age 18 years)

Skin*

Laboratory Testing

Periodic

Pap testing (yearly when sexually active or beginning at age 18 years)

*High-Risk Groups**

Hemoglobin level assessment

Bacteriuria testing

Sexually transmitted disease testing

Human immunodeficiency virus testing

Genetic testing/counseling

Rubella titer assessment

Tuberculosis skin testing

Lipid profile assessment

Fasting glucose testing

Cholesterol testing

Hepatitis C virus testing

Colorectal cancer screening†

Evaluation and Counseling

Sexuality

Development

High-risk behaviors

Preventing unwanted/unintended pregnancy

—Postponing sexual involvement

—Contraceptive options

Sexually transmitted diseases

—Partner selection

—Barrier protection

Fitness and Nutrition

Dietary/nutrition assessment (including eating disorders)

Exercise: discussion of program

Folic acid supplementation (0.4 mg/d)

Calcium intake

Psychosocial Evaluation

Interpersonal/family relationships

Sexual identity

Personal goal development

Behavioral/learning disorders

Abuse/neglect

Satisfactory school experience

Peer relationships

Cardiovascular Risk Factors

Family history

Hypertension

Dyslipidemia

Obesity

Diabetes mellitus

Health/Risk Behaviors

Hygiene (including dental); fluoride supplementation

Injury prevention

—Safety belts and helmets

—Recreational hazards

—Firearms

—Hearing

Skin exposure to ultraviolet rays

Suicide: depressive symptoms

Tobacco, alcohol, other drug use

Immunizations

Periodic

Tetanus–diphtheria booster (once between ages 11 years and 16 years)

Hepatitis B vaccine (one series for those not previously immunized)

*High-Risk Groups**

Influenza vaccine

Hepatitis A vaccine

Pneumococcal vaccine

Measles–mumps–rubella vaccine

Varicella vaccine

Leading Causes of Death‡

1. Motor vehicle accidents
2. Homicide
3. Suicide
4. Cancer
5. All other accidents and adverse effects
6. Diseases of the heart
7. Congenital anomalies
8. Chronic obstructive pulmonary diseases

Leading Causes of Morbidity‡

Acne

Asthma

Chlamydia

Depression

Dermatitis

Headaches

Infective, viral, and parasitic diseases

Influenza

Injuries

Nose, throat, ear, and upper respiratory infections

Sexual assault

Sexually transmitted diseases

Urinary tract infections

---

*See Table 1.

†Only for those with a family history of familial adenomatous polyposis or 8 years after the start of pancolitis. For a more detailed discussion of colorectal cancer screening, see Byers T, Levin B, Rothenberger D, Dodd GD, Smith RA. American Cancer Society guidelines for screening and surveillance for early detection of colorectal polyps and cancer: update 1997. American Cancer Society Detection and Treatment Advisory Group on Colorectal Cancer. CA Cancer J Clin 1997;47:154–160.

‡See box.

Periodic Assessment
Ages 19–39 Years

Screening

History
- Reason for visit
- Health status: medical, surgical, family
- Dietary/nutrition assessment
- Physical activity
- Use of complementary and alternative medicine
- Tobacco, alcohol, other drug use
- Abuse/neglect
- Sexual practices
- Urinary and fecal incontinence

Physical Examination
- Height
- Weight
- Blood pressure
- Neck: adenopathy, thyroid
- Breasts
- Abdomen
- Pelvic examination
- Skin*

Laboratory Testing

Periodic
- Pap testing (physician and patient discretion after three consecutive normal tests if low risk)

High-Risk Groups*
- Hemoglobin level assessment
- Bacteriuria testing
- Mammography
- Fasting glucose testing
- Cholesterol testing
- Sexually transmitted disease testing
- Human immunodeficiency virus testing
- Genetic testing/counseling
- Rubella titer assessment
- Tuberculosis skin testing
- Lipid profile assessment
- Thyroid-stimulating hormone testing
- Hepatitis C virus testing
- Colorectal cancer screening

Evaluation and Counseling

Sexuality
- High-risk behaviors
- Contraceptive options for prevention of unwanted pregnancy
- Preconceptional and genetic counseling for desired pregnancy
- Sexually transmitted diseases
- —Partner selection
- —Barrier protection
- Sexual function

Fitness and Nutrition
- Dietary/nutrition assessment
- Exercise: discussion of program
- Folic acid supplementation (0.4 mg/d)
- Calcium intake

Psychosocial Evaluation
- Interpersonal/family relationships
- Domestic violence
- Work satisfaction
- Lifestyle/stress
- Sleep disorders

Cardiovascular Risk Factors
- Family history
- Hypertension
- Dyslipidemia
- Obesity
- Diabetes mellitus
- Lifestyle

Health/Risk Behaviors
- Hygiene (including dental)
- Injury prevention
- —Safety belts and helmets
- —Occupational hazards
- —Recreational hazards
- —Firearms
- —Hearing
- Breast self-examination
- Chemoprophylaxis for breast cancer (for high-risk women ages 35 years or older)†
- Skin exposure to ultraviolet rays
- Suicide: depressive symptoms
- Tobacco, alcohol, other drug use

Immunizations

Periodic
- Tetanus–diphtheria booster (every 10 years)

*High-Risk Groups**
- Measles–mumps–rubella vaccine
- Hepatitis A vaccine
- Hepatitis B vaccine
- Influenza vaccine
- Pneumococcal vaccine
- Varicella vaccine

Leading Causes of Death‡
1. Accidents and adverse effects
2. Cancer
3. Human immunodeficiency virus infection
4. Diseases of the heart
5. Homicide
6. Suicide
7. Cerebrovascular diseases
8. Chronic liver disease and cirrhosis

Leading Causes of Morbidity‡
- Asthma
- Back symptoms
- Breast disease
- Deformity or orthopedic impairment
- Depression
- Diabetes
- Gynecologic disorders
- Headache/migraines
- Hypertension
- Infective, viral, and parasitic diseases
- Influenza
- Injuries
- Nose, throat, ear, and upper respiratory infections
- Sexual assault/domestic violence
- Sexually transmitted diseases
- Skin rash/dermatitis
- Substance abuse
- Urinary tract infections
- Vaginitis

*See Table 1.

†The decision to use tamoxifen should be individualized. For a more detailed discussion of risk assessment and chemoprevention therapy, see American College of Obstetricians and Gynecologists. Tamoxifen and the prevention of breast cancer in high-risk women. ACOG Committee Opinion 224. Washington, DC: ACOG, 1999.

‡See box.

Periodic Assessment
Ages 40–64 Years

Screening

History

Reason for visit

Health status: medical, surgical, family

Dietary/nutrition assessment

Physical activity

Use of complementary and alternative medicine

Tobacco, alcohol, other drug use

Abuse/neglect

Sexual practices

Urinary and fecal incontinence

Physical Examination

Height

Weight

Blood pressure

Oral cavity

Neck: adenopathy, thyroid

Breasts, axillae

Abdomen

Pelvic examination

Skin*

Laboratory Testing

Periodic

Pap testing (physician and patient discretion after three consecutive normal tests if low risk)

Mammography (every 1–2 years until age 50 years; yearly beginning at age 50 years)

Cholesterol testing (every 5 years beginning at age 45 years)

Yearly fecal occult blood testing plus flexible sigmoidoscopy every 5 years *or* colonoscopy every 10 years *or* double contrast barium enema (DCBE) every 5–10 years, with digital rectal examination performed at the time of each screening sigmoidoscopy, colonoscopy, or DCBE (beginning at age 50 years)

Fasting glucose testing (every 3 years after age 45 years)

*High-Risk Groups**

Hemoglobin level assessment

Bacteriuria testing

Fasting glucose testing

Sexually transmitted disease testing

Human immunodeficiency virus testing

Tuberculosis skin testing

Lipid profile assessment

Thyroid-stimulating hormone testing

Hepatitis C virus testing

Colorectal cancer screening

Evaluation and Counseling

Sexuality†

High-risk behaviors

Contraceptive options for prevention of unwanted pregnancy

Sexually transmitted diseases

—Partner selection

—Barrier protection

Sexual functioning

Fitness and Nutrition

Dietary/nutrition assessment

Exercise: discussion of program

Folic acid supplementation (0.4 mg/d before age 50 years)

Calcium intake

Psychosocial Evaluation

Family relationships

Domestic violence

Work satisfaction

Retirement planning

Lifestyle/stress

Sleep disorders

Cardiovascular Risk Factors

Family history

Hypertension

Dyslipidemia

Obesity

Diabetes mellitus

Lifestyle

Health/Risk Behaviors

Hygiene (including dental)

Hormone replacement therapy

Injury prevention

—Safety belts and helmets

—Occupational hazards

—Recreational hazards

—Sports involvement

—Firearms

—Hearing

Breast self-examination

Chemoprophylaxis for breast cancer (for high-risk women)‡

Skin exposure to ultraviolet rays

Suicide: depressive symptoms

Tobacco, alcohol, other drug use

Immunizations

Periodic

Influenza vaccine (annually beginning at age 50 years)

Tetanus–diphtheria booster (every 10 years)

*High-Risk Groups**

Measles–mumps–rubella vaccine

Hepatitis A vaccine

Hepatitis B vaccine

Influenza vaccine

Pneumococcal vaccine

Varicella vaccine

Leading Causes of Death§

1. Cancer
2. Diseases of the heart
3. Cerebrovascular diseases
4. Accidents and adverse effects
5. Chronic obstructive pulmonary disease
6. Diabetes mellitus
7. Chronic liver disease and cirrhosis
8. Pneumonia and influenza

Leading Causes of Morbidity§

Arthritis/osteoarthritis

Asthma

Back symptoms

Breast disease

Cardiovascular disease

Carpal tunnel syndrome

Deformity or orthopedic impairment

Depression

Diabetes

Headache

Hypertension

Infective, viral, and parasitic diseases

Influenza

Injuries

Menopause

Nose, throat, and upper respiratory infections

Obesity

Skin conditions/dermatitis

Substance abuse

Urinary tract infections

Urinary tract (other conditions, including urinary incontinence)

Vision impairment

---

*See Table 1.

†Preconceptional and genetic counseling is appropriate for certain women in this age group.

‡The decision to use tamoxifen should be individualized. For a more detailed discussion of risk assessment and chemoprevention therapy, see American College of Obstetricians and Gynecologists. Tamoxifen and the prevention of breast cancer in high-risk women. ACOG Committee Opinion 224. Washington, DC: ACOG, 1999.

§See box.

Periodic Assessment
Ages 65 Years and Older

Screening

History

Reason for visit

Health status: medical, surgical, family

Dietary/nutrition assessment

Physical activity

Use of complementary and alternative medicine

Tobacco, alcohol, other drug use, and concurrent medication use

Abuse/neglect

Sexual practices

Urinary and fecal incontinence

Physical Examination

Height

Weight

Blood pressure

Oral cavity

Neck: adenopathy, thyroid

Breasts, axillae

Abdomen

Pelvic examination

Skin*

Laboratory Testing

Periodic

Pap testing (physician and patient discretion after three consecutive normal tests if low risk)

Urinalysis

Mammography

Cholesterol testing (every 3–5 years before age 75 years)

Yearly fecal occult blood testing plus flexible sigmoidoscopy every 5 years *or* colonoscopy every 10 years *or* double contrast barium enema (DCBE) every 5–10 years, with digital rectal examination performed at the time of each screening sigmoidoscopy, colonoscopy, or DCBE

Fasting glucose testing (every 3 years)

High-Risk Groups*

Hemoglobin level assessment

Sexually transmitted disease testing

Human immunodeficiency virus testing

Tuberculosis skin testing

Lipid profile assessment

Thyroid-stimulating hormone testing

Hepatitis C virus testing

Colorectal cancer screening

Evaluation and Counseling

Sexuality

Sexual functioning

Sexual behaviors

Sexually transmitted diseases

—Partner selection

—Barrier protection

Fitness and Nutrition

Dietary/nutrition assessment

Exercise: discussion of program

Calcium intake

Psychosocial Evaluation

Neglect/abuse

Lifestyle/stress

Depression/sleep disorders

Family relationships

Work/retirement satisfaction

Cardiovascular Risk Factors

Hypertension

Dyslipidemia

Obesity

Diabetes mellitus

Sedentary lifestyle

Health/Risk Behaviors

Hygiene (general and dental)

Hormone replacement therapy

Injury prevention

—Safety belts and helmets

—Prevention of falls

—Occupational hazards

—Recreational hazards

—Firearms

Visual acuity/glaucoma

Hearing

Breast self-examination

Chemoprophylaxis for breast cancer (for high-risk women)[†]

Skin exposure to ultraviolet rays

Suicide: depressive symptoms

Tobacco, alcohol, other drug use

Immunizations

Periodic

Tetanus–diphtheria booster (every 10 years)

Influenza vaccine (annually)

Pneumococcal vaccine (once)

High-Risk Groups

Hepatitis A vaccine

Hepatitis B vaccine

Varicella vaccine

Leading Causes of Death[‡]

1. Diseases of the heart
2. Cancer
3. Cerebrovascular diseases
4. Chronic obstructive pulmonary diseases
5. Pneumonia and influenza
6. Diabetes mellitus
7. Accidents and adverse effects
8. Alzheimer's disease

Leading Causes of Morbidity[‡]

Arthritis/osteoarthritis

Back symptoms

Breast cancer

Chronic obstructive pulmonary diseases

Cardiovascular disease

Deformity or orthopedic impairment

Degeneration of macula retinae and posterior pole

Diabetes

Hearing and vision impairment

Hypertension

Hypothyroidism and other thyroid disease

Influenza

Nose, throat, and upper respiratory infections

Osteoporosis

Skin lesions/dermatoses/dermatitis

Urinary tract infections

Urinary tract (other conditions, including urinary incontinence)

Vertigo

---

*See Table 1.

[†]The decision to use tamoxifen should be individualized. For a more detailed discussion of risk assessment and chemoprevention therapy, see American College of Obstetricians and Gynecologists. Tamoxifen and the prevention of breast cancer in high-risk women. ACOG Committee Opinion 224. Washington, DC: ACOG, 1999.

[‡]See box.

Table 1. High-Risk Factors

Intervention	High-Risk Factor
Bacteriuria testing	Diabetes mellitus
Cholesterol testing	Familial lipid disorders; family history of premature coronary heart disease; history of coronary heart disease
Colorectal cancer screening*	Colorectal cancer or adenomatous polyps in first-degree relative younger than 60 years or in two or more first-degree relatives of any ages; family history of familial adenomatous polyposis or hereditary nonpolyposis colon cancer; history of colorectal cancer, adenomatous polyps, or inflammatory bowel disease
Fasting glucose testing	Obesity; first-degree relative with diabetes mellitus; member of a high-risk ethnic population (eg, African American, Hispanic, Native American, Asian, Pacific Islander); have delivered a baby weighing more than 9 lb or history of gestational diabetes mellitus; hypertensive; high-density lipoprotein cholesterol level of at least 35 mg/dL; triglyceride level of at least 250 mg/dL; history of impaired glucose tolerance or impaired fasting glucose
Fluoride supplementation	Live in area with inadequate water fluoridation (<0.7 ppm)
Genetic testing/counseling	Exposure to teratogens; considering pregnancy at age 35 years or older; patient, partner, or family member with history of genetic disorder or birth defect; African, Acadian, Eastern European Jewish, Mediterranean, or Southeast Asian ancestry
Hemoglobin level assessment	Caribbean, Latin American, Asian, Mediterranean, or African ancestry; history of excessive menstrual flow
Hepatitis A vaccination	International travelers; illegal drug users; people who work with nonhuman primates; chronic liver disease; clotting-factor disorders; sex partners of bisexual men; measles, mumps, and rubella nonimmune persons; food-service workers; health-care workers; day-care workers
Hepatitis B vaccination	Intravenous drug users and their sexual contacts; recipients of clotting factor concentrates; occupational exposure to blood or blood products; patients and workers in dialysis units; persons with chronic renal or hepatic disease; household or sexual contact with hepatitis B virus carriers; history of sexual activity with multiple partners; history of sexual activity with sexually active homosexual or bisexual men; international travelers; residents and staff of institutions for the developmentally disabled and of correctional institutions
Hepatitis C virus (HCV) testing	History of injecting illegal drugs; recipients of clotting factor concentrates before 1987; chronic (long-term) hemodialysis; persistently abnormal alanine aminotransferase levels; recipient of blood from a donor who later tested positive for HCV infection; recipient of blood or blood-component transfusion or organ transplant before July 1992; occupational percutaneous or mucosal exposure to HCV-positive blood
Human immunodeficiency virus (HIV) testing	Seeking treatment for sexually transmitted diseases; drug use by injection; history of prostitution; past or present sexual partner who is HIV positive or bisexual or injects drugs; long-term residence or birth in an area with high prevalence of HIV infection; history of transfusion from 1978 to 1985; invasive cervical cancer; pregnancy. Offer to women seeking preconceptional care.
Influenza vaccination	Anyone who wishes to reduce the chance of becoming ill with influenza; resident in long-term care facility; chronic cardiopulmonary disorders; metabolic diseases (eg, diabetes mellitus, hemoglobinopathies, immunosuppression, renal dysfunction); health-care workers; day-care workers; pregnant women who will be in the second or third trimester during the epidemic season. Pregnant women with medical problems should be offered vaccination before the influenza season regardless of stage of pregnancy.
Lipid profile assessment	Elevated cholesterol level; history of parent or sibling with blood cholesterol of at least 240 mg/dL; first-degree relative with premature (<55 years of age for men, <65 years of age for women) coronary heart disease; diabetes mellitus; smoking habit
Mammography	Women who have had breast cancer or who have a first-degree relative (ie, mother, sister, or daughter) or multiple other relatives who have a history of premenopausal breast or breast and ovarian cancer

Table 1. High-Risk Factors *(continued)*

Intervention	High-Risk Factor
Measles–mumps–rubella (MMR) vaccination	Adults born in 1957 or later should be offered vaccination (one dose of MMR) if there is no proof of immunity or documentation of a dose given after first birthday; persons vaccinated in 1963–1967 should be offered revaccination (2 doses); health-care workers, students entering college, international travelers, and rubella-negative postpartum patients should be offered a second dose.
Pneumococcal vaccination	Chronic illness such as cardiovascular disease, pulmonary disease, diabetes mellitus, alcoholism, chronic liver disease, cerebrospinal fluid leaks, functional or anatomic asplenia; exposure to an environment where pneumococcal outbreaks have occurred; immunocompromised patients (eg, HIV infection, hematologic or solid malignancies, chemotherapy, steroid therapy); pregnant patients with chronic illness. Revaccination after 5 years may be appropriate for certain high-risk groups.
Rubella titer assessment	Childbearing age and no evidence of immunity
Sexually transmitted disease (STD) testing	History of multiple sexual partners or a sexual partner with multiple contacts, sexual contact with persons with culture-proven STD, history of repeated episodes of STDs, attendance at clinics for STDs; routine screening for chlamydial and gonorrheal infection for all sexually active adolescents and other asymptomatic women at high risk for infection
Skin examination	Increased recreational or occupational exposure to sunlight; family or personal history of skin cancer; clinical evidence of precursor lesions
Thyroid-stimulating hormone testing	Strong family history of thyroid disease; autoimmune disease (evidence of subclinical hypothyroidism may be related to unfavorable lipid profiles)
Tuberculosis skin testing	Human immunodeficiency virus infection; close contact with persons known or suspected to have tuberculosis; medical risk factors known to increase risk of disease if infected; born in country with high tuberculosis prevalence; medically underserved; low income; alcoholism; intravenous drug use; resident of long-term care facility (eg, correctional institutions, mental institutions, nursing homes and facilities); health professional working in high-risk health care facilities
Varicella vaccination	All susceptible adults and adolescents, including health-care workers; household contacts of immunocompromised individuals; teachers; day-care workers; residents and staff of institutional settings, colleges, prisons, or military installations; international travelers; nonpregnant women of childbearing age

*For a more detailed discussion of colorectal cancer screening, see Byers T, Levin B, Rothenberger D, Dodd GD, Smith RA. American Cancer Society guidelines for screening and surveillance for early detection of colorectal polyps and cancer: update 1997. American Cancer Society Detection and Treatment Advisory Group on Colorectal Cancer. CA Cancer J Clin 1997;47:154–160.

Sources of Leading Causes of Mortality and Morbidity

Leading causes of mortality are provided by the Mortality Statistics Branch at the National Center for Health Statistics. Data are from 1996, the most recent year for which final data are available. The causes are ranked.

Leading causes of morbidity are unranked estimates based on information from the following sources:

- National Health Interview Survey, 1994
- National Ambulatory Medical Care Survey, 1996
- National Hospital Discharge Survey, 1996
- U.S. Department of Justice National Crime Victimization Survey
- U.S. Centers for Disease Control and Prevention Sexually Transmitted Disease Surveillance, 1996
- U.S. Centers for Disease Control and Prevention HIV/AIDS Surveillance Report, 1997
- National Nursing Home Survey, 1995

Committee on Gynecologic Practice   Number 152—March 1995

Recommendations on Frequency of Pap Test Screening

The College's current recommendations on the frequency of Pap test screening are:

All women who are or who have been sexually active or who have reached age 18 should undergo an annual Pap test and pelvic examination. After a woman has had three or more consecutive, satisfactory annual examinations with normal findings, the Pap test may be performed less frequently in a low-risk woman at the discretion of her physician.

The recognized problems of the high number of false-negative results and failure of patients to return at regular intervals raise questions about the safety of screening every 3 years as recommended by the American Cancer Society. Recent proposals for health care financing have suggested that Pap test screening may be done even less frequently or may be eliminated altogether in certain groups of women. Theoretical models may show this strategy to be cost-saving; however, a reduction in the frequency of Pap test screening in England has been accompanied by an increased incidence of cervical cancer cases and deaths from cervical carcinoma. In contrast, the Canadian province of British Columbia has had a continuing reduction in morbidity and mortality from invasive squamous cell cancers of the cervix, which is directly attributable to the province's 30-year history of performing annual Pap tests.

Certain high-risk factors have been associated with the development of cervical intraepithelial neoplasia and cervical carcinoma. The College recommends that when one or more of these risk factors is present, more frequent Pap tests may be required. High-risk factors include:

- Women who have had multiple sexual partners or whose male sexual partners have had multiple partners
- Women who began sexual intercourse at an early age
- Women whose male sexual partners have had other sexual partners with cervical cancer
- Women with current or prior human papillomavirus infection or condylomata or both
- Women with current or prior herpes simplex virus infections
- Women who are infected with the human immunodeficiency virus (HIV)
- Women with a history of other sexually transmitted diseases
- Women who are immunosuppressed (such as those who have received renal transplants)
- Smokers and abusers of other substances, including alcohol
- Women who have a history of cervical dysplasia or cervical cancer or endometrial, vaginal, or vulvar cancer
- Women of lower socioeconomic status*

The cost-effectiveness of cytologic screening for vaginal neoplasia after removal of the cervix for benign disease has not been demonstrated. Nonetheless, periodic cytologic evaluation of the vagina in such cases, based on the above risk factors, is warranted.

Physicians are encouraged to consider these risk factors when determining the frequency of Pap test screening. Annual health maintenance physical examinations and pelvic examinations continue to be encouraged even for women who appear to be at low risk for developing cervical intraepithelial neoplasia or cervical cancer. Many women may not be aware of previous or other sexual contacts of their partner, and they may be unknowingly at high risk.

---

*Low socioeconomic status appears to be a surrogate for a number of closely related risk factors that place these women at greater risk for cervical cancer.

ACOG Committee Opinion

Committee on
Obstetric Practice

The American College of Obstetricians and Gynecologists
409 12th Street, SW
PO Box 96920
Washington, DC 20090-6920

12345/43210

Number 248, December 2000

Response to Searle's Drug Warning on Misoprostol

On August 23, 2000, G.D. Searle & Co. issued a letter entitled "Important Drug Warning Concerning Unapproved Use of Intravaginal or Oral Misoprostol in Pregnant Women for Induction of Labor or Abortion." This letter cautions that Cytotec (misoprostol) is indicated for prevention of nonsteroidal-antiinflammatory-drug-induced gastric ulcers and states, "...*Cytotec administration by any route is contraindicated in women who are pregnant because it can cause abortion.*" The letter further states that Searle has become aware of the drug's use for induction of labor or as a cervical ripening agent prior to termination of pregnancy. Moreover, the letter notes serious adverse events, including uterine hyperstimulation and uterine rupture, which have resulted in fetal and maternal death. Finally, the company cautions, "*In addition to the known and unknown acute risks to the mother and fetus, the effect of Cytotec on the later growth, development, and functional maturation of the child when Cytotec is used for induction of labor or cervical ripening has not been established.*"

The American College of Obstetricians and Gynecologists (ACOG) is concerned about the content, timing, and tone of this letter. Given that misoprostol is commonly employed in conjunction with mifepristone (RU 486) to achieve nonsurgical early pregnancy terminations, the arrival of the Searle letter within weeks of the U.S. Food and Drug Administration's (FDA) approval of mifepristone could limit the use of this new option for reproductive choice. Also, although the letter correctly points out the potentially serious, but relatively rare, risks of misoprostol when employed for cervical ripening and labor induction, it fails to comment on the extensive clinical experience with this agent and the large body of published reports supporting its safety and efficacy when used appropriately. A recent review of the Cochrane Pregnancy and Childbirth group trials registry identified 26 clinical trials of misoprostol for cervical ripening or induction of labor or both (1). These studies indicate misoprostol is more effective than prostaglandin E_2 in achieving vaginal deliveries within 24 hours and reduces the need for and total amount of oxytocin augmentation. Although these studies do suggest misoprostol is associated with a higher incidence of uterine hyperstimulation and meconium-stained amniotic fluid, these complications were more common with higher doses (>25 µg) of misoprostol. Other recent reviews and clinical trials support these conclusions (2–4). No studies indicate that intrapartum exposure to misoprostol (or other prostaglandin cervical ripening agents) has any long-term adverse health consequences to the fetus in the absence of fetal distress, nor is there a plausible biologic basis for such a concern.

A review of published reports and of MedWatch, the FDA medical products reporting program, indicates the vast majority of adverse maternal and fetal outcomes associated with misoprostol therapy resulted from the use of doses greater than 25 µg, dosing intervals more frequent than 3–6 hours, addition of oxytocin less than 4 hours after the last misoprostol dose, or use of the drug in women with prior cesarean delivery or major uterine surgery. Grand multiparity also appears to be a relative risk factor for uterine rupture.

Thus, based on recently published series and a detailed review of adverse outcomes reported to the FDA, the ACOG Committee on Obstetric Practice strongly endorses its previous conclusion, published in Committee Opinion Number 228 (November 1999), *Induction of Labor with Misoprostol*, which states, *"Given the current evidence, intravaginal misoprostol tablets appear effective in inducing labor in pregnant women who have unfavorable cervices"* (5). Nonetheless, the committee would like to emphasize that the following clinical practices appear to minimize the risk of uterine hyperstimulation and rupture in patients undergoing cervical ripening or induction in the third trimester:

1. If misoprostol is to be used for cervical ripening or labor induction in the third trimester, one quarter of a 100-µg tablet (ie, approximately 25 µg) should be considered for the initial dose.

2. Doses should not be administered more frequently than every 3–6 hours.

3. Oxytocin should not be administered less than 4 hours after the last misoprostol dose.

4. Misoprostol should not be used in patients with a previous cesarean delivery or prior major uterine surgery.

The use of higher doses of misoprostol (eg, 50 µg every 6 hours) to induce labor may be appropriate in some situations, although there are reports that such doses increase the risk of complications, including uterine hyperstimulation and uterine rupture (6). There

is insufficient clinical evidence to address the safety or efficacy of misoprostol in patients with multifetal gestations or suspected fetal macrosomia.

In conclusion, the ACOG Committee on Obstetric Practice reaffirms that misoprostol is a safe and effective agent for cervical ripening and labor induction when used appropriately. Moreover, misoprostol also contributes to the obstetrician–gynecologist's resources as an effective treatment for serious postpartum hemorrhage in the presence of uterine atony (7–12).

References

1. Hofmeyr GJ, Gulmezoglu AM. Vaginal misoprostol for cervical ripening and labour induction in late pregnancy (Cochrane Review). In: The Cochrane Library, Issue 3, 2000. Oxford: Update Software

2. Wing DA. Labor induction with misoprostol. Am J Obstet Gynecol 1999;181:339–345

3. Nunes F, Rodrigues R, Meirinho M. Randomized comparison between intravaginal misoprostol and dinoprostone for cervical ripening and induction of labor. Am J Obstet Gynecol 1999;181:626–629

4. Blanchette HA, Nayak S, Erasmus S. Comparison of the safety and efficacy of intravaginal misoprostol (prostaglandin E1) with those of dinoprostone (prostaglandin E2) for cervical ripening and induction of labor in a community hospital. Am J Obstet Gynecol 1999;180: 1551–1559

5. American College of Obstetricians and Gynecologists. Induction of labor with misoprostol. ACOG Committee Opinion 228. Washington, DC: ACOG, 1999

6. American College of Obstetricians and Gynecologists. Induction of labor. ACOG Practice Bulletin 10. Washington, DC: ACOG, 1999

7. El-Refaey H, O'Brien P, Morafa W, Walder J, Rodeck C. Use of oral misoprostol in the prevention of postpartum haemorrhage. Br J Obstet Gynaecol 1997;104:336–339

8. O'Brien P, El-Refaey H, Gordon A, Geary M, Rodeck CH. Rectally administered misoprostol for the treatment of postpartum hemorrhage unresponsive to oxytocin and ergometrine: a descriptive study. Obstet Gynecol 1998; 92:212–214

9. Bamigboye AA, Hofmeyr GJ, Merrell DA. Rectal misoprostol in the prevention of postpartum hemorrhage: a placebo-controlled trial. Am J Obstet Gynecol 1998;179: 1043–1046

10. Surbek DV, Fehr PM, Hosli I, Holzgreve W. Oral misoprostol for third stage of labor: a randomized placebo-controlled trial. Obstet Gynecol 1999;94:255–258

11. Hofmeyr GJ, Nikodem VC, de Jager M, Gelbart BR. A randomised placebo controlled trial of oral misoprostol in the third stage of labour. Br J Obstet Gynaecol 1998;105: 971–975

12. Bamigboye AA, Merrell DA, Hofmeyr GJ, Mitchell R. Randomized comparison of rectal misoprostol with Syntometrine for management of third stage of labor. Acta Obstet Gynecol Scand 1998;77:178–181

ACOG Committee Opinion

Committee on
Gynecologic Practice

Requests for authorization to
make photocopies should be
directed to:

Copyright Clearance Center
222 Rosewood Drive
Danvers, MA 01923
(978) 750-8400

ISSN 1074-861X

**The American College of
Obstetricians and Gynecologists**
409 12th Street, SW
PO Box 96920
Washington, DC 20090-6920

12345/54321

Risk of breast cancer with estrogen–progestin replacement therapy.
Committee Opinion No. 262.
American College of Obstetricians
and Gynecologists. Obstet Gynecol
2001;98:1181–1183

Number 262, December 2001

Risk of Breast Cancer with Estrogen–Progestin Replacement Therapy

ABSTRACT: *Recent articles have examined the association between the use of combination estrogen–progestin regimens for hormone replacement thera-py (HRT) and the risk of breast cancer. The objective of this Committee Opinion is to evaluate critically the presented evidence. Although epidemio-logic studies suggest that the addition of progestins to estrogens may increase the risk of breast cancer, this increased risk has not been proved. The American College of Obstetricians and Gynecologists continues to recom-mend that HRT be considered as a treatment to relieve vasomotor symptoms and genitourinary tract atrophy and to reduce the risk of osteoporosis and, potentially, cardiovascular disease. Postmenopausal women should be apprised of the current understanding of the risks and benefits of HRT. When considering the use of HRT for longer than 5 years, the clinician and indi-vidual patient should weigh the benefits versus the potential side effects and risks for that particular patient.*

Breast Cancer Risk with Estrogen–Progestin Preparations

Two recent retrospective observational studies have reexamined the issue of breast cancer risk and the use of estrogen–progestin HRT regimens. Researchers have retrospectively reviewed data on 46,355 postmenopausal women who were monitored for 15 years in the Breast Cancer Detection Demonstration Project (1). In this cohort study, the authors analyzed 2,082 incident cases of breast cancer. Among women with current or recent (with-in the past 4 years) HRT use, those taking estrogen alone had a 1.2-fold (95% confidence interval [CI], 1.0–1.4) increase in risk of breast cancer, while those taking estrogen plus a progestin in a sequential regimen had a 1.4-fold increase in risk (95% CI, 1.1–1.8). A statistically significant increased risk of breast cancer was observed only in recent users with a lean body weight—those who had a body mass index of less than 24.4. Among lean women tak-ing estrogen alone, the increase was seen with at least 8 years of use. Among lean women taking estrogen–progestin, the risk was seen with at least 4 years of use. Overall limitations of the study include that data were retrospectively obtained for subjects with breast cancer who survived and that the small percentage of women with longer-term (more than 6 years) use of combined HRT resulted in wide confidence intervals.

In the other recent study, a total of 1,897 breast cancer cases were matched with a control group (2). This study found that women using combined HRT had a statistically higher risk (odds ratio [OR] = 1.24; 95% CI, 1.07–1.45) than those using estrogen alone (OR = 1.06; 95% CI, 0.97–1.15). The use of sequential progestin versus continuous progestin regimens was associated with a nonsignificantly higher risk (OR of 1.38 versus OR of 1.09). These estimates of breast cancer risk reported with HRT are consistent with those found in a previous study that reanalyzed data from 51 epidemiologic studies of more than 52,000 women with breast cancer (3).

Effects of Estrogen and Progestins on Breast Tissue

The issue of progestin use and its association with breast cancer is complex. In contrast to what happens in endometrial tissue, progestins do not oppose the action of estrogen on breast tissue. The two recent studies underscore the limited understanding of the role of medroxyprogesterone acetate in relation to the development of breast cancer. In a multinational study of more than 12,000 reproductive-aged women monitored for more than a decade, the overall relative risk of breast cancer in ever-users of depot medroxyprogesterone was not significantly increased (relative risk = 1.2; 95% CI, 1.0–1.5) (4). At present, there are no results from prospective randomized trials with menopausal women that have examined the effect of combined estrogen–progestin regimens on breast cancer risk. Instead, mammographic density of breast tissue has been used as a surrogate marker for breast cancer risk (5). Estrogen use has been shown to increase mitotic activity and mammographic density in breast tissue. More importantly, in premenopausal women with increasing progesterone secretion during the menstrual cycle, mitotic activity in breast tissue appears to increase further and peak during the mid- to late-luteal phase (6). In the Postmenopausal Estrogen/Progestin Intervention trial, mammographic breast density in women taking unopposed estrogen increased by 15%, while women on combined (cyclic or continuous) HRT regimens had a greater than 30% increase in density (7). Taken together, these data suggest that estrogen and progesterone receptors in breast tissue behave differently than do those in endometrial tissue and that progesterone does not effectively downregulate breast estrogen receptors (8).

The Effect of Age on Breast Cancer Risk

Physicians do not often discuss the age-associated increased incidence of breast cancer when counseling patients. The commonly quoted projection of the risk of breast cancer (1 in 8 women) represents a cumulative lifetime risk (9). For a woman aged 50–59 years, the lifetime risk of having a breast cancer diagnosis is 1 in 36, while for a woman aged 70–79 years the risk increases to 1 in 24 (10). In addition, although the overall incidence of breast cancer has remained steady in recent years (11), many women believe that the incidence of breast cancer is increasing. Misperceptions about the magnitude of cancer risk may prevent some women from considering HRT for the alleviation of menopausal symptoms and possible prevention of conditions with greater morbidity and mortality.

Summary

Currently, it is estimated that about 80% of U.S. women using HRT choose continuous–combined regimens. The excess risk, if any, of breast cancer in women using HRT is low. Based on the data from one study (1), the projected absolute lifetime risk for nonestrogen users is about 10 cases of breast cancer per 100 women and would increase with unopposed estrogen use to approximately 12 cases per 100 women. For combined HRT users, this risk would increase from 10 cases to 14 cases per 100 women. The differences between these projected estimates are small, so the true implications of estrogen–progestin use may not be known. The epidemiologic studies suggest that the increased risks do not become significant until after 5 years of HRT use and disappear 5 years after discontinuation of hormone treatment (3). The relevance of these findings in clinical practice remains undetermined until prospective clinical trials can be completed. Although epidemiologic studies suggest that the addition of progestins to estrogens may increase the risk of breast cancer, the increased risk has not been proven. One properly designed randomized trial may erase conclusions drawn from years of observational studies in which healthy user bias may be present.

The American College of Obstetricians and Gynecologists continues to recommend that HRT be considered as treatment to relieve vasomotor symptoms and genitourinary tract atrophy and to reduce the risk of osteoporosis and, potentially, cardiovascular disease. Postmenopausal women should be apprised of our current understanding of the risks and benefits of HRT. When considering the use of HRT for longer than 5 years, the clinician and individual patient should weigh the benefits versus the potential side effects and risks for that particular patient.

References

1. Schairer C, Lubin J, Troisi R, Sturgeon S, Brinton L, Hoover R. Menopausal estrogen and estrogen–progestin replacement therapy and breast cancer risk. JAMA 2000;283:485–491
2. Ross RK, Paganini-Hill A, Wan PC, Pike MC. Effect of hormone replacement therapy on breast cancer risk: estrogen versus estrogen plus progestin. J Natl Cancer Inst 2000;92:328–332
3. Breast cancer and hormone replacement therapy: collaborative reanalysis of data from 51 epidemiological studies of 52,705 women with breast cancer and 108,411 women without breast cancer. Collaborative Group on Hormonal Factors in Breast Cancer. Lancet 1997;350:1047–1059 [erratum in Lancet 1997;350:1484]
4. Breast cancer and depot–medroxyprogesterone acetate: a multinational study. WHO Collaborative Study of Neoplasia and Steroid Contraceptives. Lancet 1991;338:833–838
5. Oza AM, Boyd NF. Mammographic parenchymal patterns: a marker of breast cancer risk. Epidemiol Rev 1993;15:196–208
6. Pike MC, Spicer DV, Dahmoush L, Press MF. Estrogens, progestogens, normal breast cell proliferation, and breast cancer risk. Epidemiol Rev 1993;15:17–35
7. Greendale GA, Reboussin BA, Sie A, Singh HR, Olson LK, Gatewood O, et al. Effects of estrogen and estrogen–progestin on mammographic parenchymal density. Postmenopausal Estrogen/Progestin Intervention (PEPI) Investigators. Ann Intern Med 1999;130:262–269
8. Hargreaves DF, Knox F, Swindell R, Potten CS, Bundred NJ. Epithelial proliferation and hormone receptor status in the normal post-menopausal breast and the effects of hormone replacement therapy. Br J Cancer 1998;78:945–949
9. Feuer EJ, Wun LM, Boring CC, Flanders WD, Timmel MJ, Tong T. The lifetime risk of developing breast cancer. J Natl Cancer Inst 1993;85:892–897
10. National Cancer Institute. Lifetime probability of breast cancer in American women. Bethesda, Maryland: NCI, 2001. Available at: http://cis.nci.nih.gov/fact/5_6.htm. Retrieved July 26, 2001
11. Ries LA, Eisner MP, Kosary CL, Hankey BF, Miller BA, Clegg L, eds, et al. SEER cancer statistics review, 1973–1997. Bethesda, Maryland: National Cancer Institute, 2000

ACOG

Committee on
Gynecologic Practice

Committee Opinion

Number 195, November 1997

Role of Loop Electrosurgical Excision Procedure in the Evaluation of Abnormal Pap Test Results

The American College of Obstetricians and Gynecologists

409 12th Street, SW
PO Box 96920
Washington, DC 20090-6920

12345/10987

Traditionally, the evaluation of abnormal Pap test results has been done by colposcopy and directed biopsy and endocervical curettage. Once invasive cancer has been ruled out and a biopsy diagnosis of cervical intraepithelial neoplasia (CIN) has been made, treatment options might include observation, cryotherapy, laser vaporization, cone biopsy, or hysterectomy. More recently, the loop electrosurgical excision procedure (LEEP) has allowed the clinician to combine diagnosis and treatment using a relatively simple outpatient procedure done under local anesthesia. Unlike colposcopically directed biopsies, the loop excision specimen usually includes the entire transformation zone, which potentially reduces the risk of missing invasive cancer.

Loop diathermy uses a relatively inexpensive, low-current, high-frequency electrical generator and thin stainless steel or tungsten wires of various shapes and sizes to excise lesions of the transformation zone. This technique was originally described by Prendiville et al, who modified an earlier small wire loop used by Cartier (1). Other names for LEEP are large loop excision of the transformation zone (LLETZ) or loop excision of the transformation zone (LETZ).

This technique has the advantages of providing a tissue specimen for pathologic confirmation of the diagnosis, technical ease of performance, inexpensive equipment, and the ability to perform the procedure in an outpatient setting in either an office or clinic. Complications of LEEP include bleeding and infection, but they are relatively uncommon. The potential long-term sequelae of LEEP are cervical stenosis and cervical incompetence. Although several studies suggest that these risks are minimal (2), long-term evaluation of large groups of patients treated with LEEP are not yet available.

The clinician should have a broad understanding of the natural history and pathophysiology of CIN and human papillomavirus (HPV) to obtain the best results with minimum morbidity, to make management decisions, and to provide adequate and effective patient counseling. Good colposcopic skills are also necessary to identify those lesions appropriate for excision. Good surgical skill and experience are necessary to minimize complications and manage them should they occur.

In patients in whom atypical squamous cells of undetermined significance or low-grade lesions have been identified by Pap test, the appropriate sequence of diagnostic biopsy and treatment is not clear. Excision of the entire transformation zone may represent overtreatment for metaplasia, inflammation, repair, and even focal HPV changes or mild dysplasia (CIN I). Most cases of atypical squamous cells of undetermined significance and many cases of low-grade intraepithelial neoplasia of the cervix regress spontaneously. In patients who will adhere to follow-up, early cervical neoplasia (mild dysplasia, CIN I, low-grade squamous intraepithelial neoplasia) may be monitored without treatment. It should be recognized, however, that approximately 15% of these lesions may progress. Standard colposcopically directed biopsy with close follow-up, given the recurrent nature of HPV and its prevalence in the population, will reduce morbidity and costs of treatment. In most circumstances, LEEP should be reserved for cases that persist, progress, or recur after other conservative measures have been attempted and for patients thought to be unreliable for follow-up.

Women with high-grade squamous intraepithelial lesions are the most appropriate candidates for LEEP. Most patients with histologically positive margins can be followed by cytologic and colposcopic assessment safely, as long as invasive cancer is not suspected. Several large studies have identified a number of patients with occult invasive cancer found on the LEEP specimen although colposcopy with directed biopsy showed only CIN (3, 4). In those women in whom microinvasive cancer or glandular lesions are suspected, the necessity for a large enough biopsy sample to ensure an adequate diagnosis safely and satisfactorily precludes LEEP in the opinion of many experts (5). Thermal damage occurs at the margins during LEEP and may obscure precise histologic detail.

Some clinicians recommend an immediate "see-and-treat" approach in which women with abnormal Pap test results undergo colposcopic evaluation and LEEP at the same visit. They propose that this reduces the cost and the risk of patient noncompliance in returning for treatment. However, the use of LEEP for low-grade lesions and the see-and-treat approach remains controversial and awaits the results of further studies.

References

1. Prendiville W, Cullimore J, Norman S. Large loop excision of the transformation zone (LLETZ). A new method of management for women with cervical intraepithelial neoplasia. Br J Obstet Gynaecol 1989;96:1054–1060
2. Haffenden DK, Bigrigg A, Codling BW, Read MD. Pregnancy following large loop excision of the transformation zone. Br J Obstet Gynaecol 1993;100:1059–1060
3. Bigrigg MA, Codling BW, Pearson P, Read MD, Swingler GR. Colposcopic diagnosis and treatment of cervical dysplasia at a single clinic visit. Lancet 1990;336:229–231
4. Luesley DM, Cullimore J, Redman CWE, Lawton FG, Emens JM, Rollason TP, et al. Loop diathermy excision of the cervical transformation zone in patients with abnormal cervical smears. BMJ 1990;300:1690–1693
5. Gold M, Dunton CJ, Murray J, Macones G, Hanau C, Carlson JA Jr. Loop electrocautery excisional procedure: therapeutic effectiveness as an ablation and a conization equivalent. Gynecol Oncol 1996;61:241–244

Committee on
Gynecologic Practice

Committee Opinion

Number 186, September 1997 (*Replaces #140, June 1994*)

Role of the Obstetrician–Gynecologist in the Diagnosis and Treatment of Breast Disease

Obstetrician–gynecologists are in a favorable position to diagnose breast disease in their patients. The American College of Obstetricians and Gynecologists (ACOG) has adopted the goals of assisting in educating obstetrician–gynecologists in the diagnosis and treatment of benign breast disease and in reducing mortality from breast cancer. As an initial step toward these goals, ACOG has developed the following guidelines for the early diagnosis of breast disease:

1. Breast examination by visual inspection and palpation should be an integral part of initial obstetric and all complete gynecologic examinations.
2. Patients should be instructed in the technique of life-long periodic self-examination of the breast and informed of the importance of self-examination.
3. Patients should be encouraged to undergo screening by mammography in accordance with ACOG guidelines. Earlier or more frequent screening is recommended for women who have had breast cancer or who have a first-degree relative (ie, mother, sister, or daughter) or multiple other relatives who have a history of premenopausal breast or breast and ovarian cancer.
4. Obstetrician–gynecologists should perform diagnostic procedures when indicated.
5. When indicated, referrals should be made to physicians who specialize in the diagnosis and treatment of the type of breast disease that is suspected.
6. Institutions that credential physicians to perform breast surgery should apply the same criteria for clinical competence to obstetrician–gynecologists as to other physicians requesting to obtain or maintain such privileges.
7. A persistent palpable breast mass requires evaluation. Mammography alone is not sufficient to rule out malignant pathology in a patient with a palpable breast mass. Ultrasonography or magnified mammographic imaging of the breast containing the mass may provide additional information and may identify cystic structures or variations in normal breast architecture that account for the palpable abnormality.

The American College of Obstetricians and Gynecologists
409 12th Street, SW
PO Box 96920
Washington, DC 20090-6920

12345/10987

When cyst aspiration is performed, the fluid may be discarded if it is clear (transparent and not bloody) and the mass disappears. Otherwise, the patient should be considered a candidate for a breast biopsy.

Solid masses usually require histologic diagnosis. Fine-needle aspiration or stereotactic needle biopsy may be an alternative to open breast biopsy in some cases. If breast cancer or a specific benign condition is not detected by fine-needle aspiration or needle core biopsy, open biopsy is necessary. Because the incidence of breast cancer is extremely low in patients younger than 20 years of age, patients in this age group who have solid masses that appear to be benign when examined by ultrasonography can be monitored without biopsy at the discretion of the physician. These guidelines apply both to pregnant and to nonpregnant women.

8. When a patient is referred to another physician for management of a breast disorder, following are the responsibilities of the obstetrician–gynecologist:

- Explain to the patient that she needs further care
- Provide names of qualified physicians from whom the patient can receive care
- Answer the patient's questions
- Document these steps and include a detailed description of the clinical findings in the medical record

The American College of Obstetricians and Gynecologists encourages both basic and clinical research into the etiology, early diagnosis, and treatment of all breast disease. Postgraduate education, including residency training programs in obstetrics and gynecology and continuing medical education, should include education in the early diagnosis and management of all forms of breast disease. Obstetrician–gynecologists also should take advantage of opportunities to educate other physicians involved in the health care of women about the diagnosis and treatment of breast disease.

Bibliography

American College of Obstetricians and Gynecologists. Nonmalignant conditions of the breast. ACOG Technical Bulletin 156. Washington, DC: ACOG, 1991

American College of Obstetricians and Gynecologists. Carcinoma of the breast. ACOG Technical Bulletin 158. Washington, DC: ACOG, 1991

American College of Obstetricians and Gynecologists. Guidelines for women's health care. Washington, DC: ACOG, 1996

American College of Obstetricians and Gynecologists. Routine cancer screening. ACOG Committee Opinion 185. Washington, DC: ACOG, 1997

Brenner RJ, Fajardo L, Fisher PR, Dershaw DD, Evans WP, Bassett L, et al. Percutaneous core biopsy of the breast: effect of operator experience and number of samples on diagnostic accuracy. AJR Am J Roentgenol 1996;166:341–346

Mainiero MB, Philpotts LE, Lee CH, Lange RC, Carter D, Tocino I. Stereotaxic core needle biopsy of breast microcalcifications: correlation of target accuracy and diagnosis with lesion size. Radiology 1996;198:665–669

Mitnick JS, Vazquez MF, Feiner HD, Pressman P, Roses DF. Mammographically detected breast lesions: clinical importance of cytologic atypia in stereotaxic fine-needle aspiration biopsy samples. Radiology 1996;198:319–322

ACOG

Committee on
Gynecologic Practice

Committee Opinion

Number 247, December 2000   *(Replaces No. 185, September 1997)*

Routine Cancer Screening

General Health Counseling and Cancer Evaluation

For many women, the obstetrician–gynecologist is the only physician who provides them with regular health care. Therefore, the obstetrician–gynecologist should be able to provide cancer evaluation and counseling. Evaluation of risk for cancer includes questions about high-risk habits, assessment of family history of cancer, and review of symptoms pertinent to each organ system. The estimated number of women who would develop various types of cancer and the number of women estimated to die from the disease are shown in Table 1.

The Committee on Gynecologic Practice recommends that every woman undergo examination of the pelvis and breast annually, beginning at age 18 years or earlier if she is sexually active. The examination also may include the skin, lymph nodes, thyroid gland, oral cavity, anus, and rectum to detect signs of premalignant or malignant conditions. Cancer screening components currently recommended by the Committee on Gynecologic Practice, taking into consideration the recommendations of major nationally recognized experts, are summarized in Table 2. Although these guidelines apply specifically to routine cancer screening, other ACOG publications containing recommendations for high-risk groups are included in the bibliography.

Cervical Cancer

The Pap test, unlike most screening tests, is used principally to diagnose preinvasive lesions that, when treated, will result in a decrease in the incidence of and deaths from invasive cancer. The Pap test appears to have accomplished that goal.

The results of screening studies indicate that since the Pap test was introduced, the number of advanced lesions has decreased, whereas the number of early invasive lesions, as well as cervical intraepithelial neoplasia, has increased. Because of a large amount of strong indirect evidence of the effectiveness of the Pap test, it would be unethical to conduct randomized clinical trials to confirm its utility.

In the United States, 90% of women aged 18 years or older have had at least one Pap test, and more than 60% have had a Pap test within 3 years (1). Considering that cervical cancer has not been eradicated, that the incidence of cervical intraepithelial neoplasia appears to have increased over the past

Table 1. Estimated Number of Women Who Will Develop or Die from Various Types of Cancer in 2000

Type of Cancer	No. of New Cases	No. of Deaths
Cervical	12,800	4,600
Breast	182,800	40,800
Lung	74,600	67,600
Endometrial	36,100	6,500
Ovarian	23,100	14,000
Colorectal	66,600	28,500

Data from American Cancer Society. Cancer facts and figures—2000. Atlanta: ACS, 2000

decade, that the Pap test has an appreciable false-negative rate, and that women tend to extend screening intervals, the guidelines recommending annual cervical cytology screening for most women are prudent and warranted if early precursors to cervical cancer are to be detected and successfully treated.

Breast Cancer

Breast cancer is the second leading cause of death due to cancer in women (2). One in eight women will develop breast cancer during her lifetime. At present, mammography is the only screening method available to detect subclinical, or occult, breast cancer—the stage at which cancer is least likely to have spread to regional nodes and beyond.

Any recommendations concerning screening must be based on the current understanding of the risk/benefit ratio. Evidence from reports from the Breast Cancer Detection Demonstration Project of the American Cancer Society, as well as from numerous other studies, indicates that there is a decrease in mortality for all women when appropriate screening by mammography is instituted and carried out by qualified personnel.

Randomized, controlled trials have clearly demonstrated a decreased death rate from breast cancer in women who were offered mammography between the ages of 50 years and 69 years. Even among this group of women, however, less than 40% have had a mammogram in the past year.

The benefit of mammography in women ages 40–49 years is less clear. In 1993, the National Cancer Institute considered the evidence showing the benefits of screening by mammography in women 40–49 years of age and, finding it equivocal, subsequently withdrew its recommendation for routine screening of women in this age group. However, because of inadequate numbers of patients studied and length of follow-up, ACOG did not believe there were sufficient data to warrant a change in its current screening recommendations. As a result, ACOG continues to recommend offering screening by mammography every 1–2 years to women ages 40–49 years

Table 2. Suggested Cancer Screening Guidelines

Topic	Guideline
General health counseling and cancer evaluation	All women should have a general health evaluation annually or as appropriate, which should include evaluation for cancer and examination to detect signs of premalignant or malignant conditions.
Breast cancer	Mammography should be performed every 1–2 years for women 40–49 years of age and then annually thereafter.
Cervical cancer	All women who are or who have been sexually active or who have reached 18 years of age should undergo an annual Pap test and pelvic examination. After a woman has had three or more consecutive, satisfactory, annual cytologic examinations with normal findings, the Pap test may be performed less frequently on a low-risk woman at the discretion of her physician.
Endometrial cancer	Screening all women for endometrial cancer and its precursors is neither cost-effective nor warranted.
Ovarian cancer	No techniques that have proved to be effective in reducing the disease-specific mortality of ovarian cancer are currently available.
Colorectal cancer	Beginning at age 50 years one of three screening options should be selected: yearly fecal occult blood testing plus flexible sigmoidoscopy every 5 years *or* colonoscopy every 10 years *or* double contrast barium enema (DCBE) every 5–10 years. A digital rectal examination should be performed at the time of each screening sigmoidoscopy, colonoscopy, or DCBE.
Lung cancer	No available techniques are currently suitable for routine screening.

and annually to women older than 50 years. In 1997, the National Institutes of Health convened the consensus development conference "Breast Cancer Screening for Women Ages 40–49." It declined to recommend routine screening in this age group, instead advising that each woman, in consultation with her physician, decide whether to undergo screening.

Although data regarding women ages 70 years and older are insufficient to make a definitive recommendation about screening in this age group, the incidence of breast cancer does increase with age. Therefore, ACOG continues to recommend annual screening in this age group.

Clinicians should encourage screening by mammography for those women for whom benefit clearly has been established. The safety and effectiveness of mammography have been demonstrated. However, it is recognized that mammography is the most costly of all screening modalities. Dedicated equipment is essential, and considerable skill and experience are required to interpret the films. It is important, therefore, to determine the most prudent use of resources.

Lung Cancer

Among women, there has been a steady overall increase in the number of deaths from lung cancer, which now surpasses that from breast cancer; lung cancer is the major cause of cancer death in women (2). The only effective way to reduce mortality is to promote smoking cessation.

Endometrial Cancer

Endometrial cancer is the most common gynecologic cancer in women ages 45 years and older. The significant increase in the prevalence of endometrial cancer observed in the 1980s was attributed primarily to the increasing longevity of postmenopausal women, the more frequent use of unopposed estrogen replacement therapy, and the refinement of criteria for diagnosing early endometrial adenocarcinoma. In the early 1990s, there appears to have been a stabilization of the incidence of the disease. The reasons for this are unclear but may be related to the increased use of progesterone with estrogen replacement therapy.

The cost-effectiveness of screening asymptomatic women for endometrial cancer and its precursors is very low; therefore, endometrial assessment is unwarranted. Endometrial sampling is not required before or during estrogen–progestin therapy unless unexpected bleeding occurs. The Pap test has insufficient sensitivity to be used as a screening technique for endometrial cancer.

Ovarian Cancer

One woman in 70 will develop ovarian cancer during her lifetime (3). Ovarian cancer is the leading cause of death from gynecologic cancer. More women die from ovarian cancer than from cervical and endometrial cancers combined. Measuring CA 125 levels in serum and ultrasonography have not been shown to be effective in population-based screening for ovarian cancer.

Colorectal Cancer

The incidence of colorectal cancer increases with age. Because colorectal cancer is a significant risk to women, it is suggested that routine evaluation take place.

Future Screening Studies

The Prostate, Lung, Colorectal and Ovarian Cancer Screening Trial, a study sponsored by the National Institutes of Health/National Cancer Institute, is designed to identify effective ways to reduce cancer deaths in older Americans. Women participating in this study will have serial bimanual examinations, transvaginal ultrasonography, and CA 125 screening.

References

1. Trends in cancer screening—United States, 1987 and 1992. MMWR Morb Mortal Wkly Rep 1996;45:57–61
2. American Cancer Society. Cancer facts and figures—2000. Atlanta: ACS, 2000
3. Ovarian cancer: screening, treatment, and followup. NIH Consens Statement 1994 Apr 5–7;12(3):1–30

Bibliography

Cervical Cancer

American College of Obstetricians and Gynecologists. Recommendations on frequency of Pap test screening. ACOG Committee Opinion 152. Washington, DC: ACOG, 1995

Bearman DM, MacMillan JP, Creasman WT. Papanicolaou smear history of patients developing cervical cancer: an assessment of screening protocols. Obstet Gynecol 1987;69:151–155 [erratum in Obstet Gynecol 1987;69:660]

Cervical cancer screening programs: summary of the 1982 Canadian task force report. Can Med Assoc J 1982;127:581–589

Eddy DM. Screening for cervical cancer. Ann Intern Med 1990; 113:214–226

Johannesson G, Geirsson G, Day N. The effect of mass screening in Iceland, 1965–74, on the incidence and mortality of cervical carcinoma. Int J Cancer 1978;21:418–425

Mandelblatt J, Schechter C, Fahs M, Muller C. Clinical implications of screening for cervical cancer under Medicare. The natural history of cervical cancer in the elderly: what do we know? What do we need to know? Am J Obstet Gynecol 1991;164:644–651

Richart RM. Screening. The next century. Cancer 1995;76: 1919–1927

Screening for squamous cervical cancer: duration of low risk after negative results of cervical cytology and its implication for screening policies. IARC Working Group on evaluation of cervical cancer screening programmes. Br Med J (Clin Res Ed) 1986;293:659–664

Shy K, Chu J, Mandelson M, Greer B, Figge D. Papanicolaou smear screening interval and risk of cervical cancer. Obstet Gynecol 1989;74:838–843

Wilkinson EJ. Pap smears and screening for cervical neoplasia. Clin Obstet Gynecol 1990;33:817–825

Breast Cancer

American College of Obstetricians and Gynecologists. Role of the obstetrician–gynecologist in the diagnosis and treatment of breast disease. ACOG Committee Opinion 186. Washington, DC: ACOG, 1997

Bailar JC 3d. Mammography before age 50 years? JAMA 1988; 259:1548–1549

Baines CJ. The Canadian National Breast Screening Study. Why? What next? And so what? Cancer 1995;76:2107–2112

Bassett LW, Hendrick RE, Bassford TL, Butler PF, Carter D, DeBor M, et al. Quality determinants of mammography. Clinical Practice Guideline No. 13. Rockville, Maryland: Agency for Health Care Policy and Research, Public Health Service, U.S. Department of Health and Human Services, 1994; AHCPR publication no. 95-0632

Champion VL. Strategies to increase mammography utilization. Med Care 1994;32:118–129

Champion VL. The relationship of selected variables to breast cancer detection behaviors in women 35 and older. Oncol Nurs Forum 1991;18:733–739

Dawson DA, Thompson GB. Breast cancer risk factors and screening: United States, 1987. Vital Health Stat [10]1990;172: iii–iv, 1–60

Eddy DM, Hasselblad V, McGivney W, Hendee W. The value of mammography screening in women under age 50 years. JAMA 1988;259:1512–1519

Feig SA. Mammographic screening of women aged 40–49 years. Benefit, risk, and cost considerations. Cancer 1995;76:2097–2106

Feig SA. Mammography screening: published guidelines and actual practice. Recent Results Cancer Res 1987;105:78–84

Howard J. Using mammography for cancer control: an unrealized potential. CA Cancer J Clin 1987;37:33–48

Solin LJ, Fox K, August DA, Dershaw DD, Rebbeck TR, Weber BL, et al. Breast cancer. In: Hoskins WJ, Perez CA, Young RC, eds. Principles and practice of gynecologic oncology. 2nd ed. Philadelphia: Lippincott–Raven, 1997:1079–1142

Moskowitz M. Breast cancer: age specific growth rates and screening strategies. Radiology 1986;161:37–41

Screening mammography: a missed clinical opportunity? Results of the NCI Breast Cancer Screening Consortium and National Health Interview Survey Studies. JAMA 1990;264:54–58

Seidman H, Gelb SK, Silverberg E, LaVerda N, Lubera JA. Survival experience in the Breast Cancer Detection Demonstration Project. CA Cancer J Clin 1987;37:258–290

Shapiro S, Venet W, Strax P, Venet L, Roeser R. Ten- to fourteen-year effect of screening on breast cancer mortality. J Natl Cancer Inst 1982;69:349–355

Sickles EA, Kopans DB. Mammographic screening for women aged 40 to 49 years: the primary care practitioner's dilemma. Ann Intern Med 1995;122:534–538

Smart CR. The role of mammography in the prevention of mortality from breast cancer. Cancer Prev 1990;June 1–16

Tabar L, Fagerberg G, Chen HH, Duffy SW, Smart CR, Gad A, et al. Efficacy of breast cancer screening by age. New results from the Swedish Two-County Trial. Cancer 1995;75:2507–2517

Tabar L, Fagerberg G, Duffy SW, Day NE, Gad A, Grontoft O. Update of the Swedish two-county program of mammographic screening for breast cancer. Radiol Clin North Am 1992;30: 187–210

Use of mammography—United States, 1990. MMWR Morb Mortal Wkly Rep 1990;39:621, 627–630

Woolf SH. United States Preventive Services Task Force recommendations on breast cancer screening. Cancer 1992;69: 1913–1918

Wright CJ. Breast cancer screening: a different look at the evidence. Surgery 1986;100:594–598

Zapka JG, Hosmer D, Costanza ME, Harris DR, Stoddard A. Changes in mammography use: economic, need, and service factors. Am J Public Health 1992;82:1345–1351

Zapka JG, Stoddard A, Maul L, Costanza ME. Internal adherence to mammography screening guidelines. Med Care 1991;29:697–707

Lung Cancer

Berlin NI, Buncher CR, Fontana RS, Frost JK, Melamed MR. The National Cancer Institute Cooperative Early Lung Cancer Detection Program. Results of the initial screen (prevalence). Early lung cancer detection: introduction. Am Rev Respir Dis 1984;130:545–549

Epstein DM. The role of radiologic screening in lung cancer. Radiol Clin North Am 1990;28:489–495

Endometrial Cancer

American College of Obstetricians and Gynecologists. Tamoxifen and endometrial cancer. ACOG Committee Opinion 232. Washington, DC: ACOG, 2000

Chambers JT, Chambers SK. Endometrial sampling: When? Where? Why? With what? Clin Obstet Gynecol 1992;35:28–39

Ciotti MC. Screening for gynecologic and colorectal cancer: is it adequate? Womens Health Issues 1992;2:83–92; discussion 92–93

Ferenczy A, Mutter G. Endometrial hyperplasia and neoplasia: definition, diagnosis, and management principles. In: Sciarra JJ, ed. Gynecology and obstetrics. Vol 4. Philadelphia: Lippincott Williams & Wilkins, 2000:1–15

Greenwood SM, Wright DJ. Evaluation of the office endometrial biopsy in the detection of endometrial carcinoma and atypical hyperplasia. Cancer 1979;43:1474–1478

Koss LG. Diagnosis of early endometrial cancer and precancerous states. Ann Clin Lab Sci 1979;9:189–194

Koss LG, Schreiber K, Moussouris H, Oberlander SG. Endometrial carcinoma and its precursors: detection and screening. Clin Obstet Gynecol 1982;25:49–61

Koss LG, Schreiber K, Oberlander SG, Moussouris HF, Lesser M. Detection of endometrial carcinoma and hyperplasia in asymptomatic women. Obstet Gynecol 1984;64:1–11

Pritchard KI. Screening for endometrial cancer: is it effective? Ann Intern Med 1989;110:177–179

Reagan JW. Can screening for endometrial cancer be justified? Acta Cytol 1980;24:87–89

Stovall TG, Photopulos GJ, Poston WM, Ling FW, Sandles LG. Pipelle endometrial sampling in patients with known endometrial carcinoma. Obstet Gynecol 1991;77:954–956

Vuopala S. Diagnostic accuracy and clinical applicability of cytological and histological methods for investigating endometrial carcinoma. Acta Obstet Gynecol Scand Suppl 1977;70:1–72

Zucker PK, Kasdon EJ, Feldstein ML. The validity of Pap smear parameters as predictors of endometrial pathology in menopausal women. Cancer 1985;56:2256–2263

Ovarian Cancer

Bast RC Jr, Klug TL, St John E, Jenison E, Niloff JM, Lazarus H, et al. A radio-immunoassay using a monoclonal antibody to monitor the course of epithelial ovarian cancer. N Engl J Med 1983;309:883–887

Berek JS, Bast RC Jr. Ovarian cancer screening. The use of serial complementary tumor markers to improve sensitivity and specificity for early detection. Cancer 1995;76:2092–2096

Berek JS, Knapp RC, Malkasian GD, Lavin PT, Whitney C, Niloff JM, et al. CA 125 serum levels correlated with second-look operations among ovarian cancer patients. Obstet Gynecol 1986;67:685–689

Bourne TH, Whitehead MI, Campbell S, Royston P, Bhan V, Collins WP. Ultrasound screening for familial ovarian cancer. Gynecol Oncol 1991;43:92–97

Campbell S, Bhan V, Royston P, Whitehead MI, Collins WP. Transabdominal ultrasound screening for early ovarian cancer. BMJ 1989;299:1363–1367

Jacobs I, Stabile I, Bridges J, Kemsley P, Reynolds C, Grudzinskas J, et al. Multimodal approach to screening for ovarian cancer. Lancet 1988;1(8580):268–271

Jacobs I, Davies AP, Bridges J, Stabile I, Fay T, Lower A, et al. Prevalence screening for ovarian cancer in postmenopausal women by CA 125 measurement and ultrasonography. BMJ 1993;306:1030–1034

Skates SJ, Xu FJ, Yu YH, Sjovall K, Einhorn N, Chang Y, et al. Toward an optimal algorithm for ovarian cancer screening with longitudinal tumor markers. Cancer 1995;76:2004–2010

van Nagell JR Jr, DePriest PD, Puls LE, Donaldson ES, Gallion HH, Pavlik EJ, et al. Ovarian cancer screening in asymptomatic postmenopausal women by transvaginal sonography. Cancer 1991;68:458–462

van Nagell JR Jr, Gallion HH, Pavlik EJ, DePriest PD. Ovarian cancer screening. Cancer 1995;76:2086–2091

Colorectal Cancer

Byers T, Levin B, Rothenberger D, Dodd GD, Smith RA. American Cancer Society guidelines for screening and surveillance for early detection of colorectal polyps and cancer: update 1997. American Cancer Society Detection and Treatment Advisory Group on Colorectal Cancer. CA Cancer J Clin 1997; 47:154–160

Hardcastle JD, Chamberlain JO, Robinson MH, Moss SM, Amar SS, Balfour TW, et al. Randomised controlled trial of faecal-occult-blood screening for colorectal cancer. Lancet 1996; 348:1472–1477

Kronborg O, Fenger C, Olsen J, Jorgensen OD, Sondergaard O. Randomised study of screening for colorectal cancer with faecal-occult-blood test. Lancet 1996;348:1467–1471

Lang CA, Ransohoff DF. Fecal occult blood screening for colorectal cancer. Is mortality reduced by chance selection for screening colonoscopy? JAMA 1994;271:1011–1013

Mandel JS, Bond JH, Church TR, Snover DC, Bradley GM, Schuman LM, et al. Reducing mortality from colorectal cancer by screening for fecal occult blood: Minnesota Colon Cancer Control Study. N Engl J Med 1993;328:1365–1371 [erratum in N Engl J Med 1993;329:672]

Newcomb PA, Norfleet RG, Storer BE, Surawicz TS, Marcus PM. Screening sigmoidoscopy and colorectal cancer mortality. J Natl Cancer Inst 1992;84:1572–1575

Selby JV, Friedman GD, Quesenberry CP Jr, Weiss NS. A case-control study of screening sigmoidoscopy and mortality from colorectal cancer. N Engl J Med 1992;326:653–657

U.S. Preventive Services Task Force. Guide to clinical preventive services. 2nd ed. Baltimore: Williams & Wilkins, 1996

Winawer SJ, Fletcher RH, Miller L, Godlee F, Stolar MH, Malrow CD, et al. Colorectal cancer screening: clinical guidelines and rationale. Gastroenterology 1997;112:594–642 [errata in Gastroenterology 1997;112:1060 and 1998;114:625]

Committee on
Obstetric Practice

Committee
on Genetics

Committee Opinion

Number 183, April 1997

Routine Storage of Umbilical Cord Blood for Potential Future Transplantation

Reconstitution of the bone marrow can be a life-saving procedure in the treatment of hematologic disease (eg, Fanconi anemia) or advanced malignancy. The necessary hematopoietic stem and progenitor cells are usually obtained from allogeneic or autologous bone marrow. If autologous marrow is not an option, then a human leukocyte antigen (HLA)-identical sibling is the donor most likely to result in successful engraftment and minimization of the risk of graft-versus-host (GVH) disease. Most people do not have an HLA-identical sibling available, and they must look outside of their families. There is a national registry of potential bone marrow donors, but finding an identical match and convincing that individual to undergo the unpleasant donation procedure is not always easy. Many individuals who could potentially benefit from transplantation die while awaiting donors.

A recently recognized potential source for hematopoietic stem and progenitor cells is human fetal cord blood. Early results from more than 200 transplants of human cord stem cells, primarily to treat childhood malignancies, seem very encouraging for several reasons. There appears to be a relatively high success rate for the procedure even in the face of HLA mismatches at one or more loci. There also appears to be a somewhat lower risk for GVH disease than that which is true for traditional bone marrow transplantation. These encouraging preliminary reports have generated considerable enthusiasm because the 4 million births per year in the United States would appear to provide a large reservoir of genetically diverse, potentially transplantable specimens. Large volumes of cord blood are now being "wasted" as "discarded human material" that could theoretically be easily collected, typed, screened for infections, and banked cryogenically for transplantation.

The use of this technology raises a number of scientific, legal, and ethical issues that need to be addressed:

- Should cord blood specimens be collected and banked centrally for allogeneic transplantation in a system analogous to the way that we now handle blood, or would parents be well-advised to bank their own child's cord blood at birth for potential future autologous use should it ever be necessary?

The American College of Obstetricians and Gynecologists
409 12th Street, SW
PO Box 96920
Washington, DC 20090-6920

12345/10987

- What is the probability that any individual will ever need his or her own cord blood for transplantation? If that need does arise 18 years later, what is the probability that a specimen stored for 18 years will still be viable?

- Most transplants to date have been done in babies and young children. More cells are needed to reconstitute the bone marrow of persons of larger size. What percentage of cord blood specimens will have adequate numbers of cells to reconstitute the bone marrow of adults?

- Are cord blood stem and progenitor cells more efficient at reconstituting marrow than are cells obtained from adult marrow? Would fewer cells on a per-kilogram body weight basis be as effective?

- Could the number of stem and progenitor cells in a specimen of cord blood be expanded in vitro to provide enough cells for a reliable reconstitution of the bone marrow of persons of adult size?

- If the apparently lower incidence of GVH disease compared with adult marrow sources is real, it may represent reduced immunocompetence of cord stem and progenitor cells. This may be disadvantageous in treating patients with cancer. It may also permit a higher incidence of second primary cancers in transplant survivors.

- As many as 38% of cord blood specimens may be contaminated with maternal cells. What effect will this contamination with adult cells that are (presumably) immunocompetent have upon graft success rate?

- In the future, there may be other medical approaches to manage these diseases.

- Should this technology continue to show promise, and the decision is made to establish cord blood banks, should cord blood continue to be regarded as "discarded human material?"

- Could cord blood be collected routinely at deliveries without consent?

- All specimens would need to be tested for infectious and selected genetic diseases before use. Should parents be informed if their child's specimen tests positive for an infection (eg, human immunodeficiency virus) or genetic disease?

- If nonpaternity is discovered in the course of testing, should that be disclosed to the mother, father, or child?

- Physicians should resist the pressures of marketing, and they should evaluate thoroughly the potential benefits and risks—emotional as well as physical—of all new medical interventions.

Privately owned for-profit companies have been established to bank cord blood samples for potential future use by those individuals or their family members. There is a significant cost associated with the initial specimen processing (approximately $1,500) and an annual storage fee (approximately $100). Given the low probability of needing a stem cell transplant (which has been estimated at between 1 in 1,000 and 1 in 200,000 by age 18) and the other uncertainties regarding success rates with increasing body mass and time in storage, is this a "good" investment? In view of the apparent success rate, despite HLA mismatch, will there be an advantage to receiving one's own banked cells, or could one do just as well with someone else's cord blood? Once banked, to whom do the cells there belong? Do they belong to the parents who paid the fees or the child from whom they came? Do the parents have the right to give them away or sell them, or should they be held for the person from whom they came until he or she reaches the age of majority? If the cells are to be used for someone other than the person from whom they came, must both parents agree or is consent from one adequate? What happens if the parents disagree?

There are clearly many questions about this technology that remain to be answered. Some are relatively simple, such as the success rate of the procedure for various diseases and at various body weights. These simply await a larger number of cases. Some will be more difficult, such as the viability of cells in long-term storage; these questions will take time to answer. The most difficult will be the moral, ethical, and social questions, which need extensive public discussion and may never all be resolved to everyone's satisfaction. Until there is a fuller understanding of all of these issues, we must proceed with considerable circumspection. Parents should not be sold this service without a realistic assessment of their likely return on their investment. Commercial cord blood banks should not represent the service they sell as "doing everything possible" to ensure the health of children. Parents and grandparents should not be made to feel guilty if they are not eager or able to invest these considerable sums in such a highly speculative venture.

Bibliography

Broxmeyer HE. Questions to be answered regarding umbilical cord blood hematopoietic stem and progenitor cells and their use in transplantation. Transfusion 1995;35:694-702

Kurtzberg J, Laughlin M, Graham ML, Smith C, Olson JF, Halperin EC, et al. Placental blood as a source of hematopoietic stem cells for transplantation into unrelated recipients. N Engl J Med 1996;335:157-166

Laporte JP, Gorin NC, Rubinstein P, Lesage S, Portnoi MF, Barbu V, et al. Cord-blood transplantation from an unrelated donor in an adult with chronic myelogenous leukemia. N Engl J Med 1996;335:167-170

Marshall E. Clinical promise, ethical quandary. Science 1996;271:586-588

Rubinstein P, Rosenfield RE, Adamson JW, Stevens CE. Stored placental blood for unrelated bone marrow reconstitution. Blood 1993;81:1679-1690

Scaradavou A, Carrier C, Mollen N, Stevens C, Rubenstein P. Detection of maternal DNA in placental/umbilical cord blood by locus-specific amplification of the noninherited maternal HLA gene. Blood 1996;88:1494-1500

Silberstein LE, Jefferies LC. Placental-blood banking—a new frontier in transfusion medicine. N Engl J Med 1996;335:199-201

Wagner JE, Rosenthal J, Sweetman R, Shu XO, Davies SM, Ramsay NK, et al. Successful transplantation of HLA-matched and HLA-mismatched umbilical cord blood from unrelated donors: analysis of engraftment and acute graft-versus-host disease. Blood 1996:88:795-802

ACOG

Committee on
Obstetric Practice

Committee Opinion

Number 234, May 2000   *(Replaces No. 219, August 1999)*

Scheduled Cesarean Delivery and the Prevention of Vertical Transmission of HIV Infection

Prevention of transmission of the human immunodeficiency virus (HIV) from mother to fetus or newborn (vertical transmission) is a major goal in the care of pregnant women infected with HIV. An important advance in this regard was the demonstration that treatment of the mother with zidovudine (ZDV) during pregnancy and labor and of the neonate for the first 6 weeks after birth could reduce the transmission rate from 25% to 8% (1).

Continuing research into vertical transmission of HIV suggests that a substantial number of cases occur as the result of fetal exposure to the virus during labor and delivery; the precise mechanisms are not known. Transmission could occur by transplacental maternal–fetal microtransfusion of blood contaminated with the virus during uterine contractions or by exposure to the virus in maternal cervicovaginal secretions and blood at delivery. Data also indicate that the risk of vertical transmission is proportional to the concentration of virus in maternal plasma (viral load). At very low concentrations of virus in maternal plasma (viral load less than 1,000 copies per milliliter), the observed incidence of vertical transmission among 141 mother–infant pairs was 0 with a 95% upper confidence bound of about 2% (2, 3).

In theory, the risk of vertical transmission in mothers with high viral loads could be reduced by performing cesarean deliveries before the onset of labor and before rupture of membranes (termed *scheduled cesarean delivery* in this document). Early studies of the relationship between the mode of delivery and the risk of vertical transmission yielded inconsistent results. Data from two prospective cohort studies (4, 5), an international randomized trial (6), and a meta-analysis of individual patient data from 15 prospective cohort studies, including more than 7,800 mother–child pairs (7), indicate that there is a significant relationship between the mode of delivery and vertical transmission of HIV. This body of evidence, accumulated mostly before the use of highly active antiretroviral therapy (HAART) and without any data regarding maternal viral load, indicates that scheduled cesarean delivery reduces the likelihood of vertical transmission of HIV compared with either unscheduled cesarean delivery or vaginal delivery. This finding holds true whether or not the patient is receiving ZDV therapy. Whether cesarean deliv-

The American College of Obstetricians and Gynecologists
409 12th Street, SW
PO Box 96920
Washington, DC 20090-6920

12345/43210

ery offers any benefit to women on HAART or to women with low or undetectable maternal viral loads is unknown. Data are insufficient to address the question of how long after the onset of labor or rupture of membranes the benefit is lost. It is clear that maternal morbidity is greater with cesarean delivery than with vaginal delivery, as is true for women not infected with HIV (8–10). Increases in postpartum morbidity seem to be greatest among women infected with HIV who have low CD4 cell counts (9).

Although many issues remain unresolved because of insufficient data, there is consensus that the following should be recommended:

- Patients should be counseled that in the absence of antiretroviral therapy, the risk of vertical transmission is approximately 25%. With ZDV therapy, the risk is reduced to 5–8%. When care includes both ZDV therapy and scheduled cesarean delivery, the risk is approximately 2%. A similar risk of 2% or less is seen among women with viral loads of less than 1,000 copies per milliliter, even without the systematic use of scheduled cesarean delivery. No combination of therapies can guarantee that a newborn will not become infected (a 0% transmission rate).

- Women infected with HIV, whose viral loads are greater than 1,000 copies per milliliter, should be counseled regarding the potential benefit of scheduled cesarean delivery to further reduce the risk of vertical transmission of HIV beyond that achievable with antiretroviral therapy alone.

- Neonates of women at highest risk for vertical transmission, with relatively high plasma viral loads, are most likely to benefit from scheduled cesarean delivery. Data are insufficient to demonstrate a benefit for neonates of women with plasma viral loads of less than 1,000 copies per milliliter. The available data indicate no reduction in the transmission rate if cesarean delivery is performed after the onset of labor or rupture of membranes. The decision regarding the route of delivery must be individualized in these circumstances.

- The patient's autonomy in making the decision regarding route of delivery must be respected. A patient's informed decision to undergo vaginal delivery must be honored, with cesarean delivery performed only for other accepted indications and with patient consent.

- Patients should receive antiretroviral chemotherapy during pregnancy according to currently accepted guidelines for adults (11). This should not be interrupted around the time of cesarean delivery. For those patients receiving ZDV, adequate levels

of the drug in the blood should be achieved if the infusion is begun 3 hours preoperatively (1), according to the dosing schedule recommended by the Centers for Disease Control and Prevention (www.cdc.gov/hiv/treatment).

- Because morbidity is increased in HIV-infected women undergoing cesarean delivery, physicians should consider using prophylactic antibiotics during all such cesarean deliveries.

- The American College of Obstetricians and Gynecologists generally recommends that scheduled cesarean deliveries not be performed before 39 completed weeks of gestation. In women with HIV infection, however, delivery at 38 completed weeks of gestation is recommended to reduce the likelihood of onset of labor or rupture of membranes before delivery.

- Best clinical estimates of gestational age should be used for planning cesarean delivery. Amniocentesis to determine fetal lung maturity in pregnant women infected with HIV should be avoided whenever possible.

- Current recommendations for adults indicate that plasma viral load should be determined at baseline and then every 3 months or following changes in therapy (11). Plasma viral load should be monitored, according to these guidelines, during pregnancy as well. The patient's most recently determined viral load should be used to direct counseling regarding mode of delivery.

- Preoperative maternal health status affects the degree of risk of maternal morbidity associated with cesarean delivery. All women should be clearly informed of the risks associated with cesarean delivery. Ultimately, the decision to perform a cesarean delivery must be individualized in each case according to circumstances.

A skin-penetrating injury (eg, needlestick or scalpel laceration) is a risk to care providers during all deliveries, vaginal or cesarean. This risk is not greater during cesarean delivery, although there generally are more health care personnel present and, thus, at risk during a cesarean delivery than during a vaginal delivery (12). Appropriate care and precautions against such injuries always should be taken, but these concerns should not affect decisions regarding route of delivery (13).

In summary, cesarean delivery performed before the onset of labor and before rupture of membranes effectively reduces the risk of vertical transmission of HIV infection. Scheduled cesarean delivery should be discussed and recommended for women with viral loads greater than 1,000 copies per milliliter whether or not they are taking antiretroviral therapy. As with all complex clinical decisions, the choice of delivery must be individualized. Discussion of the option of scheduled cesarean delivery should begin as early as possible in pregnancy with every pregnant woman with HIV infection to give her an adequate opportunity to consider the choice and plan for the procedure. The risks, which are greater for the mother, must be balanced with the benefits expected for the neonate. The patient's autonomy must be respected when making the decision to perform a cesarean delivery, because the potential for maternal morbidity is significant.

References

1. Connor EM, Sperling RS, Gelber R, Kiselev P, Scott G, O'Sullivan MJ, et al. Reduction of maternal-infant transmission of human immunodeficiency virus type 1 with zidovudine treatment. Pediatric AIDS Clinical Trials Group Protocol 076 Study Group. N Engl J Med 1994;331:1173–1180

2. Mofenson LM, Lambert JS, Stiehm ER, Bethel J, Meyer WA 3rd, Whitehouse J, et al. Risk factors for perinatal transmission of human immunodeficiency virus type 1 in women treated with zidovudine. Pediatric AIDS Clinical Trials Group Study 185 Team. N Engl J Med 1999;341:385–393

3. Garcia PM, Kalish LA, Pitt J, Minkoff H, Quinn T, Burchett SK, et al. Maternal levels of plasma human immunodeficiency virus type 1 RNA and the risk of perinatal transmission. Women and Infants Transmission Study Group. N Engl J Med 1999;341:394–402

4. Kind C, Rudin C, Siegrist CA, Wyler CA, Biedermann K, Lauper U, et al. Prevention of vertical HIV transmission: additive protective effect of elective cesarean section and zidovudine prophylaxis. AIDS 1998;12:205–210

5. Mandelbrot L, Le Chenadec J, Berrebi A, Bongain A, Benifla JL, Delfraissy JF, et al. Perinatal HIV-1 transmission: interaction between zidovudine prophylaxis and mode of delivery in the French Perinatal Cohort. JAMA 1998;280:55–60

6. The European Mode of Delivery Collaboration. Elective caesarean-section versus vaginal delivery in prevention of vertical HIV-1 transmission: a randomized clinical trial. Lancet 1999;353:1035–1039

7. The International Perinatal HIV Group. The mode of delivery and the risk of vertical transmission of human immunodeficiency virus type 1: a meta-analysis of 15 prospective cohort studies. N Engl J Med 1999;340:977–987

8. Nielsen TF, Hakegaard KH. Postoperative cesarean section morbidity: a prospective study. Am J Obstet Gynecol 1983; 146:911–915

9. Semprini AE, Castagna C, Ravizza M, Fiore S, Savasi V, Muggiasca ML, et al. The incidence of complications after cesarean section in 156 HIV-positive women. AIDS 1996; 9:913–917

10. Bulterys M, Chao A, Dushimimana A, Saah A. Fatal complications after cesarean section in HIV-infected women. AIDS 1996;10:923–924

11. Centers for Disease Control and Prevention. Report of the NIH Panel to define principles of therapy of HIV infection and guidelines for the use of antiretroviral agents in HIV-infected adults and adolescents. MMWR Morb Mortal Wkly Rep 1998;47(RR-5):1–82

12. Duff P, Robertson AW, Read JA. Single-dose cefazolin versus cefonicid for antibiotic prophylaxis in cesarean delivery. Obstet Gynecol 1987;70:718–721

13. Centers for Disease Control. Update: universal precautions for prevention of transmission of human immunodeficiency virus, hepatitis B virus, and other bloodborne pathogens in health-care settings. MMWR Morb Mortal Wkly Rep 1988;37:377–382;387–388

Bibliography

Rodman JH, Robbins BL, Flynn PM, Fridland A. A systematic and cellular model for zidovudine plasma concentrations and intracellular phosphorylation in patients. J Infect Dis 1996;174: 490–499

ACOG

Committee on
Gynecologic Practice

Committee on
Obstetric Practice

Committee Opinion

Number 240, August 2000   *(Replaces No. 145, November 1994)*

The American College of Obstetricians and Gynecologists
409 12th Street, SW
PO Box 96920
Washington, DC 20090-6920

12345/43210

Statement on Surgical Assistants

Competent surgical assistants should be available for all major obstetric and gynecologic operations. In many cases, the complexity of the surgery or the patient's condition will require the assistance of one or more physicians to provide safe, quality care. Often, the complexity of a given surgical procedure cannot be determined prospectively. Procedures including, but not limited to, operative laparoscopy, major abdominal and vaginal surgery, and cesarean delivery may warrant the assistance of another physician to optimize safe surgical care.

The primary surgeon's judgment and prerogative in determining the number and qualifications of surgical assistants should not be overruled by public or private third-party payers. Surgical assistants should be appropriately compensated.

ACOG Committee Opinion

Committee on Gynecologic Practice

Number 232, April 2000   *(Replaces No. 169, February 1996)*

Tamoxifen and Endometrial Cancer

Tamoxifen, a nonsteroidal antiestrogen agent, is used widely as adjunctive therapy for women with breast cancer. Its efficacy has been recognized by the U.S. Food and Drug Administration, which has approved tamoxifen for the following indications:

• Adjuvant treatment of breast cancer
• Metastatic breast cancer
• Reduction in breast cancer incidence in high-risk women

As the use of tamoxifen to treat both patients with breast cancer and women at risk for the disease becomes more widespread, gynecologists will be consulted more frequently for advice on the proper follow-up of these individuals. Unfortunately, data from prospective trials are insufficient to give definitive guidelines. The purpose of this Committee Opinion is to recommend care to prevent and detect endometrial cancer in women taking tamoxifen.

Tamoxifen is one of a class of agents known as selective estrogen receptor modulators (SERMs). Although the primary therapeutic effect of tamoxifen is derived from its antiestrogenic properties, this agent also has modest estrogenic activity. In standard dosages, tamoxifen may be associated with endometrial proliferation, hyperplasia, polyp formation, and invasive carcinoma.

Most studies have found the increased relative risk of developing endometrial cancer while taking tamoxifen to be two to three times higher than that of an age-matched population (1–3). The level of risk of endometrial cancer in women treated with tamoxifen is dose and time dependent. Studies suggest that the stage, grade, histology, or biology of tumors that develop in individuals treated with tamoxifen (20 mg/d) is no different from those that arise in the general population (3, 4). However, some reports have indicated that women treated with a higher dosage of tamoxifen (40 mg/d) are more prone to develop more biologically aggressive tumors (5).

The rate of endometrial cancer occurrence among tamoxifen users who were administered 20 mg/d in the National Surgical Adjuvant Breast and Bowel Project (NSABP) was 1.6 per 1,000 patient years, compared with 0.2 per 1,000 patient years among control patients taking placebo (3). In this study, the 5-year disease-free survival rate from breast cancer was 38% higher in the tamoxifen group than in the placebo group, suggesting that the small risk of developing endometrial cancer is outweighed by the significant survival benefit provided by tamoxifen therapy for women with breast cancer (3).

The survival advantage with 5 years of tamoxifen therapy continued with long-term follow-up, but extending the duration of tamoxifen use to 10 years failed to improve the survival benefit gained from 5 years of tamoxifen use (6).

The association between tamoxifen treatment and endometrial cancer is being scrutinized because data support a chemopreventive role for tamoxifen in women at high risk for developing breast cancer. The NSABP prevention trial (P-1) data suggest their risk for both invasive and noninvasive breast cancer is reduced markedly with tamoxifen prophylaxis. In this trial, the risk ratio for developing endometrial cancer was 2.53 in women using tamoxifen compared with women receiving a placebo (7). The Pilot Breast Cancer Prevention Trial showed that 39% of healthy postmenopausal women who were administered tamoxifen at a dosage of 20 mg/d had a histologically abnormal endometrium, compared with 10% of the placebo-treated control group (8). However, no case of endometrial cancer was identified in this small cohort of 111 postmenopausal women.

Several approaches are being explored for screening asymptomatic women using tamoxifen for abnormal endometrial proliferation or endometrial cancer. Correlation may be poor between ultrasonographic measurements of endometrial thickness and abnormal pathology in asymptomatic tamoxifen users because of tamoxifen-induced subepithelial stromal hypertrophy (9). In asymptomatic women using tamoxifen, screening for endometrial cancer with routine transvaginal ultrasonography, endometrial biopsy, or both has not been shown to be effective (10–13).

Although the concurrent use of progestin reduces the risk of endometrial hyperplasia and cancer in patients receiving unopposed estrogen, the impact of progestin on the course of breast cancer and on the endometrium of women receiving tamoxifen is not known. Therefore, such use cannot be advocated as a means of lowering risk in women taking tamoxifen.

On the basis of these data, the committee recommends the following:

- Women taking tamoxifen should be monitored closely for symptoms of endometrial hyperplasia or cancer and should have a gynecologic examination at least once every year.
- Women taking tamoxifen should be educated about the risks of endometrial proliferation, endometrial hyperplasia, and endometrial cancer. Women should be encouraged to promptly report any abnormal vaginal symptoms, including bloody discharge, spotting, staining, or leukorrhea.
- Any abnormal vaginal bleeding, bloody vaginal discharge, staining, or spotting should be investigated.
- Because screening tests have not been effective in increasing the early detection of endometrial cancer in women using tamoxifen and may lead to more invasive and costly diagnostic procedures, they are not recommended.
- Tamoxifen use should be limited to 5 years' duration because a benefit beyond this time has not been documented.
- If atypical endometrial hyperplasia develops, appropriate gynecologic management should be instituted, and the use of tamoxifen should be reassessed. If tamoxifen therapy must be continued, hysterectomy should be considered in women with atypical endometrial hyperplasia. Tamoxifen use may be reinstituted following hysterectomy for endometrial carcinoma in consultation with the physician responsible for the woman's breast care.

References

1. Sismondi P, Biglia N, Volpi E, Giai M, de Grandis T. Tamoxifen and endometrial cancer. Ann N Y Acad Sci 1994;734:310–321
2. Bissett D, Davis JA, George WD. Gynaecological monitoring during tamoxifen therapy. Lancet 1994;344:1244
3. Fisher B, Costantino JP, Redmond CK, Fisher ER, Wickerham DL, Cronin WM. Endometrial cancer in tamoxifen-treated breast cancer patients: findings from the National Surgical Adjuvant Breast and Bowel Project (NSABP) B-14. J Natl Cancer Inst 1994;86:527–537
4. Barakat RR, Wong G, Curtin JP, Vlamis V, Hoskins WJ. Tamoxifen use in breast cancer patients who subsequently develop corpus cancer is not associated with a higher incidence of adverse histologic features. Gynecol Oncol 1994;55:164–168
5. Magriples U, Naftolin F, Schwartz PE, Carcangiu ML. High-grade endometrial carcinoma in tamoxifen-treated breast cancer patients. J Clin Oncol 1993;11:485–490
6. Fisher B, Dignam J, Bryant J, DeCillis A, Wickerham DL, Wolmark N, et al. Five versus more than five years of tamoxifen therapy for breast cancer patients with negative lymph nodes and estrogen receptor-positive tumors. J Natl Cancer Inst 1996;88:1529–1542
7. Fisher B, Costantino JP, Wickerham DL, Redmond CK, Kavanah M, Cronin WM, et al. Tamoxifen for prevention of breast cancer: report of the National Surgical Adjuvant Breast and Bowel Project P-1 Study. J Natl Cancer Inst 1998;90:1371–1388
8. Kedar RP, Bourne TH, Powles TJ, Collins WP, Ashley SE, Cosgrove DO, et al. Effects of tamoxifen on uterus and ovaries of postmenopausal women in a randomised breast cancer prevention trial. Lancet 1994;343:1318–1321
9. Achiron R, Lipitz S, Sivan E, Goldenberg M, Horovitz A, Frenkel Y, et al. Changes mimicking endometrial neoplasia in postmenopausal, tamoxifen-treated women with breast cancer: a transvaginal Doppler study. Ultrasound Obstet Gynecol 1995;6:116–120

10. Bertelli G, Venturini M, Del Mastro L, Garrone O, Cosso M, Gustavino C, et al. Tamoxifen and the endometrium: findings of pelvic ultrasound examination and endometrial biopsy in asymptomatic breast cancer patients. Breast Cancer Res Treat 1998;47:41–46

11. Cecchini S, Ciatto S, Bonardi R, Mazzotta A, Grazzini G, Pacini P, et al. Screening by ultrasonography for endometrial carcinoma in postmenopausal breast cancer patients under adjuvant tamoxifen. Gynecol Oncol 1996;60: 409–411

12. Love CD, Muir BB, Scrimgeour JB, Leonard RC, Dillon P, Dixon JM. Investigation of endometrial abnormalities in asymptomatic women treated with tamoxifen and an evaluation of the role of endometrial screening. J Clin Oncol 1999;17:2050–2054

13. Seoud M, Shamseddine A, Khalil A, Salem Z, Saghir N, Bikhazi K, et al. Tamoxifen and endometrial pathologies: a prospective study. Gynecol Oncol 1999;75:15–19

ACOG Committee Opinion

Committee on
Gynecologic Practice

The American College of Obstetricians and Gynecologists
409 12th Street, SW
PO Box 96920
Washington, DC 20090-6920

12345/32109

Number 224, October 1999

Tamoxifen and the Prevention of Breast Cancer in High-Risk Women

Breast cancer is a significant health problem for women in the United States. It is estimated that, in 1999, there will be 175,000 new cases of breast cancer in women and approximately 43,300 deaths as a result of the disease (1). Although gains have been made in the diagnosis and treatment of breast cancer, there has been very little success in its prevention. Recently, the Breast Cancer Prevention Trial (BCPT), initiated in 1992 by the National Surgical Adjuvant Breast and Bowel Project and funded by the National Cancer Institute, was completed. This study showed that tamoxifen administration to women at high risk of developing breast cancer was associated with a 49% reduction in the occurrence of primary disease (2).

Tamoxifen is a nonsteroidal compound with both antiestrogenic and estrogenic effects on select tissues (3, 4). The ability of tamoxifen to retard or arrest the growth of breast cancer tumor cells (antiestrogenic action) eventually led to its study as a breast cancer treatment (5 7). For the past 25 years, the drug has been used as a chemotherapeutic agent for women with advanced stages of breast cancer (8–10). In 1985, the U.S. Food and Drug Administration (FDA) recommended its use as an adjuvant or additional therapy in women receiving primary surgical or radiation treatment for early stage breast cancer (11–15). Therefore, tamoxifen has been used to treat 1) postmenopausal women with advanced or metastatic breast cancer, 2) postmenopausal women with resected node-positive disease, and 3) both premenopausal and postmenopausal women with resected node-negative disease. Subsequent follow-up studies have demonstrated that tamoxifen is effective at reducing the recurrence risk of breast cancer and prolonging survival in treated patients (15–17).

Tamoxifen's possible usefulness in preventing breast cancer was suggested by several observations. First, studies showed that tamoxifen-treated patients had a statistically significant lower incidence of contralateral breast cancer (16, 17). Second, in vitro and in vivo animal studies showed that tamoxifen blocked the initiation and progression of tumors and inhibited the growth of cancer cells by several mechanisms (5–7). Third, a great deal of information was known about the pharmacodynamics, metabolism, and antitumor effects of tamoxifen in animals and humans (18–21).

These observations resulted in the creation of the BCPT, a large, multicenter prospective breast cancer prevention study involving 13,388 women. This study was designed as a double-blind, randomized, placebo-controlled trial to test the ability of tamoxifen to reduce the incidence of breast cancer in a high-risk population, which was composed of women older than 60 years and those between 35 and 59 years of age with an increased predicted risk of breast cancer. The predicted risk was derived from a computerized program that considered a combination of variables, including number of first-degree relatives with breast cancer, nulliparity, age at first delivery, number of breast biopsies, age at menarche, and history of previous lobular carcinoma in situ (22).

The results showed that high-risk women receiving tamoxifen had a 49% reduction in the incidence of breast cancer, compared with the placebo control group. Additionally, the incidence of noninvasive in situ breast cancer was decreased by half in the treatment group. The results were so conclusive that the independent auditor (Endpoint Review, Safety Monitoring, and Advisory Committee) recommended that the National Surgical Adjuvant Breast and Bowel Project terminate the study earlier than planned. This recommendation was adopted based on the belief that any additional information from continuing the study would be outweighed by the benefit of providing therapy to women in the placebo group and other women at increased risk.

However, it must be recognized that tamoxifen was not without significant side effects. The incidence of endometrial cancers doubled in the treatment group. All endometrial cancers were stage I, except for one stage IV cancer in the placebo group, and no deaths were reported. In addition, there was a threefold increase in the number of pulmonary emboli and a 50% increase in the number of deep venous thrombi in the treatment group compared with the control group. There was an increased relative risk of cataract formation and surgery for cataracts of 1.14 and 1.57, respectively.

Following the announcement of the BCPT results, two related studies were published that showed that the incidence of breast cancer was not decreased in tamoxifen-treated women compared with those receiving a placebo. However, there were significant methodologic differences between these studies and the BCPT. One study was conducted for 5 years and involved 5,408 women 35–70 years of age who had undergone hysterectomy (23). These women were not selected for high risk of breast cancer and,

in fact, represented a low- to normal-risk population. Because of these differences in experimental design, the findings of this report do not necessarily contradict those of the BCPT. The other study occurred over 6 years and included only 2,471 women 30–70 years of age with a family history of breast cancer, thereby excluding nongenetic risk factors (24). An explanation for the disparity in results between this study and the BCPT was not readily apparent. The authors suggested that genetic differences associated with the study subjects' family histories may have affected the preventive effect of tamoxifen.

In a recent decision, the FDA granted approval of tamoxifen for the purpose of reducing the incidence of breast cancer in women at high risk for breast cancer. "High risk" is defined as women at least 35 years of age with a 5-year predicted risk of breast cancer of at least 1.67%, as calculated by the Gail model. The FDA also approved tamoxifen for the reduction of contralateral breast cancer risk in patients receiving adjuvant tamoxifen therapy for breast cancer. The FDA emphasized that patients should be informed about tamoxifen's adverse effects, including increased risk of endometrial cancer, deep vein thrombosis, pulmonary embolism, and cataracts, in addition to tamoxifen's potential benefits. The FDA Advisory Committee also emphasized that the effects of long-term treatment with tamoxifen are unknown because follow-up data are limited to 5 years.

In summary, the BCPT results are encouraging and provide an opportunity for chemoprevention in women at high risk for the development of breast cancer. However, several issues remain under consideration. For example, there are insufficient data on the long-term use of tamoxifen and subsequent occurrence of and death from breast cancer. Research addressing the associated increased risk of endometrial cancer, vascular morbidity, and potential mortality must continue. Finally, the role of tamoxifen in women at low or normal risk for breast cancer and in those individuals with genetic mutations of *BRCA1* or *BRCA2* should be defined. Some of these concerns may be addressed by continued surveillance of women receiving tamoxifen over an extended period, whereas other issues will warrant additional studies in the future.

Researchers from the National Cancer Institute and the National Surgical Adjuvant Breast and Bowel Project have developed a computer-based tool to allow clinicians to project a woman's individualized estimate of breast cancer risk. The Breast Cancer Risk Assessment Tool, currently available through a pilot program, is a computer disk that a woman and her health care professional can use to estimate her chances of developing breast cancer based on several established risk factors. The disk is available at no charge, in PC-compatible and Macintosh computer formats. To order, call the National Cancer Institute's Cancer Information Service at 1-800-422-6237 or visit the National Cancer Institute's cancer trials web site at http://cancertrials.nci.nih.gov/.

The obstetrician–gynecologist has the unique opportunity to inform high-risk patients of the need for breast cancer screening and the availability of chemopreventive therapy. However, the decision to use tamoxifen to reduce the risk of breast cancer should be individualized. Because a key factor to be considered is the woman's risk of breast cancer, it is important that clinicians take a thorough history to assess her risk adequately. Other factors to be considered include potential tamoxifen-associated side effects and risks, patient preference, clinician judgment, and clinician ability to monitor for and manage tamoxifen-related side effects, referring as necessary.

References

1. Landis SH, Murray T, Bolden S, Wingo PA. Cancer statistics, 1999. CA Cancer J Clin 1999;49:8–31
2. Fisher B, Costantino JP, Wickerham DL, Redmond CK, Kavanah M, Cronin WM, et al. Tamoxifen for prevention of breast cancer: report of the National Surgical Adjuvant Breast and Bowel Project P-1 Study. J Natl Cancer Inst 1998;90:1371–1388
3. Love RR. Antiestrogens as chemopreventive agents in breast cancer: promise and issues in evaluation. Prev Med 1989;18:661–671
4. Jordan VC. Tamoxifen: toxicities and drug resistance during the treatment and prevention of breast cancer. Annu Rev Pharmacol Toxicol 1995;35:195–211
5. Terenius L. Effect of anti-oestrogens on initiation of mammary cancer in the female rat. Eur J Cancer 1971;7:65–70
6. Jordan VC. Effect of tamoxifen (ICI 46,474) on initiation and growth of DMBA-induced rat mammary carcinomata. Eur J Cancer 1976;12:419–424
7. Jordan VC, Allen KE. Evaluation of the antitumour activity of the non-steroidal antioestrogen monohydroxytamoxifen in the DMBA-induced rat mammary carcinoma model. Eur J Cancer 1980;16:239–251
8. Heuson JC. Current overview of EORTC clinical trials with tamoxifen. Cancer Treat Rep 1976;60:1463–1466
9. Mouridsen H, Palshof T, Patterson J, Battersby L. Tamoxifen in advanced breast cancer. Cancer Treat Rev 1978;5:131–141
10. Legha SS, Buzdar AU, Hortobagyi GN, Wiseman C, Benjamin RS, Blumenschein GR. Tamoxifen. Use in treatment of metastatic breast cancer refractory to combination chemotherapy. JAMA 1979;242:49–52
11. Controlled trial of tamoxifen as adjuvant agent in management of early breast cancer. Interim analysis at four years by Nolvadex Adjuvant Trial Organisation. Lancet 1983;1:257–261
12. Controlled trial of tamoxifen as single adjuvant agent in management of early breast cancer. Analysis at six years by Nolvadex Adjuvant Trial Organisation. Lancet 1985;1:836–840
13. Fisher B, Redmond C, Brown A, Fisher ER, Wolmark N, Bowman D, et al. Adjuvant chemotherapy with and without tamoxifen in the treatment of primary breast cancer: 5-year results from the National Surgical Adjuvant Breast and Bowel Project Trial. J Clin Oncol 1986;4:459–471
14. Adjuvant tamoxifen in the management of operable breast cancer: the Scottish Trial. Report from the Breast Cancer Trials Committee, Scottish Cancer Trials Office (MRC), Edinburgh. Lancet 1987;2:171–175
15. Fisher B, Costantino J, Redmond C, Poisson R, Bowman D, Couture J, et al. A randomized clinical trial evaluating tamoxifen in the treatment of patients with node-negative breast cancer who have estrogen-receptor-positive tumors. N Engl J Med 1989;320:479–484
16. Cyclophosphamide and tamoxifen as adjuvant therapies in the management of breast cancer. CRC Adjuvant Breast Trial Working Party. Br J Cancer 1988;57:604–607
17. Rutqvist LE, Cedermark B, Glas U, Mattsson A, Skoog L, Somell A, et al. Contralateral primary tumors in breast cancer patients in a randomized trial of adjuvant tamoxifen therapy. J Natl Cancer Inst 1991;83:1299–1306
18. Furr BJ, Patterson JS, Richardson DN, Slater SR, Wakeling AE. Tamoxifen. Pharmacol Biochem Prop Drug Subst 1979;2:355–399
19. Adam HK. Pharmacokinetic studies with Nolvadex. Rev Endocr Relat Cancer 1981;9:131–143
20. Wakeling AE, Valcaccia B, Newboult E, Green LR. Non-steroidal antioestrogens-receptor binding and biological response in rat uterus, rat mammary carcinoma and human breast cancer cells. J Steroid Biochem Mol Biol 1984;20:111–120
21. Jordan VC, Fritz NF, Tormey DC. Long-term adjuvant therapy with tamoxifen: effects on sex hormone binding globulin and antithrombin III. Cancer Res 1987;47:4517–4519
22. Gail MH, Brinton LA, Byar DP, Corle DK, Green SB, Schairer C, et al. Projecting individualized probabilities of developing breast cancer for white females who are being examined annually. J Natl Cancer Inst 1989;81:1879–1886
23. Veronesi U, Maisonneuve P, Costa A, Sacchini V, Maltoni C, Robertson C, et al. Prevention of breast cancer with tamoxifen: preliminary findings from the Italian randomised trial among hysterectomised women. Italian Tamoxifen Prevention Study. Lancet 1998;352:93–97
24. Powles T, Eeles R, Ashley S, Easton D, Chang J, Dowsett M, et al. Interim analysis of the incidence of breast cancer in the Royal Marsden Hospital tamoxifen randomised chemoprevention trial. Lancet 1998;352:98–101

ACOG Committee Opinion

Committee
on Coding and
Nomenclature

Number 205, August 1998

Tubal Ligation with Cesarean Delivery

Tubal ligation at the time of cesarean delivery requires significant additional physician work even though the technical work of the procedure is brief. Informed consent by the patient requires considerably more counseling by the physician regarding potential risks and benefits of this procedure than is necessary with alternative means of sterilization and contraception. Also, many states require completion of special informed consent documents in addition to the customary consent forms required by hospitals. These forms must be completed before scheduling the procedure.

Patients have the right to change their minds. Thus, it is important to reconfirm the patient's decision shortly before the operation.

Tubal ligation with cesarean delivery involves removal of a segment of fallopian tube, which is sent for histologic confirmation. With most cesarean deliveries, tissue is not evaluated by a pathologist. Accordingly, it is important for the surgeon to verify the pathology report, which adds an additional component to post-service work.

The risk of professional liability for operative complications is increased with this procedure. This risk is low, but real. Furthermore, sterilization failure occurs in about 1 in 100 cases even though the operation was performed properly. This failure also carries a liability risk.

Because tubal ligation is a discrete extra service, it should be coded accordingly: 59510 or 59618—routine obstetric care including antepartum care, cesarean delivery, and postpartum care—and 58611—ligation or transection of fallopian tube(s) done at the time of cesarean delivery or intra-abdominal surgery.

Copyright © August 1998
ISSN 1074-861X

The American College of Obstetricians and Gynecologists

409 12th Street, SW
PO Box 96920
Washington, DC 20090-6920

12345/21098

ACOG

Committee on
Obstetric Practice

American Academy
of Pediatrics
Committee on
Fetus and Newborn

Committee Opinion

Number 174, July 1996   *(Replaces #49, November 1986)*

Use and Abuse of the Apgar Score

The Apgar score, devised in 1952 by Dr. Virginia Apgar, is a quick method of assessing the clinical status of the newborn infant (1, 2). Ease of scoring has led to its use in many studies of outcome. However, its misuse has led to an erroneous definition of asphyxia. Intrapartum asphyxia implies fetal hypercarbia and hypoxemia, which if prolonged will result in eventual metabolic acidemia. Because the intrapartum disruption of uterine or fetal blood flow is rarely, if ever, absolute, *asphyxia* is an imprecise, general term. Terms such as *hypercarbia, hypoxia,* and *metabolic, respiratory,* or *lactic acidemia* are more precise, both for immediate assessment of the newborn and for retrospective assessment of intrapartum management. Although the Apgar score continues to provide a convenient "shorthand" for reporting the status of the newborn and the effectiveness of resuscitation, the purpose of this statement is to place the Apgar score in its proper perspective.

The Apgar score comprises five components: heart rate, respiratory effort, muscle tone, reflex irritability, and color, each of which is given a score of 0, 1, or 2 (Table 1). Reliable Apgar scores require assessment of individual components of the score by trained personnel.

Factors That May Affect the Apgar Score

Although rarely stated, it is important to recognize that elements of the Apgar score such as tone, color, and reflex irritability are partially dependent on the physiologic maturity of the infant. The healthy premature infant with no evidence of anoxic insult, acidemia, or cerebral depression may thus receive a low score only because of immaturity (3, 4).

A number of maternal medications and infant conditions may influence Apgar scores, including, but not limited to, neuromuscular or cerebral malformations that may decrease tone and respiratory effort. Cardiorespiratory conditions may also decrease the infant's heart rate, respiration, and tone. Infection may interfere with tone, color, and response to resuscitative efforts. Additional information is required to interpret Apgar scores properly in infants receiving resuscitation. Thus, to equate the presence of a low Apgar score solely with asphyxia or hypoxia represents a misuse of the score.

The American College of Obstetricians and Gynecologists

409 12th Street, SW
PO Box 96920
Washington, DC 20090-6920

12345/09876

Table 1. Apgar Score: Five Components and Score Definitions

Component	Score 0	Score 1	Score 2
Heart rate	Absent	Slow (<100 beats/min)	>100 beats/min
Respirations	Absent	Weak cry, hypoventilation	Good, strong cry
Muscle tone	Limp	Some flexion	Active motion
Reflex irritability	No response	Grimace	Cry or active withdrawal
Color	Blue or pale	Body pink, extremities blue	Completely pink

Adapted from Apgar V, Holaday DA, James LS, Weisbrot IM, Berrien C. Evaluation of the newborn infant: second report. JAMA 1958;168:1985–1988

Apgar Score and Subsequent Disability

A low 1-minute Apgar score does not correlate with the infant's future outcome. The 5-minute Apgar score, and particularly the change in the score between 1 and 5 minutes, is a useful index of the effectiveness of resuscitation efforts. However, even a 5-minute score of 0–3, although possibly a result of hypoxia, is limited as an indicator of the severity of the problem and correlates poorly with future neurologic outcome (5, 6). An Apgar score of 0–3 at 5 minutes is associated with an increased risk of cerebral palsy in term infants, but this increase is only from 0.3% to 1% (5, 6). A 5-minute Apgar score of 7–10 is considered "normal." Scores of 4, 5, and 6 are intermediate and are not markers of high levels of risk of later neurologic dysfunction. As previously mentioned, such scores are affected by physiologic immaturity, medication, the presence of congenital malformations, and other factors.

Because Apgar scores at 1 and 5 minutes correlate poorly with either cause or outcome, the scores alone should not be considered evidence of or a consequence of substantial asphyxia. Therefore, a low 5-minute Apgar score alone does not demonstrate that later development of cerebral palsy was caused by perinatal asphyxia.

Correlation of the Apgar score with future neurologic outcome increases when the score remains 0–3 at 10, 15, and 20 minutes but still does not indicate the cause of future disability (5, 7). The term *asphyxia* in a clinical context should be reserved to describe a combination of damaging acidemia, hypoxia, and metabolic acidosis. A neonate who has had "asphyxia" proximate to delivery that is severe enough to result in acute neurologic injury should demonstrate all of the following:

- Profound metabolic or mixed acidemia (pH <7.00) on an umbilical cord arterial blood sample, if obtained
- An Apgar score of 0–3 for longer than 5 minutes
- Neonatal neurologic manifestations (eg, seizures, coma, or hypotonia)

- Multisystem organ dysfunction (eg, cardiovascular, gastrointestinal, hematologic, pulmonary, or renal system)

The Apgar score alone cannot establish hypoxia as the cause of cerebral palsy. A term infant with an Apgar score of 0–3 at 5 minutes whose 10-minute score improved to 4 or higher has a 99% chance of not having cerebral palsy at 7 years of age (5). Conversely, 75% of children with cerebral palsy had normal Apgar scores at birth (5).

Cerebral palsy is the only neurologic deficit clearly linked to perinatal asphyxia. Although mental retardation and epilepsy may accompany cerebral palsy, there is no evidence that they are caused by perinatal asphyxia unless cerebral palsy is also present, and even then a relationship is in doubt (8, 9).

Conclusion

Apgar scores are useful in assessing the condition of the infant at birth. Their use in other settings, such as collection of a child's Apgar score upon entry to school, is inappropriate. Low Apgar scores may be indicative of a number of maternal and infant factors. Apgar scores alone should not be used as evidence that neurologic damage was caused by hypoxia that results in neurologic damage or by inappropriate intrapartum management. In the infant who later is found to have cerebral palsy, low 1-minute or 5-minute Apgar scores are not sufficient evidence that the damage was due to hypoxia or inappropriate intrapartum management. Hypoxia as a cause of acute neurologic injury and adverse neurologic outcome occurs in infants who demonstrate the four perinatal findings listed in this Committee Opinion and in whom other possible causes of neurologic damage have been excluded. In the absence of such evidence, subsequent neurologic deficiencies cannot be ascribed to perinatal asphyxia or hypoxia (10, 11).

References

1. Apgar V. A proposal for a new method of evaluation of the newborn infant. Curr Res Anesth Analg 1953;32:260–267
2. Apgar V, Holaday DA, James LS, Weisbrot IM, Berrien C. Evaluation of the newborn infant: second report. JAMA 1958;168:1985–1988
3. Catlin EA, Carpenter MW, Brann BS IV, Mayfield SR, Shaul PW, Goldstein M, et al. The Apgar score revisited: influence of gestational age. J Pediatr 1986;109:865–868
4. Amon E, Sibai BM, Anderson GD, Mabie WC. Obstetric variables predicting survival of the immature newborn (less than or equal to 1000 gm): a five-year experience in a single perinatal center. Am J Obstet Gynecol 1987;156:1380–1389
5. Nelson KB, Ellenberg JH. Apgar scores as predictors of chronic neurologic disability. Pediatrics 1981;68:36–44
6. Stanley FJ. Cerebral palsy trends: implications for perinatal care. Acta Obstet Gynecol Scand 1994;73:5–9
7. Freeman JM, Nelson KB. Intrapartum asphyxia and cerebral palsy. Pediatrics 1988;82:240–249
8. Levene MI, Sands C, Grindulis H, Moore JR. Comparison of two methods of predicting outcome in perinatal asphyxia. Lancet 1986;1:67–69
9. Paneth N. The causes of cerebral palsy: recent evidence. Clin Invest Med 1993;16:95–102
10. Brann AW Jr, Dykes FD. The effects of intrauterine asphyxia on the full-term neonate. Clin Perinatol 1977;4:149–161
11. Nelson KB, Leviton A. How much of neonatal encephalopathy is due to birth asphyxia? Am J Dis Child 1991;145:1325–1331

committee opinion

Committee on Obstetric Practice

Number 138—April 1994
(*Replaces #91, February 1991*)

Utility of Umbilical Cord Blood Acid–Base Assessment

Despite new neonatal and obstetric technologies, the rate of cerebral palsy in term infants (1–2 cases per 1,000 births) has not been reduced over the past 20 years in Western industrialized countries. The persistent misuse of the term birth asphyxia, with the misperception that it accounts for a significant portion of infants with cerebral palsy, continues to exist, despite the fact that there is no evidence to support this misperception. A number of clinical and experimental reports confirm that only severe and prolonged hypoxia is associated with an increased risk of subsequent neurologic dysfunction. This level of hypoxia is very uncommon with birthing conditions in the United States and modern industrialized countries. When prolonged and severe hypoxia occurs, it is often followed by death or the prolonged requirement for life support systems. Most survivors develop normally.

The American College of Obstetricians and Gynecologists and the American Academy of Pediatrics have challenged the use of the Apgar score to define birth asphyxia. Umbilical cord blood acid–base assessment is a more objective measure of the acid–base status of a newborn than is the Apgar score. The exact lower limits of newborn pH (metabolic acidemia) and depression (low 5-minute Apgar score) that are predictive of subsequent neurologic dysfunction have not been determined. However, some studies have reported a significantly increased incidence of newborn morbidity associated with acidemia in term newborns with an umbilical artery pH of less than 7.00 and a 5-minute Apgar score of 3 or less and in whom the acidemia has a metabolic component. Again, most infants with this severe degree of acidemia will develop normally.

Intrapartum asphyxia implies fetal hypercarbia and hypoxemia, which, if prolonged, will result in metabolic acidemia. Because the intrapartum disruption of uterine or fetal blood flow is rarely, if ever, absolute, asphyxia is an imprecise, general term and should be reserved for the clinical context of damaging acidemia, hypoxia, and metabolic acidosis. Terms such as hypercarbia, hypoxia, metabolic acidemia, and respiratory or lactic acidemia are more precise, both for immediate assessment of the newborn and for retrospective assessment of intrapartum management.

Although fetal acidemia has been defined as an umbilical arterial blood pH of less than 7.20, this level is arbitrarily high. In normal uncomplicated pregnancies, the lower range of umbilical arterial blood pH has been reported as 7.10–7.15. Although the precise value that is required to define acidemia is not known, umbilical arterial blood pH values of less than 7.00 more realistically represent clinically significant acidosis. It should be noted that acidemia by itself is not sufficient evidence to establish that a hypoxic injury has occurred. A neonate who has had severe hypoxia proximate to delivery that is severe enough to result in hypoxic encephalopathy will show other evidence of hypoxic damage, including all of the following:

- Profound metabolic or mixed acidemia (pH less than 7.00) on an umbilical cord arterial blood sample, if obtained

- Persistent Apgar score of 0–3 for 5 minutes or longer

- Evidence of neonatal neurologic sequelae (eg, seizures, coma, prolonged hypotonia, and one or more of the following: cardiovascular, gastrointestinal, hematologic, pulmonary, or renal system dysfunction)

TECHNIQUE

Immediately after delivery of the neonate, a segment of umbilical cord should be doubly clamped, divided, and placed on the delivery table pending assignment of the 5-minute Apgar score. Values from the umbilical artery provide the most accurate information regarding fetal and newborn acid–base status. A clamped segment of cord is stable for pH and blood gas assessment for at least 60 minutes, and a cord blood sample in a syringe flushed with heparin is stable for up to 60 minutes. If the 5-minute Apgar score is satisfactory and the infant appears stable and vigorous, the segment of umbilical cord can be discarded. If a serious abnormality that arose in the delivery process or a problem with the neonate's condition or both persist at or beyond the first 5 minutes, blood can be drawn from the cord segment and sent to a laboratory for blood gas analysis. It should be noted that, occasionally, it may be difficult to obtain an adequate cord arterial blood sample.

CONCLUSION

In the depressed newborn, the documentation of umbilical blood acid–base measurements provides an objective fetal assessment and, if levels are within the normal range, can exclude intrapartum hypoxia as a proximate cause of neonatal depression. This knowledge may aid practitioners in their assessment of the depressed newborn.

BIBLIOGRAPHY

Dennis J, Johnson A, Mutch L, Yudkin P, Johnson P. Acid base status at birth and neurodevelopment at four and one-half years. Am J Obstet Gynecol 1989;161:213–220

Dorland's illustrated medical dictionary. 27th ed. Philadelphia: WB Saunders, 1988

Duerbeck NB, Chaffin DG, Seeds JW. A practical approach to umbilical artery pH and blood gas determinations. Obstet Gynecol 1992;79:959–962

Fee SC, Malee K, Deddish R, Minogue JP, Socol ML. Severe acidosis and subsequent neurologic status. Am J Obstet Gynecol 1990;162:802–806

Freeman JM, ed. Prenatal and perinatal factors associated with brain disorders. Washington, DC: U.S. Government Printing Office, 1985; NIH publication no. 85-1149

Freeman JM, Nelson KB. Intrapartum asphyxia and cerebral palsy. Pediatrics 1988;82:240–249

Gilstrap LC 3rd, Leveno KJ, Burris J, Williams ML, Little BB. Diagnosis of birth asphyxia on the basis of fetal pH, Apgar score and newborn cerebral dysfunction. Am J Obstet Gynecol 1989;161:825–830

Goldenberg RL, Huddleston JF, Nelson KG. Apgar scores and umbilical artery pH in preterm newborn infants. Am J Obstet Gynecol 1984;149:651–654

Nelson KB, Ellenberg JH. Antecedents of cerebral palsy multivariate analysis of risk. N Engl J Med 1986;315:81–86

Riley RJ, Johnson JW. Collecting and analyzing cord blood gases. Clin Obstet Gynecol 1993;36:13–23

Ruth VJ, Raivio KO. Perinatal brain damage: predictive value of metabolic acidosis and the Apgar score. BMJ 1988;297:24–27

Thorp JA, Sampson JE, Parisi VM, Creasy RK. Routine umbilical cord blood gas determinations? Am J Obstet Gynecol 1989;161:600–605

ACOG Committee Opinion

Committee on
Gynecologic Practice

ISSN 1074-861X

**The American College of
Obstetricians and Gynecologists**
409 12th Street, SW
PO Box 96920
Washington, DC 20090-6920

12345/54321

Von Willebrand's disease in gynecologic practice. ACOG Committee
Opinion No. 263. American College
of Obstetricians and Gynecologists.
Obstet Gynecol 2001;98:1185–1186

Number 263, December 2001

Von Willebrand's Disease in Gynecologic Practice

ABSTRACT: Von Willebrand's disease is one of the most common inherited bleeding disorders. Inherited and acquired disorders of coagulation and hemostasis should be considered in the differential diagnosis of menorrhagia and abnormal uterine bleeding. This Committee Opinion provides screening recommendations for von Willebrand's disease and describes treatment options.

Von Willebrand's disease is one of the most common inherited disorders. Women with von Willebrand's disease commonly experience menorrhagia, and among women with menorrhagia, von Willebrand's disease is not rare. Population prevalence studies have suggested a prevalence of approximately 1% (1, 2).

The evaluation and management of women presenting with abnormal uterine bleeding have been addressed in other ACOG publications (3). Inherited and acquired disorders of coagulation and hemostasis should be considered in the differential diagnosis of menorrhagia and abnormal uterine bleeding (4). The patient's history of past surgical procedures, injuries, fractures, and deliveries can provide useful information, along with a careful menstrual history documenting the timing of onset of heavy bleeding and a family history of abnormal bleeding, including menorrhagia. Von Willebrand's disease also may be suggested by past medical history, menstrual history, and surgical history, as well as by family history, because there is a clear genetic component. However, there is variable penetrance of type I von Willebrand's disease, so there may be little or no strong family history (5).

Recommendations regarding testing for von Willebrand's disease are as follows:

- Adolescents presenting with severe menorrhagia should be screened for von Willebrand's disease. This screening should be performed before the initiation of hormonal therapy, because oral contraceptives may mask the diagnosis. As many as one third of adolescents presenting with menorrhagia at menarche have been found to have von Willebrand's disease (6).

- Screening is warranted among adult women with significant menorrhagia without another cause, because it is not unusual to encounter adult women with menorrhagia who have a mild form of von Willebrand's disease. Studies of women with objectively documented menorrhagia have found that 13–20% meet the criteria for a diagnosis of mild von Willebrand's disease (7, 8).

• Hysterectomy for excessive menstrual bleeding should not be performed without the consideration of bleeding disorders. Women with von Willebrand's disease have in the past undoubtedly been given the diagnosis of dysfunctional uterine bleeding and have had hysterectomies for therapy, with resultant increased risks from bleeding at the time of surgery (9).

The ristocetin cofactor assay of von Willebrand's factor (vWF) function may be the best single screening test for von Willebrand's disease (10, 11). Physiologic fluctuations in vWF levels may obscure the diagnosis, so repeat testing and consultation with a hematologist regarding additional tests may be necessary for patients with strong personal and family histories of menorrhagia (5).

Von Willebrand's disease has been categorized and ranges from mild disease, type I, to severe, type III. It should be determined which type of von Willebrand's disease a particular patient has because treatment depends on type (12). Treatment options include oral contraceptive drugs, desmopressin acetate, antifibrinolytic agents, and plasma-derived concentrates rich in the high-molecular-weight multimers of vWF. Consultation with or referral to a hematologist is frequently helpful to assist in the management of patients with severe disease.

Oral contraceptive therapy has been successfully used by gynecologists as first-line therapy for the management of von Willebrand's disease for many years. Oral contraceptives have been reported to be successful in the management of menorrhagia associated with von Willebrand's disease in 88% of patients (13). Hormonally induced therapeutic amenorrhea may be appropriate for patients with severe disease.

Desmopressin acetate, which is available in parenteral form for intravenous use and in a highly concentrated intranasal spray formulation, is the treatment of choice for classic type I disease. It can be used as home therapy before the onset of menses, or only during menses (14).

References

1. Rodeghiero F, Castaman G, Dini E. Epidemiological investigation of the prevalence of von Willebrand's disease. Blood 1987;69:454–459
2. Werner EJ, Broxson EH, Tucker EL, Giroux DS, Shults J, Abshire TC. Prevalence of von Willebrand disease in children: a multiethnic study. J Pediatr 1993;123:893–898
3. American College of Obstetricians and Gynecologists. Management of anovulatory bleeding. ACOG Practice Bulletin 14. Washington, DC: ACOG, 2000
4. Brenner PF. Differential diagnosis of abnormal uterine bleeding. Am J Obstet Gynecol 1996;175:766–769
5. Ewenstein BM. The pathophysiology of bleeding disorders presenting as abnormal uterine bleeding. Am J Obstet Gynecol 1996;175:770–777
6. Claessens E, Cowell CA. Acute adolescent menorrhagia. Am J Obstet Gynecol 1981;139:277–280
7. Edlund M, Blomback M, von Schoultz B, Andersson O. On the value of menorrhagia as a predictor for coagulation disorders. Am J Hematol 1996;53:234–238
8. Kadir RA, Economides DL, Sabin CA, Owens D, Lee CA. Frequency of inherited bleeding disorders in women with menorrhagia. Lancet 1998;351:485–489
9. Chuong CJ, Brenner PF. Management of abnormal uterine bleeding. Am J Obstet Gynecol 1996;175:787–792
10. Phillips MD, Santhouse A. von Willebrand disease: recent advances in pathophysiology and treatment. Am J Med Sci 1998;316:77–86
11. Werner EJ, Abshire TC, Giroux DS, Tucker EL, Broxson EH. Relative value of diagnostic studies for von Willebrand disease. J Pediatr 1992;121:34–38
12. Lusher JM. Screening and diagnosis of coagulation disorders. Am J Obstet Gynecol 1996;175:778–783
13. Foster PA. The reproductive health of women with von Willebrand Disease unresponsive to DDAVP: results of an international survey. On behalf of the Subcommittee on von Willebrand Factor of the Scientific and Standardization Committee of the ISTH. Thromb Haemost 1995;74:784–790
14. Lethagen S, Ragnarson Tennvall G. Self-treatment with desmopressin intranasal spray in patients with bleeding disorders: effect on bleeding symptoms and socioeconomic factors. Ann Hematol 1993;66:257–260

Educational and Technical Bulletins

Educational and Technical Bulletins

ACOG EDUCATIONAL BULLETIN

Number 244, February 1998

Antiphospholipid Syndrome

Antiphospholipid syndrome is an autoimmune condition characterized by the presence of certain clinical features and moderate-to-high levels of circulating antiphospholipid antibodies. The most specific clinical features are thrombotic events (venous or arterial), autoimmune thrombocytopenia, and fetal loss (Table 1) (1–3). Other clinical features include transient ischemic attacks, amaurosis fugax, Coombs-positive hemolytic anemia, and a dermatologic condition known as livedo reticularis. "Primary" antiphospholipid syndrome occurs in patients with no other recognized autoimmune disease and is probably the most common presentation of antiphospholipid syndrome recognized by obstetrician–gynecologists. "Secondary" antiphospholipid syndrome is diagnosed when the patient has another underlying autoimmune disease such as systemic lupus erythematosus (SLE). Antiphospholipid syndrome may be seen in children, adolescents, and adults and is more prevalent in females than males.

Antiphospholipid Antibodies

Two antiphospholipid antibodies for which assays are widely available are lupus anticoagulant and anticardiolipin antibodies. The lupus anticoagulant antibody was first described in 1952 (4) and was subsequently named "lupus anticoagulant" because it was initially recognized in patients with SLE and because it prolongs clotting in vitro. Paradoxically, lupus anticoagulant (and anticardiolipin) is associated with clinical thrombosis, not bleeding. Anticardiolipin antibodies were first identified as autoantibodies in 1983 (5) using a solid phase immunoassay with the phospholipid cardiolipin as the antigen. In the assays for both lupus anticoagulant and anticardiolipin antibodies, the antiphospholipid autoantibodies bind moieties on negatively charged phospholipids or moieties formed by the interaction of negatively charged phospholipids with other lipids, phospholipids, or proteins. Some investigators have found that lupus anticoagulant and anticardiolipin antibodies may be separated in the laboratory, suggesting that they are different

This Educational Bulletin was developed under the direction of the Committee on Educational Bulletins of the American College of Obstetricians and Gynecologists as an aid to obstetricians and gynecologists. The College wishes to thank D. Ware Branch, Jr, MD, and Robert M. Silver, MD, for their assistance in the development of this bulletin. This document is not to be construed as establishing a standard of practice or dictating an exclusive course of treatment. Rather, it is intended as an educational tool that presents current information on obstetric–gynecologic issues.

121

Table 1. Clinical and Laboratory Criteria for the Diagnosis of Antiphospholipid Syndrome*

Criterion	Definition
Clinical	
Fetal loss	Three or more spontaneous abortions with no more than one live birth, or unexplained second- or third-trimester fetal death
Thrombosis	Unexplained venous or arterial thrombosis, including stroke and arterial insufficiency due to arterial thrombosis
Autoimmune thrombocytopenia	Other causes of thrombocytopenia excluded
Other features	Otherwise unexplained transient ischemic attacks or amaurosis fugax, livedo reticularis, Coombs-positive hemolytic anemia, chorea, and chorea gravidarum
Laboratory	
Lupus anticoagulant	Detected by phospholipid-dependent clotting assays, without correction with normal plasma, and confirmed by demonstration of phospholipid dependency
Anticardiolipin antibodies	IgG isotype >15–20 GPL units (medium-to-high positive) detected in standardized assay using standard serum calibrators†

*Antiphospholipid syndrome is diagnosed when the patient has (1) at least one clinical feature *and* (2) lupus anticoagulant or medium-to-high positive immunoglobulin G anticardiolipin antibodies or both. Because antiphospholipid antibodies may appear transiently following infection, positive tests should be confirmed 8 or more weeks after initial testing.

†IgM and IgA isotypes are of uncertain significance and should not be used to diagnose antiphospholipid syndrome unless patient also has lupus anticoagulant or IgG anticardiolipin antibodies (GPL units).

immunoglobulins (6–8). Others believe that these antibodies are the same immunoglobulins being detected by different methods (9). Despite this controversy, lupus anticoagulant and anticardiolipin antibodies are associated with the same set of clinical problems and are therefore likely members of the same "family" of autoantibodies. Most patients with antiphospholipid syndrome have lupus anticoagulant and anticardiolipin antibodies. However, some patients with antiphospholipid syndrome have either lupus anticoagulant or anticardiolipin antibodies, but not both. Thus, tests for both antibodies should be performed to confirm the diagnosis of antiphospholipid syndrome.

The laboratory testing for antiphospholipid antibodies remains somewhat confusing for clinicians. Part of the difficulty is that some laboratories offering antiphospholipid antibody testing use assays that are not standardized or operate with inadequate quality control analysis of results (10, 11). Underlying this problem is the fact that reliable testing for antiphospholipid antibodies is difficult. Whenever possible, clinicians should identify and use a reliable laboratory with a special interest in antiphospholipid antibody testing.

Tests for Antiphospholipid Antibodies

Indications for testing for antiphospholipid antibodies are shown in the box. Only individuals with these clinical features should be tested because the presence of antiphospholipid antibodies in the absence of these features

is of uncertain significance. In contrast to the reporting of anticardiolipin antibodies, which involves accepted international units, lupus anticoagulant is considered present or absent and is not quantified by current methodology.

Indications for Testing for Antiphospholipid Antibodies

Obstetric
  Otherwise unexplained fetal death or stillbirth
  Recurrent pregnancy loss (three or more spontaneous abortions with no more than one live birth, or unexplained second- or third-trimester fetal death)
  Severe pregnancy-induced hypertension <34 weeks of gestation
  Severe fetal growth restriction or other evidence of uteroplacental insufficiency in the second or early third trimester
Medical
  Nontraumatic thrombosis or thromboembolism (venous or arterial)
  Stroke, especially in individuals <50–55 years of age
  Autoimmune thrombocytopenia
  Transient ischemic attacks or amaurosis fugax, especially in individuals <50–55 years of age
  Livedo reticularis
  Hemolytic anemia
  Systemic lupus erythematosus
  False-positive serologic test for syphilis

Lupus Anticoagulant

Lupus anticoagulant is detected in plasma by using a sequence of phospholipid-dependent coagulation assays such as the activated partial thromboplastin time, dilute Russell viper venom time, or kaolin clotting time. In these assays, lupus anticoagulant binds to phospholipids or moieties formed by the interaction of phospholipids and clotting factors, thus interfering with the clotting cascade and delaying the time to clot formation. The result is a prolonged clotting time. In vivo, phospholipids play a dual role, facilitating both thrombotic and antithrombotic mechanisms. Though not certain, it is likely that lupus anticoagulant predisposes to clotting in vivo by interfering predominantly with the antithrombotic role of phospholipids. Lupus anticoagulant is one of the most common reasons for a prolonged activated partial thromboplastin time that does not correct with mixture of normal pooled plasma.

Anticardiolipin Antibodies

Anticardiolipin antibodies are detected by conventional immunoassays. Laboratories should use the standardized method (12) or a modified assay known to produce similar results. Standard positive serum calibrators are available from the Antiphospholipid Standardization Laboratory in Atlanta, Georgia, and should be used in each assay. Results are measured as GPL (IgG aCL), MPL (IgM aCL), or APL (IgA aCL) units and reported in semiquantitative terms as *negative*, *low-positive*, *medium-positive*, or *high-positive* (12). Most patients with antiphospholipid syndrome have medium-to-high positive anticardiolipin antibodies of IgG isotype. Low-positive results and isolated IgM aCL results (ie, IgM positive, but lupus anticoagulant negative and IgG aCL negative) are of questionable clinical significance and should not be regarded as diagnostic of antiphospholipid syndrome (13). Isolated IgA aCL results also are of uncertain clinical significance and are not diagnostic of antiphospholipid syndrome. Antiphospholipid syndrome is diagnosed when the patient has lupus anticoagulant, IgG aCL in medium-to-high levels, or both, on two occasions at least several weeks apart (1, 3).

Other Phospholipid-Binding Antibodies

Several investigators have found that anticardiolipin antibodies actually bind to β_2-glycoprotein I or a complex formed by this glycoprotein and cardiolipin (14). At present, however, tests for antibodies to β_2-glycoprotein I are still in development and are not approved for clinical use. Other antiphospholipid antibodies that may be detected include antibodies binding to phospholipid antigens other than cardiolipin (phosphatidylserine, phosphatidylethanolamine, phosphatidylinositol, phosphatidylglycerol, phosphatidylcholine, and phosphatidic acid). Although tests for such antibodies may have merit in diagnosing antiphospholipid syndrome, their status is uncertain.

Clinical Features of Antiphospholipid Syndrome

Obstetric Features

The relationship between antiphospholipid syndrome and fetal loss has been reviewed recently (15). Several important points deserve emphasis. First, positive test results for IgG or IgM aCL antibodies may be found in up to 20% of women with recurrent pregnancy loss (16–23), but many positive results are low level or only IgM isotype and therefore are not diagnostic of antiphospholipid syndrome (13). Second, antiphospholipid syndrome may present with either recurrent embryonic pregnancy loss (24) or death of the fetus at or beyond 10 weeks of gestation (25). The latter presentation may be more specific for antiphospholipid syndrome. Third, studies of general unselected populations show that lupus anticoagulant and medium-to-high positive levels of anticardiolipin antibodies (IgG or IgM) may be found in 2–4% of otherwise normal individuals (26). However, only 0.2% of IgG results are in the medium- or high-positive range.

It also is clear that sporadic miscarriage or early fetal death infrequently is associated with antiphospholipid antibodies (27, 28), a finding that is not surprising because antiphospholipid syndrome is rare. However, antiphospholipid antibodies are found in 10–15% of women with fetal deaths at or beyond 20 weeks of gestation (29, 30). The importance of identifying antiphospholipid syndrome lies not in its prevalence, but in its implications for the individual patient and its status as a potentially treatable cause of pregnancy loss.

In addition to fetal loss, other obstetric complications in women with antiphospholipid syndrome include pregnancy-induced hypertension (PIH), uteroplacental insufficiency, and preterm birth. The reported rates of these conditions vary considerably between studies, probably as a result of the differences in clinical and laboratory criteria used in patient selection (31). An unusually high rate of PIH has been noted in patients with well-characterized antiphospholipid syndrome (31–35), and PIH is a major contributor to the high rate of preterm delivery in this condition. The rate of PIH is not markedly diminished by treatment with low-dose aspirin, glucocorticoids, or heparin. In the two largest series of pregnant women with well-characterized antiphospholipid syndrome, 48% and 18%, respectively, developed PIH (31, 34).

Several studies with conflicting results have attempted to determine the rate of antiphospholipid antibodies among patients with PIH. In two studies of patients with PIH, including those with mild PIH and PIH near term, investigators did not find a relationship between antiphospholipid antibodies and PIH (1, 36). However, in four other studies, 11.7–17% of women with PIH had significant levels of antiphospholipid antibodies (37–40). In two of these studies, only patients with early-onset, severe PIH were studied (37, 39). A relationship between antiphospholipid antibodies and PIH has been confirmed by two prospective studies of unselected obstetric patients (41, 42), but not by another (43). The weight of evidence supports testing women with early-onset (<34 weeks of gestation), severe PIH for antiphospholipid antibodies. Routinely testing for antiphospholipid antibodies in women with mild or near-term PIH is not justified.

Women with antiphospholipid syndrome are at a substantial risk for placental insufficiency, which is manifested by fetal growth restriction and fetal compromise (31–34). The rate of fetal growth restriction is approximately 30% among pregnant women with well characterized antiphospholipid syndrome (31, 34). Even in women with IgG or IgM aCL antibodies, but no lupus anticoagulant, the rate of fetal growth restriction among live-born infants approaches 15% (44).

Antiphospholipid antibodies also may contribute to the overall rate of fetal growth restriction. One group of investigators found that 24% of mothers delivered of growth-restricted infants had medium- or high-positive tests for anticardiolipin antibodies, which was significantly more than controls (45). In a prospective study, 12% of women testing positive for IgG aCL antibodies had small-for-gestational age infants compared with 2% of women testing negative (42). However, in two other prospective studies, investigators did not find a relationship between antiphospholipid antibodies and fetal growth restriction (41, 43). Based on this controversy, routine testing of women with fetal growth restriction for antiphospholipid syndrome is not warranted. Instead, only those women who have severe fetal growth restriction or other evidence of uteroplacental insufficiency in the second or early third trimester should be tested for antiphospholipid antibodies.

Nonreassuring fetal heart rate patterns are relatively common in pregnant women with antiphospholipid syndrome (31–35). In the two largest studies of women treated for antiphospholipid syndrome, half of all pregnancies with successful outcomes were complicated by abnormal fetal heart rate tracings resulting in delivery (31, 34). However, as with fetal growth restriction, prospective studies do not confirm a significant relationship between nonreassuring fetal heart rate patterns and antiphospholipid antibodies in unselected patients. Thus, a nonreassuring fetal heart rate pattern is not an indication for antiphospholipid testing unless other clinical features suggest antiphospholipid syndrome.

Preterm deliveries, usually secondary to PIH and placental insufficiency (31–35), occur in approximately one third of pregnant women with antiphospholipid syndrome (31, 34). One investigator found preterm birth in 13% of 31 women with either IgG or IgM aCL antibodies, but not with lupus anticoagulant (44). In another study, 12% of 60 women testing positive for IgG aCL antibodies alone were delivered preterm as compared with 4% of those testing negative (42).

Nonobstetric Medical Problems

Thrombosis

Numerous studies confirm a link between antiphospholipid antibodies and thrombosis (5, 46, 47). Venous thrombosis accounts for about 65–70% of such episodes. The lower extremities are the most common site of involvement, but thrombosis can occur in any part of the vascular system. In particular, the diagnosis of antiphospholipid syndrome should be considered in women with venous thrombosis in unusual sites, such as the portal, mesenteric, splenic, subclavian, and cerebral veins. Antiphospholipid antibodies are detected in approximately 2% of patients with non-traumatic venous thrombosis (48), a rate similar to that of several inherited conditions of hypercoagulability such as antithrombin III deficiency and protein C deficiency. Women with nontraumatic thrombosis should be tested for antiphospholipid antibodies, as well as inherited predispositions such as activated protein C resistance, antithrombin III deficiency, and deficiencies of protein C and protein S.

Antiphospholipid antibodies also are associated with arterial thrombosis and appear to be a predisposing factor in 4–6% of cases of stroke in otherwise healthy patients under age 50 (49–51). The region of the middle cerebral artery is most commonly involved. Some events are due to thromboembolism as opposed to in situ central nervous system arterial thrombosis. As with venous thrombosis, arterial thrombosis in individuals with antiphospholipid syndrome may occur in relatively unusual locations, such as the retinal artery, subclavian or brachial artery, and digital arteries. Antiphospholipid antibodies also are associated with transient ischemic attacks and amaurosis fugax (13, 52).

Women with antiphospholipid syndrome, even those without a prior thrombotic event, are at risk for thrombosis. In a historic cohort study, investigators found that 22% of women with antiphospholipid syndrome had venous thrombosis, and 6.9% had a cerebrovascular incident over a median follow-up period of 60 months (13). Retrospective analyses of women with antiphospholipid syndrome and a history of thrombosis indicate that a very high proportion of initial thrombotic episodes occur in relationship to pregnancy or the use of combination oral contraceptives (31, 53). This observation was confirmed in the historic cohort study; in the follow-up period, 24% of thrombotic events occurred during pregnancy or the postpartum period (52). In two prospective studies of pregnancies in women with well-characterized antiphospholipid syndrome, the rates of thrombosis or stroke were 5% (31) and 12% (34). These observations suggest that women with documented antiphospholipid syndrome should not take estrogen–progestin combination oral contraceptives. Also, the risk of pregnancy-associated thrombosis in women with well-characterized antiphospholipid syndrome is substantial enough to warrant consideration of anticoagulant prophylaxis during pregnancy and the postpartum period, depending on individual circumstances.

Patients with antiphospholipid syndrome and prior thrombotic events are at very high risk for recurrent thromboses (54–57). In one study, 69% of patients with antiphospholipid syndrome and prior thrombosis had one or more recurrent thrombotic episodes; the median interval to recurrent thrombosis was only 12 months (55). Treatment with high-intensity warfarin was more effective than other therapies or no therapy in preventing recurrent thrombosis.

Thrombocytopenia

Thrombocytopenia also has been strongly associated with antiphospholipid antibodies (1, 2, 58). Anticardiolipin antibodies have been shown to correlate independently with the development of thrombocytopenia in patients with underlying connective tissue disease (1, 58). Thrombocytopenia occurs in up to 40% of individuals with primary antiphospholipid syndrome (2). The risk of thrombocytopenia is similar for patients with primary and secondary antiphospholipid syndrome (52, 59).

Thrombocytopenia associated with antiphospholipid syndrome can be difficult to distinguish from that due to other causes, and the distinction between this disorder and immune thrombocytopenic purpura (ITP [formerly known as idiopathic thrombocytopenia purpura]) is blurred. In fact, anticardiolipin antibodies have been detected in the sera of patients with ITP (60). Laboratory evidence suggests that platelet antigens associated with thrombocytopenia and antiphospholipid syndrome are different from those found in ITP (61). Unfortunately, there are no tests available to distinguish between these disorders, and antiplatelet antibodies detected in ITP also are present in some patients with antiphospholipid syndrome (61). Other causes of thrombocytopenia such as disseminated intravascular coagulation, human immunodeficiency virus (HIV) infection, drug-induced thrombocytopenia, thrombotic thrombocytopenia, gestational thrombocytopenia, PIH, and laboratory error also must be considered.

Other Associations

Because the reagents used in the Venereal Disease Research Laboratory and rapid plasma reagin tests contain cardiolipin, some patients with lupus anticoagulant or anticardiolipin antibodies also will have biologic false-positive serologic test results for syphilis (31). Also, individuals with positive serologic test results for syphilis (true-positive or false-positive) may have anticardiolipin (62). Syphilis must be excluded using appropriate methods. Women with biologic false-positive serologic test results for syphilis should be evaluated for lupus anticoagulant and anticardiolipin antibodies.

Livedo reticularis is the most widely recognized cutaneous condition linked to antiphospholipid syndrome (1, 2, 63, 64). It appears as a reticulated network of reddish blue discoloration especially evident on the extremities and intensified by exposure to cold. It is caused by dilation of the blood vessels and stagnation of blood in the capillaries or larger arterioles resulting from intravascular obstruction to flow. Other cutaneous manifestations associated with antiphospholipid syndrome include digital cyanosis, digital gangrene, and leg ulcers like those resulting from pyoderma. Antiphospholipid antibodies have been associated with a positive Coombs test and autoimmune hemolytic anemia (65, 66).

There are a number of neurologic manifestations associated with antiphospholipid syndrome. The most widely recognized is cerebrovascular stroke. Others include transient ischemic attacks, amaurosis fugax, chorea and chorea gravidarum, migraine headaches, multiinfarct dementia, and transverse myelitis. Amaurosis fugax, a condition characterized by transient, monocular visual field deficits usually lasting from a few seconds to a few minutes, is probably due to small-vessel thrombosis, thromboembolism, or spasm.

Management

Management of antiphospholipid syndrome in women should include both obstetric care and medical care. Recommended management regimens are shown in Table 2.

Obstetric Care

Patients with antiphospholipid syndrome should undergo preconceptional assessment and counseling. A detailed medical and obstetric history should be obtained, and the presence of relevant levels of antiphospholipid antibodies (ie, lupus anticoagulant, medium-to-high levels of anticardiolipin antibodies, or both) should be confirmed. The patient should be informed of potential maternal and obstetric problems, including fetal loss, thrombosis or stroke, PIH, fetal growth restriction, and preterm delivery. In those women who also have SLE, issues related to exacerbation of SLE also should be discussed. All patients with antiphospholipid syndrome should be assessed for evidence of anemia and thrombocytopenia, because both may occur in association with this syn-

Table 2. Proposed Managements for Women with Antiphospholipid Antibodies

	Management*	
Feature	Pregnant[†]	Nonpregnant[‡]
Antiphospholipid Syndrome (APS)		
APS with prior fetal death or recurrent pregnancy loss	Heparin in prophylactic doses (15,000–20,000 U of unfractionated heparin or equivalent per day) administered subcutaneously in divided doses and low-dose aspirin daily Calcium and vitamin D supplementation	Optimal management uncertain; options include no treatment or daily treatment with low-dose aspirin
APS with prior thrombosis or stroke	Heparin to achieve full anticoagulation *or* Heparin in prophylactic doses (15,000–20,000 U of unfractionated heparin or equivalent per day) administered subcutaneously in divided doses *plus* Low-dose aspirin daily Calcium and vitamin D supplementation	Warfarin administered daily in doses to maintain international normalized ratio ≥3:0
APS without prior pregnancy loss or thrombosis	Optimal management uncertain; options include no treatment, daily treatment with low-dose aspirin, daily treatment with prophylactic doses of heparin and low-dose aspirin	Optimal management uncertain. Options include no treatment or daily treatment with low-dose aspirin
Antiphospholipid Antibodies Without APS		
Lupus anticoagulant (LA) or medium-to-high-positive IgG aCL	Optimal management uncertain; options include no treatment, daily treatment with low-dose aspirin, daily treatment with prophylactic doses of heparin and low-dose aspirin	Optimal management uncertain. Options include no treatment or daily treatment with low-dose aspirin
Low levels of IgG aCL, only IgM aCL, only IgA aCL without LA, antiphospholipid antibodies other than LA, or aCL	Optimal management uncertain; options include no treatment or daily treatment with low-dose aspirin	Optimal management uncertain. Options include no treatment or daily treatment with low-dose aspirin

*The medications shown should not be used in the presence of contraindications.
[†]Close obstetric monitoring of mother and fetus is necessary in all cases.
[‡]The patient should be counseled in all cases regarding symptoms of thrombosis and thromboembolism.

drome. Evaluation for underlying renal disease may be useful.

A pregnant woman with antiphospholipid syndrome should be examined frequently and educated about the signs or symptoms of thrombosis or thromboembolism, severe PIH, or decreased fetal movement. Once the diagnosis of antiphospholipid syndrome is confirmed, serial antiphospholipid antibody determinations are not useful.

A primary goal of the antenatal visits after 20 weeks of gestation for patients with antiphospholipid syndrome is the detection of hypertension or proteinuria or both. Because of the risk of uteroplacental insufficiency, fetal ultrasonography should be performed every 4–6 weeks starting at 18–20 weeks of gestation. In patients with otherwise uncomplicated antiphospholipid syndrome, fetal surveillance should be started at 30–32 weeks of gestation. Earlier and more frequent ultrasonography and fetal

testing is indicated in patients with poor obstetric histories, evidence of PIH, or evidence of fetal growth restriction. In selected cases, fetal surveillance as early as 24–25 weeks may be justified (67).

In an attempt to improve pregnancy outcome, a number of medications and regimens have been used to treat pregnant women with antiphospholipid syndrome who have experienced pregnancy loss (Table 2). In a randomized trial, prednisone and heparin were found to be of similar efficacy for achieving successful fetal outcome (68). However, because heparin-treated patients had fewer serious side effects and obstetric complications, heparin is the preferred treatment. Most physicians prefer a thromboprophylactic dose of 15,000–20,000 U of unfractionated sodium heparin per day administered subcutaneously in two or three divided doses in women with antiphospholipid syndrome (31, 68, 69). In otherwise normal women with recurrent embryonic loss, but not thrombosis, as little as 10,000–15,000 U of heparin per day during pregnancy improves fetal outcome (44, 70). Low-molecular-weight heparin may be used in pregnancy, and it will likely replace unfractionated sodium heparin in the treatment of antiphospholipid syndrome.

It is important to counsel the patient regarding potential adverse effects of heparin. Heparin-induced osteoporosis with fracture occurs in 1–2% of women in whom full anticoagulation has been achieved during pregnancy (71). In an attempt to avoid severe osteoporosis, women treated with heparin should be encouraged to take supplemental calcium (1,500 mg calcium carbonate) and vitamin D daily. It is prudent to encourage axial skeleton weight-bearing exercise such as walking. Warfarin may be substituted for heparin during the postpartum period to limit further risk of heparin-induced osteoporosis and fracture.

Heparin also is associated with an uncommon idiosyncratic thrombocytopenia known as heparin-induced thrombocytopenia. This complication is immune mediated and usually has its onset 3–15 days after initiation of therapy. The frequency is difficult to determine, but it probably occurs in less than 5% of patients treated with heparin, with most cases being relatively mild. A more severe form of heparin-induced thrombocytopenia, paradoxically involving venous and arterial thromboses, may occur in up to 0.5% of patients treated with unfractionated sodium heparin. It has recently been shown that low-molecular-weight heparin is much less likely to be associated with heparin-induced thrombocytopenia (72), a major safety advantage over unfractionated sodium heparin.

The use of high-dose intravenous immune globulin has generated interest because of anecdotal reports of successful pregnancy outcomes (73–77). However, all but one also were treated with prednisone, heparin, or low-dose aspirin. The reported cases appear to involve more severe cases of antiphospholipid-related pregnancy loss in which other therapies had failed. Definitive evidence of the efficacy of high-dose immune globulin will be necessary before this treatment can be recommended. A prospective, randomized trial is currently being conducted.

Patients with antiphospholipid syndrome who do not have a history of thrombosis appear to have a risk of developing thrombosis during pregnancy (31, 34), and prophylaxis should be considered (16). If used, prophylaxis should be continued for about 6–8 weeks postpartum. Warfarin may be substituted for heparin during the postpartum period to limit further risk of heparin-induced osteoporosis and fracture.

Nonobstetric Care

Women with antiphospholipid syndrome are at substantial risk of developing other medical problems related to the disease. Nearly one half of women with antiphospholipid syndrome develop thrombosis, stroke, transient ischemic attacks, amaurosis fugax, new-onset SLE, or new-onset autoimmune thrombocytopenia over a median follow-up interval of 5 years (13). Thus, women with antiphospholipid syndrome require careful and close medical follow-up with a team of specialists with expertise in the management of antiphospholipid syndrome. Given the maternal and fetal risks associated with pregnancy, women with antiphospholipid syndrome should avoid unintended pregnancy.

Patients who have had prior thrombotic events are particularly prone to have recurrent thromboses. The annual risk of new thrombosis is approximately 33% for untreated patients and 20% for patients treated with low-dose aspirin alone (78). Long-term anticoagulation with warfarin to maintain the international normalized ratio of at least 3:0 is advisable for patients with antiphospholipid syndrome who have had a prior thrombotic event. In patients treated with warfarin, the risk of hemorrhage is 2–5% per year. In women taking warfarin, dysfunctional uterine bleeding and ovarian hemorrhage associated with ovulation pose unique and difficult problems. Suppression of ovulation may be beneficial, but hormonal formulations containing estrogen, including estrogen–progestin combination oral contraceptives, are contraindicated. Immunosuppressive agents should be reserved for the treatment of symptoms of SLE in patients with secondary antiphospholipid syndrome. Pending the results of further studies, women with antiphospholipid syndrome who have not had a prior thrombotic event should receive either no treatment or daily low-dose aspirin. However, such patients should receive thromboprophylaxis for thrombogenic circumstances such as abdominal or orthopedic surgery.

Summary

Antiphospholipid syndrome is a recently recognized autoimmune condition that may present with fetal loss, thrombosis, or autoimmune thrombocytopenia. Women with these clinical features should be tested for lupus anticoagulant and anticardiolipin antibodies; most patients with antiphospholipid syndrome will be found to have both lupus anticoagulant and IgG aCL antibodies. Tests for other antiphospholipid antibodies are not yet standardized, leaving the interpretation of results open to question.

Women with antiphospholipid syndrome should be treated during pregnancy with thromboprophylactic doses of heparin and low-dose aspirin. It is incumbent upon the obstetrician to be aware of the adverse effects of heparin. Close obstetric care is indicated in all cases because of an increased risk of PIH, fetal growth restriction, and a non-reassuring fetal heart rate pattern. Nonpregnant women with antiphospholipid syndrome are at increased risk for developing thrombosis, transient ischemic attacks, new-onset SLE, or new-onset autoimmune thrombocytopenia; thus, close medical follow-up is indicated. In women with antiphospholipid syndrome and one or more prior thrombotic events, lifelong anticoagulation with warfarin is advisable to avoid recurrent thrombosis.

References

1. Alarcon-Segovia D, Deleze M, Oria CV, Sanchez-Guerrero J, Gomez-Pacheco L, Cabiedes J, et al. Antiphospholipid antibodies and the antiphospholipid syndrome in systemic lupus erythematosus:a prospective analysis of 500 consecutive patients. Medicine 1989;68:353–365

2. Asherson RA, Khamashta MA, Ordi-Ros J, Derksen RHWM, Machin SJ, Barquinero J, et al. The "primary" anti-phospholipid syndrome: major clinical and serological features. Medicine 1989;68:366–374

3. Harris EN. Syndrome of the black swan. Br J Rheumatol 1987;26:324–326

4. Conley CL, Hartman RC. A hemorrhagic disorder caused by circulating anticoagulant in patients with disseminated lupus erythematosus. J Clin Invest 1952;31:621–622

5. Harris EN, Gharavi AE, Boey ML, Patel BM, Mackworth-Young CG, Loizou S, et al. Anti-cardiolipin antibodies: detection by radioimmunoassay and association with thrombosis in systemic lupus erythematosus. Lancet 1983;2: 1211–1214

6. Chamley LW, Pattison NS, McKay EJ. Separation of lupus anticoagulant from anticardiolipin antibodies by ion-exchange and gel filtration chromatography. Haemostasis 1991;21:25–29

7. Exner T, Sahman N, Trudinger B. Separation of anticardiolipin antibodies from lupus anticoagulant on a phospholipid-coated polystyrene column. Biochem Biophys Res Commun 1988;155:1001–1007

8. McNeil HP, Chesterman CN, Krillis SA. Binding specificity of lupus anticoagulants and anticardiolipin antibodies. Thromb Res 1988;52:609–619

9. Pierangeli SS, Harris EN, Gharavi AE, Goldsmith G, Branch DW, Dean WL. Are immunoglobulins with lupus anticoagulant activity specific for phospholipids? Br J Haematol 1993;85:124–132

10. Coulam CB, McIntyre JA, Wagenknecht D, Rote N. Interlaboratory inconsistencies in detection of anticardiolipin antibodies. Lancet 1990;335:865

11. Peaceman AM, Silver RK, MacGregor SN, Socol ML. Interlaboratory variation in antiphospholipid antibody testing. Am J Obstet Gynecol 1992;166:1780–1787

12. Harris EN. The second international anti-cardiolipin standardization workshop/The Kingston antiphospholipid antibody study (KAPS) group. Am J Clin Pathol 1990;94: 476–484

13. Silver RM, Porter TF, van Leeuween I, Jeng G, Scott JR, Branch DW. Anticardiolipin antibodies: clinical consequences of "low titers." Obstet Gynecol 1996;87:494–500

14. Krilis SA, Sheng YH, Kandiah DA. The role of β_2-glycoprotein I in the antiphospholid syndrome. Lupus 1996;5:150–152

15. American College of Obstetricians and Gynecologists. Early pregnancy loss. ACOG Technical Bulletin 212. Washington, DC: ACOG, 1995

16. Branch DW, Silver RM, Pierangeli S, van Leeuwen I, Harris EN. Antiphospholipid antibodies other than lupus anticoagulant and anticardiolipin antibodies in women with recurrent pregnancy loss, fertile controls, and antiphospholipid syndrome. Obstet Gynecol 1997;89:549–555

17. MacLean MA, Cumming GP, McCall F, Walker ID, Walker JJ. The prevalence of lupus anticoagulant and anticardiolipin antibodies in women with a history of first trimester miscarriages. Br J Obstet Gynaecol 1994;101:103–110

18. Out HJ, Bruinse HW, Christiaens GCML, van Vliet M, Meilof JF, de Groot PG, et al. Prevalence of antiphospholipid antibodies in patients with fetal loss. Ann Rheum Dis 1991;50:553–557

19. Parazzini F, Acaia B, Faden D, Lovotti M, Marelli G. Cortelazzo S. Antiphospholipid antibodies and recurrent abortion. Obstet Gynecol 1991;77:854–858

20. Parke AL, Wilson D, Maier D. The prevalence of anti-phospholipid antibodies in women with recurrent spontaneous abortion, women with successful pregnancies, and women who have never been pregnant. Arthritis Rheum 1991;34:1231–1235

21. Petri M, Golbus M, Anderson R, Whiting-O'Keefe Q, Corash L, Hellmann D. Antinuclear antibody, lupus anticoagulant, and anticardiolipin antibody in women with idiopathic habitual abortion. A controlled prospective study of forty-four women. Arthritis Rheum 1987;30:601–606

22. Plouffe L Jr, White EW, Tho SP, Sweet CS, Layman LC, Whitman GF, et al. Etiologic factors of recurrent abortion and subsequent reproductive performance of couples: have we made any progress in 10 years? Am J Obstet Gynecol 1992;167:313–321

23. Yetman DL, Kutteh WH. Antiphospholipid antibody panels and recurrent pregnancy loss: prevalence of anticardiolipin antibodies compared with other antiphospholipid antibodies. Fertil Steril 1996;66:540–546

24. Rai RS, Clifford K, Cohen H, Regan L. High prospective fetal loss rate in untreated pregnancies of women with recurrent miscarriage and antiphospholipid antibodies. Hum Reprod 1995;10:3301–3304

25. Oshiro BT, Silver RM, Scott JR, Yu H, Branch DW. Antiphospholipid antibodies and fetal death. Obstet Gynecol 1996;87:489–493

26. Harris EN, Spinnato JA. Should anticardiolipin tests be performed in otherwise healthy pregnant women? Am J Obstet Gynecol 1991;165:1272–1277

27. Haddow JE, Rote NS, Dostal-Johnson D, Palomaki GE, Pulkkinen AJ, Knight GJ. Lack of an association between late fetal death and antiphospholipid antibody measurements in the second trimester. Am J Obstet Gynecol 1991; 165:1308–1312

28. Infante-Rivard C, David M, Gauthier R, Rivard G-E. Lupus anticoagulants, anticardiolipin antibodies, and fetal loss. A case control study. N Engl J Med 1991;325:1063– 1066

29. Ahlenius I, Floberg J, Thomassen P. Sixty-six cases of intrauterine fetal death: a prospective study with an extensive test protocol. Acta Obstet Gynecol Scand 1995;74: 109–117

30. Bocciolone L, Meroni P, Parazzini F, Tincani A, Radici E, Tarantini M, et al. Antiphospholipid antibodies and risk of intrauterine late fetal death. Acta Obstet Gynecol Scand 1994;73:389–392

31. Branch DW, Silver RM, Blackwell JL, Reading JC, Scott JR. Outcome of treated pregnancies in women with antiphospholipid syndrome: an update of the Utah experience. Obstet Gynecol 1992;80:614–620

32. Branch DW, Scott JR, Kochenour NK, Hershgold E. Obstetric complications associated with lupus anticoagulant. N Engl J Med 1985;313:1322–1326

33. Caruso A, De Carolis S, Ferrazzani S, Valesini G, Caforio L, Manusco S. Pregnancy outcome in relation to uterine artery flow velocity waveforms and clinical characteristics in women with antiphospholipid syndrome. Obstet Gynecol 1993;82:970–976

34. Lima F, Khamashta MA, Buchanan NMM, Kerslake S, Hunt BJ, Hughes GRV. A study of sixty pregnancies in patients with the antiphospholipid syndrome. Clin Exp Rheumatol 1996;14:131–136

35. Lockshin MD, Druzin ML, Goei S, Qamar T, Magid MS, Jovanovic L, Ferenc M. Antibody to cardiolipin as a predictor of fetal distress or death in pregnant patients with systemic lupus erythematosus. N Engl J Med 1985;313: 152–156

36. Scott RAH. Anti-cardiolipin antibodies and pre-eclampsia. Br J Obstet Gynaecol 1987;94:604–605

37. Branch DW, Andres R, Digre KB, Rote NS, Scott JR. The association of antiphospholipid antibodies with severe pre-eclampsia. Obstet Gynecol 1989;73:541–545

38. Milliez J, Lelong F, Bayani N, Jannet D, El Medjadi M, Latrous H, et al. The prevalence of autoantibodies during third-trimester pregnancy complicated by hypertension or idiopathic fetal growth retardation. Am J Obstet Gynecol 1991;165:51–56

39. Moodley J, Bhoola V, Duursma J, Pudfin D, Byrne S, Kenoyer DG. The association of antiphospholipid antibodies with severe early-onset pre-eclampsia. S Afr Med J 1995;85:105–107

40. Sletnes KE, Wislof F, Moe N, Dale PO. Antiphospholipid antibodies in pre-eclamptic women: relation to growth retardation and neonatal outcome. Acta Obstet Gynecol Scand 1992;71:112–117

41. Pattison NS, Chamley LW, McKay EJ, Liggins GC, Butler WS. Antiphospholipid antibodies in pregnancy: prevalence and clinical associations. Br J Obstet Gynaecol 1993; 100: 909–913

42. Yasuda M, Takakuwa K, Tokunaga A, Tanaka K. Prospective studies of the association between anticardiolipin antibody and outcome of pregnancy. Obstet Gynecol 1995; 86:555–559

43. Lynch A, Marlar R, Murphy J, Davila G, Santos M, Rutledge J, et al. Antiphospholipid antibodies in predicting adverse pregnancy outcome. A prospective study. Ann Intern Med 1994;120:470–475

44. Kutteh WH. Antiphospholipid antibody-associated recurrent pregnancy loss: treatment with heparin and low-dose aspirin is superior to low-dose aspirin alone. Am J Obstet Gynecol 1996;174:1584–1589

45. Polzin WJ, Kopelman JN, Robinson RD, Read JA, Brady K. The association of antiphospholipid antibodies with pregnancy complicated by fetal growth restriction. Obstet Gynecol 1991;78:1108–1111

46. Bowie EJW, Thompson JH Jr, Pascuzzi CA, Owen CA Jr. Thrombosis in systemic lupus erythematosus despite circulating anticoagulants. J Lab Clin Med 1963;62:416–431

47. Lechner K, Pabinger-Fasching I. Lupus anticoagulants and thrombosis. A study of 25 cases and review of the literature. Haemostas 1985;15:254–262

48. Malm J, Laurell M, Nilsson IM, Dahlback B. Thromboembolic disease—critical evaluation of laboratory investigation. Thromb Haemost 1992;68:7–13

49. Brey RL, Hart RG, Sherman DG, Tegeler CH. Antiphospholipid antibodies and cerebral ischemia in young people. Neurology 1990;40:1190–1196

50. Ferro D, Quintarelli C, Rasura M, Antionini G, Violi F. Lupus anticoagulant and the fibrinolytic system in young patients with stroke. Stroke 1993;24:368–370

51. Hart RG, Miller VT, Coull BM, Bril V. Cerebral infarction associated with lupus anticoagulants—preliminary report. Stroke 1984;15:114–118

52. Silver RM, Draper ML, Scott JR, Lyon JL, Reading J, Branch DW. Clinical consequences of antiphospholipid antibodies: an historic cohort study. Obstet Gynecol 1994; 83:372–377

53. Branch DW, Scott JR. Clinical implication of anti-phospholipid antibodies: the Utah experience. In Harris EN, Exner T, Hughes GRV, Asherson RA, eds. Phospholipid-binding antibodies. Boca Raton, Florida: CRC Press, 1990:335–346

54. Derksen RHWM, de Groot PG, Kater L, Nieuwenhuis HK. Patients with antiphospholipid antibodies and venous thrombosis should receive a long term anticoagulant treatment. Ann Rheum Dis 1993;52:689–692

55. Khamashta MA, Cuadrado MJ, Mujic F, Taub NA, Hunt BJ, Hughes GRV. The management of thrombosis in the antiphospholipid-antibody syndrome. N Engl J Med 1995; 332:993–997

56. Levine SR, Brey RL, Joseph CLM, Havstad S. Risk of recurrent thromboembolic events in patients with focal cerebral ischemia and antiphospholipid antibodies. Stroke 1992;23 (suppl I):I-29–I-32

57. Rosove MH, Brewer PMC. Antiphospholipid thrombosis: clinical course after the first thrombotic event in 70 patients. Ann Intern Med 1992;117:303–308

58. Harris EN, Asherson RA, Gharavi AE, Morgan SH, Derue G, Hughes GRV. Thrombocytopenia in SLE and related autoimmune disorders: association with anticardiolipin antibody. Br J Haematol 1985;59:227–230

59. Italian Registry of Antiphospholipid Antibodies. Thrombosis and thrombocytopenia in antiphospholipid syndrome (idiopathic and secondary to SLE): first report from the Italian registry. Haematologica 1993;78:313–318

60. Harris EN, Gharavi AE, Hedge U, Derue G, Morgan SH, Englert H, et al. Anticardiolipin antibodies in autoimmune thrombocytopenia purpura. Br J Haematol 1985;59:231–234

61. Fabris F, Steffan A, Cordiano I, Borzini P, Luzzatto G, Randi ML, et al. Specific antiplatelet autoantibodies in patients with antiphospholipid antibodies and thrombocytopenia. Eur J Haematol 1994;53:232–236

62. Harris EN, Gharavi AE, Wasley GD, Hughes GRV. Use of an enzyme-linked immunosorbent assay and of inhibition studies to distinguish between antibodies to cardiolipin from patients with syphilis or autoimmune disorders. J Infect Dis 1988;157:23–31

63. Asherson RA, Mayou SC, Merry P, Black MM, Hughes GRV. The spectrum of livedo reticularis and anticardiolipin antibodies. Br J Dermatol 1989;120:215–221

64. Grob JJ, Bonerandi JJ. Thrombotic skin disease as a marker of the anticardiolipin syndrome: livedo vasculitis and distal gangrene associated with abnormal serum antiphospholipid activity. J Am Acad Dermatol 1989;20:1063–1069

65. Deleze M, Oria CV, Alarcon-Segovia D. Occurrence of both hemolytic anemia and thrombocytopenic purpura (Evan's syndrome) in systemic lupus erythematosus. Relationship to antiphospholipid antibodies. J Rheumatol 1988;15:611–615

66. Hazeltine M, Rauch J, Danoff D. Antiphospholipid antibodies in systemic lupus erythematosus: evidence of an association with positive Coombs' and hypocomplementemia. J Rheumatol 1988;15:80–86

67. Druzin ML, Lockshin M, Edersheim TG, Hutson JM, Krauss AL, Kogut E. Second trimester fetal monitoring and preterm delivery in pregnancies with systemic lupus erythematosus and/or circulating anticoagulant. Am J Obstet Gynecol 1987;157:1503–1510

68. Cowchock FS, Reece EA, Balaban D, Branch DW, Plouffe L. Repeated fetal losses associated with antiphospholipid antibodies: a collaborative randomized trial comparing prednisone to low-dose heparin treatment. Am J Obstet Gynecol 1992;166:1318–1323

69. Rosove MH, Tabsh K, Wasserstrum N, Howard P, Hahn BH, Kalunian KC. Heparin therapy for pregnant women with lupus anticoagulant or anticardiolipin antibodies. Obstet Gynecol 1990;75:630–634

70. Rai RS, Cohen H, Dave M, Regan L. Randomized controlled trial of aspirin and aspirin plus heparin in pregnant women with recurrent miscarriage associated with phospholipid antibodies (or antiphospholipid antibodies). BMJ 1997;314:253–257

71. Dahlman TC. Osteoporotic fractures and the recurrence of thromboembolism during pregnancy and the puerperium in 184 women undergoing thromboprophylaxis with heparin. Am J Obstet Gynecol 1993;168:1265–1270

72. Warkentin TE, Levine MN, Hirsh J, Horsewood P, Roberts RS, Gent M, et al. Heparin-induced thrombocytopia in patients treated with low-molecular-weight heparin or unfractionated heparin. N Engl J Med 1995;332:1330–1335

73. Kaaja R, Julkunen H, Ammala P, Palosuo T, Kurki P. Intravenous immunoglobulin treatment of pregnant patients with recurrent pregnancy losses associated with antiphospholipid antibodies. Acta Obstet Gynecol Scand 1993;72:63–66

74. Katz VL, Thorp JM Jr, Watson WJ, Fowler L, Heine RP. Human immunoglobulin therapy for preeclampsia associated with lupus anticoagulant and anticardiolipin antibody. Obstet Gynecol 1990;76:986–987

75. Scott JR, Branch DW, Kochenour NK, Ward K. Intravenous immunoglobulin treatment of pregnant patients with recurrent pregnancy loss caused by antiphospholipid antibodies and Rh immunization. Am J Obstet Gynecol 1988;159:1055–1056

76. Spinnato JA, Clark AL, Pierangeli SS, Harris EN. Intravenous immunoglobulin therapy for the antiphospholipid syndrome in pregnancy. Am J Obstet Gynecol 1995;172:690–694

77. Wapner RJ, Cowchock FS, Shapiro SS. Successful treatment in two women with antiphospholipid antibodies and refractory pregnancy losses with intravenous immunoglobulin infusions. Am J Obstet Gynecol 1989;161:1271–1272

78. Lockshin MD. Answers to the antiphospholipid-antibody syndrome? N Engl J Med 1995;332:1025–1027

ACOG EDUCATIONAL BULLETIN

Number 230, November 1996

Assessment of Fetal Lung Maturity

Approximately 300,000–500,000 of the deliveries in the United States each year are preterm. Preterm birth causes significant neonatal morbidity and mortality, which are often due to difficulty in providing oxygen transfer to an immature neonatal pulmonary system (1).

The pulmonary system is among the last of the fetal organ systems to become functionally mature. Thus, pulmonary maturity has been assumed to connote adequate maturation in other fetal systems. This assumption may not be true in fetuses relatively remote from term (2). Documentation of fetal pulmonary maturity should not be used as the sole indication for delivery of a preterm infant. Although preterm delivery may be indicated in many situations, delivery of fetuses with immature pulmonary systems should be avoided when possible.

Direct methods of assessing fetal pulmonary maturity have been available for more than 20 years, and a number of new tests have been introduced (3, 4). Proper use of these tests can aid the clinician in determining the optimal time for delivery.

Indications for Assessing Maturity

Fetal pulmonary maturity should be confirmed before elective delivery at less than 39 weeks of gestation unless fetal maturity can be inferred from any of the following criteria:

- Fetal heart tones have been documented for 20 weeks by nonelectronic fetoscope or for 30 weeks by Doppler.

- It has been 36 weeks since a serum or urine human chorionic gonadotropin pregnancy test was found to be positive by a reliable laboratory.

- Ultrasound measurement of the crown–rump length at 6–11 weeks of gestation supports a gestational age equal to or greater than 39 weeks.

- Ultrasound measurement at 12–20 weeks of gestation supports a clinically determined gestational age of 39 weeks or greater.

If any of the aforementioned criteria confirms a gestational age of 39 weeks or more in a patient with normal menstrual cycles (no oral contraceptive use immediately prior to conception), it is appropriate to schedule delivery at 39 weeks

This Educational Bulletin was developed under the direction of the Committee on Educational Bulletins of the American College of Obstetricians and Gynecologists as an aid to obstetricians and gynecologists. The College wishes to thank William N. P. Herbert, MD, for his assistance in the development of this bulletin. This document is not to be construed as establishing a standard of practice or dictating an exclusive course of treatment. Rather, it is intended as an educational tool that presents current information on obstetric–gynecologic issues.

of gestation or beyond in accordance with menstrual dates. Ultrasonography may be considered confirmatory of menstrual dates if there is a gestational age agreement within 1 week by crown–rump measurements obtained at 6–11 weeks of gestation or within 10 days by an average of multiple measurements obtained between 12–20 weeks of gestation. Unless circumstances preclude continued expectant management, awaiting the onset of spontaneous labor is another option for some patients (5).

Amniocentesis for fetal pulmonary assessment is rarely warranted before 33 weeks of gestation because test results confirming lung maturity are unlikely. Confirmation of a mature fetal pulmonary system does not preclude consideration of the fetal risk of intraventricular hemorrhage and necrotizing enterocolitis.

Physiology and Pathophysiology

Fetal Lung Development

Knowledge of the development of the fetal pulmonary system and the evolution of surfactant production is helpful in understanding the tests performed for fetal lung maturity. The development of the fetal pulmonary system begins about 3 weeks after conception and continues for about 8 years after birth. The pulmonary tree development begins in the glandular period, which ends at about 16 weeks of gestation. During the canalicular period (16–24 weeks of gestation), early bronchioles develop and the epithelium vascularizes and differentiates. The alveolar (or terminal sac) period is the last stage of pulmonary development, which extends from about 24 weeks of gestation well into childhood. Bronchiolar division during this period leads to the development of thin spherical saccules, known as alveoli, that are lined by type II pneumocytes. The concomitant proliferation of capillaries around these alveoli makes effective gas exchange possible after delivery.

The type II pneumocytes produce intracellular stores, or "packages," of phospholipids called lamellar bodies, which can be released into the alveolar spaces. Surfactant is the name given to this group of "surface-active" phospholipid compounds that can reduce the surface tension within the alveolar spaces following delivery. Low surface tension within the alveoli allows these sacs to remain expanded during respiratory activity permitting continuous and maximally effective gas exchange. As a result of in utero "respiratory" activity, these substances enter the amniotic fluid cavity, where they can be measured.

The most prominent of these surfactant compounds is lecithin (phosphotidylcholine). The phospholipid compound phosphatidylglycerol (PG) appears later, and documentation of its presence is the basis of several of the commonly used tests for fetal lung maturity. Other phospholipids (phosphatidylinositol, phosphatidylethanola-

mine), a variety of proteins, and cholesterol contribute to this group of surface-active substances within the lung as well.

Respiratory Distress Syndrome

A deficiency in the quantity of surfactant in premature infants leads to higher surface tension within the alveoli, which can cause alveolar collapse and make gas exchange more difficult. Impaired gas exchange can result in neonatal hypoxia, with further worsening of pulmonary status manifested by acidosis and increased shunting within the lungs. Signs of respiratory distress syndrome (RDS) include neonatal tachypnea, grunting, retractions, and cyanosis, often occuring within several hours of birth. Radiography of the infant's chest revealing atelectasis, air bronchograms, and a diffuse reticulogranular infiltrate is suggestive of RDS.

Other complications associated with RDS include necrotizing enterocolitis, patent ductus arteriosus, intraventricular hemorrhage, and infection, which can result in long-term disability or death. Some survivors of RDS will suffer long-term pulmonary sequelae in the form of bronchopulmonary dysplasia (6). The Centers for Disease Control and Prevention reports that 2,000 of the 20,000–30,000 infants who develop RDS each year will die (7). Despite the positive impact of antepartum corticosteroid therapy and neonatal administration of surfactant compounds, RDS continues to be a significant cause of neonatal morbidity and mortality.

Classification of Fetal Maturity Tests

Fetal pulmonary testing can be categorized as either indirect or direct measures of fetal lung maturation. Indirect tests do not measure pulmonary function per se but rather evaluate the age or size of the fetus. From these parameters, maturity can be inferred and neonatal respiratory function predicted. Such methods include obstetric estimation of gestational age (menstrual history, first appearance of fetal heart tones, and physical examination), ultrasound examination (identification or evaluation of gestational sac, crown–rump length, biparietal diameter, etc), and the rarely used amniotic fluid analysis for fetal fat cells or creatinine.

Direct tests of fetal maturity measure either the concentration of particular components of pulmonary surfactant (biochemical tests) or the surface-active effects of these phospholipids (biophysical tests). Biochemical tests include determining the lecithin–sphingomyelin ratio (L/S) and identifying PG. Biophysical tests include the foam stability index (FSI) and fluorescence polarization. Although these tests differ in their techniques, all predict pulmonary maturity (the absence of RDS) with much greater certainty than they predict pulmonary immaturity (the presence of RDS) (3) (Table 1).

Tests of Fetal Maturity

Lecithin–Sphingomyelin Ratio

The first widely accepted direct test for assessment of fetal pulmonary status was the L/S ratio (8). This test evaluates a change in the relative amounts of lecithin (phosphatidylcholine) and sphingomyelin (a sphingolipid of unknown origin) in amniotic fluid samples as gestational age increases. Until about 32–33 weeks of gestation, the concentrations of these two substances are quite similar; thereafter, the concentration of lecithin increases significantly compared with the relatively constant concentration of sphingomyelin. In the absence of complications, the densitometric ratio of these two components reaches 2.0 at about 35 weeks of gestation. Infants delivered after attaining an L/S ratio of 2.0 or higher rarely develop RDS. This value of 2.0 has become the commonly accepted standard value indicating maturity in the fetus of a nondiabetic woman. However, correlation with clinical outcome in individual centers should precede acceptance of this threshold for pulmonary maturity, as variations within and between laboratories can be considerable. The predictive value of a negative result (value less than 2.0) is quite low.

Determination of the L/S ratio involves thin-layer chromatography after organic solvent extraction. Commercial versions of this test are available. Identification of lecithin and sphingomyelin is accomplished by using any one of a number of different staining procedures, with planimetry or densitometry used to compare the relative amounts of lecithin and sphingomyelin. This methodology is quite cumbersome and labor intensive despite numerous modifications to the original technique.

As with many tests of fetal maturity, blood and meconium can interfere with test interpretation (4). Plasma is rich in lipids that can be difficult to distinguish from phospholipids in surfactant. A bloody amniotic fluid sample may be difficult to interpret. The L/S ratio in plasma is similar to the maturity threshold (2.0) found in amniotic fluid. Theoretically, L/S values significantly lower or higher than 2.0 should be reliable, but caution is advised in relying on results from bloody amniotic fluid samples. Likewise, the mucoid nature of meconium may obscure the thin-layer chromatography pattern and interfere with the accuracy of the L/S values. Moreover, with some L/S procedures, a heme derivative in meconium may resemble PG on the thin-layer chromatography plate.

Since amniotic fluid contains enzymes, improper storage conditions can affect the L/S ratio (9). An amniotic fluid sample should be centrifuged shortly after it is obtained. If the determination is not performed immediately or if the sample is transported to an outside laboratory, the specimen should be frozen, preferably at –20°C (9). The L/S ratio decreases if an uncentrifuged sample either remains at room temperature for at least 1 hour or is cooled but not frozen for more than 12 hours. Failure to properly handle the amniotic fluid specimen can result in invalid conclusions and difficulty in interpretation of the results.

Phosphatidylglycerol

Phosphatidylglycerol is a minor constituent of surfactant that generally appears in sufficient quantity to be measured several weeks after the increase in lecithin concentration (10). Because PG enhances the spread of phospholipids on the alveolar surface, its presence indicates a more advanced state of fetal pulmonary maturity.

Phosphatidylglycerol determination can be accomplished by thin-layer chromatography, either alone or as an extension of L/S ratio testing. In addition, a slide-agglutination test has been developed using antisera specific for PG.

An advantage of PG determination in assessing fetal maturity is the fact that it is not generally affected by blood, meconium, or other contaminants. This characteristic allows PG determination by using vaginal pool samples from patients who have experienced spontaneous rupture of membranes. A disadvantage of using PG for assessing fetal maturity is its relatively late appearance in pregnancy. Compared with results of other tests, an "immature" result (negative PG) is associated with a greater proportion of patients who will deliver infants who do not develop RDS (11).

"Shake" Test and Foam Stability Index

Prediction of pulmonary maturity based on the ability of pulmonary surfactant to generate and maintain a stable foam in the presence of ethanol was first reported in 1972 (12). In this biophysical test, the addition of ethanol to amniotic fluid eliminates foam formation caused by "nonsurfactant" substances in the amniotic fluid. The generation of a stable ring of foam by shaking amniotic fluid and ethanol in a test tube demonstrates the presence of surface-active material in the amniotic fluid. Serial dilutions with ethanol allow determination of the concentration of surfactant.

This procedure has been modified and named the FSI, which uses a series of test tubes containing successively greater amounts of 95% ethanol in an attempt to quantitate surface-active properties over a wider range of concentrations (13). In effect, a single cut-off point of 47 or 48 or greater is used to indicate fetal maturity. A commercial version of this test is available. Amniotic fluid should not be placed in a siliconized collection tube if the "shake" test or FSI is used, as stable foam will result from this contamination. The presence of blood or meconium in samples interferes with the results of these tests as well.

Table 1. Commonly Used Direct Tests of Fetal Maturity

Test*	Technique	Time/Ease of Testing†	Threshold	Typical Predictive Value (%)		Relative Cost	Notes
				Mature	Immature		
Lecithin/sphingomyelin ratio	Thin-layer chromatography	4+	2.0–3.5	95–100	33–50	High	Many variations in technique; laboratory variation significant
Phosphatidylglycerol	Thin-layer chromatography	4+	"Present" (usually means >3% of total phospholipid)	95–100	23–53	High	Not affected by blood, meconium; vaginal pool samples satisfactory
	Antisera	1+	0.5 = low positive 2.0 = high positive	95–100	23–53	Commercial version—moderate	Not affected by blood, meconium; vaginal pool samples satisfactory
Foam stability index	Ethanol added to amniotic fluid, solution shaken, presence of stable bubbles at meniscus noted	2+	≥47 or 48	95	51	Laboratory—low Commercial version—moderate	Affected by blood, meconium, vaginal pool debris, silicone-coated test tubes
Fluorescence polarization	Fluorescence polarization	1+	≥55 mg/g of albumin‡	96–100	47–61	Moderate	Minimal intraassay and interassay variability; simple testing procedure
Optical density (OD) at 650 nm	Spectrophotometric reading	1+	OD ≥0.15	98	13	Low	Simple technique
Lamellar body counts	Counts using commercial hematology counter	2+	30,000–40,000 (still investigational)	97–98	29–35	Low	Promising technique

*Commercial versions are available for all tests except optical density and lamellar body counts.

†Range in complexity: 1+ indicates procedure is simple, is available all the time, requires only short procedure time, and personnel effort is not intensive; 4+ indicates procedure is complex or difficult, time consuming, and therefore, frequently not available at all times.

‡The manufacturer has reformulated the product and revised the testing procedure. Currently, the threshold for maturity is 55; with the original assay it was 70.

Fluorescence Polarization

Fetal maturity testing using fluorescence polarization is based on competitive binding of a fluorescent probe to albumin and surfactant. When the probe is bound to albumin, net polarization values are high; when bound to surfactant, polarization values are low. In amniotic fluid samples, the fluorescence polarization measured by an automated analyzer reflects the ratio of surfactant to albumin, a value that correlates with lung maturity. Recent modifications of this concept provide a simple, automated, rapid test that is widely available and varies minimally between laboratories. In the recently modified commercial version of this assay, the ratio indicating maturity is at or above 55 mg of surfactant per gram of albumin in the nondiabetic patient. Preliminary use of this test in patients with diabetes is promising (14).

This assay compares favorably with other direct tests (15, 16), but blood and meconium contamination interfere with its interpretation. Sufficient testing on amniotic fluid samples obtained vaginally has not been done.

Optical Density at 650 nm

Measuring optical absorbance of amniotic fluid at a wavelength of 650 nm is a rapid indirect biophysical test for fetal maturity. It is based on the concept that the opalescence of mature amniotic fluid is due to an increasing number of lamellar bodies, which scatter light. After centrifugation, amniotic fluid samples are analyzed on a spectrophotometer, an instrument commonly available in hospital laboratories. An optical density reading of absorbancy of 0.15 or greater is used as the indicator of pulmonary maturity. It is a simple procedure that compares favorably with other methods of fetal maturity assessment (3, 17). The degree of centrifugation and presence of blood and meconium can alter the validity of this method.

Lamellar Body Counts

Lamellar bodies represent packages of surfactant that are extruded into the alveoli from within type II pneumocytes. The similarity of lamellar body size to platelet size permits the use of a standard hematologic counter to determine lamellar body concentrations. Values of approximately 30,000–50,000/μL appear to indicate pulmonary maturity; however, alterations in technique and determinations on different commercial hematology counters yield varying results for maturity assessment (3, 17, 18). Neither bilirubin nor meconium interferes with this test, but erythrocytes lower the lamellar body number density.

Other Amniotic Fluid Tests of Maturity

Other direct and indirect tests of fetal pulmonary status have been introduced. Direct enzymatic assays have been developed for lecithin, sphingomyelin, and PG, but their use in predicting respiratory outcome has not been evaluated adequately. The lack of commercial kits and preparation costs limit use of these assays. Surfactant proteins (apoproteins) are nonphospholipid markers of fetal maturity that have been investigated for use in maturity assessment. Immunoassay for the presence of the surfactant apoproteins SP-A and SP-B in amniotic fluid has permitted such evaluation, but further investigations are necessary to clarify the usefulness of this approach.

Imaging

Ultrasonography has replaced radiographic techniques for assessing fetal age. A biparietal diameter of 9.2 cm or more, a femur length of 7.3 cm or more, the presence and size of epiphyseal ossification centers, placental grading (classification based on chorionic convolutions and calcifications), and other imaging determinations have been evaluated as means to assess maturity (19–21). Some fetuses at term, however mature, may lack these findings, and some fetuses with these characteristics may be immature (eg, maternal diabetes complicated by macrosomia). In general, ultrasound assessment of gestational age (indirectly evaluating for maturity) in the third trimester is inferior to the other methods available.

Effect of Associated Conditions on Fetal Lung Maturity

Accelerated fetal lung maturity has been reported to occur with a number of obstetric conditions, including hypertensive disorders, hemoglobinopathies, narcotics addiction, intrauterine growth restriction, classes of diabetes that are long-standing or associated with complications, premature rupture of membranes, multiple gestation, and smoking. Conversely, a delay in fetal lung maturation has been reported in patients with certain other classes of diabetes, nonhypertensive renal disease, and isoimmunization. For virtually all of these conditions, however, conflicting results concerning their effect on pulmonary maturation and testing have been reported.

Fetal lung maturity in patients with diabetes is the condition that has been studied most extensively, yet consensus is still lacking. While some have reported altered maturity test results and an increased rate of RDS in newborns of diabetic patients, others have reported no difference in either test results or clinical outcome. Causes other than deficient surfactant may be responsible for some cases of respiratory distress (22).

Other Considerations

Administration of corticosteroids to pregnant women at risk for preterm delivery has been shown to be effective in decreasing the prevalence, severity, and complications of RDS (23). Corticosteroids accelerate pulmonary maturity by stimulation of both the synthesis and release of surfactant from the type II pneumocytes into the alveolar spaces. In general, fetal maturity test results measured soon after steroid administration are affected minimally. This is probably due in part to the time interval required between steroid administration and the synthesis and release of the surface-active materials into the alveolar spaces and subsequently into the amniotic fluid.

Amniotic fluid present in the vagina following spontaneous rupture of membranes can be used for fetal maturity assessment. As noted, PG is not present in other tissue fluids and, for this reason, has particular importance in assessing maturity in patients from whom vaginal pool specimens can be obtained. Unfortunately, PG is often absent in preterm patients with fetal pulmonary maturity and may be present in others who are not mature because of bacterial contamination. There is no consensus on the utility of other tests using vaginal samples.

Comparison Among Tests

Various characteristics of commonly used tests to assess fetal maturity are compared in Table 1. Although the L/S ratio was the first direct test used to assess fetal maturity, other tests perform equally well and, because of technical aspects of the testing procedure for L/S ratio determination, have become more widely used. Regardless of the test used, the predictive value of all mature results is over 95%. That is, if the result of any test indicates maturity, the likelihood that RDS will be diagnosed in a delivered infant is less than 5%. Conversely, all available tests share a relatively poor predictive value in assessing the likelihood of the presence of RDS. The predictive values for RDS of immature test results range from approximately 30% to 60%. Other test characteristics, including cost, ease of test performance, availability, and reproducibility, are important factors in selecting maturity tests.

Testing Strategies

With the introduction of newer tests for fetal maturity assessment, it has become a common practice to order multiple tests routinely for the assessment of fetal maturity. Results are often reported as a "lung profile" or "pulmonary profile." Since a mature result on any one of the commonly used tests of fetal lung maturity is strongly predictive of the absence of RDS, the practice of multiple testing on a routine basis should be questioned. Little additional information will be gained by the performance of multiple assays. When multiple tests are performed, discordant results are sometimes found, which is not surprising because these tests measure various components or aspects of maturity by different means. Obviously, costs are increased when multiple tests are obtained.

Because of the strong predictive value of a single mature result, the strategy of ordering tests individually, but within a defined protocol, is logical. This so-called "cascade" (24) or "sequential" (25) testing involves the performance of a rapid, inexpensive test initially, with a subsequent test ordered only if the result of the initial test is immature. Such a practice can provide clinicians with around-the-clock availability of a test for fetal maturity and yet maximizes laboratory efficiency by decreasing the overall number of tests performed. The testing sequence should be determined jointly between clinicians and laboratory personnel.

Women with diabetes are thought by some to have altered fetal lung maturation or fetal maturity test results or both; thus, some practitioners approach the assessment of these women differently from that of women who do not have diabetes. In the woman whose diabetes is well controlled, awaiting the appearance of PG may be justified, as its presence seems to provide the strongest evidence of pulmonary maturity. However, it must be remembered that PG may be absent in approximately 20% of women with gestational or overt diabetes at a gestational age as late as 38–39 weeks (26). In a recent multicenter study, only 2 of 13 patients with a mature fluorescence polarization test and absent PG delivered infants who developed RDS. Neither required intubation or prolonged oxygen therapy (14). Other strategies for managing patients with diabetes include delaying delivery until two separate tests (eg, FSI, L/S) indicate fetal lung maturity or using a higher threshold for maturity on which to proceed with delivery.

Regardless of which method of fetal lung maturity assessment is chosen, it should be emphasized that no mature result from one test or a group of tests can completely eliminate the risk of RDS or other neonatal complications (2). The risk of adverse outcome with delivery on the basis of lung maturity assessment must be weighed against the potential risk of untoward outcome by permitting the pregnancy to continue in utero.

References

1. Parilla BV, Dooley SL, Jansen RD, Socol ML. Iatrogenic respiratory distress syndrome following elective repeat cesarean delivery. Obstet Gynecol 1993;81:392–395 (Level III)

2. Wigton TR, Tamura RK, Wickstrom E, Atkins V, Deddish R, Socol ML. Neonatal morbidity after preterm delivery in the presence of documented lung maturity. Am J Obstet Gynecol 1993;169:951–955 (Level II-3)

3. Dubin SB. The laboratory assessment of fetal lung maturity. Am J Clin Pathol 1992;97:836–849 (Level III)

4. Spillman T, Cotton DB. Current perspectives in assessment of fetal pulmonary surfactant status with amniotic fluid. Crit Rev Clin Lab Sci 1989;27:341–389 (Level III)

5. American College of Obstetricians and Gynecologists. Fetal maturity assessment prior to elective repeat cesarean delivery. ACOG Committee Opinion 98. Washington, DC: ACOG, 1991 (Level III)

6. Whitsett JA, Pryhuber GS, Rice WR, Warner BB, Wert SE. Acute respiratory disorders. In: Avery GB, Fletcher MA, MacDonald MG, eds. Neonatology pathophysiology and management of the newborn. Philadelphia: JB Lippincott Company 1994;429–452 (Level III)

7. National Center for Health Statistics. Births, marriages, divorces, and deaths for 1993. Monthly vital statistics report; vol 42, no. 12. Hyattsville, Maryland: Public Health Service, 1994 (Level III)

8. Gluck L, Kulovich MV, Borer RC Jr, Brenner PH, Anderson GG, Spellacy WN. Diagnosis of respiratory distress by amniocentesis. Am J Obstet Gynecol 1971;109: 440–445 (Level II-3)

9. Blumenfeld TA. Clinical laboratory tests for fetal lung maturity. Pathol Annu 1975;10:21–36 (Level III)

10. Hallman M, Kulovich M, Kirkpatrick E, Sugarman RG, Gluck L. Phosphatidylinositol and phosphatidylglycerol in amniotic fluid: indices of lung maturity. Am J Obstet Gynecol 1976;125:613–617 (Level II-3)

11. Lewis DF, Towers CV, Major CA, Asrat T, Nageotte MP, Freeman RK, et al. Use of amniostat-FLM in detecting the presence of phosphatidylglycerol in vaginal pool samples in preterm premature rupture of membranes. Am J Obstet Gynecol 1993;169:573–576 (Level II-3)

12. Clements JA, Platzker ACG, Tierney DF, Hobel CJ, Creasy RK, Margolis AJ, et al. Assessment of the risk of the respiratory-distress syndrome by a rapid test for surfactant in amniotic fluid. N Engl J Med 1972;286:1077–1081 (Level II-3)

13. Sher G, Statland BE, Freer DE, Kraybill EN. Assessing fetal lung maturation by the foam stability index test. Obstet Gynecol 1978;52:673–677 (Level II-3)

14. Livingston EG, Herbert WNP, Hage ML, Chapman JF, Stubbs TM. Use of the TDx-FLM assay in evaluating fetal lung maturity in an insulin-dependent diabetic population. Obstet Gynecol 1995;86:826–829 (Level III)

15. Herbert WNP, Chapman JF, Schnoor MM. Role of the TDx FLM assay in fetal lung maturity. Am J Obstet Gynecol 1993;168:808–812 (Level II-3)

16. Hagen E, Link JC, Arias F. A comparison of the accuracy of the TDx-FLM assay, lecithin–sphingomyelin ratio, and phosphatidylglycerol in the prediction of neonatal respiratory distress syndrome. Obstet Gynecol 1993;82:1004–1008 (Level II-3)

17. Ashwood ER, Palmer SE, Taylor JS, Pingree SS. Lamellar body counts for rapid fetal lung maturity testing. Obstet Gynecol 1993;81:619–624 (Level II-3)

18. Delance CR, Bowie LJ, Dohnal JC, Farrell EE, Neerhof MG. Amniotic fluid lamellar body count: a rapid and reliable fetal lung maturity test. Obstet Gynecol 1995;86:235–239 (Level II-2)

19. Mahony BS, Bowie JD, Killam AP, Kay HH, Cooper C. Epiphyseal ossification centers in the assessment of fetal maturity: sonographic correlation with the amniocentesis lung profile. Radiology 1986;159:521–524 (Level II-3)

20. Goldstein I, Lockwood C, Belanger K, Hobbins J. Ultrasonographic assessment of gestational age with the distal, femoral and proximal tibial ossification centers in the third trimester. Am J Obstet Gynecol 1988;158:127–130 (Level II-3)

21. Tahilramaney MP, Platt LD, Golde SH. Use of femur length measured by ultrasonography to predict fetal maturity. J Perinatol 1991;11:157–160 (Level II-3)

22. Kjos SL, Walther FJ, Montoro M, Paul RH, Diaz F, Stabler M. Prevalence and etiology of respiratory distress in infants of diabetic mothers: predictive value of fetal lung maturation tests. Am J Obstet Gynecol 1990;163:898–903 (Level II-3)

23. Effect of corticosteroids for fetal maturation on perinatal outcomes. NIH Consens Statement 1994 Feb 28–Mar 2; 12(2):1–24 (Level III)

24. Garite TJ, Freeman RK, Nageotte MP. Fetal maturity cascade: a rapid and cost-effective method for fetal lung maturity testing. Obstet Gynecol 1986;67:619–622 (Level II-3)

25. Herbert WNP, Chapman JF. Clinical and economic considerations associated with testing for fetal lung maturity. Am J Obstet Gynecol 1986;155:820–823 (Level II-3)

26. Ojomo EO, Coustan DR. Absence of evidence of pulmonary maturity at amniocentesis in term infants of diabetic mothers. Am J Obstet Gynecol 1990;163:954–957 (Level II-3)

The references in this bulletin are graded according to the method outlined by the U.S. Preventive Services Task Force:

I   Evidence obtained from at least one properly designed randomized controlled trial

II-1   Evidence obtained from well-designed controlled trials without randomization

II-2   Evidence obtained from well-designed cohort or case–control analytic studies, preferably from more than one center or research group

II-3   Evidence obtained from multiple time series, with or without intervention, or dramatic results in uncontrolled experiments

III   Opinions of respected authorities, based on clinical experience, descriptive studies, or reports of expert committees

Other publications from ACOG:

- **Committee Opinions**, focused updates on emerging areas

- **Practice Patterns**, evidence-based guidelines

- **Criteria Sets**, baseline guidelines for review of diagnostic and management procedures

Copyright © November 1996
ISSN 1074-8628

**The American College of Obstetricians and Gynecologists
409 12th Street, SW
PO Box 96920
Washington, DC 20090-6920**

12345/09876

ACOG EDUCATIONAL BULLETIN

Number 258, July 2000

Breastfeeding: Maternal and Infant Aspects

Breastfeeding rates decreased significantly in the past half century as formula feeding gained popularity. In 1971, only 24.7% of mothers left the hospital breastfeeding. Recently, breastfeeding initiation rates have been increasing, reaching 64.3% in 1998, according to the Mothers' Survey (Ross Products Division, Abbott Laboratories, Inc., Columbus, Ohio). These increases reflect a growing awareness of the advantages of breast milk over formula. Improvement in breastfeeding initiation rates, however, has been uneven, as women attempt to overcome practical obstacles.

Evidence continues to mount regarding the value of breastfeeding for both women and their infants. Human milk provides developmental, nutritional, and immunologic benefits to the infant that cannot be duplicated by formula feeding. Breastfeeding also provides significant benefits to women. It is critical that women be prepared to make an informed choice in deciding what is best for them, their families, and their babies. Obstetrician–gynecologists and other health professionals caring for pregnant women should regularly impart accurate information about breastfeeding to expectant mothers and be prepared to support them should any problems arise while breastfeeding.

This document will focus primarily on breastfeeding by healthy mothers with healthy infants born at term. Human milk and breastfeeding are recommended for premature newborns and mother–infant pairs with other special needs; however, specific information in this regard is beyond the scope of this document.

Benefits of Breastfeeding

Research in the United States and throughout the world indicates that breastfeeding and human milk provide benefits to infants, women, families, and society. These studies have been done in a variety of settings, resulting in information derived from culturally and economically diverse populations.

Infants

The benefits of breastfeeding for the infant have been established in the following areas. Human milk provides species-specific and age-specific nutrients for the infant (1). Colostrum, the fluid secreted immediately following

This Educational Bulletin was developed under the direction of the Committees on Health Care for Underserved Women and Obstetric Practice of the American College of Obstetricians and Gynecologists. The college wishes to thank John T. Queenan, MD, for his assistance in the development of this bulletin. This document is not to be construed as establishing a standard of practice or dictating an exclusive course of treatment. Rather, it is intended as an educational tool that presents current information on obstetric–gynecologic issues.

the infant's birth, conveys a high level of immune protection, particularly secretory immunoglobulin A (IgA). During the first 4–7 days following delivery, protein and mineral concentrations decrease and water, fat, and lactose increase. Milk composition continues to change to match infant nutritional needs. In addition to the right balance of nutrients and immunologic factors, human milk contains factors that act as biologic signals for promoting cellular growth and differentiation. It also contains multiple substances with antimicrobial properties, which protect against infection (1, 2). Human milk alone, however, may not provide adequate iron for premature newborns, infants whose mothers have low iron stores, and infants older than 6 months.

In 1997, the American Academy of Pediatrics (AAP) published a policy statement, "Breastfeeeding and the Use of Human Milk" (3). The statement was developed by the AAP Work Group on Breastfeeding, which evaluated the research literature on relationships between breastfeeding and infant health and development. The statement's summary paragraph (see the box below) on established infant protective effects, as well as positive associations (which require further study), is well referenced. Obstetrician–gynecologists who review these sources of evidence for infant benefit will be better prepared to care for the women in their practices.

Women

The benefits of breastfeeding for women are well documented. During the immediate postpartum period, the oxytocin released during milk let-down causes increased uterine contractions and lessens maternal blood loss (4). Evidence exists that the hormones of lactation (oxytocin and prolactin) contribute to feelings of relaxation and attachment (5). Breastfeeding is associated with a decreased risk of developing ovarian and premenopausal breast cancer (6, 7). Breastfeeding also delays postpartum ovulation, supporting birth spacing (8–10). Although breastfeeding causes some bone demineralization, studies indicate that "catch-up" remineralization occurs following weaning; some studies also show a lower incidence of osteoporosis and hip fracture after menopause (11, 12). The incidence of pregnancy-induced long-term obesity also is reduced (13).

There are psychologic benefits as well. A woman who breastfeeds her baby is able to take advantage of the natural dynamics of nurturing and bonding.

Families and Society

Studies indicate that the breastfed child has fewer illnesses and, therefore, fewer visits to the doctor and hospital (14). This translates into less absenteeism from work for the mother and lower medical expenses. The improvement in work productivity may be significant for society as well, because women now constitute a large portion of the workforce. More than 60% of all women return to outside employment during the first year following birth of a child.

Breastfeeding, while demanding maternal time and attention, can save individual families and society considerable money compared with formula feeding (15). On a national scale, disposal of formula cans, bottles, and bottle liners may be an ecologic consideration.

Obstacles to Breastfeeding

Women need to know that breastfeeding, like other aspects of having a new baby, may be demanding as well as rewarding. They should be assured that they will have support and that there are options for problem solving and for addressing the practical obstacles they may face. Some women will decide the challenges outweigh the benefits for themselves and their babies, given the overall circumstances of their lives. However, physicians and other health professionals should recognize the potential effectiveness of applying their knowledge and skills to encourage and support women in initiating and continuing breastfeeding.

Modern society creates some of the obstacles to breastfeeding. Short hospital stays make the teaching of breastfeeding a challenge. Lack of spousal or partner support and family custom may discourage breastfeeding. Having to return to work is an obstacle, which is being diminished for some women as more employers learn that

---

Research on Established and Potential Protective Effects of Human Milk and Breastfeeding on Infants

Research in the United States, Canada, Europe and other developed countries, among predominantly middle-class populations, provides strong evidence that human milk feeding decreases the incidence and/or severity of diarrhea, lower respiratory infection, otitis media, bacteremia, bacterial meningitis, botulism, urinary tract infection, and necrotizing enterocolitis. There are a number of studies that show a possible protective effect of human milk feeding against sudden infant death syndrome, insulin-dependent diabetes mellitus, Crohn's disease, ulcerative colitis, lymphoma, allergic diseases, and other chronic digestive diseases. Breastfeeding has also been related to possible enhancement of cognitive development.

American Academy of Pediatrics, Work Group on Breastfeeding. Breastfeeding and the use of human milk. Pediatrics 100;1997: 1035–1039 (Paragraph includes 39 citations.)

encouraging breastfeeding as a policy improves employee morale and decreases absenteeism (16, 17). An unfriendly social environment may make it difficult to breastfeed in public. The effect of these obstacles can be mitigated by educating the families, employers, and society. All share in the benefits and, through positive attitudes and workplace and public policies, also can support women who are willing to breastfeed.

Who Can Breastfeed

Breastfeeding is a natural function; nearly every woman can breastfeed her child. Mother and newborn can more easily learn the basics and how to deal with the challenges if they have skilled and experienced support. Mothers who have cesarean deliveries should be reassured that they can breastfeed their newborns as well as those women having vaginal deliveries. Specific infections such as endometritis or mastitis are not contraindications to breastfeeding.

Women with structural problems such as hypoplastic or tubular breasts may have difficulty producing sufficient milk. True inverted nipples are rare but generally preclude nursing; most women with nipples that appear flat or inverted can breastfeed, given appropriate assistance in the early days of lactation. Pumping for a minute or two before offering the breast to the newborn has been shown to facilitate latch-on (1). Lactation is not possible for women who have had breast surgery involving the complete severing of the lactiferous ducts. However, some women may breastfeed after reduction mammoplasty or augmentation mammoplasty with implants, and most women can breastfeed after breast biopsies.

Mothers with premature infants also can breastfeed. A mother's milk has specific properties that match the needs of her premature newborn. However, nutrition requirements for the premature newborn are different and require special attention. Some babies with cleft lips or palate may be able to breastfeed. The soft breast tissue may fill the defect and enable the infant to develop a seal. Sometimes a palatal obturator allows the infant to breastfeed and not aspirate milk. A newborn that is premature or has other special needs may benefit from breastfeeding but requires individual evaluation by appropriate experts.

Who Should Not Breastfeed

Although it is true that most women can breastfeed, there are exceptions. These exceptions should be understood by all clinicians so that a patient's frustration and disappointment can be minimized. The number of contraindi-

cations is small (18). Women who should not breastfeed are those who:

- Take street drugs or do not control alcohol use
- Have an infant with galactosemia
- Are infected with the human immunodeficiency virus (HIV)
- Have active, untreated tuberculosis
- Take certain medications
- Are undergoing treatment for breast cancer (1)

Women who use illegal drugs should not breastfeed because it is unknown which agent or how much of the agent the infant will be exposed to. Alcohol is a toxin, so a breastfeeding woman should minimize or avoid it, and a mother who drinks significant amounts of alcohol should not breastfeed (2).

Infants with galactosemia should neither breastfeed, because this will exacerbate the condition, nor consume any formula containing lactose (eg, cows' milk). They need special lactose-free formula.

Some infections contraindicate breastfeeding; others require precautions. Approaches to breastfeeding vary according to the infection and the environment. Comprehensive information about breastfeeding in relation to the following common maternal infections and others is available for further reference (1). Women in the United States who have HIV infections should not breastfeed because breast milk can carry HIV and pass the infection to the infant. In some countries with high infant mortality rates, however, the benefits of breastfeeding in providing nutrition and preventing infections may still outweigh the risks of transmitting HIV.

If a woman has active pulmonary tuberculosis, the repeated and prolonged close contact involved in feeding exposes the infant to risk of airborne infection. Therefore the woman should neither breastfeed nor bottle feed her newborn until she has been appropriately treated for at least 2 weeks and is otherwise considered to be noncontagious. The infant can be given the mother's expressed breast milk because it does not contain *Mycobacterium tuberculosis* (1).

Similarly, if a woman has varicella, she should be isolated from the infant and neither breastfeed nor bottle feed while she is clinically infectious. Once the infant has received varicella-zoster immune globulin (1), the woman can provide expressed breast milk for the infant if there are no skin lesions on the breasts. An immunocompetent woman who develops herpes zoster infection (shingles) can continue breastfeeding if lesions are covered and are not on the breast. Maternal antibodies delivered through the placenta and breast milk will prevent the disease or diminish its severity. An infant may be given varicella-zoster immune globulin in these circumstances as an added precaution (1).

Breastfeeding also is contraindicated in women who have active herpes simplex infections on the breast until the lesion is cleared. In women with cytomegalovirus infection, both the virus and maternal antibodies are present in breast milk. Because of the antibodies, otherwise healthy infants born at term with congenital or acquired cytomegalovirus infections usually do better if they are breastfed. A study of infants who developed infections during breastfeeding found the infants also developed an immune response, did not develop the disease, and rarely manifested symptoms (18).

Hepatitis infections do not preclude breastfeeding. With appropriate immunoprophylaxis, including hepatitis B immune globulin (HBIG) and hepatitis vaccine, breastfeeding of babies born to women positive for hepatitis B surface antigen poses no additional risk for the transmission of hepatitis B virus (19). If a woman has acute hepatitis A infection, her infant can breastfeed after receiving immune serum globulin and vaccine (1). The average rate of hepatitis C virus (HCV) infection reported in infants born to HCV-positive women is 4% for both breastfed and bottle-fed infants. Therefore maternal HCV is not considered a contraindication to breastfeeding (20).

Many medications are compatible with breastfeeding. The AAP Committee on Drugs reviewed the current data on the transfer of drugs and other chemicals in human milk. The committee classified drugs for safety in breastfeeding on a scale of 1 (contraindicated) to 6 (compatible) (21). Generally, breastfeeding is contraindicated for women taking antineoplastic, thyrotoxic, and immunosuppressive agents (Table 1) (19). Medications with relative contraindications may sometimes be used cautiously by timing doses to immediately follow a feeding.

Education on Breastfeeding

Teaching the pregnant woman and her partner about childbirth and breastfeeding is an integral part of good prenatal care. Other family members who could support breastfeeding may be included. Education can occur in the physician's office or clinic. Alternatively, hospitals and other organizations provide education for pregnant women and their partners. The advice and encouragement of the obstetrician–gynecologist are critical in making the decision to breastfeed. Other health professionals such as pediatricians, nurses, and certified lactation specialists play an important role, as do mother-to-mother groups and other lay organizations. The health benefits of breastfeeding warrant efforts in professional cooperation and

Table 1. Medications Contraindicated During Breastfeeding

Medication	Reason
Bromocriptine	Suppresses lactation; may be hazardous to the mother
Cocaine	Cocaine intoxication
Cyclophosphamide	Possible immune suppression; unknown effect on growth or association with carcinogenesis; neutropenia
Cyclosporine	Possible immune suppression; unknown effect on growth or association with carcinogenesis
Doxorubicin*	Possible immune suppression; unknown effect on growth or association with carcinogenesis
Ergotamine	Vomiting, diarrhea, convulsions (at doses used in migraine medications)
Lithium	One third to one half of therapeutic blood concentration in infants
Methotrexate	Possible immune suppression; unknown effect on growth or association with carcinogenesis; neutropenia
Phencyclidine	Potent hallucinogen
Phenindione	Anticoagulant; increased prothrombin and partial thromboplastin time in one infant; not used in United States
Radioactive iodine and other radiolabeled elements	Contraindications to breastfeeding for various periods

*Medication is concentrated in human milk.

American Academy of Pediatrics, American College of Obstetricians and Gynecologists. Guidelines for perinatal care. 4th ed. Elk Grove Village, Illinois: AAP; Washington, DC: ACOG, 1997

coordination among all health care workers to educate and encourage women and their families to choose breastfeeding. Patient education materials can reinforce the message (see the boxes, "Patient Education Materials" and "References for Health Care Workers and Patients Seeking In-depth Information").

Some women who choose to breastfeed were breastfed themselves or had a sibling who was breastfed, which established it as normal behavior in their household. These women would probably benefit from some education and reinforcement concerning breastfeeding. Women whose family and friends have not shared breastfeeding experiences also approach pregnancy with a desire to do what is healthiest for their babies. Guidance and consideration of life situations are important in helping these women and their families make a decision about feeding their infants. Information about the benefits and challenges of breastfeeding compared with the use of formula will help them make good decisions. The obstetrician–gynecologist often

---

Patient Education Materials

Breast-feeding your baby. Patient Education Pamphlet AP029. Washington, DC: American College of Obstetricians and Gynecologists, 1997

Breastfeeding: loving support for a bright future. Q & A. Physicians' breastfeeding support kit. Tampa, Florida: Best Start Social Marketing, 1998

Working & breastfeeding. Can you do it? Yes, you can! Alexandria, Virginia: National Healthy Mothers, Healthy Babies Coalition, 1997

Ten steps to support parents' choice to breastfeed their baby. American Academy of Pediatrics Task Force on Breastfeeding. Elk Grove Village, Illinois: AAP, 1999

References for Health Care Workers and Patients Seeking In-depth Information

American Academy of Pediatrics and the American College of Obstetricians and Gynecologists. Guidelines for perinatal care. 4th ed. Elk Grove Village, Illinois: AAP, and Washington, DC: ACOG, 1997

American Academy of Pediatrics Committee on Drugs. The transfer of drugs and other chemicals into human milk. Pediatrics 1994;93:137–150.

American Academy of Pediatrics, Work Group on Breastfeeding. Breastfeeding and the use of human milk. Pediatrics 1997;100:1035–1039

ABM News and Views. The Newsletter of The Academy of Breastfeeding Medicine. Lenexa, Kansas: ABM

Lawrence RA. A review of the medical benefits and contraindications to breastfeeding in the United States. Maternal and Child Health Technical Information Bulletin. Arlington, Virginia: National Center for Education in Maternal and Child Health, 1997

Lawrence RA, Lawrence RM. Breastfeeding: a guide for the medical profession. 5th ed. St. Louis, Missouri: Mosby, 1999

U.S. Department of Health and Human Services, Health Resources & Services Administration, Maternal and Child Health Bureau, U.S. Department of Agriculture, Food and Nutrition Service. Physicians' breastfeeding support kit. Tampa, Florida: Best Start Social Marketing, 1998

---

can allay a woman's anxieties and suggest solutions or resources to make breastfeeding a practical choice for her and her family.

Periodic Gynecologic Examinations

Obstetrician–gynecologists can begin to educate women who have their reproductive lives ahead of them by mentioning breastfeeding during the breast examination portion of routine gynecologic visits, if appropriate. Women whose anatomy appears to be normal can be told that if they decide to have a baby, there are no structural impediments to breastfeeding.

First Obstetric Visit

The initial prenatal visit is the optimal time to encourage or reinforce the decision to breastfeed. It is also an ideal time to let the patient know the advantages of breastfeeding over formula feeding. Most patients seek information and guidance from their doctors. The importance of the physician's recommendation should never be underestimated. If a woman has not yet made a decision to breastfeed, this and subsequent visits may provide an opportunity for her to do so. During the breast examination, the physician can perform a breastfeeding-specific examination and answer any questions about the usual pattern of changes in the breasts during pregnancy and breastfeeding. If there are no structural problems, the woman can be reassured about her ability to breastfeed. If her nipples appear to be inverted, she should know that appearance is not necessarily prognostic and she may be able to breastfeed, but that techniques to assist in nipple eversion are not recommended during pregnancy because of the potential for stimulating contractions.

Antenatal Breastfeeding Instruction

In the past, when hospital stays were longer, women could receive fairly adequate education about breastfeeding before discharge. Today, with shorter hospital stays, it is imperative that pregnant women come to the hospital for delivery with a good foundation of knowledge gained during the antepartum period. Prenatal education groups have been shown to be particularly effective in increasing duration of breastfeeding (22). Education in the hospital can then focus on operational aspects of breastfeeding such as latch-on and feeding techniques.

The woman who is appropriately counseled on breastfeeding options and chooses not to breastfeed should be reassured that her milk production will abate during the first few days after delivery. Hormone treatment to stop milk production is no longer recommended. She should be treated with a well-fitted support bra, analgesics, and ice packs to relieve the pain. She also can be assured that if she changes her mind, she may still be able to initiate breastfeeding within the first few days.

Hospital Stay

Shortened hospital stays for childbirth have made the teaching of breastfeeding difficult. Certain protocols and practices, however, will increase rates of successful breastfeeding (see the box, "Ten Hospital Practices to Encourage and Support Breastfeeding") (23).

Delivery

The immediate postpartum period should allow the woman and her newborn to experience optimal bonding with immediate physical contact, preferably skin to skin. The initial feeding should occur as soon after birth as possible, preferably in the first hour when the baby is awake,

---

Ten Hospital Practices to Encourage and Support Breastfeeding*

- Maintain a written breastfeeding policy that is communicated to all health care staff.

- Train all pertinent health care staff in skills necessary to implement this policy.

- Inform all pregnant women about the benefits of breastfeeding.

- Offer all mothers the opportunity to initiate breastfeeding within 1 hour of birth.

- Show breastfeeding mothers how to breastfeed and how to maintain lactation even if they are separated from their infants.

- Give breastfeeding infants only breast milk unless medically indicated.

- Facilitate rooming-in; encourage all mothers and infants to remain together during their hospital stay.

- Encourage unrestricted breastfeeding when baby exhibits hunger cues or signals or on request of mother.

- Encourage exclusive suckling at the breast by providing no pacifiers or artificial nipples.

- Refer mothers to established breastfeeding and mother's support groups and services, and foster the establishment of those services when they are not available.

*The 1994 report of the Healthy Mothers, Healthy Babies National Coalition Expert Work Group recommended that the UNICEF-WHO Baby Friendly Hospital Initiative be adapted for use in the United States as the United States Breastfeeding Health Initiative, using the adapted 10 steps above.

Randolph L, Cooper L, Fonseca-Becker F, York M, McIntosh M. Baby Friendly Hospital Initiative feasibility study: final report. Healthy Mothers, Healthy Babies National Coalition Expert Work Group. Alexandria, Virginia: HMHB, 1994

---

alert, and ready to suck. Newborn eye prophylaxis, weighing, measuring, and other such examinations can be done after the feeding. Such procedures usually can be performed later in the woman's room.

Rooming-In

Today, all hospitals should make trained personnel available to provide breastfeeding support and should offer 24-hour rooming-in to maximize the interaction between the woman and her newborn. Separation of a breastfeeding woman and newborn should be avoided whenever possible. Most newborn care and procedures, including bathing, blood drawing, physical examinations, and administration of medication and phototherapy, can be performed in the mother's room. In this way, mother and baby can benefit together from the nursing care available (3).

The rooming-in experience allows a woman and her newborn to start the adjustment to a breastfeeding routine. Normally a newborn will show signs of hunger, such as increased alertness or activity, mouthing, or rooting. Crying is a late sign of hunger. Newborns should be nursed approximately 8–12 times every 24 hours until satiety; time at breast varies but may be 10 to 15 minutes on each breast (3).

Instruction

Hospital personnel should have adequate time allotted to each patient, no matter when the delivery occurs, and provide a specific program on practical aspects of breastfeeding that women master before discharge. Trained staff should assess breastfeeding behavior of the woman and newborn during the first 24–48 hours after birth for correct nursing positions, latch-on, and adequacy of newborn swallowing. They also should ensure that the woman is skilled in the technique of manual expression of milk (3).

Before discharge the woman should be educated about age-appropriate elimination patterns of her newborn during the first week after birth. At least six urinations per day and three to four stools per day are to be expected by 5–7 days of age. She can be shown how to keep simple records for the first few weeks, noting the frequency and length of feedings and the number of stools and wet diapers, for discussion with her care providers. She should understand expected patterns of newborn weight loss and gain (3). Before gaining, the breastfeeding newborn may lose 5–7% of birth weight in the first week. When the loss is greater than 5–7% or reaches that level in the first 3 days, a clinician should evaluate the breastfeeding process to address any problems before they become serious. A loss of up to 10% is the maximum acceptable. Follow-up should confirm that the newborn is beginning to regain weight after the first week (1).

Latch-On

Breastfeeding should not be painful, but minor discomfort is common during the first 2 weeks. Painful breastfeeding almost always results from poor positioning or latch-on, which should be immediately corrected. ACOG's "Breast-feeding Your Baby" pamphlet is an example of a resource that can be used to help women with positioning and latch-on (24). Discomfort may occur temporarily as the woman's milk supply is beginning to be established. Any significant pain or tenderness should be assessed promptly by a physician.

Latch-on is one of the most important steps to successful breastfeeding. There are several helpful approaches, including gently stroking the newborn's lower lip with the nipple to get the baby to open his or her mouth wide, or gently pulling the newborn's chin down. The newborn should take a large amount of breast into his or her mouth, generally an inch or more of the areola with the nipple pointing toward the soft palate. The mother may hold her breast to facilitate this position, using a hand position comfortable for her. The nipple and the areola elongate into a teat, and the baby's tongue should be slightly cupped beneath it. The mother should adopt a comfortable position and draw the baby to the breast. The newborn should be held close, facing the mother, with his chin and the tip of his nose touching but not completely occluded by the breast. Usually, it is wise to alternate the breast used to initiate the feeding and to equalize the time spent at each breast over the day. The mother can break the suction by gently inserting her finger in the newborn's mouth before taking him off the breast.

Home

All breastfeeding women and their babies who are discharged from the hospital in less than 48 hours after delivery should be seen by a pediatrician or other knowledgeable health care practitioner when the baby is 2–4 days old. This is important in order to evaluate health status of the newborn (eg, weight, hydration, and hyperbilirubinemia) at this critical age, as well as to observe the woman and newborn during breastfeeding (3).

Women can be reassured that eating a well-balanced diet generally will provide the nutrients their infants need. On average, it is estimated that women will need approximately 500 kcal per day more than nonpregnant and nonlactating recommended levels, and the additional maternal food intake generally will provide additional needed vitamins and minerals (with the possible exceptions of calcium and zinc). Women of childbearing age need to maintain a calcium intake of 1,000 mg per day at all times, including during pregnancy and lactation

(1,300 for adolescents through 18 years of age). Dietary intake is the preferred source of all needed nutrients. However, many women breastfeed on a lower calorie intake level than suggested, consuming bodily stores instead. This will result in gradual weight loss and is not likely to affect breastfeeding, but further questions may need to be asked about sources of magnesium, vitamin B_6, folate, calcium, and zinc (2, 25, 26). Corrective measures can be suggested for improving nutrient intakes of women with restrictive eating patterns (2). Women should be encouraged to drink plenty of fluids to satisfy their thirst and maintain adequate hydration. They need not avoid certain foods (spicy or strong flavored) because of breastfeeding unless the infant seems to react negatively to specific foods.

The spouse or partner can play a vital support role for the breastfeeding woman by encouraging her, bringing the newborn to her for feeding, changing the newborn, and holding the newborn. Couples may find that caring for a baby can complicate their own relationship, including a desired resumption of sexual intercourse. They may be encouraged to discuss emotional adjustments to their new family status as well as physical problems of soreness, fatigue, and vaginal dryness secondary to lactation. When a woman is ready to resume sexual intercourse, prelubricated latex condoms can be recommended to prevent infection and ease vaginal dryness.

Phone-In Resource

The departure of a woman and her newborn from the hospital can be a joyous but daunting experience. The family is now responsible for the care and feeding of the newborn. Whether or not they have a support system at home, a phone-in resource is needed for ongoing instruction and advice. The obstetrician–gynecologist's office, the place where the woman has received most of her care, should be that resource or at least provide links to other resources in the community, such as lactation specialists and support groups.

Contraception

Women should be encouraged to consider their future plans for additional childbearing during prenatal care and be given information and services that will help them meet their goals. This is especially important for a woman who breastfeeds, because there are fewer variables in her nutrition status if the next pregnancy is delayed until she has completed breastfeeding.

In nonbreastfeeding women, the average time to first ovulation is 45 days (range, 25–72 days) (27). Many women resume intercourse well before they return for their postpartum checkup, thus some women are at risk of becoming pregnant.

For breastfeeding women, however, the situation is different. Exclusive breastfeeding helps prevent pregnancy for the first 6 months after delivery, but should be relied on only temporarily and when it meets carefully observed criteria of the lactational amenorrhea method (LAM) (see "Lactational Amenorrhea Method").

Nonhormonal Methods

If a breastfeeding woman needs or wants more protection from pregnancy, options are available that do not affect breastfeeding or pose even a theoretical risk to the infant. *She should first consider the nonhormonal methods such as copper intrauterine contraceptive devices, condoms, or other barrier methods* (see the box, "ACOG Recommendations for Nonhormonal Contraception for Breastfeeding Women"). Condoms have additional, noncontraceptive advantages. Female sterilization or vasectomy may be considered by couples desiring permanent methods of birth control (27).

Hormonal Methods

Hormonal contraception offers effective protection from becoming pregnant. Several factors should be considered before prescribing hormonal contraception for the lactating woman. Contradictory lines of thought have resulted in conflicting recommendations that have been put forward by generally authoritative sources. The ACOG recommendations represent a more practical approach to the woman's needs, based on relevant research.

Progestin-Only Contraceptives

Progestin-only contraceptives, including progestin-only tablets (minipills), depot medroxyprogesterone acetate

---

ACOG Recommendations for Nonhormonal Contraception for Breastfeeding Women

Exclusive breastfeeding up to 6 months meeting lactational amenorrhea method criteria (see "Lactational Amenorrhea Method")

Additional protection if desired

- Prelubricated latex condoms
- Other barrier methods
- Copper intrauterine contraceptive devices
- Male or female sterilization if permanent contraception is desired

---

(DMPA), and levonorgestrel implants, do not affect the quality of breast milk and may slightly increase the volume of milk and duration of breastfeeding compared with nonhormonal methods (28–32). Accordingly, progestin-only methods are the hormonal contraceptives of choice for breastfeeding women. Nonetheless, some authorities have recommended delays of various lengths before introduction of progestin-only contraceptives on the basis of two sets of theoretical concerns:

- The normal 2–3-day postdelivery decrease of progesterone is part of the process that initiates lactation. There is theoretical concern that giving progestins in the first few days before lactation is established could interfere with optimal lactation. Note that DMPA enters the milk at approximately the same level found in the woman's blood; by contrast norgestrel and norethindrone enter the milk at only one tenth the level in the woman's blood. The injectable route of administration also may result in a comparatively high initial dose (27).

- Progestin methods carry a theoretical risk to the newborn because of exposure to exogenous steroids at a time when the newborn's system is very immature in its ability to metabolize drugs. Because of this concern, research studies presented to the FDA for drug approval investigated only the effects of these methods administered several weeks after birth. Because documentation of experience with earlier initiation was not presented to the FDA, package inserts recommend initiation of progestin-only oral contraceptives at 6 weeks for women who are exclusively breastfeeding and at 3 weeks for those who are breastfeeding with supplementation. Most authorities recommend introduction of long-acting progestin-only injectables or implants 6 weeks after delivery for breastfeeding women (27, 33, 34).

To balance these conservative recommendations, it is important to understand that the few studies that included early administration of progestin-only methods—oral contraceptives at 1 week postpartum (35, 36) and injectable medroxyprogesterone acetate at 2 days (37) and 7 days (38)—found no adverse effects on the newborn or on breastfeeding. In the absence of evidence that earlier introduction of progestin-only contraceptives has adverse effects on the newborn and on breastfeeding, the labeling for progestin-only oral contraceptives focuses instead on what is known about fertility after childbirth. Taking only biologic factors into account, contraception is not needed in the first 3 weeks postpartum because of a delay in return of ovulation in all women. And this delay is extended for women who breastfeed exclusively. An implied prohibition on earlier administration is more in the nature of a pragmatic rather than a scientific resolution of the question. From the perspective of routine clinical practice, it would appear reasonable to apply the same rationale, even though conservative, to the initiation of DMPA and implants in postpartum breastfeeding women. However, the package labeling for these methods has the effect of being even more conservative as noted, outlining a 6-week start for all breastfeeding women, with no flexibility. Sometimes, however, there are practical reasons a breastfeeding woman may consider initiating hormonal contraception while in the hospital or shortly after. For example, there may be uncertainty about opportunities for follow-up visits. The breastfeeding woman and her physician can then weigh the reasons for early use of these contraceptives against potential disadvantages, make an appropriate decision, and continue to evaluate the woman's individual breastfeeding experience if hormonal contraceptives are chosen.

Combination Estrogen–Progestin Contraceptives

The postpartum patient has a hypercoagulable state that predisposes her to venous thrombosis (39). The use of estrogen-containing contraceptives during this phase of approximately 3 weeks after childbirth could contribute to this state. Furthermore, estrogen–progestin contraceptives have been shown to reduce the quantity and quality of breast milk. The World Health Organization recommends that the breastfeeding woman wait at least 6 months after childbirth to start using them (33). Labeling required by the FDA for combined oral contraceptives states, "If possible, the nursing mother should be advised not to use oral contraceptives but to use other forms of contraception until she has completely weaned her child" (34). These conservative approaches emanate for the most part from earlier combination oral contraceptive studies using higher doses of estrogens. Low-dose tablets (35 µg or lower) probably have a lesser effect on quality and quantity of breast milk. Effects are variable and if there are strong reasons the woman wishes to start combined estrogen–progestin contraceptive use earlier, she should understand and weigh the potential disadvantages. If estrogen–progestin contraceptives are prescribed, they should not be started before 6 weeks postpartum, and the physician should continue to evaluate the woman's individual breastfeeding experience.

The summary recommendations given in the box, "ACOG Recommendations for Hormonal Contraception If Used by Breastfeeding Women," with regard to progestin-only methods are based on the conservative timing outlined in labeling. Exceptions may be considered for earlier use on an individual basis. With combined estrogen–progestin contraceptives, a minimum 6-week delay is prudent because practical obstacles in developing successful breastfeeding techniques are likely to be resolved by 6 weeks. Most women experience reduced milk volume as a result of estrogen ingestion; this may be dealt with more easily after breastfeeding skills and patterns are established, should combined contraceptives be chosen despite this disadvantage. FDA labeling, however, is more conservative than the summary recommendation offered for combined estrogen–progestin contraceptives here. As noted earlier, prelubricated condoms are a good interim contraceptive choice and will address vaginal dryness associated with breastfeeding as well as help prevent infection.

Lactational Amenorrhea Method

Women who breastfeed can make use of the natural contraceptive effect of lactation. The LAM is most appropriate for women who plan to fully breastfeed 6 months or longer. If the baby is fed only mother's milk or is given supplemental nonbreast-milk feedings only to a minor extent and the woman has not experienced her first postpartum menses, then breastfeeding provides more than 98% protection from pregnancy in the first 6 months following delivery (27, 40, 41). Four prospective clinical trials of the contraceptive effect of LAM demonstrated cumulative 6-month life-table, perfect-use pregnancy rates of 0.5%, 0.6%, 1.0%, and 1.5% among women who relied solely on it. Women should be advised that for significant fertility impact, intervals between feedings should not exceed 4 hours during the day or 6 hours at night (Fig. 1). Supplemental feedings should not exceed 5–10% of the total (42–46). For example, more than one supplemental feeding out of every 10 might increase the

---

ACOG Recommendations for Hormonal Contraception If Used by Breastfeeding Women

- Progestin-only oral contraceptives prescribed or dispensed at discharge from the hospital to be started 2–3 weeks postpartum (eg, the first Sunday after the newborn is 2 weeks old)

- Depot medroxyprogesterone acetate initiated at 6 weeks postpartum*

- Hormonal implants inserted at 6 weeks postpartum*

- Combined estrogen–progestin contraceptives, if prescribed, should not be started before 6 weeks postpartum, and only when lactation is well established and the infant's nutritional status well-monitored

*There are certain clinical situations in which earlier initiation might be considered.

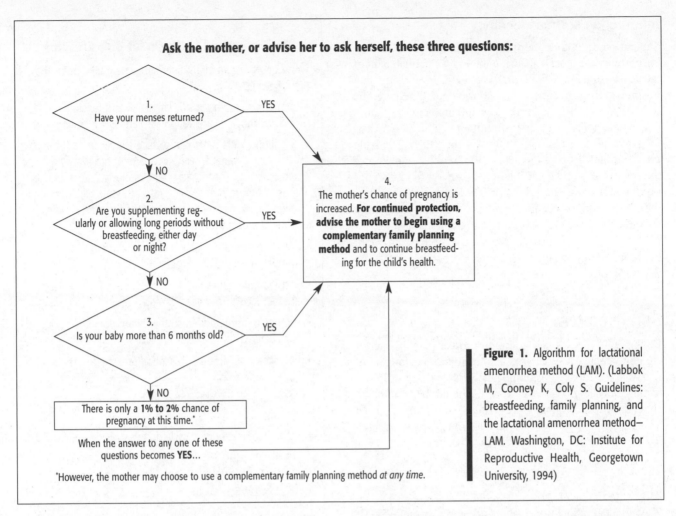

Ask the mother, or advise her to ask herself, these three questions:

1. Have your menses returned? — YES

NO

2. Are you supplementing regularly or allowing long periods without breastfeeding, either day or night? — YES

NO

3. Is your baby more than 6 months old? — YES

NO

There is only a **1% to 2%** chance of pregnancy at this time.*

When the answer to any one of these questions becomes **YES**...

4. The mother's chance of pregnancy is increased. **For continued protection, advise the mother to begin using a complementary family planning method** and to continue breastfeeding for the child's health.

*However, the mother may choose to use a complementary family planning method *at any time*.

Figure 1. Algorithm for lactational amenorrhea method (LAM). (Labbok M, Cooney K, Coly S. Guidelines: breastfeeding, family planning, and the lactational amenorrhea method—LAM. Washington, DC: Institute for Reproductive Health, Georgetown University, 1994)

likelihood of returning fertility. Feeding practices other than direct breastfeeding, insofar as they may reduce the vigor and frequency of suckling and the maternal neuroendocrine response, increase the probability of returning ovulation (47). If there is uncertainty regarding the extent to which a given woman is breastfeeding, it would be prudent to recommend additional contraception.

Maintaining Milk Supply

Regular breastfeeding generally ensures adequate milk supply. As the baby grows and requires more milk, the woman's supply, which is demand driven, increases to accommodate the baby's needs.

Bottle Supplements and Pacifiers

The use of pacifiers and supplemental bottle feeding have been considered deterrents to sustained breastfeeding. Studies do not provide clear evidence that bottle feeding and pacifiers directly interfere with breastfeeding. A recent prospective cohort study indicated that pacifier use in the first 6 weeks was independently associated with declines in the duration of full and overall breastfeeding in the long term, but not short term (during the first 3 months of life). Women who introduced pacifiers early tended to breastfeed fewer times per day. The authors suggested that maternal behavior, such as extending intervals between feedings and decisions to begin weaning, may lead to introduction of pacifiers. They suggested that pacifier use, through an association with infrequent breastfeeding, may mediate (rather than cause) the declines observed in breastfeeding duration (48). It is important to help mothers understand that substituting for or delaying breastfeedings may ultimately reduce milk supply because of the reduction in stimulation of milk production that depends on infant suckling. Another study found that fluid supplements offered by bottle with or without the use of pacifiers during the first 5 days of life were not associated with a lower frequency or shorter duration of breastfeeding during the first 6 months of life (49).

Interruption of Breastfeeding

Separation of mother and infant should be avoided whenever possible, especially during the early establishment of lactation (first 3 weeks). If it is known in advance that hospitalization or a trip, for example, will require the mother to be separated from the infant for more than a day, careful planning can ensure that the ability to breastfeed will be preserved and breast milk will be available for the infant. During the separation, regular pumping of the breasts should be sufficient to maintain the milk supply. The milk may be saved for feeding the infant. When the separation is because of hospitalization, the milk should be discarded if it is judged to contain anesthetic or contraindicated medications. When the mother and infant are reunited, the reestablishment of normal breastfeeding generally progresses well.

Sore Nipples

Having sore nipples is a common problem for the breastfeeding woman. It usually results from poor positioning or latch-on (see box, "Positioning and Latch-On for Breastfeeding"). The first-line treatment should be counseling about these basic techniques (24). Purified lanolin cream and breast shells (to protect the nipples from friction between feedings) may be initiated to facilitate healing (50).

Mastitis

Mastitis occurs in 1–2% of breastfeeding women (51). It most commonly occurs between the first and fifth weeks postpartum but may be seen any time throughout the first year (52). Mastitis is manifested by a sore, reddened area on one breast and often is accompanied by chills, fever, and malaise. A segment of the breast becomes hard and erythematous, the fever can be as high as 40°C, and the mother feels ill.

The differential diagnosis includes clogged milk duct, marked engorgement, and a rare condition, inflammatory breast carcinoma. Clogged milk ducts present as localized tender masses. They respond to warm wet compresses and manually massaging the loculated milk towards the nipple. Breast engorgement is always bilateral with generalized involvement. It occurs most commonly in the first 2 weeks postpartum. The major feature that differentiates it from inflammatory breast cancer is the knowledge of previous negative breast examination results during the pregnancy. If examination results have been normal, breast engorgement is the more likely diagnosis (51). Inflammatory breast cancer is a lethal form of breast cancer. It presents as unilateral erythema, heat, and induration that is more diffuse and recurrent (53).

Positioning and Latch-On for Breastfeeding

When observing an infant being breastfed, take note of the following:

- Position of mother, body language, and tension. Pillows may provide support for arms or infant.

- Position of infant. Ventral surface should be to mother's ventral surface, with lower arm, if not swaddled, around mother's thorax. Infant cannot swallow if head has to turn to breast, and grasp of areola will be poor. Infant's head should be in crook of arm and moved toward breast by arm movement.

- Position of mother's hand on breast not in way of proper grasp by infant

- Position of infant's lips on areola about 1–1½ inches (2.5–3.7 cm) from base of nipple

- Lower lip not folded in so that infant does not suck it; lips flanged

- Actual events around presenting breast and assisting infant to latch on

- Response of infant to lower lip stimulus by opening mouth wide

- Motion of masseter muscle during suckling and sounds of swallowing

- Mother comfortable with no breast pain

Lawrence RA, Lawrence RM. Breastfeeding: a guide for the medical profession. 5th ed. St. Louis, Missouri: Mosby, 1999

The most common causative agent in mastitis is *Staphylococcus aureus,* occurring in 40% of cases (54). It is also the most common cause of abscess. Other common organisms in mastitis are *Hemophilus influenzae* and *H parainfluenzae, Escherichia coli, Enterococcus faecalis, Klebsiella pneumoniae, Enterobacter cloacae, Serratia marcescens,* and *Pseudomonas pickettii* (53).

The condition usually can be treated successfully with narrow-spectrum antibiotic therapy (first choice for women who are not allergic is dicloxacillin, 500 mg four times daily), hydration, bedrest, and acetaminophen. The mother should continue to breastfeed or express the milk from both breasts because it is important to empty the affected breast. In some cases, the woman may be advised to discard the milk until she has been treated for 24 hours.

If mastitis is not treated aggressively, an abscess may develop. Treatment is successful in curing mastitis if started early; the most common cause of recurrent mastitis is inadequate treatment. Delayed administration of antibiotics is associated with an increased incidence of breast abscess. Many staphylococcal infections are caused by organisms sensitive to penicillin or a cephalosporin. Dicloxacillin may be started empirically (55). Women who are allergic to penicillin may be given erythromycin. If the infection is caused by resistant, penicillinase-producing staphylococci, an antibiotic such as vancomycin or cefotetan should be given and continued until 2 days after the infection subsides, a minimum of 10–14 days.

Abscess

Abscess is diagnosed by a palpable mass or failure to defervesce within 48–72 hours of antibiotic therapy. Generally, abscesses are treated with incision and drainage. Multiple abscesses may require multiple incisions, with a finger inserted to break down the locules. Breast milk should be discarded for the first 24 hours after surgery, with breastfeeding resuming thereafter if there is no drainage into the breast milk (1). Recently, ultrasonographically guided needle aspiration was shown to be successful in treating abscesses in 18 of 19 women (56).

Working Mothers and Time Away

Over half of mothers are employed outside the home. In some situations, the mother is able to feed her infant at work, but this is not common. Health professionals can help the mother consider the method by which she plans to feed her infant when she returns to work. Employers are increasingly supportive of accommodating the needs of their breastfeeding employees (16). If a woman wants to continue to breastfeed or breast-milk feed, she should plan to pump her breasts to maintain her milk supply and to provide stored milk for the caregiver to feed the infant in her absence. A mother can be reassured that continuing breastfeeding and use of breast milk to whatever degree she finds possible will benefit her infant.

Expressing Milk

Several methods are available to collect milk. Health professionals should ensure that breastfeeding women can successfully express milk by hand. Because use of a breast pump is more efficient, rental or purchase of a pump can be considered. In general, electric pumps are more efficient than hand pumps. Pumping both breasts simultaneously is more effective and saves time.

On occasion, women have to educate employers about the necessity of time and location to pump breasts during the workday. The influence of the physician in creating a better environment should not be underestimated. A physician's letter or phone call to the employer explaining how simple but vital the breastfeeding employee's needs are can be effective.

Storage of Milk

Breast milk can be stored in the refrigerator or on ice in glass or plastic containers. The use of refrigerated milk within 2 days is recommended, which is well before appreciable bacterial growth usually occurs. Breast milk intended for longer storage should be frozen as soon as possible and kept at the lowest and most constant temperatures available; for example, a deep freezer is preferable to a refrigerator freezer with a self-defrost cycle. Milk should be dated and used in date order to avoid loss of beneficial properties over time. Frozen milk can be thawed quickly under running water or gradually in the refrigerator. It should not be left out at room temperature for more than 4–8 hours, exposed to very hot water, or put in the microwave. Once the milk has thawed, it can be kept in the refrigerator for 24 hours (1, 57).

Breastfeeding Expectations in Daily Life

Despite sporadic instances of authorities forbidding breastfeeding in public, there is an increased level of acceptance of breastfeeding nationally. Supportive laws and policies are becoming the trend. Recently, breastfeeding mothers have had increasing success in leading active lives. Couples commonly take their babies with them to meetings, outings, restaurants, and while traveling. Women can be skillful at unobtrusively feeding their babies in public. There are many baby-friendly restaurants that welcome families and have a positive approach to breastfeeding.

Physicians' offices and other health facilities should welcome and encourage breastfeeding by providing educational material and an atmosphere receptive to breastfeeding women. All staff members should be aware of the value and importance of breastfeeding and understand that their contacts with patients can help them decide to breastfeed and encourage them to continue (see the box, "Office Tips").

Formula companies try to attract the interest of pregnant women with gift packs. Care providers should be aware that the giving of gift packs with formula to breastfeeding women is commonly a deterrent to continuation of breastfeeding (58, 59). A professional recommendation of the care and feeding products in the gift pack is implied. Physicians may conclude that noncommercial educational alternatives or gift packs without health-related items are preferable.

Office Tips

- Make ACOG Patient Education Pamphlets and other patient education materials available in waiting and examination rooms.

- Offer a call-in telephone number for advice—yours or another health care resource available in the community or hospital of birth.

- Provide information about and phone numbers of lactation consultants, such as La Leche League, in your community.

- Show videos on breastfeeding; if women's health videos normally play in waiting room, include those on breastfeeding so all patients see them, not just pregnant or breastfeeding patients.

- Provide seating, such as pillows and a rocking chair for women with infants, that keeps breastfeeding in mind.

- Have pumps and an appropriate room for employees and patients. If in a medical office complex with other practices, make its availability known to other employees (they may be your patients) or collaborate in setting up a room elsewhere in the building.

- Identify a staff member interested in being a special resource on breastfeeding in the office and facilitate further training for the individual in order to assist you, other staff, and patients.

- Develop breastfeeding statistics for your practice and encourage staff by showing changes over time on displays in staff areas.

- Ask about hospital policies and practices and offer to help with staff training and patient orientation materials.

- Find out about breastfeeding skills, interests, and services of family physician and pediatric colleagues in the community. Encourage women and parents to choose a supportive caregiver for the infant and meet with him or her during pregnancy.

How Long to Breastfeed

During the first 6 months of life, exclusive breastfeeding is the preferred feeding approach for the healthy infant born at term. It provides optimal nutrients for growth and development of the infant. The ACOG recommends that exclusive breastfeeding be continued until the infant is about 6 months old. A longer breastfeeding experience is, of course, beneficial. The professional objectives are to encourage and enable as many women as possible to breastfeed and to help them continue as long as possible.

Gradual introduction of iron-enriched solid foods in the second half of the first year should complement the breast milk diet (3). The AAP recommends that breastfeeding continue for at least 12 months, and thereafter for as long as is mutually desired (3). "Vitamin D and iron may need to be given before 6 months of age in selected groups of infants (vitamin D for infants whose mothers are vitamin D-deficient or those infants not exposed to adequate sunlight, iron for those who have low iron stores or anemia)" (3).

Weaning

The weaning process should be gradual. Eliminating a feeding every 2–3 days will achieve a comfortable transition for the infant and prevent engorgement in the mother. An infant weaned before 12 months should receive iron-fortified infant formula rather than cows' milk (3). If an infant is less than 9 months, weaning can be accomplished by substituting a bottle or cup for a breastfeeding. If an infant is 9 months or older, he or she may use a cup and substitute other foods for breastfeeding.

Abrupt weaning can be difficult for the mother and the baby. When this is necessary, certain measures can be helpful. The mother should wear a support bra. She does not need to restrict fluids. She may manually express sufficient milk to relieve the engorgement, but not so much that more milk production is stimulated. Cool compresses will reduce engorgement. Hormonal therapy is not recommended.

Weaning creates a hormonal milieu conducive to remineralization of bone and maternal replenishment. This may be a consideration favoring delay of the next pregnancy until the mother has completed breastfeeding.

Breast Cancer Detection

Because of normal changes in the breasts during pregnancy and lactation, cancer detection by palpation becomes more difficult. Breast self-examination is recommended, as it is for all women; however, in general, significant changes are difficult to distinguish from the normal changes in the breast during breastfeeding. Any suspicious lesion should be investigated. Studies indicate there are delays in diagnosis of breast cancer during pregnancy and lactation, including greater intervals between palpation of a lesion and diagnosis. These delays result in an increased risk of metastatic disease at diagnosis and a reduced chance of diagnosis at stage I (60). If a mass or other abnormality is detected during lactation, it should be fully evaluated, including biopsy, if indicated. Breastfeeding can continue during the evaluation. During lactation, mammograms are less reliable because of the associated increase in breast tissue density, which may make the test more difficult to interpret (53).

With these difficulties in detection during pregnancy and lactation as a backdrop, clinical breast examinations of women who may become pregnant are especially important. In addition, increasing age is one of many risk factors for breast cancer. Women are having babies in their late 30s and early 40s, and screening may be difficult during a 1- or 2-year period of pregnancy and lactation. This may influence some women who would not otherwise be candidates for mammography to consider it with their physicians as part of the total clinical evaluation before pregnancy.

Healthy People 2010

The goal set by the U.S. Public Health Service for *Healthy People 2010* is to "increase the proportion of mothers who breastfeed their babies" with specific targets for breastfeeding of 75% in the early postpartum period, 50% at 6 months, and 25% at 12 months (61). These are basically the same levels that were called for in *Healthy People 2000* except that the 12-month target has been added. Significant progress has been made from the rates of the early 90s. By 1998, the most recent year for which data are available, the proportion of mothers choosing to breastfeed reached a high of 64.3% after a concerted effort on the part of health professionals and support people. The highest breastfeeding rates are among college-educated women, those older than the age of 30, those living in the Mountain or Pacific census regions, and those not enrolled in WIC (Special Supplemental Nutrition Program for Women, Infants, and Children). Breastfeeding initiation rates are lowest among black women, women younger than 20 years old, women enrolled in WIC, those who did not complete high school, and those living in the East South Central census region (Mothers' Survey, Ross Products Division, Abbott Laboratories, Inc., Columbus, Ohio).

Some concentrated educational efforts also have had a statistical impact in specific populations (62). Women enrolled in WIC, because of increased breastfeeding support, are among those with the most rapid increases in rates of breastfeeding, although their rates remain well below national averages. Between 1990 and 1998, the most rapidly increasing initiation rate was among black women, the demographic group with the lowest breastfeeding rate (44.9% in-hospital compared with 64.3% nationally) in 1998 despite this increase (Mothers' Survey).

In 1998, the breastfeeding rate at 6 months reached 28.6%, the highest rate in the nearly 30 years such data have been collected. The highest 6-month rates are among mothers with the same demographic and socioeconomic characteristics as those who have the highest in-hospital breastfeeding rates. Younger women, black women, WIC participants, women in the East South Central census region, and women who are employed full time outside the home have the lowest 6-month breastfeeding rates (Mothers' Survey).

With the cooperation of many dedicated caregivers, it appears that the 2010 goals may be achievable. However, even if 75% of women initiate breastfeeding, two thirds of them will need to continue breastfeeding, to reach the proposed 6-month target of 50% of all women breastfeeding. Obstetrician–gynecologists should ensure that women have the correct information to make an informed decision and, together with pediatricians, they should ensure that each woman has the help and support necessary to continue to breastfeed successfully (63). The combined efforts of all health care providers will be necessary to meet this goal.

References

1. Lawrence RA, Lawrence RM. Breastfeeding: a guide for the medical profession. 5th ed. St. Louis, Missouri: Mosby, 1999

2. Institute of Medicine. Subcommittee on Nutrition During Lactation, Committee on Nutritional Status During Pregnancy and Lactation, Food and Nutrition Board. Nutrition during lactation. Washington, DC: National Academy Press, 1991

3. American Academy of Pediatrics, Work Group on Breastfeeding. Breastfeeding and the use of human milk. Pediatrics 1997;100:1035–1039

4. Chua S, Arulkumaran S, Lim I, Selamat N, Ratham SS. Influence of breastfeeding and nipple stimulation on postpartum uterine activity. Br J Obstet Gynaecol 1994;101:804–805

5. Carter CS, Altemus M. Integrative functions of lactational hormones in social behavior and stress management. Ann N Y Acad Sci 1997;807:164–174

6. Rosenblatt KA, Thomas DB. Lactation and the risk of epithelial ovarian cancer. The WHO Collaborative Study of Neoplasia and Steroid Contraceptives. Int J Epidemiol 1993;22:192–197

7. Newcomb PA, Storer BE, Longnecker MP, Mittendorf R, Greenberg ER, Clapp RW, et al. Lactation and a reduced risk of premenopausal breast cancer. N Engl J Med 1994;330:81–87

8. Kennedy KI, Visness CM. Contraceptive efficacy of lactational amenorrhoea. Lancet 1992;339:227–230

9. Gray RH, Campbell OM, Apelo R, Eslami SS, Zacur H, Ramos RM, et al. Risk of ovulation during lactation. Lancet 1990;335:25–29

10. Labbok MH, Colie C. Puerperium and breast-feeding. Curr Opin Obstet Gynecol 1992;4:818–825

11. Melton LJ 3d, Bryant SC, Wahner HW, O'Fallon WM, Malkasian GD, Judd HL, et al. Influence of breastfeeding and other reproductive factors on bone mass later in life. Osteoporos Int 1993;3:76–83

12. Cumming RG, Klineberg RJ. Breastfeeding and other reproductive factors and the risk of hip fractures in elderly women. Int J Epidemiol 1993;22:684–691

13. Dewey KG, Heinig MJ, Nommsen LA. Maternal weight-loss patterns during prolonged lactation. Am J Clin Nutr 1993;58:162–166

14. Ball TM, Wright AL. Health care costs of formula-feeding in the first year of life. Pediatrics 1999;103:870–876

15. Montgomery DL, Splett PL. Economic benefit of breast-feeding infants enrolled in WIC. J Am Diet Assoc 1997; 97:379–385

16. Jacobson M, Kolarek MH, Newton B. Business, babies and the bottom line: corporate innovations and best practices in maternal and child health. Washington, DC: Washington Business Group on Health, 1996

17. Cohen R, Mrtek MB, Mrtek RG. Comparison of maternal absenteeism and infant illness rates among breast-feeding and formula-feeding women in two corporations. Am J Health Promot 1995;10:148–153

18. Lawrence RA. A review of the medical benefits and contraindications to breastfeeding in the United States. Maternal and Child Health Technical Information Bulletin. Arlington, Virginia: National Center for Education in Maternal and Child Health, 1997

19. American Academy of Pediatrics, American College of Obstetricians and Gynecologists. Guidelines for perinatal care. 4th ed. Elk Grove Village, Illinois: AAP; Washington, DC: ACOG, 1997

20. Recommendations for prevention and control of hepatitis C virus (HCV) infection and HCV-related chronic disease. Centers for Disease Control and Prevention. MMWR Morb Mortal Wkly Rep 1998;47(RR-19):1–39

21. American Academy of Pediatrics Committee on Drugs. The transfer of drugs and other chemicals into human milk. Pediatrics 1994;93:137–150

22. Pugin E, Valdes V, Labbok MH, Perez A, Aravena R. Does prenatal breastfeeding skills group education increase the effectiveness of a comprehensive breastfeeding promotion program? J Hum Lact 1996;12(1):15–19

23. Randolph L, Cooper L, Fonseca-Becker F, York M, McIntosh M. Baby friendly hospital initiative feasibility study: final report. Healthy Mothers Healthy Babies National Coalition Expert Work Group. Alexandria, Virginia: HMHB, 1994

24. American College of Obstetricians and Gynecologists. Breast-feeding your baby. ACOG Patient Education Pamphlet AP029. Washington, DC: ACOG, 1997

25. Institute of Medicine. Standing Committee on the Scientific Evaluation of Dietary Reference Intakes, Food and Nutrition Board. Dietary reference intakes for calcium, phosphorus, magnesium, vitamin D, and fluoride. Washington, DC: National Academy Press, 1997

26. Institute of Medicine. Committee on Nutritional Status During Pregnancy and Lactation, Food and Nutrition Board. Nutrition services in perinatal care. 2nd ed. Washington, DC: National Academy Press, 1992

27. Hatcher RA, Trussell J, Stewart F, Cates W Jr, Stewart GK, Guest F, et al. Contraceptive technology. 17th rev. ed. New York: Ardent Media, Inc, 1998

28. Tankeyoon M, Dusitsin N, Chalapati S, Koetsawang S, Saibiang S, Sas M, et al. Effects of hormonal contraceptives on milk volume and infant growth. WHO Special Programme of Research, Development, and Research Training in Human Reproduction, Task Force on Oral Contraceptives. Contraception 1984;30:505–522

29. World Health Organization (WHO) Task Force on Oral Contraceptives. Effects of hormonal contraceptives on milk composition and infant growth. Stud Fam Plann 1988;19:361–369

30. Speroff L, Darney P. A clinical guide for contraception. 2nd ed. Baltimore, Maryland: Williams & Wilkins, 1996

31. Abdulla KA, Elwan SI, Salem HS, Shaaban MM. Effect of early postpartum use of the contraceptive implants, NOR-PLANT, on the serum levels of immunoglobulins of the mothers and their breastfed infants. Contraception 1985; 32:261–266

32. Shaaban MM, Salem HT, Abdullah KA. Influence of levonorgestrel contraceptive implants, NORPLANT, initiated early postpartum upon lactation and infant growth. Contraception 1985;32:623–635

33. World Health Organization. Division of Family and Reproductive Health. Improving access to quality care in family planning: medical eligibility criteria for contraceptive use. Geneva: WHO, 1996

34. Physicians' Desk Reference. 53rd ed. Montvale, New Jersey: Medical Economics, Inc, 1999

35. McCann MF, Moggia AV, Higgins JE, Potts M, Becker C. The effects of a progestin-only oral contraceptive (levonorgestrel 0.03 mg) on breast-feeding. Contraception 1989;40:635–648

36. Moggia AV, Harris GS, Dunson TR, Diaz R, Moggia MS, Ferrer MA, et al. A comparative study of a progestin-only oral contraceptive versus non-hormonal methods in lactating women in Buenos Aires, Argentina. Contraception 1991;44:31–43

37. Guiloff E, Ibarra-Polo A, Zañartu J, Toscanini C, Mischler TW, Gómez-Rogers C. Effect of contraception on lactation. Am J Obstet Gynecol 1974;118:42–45

38. Karim M, Ammar R, el Mahgoub S, el Ganzoury B, Fikri F, Abdou I. Injected progestogen and lactation. BMJ 1971; 1:200–203

39. WHO Task Force on Oral Contraceptives. Contraception during the postpartum period and during lactation: the effects on women's health. Int J Gynaecol Obstet 1987;25 (suppl):13–26

40. Kennedy KI, Rivera R, McNeilly AS. Consensus statement on the use of breastfeeding as a family planning method. Contraception 1989;39:477–496

41. World Health Organization. Task Force on Methods for the Natural Regulation of Fertility. The WHO multinational study of breast-feeding and lactational amenorrhea. III. Pregnancy during breast-feeding. Fertil Steril 1999;72:431–440

42. Perez A, Labbok MH, Queenan JT. Clinical study of the lactational amenorrhoea method for family planning. Lancet 1992;339:968–970

43. Ramos R, Kennedy KI, Visness CM. Effectiveness of lactational amenorrhea in prevention of pregnancy in Manila, the Philippines: non-comparative prospective trial. BMJ 1996;313:909–912

44. Labbok MH, Hight-Laukaran V, Peterson AE, Fletcher V, von Hertzen H, Van Look PF. Multicenter study of the Lactational Amenorrhea Method (LAM): I. Efficacy, duration and implications for clinical application. Contraception 1997;55:327–336

45. Kazi A, Kennedy KI, Visness CM, Khan T. Effectiveness of the lactational amenorrhea method in Pakistan. Fertil Steril 1995;64:717–723

46. Labbok M, Cooney K, Coly S. Guidelines: breastfeeding, family planning, and the lactational amenorrhea method—LAM. Washington, DC: Institute for Reproductive Health, Georgetown University, 1994

47. Campbell OM, Gray RH. Characteristics and determinants of postpartum ovarian function in women in the United States. Am J Obstet Gynecol 1993;169:55–60

48. Howard CR, Howard FM, Lanphear B, deBlieck EA, Eberly S, Lawrence RA. The effects of early pacifier use on breastfeeding duration. Pediatrics 1999;103:E33

49. Schubiger G, Schwarz U, Tonz O. UNICEF/WHO baby-friendly hospital initiative: does the use of bottles and pacifiers in the neonatal nursery prevent successful breastfeeding? Neonatal Study Group. Eur J Pediatr 1997;156:874–877

50. Brent N, Rudy SJ, Redd B, Rudy TE, Roth LA. Sore nipples in breast-feeding women: a clinical trial of wound dressings vs conventional care. Arch Pediatr Adolesc Med 1998;152:1077–1082

51. Stehman FB. Infections and inflammations of the breast. In: Hindle WH, ed. Breast disease for gynecologists. Norwalk, Connecticut: Appleton & Lange, 1990:151

52. Niebyl JR, Spence MR, Parmley TH. Sporadic (nonepidemic) puerperal mastitis. J Reprod Med 1978;20: 97–100

53. Hankins GD, Clark SL, Cunningham FG, Gilstrap LC III. Breast disease during pregnancy and lactation. In: Hankins GD, Clark SL, Cunningham FG, Gilstrap LC III, eds. Operative obstetrics. Norwalk, Connecticut: Appleton & Lange, 1995:667–694

54. Matheson I, Aursnes I, Horgen M, Aabo O, Melby K. Bacteriological findings and clinical symptoms in relation to clinical outcome in puerperal mastitis. Acta Obstet Gynecol Scand 1988;67:723–726

55. Hindle WH. Other benign breast problems. Clin Obstet Gynecol 1994;37:916–924

56. Karstrup S, Solvig J, Nolsoe CP, Nilsson P, Khattar S, Loren I, et al. Acute puerperal breast abscesses: US-guided drainage. Radiology 1993;188:807–809

57. Arnold LDW. Recommendations for collection, storage and handling of a mother's milk for her own infant in the hospital setting. 3rd ed. Denver: Human Milk Banking Association of North America, 1999

58. Howard C, Howard F, Lawrence R, Andresen E, DeBlieck E, Weitzman M. Office prenatal formula advertising and its effect on breast-feeding patterns. Obstet Gynecol 2000;95:296–303

59. Pérez-Escamilla R, Pollitt E, Lönnerdal B, Dewey KG. Infant feeding policies in maternity wards and their effect on breast-feeding success: an analytical overview. Am J Public Health 1994;84:89–97

60. Zemlickis D, Lishner M, Degendorfer P, Panzarella T, Burke B, Sutcliffe SB, et al. Maternal and fetal outcome after breast cancer in pregnancy. Am J Obstet Gynecol 1992;166:781–787

61. Healthy people 2010, volume II. Washington, DC: U.S. Department of Health and Human Services, 2000: 16-46–16-48

62. Ryan AS. The resurgence of breastfeeding in the United States. Pediatrics 1997;99:E12

63. Freed GL, Clark SJ, Cefalo RC, Sorenson JR. Breast-feeding education of obstetrics-gynecology residents and practitioners. Am J Obstet Gynecol 1995;173:1607–1613

Number 218—December 1995
(Replaces #137, December 1989,
and #157, July 1991)

Technical Bulletin

An Educational Aid to Obstetrician–Gynecologists

Dystocia and the Augmentation of Labor

The dramatic increase in the number of cesarean births among U.S. women in the past 25 years is due mainly to the number of repeat cesarean deliveries and cesarean deliveries performed for dystocia. Dystocia is the most common indication for primary cesarean delivery, accounting for more than three times as many primary cesarean births as either "nonreassuring fetal status" or malpresentations (1). Reducing the rate of cesarean deliveries for dystocia would therefore decrease the overall rate of cesarean birth quite substantially.

Central to the management of dystocia is augmentation of labor, that is, correcting ineffective uterine contractions. Despite vast experience with labor augmentation, considerable variability in practice exists regarding criteria for initiating oxytocin and for the oxytocin dosage regimen prescribed. The purpose of this Technical Bulletin is to describe an approach to the diagnosis and management of dystocia, including a range of acceptable methods of augmentation of labor.

Normal Labor

Labor commences when uterine contractions of sufficient frequency, intensity, and duration result in effacement and dilation of the cervix. The first stage of labor has been divided into a latent and an active phase (Fig. 1). During the latent phase, uterine contractions typically are infrequent and irregular and often result in only modest discomfort; however, they do result in gradual effacement and dilation of the cervix. Although the onset of the latent phase of labor is often difficult to define precisely, a prolonged latent phase is considered as one exceeding 20 hours in the nullipara and 14 hours in the multipara (2).

The active phase of labor is characterized both by an increased rate of cervical dilation and, ultimately, by descent of the presenting fetal part. The beginning of the active phase of labor is signaled by an abrupt change in the slope of the curve that results when cervical dilata-

tion is plotted against time; this generally occurs when the cervix reaches 3–4 cm of dilatation. The active phase of labor has been further subdivided into an acceleration phase, a phase of maximum slope, and a deceleration phase.

The second stage of labor is usually brief, averaging 20 minutes for parous women and 50 minutes for nulliparous women. Older studies demonstrated increased perinatal and maternal morbidity associated with a second stage of labor in excess of 2 hours. Consequently, 2 hours became the accepted point at which a prolonged second stage of labor was diagnosed in nulliparous patients, with 3 hours considered abnormal if epidural anesthesia was used. For multiparous patients, the definition of a prolonged second stage of labor was 1 or 2 hours depending on the use of epidural anesthesia. Other data, however, have shown the duration of the second stage of labor to be unrelated to perinatal outcome in the absence of a nonreassuring fetal heart rate pattern or traumatic delivery as long as progress occurs, however slowly (3).

Abnormal Labor

Dystocia is defined as difficult labor or childbirth. It can result from abnormalities primarily involving the cervix and uterus, the fetus, the maternal pelvis, or combinations of these factors.

The term cephalopelvic disproportion has been used to describe a disparity between the size of the maternal pelvis and the fetal head that precludes vaginal delivery. This condition can rarely be diagnosed with certainty; in fact, it is often given as an indication for operative delivery when the true abnormality is malposition of the fetal head (ie, asynclitism or extension of the fetal head that presents bony diameters too great to allow passage through the maternal pelvis). Similarly, the term failure to progress is imprecise and has been used to include lack of progressive cervical dilation or lack of descent of the fetal

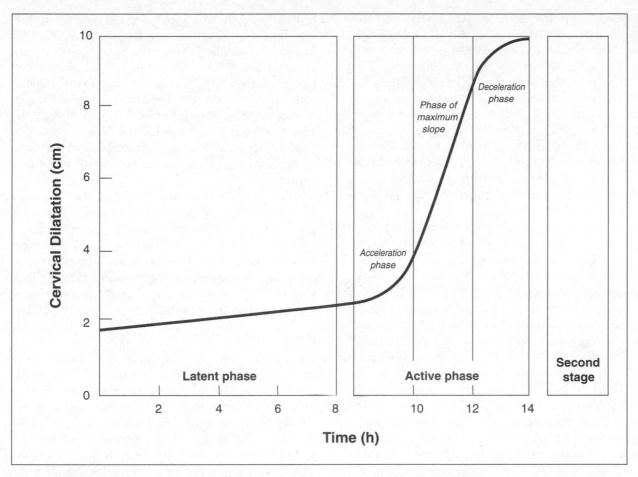

FIG. 1. Composite graph of cervical dilatation for nulliparous women. The first stage is divided into a Flat latent phase and a rapidly progressive active phase. (Modified from Friedman EA. Labor: clinical evaluation and management. 2nd ed. New York: Appleton–Century–Crofts, 1978)

head or both. Often, the diagnosis of failure to progress is made before the active phase of labor and before an adequate trial of labor has been achieved.

A more practical classification is to categorize labor abnormalities as either slower-than-normal (protraction disorders) or complete cessation of progress (arrest disorder) (2). These disorders require the parturient to have entered the active phase of labor. A prolonged latent phase of labor is not indicative of dystocia as this diagnosis cannot be made in the latent phase of labor. Criteria for diagnosis are listed in Table 1.

Abnormalities of the first stage of labor complicate 8–11% of all cephalic deliveries (4). Second-stage abnormalities may be at least as common. Identification of an abnormal labor and institution of the proper management for dystocia require assessment of the *powers* (uterine contractility and expulsive effort), the *passenger* (the fetus), and the *passage* (the pelvis).

Powers

Assessment of powers during the active phase of the first stage of labor involves the investigation of uterine con-

TABLE 1. ABNORMAL LABOR PATTERNS AND DIAGNOSTIC CRITERIA

Labor Pattern	Nulligravida	Multipara
Protraction disorders		
Dilation	<1.2 cm/h	<1.5 cm/h
Descent	<1.0 cm/h	<2.0 cm/h
Arrest disorders		
Dilation	>2 h	>2 h
Descent	>1 h	>1 h

tractility. The minimal contractile pattern of 95% of women in spontaneous labor consists of three to five contractions in a 10-minute window (5). Uterine activity may be quantified by palpation, external tocodynamometry, or internal uterine pressure sensors.

Several methods of quantifying uterine activity with internal monitors have been described (6–10). In a retrospective report of induction of labor with oxytocin, 91% of women achieved at least 200–224 Montevideo units (the strength of contractions in millimeters of mercury multiplied by the frequency per 10 minutes), and 40% achieved at least 300 Montevideo units (11). Accordingly, it has been suggested that before the arrest disorder can be diagnosed in the first stage of labor the following criteria should be met: 1) the latent phase is completed (ie, cervical dilatation is a minimum of 4 cm), and 2) a uterine contraction pattern exceeds 200 Montevideo units for 2 hours without cervical change. However, there is no convincing evidence to demonstrate a reduction in the rate of cesarean deliveries or improvement in perinatal outcome attributable to the use of the sophisticated measurements of uterine activity as compared with external tocodynamometry.

In assessing the optimal uterine contraction pattern, the effects of anesthesia should be considered. One randomized study suggested that epidural bupivacaine analgesia administered before 5 cm of dilatation prolonged the first stage of labor and increased the incidence of cesarean delivery in nulliparous women (12). An increased incidence of malpresentations and operative vaginal delivery has also been reported with the use of epidural anesthesia (13). Two randomized trials compared early versus late administration of epidural anesthesia. The early administration group consisted of nulliparous women who were in spontaneous labor or who were receiving intravenous oxytocin for induction or augmentation of early labor. The late administration group consisted of similar women who received intravenous nalbuphine followed by late administration of epidural analgesia (14, 15). These studies demonstrated that early administration of epidural analgesia (ie, before 3 and 5 cm of cervical dilatation) did not prolong labor or increase the incidence of cesarean delivery.

Passenger

Assessment of the passenger—the fetus—in cephalic presentation consists of estimating fetal weight, position, and attitude and judging their respective roles in dystocia. Estimations of fetal size, even those obtained by ultrasonography, are frequently inaccurate, especially in fetuses weighing more than 4–4.5 kg. Consequently, with cephalic presentation in the first stage of labor, excluding obvious pelvic deformity, the diagnosis of dystocia first requires progression into the active phase of labor and adequate uterine contractile forces.

Although in some cases the relationship between the size of the fetus and the adequacy of the pelvis may appear appropriate on physical examination, poor progress of labor may occur as a result of the influence of excessive degrees of asynclitism or extension of the fetal head, thereby presenting an unusually large diameter to the pelvis. When the presenting part is at +2 station or below in the second stage of labor, abnormalities of fetal head position or asynclitism can be approached either manually or by forceps application and rotation, depending on the experience and skills of the physician. With traction, the vacuum extractor may also result in spontaneous rotation. When a positional dystocia cannot be corrected manually or with instruments or when personnel with such skills are not available, cesarean delivery is appropriate. Such instrument-assisted vaginal deliveries after a prolonged second stage should be preceded by careful assessment, especially in a fetus with suspected macrosomia, because of the increased risk of shoulder dystocia (16, 17).

Fetal anomalies such as hydrocephaly, encephalocele, and soft tissue tumors may obstruct labor. Fetal imaging should be considered when malpresentation or anomalies are suspected based on vaginal or abdominal examination or when the presenting fetal part is persistently high. Further management is dictated by the location and size of the specific anomaly as well as the ultimate prognosis for the fetus.

Passage

Inefficient uterine action should be corrected before attributing dystocia to a pelvic problem. With rare exceptions, the bony pelvis is not the factor that limits vaginal delivery of a fetus in cephalic presentation. Although grossly misshapen pelves may infrequently result from severe malnutrition or trauma, radiographic pelvimetry is of limited value in managing most cephalic presentations. Moreover, X-rays provide no information regarding soft tissue resistance. On the other hand, clinical pelvimetry can be useful to qualitatively identify the general architectural features of the pelvis and assist in the performance of operative vaginal delivery. For example, the deeply engaged head with occiput posterior and a narrow maternal pubic arch may best be delivered without rotation.

Extrinsic Factors

A number of extrinsic factors may influence the likelihood of cesarean birth. Social support and childbirth preparation classes may lead to a reduction in fear, pain, and anxiety (18). Consequently, whether through an effect on uterine activity or other means, operative delivery appears to be decreased. Although some studies suggest that epidural anesthesia may predispose to desultory labor and fetal malpresentations, others have refuted this. Prospective randomized trials of electronic fetal monitoring versus intermittent auscultation have not identified a decline in operative deliveries with electronic monitoring. To the contrary, electronic monitoring has been associated with a comparable or even a higher incidence of abdominal deliveries without improvement in neonatal outcome (19–22). Explanations for the increase in cesarean births include the restrictive postures and activity for parturients and the overinterpretation of fetal heart rate patterns. Many practitioners feel that changes in maternal position may be helpful in aiding descent and rotations in fetuses with occiput transverse or occiput posterior positions (23–25).

Labor Augmentation

Uterine hypocontractility should be augmented only after both the maternal pelvis and fetal presentation have been assessed. Contraindications to augmentation are similar to those for labor induction and may include placenta or vasa previa, umbilical cord presentation, prior classical uterine incision, active genital herpes infection, pelvic structural deformities, or invasive cervical cancer.

Amniotomy has been used for years to augment labor; however, whether amniotomy confers more benefit than harm has been a matter of debate (26). In the latent phase of labor or once the diagnosis of dystocia secondary to uterine hypocontractility is made in the active phase of labor, it may be reasonable to perform amniotomy, initiate oxytocin therapy, or both. A theoretical advantage of amniotomy includes correction of hypocontractility without the need for oxytocin; on the other hand, administration of oxytocin with intact membranes may be protective against infectious morbidity (27). A randomized trial of elective amniotomy on admission to the labor and delivery suite for patients with cervical dilatation of 4–6 cm found that this procedure shortened the active phase of labor and decreased the need for oxytocin augmentation. A greater number of mild and moderate variable decelerations were observed in patients who had amniotomy as compared with control patients, but the incidence of severe abnormal fetal heart rate patterns or operative intervention was not increased (28). In another randomized trial of elective amniotomy in nulliparous patients, rupture of membranes was associated with a shortened duration of labor, but the rate of cesarean delivery was not reduced (29).

Oxytocin

Oxytocin is an octapeptide whose pharmacokinetics are still incompletely understood. The mean in vitro half-life of oxytocin has been reported to be 3–5 minutes (30), and this is consistent with the observation that oxytocin-induced hyperstimulation usually resolves quickly with discontinuation of the oxytocin infusion. Investigators have pointed out that the half-life may vary with the infusion rate (31) and have found that the interval to reach a steady-state concentration of oxytocin in plasma is between 20 and 40 minutes (32).

Clinically, the response to oxytocin depends on pre-existing uterine activity, uterine sensitivity, gestational age, and cervical status. One study identified cervical dilatation, parity, and gestational age as clinical variables related to the maximum dose of oxytocin required for labor augmentation (33). However, despite analysis of nearly 2,000 cases of augmented labors, individual variability precluded the ability to predict confidently the dosage of oxytocin needed to successfully augment a given patient's labor.

The goal of oxytocin administration is to effect uterine activity that is sufficient to produce cervical change and fetal descent while avoiding uterine hyperstimulation and fetal compromise. Minimally effective uterine activity has been defined as three contractions per 10 minutes averaging greater than 25 mm Hg above baseline. However, adequate labor describes a wide range of uterine activity, as previously noted. The amplitude of each contraction may vary from 25 to 75 mm Hg, and contractions may occur for a total of 2–4.5 minutes in every 10-minute window achieving from 95 to 395 Montevideo units. Typically, a goal of a maximum of five contractions in a 10-minute period with resultant cervical dilatation is considered adequate. As a general guideline, hyperstimulation may be defined as a persistent pattern of more than five contractions in 10 minutes, contractions lasting 2 minutes or more, or contractions of normal duration occurring within 1 minute of each other.

Oxytocin should be administered when a patient is progressing slowly through the latent phase of labor or has a protraction or arrest disorder of labor, when a hypotonic uterine contraction pattern is identified, and when there are no maternal or fetal contraindications. A physician or qualified nurse should perform an examination in reasonable proximity to the initiation of oxytocin infusion. Oxytocin is usually diluted (10 units USP) in 1,000 ml of a balanced salt solution administered via a controlled infusion device. To avoid bolus administration, the infusion should be inserted as a secondary line into the main intravenous line close to the venous puncture site. Personnel who are familiar with the effects of oxytocin and who are able to identify both maternal and fetal complications should be in attendance during the administration of oxytocin. The resting uterine tone and frequency and duration of uterine contractions should be monitored appropriately, either by electronic monitoring or palpation. Fetal well-being should be assessed electronically or by auscultation and recorded every 15 minutes during the first stage of labor and every 5 minutes during the second stage of labor. A physician who has privileges to perform cesarean delivery should be readily available.

Adverse effects of oxytocin are primarily dose related. The most common adverse effect is fetal heart rate deceleration associated with uterine hyperstimulation. Decreasing the oxytocin dose rather than stopping it may correct the abnormal pattern yet prevent an unwarranted delay in delivery. Additional measures may include changing the patient's position and administering oxygen or more intravenous fluid. If it is necessary to discontinue oxytocin, it may be restarted once fetal heart rate and uterine activity return to acceptable levels. When restarting the oxytocin, it may be necessary to lower the dose and lengthen the interval between increases. If oxytocin-induced uterine hyperstimulation does not respond to conservative measures, intravenous terbutaline (0.125–0.25 mg) or magnesium sulfate (2–6 g in 10–20% dilution) may be used for uterine relaxation (34, 35).

Numerous protocols for oxytocin augmentation of labor varying with respect to the initial dose, incremental dose increases, and intervals between dose increases have been studied, and a few are listed in Table 2. Low-dose oxytocin regimens were developed based on the knowledge that it takes oxytocin up to 40 minutes to reach steady-state concentration in maternal serum. Low-dose regimens have been reported to be associated with a lower incidence of uterine hyperstimulation. In Ireland and the United States, high-dose protocols have been applied. In the United States, these protocols were in response to rising cesarean delivery rates and have been credited with shortening time in labor and reducing the number of cesarean deliveries for dystocia. Thus, there are advantages and disadvantages of using high- and low-dose oxytocin regimens. Any of the oxytocin regimens outlined in Table 2, as well as many others, are appropriate for labor stimulation provided proper precautions are met (5, 11, 32, 36, 37).

Active Management

A system of labor management for nulliparous women, termed active management of labor, has been developed and practiced in Ireland. The active management of labor has been associated with a cesarean delivery rate of 4.8% (36). This approach is beginning to gain acceptance in the United States. Although many American obstetricians have focused on the use of a high-dose oxytocin regimen as a means to reduce the high cesarean delivery rate, it is important to emphasize that high-dose oxytocin is just one part of the active management of labor. In fact, many women who undergo active management of labor do not even receive oxytocin.

Active management of labor is confined to nulliparous women with singleton, cephalic presentations at term who show no evidence of fetal compromise. Active management of labor, as developed and practiced in Ireland, involves several distinct entities:

■ Patient education

■ Strict criteria for the diagnosis of labor

■ Strict criteria for the determination of abnormal progress in labor

■ High-dose oxytocin infusion

■ The presence of a personal nurse in labor

■ Strict criteria for interpretation of fetal compromise

■ Peer review of operative deliveries

Women are instructed during pregnancy as to the signs and symptoms of labor, and they are encouraged to go to the hospital early in labor. Confirmation of labor depends on the presence of regular, painful uterine contractions and one of the following: passage of a mucus plug, complete effacement, or spontaneous rupture of membranes. Patients not meeting the criteria of labor are not admitted to the labor suite. For patients in labor with intact membranes, artificial rupture of membranes is performed within the first hour of admission. A vaginal examination is performed hourly, and oxytocin infusion is begun if there has not been at least 1 cm of dilation since the last examination. Thus, the active management of labor does not differentiate latent phase and active phase of labor, and the diagnosis and treatment of a protraction disorder requires only 1 hour without progress in labor.

According to the active management protocol, oxytocin infusion is begun with 6 mU/min and increased by 6 mU/min every 15 minutes to a maximum of about 40 mU/min to achieve a labor pattern of no more than seven uterine contractions per 15 minutes (36). As practiced in Ireland, a nurse attends each woman in labor, and the

TABLE 2. LABOR STIMULATION WITH OXYTOCIN: EXAMPLES OF LOW-DOSE AND HIGH-DOSE REGIMENS

Regimen	Starting Dose (mU/min)	Incremental Increase	Dosage Interval (mU/min)	Maximum Dose (min) (mU/min)
Low-Dose	0.5–1	1	30–40	20
	1–2	2	15	40
High-Dose	≈ 6	≈ 6	15	≈ 40
	6	6*, 3, 1	20–40	42

* The incremental increase is reduced to 3 mU/min in presence of hyperstimulation and reduced to 1 mU/min with recurrent hyperstimulation.

Data from references 5, 11, 32, 36, and 37.

fetus is monitored by intermittent auscultation. Electronic monitors are restricted to cases in which fetal blood sampling is deemed necessary, such as when meconium is present or an abnormal heart rate is auscultated. Fetal compromise is mainly diagnosed by fetal scalp pH sampling, not the interpretation of continuous electronic fetal heart rate tracings. Cesarean delivery is performed if delivery has not occurred or is not imminent 12 hours after admission or, rarely, for fetal compromise.

The Irish experience with active management of labor includes a low cesarean delivery rate without untoward events. In the United States, a randomized trial of the active management of labor (that did not include one-on-one nursing care or peer review of operative deliveries but did include electronic fetal monitoring) as compared with a traditional approach to labor management was associated with decreases in cesarean births, length of labor, and infectious morbidity (38). It is important to emphasize that this disciplined approach to labor management involves several distinct facets in addition to the higher doses of oxytocin. It is uncertain which of these is responsible for the low cesarean delivery rate. In a subsequent American investigation, active management of labor did not reduce the rate of cesarean delivery in nulliparous women but was associated with shorter labors and less maternal fever (39). Interestingly, the cesarean delivery rate with the active management of labor in Ireland has doubled, and this change has been attributed to more widespread use of epidural analgesia (40).

Summary

The diagnosis of dystocia is currently a leading indication for cesarean delivery in the United States. Efforts to identify abnormal labor and correct abnormal contraction patterns, fetal malposition, and inadequate expulsive efforts may help eliminate many cesarean deliveries without compromising the outcome for either mother or fetus. Cesarean deliveries for dystocia should not be performed in the latent phase of labor or in the active phase of labor unless adequate uterine activity has been achieved. Cesarean deliveries in the second stage of labor may be reduced if, after reevaluation of the fetus and pelvis, there is potential for correction of uterine forces with oxytocin, correction of malposition, operative vaginal delivery, or safe continued observation. Use of either a low-dose or high-dose oxytocin regimen is appropriate for augmentation of labor. Regardless of the regimen used, oxytocin should be administered by trained personnel capable of responding to complications. A physician who has privileges to perform cesarean delivery should be readily available.

REFERENCES

1. Shiono PH, McNellis D, Rhoads GG. Reasons for the rising cesarean delivery rates: 1978–1984. Obstet Gynecol 1987;69:696–700

2. Friedman EA, ed. Labor: clinical evaluation and management. 2nd ed. New York: Appleton-Century-Crofts, 1978

3. Cohen WR. Influence of the duration of second stage labor on perinatal outcome and puerperal morbidity. Obstet Gynecol 1977;49:266–269

4. Cohen WR, Friedman EA, Acker DB, eds. Management of labor. 2nd ed. Rockville, Maryland: Aspen Publishers, 1988

5. Seitchik J, Castillo M. Oxytocin augmentation of dysfunctional labor. II. Uterine activity data. Am J Obstet Gynecol 1983;145:526–529

6. Caldeyro-Barcia R, Poseiro JJ. Oxytocin and contractility of the pregnant human uterus. Ann N Y Acad Sci 1959;75:813–830

7. El-Sahwi S, Gaafar AA, Toppozada HK. A new unit for evaluation of uterine activity. Am J Obstet Gynecol 1967;98:900–903

8. Hon EH, Paul RH. Quantitation of uterine activity. Obstet Gynecol 1973;42:368–370

9. Steer PJ. The measurement and control of uterine contractions. In: Beard RW, Campbell S, eds. The current status of fetal heart rate monitoring and ultrasound in obstetrics. London: Royal College of Obstetricians and Gynaecologists, 1977:48–70

10. Phillips GF, Calder AA. Units for the evaluation of uterine contractility. Br J Obstet Gynaecol 1987;94:236–241

11. Hauth JC, Hankins GDV, Gilstrap LC III, Strickland DM, Vance P. Uterine contraction pressures with oxytocin induction/augmentation. Obstet Gynecol 1986;68:305–309

12. Thorp JA, Hu DH, Albin RM, McNitt J, Meyer BA, Cohen GR, et al. The effect of intrapartum epidural analgesia on nulliparous labor: A randomized, controlled, prospective trial. Am J Obstet Gynecol 1993;169:851-858

13. Thorp JA, Parisi VM, Boylan PC, Johnston DA. The effect of continuous epidural analgesia on cesarean section for dystocia in nulliparous women. Am J Obstet Gynecol 1989;161:670–675

14. Chestnut DH, Vincent RD Jr, McGrath JM, Choi WW, Bates JN. Does early administration of epidural analgesia affect obstetric outcome in nulliparous women who are receiving intravenous oxytocin? Anesthesiology 1994;80:1193–1200

15. Chestnut DH, McGrath JM, Vincent RD Jr, Penning DH, Choi WW, Bates JN, et al. Does early administration of epidural analgesia affect obstetric outcome in nulliparous women who are in spontaneous labor? Anesthesiology 1994;80:1201–1208

16. Benedetti TJ, Gabbe SG. Shoulder dystocia: a complication of fetal macrosomia and prolonged second stage of labor with midpelvic delivery. Obstet Gynecol 1978;52:526–529

17. American College of Obstetricians and Gynecologists. Fetal macrosomia. ACOG Technical Bulletin 159. Washington, DC: ACOG, 1991

18. Sosa R, Kennell J, Klaus M, Robertson S, Urrutia J. The effect of a supportive companion on perinatal problems, length of labor, and mother–infant interaction. New Engl J Med 1980;303:597–600

19. Kelso IM, Parsons RJ, Lawrence GF, Arora SS, Edmonds DK, Cooke ID. An assessment of continuous fetal heart rate monitoring in labor: a randomized trial. Am J Obstet Gynecol 1978;131:526–532

20. Haverkamp AD, Orleans M, Langendoerfer S, McFee J, Murphy J, Thompson HE. A controlled trial of the differential effects of intrapartum fetal monitoring. Am J Obstet Gynecol 1979;134:399–412

21. Macdonald D, Grant A, Sheriden-Pereira M, Boylan P, Chalmers I. The Dublin randomized controlled trial of intrapartum fetal heart rate monitoring. Am J Obstet Gynecol 1985;152:524–539

22. Luthy DA, Shy KK, van Belle G, Larson EB, Hughes JP, Benedetti TJ, et al. A randomized trial of electronic fetal monitoring in preterm labor. Obstet Gynecol 1987;69:687–695

23. Fenwick L, Simkin P. Maternal positioning to prevent or alleviate dystocia in labor. Clin Obstet Gynecol 1987;30:83–89

24. Johnson N, Johnson VA, Gupta JK. Maternal positions during labor. Obstet Gynecol Surv 1991;46:428–434

25. Gardosi J, Sylvester S, B-Lynch C. Alternative positions in the second stage of labour: a randomized controlled trial. Br J Obstet Gynaecol 1989;96:1290–1296

26. Keirse MJNC. Augmentation of labour. In: Chalmers I, Enkin M, Keirse MJNC, eds. Effective care in pregnancy and childbirth. Vol 2. Childbirth, parts VI–X. Oxford: Oxford University Press, 1989

27. Rouse DJ, McCullough C, Wren AL, Owen J, Hauth JC. Active-phase labor arrest: a randomized trial of chorioamnion management. Obstet Gynecol 1994;83:937–940

28. Garite TJ, Porto M, Carlson NJ, Rumney PJ, Reimbold PA. The influence of elective amniotomy on fetal heart rate patterns and the course of labor in term patients: a randomized study. Am J Obstet Gynecol 1993;168:1827–1832

29. Fraser WD, Marcoux S, Moutquin J-M, Christen A, and the Canadian Early Amniotomy Study Group. Effect of early amniotomy on the risk of dystocia in nulliparous women. N Engl J Med 1993;328:1145–1149

30. Rydén G, Sjöholm I. The metabolism of oxytocin in pregnant and non–pregnant women. Acta Obstet Gynecol Scand 1971;50:37

31. Seitchik J, Amico JA, Castillo M. Oxytocin augmentation of dysfunctional labor. V. An alternative oxytocin regimen. Am J Obstet Gynecol 1985;151:757–761

32. Seitchik J, Amico J, Robinson AG, Castillo M. Oxytocin augmentation of dysfunctional labor. IV. Oxytocin pharmacokinetics. Am J Obstet Gynecol 1984;150:225–228

33. Satin AJ, Leveno KJ, Sherman ML, McIntire DD. Factors affecting the dose response to oxytocin for labor stimulation. Am J Obstet Gynecol 1992;166:1260–1261

34. Reece EA, Chervenak FA, Romero R, Hobbins JC. Magnesium sulfate in the management of acute intrapartum fetal distress. Am J Obstet Gynecol 1984;148:104–107

35. Patriarco MS, Viechnicki BM, Hutchinson TA, Klasko SK, Yeh S-Y. A study on intrauterine fetal resuscitation with terbutaline. Am J Obstet Gynecol 1987;157:384–387

36. O'Driscoll K, Foley M, MacDonald D. Active management of labor as an alternative to cesarean section for dystocia. Obstet Gynecol 1984;63:485–490

37. Satin AJ, Leveno KJ, Sherman ML, Brewster DS, Cunningham FG. High- versus low-dose oxytocin for labor stimulation. Obstet Gynecol 1992;80:111–116

38. López-Zeno JA, Peaceman AM, Adashek JA, Socol ML. A controlled trial of a program for the active management of labor. N Engl J Med 1992;326:450–454

39. Frigoletto FD Jr, Lieberman E, Lang JM, Cohen A, Barss V, Ringer S, et al. A clinical trial of active management of labor. N Engl J Med 1995;333:745–750

40. Boylan P, Robson M, McParland P. Active management of labor 1963–1993. Am J Obstet Gynecol 1993;168:295

This Technical Bulletin was developed under the direction of the Committee on Technical Bulletins of the American College of Obstetricians and Gynecologists as an educational aid to obstetricians and gynecologists. The committee wishes to thank Andrew J. Satin, MD, for his assistance in the development of this bulletin. The opinions expressed in this manuscript are those of the author and not necessarily those of the United States Air Force or the Department of Defense. This Technical Bulletin does not define a standard of care, nor is it intended to dictate an exclusive course of management. It presents recognized methods and techniques of clinical practice for consideration by obstetrician–gynecologists for incorporation into their practices. Variations of practice taking into account the needs of the individual patient, resources, and limitations unique to the institution or type of practice may be appropriate. Requests for authorization to make photocopies should be directed to the Copyright Clearance Center, 222 Rosewood Drive, Danvers, MA 01923; telephone (508) 750-8400.

Number 207—July 1995
(Replaces #132, September 1989)

Technical Bulletin

An Educational Aid to Obstetrician–Gynecologists

Fetal Heart Rate Patterns:
Monitoring, Interpretation, and Management

Intrapartum fetal heart rate (FHR) monitoring can help the physician identify and interpret changes in FHR patterns that may be associated with such fetal conditions as hypoxia, umbilical cord compression, tachycardia, and acidosis. The ability to interpret FHR patterns and understand their correlation with the fetus' condition allows the physician to institute management techniques, including maternal oxygenation, amnioinfusion, and tocolytic therapy. Current data indicate that FHR monitoring is equally effective whether done electronically or by auscultation.

Intrapartum fetal assessment by FHR monitoring is only one parameter of fetal well-being. It involves evaluation of the pattern as well as the rate, but it is not a substitute for informed clinical judgment.

Transient and repetitive episodes of hypoxemia and hypoxia, even at the level of the central nervous system (CNS), are extremely common during normal labor and are generally well tolerated by the fetus. Further, a progressive intrapartum decline in baseline fetal oxygenation and pH is virtually universal; levels of acidemia that would be ominous in an infant or adult are commonly seen in normal newborns. Only when hypoxia and resultant metabolic acidemia reach extreme levels is the fetus at risk for long-term neurologic impairment (1).

For the purposes of this bulletin, the following definitions will be used:

Hypoxemia: Decreased oxygen content in blood

Hypoxia: Decreased level of oxygen in tissue

Acidemia: Increased concentration of hydrogen ions in the blood

Acidosis: Increased concentration of hydrogen ions in tissue

Asphyxia: Hypoxia with metabolic acidosis

Physiologic Basis

The fetus is well adapted to extracting oxygen from the maternal circulation even with the additional stress of normal labor and delivery. However, alterations in the fetoplacental unit resulting from labor or intrapartum complications may subject the fetus to decreased oxygenation, leading to potential damage to any susceptible organ systems or even fetal death.

Oxygen delivery is critically dependent on uterine blood flow. Uterine contractions decrease placental blood flow and result in intermittent episodes of decreased oxygen delivery. Normally, the fetus tolerates contractions without difficulty, but if the frequency, duration, or strength of contractions becomes excessive, fetal hypoxemia may result. Maternal position and the use of conduction anesthesia can also alter uterine blood flow and oxygen delivery during labor. Finally, labor may be complicated by conditions such as preeclampsia, abruptio placentae, chorioamnionitis, and other pathologic situations that can further alter blood flow and oxygen exchange within the placenta.

The umbilical cord is particularly vulnerable during labor because it can prolapse once membranes rupture or become compressed either through cord entanglement or secondary to oligohydramnios. While umbilical cord compression is common during labor, prolonged compression is infrequent but can seriously disrupt oxygen delivery and carbon dioxide removal and lead to acidosis or death.

Some fetuses are unusually susceptible to the effects of intrapartum hypoxemia, such as fetuses with growth retardation and those who are delivered prematurely. In these circumstances, hypoxia tends to progress more rapidly and is more likely to cause or aggravate metabolic acidemia which, in extreme cases, correlates with poor long-term outcome. In severe cases, such hypoxia may lead to death (2, 3).

Experimentally induced hypoxia has been associated with consistent, predictable changes in the FHR (4). The fetal CNS is susceptible to hypoxia. Since the FHR and its alterations are most directly under CNS control through sympathetic and parasympathetic reflexes, alterations in the FHR can be sensitive indicators of fetal hypoxia (4, 5).

In some instances of decreased oxygenation, the pattern of the FHR change can identify the mechanism. Umbilical cord compression or, occasionally, head compression coincides with variable decelerations (6). These are defined as slowing of the FHR with abrupt onset and return and are frequently preceded and followed by small accelerations of the FHR. These decelerations vary in depth, duration, and shape on the tracing but generally coincide in timing and duration with the compression of the cord which, in turn, usually coincides with the timing of the uterine contractions.

Uterine contractions that result in decreases in fetal oxygenation exceeding that usually seen in labor may result in delayed or late decelerations. These are U-shaped decelerations of gradual onset and gradual return that are usually shallow (10–30 beats per minute [bpm]) and that reach their nadir after the peak of the contraction. In milder cases, they can be a reflex and the result of CNS hypoxia; in more severe cases, it has been postulated that they may be the result of direct myocardial depression.

Early decelerations are shallow and symmetrical with a pattern similar to that of late decelerations but reach their nadir at the same time as the peak of the contraction. They are seen in the active phase of labor, albeit infrequently. They are benign changes caused by fetal head compression.

Changes in the baseline FHR may also indicate the response of the fetus to an episode of hypoxia. Two specific parameters of the baseline FHR are important: rate and variability. The FHR at term usually ranges from 120–160 bpm. The initial response of the FHR to intermittent hypoxia is deceleration, but baseline tachycardia may develop if the hypoxia is prolonged and severe. Tachycardia also may be associated with conditions other than hypoxia (such as maternal fever, intraamniotic infection, and congenital heart disease). The presence of variability—or variation of successive beats in the FHR—is a useful indicator of fetal CNS integrity. In the absence of maternal sedation or extreme prematurity, decreasing variability—or flattening of the FHR baseline—may serve as a barometer of the fetal response to hypoxia. Because this is presumed to be a CNS response, in most situations, decelerations of the FHR will precede the loss of variability, indicating the cause of neurologic depres-

sion. Many other factors, such as a fetal sleep cycle or medications, may decrease the activity of the CNS and the variability of the FHR. The development of decreased variability in the absence of decelerations is unlikely to be due to hypoxia (7).

Accelerations are common periodic changes in labor and are nearly always associated with fetal movement. These changes are virtually always reassuring and almost always confirm that the fetus is not acidotic at that time (8).

Guidelines for Performing Fetal Heart Rate Monitoring

The FHR may be evaluated by auscultation or by electronic monitoring. Auscultation is usually performed with a DeLee stethoscope or a Doppler ultrasound device.

Continuous FHR and contraction monitoring may be performed externally or internally. Most external monitors use a Doppler device with computerized logic to interpret and count the Doppler signals. Internal FHR monitoring is accomplished with a fetal electrode, which is a spiral wire placed directly on the fetal scalp or other presenting part. This method records the fetal electrocardiogram. In either case, the FHR is recorded continuously on the upper portion of a paper strip and every beat-to-beat interval is recorded as a rate. The lower portion of the strip records uterine contractions, which also may be monitored externally or internally. The most common paper speed in the United States is 3 cm/min.

Well-controlled studies have shown that intermittent auscultation of the FHR is equivalent to continuous electronic monitoring in assessing fetal condition when performed at specific intervals with a 1:1 nurse-to-patient ratio (9–14).

The intensity of FHR monitoring used during labor should be based on risk factors. When intensified monitoring is undertaken, such as when risk factors are present during labor, the fetal heart rate should be assessed according to the following guidelines:

- During the active phase of the first stage of labor: If auscultation is used the FHR should be evaluated and recorded at least every 15 minutes after a uterine contraction. If continuous electronic monitoring is used, the tracing should be evaluated at least every 15 minutes.

- During the second stage of labor: With auscultation, the FHR should be evaluated and recorded at least every 5 minutes. When electronic monitoring is used, FHR should also be evaluated at least every 5 minutes.

There are no comparative data indicating the optimal frequency at which intermittent auscultation should be performed in the absence of risk factors. One method is to evaluate and record the fetal heart rate at least every 30 minutes in the active phase of the first stage of labor and at least every 15 minutes in the second stage of labor.

With either auscultation or electronic monitoring, documentation of the evaluation is required. Auscultated FHR should be recorded in the chart after each observation. With electronic FHR monitoring, the monitor strip should be carefully labeled and the complete strip is usually retained, as with other medical records. Computer storage of fetal monitor records on devices such as laser discs which do not permit overwriting or revision appears to be a reasonable alternative, as do various methods of microfilm recording.

Documentation may consist of narrative notes or the use of comprehensive flow sheets detailing the periodic assessment. Specific responses to an abnormal FHR pattern such as further diagnostic procedures or therapeutic interventions also should be documented, as should the nature, date, and time of other pertinent events (eg, administration of medication or anesthesia).

Risks and Benefits

Currently, neither the most effective method of FHR monitoring nor the specific frequency or duration of monitoring to ensure optimal perinatal outcome has been identified by a significant body of scientific evidence. With the advent and liberal use of electronic FHR monitoring in the 1970s, there was great hope that intrapartum fetal death and morbidity associated with intrapartum asphyxia could be virtually eliminated. Retrospective studies of electronic FHR monitoring in both high- and low-risk populations were encouraging. A review of 11 studies including almost 40,000 electronically monitored patients and nearly 100,000 historical controls suggested a reduction in the intrapartum fetal death rate from 1.76/1,000 births in controls to 0.54/1,000 births in monitored patients (15). Similar reductions in neonatal death rates were also observed.

Subsequently, seven randomized, controlled trials have compared continuous electronic FHR monitoring with intermittent auscultation in both high- and low-risk patients; no differences in intrapartum fetal death rates were found (9–14, 16). It is significant that the intermittent auscultation groups in all but one of the seven studies had a dedicated 1:1 nurse-to-patient ratio. Nurses auscultated the FHR at least every 15 minutes in the first stage of labor and every 5 minutes in the second stage. If only the results of the studies with this intensity of FHR auscultation are included, the intrapartum fetal death rate in auscultated women was only 0.5/1,000. This rate is nearly identical to those seen with electronic FHR monitoring in both prospective, randomized, controlled trials and retrospective, controlled studies (9–14).

In contrast, the most recently published randomized, controlled trial did show a significant reduction in perinatal deaths due to asphyxia in the electronically monitored group (17). It is not clear why this single study is so discordant with the others, but it does provide some promise that further studies may yet elucidate the real value of electronic FHR monitoring.

Likewise, a substantial body of evidence disproves the hypothesis that electronic fetal monitoring would reduce long-term neurologic impairment and cerebral palsy in newborns so monitored. Electronic FHR monitoring has been no more effective in reducing the rates of low Apgar scores at birth and long-term neurologic morbidity than has intensive intrapartum auscultative monitoring (as described here). One study did suggest that electronic FHR monitoring may decrease the rate of seizures in the newborn (14); however, this reduction did not persist into late childhood. On the other hand, another study showed a significant increase in cerebral palsy among premature infants monitored electronically during labor (18).

Certainly a correlation exists between abnormal FHR patterns and neurologic depression at birth; similarly, neonatal depression is correlated to some extent with adverse long-term neurologic outcome. It must be emphasized, however, that this correlation occurs only with prolonged and severe intrapartum fetal compromise. Indeed, the various methods of intrapartum fetal assessment currently used are not effective in predicting or preventing adverse long-term neurologic outcomes. Management of nonreassuring FHR patterns does not appear to affect the risk of subsequent cerebral palsy (19). This is due to the facts that neurologic abnormalities infrequently result from subtle events occurring during labor and delivery and, conversely, that most hypoxic and asphyxic episodes do not result in irreversible neurologic damage (19, 20).

The primary risk of electronic FHR monitoring is a potential increase in the cesarean delivery rate. This effect has been observed in both retrospective trials and the majority of prospective, randomized, controlled trials. More accurate interpretation of FHR monitoring, the use of fetal scalp blood pH monitoring, and possibly, the use of acoustic or scalp stimulation to elicit FHR accelerations can lead tomoreprecisediagnosis of the condition of the fetus and, by inference, may lead to a decrease in the cesarean delivery rate. The use of amnioinfusion has also been shown in randomized, controlled trials to lower the cesarean delivery rate for those patients with FHR patterns consistent with umbilical cord compression (21–23).

Interpretation and Management

A normal FHR pattern is reassuring and, when obtained by careful auscultation or electronic monitoring, is nearly always associated with a newborn who is vigorous at birth. Therefore, the terminology of *reassuring* implies that in the absence of patterns defined as nonreassuring, the fetus can be assumed—with a great deal of reliability—to have normal oxygen and acid–base status.

Conversely, nonreassuring patterns are quite nonspecific and cannot reliably predict whether a fetus will be well oxygenated, depressed, or acidotic. However, factors other than hypoxia may lead to a nonreassuring FHR. In addition, an abnormal FHR pattern associated with hypoxia may neither depict the severity of hypoxia nor predict how it will progress if labor is allowed to proceed.

The term *fetal distress*, while imprecise and inaccurate, has been applied so commonly to abnormal FHR patterns in labor that it is difficult to abandon. It is more helpful clinically to describe the fetal heart rate patterns in terms of type and severity, and to outline a management plan accordingly.

Interpretation of Fetal Heart Rate Patterns

The initial FHR pattern should be carefully evaluated for the presence or absence of accelerations, decelerations, and abnormalities of the baseline. In one study, the first 30 minutes of electronic FHR monitoring identified about 50% of all fetuses for whom cesarean delivery will be required for a nonreassuring FHR pattern or "fetal distress" (24). While the progression of decelerations will usually explain changes in the baseline later in labor, abnormalities of the baseline on admission, such as fetal tachycardia or loss of variability, are the most difficult to interpret, as data regarding previous changes are lacking.

Periodic changes in FHR are common in labor; they occur in response to contractions or fetal movement and include accelerations and decelerations. Variable decelerations are the most common decelerations seen in labor and indicate umbilical cord compression; they are generally associated with a favorable outcome (25). Only when they become persistent, progressively deeper, and longer lasting are they considered nonreassuring. Although progression is more important than absolute parameters, persisting variable decelerations to less than 70 bpm lasting greater than 60 seconds are generally concerning. In addition to prolonged and deep variable decelerations, those with persistently slow return to baseline are also considered nonreassuring, as these reflect hypoxia persistent beyond the relaxation phase of the contraction (26). The response of the baseline FHR to the variable decelerations and the presence or absence of accelerations are important in formulating a management plan for the patient with significant variable decelerations. When nonreassuring variable decelerations are associated with the development of tachycardia and loss of variability, one begins to see substantial correlation with fetal acidosis.

Late decelerations may be secondary to transient fetal hypoxia in response to the decreased placental perfusion associated with uterine contractions. Occasional or intermittent late decelerations are not uncommon during labor. When late decelerations become persistent (ie, present with most contractions), they are considered nonreassuring, regardless of the depth of the deceleration. Late decelerations caused by reflex—those mediated by the CNS—generally become deeper as the degree of hypoxia becomes more severe. However, as metabolic acidosis develops from tissue hypoxia, late decelerations are believed to be the result of direct myocardial depression, and at this point, the depth of the late deceleration will not indicate the degree of hypoxia (27).

A prolonged deceleration, often incorrectly referred to as bradycardia, is an isolated, abrupt decrease in the FHR to levels below the baseline that lasts at least 60–90 seconds. These changes are always of concern and may be caused by virtually any mechanism that can lead to fetal hypoxia. The severity of the event causing the deceleration is usually reflected in the depth and duration of the deceleration, as well as the degree to which variability is lost during the deceleration. When such a deceleration returns to the baseline, especially with more profound episodes, a transient fetal tachycardia and loss of variability may occur while the fetus is recovering from hypoxia. The degree to which such decelerations are nonreassuring depends on their depth and duration, loss of variability, response of the fetus during the recovery period, and, most importantly, the frequency and progression of recurrence.

A sinusoidal heart rate pattern consists of a regular oscillation of the baseline long-term variability resembling a sine wave. This smooth, undulating pattern, lasting at least 10 minutes, has a relatively fixed period of three to five cycles per minute and an amplitude of 5–15 bpm above and below the baseline. Short-term variability is usually absent. This pattern may be associated with severe chronic, as opposed to acute, fetal anemia. It has also been described following the use of alphaprodine or other medications and, in such circumstances, may not represent fetal compromise. Additionally, severe hypoxia and acidosis occasionally manifest as a sinusoidal FHR; the reason for this is as yet not understood. True sinusoidal patterns are quite rare. Unfortunately, small, frequent accelerations of low amplitude are easy to confuse with sinusoidal patterns. The former are benign and occur more frequently while the latter, if they meet the strict criteria of a sinusoidal FHR, are always nonreassuring (28).

Evaluation and Management of Nonreassuring Patterns

With a persistently nonreassuring FHR pattern in labor, the clinician should approach the evaluation and management in a four-step plan as follows:

1. When possible, determine the etiology of the pattern.
2. Attempt to correct the pattern by specifically correcting the primary problem or by instituting general measures aimed at improving fetal oxygenation and placental perfusion.

3. If attempts to correct the pattern are not successful, fetal scalp blood pH assessment may be considered.

4. Determine whether operative intervention is warranted and, if so, how urgently it is needed.

The search for the cause of the nonreassuring FHR pattern should be directed by the clinician's interpretation of the pattern. If there are late decelerations, then excessive uterine contractions, maternal hypotension, or maternal hypoxemia should be considered. For severe variable or prolonged decelerations, a pelvic examination should be performed immediately to rule out umbilical cord prolapse or rapid descent of the fetal head. If no causes of such decelerations are found, one can usually conclude that umbilical cord compression is responsible.

General measures that may improve fetal oxygenation and placental perfusion include administering maternal oxygen by a tight-fitting face mask, ensuring that the woman is in the lateral recumbent position, discontinuing oxytocin, and, if maternal intravascular volume status is in question, beginning intravenous hydration.

Oxygen Therapy

The arterial Po_2 in the fetus is normally about one fourth of the arterial Po_2 in the mother. Despite this low Po_2, the fetal blood can carry a large amount of oxygen from the placenta because of the high concentration of fetal hemoglobin and its high affinity for oxygen. Oxygen is constantly and rapidly consumed and cannot be stored by the fetus. The fetus is thus dependent upon a constant supply of oxygen; a reduction in this supply cannot be tolerated for more than brief intervals.

When there is evidence of a nonreassuring pattern, administration of supplemental oxygen to the mother is indicated. A significant increase in maternal oxygenation is accomplished with a tight-fitting face mask and an oxygen flow rate of 8–10 L/min. Although such administration results in only a small increase in fetal Po_2, animal studies have suggested that a significant increase in fetal oxygen content may occur. Assuming both adequate placental exchange and delivery of oxygen through unobstructed umbilical cord circulation, the resultant increase in total fetal blood oxygen content is 30–40% or greater in animal studies, depending upon the degree to which the fetal Po_2 has fallen (29). When given for the usual duration of labor, maternal oxygen therapy has no known harmful effects on the fetus.

Maternal Position

Maternal position during labor can affect uterine blood flow and placental perfusion. In the supine position, there is an exaggeration of the lumbar lordotic curvature of the maternal spine facilitating compression of the vena cava and aortoiliac vessels by the gravid uterus. This results in decreased return of blood to the maternal heart leading directly to a fall in cardiac output, blood pressure, and uterine blood flow. In the supine position, aortic compression by the uterus may result in an increase in the incidence of late decelerations and a decrease in fetal scalp pH (30). The lateral recumbent position (either side) is best for maximizing cardiac output and uterine blood flow and is often associated with improvement in the FHR pattern (31). Other maternal positions may accomplish similar uterine displacement.

Epidural Block

Some degree of maternal hypotension is a relatively common complication of epidural block, occurring in 5–25% of procedures (32). Prophylactic intravascular volume expansion with 500–1,000 ml of lactated Ringer's injection is recommended prior to administration of an epidural anesthetic in order to diminish the likelihood of this complication. Treatment with an increase in intravenous fluids, left uterine displacement, or 2.5–10 mg of ephedrine intravenously or intramuscularly is recommended for hypotension occurring with administration of an epidural block. During the period of hypotension, uteroplacental perfusion may be compromised. This may be manifested by fetal tachycardia, prolonged decelerations, decreased beat-to-beat variability, late decelerations, or some combination of these.

The frequency of prolonged decelerations after administration of epidural analgesia has been reported to be 7.9–12.5% (33, 34). Uterine hypertonia with resultant prolonged decelerations has been observed in patients receiving epidural block during labor even in the absence of systemic hypotension (35). Management of epidural-associated decelerations should focus on treatment of the specific cause—either the increased uterine tone or maternal hypotension.

Oxytocin

Careful use of oxytocin is necessary to minimize uterine hyperstimulation and potential maternal and fetal morbidity. If nonreassuring FHR changes occur in patients receiving oxytocin, the infusion should be decreased or discontinued. Restarting the infusion at a lower rate or increasing it in smaller increments may be better tolerated.

Amnioinfusion

Variable decelerations are frequently encountered in both the first and second stages of labor. Those occurring prior to fetal descent at 8–9 cm of dilatation are most frequently seen in patients with oligohydramnios.

In patients with decreased amniotic fluid volume in either preterm or term pregnancies, replacement of amniotic fluid with normal saline infused through a transcervical intrauterine pressure catheter has been reported to decrease both the frequency and severity of variable decelerations (22, 23, 36). Replacement of amniotic fluid may be elected therapeutically in patients with progressive variable decelerations. Although randomized, controlled trials are lacking, it is reasonable to replace amniotic fluid prophylactically at the onset of labor in patients with known oligohydramnios. Studies also have demonstrated that amnioinfusion results in reductions in rates of cesarean delivery for "fetal distress," primarily due to variable decelerations, and fewer low Apgar scores at birth. Acute saline amnioinfusion has been reported to be an effective therapy that relieves most repetitive variable or prolonged intrapartum decelerations and is without apparent maternal or fetal risk (21). Investigators have also reported a decrease in newborn respiratory complications from meconium in patients who receive amnioinfusion. This results presumably from the dilutional effect of amnioinfusion and possibly from prevention of in utero fetal gasping that may occur during episodes of hypoxia caused by umbilical cord compression (37–39).

Generally, two techniques of amnioinfusion have been described: bolus infusion and continuous infusion. Originally described for patients requiring therapeutic amnioinfusion, bolus infusion of up to 800 ml can be administered at a rate of 10–15 ml/min until the decelerations abate; then, an extra 250 ml can be added (21). The infusion can be repeated when there is sudden or large fluid loss due to maternal position change or performance of the Valsalva maneuver or when an abnormal FHR tracing recurs. Ultrasound assessment of amniotic fluid volume can also be used to determine the need for repeat infusion (39).

Alternatively, a continuous infusion may be performed. While this was originally described for prophylactic amnioinfusion (22), it may also be used therapeutically. Continuous amnioinfusion usually begins with a loading dose of 10 ml/min for 1 hour followed by a maintenance dose of 3 ml/min. Use of an infusion pump, although not essential, can more accurately control both the volume and rate of infusion.

Warmed saline has been used in prophylactic amnioinfusions of preterm patients, but warming of infusate has not been shown to be of any specific value in term or preterm patients. For the term patient, there do not appear to be any adverse effects on maternal or newborn temperature or electrolytes when room temperature saline amnioinfusion is administered (36).

Care should be taken to avoid overdistending the uterine cavity. Increased basal uterine tone and sudden deterioration of FHR has been reported with infusion volumes of as little as 250 ml; abnormal FHR secondary to polyhydramnios has been reported following prolonged continuous amnioinfusion (40). With continuous amnioinfusion, intermittent discontinuation to assess basal uterine tone or the use of double-lumen uterine pressure catheters is recommended.

The onset of beneficial effects of amnioinfusion requires at least 20–30 minutes, so care should be taken when performing saline amnioinfusion to avoid delaying surgical intervention if there is no improvement in a significantly abnormal FHR. Preparations for expeditious delivery should be made simultaneously with saline amnioinfusion when worsening variable or prolonged decelerations occur.

Tocolytic Agents

Tocolytic agents are a potentially valuable tool in the management of certain intrapartum events. Changes in the FHR suggesting possible nonreassuring FHR patterns may accompany excessive uterine contractions. If a nonreassuring FHR pattern results from such excessive contractions, specific measures can be taken to decrease uterine activity. If oxytocin is being administered, the dose should be decreased or discontinued. In addition, a tocolytic agent sometimes may be injected. Terbutaline, 0.25 mg subcutaneously or 0.125–0.25 mg intravenously, has been used for this purpose. Both beta agonists and magnesium sulfate have been reported to be of value in rapidly improving fetal condition secondary to uterine relaxation during active labor (41, 42).

Even in the absence of uterine hypertonus, abnormal FHR patterns occurring in response to uterine contractions may be improved and newborn condition benefitted by the administration of tocolytic agents (43). This is especially true when unavoidable delays in effecting operative delivery are encountered.

Certain potential maternal and fetal side effects need to be considered when tocolytic agents are administered for a nonreassuring FHR. Beta agonists elevate both serum glucose levels and maternal and fetal heart rate. However, the direct effect on FHR is minor, and any improvement in FHR from a nonreassuring pattern following acute beta agonist therapy is not due to a direct effect of therapy on the fetal heart, but rather the result of a decrease in the uterine activity. Maternal pulse pressure is widened, and peripheral vascular resistance decreases. Additionally, reinstituting or augmenting uterine activity with oxytocin following acute administration of tocolytic agents may be necessary to reestablish a normal labor pattern. The administration of tocolytic therapy for nonreassuring FHR patterns should not delay necessary interventions.

Management of Persistent Nonreassuring Fetal Heart Rate Patterns

If the FHR pattern remains uncorrected, the decision to intervene depends on the clinician's assessment of the likelihood of severe hypoxia and the possibility of metabolic acidosis, as well as the estimated time to spontaneous delivery. For the fetus with persistent nonreassuring decelerations, normal FHR variability and the absence of tachycardia generally indicate the lack of acidosis. However, variability is difficult to quantify except in the extremes.

Persistent late decelerations or severe variable decelerations associated with the absence of variability are always nonreassuring and generally require prompt intervention unless they spontaneously resolve or can be corrected rapidly with immediate conservative measures (ie, oxygen, hydration, or maternal repositioning). The absence of variability or markedly decreased variability demonstrated on an external monitor is generally reliable. The presence of FHR variability is not confirmatory, however, and, in the presence of nonreassuring decelerations, a fetal electrode should be placed when possible.

The presence of spontaneous accelerations of greater than 15 bpm lasting at least 15 seconds virtually always ensures the absence of fetal acidosis. Fetal scalp stimulation or vibroacoustic stimulation can be used to induce accelerations; these also indicate the absence of acidosis (44, 45). Conversely, there is about a 50% chance of acidosis in the fetus who fails to respond to stimulation in the presence of an otherwise nonreassuring pattern (44, 45). In these fetuses, assessment of scalp blood pH, if available, may be used to clarify the acid–base status. This technique, while occasionally helpful, is used uncommonly in current obstetric practice (46). If the FHR pattern remains worrisome, either induced accelerations or repeat assessment of scalp blood pH is required every 20–30 minutes for continued reassurance. In cases in which the FHR patterns are persistently nonreassuring and acidosis is present or cannot be ruled out, the fetus should be promptly delivered by the most expeditious route, whether abdominal or vaginal.

Summary

Because alterations in fetal oxygenation occur during labor and because many complications can occur during this critical period, some form of FHR evaluation should be provided for all patients. The choice of technique is based on various factors, including the resources available. Nonreassuring FHR patterns are common and quite nonspecific. By understanding the physiologic and pathophysiologic basis of FHR monitoring, as well as its capabilities and limitations, the clinician can reduce the need for interventions.

REFERENCES

1. American College of Obstetricians and Gynecologists. Fetal and neonatal neurologic injury. ACOG Technical Bulletin 163. Washington, DC: ACOG, 1992

2. Low JA, Boston RW, Pancham SR. Fetal asphyxia during the intrapartum period in intrauterine growth-retarded infants. Am J Obstet Gynecol 1972;113:351–357

3. Westgren LMR, Malcus P, Svenningsen NW. Intrauterine asphyxia and long-term outcome in preterm fetuses. Obstet Gynecol 1986;67:512–516

4. Myers RE, Mueller-Huebach E, Adamsons K. Predictability of the state of fetal oxygenation from quantitative analysis of the components of late deceleration. Am J Obstet Gynecol 1973;115:1083–1094

5. Wakatsuki A, Murata Y, Ninomiya Y, Masaoka N, Tyner JG, Kutty KK. Autonomic nervous system regulation of baseline heart rate in the fetal lamb. Am J Obstet Gynecol 1992;167:519–523

6. Ball RH, Parer JT. The physiologic mechanisms of variable decelerations. Am J Obstet Gynecol 1992; 166:1683–1689

7. Davidson SR, Rankin JHG, Martin CB Jr, Reid DL. Fetal heart rate variability and behavioral state: analysis by power spectrum. Am J Obstet Gynecol 1992;167:717–722

8. Clark SL, Gimovsky ML, Miller FC. Fetal heart rate response to scalp blood sampling. Am J Obstet Gynecol 1982;44:706–708

9. Haverkamp AD, Orleans M, Langendoerfer S, McFee J, Murphy J, Thompson HE. A controlled trial of the differential effects of intrapartum fetal monitoring. Am J Obstet Gynecol 1979;134:399–412

10. Haverkamp AD, Thompson HE, Mcfee JG, Cetrulo C. The evaluation of continuous fetal heart rate monitoring in high-risk pregnancy. Am J Obstet Gynecol 1976;125: 310–320

11. Renou P, Chang A, Anderson I, Wood C. Controlled trial of fetal intensive care. Am J Obstet Gynecol 1976;126: 470–476

12. Kelso IM, Parsons RJ, Lawrence GF, Arora SS, Edmonds DK, Cooke ID. An assessment of continuous fetal heart rate monitoring in labor: a randomized trial. Am J Obstet Gynecol 1978;131:526–532

13. Wood C, Renou P, Oats J, Farrell E, Beischer N, Anderson I. A controlled trial of fetal heart rate monitoring in a low-risk obstetric population. Am J Obstet Gynecol 1981;141:527–534

14. MacDonald D, Grant A, Sheridan-Pereira M, Boylan P, Chalmers I. The Dublin randomized controlled trial of intrapartum fetal heart rate monitoring. Am J Obstet Gynecol 1985;152:524–539

15. National Institutes of Health. Antenatal diagnosis. Report of a consensus development conference. NIH publication #79-1973. Bethesda, Maryland: NIH, 1979

16. Leveno KJ, Cunningham FG, Nelson S, Roark M, Williams ML, Guzick D, et al. A prospective comparison of selective and universal electronic fetal monitoring in 34,995 pregnancies. N Engl J Med 1986;315;615–619

17. Vintzileos AM, Antsaklis A, Varvarigos I, Papas C, Sofatzis I, Montgomery JT. A randomized trial of intrapartum electronic fetal heart rate monitoring versus intermittent auscultation. Obstet Gynecol 1993;81:899–907

18. Shy KK, Luthy DA, Bennett FC, Whitfield M, Larson EB, van Belle G, et al. Effects of electronic fetal-heart-rate monitoring, as compared with periodic auscultation, on the neurologic development of premature infants. N Engl J Med 1990;322:588–593

19. Melone PJ, Ernest JM, O'Shea MD Jr, Klinepeter KL. Appropriateness of intrapartum fetal heart rate management and risk of cerebral palsy. Am J Obstet Gynecol 1991;165:272–277

20. Colditz PB, Henderson-Smart DJ. Electronic fetal heart rate monitoring during labour: does it prevent perinatal asphyxia and cerebral palsey? Med J Austr 1990;153:88–90

21. Miyazaki FS, Nevarez F. Saline amnioinfusion for relief of repetitive variable decelerations: a prospective randomized study. Am J Obstet Gynecol 1985;153:301–306

22. Nageotte MP, Freeman RK, Garite TJ, Dorchester W. Prophylactic intrapartum amnioinfusion in patients with preterm premature rupture of membranes. Am J Obstet Gynecol 1985;153:557–562

23. Strong TH Jr, Hetzler G, Sarno AP, Paul RH. Prophylactic intrapartum amnioinfusion: a randomized clinical trial. Am J Obstet Gynecol 1990;162:1370–1375

24. Ingemarsson I, Arulkumaran S, Ingemarsson E, Tambyraja RL, Ratnam SS. Admission test: a screening test for fetal distress in labor. Obstet Gynecol 1986;68: 800–806

25. Bissonnette JM. Relationship between continuous fetal heart rate patterns and Apgar score in the newborn. Br J Obstet Gynaecol 1975;82:24–28

26. Freeman RK, Garite TJ, Nageotte MP. Fetal heart rate monitoring. 2nd ed. Baltimore, Maryland: Williams and Wilkins, 1991

27. Martin CB Jr, de Haan J, van der Wildt B, Jongsma HW, Dieleman A, Arts THM. Mechanisms of late decelerations in the fetal heart rate. A study with autonomic blocking agents in fetal lambs. Eur J Obstet Gynecol Reprod Biol 1979;9:361–373

28. Modanlou HD, Freeman RK. Sinusoidal fetal heart rate pattern: its definition and clinical significance. Am J Obstet Gynecol 1982;142:1033–1038

29. Meschia G. Placental respiratory gas exchange and fetal oxygenation. In: Creasy RK, Resnik R, eds. Maternal fetal medicine: principles and practice. Philadelphia, Pennsylvania: WB Saunders, 1989:303–313

30. Abitbol MM. Supine position in labor and associated fetal heart rate changes. Obstet Gynecol 1985;65:481–486

31. Clark SL, Cotton DB, Pivarnik JM, Lee W, Hankins GDV, Benedetti TJ, et al. Position change and central hemodynamic profile during normal third-trimester pregnancy and post partum. Am J Obstet Gynecol 1991;164:883–887

32. Hood DD. Obstetric anesthesia: complications and problems. In: Problems in anesthesia. Philadelphia, Pennsylvania: JB Lippincott Co, 1989:1–17

33. Vroman S, Sian AYL, Thiery M, de Hemptinne D, Vanderheyden K, Van Kets H, et al. Elective induction of labor conducted under lumbar epidural block. I. Labor induction by amniotomy and intravenous oxytocin. Eur J Obstet Gynecol Reprod Biol 1977;7:159–180

34. Abboud TK, Afrasiabi A, Sarkis F, Daftarian F, Nagappala S, Noueihed R, et al. Continuous infusion epidural analgesia in parturients receiving bupivacaine, chloroprocaine, or lidocaine—maternal, fetal, and neonatal effects. Anesth Analg 1984;63:421–428

35. Steiger RM, Nageotte MP. Effect of uterine contractility and maternal hypotension on prolonged decelerations after bupivacaine epidural anesthesia. Am J Obstet Gynecol 1990;163:808–812

36. Nageotte MP, Bertucci L, Towers CV, Lagrew DL, Modanlou H. Prophylactic amnioinfusion in pregnancies complicated by oligohydramnios: a prospective study. Obstet Gynecol 1991;77:677–680

37. Sadovsky Y, Amon E, Bade ME, Petrie RH. Prophylactic amnioinfusion during labor complicated by meconium: a preliminary report. Am J Obstet Gynecol 1989;161:613–617

38. Wenstrom KD, Parsons MT. The prevention of meconium aspiration in labor using amnioinfusion. Obstet Gynecol 1989;73:647–651

39. Macri CJ, Schrimmer DB, Leung A, Greenspoon JS, Paul RH. Prophylactic amnioinfusion improves outcome of pregnancy complicated by thick meconium and oligohydramnios. Am J Obstet Gynecol 1992;167:117–121

40. Tabor BL, Maier JA. Polyhydramnios and elevated intrauterine pressure during amnioinfusion. Am J Obstet Gynecol 1987;156:130–131

41. Arias F. Intrauterine resuscitation with terbutaline: a method for the management of acute intrapartum fetal distress. Am J Obstet Gynecol 1978;131:39–43

42. Reece EA, Chervenak FA, Romero R, Hobbins JC. Magnesium sulfate in the management of acute intrapartum fetal distress. Am J Obstet Gynecol 1984;148:104–107

43. Tejani NA, Verma UL, Chatterjee S, Mittelmann S. Terbutaline in the management of acute intrapartum acidosis. J Reprod Med 1983;28:857–861

44. Clark SL, Gimovsky ML, Miller FC. The scalp stimulation test: a clinical alternative to fetal scalp blood sampling. Am J Obstet Gynecol 1984;148:274–277

45. Smith CV, Nguyen HN, Phelan JP, Paul RH. Intrapartum assessment of fetal well-being: a comparison of fetal acoustic stimulation with acid–base determinations. Am J Obstet Gynecol 1986;155:726–728

46. Clark SL, Paul RH. Intrapartum fetal surveillance: the role of fetal scalp blood sampling. Am J Obstet Gynecol 1985;153:717–720

This Technical Bulletin was developed under the direction of the Committee on Technical Bulletins of the American College of Obstetricians and Gynecologists as an educational aid to obstetricians and gynecologists. The committee wishes to thank Thomas J. Garite, MD, and Michael P. Nageotte, MD, for their assistance in the development of this bulletin. This Technical Bulletin does not define a standard of care, nor is it intended to dictate an exclusive course of management. It presents recognized methods and techniques of clinical practice for consideration by obstetrician–gynecologists for incorporation into their practices. Variations of practice taking into account the needs of the individual patient, resources, and limitations unique to the institution or type of practice may be appropriate. Requests for authorization to make photocopies should be directed to the Copyright Clearance Center, 222 Rosewood Drive, Danvers, MA 01923; telephone (508) 750-8400.

Number 210—August 1995

Technical Bulletin

An Educational Aid to Obstetrician–Gynecologists

Health Maintenance for Perimenopausal Women

Since 1960, the U.S. population has been increasing in age. As growing numbers of women of the post–World War II, baby-boom generation approach menopause, they will be faced with the transition from reproductive to postreproductive status. Attention to the special needs of these women can help prepare them for this transition and promote early interventions to improve health and well-being in the years to follow.

Transition

Menopause is the permanent cessation of menstruation following the decline of ovarian estrogen production. Perimenopause, or the climacteric, is the period extending from immediately before to after the menopause (generally around 45–55 years of age). For most women, this transition lasts approximately 4 years. This period is marked by altered ovarian function.

Prior to menopause when women are in their 40s, menstrual cycle length may begin to increase or decrease, and episodes of anovulation become more prevalent. Menstrual cycle changes during this time are associated with fluctuations in circulating follicle-stimulating hormone (FSH) levels which may be elevated or normal. Although measurement of circulating levels of FSH can be used to identify whether a woman is postmenopausal, it is not useful for monitoring the status of women taking postmenopausal hormone therapy because of failure of exogenous estrogen to suppress FSH.

Because ovarian function waxes and wanes during the perimenopausal years, contraception is necessary until the woman is amenorrheic for one year. Measurement of early follicular phase FSH may be clinically useful as a predictor of fecundity in perimenopausal women attempting to conceive. In women who have had a hys-

terectomy with their ovaries retained, serum FSH measurement can help to determine their menopausal status.

Screening and Counseling

The perimenopausal period offers an opportunity for counseling about factors that affect a woman's health. Physicians should develop preventive health programs based on each patient's needs and circumstances. The goal of a preventive health program is identification of an unhealthy life style that would benefit from intervention. Patients should undergo a complete medical history, physical examination, and selected laboratory studies and immunizations yearly or as appropriate based on risk factors (see the box).

Screening for Medical Disorders

Certain medical conditions are more prevalent in the perimenopausal woman. Routine assessments for these conditions improve the likelihood of early detection. Once identified, several of these conditions lend themselves to management by the obstetrician–gynecologist. Others may require referral.

Thyroid Disease

Thyroid disorders are common in women, and the incidence of hypothyroidism increases after age 65. Symptomatic women who have a strong family history of thyroid disorders or who have autoimmune dysfunction should be assessed by use of sensitive thyroid-stimulating hormone assays. Thyroid function tests can be misleading in women with systemic illness or those taking certain drugs. In healthy women, menopause and aging do not alter full thyroid hormone concentrations. Women being treated with thyroid replacement should also be moni-

---

Perimenopausal Health Maintenance

As a woman approaches age 45, her annual examination can be used as an opportunity for a perimenopausal assessment covering the following components, which relate to both menopause and routine health maintenance.

History
- Family history
  - Cardiovascular disease
  - Cancer
  - Diabetes
  - Osteoporosis
  - Other (Alzheimer disease, mental illness, obesity)
- Personal history
  - Health status (including symptoms of menopause)
  - Dietary/nutritional assessment
  - Physical activity
  - Substance use/abuse
  - Abuse or family violence
  - Sexual practices
  - Mental attitude (depression, anxiety, stress)
  - Psychosocial factors (marital status, work, family dynamics)

Physical Examination
- Height
- Weight
- Blood pressure
- Oral cavity
- Neck: adenopathy, thyroid gland
- Breasts, axillae
- Abdomen
- Pelvic and rectovaginal examination
- Skin

Laboratory Tests
- Pap test (physician discretion after three consecutive normal tests if patient is considered to be low risk)
- Mammography (every 1–2 years until age 50; yearly beginning at age 50)
- Cholesterol (every 5 years)
- Fecal occult blood test
- Sigmoidoscopy (every 3–5 years after age 50)
- Other tests (based on risk factors)

Immunizations
- Tetanus–diphtheria booster every 10 years
- Influenza vaccine (yearly beginning at age 55)
- Other (based on risk factors)

Education and Counseling
- Sexuality
  - High-risk behaviors
  - Contraceptive options
  - Sexually transmitted disease
  - Sexual function
- Fitness
  - Hygiene (including dental care)
  - Diet and weight control
  - Exercise
- Psychosocial
  - Family relationships
  - Domestic violence
  - Job/work satisfaction
  - Life style/stress
  - Sleep disorders
- Cardiovascular risk factors
  - Hypertension
  - Hyperlipidemia
  - Obesity/diabetes mellitus
- Health/Risk behaviors
  - Injury prevention
  - Breast self-examination
  - Exposure to ultraviolet rays
  - Suicide prevention
  - Substance abuse
- Hormone therapy
  - Risks versus benefits
  - Side effects
  - Therapeutic regimens

---

tored annually by thyroid-stimulating hormone assay; overtreatment is associated with osteoporosis.

Diabetes Mellitus

Fasting plasma glucose measurements are recommended every 3–5 years for women with one or more of the following risk factors:

- Family history of diabetes in parents or siblings
- Obesity (body weight greater than 120% of ideal)
- History of gestational diabetes

Diabetes can be diagnosed by assessment of fasting blood glucose levels or random blood glucose levels or use of a 2-hour oral glucose tolerance test. Screening should consist of fasting serum or plasma glucose measurement.

Concentrations of less than 115 mg/dl are normal. Concentrations of at least 140 mg/dl are consistent with diabetes and should be repeated to confirm the diagnosis. Concentrations of 115–139 mg/dl are abnormal, but they are not diagnostic for diabetes.

When diabetes has been diagnosed, it can be categorized as Type I (insulin dependent) or Type II (non-insulin dependent). If diabetes is overt and symptomatic, immediate drug therapy may be necessary. If it is not, dietary control, weight loss, and active exercise programs should be instituted and the patient educated about her disease. The patient's condition should be assessed to detect complications of the disease, such as organ damage from vascular changes. The goal of management is to ensure adequate glucose control.

Nutritional control for secondary and primary prevention (in the presence of insulin resistance with or without carbohydrate intolerance) is an integral component of care for women with overt or potential diabetes. Patients should be educated about the importance of fiber and limiting saturated fats and refined sugars. Women with overt diabetes need the services of a knowledgeable dietician with experience in diabetic diet education.

Insulin resistance can be a factor in diabetes and hypertension and is often linked to obesity. Regular physical exercise promotes weight loss and can improve insulin sensitivity and dyslipidemia in those people who are in high risk groups for cardiovascular and microvascular disease (1).

Breast Cancer

One of every nine American women who lives to 85 years of age will develop breast cancer. The incidence has increased over the past two decades but in 1987 reached a plateau at about 182,000 new cases per year. Mortality rates have remained constant at about 46,000 deaths per year. However, in view of an increasing incidence, a steady mortality rate may indicate an improvement in early diagnosis or therapy. The 5-year survival rate for women with localized breast cancer has risen from 78% in the 1940s to 93% in 1993. This is attributed to earlier diagnosis as a result of greater use of screening mammography. The breast is the leading site of cancer in women (32% of all cancers) and is the second leading cause of death from cancer in women, exceeded only by lung cancer.

Randomized, controlled trials have clearly demonstrated a decreased death rate from breast cancer in women who were offered mammography between the ages of 50 and 69 years old. After a review of the evidence showing the benefit of screening by mammography in women between 40 and 49 years old, the National Cancer Institute withdrew its recommendation for screening these women. It is ACOG's conclusion however, that the data are limited; thus ACOG guidelines continue to recommend offering screening by mammography every 1–2 years to women 40–49 years of age and annually to women over 50 years of age (2).

All women should have a thorough annual breast examination and perform monthly breast self-examination. Because of breast changes in response to the hormonal sequence of a normal menstrual cycle, self-breast examination is most effective during the follicular phase of the cycle.

Hypertension

Hypertension is the most common chronic disease in older women and a significant risk factor for stroke, congestive heart disease, and renal disease. Beginning at age 50, hypertension is more common in women than in men and more common in African Americans than in other racial groups.

The history and physical examination provide an opportunity to seek information regarding the following risk factors:

- Previous history of hypertension
- Previous history of antihypertensive treatment
- Family history of cardiovascular disease, especially with early age of onset
- Dietary history, especially excessive sodium or alcohol intake
- Relevant medications, such as glucocorticosteroids, sympathomimetic amines, or nasal decongestants
- Medical information of specific interest: headaches, coronary artery disease, chest pain, prior stroke, renal disease
- Other cardiovascular risk factors: smoking, high cholesterol or problematic lipid profile, obesity, diabetes mellitus, stress

The blood pressure classification for adults established in 1993 is shown in Table 1. A single elevated diastolic pressure less than 100 mm Hg should not be treated but should be rechecked within 2 months. When the diastolic pressure is 100 mm Hg or greater, the patient should be evaluated. A diastolic pressure greater than 120 mm Hg requires immediate attention. Malignant hypertension is a diastolic pressure greater than 140 mm Hg with papilledema. Evidence suggests that patients with a systolic blood pressure greater than 160 mm Hg will benefit from treatment (3).

The initial assessment of patients with hypertension should include at least the following laboratory evaluation: urinalysis; determination of levels of hemoglobin or hematocrit, creatinine, potassium, and fasting glucose; lipid profile; and electrocardiography. The first line of treatment for hypertension is dietary and life style changes. Weight loss, control of sodium and alcohol intake, exercise, stress management, and smoking cessation are all important treatment interventions for hypertension. If after 3 months these efforts have failed, pharmacologic

TABLE 1. CLASSIFICATION OF BLOOD PRESSURE FOR ADULTS AGED 18 YEARS AND OLDER

Category	Systolic (mm Hg)	Diastolic (mm Hg)
Normal	<130	<85
High normal	130–139	85–89
Hypertension		
Stage 1 (mild)	140–159	90–99
Stage 2 (moderate)	160–179	100–109
Stage 3 (severe)	180–209	110–119
Stage 4 (very severe)	210 or greater	120 or greater

Joint National Committee on the Detection, Evaluation, and Treatment of High Blood Pressure. The fifth report of the Joint National Committee on the Detection, Evaluation, and Treatment of High Blood Pressure (JNC V). Arch Intern Med 1993;153:161

therapy should be considered. Patients who respond to nonpharmacologic treatment require close monitoring, however, because a significant percentage will progress to higher levels of blood pressure and require pharmacologic therapy.

Women with diastolic blood pressures greater than 100 mm Hg should be treated with pharmacologic methods if nonpharmacologic methods fail to reduce blood pressures. Women with diastolic blood pressures of 90–100 mm Hg should be treated with medication if they are African American, have a systolic blood pressure greater than 160 mm Hg, or have other specific cardiovascular risk factors.

A Healthy Life Style

Maintaining a healthy life style is beneficial to women of all ages. For perimenopausal women, a healthy life style can also reduce the risk of several disorders prevalent in this age group. By making certain life style changes, these women can improve both their overall health and their quality of life.

Smoking

Certain health conditions that are more prevalent in perimenopausal women have been linked to smoking. The relationship of cigarette smoking to coronary heart disease, chronic obstructive pulmonary disease, lung cancer, and a number of other chronic diseases is well established. Smoking has a greater adverse effect on women when compared with men (4). Women who smoke only one to four cigarettes per day have a 2.5-fold increased risk of fatal coronary heart disease (5). In 1994, the incidence of lung cancer among women was estimated to be 72,000 cases, with an estimated 59,000 deaths (6).

Smokers should be repeatedly counseled to quit smoking, and follow-up visits just for this purpose are worthwhile. Approximately 65% of those who stop smoking relapse within 3 months, and another 10% resume smoking between 3 and 6 months, whereas only 3% relapse from 6 to 12 months (7). Nicotine replacement therapy, in the form of chewing gum or a transdermal patch, has been demonstrated to increase the effectiveness of smoking cessation programs when evaluated 6 months after the intervention. One study has demonstrated that smoking cessation at any age improves the health of the lungs, regardless of how long one has smoked (8).

Exercise

Although data in women are scarce, lack of physical activity is recognized as a risk factor for coronary artery disease in men. There is a significant positive relationship between levels of high-density lipoprotein (HDL) cholesterol and physical activity in postmenopausal women. Furthermore, in women with low levels of HDL cholesterol, aerobic exercise provides a greater increase in HDL cholesterol than it does in women with normal to high levels.

Vigorous exercise at least three times a week for 20 minutes should be strongly encouraged as part of an overall health plan for both cardiovascular health promotion and protection against osteoporosis. Cardiovascular training can be accomplished with aerobic exercise that elevates the heart rate into the patient's target heart rate. If this exercise is not weight bearing, strength training should be added two times per week. Weight-bearing physical activity, as little as 30 minutes a day for 3 days a week, may increase the mineral content of bone in older women. The exercise need not be extreme; walking 1.5 miles and performing ordinary calisthenics are sufficient to increase mineral content. More detailed information on exercise recommendations for women has been published elsewhere (9).

Alcohol Abuse

It is estimated that alcoholism occurs in up to 10% of older women, contributing significantly to functional disability (10). However, alcohol abuse is often overlooked and misdiagnosed. Women are at high risk for alcoholism if there is a family history of alcoholism or personal habitual alcohol use. The CAGE questionnaire may be helpful in detecting problem drinking (see the box).

Weight Control, Nutrition, and Diet

Weight control, exercise, and nutrition are keystones for good health, and there are some specific issues for perimenopausal women. Women in this age group commonly report weight gain, and this observation is validated by epidemiologic studies. Such studies indicate that 38% of women aged 40–49 and 52% of women aged 50–59 are overweight (11).

The traditionally recommended method for weight control is simple caloric reduction, although there is ample evidence that caloric reduction alone is ineffective for

---

The CAGE Questions

C   Have you ever felt you ought to **C**ut down on your drinking?

A   Have people **A**nnoyed you by criticizing your drinking?

G   Have you ever felt bad or **G**uilty about your drinking?

E   Have you ever had a drink first thing in the morning to steady your nerves or get rid of a hangover (**E**ye opener)?

Ewing JA. Detecting alcoholism: the CAGE questionnaire. JAMA 1984;252:1907; Copyright 1984, American Medical Association

---

maintaining long-term weight reduction. Of particular concern are regimens requiring marked caloric restriction. Efforts at weight reduction are optimized when dietary changes are combined with moderate cardiovascular exercise (30 minutes, three times per week) (12) and strength training (two sessions per week). Life style regimens that are most effective in reducing bone loss include weight-bearing cardiovascular exercise (13, 14), strength training, hormone therapy, and calcium supplementation. The best results occur in patients using more than one regimen (15–18). Use of hormone therapy, however, is the most important factor in reducing bone loss.

Strength training is assuming increasing importance in providing health benefits, particularly for perimenopausal women (19). In addition to conferring strength (20) and bone protection, strength training increases muscle mass, which in turn increases the metabolic rate and enhances weight control efforts (21, 22).

Good nutrition is an essential part of preventive health care. All evidence indicates that diet influences the risk of several major chronic diseases, especially atherosclerotic cardiovascular disease and hypertension. Diet may also play a positive role in preventing some cancers. Other health problems influenced by diet include dental caries, chronic liver disease, diabetes mellitus, and obesity.

While many clinicians do not routinely review dietary histories, it is important to assess calcium supplementation. In the absence of dietary calcium intake, 1,200–1,600 mg of elemental calcium should be ingested. Calcium carbonate has 40% elemental calcium; lactate, 13%; and gluconate, 9%. Although lactose intolerance increases with age, many patients consume some calcium in their diet. Dairy sources are calcium rich, but other foods, such as fortified orange juice, may also be excellent sources.

Even patients who appear well nourished may be malnourished. A 24-hour diet and fluid recall history is helpful to assess a patient's dietary habits.

Domestic Violence

Domestic violence includes both physical and mental abuse. It occurs in all segments of society. Obstetrician–gynecologists can play a vital role in identifying women who are the victims of abuse and offering them appropriate care.

Recognition of this problem requires a high index of suspicion; direct questioning is appropriate and recommended. Questions such as "Has anyone at home hit you or tried to injure you?" and "Have you ever been physically abused, either recently or in the past?" are appropriate ways in which to raise the subject. Physical examination may show evidence of injury, either recent or remote. Any such injuries should be noted in the medical record, and the patient should be asked how they occurred.

In addition to treating the patient's injuries, the physician should assess her emotional status. The physician should provide counseling and referral to legal and social resources and psychologic therapy.

Emotional Problems

Mood disorders, particularly depression, are among the most common psychiatric illnesses in women. Although depression can occur at any age, in 50% of patients the onset is between 20 and 50 years of age, with the mean being about 40 years. Depression can be overdiagnosed in women who have experienced grief reactions or who are undergoing situational stress (23).

Epidemiologic studies of the prevalence of depression in women have dispelled the notion of an increase in depression at the time of menopause or so-called *involutional melancholia*. The complex experience of menopause and midlife adjustment disorders must be considered within social, cultural, and psychologic contexts. Aging involves additional and unexpected losses of family and friends, physical changes, and concerns about premature aging or a loss of sexuality and femininity. The successful adjustment to living with chronic illness, uncertainties about developing cancer, or aging in general depends on the woman's past history of depression, her emotional resources, and the extended family and community support available to her. The obstetrician–gynecologist should be cognizant of the various factors that influence the presentation, diagnosis, and treatment of depression in women and refer patients for treatment as needed.

Reproductive Concerns

Perimenopausal women have reproductive concerns relating to fertility and infertility. Contraception may involve some adjustment in response to changing hormone levels. Those women who desire pregnancy may require special care.

Contraception

Prevention of unwanted pregnancy assumes increasing importance during the perimenopausal years. About 75% of pregnancies in women over age 40 are unintended (24). It may be difficult to know when it is safe to change from oral contraception to postmenopausal hormone treatment. Contraception can be discontinued when the FSH level is greater than 30 IU/L (measured at the end of the pill-free week in women on estrogen/progestin oral contraceptives).

Except for women who smoke, there is no limitation of contraceptive choice. The health risks and benefits of the contraceptive method should be discussed. Combination oral contraceptive pills are safe for women over 40 who don't smoke. Progestin-only methods, including the minipill, injectables (depot medroxyprogesterone acetate), or implants (Norplant), are excellent alternatives. The intrauterine device (IUD) is also an option, particularly the copper IUD, which is now approved for a 10-year duration of use. The progesterone IUD has an added benefit of reduced menstrual bleeding but requires replacement every year. Barrier methods that use nonoxynol-9 appear effective in reducing pregnancy and may reduce some sexually transmitted diseases as well.

Pregnancy

The proportion of births among women aged 35–49 is predicted to rise from 5% in 1982 to 8.6% in 2000, an increase of about 72% (25). Women considering pregnancy as they approach their perimenopausal years are faced with two concerns: the difficulty of achieving pregnancy later in life and the complications associated with being pregnant later in life.

There is a decline in fecundity with advancing age. A major contributor to the decline in delivery rates associated with increasing age is the risk of spontaneous abortion. The frequency of both euploid (normal) and aneuploid (abnormal) abortuses increases with maternal age. Clinically recognized abortion occurs in only 12% of women under age 20, but increases to at least 26% in women over age 40.

Traditionally, increased maternal age has been associated with an increased risk of obstetric complications. Statistics indicate that older women have a higher mortality rate with pregnancy. There is reason to believe, however, that the obstetric risks associated with advanced age can be minimized by attention to screening and modern obstetric care.

Hypoestrogenic Changes

Data from longitudinal studies uniformly indicate that approximately 80% of women experience menopause without significant difficulty as a normal physiologic event in their lives (26). Most women do experience some symptoms related to menopause, although the causal relation to estrogen deficiency is uncertain. The vasomotor flush is experienced to some degree by most menopausal women (26–28). Frequent problems include fatigue, nervousness, headaches, insomnia, depression, irritability, joint and muscle pain, dizziness, and palpitations. Emotional stability during the perimenopausal period can be disrupted by poor sleep patterns. The nature and severity of these symptoms vary considerably, so it can be difficult to differentiate among social, cultural, and biologic factors. Certain physiologic effects of estrogen deficiency can lead to long-term health problems such as osteoporosis and coronary heart disease.

Genitourinary Changes

Low levels of estrogen cause atrophy of mucosal surfaces accompanied by vaginitis, pruritus, dyspareunia, and stenosis. Genitourinary atrophy leads to a variety of symptoms that affect the ease and quality of living. Urethritis, urge incontinence, and urinary frequency are related to hypoestrogenism in the lower urinary tract. In discussing hypoestrogenic changes with patients, physicians should be sensitive to use of the term *atrophy* as patients may react negatively to its connotation of wasting away or decline.

Sexuality

Sexuality is an integral component of quality of life. Physicians should be prepared to bring up the subject of sexuality, because women may have questions but may be reluctant to ask them.

The major physical changes affecting sexuality that occur in perimenopausal women are a reduction in the rate of production and volume of vaginal fluid, some loss of vaginal elasticity, and thinning of vaginal tissues, which result in a decreased ability to tolerate deep thrusting or long-continuing thrusting. The dyspareunia associated with postmenopausal urogenital atrophy includes a feeling of dryness and tightness, vaginal irritation and burning with coitus, and postcoital spotting and soreness.

Coital activity correlates more closely with a woman's relationship with her partner than with hormone levels. Less vaginal atrophy is noted in sexually active women compared with inactive women; presumably, sexual activity maintains vaginal vasculature and circulation. However, objective measurements of the degree of lubrication have demonstrated that the vaginal factors that influence the enjoyment of sexual intercourse can be maintained by estrogen therapy (29).

Osteoporosis

Women who are thin, white, or of Asian descent; are hypoestrogenic with small frames; or have a family history of osteoporosis are considered to have an increased risk for the development of osteoporosis. Osteoporosis can also occur secondary to other disease processes. Other factors that have been implicated include alcohol, tobacco, and caffeine.

Measuring Bone Density

Screening bone density may be warranted in those women who are at high risk for osteoporosis and who cannot or will not take estrogen. If testing identifies rapid bone loss, referral to an appropriate specialist may be indicated. There is a 50–100% increase in the risk of fracture for each standard deviation decline in bone mass. Measurement of lower bone mass in the hip is even more predictive; one standard deviation is associated with a nearly threefold increase in risk of fracture (30). Despite the impressive correlation between fracture risk and bone density, it is not cost-effective to screen all postmenopausal women.

Preventing Osteoporosis

Preventive health efforts in this age group should be directed toward those factors that influence accumulation and loss of bone. Patients should be counseled about adequate calcium intake, weight-bearing exercise, and the elimination of risk factors to attain the best possible maximal bone density.

While exercise can have a beneficial effect on bone density, the impact of exercise on bone is significantly less than that achieved by hormone therapy (17). Women require a combination of hormone therapy, calcium supplementation, and exercise in order to fully minimize the risk of fractures. Women who do not take hormone therapy need higher levels of calcium supplementation.

Cardiovascular Disease

Cardiovascular disease is the leading cause of death for women in the United States; of the 550,000 people in the United States who die each year of heart disease, 250,000 are women (31). The risk factors are high blood pressure, smoking, high cholesterol levels, diabetes mellitus, and obesity. Men have a higher risk of developing coronary heart disease than women. With increasing age, however, the death rate of women approaches that of men.

Preventive measures—smoking cessation, blood pressure reduction, and lowered cholesterol levels—have helped improve mortality rates from coronary heart disease. It has also been shown that estrogen therapy protects against cardiovascular disease in women. Hormone therapy does not cause hypertension (except in very rare cases of idiosyncratic reaction) (32) and may provide cardiovascular protection to hypoestrogenic women with well-controlled hypertension.

In women, HDL cholesterol is an indicator of risk for coronary heart disease. For every increase in HDL cholesterol of 10 mg/dl there appears to be a 50% decrease in risk (33). After menopause, however, the ratio of low-density lipoprotein (LDL) cholesterol to HDL cholesterol rises. Estrogens increase HDL cholesterol and lower LDL cholesterol, and progestins are thought to have the opposite effect. It is unclear at present whether the addition of progestin to estrogen therapy diminishes the cardiovascular protection of estrogen.

Triglycerides are also an important risk factor for coronary heart disease in women. However, an increased rate of cardiovascular disease is observed only when increased triglyceride levels are present in association with low HDL cholesterol levels (34).

The correlation between total cholesterol and coronary heart disease rates is similar for men and women. Therefore, the National Cholesterol Education Program and the National Cholesterol Consensus Conference have concluded that the same levels of total cholesterol and HDL cholesterol should be used in assigning risk in both women and men (Table 2). If high levels of cholesterol are detected, the first steps in treatment are diet and exercise (35).

Abnormal Uterine Bleeding

Throughout the perimenopause, there is a significant incidence of abnormal uterine bleeding. Although the greatest concern provoked by this symptom is endometrial neoplasia, the usual finding is tissue that displays the effects of estrogen unopposed by progesterone. In premenopausal women, this results from anovulation, and in postmenopausal women, it results from extragonadal endogenous estrogen production or estrogen administration. Abnormal uterine bleeding should be evaluated and treated according to previously published guidelines (36).

Hormone Therapy

The issues of menopause and hormone therapy should be reviewed annually with perimenopausal patients. The variability in the symptoms and time course of the perimenopause, as well as the benefits, side effects, and risks of estrogen therapy, should be discussed.

If the patient has significant symptoms of hypoestrogenism, estrogen therapy can be offered even if the patient is menstruating. Measurement of FSH levels may be useful to document estrogen deficiency as the cause of symptoms when the clinical situation is not clear. In the asymptomatic patient who has been amenorrheic for 6 months, hormone therapy should be considered for its protective benefits. In the patient who has undergone hysterectomy with intact ovaries, the timing of initiation of therapy can be based on symptoms, signs, or the vaginal maturation index.

TABLE 2. INITIAL CLASSIFICATION BASED ON TOTAL CHOLES-
TEROL AND HDL CHOLESTEROL LEVELS*

Cholesterol Level	Initial Classification
Total Cholesterol	
<200 mg/dl (5.2 mmol/L)	Desirable blood cholesterol
200–239 mg/dl (5.2–6.2 mmol/L)	Borderline-high blood cholesterol
≥ 240 mg/dl (6.2 mmol/L)	High blood cholesterol
HDL Cholesterol	
<35 mg/dl (0.9 mmol/L)	Low HDL cholesterol

*HDL indicates high-density lipoprotein.

National Cholesterol Education Program. Expert panel on detection, evaluation, and treatment of high blood cholesterol in adults. Summary of the Second Report of the National Cholesterol Education Program (NCEP) Expert Panel on Detection, Evaluation, and Treatment of High Blood Cholesterol in Adults (Adult Treatment Panel II). JAMA 1993;269:3017

When considering the use of estrogen, the clinician should weigh benefits against side effects and risks for the individual patient. A full discussion of these factors is presented elsewhere (37). Areas of controversy include assessing the level of altered risk (if any) of breast cancer with low-dose estrogen, the level of cardiovascular protection with the addition of progestin, and the use of estrogen in women who have had endometrial or breast cancer.

Summary

Perimenopausal women are assuming increasing importance in the practice of obstetrics and gynecology. While continuing to have reproductive concerns, such as attaining or preventing pregnancy, these women are confronted with a decline in estrogen levels and the inherent protection estrogen provides against osteoporosis and cardiovascular disease. Preventive care, life style modification, and early diagnosis and intervention can play a valuable role in maintaining patients' overall health and quality of life.

REFERENCES

1. Kitabchi AE, Ghawji M. Diabetes in the nonpregnant patient. Prim Care Update Ob/Gyns 1994;1:86–94

2. American College of Obstetricians and Gynecologists. Routine cancer screening. ACOG Committee Opinion 128. Washington, DC: ACOG, 1993

3. Joint National Committee on Detection, Evaluation, and Treatment of High Blood Pressure. The Fifth Report of the Joint National Committee on Detection, Evaluation, and Treatment of High Blood Pressure (JNC V). Arch Intern Med 1993;153:154–183

4. Davis DL, Dinse GE, Hoel DG. Decreasing cardiovascular disease and increasing cancer among whites in the United States from 1973 through 1987. JAMA 1994; 271:431–437

5. Willett WC, Green A, Stampfer MJ, Speizer FE, Colditz GA, Rosner B, et al. Relative and absolute excess risks of coronary heart disease among women who smoke cigarettes. N Engl J Med 1987;317:1303–1309

6. American Cancer Society. Cancer facts and figures—1994. Atlanta, Georgia: ACS, 1994

7. U.S. Department of Health and Human Services. The health benefits of smoking cessation: a report of the Surgeon General. Rockville, Maryland: U.S. Department of Health and Human Services, 1990; publication no. (CDC)90-8416:595

8. Anthonisen NR, Connett JE, Kiley JP, Altose MD, Bailey WC, Buist AS, et al. Effects of smoking intervention and the use of an inhaled anticholinergic bronchodilator on the rate of decline of FEV_1. The lung health study. JAMA 1994;272:1497–1505

9. American College of Obstetricians and Gynecologists. Women and exercise. ACOG Technical Bulletin 173. Washington, DC: ACOG, 1992

10. A federal response to a hidden epidemic: alcohol and other drug problems among women. Washington, DC: National Council on Alcoholism, 1987

11. Kuczmarski RJ, Flegal KM, Campbell SM, Johnson CL. Increasing prevalence of overweight among US adults. JAMA 1994;272:205–211

12. Johannessen S, Lui H. High-frequency, moderate-intensity training in sedentary middle-aged women. Physician Sportsmed 1986;14:99–102

13. Shimegi S, Yanagita M, Okano H, Yamada M, Fukui H, Fukumura Y, et al. Physical exercise increases bone mineral density in postmenopausal women. Endocrine Journal 1994;41:49–56

14. Michel BA, Lane NE, Block DA, Jones HH, Fries JF. Effect of changes in weight-bearing exercise on lumbar bone mass after age fifty. Ann Med 1991;23:397–401

15. Chestnut CH III. Bone mass and exercise. Am J Med 1993;95(5A):34S–36S

16. Gutin B, Kasper MJ. Can vigorous exercise play a role in osteoporosis prevention? A review. Osteoporos Int 1992;2(2):55–69

17. Prince RL, Smith M, Dick IM, Price RI, Webb PG, Henderson NK, et al. Prevention of postmenopausal osteoporosis. A comparative study of exercise, calcium supplementation, and hormone-replacement therapy. N Engl J Med 1991;325:1189–1195

18. Whatley JE, Gillespie WJ, Honig J, Walsh MJ, Blackburn AL, Blackburn GL. Does the amount of endurance exercise in combination with weight training and a very-low-energy diet affect resting metabolic rate and body composition? Am J Clin Nutr 1994;59:1088–1092

19. Mortell R, Tucker L. Effects of a 12-week resistive training program in the home using the body bar on dynamic and absolute strength of middle-age women. Percept Mot Skills 1993;76:1131–1138

20. Manning JM, Dooly Manning CF, White K, Kampa I, Silas S, Kesselhaut M, et al. Effects of a resistive training pro-

gram on lipoprotein–lipid levels in obese women. Med Sci Sports Exerc 1991;23:1222–1226

21. Heislein DM, Harris BA, Jette AM. A strength training program for postmenopausal women: a pilot study. Arch Phys Med Rehabil 1994;75:198–204

22. Butts NK, Price S. Effects of a 12-week weight training program on the body composition of women over 30 years of age. J Strength Conditioning Res 1994;8:265–269

23. American College of Obstetricians and Gynecologists. Depression in women. ACOG Technical Bulletin 182. Washington, DC: ACOG, 1993

24. Brown SS, Eisenberg L, eds. The best intentions: unintended pregnancy and the well-being of children and families. Washington, DC: National Academy Press, 1995

25. Spencer G. Projections of the population of the United States, by age, sex, and race: 1983–2080. Current population reports—population estimates and projections; series P025, no. 952. Washington, DC: U.S. Department of Commerce, 1984

26. McKinlay SM, Brambilla DJ, Posner JG. The normal menopause transition. Maturitas 1992;14:103–115

27. Hunter M. The South-East England longitudinal study of the climacteric and postmenopause. Maturitas 1992;14:117–126

28. Oldenhave A, Jaszmann LJB, Haspels AA, Everaerd WTAM. Impact of climacteric on well-being. A survey based on 5213 women 39 to 60 years old. Am J Obstet Gynecol 1993;168:772–780

29. Semmens JP, Tsai CC, Semmens EC, Loadholt CB. Effects of estrogen therapy on vaginal physiology during menopause. Obstet Gynecol 1985;66:15–23

30. Cummings SR, Black DM, Nevitt MC, Browner W, Cauley J, Ensrud K, et al. Bone density at various sites for prediction of hip fractures. Lancet 1993;341:72–75

31. Wenger NK, Speroff L, Packard B. Cardiovascular health and disease in women. N Engl J Med 1993;329:247–256

32. Lip GY, Beevers M, Churchill D, Beevers DG. Hormone replacement therapy and blood pressure in hypertensive women. J Hum Hypertens 1994;8:491–494

33. Kannel WB. Metabolic risk factors for coronary heart disease in women: perspective from the Framingham Study. Am Heart J 1987;114:413–419

34. Bass KM, Newschaffer CJ, Klag MJ, Bush TL. Plasma lipoprotein levels as predictors of cardiovascular deaths in women. Circulation 1993;153:2209

35. National Cholesterol Education Program. Expert panel on detection, evaluation, and treatment of high blood cholesterol in adults. Summary of the Second Report of the National Cholesterol Education Program (NCEP) Expert Panel on Detection, Evaluation, and Treatment of High Blood Cholesterol in Adults (Adult Treatment Panel II). JAMA 1993;269:3015–3023

36. American College of Obstetricians and Gynecologists. Dysfunctional uterine bleeding. ACOG Technical Bulletin 134. Washington, DC: ACOG, 1989

37. American College of Obstetricians and Gynecologists. Hormone replacement therapy. ACOG Technical Bulletin 166. Washington, DC: ACOG, 1992

SUGGESTED READING

American College of Obstetricians and Gynecologists. The battered woman. ACOG Technical Bulletin 124. Washington, DC: ACOG, 1989

American College of Obstetricians and Gynecologists. Carcinoma of the breast. ACOG Technical Bulletin 158. Washington, DC: ACOG, 1991

American College of Obstetricians and Gynecologists. Hormonal contraception. ACOG Technical Bulletin 198. Washing-ton, DC: ACOG, 1994

American College of Obstetricians and Gynecologists. The intrauterine device. ACOG Technical Bulletin 164. Washington, DC: ACOG, 1992

American College of Obstetricians and Gynecologists. Management of medical disorders. In: Precis V. An update in obstetrics and gynecology. Washington, DC: ACOG, 1994:15–54

American College of Obstetricians and Gynecologists. Nonmalignant conditions of the breast. ACOG Technical Bulletin 156. Washington, DC: ACOG, 1991

American College of Obstetricians and Gynecologists. Osteoporosis. ACOG Technical Bulletin 167. Washington, DC: ACOG, 1992

American College of Obstetricians and Gynecologists. The role of the obstetrician–gynecologist in the diagnosis and treatment of breast disease. ACOG Committee Opinion 140. Washington, DC: ACOG, 1994

This Technical Bulletin was developed under the direction of the Committee on Technical Bulletins of the American College of Obstetricians and Gynecologists as an educational aid to obstetricians and gynecologists. The committee wishes to thank Leon Speroff, MD, for his assistance in the development of this bulletin. This Technical Bulletin does not define a standard of care, nor is it intended to dictate an exclusive course of management. It presents recognized methods and techniques of clinical practice for consideration by obstetrician–gynecologists for incorporation into their practices. Variations of practice taking into account the needs of the individual patient, resources, and limitations unique to the institution or type of practice may be appropriate. Requests for authorization to make photocopies should be directed to the Copyright Clearance Center, 222 Rosewood Drive, Danvers, MA 01923; telephone (508) 750-8400.

ACOG EDUCATIONAL BULLETIN

Number 247, May 1998

Hormone Replacement Therapy

It has been estimated that more than 36 million women in the United States will become menopausal during the next decade. With the onset of menopause, ovarian production of estrogen is significantly reduced, leading to dramatic physiologic changes including:

- Hot flushes
- Mood disturbances
- Thinning of genitourinary tissues and a decrease in tissue elasticity
- Loss of calcium from the skeleton
- Metabolic shift to a more atherogenic lipoprotein profile

Previous studies have demonstrated unequivocally that estrogen replacement therapy can reduce significantly the incidence of osteoporotic fractures and vasomotor symptoms and improve genital atrophy (1, 2). Because estrogen receptors have been identified in almost all tissues in the body, it has been proposed that estrogen replacement can delay many of the undesired effects of aging. The results of a number of observational studies have suggested that estrogen replacement therapy is associated with reduced cardiovascular morbidity (3). Nevertheless, currently there is only one large-scale, long-term randomized trial under way to examine the effects of estrogen replacement therapy on cardiovascular disease. In this trial, the Women's Health Initiative, 25,000 menopausal women are being randomly selected to receive either estrogen replacement therapy or placebo. If the results of this 10-year trial support current observational data, hormone replacement therapy will be considered a major preventive public health strategy for all postmenopausal women.

Despite the many documented benefits of estrogen replacement therapy, compliance remains a significant problem. A substantial number of women who are prescribed estrogen either do not fill the prescription or discontinue therapy within less than 5 years because of perceived cancer risks (primarily breast cancer) or adverse side effects. In a study of 685 women who were screened, designated "at risk" for osteoporosis, and given estrogen therapy,

This Educational Bulletin was developed under the direction of the Committee on Educational Bulletins of the American College of Obstetricians and Gynecologists as an aid to obstetricians and gynecologists. The College wishes to thank James H. Liu, MD, for his assistance in the development of this bulletin. This document is not to be construed as establishing a standard of practice or dictating an exclusive course of treatment. Rather, it is intended as an educational tool that presents current information on obstetric–gynecologic issues.

Replaces Number 166, April 1992

only 49% were still taking estrogen at the end of 1 year (4). The compliance rate was only marginally better in women who had undergone hysterectomy (59%). Even in prospective clinical trials where women were closely monitored, compliance rates were only in the 80% range (5). Widespread and long-term use will require coordinated strategies to educate physicians and women regarding the benefits and adverse effects of estrogen replacement therapy.

The use of antiestrogens, such as tamoxifen as adjuvant chemotherapy for breast cancer in menopausal women and as prophylactic treatment for women at high risk for breast cancer, is associated with improved lipid profiles and increased bone density (6). These unexpected beneficial effects suggest that certain estrogen analogs such as tamoxifen may function as weak estrogen agonists in specific tissues such as bone, liver, and endometrium. These differences in estrogen activity may be explained in part by the recent discovery of a second type of estrogen receptor, the estrogen beta receptor. Clinical trials are being conducted with other estrogen analogs (now called selective estrogen receptor modulators or SERMs) such as raloxifene to assess their use as an alternative to traditional estrogen replacement therapy. Raloxifene has been approved by the Food and Drug Administration for the prevention of postmenopausal osteoporosis. The effect of these agents on cognitive function has not been determined.

Substantial decreases in other circulating hormones besides estrogen occur during the transition into menopause or with aging. These hormones include progesterone, growth hormone (GH), and dehydroepiandrosterone sulfate (DHEAS) (7–10). Physiologic replacement therapies of these hormones are being evaluated in older men and postmenopausal women; however, a detailed discussion is beyond the scope of this bulletin. In contrast to estrogen, the postmenopausal ovary continues to secrete testosterone in significant amounts. The mean concentrations of circulating testosterone levels in postmenopausal women is approximately 250 pg/mL, which is only slightly less than in reproductive-age women (11).

Indications

Central Nervous System Symptoms

Changes in neurologic function such as increased irritability, mood disorders, mild depression, hot flushes, and sleep disturbances may arise during the perimenopausal transition even before the onset of menopause. Decreases in memory and other cognitive changes also have been reported in some menopausal women and younger women in whom menopause has been surgically induced (12–14). Estrogen replacement therapy is the most effective treatment for the relief of hot flushes. In a short-term crossover placebo study, treatment with 1.25 mg per day of conjugated estrogens was found to be significantly more effective than placebo in reducing central nervous system symptoms (ie, hot flushes, insomnia, irritability, poor memory, anxiety, and headaches) (15). Hormone replacement with adequate doses of estrogen can in many cases effectively reverse cognitive changes and improve function (16, 17).

In elderly menopausal women, recent observational and cross-sectional data suggest that estrogens may retard the progression of senile-associated dementia, especially Alzheimer's disease (18–21). The mechanism of estrogen action on brain function is unclear. However, estrogen can increase cerebral perfusion (22), and estrogen and other steroid receptors have been localized to multiple neuronal tissues (23). The impact of estrogen replacement therapy on senile-onset dementias will be evaluated in a prospective estrogen replacement randomized trial within the Women's Health Initiative study.

Progestins such as megestrol acetate, norethindrone, and medroxyprogesterone acetate can be effective in reducing vasomotor symptoms in women who are unable to take estrogens. However, these medications are less effective than estrogen in relieving hot flushes, must be administered in large doses to be effective, and have side effects. Other nonhormonal medications used to treat vasomotor symptoms include clonidine hydrochloride (0.1–0.3 mg patch) and a combination preparation containing phenobarbital, ergotamine, and belladonna alkaloids (24).

Sexual Function

There is no clear-cut evidence that sex drive is reduced significantly at the time of the menopause. For an interval of a few years, postmenopausally, the ovary remains a significant source of circulating androgens (11). Sexual function may be affected by other factors that may occur at the time of menopause, such as changes in body image, stress, or loss of a spouse. The use of combination estrogen and androgen therapy to increase libido is controversial because libido is affected by many variables and is difficult to quantitate objectively. Nevertheless, available literature suggests that the use of androgen alone or androgen with estrogen may induce a positive effect on mood and overall sense of well-being, particularly in women who have had their ovaries removed (14, 16, 17). The long-term use of estrogen and androgen in combination is not without risks.

Cardiovascular Symptoms

Coronary heart disease is the leading cause of death in women. Between the ages of 50 and 79 years, the incidence of coronary heart disease increases significantly. It accounts for approximately 400,000 deaths annually in the United States, with almost all deaths occurring in postmenopausal women. Many observational studies suggest that one mechanism by which estrogens protect against coronary heart disease is by lowering LDL cholesterol and increasing HDL cholesterol concentrations (25, 26). Currently, only one large randomized trial, the Postmenopausal Estrogen/Progestin Interventions (PEPI) study, has examined the effects of estrogen replacement therapy on risk factors for heart disease. This 3-year trial of 875 women demonstrated that conjugated estrogen (0.625 mg) given either alone or with progestin (medroxyprogesterone acetate [10 mg for 12 days per month], medroxyprogesterone acetate [2.5 mg per day], or oral micronized progesterone [200 mg for 12 days per month]) improves the lipoprotein profile by lowering LDL cholesterol and increasing HDL cholesterol levels (5). Although medroxyprogesterone acetate tended to reduce the magnitude of the increased HDL cholesterol levels, results of the PEPI trial indicate that this beneficial increase in HDL cholesterol remained significant when compared with placebo use. In contrast with medroxyprogesterone acetate, the administration of micronized progesterone did not reduce the beneficial lipid effects of estrogens. Fibrinogen levels, another marker for cardiovascular risk, also were decreased significantly in estrogen-treated groups relative to placebo.

It is estimated that the alteration in lipoprotein metabolism induced by estrogen therapy probably accounts for less than 50% of the cardioprotective effect of estrogens. It is postulated that estrogen may provide additional protection through other mechanisms such as its direct effect on arterial vasodilation and increased perfusion (19, 27), its intrinsic antioxidant properties (28), or its action on reducing the circulating levels of oxidized LDL (29).

Osteoporosis

A gradual loss of bone mineral density is associated with aging in both men and women. In contrast to bone loss in men, bone loss in women accelerates at the onset of menopause on average at a rate of approximately 3% per year for the first 5 years and 1% per year thereafter. However, in some women bone loss at this time may exceed 5% per year. Hip fractures frequently occur 15–25 years after menopause and result from the combination of severely reduced bone mass and falls. It is estimated that women hospitalized for hip fractures will have an overall mortality rate of 30% within 1 year of hip fracture. The projected health care costs for hip fractures alone is more than 7 billion dollars annually. Other fractures associated with osteoporosis include fractures of the vertebrae, distal forearm, and proximal humerus.

The loss of bone mineral density is the result of an alteration in the bone remodeling process. The rate of bone resorption increases, exceeding the rate of bone formation. Osteoporosis is diagnosed when bone mineral density decreases to less than 2.5 standard deviations below the young adult peak mean.

Estrogen therapy has been shown to be effective in preventing further bone loss by inhibiting osteoclastic activity in the bone remodeling process, thereby reducing bone resorption. Effective doses of estrogen for the prevention of osteoporosis are: 0.625 mg of conjugated estrogen, 0.5 mg of micronized estradiol, and 0.3 mg of esterified estrogen. Other therapies that are effective in preventing bone loss include alendronate, sodium fluoride (30), and intranasal use of calcitonin (31).

Genitourinary Symptoms

The tissues of the urethra and vagina are derived embryologically from the urogenital sinus and are classic examples of estrogen-responsive tissues. Withdrawal of estradiol during menopause results in a reduction in overall mitotic activity of vaginal and urethral mucosal epithelium, a decrease in exfoliation of surface cells, a decrease in tissue vascularity, and thinning of the mucosal layer. The vaginal and urethral mucosa appear pale, dry, and flattened. These hypoestrogenic changes in the vaginal mucosa are associated with vaginal dryness, dyspareunia, and a greater incidence of atrophic vaginitis. Atrophy of the urethral mucosa is associated with a greater incidence of urethritis, decreased urethral pressure, and a possible increased incidence of urinary incontinence.

Use of systemic estrogen replacement or local estrogen creams and urethral suppositories can reverse many if not all of these changes. Hormone replacement therapy can decrease the risk of urinary tract infection and microscopic hematuria (32). Even small amounts of estrogen preparations introduced onto the vaginal mucosa are more readily absorbed than oral preparations and can lead to significant increases in circulating levels of estrogen. For women who are unable to take estrogen but experience urogenital atrophy, there are estrogen creams or a polysiloxane estradiol-impregnated vaginal ring. The ring delivery system has been shown to relieve vaginal and urinary tract symptoms without increasing systemic estradiol levels; the device needs to be changed every three months.

Hypogonadal Conditions

Individuals who do not undergo pubertal maturation (ovarian failure secondary to cancer treatment, gonadal dysgenesis, isolated gonadotropin deficiency) require estrogen replacement therapy to induce the normal adult female phenotype. Treatment of these individuals generally requires gradually increasing estrogen doses to mimic the same pattern of changes that occurs during puberty. At reproductive age, these women may require twice as much estrogen as women of postmenopausal age. For women with a diagnosis of premature ovarian failure, hypothalamic amenorrhea, exercise-associated amenorrhea, anorexia nervosa, or hyperprolactinemia, estrogen replacement therapy should be considered for the same indications as for postmenopausal women.

Risk Factors

Thromboembolic Disease

Recent studies have shown a twofold to fourfold increase in the risk of venous thromboembolism in users of estrogen-only and combined estrogen–progestin hormone replacement therapy (33–35). Because the absolute risk of venous thromboembolism in both users and nonusers of estrogen is low, there is only a modest increase in the morbidity associated with hormone replacement therapy, and this increased risk must be weighed against documented benefits. At the least, however, the risk factors for venous thromboembolism—such as family history of venous thrombosis, gross obesity, an earlier episode of thromboembolism and intercurrent illness associated with immobilization—should be considered in weighing the benefits and risks of hormone replacement therapy for any individual.

Endometrial Hyperplasia and Endometrial Cancer

Long-term use of estrogen alone has been associated with the development of endometrial hyperplasia and endometrial cancer. The PEPI trial was the first large, prospective randomized study to examine the effects of unopposed estrogen over a 3-year follow-up period (36). During the trial, women who took conjugated estrogen (0.625 mg) only were more likely to develop simple cystic hyperplasia (27.7%), adenomatous hyperplasia (22.7%), or atypical adenomatous hyperplasia (11.8%) than the placebo group (<0.8%). Women who took conjugated estrogen (0.625 mg) in combination with either cyclic (10 mg of medroxyprogesterone acetate per day for 12 days or 200 mg of micronized oral progesterone per day for 12 days) (ie, 200 mg given as a single dose once daily for 12 days) or continuous progestin therapy (2.5 mg of medroxyprogesterone acetate per day) had the same rate of hyperplasia as the placebo group. In those developing adenomatous or atypical adenomatous hyperplasia, the endometrium reverted to normal in 94% of women after treatment with progestin therapy (10 mg of medroxyprogesterone acetate per day for 3 months). Thus, in women with a uterus,

cyclic or continuous progestin therapy is required to protect the endometrium from hyperplastic transformation during estrogen replacement therapy (36).

For women with previously diagnosed endometrial cancer, hormone replacement therapy remains an option that should be viewed cautiously. In a survey of members of the Society of Gynecologic Oncologists, 83% of respondents approved the use of estrogen replacement therapy in patients with stage I, grade I, endometrial cancer; 56% favored using estrogen in cases of stage I, grade 2 cancer; and 39% would use estrogen in cases of stage I, grade 3 cancer. In women with a history of endometrial carcinoma, estrogens can be used for the same indications as for other women, except the selection of appropriate candidates should be based on prognostic indicators and the risk the patient is willing to assume. If the patient is free of tumor, the use of estrogen replacement therapy cannot result in recurrence. If an estrogen-dependent neoplasm is harbored somewhere in her body, it will eventually recur; however, the use of estrogen replacement therapy may result in an earlier recurrence (37).

Endometriosis

For women with a history of endometriosis, treatment with estrogen-only regimens is not contraindicated. However, because these women often are younger than most menopausal women and may have undergone bilateral oophorectomy, higher doses of estrogen may induce the recurrence of endometriosis (38). If this occurs, discontinuing the estrogen therapy and beginning a progestin-only regimen can be an option (see Table 1).

Breast Cancer

An increased risk of breast cancer has been associated with the extended duration of endogenous estrogen exposure such as that which occurs with early menarche, late menopause, and obesity. Although some studies have suggested that hormone replacement therapy is linked to an increased risk of breast cancer in postmenopausal wo-

TABLE 1. Commonly Used Progestin Preparations, Their Estimated Relative Potencies for Ability to Induce Endometrial Secretory Changes, and Recommended Progestin-Only Therapeutic Doses

Progestin	Relative Potency	Progestin-Only Dose
Medroxyprogesterone acetate (10 mg)	1.0	10–30 mg
Norethindrone (5 mg)	>6.0	1–5.0 mg
(0.35 mg)	~0.5	
Micronized progesterone (200 mg)	1.0	Not reported
Progesterone vaginal suspension (90 mg)	1.0	Not reported
Megestrol acetate		40–80 mg

men (39, 40), other studies have shown little or no relationship between estrogen use and breast cancer (41, 42). Despite the more than 50 epidemiologic studies published on this topic, no consistent link between hormone replacement therapy and breast cancer has been found. One possible interpretation of the data is that either there is no increased risk or the risk is too small to be shown clearly by epidemiologic studies. As for all women, those taking hormone replacement therapy should be encouraged to perform monthly breast self-examinations, have regular physical examinations, and have mammography every 1–2 years after age 40 and annually after age 50.

Because progestins potentially may stimulate the growth of breast tumors, the effects of the combination of estrogen and progestin on breast cancer risk also should be considered. The results of studies that have examined this issue have been inconsistent (43). Various studies have shown estrogen–progestin therapy to increase, have no effect, or actually protect against breast cancer. The results of the Women's Health Initiative trial may help to reveal whether there is truly an increased breast cancer risk associated with long-term use of estrogen and estrogen–progestin therapy.

There are concerns that in women with previously diagnosed breast cancer, estrogen use may stimulate residual cancer cells to proliferate. However, there are no studies that support the concept that estrogen use leads to an increased risk of breast cancer recurrence or a change in the survival rate of these patients. Because women with prior breast cancer have an increased risk for a second primary breast cancer (44), close surveillance is warranted. Despite the well-recognized short-term and potential long-term benefits of hormone replacement therapy, it should be considered cautiously in women who have had breast cancer. Before starting this therapy, the patient should receive extensive counseling with input from her oncologist (45).

Hypertension and Weight Gain

In a large, randomized, prospective trial of women taking hormone replacement therapy, there were no significant differences in the mean systolic or diastolic blood pressures during the 3-year period of monitoring (5). Mean waist-to-hip ratios increased slightly over time for both the placebo and estrogen-treated groups. During the 3-year trial, the greatest weight gain (2.1 kg) occurred in the placebo group while the unopposed estrogen group had the lowest weight gain (0.7 kg).

Therapeutic Options

Hormone replacement therapy should be considered to relieve vasomotor symptoms, genital urinary tract atrophy, and mood and cognitive disturbances, as well as to prevent osteoporosis and cardiovascular disease. It also may be considered to help prevent colon cancer, Alzheimer's disease, and adult tooth loss. Before therapy is instituted, a thorough medical evaluation is appropriate. The medical history should focus on contraindications to estrogen and precautions against risk factors and side effects.

Estrogen Component

Although many estrogen preparations are available, the lowest effective estrogen dose that will relieve the patient's symptoms and provide cardiovascular and bone protection should be used. Table 2 outlines several of the more commonly used estrogen preparations and their relative potencies. Because oral estrogen preparations are initially transported to the liver via portal circulation, liver conversion and degradation will alter the expected ratio of estradiol to estrone. In contrast, transdermal, buccal, or vaginally administered estrogens are not subject to the hepatic "first pass" effect, and circulating estrogen levels will mimic a steady state. Because the impact on liver metabolism is greater with oral than with transdermal administration of estrogen, at equivalent doses, oral therapy results in greater increases in HDL cholesterol, decreases in LDL cholesterol, and increases in triglycerides. Measurement of circulating estradiol levels may be useful as an estimate of estrogen effects on symptoms for those taking transdermal or vaginal estradiol preparations. For those taking oral preparations, particularly conjugated estrogens, measurement of estradiol levels does not accurately reflect estrogen activity (see Table 2). Follicle-stimulating hormone (FSH) levels remain in the postmenopausal range (>40 mIU/mL) for women taking hormone replacement therapy.

Dietary sources of estrogen such as phytoestrogens are available from legumes (primarily soy-based products). Because phytoestrogens are weak estrogen agonists, relatively high doses must be taken to achieve the therapeutic effects derived from hormone replacement therapy. Preliminary studies suggest that a soy protein extract can reduce hot flushes by 45%, compared with a placebo response of 30% (46). Therefore, the estimated amounts of soy products that would need to be consumed to achieve therapeutic concentrations of phytoestrogens would be enormous.

Progestin Component

There are several types of progestins that can be used in hormone replacement therapy (see Table 1). The most commonly used progestin, medroxyprogesterone acetate, is a 21-carbon derivative of progesterone. A dose of 5–10 mg of medroxyprogesterone acetate during the last 12–14 days of estrogen administration is recommended to reduce

Table 2. Commonly Used Estrogen Preparations with Estimated Relative Potencies and Approximate Circulating Levels of Estradiol and Estrone

Estrogen	Relative Potency	Estradiol (pg/mL)	Estrone (pg/mL)
Oral conjugated estrogen			
0.625 mg*	1.0	40	150
0.3 mg	0.5	<40	<150
Oral micronized estradiol			
1 mg	1.0	30	260
0.5 mg*		<30	<260
Oral piperazine estrone sulfate			
0.75 mg estropipate*	1.0	~30–40	~120
Transdermal estradiol			
0.05 mg/day*	1.0	60	50
Oral esterified estrogen			
0.3 mg	0.5	<30	~60
Estradiol vaginal ring	<0.5	No detectable change	No detectable change

*Minimal effective dose for prevention of bone loss.

Modified from Lobo R, Mishell DR, Budoff PW, et al: Estrogen Replacement Therapy, Symposium Proceedings, San Francisco, May 9–10, 1984. Abbott Pharmaceuticals, Inc, p 9.

the incidence of hyperplasia and endometrial cancer. Lower doses (2.5 mg) will provide similar protection when given continuously with estrogen.

Oral micronized progesterone preparations are not standardized but are available from individual pharmacies. Absorption is affected by progesterone particle size, food intake, the use of oil vehicles, and the type of capsules (47–49). It appears that oral micronized progesterone in the dose range of 200–300 mg per day for 12 days per month (given in divided doses) is sufficient to protect against endometrial hyperplasia (50–52).

Norethindrone, a 19-carbon compound, is the most potent oral progestin compound available for hormone replacement therapy. Doses of 1 mg are sufficient to induce endometrial secretory changes. Higher doses of norethindrone have been associated with elevations in LDL cholesterol.

Therapeutic Regimens

In women who elect to begin hormone replacement therapy, annual physical examinations, including breast and pelvic examinations, should be performed. Routine assessments such as blood pressure evaluation, Pap tests, lipid profile assessment, and mammography should be performed. In those women with a uterus, a progestin should be given either in a sequential fashion (5–10 mg of medroxyprogesterone acetate for 12–14 days each month) or continuously (2.5 mg of medroxyprogesterone acetate per day). A baseline endometrial biopsy is not necessary unless there is irregular bleeding, but a biopsy should be considered for women with unexpected or excessive bleeding.

Estrogen–Progestin Combinations

For perimenopausal women (around ages 45–50) who use low-dose oral contraceptives, it is difficult to determine whether menopause has actually occurred. Two practical approaches can be considered. In women 50 years of age or older, evaluating FSH levels at the end of the placebo week will provide an assessment of residual ovarian function. Women with FSH levels >40 mIU/mL can be started on hormone replacement therapy. Alternatively, switching from oral contraceptives to hormone replacement therapy can be tried empirically between the ages of 50 and 51 years. Because hormone replacement therapy will not effectively suppress ovarian function, those women with ovarian activity will experience episodes of intermenstrual bleeding and increased breast tenderness.

In women who have an intact uterus, the addition of a progestin to the estrogen is necessary to prevent endometrial hyperplasia or endometrial cancer. In general, administration of progestins in sequential regimen is associated with cyclic, uterine withdrawal bleeding in a fairly predictable pattern. More recently, continuous administration of progestins has been studied in large multicenter trials. This approach results in a thin, atrophic endometrium, which can be associated with amenorrhea in up to 75% of individuals after 1 year. However, this amenorrheal response is not uniform, and many women will experience unpredictable vaginal spotting. Figure 1 shows several of the more common estrogen–progestin regimens.

Progestin-Only Regimens

For women who cannot take estrogens for various reasons but who are symptomatic with hot flushes or are con-

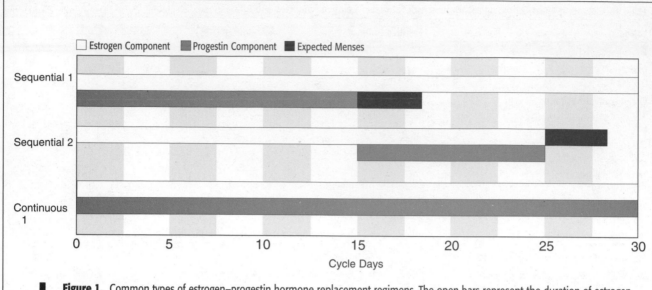

Figure 1. Common types of estrogen–progestin hormone replacement regimens. The open bars represent the duration of estrogen therapy, the diagonal-patterned bars represent duration of progestin administration, and the solid bars indicate when vaginal bleeding is expected.

cerned about osteoporosis, a progestin-only regimen is an option. The lowest doses of progestin that are effective for the treatment of vasomotor flushes are provided in Table 1.

Estrogen-Only Regimens

In women who do not have a uterus, there is no evidence that the addition of a progestin to estrogen replacement therapy provides any additional advantages or has any effect on the risk of breast cancer. For women who do not tolerate estrogen–progestin or progestin-only regimens, estrogen-only therapy can be considered if the patient can be monitored by endometrial biopsy to detect endometrial proliferation. In these circumstances, the risk of endometrial hyperplasia can approach 20% per year and require the addition of progestin therapy to reverse endometrial changes.

Estrogen–Androgen Regimens

Two estrogen–androgen dose preparations that contain 2.5 mg and 1.25 mg of methyltestosterone, respectively, are available. Absorption of methyltestosterone is excellent, allowing supraphysiologic levels of testosterone to be achieved. The use of androgens has been shown to increase total cholesterol (increase LDL cholesterol and decrease HDL cholesterol). Other side effects can include hirsutism, acne, and weight gain.

Selective Estrogen Modulators

A daily dose of 60 mg of raloxifene is currently recommended for osteoporosis prevention. In a prospective randomized multicenter trial of over 600 menopausal women,

raloxifene was shown to effectively protect against bone loss and reduce LDL cholesterol levels without inducing endometrial proliferation (53). In contrast to oral estrogens, levels of HDL cholesterol and triglycerides were unchanged during treatment. The risk of venous thromboembolic phenomena associated with raloxifene use appears to be similar to that of estrogen. In this study, there were no significant differences in the proportions of women reporting hot flashes between the group receiving 60 mg of raloxifene daily and those taking placebo (26.3% and 22.7%). Thus, raloxifene would probably not be used in early menopausal women who are more likely to have hot flashes and other hypoestrogenic symptomatology.

Growth Hormone and Dehydroepiandrosterone Sulfate Replacement

Although GH and DHEAS decrease with aging, it has not been demonstrated that long-term empiric exogenous replacement of these compounds is effective in ameliorating the physiologic changes of aging. Several small studies have examined the short-term effects of GH replacement in older men and women (54). In general, short-term GH treatment will decrease body fat, increase muscle mass, and increase exercise capacity. However, the side effects of this treatment include decreased glucose tolerance, peripheral edema, and carpal tunnel syndrome. Preliminary studies suggest that short-term DHEAS therapy can increase circulating DHEAS levels in older women and by metabolic interconversion lead to increased testosterone levels (55). Both of these therapies should be considered investigational.

Strategies to Improve Compliance

Once a woman begins hormone replacement therapy, long-term compliance will become the major challenge if long-term benefits are to be realized. In a study of menopausal women between 46 and 63 years of age enrolled in a prescription plan, the stopping rate for estrogen replacement therapy was reported to be 20% at 6 months, 38% at 1 year, 51% at 18 months, and 59% at 2 years (56).

Several strategies proposed by the Women's Health Initiative may improve compliance significantly. A follow-up phone call at 6 weeks from a nurse inquiring about patient concerns seems to increase adherence. Women should be counseled regarding the development of breast tenderness, breast engorgement, and the timing of vaginal bleeding. The use of pill packs may reduce confusion of when to take estrogen–progestin regimens. For women who experience persistent or unpredictable vaginal spotting while on a continuous estrogen–progestin regimen, a switch to a cyclic regimen may increase compliance. A follow-up visit at 6 months after beginning hormone replacement therapy may help to identify any side effects. As with many compliance issues, establishing good rapport with ongoing communication between the patient and medical provider is key.

Summary

Traditionally, hormone replacement therapy has been started in menopausal women for treatment of vasomotor symptoms, mood disturbances, vaginal dryness, and osteoporosis prevention. However, because an increasing number of menopausal women are now better informed regarding menopausal changes and are beginning to embrace the concept of preventive health care, other additional benefits of hormone replacement therapy such as protection against cardiovascular disease and possible protection or delay in the onset of senile dementias make this option even more appealing. Alternatively, these perceived benefits must be assessed against the potential increased risk of breast cancer. Once the decision is made to begin hormone replacement therapy, it is important that patients continue treatment so that these long-term benefits are realized.

References

1. Cummings SR, Kelsey JL, Nevitt MC, O'Dowd KJ. Epidemiology of osteoporosis and osteoporotic fractures. Epidemiol Rev 1985;7:178–208
2. Steingold KA, Laufer L, Chetkowski RJ, DeFazio JD, Matt DW, Meldrum DR, et al. Treatment of hot flashes with transdermal estradiol administration. J Clin Endocrinol Metab 1985;61:627–632
3. Barrett-Connor E, Bush T. Estrogen and coronary heart dis-ease in women. JAMA 1991;265:1861–1867
4. Torgerson DJ, Donaldson C, Russell IT, Reid DM. Hormone replacement therapy: compliance and cost after screening for osteoporosis. Eur J Obstet Gynecol Reprod Biol 1995;59:57–60
5. The Writing Group for the PEPI Trial. Effects of estrogen or estrogen/progestin regimens on heart disease risk factors in postmenopausal women. JAMA 1995;273:199–208
6. Love RR, Mazess RB, Barden HS, Epstein S, Newcomb PA, Jordan VC, et al. Effects of tamoxifen on bone mineral density in postmenopausal women with breast cancer. N Engl J Med 1992;326:852–856
7. Barrett-Connor E, Khaw KT. Absence of an inverse relation of dehydroepiandrosterone sulfate with cardiovascular mortality in postmenopausal women. N Engl J Med 1987;317:711
8. Musey VC, Collins DC, Musey PI, Martino-Saltzman D, Preedy JRK. Age-related changes in the female hormonal environment during reproductive life. Am J Obstet Gynecol 1987;157:312–317
9. Prior JC. Progesterone as a bone-trophic hormone. Endocr Rev 1990;11:386–398
10. Thompson JL, Butterfield GE, Marcus R, Hintz RL, Loan MV, Ghiron L, et al. The effects of recombinant human insulin-like growth factor-I and growth hormone on body composition in elderly women. J Clin Endocrinol Metab 1995;80:1845–1852
11. Judd HL, Judd GE, Lucas WE, Yen SS. Endocrine function of the postmenopausal ovary: concentration of androgens and estrogens in ovarian and peripheral vein blood. J Clin Endocrinol Metab 1974;39:1020–1024
12. Kampen DL, Sherwin BB. Estrogen use and verbal memory in healthy postmenopausal women. Obstet Gynecol 1994;83:979–983
13. Sherwin BB. The impact of different doses of estrogen and progestin on mood and sexual behavior in postmenopausal women. J Clin Endocrinol Metab 1991;72:336–343
14. Sherwin BB. Affective changes with estrogen and androgen replacement therapy in surgically menopausal women. J Affect Disord 1988;14:177–187
15. Campbell S, Whitehead M. Oestrogen therapy and the menopausal syndrome. Clin Obstet Gynaecol 1977;4:31–47
16. Sherwin BB, Gelfand MM. Differential symptom response to parenteral estrogen and/or androgen administration in the surgical menopause. Am J Obstet Gynecol 1989;151:153–160
17. Sherwin BB. Estrogen and/or androgen replacement therapy and cognitive functioning in surgically menopausal women. Psychoneuroendocrinology 1988;13:345–357
18. Fillit H, Weinreb H, Cholst I, Luine V, McEwen B, Amador R, et al. Observations in a preliminary open trial of estradiol therapy for senile dementia-Alzheimer's type. Psychoneuroendocrinology 1986;11:337–345

19. Funk JL, Mortel KF, Meyer JS. Effects of estrogen replacement therapy on cerebral perfusion and cognition among postmenopausal women. Dementia 1991;2:268–272

20. Henderson VW, Paganini-Hill A, Emanuel CK, Dunn ME, Buckwalter JG. Estrogen replacement therapy in older women. Arch Neurol 1994;51:896–900

21. Honjo H, Tanaka K, Kashiwagi T, Urabe M, Okada H, Hayashi M, et al. Senile dementia-Alzheimer's type and estrogen. Horm Metab Res 1995;27:204–207

22. Gangar KF, Vyas S, Whitehead M, Crook D, Meire H, Campbell S. Pulsatility index in internal carotid artery in relation to transdermal oestradiol and time since menopause. Lancet 1991;338:839–842

23. Sheridan PJ. Autoradiographic localization of steroid receptors in the brain. Clin Neuropharmacol 1984;7:281–295

24. Lebherz TB, French L. Nonhormonal treatment of the menopausal syndrome: a double-blind evaluation of an autonomic system stabilizer. Obstet Gynecol 1969; 33:795–799

25. Bush TL, Cowan LD, Barrett-Connor E, Criqui MH, Karon JM, Wallace RB, et al. Estrogen use and all-cause mortality. JAMA 1983;249:903–906

26. Stampfer MJ, Colditz GA. Estrogen replacement therapy and coronary heart disease: a quantitative assessment of the epidemiologic evidence. Prev Med 1991;20:47–63

27. Mikkola T, Turunen P, Avela K, Orpana A, Viinikka L, Ylikorkala O. 17 β-estradiol stimulates prostacyclin, but not endothelin-1, production in human vascular endothelial cells. J Clin Endocrinol Metab 1995;80:1832–1836

28. Tang M, Subbiah R. Estrogens protect against hydrogen peroxide and arachidonic acid induced DNA damage. Biochim Biophys Acta 1996;1299:155–159

29. Subbiah MT, Kessel B, Agrawal M, Rajan R, Abplanalp W, Rymaszewski Z. Antioxidant potential of specific estrogens on lipid peroxidation. J Clin Endocrinol Metab 1993;77: 1095–1097

30. Kleerekoper M, Mendlovic B. Sodium fluoride therapy of postmenopausal osteoporosis. Endocr Rev 1993;14:312–323

31. Reginster JY, Deroisy R, Lecart MP, Sarlet N, Zegels B, Jupsin I, et al. A double-blind, placebo-controlled, dose-finding trial of intermittent nasal salmon calcitonin for prevention of postmenopausal lumbar spine bone loss. Am J Med 1995;98:452–458

32. Bergman A, Brenner PF. Beneficial effects of pharmacologic agents—genitourinary. In: Mishell DR, Jr, ed. Menopause: physiology and pharmacology. Chicago: Year Book Medical Publishers, Inc, 1987:151–164

33. Daly E, Vessey MP, Hawkins MM, Carson JL, Gough P, Marsh S. Risk of venous thromboembolism in users of hormone replacement therapy. Lancet 1996;348:977–980

34. Grodstein F, Stampfer MJ, Goldhaber SZ, Manson JE, Colditz GA, Speizer FE, et al. Prospective study of exoge-nous hormones and risk of pulmonary embolism in women. Lancet 1996; 348:983–987

35. Jick H, Derby LE, Myers MW, Vasilakis C, Newtom KM. Risk of hospital admission for idiopathic venous thromboembolism among users of postmenopausal oestrogens. Lancet 1996;348:981–983

36. The Writing Group for the PEPI Trial. Effects of hormone replacement therapy on endometrial histology in postmenopausal women. JAMA 1996;275:370–375

37. American College of Obstetricians and Gynecologists. Estrogen replacement therapy and endometrial cancer. ACOG Committee Opinion 126. Washington, DC: ACOG, 1993

38. Barbieri RL. Hormone treatment of endometriosis: the estrogen threshold hypothesis. Am J Obstet Gynecol 1992; 166:740–745

39. Colditz GA, Hankinson SE, Hunter DJ, Willett WC, Manson JE, Stampfer MJ, et al. The use of estrogens and progestins and the risk of breast cancer in postmenopausal women. N Engl J Med 1995;332:1589–1593

40. Steinberg KK, Thacker SB, Smith SJ, Stroup DF, Zack MM, Flanders WD, et al. A meta-analysis of the effect of estrogen replacement therapy on the risk of breast cancer. JAMA 1991;265:1985–1990

41. Dupont WD, Page DL. Menopausal estrogen replacement therapy and breast cancer. Arch Intern Med 1991;151: 67–72

42. Henrich JB. The postmenopausal estrogen/breast cancer controversy. JAMA 1992;268:1900–1902

43. Bergkvist L, Adami H, Persson I, Hoover R, Schairer C. The risk of breast cancer after estrogen and estrogen-progestin replacement. N Engl J Med 1989;321:293–297

44. Fornander T, Rutquist LE, Cedermark B, Glas U, Mattsson A, Silfversward C, et al. Adjuvant tamoxifen in early breast cancer: occurrence of new primary cancers. Lancet 1989;1: 117–120

45. American College of Obstetricians and Gynecologists. Estrogen replacement therapy in women with previously treated breast cancer. ACOG Committee Opinion 135. Washington, DC: ACOG, 1994

46. Albertazzi P, Pansini F, Bonaccorsi G, Zanotti L, Forini E, de Aloysio D. The effect of dietary soy supplementation on hot flushes. Obstet Gynecol 1998;91:6–11

47. Hargrove JT, Maxson WS, Wentz AC. Absorption of oral progesterone is influenced by vehicle and particle size. Am J Obstet Gynecol 1989;161:948–951

48. Nakajima ST, Gibson M. The effect of a meal on circulating steady-state progesterone levels. J Clin Endocrinol Metab 1989;69:917–919

49. Simon JA, Robinson DE, Andrews MC, Hildebrand JR, Rocci ML Jr, Blake RE, et al. The absorption of oral micronized progesterone: the effect of food, dose proportion-

ality, and comparison with intramuscular progesterone. Fertil Steril 1993;60:26–33

50. Gillet JY, Andre G, Faguer B, Erny R, Buvat-Herbaut M, Domin MA, et al. Induction of amenorrhea during hormone replacement therapy: optimal micronized progesterone dose. A multicenter study. Maturitas 1994;19:103–115

51. Hargrove JT, Maxon WS, Wentz AC, Burnett LS. Menopausal hormone replacement therapy with continuous daily oral micronized estradiol and progesterone. Obstet Gynecol 1989;73:606–612

52. Lane G, Siddle NC, Ryder TA, Pryse-Davies J, King RJB, Whitehead MI. Dose dependent effects of oral progesterone on oestrogenised postmenopausal endometrium. BMJ 1983;287:1241–1245

53. Delmas PD, Bjarnason NH, Mitlak BH, Ravoux A-C, Shah AS, Huster WJ, et al. Effects of raloxifene on bone mineral density, serum cholesterol concentrations, and uterine endometrium in postmenopausal women. N Engl J Med 1997;337:1641–1647

54. Corpas E, Harman SM, Blackman MR. Human growth hormone and human aging. Endocr Rev 1993;14:20–39

55. Morales AJ, Nolan JJ, Nelson JC, Yen SSC. Effects of replacement dose of dehydroepiandrosterone in men and women of advancing age. J Clin Endocrinol Metab 1994;78:1360–1367

56. Berman RS, Epstein RS, Lydick EG. Compliance of women in taking estrogen replacement therapy. J Womens Health 1996;5:213–220

ACOG EDUCATIONAL BULLETIN

Number 227, August 1996

Management of Isoimmunization in Pregnancy

This Educational Bulletin was developed under the direction of the Committee on Educational Bulletins of the American College of Obstetricians and Gynecologists as an aid to obstetricians and gynecologists. The College wishes to thank Michael L. Socol, MD, for his assistance in the development of this bulletin. This document is not to be construed as establishing a standard of practice or dictating an exclusive course of treatment. Rather, it is intended as an educational tool that presents current information on obstetric–gynecologic issues.

When any fetal blood group factor inherited from the father is not possessed by the mother, antepartum or intrapartum fetal–maternal bleeding may stimulate an immune reaction by the mother. Maternal immune reactions can also occur from blood product transfusion. The formation of maternal antibodies to a foreign antigen may be followed by various degrees of transplacental passage of these antibodies into the fetal circulation. Depending on the degree of antigenicity and the amount and type of antibody involved, this transplacental passage may lead to hemolytic disease of the newborn.

The reproductive history of a woman with isoimmunization is of considerable importance in recognizing and determining the prognosis for a subsequent isoimmunized pregnancy. For example, if a D-negative, isoimmunized woman becomes pregnant with a D-positive fetus, the severity of the hemolytic disease will usually be equal to or greater than that of the previous pregnancy. Occasionally, the disease progression may be such that early-onset fetal hydrops may occur in a patient who experienced only mildly affected prior pregnancies. In rare cases, hemolytic disease in the current pregnancy may be less severe than in a prior pregnancy. Regardless of obstetric history, all pregnant women should undergo laboratory examinations at the first prenatal visit to determine the possibility of isoimmunization. Tests should include determination of ABO and D types as well as a screen for the presence of antibodies by an indirect Coombs test (antibody screen).

Factors that minimize the chance of isoimmunization to the D antigen are detailed elsewhere (1). There are no preventive strategies against sensitization to blood factors other than the D antigen. Although some of these antibodies are not clinically significant, most do gain access to the fetus across the placenta and can potentially cause fetal anemia and hydrops. Fortunately, ABO incompatibility, which is a common cause of subclinical and mild hemolytic disease of the newborn, does not cause clinical or severe erythroblastosis. Therefore, no antenatal testing, either by titer or by amniocentesis, is necessary when there is a history of ABO incompatibility.

Replaces Number 148, October 1990

Clinically Significant Antibodies

CDE System

Anti-D isoimmunization remains the most common cause of erythroblastosis fetalis. Antibodies formed in response to the D antigen are of the immunoglobulin G (IgG) type. Consequently, they can cross the placenta and hemolyze fetal erythrocytes. Whereas most clinically significant blood group sensitizations noted during pregnancy are still secondary to anti-D incompatibility, sensitization to antigens other than D in the CDE system is not uncommon and can cause severe disease.

Other Antibodies

The most frequently encountered antibodies other than D are Lewis antibodies (Le[a] and Le[b]). Like most cold agglutinins, Lewis antigens do not cause erythroblastosis fetalis because they are predominantly of the IgM type and they are poorly expressed on fetal and newborn erythrocytes. In contrast, Kell antibodies (k, K, Kp[a], Kp[b], Js[a], Js[b]) can produce erythroblastosis fetalis. Kell isoimmunization is often caused by prior transfusion, since Kell compatibility is usually not considered when blood is crossmatched. Fortunately, 90% of partners of Kell-immunized women are Kell negative themselves. Less common, but just as likely to cause erythroblastosis fetalis, are some of the Duffy antigens. Additional antibodies known to cause hemolytic disease are listed in Table 1. Care of patients with sensitization to antigens other than D that are known to cause hemolytic disease should be the same as that for

TABLE 1. ISOIMMUNIZATION RESULTING FROM IRREGULAR ANTIBODIES*

Blood Group System	Antigen
Rh	C, c, e, E
Kell	K, k, Ko, Kp[a], Kp[b], Js[a], Js[b]
Duffy	Fy[a], Fy[b], Fy[3]
Kidd	Jk[a], Jk[b], Jk[3]
MNSs	M, N, S, s, U, Mi[a], Mt[a], Vw, Mur, Hil, Hut
Lutheran	Lu[a], Lu[b]
Diego	Di[a], Di[b]
Xg	Xg[a]
P	PP[1]P[k](Tj[a])
Public antigens	Yt[a], Yt[b], Lan, En[a], Ge, Jr[a], Co[a], Co[a-b-]
Private antigens	Batty, Becker, Berrens, Biles, Evans, Gonzales, Good, Heibel, Hunt, Jobbins, Radin, Rm, Ven, Wright[a], Wright[b], Zd

* Lewis (Le[a], Le[b]) and I antigens are not causes of hemolytic disease of the newborn.

Modified from Socol ML. Management of blood group isoimmunization. In: Gleicher N. Principles and practice of medical therapy in pregnancy. 2nd ed. Norwalk, Connecticut: Appleton and Lange, 1992:1051

patients with D isoimmunization. A possible exception is Kell sensitization, in which amniotic fluid analysis has been reported to correlate poorly with the severity of fetal anemia (2). These patients may benefit from more aggressive fetal assessment; however, optimal management of Kell-sensitized patients is controversial (3).

Clinical Management

Once it has been established that a pregnant woman is sensitized to an antigen that may cause erythroblastosis, the genotype of the fetus's father should be determined. This is most useful for the atypical antigens because isoimmunization is often secondary to a transfusion. If the father of the fetus does not possess the antigen, the fetus is not at risk. If the father is a heterozygote there is only a 50% chance that the fetus has inherited the blood group antigen and the pregnancy is affected. The most likely zygosity for the D antigen can also be predicted as the alleles at the C, D, and E loci are inherited together, and some combinations are more frequent than others. Because it is not possible to test for the presence of D antigens, zygosity can be determined only by looking at the combination. Clinically, however, determining this genotype is of limited value for the couple receiving counseling after a severely affected pregnancy. Unless the D-positive partner has previously fathered a D-negative child, it is impossible to state with certainty that he is a heterozygote.

Antibody Titers

Maternal serum antibody titers can be measured by a variety of techniques (4). Agglutination of erythrocytes in saline measures maternal IgM antibody, and this is too large a molecule to cross the placenta. Albumin is a more viscous medium; therefore, the smaller IgG molecules are capable of agglutinating erythrocytes, but the contribution by IgM is not eliminated. The most sensitive and accurate barometer for clinical practice is the indirect Coombs test.

The usefulness of maternal serum antibody titers is determined by the patient's reproductive history. If a patient has never had a pregnancy complicated by Rh-related neonatal morbidity other than hyperbilirubinemia treated by phototherapy, antibody titers are the initial step of management. An antibody titer should be determined at the first prenatal visit, at 20 weeks of gestation, and approximately every 4 weeks thereafter. When the antibody titer is ≤ 1:8, whether directed to D or another paternal antigen capable of causing severe erythroblastosis, no intervention is necessary; when the titer is ≥ 1:16 in albumin or 1:32 by indirect antiglobulin (indirect Coombs test), amniocentesis or percutaneous umbilical cord blood sampling (cordocentesis) should be considered (5).

If a patient has had a prior affected pregnancy (neonatal exchange transfusion, early delivery, or intrauterine transfusion), antibody titers are not necessary because amniocentesis or percutaneous umbilical cord blood sampling will be required. The timing of the initial procedure is determined by past clinical history. It is usually performed at least 4–8 weeks earlier than the prior gestational age at which significant morbidity occurred, with some clinicians beginning at 20 weeks or even earlier.

Amniocentesis and Percutaneous Umbilical Cord Blood Sampling

Since the mid-1960s, amniocentesis with spectrophotometric examination of the amniotic fluid has been the accepted method for assessing the severity of erythroblastosis in utero. Amniotic fluid bilirubin is most likely derived from fetal tracheal and pulmonary secretions. It can be quantitated by spectrophotometrically measuring absorbance at the 450-nm wavelength in a specimen of amniotic fluid that has been shielded from light. The deviation from linearity (change in optical density at 450 nm [ΔOD_{450}]) is determined by measuring the difference between this absorbance and a straight line drawn from points 365 nm to 535 nm on the spectrophotometric curve. Contamination of amniotic fluid by meconium and by erythrocytes and their porphyrin breakdown products can significantly alter spectrophotometric analysis at 450 nm, but these problems can be largely overcome by chloroform extraction of the amniotic fluid (6). Heme pigment will also generate a peak at the 405-nm wavelength, and in the absence of blood contamination this may be indicative of severe hemolysis (4).

Fetal status is determined by plotting the ΔOD_{450} measurement on a Liley graph (Fig. 1) (7). Readings in zone III (uppermost zone) suggest severe hemolytic disease with a high probability of fetal death within 7–10 days. Readings in zone I (lowest zone) are reassuring although neonatal exchange transfusion may be necessary occasionally. There are no reliable data concerning the optimal frequency for repeated sampling. In general, amniocentesis is repeated every 1–4 weeks if the ΔOD_{450} measurement is in zone II (middle zone) and every 3–4 weeks if it has dropped into zone I. The frequency depends on where in zone II the value falls and the pattern established in previous procedures. Declining values are encouraging although they do not preclude mild hemolytic disease. Stable or rising ΔOD_{450} measurements are causes of concern.

Patients with results in zone I or low zone II can be allowed to proceed to term, at which point labor should be induced. In most cases, patients in the middle of zone II can progress to 36–38 weeks of gestation, at which time delivery should be accomplished, by induction of labor if possible. Depending on gestational age, patients in zone III should either be delivered or should receive intrauterine fetal transfusion. Similar considerations may apply to a rising titer in upper zone II. Delivery is often by cesarean birth because of an unfavorable cervix, but a trial of labor is not contraindicated.

Percutaneous umbilical cord blood sampling has improved the obstetric care of isoimmunized patients because of the ability to evaluate fetal status precisely. This is particularly true in the middle trimester, when amniotic fluid from unaffected fetuses will also contain bilirubin. Peak values of bilirubin are present between 20 and 24 weeks of gestation. The Liley curve was generated from pregnancies of at least 28 weeks of gestation. In the past, obstetricians have derived values for pregnancies of 20–27 weeks of gestation by extrapolating backwards from the Liley curve; however, such extrapolations may be inappropriate (8). In either the second or the third trimester, knowledge of the specific fetal hematocrit enables the physician to take a more rational approach to the need for, volume of, and timing of fetal transfusions. Hematologic values for normal fetuses from 15 to 30 weeks of gestation are shown in Table 2 (9, 10). In some instances, findings may even indicate that the fetus does not possess the blood group antigen in question and therefore requires no further evaluation. Perhaps most importantly, the use of amniocentesis in conjunction with percutaneous umbilical cord blood sampling allows a more aggressive approach at an earlier gestational age.

In spite of the enthusiasm that percutaneous umbilical cord blood sampling has generated for fetal diagnosis and therapy, some caution should be exercised. First, a chart of spectrophotometric measurements from sensitized pregnancies in the middle trimester has been constructed that may minimize the benefit of fetal blood sampling as the primary assessment of fetal status (11). Second, determination of fetal blood type, particularly for the D antigen, can be accomplished by polymerase chain reaction on fetal amniocytes and therefore does not always require a fetal blood sample (12). It should be emphasized, however, that these tests should be done in specialized laboratories with considerable experience in polymerase chain reaction testing. Third, liberal use of percutaneous umbilical cord blood sampling may induce an anamnestic immune response in the mother secondary to fetal–maternal hemorrhage, thereby accelerating the disease process (13, 14). Fourth, the loss rate with percutaneous umbilical cord blood sampling is generally agreed to be greater than that with amniocentesis. Consequently, whereas fetal blood sampling as the principal means of fetal assessment in isoimmunized pregnancies appears safe and effective in experienced hands (15, 16), most clinicians continue to rely primarily on amniocentesis.

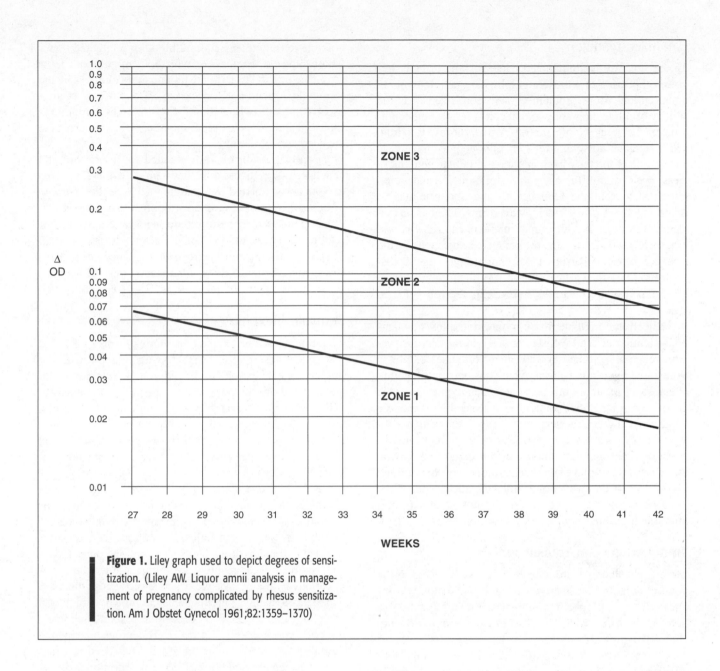

Figure 1. Liley graph used to depict degrees of sensitization. (Liley AW. Liquor amnii analysis in management of pregnancy complicated by rhesus sensitization. Am J Obstet Gynecol 1961;82:1359–1370)

TABLE 2. HEMATOLOGIC VALUES FOR NORMAL FETUSES*

Hematologic Value†	Gestational Age (Weeks)					
	15	**16–17**	**18–20**	**21–22**	**23–25**	**26–30**
Hgb (g/100 ml)	10.9 ± 0.7	12.5 ± 0.8	11.48 ± 0.78	12.29 ± 0.89	12.4 ± 0.77	13.36 ± 1.18
RBC (×10⁹/L)	2.43 ± 0.26	2.68 ± 0.21	2.66 ± 0.29	2.97 ± 0.27	3.06 ± 0.27	3.52 ± 0.32
MCV (±1)	143 ± 8	143 ± 12	133.9 ± 8.83	130 ± 6.17	126.2 ± 6.23	118.2 ± 5.7

* Values are for normal fetuses from 15 to 30 weeks of estimated gestational age.

† Hgb indicates hemoglobin; RBC, red blood cells; MCV, mean corpuscular volume.

Ancillary Testing

In the severely isoimmunized patient, signs of early hydrops appearing on ultrasonography may facilitate timely intervention. More problematic and controversial is the ability of ultrasonography to detect a deteriorating condition in the fetus before the onset of hydrops. Reported early signs of worsening fetal anemia include an increase in the size of the fetal liver, an increase in placental thickness, pericardial effusion, polyhydramnios, visualization of both sides of the fetal bowel, and abnormalities of pulsed Doppler flow-velocity waveforms. There is no evidence, however, that ultrasound markers can reliably distinguish mild from severe hemolytic disease in the absence of fetal hydrops (17). One study suggests that hydramnios is the earliest sign of significant fetal anemia (18), but it is not invariably present in severely affected cases.

Electronic fetal heart rate monitoring allows dynamic evaluation of fetal well-being and central nervous system reactivity. Some severely anemic fetuses exhibit a sinusoidal heart rate pattern, which has been attributed to the absence of autonomic nervous system control over the heart, high-output cardiac failure, or tissue hypoxia of the fetal heart and central nervous system. Nonreactive, suboptimal, or pathologic fetal heart rate patterns have also been reported more commonly in sensitized fetuses who were hypoxic and anemic than in those who had normal oxygen levels and were not anemic. Characteristics of the fetal heart rate pattern, however, did not accurately predict the degree of anemia or oxygenation (19).

Intrauterine Fetal Transfusion

Before physicians were able to gain direct access to the fetal circulation, intraperitoneal fetal transfusion was indicated if serial spectrophotometric measurements rose into upper zone II before 30 weeks of gestation or into zone III before 32–34 weeks of pregnancy. The infused blood was absorbed into the fetal circulation via the subdiaphragmatic lymphatic system. In the nonhydropic fetus, the rate of absorption was estimated to be 10–15% per 24 hours. Absorption was slower if hydrops was already evident (4).

Because of erratic absorption, especially in hydropic fetuses, intravascular fetal transfusion (20, 21) has largely replaced the intraperitoneal technique, although some investigators advocate a combined intravascular and intraperitoneal approach in select circumstances (22, 23). The fetal hematocrit level at which to initiate transfusion is somewhat arbitrary, but the value of 25% seems reasonable (24). Transfusions are performed using type O, Rh-negative, cytomegalovirus-negative, washed, irradiated packed cells cross-matched against maternal blood. After the fetal blood type is determined, it may occasionally be possible to use either maternal blood or a targeted donor whose blood is compatible with both mother and fetus (25). One method to estimate transfusion volume is by the formula described by Rodeck (26). Transfusion volumes usually range between 30 and 100 ml, and fetal blood is aspirated at the conclusion of the transfusion to determine the adequacy of therapy.

Repeat transfusions are planned for when the fetal hematocrit is predicted to be between 20% and 25%. This may be approximated by assuming a 1% decline per day or by using one of a number of published equations (27, 28). In fetuses with more severe hemolytic anemia, few fetal erythrocytes survive the initial transfusion interval. Therefore, the interval between first and second transfusions is usually 7–14 days, whereas the interval between subsequent transfusions or birth is 21–28 days.

Perinatal Outcome

Direct intravascular transfusion eliminates the erratic and incomplete absorption of erythrocytes inherent with the intraperitoneal approach. In addition, the intravascular technique allows more precise evaluation of the need for and adequacy of therapy by measurements of the initial and final fetal hematocrits. Consequently, it is not surprising that perinatal survival rates for severely isoimmunized fetuses following intravascular transfusion are now reported in excess of 80% (16, 21, 29–32). The improved survival rate is especially noteworthy when the early gestational ages at which therapy is being attempted are considered. Also encouraging is the improved outcome for hydropic fetuses. In one series, 16 of 20 pregnancies complicated by fetal hydrops had successful outcomes (33).

Although these results are promising, there are complications with any invasive procedure. Even in the most experienced hands, percutaneous umbilical cord blood sampling alone results in procedure-related pregnancy loss of approximately 1% (34). The procedure-related mortality for intravascular transfusion has been reported to be between 4% and 9% (29–31, 33). Additional significant morbidity has included nonremediable prolonged fetal heart rate decelerations that required emergent cesarean delivery (35) and increases in maternal antibody titer, presumably secondary to fetal–maternal hemorrhage (13, 14). When weighing the procedure-related risks against those for the neonate in the nursery, one should seriously consider delivery rather than performing an intravascular transfusion after 34 completed weeks of pregnancy.

Summary

Isoimmunization is diagnosed by a positive antibody screen and requires identification of the specific antigen responsible, classification of the antigen into either a clinically significant or a benign group, and titration of the level of antibody response. The paternal antigen status and zygosity should be determined whenever possible. Repetitive amniocentesis or fetal blood sampling may be required to monitor the fetal condition adequately. Early and continued consultation with experts in the management of this condition is key to developing an appropriate therapeutic plan that includes proper management at delivery and optimal neonatal support. New technologies and expertise now allow better outcome for severely affected fetuses.

References

1. American College of Obstetricians and Gynecologists. Prevention of D isoimmunization. ACOG Technical Bulletin 147. Washington, DC: ACOG, 1990 (Level III)

2. Caime ME, Mueller-Heubach E. Kell sensitization in pregnancy. Am J Obstet Gynecol 1986;154:85–90 (Level III)

3. Weiner CP, Widness JA. Decreased fetal erythropoiesis and hemolysis in Kell hemolytic anemia. Am J Obstet Gynecol 1996;174:547–551 (Level II-3)

4. Bowman JM. Maternal blood group isoimmunization. In: Creasy RK, Resnik R, eds. Maternal–fetal medicine: principles and practice. 3rd ed. Philadelphia: WB Saunders, 1994:711–743 (Level III)

5. Bowman JM, Pollock JM. Transplacental fetal hemorrhage after amniocentesis. Obstet Gynecol 1985;66:749–754 (Level II-3)

6. Brazie JV, Bowes WA Jr, Ibbott FA. An improved, rapid procedure for the determination of amniotic fluid bilirubin and its use in the prediction of the course of Rh-sensitized pregnancies. Am J Obstet Gynecol 1969;104:80–86 (Level III)

7. Liley AW. Liquor amnii analysis in the management of pregnancy complicated by rhesus sensitization. Am J Obstet Gynecol 1961;82:1359–1370 (Level III)

8. Nicolaides KH, Rodeck CH, Mibashan RS, Kemp JR. Have Liley charts outlived their usefulness? Am J Obstet Gynecol 1986;155:90–94 (Level III)

9. Forestier F, Daffos F, Galacteros F, Bardakjian J, Rainaut M, Beuzard Y. Hematological values of 163 normal fetuses between 18 and 30 weeks of gestation. Pediatr Res 1986; 20:342–346 (Level II-3)

10. Millar DS, Davis LR, Rodeck CH, Nicolaides KH, Mibashan RS. Normal blood cell values in the early midtrimester fetus. Prenat Diagn 1985;5:367–373 (Level III)

11. Queenan JT, Tomai TP, Ural SH, King JC. Deviation in amniotic fluid optical density at a wavelength of 450 nm in Rh-immunized pregnancies from 14 to 40 weeks' gestation: a proposal for clinical management. Am J Obstet Gynecol 1993;168:1370–1376 (Level III)

12. Fisk NM, Bennett P, Warwick RM, Letsky EA, Welch R, Vaughan JI, et al. Clinical utility of fetal RhD typing in alloimmunized pregnancies by means of polymerase chain reaction on amniocytes or chorionic villi. Am J Obstet Gynecol 1994;171:50–54 (Level III)

13. Nicolini U, Kochenour NK, Greco P, Letsky EA, Johnson RD, Contreras M, et al. Consequences of fetomaternal haemorrhage after intrauterine transfusion. BMJ 1988;297: 1379–1381 (Level III)

14. MacGregor SN, Silver RK, Sholl JS. Enhanced sensitization after cordocentesis in a rhesus-isoimmunized pregnancy. Am J Obstet Gynecol 1991;165:382–383 (Level III)

15. Weiner CP, Williamson RA, Wenstrom KD, Sipes SL, Grant SS, Widness JA. Management of fetal hemolytic disease by cordocentesis. I. Prediction of fetal anemia. Am J Obstet Gynecol 1991;165:546–553 (Level II-3)

16. Weiner CP, Williamson RA, Wenstrom KD, Sipes SL, Widness JA, Grant SS, et al. Management of fetal hemolytic disease by cordocentesis. II. Outcome of treatment. Am J Obstet Gynecol 1991;165:1302–1307 (Level II-3)

17. Nicolaides KH, Fontanarosa M, Gabbe SG, Rodeck CH. Failure of ultrasonographic parameters to predict the severity of fetal anemia in Rhesus isoimmunization. Am J Obstet Gynecol 1988;158:920–926 (Level II-2)

18. Chitkara U, Wilkins I, Lynch L, Mehalek K, Berkowitz RL. The role of sonography in assessing severity of fetal anemia in Rh- and Kell-isoimmunized pregnancies. Obstet Gynecol 1988;71:393–398 (Level III)

19. Nicolaides KH. Studies on fetal physiology and pathophysiology in Rhesus disease. Semin Perinatol 1989;13:328–337 (Level III)

20. Socol ML, MacGregor SN, Pielet BW, Tamura RK, Sabbagha RE. Percutaneous umbilical transfusion in severe rhesus isoimmunization: resolution of fetal hydrops. Am J Obstet Gynecol 1987;157:1369–1375 (Level III)

21. Harman CR, Bowman JM, Manning FA, Menticoglou SM. Intrauterine transfusion—intraperitoneal versus intravascular approach: a case–control comparison. Am J Obstet Gynecol 1990;162:1053–1059 (Level II-2)

22. Pattison N, Roberts A. The management of severe erythroblastosis fetalis by fetal transfusion: survival of transfused adult erythrocytes in the fetus. Obstet Gynecol 1989; 74:901–904 (Level II-3)

23. Moise KJ, Giancarlo M, Fisher DJ, Huhta JC, Cano LE, Carpenter RJ Jr. Acute fetal hemodynamic alterations after intrauterine transfusion for treatment of severe red blood cell alloimmunization. Am J Obstet Gynecol 1990;163: 776–784 (Level II-3)

24. Reece EA, Copel JA, Scioscia AL, Grannum PAT, DeGennaro N, Hobbins JC. Diagnostic fetal umbilical blood sampling in the management of isoimmunization. Am J Obstet Gynecol 1988;159:1057–1062 (Level III)

25. Gonsoulin WJ, Moise KJ Jr, Milam JD, Sala JD, Weber VW, Carpenter RJ Jr. Serial maternal blood donations for intrauterine transfusion. Obstet Gynecol 1990;75:158–162 (Level II-3)

26. Rodeck CH, Nicolaides KH, Warsof SL, Fysh WJ, Gamsu HR, Kemp JR. The management of severe rhesus iso-immunization by fetoscopic intravascular transfusions. Am J Obstet Gynecol 1984;150:769–774 (Level III)

27. Plecas DV, Chitkara U, Berkowitz GS, Lapinski RH, Alvarez M, Berkowitz RL. Intrauterine intravascular transfusion for severe erythroblastosis fetalis: how much to transfuse? Obstet Gynecol 1990;75:965–969 (Level II-3)

28. MacGregor SN, Socol ML, Pielet BW, Sholl JS, Silver RK. Prediction of hematocrit decline after intravascular fetal transfusion. Am J Obstet Gynecol 1989;161:1491–1493 (Level II-3)

29. Ney JA, Socol ML, Dooley SL, MacGregor SN, Silver RK, Millard DD. Perinatal outcome following intravascular transfusion in severely isoimmunized fetuses. Int J Gynaecol Obstet 1991;35:41–46 (Level II-3)

30. Berkowitz RL, Chitkara U, Wilkins IA, Lynch L, Plosker H, Bernstein HH. Intravascular monitoring and management of erythroblastosis fetalis. Am J Obstet Gynecol 1988;158: 783–795 (Level III)

31. Barss VA, Benacerraf BR, Frigoletto FD, Greene MF, Penso C, Saltzman DH, et al. Management of isoimmunized pregnancy by use of intravascular techniques. Am J Obstet Gynecol 1988;159:932–937 (Level III)

32. Parer JT. Severe Rh isoimmunization—current methods of in utero diagnosis and treatment. Am J Obstet Gynecol 1988;158:1323–1329 (Level III)

33. Grannum PAT, Copel JA, Moya FR, Scioscia AL, Robert JA, Winn HN, et al. The reversal of hydrops fetalis by intravascular intrauterine transfusion in severe isoimmune fetal anemia. Am J Obstet Gynecol 1988;158:914–919 (Level III)

34. Daffos F, Capella-Pavlovsky M, Forestier F. Fetal blood sampling during pregnancy with use of a needle guided by ultrasound: a study of 606 consecutive cases. Am J Obstet Gynecol 1985;153:655–660 (Level III)

35. Pielet BW, Socol ML, MacGregor SN, Ney JA, Dooley SL. Cordocentesis: an appraisal of risks. Am J Obstet Gynecol 1988;159:1497–1500 (Level III)

The references in this bulletin are graded according to the method outlined by the U.S. Preventive Services Task Force:

I   Evidence obtained from at least one properly designed randomized controlled trial

II-1 Evidence obtained from well-designed controlled trials without randomization

II-2 Evidence obtained from well-designed cohort or case–control analytic studies, preferably from more than one center or research group

II-3 Evidence obtained from multiple time series, with or without intervention, or dramatic results in uncontrolled experiments

III   Opinions of respected authorities, based on clinical experience, descriptive studies, or reports of expert committees

Other publications from ACOG:

- **Committee Opinions**, focused updates on emerging areas

- **Practice Patterns**, evidence-based guidelines

- **Criteria Sets**, baseline guidelines for review of diagnostic and management procedures

Copyright © August 1996
ISSN 1074-8628

The American College of Obstetricians and Gynecologists
409 12th Street, SW
PO Box 96920
Washington, DC 20090-6920

12345/09876

ACOG EDUCATIONAL BULLETIN

Number 251, September 1998

Obstetric Aspects of Trauma Management

Trauma has become one of the leading causes of morbidity and mortality of women in the world, resulting in nearly one million deaths each year. It also has become one of the leading causes of morbidity and mortality during pregnancy (1, 2). It is estimated that physical trauma complicates approximately 1 in every 12 pregnancies, with motor vehicle crashes being the most significant contributor to fetal death due to trauma (3). Nearly 50,000 of the estimated 250 million people in the United States die each year from motor vehicle crashes. This rate is equivalent to approximately 20 deaths due to motor vehicle crashes for every 100,000 persons in the United States.

The incidence and severity of injuries can be lessened by the appropriate use of automobile safety restraints. Physicians should counsel patients about such use and reassure them of the safety of these devices during pregnancy. Despite these precautions, injuries will occur during pregnancy and obstetrician–gynecologists should be equipped to handle them.

Optimum management of the seriously injured pregnant woman requires an integrated effort of multiple specialties, starting with emergency medical technicians, emergency medicine physicians, trauma surgeons, and other specialists, depending on the type of injury. Obstetricians play a central role in the management of injured pregnant women. Their knowledge and expertise are vital to management decisions regarding both the woman and the fetus. The effects of various drugs on uterine blood flow, potential teratogenic and mutagenic effects of diagnostic radiation and medications, the effect of surgery on pregnancy, and the assessment of gestational age are critical management issues. In addition, complications of pregnancy unrelated to the trauma may be superimposed in the injured gravida (eg, pregnancy-induced hypertension, placenta previa) and are best managed by the obstetrician. The obstetrician may be consulted regarding the condition of a pregnant trauma patient or, more commonly, may be the primary physician caring for the patient following trauma. In either case, the approach must be systematic, ensuring that the woman is medically stable prior to evaluation of the fetus.

Obstetricians who are involved with the care of pregnant trauma patients should seek consultation with experienced trauma surgeons. It also is helpful for all physicians to be knowledgeable about advanced trauma life-support measures.

This Educational Bulletin was developed under the direction of the Committee on Educational Bulletins of the American College of Obstetricians and Gynecologists as an aid to obstetricians and gynecologists. The College wishes to thank Mark Pearlman, MD, and Cosmas van de Ven, MD, for their assistance in the development of this bulletin. This document is not to be construed as establishing a standard of practice or dictating an exclusive course of treatment. Rather, it is intended as an educational tool that presents current information on obstetric–gynecologic issues.

Replaces Number 151, January 1991, and Number 161, November 1991

Incidence

In industrialized nations, approximately two thirds of all trauma during pregnancy results from motor vehicle crashes. Other frequent causes of trauma during pregnancy are falls and direct assaults to the abdomen (3, 4). According to the National Safety Council, female drivers are more likely to be involved in automobile accidents than male drivers (84 female drivers versus 73 male drivers per 10 million miles driven) (5).

Domestic violence has reached epidemic proportion in the United States. It is estimated that approximately 2 million women per year are reported to have been assaulted by their male partners (6). Researchers have found a prevalence of violence against pregnant women ranging from 1% to 20% (7). Domestic violence and battery were found to occur in 1 of every 12 pregnant women in an inner-city setting (8). Among victims of physical abuse, moderate or severe violence during pregnancy was reported by 20% of women in the Baltimore area, 17% in Houston, 7% in Galveston, and 7% in Toronto (9, 10). Sixty percent of victims report two or more episodes of physical assault during pregnancy (11). This latter statistic emphasizes the importance of early identification of physical abuse during pregnancy and implementation of effective intervention methods, which are discussed elsewhere (6).

Maternal Mortality

Trauma, either accidental (as in traffic accidents) or intentional (as in homicide or domestic violence), is a leading cause of death in women of reproductive age (1). Trauma also is the leading cause of nonobstetric maternal death (12); for example, it accounted for an average of 22% of all maternal deaths in Iowa and caused nearly one half of 95 maternal deaths from 1986 to 1989 in Cook County, Illinois (2).

Fetal Mortality

Accurate statistics on the number of fetal losses due to trauma each year are not available. Estimates extrapolated from published case series suggest that between 1,300 and 3,900 pregnancies are lost each year in the United States as a result of trauma (13).

Life-threatening maternal trauma (eg, maternal shock, head injury resulting in coma, emergency laparotomy for maternal indications) is associated with a 40–50% fetal loss rate, whereas minor or non–life-threatening injuries resulted in a 1–5% pregnancy loss (14). Because minor injuries are more common, most fetal losses result from minor maternal injuries (4, 15, 16). It is estimated that abruptio placentae is a complication in 40–50% of pregnant women who sustain severe trauma, compared with the 1–5% incidence in pregnant women who experience non–life-threatening trauma (4, 16–19). Several series of fetal losses resulting from trauma indicate that more than 50% of fetal losses occur in association with seemingly minor or insignificant maternal trauma (4, 15, 16, 18, 20).

Numerous retrospective studies have attempted to predict fetal or neonatal outcome based on an injury severity score. However, one study suggests that injury severity scoring is not a good predictor of adverse fetal outcome (21).

Types of Trauma

Blunt Abdominal Trauma

The evaluation and management of blunt abdominal trauma during pregnancy involves several key issues. Gestational age at the time of injury, extent and severity of maternal injury, and mechanism of injury should be considered.

The gestational age at the time of injury is valuable in determining the need for fetal assessment as well as in managing the mother's condition. The possibility of fetal viability in an extrauterine environment (ie, beyond 24–26 weeks of gestation) can significantly change management decisions if there is evidence of fetal compromise. Furthermore, enlargement of the uterus beyond 18–20 weeks of gestation compresses both the inferior vena cava and aorta in the supine position, increasing the likelihood of hypotension and decreased uterine perfusion. Finally, the type of maternal and fetal injury patterns may depend to a great extent on gestational age at the time of injury. For example, direct injury to the uterus and fetus prior to 13 weeks of gestation is extremely unlikely because they are protected by the bony pelvis. Generally, trauma in the first trimester does not cause pregnancy loss, with the exception of profound hypotension and associated hypoperfusion of the uterus and its contents. Although it is not the highest priority in managing the injured gravida, gestational age should be assessed as soon as feasible.

Fetal loss resulting from blunt abdominal trauma may result from abruptio placentae or other placental injury, direct fetal injury, uterine rupture, maternal shock, or death or some combination thereof. Several studies of trauma and fetal loss show that at least 50% of fetal losses with known etiology were the result of abruptio placenta (4, 15, 16, 18). In one report of severe car crashes involving pregnant women, maternal loss of life was the most frequent cause of fetal death (17).

There are several potential mechanisms of abruptio placentae due to trauma. Differences in tissue properties between the elastic myometrium and the relatively inelastic placenta can result in a shearing at the tissue interface. Because fluid is noncompressible, intrusion of the elastic uterine wall will result in displacement of amniotic fluid and distention of the other parts of the uterus. Therefore, a shear force can occur regardless of placental location. The risk of abruptio placentae appears to be independent of the placental location (3).

Direct fetal injury (eg, skull fracture) complicates less than 1% of all pregnancies in which trauma occurs. Although case reports of fetal skull fractures have been described following relatively minor trauma, most cases result from significant maternal injury later in gestation (22, 23).

Uterine rupture is an infrequent but life-threatening complication of trauma. It occurs in only 0.6% of all injuries during pregnancy and tends to complicate trauma resulting from direct abdominal impact associated with substantial force (24, 25). The extent of uterine injury can be variable, and it may result in serosal hemorrhage or abrasions; avulsion of the uterine vasculature with hemorrhage; complete disruption of the myometrial wall with extrusion of the fetus, placenta, or umbilical cord into the abdominal cavity; or complete uterine avulsion. Approximately 75% of reported cases of uterine rupture involve the fundus. The presentation of uterine rupture can range from subtle findings (eg, uterine tenderness, nonreassuring fetal heart rate patterns) without changes in maternal vital signs, to rapid onset of maternal hypovolemic shock. Signs of peritoneal irritation, such as distention, rebound tenderness, guarding, and rigidity are frequently detected upon examination but may be less pronounced during pregnancy.

Pelvic Fractures

Pelvic fractures may result in significant retroperitoneal bleeding, which is associated with substantial morbidity and mortality. When combined with the possibility of intraperitoneal bleeding, pelvic fractures are frequently associated with hypovolemic shock. Associated injuries of the bladder or urethral disruption can result in hematuria and also may pose difficulty in placing a urinary catheter.

Pelvic fracture is not a definite contraindication for vaginal delivery. Even in the presence of a slightly displaced pelvic fracture, safe vaginal delivery can be accomplished. However, a severe, dislocated, or unstable fracture or a large healing callus may preclude an attempt at vaginal delivery.

Penetrating Trauma

Most penetrating abdominal trauma results from gunshot wounds or stab wounds. Penetrating abdominal trauma during pregnancy has a remarkably disparate prognosis for the fetus and the woman (26, 27). Fetal loss due to penetrating trauma usually occurs through direct injury or by injury to the cord or placenta. Maternal outcome generally is more favorable because the maternal viscera are shielded by the uterus and its contents, which absorbs much of the projectile energy.

The extent and severity of maternal and fetal injury due to gunshot wounds depends on a number of factors including the size and velocity of the bullet; the anatomic region penetrated; the angle of entry; deflection of the bullet's trajectory by muscle, bone, or viscera; the gestational age of the fetus; and the distance from which the bullet was fired. Frequently, more internal damage occurs than that suggested by the appearance of the entrance wound.

The enlarged uterus tends to protect the bowel from injury when stab wounds penetrate the lower abdomen because the bowel is displaced into the upper abdomen. However, as a result of cephalad displacement of the bowel by the enlarging uterus, stab wounds to the upper abdomen can frequently result in more complex bowel injury than in the nonpregnant woman.

Management

The primary goal and initial efforts in managing the injured pregnant woman should be evaluation and stabilization of maternal vital signs. If attention is drawn to the fetus before the woman is stabilized, serious or life-threatening maternal injuries may be overlooked, or circumstances that can compromise fetal oxygenation (eg, maternal hypoxemia, hypovolemia, or supine hypotension) may be ignored, lessening the likelihood of both maternal and fetal survival.

A systematic approach begins with a primary survey of the woman by securing and maintaining an airway, ensuring adequate breathing, and maintaining adequate circulatory volume. The placement of two large-bore (14–16 gauge) intravenous lines is necessary in most seriously injured trauma patients. Supplemental oxygen should be administered by nasal cannula, mask, or endotracheal intubation as required to maintain a hemoglobin saturation of 90% or greater. Crystalloid in the form of lactated Ringer's solution or normal saline should be given over the first 30–60 minutes of acute resuscitation as a 3:1 replacement based on blood loss. The use of vasopressors to restore maternal blood pressure should be avoided until appropriate volume replacement has been administered. Although these agents may reduce uterine blood flow in normovolemic patients, they should not be withheld if needed in the resuscitation of the mother. Displacement of the uterus off the inferior vena cava and abdominal aorta with the patient in a supine position is helpful in trauma patients beyond midpregnancy. This can be effected by having the patient lie in the lateral decubitus position. If the patient must remain supine (eg, if a spinal injury is suspected or if cardiopulmonary resuscitation is being administered), manual displacement of the uterus laterally with a hand or placement of a wedge under a backboard will accomplish this goal.

Following stabilization, a more detailed secondary survey of the patient, including fetal evaluation, should be performed. All body regions must be thoroughly examined. Pregnancy should not alter necessary treatment and evaluation of the trauma patient. The abdomen is of particular importance, because a substantial percentage of serious injuries involve the uterus, intraperitoneal structures, and retroperitoneum. The uterus should be examined for evidence of gross deformity, tenderness, or contractions.

Computed tomography can be used to evaluate patients who have suffered significant trauma. Computed tomographic scanning of the abdomen exposes the fetus to approximately 3.5 rad, depending on the number and thickness of the images and the equipment used. As with any procedure involving ionizing radiation, scanning closer to the uterus increases fetal exposure. Fetal exposure exceeding 20 rad may be sufficient to induce adverse effects in early pregnancy (28).

Open peritoneal lavage can be effective in the diagnosis of intraperitoneal hemorrhage during pregnancy (29). Open lavage with sharp dissection and opening of the anterior abdominal peritoneum under direct vision, usually periumbilically, is advocated over a blind needle insertion to lessen the likelihood of injury to the uterus or to other displaced intraabdominal organs. Peritoneal lavage is unnecessary if clinically obvious intraperitoneal bleeding is present. Following are some indications for peritoneal lavage after trauma during pregnancy:

- Abdominal signs or symptoms suggestive of intraperitoneal bleeding
- Altered sensorium
- Unexplained shock
- Major thoracic injuries
- Multiple major orthopedic injuries

Penetrating trauma requires the complete undressing of the patient for careful inspection of all entrance and exit wounds because occasionally victims are shot or stabbed multiple times, and entrance and exit wounds of high-velocity projectiles are unpredictable. Radiographs of the area in multiple projections often are helpful to localize a bullet if an exit wound is not seen. The uterus and its contents can often stop the progression of a projectile, limiting the extent of maternal injury to the abdominal wall and the uterus. Signs of peritoneal irritation are less reliable during pregnancy, however, and changes in vital signs due to blood loss may occur rela-

tively late because of the increase in blood volume related to pregnancy. The general approach to management of abdominal gunshot wounds involves exploratory laparotomy, although laparotomy can be used selectively (26). Although stab wounds that do not appear to penetrate beyond the abdominal wall have been managed nonoperatively, evidence of peritoneal penetration usually requires exploratory laparotomy, particularly if there are signs of intraperitoneal hemorrhage or bowel perforation (30). The indications for tetanus prophylaxis do not change in pregnancy, and appropriate candidates should be vaccinated.

If adequate oxygenation and uterine perfusion are maintained, the fetus usually tolerates surgery and anesthesia well. Intraoperative fetal heart rate monitoring should be considered if the fetus is viable. A Doppler device or ultrasound transducer wrapped in a sterile plastic bag may be used for this purpose. When the uterus has been penetrated by an object or projectile, the fetus probably has been injured. If the fetus is alive, the decision to perform cesarean delivery should be weighed against the likelihood of fetal survival. Factors involved in this decision include gestational age, the condition of the fetus based on any antenatal testing that may have been performed, the extent of injury to the uterus (ie, a cesarean hysterectomy may be necessary with extensive injuries), and whether the gravid uterus allows adequate exploration of the peritoneal cavity. These decisions often are made jointly with the trauma surgeon. The need to perform a laparotomy, by itself, is not an indication to proceed with cesarean delivery. If the uterus has been penetrated and delivery must proceed, a pediatric surgeon and a neonatologist should be available if possible.

Fetal Assessment

The use of electronic fetal cardiac and uterine activity monitoring in pregnant trauma victims beyond 20 weeks of gestation may be predictive of abruptio placentae. Placental abruption did not occur in trauma patients in whom uterine contractions occurred at a frequency of less than one every 10 minutes during 4 hours of monitoring (16, 18). Of those women who had uterine contractions of greater frequency, however, almost 20% had placental abruption (16). Abnormal fetal heart tracings, including tachycardia and late deceleration, were seen frequently in cases of abruptio placentae.

Because abruption usually becomes apparent shortly after injury, monitoring should be initiated as soon as the woman is stabilized. Recommended minimum time of posttrauma monitoring includes 4 hours (3, 18) and 2–6 hours (31). However, none of these times have been validated by large, prospective studies. Monitoring should be continued and further evaluation carried out if uterine contractions, a nonreassuring fetal heart rate pattern, vaginal bleeding, significant uterine tenderness or irritability, serious maternal injury, or rupture of the amniotic membranes is present. If these findings are not present, the patient may be discharged or transferred (20). Upon discharge, the patient should be instructed to return if she develops vaginal bleeding, leakage of fluid, decreased fetal movement, or severe abdominal pain.

The use of ultrasonography following trauma during pregnancy does not appear to be as sensitive as cardiotocographic monitoring for diagnosing abruptio placentae (4, 16, 18, 20). However, ultrasonography is useful in the setting of trauma during pregnancy for establishing gestational age, locating the placenta, determining fetal wellbeing and extent of fetal injury or demise, and estimating amniotic fluid volume. In the woman, ultrasonography also may reveal the presence of intraabdominal fluid and increase the index of suspicion for intraperitoneal hemorrhage.

Fetal–Maternal Hemorrhage

Complications of fetal–maternal hemorrhage in trauma patients include fetal and neonatal anemia, fetal cardiac arrhythmias, and fetal death. There is no evidence that laboratory testing for fetal–maternal hemorrhage (eg, Kleihauer–Betke test) can predict adverse immediate sequelae due to hemorrhage (32). Among women who exhibit signs of fetal–maternal hemorrhage due to trauma, the mean estimated blood volume of injected fetal blood usually is less than 15 mL, and more than 90% of the hemorrhages are less than 30 mL (4, 16). Therefore, administration of 300 µg (one ampule) of D immune globulin would protect nearly all D-negative trauma victims from D alloimmunization. The routine use of the Kleihauer–Betke assay or other similar quantitative assays of fetal–maternal hemorrhage may be useful in identifying those few unsensitized, D-negative trauma patients who are found to have more than 30 mL transfusion. Additional D immune globulin (300 µg for every 30 mL of whole blood transfused) may be administered to these patients. Administration of D immune globulin at any time within the first 72 hours following fetal–maternal hemorrhage appears to provide protection from alloimmunization. Consideration should be given to administering D immune globulin to all unsensitized D-negative pregnant patients who have experienced abdominal trauma.

Special Considerations

Perimortem Cesarean Delivery

Although there are no clear guidelines regarding perimortem cesarean delivery, fetal survival is unlikely if more than 15–20 minutes have transpired since the loss of maternal vital signs. There are insufficient data on which to base conclusions regarding the appropriateness of abdominal delivery when efforts at resuscitation have failed. Based on isolated case reports, cesarean delivery should be considered for both maternal and fetal benefit 4 minutes after a woman has experienced cardiopulmonary arrest in the third trimester (33).

Safety Restraint Use During Pregnancy

There is substantial evidence that seat belt use during pregnancy protects both the mother and the fetus (17, 34, 35). Nonetheless, many pregnant women do not wear seat belts properly (13). Prenatal education on the use of seat belts improves compliance of seat belt use as well as improves knowledge of proper use (13). Current recommendations indicate that throughout pregnancy, safety belts should be used with both the lap belt and shoulder harness in place. The lap belt portion should be placed under the pregnant woman's abdomen, over both anterior superior iliac spines and the pubic symphysis. The shoulder harness should be positioned between the breasts. There should not be excessive slack in either belt, and both the lap and shoulder restraints should be applied as snugly as comfort will allow. Placement of the lap belt over the dome of the uterus significantly increases pressure transmission to the uterus and has been associated with significant uterine and fetal injury (36, 37). Based on preliminary data using a crash dummy that simulates a pregnant woman, there does not appear to be extraordinary force transmission to the pregnant uterus when seat belts are properly placed (37).

Airbag deployment during pregnancy does not appear to be associated with an increased risk for either maternal or fetal injury. Based on limited existing information, it does not appear reasonable to recommend disabling airbags during pregnancy.

Summary

Trauma is one of the leading causes of death of young people in this country; in many cases, it is preventable. The appropriate use of safety restraint systems in automobiles, compliance with traffic laws, and early identification and intervention in suspected cases of domestic violence are all preventive measures that may reduce the likelihood of both maternal and fetal morbidity and mortality. The obstetrician–gynecologist plays a central role both in the education of pregnant women and in the early identification of suspected abuse.

When trauma has occurred, an organized approach to management is critically important to optimize outcome. The first priority is treatment and stabilization of the woman; only then should attention be directed to the fetus. Electronic fetal and uterine monitoring is an important component of management beyond midtrimester trauma.

References

1. Dannenberg AL, Carter DM, Lawson HW, Ashton DM, Dorfman SF, Graham EH. Homicide and other injuries as causes of maternal death in New York City, 1987 through 1991. Am J Obstet Gynecol 1995;172:1557–1564

2. Fildes J, Reed L, Jones N, Martin M, Barrett J. Trauma: the leading cause of maternal death. J Trauma 1992;32:643–645

3. Pearlman MD, Tintinalli JE, Lorenz RP. A prospective controlled study of outcome after trauma during pregnancy. Am J Obstet Gynecol 1990;162:1502–1510

4. Goodwin TM, Breen MT. Pregnancy outcome and fetomaternal hemorrhage after noncatastrophic trauma. Am J Obstet Gynecol 1990;162:665–671

5. National Safety Council. Accident facts. Chicago: National Safety Council, 1997

6. American College of Obstetricians and Gynecologists. Domestic violence. ACOG Technical Bulletin 209. Washington, DC: ACOG, 1995

7. Gazamararian JA, Lazorick S, Spitz AM, Ballard TJ, Saltzman LE, Marks JS. Prevalence of violence against pregnant women. JAMA 1996;275:1915–1920

8. Helton AS, McFarlane J, Anderson ET. Battered and pregnant: a prevalence study. Am J Public Health 1987;77:1337–1339

9. Berenson AB, Stiglich NJ, Wilkinson GS, Anderson GD. Drug abuse and other risk factors for physical abuse in pregnancy among white non-Hispanic, black, and Hispanic women. Am J Obstet Gynecol 1991;164:1491–1499

10. McFarlane J, Parker B, Soeken K, Bullock L. Assessing for abuse during pregnancy. Severity and frequency of injuries and associated entry into prenatal care. JAMA 1992;267:3176–3178

11. Stewart DE, Cecutti A. Physical abuse in pregnancy. Can Med Assoc J 1993;149:1257–1263

12. Varner MW. Maternal mortality in Iowa from 1952 to 1986. Surg Gynecol Obstet 1989;168:555–562

13. Pearlman MD, Phillips ME. Safety belt use during pregnancy. Obstet Gynecol 1996;88:1026–1029

14. Pearlman MD, Tintinalli JE. Evaluation and treatment of the gravida and fetus following trauma during pregnancy. Obstet Gynecol Clin North Am 1991;18:371–381

15. Fries MH, Hankins GDV. Motor vehicle accident associated with minimal maternal trauma but subsequent fetal demise. Ann Emerg Med 1989;18:301–304

16. Pearlman MD, Tintinalli JE, Lorenz RP. Blunt trauma during pregnancy. N Engl J Med 1990;323:1609–1613

17. Crosby WM, Costiloe JP. Safety of lap-belt restraint for pregnant victims of automobile collisions. N Engl J Med 1971;284:632–636

18. Dahmus MA, Sibai BM. Blunt abdominal trauma: are there predictive factors for abruptio placentae or maternal–fetal distress? Am J Obstet Gynecol 1993;169:1054–1059

19. Rothenberger D, Quattlebaum FW, Perry JF Jr, Zabel J, Fischer RP. Blunt maternal trauma: a review of 103 cases. J Trauma 1978;18:173–179

20. Williams JK, McClain L, Rosemurgy AS, Colorado NM. Evaluation of blunt abdominal trauma in the third trimester of pregnancy: maternal and fetal considerations. Obstet Gynecol 1990;75:33–37

21. Biester EM, Tomich PG, Esposito TJ, Weber L. Trauma in pregnancy: normal revised trauma score in relation to other markers of maternofetal status—a preliminary study. Am J Obstet Gynecol 1997;176:1206–1212

22. Evrard JR, Sturner WQ, Murray EJ. Fetal skull fracture from an automobile accident. Am J Forensic Med Pathol 1989;10:232–234

23. Hartl R, Ko K. In utero skull fracture: case report. J Trauma 1996;41:549–552

24. Astarita DC, Feldman B. Seat belt placement resulting in uterine rupture. J Trauma 1997;42:738–740

25. Buchsbaum HJ. Accidental injury complicating pregnancy. Am J Obstet Gynecol 1968;102:752–769

26. Awwad JT, Azar GB, Seoud MA, Mroueh AM, Karam KS. High-velocity penetrating wounds of the gravid uterus: review of 16 years of civil war. Obstet Gynecol 1994;83:259–264

27. Kissinger DP, Rozycki GS, Morris JA Jr, Knudson M, Copes WS, Bass SM, et al. Trauma in pregnancy: predicting pregnancy outcome. Arch Surg 1991;126:1079–1086

28. American College of Obstetricians and Gynecologists. Guidelines for diagnostic imaging during pregnancy. ACOG Committee Opinion 158. Washington, DC: ACOG, 1995

29. Esposito TJ, Gens DR, Smith LG, Scorpio R. Evaluation of blunt abdominal trauma occurring during pregnancy. J Trauma 1989;29:1628–1632

30. Grubb DK. Nonsurgical management of penetrating uterine trauma in pregnancy: a case report. Am J Obstet Gynecol 1992;166:583–584

31. American Academy of Pediatrics, American College of Obstetricians and Gynecologists. Guidelines for perinatal care. 4th ed. Elk Grove Village, Illinois: AAP; Washington, DC: ACOG, 1997

32. Boyle J, Kim J, Walerius H, Samuels P. The clinical use of the Kleihauer–Betke test in Rh positive patients. Am J Obstet Gynecol 1996;174:343

33. Katz VL, Dotters DJ, Droegemueller W. Perimortem cesarean delivery. Obstet Gynecol 1986;68:571–576

34. Crosby WM, King AI, Stout LC. Fetal survival following impact: improvement with shoulder harness restraint. Am J Obstet Gynecol 1972;112:1101–1106

35. Wolf ME, Alexander BH, Rivara FP, Hickok DE, Maier RV, Starzyk PM. A retrospective cohort study of seatbelt use and pregnancy outcome after a motor vehicle crash. J Trauma 1993;34:116–119

36. McCormick RD. Seat belt injury: case of complete transection of pregnant uterus. J Am Osteopath Assoc 1968;67: 1139–1141

37. Pearlman MD, Viano D. Automobile crash simulation with the first pregnant crash test dummy. Am J Obstet Gynecol 1996;175:977–981

ACOG EDUCATIONAL BULLETIN

Number 246, April 1998

Osteoporosis

This Educational Bulletin was developed under the direction of the Committee on Educational Bulletins of the American College of Obstetricians and Gynecologists as an aid to obstetricians and gynecologists. The College wishes to thank Robert L. Barbieri, MD, for his assistance in the development of this bulletin. This document is not to be construed as establishing a standard of practice or dictating an exclusive course of treatment. Rather, it is intended as an educational tool that presents current information on obstetric–gynecologic issues.

Osteoporosis is an important health problem affecting mature women. The health care costs of osteoporosis are staggering and estimated to be in the range of $14 billion annually. Of the 28 million Americans with osteoporosis or with low bone mass, approximately 80% are women. Osteoporosis-related fractures will occur in more than 40% of women over the age of 50 (1). An estimated 1.3 to 1.5 million fractures occurring annually are attributed to osteoporosis and disproportionately affect women. Hip fracture, a serious manifestation of osteoporosis, accounts for about 15% of the total. Within 1 year after a hip fracture, up to 20% of the victims will die, 25% of the survivors will be confined to long-term care facilities, and 50% will experience long-term loss of mobility. Hip fractures are associated with more death, greater disability, and higher costs than all other types of osteoporotic fractures combined. Spinal fractures can be associated with pain, loss of height, and deformities (Dowager hump). Osteoporosis also is associated with tooth loss and the resorption of the alveolar ridge. Numerous studies suggest that osteoporosis increases the risk of edentia. Obstetrician–gynecologists play a major role in the prevention, diagnosis, and treatment of osteoporosis as outlined in this bulletin.

Definition

Osteoporosis is a systemic skeletal disease characterized by low bone mass and microarchitectural deterioration of bone tissue, with a consequent increase in bone fragility and susceptibility to fracture (2). Until recently, the diagnosis of osteoporosis usually was made after a woman had suffered a clinically significant fracture. Advances in the measurement of bone mass now make the diagnosis of osteoporosis possible prior to the occurrence of clinically significant fractures. The World Health Organization suggests that low bone density, or osteopenia, be defined as a bone mineral density between 1 and 2.5 standard deviations below the young adult mean and that osteoporosis be defined as a bone mineral density 2.5 standard deviations or more below the young adult peak mean (3). Other authorities define osteoporosis as a bone mineral density more than 2 standard deviations below the young adult peak mean (4). At the spine and hip, a 1 standard deviation decrease in bone mass is associated with approximately a twofold increase in fracture risk.

Replaces Number 167, May 1992

Pathophysiology

The functional part of bone is the remodeling unit. The bone-remodeling unit is the site on the surface of the bone where osteoblasts and osteoclasts work to make and resorb bone. Bone is constantly being remodeled in order to provide optimal support and to repair damage occurring from daily activities. The remodeling cycle can be conveniently divided into four phases: resting, resorption, reversal, and formation. Each remodeling cycle may take several months to complete.

During the resting phase, stem cells from the bone marrow are attracted to the bone surface and differentiate into osteoclasts. During the resorption phase, the osteoclasts remove bone using an acid pH to dissolve the minerals and proteolytic enzymes to digest the bone proteins. During the reversal phase, the osteoclasts cease removing the bone and mesenchymal stem cells are attracted to the bone surface and differentiate into osteoblasts. During the formation phase, osteoblasts make new bone by first laying down a protein matrix (osteoid), which is then mineralized. Type I collagen constitutes 90% of the osteoid. The protein matrix accounts for much of the tensile strength, and the minerals provide compressional strength. Cytokines (interleukin-1, -3, -6, and -11) and growth factors (transforming growth factor-beta, platelet derived growth factor, and insulinlike growth factors I and II) may modulate osteoclast and osteoblast function and mediate the coordination of these two cell types.

Bone conveniently can be divided into two major types: cortical and trabecular. Cortical bone forms the outer shell of all bones and accounts for 75% of total bone mass. Trabecular bone is the spongy, interlacing network of struts that forms the internal support within the cortical bone. Trabecular bone is concentrated in the vertebral bodies and pelvis and at the ends of the long bones. Trabecular bone accounts for 25% of total bone mass, but because of its spongy, open architectural structure it accounts for most of the surface area of the bone. Bone remodeling units are limited to the bone surface. Because trabecular bone has a large surface area, it has a higher turnover rate than cortical bone.

Bone formation and resorption is an ongoing process that usually is balanced in young adults who have adequate nutrition and exercise and normal puberty (5). Bone mass peaks at approximately 30 years in both men and women. After reaching peak bone mass, about 0.4% of bone is lost per year in both sexes. In addition to this loss, women also lose approximately 2% of cortical bone and 5% of trabecular bone per year for the first 5 to 8 years following menopause. With aging, the coordinated balance between osteoclasts and osteoblasts may be disturbed, resulting in excessive bone loss. In women who are recently menopausal, excess bone loss is commonly due to excessive osteoclast resorption. In later postmenopausal years, suppressed osteoblast activity and inadequate formation of bone may play a major role in the progression of osteoporosis. The excessive number of women as compared to men with osteoporosis is due in part to the accelerated loss of bone that occurs following menopause.

Factors Affecting Bone Mass

Bone mass is influenced by numerous factors. These factors include: family history, hormone levels, lifestyle and habits, nutrition, medications, and diseases that affect bone metabolism.

Many studies have shown that the risk of osteoporosis is greater for white and Asian women than for African American women. Mexican American women have an intermediate risk. These racial differences are probably due, in part, to genetic determinants of body size, body composition, and bone metabolism. Family studies also suggest that genetic factors play a role in determining bone mass. Female children and relatives of women with osteoporosis have lower bone mass than children and relatives of women without osteoporosis.

Estradiol, testosterone, progesterone, cortisol, parathyroid hormone, thyroxine, growth hormone, and insulin all can influence bone mass. The effect of estradiol on bone mass is probably both dose and time dependent. Marked deficiency in circulating estradiol (<20 pg/mL) appears to produce greater bone loss than modest deficiencies in estradiol (in the range of 40 pg/mL). Short periods of estrogen deficiency appear to be associated with less total bone loss than long periods of estradiol deficiency. Estrogen deficiency also is associated with many physiologic conditions and disease states (breastfeeding; menopause; surgical oophorectomy; and hypothalamic and pituitary causes of hypogonadotropic hypogonadism, such as nutritional and weight loss-associated amenorrhea, stress-associated amenorrhea, and amenorrhea associated with prolactin-secreting pituitary tumors). The mechanisms by which estradiol regulates bone mass are not completely defined.

Many lifestyle factors and habits influence bone mass. Cigarette smoking, excessive use of alcohol, and high caffeine intake may be associated with decreased bone mass and an increased risk of hip fracture (6). Most studies show that women who smoke cigarettes have lower bone mass than nonsmokers and a twofold increased risk of hip fracture. Alcohol consumption of 7 ounces or more per week has been associated with low bone mass and increased fracture rate (7).

Dietary calcium intake is an important modulator of bone mass, especially during childhood, adolescence, and advanced age (8). Childhood calcium intake appears to influence adult hipbone mass (9). In elderly hypoestrogenic women, the efficiency of gastrointestinal absorption of calcium may be reduced, requiring greater calcium intake to maintain calcium balance.

Vitamin D and its metabolites are essential to calcium metabolism and maintenance of mineral balance. In the United States, vitamin D deficiency rarely occurs except in select populations, such as those who are institutionalized with inadequate dietary intake and insufficient exposure to the sun. High protein diets acutely increase calcium excretion, but long-term, high-protein diets are not associated with excess bone loss. Diets high in phosphorus can result in excess calcium loss, but daily phosphorus intake less than 2,000 mg is not harmful to bone (recommended daily allowance in menopausal women is 700 mg [10]).

Systemic medications such as glucocorticoids, thyroxine, and heparin can cause decreased bone mass. Glucocorticoids are commonly used to treat rheumatic, allergic, and pulmonary diseases and to reduce rejection in patients with organ transplants. They have a direct effect on bone, causing inhibition of bone formation and enhancing bone resorption, and also decrease calcium absorption from the intestine and increase renal excretion of calcium. A dose of less than 10 mg daily of prednisone or equivalent is associated with minimal bone loss. At high doses, glucocorticoids are associated with bone loss in the range of 10% in the first year of treatment. Hyperthyroidism is associated with decreased bone mass. The effect may persist for many years after the hyperthyroidism is successfully treated. Thyrox-ine replacement at doses of 200 μg or more daily also is associated with osteoporosis. Thyroxine replacement that normalizes thyroid-stimulating hormone but does not completely suppress it appears to be associated with normal bone density (11). Chronic heparin therapy (12,000–50,000 U/d) is associated with bone loss in approximately one third of women.

Many metabolic bone diseases are associated with bone loss. These diseases often can be differentiated based on the measurement of serum calcium, phosphorus, and alkaline phosphatase (Table 1). The clinician should be aware that serum calcium rises slightly in hypoestrogenic states. Menopausal women may have a different normal range, with a higher upper normal limit, than women who are premenopausal or than men. Many laboratories do not account for this observation in their published normal ranges for serum calcium.

Osteoporosis can be caused by systemic diseases of the endocrine, hematopoietic, gastrointestinal, and connective tissue systems. When osteoporosis is caused by a systemic disease it often is referred to as secondary osteoporosis. The endocrine diseases most commonly associated with secondary osteoporosis are Cushing's disease, hyperthyroidism, hyperparathyroidism, and diabetes mel-

Table 1. Summary of Clinical Laboratory Data in Common Metabolic Diseases of the Bone

Bone Disorder	Serum Calcium	Serum Phosphorus	Alkaline Phosphatase
Osteoporosis	Normal	Normal	Normal
Osteomalacia	Low	Low	Elevated
Hyperparathyroid	Elevated	Low	Elevated
Renal failure, renal osteodystrophy	Low	Elevated	
Paget's disease	Normal	Normal	Very elevated

litus. The diseases of the hematopoietic system most commonly associated with secondary osteoporosis are lymphoma and multiple myeloma. Gastrointestinal diseases can cause osteoporosis by impairing the action of vitamin D and reducing calcium absorption. Gastrointestinal diseases that can cause osteoporosis include malabsorption syndromes due to systemic diseases (celiac disease) or surgical resection of stomach or bowel. Connective tissue disease such as Marfan syndrome and Ehlers–Danlos syndrome also can be associated with osteoporosis.

Screening

Development of screening guidelines for osteoporosis raises many complex issues. There is no single guideline for testing bone density. Figure 1 illustrates one possible screening algorithm for osteoporosis. In this algorithm, menopausal women taking hormone replacement therapy are not routinely offered bone mass measurements. Women who decline hormone replacement therapy are offered bone mass measurements if clinical risk factors for osteoporosis are present. In contrast, one consensus development conference concluded that: "assessment of clinical risk factors does not accurately predict the likelihood of fracture. Hence, bone mass measurement is recommended as the best approach to screen individuals for their risk of developing osteoporosis" (2). However, not all authorities support population-wide screening for osteoporosis.

Diagnosis

Imaging technology is now available to determine bone mass with minimal radiation exposure, high accuracy, and high precision. For measurement of the axial, proximal appendicular, and total body bone mass, dual X-ray absorptiometry (DXA) is preferred by most authorities. The precision of the measurement is approximately 1%. The radiation dose is less than 5 mrem (12). Almost all

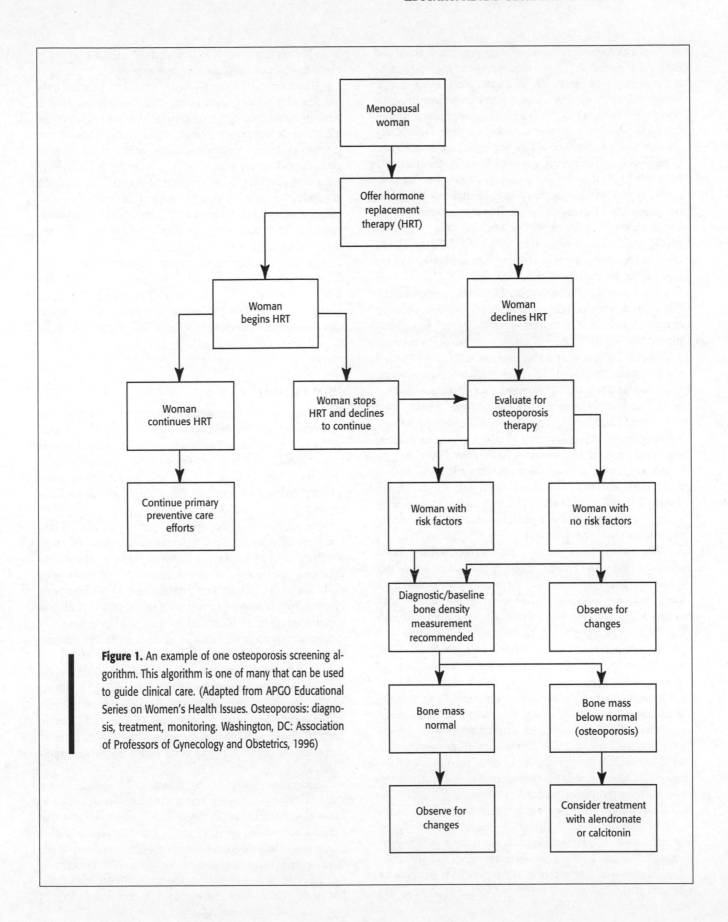

Figure 1. An example of one osteoporosis screening algorithm. This algorithm is one of many that can be used to guide clinical care. (Adapted from APGO Educational Series on Women's Health Issues. Osteoporosis: diagnosis, treatment, monitoring. Washington, DC: Association of Professors of Gynecology and Obstetrics, 1996)

modern DXA devices have an examination time in the range of 5 minutes. The fastest devices use high-power X-ray generators or fan beams and can complete an examination in 2 minutes. For clinical purposes in identifying a population at high risk for fracture, the reproducibility of DXA measurement of bone mass is excellent. Dual X-ray absorptiometry instruments are available, which measure bone mass at peripheral sites such as in the forearm. Measurement of forearm, wrist, or hand bone density may not predict hip fractures as accurately as the direct measurement of hipbone mass. However, some authorities state that "measurement at any site is a competent predictor of fracture at all sites" (2). One disadvantage of DXA is that bone spurs, aortic calcium, and arthritis may falsely elevate the reported bone density.

Dual-photon absorptiometry utilizes a gadolinium 135 source, which emits gamma photons at two different energy levels. Dual X-ray absorptiometry has largely replaced dual-photon absorptiometry instruments because of higher resolution and the avoidance of the cost and maintenance required for the radionuclide source. Quantitative computed tomography has been adapted for bone mass measurements, but radiation dosage, cost issues, and accessibility have limited its widespread use. Single-photon absorptiometry at peripheral sites such as the wrist or heel has less precision than DXA and, as noted previously, measurements at the wrist may not predict hip fracture as well as direct measurement of hipbone density. Ultrasound bone mass measurement is a new technique that offers the potential advantage of avoiding exposure to ionizing radiation.

Bone mass tests typically report three values: 1) an absolute value for the bone mass expressed as grams per square centimeter, 2) a value for bone mass relative to a sex- and age-matched reference population, usually called a Z-score, and 3) a value for bone mass relative to the mean peak bone mass, usually called a T-score or a young adult Z-score (13). The T-score describes bone mass compared with the mean peak bone mass of a young adult reference population using standard deviations as the measure. A T-score of -2 indicates that the bone mass is 2 standard deviations below the mean peak bone mass. A T-score of –2 is associated with an approximate four-fold increased fracture risk. Some authorities contend that measurement of bone mass is a better predictor of fracture than blood pressure measurement is of stroke, or blood cholesterol is of heart disease (4).

In addition to bone density instruments, bone mass can be estimated through serial height measurements. Measurement of current height and comparison to reported maximal adult height can help establish the presumptive diagnosis of osteoporosis. Osteoporosis is likely to be present if the patient has lost more than 1 inch in height from her maximal adult height and the clinical setting is consistent with a diagnosis of osteoporosis.

Biochemical markers can be useful to help identify women with high bone turnover. Biochemical markers of bone turnover also may prove to be useful to monitor the effects of osteoporosis treatment. Markers that measure the rate of bone formation include serum bone alkaline phosphatase, serum osteocalcin, and serum procollagen I extension peptides. Markers that show the rate of bone resorption include urinary N-telopeptide collagen cross-links, urinary deoxypyridinoline, and urinary hydroxyproline. The technology for measurement of bone biochemical markers is evolving rapidly.

For premenopausal and postmenopausal women who have osteoporosis documented by bone mass measurement or who have lost significant height or who have had a fracture, the presence of metabolic bone disease should be considered. Common secondary causes of metabolic bone disease are shown in Table 1.

Prevention

The most effective approach to osteoporosis prevention is to ensure each woman reaches her genetically endowed peak bone mass and to minimize the amount of bone loss during menopause. Interventions to prevent osteoporosis span the continuum of life and extend into menopause with the addition of estrogen. Several options are outlined in Table 2.

Prevention of osteoporosis begins in childhood and adequate calcium intake is important. Recommendations for daily calcium intake are listed in Table 3. Many children and adolescents do not achieve the recommended daily intake of calcium. For children and adolescents, calcium supplementation is not widely practiced. Calcium supplementation is indicated to ensure that genetically determined peak bone mass is achieved (9). Insufficient calcium intake also can accelerate age-associated bone loss. Calcium supplementation may provide a convenient means for reaching the daily dietary calcium goal without adding significant calories to the diet. Elemental calcium is present in various preparations (Table 4). Calcium citrate is more soluble and better absorbed than calcium carbonate in both fasting normal and achlorhydric individuals.

Sedentary lifestyle is associated with reduced bone mass. Weight-bearing exercise stimulates osteoblasts to form new bone (14). Observational studies suggest that exercise stimulates an increase in muscle mass and that exercise and increased muscle mass both contribute to the development of an increased bone mass. The benefits of exercise can be demonstrated into the ninth decade of life, but persist only when the exercise is continued (15). In

Table 2. Options for Osteoporosis Prevention and Treatment

Agent	Mechanism of Action	Effect on Bone	Effect on Fractures	Recommended for	Risks	Comment
Calcium	Increased availability	Deficiency causes loss; supplements reduce loss	Reduction in fracture risk by use of calcium with vitamin C	Adolescents, lactating women, hypoestrogenic women, osteoporosis risk factors including age	Should not exceed 2,000 mg/d; hypercalciuria, hypercalcemia	Revised daily requirement
Vitamin D	Increased intestinal absorption of CA++	Direct effect unknown; increases mass when combined with calcium	Reduction in fracture risk by use of calcium with vitamin D	Institutionalized elderly and women over 70	Hypercalciuria and hypercalcemia with increased doses	Overdosage in elderly can lead to renal failure
Estrogen	Reduces bone resorption by inhibiting osteoclasts	Slows bone loss; increases mass slightly; affects all types of bones	Documented reduction of all fractures; as high as 50% reduction of hip fractures	First-line choice for prevention in absence of contraindication; indicated for proven osteoporosis or abnormal bone density	Uterine bleeding, endometrial hyperplasia, endometrial carcinoma	Additional cardiovascular and other benefits have been described
Alendronate	Reduces bone resorption by inhibiting osteoclasts	Slows bone loss; increases bone mass	Significant reduction (48%) in new vertebral fractures	Treatment of osteoporosis (10 mg dose); prevention of repeat vertebral fractures	Not recommended for patients with renal insufficiency or upper gastrointestinal problems	Use as a preventive in normal population (5 mg dose)
Calcitonin	Reduces bone resorption by inhibiting osteoclasts	Increases vertebral bone mass	Significant reduction in new vertebral fractures	Alternative to estrogen therapy	Development of neutralizing antibodies—effect unknown	Objection to injections now avoided by intranasal spray; absorption is variable
Raloxifene	Reduces bone resorption by inhibiting osteoclasts	Slight increase in bone mass over 2–3 years of use	—	Prevention of osteoporosis	—	Low rate of uterine bleeding
Progestogens	Reduces bone resorption by inhibiting osteoclasts	Slows bone loss	Long-term study of progestins alone unavailable	Women on estrogen replacement therapy unless hysterectomized; not recommended as sole agent	Doses required to positively affect bone; causes reduction in high-density lipoprotein and elevation of low-density lipoprotein	—
Fluoride	Deposited and concentrated in bone; slowly reabsorbed	Increases bone mass in continuous manner; new bone is structurally abnormal	No demonstrated reduction in vertebral fracture; may increase nonvertebral fractures	Not recommended in the United States	New bone may be weaker and increase fracture risk	Slow-release formulations may improve effectiveness of fluoride
Etidronate	Inhibits bone resorption by reducing ability of osteoclasts to reabsorb bone	Increases bone mass; reduces bone remodeling	Reduction not clearly demonstrated	Not FDA approved for this purpose	Inhibits mineralization at slightly higher doses; long-term effects unknown	Approved for osteoporosis treatment in Canada
Tamoxifen	Assumed to be an antiabsorptive agent with an effect of a weak estrogen	Laboratory evidence of reduced bone loss in rats	No long-term data	Not recommended as an agent specific for osteoporosis prevention	Endometrial carcinoma incidence is reportedly increased	Level of protection against osteoporosis unknown; other agents should be added

Table 3. Optimal Calcium Requirements

Age or Clinical State	Recommended Elemental Calcium Intake (mg)
Children	
Age 1–5 years	800
Age 6–10 years	800–1,200
Adolescents	1,200–1,500
Adult women (premenopausal)	1,000
Adult women (menopausal or hypo-estrogenic on estrogen replacement therapy)	1,000
Adult women (menopausal or hypo-estrogenic not on estrogen replacement therapy)	1,500

Adapted from Optimal Calcium Intake. NIH Consensus Statement 1994;12(4):7

menopausal women, weight-bearing exercise for 22 months was shown to result in a 6.1% increase in bone density of the lumbar spine (16). The benefits of physical exercise include maintenance of bone mass and an increase in muscle strength and coordination.

The risk of falling increases substantially with aging. Diseases and sensory impairments that can promote falling should be treated. Medications that reduce strength and balance should be avoided, if possible. Most falls that result in hip fractures occur indoors. The living environment should be monitored to reduce the risk of falling. Cessation of smoking and reducing alcohol and caffeine intake may all contribute to a decreased risk of developing a fracture.

Raloxifene, a nonsteroidal benzothiophene, has been approved by the Food and Drug Administration for the prevention of osteoporosis at a dose of 60 mg daily. Raloxifene is a selective estrogen receptor modulator, which displays estrogen agonist properties in the bone (inhibits osteoclast function) and the liver (decreases low-density lipoprotein cholesterol). Because raloxifene has no estrogen agonist activity in the endometrium, raloxifene treatment is associated with minimal uterine bleeding. At doses of 60 mg daily for 24 months, raloxifene is associated with a 1–2% increase in lumbar spine and hip bone density (17).

Treatment

In women with established osteoporosis, calcium, vitamin D supplementation, and an exercise program should be considered. As outlined in Figure 1, estrogen replacement therapy is the primary preventive and therapeutic modality for hypoestrogenic women with osteoporosis.

Many women who start estrogen replacement therapy discontinue the treatment. For menopausal women with established osteoporosis who decline estrogen replacement, alendronate and calcitonin are effective treatment options. All women with osteoporosis should be offered estrogen replacement as the first line of therapy, which decreases bone loss, reduces the incidence of fracture, and prevents height loss (18–20). Estrogen replacement initiated during perimenopause or soon after the onset of menopause prevents the early phase of menopausal bone loss and decreases the subsequent risk of fracture by approximately 50%. Estrogen also is effective if initiated many years after the onset of menopause (19, 21, 22). For menopausal women taking estrogen replacement therapy, the addition of a progestin does not significantly increase bone mass; the optimum duration of this therapy is not well established. When estrogen replacement therapy is discontinued, bone loss can increase to a rate similar to that seen following oophorectomy (23).

Alendronate is a bisphosphonate that has been demonstrated to increase bone mineral density and reduce the fracture rate in menopausal women with osteoporosis. Biphosphonates are analogues of inorganic pyrophosphate, and a number of other biphosphonates are currently under development. Alendronate binds tightly to the bone's hydroxyapatite crystal surface and inhibits the function of nearby osteoclasts, reducing bone resorption. At the doses used to treat osteoporosis, alendronate does not significantly inhibit osteoblast function. Menopausal women treated with alendronate for 3 years gained significant bone mass at the hip trochanter (6–8%) and the spine (6–9%) (24). Vertebral fractures were reduced by 48% in the women treated with alendronate. Loss of height was greater in the women who were treated with

Table 4. Amount of Elemental Calcium Present in Various Preparations

Generic Name	Amount of Elemental Calcium (%)	Dose	Elemental Calcium Present in Preparation (mg)
Calcium carbonate	40	600–1,500 mg tablet	600
		500–1,250 mg tablet	500
		500 mg tablet	200
Calcium citrate	21.2	950 mg tablet	200
Calcium lactate	13	325 mg tablet	42.2
		650 mg tablet	84.5

placebo plus 500 mg of calcium than in the women treated with alendronate.

Alendronate is approved by the Food and Drug Administration for the prevention of osteoporosis (5 mg daily) and for the treatment of established osteoporosis (10 mg daily). Alendronate is poorly absorbed from the gastrointestinal tract (1% absorption). It is recommended that alendronate be taken in the morning with 8 ounces of water, prior to any food or beverage. No food or beverage should be taken for the next 30 minutes to allow the alendronate to be absorbed. After taking alendronate, the woman should remain in an upright position, either sitting or standing, to minimize the possibility of abdominal discomfort. The major side effects associated with alendronate treatment are abdominal pain and musculoskeletal pain. Alendronate use can be associated with upper gastrointestinal bleeding. One potential advantage of alendronate is that it remains tightly bound to the surface of the bone for many years. Because of the long half-life of alendronate, estimated to be greater than 10 years, there may not be rapid bone loss during the period just after discontinuation of the drug that occurs after the discontinuation of estrogen.

Calcitonin is produced endogenously by the parafollicular C cells of the thyroid gland. Calcitonin inhibits bone resorption. Currently, the most convenient route of administration of calcitonin is as a nasal spray. One spray in one nostril delivers the recommended dose of 200 IU of salmon calcitonin. Intranasal calcitonin has been demonstrated to increase bone mass and reduce the risk of vertebral fractures (25, 26). The most frequent side effect of nasal salmon calcitonin is rhinitis.

Progestins, fluoride, androgens, and parathyroid hormone have been demonstrated to be effective in the treatment of osteoporosis. In a hypoestrogenic state, progestins can decrease biochemical markers of bone resorption and preserve bone density. Progestins, used as monotherapy for osteoporosis may be more effective at preserving bone in the wrist than the spine.

Fluoride is a mineral that stimulates osteoblasts to produce new bone. When fluoride is administered at doses of 75 mg daily or more, the new bone formed is dense but may be structurally weak and susceptible to fracture (27). Lower doses of fluoride, administered in a slow-release formulation for 28 months, have been demonstrated to both improve bone density and simultaneously decrease fracture risk (28). The most common side effects of treatment with fluoride are gastric irritation and lower extremity pain. Currently, there is insufficient evidence to support the safety and efficacy of sodium fluoride therapy for the treatment of osteoporosis (29).

Parathyroid hormone is not approved by the Food and Drug Administration for the treatment of osteoporosis. On an experimental basis, exogenously administered parathyroid hormone and biologically active fragments of parathyroid hormone appear to stimulate bone growth if given intermittently or at low doses (30).

Summary

Advances in imaging technology allow clinicians to diagnose osteoporosis before a clinically significant fracture occurs. In addition, advances in pharmacology give clinicians a broad range of estrogens and nonestrogen treatments for osteoporosis. These advances in imaging technology and treatment are timely. As the population ages, a large increase in osteoporotic fractures is expected. It is key that women at increased risk are identified. Premenopausal and menopausal women should be encouraged to exercise and maintain adequate calcium intake. Menopausal women should be encouraged to consider estrogen replacement therapy, and those with risk factors who decline estrogen replacement therapy should be recommended for bone density measurements. Women with low bone density or established osteoporosis should be offered estrogen replacement, alendronate, or calcitonin therapy. Application of these new tools and treatments by obstetrician–gynecologists may reduce the number of osteoporotic fractures experienced by our aging population.

References

1. Genant HK, Jergas M, Palermo L, Nevitt M, Valentin RS, Black D, et al. Comparison of semiquantitative visual and quantitative morphometric assessment of prevalent and incident vertebral fractures in osteoporosis. The Study of Osteoporotic Fractures Research Group. J Bone Miner Res 1996;11:984–996

2. Consensus Development Conference: Diagnosis, prophylaxis, and treatment of osteoporosis. Am J Med 1993; 94:646–650

3. World Health Organization. Assessment of fracture risks and its application to screening for postmenopausal osteoporosis. WHO Technical Report Series. Geneva: WHO, 1994

4. Nordin BEC. Guidelines for bone densitometry. Med J Aust 1994;160:517–520

5. Boot AM, DeRidder MAJ, Pols HAP, Krenning EP, DeMuinck Keizer-Schrama SMPF. Bone mineral density in children and adolescents: relation to puberty, calcium intake, and physical activity. J Clin Endocrinol Metab 1997;82:57–62

6. Hernandez-Avila M, Colditz GA, Stampfer MJ, Rosner B, Speizer FE, Willett WC. Caffeine, moderate alcohol intake, and risk of fractures of the hip and forearm in middle-aged women. Am J Clin Nutr 1991;54:157–163

7. Felson DT, Kiel DP, Anderson JJ, Kannel WB. Alcohol consumption and hip fractures: the Framingham study. Am J Epidemiol 1988;128:1102–1110

8. Matkovic V, Illich J. Calcium requirements for growth: are current recommendations adequate? Nutr Rev 1993;51: 171–180

9. Nieves JW, Golden AL, Siris E, Kelsey JL, Lindsay R. Teenage and current calcium intake are related to bone mineral density of the hip and forearm in women aged 30–39 years. Am J Epidemiol 1995;141:342–351

10. Institute of Medicine. Standing Committee on the Scientific Evaluation of Dietary Reference Intakes. Dietary reference intakes for calcium, phosphorus, magnesium, vitamin D, and fluoride. Washington, DC: National Academy Press, 1997 (prepublication copy)

11. Marcocci C, Golia F, Bruno-Bossio G, Vignali E, Pinchera A. Carefully monitored levothyroxine suppressive therapy is not associated with bone loss in premenopausal women. J Clin Endocrinol Metab 1994;78:818–823

12. Jergas M, Genant HK. Current methods and recent advances in the diagnosis of osteoporosis. Arthritis Rheum 1993;36:1649–1662

13. Compston JE, Cooper C, Kanis JA. Bone densitometry in clinical practice. BMJ 1995;310:1507–1510

14. Gutin B, Kasper MJ. Can vigorous exercise play a role in osteoporosis prevention? A review. Osteoporos Int 1992;2: 55–69

15. Fiatarone MA, Marks EC, Ryan ND, Meredith CN, Lipsitz LA, Evans WJ. High-intensity strength training in nonagenarians: effects on skeletal muscle. JAMA 1990;263: 3029–3034

16. Dalsky GP, Stocke KS, Ehsani AA, Slatopolsky E, Lee WC, Birge SJ Jr. Weight-bearing exercise training and lumbar bone mineral content in postmenopausal women. Ann Intern Med 1988;108:824–828

17. Delmas PD, Bjarnason NH, Mitlak BH, Ravoux A-C, Shah AS, Huster WJ, et al. Effects of raloxifene on bone mineral density, serum cholesterol concentrations, and uterine endometrium in postmenopausal women. N Engl J Med 1997;337:1641–1647

18. Ettinger B, Genant HK, Cann CE. Long-term estrogen replacement therapy prevents bone loss and fractures. Ann Intern Med 1985;102:319–324

19. Lindsay R, Tohme JF. Estrogen treatment of patients with established postmenopausal osteoporosis. Obstet Gynecol 1990;76:290–295

20. Nachtigall LE, Nachtigall RH, Nachtigall RD, Beckman EM. Estrogen replacement therapy; I: a 10-year prospective study in the relationship to osteoporosis. Obstet Gynecol 1979;53:277–281

21. Lufkin EG, Wahner HW, O'Fallon WM, Hodgson SF, Kotowitcz MA, Lane AW, et al. Treatment of postmenopausal osteoporosis with transdermal estrogen. Ann Intern Med 1992;117:1–9

22. Schneider DL, Barrett-Connor EL, Morton DJ. Timing of postmenopausal estrogen for optimal bone mineral density: the Rancho Bernardo study. JAMA 1997;277:543–547

23. Christiansen C, Christensen MS, Transbol I. Bone mass in postmenopausal women after withdrawal of oestrogen/ gestagen replacement therapy. Lancet 1981;1:459–461

24. Liberman UA, Weiss SR, Broll J, Minne HW, Quan H, Bell NH, et al. Effect of oral alendronate on bone mineral density and the incidence of fractures in postmenopausal osteoporosis. The Aldendronate Phase III Osteoporosis Treatment Study Group. N Engl J Med 1995;333: 1437–1443

25. Overgaard K, Hansen MA, Jensen SB, Christiansen C. Effect of salcatonin given intranasally on bone mass and fracture rates in established osteoporosis: a dose-response study. BMJ 1992;305:556–561

26. Rico H, Hernandez ER, Revilla M, Gomez-Castresana F. Salmon calcitonin reduces vertebral fracture rate in postmenopausal crush fracture syndrome. Bone Miner 1992;16:131–138

27. Riggs BL, Hodgson SF, O'Fallon WM, Chao EYS, Wahner HW, Muhs JM, et al. Effect of fluoride treatment on the fracture rate in postmenopausal women with osteoporosis. N Engl J Med 1990;322:802–809

28. Pak CYC, Sakhaee K, Piziak V, Peterson RD, Breslau NA, Boyd P, et al. Slow-release sodium fluoride in the management of postmenopausal osteoporosis: a randomized controlled trial. Ann Intern Med 1994;120:625–632

29. American Medical Association. Drug evaluations annual. Chicago: AMA, 1995.

30. Finkelstein JS, Klibanski A, Schaefer EH, Hornstein MD, Schiff I, Neer RM. Parathyroid hormone for the prevention of bone loss induced by estrogen deficiency. N Engl J Med 1994;331:1618–1623

ACOG EDUCATIONAL BULLETIN

Number 255, November 1999

Psychosocial Risk Factors: Perinatal Screening and Intervention

The American College of Obstetricians and Gynecologists has long been concerned about the psychosocial issues faced by women and their families during the childbearing years that affect their mental and physical well being. Many of these issues are more prevalent in the adolescent population. Screening for psychosocial risk factors may help predict a woman's attentiveness to personal health matters, her use of prenatal services, and the health status of her offspring (1).

Many physicians who care for women have had little training in managing the psychosocial issues that women encounter (2). An emerging body of evidence indicates that patients place high value on attention to these issues and report greater satisfaction with physician visits when there is more "psychosocial talk" and less "biomedical talk" (3). Health care providers, therefore, need to be encouraged to screen for psychosocial risk factors and to provide or refer patients for essential services to manage psychosocial problems. This can be accomplished through training to increase provider awareness of and interest in these issues as well as ways to respond to them. Adequate reimbursement by third-party payers for the necessary services also is essential.

Background

Although it is acknowledged that addressing psychosocial issues during pregnancy is important and has the potential to reduce costs to the individual and society (4), there are no screening tools widely available that have been shown to have high degrees of sensitivity and specificity. The Healthy Start Program of the Florida Department of Health, however, has designed one particularly well-regarded screening system, which has been used and refined by this program since 1992. Other tools exist, but none have been identified that have been evaluated as extensively as the Healthy Start tool. In addition, the Healthy Start tool provides a more concise and simple

Psychosocial Screening Tool

1. Do you have any problems that prevent you from keeping your health care appointments?

2. How many times have you moved in the past 12 months? 0 1 2 3 >3

3. Do you feel unsafe where you live?

4. Do you or any members of your household go to bed hungry?

5. In the past 2 months, have you used any form of tobacco?

6. In the past 2 months, have you used drugs or alcohol (including beer, wine, or mixed drinks)?

7. In the past year, has anyone hit you or tried to hurt you?

8. How do you rate your current stress level—low or high?

9. If you could change the timing of this pregnancy, would you want it earlier, later, not at all, or no change?

Modified and reprinted with permission from Florida's Healthy Start Prenatal Risk Screening Instrument. Florida Department of Health. DH 3134. September 1997

means of collecting psychosocial data that can be used for self-reporting or interview style information retrieval (see the box for a modified version of this screening tool). Each topic identified in this tool will be discussed in this Educational Bulletin. Many of the topics are discussed more fully in various ACOG documents (see ACOG Resources).

Even though at first glance some of the questions appear to be relevant only for low-income populations, psychosocial screening of all patients presenting for pregnancy evaluation or prenatal care is an important step toward improving women's health and birth outcomes. When screening is done, every effort should be made to provide the brief interventions that are described in the following discussion. Through a brief intervention, the provider can identify areas of concern, validate major issues with the patient, provide information and, if indicated, make suggestions for possible changes. If necessary, the provider can refer the patient for further evaluation or intervention. For screening to be effective, a well-developed process for referrals is necessary. If assistance is needed with locating appropriate referral sites, local or state health officials can be contacted.

Given the sensitive nature of psychosocial assessment, every effort should be made to screen in private, especially when inquiring about domestic or intimate partner violence. Even then, patients may not be comfortable discussing problems with physicians until a trusting relationship has been formed. Because problems may arise during the pregnancy that were not present at the initial visit, it is best to perform psychosocial screening once each trimester to increase the likelihood of identifying important issues and reducing poor birth outcomes. A recent study indicates that women who were screened for psychosocial issues once each trimester were half as likely as women who were not screened to have a low-birth-weight or preterm baby (5). Documentation should include the nature of any problems identified, the chosen intervention(s), and plans for follow-up. A suggested format for this documentation can be found at the end of this document.

Psychosocial risk factors also should be considered in discharge planning after delivery. Many of the psychosocial issues that increase the risk for poor pregnancy outcome also can affect the health and welfare of the newborn. It is essential that women with significant psychosocial problems stay in the hospital after delivery as long as necessary to assess adequately the health of the mother and the newborn; education of the woman about postpartum and infant care also occurs during this time. In the absence of complications, a 48-hour hospital stay after a normal vaginal delivery and a 96-hour stay after a cesarean delivery is recommended (6).

Barriers to Care

Inadequate insurance coverage, inability to pay for health care services, and not knowing where to go to receive care are a few of the most common barriers to health care. Others include lack of transportation and day care and language difficulties (7). These barriers are especially problematic for adolescents. For individuals faced with these barriers, referral to an appropriate social service agency may be useful. These agencies can sometimes help women navigate the health care system. In particular, they can help her enroll in Medicaid, which covers the costs of medical care and transportation to and from medical and social service appointments and also subsidizes or provides free day care. Through flexible scheduling of appointments, inquiring about difficulties a patient may have with keeping appointments, and assisting with solutions, the provider increases the likelihood of compliance with prenatal care recommendations. Following are brief interventions for several of the most common barriers to care.

Transportation

Transportation difficulties are commonly cited as a barrier to prenatal visits (8), particularly for women residing in rural areas (9). Many women lack transportation to and from health care appointments and rely on either public transportation or the willingness of friends and family to transport them. If a patient is not certain how she will get to appointments, the health care provider should discuss options available to her.

Day Care

For a patient who already has children, finding and paying for appropriate child care while attending appointments can be another barrier to care (10). Caring for elderly or disabled family members may pose a similar challenge. For patients who cannot arrange day care, establishing an office setting that can accommodate children and relatives is helpful.

Interference by Others

Sometimes a patient's spouse, partner, or parent may not want her to keep medical appointments. Although patients often are not directly forthcoming with this information, providers can obtain important details about the patient by asking about interference from family members, domestic or family violence, and safety issues when patients miss appointments. Flexible scheduling, assistance with transportation, or social service assistance may improve compliance with ongoing perinatal care.

Language

Because barriers to care are magnified when the patient does not speak English, it is important to use translators when possible. If this is not possible, providers can ask the patient to identify a family member or friend who can act as a translator. This may be a less desirable choice, however, because information may be intentionally or unintentionally translated incorrectly. For example, in cases of domestic violence, if the abusive spouse is translating, he might omit a question about safety in the home, misrepresent the patient's response, or retaliate. Another partial solution is to provide written materials in appropriate languages for patients who do not speak English. If communication is not adequate, it must be decided whether the patient should remain in the practice or be referred to a facility with better access to translators.

Frequent Moves

Frequent moves can indicate a variety of problems. For example, the patient may be having difficulty finding acceptable housing that is affordable. If this is the case, the patient can be referred to the appropriate social service agency for assistance. These local agencies also can provide information about other resources in the area, including health services, social support groups, and child care resources. Inquiring about the patient's feelings of isolation also is important. If this is a problem, referral to any available neighborhood support groups or a counselor can be helpful. In addition, frequent moves may reflect violence in the home or may indicate problems with the law that can cause stress.

Safety

Safety concerns can pertain to either safety in the house or safety in the neighborhood. In either case, if there is immediate danger to the patient, alternative housing should be discussed. If there are children who are not safe in the household, a referral to the state's child protection agency may be required. The state agency can be contacted for specific reporting requirements. If the safety concern relates specifically to the house, such as structural defects, rat or insect infestation, or sanitation issues, further inquiry can determine the necessary referral or intervention.

If the danger is a result of intimate partner violence, referrals, including one to a battered women's shelter, should be made. If there are no shelters or safe houses available, hospital beds may be provided on an emergency basis in some cases. It is important to assess the potential for life-threatening situations and develop safety plans with the patient, understanding that the likelihood of serious injury often is highest when the woman attempts to leave her abuser. Physicians need to be aware that the patient is the best judge of her own safety. She, therefore, may choose to return home despite receiving advice to the contrary, and the physician must honor her decision.

Nutrition

Nutritional problems can be found in women of every socioeconomic status and range from an inability to acquire and prepare food to eating disorders. If the woman cannot afford a sufficient supply of food, she should be referred to food pantries and soup kitchens in her area. All low-income women should receive information about the Special Supplemental Food Program for Women, Infants and Children (WIC) and food stamp programs. Referrals to the appropriate social service agency to apply for these or other available benefits can be helpful.

Women of low socioeconomic status often live in environments that do not allow for the storage, refrigeration, or preparation of food. Many nutritionists are trained in alternative methods of food storage and preparation and would, therefore, be able to assist the patient upon referral. The nutritionist also could assess the patient's diet and suggest healthy foods that are inexpensive.

Additional questions should be asked, especially of adolescents and young women, about eating habits such as fasting or meal skipping, which are indicative of anorexia and bulimia. If it is determined that the patient has an eating disorder, referral to a psychiatrist who specializes in this issue and a nutritionist for counseling about food management is essential. All WIC programs have nutritionists who are required to counsel patients on these matters. Hospitalization also may be required for patients with eating disorders. Poor weight gain also may reflect substance abuse, domestic violence, or depression.

Tobacco Use

Smoking tobacco is associated with increased perinatal mortality; bleeding complications of pregnancy; and a higher incidence of small-for-gestational age babies, low-birth-weight babies, and preterm delivery (11). It is estimated that a 10% reduction in fetal and infant deaths would be achieved if all pregnant women stopped smoking (12). There also is increasing evidence that Attention Deficit Hyperactivity Disorder (ADHD) and other behavioral or learning problems that affect school-aged children may be linked to maternal smoking during pregnancy (13). Therefore, it is essential that patients be screened for tobacco use and provided information on smoking cessation and why it is necessary to stop smoking during pregnancy. Interventions by clinicians that are as brief as 5–15 minutes have been shown to be effective at increasing smoking cessation rates (14).

Substance Use

Women who use substances have increased risks of preterm delivery, fetal growth restriction, fetal alcohol syndrome, fetal death, and possible long-term neurobehavioral effects (15). They also are at increased risk for sexually transmitted diseases, including human immunodeficiency virus (HIV). Women who use substances often obtain prenatal care late in the pregnancy, achieve poor weight gain, and frequently miss appointments, all of which can have negative effects on the health of the woman and the fetus. Substance abuse, by either the woman or her partner, also is associated with domestic violence. Asking patients about substance abuse at the time of the first prenatal visit is essential; questions about her partner's use of substances also may be helpful. If

either inquiry indicates an area of concern, additional assessment is required (15).

Intimate Partner Violence

The incidence of abuse during pregnancy is high, with reports ranging from 1% to 20% of all pregnant women (16). Many studies report that violence often begins in pregnancy; if already present, it may escalate (17). Research also suggests that violence may increase during the postpartum period (18). Given these findings, it would be useful to screen every woman for intimate partner violence at least once in each trimester; whenever bruising, improbable injury, or depressed mood is noted; and at the postpartum visit. It also is important to know the various characteristics that may serve as markers for abuse. Women who are abused are more likely to receive inadequate prenatal care. In particular, abused pregnant women seek prenatal care later in pregnancy (19), miss more appointments, and are more likely to cancel appointments on short notice than nonabused pregnant women (20).

Stress

Stress is defined as any real or perceived trauma—whether it is physical or psychologic—that results in the release of stress hormones. Folklore has always taken it for granted that stress, such as acute anxiety, sorrow, or worry disturbs the fetus and causes physical harm (21). The observation that maternal stress is measurably related to neonatal activity and irritability in both lower animals and in humans has been documented by research during the past 30 years (22). Recent studies support that women who are anxious during pregnancy tend to have smaller babies and that women with high levels of stress hormones are more likely to deliver preterm (23, 24).

Practitioners should identify patients under stress. The stress associated with pregnancy itself, concerns about labor and delivery, and projected fears about parenting can sometimes be reduced by providing counseling and information during the course of prenatal care. Other patients may require evaluation and treatment by mental health practitioners to help identify and resolve distress.

Unintended Pregnancy

Approximately 49% of all pregnancies are unintended at the time of conception (25). This percentage is considerably higher among adolescents. An unintended pregnancy generally is defined as a pregnancy that was mistimed or unwanted at the time of conception. Research has shown that having an unintended pregnancy is a predictor of insufficient prenatal care, which results in an increased risk of a poor birth outcome. Women with unintended pregnancies are more likely to smoke and drink and have a greater likelihood of delivering a low-birth-weight infant. Their infants are more likely to die within the first year of life (26). In addition, the incidence of unintended pregnancy is higher among women who have been battered (27) and battering is more common during an unplanned pregnancy (28).

Unintended pregnancies often become accepted pregnancies that produce much-loved and wanted children. However, women with pregnancies that remain unwanted should be counseled about the full range of reproductive options, which include abortion and adoption. Women must be allowed to make independent decisions about their own pregnancies. This choice remains a woman's right and must be respected.

Summary

Addressing the broad range of psychosocial issues with which pregnant women are confronted is an essential step toward improving women's health and birth outcomes. This may be difficult to do completely in a private physician's office setting, therefore, an effective system of referrals is helpful. To increase the likelihood of successful interventions, psychosocial screening should be performed on a regular basis and documented in the patient's prenatal record.

ACOG Resources

American College of Obstetricians and Gynecologists. Depression in women. ACOG Technical Bulletin 182. Washington, DC: ACOG, 1993

American College of Obstetricians and Gynecologists. Domestic violence: the role of the physician in identification, intervention, and prevention. Slide lecture kit. Washington, DC: ACOG, 1995

American College of Obstetricians and Gynecologists. Domestic violence. ACOG Educational Bulletin 209. Washington, DC: ACOG, 1995

American College of Obstetricians and Gynecologists. Mandatory reporting of domestic violence. ACOG Committee Opinion 200. Washington, DC: ACOG, 1998

American College of Obstetricians and Gynecologists. Nutrition and women. ACOG Educational Bulletin 229. Washington, DC: ACOG, 1996

American College of Obstetricians and Gynecologists. Smoking and women's health. ACOG Educational Bulletin 240. Washington, DC: ACOG, 1997

American College of Obstetricians and Gynecologists. Substance abuse. ACOG Technical Bulletin 194. Washington, DC: ACOG, 1994

American College of Obstetricians and Gynecologists. Substance abuse in pregnancy. ACOG Technical Bulletin 195. Washington, DC: ACOG, 1994

Bibliography

American Academy of Pediatrics Committee on Drugs. The transfer of drugs and other chemicals into human milk. Pediatrics 1994;93:137–150

Briggs GG, Freeman RK, Yaffe SJ. Drugs in pregnancy and lactation. 5th ed. Baltimore: Williams & Wilkins, 1998

Dolan-Mullen P, Ramirez G, Groff JY. A meta-analysis of randomized trials of prenatal smoking cessation interventions. Am J Obstet Gynecol 1994;171:1328–1334

Haller E. Eating disorders. A review and update. West J Med 1992;157:658–662

Henningfield JE. Nicotine medications for smoking cessation. N Engl J Med 1995;333:1196–1203

Hutchins E, DiPietro J. Psychosocial risk factors associated with cocaine use during pregnancy: a case-control study. Obstet Gynecol 1997;90:142–147

Laken MP, Hutchins E. Building and sustaining systems of care for substance-using pregnant women and their infants: Lessons learned. Arlington, Virginia: National Center for Education in Maternal and Child Health, 1995

MacGregor SN, Keith LG, Bachicha JA, Chasnoff IJ. Cocaine abuse during pregnancy: correlation between prenatal care and perinatal outcome. Obstet Gynecol 1989;74:882–885

Morse B, Gehshan S, Hutchins E. Screening for substance abuse during pregnancy: improving care, improving health. Arlington, Virginia: National Center for Education in Maternal and Child Health, 1997

Tofler IR, Stryer BK, Micheli LJ, Herman LR. Physical and emotional problems of elite female gymnasts. N Engl J Med 1996;335:281–283

Working Group on Nicotine Dependence. Practice guideline for the treatment of patients with nicotine dependence. American Psychiatric Association. Am J Psychiatry 1996;153:1–31

References

1. Goldenberg RL, Patterson ET, Freese MP. Maternal demographic, situational and psychosocial factors and their relationship to enrollment in prenatal care: a review of the literature. Women Health 1992;19:133–151

2. Goldberg D. A classification of psychological distress for use in primary care setting. Soc Sci Med 1992;35:189–193

3. Bertakis KD, Roter D, Putnam SM. The relationship of physician medical interview style to patient satisfaction. J Fam Pract 1991;32:175–181

4. Curry MA. Nonfinancial barriers to prenatal care. Women Health 1989;15:85–99

5. Wilkinson DS, Korenbrot CC, Greene J. A performance indicator of psychosocial services in enhanced prenatal care of Medicaid-eligible women. Matern Child Health J 1998;2:131–143

6. American Academy of Pediatrics, American College of Obstetricians and Gynecologists. Guidelines for perinatal care. 4th ed. Elk Grove Village, Illinois: AAP; Washington, DC: ACOG, 1997

7. Brown SS. Drawing women into prenatal care. Fam Plann Perspect 1989;21:73–80

8. Aved BM, Irwin MM, Cummings LS, Findeisen N. Barriers to prenatal care for low-income women. West J Med 1993;158:493–498

9. McDonald TP, Coburn AF. Predictors of prenatal care utilization. Soc Sci Med 1988;27:167–172

10. Kugler JP, Yeash J, Rumbaugh PC. The impact of sociodemographic, health care system, and family function variables on prenatal care utilization in a military setting. J Fam Pract 1993;37:143–147

11. American College of Obstetricians and Gynecologists. Smoking and women's health. ACOG Educational Bulletin 240. Washington, DC: ACOG, 1997

12. Kleinman JC, Pierre MB Jr, Madans JH, Land GH, Schramm WF. The effects of maternal smoking on fetal and infant mortality. Am J Epidemiol 1988;127:274–282

13. Milberger S, Biederman J, Faraone SV, Chen L, Jones J. Is maternal smoking during pregnancy a risk factor for attention deficit hyperactivity disorder in children? Am J Psychiatry 1996;153:1138–1142

14. Dolan Mullen P, Melvin CL, Windsor RA. A Review of the Evidence to Recommend Cessation Counseling for Pregnant Women Who Smoke. Smoke-Free Families Program, Department of Obstetrics and Gynecology, School of Medicine, University of Alabama at Birmingham, Birmingham, Alabama, 1999

15. American College of Obstetricians and Gynecologists. Substance abuse in pregnancy. ACOG Technical Bulletin 195. Washington, DC: ACOG, 1994

16. Gazmararian JA, Lazorick S, Spitz AM, Ballard TJ, Saltzman LE, Marks JS. Prevalence of violence against pregnant women. JAMA 1996:1915–1920

17. Hillard PJ. Physical abuse in pregnancy. Obstet Gynecol 1985;66:185–190

18. Stewart DE. Incidence of postpartum abuse in women with a history of abuse during pregnancy. CMAJ 1994;151: 1601–1604

19. McFarlane J, Parker B, Soeken K, Bullock L. Assessing for abuse during pregnancy. Severity and frequency of injuries and associated entry into prenatal care. JAMA 1992; 267:3176–3178

20. American Medical Association. Diagnostic and treatment guidelines on domestic violence. Chicago: AMA, 1994

21. Benedek T. The psychobiology of pregnancy. In: Anthony EJ, Benedek T, eds. Parenthood: Its psychology and psychopathology. London: J & A Churchill Ltd., 1970: 137–151

22. Herrenkohl LR. The impact of prenatal stress on the developing fetus and child. In: Cohen RL, ed. Psychiatric consultation in childbirth settings. New York: Plenum, 1988:21–35

23. Teixeira JM, Fisk NM, Glover V. Association between maternal anxiety in pregnancy and increased uterine artery resistance index: cohort based study. BMJ 1999;318: 153–157

24. Wadhwa PD, Porto M, Garite TJ, Chicz-DeMet A, Sandman CA. Maternal corticotropin-releasing hormone levels in the early trimester predict length of gestation in human pregnancy. Am J Obstet Gynecol 1998;179: 1079–1085

25. National Center for Health Statistics. Healthy People 2000 review, 1998-99. Hyattsville, Maryland: Public Health Service, 1999

26. The best intentions: unintended pregnancy and the well-being of children and families. Committee on Unintended Pregnancy, Institute of Medicine, National Academy of Sciences. Washington, DC: National Academy Press, 1995

27. Stewart DE, Cecutti A. Physical abuse in pregnancy. CMAJ 1993;149:1257–1263

28. Fergusson DM, Horwood LJ, Kershaw KL, Shannon FT. Factors associated with reports of wife assault in New Zealand. J Marriage Fam 1986;48:407–412

Psychosocial Risk Assessment

YES **NO**

☐ ☐ 1. Do you have any problems that prevent you from keeping your health care appointments?

0 1 2 3 >3 2. How many times have you moved in the past 12 months?

☐ ☐ 3. Do you feel unsafe where you live?

☐ ☐ 4. Do you or any members of your household go to bed hungry?

☐ ☐ 5. In the past 2 months, have you used any form of tobacco?

☐ ☐ 6. In the past 2 months, have you used drugs or alcohol (including beer, wine, and mixed drinks)?

☐ ☐ 7. In the past year, has anyone hit you or tried to hurt you?

low   high 8. How do you rate your current stress level—low or high?

a b c d 9. If you could change the timing of this pregnancy, would you want it (a) earlier, (b) later, (c) not at all, (d) no change?

Patient Name: _____

Patient No.: _____

Date	Area of Concern	Intervention	Recommendation/Referral	Follow-up	Initials

Modified and reprinted with permission from Florida's Healthy Start Prenatal Risk Screening Instrument. Florida Department of Health. DH 3134. October 1996

ACOG EDUCATIONAL BULLETIN

Number 260, September 2000

Smoking Cessation During Pregnancy

Smoking during pregnancy is associated with maternal, fetal, and infant morbidity and mortality (1). An office-based protocol that systematically identifies pregnant women who smoke and offers treatment has been proven to increase quit rates (2). For pregnant women who smoke less than 20 cigarettes per day, the provision of a 5–15 minute, five-step counseling session and pregnancy-specific educational materials increases cessation by 30–70% (3). This bulletin outlines this office-based intervention and addresses treatment issues pertaining to pregnant women who smoke heavily, smoking reduction, pharmacotherapy, health care support systems, and coding.

Epidemiology

Between 15% and 29% of pregnant women smoke during pregnancy (4). Health risks associated with smoking during pregnancy include ectopic pregnancy, intrauterine growth restriction, placenta previa, and abruptio placentae (1). Adverse pregnancy outcomes include preterm birth, low birth weight, and perinatal mortality (1). It is estimated that there would be a 10% reduction in perinatal mortality (5) and an 11% reduction in the incidence of low birth weight (6) if smoking during pregnancy were eliminated. Infant health risks include sudden infant death syndrome (SIDS), hospitalization, and neurodevelopmental abnormalities (1).

Intervention

The 5–15 minute intervention is most effective with pregnant women who smoke less than 20 cigarettes per day (3). The intervention is appropriate for use during routine prenatal office visits and includes the following five steps: **Ask, Advise, Assess, Assist,** and **Arrange** (2). It is adapted from the U.S. Public Health Service clinical practice guideline, Treating Tobacco Use and Dependence (2) and is based, in part, on earlier work by the

This Educational Bulletin was developed under the direction of the Committees on Obstetric Practice and Health Care for Underserved Women of the American College of Obstetricians and Gynecologists as an aid to obstetricians and gynecologists. This document is not to be construed as establishing a standard of practice or dictating an exclusive course of treatment. Rather, it is intended as an educational tool that presents current information on obstetric–gynecologic issues.

National Cancer Institute (7). The obstetrician–gynecologist or auxiliary health care provider, after appropriate training, can perform the five steps with pregnant women who smoke. The steps are outlined as follows and on the chart (see the box). The chart guides the provider through the interaction and documents the treatment (3).

1. **Ask** about smoking status. Providers should ask the patient at the first prenatal visit to choose a statement that best describes her smoking status from a list of statements on smoking behavior (see the box). Using this multiple-choice method is more likely to elicit an accurate response than asking a simple "Yes or No" question. The smoking cessation chart, a tobacco use sticker, or a vital signs stamp that includes smoking status should be used in the medical record to remind providers to ask patients about smoking status at follow-up visits.

2. **Advise** patients who smoke to stop by providing clear, strong advice to quit with personalized messages about the benefits of quitting and the impact of continued smoking on the woman, fetus, and newborn. Congratulate patients who report having stopped smoking and affirm their efforts with a statement about the benefits of quitting.

3. **Assess** patients' willingness to attempt to quit smoking within the next 30 days. One approach to this assessment is to say, "Quitting smoking is one of the most important things you can do for your health and your baby's health. If we can give you some help, are you willing to try?" If the patient is willing, then the provider can move to the next step. If the patient is unwilling to try, providers may consider having a brief discussion with the patient to educate and reassure her about quitting (2). Quitting advice, assessment, and assistance should be offered at subsequent prenatal care visits.

4. **Assist** patients who are interested in quitting by providing pregnancy-specific, self-help smoking cessation materials. Enhance the patient's problem-solving skills by asking when and where she typically smokes and suggesting how she might avoid these "trigger situations." Offer support around the importance of having smoke-free space at home; seeking out a "quitting buddy" such as a former smoker or nonsmoker both at work and at home; and what to expect in terms of nicotine withdrawal, such as irritability and cravings. Communicate caring and concern and encourage the patient to talk about the process of quitting.

5. **Arrange** during regular follow-up visits to track the progress of the patient's attempt to quit smoking. Smoking status should be monitored throughout pregnancy, providing opportunities to congratulate and support success, reinforce steps taken towards quitting, and advise those still considering a cessation attempt.

Although counseling and pregnancy-specific materials are effective cessation aids for many pregnant women, some women continue to smoke. These women often are heavily addicted and should be encouraged at follow-up visits to stop smoking. Clinicians also may consider offering or referring patients for additional psychosocial treatment (2). Although quitting smoking early in pregnancy yields the greatest benefits for the pregnant woman and fetus, quitting at any point can be beneficial (2). For instance, pregnant women who stop smoking at any time up to the 30th week of gestation have infants with higher birth weights than women who smoke throughout pregnancy (8). The benefits of "cutting down" are difficult to measure or verify. So, the effort of women who cut down should be reinforced, but they also should be reminded that quitting entirely brings the best results for their health and that of their babies (3).

Pharmacotherapy

The use of nicotine replacement products or other pharmaceuticals as smoking cessation aids during pregnancy has not been sufficiently evaluated to determine its efficacy or safety. Nicotine gum and patches should be considered for use during pregnancy only when nonpharmacologic treatments (eg, counseling) have failed, and if the increased likelihood of smoking cessation, with its potential benefits, outweighs the unknown risk of nicotine replacement and potential concomitant smoking. Research to determine the safety and efficacy of pharmacotherapy is strongly recommended because potential benefits seem to outweigh potential risks. Optimally, smokers can be treated with these pharmacotherapies before conception.

Support Systems

The Agency for Healthcare Research and Quality has recommended systems changes to help health care providers identify and treat tobacco users (2). These changes require the partnership of health care administrators, insurers, and purchasers and include the following strategies: 1) provide education, resources, and feedback to promote provider involvement in smoking cessation; 2) promote hospital policies that support and provide smoking cessation services; 3) include effective smoking cessation treatments as paid or covered services in all health benefits packages; and 4) reimburse clinicians and specialists for delivery of effective tobacco dependence treatments and include these interventions among the defined duties of the clinicians (2).

Smoking Cessation Intervention for Pregnant Patients

ASK–1 minute

- Ask the patient to choose the statement that best describes her smoking status:

  A.   I have NEVER smoked or have smoked LESS THAN 100 cigarettes in my lifetime.   ❏

  B.   I stopped smoking BEFORE I found out I was pregnant, and I am not smoking now.   ❏

  C.   I stopped smoking AFTER I found out I was pregnant, and I am not smoking now.   ❏

  D.   I smoke some now, but I have cut down on the number of cigarettes I smoke
     SINCE I found out I was pregnant.   ❏

  E.   I smoke regularly now, about the same as BEFORE I found out I was pregnant.   ❏

  If the patient stopped smoking before or after she found out she was pregnant (B or C), reinforce her decision to quit, congratulate her on success in quitting, and encourage her to stay smoke free throughout pregnancy and postpartum.

  If the patient is still smoking (D or E), document smoking status in her medical record, and proceed to Advise, Assess, Assist, and Arrange.

ADVISE–1 minute

- Provide clear, strong advice to quit with personalized messages about the benefits of quitting and the impact of smoking and quitting on the woman and fetus.   ❏

ASSESS–1 minute

- Assess the willingness of the patient to attempt to quit within 30 days.   ❏

  If the patient is ready to quit, proceed to Assist.

  If the patient is not ready, provide information to motivate the patient to quit and proceed to Arrange.

ASSIST–3 minutes +

- Suggest and encourage the use of problem-solving methods and skills for smoking cessation (eg, identify "trigger" situations).   ❏

- Provide social support as part of the treatment (eg, "we can help you quit").   ❏

- Arrange social support in the smoker's environment (eg, identify "quit buddy" and smoke-free space).   ❏

- Provide pregnancy-specific, self-help smoking cessation materials.   ❏

ARRANGE–1 minute +

- Assess smoking status at subsequent prenatal visits and, if patient continues to smoke, encourage cessation.

Data from Melvin C, Dolan Mullen P, Windsor RA, Whiteside HP, Goldenberg RL. Recommended cessation counselling for pregnant women who smoke: a review of the evidence. Tobacco Control 2000;9:1–5

Coding

Office visits specifically addressing smoking cessation may be coded as follows (note that not all payers reimburse for counseling outside of the global package and some do not cover preventive services at all):

- International Classification of Diseases, Ninth Revision, Clinical Modification (ICD-9-CM) code 305.1 (tobacco use disorder, tobacco dependence from the Mental Health section) *with* Current Procedural Terminology* (CPT) code 99401 *or* 99211

  — CPT code 99401 (preventive medicine counseling lasting approximately 15 minutes): If counseling is done by the physician at the time of a regular antepartum visit, use modifier 25 on code 99401. If counseling is done by the physician at another encounter, separate from the antepartum visit, no modifier is needed with code 99401.

  — CPT code 99211: If a nurse counsels the patient, and if nurses are recognized by the insurance company as "qualified" providers of the service, then code 99211 would be used instead of code 99401. If the nurse is not recognized as a caregiver, the services will not be covered unless provided by the physician.

---

*CPT codes, descriptions, and material only are copyright 1999 American Medical Association. All rights reserved. No fee schedules, basic units, relative values or related listings are included in CPT. The AMA assumes no liability for the data contained herein.

References

1. American College of Obstetricians and Gynecologists. Smoking and women's health. ACOG Educational Bulletin 240. Washington, DC: ACOG, 1997

2. Fiore MC, Bailey WC, Cohen SJ, et al. Treating tobacco use and dependence. Clinical practice guideline. Rockville, MD: U.S. Department of Health and Human Services. Public Health Service, June 2000

3. Melvin C, Dolan Mullen P, Windsor RA, Whiteside HP, Goldenberg RL. Recommended cessation counselling for pregnant women who smoke: a review of the evidence. Tobacco Control 2000;9:1–5

4. Ventura SJ, Martin JA. Report of final natality statistics, 1996. Monthly vital statistics report; vol 46, no. 11 (suppl). Hyattsville, Maryland: National Center for Health Statistics, June 30, 1998

5. Kleinman JC, Pierre MB, Madans JH, Land GH, Schramm WF. Effects of maternal smoking on fetal and infant mortality. Am J Epidemiol 1998;127:274–282

6. DiFranza JR, Lew RA. Effect of maternal cigarette smoking on pregnancy complications and sudden infant death syndrome. J Fam Pract 1995;40:385–394

7. Glynn TJ, Manley MW. How to help your patients stop smoking: a National Cancer Institute manual for physicians. Smoking and Tobacco Control Program, Division of Cancer Prevention, NCI, U.S. Department of Health and Human Services, Washington, DC, November 1990; NIH publication no. 90-3064

8. U.S. Department of Health and Human Services. The health benefits of smoking cessation. U.S. Department of Health and Human Services, Public Health Service, Centers for Disease Control, Center for Chronic Disease Prevention and Health Promotion, Office on Smoking and Health, 1990; DHHS publication no. (CDC) 90-8416

ISSN 1074-8628

The American College of Obstetricians and Gynecologists
409 12th Street, SW
PO Box 96920
Washington, DC 20090-6920

12345/43210

ACOG EDUCATIONAL BULLETIN

Number 253, November 1998

Special Problems of Multiple Gestation

The incidence of twin and higher-order multiple gestations has increased significantly over the past 15 years primarily because of the availability and increased use of ovulation-inducing drugs and newly developed assisted reproductive technologies such as in vitro fertilization. Multiple pregnancies and their various complications have, therefore, become more common (1). The incidence of twins, triplets, and higher-order multiple gestations now has reached approximately 3% of all pregnancies (2). When considering only those pregnancies resulting from assisted reproductive techniques, the rate of twin deliveries is from 25% to 30%; triplets account for 5% of deliveries, whereas the rate of higher-order multiple gestations is 0.5–1% of deliveries (3). Significant maternal and neonatal consequences are affected by this increase in multiple births.

Multifetal gestation is associated with an increased risk of perinatal morbidity and mortality (see Tables 1–3). Women who are undergoing treatment for infertility should be aware of the risks and potential fetal and maternal complications of multiple gestation. Such women can benefit from preconceptional counseling.

Obstetrician–gynecologists should be prepared to manage, with consultation when necessary, the special problems and complications of twin and higher-order multiple gestations. Because of the many variables associated with higher-order gestations and the need for specialized care based on individual circumstances, this Educational Bulletin will focus on twin gestations.

Antepartum Management

Nutritional Considerations

It is recommended that maternal dietary intake in a multiple gestation be increased daily by approximately 300 kcal above that for a singleton pregnancy (4). Supplementation should include iron and folic acid. Although optimal weight gain for women with multiple gestations has not been deter-

Replaces Number 131, August 1989

Table 1. Singleton Fetal Death Rates (per 1,000 conceptions)

Birth Weight (g)	Weeks of Gestation										Birth Weight Alone
	24–25	26–27	28–29	30–31	32–33	34–35	36–37	38–39	40–41	≥ 42	
≥ 4,900	—	—	—	—	—	—	—	—	—	—	—
4,600 < 4,900	—	—	—	—	—	—	—	3.6	1.9	2.1	2.3
4,300 < 4,600	—	—	—	—	—	—	—	1.7	1.2	1.6	1.4
4,000 < 4,300	—	—	—	—	—	—	3.0	1.1	1.0	1.3	1.1
3,700 < 4,000	—	—	—	—	—	—	2.2	0.9*	0.9	1.4	1.0†
3,400 < 3,700	—	—	—	—	—	—	2.2	1.0	1.1	1.5	1.2
3,100 < 3,400	—	—	—	—	—	2.9	2.6	1.3	1.4	1.8	1.5
2,800 < 3,100	—	—	—	—	6.4	5.0	3.5	2.0	2.2	2.6	2.5
2,500 < 2,800	—	—	—	—	12.1	8.8	6.5	4.1	4.5	4.8	5.3
2,200 < 2,500	—	—	—	21.4	19.4	14.2	13.9	10.3	11.2	12.0	12.9
1,900 < 2,200	—	—	49.2	37.1	29.6	27.8	31.1	26.2	24.4	—	29.1
1,600 < 1,900	—	68.9	72.1	43.7	49.8	61.8	72.3	—	—	—	57.0
1,300 < 1,600	150.2	99.2	66.2	68.4	103.2	127.3	—	—	—	—	89.4
1,000 < 1,300	193.2	93.5	95.1	142.9	212.5	—	—	—	—	—	128.6
700 < 1,000	173.7	151.5	221.7	287.9	353.4	—	—	—	—	—	200.7
500 < 700	318.1	355.2	447.0	509.7	—	—	—	—	—	—	361.2
Gestational Age Alone	231.3	157.3	126.7	86.8	45.2	15.1	5.9	1.9	1.6‡	1.9	4.3§

*Lowest fetal death rate by birth weight and gestational age: 0.9.
†Lowest fetal death rate by birth weight alone: 1.0.
‡Lowest fetal death rate by gestational age alone: 1.6.
§Overall fetal death rate: 4.3.
Modified from Luke B. Reducing fetal deaths in multiple births: optimal birthweights and gestational ages for infants of twin and triplet births. Acta Genet Med Gemellol 1996;45:333–348.

mined, it has been suggested that women with twins gain 35–45 pounds (5).

Prenatal Diagnosis

The usual indications for prenatal diagnosis and counseling in a singleton pregnancy apply to twin and higher-order gestations. Because the incidence of twin gestation increases with maternal age, women with multiple gestations often are candidates for prenatal genetic diagnosis. Genetic counseling should make clear to the patient the need to obtain a sample from each fetus, the risk of a chromosomal abnormality, potential complications of the procedure, the possibility of discordant results, and the ethical and technical concerns when one fetus is found to be abnormal. Some research has shown that the combined risk of fetal chromosome abnormality is higher in dizygotic twin gestations than in a singleton gestation (6, 7).

Structural anomalies are more common in monozygotic twins.

Maternal Serum Screening

Maternal serum alpha-fetoprotein (MSAFP) screening programs contribute to the detection of multiple gestations. Multiple gestation is the second most common reason after incorrect dating for the reported increase in the MSAFP level during the second trimester. Maternal serum alpha-fetoprotein screening will identify approximately 60% of unsuspected twin gestations and virtually all higher-order gestations. About 10% of pregnancies with an elevated MSAFP level will be explained by the presence of more than one fetus. The median value of MSAFP levels in twins from 14 to 20 weeks of gestation is 2.5 times that for singleton pregnancies (8). The levels in triplets and quadruplets are three and four times as high, respectively (9). Genetic screening programs, there-

Table 2. Twin Fetal Death Rates (per 1,000 conceptions)

Birth Weight (g)	Weeks of Gestation										Birth Weight Alone
	24–25	26–27	28–29	30–31	32–33	34–35	36–37	38–39	40–41	≥ 42	
≥ 4,900	—	—	—	—	—	—	—	—	—	—	—
4,600 < 4,900	—	—	—	—	—	—	—	—	—	—	—
4,300 < 4,600	—	—	—	—	—	—	—	—	—	—	—
4,000 < 4,300	—	—	—	—	—	—	—	—	—	—	—
3,700 < 4,000	—	—	—	—	—	—	—	—	—	—	—
3,400 < 3,700	—	—	—	—	—	—	7.7	6.2	7.6	13.6	7.3
3,100 < 3,400	—	—	—	—	—	8.9	4.5	5.8	5.7	11.6	5.9
2,800 < 3,100	—	—	—	—	11.1	6.2	3.6	4.8	4.8	9.7	4.8
2,500 < 2,800	—	—	—	—	9.5	4.3	3.3*	4.1	7.7	11.4	4.7†
2,200 < 2,500	—	—	—	22.0	9.4	5.2	5.9	9.1	12.2	17.5	7.8
1,900 < 2,200	—	—	29.9	19.8	9.3	9.1	12.4	19.4	22.2	30.1	13.4
1,600 < 1,900	—	—	22.5	17.5	14.2	17.3	33.1	42.4	58.3	76.2	23.8
1,300 < 1,600	—	55.8	24.0	26.0	35.7	60.0	90.7	105.5	73.8	—	44.6
1,000 < 1,300	142.9	57.4	41.5	58.0	97.2	126.2	—	—	—	—	65.1
700 < 1,000	86.4	68.5	106.7	180.8	185.4	—	—	—	—	—	99.6
500 < 700	157.1	187.6	214.7	191.7	—	—	—	—	—	—	176.2
Gestational Age Alone	123.4	85.5	57.0	41.0	21.5	11.7	8.1‡	8.2	10.1	16.7	15.5§

*Lowest fetal death rate by birth weight and gestational age: 3.3.
†Lowest fetal death rate by birth weight alone: 4.7.
‡Lowest fetal death rate by gestational age alone: 8.1.
§Overall fetal death rate: 15.5.

Modified from Luke B. Reducing fetal deaths in multiple births: optimal birthweights and gestational ages for infants of twin and triplet births. Acta Genet Med Gemellol 1996;45:333–348.

fore, redefine an elevated MSAFP level for a twin gestation because there are two fetuses and a larger volume of placenta. Depending on the laboratory, a value greater than 4.5 multiples of the median in an uncomplicated twin gestation is abnormal, requiring further comprehensive ultrasound evaluation by an experienced ultrasonographer and possible amniocentesis for the detection of amniotic fluid alpha-fetoprotein and acetylcholinesterase.

Although maternal serum screening for neural tube defects can be useful in the twin pregnancy, its effectiveness in screening for trisomy 21 is not well defined (10). Further investigation is necessary to determine the clinical usefulness of multiple marker screening for Down syndrome in twin and higher-order pregnancies.

Amniocentesis

Although the risks may be increased, amniocentesis, using continuous ultrasound guidance, of both sacs can be performed successfully in most patients with a twin gestation (11). One technique is ultrasound-guided amnio-

centesis of each sac with approximately 1–2 mL of a dilute (approximately 0.08%) indigo carmine dye instilled into the first amniotic sac (12). A second amniocentesis of clear fluid confirms specimens from each sac. Methylene blue dye, which is associated with fetal bowel atresia and other complications, should not be used (13). If the twins are without question monozygotic, there is no reason to tap more than one sac.

Chorionic Villus Sampling

Chorionic villus sampling (CVS) is an appropriate method of first-trimester prenatal diagnosis in multiple gestations (14). The procedure is best performed by or under the supervision of an experienced operator who samples both placentas under ultrasound guidance between 10.0 and 12.9 weeks of gestation. Difficulties that can arise with CVS in twin gestations include the inability to obtain an adequate sample and contamination of one sample with tissue from the second. In approximately 1% of patients, tissue can be obtained only from

Table 3. Triplet Fetal Death Rates (per 1,000 conceptions)

Birth Weight (g)	Weeks of Gestation										Birth Weight Alone
	24–25	26–27	28–29	30–31	32–33	34–35	36–37	38–39	40–41	≥ 42	
≥ 4,900	—	—	—	—	—	—	—	—	—	—	—
4,600 < 4,900	—	—	—	—	—	—	—	—	—	—	—
4,300 < 4,600	—	—	—	—	—	—	—	—	—	—	—
4,000 < 4,300	—	—	—	—	—	—	—	—	—	—	—
3,700 < 4,000	—	—	—	—	—	—	—	—	—	—	—
3,400 < 3,700	—	—	—	—	—	—	—	—	—	—	—
3,100 < 3,400	—	—	—	—	—	—	—	—	—	—	—
2,800 < 3,100	—	—	—	—	—	27.8	22.2	39.0	117.6	—	34.0
2,500 < 2,800	—	—	—	—	41.7	14.3	9.5	32.0	78.9	200.0	23.0
2,200 < 2,500	—	—	—	—	15.2	6.8	9.0	18.8	59.7	130.4	13.8
1,900 < 2,200	—	—	—	16.7	7.0	5.2*	8.1	15.5	40.8	100.0	9.3†
1,600 < 1,900	—	—	22.7	11.0	7.0	7.2	21.8	46.2	76.9	125.0	13.4
1,300 < 1,600	—	29.4	15.7	11.4	12.0	24.6	54.3	60.6	93.8	272.7	21.5
1,000 < 1,300	—	37.4	15.9	24.2	34.7	54.8	80.0	133.3	—	—	29.1
700 < 1,000	31.3	30.4	32.6	25.0	153.8	214.3	—	—	—	—	41.0
500 < 700	73.8	105.3	172.4	—	—	—	—	—	—	—	94.5
Gestational Age Alone	54.2	43.8	25.5	15.5	14.2	11.4‡	15.0	31.5	69.9	147.7	21.0§

*Lowest fetal death rate by birth weight and gestational age: 5.2.

†Lowest fetal death rate by birth weight alone: 9.3.

‡Lowest fetal death rate by gestational age alone: 11.4.

§Overall fetal death rate: 21.0.

Modified from Luke B. Reducing fetal deaths in multiple births: optimal birthweights and gestational ages for infants of twin and triplet births. Acta Genet Med Gemellol 1996;45:333–348.

one placenta. When CVS is performed at centers with experienced operators, twin–twin contamination occurs in approximately 4–6% of samples, causing prenatal diagnostic errors. When CVS or amniocentesis is performed in the twin gestation, documentation of the location of the fetuses and the membrane separating the sacs is important because discordant results can occur, and the location of the abnormal fetus may need to be known for future management.

Multifetal Reduction

The greater the number of fetuses within the uterus, the greater the risk for preterm delivery and adverse perinatal outcome. Multifetal pregnancy reduction may be performed to decrease the risk of serious perinatal morbidity and mortality associated with preterm delivery by reducing the number of fetuses (15, 16). Preferably, this problem can be avoided by carefully monitoring patients receiving ovulation-inducing drugs and by minimizing the number of embryos transferred during in vitro fertilization or embryo transfer programs. The ethical dilem-

mas can be considerable (17). Patients with higher-order multiple gestations may be faced with the possibility of terminating the entire pregnancy, continuing the pregnancy and taking the risk of delivering severely preterm infants, or reducing the pregnancy in an effort to decrease the risk of perinatal morbidity and mortality.

Pregnancy loss is the main risk of multifetal pregnancy reduction and ranges from 10% to 26%. The benefit of this procedure is most clear in quadruplet and higher-order gestations because it increases the length of gestation of the surviving fetuses (18). It is unclear and remains to be determined whether multifetal pregnancy reduction improves long-term neonatal outcome of a triplet gestation reduced to twins. Elevations in MSAFP levels occur after selective reduction to twins (19); nonetheless, these patients should undergo a detailed ultrasound examination of the surviving fetuses in the middle of the second trimester.

Dizygotic twins can be discordant for congenital anomalies. Selective fetal termination allows a pregnancy to continue with a normal twin after the termination of an abnormal twin. In one study, selective fetal termination was performed successfully in 183 multifetal pregnancies, most of which were twin gestations (20). Indications for selective fetal termination were twins discordant for chromosomal abnormalities, fetal structural anomalies, or one twin affected by a Mendelian disorder. The preferred method for selective fetal termination was intracardiac injection of potassium chloride. The procedure caused loss of the entire pregnancy if there was a monochorionic placentation. The pregnancy loss rate before 24 weeks of gestation was 12.6%; an additional 3.8% of patients gave birth between 24 and 28 weeks of gestation. The authors of this study concluded that selective fetal termination for an abnormal pregnancy is a safe procedure when performed by experienced physicians provided there is a dichorionic placentation. Ligation of the umbilical cord under endoscopic visualization has been performed for selective termination in a monochorionic pregnancy, but the safety and efficacy of this procedure requires further study (21).

Ultrasonography

Ultrasonography can be useful in both prenatal diagnosis and antepartum surveillance. With its use, less than 10% of twin gestations are undiagnosed before labor and delivery. Although the value of routine screening to promote early diagnosis is subject to debate, ultrasonography has a role in evaluating the progress of pregnancy once the diagnosis is established.

Screening

In the randomized clinical Routine Antenatal Diagnostic Imaging With Ultrasound (RADIUS) trial, special attention was given to multiple gestation. In the study, 129 multiple gestations were included. The RADIUS study concluded that multiple pregnancies were consistently diagnosed at an earlier gestational age in the screened group; however, this finding did not result in any overall alteration in management improving adverse perinatal outcome. This conclusion is not consistent with findings of other studies. In a 10-year study of 22,400 women having 43,000 routine ultrasound examinations involving 249 multiple gestations, earlier detection improved perinatal outcome (22). When multiple gestation is suspected on the basis of clinical examination, family history, a history of assisted reproduction, or an elevated MSAFP value, an ultrasound examination should be performed. Often, ultrasound examinations are performed early in gestation in twins to document viability; this examination also can be helpful in defining chorionicity.

Evaluation

A detailed ultrasound evaluation of a multiple gestation should be performed during the second trimester. This examination should include determination of placentation, amnionicity, and chorionicity; the number of fetuses; evaluation for fetal amniotic fluid or placental abnormalities; and an assessment of the growth of each fetus. If two separate placentas are identified or if the fetuses are of different sex, the placentation is dichorionic. A thick membrane also suggests dichorionicity. When a thin, wispy membrane is seen between two sacs with a single placenta, and the fetuses are of the same sex, monochorionicity is suggested. "Stuck twin syndrome," where there is polyhydramnios for one twin and extreme oligohydramnios for the other, can be very difficult to differentiate from a monochorionic pregnancy because the membrane may be so near the stuck twin that it is difficult to detect. Determination of chorionicity is most accurate in the first trimester; as the pregnancy pro-gresses, it becomes less accurate (23, 24).

Visualization of a membrane confirms the diagnosis of a diamniotic gestation. When dichorionicity is diagnosed, the pregnancy must also be diamniotic. The number of fetuses should be identified; this number, however, may decrease as the pregnancy progresses. Until the third trimester, twins follow the same growth curves that apply to singleton pregnancies. There is no clear clinical advantage to the use of twin- or triplet-specific ultrasound growth tables. Evaluation of serial fetal growth should include estimated fetal weight of each fetus and appropriate and concordant interval growth.

Routine Cervical Evaluation

Routine cervical evaluation by either clinical or ultrasonographic assessment has been investigated as an approach to predict preterm birth in the multiple gestation. A cervical scoring system, calculated as cervical length (in centimeters) minus cervical dilatation at the internal os (in centimeters) has been used (25). This system has been associated with a positive predictive value of 75%, which is associated with a fourfold increased relative risk of preterm delivery (26). Weekly digital cervical examination for clinical assessment of the cervix has not been associated with adverse maternal or fetal outcome (27).

Vaginal ultrasonography has been used to measure cervical width, length, and funneling and to examine the relationship of these measurements to the risk of preterm birth (28). In this study, the risk of spontaneous preterm delivery was increased in women who were found to have a short cervix. Although this is a promising technique, further evaluation of transvaginal ultrasonography by a prospective randomized study is necessary to determine its role in the prevention of preterm birth.

Several investigators have studied the use of cervical cerclage in multiple gestations to prevent preterm birth (29). Because there is no clear-cut benefit to this approach, and its use is associated with both maternal and fetal risks, this procedure is not recommended for multiple gestations.

Bed Rest

The role and value of bed rest at home or in the hospital in the prevention of preterm delivery of a multiple gestation remains controversial. Not only is hospital bed rest costly, stressful, and disruptive, there is no clear consensus that it is of any benefit. Numerous studies have failed to show that bed rest decreases the incidence of preterm delivery, lengthens gestation, or improves neonatal morbidity in multiple gestation (30). Also, there are little data to support activity reduction in multiple or singleton gestations. Antepartum hospitalization may be necessary in the multiple gestation for managing complications such as preterm labor and abnormal fetal growth.

Antepartum Surveillance

The routine use and benefit of antepartum fetal surveillance in the uncomplicated multifetal gestation has not been shown to be of benefit. When intrauterine growth restriction, abnormal fluid volumes, growth discordance, pregnancy-induced hypertension, fetal anomalies, monoamnionicity, or other pregnancy complications occur, fetal surveillance, including nonstress testing or the modified or standard biophysical profile, is indicated (31). The biophysical profile is as reliable in multiple gestations as in singleton gestations (32).

Although some patients may find it difficult to distinguish between fetal movement of each twin, fetal movement counting can be an adjunct to these antepartum surveillance techniques. Umbilical cord velocimetry may be helpful in evaluating the severely growth-restricted fetus, but its role in antepartum fetal surveillance of the singleton or multiple gestation is yet to be determined (33).

Home Uterine Activity Monitoring

The use of the home uterine activity monitor has been advocated by some to prevent or manage preterm labor in singleton or multiple gestations. There are, however, no data to support its use (34–36).

Management of Complications
Preterm Labor

The most significant and common complication of multiple pregnancy is preterm labor resulting in preterm delivery. Perinatal morbidity and mortality are affected by gestational age and weight at delivery as well as by the number of fetuses. The presence of a single anomalous fetus in a twin gestation increases the risk of preterm delivery compared with nonanomalous twin gestations (37). Patient education, risk assessment, serial cervical evaluation by manual or transvaginal ultrasound examinations, specialized antepartum clinics, and home uterine activity monitoring have been used with mixed results to detect preterm labor early and prevent preterm birth in multiple gestations.

Preterm labor in twins is preceded by an increase in uterine contraction frequency; however, this does not hold true with triplets (38). Women with triplet gestations have more uterine irritability than do those with twin or singleton pregnancies. The management of preterm labor is discussed elsewhere (39).

A number of medications are available for inhibition of preterm labor. These agents include magnesium sulfate, beta-adrenergic agents, indomethacin, and the calcium channel blockers. Whenever tocolysis is used, recognition of contraindications and close maternal and fetal monitoring are necessary to detect complications. Women pregnant with multiple gestations are at a higher risk for the development of pulmonary edema because of higher blood volume, lower colloid osmotic pressure, and anemia. Older women with multiple gestations also are at increased risk for myocardial ischemia and cardiac arrhythmias as a result of tocolytic therapy. No benefit has been shown from the use of oral tocolysis in multiple gestations to prevent the onset of preterm labor or preterm birth (40, 41).

Corticosteroids should be administered for induction of fetal lung maturation to women with multiple pregnancies who are experiencing preterm labor (less than 34 weeks of gestation) (42). The National Institutes of Health also recommends corticosteroid therapy for women with preterm premature rupture of membranes at less than 30–32 weeks of gestation. Because steroid administration in triplet and higher-order multiple gestation may actually increase contractions, close surveillance of uterine activity following administration of corticosteroids is recommended (43).

Preterm Rupture of Membranes

Preterm premature rupture of membranes occurs more frequently in twin gestations than in singleton gestations (44). A matched-control study of preterm premature rupture of membranes in twins concluded that the nonpresenting twin more frequently had hyaline membrane disease, respiratory complications, and required more oxygen therapy than the presenting infant. There were no significant differences between twin and singleton gestations in infectious morbidity, cord prolapse, abruptio placentae, or latency to delivery. Infant morbidity and mortality were high for the nonpresenting infant at significantly increased risk of respiratory complications (44).

Preterm rupture of the presenting sac occurs most frequently. Although the incidence is unknown, membrane rupture of the nonpresenting sac also can occur. When preterm rupture of membranes occurs in the multiple gestation, it most frequently occurs prior to fetal lung maturation. Preterm premature rupture of membranes occurs more frequently in the triplet gestation than in the twin gestation, resulting in a higher incidence of preterm labor, delivery, and perinatal mortality (45). The management of the multifetal gestation complicated by preterm premature rupture of membranes depends on the gestational age, fetal lung maturation, number of fetuses, and the presence of maternal or fetal complications. The use of tocolysis, antibiotics, and glucocorticoids when preterm premature rupture of membranes occurs remains controversial. When there is evidence of fetal lung maturation, delivery may be indicated. In rare cases, prolongation of pregnancy after preterm premature rupture of membranes after delivery of the first twin may be considered.

Fetal Disorders

Intrauterine Growth Restriction

Intrauterine growth restriction occurs more frequently in twins and higher-order multiple gestations than in a singleton pregnancy and is a significant cause of increased neonatal morbidity and mortality. Antepartum management of the multiple gestation should include early identification of intrauterine growth restriction by ultrasonography and increased fetal surveillance to improve perinatal outcome. There is no single definition for the diagnosis of intrauterine growth restriction or discordant growth in twins. Estimated fetal weight is helpful in making the diagnosis of intrauterine growth restriction and discordance between fetuses.

Intrauterine growth restriction usually is diagnosed either when the estimated fetal weight decreases below the 10th percentile for a singleton gestation or when there is discordance (ie, a difference in estimated fetal weight of greater than 20% between twin A and twin B expressed as a percentage of the larger twin's weight). Once intrauterine growth restriction has been diagnosed, the multiple gestation should be monitored more closely with serial ultrasonography every 2–3 weeks to assess fetal growth and amniotic fluid volume. Frequent fetal antenatal surveillance by the nonstress test or biophysical profile is necessary. Early delivery should be considered. When amniocentesis is necessary to assess fetal lung maturity, results obtained from amniotic fluid of either twin usually will represent lung maturity of both twins (46).

Other Complications

Twin–twin transfusion syndrome, monoamniotic twinning, conjoined twins, and acardia (or twin reversed arterial perfusion sequence) are fetal complications of monochorionic

gestations that are rarely encountered by the obstetrician–gynecologist. Patients with these complications should be cared for by or in collaboration with specialists familiar with their management.

Death of One Twin

Death of one fetus of a multiple gestation can occur at any time during pregnancy although it is more common in the first trimester. These patients can benefit from perinatal grief counseling. Only 50% of twin gestations diagnosed in the first trimester result in delivery of two live infants. Early fetal demise of one twin may not be recognized clinically but may be diagnosed by first-trimester ultrasonography. A documented multiple gestation that spontaneously loses one or more fetuses during the first trimester is called the vanishing twin phenomenon. This occurs most commonly in the twin gestation, but also has been reported in the higher-order multiple pregnancy (47). The true incidence of this phenomenon is unknown, but one study reported a vanishing twin rate of 21.2% (48). Another study reported a 25% loss rate of a single twin in multiple gestations arising from assisted reproductive procedures (49). No adverse maternal outcome occurs as the result of a vanishing embryo, and the prognosis for the surviving twin is excellent (48).

Single fetal demise after the first trimester is more common with monochorionic placentation, ranging in incidence from 0.5% to 6.8% (50). When death of one fetus occurs, the probability of harm to the surviving twin or to the mother is low. Death or damage in the remaining twin was previously thought to be caused by intravascular coagulation. Recent evidence, however, suggests that acute hypotension in the surviving twin with partial exsanguination into the dying twin through anastomoses within the placenta is more likely responsible. The surviving twin can develop fetal morbidity consisting more often of renal cortical necrosis and multicystic encephalomalacia. The incidence of morbidity and mortality in the surviving co-twin is highest with monochorionic twins compared with dichorionic twins, in whom the risk is negligible (51). Preterm birth is one of the greatest risks to the surviving co-twin (52, 53).

Once a single fetal demise is diagnosed, the gestational age of the pregnancy and the condition of the surviving fetus will dictate clinical management. When death of one fetus occurs prior to 34 weeks of gestation, fetal movement counting and increased antepartum fetal surveillance of the surviving twin should be undertaken. Fetal compromise or the presence of fetal lung maturation suggest a need for delivery. Maternal consumptive coagulopathy with hypofibrinogenemia occasionally may develop under these circumstances (54, 55). Delivery may be appropriate if the death of one twin occurs after 34 weeks of gestation.

Intrapartum Management

Timing

Ideally, women with multiple pregnancies should undergo delivery by 40 weeks of gestation; however, the clinician must frequently weigh the risks to the fetuses if intrauterine life is continued versus the risk to the mother if the pregnancy is continued. For example, preterm labor, discordance, abnormal fetal surveillance, or pregnancy-induced hypertension may mandate earlier intervention. The ideal time of delivery for uncomplicated pregnancies is uncertain; however, if elective delivery is considered before 38 weeks of gestation, fetal lung maturity should be assessed. Although there are few data pertaining to multiple gestations beyond 40 weeks of gestation, delivery should probably be effected by this time.

Labor and Delivery

When a woman with a known or suspected multiple gestation presents in labor, confirmation as soon as possible by ultrasound examination of fetal number and presentations is indicated. Both twins should be monitored continuously during labor. Ultrasonography should be available to determine the heart rate of the second twin as well as its orientation following delivery of the first twin. Appropriate, experienced pediatric and anesthesia personnel should be notified and available at delivery. Capability for emergency cesarean delivery is necessary and blood should be available because the likelihood of operative intervention, as well as postpartum hemorrhage, is increased.

Route of Delivery

Controversy surrounds the preferred route of delivery for some multiple gestations, especially twins. Delivery should be based on individual needs and may depend on the clinician's practice and experience. The various twin presentations should be taken into account. All combinations of twin presentations and their frequency essentially can be classified into the following groups (56):

Twin A–Vertex with Twin B–Vertex. Vaginal delivery is anticipated for vertex–vertex twins. Cesarean delivery should only be performed for the same indications applied to singleton gestations. In one series, 81.2% of the vertex–vertex twin gestations were successfully delivered vaginally (57).

Twin A–Vertex with Twin B–Nonvertex. There are conflicting data on the management of twins in vertex–breech or vertex–transverse presentation. Because depressed Apgar scores and an increased perinatal mortality rate have been associated with vaginal delivery of the second twin, cesarean delivery has been advocated by some whenever the second twin is in a nonvertex presentation (58). Cesarean delivery, however, is not always necessary. Vaginal delivery of twin B in the nonvertex presentation is a reasonable option for a neonate with an estimated weight greater than 1,500 g. Under these circumstances, it has been reported that perinatal mortality and low 5-minute Apgar scores are not increased when a second breech twin is delivered vaginally after the criteria for vaginal delivery of a singleton breech are met (57, 59–61). There are insufficient data to advocate a specific route of delivery (vaginal or abdominal) of twin B whose birth weight is less than 1,500 g, although cesarean delivery is performed frequently (57, 62).

Twin A–Nonvertex. In general, cesarean delivery is the method of choice when the first twin is nonvertex, such as a breech or transverse presentation. The safety of vaginal delivery for this group has not been documented. When the first twin is breech and the second is in a vertex presentation, the possibility of locked twins exists, in which case vaginal delivery would be contraindicated, if not impossible. Locked twins, however, appear to be exceedingly rare.

Interval Between Deliveries

The interval between delivery of each twin is not critical in determining the outcome of twin B (57, 63). Surveillance of twin B with real-time ultrasonography and continuous monitoring of the fetal heart rate, however, are advised after the delivery of twin A. Rapid delivery may be required because of complications, such as abruptio placentae, cord prolapse, or a decrease in the fetal heart rate. If labor has not resumed within a reasonable time after the delivery of twin A, oxytocin augmentation with careful fetal heart rate surveillance can be initiated. Once the vertex is in the pelvic inlet, amniotomy can be performed. When fetal condition dictates the need to expedite delivery, internal podalic version and breech extraction may be an acceptable alternative.

There are insufficient data to assess the safety of vaginal delivery of twins after previous cesarean delivery. The modes of delivery used for twins and higher-order multiple gestations in the presence of a prior cesarean delivery are areas under study (64, 65). Obstetricians should select the delivery technique with which they are most comfortable.

Summary

The incidence of twins, triplets, and higher-order multiple gestations has increased dramatically because of widespread use of ovulation-inducing drugs and advanced assisted reproductive techniques. There is considerable perinatal/maternal morbidity and mortality associated with multifetal gestations. The practicing obstetrician managing these high-risk patients should be familiar with their special antepartum and intrapartum problems. The obstetrician–gynecologist unaccustomed to caring for patients with a multifetal gestation should consult with maternal–fetal medicine specialists who have expertise in managing these pregnancies. Better use of infertility modalities, early diagnosis of the multiple pregnancy, prevention of preterm birth, close fetal surveillance, and atraumatic labor and delivery can improve perinatal outcome in the multifetal gestation.

References

1. Luke B. The changing pattern of multiple births in the United States: maternal and infant characteristics, 1973 and 1990. Obstet Gynecol 1994;84:101–106

2. Ventura SJ, Martin JA, Curtin SC, Mathews TJ. Report of final natality statistics, 1996. Monthly vital statistics report; vol 46, no. 11 (suppl). Hyattsville, Maryland: National Center for Health Statistics, 1998

3. American Fertility Society, Society for Assisted Reproductive Technology. Assisted reproductive technology in the United States and Canada: 1992 results generated from the American Fertility Society/Society for Assisted Reproductive Technology registry. Fertil Steril 1994;62:1121–1128

4. National Research Council. Subcommittee on the Tenth Edition of the RDAs, Food and Nutrition Board, Commission on Life Sciences. Recommended dietary allowances. 10th ed. Washington, DC: National Academy Press, 1989

5. Abrams B. Maternal nutrition. In: Creasy RK, Resnick R, eds. Maternal-fetal medicine, principles and practice. 3rd ed. Philadelphia: WB Saunders, 1994:162–170

6. Rodis JF, Egan JFX, Craffey A, Ciarleglio L, Greenstein RM, Scorza WE, et al. Calculated risk of chromosomal abnormalities in twin gestations. Obstet Gynecol 1990; 76:1037–1041

7. Meyers C, Adam R, Dungan J, Prenger V. Aneuploidy in twin gestations: when is maternal age advanced? Obstet Gynecol 1997;89:248–251

8. Johnson JM, Harman CR, Evans JA, MacDonald K, Manning FA. Maternal serum alpha-fetoprotein in twin pregnancy. Am J Obstet Gynecol 1990;162:1020–1025

9. Wald N, Cuckle H. Maternal serum alpha-fetoprotein levels in triplet and quadruplet pregnancy. Br J Obstet Gynaecol 1978;85:124–126

10. Wald N, Cuckle H, Wu T, George L. Maternal serum unconjugated oestriol and human chorionic gonadotrophin levels in twin pregnancies: implications for screening for Down's syndrome. Br J Obstet Gynaecol 1991;98:905–908

11. Tabsh KM, Crandall B, Lebherz TB, Howard J. Genetic amniocentesis in twin pregnancy. Obstet Gynecol 1985; 65:843–845

12. Elias S, Gerbie AB, Simpson JL, Nader HL, Sabbagha RE, Shkolnik A. Genetic amniocentesis in term gestation. Am J Obstet Gynecol 1980;138:169–174

13. Van der Pol JG, Wolf H, Boer K, Treffers PE, Leschot NJ, Hey HA, et al. Jejunal atresia related to the use of methylene blue in genetic amniocentesis in twins. Br J Obstet Gynaecol 1992;99:141–143

14. Wapner RJ, Johnson A, Davis G, Urban A, Morgan P, Jackson L. Prenatal diagnosis in twin gestations: a comparison between second-trimester amniocentesis and first-trimester chorionic villus sampling. Obstet Gynecol 1993; 82:49–56

15. Berkowitz RL, Lynch L, Chitkara U, Wilkins IA, Mehalek KE, Alvarez E. Selective reduction of multifetal pregnancies in the first trimester. N Engl J Med 1988;318:1043–1047

16. American College of Obstetricians and Gynecologists. Multifetal pregnancy reduction and selective termination. Committee Opinion 94. Washington, DC: ACOG, 1991

17. Evans MI, May M, Drugan A, Fletcher JC, Johnson MP, Sokol RJ. Selective termination: clinical experience and residual risks. Am J Obstet Gynecol 1990;162:1568–1575

18. Evans MI, Dommergues M, Wapner RJ, Lynch L, Dumez Y, Goldberg JD, et al. Efficacy of transabdominal multifetal pregnancy reduction: collaborative experience among the world's largest centers. Obstet Gynecol 1993;82:61–66

19. Lynch L, Berkowitz RL. Maternal serum alpha-fetoprotein and coagulation profiles after multifetal pregnancy reduction. Am J Obstet Gynecol 1993;169:987–990

20. Evans MI, Goldberg JD, Dommergues M, Wapner RJ, Lynch L, Dock BS, et al. Efficacy of second-trimester selective termination for fetal abnormalities: international collaborative experience among the world's largest centers. Am J Obstet Gynecol 1994;171:90–94

21. Quintero RA, Reich H, Puder KS, Bardicef M, Evans MI, Cotton DB, et al. Brief report: umbilical-cord ligation of an acardiac twin by fetoscopy at 19 weeks of gestation. N Engl J Med 1994;330:469–471

22. Persson PH, Kullander S. Long-term experience of general ultrasound screening in pregnancy. Am J Obstet Gynecol 1983;146:942–947

23. D'Alton ME, Dudley DK. The ultrasonographic prediction of chorionicity in twin gestation. Am J Obstet Gynecol 1989;160:557–561

24. Kurtz AB, Wapner RJ, Mata J, Johnson A, Morgan P. Twin pregnancies: accuracy of first-trimester abdominal US in predicting chorionicity and amnionicity. Radiology 1992; 185:759–762

25. Houlton MCC, Marivate M, Philpott RH. Factors associated with preterm labour and changes in the cervix before labour in twin pregnancy. Br J Obstet Gynaecol 1982; 89:190–194

26. Newman RB, Godsey RK, Ellings JM, Campbell BA, Eller DP, Miller MC. Quantification of cervical change: relationship to preterm delivery in the multifetal gestation. Am J Obstet Gynecol 1991;165:264–269

27. Bivins HA Jr, Newman RB, Ellings JM, Hulsey TC, Keenan A. Risks of antepartum cervical examination in multifetal gestations. Am J Obstet Gynecol 1993;169:22–25

28. Iams JD, Goldenberg RL, Meis PJ, Mercer BM, Moawad A, Das A, et al. The length of the cervix and the risk of spon-taneous premature delivery. N Engl J Med 1996;334: 567–572

29. Mordel N, Zajicek G, Benshushan A, Schenker JG, Laufer N, Sadovsky E. Elective suture of uterine cervix in triplets. Am J Perinatol 1993;10:14–16

30. Andrews WW, Leveno KJ, Sherman ML, Mutz J, Gilstrap LC, Whalley PJ. Elective hospitalization in the management of twin pregnancies. Obstet Gynecol 1991;77:826–831

31. American College of Obstetricians and Gynecologists. Antepartum fetal surveillance. ACOG Technical Bulletin 188. Washington, DC: ACOG, 1994

32. Newman RB, Ellings JM. Antepartum management of the multiple gestation: the case for specialized care. Semin Perinatol 1995;19:387–403

33. American College of Obstetricians and Gynecologists. Utility of antepartum umbilical artery Doppler velocimetry in intrauterine growth restriction. Committee Opinion 188. Washington, DC: ACOG, 1997

34. Dyson DC, Crites YM, Ray DA, Armstrong MA. Prevention of preterm birth in high-risk patients: the role of education and provider contact versus home uterine monitoring. Am J Obstet Gynecol 1991;164:756–762

35. Dyson DC, Danbe KH, Bamber JA, Crites YM, Field DR, Maier JA, et al. Monitoring women at risk for preterm labor. N Engl J Med 1998;338:15–19

36. American College of Obstetricians and Gynecologists. Home uterine activity monitoring. Committee Opinion 172. Washington, DC: ACOG, 1996

37. Malone FD, Craigo SD, Chelmow D, D'Alton ME. Outcome of twin gestations complicated by a single anomalous fetus. Obstet Gynecol 1996;88:1–5

38. Newman RB, Gill PJ, Campion S, Katz M. The influence of fetal number on antepartum uterine activity. Obstet Gynecol 1989;73:695–699

39. American College of Obstetricians and Gynecologists. Preterm labor. ACOG Technical Bulletin 206. Washington, DC: ACOG, 1995

40. Newton ER. Antepartum care in multiple gestation. Semin Perinatol 1986;10:19–29

41. Ashworth MF, Spooner SF, Verkuyl DAA, Waterman R, Ashurst HM. Failure to prevent preterm labour and delivery in twin pregnancy using prophylactic oral salbutamol. Br J Obstet Gynaecol 1990;97:878–882

42. National Institutes of Health. Consensus development conference statement. Effect of corticosteroids for fetal maturation on perinatal outcomes. Bethesda, Maryland: NIH Office of Medical Applications of Research, 1994

43. Elliott JP, Radin TG. The effect of corticosteroid administration on uterine activity and preterm labor in high-order multiple gestations. Obstet Gynecol 1995;85:250–254

44. Mercer BM, Crocker LG, Pierce WF, Sibai BM. Clinical characteristics and outcome of twin gestation complicated by preterm premature rupture of the membranes. Am J Obstet Gynecol 1993;168:1467–1473

45. Sassoon DA, Castro LC, Davis JL, Hobel CJ. Perinatal outcome in triplet versus twin gestations. Obstet Gynecol 1990;75:817–820

46. Leveno KJ, Quirk JG, Whalley PJ, Herbert WNP, Trubey R. Fetal lung maturation in twin gestation. Am J Obstet Gynecol 1984;148:405–411

47. Seoud MA-F, Toner JP, Kruithoff C, Muasher SJ. Outcome of twin, triplet, and quadruplet in vitro fertilization pregnancies: the Norfolk experience. Fertil Steril 1992;57: 825–834

48. Landy HJ, Weiner S, Corson SL, Batzer FR, Bolognese RJ. The "vanishing twin": ultrasonographic assessment of fetal disappearance in the first trimester. Am J Obstet Gynecol 1986;155:14–19

49. Corson SL, Dickey RP, Gocial B, Batzer FR, Eisenberg E, Huppert L, et al. Outcome in 242 in vitro fertilization-embryo replacement or gamete intrafallopian transfer-induced pregnancies. Fertil Steril 1989;51:644–650

50. Dudley DKL, D'Alton ME. Single fetal death in twin gestation. Semin Perinatol 1986;10:65–72

51. Burke MS. Single fetal demise in twin gestation. Clin Obstet Gynecol 1990;33:69–78

52. Fusi L, Gordon H. Twin pregnancy complicated by single intrauterine death. Problems and outcome with conservative management. Br J Obstet Gynaecol 1990;97:511–516

53. Eglowstein MS, D'Alton ME. Single intrauterine demise in twin gestation. J Matern Fetal Med 1993;2:272–275

54. Romero R, Duffy TP, Berkowitz RL, Chang E, Hobbins JC. Prolongation of a preterm pregnancy complicated by death of a single twin in utero and disseminated intravascular coagulation. Effects of treatment with heparin. N Engl J Med 1984;310:772–774

55. Landy HJ, Weingold AB. Management of a multiple gestation complicated by an antepartum fetal demise. Obstet Gynecol Surv 1989;44:171–176

56. Hays PM, Smeltzer JS. Multiple gestation. Clin Obstet Gynecol 1986;29:264–285

57. Chervenak FA, Johnson RE, Youcha S, Hobbins JC, Berkowitz RL. Intrapartum management of twin gestation. Obstet Gynecol 1985;65:119–124

58. Cetrulo CL. The controversy of mode of delivery in twins: the intrapartum management of twin gestation. Part I. Semin Perinatol 1986;10:39–43

59. Acker D, Lieberman M, Holbrook RH, James O, Phillipe M, Edelin KC. Delivery of the second twin. Obstet Gynecol 1982;59:710–711

60. Chervenak FA, Johnson RE, Berkowitz RL, Grannum P, Hobbins JC. Is routine cesarean section necessary for vertex-breech and vertex-transverse gestations? Am J Obstet Gynecol 1984;148:1–5

61. Gocke SE, Nageotte MP, Garite T, Towers CV, Dorcester W. Management of the nonvertex second twin: primary cesarean section, external version, or primary breech extraction. Am J Obstet Gynecol 1989;161:111–114

62. Barrett JM, Staggs SM, Van Hooydonk JE, Growdon JH, Killam AP, Boehm FH. The effect of type of delivery upon neonatal outcome in premature twins. Am J Obstet Gynecol 1982;143:360–367

63. Rayburn WF, Lavin JP Jr, Miodovnik M, Varner MW. Multiple gestation: time interval between delivery of the first and second twins. Obstet Gynecol 1984;63:502–506

64. Miller DA, Mullin P, Hou D, Paul RH. Vaginal birth after cesarean section in twin gestation. Am J Obstet Gynecol 1996;175:194–198

65. Essel JK, Opai-Tetteh ET. Twin delivery after a cesarean section—always a section? S Afr Med J 1996;86:279–280

Suggested Reading

American College of Obstetricians and Gynecologists. Antepartum fetal surveillance. ACOG Technical Bulletin 188. Washington, DC: ACOG, 1994

American College of Obstetricians and Gynecologists. Hypertension in pregnancy. ACOG Technical Bulletin 219. Washington, DC: ACOG, 1996

American College of Obstetricians and Gynecologists. Maternal serum screening. ACOG Educational Bulletin 228. Washington, DC: ACOG, 1996

American College of Obstetricians and Gynecologists. Preconceptional care. ACOG Technical Bulletin 205. Washington, DC: ACOG, 1995

Berkowitz RL, Lynch L, Stone J, Alvarez M. The current status of multifetal pregnancy reduction. Am J Obstet Gynecol 1996; 174:1265–1272

Chervenak FA, D'Alton ME, eds. Multiple gestation. Semin Perinatol 1995;19:341–434

Gall SA. Multiple pregnancy and delivery. St. Louis, Missouri: Mosby-Year Book, 1996

Keith LG, Papiernik E, Keith DM, Luke B. Multiple pregnancy: epidemiology, gestation and perinatal outcome. New York: The Parthenon Publishing Group, 1995

Number 222—April 1996
(Replaces #113, February 1988)

Technical Bulletin

An Educational Aid to Obstetrician–Gynecologists

Sterilization

Over 170 million couples worldwide use surgical sterilization as a safe and reliable method of contraception. In the United States, sterilization is the most commonly used method among married or formerly married women. An estimated 640,000 female sterilization procedures and 500,000 male sterilization procedures are performed each year (1, 2). In 1988, sterilizations accounted for 39% of contraceptive method use by all women 15–44 years old; 27.5% of women using contraception had undergone tubal sterilization, and 11.7% reported that their partners had undergone vasectomy (3).

Patient Counseling and Selection

Patients should be informed about both male and female sterilization as well as the risks and benefits of alternative long-acting, temporary contraceptive methods (see the box). When appropriate, the male partner can be included in such initial counseling. Many men and women have the impression that sterilization operations are easily reversible. The clinician should make clear to the patient that all operative sterilizations are intended to be permanent. Counseling should take into account risk factors that affect regret of sterilization. In the United States, the strongest indicator of future regret is young age at the time of sterilization, regardless of parity or marital status. Women between the ages of 20 and 24 years at sterilization are twice as likely to experience poststerilization regret as women sterilized between the ages of 30 and 34 years (4). Marital instability increases the probability of regret. Approximately 6% of sterilized women report regret or request information about sterilization reversal within 5 years of the procedure; urologists estimate that close to 1–2% of the total number of men they sterilize seek information on vasectomy reversal (4, 5). Although success rates in vas and tubal reanastomosis have improved dramatically in recent years, successful reversal and subsequent pregnancy depend on many factors, including the type of sterilization, interval between sterilization and reversal, age, and length of the remaining tube.

Preoperative counseling should include an explanation of the causes and probability of sterilization failure. When the patient has considered and accepted the risks of regret or failure, the physician can provide information about operative approaches, including a review of the possible complications from both the operation and the anesthesia. The patient should be informed about the advantages and disadvantages of local and general anesthesia, pain likely to be associated with the operation, and possible complications, including damage to organs or

---

Components of Presterilization Counseling

Alternative methods available, including male sterilization

Reasons for choosing sterilization

Screening for risk indicators for regret

Details of the procedure, including anesthesia with attendant risks and benefits

The permanent nature of the procedure and information on reversal

The possibility of failure, including ectopic pregnancy

Post tubal ligation physiology, including the possibility of unrelated change in menstruation

The need to use condoms for protection against sexually transmitted diseases and human immunodeficiency virus infection if at risk of exposure

Answers to all questions to the satisfaction of the patient

Completion of informed consent document

Modified from Pollack AE, Soderstrom RM. Female tubal sterilization. In: Corson SL, Derman RJ, Tyrer LB, eds. Fertility control. 2nd ed. London, Ontario: Goldin Publishers, 1994:295–296

major vessels, infection, and subsequent ectopic pregnancy. The patient should be informed of her need for adequate postoperative care and support, and she should plan accordingly.

The patient should be given an opportunity to ask questions about the procedure. Both this discussion and the fact that the patient was given the opportunity to ask questions should be noted in the patient's record by the physician. All this is best accomplished at a preoperative visit scheduled far enough in advance of the operation to allow the patient ample time to weigh the factors involved in the decision. Physicians should be aware of state laws or insurance regulations that may require a specific interval between obtaining consent and performance of sterilization procedures. State law may mandate the use of special consent forms. Written informed consent should be obtained following counseling in a relaxed and unpressured environment. It is best not to obtain consent concurrent with labor or an abortion procedure because these events are associated with stress and a high incidence of regret of sterilization.

Patients should be advised that female and male sterilization offer no protection against sexually transmitted diseases (STDs) such as human immunodeficiency virus (HIV) infection. Patients should be encouraged to use condoms or have their partners use condoms when they are at risk of exposure. In the United States, studies indicate that sterilized women with risk factors for STDs have low rates of condom use and infrequently attend clinics for preventive reproductive health services (6, 7).

Tubal Sterilization

Timing

Tubal sterilization can be performed postpartum, postabortion, or as an interval procedure (unrelated in time to a pregnancy). The timing of the procedure will influence both the surgical approach and the method of tubal occlusion used.

Postpartum sterilizations are performed at the time of cesarean delivery while the abdomen is open or following a vaginal delivery using a 2–5-cm subumbilical minilaparotomy incision. The subumbilical minilaparotomy approach allows for easy entry into the abdomen and access to the tubes because the anterior abdominal wall is thin just below the umbilicus over the fundus. It is best to perform postpartum minilaparotomy before the onset of significant uterine involution but following full assessment of maternal and neonatal well being. The likelihood of postpartum hemorrhage in multiparous women subsides after the first 12 hours postpartum. Postpartum minilaparotomy may be performed safely and comfortably using local anesthesia with sedation or regional or general anesthesia.

Postabortion sterilizations can be performed safely following uncomplicated spontaneous or induced abortion. Following a first-trimester abortion, laparoscopic sterilization or minilaparotomy using a suprapubic approach are both acceptable. In either case, a single anesthetic for the abortion and the sterilization may be used to avoid additional risk. Following a second-trimester abortion, minilaparotomy via a small midline vertical incision at the level of the fundus can be used safely. Open laparoscopy or the Hasson cannula may be used, thereby avoiding the risk of perforation of the soft, enlarged uterus associated with introduction of the laparoscopic trocar. Alternatively, an interval procedure can be performed once complete uterine involution has occurred.

Tubal sterilization can be performed as an interval procedure at any time during the menstrual cycle. Although performance of the sterilization procedure during the patient's estimated follicular phase and confirmation of patient use of a highly effective method of contraception before sterilization will reduce the risk of luteal phase pregnancy (a pregnancy diagnosed after sterilization in which conception occurred before sterilization), highly sensitive pregnancy testing will further reduce the risk. A same-day presterilization urine test capable of detecting human chorionic gonadotropin levels as low as 20 mIU/ml or a qualitative serum assay for the beta subunit of human chorionic gonadotropin will suffice (8). Tests this sensitive will allow for pregnancy detection as early as 1 week after conception. Performance of dilation and curettage concurrent with all interval sterilizations as a routine practice is not recommended on the basis of effectiveness, cost, and morbidity (9). Interval sterilization is usually performed using laparoscopy or minilaparotomy with local, regional, or general anesthesia. Transvaginal approaches have been described, and transcervical hysteroscopic approaches are being investigated.

Surgical Approach

Laparoscopy

Modern laparoscopy was first developed in Europe in the 1960s and became a popular method for direct visualization of the abdominal and pelvic organs. In the 1970s, it was introduced in the United States for tubal sterilization. In 1987, approximately one third of all tubal sterilizations in the United States were laparoscopic procedures. Most of these were performed under short-acting, general anesthesia in an outpatient setting.

In the United States, closed laparoscopy is used more often than open laparoscopy. In laparoscopic sterilization, an endoscope is inserted through a small incision made just below the umbilicus. Closed laparoscopy is performed through a small subumbilical skin incision just large enough to admit a sharp trocar. The trocar is used to puncture the abdominal wall, gaining entry into the peritoneal cavity blindly. Open laparoscopy is performed through a 1.5-cm semilunar or vertical subumbilical incision made through the layers of the abdominal wall until the peritoneal cavity has been entered under direct visualization (10).

Advantages of laparoscopy over other surgical approaches for sterilization include the opportunity to inspect the abdominal and pelvic organs, barely visible incision scars, and a rapid return to full activity for the patient. The disadvantages of laparoscopic sterilization include the cost and the fragility of the equipment, the special training required, and the risk of bowel, bladder, or major vessel injury following insertion of the needle or trocar.

With special training and experience, both closed and open laparoscopy can be performed with local anesthesia while maintaining a high level of patient comfort. Small studies have indicated that many women prefer the use of local anesthesia for sterilization procedures (11).

Minilaparotomy

The minilaparotomy approach may be performed by using local anesthesia with sedation, regional anesthesia, or general anesthesia. In contrast to laparoscopy, minilaparotomy requires only basic surgical instruments and training. Minilaparotomy is performed by using a 2–3-cm incision placed in relation to the uterine fundus. For interval sterilization, a uterine manipulator may be used to bring the uterine fundus toward the incision. For women undergoing either laparoscopic or minilaparotomy procedures with local anesthesia, placement of a paracervical block before insertion of the uterine manipulator reduces discomfort (12). Although most surgeons prefer to perform tubal occlusion using suture ligation and excision techniques, clips or rings may be applied through the minilaparotomy incision. With minilaparotomy, a segment of the tube can be removed for pathologic confirmation that both tubes were sterilized.

Methods of Occlusion

Electrocoagulation

Electrocoagulation for tubal occlusion is used exclusively with laparoscopic sterilization. Unipolar electrocoagulation with or without tubal excision was the first laparoscopic method of tubal occlusion. However, because uncommon but serious complications, including thermal bowel injury, were reported, bipolar coagulation was introduced and is now the most commonly used laparoscopic method in the United States. Bipolar coagulation also results in a more localized injury to the fallopian tube than does the unipolar method. Therefore, to maximize its effectiveness, at least 3 cm of the isthmic portion of the fallopian tube must be completely coagulated. Adequate coagulation requires sufficient energy of 25 W delivered in a cutting waveform (13). Use of a current meter, rather than a visual endpoint or a defined period of time, more accurately indicates complete coagulation.

Mechanical Methods

Mechanical occlusion devices commonly used in the United States include the silicone rubber band (Falope ring) and the spring-loaded clip (Hulka-Clemens clip). A new titanium clip lined with silicone rubber (Filshie clip) has been widely used in Great Britain with low reported failure rates (14, 15).

Special applicators are necessary for each of the mechanical occlusive devices, and each requires skill for proper application. The band can only be applied to a fallopian tube that is sufficiently mobile to allow it to be drawn into the applicator. Both types of clips should be applied perpendicular to the long axis of the proximal isthmus of the fallopian tube. Both types of clips and the silicone rubber band are most likely to be effective when used to occlude a normal tube. Tubal adhesions or a thickened or dilated fallopian tube increase the risk of misapplication and subsequent failure (16).

All of the mechanical methods of tubal occlusion destroy much less oviduct (about 5 mm for clips and 2 cm for rings) than do electrocoagulation methods. Therefore, if reversal is attempted, there is a greater chance of success.

Ligation Methods

Tubal occlusion at the time of cesarean delivery, laparotomy for other indications, or minilaparotomy is usually performed by using ligation techniques. A variety of techniques have been well described (17). Care should be taken to excise a sufficient section of fallopian tube to ensure complete transection of the tubal lumen.

Efficacy

Failure

Precise failure rates for each method of tubal occlusion and long-term cumulative failure rates have been difficult to measure because of the methods' high effectiveness rates. A generally accepted failure rate of less than 1% is based on combined small studies in which different occlusion methods were used (18). Preliminary findings from the U.S. Collaborative Review of Sterilization indicate that cumulative failure rates are higher than expected, with significant differences between methods (19). The risk of failure persists for years after the procedure and varies by method of tubal occlusion and age. In a total of 143 sterilization failures, cumulative 10-year probabilities of pregnancy were highest after spring-loaded clip sterilization (36.5 per 1,000 procedures) and lowest after unipolar coagulation (7.5 per 1,000) and postpartum partial salpingectomy (7.5 per 1,000). The cumulative risk of pregnancy was highest among women sterilized at a young age with bipolar coagulation (54.3 per 1,000) and spring-loaded clip application (52.1 per 1,000). It is important to note, however, that in another study of sterilization failures, all spring-loaded clip failures were found to be due to misapplication (16).

Fecundity declines significantly after the age of 35 years. In one study, patients younger than 35 years were 1.7 times more likely to become pregnant following sterilization than women over the age of 35 years (20). In another study, among women 18–27 years of age who underwent bipolar coagulation, 2.8% became pregnant between 5 and 10 years after the procedure (19).

Pregnancies after sterilization may occur without any technical error. Technical error leading to failure occurs less frequently with minilaparotomy regardless of the occlusion method used (21). In one study, the location of the suture on the ligated tube affected estimated minilaparotomy failure rates, which were approximately 3% in 3 years for fimbriectomy with infundibular ligation, approximately 1.7% for ampullary ligation, and approximately 0.34% for isthmic ligation (20).

Ectopic Pregnancy

When sterilization failure occurs, the subsequent pregnancy is more likely to be ectopic than intrauterine. The degree of increased risk depends on the occlusion method used. The results of several reports suggest that over half of the pregnancies that occur after electrocoagulation sterilization procedures may be ectopic (22, 23). If an ectopic pregnancy occurs, the physician should evaluate both proximal tubes and manage any acute problems that are present.

Complications

In the United States, female sterilization has a mortality rate of 1–2 deaths per 100,000 procedures (24). Complications of general anesthesia are the leading cause of death from tubal sterilization. Other causes include sepsis and hemorrhage. Between 1977 and 1981, most of those deaths from sepsis resulted from thermal bowel injury following unipolar electrocoagulation, while most of those deaths from hemorrhage followed major vessel lacerations associated with abdominal entry for laparoscopic sterilization (25).

Studies in the United States indicate that women undergoing interval minilaparotomy are at approximately twice the risk of having any complication than are women undergoing interval laparoscopic sterilization. However, women who undergo minilaparotomy often have medical risk factors, including certain cardiac and pulmonary problems, that are contraindications to laparoscopy and therefore are intrinsically at greater surgical risk (26, 27).

Late Sequelae

The long-term health effects of tubal sterilization on menstrual pattern disturbance, pelvic pain, and the need for pelvic surgery are controversial. Early studies of menstrual disturbance following sterilization failed to account for confounding variables such as presterilization use of hormonal contraceptives that generally mask underlying menstrual dysfunction. Most recent prospective studies that account for these factors have found little or no difference in menstrual function between women before and after sterilization, or between sterilized women and nonsterilized control subjects in the first 2 years of follow up. Findings from reports that include follow up for more than 2 years have been less consistent, yet no single method of occlusion, regardless of the amount of tubal destruction, has been associated with an increase in risk for poststerilization menstrual disturbance (28).

Two studies have evaluated the likelihood of hospitalization for menstrual disorders in women who have undergone sterilization. A U.S. population-based cohort study showed an increased relative risk of 1.6 (95% confidence interval of 1.3–2.1) for hospitalization for menstrual disorders compared with a control group of wives of men who have had vasectomies (29). Follow up of a large British cohort for 6 years failed to identify a significant increase in risk (30).

Some sterilized women may be more likely to undergo subsequent hysterectomy. Women who have been sterilized before age 30 have a higher risk of a hysterectomy than women sterilized after age 30. This risk has not been related to an increase in menstrual disturbance or the extent of tissue damage based on the method of occlusion used (31).

Ovarian Cancer

In several older studies, an inverse relationship between tubal occlusion and subsequent ovarian cancer has been found, although the strength of this relationship has varied widely (32, 33, 34). A controlled, prospective study reported a reduced risk of ovarian cancer among women who had tubal occlusion or hysterectomy (35). The study monitored 77,544 women for 12 years. For those women who had a tubal ligation, the relative risk of ovarian cancer was 0.33. The reduced risk persisted after the investigators controlled for risk factors such as smoking and protective factors (eg, use of oral contraceptives). Cases of reported ovarian cancer, identified within the first 4 years after sterilization, were excluded to eliminate possible screening bias (32, 33).

Pelvic Inflammatory Disease

It has long been believed that tubal sterilization protects against pelvic inflammatory disease. This would seem to make intuitive sense, as this condition is thought to be caused by the ascent of bacteria through the cervix, uterus, and fallopian tubes and into the peritoneal cavity. This protection is, however, not absolute. Case reports of pelvic inflammatory disease and tuboovarian abscess in women who have undergone sterilization are rare but do exist in the literature (36, 37).

Sterilization in Men

Vasectomy performed as an outpatient procedure has been popular in the United States since 1965. More than 5 million men in the United States have had a vasectomy (38). When compared with tubal sterilization, vasectomy is safer, less expensive, and equally as effective. In the United States, urologists, general surgeons, and family physicians perform vasectomy procedures in their offices using local anesthesia.

Traditionally, vasectomy was performed through two incisions in the scrotum, one overlying each vas deferens. The incisions were then closed with a suture. In 1985, the no-scalpel vasectomy technique was introduced (39). This method makes use of two specially designed instruments: one allows the vas to be fixed externally, while the second is used to puncture the scrotal skin without using a scalpel (40). The technique was developed to increase acceptability of vasectomy by reducing the apprehension related to making an incision on the scrotum (41, 40). It reduces the already low rate of minor complications (less than 3%) seen with traditional vasectomy, such as wound hematoma and infection (42).

Both traditional and no-scalpel vasectomy use the same methods to occlude the vas. These include excising a segment of the vas and sealing the ends via ligation, electrocoagulation or thermocoagulation, or clips. To decrease the incidence of recanalization, some surgeons further separate the severed ends by folding them back on one another or burying one end in the scrotal fascia.

Pregnancy rates following vasectomy are less than 1% in most studies and usually result from failure to occlude the correct structure, unprotected intercourse too soon after the operation, or spontaneous recanalization. Unlike tubal occlusion in women, vasectomy is not immediately effective: about 3 months or 20 ejaculations are needed to flush the vasa of viable sperm. Postvasectomy semen analysis should be performed to determine the effectiveness of the procedure.

The possibility of long-term side effects from vasectomy has received considerable attention. Nine separate epidemiological studies in men have failed to show a relationship between atherosclerosis and vasectomy (43). An original study in monkeys that suggested such a relationship has not been confirmed (44, 45). Other consequences of vasectomy have been suggested, but none has been proven. In addition, several studies report that in the United States, men who have chosen vasectomies are often healthier than control counterparts (46, 47).

In Western countries, white, upper-middle-class men are more likely to choose vasectomy and are also the group more likely to have testicular cancer. A study of nearly 74,000 men who have had vasectomies showed the incidence of testicular cancer in this group to be no higher than that of the general population (48). It also showed that vasectomy does not accelerate the growth of preexisting testicular tumors.

In 1993, researchers published the first large cohort studies to show a weak but statistically significant increased risk for prostate cancer in a subgroup of men at least 20 years after vasectomy (49, 47). Two subsequent studies have failed to support these findings (50, 51).

The U.S. National Institutes of Health convened a group of experts in 1993 to review the published reports on prostate cancer. The committee found that although additional research into a possible causal relationship between vasectomy and prostate cancer should be conducted, a change in the current practice of vasectomy was not warranted. The National Institutes of Health made the following recommendations (52):

- Providers should continue to offer vasectomy and perform the procedure
- Vasectomy reversal is not warranted to prevent prostate cancer
- Screening for prostate cancer should not be any different for men who have had a vasectomy than for those who have not

Summary

Sterilization provides a safe and effective contraceptive method. Both female and male sterilization have few long-term sequelae. Several new methods of transcervical sterilization are under development, but laparoscopy and minilaparotomy are likely to remain the most popular methods of female sterilization.

REFERENCES

1. Schwartz DB, Wingo PA, Antarsh L, Smith JC. Female sterilizations in the United States, 1987. Fam Plann Perspect 1989;21:209–212

2. Marquette CM, Koonin LM, Antarsh L, Gargiullo PM, Smith JC. Vasectomy in the United States, 1991. Am J Public Health 1995;85:644–649

3. Mosher WD. Contraceptive practice in the United States, 1982–1988. Fam Plann Perspect 1990;22:198–205

4. Wilcox LS, Chu SY, Eaker ED, Zeger SL, Peterson HB. Risk factors for regret after tubal sterilization: 5 years of follow-up in a prospective study. Fertil Steril 1991; 55:927–933

5. Wilcox LS, Chu SY, Peterson HB. Characteristics of women who considered or obtained tubal reanastomosis: results from a prospective study of tubal sterilization. Obstet Gynecol 1990;75:661–665

6. Centers for Disease Control. HIV-risk behaviors of sterilized and nonsterilized women in drug-treatment programs—Philadelphia, 1989–1991. MMWR 1992;41: 149–152

7. Centers for Disease Control. Surgical sterilization among women and use of condoms-Baltimore, 1989–1990. MMWR 1992;41:568–575

8. Lipscomb GH, Spellman JR, Ling FW. The effect of same-day pregnancy testing on the incidence of luteal phase pregnancy. Obstet Gynecol 1993;82:411–413

9. Lichter ED, Laff SP, Friedman EA. Value of routine dilation and curettage at the time of interval sterilization. Obstet Gynecol 1986;67:763–765

10. Penfield AJ. Female sterilization by minilaparotomy or open laparoscopy. Baltimore, Maryland: Urban & Schwarzenberg, 1980

11. Handa VL, Berlin M, Washington AE. A comparison of local and general anesthesia for laparoscopic tubal sterilization. Journal of Women's Health 1994;3:135–141

12. Poindexter AN III, Abdul-Malak M, Fast JE. Laparoscopic tubal sterilization under local anesthesia. Obstet Gynecol 1990;75:5–8

13. Soderstrom RM, Levy BS, Engel T. Reducing bipolar sterilization failures. Obstet Gynecol 1989;74:60–63

14. Filshie GM, Casey D, Pogmore JR, Dutton AGB, Symonds EM, Peake ABL. The titanium/silicone rubber clip for female sterilization. Br J Obstet Gynaecol 1981;88:655–662

15. Green-Thompson RW, Popis M, Cairncross NWA. Outpatient laparoscopic tubal sterilization under local anaesthesia: a review of three years at King George V Hospital, Durban. Obstet Gynecol Forum August 1993:4–14,44

16. Stovall TG, Ling FW, O'Kelley KR, Coleman SA. Gross and histologic examination of tubal ligation failures in a residency training program. Obstet Gynecol 1990;76: 461–465

17. Wheeless CR Jr. Tubal sterilization. In: Thompson JD, Rock JA. Te Linde's operative gynecology. 7th ed. Philadelphia: JB Lippincott Co, 1992:343–359

18. The Johns Hopkins University. Population Information Program. Minilaparotomy and laparoscopy: safe, effective, and widely used. Popul Rep C 1985;9:C-125–C-167

19. Peterson HB, Xia Z, Hughes JM, Wilcox LS, Tylor LR, Trussel J. The risk of pregnancy after tubal sterilization: findings from the U.S. Collaborative Review of Sterilization. Am J Obstet Gynecol 1996;174:1161–1170

20. Cheng MCE, Wong YM, Rochat RW, Ratnam SS. Sterilization failures in Singapore: an examination of ligation techniques and failure rates. Stud Fam Plann 1977; 8:109–115

21. Chi I-C, Laufe LE, Gardner SD, Tolbert MA. An epidemiologic study of risk factors associated with pregnancy following female sterilization. Am J Obstet Gynecol 1980;136:768–773

22. McCausland A. High rate of ectopic pregnancy following laparoscopic tubal coagulation failures: incidence and etiology. Am J Obstet Gynecol 1980;136:97–101

23. Kjer JJ, Knudsen LB. Ectopic pregnancy subsequent to laparoscopic sterilization. Am J Obstet Gynecol 1989; 160:1202–1204

24. Escobedo LG, Peterson HB, Grubb GS, Franks AL. Case-fatality rates for tubal sterilization in U.S. hospitals, 1979 to 1980. Am J Obstet Gynecol 1989;160:147–150

25. Peterson HB, DeStefano F, Rubin GL, Greenspan JR, Lee NC, Ory HW. Deaths attributable to tubal sterilization in the United States, 1977 to 1981. Am J Obstet Gynecol 1983;146:131–136

26. DeStefano F, Greenspan JR, Dicker RC, Peterson HB, Strauss LT, Rubin GL. Complications of interval laparoscopic tubal sterilization. Obstet Gynecol 1983;61: 153–158

27. Layde PM, Peterson HB, Dicker RC, DeStefano F, Rubin GL, Ory HW. Risk factors for complications of interval tubal sterilization by laparotomy. Obstet Gynecol 1983;62:180–184

28. Wilcox LS, Martinez-Schnell B, Peterson HB, Ware JH, Hughes JM. Menstrual function after tubal sterilization. Am J Epidemiol 1992;135:1368–1381

29. Shy KK, Stergachis A, Grothaus LG, Wagner EH, Hecht J, Anderson G. Tubal sterilization and risk of subsequent hospital admission for menstrual disorders. Am J Obstet Gynecol 1992;166:1698–1706

30. Vessey M, Huggins G, Lawless M, McPherson K, Yeates D. Tubal sterilization: findings in a large prospective study. Br J Obstet Gynaecol 1983;90:203–209

31. Rulin MC, Davidson AR, Philliber SG, Graves WL, Cushman LF. Long-term effect of tubal sterilization on menstrual indices and pelvic pain. Obstet Gynecol 1993;82:118–121

32. Irwin KL, Weiss NS, Lee NC, Peterson HB. Tubal sterilization, hysterectomy, and the subsequent occurrence of epithelial ovarian cancer. Am J Epidemiol 1991;134:362–369

33. Whittemore AS, Wu ML, Paffenbarger RS Jr, Sarles DL, Kampert JB, Grosser S, et al. Personal and environmental characteristics related to epithelial ovarian cancer. II. Exposures to talcum powder, tobacco, alcohol, and coffee. Am J Epidemiol 1988;128:1228–1240

34. Mori M, Harabuchi I, Miyake H, Casagrande JT, Henderson BE, Ross RK. Reproductive, genetic, and dietary risk factors for ovarian cancer. Am J Epidemiol 1988;128:771–777

35. Hankinson SE, Hunter DJ, Colditz GA, Willett WC, Stampfer MJ, Rosner B, et al. Tubal ligation, hysterectomy,

and risk of ovarian cancer: a prospective study. JAMA 1993;270:2813–2818

36. Vermesh M, Confino E, Boler LR, Friberg J, Gleicher N. Acute salpingitis in sterilized women. Obstet Gynecol 1987;69:265–267

37. Huggins GR, Sondheimer SJ. Complications of female sterilization: immediate and delayed. Fertil Steril 1984;41:337–355

38. Mosher WD, Pratt WF. Contraceptive use in the United States, 1973–88. Advance data from vital and health statistics; no. 182. Hyattsville, Maryland: National Center for Health Statistics, 1990

39. Huber D. No-scalpel vasectomy: the transfer of a refined surgical technique from China to other countries. Adv Contracept 1989;5:217–218

40. Schlegel PN, Goldstein M. No-scalpel vasectomy. Semin Urol 1992;10:252–256

41. Nirapathpongporn A, Huber DH, Krieger JN. No-scalpel vasectomy at the King's birthday vasectomy festival. Lancet 1990;335:894–895

42. Li S, Goldstein M, Zhu J, Huber D. The no-scalpel vasectomy. J Urol 1991;145:341–344

43. Peterson HB, Huber DH, Belker AM. Vasectomy: an appraisal for the obstetrician-gynecologist. Obstet Gynecol 1990;76:568–572

44. Alexander NJ, Clarkson TB. Vasectomy increases the severity of diet-induced atherosclerosis in *Macaca fascicularis*. Science 1978;201:538–541

45. Clarkson TB, Alexander NJ, Morgan TM. Atherosclerosis of cynomolgus monkeys hyper- and hyporesponsive to dietary cholesterol: lack of effect on vasectomy. Arteriosclerosis 1988;8:488–498

46. Massey FJ Jr, Bernstein GS, O'Fallon WM, Schuman LM, Coulson AH, Crozier R, et al. Vasectomy and health: results from a large cohort study. JAMA 1984; 252:1023–1029

47. Giovannucci E, Tosteson TD, Speizer FE, Ascherio A, Vessey MP, Colditz GA. A retrospective cohort study of vasectomy and prostate cancer in US men. JAMA 1993;269:878–882

48. Møller H, Knudsen LB, Lynge E. Risk of testicular cancer after vasectomy: cohort study of over 73 000 men. BMJ 1994;309:295–299

49. Giovannucci E, Ascherio A, Rimm EB, Colditz GA, Stampfer MJ, Willett WC. A prospective cohort study of vasectomy and prostate cancer in US men. JAMA 1993;269:873–877

50. Hayes RB, Pottern LM, Greenberg R, Schoenberg J, Swanson GM, Liff J, et al. Vasectomy and prostate cancer in US blacks and whites. Am J Epidemiol 1993;137:263–269

51. Coulson AH, Crozier R, Massey FJ Jr, O'Fallon WM, Schuman LM, Spivey GH. Health status of american men—a study of post-vasectomy sequelae: results. J Clin Epidemiol 1993;46:857–920

52. Healy B. Does vasectomy cause prostate cancer? JAMA 1993;269:2620

This Technical Bulletin was developed under the direction of the Committee on Technical Bulletins of the American College of Obstetricians and Gynecologists as an educational aid to obstetricians and gynecologists. The committee wishes to thank Amy E. Pollack, MD, MPH, for her assistance in the development of this bulletin. This Technical Bulletin does not define a standard of care, nor is it intended to dictate an exclusive course of management. It presents recognized methods and techniques of clinical practice for consideration by obstetrician–gynecologists for incorporation into their practices. Variations of practice taking into account the needs of the individual patient, resources, and limitations unique to the institution or type of practice may be appropriate. Requests for authorization to make photocopies should be directed to the Copyright Clearance Center, 222 Rosewood Drive, Danvers, MA 01923; telephone (508) 750-8400.

ACOG EDUCATIONAL BULLETIN

Number 248, July 1998

Viral Hepatitis in Pregnancy

Viral hepatitis is one of the most serious infections that can occur in pregnant women. Six different forms of viral hepatitis have now been defined. This bulletin describes the various types of hepatitis, their implications during pregnancy, the risk of perinatal transmission, and treatment.

Etiology, Epidemiology, and Natural History

Hepatitis A

This Educational Bulletin was developed under the direction of the Committee on Educational Bulletins of the American College of Obstetricians and Gynecologists as an aid to obstetricians and gynecologists. This document is not to be construed as establishing a standard of practice or dictating an exclusive course of treatment. Rather, it is intended as an educational tool that presents current information on obstetric–gynecologic issues.

In the United States, approximately one third of cases of acute hepatitis are caused by hepatitis A virus. The virus usually is transmitted by person-to-person contact through fecal–oral contamination. Poor hygiene, poor sanitation, and intimate personal or sexual contact facilitate transmission. Epidemics frequently result from exposure to contaminated food and water. In obstetric populations in the United States, the patients at greatest risk for hepatitis A infection are those who recently have emigrated from, or traveled to, developing nations where hepatitis A is endemic, particularly in Southeast Asia, Africa, Central America, Greenland, Mexico, and the Middle East. In the United States, the incidence of acute hepatitis A in pregnancy is approximately 1/1,000.

Hepatitis A is caused by an RNA virus. Its incubation period ranges from 15 to 50 days; the mean is 28–30 days. Feces contain the highest concentration of virus particles, and virus excretion reaches its maximum late in the incubation period and early in the prodromal phase of the illness. The duration of viremia is short, and the virus normally is not excreted in urine or other body fluids.

Serious complications of hepatitis A are uncommon. Among all acutely ill patients who require hospitalization, the overall fatality rate does not exceed 2/1,000 cases in the United States. A chronic carrier state of hepatitis A does not exist. In addition, perinatal transmission of the virus has not been demonstrated (1). Hepatitis A immune globulin is recommended for household contacts and contacts in day care centers and custodial institutions. It should be given as soon as possible after exposure; it is ineffective if given more than 2 weeks after exposure. A vaccine is available, which may be taken during pregnancy (2).

Replaces Number 174, November 1992

Hepatitis B

Hepatitis B is caused by a small DNA virus. The intact virus is termed the Dane particle. Hepatitis B virus contains three principal antigens. Hepatitis B surface antigen (HBsAg) is present on the surface of the virus and also circulates freely in the serum in spherical and filamentous forms. The middle portion of the Dane particle contains hepatitis B core antigen (HBcAg). The core antigen is present only in hepatocytes and does not circulate in the serum. Hepatitis B e antigen (HBeAg) is encoded by the same portion of the viral genome that codes for the core antigen. The presence of HBeAg indicates an extremely high viral inoculum and active virus replication (1, 3).

Hepatitis B infection occurs throughout the world. In the United States, it is responsible for 40–45% of all cases of hepatitis. Approximately 300,000 new cases of hepatitis B occur annually, and more than 1 million Americans are chronic carriers. Acute hepatitis B occurs in 1–2/1,000 pregnancies. Chronic infection is present in 5–15/1,000 pregnancies (3, 4), but is more prevalent among certain ethnic groups (ie, Asians, Inuits).

Hepatitis B virus is transmitted by parenteral and sexual contact. Individuals at greatest risk of becoming infected are those who have multiple sexual partners, inject drugs percutaneously, or have sexual partners who engage in these risk-taking behaviors. Other important risk factors are receipt of blood products and household or institutional contact.

All blood donors are screened routinely for HBsAg. Thus, transmission of hepatitis B virus by transfusion of blood or blood products is rare (1). Drug addiction is an important risk factor for horizontal transmission of hepatitis B virus. Sexual contact is an efficient mechanism for spreading the virus. Approximately 25% of the regular sexual contacts of infected individuals will themselves become seropositive.

The mortality associated with acute hepatitis B is approximately 1%. Of patients who become infected, 85–90% experience complete resolution of their physical findings and develop protective levels of the antibody. The other 10–15% of patients become chronically infected; they continue to have detectable serum levels of HBsAg but are asymptomatic and have no biochemical evidence of hepatic dysfunction. In 15–30% of those chronically infected, viral replication continues and is manifested by persistence of the e antigen and active viral DNA synthesis. These individuals are at risk for the subsequent development of chronic or persistent hepatitis and cirrhosis, and approximately 4,000–5,000 die annually of complications of chronic liver disease (5, 6), including hepatocellular carcinoma.

Because hepatitis B virus is highly pathogenic and infectious, perinatal transmission of infection occurs with disturbing regularity. Approximately 10–20% of women who are seropositive for HBsAg transmit the virus to their neonates in the absence of immunoprophylaxis. In women who are seropositive for both HBsAg and HBeAg, the frequency of vertical transmission increases to approximately 90%.

In patients with acute hepatitis B, the frequency of vertical transmission also depends on the time during gestation that maternal infection occurs. When maternal infection occurs in the first trimester, up to 10% of neonates will be seropositive for HBsAg (1, 3). In women acutely infected in the third trimester, 80–90% of offspring will be infected (3).

Between 85% and 95% of cases of perinatal transmission of hepatitis B virus occur as a consequence of intrapartum exposure of the infant to contaminated blood and genital tract secretions. The remaining cases result from hematogenous transplacental dissemination, breastfeeding, and close postnatal contact between the infant and the infected parent. Infants of women who are HBsAg positive at the time of delivery should receive both hepatitis B immune globulin (HBIG) and hepatitis B vaccine within 12 hours of birth, followed by two more injections of hepatitis B vaccine in the first 6 months of life.

Hepatitis C

Hepatitis C virus (previously termed nonA, nonB hepatitis) is a single-stranded RNA virus that appears to infect as much as 0.6% of the pregnant population (7, 8). The principal risk factors for acquiring hepatitis C virus are the same as for hepatitis B.

Approximately 50% of patients with acute hepatitis C develop biochemical evidence of chronic liver disease. Of these individuals, at least 20% subsequently have chronic active hepatitis or cirrhosis. Vertical transmission has been well documented and is proportional in likelihood to the titer of hepatitis C virus RNA present in the mother's blood (7, 9). Approximately 7–8% of hepatitis C virus-positive women transmit hepatitis C virus to their offspring (7, 8). Vertical transmission of hepatitis C may be more likely if the mother also is infected with human immunodeficiency virus (HIV) (8, 10). Currently, no method has been found to prevent prenatal transmission. Many experts believe that hepatitis C virus-positive women should not breastfeed because there is a 2–3% risk of vertical transmission. Unlike hepatitis B, antibodies to hepatitis C are not protective.

Hepatitis D

Hepatitis D requires hepatitis B virus for replication and expression and so occurs only in people already infected with hepatitis B. In acute hepatitis B, once HBsAg clears the bloodstream, so does hepatitis D. Approximately 20–25% of chronic hepatitis B virus carriers ultimately are coinfected with hepatitis D virus (11, 12). In acute hepatitis D, immunoglobulin M (IgM) antibodies against hepatitis D predominate, whereas IgG antibodies may be found in chronic infections.

Chronic hepatitis D produces severe disease more often than other forms of chronic hepatitis. Of patients with chronic hepatitis D, 70–80% ultimately develop cirrhosis and portal hypertension, 15% of whom suffer an unusually rapid progression to cirrhosis within 2 years of the initial onset of acute illness. Mortality due to hepatic failure approaches 25% (11–13). In contrast, only 15–30% of patients with chronic hepatitis B virus infection develop cirrhosis and portal hypertension, and the disease progression typically is much slower.

Vertical transmission of hepatitis D virus has been documented. Transmission is uncommon, however, because the measures used to prevent perinatal infection with hepatitis B virus are almost uniformly effective in preventing infection by hepatitis D.

Hepatitis E

The epidemiologic features of hepatitis E are similar to those of hepatitis A. Although the disease has been reported only rarely in the United States, it is endemic in several developing nations, similar to those mentioned for hepatitis A. In these regions, maternal mortality often has been alarmingly high. In the 1980s, India and Burma reported 10–18% of pregnant women with hepatitis E died as a complication of their infection (14). Most of these women lived under conditions of extreme poverty. Women who have a higher standard of living and greater access to medical care are unlikely to have the same high rate of mortality.

Although acute hepatitis E can be a serious disease, it usually is self-limited and does not result in a chronic carrier state (14, 15). As with hepatitis A, hepatitis E is transmitted via contaminated food or water, though less efficiently. Vertical transmission of hepatitis E has been reported (16).

Hepatitis G

Hepatitis G infection is more likely in people already infected with hepatitis B or C or who have a history of intravenous drug use (17). In a study of 47 women infected with HIV or hepatitis C virus, 9 of whom also were infected with the hepatitis G virus, the risk of vertical transmission was higher for hepatitis G than it was for the other two agents (18). Hepatitis G probably does not cause chronic active hepatitis or cirrhosis.

Clinical Manifestations

The usual subjective symptoms in patients with acute viral hepatitis are malaise, fatigue, anorexia, nausea, and right upper quadrant or epigastric pain. Typical physical findings include jaundice, upper abdominal tenderness, and hepatomegaly, although many cases of hepatitis are anicteric. The patient's urine usually is darkened, and the stool may be acholic. In cases of fulminant hepatitis, signs of coagulopathy and encephalopathy may be evident.

In patients with hepatitis A or E, these clinical manifestations usually are temporally related to recent travel to an endemic area or exposure to an infected person. Similarly, hepatitis B, C, D, or G typically ensues after parenteral exposure to contaminated blood or sexual contact with an infected partner. The evolution of acute clinical illness in patients with hepatitis D often follows a biphasic course. In the initial phase of infection, patients with hepatitis D are indistinguishable from individuals with acute hepatitis B. Two to four weeks after apparent resolution of symptoms, patients have a relapse, which usually is of a milder nature and is associated with a second episode of elevation in serum transaminases. At this time serologic assays for hepatitis D virus usually are positive.

As noted previously, among those patients originally infected with hepatitis B, C, or D virus whose acute symptoms resolve, some become chronic carriers of viral antigens. The same may be true for hepatitis G, although a carrier state has yet to be identified. Although most viral hepatitis carriers initially are asymptomatic, up to one third subsequently develop chronic active or persistent hepatitis or cirrhosis. Once cirrhosis ensues, patients demonstrate the typical signs of end-stage liver disease, such as jaundice, muscle wasting, ascites, spider angioma, palmar erythema, and, ultimately, hepatic encephalopathy. Hepatitis C is probably the leading cause of hepatocellular carcinoma in the United States, whereas hepatitis B virus is the leading cause worldwide.

Diagnosis

Jaundice, a primary symptom of hepatitis infection, also occurs with numerous other disorders. The principal disorders that should be considered in the differential diagnosis of jaundice in pregnancy are shown in Table 1. Testing strategies should be directed toward discriminating among clinically likely diagnoses.

General Tests

Coincident with the onset of symptoms, patients with acute hepatitis usually have a marked increase in the serum concentration of alanine aminotransferase (ALT, previously SGPT) and aspartate aminotransferase (AST, previously SGOT). In addition, the serum bilirubin concentration often is increased. In patients who are mod-

Table 1. Disorders to Consider in the Differential Diagnosis of Jaundice in Pregnancy

Condition	Distinguishing Characteristics
Viral hepatitis	Mild to marked elevation in serum transaminases Positive viral serology Prominent inflammatory infiltrate with hepatocellular disarray
Acute fatty liver of pregnancy	Minimal elevation in transaminases Little if any inflammatory infiltrate with prominent microvesicular fat deposition
Toxic injury	History of drug exposure (eg, tetracycline, isoniazid, erythromycin estolate, alpha methyldopa)
Cholestasis of pregnancy	Pruritus Elevation of bile salts Cholestasis with little inflammation
Severe preeclampsia	Hypertension, edema, proteinuria, oliguria Elevated blood urea nitrogen, creatinine, uric acid, transaminases, and lactate dehydrogenase Thrombocytopenia
Mononucleosis	Flulike illness Positive heterophile antibody Elevated transaminases
Cytomegalovirus (CMV) hepatitis	CMV antibodies Positive viral culture or polymerase chain reaction Elevated transaminases
Autoimmune hepatitis	Antinuclear antibodies, liver–kidney microsomal antibodies Elevated transaminases

erately to severely ill, coagulation abnormalities and hyperammonemia also may be present. Although liver biopsy is rarely indicated in pregnancy, viral hepatitis may be distinguished histologically from other causes of hepatic injury by its characteristic pattern of extensive hepatocellular injury and inflammatory infiltrate. Initial evaluation of the patient with suspected viral hepatitis should include tests for: anti-HA IgM, HBsAg, and HC PCR. In selected patients, additional testing can include anti-HBc IgM, HD PCR, anti-HE, and anti-HG.

Specific Tests

If hepatitis is suspected based on the initial evaluation and general tests, the type of virus is determined through laboratory analysis.

Hepatitis A

The diagnosis of acute hepatitis A is confirmed by detecting IgM antibodies to the virus. A chronic carrier state for this infection does not exist, but IgG antibodies to hepatitis A virus will persist in patients with previous exposure to the virus (1).

Hepatitis B

In the acute stage of hepatitis B virus infection, the diagnosis is confirmed by the identification of the surface antigen and the IgM antibody to the core antigen. The presence of e antigen is indicative of an exceptionally high viral inoculum and active virus replication, and implies a high degree of infectivity. Chronic hepatitis B virus infection is characterized by the persistence of the surface antigen in the liver and serum. The time of infection can be evaluated by measuring IgG and IgM antibodies to HBcAg. Typically, the IgG hepatitis B core antibody (HBcAb) appears 6 months or more after infection, with the IgM moiety being predominant prior to that time.

Occasionally patients with acute hepatitis B will demonstrate HBsAg only briefly and will develop anti-HBc (IgM) as their only marker of acute hepatitis B infection. Anti-HBc (IgM) may be helpful in HBsAg-negative patients in whom hepatitis B is strongly suspected (19).

Hepatitis C

The diagnosis of hepatitis C is confirmed by the identification of the antibody to hepatitis C virus. However, the antibody may not be present until 6–16 weeks after the onset of clinical illness. Hepatitis C viral RNA can be detected by polymerase chain reaction assay of serum soon after infection as well as in chronic disease.

Hepatitis D

Laboratory tests that may be used to confirm the diagnosis of acute hepatitis D are detection of D antigen in hepatic tissue or serum and identification of the IgM antibody to hepatitis D virus. D antigenemia usually persists in patients with chronic hepatitis D despite the appearance of the IgG antibody to the virus. Thus, as in hepatitis C and HIV infection, viremia and end-organ damage can continue despite the presence of the antibody to the virus (11, 12).

Hepatitis E and G

The diagnoses of infection with hepatitis E and hepatitis G are similar. In both cases, the infection is documented by the presence of virus-specific antibodies.

Management

General Supportive Measures

Patients with acute hepatitis should be hospitalized if they have encephalopathy, coagulopathy, or severe debilitation. Nutritional needs should be addressed within the context of the severity of the disease. Fluid and electrolyte abnormalities should be corrected. If a coagulopathy is present, administration of erythrocytes, platelets, and clotting factors such as fresh frozen plasma or cryoprecipitate may be necessary. Activity should be limited, and the patient should be protected from upper abdominal trauma.

Women who are less severely ill may be treated as outpatients. They should reduce their level of activity, avoid upper abdominal trauma, and maintain good nutrition as well. Infected women also should avoid intimate contact with household members and sexual partners until these individuals receive appropriate prophylaxis outlined as follows.

Specific Immunotherapy

Hepatitis A

Currently, no antiviral agent is available for treatment of acute hepatitis A. An inactivated-virus vaccine that is safe in pregnancy is available. Women at risk for infection with hepatitis A, such as those traveling to endemic areas, should be vaccinated (2).

Patients who have close personal or sexual contact with an individual who has hepatitis A should receive immune globulin if they have not been immunized. Immune globulin does not pose a risk to either a pregnant woman or her fetus, and therefore the preparation should be administered during pregnancy if indicated. For postexposure prophylaxis, a single intramuscular dose of 1 mL should be administered as soon as possible after contact with the infected individual. Administration of immune globulin more than 2 weeks after exposure is not effective in preventing or ameliorating the severity of hepatitis A (1).

Hepatitis B

Although interferon alfa has been shown to alter the natural history of acute hepatitis B, C, and D virus infection, it has multiple side effects including myelosuppression, autoantibody formation, thyroid disturbances, and possible cardiotoxicity. Interferon alfa should be avoided during pregnancy because of its possible abortifacient effects. Accordingly, prevention of infection is of paramount importance. Specific immunotherapy with hepatitis B immune globulin (HBIG) has been effective (20).

Vaccination. Individuals who have risk factors should be vaccinated against infection. In general, it is cost-effective to screen for the antibody to hepatitis B virus in women who belong to groups with a high risk of infection. In most other risk groups, antibody screening prior to vaccination is probably not indicated.

Two vaccines for hepatitis B virus, Recombivax HB and Engerix-B, have been developed. The original vaccine (Heptavax-B), licensed in 1982 but not currently available, was prepared by purification of surface antigen extracted from the serum of hepatitis B virus carriers. Because of concerns, later disproven, that this vaccine might transmit HIV infection, many individuals who were appropriate candidates for the vaccine refused to receive it. Currently available vaccines prepared from yeast cultures by using recombinant DNA technology clearly pose no risk of transmission of HIV infection. They are highly immunogenic and result in seroconversion in more than 95% of recipients (1).

The vaccine should be administered into the deltoid muscle. Intragluteal and intradermal injections result in lower rates of seroconversion. Pregnancy is not a contraindication to vaccination. In fact, susceptible pregnant women who are at risk for hepatitis B infection should be specifically targeted for vaccination.

Individuals who have been exposed to hepatitis B virus before they are vaccinated should receive passive immunization with HBIG and undergo the immunization series—preferably in the contralateral arm. Hepatitis B immune globulin is prepared from pooled plasma that has an HBsAg antibody titer of at least 1/100,000, as determined by radioimmunoassay. The preparation is administered intramuscularly in a dose of 0.06 mL/kg. When exposure has occurred as a result of sexual contact, the patient should receive a single dose of HBIG within 14 days of contact. For prophylaxis after percutaneous or mucous membrane injury, treatment should include an initial injection of HBIG, followed by a second dose 1 month later. These regimens are approximately 75% effective in preventing hepatitis B virus infection. If an antibody response is documented, clinical hepatitis B virus infection is rare (1). However, because of the high rate of usually conferred protection, evaluation of immune status at any interval is not deemed necessary (1). Human immunodeficiency virus infection has not been transmitted by HBIG. In addition, pregnancy is not a contraindication to administration of HBIG (1).

Perinatal Management. The combination of passive and active immunization, as outlined here, has been particularly effective in reducing the frequency of perinatal transmission of hepatitis B virus. Several investigations conducted in Asian nations have shown that passive and active immunization of the newborn is 85–95% effective in preventing perinatal transmission of hepatitis B virus.

The Centers for Disease Control and Prevention and the American College of Obstetricians and Gynecologists recommend hepatitis B virus screening for all pregnant women. Pregnant women should be routinely tested for HBsAg during an early prenatal visit. If, at the time of admission to the hospital for delivery, the test has not been performed or the results are not available, the HBsAg test should be done. Women in high-risk groups who initially test negative for hepatitis B virus should be targeted for vaccination if they have not been vaccinated previously. Seropositive women should be encouraged to inform their children and sexual partners of the need for testing and vaccination. Serum transaminases should be measured in seropositive women to detect biochemical evidence of chronic active hepatitis. If the test results are abnormal or if the liver is palpable, the patient should be evaluated further to determine whether the disease is acute or chronic.

The Centers for Disease Control and Prevention recommends universal active immunization of all infants born in the United States (6). The immunization schedule for infants of women who have been screened and are negative should be started preferably before discharge, but by no later than 2 months of age. Infants of women who are known to be HBsAg positive or whose status is unknown should have both passive and active immunization treatment. It should be given simultaneously at different sites intramuscularly and started within 12 hours after birth. Such a strategy will prevent postnatal and neonatal acquisition of hepatitis B virus in most cases. The physician responsible for the care of a newborn delivered to a mother with chronic hepatitis B should be informed of the mother's carrier status so that the appropriate doses of hepatitis B virus vaccine and HBIG can be given as soon as possible following delivery.

Hepatitis C and D
Treatment with interferon alfa produced clinical improvement in 28–46% of patients with chronic hepatitis C. Unfortunately, however, approximately 50% of patients who initially improved suffered a relapse within 6 months of the cessation of therapy. In addition, pregnant women were specifically excluded from the investigation (21). Similar results are seen with hepatitis D.

Precautions for Health Care Workers
Each year, approximately 12,000 health care workers in the United States contract hepatitis B virus infection as a result of an occupational injury. Of these individuals, about 200 experience a fulminant course and die. Another 1,000–1,200 become chronic carriers of the surface antigen (22).

The principal mechanism of transmission of hepatitis B virus from patient to health care worker is through injury from a sharp object, such as a needle or scalpel, that is contaminated with infected blood. Of the individuals exposed in these ways, 10–20% subsequently become seropositive for HBsAg. Although most remain asymptomatic, they are still at increased risk for development of chronic liver disease (1, 22). Another important, but less frequent, mechanism of transmission is a splash injury, resulting in contact between skin or mucosal surfaces and contaminated secretions or blood.

Physicians and other health care workers should use standard precautions to reduce their risk of acquiring hepatitis B virus infection (23). The primary element of universal precautions is the use of appropriate barrier precautions by all health care personnel to prevent the exposure of their skin and mucous membranes to the blood or other body fluids of any patient. Most important, all health care workers who may have direct or indirect exposure to patients should be immunized.

Reports have been published documenting transmission of hepatitis B from infected health care workers, including obstetrician–gynecologists, to patients during invasive procedures (24). In each instance in which complete serologic testing has been performed, the health care workers were seropositive for both surface and e antigens.

Summary
Hepatitis A is an uncommon complication of pregnancy and is not associated with perinatal transmission. In contrast, hepatitis B virus infection is more common and

clearly poses a serious risk to the household contacts and neonates of infected mothers. Accordingly, all pregnant women should be tested for hepatitis B virus. Universal vaccination of all neonates with hepatitis B vaccine is now recommended. Infants delivered to HBsAg seropositive mothers also should receive HBIG and vaccination immediately after birth. Hepatitis E is extremely rare in the United States and is quite similar to hepatitis A, although perinatal transmission does occur with hepatitis E. Hepatitis C and D, which are transmitted parenterally and by sexual contact, have been associated with vertical transmission. No immunoprophylaxis currently is available for neonates of mothers with hepatitis C or E virus. Immunization against hepatitis B is protective against vertical transmission of hepatitis D.

References

1. Centers for Disease Control. Protection against viral hepatitis. Recommendations of the Immunization Practices Advisory Committee (ACIP). MMWR 1990;39(RR-2):1–26

2. Totos G, Gizaris V, Papaevangelou G. Hepatitis A vaccine: persistence of antibodies 5 years after the first vaccination. Vaccine 1997;15:1252–1253

3. Sweet RL. Hepatitis B infection in pregnancy. Obstetrics/Gynecology Report 1990;2:128–139

4. Snydman DR. Hepatitis in pregnancy. N Engl J Med 1985;313:1398–1401

5. Hoofnagle JH. Chronic hepatitis B. N Engl J Med 1990;323:337–339

6. Centers for Disease Control. Hepatitis B virus: A comprehensive strategy for eliminating transmission in the United States through universal childhood vaccination: recommendations of the Immunization Practices Advisory Committee (ACIP). MMWR 1991;40(RR-13):1–25

7. Ohto H, Terazawa S, Sasaki N, Sasaki N, Hino K, Ishiwata C, et al. Transmission of hepatitis C virus from mothers to infants. N Engl J Med 1994;330:744–750

8. Silverman NS, Snyder M, Hodinka RL, McGillen P, Knee G. Detection of hepatitis C virus antibodies and specific hepatitis C virus ribonucleic acid sequences in cord bloods from a heterogeneous prenatal population. Am J Obstet Gynecol 1995;173:1396–1400

9. Matsubara T, Sumazaki R, Takita H. Mother-to-infant transmission of hepatitis C virus: a prospective study. Eur J Pediatr 1995;154:973–978

10. Zucotti GV, Ribero ML, Giovannini M, Fasola M, Riva E, Portera G, et al. Effect of hepatitis C genotype on mother-to-infant transmission of virus. J Pediatr 1995;127:278–280

11. Hoofnagle JH. Type D (delta) hepatitis. JAMA 1989;261:1321–1325 [Erratum in JAMA 1989;261:3552]

12. Rizzetto M. The delta agent. Hepatology 1983;3:729–737

13. Shattock AG, Irwin FM, Morgan BM, Hillary IB, Kelly MG, Fielding JF, et al. Increased severity and morbidity of acute hepatitis in drug abusers with simultaneously acquired hepatitis B and hepatitis D virus infections. BMJ 1985;290:1377–1380

14. Bradley DW, Maynard JE. Etiology and natural history of post-transfusion and enterically-transmitted non-A, non-B hepatitis. Semin Liver Dis 1986;6:56–66

15. Velázquez O, Stetler HC, Avila C, Ornelas G, Alvarez C, Hadler SC, et al. Epidemic transmission of enterically transmitted non-A, non-B hepatitis in Mexico, 1986-1987. JAMA 1990;263:3281–3285

16. Khuroo MS, Kamill S, Jameel S. Vertical transmission of hepatitis E virus. Lancet 1995;345:1025–1026

17. Linnen J, Wages J Jr, Zhang-Keck Z-Y, Fry KE, Krawzynski KZ, Alter H, et al. Molecular cloning and disease association of hepatitis G virus: a transfusion-transmissible agent. Science 1996;271:505–508

18. Feucht HH, Zollner B, Polywka S, Laufs R. Vertical transmission of hepatitis G. Lancet 1996;347:615–616

19. Kryger P. Significance of anti-HBc IgM in the differential diagnosis of viral hepatitis. J Virol Methods 1985;10:283–289

20. Vassiliadis S, Athanassakis I. Type II interferon may be a potential hazardous therapeutic agent during pregnancy. Br J Haematol 1992;82:782–783

21. Davis GL, Balart LA, Schiff ER, Lindsay K, Bodenheimer HC Jr, Perillo RP, et al. Treatment of chronic hepatitis C with recombinant interferon alfa. N Engl J Med 1989;321:1501–1506

22. Jagger J, Hunt EH, Brand-Elnaggar J, Pearson RD. Rates of needle-stick injury caused by various devices in a university hospital. N Engl J Med 1988;319:284–288

23. Occupational Safety and Health Administration. Blood-borne pathogens (29 CFR 1910.1030). Fed Regis. December 6, 1991; 56:64004–64182

24. Welch J, Webster M, Tilzey AJ, Noah ND, Banatvala JE. Hepatitis B infections after gynaecological surgery. Lancet 1989;1:205–206

Practice Bulletins

Practice Bulletins

Reading the Medical Literature

Applying Evidence to Practice

Developed under the direction
of the ACOG Committee on
Practice Patterns:

James R. Scott, MD, Chair

Daniel W. Cramer, MD, ScD

Herbert B. Peterson, MD

Benjamin P. Sachs, MD

Mary L. Segars Dolan, MD, MPH

Stanley Zinberg, MD
    Director of Practice Activities

Nancy E. O'Reilly, MHS
    Manager, Practice Activities

Peter J. Sebeny
    Research Associate

Reading the Medical Literature is designed as a resource for Fellows of the American College of Obstetricians and Gynecologists (ACOG) and others to offer a better understanding of evidence-based medicine, particularly as it relates to the development of ACOG's clinical practice guidelines. As evidence-based medicine continues to develop and to be integrated into clinical practice, an understanding of its basic elements is critical in translating the medical literature into appropriate clinical practice. The emphasis on evidence-based medicine has taken on new and greater importance as the environment of clinical practice grows more diverse, with increased access to more information by both physicians and patients and the changing allocation of resources. Practice guidelines are a formal synthesis of evidence, developed according to a rigorous research and review process. This document provides an overview of ACOG's guideline development process, including elements of study design that are linked to the strength of the evidence. Reading the Medical Literature *is not intended to serve as a comprehensive overview of the scientific methods of epidemiology and study design. Rather, it is provided to serve as a readily available introduction to and overview of the topic.*

In 1995, ACOG began developing scientifically based practice guidelines, formerly known as Practice Patterns and subsequently as Practice Bulletins. The guidelines are derived from the best available evidence of clinical efficacy and consideration of costs, with recommendations explicitly linked to the evidence. These evidence-based practice guidelines are intended to be a means of improving the quality of health care, decreasing its cost, and diminishing professional liability. They are proscriptive in nature and, therefore, directive in their approach.

This document describes how ACOG Practice Committees identify, evaluate, and synthesize evidence from the medical literature to produce practice guidelines. In particular, this document briefly describes various study designs evaluated in the production of evidence-based guidelines and the decision-making steps used to construct evidence-based recommendations on clinical issues. Also highlighted are potential major flaws in study design that affect the validity and applicability of study results, as well as the strength of the evidence. This document includes a glossary of commonly encountered epidemiologic and bio-statistic terms found in reports of scientific evidence, as well as suggestions for further reading.

Selection of Topics

Topics developed into evidence-based practice guidelines are selected based on clinical issues in obstetrics and gynecology with unexplained variations in practice or because there are differences between what is known scientifically and what is practiced. Once a topic has been identified, objectives of the guideline are developed and research questions are formulated to guide the literature search. The research questions highlight the most important aspects of a particular clinical issue, focusing on areas relevant to practice and useful in patient management.

Searching the Literature

In the ACOG Resource Center, medical librarians with extensive subject expertise perform a literature search based on the clinical questions and objectives. The search includes a review of the MEDLINE database, the Cochrane Library, ACOG's internal resources and documents, and other databases as appropriate. In addition, ACOG librarians review more than 200 journals. This process locates relevant articles from journals not indexed in MEDLINE and those not yet indexed.

The search is limited to documents published in English, and a specific strategy may be used to refine the search further. This filter strategy restricts the search by study design or publication type and is similar to the process used by the Cochrane Library. No further screening or elimination of records is done by the librarians. Updated searches are conducted as the topic is developed or further revised.

Literature Analysis

After results of the literature search are compiled, the study abstracts are reviewed to assess the relevance of each study or report. Those articles appropriate for further critical appraisal are obtained and subdivided according to the research question they address. The bibliographies of these articles are also reviewed to identify additional studies that may not have been identified in the initial literature search.

The data in the literature are evaluated to provide answers to the clinical questions. The articles obtained for review are organized by study design to ascertain the possible strengths and weaknesses inherent in each study, as well as the quality of evidence they may provide. Certain aspects of a clinical issue may not be addressed in research studies, and expert opinion may be used and identified as such.

The levels of evidence used are based on the method used by the U.S. Preventive Services Task Force. The U.S. Preventive Services Task Force was a 20-member panel of scientific and medical experts charged with developing recommendations on appropriate use of clinical interventions. Their recommendations were based on a systematic review of the evidence of clinical effectiveness.

Types of Study Designs

Intervention Studies

Level I Evidence

Commonly referred to as clinical trials, intervention studies are characterized by the investigators' roles in assigning subjects to exposed and nonexposed groups and following the subjects to assess outcome. Intervention studies may involve the use of a comparison group, which may include subjects under another treatment, drug, test, or placebo.

Randomized controlled trials are characterized by the prospective assignment of subjects, through a random method, into an experimental group and a control (placebo) group. The experimental group receives the drug or treatment to be evaluated, while the control group receives a placebo, no treatment, or the standard of care. Both groups are followed for the outcome(s) of interest. Randomization is the most reliable method to ensure that the participants in both groups are as similar as possible with respect to all known or unknown factors that might affect the outcome.

 Example

Postmenopausal women are identified from a population and randomly assigned either to a study group that will be prescribed hormone replacement therapy or to a control group that will be prescribed a placebo. Both groups of women are observed prospectively to determine who in each group subsequently develops endometrial cancer. The rate at which women prescribed hormone replacement therapy develop endometrial cancer is compared to that of women in the control group.

Major Study Flaws

- Randomization was not valid and resulted in a differential assignment of treatment that affected the outcomes.
- The sample size was too small to detect a clinically important difference.
- Poor compliance or loss to follow-up was significant enough to affect the outcomes.

Level II-1 Evidence

Controlled trials without randomization are intervention studies in which allocation to either the experimental or control group is not based on randomization, making assignment subject to biases that may influence study results. Conclusions drawn from these types of studies are considered to be less reliable than those from randomized controlled trials.

Example

Postmenopausal women are identified from a population and assigned in a nonrandomized manner either to a study group that will be prescribed hormone replacement therapy or to a control group that will be prescribed a placebo. Both groups of women are observed prospectively to determine who subsequently develops endometrial cancer. The rate at which women prescribed hormone replacement therapy develop endometrial cancer is compared to that of women in the control group.

Major Study Flaws

- Nonrandom group assignment resulted in unequal distribution of known and unknown factors that may influence the outcome.
- Other potential flaws are the same as those for randomized controlled trial (Level I).

Observational Studies

Level II-2 Evidence

There are two types of observational studies in this category: cohort and case-control. In these studies, the investigator has no role in assignment of study exposures but, rather, observes the natural course of events of exposure and outcome.

The starting point for a *cohort study* is exposure status. Subjects are classified on the basis of the presence or absence of exposure to a risk factor, a treatment, or an intervention and then followed for a specified period to determine the presence or absence of disease. Cohort studies can be of two different types determined by the timing

of initiation of the study: retrospective (nonconcurrent) or prospective (concurrent) studies. In a *prospective cohort study*, the groups of exposed and unexposed subjects have been identified and the investigator must conduct follow-up for an adequate period to ascertain the outcome of interest. In a *retrospective cohort study*, both the exposure and outcomes of interest already have occurred by the initiation of the study. The rate of disease in the exposed group is divided by the rate of disease in the unexposed group, yielding a rate ratio or relative risk.

Example

A group of postmenopausal women who have been prescribed hormone replacement therapy is identified (study group), as is an otherwise similar group of postmenopausal women who have not been prescribed hormone replacement therapy (control group). The study and control groups are observed to determine who subsequently develops endometrial cancer. The rate at which women using hormone replacement therapy develop endometrial cancer is compared with that of women not using hormone replacement therapy who also develop endometrial cancer.

Major Study Flaws

- Criteria for determining exposure status were inadequately defined.
- The assessments of the outcome for the exposed and nonexposed groups differed in a biased manner.
- The nonexposed comparison group was inappropriate.

A *case-control study* is a retrospective study in which a group of subjects with a specified outcome (cases) and a group without that same outcome (controls) are identified. Thus, the starting point for a case-control study is disease status. Investigators then compare the extent to which each subject was previously exposed to the variable of interest such as a risk factor, a treatment, or an intervention. A disadvantage of this study type is that assessment of exposure may have been influenced by disease status, including the possibility that cases recalled their exposure differently than controls. The odds of exposure in the case group compared with the odds of exposure in the control group provide the measure of association between the disease and exposure (odds ratio).

Example

Researchers conduct a case-control study to assess the relationship between hormone replacement therapy and endometrial cancer. A group of women who have recently developed endometrial cancer (cases) and a group of women with similar characteristics who did not develop endometrial cancer (controls) are identified. The use of hormone replacement therapy for each woman in the case group and the control group is determined to assess exposure history. The odds that women who developed endometrial cancer had used hormone replacement therapy are compared with the odds that women who did not develop endometrial cancer had used hormone replacement therapy. These odds are calculated to determine any association of hormone replacement therapy to endometrial cancer.

 Major Study Flaws

- The case or control group preferentially included or excluded subjects with a particular exposure history.
- Cases or controls were selectively more likely to recall or admit to a particular exposure.
- The possibility of known or unknown factors that may have been related to both exposure status and outcome were not adequately considered and assessed.

Level II-3 Evidence

Cross-sectional studies are observational studies that assess the status of individuals with respect to the presence or absence of both exposure and outcome at a particular time. In this type of study, one is unlikely to be able to discern the temporal relationship between an exposure and outcome. Results from cross-sectional studies can yield correlations and disease prevalence. Prevalence is defined as the proportion of individuals with a disease at a specific time; in contrast, incidence is the number of new cases occurring over a specified period.

Uncontrolled investigational studies report the results of treatment or interventions in a particular group, but lack a control group for comparison. They may demonstrate impressive results, but in the absence of a control group the results may be attributable to factors other than the intervention or treatment.

Of all observational studies, cross-sectional and uncontrolled investigational studies provide the least evidence of causation.

 Example

Postmenopausal women are identified from a population and surveyed at a particular time about their current intake of calcium. Bone densitometry is evaluated in these women at the same time to identify signs of osteoporosis. In this cross-sectional study, a measure of calcium intake in women with and without signs of osteoporosis is compared.

 Major Study Flaws

- It is usually not possible to determine the temporal relationship between disease and exposure.
- Other factors that may contribute to the disease, particularly past exposure to factors other than the factor under study, are not taken into consideration.

Level III Evidence

These studies provide limited information about the relationship between exposure and the outcome of interest. This category includes *descriptive studies*, such as case reports and case series, and *expert opinion*, which is often based on clinical experience.

A *case study* describes clinical characteristics or other interesting features of a single patient or a series of patients. The latter is referred to as a *case series*.

Expert opinion often is used to make recommendations. This type of evidence includes findings from expert panels and committees and the opinions of respected experts in a particular field.

Other Study Designs

A *meta-analysis* is a systematic structured process, not merely a literature review. It combines results from more than one investigation to obtain a weighted average of the effect of a variable or intervention on a defined outcome. This approach can increase precision of the exposure to the outcome measured, although it is important to add that the validity of the conclusions of the meta-analysis depends largely on the quality of its component studies. Results are usually presented in a graph that illustrates the measure of association by each study type and the overall summary association (Fig. 1).

A *decision analysis* is a type of study that uses mathematical models of the sequences of multiple strategies to determine which are optimal. The basic framework is the decision tree in which branches of the tree represent key probabilities or decisions. Decision analysis is driven by key assumptions. Ideally the assumptions are based on data that may include findings from meta-analyses. Often a decision analysis is undertaken when there are inadequate data to perform a meta-analysis (Fig. 2).

Cost-benefit analysis and *cost-effectiveness analysis* are related analytic methods that compare health care practices or techniques in terms of their relative economic efficiencies

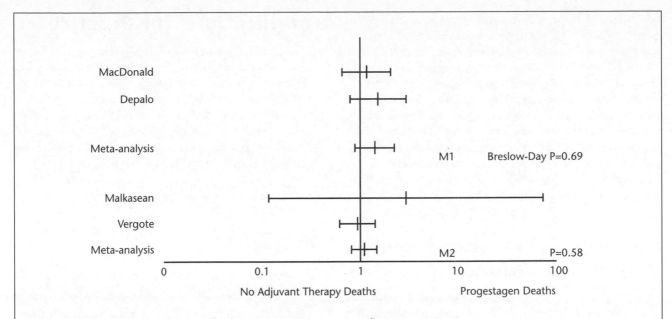

Fig. 1. Effects on endometrial cancer deaths: progestagen versus no adjuvant treatment.

(Reprinted from the European Journal of Obstetrics, Gynecology, and Reproductive Biology, Vol. 65. Martin-Hirsch PL, Lilford RJ, Jarvis GJ. Adjuvant progestagen therapy for the treatment of endometrial cancer: review and meta-analyses of published randomized controlled trials, p. 205, © 1996, with permission from Elsevier Science Ireland Ltd, Bay 15K, Shannon Industrial Estate, Co. Clare, Ireland.)

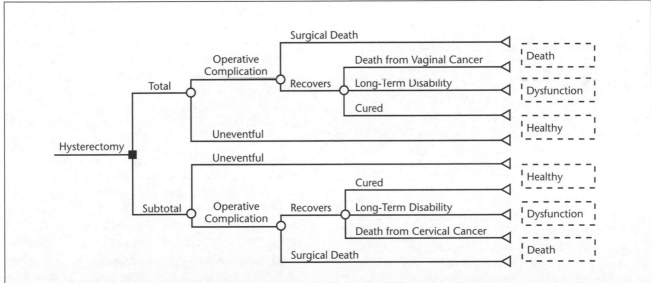

Fig. 2. Decision model. Square at far left, choice between two treatment options: total or subtotal hysterectomy. Round nodes, chance outcomes; end branches, final outcome states.

(Scott JR, Sharp HT, Dodson MK, Norton PA, Warner HR. Subtotal hysterectomy in modern gynecology: a decision analysis. Am J Obstet Gynecol 1997;176:1187. Reprinted with permission.)

in providing health benefits. In a *cost-effectiveness analysis*, the net monetary costs of a health care intervention are compared with some measure of clinical outcome or effectiveness. In a *cost-benefit analysis*, the net monetary costs of a health care intervention typically are compared with the net monetary costs of the clinical outcome or effectiveness. Therefore, a cost-benefit analysis compares costs associated with an intervention with monetary benefits from the use of that intervention. The advantage of a cost-benefit analysis is the ability to use dollars for comparison across interventions. The disadvantage is the difficulty in assigning a monetary value to health status or quality of life.

Developing Evidence-Based Recommendations

Having stated the clinical question and assembled and graded the literature using the levels just outlined, recommendations are formulated according to the quality and quantity of evidence. Based on the highest available level of evidence, recommendations are provided and graded according to the following categories:

A   There is good evidence to support the recommendation.

B   There is fair evidence to support the recommendation.

C   There is insufficient evidence to support the recommendation; however, the recommendation may be made on other grounds.

D   There is fair evidence against the recommendation.

E   There is good evidence against the recommendation.

This method explicitly links recommendations to the evidence. Determination of the quality of the evidence and the strength of recommendations are based on good, fair, or insufficient evidence. These descriptors address the levels of evidence and also provide a qualitative review of the evidence in terms of its methodologic strengths and weaknesses. A prerequisite for inclusion of each study in the analysis is that it provides overall evidence of "good quality."

It is important to note that an exact correlation does not exist between the strength of the recommendation and the level of evidence (ie, an "A" grade does not necessarily require Level I evidence, nor does Level I evidence necessarily lead to an "A" grade). For example, for some clinical issues a randomized trial is not possible for medical or ethical reasons, and recommendations must be based on evidence from other types of studies (Level II-2, II-3). In other cases, high-quality studies have produced conflicting results, or evidence of significant benefit is offset by evidence of important harm from the intervention. Although these studies may be randomized controlled trials (Level I), insufficient or conflicting evidence would result in a "C" recommendation.

Implications for Practice

Medicine will continue to face the rapid introduction of new technologies, rationing of health resources, and increasing attention to the quality and outcomes of medical care. Physicians will have to acquire the skills necessary to review the medical literature critically to identify the best evidence in managing patients. This process for developing practice guidelines identifies available evidence and constructs recommendations based on the best evidence so that obstetrician–gynecologists can continue to provide the highest quality of care.

 Glossary*

Accuracy: The degree to which a measurement or an estimate based on measurements represents the true value of the attribute that is being measured.

Bias: Deviation of results or inferences from the truth, or processes leading to such deviation; it is any trend in the collection, analysis, interpretation, publication, or review of data that can lead to conclusions that are systematically different from the truth. Three frequently occurring types of bias include selection bias, information bias, and confounding. *Selection bias* is error due to systematic differences in characteristics between those who are selected for study and those who are not. *Information bias*, also called observational bias, is a flaw in measuring exposure or outcome data that results in different quality (accuracy) of information between comparative groups. Recall bias is an example of information bias. The third example of bias, *confounding*, describes a situation in which the effects of two processes are not separated; it is the distortion of the apparent effect of an exposure on risk brought about by the association with other factors that can influence the outcome.

Confidence interval: An indication of the variability of a point estimate, such as an odds ratio or relative risk. In general, the wider the confidence interval, the less precise the point estimate. The 95% confidence interval is often used. As an example, if the 95% confidence interval does not overlap 1.0, then one would reject the null hypothesis.

Confounding variable (syn: confounder): A variable that can cause or prevent the outcome of interest, is not an intermediate variable, and is associated with the factor under investigation. Unless it is possible to adjust for confounding variables, their effects cannot be distinguished from those factor(s) being studied. Bias can occur when adjustment is made for any factor that is caused in part by the exposure and is also correlated with the outcome.

*Adapted from *A Dictionary of Epidemiology*, third edition. Last JM, ed. Used by permission of Oxford University Press.

Incidence: The number of instances of illness commencing, or persons falling ill, during a given period in a specified population. More generally, the number of new events (eg, new cases of a disease in a defined population) within a specified period.

Null hypothesis (test hypothesis): The statistical hypothesis that one variable has no association with another variable or set of variables, or that two or more population distributions do not differ from one another. In simplest terms, the null hypothesis states that the results observed in a study, experiment, or test are no different from what might have occurred as a result of the operation of chance alone.

Odds ratio (syn: cross product ratio, relative odds): The ratio of two odds. The exposure odds ratio for a set of case control data is the ratio of the odds in favor of exposure among the cases (a/b) to the odds in favor of exposure among noncases (c/d). A 2×2 table (Table 1) can be used to illustrate this calculation of odds ratios.

Table 1. Odds Ratio Calculations*

	Exposed	Unexposed
Disease	a	b
No disease	c	d

*The odds ratio is *ad/bc*.

P-value: The probability that a test statistic would be as extreme or more extreme than observed if the null hypothesis were true. The letter *P*, followed by the abbreviation n.s. (not significant) or by the symbol < (less than) and a decimal notation such as 0.01 or 0.05, is a statement of the probability that the difference observed could have occurred by chance if the groups were really alike (ie, under the null hypothesis). Investigators may arbitrarily set their own significance levels, but in most biomedical and epidemiologic work, a study result whose probability value is less than 5% ($P < 0.05$) or 1% ($P < 0.01$) is considered sufficiently unlikely to have occurred by chance and would justify the designation "statistically significant." By convention, most investigators choose $P < 0.05$ as statistically significant.

Power (statistical power): The ability of a study to demonstrate an association if one exists. The power of the study is determined by several factors, including the frequency of the condition under study, the magnitude of the effect, the study design, and sample size.

Prevalence: The number of events (eg, instances of a given disease or other condition) in a given population at a des-

ignated time; sometimes used to mean prevalence rate. When used without qualification, the term usually refers to the situation at a specified time (point prevalence).

Relative risk: The ratio of risk of disease or death among the exposed to that of the risk among the unexposed; this usage is synonymous with risk ratio. If the relative risk is above 1.0, then there is a positive association between the exposure and the disease; if it is less than 1.0, then there is a negative association.

Sensitivity and specificity: Sensitivity is the proportion of truly diseased persons in the screened population who are identified as diseased by the screening test. Specificity is the proportion of truly nondiseased persons who are so identified by the screening test. Table 2 illustrates these quantities.

In screening and diagnostic tests, the probability that a person with a positive test is a true positive (ie, does have the condition) is referred to as the *predictive value* of a positive test. The *predictive value* of a negative test is the probability that a person with a negative test does not have the condition. The predictive value of a screening test is determined by the sensitivity and specificity of the test and by the prevalence of the condition for which the test is being used.

$$\text{Positive predictive value} = a/a+b$$
$$\text{Negative predictive value} = d/c+d$$

Table 2. Sensitivity and Specificity Calculations

Screening Test Results	True Status		
	Diseased	Not Diseased	Total
Positive	a	b	a + b
Negative	c	d	c + d
Total	a + c	b + d	a + b + c + d

a = Diseased individuals detected by the test (true positives)

b = Nondiseased individuals positive by the test (false positives)

c = Diseased individuals not detected by the test (false negatives)

d = Nondiseased individuals negative by the test (true negatives)

Sensitivity = *a/a+c*; specificity = *d/b+d*.

Type I error: The error of rejecting a true null hypothesis (ie, declaring that a difference exists when it does not).

Type II error: The error of failing to reject a false null hypothesis (ie, declaring that a difference does not exist when in fact it does).

▶ Suggested Reading

Asilomar Working Group on Recommendations for Reporting of Clinical Trials in the Biomedical Literature. Checklist of information for inclusion in reports of clinical trials. Ann Intern Med 1996;124:741–743

Chalmers TC, Smith H Jr, Blackburn B, Silverman B, Schroeder B, Reitman D, et al. A method for assessing the quality of a randomized control trial. Control Clin Trials 1981; 2:31–49

DuRant RH. Checklist for the evaluation of research articles. J Adolesc Health 1994;15:4–8

Grisso JA. Making comparisons. Lancet 1993;342:157–160

Guyatt GH, Sackett DL, Cook DJ. Users' guides to the medical literature. II. How to use an article about therapy or prevention. A. Are the results of the study valid? Evidence-Based Medicine Working Group. JAMA 1993;270:2598–2601

Guyatt GH, Sackett DL, Cook DJ. Users' guides to the medical literature. II. How to use an article about therapy or prevention. B. What were the results and will they help me in caring for my patients? Evidence-Based Medicine Working Group. JAMA 1994;271:59–63

Guyatt GH, Sackett DL, Sinclair JC, Hayward R, Cook DJ, Cook RJ. Users' guides to the medical literature. IX. A method for grading health care recommendations. Evidence-Based Medicine Working Group. JAMA 1995;274:1800–1804

Hadorn DC, Baker D, Hodges JS, Hicks N. Rating the quality of evidence for clinical practice guidelines. J Clin Epidemiol 1996;49:749–754

Hayward RS, Wilson MC, Tunis SR, Bass EB, Guyatt G. Users' guides to the medical literature. VIII. How to use clinical practice guidelines. A. Are the recommendations valid? The Evidence-Based Medicine Working Group. JAMA 1995; 274:570–574

Jaeschke R, Guyatt GH, Sackett DL. Users' guides to the medical literature. III. How to use an article about a diagnostic test. B. What are the results and will they help me in caring for my patients? The Evidence-Based Medicine Working Group. JAMA 1994;271:703–707

Laupacis A, Wells G, Richardson WS, Tugwell P. Users' guides to the medical literature. V. How to use an article about prognosis. Evidence-Based Medicine Working Group. JAMA 1994;272:234–237

Naylor CD, Guyatt GH. Users' guides to the medical literature. X. How to use an article reporting variations in the outcomes of health services. The Evidence-Based Medicine Working Group. JAMA 1996;275:554–558

Naylor CD, Guyatt GH. Users' guides to the medical literature. XI. How to use an article about a clinical utilization review. Evidence-Based Medicine Working Group. JAMA 1996;275: 1435–1439

Oxman AD. Checklists for review articles. BMJ 1994;309: 648–651

Oxman AD, Cook DJ, Guyatt GH. Users' guides to the medical literature. VI. How to use an overview. Evidence-Based Medicine Working Group. JAMA 1994;272:1367–1371

Oxman AD, Sackett DL, Guyatt GH. Users' guides to the medical literature. I. How to get started. The Evidence-Based Medicine Working Group. JAMA 1993;270:2093–2095

Peipert JF, Gifford DS, Boardman LA. Research design and methods of quantitative synthesis of medical evidence. Obstet Gynecol 1997;90:473–478

Richardson WS, Detsky AS. Users' guides to the medical literature. VII. How to use a clinical decision analysis. A. Are the results of the study valid? Evidence-Based Medicine Working Group. JAMA 1995;273:1292–1295

Wilson MC, Hayward RS, Tunis SR, Bass EB, Guyatt G. Users' guides to the medical literature. VIII. How to use clinical practice guidelines. B. What are the recommendations and will they help you in caring for your patients? The Evidence-Based Medicine Working Group. JAMA 1995;274:1630–1632

ACOG PRACTICE BULLETIN

CLINICAL MANAGEMENT GUIDELINES FOR
OBSTETRICIAN–GYNECOLOGISTS

NUMBER 9, OCTOBER 1999

(Replaces Technical Bulletin Number 188, January 1994)

This Practice Bulletin was developed by the ACOG Committee on Practice Bulletins—Obstetrics with the assistance of Dwight J. Rouse, MD. The information is designed to aid practitioners in making decisions about appropriate obstetric and gynecologic care. These guidelines should not be construed as dictating an exclusive course of treatment or procedure. Variations in practice may be warranted based on the needs of the individual patient, resources, and limitations unique to the institution or type of practice.

Antepartum Fetal Surveillance

The goal of antepartum fetal surveillance is to prevent fetal death. Antepartum fetal surveillance techniques based on assessment of fetal heart rate patterns have been in clinical use for almost three decades. More recently, real-time ultrasonography and Doppler velocimetry have been used to evaluate fetal well-being. Antepartum fetal surveillance techniques are now routinely used to assess the risk of fetal death in pregnancies complicated by preexisting maternal conditions (eg, type 1 diabetes mellitus) as well as those in which complications have developed (eg, intrauterine growth restriction). This document will review the current indications for and techniques of antepartum fetal surveillance and outline management guidelines for antepartum fetal surveillance, consistent with the best contemporary scientific evidence.

Background

Physiology of Fetal Heart Response and Fetal Behavioral State Alteration

In both animals and humans, fetal heart rate pattern, level of activity, and degree of muscular tone are sensitive to hypoxemia and acidemia (1–4). Redistribution of fetal blood flow in response to hypoxemia may result in diminished renal perfusion and oligohydramnios (5). Surveillance techniques such as cardiotocography, real-time ultrasonography, and maternal perception of fetal movement can identify the fetus that is either suboptimally oxygenated or, with increasing degrees of placental dysfunction, acidemic. Identification of suspected fetal compromise provides the opportunity to intervene before progressive metabolic acidosis can lead to fetal death. However, acute, catastrophic changes in fetal status, such as those that can occur with abruptio placentae or an umbilical cord accident, are generally not predicted by tests of fetal well-being. Therefore, fetal deaths from such events are not as amenable to prevention.

In humans, the range of normal umbilical blood gas parameters has been established by cordocentesis performed in pregnancies in which the fetus ultimately proved to be healthy, and ranges vary by gestational age (6). Although the degree of hypoxemia and acidemia at which various indices of fetal well-being become abnormal is not known with precision, it can be estimated, based on data from published studies. In one investigation, the fetal biophysical profile (BPP) was performed immediately before cordocentesis. Fetuses with a nonreactive nonstress test (NST) were found to have a mean (± standard deviation) umbilical vein pH of 7.28 ± 0.11. Cessation of fetal movement appears to occur at lower pH levels; fetuses with abnormal movement were found to have an umbilical vein pH of 7.16 ± 0.08 (7). Thus, a reasonable correlation between certain measurable aspects of fetal heart rate and behavior and evidence of fetal metabolic compromise can be inferred.

However, when abnormal antepartum fetal surveillance results are compared with evidence of hypoxia or acidemia, the degree of acid–base disturbance may range from mild to severe. Furthermore, factors other than acid–base and oxygenation status (eg, prematurity, fetal sleep–wake cycle, maternal medication exposure, and fetal central nervous system abnormalities) can adversely affect biophysical parameters. Finally, neither the degree nor the duration of intrauterine hypoxemia and acidemia necessary to adversely affect short- and long-term neonatal outcome has been established with any precision.

Antepartum Fetal Surveillance Techniques

Several antepartum fetal surveillance techniques (tests) are in use. These include fetal movement assessment, NST, contraction stress test (CST), BPP, modified BPP, and umbilical artery Doppler velocimetry.

Fetal Movement Assessment

A diminution in the maternal perception of fetal movement often but not invariably precedes fetal death, in some cases by several days (8). This observation provides the rationale for fetal movement assessment by the mother ("kick counts") as a means of antepartum fetal surveillance.

Although several counting protocols have been employed, neither the optimal number of movements nor the ideal duration for counting movements has been defined. Thus, numerous protocols have been reported and appear to be acceptable. In one approach, the woman lies on her side and counts distinct fetal movements (9). Perception of 10 distinct movements in a peri-

od of up to 2 hours is considered reassuring. Once 10 movements have been perceived, the count may be discontinued. In another approach, women are instructed to count fetal movements for 1 hour three times per week (10). The count is considered reassuring if it equals or exceeds the woman's previously established baseline count. In the absence of a reassuring count, further fetal assessment is recommended.

Contraction Stress Test

The CST is based on the response of the fetal heart rate to uterine contractions. It relies on the premise that fetal oxygenation will be transiently worsened by uterine contractions. In the suboptimally oxygenated fetus, the resultant intermittent worsening in oxygenation will, in turn, lead to the fetal heart rate pattern of late decelerations. Uterine contractions also may provoke or accentuate a pattern of variable decelerations caused by fetal umbilical cord compression, which in some cases is associated with oligohydramnios.

With the patient in the lateral recumbent position, the fetal heart rate and uterine contractions are simultaneously recorded with an external fetal monitor. If at least three spontaneous contractions of 40 seconds' duration each or longer are present in a 10-minute period, no uterine stimulation is necessary. If fewer than three contractions of at least 40 seconds' duration occur in 10 minutes, contractions are induced with either nipple stimulation or intravenous administration of dilute oxytocin.

Nipple stimulation usually is successful in inducing an adequate contraction pattern and allows completion of testing in approximately half the time required when intravenous oxytocin is given (11). In one nipple stimulation technique, the woman is instructed to rub one nipple through her clothing for 2 minutes or until a contraction begins (11). If by that time the contraction frequency has not become adequate (as defined previously), stimulation is stopped and restarted again after 5 minutes. If nipple stimulation is unsuccessful, or if the use of oxytocin is preferred, an intravenous infusion of dilute oxytocin may be initiated at a rate of 0.5 mU/min and doubled every 20 minutes until an adequate contraction pattern is achieved (12).

The CST is interpreted according to the presence or absence of late fetal heart rate decelerations (13), which are defined as decelerations that reach their nadir after the peak of the contraction and that usually persist beyond the end of the contraction. The results of the CST are categorized as follows:

- Negative: no late or significant variable decelerations

- Positive: late decelerations following 50% or more of contractions (even if the contraction frequency is fewer than three in 10 minutes)

- Equivocal–suspicious: intermittent late decelerations or significant variable decelerations

- Equivocal–hyperstimulatory: fetal heart rate decelerations that occur in the presence of contractions more frequent than every 2 minutes or lasting longer than 90 seconds

- Unsatisfactory: fewer than three contractions in 10 minutes or an uninterpretable tracing

Relative contraindications to the CST generally include conditions associated with an increased risk of preterm labor and delivery, uterine rupture, or uterine bleeding. These include the following (12):

- Preterm labor or certain patients at high risk of preterm labor

- Preterm membrane rupture

- History of extensive uterine surgery or classical cesarean delivery

- Known placenta previa

Nonstress Test

The NST is based on the premise that the heart rate of the fetus that is not acidotic or neurologically depressed will temporarily accelerate with fetal movement. Heart rate reactivity is thought to be a good indicator of normal fetal autonomic function. Loss of reactivity is associated most commonly with a fetal sleep cycle but may result from any cause of central nervous system depression, including fetal acidosis.

With the patient in the lateral tilt position, the fetal heart rate is monitored with an external transducer. Ideally, the patient should not have smoked recently, because this may adversely affect test results (14). The tracing is observed for fetal heart rate accelerations that peak (but do not necessarily remain) at least 15 beats per minute above the baseline and last 15 seconds from baseline to baseline. It may be necessary to continue the tracing for 40 minutes or longer to take into account the variations of the fetal sleep–wake cycle. Acoustic stimulation of the nonacidotic fetus may elicit fetal heart rate accelerations that appear to be valid in the prediction of fetal well-being. Such stimulation offers the advantage of safely reducing overall testing time without compromising detection of the acidotic fetus (15–17). To perform acoustic stimulation, an artificial larynx (ideally one of the commercially available models especially designed for this purpose) is positioned on the maternal abdomen and a stimulus of 1–2 seconds is applied. This may be

repeated up to three times for progressively longer durations of up to 3 seconds to elicit fetal heart rate accelerations.

Nonstress test results are categorized as reactive or nonreactive. Various definitions of reactivity have been used. Using the most common definition, the NST is considered reactive (normal) if there are two or more fetal heart rate accelerations (as defined previously) within a 20-minute period, with or without fetal movement discernible by the woman (18). A nonreactive NST is one that lacks sufficient fetal heart rate accelerations over a 40-minute period. The NST of the noncompromised preterm fetus is frequently nonreactive: from 24 to 28 weeks of gestation, up to 50% of NSTs may not be reactive (19), and from 28 to 32 weeks of gestation, 15% of NSTs are not reactive (20, 21).

Variable decelerations may be observed in up to 50% of NSTs (22). If nonrepetitive and brief (<30 seconds), they indicate neither fetal compromise nor the need for obstetric intervention (22). Repetitive variable decelerations (at least 3 in 20 minutes), even if mild, have been associated with an increased risk of cesarean delivery for a nonreassuring intrapartum fetal heart rate pattern (23, 24). Fetal heart rate decelerations during an NST that persist for 1 minute or longer are associated with a markedly increased risk of both cesarean delivery for a nonreassuring fetal heart rate pattern and fetal demise (25–27).

Biophysical Profile

The BPP consists of an NST combined with four observations made by real-time ultrasonography (28). Thus, the BPP comprises five components:

1. Nonstress test (which, if all four ultrasound components are normal, may be omitted without compromising the validity of the test results) (28)

2. Fetal breathing movements (one or more episodes of rhythmic fetal breathing movements of 30 seconds or more within 30 minutes)

3. Fetal movement (three or more discrete body or limb movements within 30 minutes)

4. Fetal tone (one or more episodes of extension of a fetal extremity with return to flexion, or opening or closing of a hand)

5. Determination of the amniotic fluid volume (a single vertical pocket of amniotic fluid exceeding 2 cm is considered evidence of adequate amniotic fluid) (29, 30)

Each of the five components is assigned a score of either 2 (normal or present as defined previously) or 0 (abnormal, absent, or insufficient). A composite score of 8 or 10 is normal, a score of 6 is considered equivocal, and a score of 4 or less is abnormal. Regardless of the composite score, in the presence of oligohydramnios (largest vertical pocket of amniotic fluid volume ≤ 2 cm), further evaluation is warranted (30).

Modified Biophysical Profile

In the late second- or third-trimester fetus, amniotic fluid reflects fetal urine production. Placental dysfunction may result in diminished fetal renal perfusion, leading to oligohydramnios (5). Amniotic fluid volume assessment can therefore be used to evaluate long-term uteroplacental function. This observation fostered the development of what has come to be termed the "modified BPP" as a primary mode of antepartum fetal surveillance. The modified BPP combines the NST (with the option of acoustic stimulation), as a short-term indicator of fetal acid–base status, with the amniotic fluid index (AFI), which is the sum of measurements of the deepest cord-free amniotic fluid pocket in each of the abdominal quadrants, as an indicator of long-term placental function (15). An AFI greater than 5 cm generally is considered to represent an adequate volume of amniotic fluid (31). Thus, the modified BPP is considered normal if the NST is reactive and the AFI is more than 5, and abnormal if either the NST is nonreactive or the AFI is 5 or less.

Umbilical Artery Doppler Velocimetry

Doppler ultrasonography is a noninvasive technique used to assess the hemodynamic components of vascular impedance. Umbilical artery Doppler flow velocimetry has been adapted for use as a technique of fetal surveillance, based on the observation that flow velocity waveforms in the umbilical artery of normally growing fetuses differ from those of growth-restricted fetuses. Specifically, the umbilical flow velocity waveform of normally growing fetuses is characterized by high-velocity diastolic flow, whereas with intrauterine growth restriction, there is diminution of umbilical artery diastolic flow (32–34). In some cases of extreme intrauterine growth restriction, flow is absent or even reversed. The perinatal mortality rate in such pregnancies is quite high (35). Abnormal flow velocity waveforms have been correlated histopathologically with small-artery obliteration in placental tertiary villi (36) and functionally with fetal hypoxia and acidosis (37), as well as with perinatal morbidity and mortality (35). Commonly measured flow indices, based on the characteristics of peak systolic frequency shift (S), end-diastolic frequency shift (D), and mean peak frequency shift over the cardiac cycle (A), include the following:

- Systolic to diastolic ratio (S/D)
- Resistance index (S-D/S)
- Pulsatility index (S-D/A)

Randomized studies (38–44) of the utility of umbilical artery Doppler velocimetry generally have defined abnormal flow as either absent end diastolic flow, or a flow index greater than two standard deviations above the mean for gestational age. To maximize interpretability, multiple waveforms should be assessed, and wall-filter settings should be set low enough (typically <150 Hz) to avoid masking diastolic flow.

Clinical Considerations and Recommendations

▶ *Is there compelling evidence that any form of antepartum fetal surveillance decreases the risk of fetal demise or otherwise improves perinatal outcome?*

There is a dearth of evidence from randomized controlled trials that antepartum fetal surveillance decreases the risk of fetal death (45). Moreover, in one comprehensive review, antepartum fetal surveillance was categorized as a form of care "likely to be ineffective or harmful" (46). In spite of its unproven value, antepartum fetal surveillance is widely integrated into clinical practice in the developed world. Therefore, a definitive evaluation of antepartum fetal surveillance (which would require the random allocation of gravidas to prenatal care that included some form of antepartum fetal surveillance versus prenatal care that did not include any form of antepartum fetal surveillance) is unlikely to be conducted in a setting that can be generalized to current U.S. obstetric practice. In the absence of a definitive, relevant randomized clinical trial, evidence for the value of antepartum fetal surveillance will remain circumstantial and rest principally on the observation that antepartum fetal surveillance has been consistently associated with rates of fetal death that are substantially lower than the rates of fetal death in both untested (and presumably lower-risk) contemporaneous pregnancies from the same institutions (15, 16, 47) and pregnancies with similar complicating factors that were managed before the advent of currently employed techniques of antepartum fetal surveillance (historic controls). However, these perceived benefits of antepartum fetal surveillance may be influenced by the low incidence of adverse fetal outcome in the general population. The lower the incidence of adverse outcomes, the more likely favorable outcomes will be achieved regardless of test performance.

▶ *What are the indications for antepartum fetal surveillance?*

Because antepartum fetal surveillance results have not been definitively demonstrated to improve perinatal outcome, all indications for antepartum testing must be considered somewhat relative. In general, antepartum fetal surveillance has been employed in pregnancies in which the risk of antepartum fetal demise is increased. Accordingly, some of the conditions under which testing may be appropriate include the following:

- Maternal conditions
  - Antiphospholipid syndrome
  - Hyperthyroidism (poorly controlled)
  - Hemoglobinopathies (hemoglobin SS, SC, or S-thalassemia)
  - Cyanotic heart disease
  - Systemic lupus erythematosus
  - Chronic renal disease
  - Type 1 diabetes mellitus
  - Hypertensive disorders
- Pregnancy-related conditions
  - Pregnancy-induced hypertension
  - Decreased fetal movement
  - Oligohydramnios
  - Polyhydramnios
  - Intrauterine growth restriction
  - Postterm pregnancy
  - Isoimmunization (moderate to severe)
  - Previous fetal demise (unexplained or recurrent risk)
  - Multiple gestation (with significant growth discrepancy)

▶ *When during gestation should antepartum fetal surveillance be initiated?*

Choosing the appropriate point in gestation to begin antepartum testing depends on balancing several considerations, including the prognosis for neonatal survival, the severity of maternal disease, the risk of fetal death, and the potential for iatrogenic prematurity complications resulting from false-positive test results. The importance of the last consideration is illustrated by the experience of one large center, in which 60% of infants delivered because of an abnormal antepartum test result had no evidence of short-term or long-term fetal compromise (16). Both theoretic models (48) and large clinical studies (49, 50) confirm that initiating testing at 32–34 weeks of gestation is appropriate for most at-risk patients. However, in pregnancies with multiple or particularly worrisome high-risk conditions (eg, chronic hypertension

with suspected intrauterine growth restriction), testing might begin as early as 26–28 weeks of gestation.

▶ *What is the proper frequency of testing?*

How frequently to perform fetal testing depends on several factors, including clinical judgment. If the indication for testing is not persistent (eg, a single episode of decreased fetal movement followed by reassuring testing in an otherwise uncomplicated pregnancy), it need not be repeated. When the clinical condition that prompted testing persists, the test should be repeated periodically until delivery to monitor for continued fetal well-being. If the maternal medical condition is stable and CST results are negative, the CST is typically repeated in 1 week (12). Other tests of fetal well-being (NST, BPP, or modified BPP) are typically repeated at weekly intervals (16), but in the presence of certain high-risk conditions, such as postterm pregnancy, type 1 diabetes, intrauterine growth restriction, or pregnancy-induced hypertension, some investigators have performed twice-weekly NST, BPP, or modified BPP testing. Any significant deterioration in the maternal medical status requires fetal reevaluation, as does any acute diminution in fetal activity, regardless of the amount of time that has elapsed since the last test.

▶ *How reassuring is a normal test result?*

In most cases, a normal test result is highly reassuring, as reflected in the false-negative rate of antepartum fetal surveillance, defined as the incidence of stillbirth occurring within 1 week of a normal test result. The stillbirth rate, corrected for lethal congenital anomalies and unpredictable causes of demise, was 1.9 per 1,000 in the largest series of NSTs (5,861) versus 0.3 per 1,000 in 12,656 CSTs (13), 0.8 per 1,000 in 44,828 BPPs (51), and 0.8 per 1,000 in 54,617 modified BPPs (16). Based on these data, the negative predictive value of the NST is 99.8%, and greater than 99.9% for the CST, BPP, and modified BPP. Although similar data from a large series are not available for umbilical artery Doppler velocimetry, in one randomized clinical trial among women with pregnancies complicated by intrauterine growth restriction (38), no stillbirths occurred in 214 pregnancies in which umbilical artery Doppler velocimetry was the primary means of antepartum fetal surveillance (negative predictive value of 100%). The low false-negative rate of these tests depends on an appropriate response to any significant deterioration in the maternal clinical status, including retesting of the fetal condition. As mentioned previously, these tests generally do not predict stillbirths related to acute changes in maternal–fetal status, such as those that occur with abruptio placentae or an umbilical cord accident. Moreover, recent, normal antepartum fetal test results should not preclude the use of intrapartum fetal monitoring.

▶ How should one respond to an abnormal test result?

An abnormal fetal test result should always be considered in the context of the overall clinical picture, taking into account the substantial possibility that the test result is falsely positive. Certain acute maternal conditions (eg, diabetic ketoacidosis, pneumonia with hypoxemia) can result in abnormal test results, which generally will become normal as the maternal condition improves. In these circumstances, stabilizing the maternal condition and retesting the fetus may be appropriate.

In cases where an abnormal test result is not associated with any clinical evidence of worsening in the maternal status, a sequenced approach to the investigation of the fetal condition should be undertaken. Such an approach takes advantage of the high negative predictive value generally exhibited by all commonly used antepartum tests (see above), and minimizes the potential for unnecessary delivery based on a false-positive (ie, abnormal) test result. False-positive rates, in contrast to false-negative rates, have typically not been calculated using the outcome of stillbirth. This is because most antepartum tests were introduced into clinical practice before an unbiased evaluation of their sensitivity and specificity. In clinical practice, abnormal test results usually are followed by another test or delivery is effected, which obscures the relationship between a positive test result and the subsequent risk of stillbirth. Therefore, in the absence of unbiased evaluations, the positive predictive value of antepartum tests has been estimated using surrogate markers, such as the rate of positive follow-up test results when the primary test result is positive. For example, it has been observed that up to 90% of nonreactive NSTs are followed by a negative CST result (18). Based on this observation, the positive predictive value of an NST is only 10%. Another way that the false-positive rate of fetal testing has been estimated is to calculate the incidence of abnormal test results that prompt delivery but are not associated with evidence of fetal compromise, as manifested by a nonreassuring intrapartum fetal heart rate, meconium-stained amniotic fluid, 5-minute Apgar scores of less than 7, or birth weight greater than the 10th percentile for gestational age. By this latter definition, in one large series, a testing scheme in which abnormal modified BPPs were followed by full BPPs had a false-positive rate of 60% (positive predictive value = 40%) (18). In another study in which the physicians were blinded to test results, a CST was found to have a positive predictive value of less than 35% (52).

Therefore, the response to an abnormal test result should be tailored to the clinical situation. Maternal reports of decreased fetal movement should be evaluated by an NST, CST, BPP, or modified BPP; these results, if normal, usually are sufficient to exclude imminent fetal jeopardy. A nonreactive NST or an abnormal modified BPP generally should be followed by additional testing (either a CST or a full BPP). A positive CST result suggests that NST nonreactivity is a consequence of hypoxia-induced acidosis, whereas a negative result implies that the NST nonreactivity exists for another reason, such as a premature fetus, maternal exposure to certain drugs or medications, a fetal sleep cycle, or preexisting neurologic damage. In many circumstances, a positive CST result generally indicates that delivery is warranted. However, the combination of a nonreactive NST and a positive CST result is associated frequently with serious fetal malformation and justifies ultrasonographic investigation for anomalies whenever possible (53). Indeed, evaluation for grossly abnormal fetal anatomy should precede any intervention for suspected fetal compromise whenever possible.

A BPP score of 6 is considered equivocal; in the term fetus, this score generally should prompt delivery, whereas in the preterm fetus, it should result in a repeat BPP in 24 hours (30). In the interim, maternal corticosteroid administration should be considered for pregnancies of less than 34 weeks of gestation. Repeat equivocal scores should result either in delivery or continued intensive surveillance. A BPP score of 4 usually indicates that delivery is warranted, although in extremely premature pregnancies, management should be individualized. Biophysical profiles less than 4 should result in expeditious delivery. Regardless of the overall score, oligohydramnios always requires further evaluation.

In the absence of obstetric contraindications, delivery of the fetus with an abnormal test result often may be attempted by induction of labor, with continuous monitoring of both the fetal heart rate and contractions.

▶ Are there clinical circumstances in which one test is distinguished by its utility or lack thereof?

A large-scale, definitive randomized trial comparing the relative efficacy of one technique of antepartum fetal testing to another has not yet been performed. Accordingly, in most clinical situations, no single antepartum fetal test can be considered superior to any other.

As mentioned previously, in certain clinical situations, the CST is considered relatively contraindicated (increased risk of preterm labor and delivery, uterine rupture, and uterine bleeding), although even in these situations the value of the information provided by the test may outweigh its potential risks.

▶ *When should oligohydramnios prompt delivery?*

Amniotic fluid volume is estimated using ultrasonography. One widely used definition of oligohydramnios is no measurable vertical pocket of amniotic fluid greater than 2 cm (29), and another is an AFI of 5 cm or less (31). Nevertheless, from a clinical standpoint, an ideal cutoff level for intervention using the AFI has yet to be established. Determining when to intervene for oligohydramnios depends on several factors, including gestational age, the maternal and fetal clinical condition as determined by other indices of fetal well-being, and the actual measured AFI value. Because rupture of the fetal membranes can cause diminished amniotic fluid volume, an evaluation for membrane rupture may be appropriate.

In postterm pregnancy, oligohydramnios is common and is associated with an increased risk of meconium staining of the amniotic fluid and cesarean delivery for nonreassuring fetal heart rate (54, 55). Thus, oligohydramnios has been considered an indication for delivery of the postterm pregnancy (15), although the effectiveness of this approach in improving perinatal outcome has not been established by randomized investigation.

In a term pregnancy complicated by oligohydramnios, delivery often is the most appropriate course of action. However, management should be individualized, and in certain situations, delivery may be safely postponed (eg, an uncomplicated pregnancy with an AFI of 5 cm but otherwise reassuring fetal testing and an unfavorable cervix at 37 weeks of gestation).

In the preterm fetus, depending on the maternal and fetal condition, expectant management may be the most appropriate course of action (eg, with preterm premature rupture of membranes or in the presence of fetal anomalies). Once oligohydramnios is diagnosed, if delivery is not undertaken, follow-up amniotic fluid volume and fetal growth assessments are indicated. If the oligohydramnios is persistent, close monitoring of the maternal condition and ongoing antepartum fetal surveillance should be performed to guide further management. If the oligohydramnios results from fetal membrane rupture, follow-up amniotic fluid volume assessment often may be safely omitted.

▶ *What is the role of Doppler velocimetry?*

At least three randomized trials (38, 56, 57) have evaluated the utility of umbilical artery Doppler velocimetry as a technique of antepartum fetal surveillance in pregnancies complicated by suspected intrauterine growth restriction.

In the first and largest of these trials (38), 214 pregnancies were allocated to Doppler umbilical artery velocimetry as the primary technique of fetal surveillance, and 212 were allocated to cardiotocography (NST). Overall, women in the Doppler group were significantly less likely to undergo obstetric intervention, including antepartum hospital admission, labor induction, and emergency cesarean delivery for nonreassuring fetal status. On average, women in the Doppler group underwent antenatal testing less frequently (4 times) than women in the cardiotocography group (8 times). Other perinatal outcomes, such as gestational age at birth, birthweight, Apgar scores, and cesarean birth rates, did not differ between the groups.

Subsequent trials (56, 57) have supported the findings of less frequent antenatal monitoring (56) and shorter durations of maternal hospitalization (56, 57) in the Doppler group. However, rates of obstetric interventions, such as antepartum admission and labor induction, were not lower in the Doppler groups, and perinatal outcome was not improved. On balance, the available evidence suggests that primary antepartum surveillance of suspected intrauterine growth restriction with umbilical artery Doppler velocimetry can achieve at least equivalent (and possibly better) fetal and neonatal outcomes as primary antepartum surveillance based on results of the NST. Furthermore, frequency of antepartum testing and certain aspects of obstetric intervention are reduced with use of Doppler (58). If umbilical artery Doppler velocimetry is used, decisions regarding timing of delivery should be made using a combination of information from the Doppler ultrasonography and other tests of fetal well-being, such as amniotic fluid volume assessment, NST, CST, and BPP, along with careful monitoring of maternal status.

No benefit has been demonstrated for umbilical artery velocimetry for conditions other than suspected intrauterine growth restriction, such as postterm gestation, diabetes mellitus, systemic lupus erythematosus, or antiphospholipid syndrome. Doppler ultrasonography has not been shown to be of value as a screening test for detecting fetal compromise in the general obstetric population, and its use for this purpose cannot be recommended (59). In addition to the umbilical artery, it is possible to evaluate blood flow in major fetal vessels. Multiple investigators have observed a correlation between increased flow resistance (elevated S/D ratio) in the umbilical artery and decreased resistance to flow (reduced S/D ratio) in the middle cerebral artery. This phenomenon has been attributed to a "brain sparing" adaptive response to fetal hypoxemia, and it has been suggested that the ratio of middle cerebral artery S/D ratio to umbilical artery S/D ratio might serve as a useful predictor of fetal compromise (60). However, the only randomized clinical trial of middle cerebral artery Doppler velocimetry failed to demonstrate any clinical benefit to assessing this parameter (61). Moreover, women in this trial who were allocated to standard fetal evaluation plus assessment of the ratio of middle cerebral artery or umbilical artery Doppler flow, or both, were delivered on average 5.7 days earlier after the institution of fetal testing than women who were allocated to standard fetal evaluation without assessment of middle cerebral artery blood flow. This suggests that incorporation of middle cerebral artery Doppler flow assessment into clinical practice might increase unnecessary intervention. Therefore, at present, middle cerebral artery Doppler flow measurement should be considered investigational.

▶ *Should all women perform daily fetal movement assessment?*

Whether programs of fetal movement assessment actually can reduce the risk of stillbirth is not clear. Only two randomized trials have addressed this issue. The first was conducted in a mixed high-risk (39%) and low-risk (61%) population of 3,111 Danish women who, after 32 weeks of gestation, were randomly assigned to an experimental (counting) group or a control group (10). Women in the experimental group were asked to count fetal movements for 1 hour three times a week and to contact their hospital immediately if they detected fewer movements than their previously established baseline. The control group of women were given no special fetal movement assessment instructions but were asked about fetal movement at their prenatal visits. Of the 1,583 women in the counting group, three experienced stillbirths of normally formed infants weighing more than 1,500 g, versus 12 stillbirths among the 1,569 women in the control group (*P*<0.05). Of women allocated to the counting group, 80% complied well with the protocol for counting, and 4% were evaluated for decreased fetal movement. The rates of operative vaginal birth and cesarean delivery did not differ significantly between the groups.

The second randomized study to evaluate fetal movement allocated 68,000 women at 28–32 weeks of gestation to a counting policy (in which normal fetal movement was defined as the perception of 10 movements within 10 hours) or to routine care in which no special counting policies were employed (62). Women in the counting group with fewer than 10 movements in 10 hours for two successive days were instructed to alert their care provider, at whose discretion further evaluation was undertaken. Overall fetal death rates were low in this trial and did not differ significantly between the two groups (2.9/1,000 in the counting group versus 2.7/1,000 in the control group). More women in the counting group

(7% versus 5%) underwent fetal heart rate testing, and more (5% versus 4%) were admitted antenatally to the hospital. However, the rates of labor induction and elective cesarean delivery did not differ significantly between the two groups. It should be noted that in the counting group, only 46% of women with decreased fetal movement alerted their care providers. Compliance for both recording fetal movements and reporting when they were diminished was even lower for women who experienced a stillbirth.

Consistent evidence that a formal program of fetal movement assessment will result in a reduction in fetal deaths is lacking. Moreover, whether fetal movement assessment adds benefit to an established program of regular fetal surveillance has not been evaluated. One of the two randomized studies of fetal movement assessment suggests that its use may reduce stillbirths; the other does not. Formal movement assessment may increase, by a small degree, the number of antepartum visits and fetal evaluations. In the randomized trials, however, this increased surveillance did not result in a higher rate of intervention (10, 62).

Summary

The following recommendations are based on limited or inconsistent scientific evidence (Level B):

▶ Women with high-risk factors for stillbirth should undergo antepartum fetal surveillance using the NST, CST, BPP, or modified BPP.

▶ Initiating testing at 32–34 weeks of gestation is appropriate for most pregnancies at increased risk of stillbirth, although in pregnancies with multiple or particularly worrisome high-risk conditions, testing may be initiated as early as 26–28 weeks of gestation.

▶ When the clinical condition that has prompted testing persists, a reassuring test should be repeated periodically (either weekly or, depending on the test used and the presence of certain high-risk conditions, twice weekly) until delivery. Any significant deterioration in the maternal medical status or any acute diminution in fetal activity requires fetal reevaluation, regardless of the amount of time that has elapsed since the last test.

▶ An abnormal NST or modified BPP usually should be further evaluated by either a CST or a full BPP. Subsequent management should then be predicated on the results of the CST or BPP, the gestational age, the degree of oligohydramnios (if assessed), and the maternal condition.

▶ Oligohydramnios, defined as either no ultrasonographically measurable vertical pocket of amniotic fluid greater than 2 cm or an AFI of 5 cm or less, requires (depending on the degree of oligohydramnios, the gestational age, and the maternal clinical condition) either delivery or close maternal or fetal surveillance.

▶ In the absence of obstetric contraindications, delivery of the fetus with an abnormal test result often may be attempted by induction of labor with continuous monitoring of the fetal heart rate and contractions. If repetitive late decelerations are observed, cesarean delivery generally is indicated.

▶ Recent, normal antepartum fetal test results should not preclude the use of intrapartum fetal monitoring.

▶ Umbilical artery Doppler velocimetry has been found to be of benefit only in pregnancies complicated by intrauterine growth restriction. If used in this setting, decisions regarding timing of delivery should be made using a combination of information from the Doppler ultrasonography and other tests of fetal well-being, along with careful monitoring of maternal status.

▶ Middle cerebral artery Doppler velocimetry should be considered an investigational approach to antepartum fetal surveillance.

References

1. Boddy K, Dawes GS, Fisher R, Pinter S, Robinson JS. Foetal respiratory movements, electrocortical and cardiovascular responses to hypoxaemia and hypercapnia in sheep. J Physiol 1974;243:599–618 (Level III)

2. Manning FA, Platt LD. Maternal hypoxemia and fetal breathing movements. Obstet Gynecol 1979;53:758–760 (Level III)

3. Murata Y, Martin CB Jr, Ikenoue T, Hashimoto T, Taira S, Sagawa T, et al. Fetal heart rate accelerations and late decelerations during the course of intrauterine death in chronically catheterized rhesus monkeys. Am J Obstet Gynecol 1982;144:218–223 (Level III)

4. Natale R, Clewlow F, Dawes GS. Measurement of fetal forelimb movements in the lamb in utero. Am J Obstet Gynecol 1981;140:545–551 (Level III)

5. Seeds AE. Current concepts of amniotic fluid dynamics. Am J Obstet Gynecol 1980;138:575–586 (Level III)

6. Weiner CP, Sipes SL, Wenstrom K. The effect of fetal age upon normal fetal laboratory values and venous pressure. Obstet Gynecol 1992;79:713–718 (Level III)

7. Manning FA, Snijders R, Harman CR, Nicolaides K, Menticoglou S, Morrison I. Fetal biophysical profile score. VI. Correlation with antepartum umbilical venous fetal pH. Am J Obstet Gynecol 1993;169:755–763 (Level II-2)

8. Pearson JF, Weaver JB. Fetal activity and fetal wellbeing: an evaluation. BMJ 1976;1(6021):1305–1307 (Level III)

9. Moore TR, Piacquadio K. A prospective evaluation of fetal movement screening to reduce the incidence of antepartum fetal death. Am J Obstet Gynecol 1989;160: 1075–1080 (Level II-2)

10. Neldam S. Fetal movements as an indicator of fetal wellbeing. Dan Med Bull 1983;30:274–278 (Level II-1)

11. Huddleston JF, Sutliff G, Robinson D. Contraction stress test by intermittent nipple stimulation. Obstet Gynecol 1984;63:669–673 (Level II-3)

12. Freeman RK. The use of the oxytocin challenge test for antepartum clinical evaluation of uteroplacental respiratory function. Am J Obstet Gynecol 1975;121:481–489 (Level III)

13. Freeman RK, Anderson G, Dorchester W. A prospective multi-institutional study of antepartum fetal heart rate monitoring. I. Risk of perinatal mortality and morbidity according to antepartum fetal heart rate test results. Am J Obstet Gynecol 1982;143:771–777 (Level II-3)

14. Graca LM, Cardoso CG, Clode N, Calhaz-Jorge C. Acute effects of maternal cigarette smoking on fetal heart rate and fetal body movements felt by the mother. J Perinat Med 1991;19:385–390 (Level III)

15. Clark SL, Sabey P, Jolley K. Nonstress testing with acoustic stimulation and amniotic fluid volume assessment: 5973 tests without unexpected fetal death. Am J Obstet Gynecol 1989;160:694–697 (Level II-3)

16. Miller DA, Rabello YA, Paul RH. The modified biophysical profile: antepartum testing in the 1990s. Am J Obstet Gynecol 1996;174:812–817 (Level II-3)

17. Smith CV, Phelan JP, Platt LD, Broussard P, Paul RH. Fetal acoustic stimulation testing. II. A randomized clinical comparison with the nonstress test. Am J Obstet Gynecol 1986;155:131–134 (Level I)

18. Evertson LR, Gauthier RJ, Schifrin BS, Paul RH. Antepartum fetal heart rate testing. I. Evolution of the nonstress test. Am J Obstet Gynecol 1979;133:29–33 (Level II-3)

19. Bishop EH. Fetal acceleration test. Am J Obstet Gynecol 1981;141:905–909 (Level II-2)

20. Lavin JP Jr, Miodovnik M, Barden TP. Relationship of nonstress test reactivity and gestational age. Obstet Gynecol 1984;63:338–344 (Level II-3)

21. Druzin ML, Fox A, Kogut E, Carlson C. The relationship of the nonstress test to gestational age. Am J Obstet Gynecol 1985;153:386–389 (Level III)

22. Meis PJ, Ureda JR, Swain M, Kelly RT, Penry M, Sharp P. Variable decelerations during nonstress tests are not a sign of fetal compromise. Am J Obstet Gynecol 1986;154: 586–590 (Level II-3)

23. Anyaegbunam A, Brustman L, Divon M, Langer O. The significance of antepartum variable decelerations. Am J Obstet Gynecol 1986;155:707–710 (Level II-2)

24. O'Leary JA, Andrinopoulos GC, Giordano PC. Variable decelerations and the nonstress test: an indication of cord compromise. Am J Obstet Gynecol 1980;137:704–706 (Level III)

25. Bourgeois FJ, Thiagarajah S, Harbert GM Jr. The significance of fetal heart rate decelerations during nonstress testing. Am J Obstet Gynecol 1984;150:213–216 (Level III)

26. Druzin ML, Gratacos J, Keegan KA, Paul RH. Antepartum fetal heart rate testing. VII. The significance of fetal bradycardia. Am J Obstet Gynecol 1981;139:194–198 (Level III)

27. Pazos R, Vuolo K, Aladjem S, Lueck J, Anderson C. Association of spontaneous fetal heart rate decelerations during antepartum nonstress testing and intrauterine growth retardation. Am J Obstet Gynecol 1982;144:574–577 (Level II-2)

28. Manning FA, Morrison I, Lange IR, Harman CR, Chamberlain PF. Fetal biophysical profile scoring: selective use of the nonstress test. Am J Obstet Gynecol 1987;156:709–712 (Level II-3)

29. Chamberlain PF, Manning FA, Morrison I, Harman CR, Lange IR. Ultrasound evaluation of amniotic fluid volume. I. The relationship of marginal and decreased amniotic fluid volumes to perinatal outcome. Am J Obstet Gynecol 1984;150:245–249 (Level II-3)

30. Manning FA, Harman CR, Morrison I, Menticoglou SM, Lange IR, Johnson JM. Fetal assessment based on fetal biophysical profile scoring. IV. An analysis of perinatal morbidity and mortality. Am J Obstet Gynecol 1990;162:703–709 (Level II-3)

31. Rutherford SE, Phelan JP, Smith CV, Jacobs N. The four-quadrant assessment of amniotic fluid volume: an adjunct to antepartum fetal heart rate testing. Obstet Gynecol 1987;70:353–356 (Level III)

32. Erskine RL, Ritchie JW. Umbilical artery blood flow characteristics in normal and growth-retarded fetuses. Br J Obstet Gynaecol 1985;92:605–610 (Level II-2)

33. Gudmundsson S, Marsal K. Umbilical and uteroplacental blood flow velocity waveforms in pregnancies with fetal growth retardation. Eur J Obstet Gynecol Reprod Biol 1988;27:187–196 (Level III)

34. Reuwer PJ, Bruinse HW, Stoutenbeek P, Haspels AA. Doppler assessment of the fetoplacental circulation in normal and growth-retarded fetuses. Eur J Obstet Gynecol Reprod Biol 1984;18:199–205 (Level II-2)

35. Karsdorp VH, van Vugt JM, van Geijn HP, Kostense PJ, Arduini D, Montenegra N, et al. Clinical significance of absent or reversed end diastolic velocity waveforms in umbilical artery. Lancet 1994;344:1664–1668 (Level II-2)

36. Giles WB, Trudinger BJ, Baird PJ. Fetal umbilical artery flow velocity waveforms and placental resistance: pathological correlation. Br J Obstet Gynaecol 1985;92:31–38 (Level II-2)

37. Nicolaides KH, Bilardo CM, Soothill PW, Campbell S. Absence of end diastolic frequencies in umbilical artery: a sign of fetal hypoxia and acidosis. BMJ 1988;297:1026–1027 (Level III)

38. Almstrom H, Axelsson O, Cnattingius S, Ekman G, Maesel A, Ulmsten U, et al. Comparison of umbilical-artery velocimetry and cardiotocography for surveillance of small-for-gestational-age fetuses. Lancet 1992;340:936–940 (Level I)

39. Johnstone FD, Prescott R, Hoskins P, Greer IA, McGlew T, Compton M. The effect of introduction of umbilical Doppler recordings to obstetric practice. Br J Obstet Gynaecol 1993;100:733–741 (Level I)

40. Newnham JP, O'Dea MR, Reid KP, Diepeveen DA. Doppler flow velocity waveform analysis in high risk pregnancies: a randomized controlled trial. Br J Obstet Gynaecol 1991;98:956–963 (Level I)

41. Omtzigt AM, Reuwer PJ, Bruinse HW. A randomized controlled trial on the clinical value of umbilical Doppler velocimetry in antenatal care. Am J Obstet Gynecol 1994;170:625–634 (Level I)

42. Pattinson RC, Norman K, Odendaal HJ. The role of Doppler velocimetry in the management of high risk pregnancies. Br J Obstet Gynaecol 1994;101:114–120 (Level I)

43. Trudinger BJ, Cook CM, Giles WB, Connelly A, Thompson RS. Umbilical artery flow velocity waveforms in high-risk pregnancy. Randomised controlled trial. Lancet 1987;1(8526):188–190 (Level I)

44. Tyrrell SN, Lilford RJ, Macdonald HN, Nelson EJ, Porter J, Gupta JK. Randomized comparison of routine vs highly selective use of Doppler ultrasound and biophysical scoring to investigate high risk pregnancies. Br J Obstet Gynaecol 1990;97:909–916 (Level I)

45. Thacker SB, Berkelman RL. Assessing the diagnostic accuracy and efficacy of selected antepartum fetal surveillance techniques. Obstet Gynecol Surv 1986;41:121–141 (Level III)

46. Enkin M, Keirse MJNC, Renfrew M, Neilson J. A guide to effective care in pregnancy and childbirth. 2nd ed. Oxford: Oxford University Press, 1995:410 (Level III)

47. Nageotte MP, Towers CV, Asrat T, Freeman RK. Perinatal outcome with the modified biophysical profile. Am J Obstet Gynecol 1994;170:1672–1676 (Level I)

48. Rouse DJ, Owen J, Goldenberg RL, Cliver SP. Determinants of the optimal time in gestation to initiate antenatal fetal testing: a decision-analytic approach. Am J Obstet Gynecol 1995;173:1357–1363 (Decision Analysis)

49. Lagrew DC, Pircon RA, Towers CV, Dorchester W, Freeman RK. Antepartum fetal surveillance in patients with diabetes: when to start? Am J Obstet Gynecol 1993;168:1820–1826 (Level III)

50. Pircon RA, Lagrew DC, Towers CV, Dorchester WL, Gocke SE, Freeman RK. Antepartum testing in the hypertensive patient: when to begin. Am J Obstet Gynecol 1991;164:1563–1570 (Level III)

51. Manning FA, Morrison I, Harman CR, Lange IR, Menticoglou S. Fetal assessment based on fetal biophysical profile scoring: experience in 19,221 referred high-risk pregnancies. II. An analysis of false-negative fetal deaths. Am J Obstet Gynecol 1987;157:880–884 (Level II-3)

52. Staisch KJ, Westlake JR, Bashore RA. Blind oxytocin challenge test and perinatal outcome. Am J Obstet Gynecol 1980;138:399–403 (Level II-2)

53. Garite TJ, Linzey EM, Freeman RK, Dorchester W. Fetal heart rate patterns and fetal distress in fetuses with congenital anomalies. Obstet Gynecol 1979;53:716–720 (Level II-2)

54. Leveno KJ, Quirk JG Jr, Cunningham FG, Nelson SD, Santos-Ramos R, Toofanian A, et al. Prolonged pregnancy. I. Observations concerning the causes of fetal distress. Am J Obstet Gynecol 1984;150:465–473 (Level III)

55. Phelan JP, Platt LD, Yeh SY, Broussard P, Paul RH. The role of ultrasound assessment of amniotic fluid volume in the management of the postdate pregnancy. Am J Obstet Gynecol 1985;151:304–308 (Level II-2)

56. Haley J, Tuffnell DJ, Johnson N. Randomised controlled trial of cardiotocography versus umbilical artery Doppler in the management of small for gestational age fetuses. Br J Obstet Gynaecol 1997;104:431–435 (Level I)

57. Nienhuis SJ, Vles JS, Gerver WJ, Hoogland HJ. Doppler ultrasonography in suspected intrauterine growth retardation: a randomized clinical trial. Ultrasound Obstet Gynecol 1997;9:6–13 (Level I)

58. Neilson JP, Alfirevic Z. Doppler ultrasound for fetal assessment in high risk pregnancies (Cochrane Review). In: The Cochrane Library, Issue 3, 1999. Oxford: Update Software (Meta-analysis)

59. Mason GC, Lilford RJ, Porter J, Nelson E, Tyrell S. Randomised comparison of routine versus highly selective use of Doppler ultrasound in low risk pregnancies. Br J Obstet Gynaecol 1993;100:130–133 (Level I)

60. Mari G, Deter RL. Middle cerebral artery flow velocity waveforms in normal and small-for-gestational-age fetuses. Am J Obstet Gynecol 1992;166:1262–1270 (Level II-2)

61. Ott WJ, Mora G, Arias F, Sunderji S, Sheldon G. Comparison of the modified biophysical profile to a "new" biophysical profile incorporating the middle cerebral artery to umbilical artery velocity flow systolic/diastolic ratio. Am J Obstet Gynecol 1998;178:1346–1353 (Level I)

62. Grant A, Elbourne D, Valentin L, Alexander S. Routine formal fetal movement counting and risk of antepartum late death in normally formed singletons. Lancet 1989;2(8659):345–349 (Level I)

The MEDLINE database, the Cochrane Library, and ACOG's own internal resources and documents were used to conduct a literature search to locate relevant articles published between January 1985 and February 1999. The search was restricted to articles published in the English language. Priority was given to articles reporting results of original research, although review articles and commentaries also were consulted. Abstracts of research presented at symposia and scientific conferences were not considered adequate for inclusion in this document. Guidelines published by organizations or institutions such as the National Institutes of Health and the American College of Obstetricians and Gynecologists were reviewed, and additional studies were located by reviewing bibliographies of identified articles. When reliable research was not available, expert opinions from obstetrician–gynecologists were used.

Studies were reviewed and evaluated for quality according to the method outlined by the U.S. Preventive Services Task Force:

I Evidence obtained from at least one properly designed randomized controlled trial.
II-1 Evidence obtained from well-designed controlled trials without randomization.
II-2 Evidence obtained from well-designed cohort or case–control analytic studies, preferably from more than one center or research group.
II-3 Evidence obtained from multiple time series with or without the intervention. Dramatic results in uncontrolled experiments also could be regarded as this type of evidence.
III Opinions of respected authorities, based on clinical experience, descriptive studies, or reports of expert committees.

Based on the highest level of evidence found in the data, recommendations are provided and graded according to the following categories:

Level A—Recommendations are based on good and consistent scientific evidence.

Level B—Recommendations are based on limited or inconsistent scientific evidence.

Level C—Recommendations are based primarily on consensus and expert opinion.

ISSN 1099-3630

The American College of
Obstetricians and Gynecologists
409 12th Street, SW
PO Box 96920
Washington, DC 20090-6920

12345/32109

ACOG PRACTICE BULLETIN

CLINICAL MANAGEMENT GUIDELINES FOR
OBSTETRICIAN–GYNECOLOGISTS

NUMBER 23, JANUARY 2001

(Replaces Educational Bulletin Number 237, June 1997)

This Practice Bulletin was developed by the ACOG Committee on Practice Bulletins—Gynecology with the assistance of David Soper, MD. The information is designed to aid practitioners in making decisions about appropriate obstetric and gynecologic care. These guidelines should not be construed as dictating an exclusive course of treatment or procedure. Variations in practice may be warranted based on the needs of the individual patient, resources, and limitations unique to the institution or type of practice.

Antibiotic Prophylaxis for Gynecologic Procedures

Antibiotic use, especially prophylactic antibiotic use, has been associated with the selection of antibiotic-resistant bacteria. Indiscriminate use of antimicrobial prophylaxis promotes this dangerous side effect. There are acknowledged consequences of prophylactic antibiotics for institutions as well as for individual patients. It is important for clinicians to understand when antibiotic prophylaxis is indicated and when it is inappropriate. The purpose of this document is to review the evidence for appropriate antibiotic prophylaxis for gynecologic surgery and other procedures.

Background

Pathophysiology and Microbiology of Gynecologic Infections

As the number and virulence of contaminating bacteria increase in a surgical site, so does the risk for postoperative infection. Surgery and the use of foreign material, such as sutures, further potentiate the risk of infection. At the same time, systemic and local host immune mechanisms function to contain inoculated bacteria and prevent infection. Antibiotics in the tissues provide a pharmacologic means of defense that augments the natural host immunity. Bacterial resistance mechanisms may contribute to the pathogenesis of operative-site infection by enabling organisms to evade the prophylactically administered antibiotics (1).

Operative-site infections after a hysterectomy result from the ascending spread of microorganisms from the upper vagina and endocervix to the vaginal cuff and paravaginal tissues dissected during the procedure (2). Bacterial vaginosis, a complex alteration of vaginal flora resulting in an increased concentration of potentially pathogenic anaerobic bacteria, is associated with an increased risk of posthysterectomy cuff cellulitis (3). However, there is a lack of data showing that pretreatment for bacterial vaginosis before hysterectomy reduces the rate of postoperative cuff cellulitis. These microorganisms also can be spread to the abdominal incision at the time of surgery; in addition, the skin microorganisms *Staphylococcus epidermidis* and *Staphylococcus aureus* may lead to an abdominal-incision infection. Gynecologic surgical procedures, such as laparotomy or laparoscopy, do not breach surfaces colonized with bacteria from the vagina, and infections following these procedures more commonly result from contaminating skin bacteria only.

Procedures breaching the endocervix, such as hysterosalpingogram, sonohysterography, intrauterine device (IUD) insertion, endometrial biopsy, and dilation and curettage, may seed the endometrium and the fallopian tubes with microorganisms found in the upper vagina and endocervix. Prevention and treatment of these postoperative infections, either endometritis or pelvic inflammatory disease (PID), should take into consideration the polymicrobial nature of these infections.

The risk of developing bacterial endocarditis is related to a patient's risk of bacteremia and the significance of an underlying cardiac lesion. Most cases of infective endocarditis are caused by gram-positive cocci that originate from the mouth or the skin.

Theory of Antimicrobial Prophylaxis

State-of-the-art aseptic technique has been associated with a dramatic decrease in operative-site infections, but bacterial contamination of the operative site is inevitable. The in vivo interaction between the inoculated bacteria and prophylactically administered antibiotic is one of the most important determinants of the state of the surgical site. Systemic antibiotic prophylaxis is based on the belief that antibiotics in the host tissues can augment natural immune-defense mechanisms and help to kill bacteria that are inoculated into the wound. Only a narrow window of antimicrobial efficacy is available, requiring the administration of antibiotics either shortly before or at the time of bacterial inoculation (eg, when the incision is made, viscus entered, or pedicles clamped). A delay of only 3–4 hours can result in ineffective prophylaxis (4). The induction of anesthesia represents a convenient time for initiating antibiotic prophylaxis in major gynecologic procedures. Current data indicate that for lengthy procedures, additional, intraoperative doses of an antibiotic, given at intervals of one or two times the half-life of the drug, maintain adequate levels throughout the operation (5). A second dose of the prophylactic antibiotic also may

be appropriate in surgical cases with an increased blood loss (>1,500 mL). Neither subsequent doses nor treatment for several days before a procedure is indicated for prophylaxis. The use of prophylaxis implies that the patient is presumed to be free of infection at the time of the procedure. During a procedure when a patient is found to be at greater risk for disease, use of therapeutic antibiotics should be considered.

Pharmacology and Spectrum of Activity of Antibiotics Used in Prophylaxis

The cephalosporins have emerged as the drugs of choice for the vast majority of operative procedures because of their broad antimicrobial spectrum and low incidence of allergy and side effects. Cefazolin (1 g) is the most commonly used agent because of its reasonably long half-life (1.8 hours) and low cost. It is the frequent choice for clean procedures, and most clinical studies indicate that it is equivalent to cephalosporins which have improved in vitro activity against anaerobic bacteria in clean-contaminated procedures such as hysterectomy. Table 1 lists antibiotic regimens by procedure.

Table 1. Antimicrobial Prophylactic Regimens by Procedure

Procedure	Antibiotic	Dose
Vaginal/abdominal hysterectomy*	Cefazolin	1 or 2 g single dose IV
	Cefoxitin	2 g single dose IV
	Cefotetan	1 or 2 g single dose IV
	Metronidazole	500 mg single dose IV
Laparoscopy	None	
Laparotomy	None	
Hysteroscopy	None	
Hysterosalpingogram	Doxycycline†	100 mg twice daily for 5 days orally
IUD insertion	None	
Endometrial biopsy	None	
Induced abortion/D&C	Doxycycline	100 mg orally 1 hour before procedure and 200 mg orally after the procedure
	Metronidazole	500 mg twice daily orally for 5 days
Urodynamics	None	

Abbreviations: IV, intravenously; IUD, intrauterine device; D&C, dilation and curettage.

*A convenient time to administer antibiotic prophylaxis is just before induction of anesthesia.

†If hysterosalpingogram demonstrates dilated tubes. No prophylaxis is indicated for a normal study.

Adverse Reactions to Antibiotics

Adverse effects for the patient include allergic reactions ranging in severity from minor skin rashes to anaphylaxis. Pseudomembranous colitis is an uncommon complication of prophylactic antibiotics. Overall, attack rates for antibiotic-associated diarrhea in hospitals range from 3.2% to 29% (6, 7). Nearly 15% of hospitalized patients receiving β-lactam antibiotics develop diarrhea (7), and rates for those receiving clindamycin range from 10% to 25% (8). Predisposing host factors and circumstances affecting the frequency and severity of disease include advanced age, underlying illness, recent surgery, and recent administration of bowel motility-altering drugs (9).

Anaphylaxis, the most immediate and most life-threatening risk of prophylaxis, is rare. Anaphylactic reactions to penicillin reportedly occur in 0.2% of courses of treatment, with a fatality rate of 0.0001% (10). The induction of bacterial resistance may be a consequence of prophylactic antibiotic use. The most common example of this is the selection of *Enterococcus* sp. as a result of cephalosporin use. However, no clinically relevant ill effects have been reported as a result of this particular type of alteration in the flora of the lower genital tract (11).

Patients with a history of an adverse reaction or allergy to an antibiotic recommended for prophylaxis should not be administered that particular drug. However, given the wide range of antibiotics available for prophylaxis, it would be unlikely to have to avoid giving antibiotic prophylaxis because of the inability to find an appropriate agent.

Clinical Considerations and Recommendations

▶ *What constitutes appropriate antibiotic prophylaxis for the following situations?*

When choosing a prophylactic antimicrobial agent, the practitioner should consider the following factors. The agent selected must: 1) be of low toxicity, 2) have an established safety record in patients, 3) not be routinely used for the treatment of serious infections, 4) have a spectrum of activity that includes the microorganisms most likely to cause infection, 5) reach a useful concentration in relevant tissues during the procedure, 6) be administered for a short duration, and 7) be administered in a manner that will ensure it is present in surgical sites at the time of the incision (11).

Hysterectomy—Vaginal, Abdominal, or Laparoscopically Assisted. More than 25 prospective randomized clinical trials and two meta-analyses support the use of prophylactic antibiotics to significantly reduce postoperative infectious morbidity and decrease length of hospitalization in women undergoing abdominal hysterectomy (12, 13). Most studies show no particular antibiotic regimen to be superior to all others. A single study performed in women undergoing abdominal hysterectomy showed that, when compared with cefotetan, cefazolin prophylaxis was associated with a significantly increased risk for major operative-site infection and postoperative pelvic abscess (14). Patients undergoing vaginal or abdominal hysterectomy should receive antibiotic prophylaxis.

Laparoscopy and Laparotomy. No data are available to recommend antibiotic prophylaxis in clean abdominal surgery not involving vaginal or intestinal operations. Studies evaluating the use of antibiotics to prevent wound infections after hernia repair and total or partial mastectomy fail to show a benefit. Antibiotic prophylaxis is not recommended in patients undergoing diagnostic laparoscopy or exploratory laparotomy.

Hysterosalpingography, Sonohysterography, and Hysteroscopy. Hysterosalpingography (HSG) is a commonly performed procedure to evaluate infertile couples for tubal factor infertility. Post-HSG PID is an uncommon (1.4–3.4%) but potentially serious complication in this patient population (15, 16). Patients with dilated tubes at the time of HSG have a higher rate (11%) of post-HSG PID (15). The possibility of lower genital tract infection with chlamydia should be considered before performing this procedure (16). In a retrospective review, investigators observed no cases of post-HSG PID in patients with nondilated tubes (0/398) (15). In 56 women with dilated tubes, doxycycline was effective in preventing infection. In 51 of these 56 cases, after dilated tubes were noted during the HSG, the antibiotic was administered. The other five patients received their doxycycline before the HSG.

In patients with no history of pelvic infection, HSG can be performed without prophylactic antibiotics. If HSG demonstrates dilated tubes, the patient should be given doxycycline, 100 mg twice daily for 5 days, to reduce the incidence of post-HSG PID (17). In patients with a history of pelvic infection, doxycycline can be started before the procedure and continued if dilated tubes are found. Another option in patients with a history of pelvic infection is to begin antibiotics if dilated tubes are discovered. In patients thought to have an active pelvic infection, HSG should not be performed.

No data are available on which to base a recommendation for prophylaxis in patients undergoing sonohysterography, but reported rates of postprocedure infection are negligible (0/300 in one series) (18). Sonohysterography is a relatively new procedure, technically similar to HSG. The risks probably are similar to those of HSG, and the same considerations should be taken into account. Prophylaxis should be based on the individual patient's risk of PID; routine use of antibiotic prophylaxis is not recommended.

Infectious complications following hysteroscopic surgery are uncommon and estimated to occur in 0.18–1.5% of cases (19). A single prospective study has evaluated the utility of amoxicillin/clavulanate antibiotic prophylaxis in preventing bacteremia associated with hysteroscopic endometrial laser ablation or endometrial resection (20). Although the incidence of bacteremia was lower in the antibiotic group than in the placebo group (2% versus 16%), most of the microorganisms isolated were of dubious clinical significance (anaerobic staphylococci) and may have resulted from contamination. Interestingly, postoperative fever was noted twice as often in the patients receiving antimicrobial prophylaxis. Postoperative infection requiring antibiotic therapy was not significantly different between the two groups, with 11.4% and 9% of patients requiring antibiotics in the placebo and antibiotic groups, respectively.

Other retrospective case series evaluating endometrial ablation reported similarly low rates of infection. In a series of 568 patients treated without antimicrobial prophylaxis, one woman (0.18%) developed endometritis (21). A second series reported 2 of 600 women (0.3%) developed mild pelvic infections, of whom one received antimicrobial prophylaxis and one did not (22). However, in a series of 200 women undergoing operative hysteroscopy without prophylactic antibiotics, investigators reported three cases of severe pelvic infection, although all three of these women had a history of PID (23). Given the low risk of infection and lack of evidence of efficacy, antibiotics are not of value for the general patient population undergoing these procedures.

Intrauterine Device Insertion, Endometrial Biopsy. The IUD is a highly effective contraceptive, but concern about the perceived risk of PID limits its use. Most of the risk of IUD-related infection occurs in the first few weeks to months after insertion, suggesting that contamination of the endometrial cavity at the time of insertion is the infecting mechanism rather than the IUD or string itself. Four randomized clinical trials have now been performed using doxycycline or azithromycin as antibiotic prophylaxis (24–27). Pelvic inflammatory disease occurred uncommonly with or without the use of antibiotic prophylaxis. A Cochrane Collaboration review concluded that either doxycycline or azithromycin before IUD insertion confers little benefit (28). When the results of the four studies were combined, a reduction in unscheduled visits to the provider was seen but not in the only trial performed in the United States. In the U.S. trial, however, all patients were screened for gonorrhea and chlamydia, and some with positive results were excluded from the study. The cost-effectiveness of screening for sexually transmitted diseases (STDs) before IUD insertion remains unclear because of limited data. The only randomized controlled trial performed in the United States concluded that in women screened for STDs before IUD insertion, prophylactic antibiotics provide no benefit (27).

No data are available on infectious complications of endometrial biopsy. The incidence is presumed to be negligible. It is recommended that this procedure be performed without the use of antimicrobial prophylaxis.

Induced Abortion and Dilation and Curettage. Eleven of 15 randomized clinical trials support the use of antibiotic prophylaxis at the time of suction curettage abortion. In a meta-analysis of 11 placebo-controlled, blinded clinical trials, the overall summary relative risk (RR) estimate for developing postabortal infection of the upper genital tract in women receiving antibiotic therapy compared with those receiving placebo was 0.58 (95% confidence interval [CI], 0.47–0.71) (29). Of high-risk women, those with a history of PID had a summary RR of 0.56 (CI, 0.37–0.84); women with a positive chlamydia culture at abortion had a summary RR of 0.38 (CI, 0.15–0.92). Of low-risk women, those with no reported history of PID had a summary RR of 0.65 (CI, 0.47–0.90); in women with a negative chlamydia culture, the RR was 0.63 (CI, 0.42–0.97). The overall 42% decreased risk of infection in women given periabortal antibiotics confirms that prophylactic antibiotics are effective for these women, regardless of risk.

The optimal antibiotic and dosing regimens remain unclear. Both tetracyclines and nitro-imidazoles provide significant and comparable protection against postabortal PID. One of the most effective and inexpensive regimens reported in a meta-analysis was doxycycline, 100 mg orally 1 hour before the abortion followed by 200 mg after the procedure. It is estimated that the cost of treating a single case of postabortal PID as an outpatient far exceeds the cost of doxycycline prophylaxis (29). In a prospective, randomized trial, antibiotic prophylaxis showed no benefit before treatment of incomplete abortion (30).

Preoperative Bowel Preparation. Occasionally the gynecologic surgeon runs the risk of both small- and large-bowel injuries because of the presence of pelvic adhesions resulting from either previous surgery or an inflammatory process, such as PID or endometriosis. In these cases, it is reasonable to consider preparing the bowel for surgery with a mechanical bowel preparation and using an antibiotic regimen that is effective in preventing infection among patients undergoing elective bowel surgery. Eight randomized clinical trials confirm the effectiveness of prophylactic parenteral antibiotics administered preoperatively with or without a prior oral antibiotic bowel preparation in decreasing the rate of postoperative infection, such as wound and intraabdominal infections (5). It is unclear whether any one regimen is superior, but broad-spectrum cephalosporins, such as cefotetan or cefoxitin, were commonly used.

Endocarditis Prophylaxis. As many as 75% of patients who develop endocarditis after undergoing a surgical procedure have preexisting cardiac abnormalities. To date, no randomized controlled trials have definitively established the efficacy of endocarditis prophylaxis, but most authorities agree that prophylaxis should be offered to susceptible patients. Patients with high- and moderate-risk structural cardiac defects may benefit from antimicrobial prophylaxis (see the box, right). In addition, bacteremia is associated with certain surgical procedures; therefore, in patients with underlying cardiac structural defects who are undergoing these procedures, antimicrobial prophylaxis is recommended (see the box, next page). Suggested regimens are listed in Table 2.

In the absence of obvious infection, bacteremia is uncommon after cervical biopsy or IUD insertion or removal, and prophylaxis is not indicated. In the presence of infection, removal of an IUD or other genitourinary procedures require endocarditis prophylaxis. Antibiotics administered for prevention of surgical-site infection are not sufficient for endocarditis prophylaxis. However, most experts agree that prophylactic agents for endocarditis provide sufficient coverage against surgical-site infection. For patients with significant heart disease being treated by a specialist, it may be helpful to consult the specialist for additional information if necessary.

Urodynamic Studies or Bladder Catheterization. Several studies suggest that prophylactic antibiotics are not effective in preventing urinary tract infections resulting from urodynamic testing. One study identified 2 of 45 women (4%) not given antibiotics following urodynamic testing whose postprocedure urine cultures were positive, compared with 0 of 51 women given macrodantin, 50 mg three times a day for 3 days after testing (31). A second study identified 10 of 49 women (18.9%) not given antibiotics after urodynamic testing whose urine

cultures were positive, compared with 4 of 49 women (8.9%) who received prophylaxis and had positive urine cultures (32). The differences in both studies were not statistically significant. Because neither study reported on "symptomatic infection" nor the microbiology of the postprocedure bacteriuria, the site could have been contaminated with a nonuropathogen. However, given the prevalence of asymptomatic bacteriuria in women, approximately 8% of women had unsuspected bacteriuria at the time of urodynamic testing. Because bacteriuria and urinary tract infection can be a cause of detrusor instability, pretest screening by urine culture or urinalysis, or both, is recommended.

Cardiac Conditions Associated with Endocarditis

Endocarditis Prophylaxis Recommended

High-Risk Category

Prosthetic cardiac valves, including bioprosthetic and homograft valves
Previous bacterial endocarditis
Complex cyanotic congenital heart disease (eg, single-ventricle states, transposition of the great arteries, tetralogy of Fallot)
Surgically constructed systemic pulmonary shunts or conduits

Moderate-Risk Category

Most other congenital cardiac malformations (other than those listed above and below)
Acquired valvar dysfunction (eg, rheumatic heart disease)
Hypertrophic cardiomyopathy
Mitral valve prolapse with valvar regurgitation, thickened leaflets, or both

Endocarditis Prophylaxis Not Recommended

Negligible-Risk Category (Risk No Greater Than That of the General Population)
Isolated secundum atrial septum defect
Surgical repair of atrial septal defect, ventricular septal defect, or patent ductus arteriosus (without residua beyond 6 months)
Previous coronary artery bypass graft surgery
Mitral valve prolapse without valvar regurgitation
Physiologic, functional, or innocent heart murmurs
Previous Kawasaki syndrome without valvar dysfunction
Previous rheumatic fever without valvar dysfunction
Cardiac pacemakers (intravascular and epicardial) and implanted defibrillators

Dajani AS, Taubert KA, Wilson W, Bolger AF, Bayer A, Ferrieri P, et al. Prevention of bacterial endocarditis: recommendations by the American Heart Association. JAMA 1997;277:1795. Copyrighted 1997, American Medical Association.

Endocarditis Prophylaxis by Surgical Procedure

Endocarditis Prophylaxis Recommended

Gastrointestinal Tract*
  Surgical operations that involve intestinal mucosa
Genitourinary Tract
  Cystoscopy
  Urethral dilation
  Other genitourinary procedures only in presence of
    infection

Endocarditis Prophylaxis Not Recommended

Genitourinary Tract
  Vaginal hysterectomy†
  In uninfected tissue:
    Urethral catheterization
    Uterine dilation and curettage
    Therapeutic abortion
    Sterilization procedures
    Insertion or removal of intrauterine devices

*Prophylaxis is recommended for high-risk patients; optional for medium-risk patients.

†Prophylaxis is optional for high-risk patients.

Adapted from Dajani AS, Taubert KA, Wilson W, Bolger AF, Bayer A, Ferrieri P, et al. Prevention of bacterial endocarditis: recommendations by the American Heart Association. JAMA 1997;277:1797. Copyrighted 1997, American Medical Association.

Urinary tract infection after one-time bladder catheterization has been reported to be approximately 2% (33). No randomized trials have compared antibiotic prophylaxis with placebo in trying to further decrease the incidence of urinary tract infection. Therefore, given the low risk of infection, antibiotic prophylaxis is not indicated for this procedure.

▶ *Which antibiotics should be used in the patient with penicillin allergy?*

Allergic reactions occur in 0.7–4% of courses of treatment with penicillin (34). Four types of immunopathologic reactions have been described, all of which have been seen with β-lactam antibiotics: 1) immediate hypersensitivity reactions, 2) cytotoxic antibodies, 3) immune complexes, and 4) cell-mediated hypersensitivity (35). Approximately 5–20% of patients indicate a history of reactions to β-lactam antibiotics.

Like penicillins, cephalosporins possess a β-lactam ring; however, the five-membered thiazolidine ring is replaced by a six-membered dihydrothiazine ring. The overall incidence of adverse reactions from cephalosporins ranges from 1% to 10%, with rare anaphylaxis (<0.02%). In patients with histories of penicillin allergy, the incidence of cephalosporin reactions is increased minimally. Postmarketing studies of second- and third-generation cephalosporins showed no increase in allergic reactions to cephalosporins in patients with histories of penicillin allergy. One reaction occurred in 98 patients (1%) with positive penicillin skin test results, and six reactions occurred in 310 patients (2%) with negative test results (36). The incidence of clinically relevant cross-reactivity between the penicillins and cephalosporins is

Table 2. Prophylactic Regimens for Prevention of Endocarditis in Susceptible Patients Undergoing Genitourinary or Gastrointestinal Procedures

Situation	Agents	Regimen*
High-risk patients	Ampicillin plus gentamicin	Ampicillin, 2 g IM or IV, plus gentamicin, 1.5 mg/kg (not to exceed 120 mg) within 30 minutes of starting the procedure; 6 hours later, ampicillin, 1 g IM/IV, or amoxicillin, 1 g orally
High-risk patients allergic to ampicillin/amoxicillin	Vancomycin plus gentamicin	Vancomycin, 1 g IV over 1 to 2 hours, plus gentamicin, 1.5 mg/kg IV/IM (not to exceed 120 mg); complete injection/infusion within 30 minutes of starting the procedure
Moderate-risk patients	Amoxicillin or ampicillin	Amoxicillin, 2 g orally 1 hour before procedure, or ampicillin, 2 g IM/IV within 30 minutes of starting the procedure
Moderate-risk patients allergic to ampicillin/amoxicillin	Vancomycin	Vancomycin, 1 g IV over 1 to 2 hours; complete infusion within 30 minutes of starting the procedure

Abbreviations: IM, intramuscularly; IV, intravenously.

*No second dose of vancomycin or gentamicin is recommended.

Adapted from Dajani AS, Taubert KA, Wilson W, Bolger AF, Bayer A, Ferrieri P, et al. Prevention of bacterial endocarditis: recommendations by the American Heart Association. JAMA 1997;277:1799. Copyrighted 1997, American Medical Association.

small, but rare anaphylactic reactions have occurred (37). Patients with a history of an immediate hypersensitivity reaction to penicillin should not receive cephalosporin antibiotics, given that alternative drugs are available for prophylaxis. Alternative agents include metronidazole, doxycycline, clindamycin, and the quinolones. Cephalosporin prophylaxis is acceptable in those patients with a history of penicillin allergy not felt to be immunoglobulin-E (IgE) mediated (immediate hypersensitivity).

▶ *How cost-effective is antibiotic prophylaxis?*

Prophylactic antibiotics add considerable cost to the routine care of surgical patients. However, the prevention of postoperative infection decreases hospital stay and the use of other resources to assess and treat infections not otherwise prevented by antimicrobial prophylaxis. A 1983 study found an average net savings of $102 per patient in women undergoing hysterectomy who received prophylactic antibiotics (38). This savings would be eroded by use of the more expensive cephalosporins unless they were considerably more effective than cefazolin or cefotetan. Likewise, the inexpensive prophylactic regimens used for the prevention of postabortal PID are cost-effective as noted previously. It is estimated that more than $500,000 would be saved each year in the United States in direct treatment costs alone by providing antibiotic prophylaxis to women at average risk undergoing induced abortion (29).

Summary

The following recommendations are based on good and consistent scientific evidence (Level A):

▶ Patients undergoing hysterectomy should receive antimicrobial prophylaxis.

▶ Pelvic inflammatory disease complicating IUD insertion is uncommon. The cost-effectiveness of screening for gonorrhea and chlamydia before insertion is unclear; in women screened and found to be negative, prophylactic antibiotics appear to provide no benefit.

▶ Women undergoing surgically induced abortion are candidates for antibiotic prophylaxis.

▶ Appropriate prophylaxis for women undergoing surgery that may involve the bowel includes a mechanical bowel preparation with or without oral antibiotics and the use of a broad-spectrum parenteral antibiotic, given preoperatively.

The following recommendations are based on limited or inconsistent scientific evidence (Level B):

▶ In patients with no history of pelvic infection, HSG can be performed without prophylactic antibiotics. If HSG demonstrates dilated tubes, antibiotic prophylaxis should be given to reduce the incidence of post-HSG PID.

▶ Routine antibiotic prophylaxis is not recommended in patients undergoing hysteroscopic surgery.

▶ Cephalosporin antibiotics may be used for antimicrobial prophylaxis in women with a history of penicillin allergy not manifested by an immediate hypersensitivity reaction.

The following recommendations are based primarily on consensus and expert opinion (Level C):

▶ Antibiotic prophylaxis is not recommended in patients undergoing exploratory laparotomy or diagnostic laparoscopy.

▶ Use of antibiotic prophylaxis with saline infusion sonography should be based on clinical considerations, including individual risk factors.

▶ Patients with high- and moderate-risk structural cardiac defects undergoing certain surgical procedures may benefit from antimicrobial prophylaxis.

▶ Patients with a history of anaphylactic reaction to penicillin should not receive cephalosporins.

▶ Pretest screening for bacteriuria or urinary tract infection by urine culture or urinalysis, or both, is recommended in women undergoing urodynamic testing. Those with positive results should be given antibiotic treatment.

References

1. Kernodle DS, Kaiser AB. Postoperative infections and antimicrobial prophylaxis. In: Mandell GL, Bennett JE, Dolin R, eds. Mandell, Douglas, and Bennett's principles and practice of infectious diseases. 5th ed. Philadelphia: Churchill Livingstone, 2000:3177–3191 (Level III)

2. Hemsell DL. Gynecologic postoperative infections. In: Pastorek JG II, ed. Obstetric and gynecologic infectious disease. New York: Raven Press, 1994:141–149 (Level III)

3. Soper DE, Bump RC, Hurt WG. Bacterial vaginosis and trichomoniasis vaginitis are risk factors for postoperative cuff cellulitis after abdominal hysterectomy. Am J Obstet Gynecol 1990;163:1016–1021; discussion 1021–1023 (Level II-2)

4. Burke JF. The effective period of preventive antibiotic action in experimental incisions and dermal lesions. Surgery 1961;50:161–168; discussion 184–185 (Level II-2)

5. Dellinger EP, Gross PA, Barrett TL, Krause PJ, Martone WJ, McGowan JE, et al. Quality standard for antimicrobial prophylaxis in surgical procedures. Infectious Disease Society of America. Clin Infect Dis 1994;18:422–427 (Level III)

6. McFarland LV. Diarrhea acquired in the hospital. Gastroenterol Clin North Am 1993;22:563–577 (Level III)

7. McFarland LV, Surawicz CM, Greenberg RN, Elmer GW, Moyer KA, Melcher SA, et al. Prevention of beta-lactam-associated diarrhea by Saccharomyces boulardii compared with placebo. Am J Gastroenterol 1995;90:439–448 (Level I)

8. Bartlett JG. Antibiotic-associated diarrhea. Clin Infect Dis 1992;15:573–581 (Level III)

9. Thielman NM. Antibiotic-associated colitis. In: Mandell GL, Bennett JE, Dolin R, eds. Mandell, Douglas, and Bennett's principles and practice of infectious diseases. 5th ed. Philadelphia: Churchill Livingstone, 2000: 1111–1126 (Level III)

10. Idsoe O, Guthe T, Willcox RR, Weck AL de. Nature and extent of penicillin side-reactions, with particular reference to fatalities from anaphylactic shock. Bull World Health Organ 1968;38:159–188 (Level III)

11. Hemsell DL. Prophylactic antibiotics in gynecologic and obstetric surgery. Rev Infect Dis 1991;13(Suppl 10): S821–S841 (Level III)

12. Tanos V, Rojansky N. Prophylactic antibiotics in abdominal hysterectomy. J Am Coll Surg 1994;179:593–600 (Meta-analysis)

13. Mittendorf R, Aronson MP, Berry RE, Williams MA, Kupelnick B, Klickstein A, et al. Avoiding serious infections associated with abdominal hysterectomy: a meta-analysis of antibiotic prophylaxis. Am J Obstet Gynecol 1993;169:1119–1124 (Meta-analysis)

14. Hemsell DL, Johnson ER, Hemsell PG, Nobles BJ, Little BB, Heard MC. Cefazolin is inferior to cefotetan as single-dose prophylaxis for women undergoing elective total abdominal hysterectomy. Clin Infect Dis 1995;20: 677–684 (Level I)

15. Pittaway DE, Winfeld AC, Maxson W, Daniell J, Herbert C, Wentz AC. Prevention of acute pelvic inflammatory disease after hysterosalpingography: efficacy of doxycycline prophylaxis. Am J Obstet Gynecol 1983;147:623–626 (Level II-2)

16. Moller BR, Allen J, Toft B, Hansen KB, Taylor-Robinson D. Pelvic inflammatory disease after hysterosalpingography associated with Chlamydia trachomatis and Mycoplasma hominis. Br J Obstet Gynaecol 1984;91: 1181–1187 (Level III)

17. Speroff L, Glass RH, Kase NG. Female infertility. In: Clinical gynecologic endocrinology and infertility. 5th ed. Baltimore: Williams & Wilkins, 1994:809–839 (Level III)

18. Goldstein SR. Sonohysterography. In: Goldstein SR, Timor-Tritsch IE. Ultrasound in gynecology. New York: Churchill Livingstone, 1995:203–221 (Level III)

19. Baggish MS. Complications of hysteroscopic surgery. In: Baggish MS, Barbot J, Valle RF, eds. Diagnostic and operative hysteroscopy. 2nd ed. St. Louis: Mosby, 1999: 367–379 (Level III)

20. Bhattacharya S, Parkin DE, Reid TM, Abramovich DR, Mollison J, Kitchener HC. A prospective randomised study of the effects of prophylactic antibiotics on the incidence of bacteraemia following hysteroscopic surgery. Eur J Obstet Gynecol Reprod Biol 1995;63:37–40 (Level I)

21. Baggish MS, Sze EH. Endometrial ablation: a series of 568 patients treated over an 11-year period. Am J Obstet Gynecol 1996;174:908–913 (Level II-3)

22. Garry R, Shelley-Jones D, Mooney P, Phillips G. Six hundred endometrial laser ablations. Obstet Gynecol 1995; 85:24–29 (Level II-2)

23. McCausland VM, Fields GA, McCausland AM, Townsend DE. Tuboovarian abscesses after operative hysteroscopy. J Reprod Med 1993;38:198–200 (Level II-3)

24. Walsh T, Grimes D, Frezieres R, Nelson A, Bernstein L, Coulson A, et al. Randomised controlled trial of prophylactic antibiotics before insertion of intrauterine devices. IUD Study Group. Lancet 1998;351:1005–1008 (Level I)

25. Walsh TL, Bernstein GS, Grimes DA, Frezieres R, Bernstein L, Coulson AH. Effect of prophylactic antibiotics on morbidity associated with IUD insertion: results of a pilot randomized controlled trial. IUD Study Group. Contraception 1994;50:319–327 (Level I)

26. Ladipo OA, Farr G, Otolorin E, Konje JC, Sturgen K, Cox P, et al. Prevention of IUD-related pelvic infection: the efficacy of prophylactic doxycycline at IUD insertion. Adv Contracept 1991;7:43–54 (Level I)

27. Sinei SK, Schulz KF, Lamptey PR, Grimes DA, Mati JK, Rosenthal SM, et al. Preventing IUCD-related pelvic infection: the efficacy of prophylactic doxycycline at insertion. Br J Obstet Gynaecol 1990;97:412–419 (Level I)

28. Grimes DA, Schulz KF. Antibiotic prophylaxis for intrauterine contraceptive device insertion (Cochrane Review). In: The Cochrane Library, Issue 4, 2000. Oxford: Update Software.

29. Sawaya GF, Grady D, Kerlikowske K, Grimes DA. Antibiotics at the time of induced abortion: the case for universal prophylaxis based on a meta-analysis. Obstet Gynecol 1996;87:884–890 (Meta-analysis)

30. Prieto JA, Eriksen NL, Blanco JD. A randomized trial of prophylactic doxycycline for curettage in incomplete abortion. Obstet Gynecol 1995;85:692–696 (Level I)

31. Bergman A, McCarthy TA. Antibiotic prophylaxis after instrumentation for urodynamic testing. Br J Urol 1983; 55:568–569 (Level II-1)

32. Baker KR, Drutz HP, Barnes MD. Effectiveness of antibiotic prophylaxis in preventing bacteriuria after multichan-

nel urodynamic investigations: a blind, randomized study in 124 female patients. Am J Obstet Gynecol 1991;165:679–681 (Level I)

33. Walter S, Vejlsgaard R. Diagnostic catheterization and bacteriuria in women with urinary incontinence. Br J Urol 1978;50:106–108 (Level II-3)

34. Parker CW. Drug allergy (first of three parts). N Engl J Med 1975;292:511–514 (Level III)

35. Gell PG, Coombs RR. Classification of allergic reactions responsible for clinical hypersensitivity and disease. In: Gell PG, Coombs RR, Hachmann PJ, eds. Clinical aspects of immunology. Oxford: Blackwell Scientific Publications, 1975:761–781 (Level III)

36. Anne S, Reisman RE. Risk of administering cephalosporin antibiotics to patients with histories of penicillin allergy. Ann Allergy Asthma Immunol 1995;74:167–170 (Level III)

37. Weiss ME, Adkinson NF Jr. β-lactam allergy. In: Mandell GL, Bennett JE, Dolin R, eds. Mandell, Douglas, and Bennett's principles and practice of infectious diseases. 5th ed. Philadelphia: Churchill Livingstone, 2000:299–305 (Level III)

38. Shapiro M, Schoenbaum SC, Tager IB, Munoz A, Polk BF. Benefit-cost analysis of antimicrobial prophylaxis in abdominal and vaginal hysterectomy. JAMA 1983;249:1290–1294 (Cost-benefit analysis)

The MEDLINE database, the Cochrane Library, and ACOG's own internal resources and documents were used to conduct a literature search to locate relevant articles published between January 1985 and May 2000. The search was restricted to articles published in the English language. Priority was given to articles reporting results of original research, although review articles and commentaries also were consulted. Abstracts of research presented at symposia and scientific conferences were not considered adequate for inclusion in this document. Guidelines published by organizations or institutions such as the National Institutes of Health and the American College of Obstetricians and Gynecologists were reviewed, and additional studies were located by reviewing bibliographies of identified articles. When reliable research was not available, expert opinions from obstetrician–gynecologists were used.

Studies were reviewed and evaluated for quality according to the method outlined by the U.S. Preventive Services Task Force:

I   Evidence obtained from at least one properly designed randomized controlled trial.

II-1   Evidence obtained from well-designed controlled trials without randomization.

II-2   Evidence obtained from well-designed cohort or case–control analytic studies, preferably from more than one center or research group.

II-3   Evidence obtained from multiple time series with or without the intervention. Dramatic results in uncontrolled experiments also could be regarded as this type of evidence.

III   Opinions of respected authorities, based on clinical experience, descriptive studies, or reports of expert committees.

Based on the highest level of evidence found in the data, recommendations are provided and graded according to the following categories:

Level A—Recommendations are based on good and consistent scientific evidence.

Level B—Recommendations are based on limited or inconsistent scientific evidence.

Level C—Recommendations are based primarily on consensus and expert opinion.

ISSN 1099-3630

The American College of Obstetricians and Gynecologists
409 12th Street, SW, PO Box 96920
Washington, DC 20090-6920

12345/54321

ACOG PRACTICE BULLETIN

CLINICAL MANAGEMENT GUIDELINES FOR
OBSTETRICIAN–GYNECOLOGISTS

NUMBER 31, OCTOBER 2001

(Replaces Technical Bulletin Number 206, June 1995; Committee Opinion Number 172, May 1996; Committee Opinion Number 187, September 1997; Committee Opinion Number 198, February 1998; and Committee Opinion Number 251, January 2001)

This Practice Bulletin was developed by the ACOG Committee on Practice Bulletins— Obstetrics with the assistance of Jodi F. Abbott, MD. The information is designed to aid practitioners in making decisions about appropriate obstetric and gynecologic care. These guidelines should not be construed as dictating an exclusive course of treatment or procedure. Variations in practice may be warranted based on the needs of the individual patient, resources, and limitations unique to the institution or type of practice.

Assessment of Risk Factors for Preterm Birth

Preterm birth is the second leading cause of neonatal mortality in the United States (1) (second only to birth defects), and preterm labor is the cause of most preterm births (2). Neonatal intensive care has improved the survival rate for babies at the cusp of viability, but it also has increased the proportion of survivors with disabilities (3). The incidence of multiple births also has increased along with the associated risk of preterm delivery (4). Interventions to delay preterm delivery in these settings have not shown conclusive effectiveness. Because the morbidity of babies born after 34–35 weeks of gestation has diminished, most efforts to identify preterm deliveries have focused on deliveries before this age. This document describes the various methods proposed for predicting preterm birth and the evidence for their roles in clinical practice.

Background

Preterm labor is defined as regular contractions associated with cervical change before the completion of 37 weeks of gestation. Spontaneous preterm birth includes preterm labor, preterm spontaneous rupture of membranes, and cervical incompetence; it does not include indicated preterm delivery for maternal or fetal conditions (5). Preterm delivery accounted for 11.8% of births in the United States in 1999; this figure has increased steadily from 9.4% in 1981 (6).

The pathophysiologic events that trigger preterm parturition are largely unknown but may include decidual hemorrhage (abruption), mechanical factors (uterine overdistention or cervical incompetence), and hormonal changes (perhaps mediated by fetal or maternal stress) (7–9). In addition, several bacterial infections have been associated with preterm labor. Commonly identified organisms are *Ureaplasma urealyticum, Mycoplasma hominis, Gardnerella vaginalis, Peptostreptococcus,* and *Bacteroides* species (10). Because these bacteria usually are of low virulence, it is unclear whether they are truly etiologic or are associated with an acute inflammatory response of another etiology.

Value of Predicting Risk

The ability to predict whether a woman is at risk of preterm delivery has value only if an intervention is available that is likely to improve the outcome. The opportunity to administer maternal corticosteroid ther-apy is an important intervention recommended by the National Institutes of Health because it is strongly associated with decreased morbidity and mortality (11–13). In addition, maternal tocolytic therapy may prolong pregnancy for up to 48 hours in some women, during which time corticosteroids can be administered (14). Because tocolytic and steroid therapy may result in untoward maternal and fetal consequences, use of these therapies should be limited to women with true preterm labor at high risk for spontaneous preterm birth. Finally, in women being managed at hospitals without appropriate neonatal resources, identifying women at risk allows for appropriate maternal transport to a tertiary care center. Conversely, identifying those women at low risk for preterm delivery would avert the use of unnecessary interventions.

Risk Factors

Risk factors for preterm birth include demographic characteristics, behavioral factors, and aspects of obstetric history. Demographic characteristics that carry a high risk for preterm birth include nonwhite race (African American relative risk [RR]=3.3), age younger than 17 years or older than 35 years (RR=1.47–1.95), low socioeconomic status (RR=1.83–2.65), and low prepregnancy weight (odds ratio=2.72) (15, 16). Maternal his-tory of preterm birth, particularly in the second trimester, has a strong statistical association with the risk of preterm delivery (17); this risk appears to be associated with prior spontaneous preterm birth with or without rupture of membranes and increases the relative risk sixfold to eightfold. Risk also increases with vaginal bleeding in more than one trimester (18). Controversy exists as to whether an excessively physically stressful job can lead to early delivery; one study has shown an increase in spontaneous preterm birth associated with long periods of standing (>40 hours per week) (19). Smoking increases the risk of preterm birth (20) and low birth weight, and some evidence suggests it increases the risk for spontaneous abortion (21). Despite the identification of a number of risk factors, attempts to determine the risk of preterm delivery based on historic and epidemiologic risk scoring systems (22–24) have been unable to reliably identify women who will give birth preterm.

Biologic Markers for Predicting Preterm Birth

Home Uterine Activity Monitoring

Tocodynamometry has long been used for hospital-based evaluation of uterine contractions. Home uterine activity monitoring (HUAM) has been proposed as a method for predicting preterm birth in high-risk women. It consists of a combination of telemetric recordings of uterine contractions with the use of a tocodynamometer and daily telephone calls from a health care practitioner to offer patient support and advice. Uterine activity beyond an arbitrary cutoff triggers notification of the patient's health care practitioner. This approach was based on the observation that some women who subsequently give birth before term have an increase in uterine activity earlier in pregnancy than women who give birth at term (25) and that these prodromal uterine contractions otherwise may not be recognized by the patient.

Salivary Estriol

Activation of the fetal hypothalamic pituitary–adrenal axis precedes some spontaneous preterm births. Adrenal production of dehydroepiandrosterone results in increased placental estrogen synthesis. Observational studies have shown that maternal levels of serum estradiol and salivary estriol increase before the onset of spontaneous term and preterm labor (26). These findings prompted the design of a test to predict preterm delivery by measuring salivary estriol; however, maternal estriol levels show diurnal variation, peaking at night (27). Also, estriol levels may be suppressed by betamethasone administration (28).

Bacterial Vaginosis

Bacterial vaginosis (BV) is a common alteration of the normal vaginal flora and has been found in 10–25% of patients in general gynecologic and obstetric clinics and in up to 64% of patients in clinics for sexually transmitted diseases (29). Fifty percent of women with BV are asymptomatic (30). Bacterial vaginosis also has been found more frequently in African-American women (22%) than in white women (8%) (10, 31). The presence of BV has been associated with preterm delivery independent of other known risk factors (32, 33).

Fetal Fibronectin Screening

Fetal fibronectin (fFN) is a basement membrane protein produced by the fetal membranes that functions as an adhesion binder of the placenta and membranes to the decidua (34, 35). It is normally present in cervical secretions until 16–20 weeks of gestation. Numerous trials have shown both an association with the presence of fFN and preterm birth (5, 34, 36) and a decrease in the risk of preterm birth when the test result for the presence of this protein is negative. The basis for the association of fFN and preterm birth is unclear. It has been hypothesized that fFN is a marker for the disruption of the chorioamnion and underlying decidua due to inflammation with or without infection (34). A positive midtrimester fFN test result has been associated with subsequently diagnosed maternal and fetal infection (37).

Cervical Ultrasonography

Transvaginal cervical ultrasonography has been shown to be a reliable and reproducible way to assess the length of the cervix (38). A prospective blinded trial showed an association between cervical length and preterm delivery (39). This study established the normal distribution of cervical length in pregnancy after 22 weeks of gestation. It also looked at various cervical measurements as criteria for the prediction of preterm delivery.

Clinical Considerations and Recommendations

▶ *Does the use of HUAM predict preterm birth?*

The usefulness of HUAM as a screening test depends on both its ability to detect women at higher risk for preterm birth as well as the effectiveness of any intervention to then prevent preterm birth. At least 13 randomized controlled trials examining the efficacy of HUAM have published results (40–52). The studies vary in design, criteria for inclusion of patients, and measurements of endpoints and outcomes. These differences make comparisons difficult. Furthermore, many of these studies had limitations with their research design, including sample size (power) or numbers of patients, that preclude reaching conclusions about the usefulness of HUAM. Results vary, with some trials reporting no difference and some reporting a difference in outcome in monitored and unmonitored women. The largest study involved 2,422 women at risk and showed no improvement in outcome (41).

Earlier studies that showed a reduction in the incidence of preterm birth with HUAM have been criticized for their flawed design (53, 54); some studies have been identified as having biases and errors sufficient to warrant dismissing the results (55). The U.S. Preventive Services Task Force performed an independent review and concluded the device was not effective (56). Although the U.S. Food and Drug Administration has approved a HUAM device for women with a prior preterm birth, there is no demonstrated role for HUAM in the prevention of preterm birth. Data are insufficient to support a benefit from HUAM in preventing preterm birth (13, 57, 58); therefore, this system of care is not recommended.

▶ *Does salivary estriol determination predict preterm birth?*

There have been two prospective trials evaluating whether salivary estriol levels can predict preterm delivery (59, 60); they showed that salivary estriol was more predictive than traditional risk assessment. However, the results of the second trial showed a relatively poor sensitivity of 71%, specificity of 77%, and a false-positive rate of 23% (using delivery before 37 weeks of gestation as the outcome measure) (60). Because the test carries a high percentage of false-positive results, its use could add significantly to the cost of prenatal care, particularly if used in a low-risk population. Although the hormonal pathway etiology for some cases of preterm birth is intriguing, trials with salivary estriol testing to predict preterm birth have failed to establish its usefulness for anything more than investigational purposes at present.

▶ *Do screening and treatment for BV affect the likelihood of preterm birth?*

Trials of screening and treatment for BV in pregnant women to reduce the incidence of preterm delivery have been conducted in mixed populations with varying results. Some small studies found screening and treatment of women at risk for preterm birth reduced the risk of preterm birth (61, 62), but other studies have not confirmed these findings (63, 64).

A recent meta-analysis reviewed five trials involving 1,504 women (65). The analysis included trials of women without risk factors for preterm birth as well as studies that screened general obstetric populations. Treatments used in these trials included amoxicillin, clindamycin, and metronidazole. Although investigators found antibiotic therapy effective at eradicating BV, the difference in the rate of preterm birth between the two groups was not statistically significant. However, looking at the subgroup of women with a previous preterm birth, the difference was significant, with an odds ratio of 0.37 (95% confidence interval, 0.23–0.60). This meta-analysis did not include results from the most recent and largest double-blind, randomized controlled trial. This trial of 1,953 women found no difference in the rates of preterm birth between the treatment and placebo groups, and no subgroup demonstrated a statistically significant difference in preterm birth rates (64).

Although some trials have shown an association with the presence of BV and preterm birth, most large trials designed to determine whether treatment of BV can prevent preterm birth have failed. Currently, there are insufficient data to suggest screening and treating women at either low or high risk will reduce the overall rate of preterm birth (66). There is speculation that BV could be either a marker or a cause of choriodecidual inflammation without intraamniotic infection (24). However, research testing this hypothesis by serial fFN screening in women with BV was unable to confirm an association (67).

▶ *Does screening for fFN predict preterm birth?*

A meta-analysis of 27 studies showed consistent moderate success using fFN screening to predict preterm birth (68). Using delivery at less than 34 weeks of gestation as the outcome, sensitivity was 61% and specificity was 83% (68). A study that analyzed the relationship between fFN, short cervix, BV, and designated traditional risk factors for spontaneous preterm birth showed the highest association of preterm birth with positive fFN test result, followed by a cervical length less than 25 mm and a history of preterm birth (69). The negative predictive value of the fFN test to identify symptomatic women who are actually at low risk for imminent preterm delivery ranges from 69% to 92% before 37 weeks of gestation, with a greater than 95% likelihood of not delivering within 14 days of a negative test result (13, 70, 71).

Although a negative test result appears to be useful in ruling out preterm delivery that is imminent (ie, within 2 weeks) (13, 72, 73), the clinical implications of a positive test result have not been evaluated fully because no obstetric intervention has been shown to decrease the risk of preterm delivery. The test should not be routinely used to screen low-risk, asymptomatic women, because the incidence of preterm birth in this population is low and the test, therefore, has limited usefulness (68).

If the test is to be used in specific high-risk groups, the following criteria should be met: intact amniotic membranes, minimal cervical dilatation (<3 cm), and sampling performed no earlier than 24 weeks and 0 days of gestation and no later than 34 weeks and 6 days of gestation (74). If the test is to be clinically useful, the results must be available from a laboratory within a time frame that allows for clinical decision making (ideally within 24 hours).

▶ *Does cervical ultrasonography predict preterm birth?*

Numerous studies have confirmed the association of cervical shortening with preterm delivery, but they have varied widely in their predictive value (13, 75–77). A review of 35 studies using cervical length (determined by ultrasonography) to predict preterm delivery found sensitivities ranging from 68% to 100%, with specificities from 44% to 79% (78).

A prospective trial of more than 2,900 women evaluated by serial transvaginal ultrasonography at 24 weeks of gestation and again at 28 weeks of gestation showed the RR of preterm delivery increased as the cervical length decreased. Specifically, at 28 weeks of gestation, when cervical lengths were 40 mm or less, RR was 2.80; at 35 mm or less, RR was 3.52; at 30 mm or less, RR was 5.39; at 26 mm or less, RR was 9.57; at 22 mm or less, RR was 13.88; and at 13 mm or less, RR was 24.94 (39).

Despite the usefulness of cervical length determination by ultrasonography as a predictor of preterm labor, routine use is not recommended because of the lack of proven treatments affecting outcome (79). Until effective treatment options are identified, cervical length measurement has limited clinical application.

▶ *Should fFN and cervical ultrasonography be used together to better identify those at highest risk?*

In a multicenter trial, investigators found a short cervix (defined as <25 mm), particularly if associated with a positive fFN test result, to be a strong predictor of preterm birth (80). A more recent trial by the National Institute of Child Health and Human Development looked at the sequential use of both methods to try to stratify risk groups as well as discern etiologies of preterm birth (69) (see Table 1). The presence of either a cervix less than 25 mm in length at less than 35 weeks of gestation or a positive fFN test result was strongly associated with preterm birth, especially in women with a history of preterm birth. These data were particularly useful in decreasing the assessed risk of preterm birth in women with classic risk factors and negative results of one or both tests. The success of interventions once a short cervix is identified or positive fFN test result is determined remains uncertain (13).

Table 1. Recurrence Risk of Spontaneous Preterm Birth at <35 Weeks of Gestation According to Cervical Length and Fetal Fibronectin in Women with a Prior Preterm Birth

Cervical Length (mm)	Fetal Fibronectin + (%)	Fetal Fibronectin – (%)
25	65	25
26–35	45	14
>35	25	7

Fetal fibronectin and cervical length assessed at 24 weeks of gestation. Cervical length assessed by transvaginal ultrasonography.

Data from: Iams JD, Goldenberg RL, Mercer BM, Moawad A, Thom E, Meis PJ, et al. The Preterm Prediction Study: recurrence risk of spontaneous preterm birth. National Institute of Child Health and Human Development Maternal-Fetal Medicine Units Network. Am J Obstet Gynecol 1998;178:1035–1040

Summary of Recommendations

The following recommendation is based on good and consistent scientific evidence (Level A):

▶ There are no current data to support the use of salivary estriol, HUAM, or BV screening as strategies to identify or prevent preterm birth.

The following recommendations are based on limited or inconsistent scientific evidence (Level B):

▶ Screening for risk of preterm labor by means other than historic risk factors is not beneficial in the general obstetric population.

▶ Ultrasonography to determine cervical length, fFN testing, or a combination of both may be useful in determining women at high risk for preterm labor. However, their clinical usefulness may rest primarily with their negative predictive value given the lack of proven treatment options to prevent preterm birth.

▶ Fetal fibronectin testing may be useful in women with symptoms of preterm labor to identify those with negative values and a reduced risk of preterm birth, thereby avoiding unnecessary intervention.

References

1. Murphy SL. Deaths: final data for 1998. Natl Vital Stat Rep 2000:48(11):1–108 (Level III)

2. Tucker JM, Goldenberg RL, Davis RO, Copper RL, Winkler CL, Hauth JC. Etiologies of preterm birth in an indigent population: is prevention a logical expectation? Obstet Gynecol 1991;77:343–347 (Level II-3)

3. Wood NS, Marlow N, Costeloe K, Gibson AT, Wilkinson AR. Neurologic and developmental disability after extremely preterm birth. EPICure Study Group. N Engl J Med 2000;343:378–384 (Level II-2)

4. Preterm singleton births—United States, 1989–1996. MMWR Morb Mortal Wkly Rep 1999;48:185–189 (Level III)

5. Iams JD. Preterm birth. In: Gabbe SG, Niebyl JR, Simpson JL, eds. Obstetrics: normal and problem pregnancies. 3rd ed. New York: Churchill Livingstone, 1996:743–820 (Level III)

6. Ventura SJ, Martin JA, Curtin SC, Menacker F, Hamilton BE. Births: final data for 1999. Nat Vital Stat Rep 2001;49(1):1–100 (Level III)

7. Goldenberg RL, Iams JD, Mercer BM, Meis PJ, Moawad AH, Copper RL, et al. The preterm prediction study: the value of new vs. standard risk factors in predicting early

8. and all spontaneous preterm births. NICHD MFMU Network. Am J Public Health 1998;88:233–238 (Level III)

8. Norwitz ER, Robinson JN, Challis JR. The control of labor. N Engl J Med 1999;341:660–666 (Level III)

9. Lockwood CJ. Stress-associated preterm delivery: the role of corticotropin-releasing hormone. Am J Obstet Gynecol 1999;180:S264–S266 (Level III)

10. Goldenberg RL, Hauth JC, Andrews WW. Intrauterine infection and preterm delivery. N Engl J Med 2000; 342:1500–1507 (Level III)

11. Effect of corticosteroids for fetal maturation on perinatal outcomes. NIH Consens Statement 1994;12(2):1–24 (Level III)

12. Antenatal corticosteroids revisited: repeat courses. NIH Consens Statement 2000;17(2):1–10 (Level III)

13. Agency for Healthcare Research and Quality. Management of preterm labor. Evidence Report/Technology Assessment no. 18. Rockville, Maryland: AHRQ, 2000. AHRQ publication no. 00-E021 (Level III)

14. Gyetvai K, Hannah ME, Hodnett ED, Ohlsson A. Any tocolytic drug for preterm labour (Protocol for a Cochrane Review). In: The Cochrane Library, Issue 2, 2001. Oxford: Update Software (Level III)

15. Lumley J. The epidemiology of preterm birth. Baillieres Clin Obstet Gynaecol 1993;7:477–498 (Level III)

16. Wen SW, Goldenberg RL, Cutter GR, Hoffman HJ, Cliver SP. Intrauterine growth retardation and preterm delivery: perinatal risk factors in an indigent population. Am J Obstet Gynecol 1990;162:213–218 (Level II-2)

17. Ekwo EE, Gosselink CA, Moawad A. Unfavorable outcome in penultimate pregnancy and premature rupture of membranes in successive pregnancy. Obstet Gynecol 1992;80:166–172 (Level II-2)

18. Strobino B, Pantel-Silverman J. Gestational vaginal bleeding and pregnancy outcome. Am J Epidemiol 1989;129:806–815 (Level II-2)

19. Luke B, Mamelle N, Keith L, Munoz F, Minogue J, Papiernik E, et al. The association between occupational factors and preterm birth: a United States nurses' study. Research Committee of the Association of Women's Health, Obstetric and Neonatal Nurses. Am J Obstet Gynecol 1995;173:849–862 (Level II-2)

20. Cnattingius S, Granath F, Petersson G, Harlow BL. The influence of gestational age and smoking habits on the risk of subsequent preterm deliveries. N Eng J Med 1999;341:943–948 (Level II-2)

21. Walsh RA. Effects of maternal smoking on adverse pregnancy outcomes: examination of the criteria of causation. Hum Biol 1994;66:1059–1092 (Level II-3)

22. Creasy RK, Gumer BA, Liggins GC. System for predicting spontaneous preterm birth. Obstet Gynecol 1980;55:692–695 (Level II-3)

23. Main DM, Gabbe SG, Richardson D, Strong S. Can preterm deliveries be prevented? Am J Obstet Gynecol 1985;151:892–898 (Level I)

24. Mercer BM, Goldenberg RL, Dao A, Moawad AH, Iams JD, Meis PJ, et al. The preterm prediction study: a clinical

risk assessment system. Am J Obstet Gynecol 1996;174:1885–1893; discussion 1893–1895 (Level II-2)

25. Nageotte MP, Dorchester W, Porto M, Keegan KA Jr, Freeman RK. Quantitation of uterine activity preceding preterm, term and postterm labor. Am J Obstet Gynecol 1988;158:1254–1259 (Level II-2)

26. Goodwin TM. A role for estriol in human labor, term and preterm. Am J Obstet Gynecol 1999;180:S208–S213 (Level III)

27. McGregor JA, Hastings C, Roberts T, Barrett J. Diurnal variation in salivary estriol level during pregnancy: a pilot study. Am J Obstet Gynecol 1999;180:S223–S225 (Level III)

28. Hendershott CM, Dullien V, Goodwin TM. Serial betamethasone administration: effect on maternal salivary estriol levels. Am J Obstet Gynecol 1999;180:S219–S222 (Level II-2)

29. Hallen A, Pahlson C, Forsum U. Bacterial vaginosis in women attending STD clinic: diagnostic criteria and prevalence of mobiluncus spp. Genitourin Med 1987;63:386–389 (Level III)

30. Eschenbach DA. History and review of bacterial vaginosis. Am J Obstet Gynecol 1993;169:441–445 (Level III)

31. Royce RA, Jackson TP, Thorp JM Jr, Hillier SL, Rabe LK, Pastore LM, et al. Race/ethnicity, vaginal flora patterns, and pH during pregnancy. Sex Transm Dis 1999;26:96–102 (Level II-2)

32. Meis PJ, Goldenberg RL, Mercer B, Moawad A, Das A, McNellis D, et al. The preterm prediction study: significance of vaginal infections. National Institute of Child Health and Human Development Maternal-Fetal Medicine Units Network. Am J Obstet Gynecol 1995;173:1231–1235 (Level II-2)

33. Hillier SL, Nugent RP, Eschenbach DA, Krohn MA, Gibbs RS, Martin DH, et al. Association between bacterial vaginosis and preterm delivery of a low-birth-weight infant. The Vaginal Infections and Prematurity Study Group. N Engl J Med 1995;333:1737–1742 (Level II-2)

34. Lockwood CJ, Senyei AE, Dische MR, Casal D, Shah KD, Thung SN, et al. Fetal fibronectin in cervical and vaginal secretions as a predictor of preterm delivery. N Engl J Med 1991;325:669–674 (Level II-2)

35. Feinberg RF, Kliman HJ, Lockwood CJ. Is oncofetal fibronectin a trophoblast glue for human implantation? Am J Pathol 1991;138:537–543 (Level II-2)

36. Lockwood CJ, Wein R, Lapinski R, Casal D, Berkowitz G, Alvarez M, et al. The presence of cervical and vaginal fetal fibronectin predicts preterm delivery in an inner-city obstetric population. Am J Obstet Gynecol 1993;169:798–804 (Level II-2)

37. Goldenberg RL, Thom E, Moawad AH, Johnson F, Roberts J, Caritis SN. The preterm prediction study: fetal fibronectin, bacterial vaginosis, and peripartum infection. NICHD Maternal Fetal Medicine Units Network. Obstet Gynecol 1996;87:656–660 (Level II-2)

38. Sonek JD, Iams JD, Blumenfeld M, Johnson F, Landon M, Gabbe S. Measurement of cervical length in preg-nancy: comparison between vaginal ultrasonography and digital examination. Obstet Gynecol 1990;76:172–175 (Level II-2)

39. Iams JD, Goldenberg RL, Meis PJ, Mercer BM, Moawad A, Das A, et al. The length of the cervix and the risk of spontaneous premature delivery. National Institute of Child Health and Human Development Maternal Fetal Medicine Unit Network. N Engl J Med 1996;334:567–572 (Level II-2)

40. Brown HL, Britton KA, Brizendine EJ, Hiett AK, Ingram D, Turnquest MA, et al. A randomized comparison of home uterine activity monitoring in the outpatient management of women treated for preterm labor. Am J Obstet Gynecol 1999;180:798–805 (Level I)

41. Dyson DC, Crites YM, Ray DA, Armstrong MA. Prevention of preterm birth in high-risk patients: the role of education and provider contact versus home uterine monitoring. Am J Obstet Gynecol 1991;164:756–762 (Level I)

42. Dyson DC, Danbe KH, Bamber JA, Crites YM, Rield DR, Maier JA, et al. Monitoring women at risk for preterm labor. N Engl J Med 1998;338:15–19 (Level I)

43. Iams JD, Johnson FF, O'Shaugnessy RW, West LC. A prospective random trial of home uterine monitoring in pregnancies at increased risk of preterm labor. Part II. Am J Obstet Gynecol 1987;157:638–643 (Level I)

44. Iams JD, Johnson FF, O'Shaughnessy RW. A prospective random trial of home uterine activity monitoring in pregnancies at increased risk of preterm labor. Am J Obstet Gynecol 1988;159:595–603 (Level I)

45. Blondel B, Breat G, Berthoux Y, Berland M, Melher B, Rudigoz RC, et al. Home uterine activity monitoring in France: a randomized controlled trial. Am J Obstet Gynecol 1992;167:424–429 (Level I)

46. Hill WC, Fleming AD, Martin RW, Hamer C, Knuppel RA, Lake MF, et al. Home uterine activity monitoring is associated with a reduction in preterm birth. Obstet Gynecol 1990;76:13S–18S (Level I)

47. Knuppel RA, Lake MF, Watson DL, Welch RA, Hill WC, Fleming AD, et al. Preventing preterm birth in twin gestation: home uterine activity monitoring and perinatal nursing support. Obstet Gynecol 1990;76:24S–27S (Level II-1)

48. Morrison JC, Martin JN Jr, Martin RW, Gookin KS, Wiser WL. Prevention of preterm birth by ambulatory assessment of uterine activity: a randomized study. Am J Obstet Gynecol 1987;156:536–543 (Level I)

49. Mou SM, Sunderji SG, Gall S, How H, Patel V, Gray M, et al. Multicenter randomized clinical trial of home uterine activity monitoring for the detection of preterm labor. Am J Obstet Gynecol 1991;165:858–866 (Level I)

50. Nagey DA, Bailey-Jones C, Herman AA. Randomized comparison of home uterine activity monitoring and routine care in patients discharged after treatment for preterm labor. Obstet Gynecol 1993;82:319–323 (Level II-1)

51. Wapner RJ, Cotton DB, Artal R, Librizzi RJ, Ross MG. A randomized multicenter trial assessing a home uterine activity monitoring device used in the absence of daily nursing contact. Am J Obstet Gynecol 1995;172:1026–1034 (Level I)

52. Watson DL, Welch RA, Mariona FG, Lake MF, Knuppel RA, Martin RW, et al. Management of preterm labor patients at home: does daily uterine activity monitoring

and nursing support make a difference? Obstet Gynecol 1990;76:32S–35S (Level I)

53. Grimes DA, Schulz KF. Randomized controlled trials of home uterine activity monitoring: a review and critique. Obstet Gynecol 1992;79:137–142 (Level III)

54. Sachs BP, Hellerstein S, Freeman R, Frigoletto F, Hauth JC. Home monitoring of uterine activity. Does it prevent prematurity? N Engl J Med 1991;325:1374–1377 (Level III)

55. Keirse MJ, Van Hoven M. Reanalysis of a multireported trial on home uterine activity monitoring. Birth 1993;20:117–122 (Level III)

56. Home uterine activity monitoring for preterm labor. Review article. US Preventive Services Task Force. JAMA 1993;270:371–376 (Level III)

57. A multicenter randomized controlled trial of home uterine monitoring: active versus sham device. The Collaborative Home Uterine Monitoring Study Group (CHUMS). Am J Obstet Gynecol 1995;173:1120–1127 (Level I)

58. Colton T, Kayne HL, Zhang Y, Heeren T. A metaanalysis of home uterine activity monitoring. Am J Obstet Gynecol 1995;173:1499–1505 (Meta-analysis)

59. McGregor JA, Jackson GM, Lachelin GC, Goodwin TM, Artal R, Hastings C, et al. Salivary estriol as risk assessment for preterm labor: a prospective trial. Am J Obstet Gynecol 1995;173:1337–1342 (Level II-2)

60. Heine RP, McGregor JA, Dullien VK. Accuracy of salivary estriol testing compared to traditional risk factor assessment in predicting preterm birth. Am J Obstet Gynecol 1999;180:S214–S218 (Level II-2)

61. Morales WJ, Schorr S, Albritton J. Effect of metronidazole in patients with preterm birth in preceding pregnancy and bacterial vaginosis: a placebo-controlled, double-blind study. Am J Obstet Gynecol 1994;171:345–347; discussion 348–349 (Level I)

62. Hauth JC, Goldenberg RL, Andrews WW, DuBard MB, Copper RL. Reduced incidence of preterm delivery with metronidazole and erythromycin in women with bacterial vaginosis. N Engl J Med 1995;333:1732–1736 (Level I)

63. Joesoef MR, Schmid GP, Hillier SL. Bacterial vaginosis: review of treatment options and potential clinical indications for therapy. Clin Infect Dis 1999;28:S57–S65 (Level III)

64. Carey JC, Klebanoff MA, Hauth JC, Hillier SL, Thom EA, Ernest JM, et al. Metronidazole to prevent preterm delivery in pregnant women with asymptomatic bacterial vaginosis. National Institute of Child Health and Human Development Network of Maternal-Fetal Medicine Units. N Engl J Med 2000;342:534–540 (Level I)

65. Brocklehurst P, Hannah M, McDonald H. Interventions for treating bacterial vaginosis in pregnancy (Cochrane Review). In: The Cochrane Library, Issue 2, 2001. Oxford: Update Software (Meta-analysis)

66. Berg AO. Screening for bacterial vaginosis in pregnancy. Recommendations and rationale. Am J Prev Med 2001;20(3 Suppl):59–61 (Level III)

67. Goldenberg RL, Andrews WW, Guerrant RL, Newman M, Mercer B, Iams J, et al. The preterm prediction study: cer-

vical lactoferin concentration, other markers of lower genital tract infection, and preterm birth. National Institute of Child Health and Human Development Maternal-Fetal Medicine Units Network. Am J Obstet Gynecol 2000;182:631–635 (Level II-2)

68. Leitich H, Egarter C, Kaider A, Hohlagschwandtner M, Berghammer P, Hussein P. Cervicovaginal fetal fibronectin as a marker for preterm delivery: a meta-analysis. Am J Obstet Gynecol 1999;180:1169–1176 (Meta-analysis)

69. Goldenberg RL, Iams JD, Das A, Mercer BM, Meis PJ, Moawad AH, et al. The Preterm Prediction Study: sequential cervical length and fetal fibronectin testing for the prediction of spontaneous preterm birth. National Institute of Child Health and Human Development Maternal-Fetal Medicine Network. Am J Obstet Gynecol 2000;182:636–643 (Level III)

70. Inglis SR, Jeremias J, Kuno K, Lescale K, Peeper Q, Chervenak FA, et al. Detection of tumor necrosis factor-alpha, interleukin-6, and fetal fibronectin in the lower genital tract during pregnancy: relation to outcome. Am J Obstet Gynecol 1994;171:5–10 (Level II-3)

71. Malak TM, Sizmur F, Bell SC, Taylor DJ. Fetal fibronectin in cervicovaginal secretions as a predictor of preterm birth. Br J Obstet Gynaecol 1996;103:648–653 (Level II-3)

72. Revah A, Hannah ME, Sue-A-Quan AK. Fetal fibronectin as a predictor of preterm birth: an overview. Am J Perinatol 1998;15:613–621 (Level III)

73. Benattar C, Taieb J, Fernandez H, Lindendaum A, Frydman R, Ville Y. Rapid fetal fibronectin swab-test in preterm labor patients treated by betamimetics. Eur J Obstet Gynecol Reprod Biol 1997;72:131–135 (Level II-3)

74. Peaceman AM, Andrews WW, Thorp JM, Cliver SP, Lukes A, Iams JD, et al. Fetal fibronectin as a predictor of preterm birth in patients with symptoms: a multicenter trial. Am J Obstet Gynecol 1997;177:13–18 (Level II-2)

75. Crane JM, Van den Hof M, Armson BA, Liston R. Transvaginal ultrasound in the prediction of preterm delivery: singleton and twin gestations. Obstet Gynecol 1997;90:357–363 (Level II-2)

76. Berghella V, Tolosa JE, Kuhlman K, Weiner S, Bolognese RJ, Wapner RJ. Cervical ultrasonography compared with manual examination as a predictor of preterm delivery. Am J Obstet Gynecol 1997;177:723–730 (Level II-2)

77. Watson WJ, Stevens D, Welter S, Day D. Observations on the sonographic measurement of cervical length and the risk of preterm birth. J Matern Fetal Med 1999;8:17–19 (Level II-2)

78. Leitich H, Brunbauer M, Kaider A, Egarter C, Husslein P. Cervical length and dilatation of the internal cervical os detected by vaginal ultrasonography as markers for preterm delivery: a systematic review. Am J Obstet Gynecol 1999;181:1465–1472 (Level III)

79. Ultrasound cervical assessment in predicting preterm birth. SOGC Clinical Practice Guidelines 102. J SOGC 2001;23:418–421 (Level III)

80. Iams JD, Goldenberg RL, Mercer BM, Moawad A, Thom E, Meis PJ, et al. The Preterm Prediction Study: recurrence

risk of spontaneous preterm birth. National Institute of Child Health and Human Development Maternal-Fetal Medicine Units Network. Am J Obstet Gynecol 1998;178:1035–1040 (Level II-2)

The MEDLINE database, the Cochrane Library, and ACOG's own internal resources and documents were used to conduct a literature search to locate relevant articles published between January 1985 and May 2000. The search was restricted to articles published in the English language. Priority was given to articles reporting results of original research, although review articles and commentaries also were consulted. Abstracts of research presented at symposia and scientific conferences were not considered adequate for inclusion in this document. Guidelines published by organizations or institutions such as the National Institutes of Health and the American College of Obstetricians and Gynecologists were reviewed, and additional studies were located by reviewing bibliographies of identified articles. When reliable research was not available, expert opinions from obstetrician–gynecologists were used.

Studies were reviewed and evaluated for quality according to the method outlined by the U.S. Preventive Services Task Force:

I   Evidence obtained from at least one properly designed randomized controlled trial.

II-1 Evidence obtained from well-designed controlled trials without randomization.

II-2 Evidence obtained from well-designed cohort or case–control analytic studies, preferably from more than one center or research group.

II-3 Evidence obtained from multiple time series with or without the intervention. Dramatic results in uncontrolled experiments could also be regarded as this type of evidence.

III   Opinions of respected authorities, based on clinical experience, descriptive studies, or reports of expert committees.

Based on the highest level of evidence found in the data, recommendations are provided and graded according to the following categories:

Level A—Recommendations are based on good and consistent scientific evidence.

Level B—Recommendations are based on limited or inconsistent scientific evidence.

Level C—Recommendations are based primarily on consensus and expert opinion.

ISSN 1099-3630

The American College of Obstetricians and Gynecologists
409 12th Street, SW, PO Box 96920
Washington, DC 20090-6920

12345/54321

Assessment of risk factors for preterm birth. ACOG Practice Bulletin No. 31. American College of Obstetricians and Gynecologists. Obstet Gynecol 2001;98:709–716

ACOG PRACTICE BULLETIN

CLINICAL MANAGEMENT GUIDELINES FOR
OBSTETRICIAN–GYNECOLOGISTS
NUMBER 29, JULY 2001

(Replaces Technical Bulletin Number 219, January 1996)

This Practice Bulletin was developed by the ACOG Committee on Practice Bulletins—Obstetrics with the assistance of Larry C. Gilstrap III, MD and Susan M. Ramin, MD. The information is designed to aid practitioners in making decisions about appropriate obstetric and gynecologic care. These guidelines should not be construed as dictating an exclusive course of treatment or procedure. Variations in practice may be warranted based on the needs of the individual patient, resources, and limitations unique to the institution or type of practice.

Chronic Hypertension in Pregnancy

Chronic hypertension occurs in up to 5% of pregnant women; rates vary according to the population studied and the criteria used for confirming the diagnosis (1, 2). This complication may result in significant maternal, fetal, and neonatal morbidity and mortality. There has been confusion over the terminology and criteria used to diagnose this complication, as well as the benefit and potential harm of treatment during pregnancy. The purpose of this document is to review the effects of chronic hypertension on pregnancy, to clarify the terminology and criteria used to define and diagnose it during pregnancy, and to review the available evidence for treatment options.

Background

Definition

According to the National High Blood Pressure Education Program Working Group on High Blood Pressure in Pregnancy, chronic hypertension is defined as hypertension present before the 20th week of pregnancy or hypertension present before pregnancy (3). The blood pressure (BP) criteria used to define hypertension are a systolic pressure of ≥140 mmHg, a diastolic pressure of ≥90 mmHg, or both (see the box). Chronic hypertension during pregnancy is most commonly classified as mild (BP >140/90 mmHg) or as severe (BP ≥180/110 mmHg) (4). The diagnosis is relatively easy to make in women taking antihypertensive medications before conception. However, the diagnosis can be difficult to establish or distinguish from preeclampsia when the woman presents with hypertension late in gestation. In this latter scenario, hypertension that persists longer than the postpartum period (12 weeks post delivery) is classified as chronic.

Hypertension should be documented on more than one occasion. According to the National High Blood Pressure Education Program Working

---

Criteria for Diagnosis of Chronic Hypertension in Pregnancy

- Mild: Systolic blood pressure ≥140 mmHg
           Diastolic blood pressure ≥90 mmHg
- Severe: Systolic blood pressure ≥180 mmHg
          Diastolic blood pressure ≥110 mmHg
- Use of antihypertensive medications before pregnancy
- Onset of hypertension before 20th week of gestation
- Persistence of hypertension beyond the usual postpartum period

---

Group on High Blood Pressure in Pregnancy, the diastolic blood pressure is that pressure at which the sound disappears (Korotkoff phase V) (3). In order to reduce inaccurate readings, an appropriate size cuff should be used (length 1.5 times upper arm circumference or a cuff with a bladder that encircles 80% or more of the arm). Pressure should be taken with the patient in an upright position, after a 10-minute or longer rest period. For patients in the hospital, the blood pressure can be taken with either the patient sitting up or in the left lateral recumbent position with the patient's arm at the level of the heart (5). The patient should not use tobacco or caffeine for 30 minutes preceding the measurement (6, 7). Although validated electronic devices can be used, a mercury sphygmomanometer is preferred (6, 7).

Chronic hypertension usually can be distinguished from preeclampsia because preeclampsia typically appears after 20 weeks of gestation in a woman who was normotensive before pregnancy. Moreover, preeclampsia resolves during the postpartum period. Additionally, preeclampsia is frequently associated with proteinuria and characteristic symptoms such as headache, scotomata, or epigastric pain. Women with preeclampsia also may have hemolysis, elevated liver enzymes, and low platelet count (HELLP syndrome). However, the development of superimposed preeclampsia in pregnant women with chronic hypertension is relatively common and is often difficult to diagnose. The acute onset of proteinuria and worsening hypertension in women with chronic hypertension is suggestive of superimposed preeclampsia.

An additional diagnostic complication may arise in women with chronic hypertension who begin prenatal care after 20 weeks of gestation. A physiologic decrease in blood pressure normally occurs early in the second trimester, and may be exaggerated in women with chronic hypertension. This decrease may lead to an erroneous assumption that the blood pressure is normal at this stage of gestation (3). By the third trimester, the blood pressure usually returns to its prepregnancy level (5).

Effects of Chronic Hypertension on Pregnancy

Chronic hypertension complicates pregnancy and is associated with several adverse outcomes, including premature birth, intrauterine growth restriction (IUGR), fetal demise, placental abruption, and cesarean delivery (4). The incidence of these potential adverse effects is related to the degree and duration of hypertension and to the association of other organ system involvement or damage. As many as one third of women with severe chronic hypertension may have a small-for-gestational-age (SGA) infant, and two thirds may have a preterm delivery (8). In a study of 211 pregnant women with mild chronic hypertension, the uncorrected perinatal mortality rate was 28 per 1,000 and was highest in the 21 pregnancies complicated by superimposed preeclampsia. The perinatal mortality rate was 5 per 1,000 in the 190 pregnancies not complicated by preeclampsia (9).

In another study, pregnancy outcomes were reviewed in 44 pregnant women with severe chronic hypertension in the first trimester (10). Slightly more than half developed superimposed preeclampsia; in this subgroup of patients, perinatal death and neonatal morbidity were significantly increased. Comparing women who developed superimposed preeclampsia with women who did not, the incidence of prematurity was 100% versus 38%, the incidence of SGA infants was 78% versus 15%, and the perinatal mortality rate was 48% versus 0%.

Other studies also have reported an increase in perinatal mortality of 2–4 times more than the general population (11–13). For example, a study of 337 pregnancies complicated by chronic hypertension reported a perinatal mortality rate of 45 per 1,000 compared with a rate of 12 per 1,000 in the general population (11).

A study of outcomes in 763 pregnant women with chronic hypertension indicated that women with baseline proteinuria (300 mg or greater of urinary protein in 24 hours at initial evaluation at 13–26 weeks of gestation) were at significant risk of preterm delivery (odds ratio [OR], 3.1; 95% confidence interval [CI], 1.8–5.3) and SGA infants (OR, 2.8; 95% CI, 1.6–5.0) independent of superimposed preeclampsia (14). The development of preeclampsia (defined as new-onset proteinuria) was significantly associated with perinatal death (OR, 2.3; 95% CI, 1.1–4.8). Preeclampsia also was associated with an increase in placental abruption (3% versus 1%). In a meta-analysis of seven case–control and six cohort studies, the risk of placental abruption was related to both cigarette smoking and chronic hypertension, as well as preeclampsia (15). A systematic review of the management of chronic hypertension during pregnancy revealed that chronic hypertension doubled the risk for placental abruption (OR, 2.1; 95% CI, 1.1, 3.9) and tripled the risk for perinatal mortality (OR, 3.4; 95% CI, 3.0, 3.7) (4, 16). Several of the studies included in this review also showed an association between chronic hypertension and preeclampsia (variously defined) and preterm, SGA, or low-birth-weight infants when compared with normotensive women or the general obstetric population. The risk of these complications was increased even in the absence of superimposed preeclampsia, although the absolute increased risk from mild hypertension could not be calculated from the available data (4).

Effects of Pregnancy on Hypertension

Several physiologic changes occur in pregnant women that can affect chronic hypertension. One of the most significant changes is the increase in blood volume, which may further burden an already stressed heart and, along with the decrease in colloid oncotic pressure, may lead to cardiac decompensation. Another important change is the physiologic decrease in blood pressure, which begins by the end of the first trimester and reaches its lowest level at 16–18 weeks of gestation (16). This change can mask either the course or the detection of chronic hypertension in early pregnancy (3). Besides superimposed preeclampsia or eclampsia, pregnancy complicated by chronic hypertension (especially if severe) may be associated with worsening or malignant hypertension, central nervous system hemorrhage, cardiac decompensation, and renal deterioration or failure.

Clinical Considerations and Recommendations

▶ *In the initial evaluation of a pregnant woman with hypertension, which clinical tests are useful?*

The age of onset, results of previous evaluation, severity and duration of hypertension, and physical examination are important determinants of which clinical tests may be useful. Ideally, a woman with chronic hypertension should be evaluated before conception to ascertain potentially reversible causes and possible end-organ involvement (eg, heart or kidney). Women who have had hypertension for several years are more likely to have cardiomegaly, ischemic heart disease, renal involvement, and retinopathy (3). Thus, these women are more likely to benefit from various specialized clinical tests at the initial evaluation during pregnancy or preconceptionally. Tests may include electrocardiography, echocardiography, ophthalmologic examination, and renal ultrasonography (7). The information obtained from these tests may prove useful in assessing risks of hypertension during pregnancy, as well as providing information for prenatal counseling. Women with significant left ventricular hypertrophy secondary to

hypertension may experience cardiac decompensation and heart failure as pregnancy progresses.

Women with significant renal disease (serum creatinine >1.4 mg/dL) may experience deterioration of renal function, although it may be difficult to separate the effects of pregnancy from the disease process (3, 17, 18). Many women with the diagnosis of peripartum cardiomyopathy are found to have underlying causes, chronic hypertension being one of the most common (19, 20). However, most pregnant women with mild chronic hypertension have uneventful pregnancies with no end-organ involvement.

▶ *Are other adjunctive tests useful in evaluating a pregnant woman with hypertension?*

Many women with chronic hypertension are under the care of a primary care physician and already have been evaluated for causes of secondary hypertension, such as pheochromocytoma or Cushing's disease. However, young women in whom hypertension has been diagnosed for the first time in early pregnancy, especially those with severe hypertension (systolic pressure ≥180 mmHg or diastolic pressure ≥110 mmHg), are more likely to have secondary hypertension and to benefit from further evaluation for potentially reversible causes (3). Women with paroxysmal hypertension, frequent "hypertensive crisis," seizure disorders, or anxiety attacks should be evaluated for pheochromocytoma with measurements of 24-hour urine vanillylmandelic acid, metanephrines, or unconjugated catecholamines (21). Magnetic resonance imaging after the first trimester or computed tomography also may be useful for adrenal tumor localization (19).

Cushing's syndrome is rare in pregnancy and is difficult to diagnose because of pregnancy related changes in steroids (22). Fortunately, this condition is diagnosed in most women before pregnancy. Primary aldosteronism also is rare in pregnancy. Women with this disorder may present with severe hypertension and hypokalemia. Imaging studies may be helpful in demonstrating an adrenal adenoma.

A young woman (younger than 30 years) with severe hypertension (especially with no family history) who has not been previously evaluated may benefit from Doppler flow studies or magnetic resonance angiography to detect renal artery stenosis (7). Renal artery stenosis appears to be more prevalent in patients with type-2 diabetes and coexistent hypertension (23, 24). Negative results from renal ultrasonography do not rule out renal artery stenosis.

▶ *Are laboratory tests useful in evaluating a pregnant woman with essential hypertension?*

In pregnant women with known essential hypertension (primary hypertension or hypertension not secondary to underlying renal or adrenal disease), baseline laboratory evaluations that may prove clinically useful include tests of renal function such as serum creatinine, blood urea nitrogen, and 24-hour urine evaluation for total protein and creatinine clearance (1, 7, 25). This initial laboratory assessment is important in identifying women with underlying renal disease because this complication may adversely affect pregnancy outcome (26). The subsequent development of proteinuria in a woman with essential hypertension also may be helpful in identifying the development of superimposed preeclampsia.

As pregnancy progresses, other laboratory tests—in addition to repeating those mentioned previously—may be clinically useful in evaluating worsening renal disease and in diagnosing superimposed preeclampsia. These include liver function tests, hemoglobin/hematocrit evaluation, and platelet count (27). Periodic measurement of urine protein may be useful in detecting worsening renal disease or the development of superimposed preeclampsia (28). It has been reported that the random protein-creatinine ratio may be useful for the quantitation of proteinuria during pregnancy. The correlation coefficient between this ratio and the 24-hour urine total protein was 0.94 (29). Investigators also reported high sensitivity and specificity between the protein/creatinine ratio from a single urine sample and proteinuria of 300 mg or greater in a 24-hour specimen (30).

Although an elevated serum uric acid level represents a useful confirmatory test for the diagnosis of preeclampsia, it has very poor predictive value among patients without preexisting hypertension. However, when the patient has chronic hypertension, the serum uric acid level may be of some value. One investigator has reported that a serum uric acid level of ≥ 5.5 mg/dL could identify women with an increased likelihood of having superimposed preeclampsia (31).

▶ *Who are candidates for treatment of chronic hypertension in pregnancy?*

Women with mild hypertension (140–179 mmHg systolic or 90–109 mmHg diastolic pressure) generally do well during pregnancy and do not, as a rule, require antihypertensive medication (3). There is, to date, no scientific evidence that antihypertensive therapy will improve perinatal outcome (25, 32–34). In a review of 263 women with mild hypertension randomized to methyldopa, labetalol, or no treatment at 6–13 weeks of gestation, treatment with antihypertensive medications did not decrease the incidence of complications such as IUGR, superimposed preeclampsia, placental abruption, or perinatal mortality (25).

There also is a paucity of scientific data regarding the most appropriate management of women with well-con-

trolled or mild hypertension already taking antihypertensive medications at the time of pregnancy. Although such therapy may offer long-term benefits to the mother, such therapy is of unproven short-term benefit and could interfere with uteroplacental blood flow and fetal growth (3, 35). In one review of 298 pregnant women in whom antihypertensive medications were stopped or whose dosage was reduced, there was no difference in the incidence of preeclampsia, placental abruption, or perinatal death compared with untreated groups (11). In a meta-analysis of 623 women with mild chronic hypertension from 7 trials comparing antihypertensive treatment to no treatment, treatment was associated with a decrease in the incidence of severe hypertension but did not improve perinatal outcomes (36). In a follow-up meta-analysis that included these 7 trials of pregnant women with chronic hypertension and 38 trials of women with late-onset hypertension receiving therapy versus no therapy, there was an increase in the frequency of SGA infants associated with treatment-induced reduction in mean arterial pressure (35).

Thus, the data are inconclusive with regard to both the benefits and potential adverse fetal effects of treatment of mild chronic hypertension during pregnancy. It would seem reasonable not to start antihypertensive therapy in women with mild hypertension who become pregnant unless they have other complicating factors (eg, cardiovascular or renal disease) and to either stop or reduce medication in women who are already taking antihypertensive therapy. As suggested by the National High Blood Pressure Education Program Working Group on High Blood Pressure in Pregnancy, therapy could be increased or reinstituted for women with blood pressures exceeding 150–160 mmHg systolic or 100–110 mmHg diastolic (3). In women with severe chronic hypertension (systolic pressure ≥ 180 mmHg or diastolic pressure ≥ 110 mmHg), antihypertensive therapy should be initiated or continued (10).

In addition, a systematic review of management of chronic hypertension during pregnancy concluded that "the evidence base regarding pharmacologic management of chronic hypertension during pregnancy is too small to either prove or disprove moderate to large benefits (>20 percent improvements) of antihypertensive therapy" (16). The report further concluded that the efficacy of antihypertensive therapy for chronic hypertension in pregnant women was still uncertain. In this latter systematic review, the authors also were unable to identify trials that compared nonpharmacologic interventions with antihypertensive agents or with no interventions for chronic hypertension.

▶ *What medications are most often prescribed for the treatment of chronic hypertension in pregnancy?*

Although there are numerous antihypertensive agents that have been used for the treatment of chronic hypertension during pregnancy, methyldopa has been commonly used. It is preferred by most practitioners, and it appears to be relatively safe (3, 16, 37, 38). Methyldopa appears to have limited effects on uteroplacental blood flow (3, 32, 33, 38).

Labetalol, a combined alpha- and beta-blocker, also can be used during pregnancy as an alternative to methyldopa. In one study on the treatment of chronic hypertension with labetalol versus methyldopa, the authors reported no differences in outcomes between the two medications (25).

In a meta-analysis of beta-receptor blockers prescribed for pregnancies complicated by hypertension, there was an increase in SGA infants born to those women who took oral beta-blockers for mild hypertension (OR, 2.46; 95% CI, 1.02, 5.92) (39). Calcium-channel blockers or antagonists also have been used with limited experience (1, 3). In one randomized study that compared nifedipine (n=145) versus expectant management (n=138) for mild hypertension in pregnancy, there was no benefit to pregnancy outcome but also no increase in adverse effects (34).

Diuretics also have been used to treat chronic hypertension, but there has been concern regarding the potential effect of these medications on normal blood volume expansion associated with pregnancy. In one study of 20 women with mild hypertension, diuretics prevented normal expansion of the blood volume but did not adversely affect perinatal outcome (40). Moreover, a meta-analysis of 9 trials involving diuretics during pregnancy reported no increase in adverse perinatal effects (41). The National High Blood Pressure Education Program Working Group on High Blood Pressure in Pregnancy concluded, "If diuretics are indicated, they are safe and efficacious agents that can markedly potentiate the response to other antihypertensive agents and are not contraindicated in pregnancy except in settings in which uteroplacental perfusion is already reduced (preeclampsia and IUGR)" (3).

▶ *Are certain medications used to treat chronic hypertension contraindicated during pregnancy?*

Angiotensin–converting enzyme (ACE) inhibitors are contraindicated during the second and third trimesters of pregnancy. Although the data regarding their use during pregnancy are limited to captopril, enalapril, and lisino-pril, the teratogenic risk appears to be similar for the entire drug class. These ACE inhibitors have been associated with severely underdeveloped calvarial bone, renal failure, oligohydramnios, anuria, renal dysgenesis, pulmonary hypoplasia, IUGR, fetal death, neonatal renal failure, and neonatal death (42–46). Fetal risks with ACE inhibitors depend on timing and dose. For example, the use of ACE inhibitors during the first trimester (before renal tubular function begins) has not been associated with an increase in birth defects (47, 48).

▶ *Is there a role for fetal surveillance in pregnancies complicated by hypertension?*

There is no consensus as to the most appropriate fetal surveillance test(s) or the interval and timing of testing in women with chronic hypertension. Thus, such testing should be individualized and based on clinical judgment and on severity of disease. A recent systematic review concluded that there are no conclusive data to address either the benefits or the harms of various monitoring strategies for pregnant women with chronic hypertension (16). However, other studies have indicated that most of the increased morbidity associated with this condition is secondary to superimposed preeclampsia or IUGR (3). Thus, these investigators recommend that baseline ultrasonography be obtained at 18–20 weeks of gestation and that ultrasonography should be repeated at 28–32 weeks of gestation and monthly thereafter until delivery to monitor fetal growth. If growth restriction is detected or suspected, fetal status should be monitored frequently with nonstress testing or biophysical profile testing (3). If growth restriction is not present and superimposed preeclampsia is excluded, these tests are not indicated (3).

▶ *Should patients with chronic hypertension be delivered before term?*

Pregnant women with uncomplicated chronic hypertension of a mild degree generally can be delivered vaginally at term (25); most have good maternal and neonatal outcomes (3). Cesarean delivery should be reserved for other obstetric indications. Women with mild hypertension during pregnancy and a prior adverse pregnancy outcome (eg, stillbirth) may be candidates for earlier delivery after documentation of fetal lung maturity (as long as fetal status is reassuring). Women with severe chronic hypertension during pregnancy most often either deliver prematurely or have to be delivered prematurely for fetal or maternal indications (10).

There are no randomized clinical trials that specifically address the timing of delivery in women with chronic hypertension and superimposed preeclampsia. However, the combination of chronic hypertension and superimposed preeclampsia represents a complicated situation, and the clinician should consider consultation with someone who has expertise in such clinical matters. Delivery should be considered in all women with superimposed severe preeclampsia at or beyond 28 weeks of gestation and in women with mild superimposed preeclampsia at or beyond 37 weeks of gestation (49). Women with superimposed severe preeclampsia in whom it is elected to continue the pregnancy should be monitored in a center with maternal and neonatal intensive care capability (49). In women with superimposed severe preeclampsia and the HELLP syndrome (a form of severe preeclampsia) delivery should be considered, even remote from term.

▶ *Are there intrapartum concerns unique to pregnant women with chronic hypertension?*

The majority of pregnant women with chronic hypertension have uncomplicated mild hypertension and can be managed the same as normal, nonhypertensive women during the intrapartum period. In contrast, women with severe hypertension or hypertension that is complicated by cardiovascular or renal disease may present special problems during the intrapartum period. Women with severe hypertension may require antihypertensive medications for acute elevation of blood pressure. Although no well-designed studies specifically address the treatment of severe chronic hypertension during the intrapartum period, it is generally recommended that antihypertensive medications be given to women with preeclampsia for systolic blood pressure of >160 mmHg or diastolic blood pressure of 105–110 mmHg or greater (3).

Women with chronic hypertension complicated by significant cardiovascular or renal disease require special attention to fluid load and urine output because they may be susceptible to fluid overload with resultant pulmonary edema. There are insufficient data to address the benefits and potential harm of central invasive hemodynamic monitoring in women with pregnancy related hypertensive disorders (3, 50).

There are limited data to address the issue of analgesia or anesthesia in pregnant women with chronic hypertension. In one study of 327 women with severe hypertension in labor (158 of whom had chronic hypertension), there was no increase in maternal pulmonary edema, renal failure, or cesarean delivery in women with an epidural (n=209) or without an epidural (n=118). However, there was a higher cesarean delivery rate in the subgroup of women with chronic hypertension who received an epidural (51). There also were no significant differences in neonatal outcomes between the two groups. Mild hypertension was not addressed in this cohort. The authors

concluded that the data regarding safety of epidural anesthesia in women with severe hypertension are limited by both the heterogeneity of diagnoses and the uncontrolled nature of the study. It would seem reasonable to conclude that if regional anesthetic techniques are used in women with severe hypertension, clinicians with specialized training in obstetric anesthesia should be available.

General anesthesia may pose a risk in pregnant women with severe hypertension or superimposed preeclampsia. Intubation and extubation may be associated with acute and significant elevations in blood pressure and an agent such as labetalol usually is given acutely to minimize this effect (3). Ketamine, because of its association with hypertension, is not considered first line therapy for the induction of general anesthesia (52).

Magnesium sulfate should be used for women with superimposed severe preeclampsia to prevent seizures. However, its benefit in women with mild preeclampsia is unclear (3).

▶ *How is chronic hypertension distinguished from preeclampsia when the woman presents late in pregnancy?*

It is often difficult, if not impossible, to distinguish worsening chronic hypertension from superimposed severe preeclampsia, especially when the patient presents late in pregnancy. In the woman with chronic hypertension and renal disease, it may not be possible to distinguish between the two entities. If the same woman has only hypertension without proteinuria and no symptoms of preeclampsia, such as headache, epigastric pain, or scotomata, the diagnosis may be more difficult. However, the vast majority of young, nulliparous women presenting with hypertension for the first time during late pregnancy will have preeclampsia. In addition to testing for proteinuria, other tests that may be helpful include hemoglobin and hematocrit evaluation, platelet count, and liver function tests. These latter tests are useful in the diagnosis of the HELLP syndrome. Oliguria and an elevated hemoglobin/hematocrit level usually indicate hemoconcentration—more indicative of preeclampsia. Serum creatinine levels also may be elevated in women with preeclampsia.

Summary of Recommendations

The following recommendation is based on good and consistent scientific evidence (Level A):

▶ Angiotensin-converting enzyme inhibitors are contraindicated during pregnancy and are associated with fetal and neonatal renal failure and death.

The following recommendations are based on limited or inconsistent scientific evidence (Level B):

▶ Antihypertensive therapy should be used for pregnant women with severe hypertension for maternal benefit.

▶ Methyldopa and labetalol are appropriate first-line antihypertensive therapies.

▶ Treatment of women with uncomplicated mild chronic hypertension is not beneficial because it does not improve perinatal outcome.

▶ The beta-blocker atenolol may be associated with growth restriction and is not recommended for use in pregnancy.

The following recommendations are based primarily on consensus and expert opinion (Level C):

▶ Women with chronic hypertension should be evaluated for potentially reversible etiologies, preferably prior to pregnancy.

▶ Women with long-standing hypertension should be evaluated for end-organ disease, including cardiomegaly, renal insufficiency, and retinopathy, preferably prior to pregnancy.

▶ When chronic hypertension is complicated by IUGR or preeclampsia, fetal surveillance is warranted.

References

1. Haddad B, Sibai BM. Chronic hypertension in pregnancy. Ann Med 1999;31:246–252 (Level III)

2. National High Blood Pressure Education Program Working Group Report on High Blood Pressure in Pregnancy. Am J Obstet Gynecol 1990;163:1691–1712 (Level III)

3. Report of the National High Blood Pressure Education Program Working Group on High Blood Pressure in Pregnancy. Am J Obstet Gynecol 2000;183:S1–S22 (Level III)

4. Ferrer RL, Sibai BM, Mulrow CD, Chiquette E, Stevens KR, Cornell J. Management of mild chronic hypertension during pregnancy: a review. Obstet Gynecol 2000;96:849–860 (Level III)

5. Garovic VD. Hypertension in pregnancy: diagnosis and treatment. Mayo Clin Proc 2000;75:1071–1076 (Level III)

6. Helewa MF, Burrows RF, Smith J, Williams K, Brain P, Rabkin SW. Report of the Canadian Hypertension Society Consensus Conference: 1. Definitions, evaluation and classification of hypertensive disorders in pregnancy. CMAJ 1997;157:715–725 (Level III)

7. The sixth report of the Joint National Committee on prevention, detection, evaluation, and treatment of high blood pressure. Arch Intern Med 1997;157:2413–2446 [erratum in Arch Intern Med 1998;158:573] (Level III)

8. McCowan LM, Buist RG, North RA, Gamble G. Perinatal morbidity in chronic hypertension. Br J Obstet Gynaecol 1996;103:123–129 (Level II-2)

9. Sibai BM, Abdella TN, Anderson GD. Pregnancy outcome in 211 patients with mild chronic hypertension. Obstet Gynecol 1983;61:571–576 (Level II-3)

10. Sibai BM, Anderson GD. Pregnancy outcome of intensive therapy in severe hypertension in first trimester. Obstet Gynecol 1986;67:517–522 (Level II-2)

11. Rey E, Couturier A. The prognosis of pregnancy in women with chronic hypertension. Am J Obstet Gynecol 1994;171:410–416 (Level II-3)

12. Ananth CV, Savitz DA, Bowes WA Jr. Hypertensive disorders of pregnancy and stillbirth in North Carolina, 1988 to 1991. Acta Obstet Gynecol Scand 1995;74:788–793 (Level II-3)

13. Jain L. Effect of pregnancy-induced and chronic hypertension on pregnancy outcome. J Perinatol 1997;17:425–427 (Level II-3)

14. Sibai BM, Lindheimer M, Hauth J, Caritis S, VanDorsten P, Klebanoff M, et al. Risk factors for preeclampsia, abruptio placentae, and adverse neonatal outcomes among women with chronic hypertension. National Institute of Child Health and Human Development Network of Maternal-Fetal Medicine Units. N Engl J Med 1998;339:667–671 (Level I)

15. Ananth CV, Smulian JC, Vintzileos AM. Incidence of placental abruption in relation to cigarette smoking and hypertensive disorders during pregnancy: a meta-analysis of observational studies. Obstet Gynecol 1999;93:622–628 (Meta-analysis)

16. Agency for Healthcare Research and Quality. Manage-ment of chronic hypertension during pregnancy. Evidence Report/Technology Assessment no. 14. AHRQ Publication No. 00-E011. Rockville, Maryland: AHRQ, 2000 (Level III)

17. Cunningham FG, Cox SM, Harstad TW, Mason RA, Pritchard JA. Chronic renal disease and pregnancy outcome. Am J Obstet Gynecol 1990;163:453–459 (Level II-3)

18. Jones DC. Pregnancy complicated by chronic renal disease. Clin Perinatol 1997;24:483–496 (Level III)

19. Cunningham FG, Pritchard JA, Hankins GD, Anderson PL, Lucas MK, Armstrong KF. Peripartum heart failure: idiopathic cardiomyopathy or compounding cardiovascular events? Obstet Gynecol 1986;67:157–168 (Level III)

20. Mabie WC, Hackman BB, Sibai BM. Pulmonary edema associated with pregnancy: echocardiographic insights and implications for treatment. Obstet Gynecol 1993;81:227–234 (Level II-3)

21. Botchan A, Hauser R, Kupfermine M, Grisaru D, Peyser MR, Lessing JB. Pheochromocytoma in pregnancy: case report and review of the literature. Obstet Gynecol Surv 1995;50:321–327 (Level III)

22. Buescher MA, McClamrock HD, Adashi EY. Cushing syndrome in pregnancy. Obstet Gynecol 1992;79:130–137 (Level III)

23. Valabhji J, Robinson S, Poulter C, Robinson AC, Kong C, Henzen C, et al. Prevalence of renal artery stenosis in subjects with type 2 diabetes and coexistent hypertension. Diabetes Care 2000;23:539–543 (Level II-3)

24. Courreges JP, Bacha J, Aboud E, Pradier P. Prevalence of renal artery stenosis in type 2 diabetes. Diabetes Metab 2000;26 Suppl 4:90–96 (Level II-3)

25. Sibai BM, Mabie WC, Shamsa F, Villar MA, Anderson GD. A comparison of no medication versus methyldopa or labetalol in chronic hypertension during pregnancy. Am J Obstet Gynecol 1990;162:960–966; discussion 966–967 (Level I)

26. Katz AL, Davison JM, Hayslett JP, Singson E, Lindheimer MD. Pregnancy in women with kidney disease. Kidney Intl 1980;18:192–206 (Level II-3)

27. Weinstein L. Syndrome of hemolysis, elevated liver enzymes, and low platelet count: a severe consequence of hypertension in pregnancy. Am J Obstet Gynecol 1982: 142:159–167 (Level II-3)

28. Evans W, Lensmeyer JP, Kirby RS, Malnory ME, Broekhuizen FF. Two-hour urine collection for evaluating renal function correlates with 24-hour urine collection in pregnant patients. J Matern Fetal Med 2000;9:233–237 (Level II-3)

29. Robert M, Sepandj F, Liston RM, Dooley KC. Random protein-creatinine ratio for the quantitation of proteinuria in pregnancy. Obstet Gynecol 1997;90:893–895 (Level II-2)

30. Ramos JG, Martins-Costa SH, Mathias MM, Guerin YL, Barros EG. Urinary protein/creatinine ratio in hypertensive pregnant women. Hypertens Pregnancy 1999;18:209–218 (Level II-3)

31. Lim KH, Friedman SA, Ecker JL, Kao L, Kilpatrick SJ. The clinical utility of serum uric acid measurements in hypertensive diseases of pregnancy. Am J Obstet Gynecol 1998;178:1067–1071 (Level II-2)

32. Cunningham FG, MacDonald PC, Gant NF, Leveno KJ, Gilstrap LC III, Hankins GD, et al. Endocrine disorders. In: Williams obstetrics. 20th ed. Stamford, Connecticut: Appleton & Lange, 1997:1223–1238 (Level III)

33. Sibai BM. Treatment of hypertension in pregnant women. N Engl J Med 1996;335:257–265 (Level III)

34. Nifedipine versus expectant management in mild to moderate hypertension in pregnancy. Gruppo di Studio Ipertensione in Gravidanza. Br J Obstet Gynaecol 1998; 105:718–722 (Level I)

35. von Dadelszen P, Ornstein MP, Bull SB, Logan AG, Koren G, Magee LA. Fall in mean arterial pressure and fetal growth restriction in pregnancy hypertension: a meta-analysis. Lancet 2000;355:87–92 (Meta-analysis)

36. Magee LA, Ornstein MP, von Dadelszen P. Fortnightly review: management of hypertension in pregnancy. BMJ 1999;318:1332–1336 (Meta-analysis)

37. Ounsted M, Cockburn J, Moar VA, Redman CW. Maternal hypertension with superimposed pre-eclampsia: effects on child development at 7 1/2 years. Br J Obstet Gynaecol 1983;90:644–649 (Level II-2)

38. Montan S, Anandakumar C, Arulkumaran S, Ingemarsson I, Ratnam SS. Effects of methyldopa on uteroplacental and fetal hemodynamics in pregnancy-induced hypertension. Am J Obstet Gynecol 1993;168:152–156 (Level III)

39. Magee LA, Elran E, Bull SB, Logan A, Koren G. Risks and benefits of beta-receptor blockers for pregnancy hypertension: overview of the randomized trials. Eur J Obstet Gynecol Reprod Biol 2000;88:15–26 (Meta-analysis)

40. Sibai BM, Grossman RA, Grossman HG. Effects of diuretics on plasma volume in pregnancies with long-term hypertension. Am J Obstet Gynecol 1984;150:831–835 (Level II-1)

41. Collins R, Yusuf S, Peto R. Overview of randomized trials of diuretics in pregnancy. Br Med J (Clin Res Ed) 1985; 290:17–23 (Meta-analysis)

42. Barr M Jr, Cohen MM Jr. ACE inhibitor fetopathy and hypocalvaria: the kidney-skull connection. Teratology 1991;44:485–495 (Level III)

43. Hanssens M, Keirse MJ, Vankelecom F, Van Assche FA. Fetal and neonatal effects of treatment with angiotensin-converting enzyme inhibitors in pregnancy. Obstet Gynecol 1991;78:128–135 (Level III)

44. Briggs GG, Freeman RK, Yaffe SJ. Drugs in pregnancy and lactation: a reference guide to fetal and neonatal risk. 5th ed. Baltimore: Williams & Wilkins, 1998 (Level III)

45. Buttar HS. An overview of the influence of ACE inhibitors on fetal-placental circulation and perinatal development. Mol Cell Biochem 1997;176:61–71 (Level III)

46. Pryde PG, Sedman AB, Nugent CE, Barr M Jr. Angiotensin-converting enzyme inhibitor fetopathy. J Am Soc Nephrol 1993;3:1575–1582 (Level III)

47. Postmarketing surveillance for angiotensin-converting enzyme inhibitor use during the first trimester of pregnancy—United States, Canada, and Israel, 1987–1995. MMWR Morb Mortal Wkly Rep 1997;46:240–242 (Level III)

48. Bar J, Hod M, Merlob P. Angiotensin converting enzyme inhibitors use in the first trimester of pregnancy. Int J Risk Saf Med 1997;10:23–26 (Level III)

49. Sibai BM. Management of pre-eclampsia remote from term. Eur J Obstet Gynecol Reprod Biol 1991;42:S96–S101 (Level III)

50. Practice guidelines for obstetrical anesthesia: a report by the American Society of Anesthesiologists Task Force on Obstetrical Anesthesia. Anesthesiology 1999;90:600–611 (Level III)

51. Hogg B, Hauth JC, Caritis SN, Sibai BM, Lindheimer M, Van Dorsten JP, et al. Safety of labor epidural anesthesia for women with severe hypertensive disease. National Institute of Child Health and Human Development Maternal-Fetal Medicine Units Network. Am J Obstet Gynecol 1999;181:1096–1101 (Level II-3)

52. Cheek TG, Samuels P. Pregnancy-induced hypertension. In: Datta S, ed. Anesthetic and obstetric management of high-risk pregnancy. 2nd ed. St. Louis: Mosby, 1996: 386–411 (Level III)

The MEDLINE database, the Cochrane Library, and ACOG's own internal resources and documents were used to conduct a literature search to locate relevant articles published between January 1985 and August 2000. The search was restricted to articles published in the English language. Priority was given to articles reporting results of original research, although review articles and commentaries also were consulted. Abstracts of research presented at symposia and scientific conferences were not considered adequate for inclusion in this document. Guidelines published by organizations or institutions such as the National Institutes of Health and the American College of Obstetricians and Gynecologists were reviewed, and additional studies were located by reviewing bibliographies of identified articles. When reliable research was not available, expert opinions from obstetrician–gynecologists were used.

Studies were reviewed and evaluated for quality according to the method outlined by the U.S. Preventive Services Task Force:

I   Evidence obtained from at least one properly designed randomized controlled trial.

II-1 Evidence obtained from well-designed controlled trials without randomization.

II-2 Evidence obtained from well-designed cohort or case–control analytic studies, preferably from more than one center or research group.

II-3 Evidence obtained from multiple time series with or without the intervention. Dramatic results in uncontrolled experiments could also be regarded as this type of evidence.

III   Opinions of respected authorities, based on clinical experience, descriptive studies, or reports of expert committees.

Based on the highest level of evidence found in the data, recommendations are provided and graded according to the following categories:

Level A—Recommendations are based on good and consistent scientific evidence.

Level B—Recommendations are based on limited or inconsistent scientific evidence.

Level C—Recommendations are based primarily on consensus and expert opinion.

ISSN 1099-3630

The American College of Obstetricians and Gynecologists
409 12th Street, SW,
PO Box 96920
Washington, DC 20090-6920

12345/54321

Chronic Hypertension in Pregnancy. ACOG Practice Bulletin No. 29. American College of Obstetricians and Gynecologists. Obstet Gynecol 2001;98:177–185

ACOG PRACTICE BULLETIN

CLINICAL MANAGEMENT GUIDELINES FOR
OBSTETRICIAN–GYNECOLOGISTS

NUMBER 25, MARCH 2001

(Replaces Practice Pattern Number 3, December 1996)

This Practice Bulletin was developed by the ACOG Committee on Practice Bulletins— Gynecology with the assistance of Ronald A. Chez, MD. The information is designed to aid practitioners in making decisions about appropriate obstetric and gynecologic care. These guidelines should not be construed as dictating an exclusive course of treatment or procedure. Variations in practice may be warranted based on the needs of the individual patient, resources, and limitations unique to the institution or type of practice.

Emergency Oral Contraception

Emergency contraception is a therapy for women who have had unprotected sexual intercourse, including sexual assault. It also has been called the "morning-after pill," interception, and postcoital contraception. Methods of emergency contraception include use of combination or progestin-only oral contraceptives, danazol, synthetic estrogens and conjugated estrogens, antiprogestins, and the insertion of an intrauterine device. One particular combination oral-contraceptive regimen is the Yuzpe method. This document addresses only combination and progestin-only oral contraceptives because they are the most frequently used methods.

This document will present evidence regarding the safety, efficacy, risks, and benefits of the use of oral contraceptives for emergency contraception. For widespread use of this therapy, physician familiarity with the method, public awareness of the method's availability, prompt availability of these methods (because of their time-sensitive nature), and access to a physician who is available to prescribe the method must be increased.

Background

Women seeking postcoital contraception typically are younger than 25 years, have never been pregnant, have been sexually active for an average of 2 years, and have used some form of contraception in the past (1, 2). The two most common reasons given for seeking treatment are failure of a barrier method of contraception (usually condoms) and failure to use any method (3–19).

The combination oral-contraceptive method of emergency contraception consists of the ingestion of 0.1 mg of ethinyl estradiol and 1.0 mg DL-norgestrel (equivalent to 0.5 mg levonorgestrel) in two doses 12 hours apart starting within 72 hours of unprotected sexual intercourse. The progestin-only method consists of the ingestion of 0.75 mg of levonorgestrel in two doses taken in the same manner. Products designated specifically for this use are available.

Method of Action

A single mechanism of action of emergency contraception has not been established. Inhibition or delay in ovulation and insufficient corpus luteum function have been reported in some women (20). Some studies have reported histologic or biochemical changes within the endometrium, which may result in failure of nidation (21, 22). Another study suggested the mechanism of action is interference with tubal transport of sperm, egg, or embryo (23). There is no evidence that emergency contraception increases the incidence of ectopic pregnancy; however, no studies specifically focus on this issue. This method does not interrupt an implanted pregnancy.

Up to 98% of patients will menstruate by 21 days after the treatment (3, 8, 16–18). In more than half of the patients, menses will occur at the expected time (24). In more than 90% of cases, menses will be of normal duration for that patient (11, 14, 18). Whether the patient has a history of regular or irregular menstrual cycles does not appear to be a factor (17, 18). If the treatment is given before ovulation, the onset of menstrual bleeding may be 3–7 days earlier than expected. If the treatment is given after ovulation, the onset of menstrual bleeding may be at the expected time or delayed (6, 7, 10–12, 14–16). It is important for the patient to seek medical care promptly if menses have not begun within 21 days of treatment.

Teratogenic Effects

There are a relatively small number of reports in which treatment failed and the women elected to continue the pregnancy. No evidence exists of a specific syndrome of anomalies or an apparent increase in the incidence of major or minor anomalies (15, 19). It is important to acknowledge that no studies have investigated teratogenic effects associated with the use of oral emergency contraception. However, numerous studies of the teratogenic risk of conception during the regular, daily use of oral contraceptives (including use of older, higher-dose preparations) found no increase in risk (25).

Cost Considerations

The purpose of emergency contraception is to avoid unintended pregnancy. Many of these pregnancies also are unwanted. The therapy described herein will prevent most pregnancies resulting from a single act of unprotected intercourse. Thus, the treatment costs of any sub-

sequent induced abortions, spontaneous abortions, ectopic pregnancies, and pregnancies carried to fetal viability will be avoided (26).

Prevention Counseling

Patients who request emergency contraception also may be in need of and motivated toward counseling about sexually transmitted disease prevention, a reliable method of birth control, and preconception care. Physicians may find this an opportune time to institute this type of comprehensive health care.

Clinical Considerations and Recommendations

▶ **Who are candidates for emergency contraception?**

A potential candidate for emergency contraception is a woman of reproductive age who has had unprotected sexual intercourse within the previous 72 hours, independent of the time in the menstrual cycle (3).

▶ **How is the emergency oral contraceptive method prescribed?**

The U.S. Food and Drug Administration has approved two prescription methods specifically for emergency contraception. The Preven Emergency Contraceptive Kit consists of four pills, each containing 0.25 mg of levonorgestrel and 0.05 mg of ethinyl estradiol; a urine pregnancy test; and a patient information book. To use this method, the patient ingests two pills within 72 hours of unprotected intercourse, followed by a second dose of two pills 12 hours later.

The Plan B method consists of two tablets, each containing 0.75 mg of levonorgestrel. (Note that this dose differs from the 0.075-mg dose of norgestrel found in certain progestin-only pills.) The second pill is ingested 12 hours after the first. Detailed physician and patient labeling accompany both methods. Table 1 describes equivalent dosing between certain oral contraceptives and the currently available prepackaged emergency contraception kits.

▶ **Are antiemetics useful as an adjunct to treatment?**

Nausea occurs in 30–66% of patients who use combination oral contraceptives for emergency contraception (11). It may occur after either dose of medication and tends to last for 2 days or less. Emesis occurs in 12–22%

of patients. The incidence and severity of nausea and the incidence of vomiting are decreased when antiemetic

Table 1. Prescriptive Equivalents of Dedicated Products and Common Oral Contraceptives for Use as Emergency Contraception

Trade Name	Formulation	No. of Pills/Dose*
Dedicated Products		
Plan B	0.75 mg of levonorgestrel	1
Preven	0.05 mg of ethinyl estradiol 0.25 mg of levonorgestrel	2
Common Oral Contraceptives		
Ovrette	0 mg of ethinyl estradiol 0.075 mg of levonorgestrel	20
Ogestrel[†]	0.05 mg of ethinyl estradiol 0.50 mg norgestrel	2
Ovral[†]	0.05 mg of ethinyl estradiol 0.50 mg of norgestrel	2
Low-Ogestrel[†]	0.03 mg ethinyl estradiol 0.30 mg norgestrel	4
Lo/Ovral[†]	0.03 mg of ethinyl estradiol 0.30 mg of norgestrel	4
Nordette	(light orange pills) 0.03 mg of ethinyl estradiol 0.15 mg of levonorgestrel	4
Levlen	(light orange pills) 0.03 mg of ethinyl estradiol 0.15 mg of levonorgestrel	4
Levora	0.03 mg of ethinyl estradiol 0.15 mg of levonorgestrel	4
TriLevlen	(yellow pills only) 0.03 mg of ethinyl estradiol 0.125 mg of levonorgestrel	4
Triphasil	(yellow pills only) 0.03 mg of ethinyl estradiol 0.125 mg of levonorgestrel	4
Trivora	(pink pills only) 0.03 mg of ethinyl estradiol 0.125 mg of levonorgestrel	4
Alesse	0.02 mg of ethinyl estradiol 0.1 mg of levonorgestrel	5
Levlite	0.02 mg of ethinyl estradiol 0.1 mg of levonorgestrel	5

* Treatment consists of two doses taken 12 hours apart. Use of an antiemetic agent before taking the medication will lessen the risk of nausea, a common side effect.

† When compared with products containing levonorgestrel, norgestrel was associated with higher rates of side effects (Sanchez-Borrego R, Balasch J. Ethinyl oestradiol plus dl-norgestrel or levonorgestrel in the Yuzpe method for postcoital contraception: results of an observational study. Hum Reprod 1996;11:2449–2453).

agents are taken 1 hour before the first contraceptive dose (3, 14, 27). Such medications do not seem to be effective if taken after the onset of symptoms (10).

Compared with the combination method, the frequency of vomiting with the progestin-only method is significantly less. This difference is also true for nausea, dizziness, and fatigue (24).

There is no evidence that emesis within 3 hours of ingesting the dose is associated with an increased failure rate; however, none of the studies reported was designed specifically to measure this effect. There is no evidence on which to base a recommendation for repeating the dose if emesis occurs. However, it seems reasonable to infer that if gastrointestinal symptoms are estrogen mediated secondary to an effect on the central nervous system, absorption of the dose should have occurred by the time of emesis.

In addition to nausea, another side effect is breast tenderness. This occurs in anywhere from 1% to 47% of patients (3, 4, 6–19).

▶ *How effective is levonorgestrel alone and in combination with ethinyl estradiol in preventing pregnancy?*

Many studies have examined the failure rate of emergency contraception with combination pills containing ethinyl estradiol and DL-norgestrel or levonorgestrel after a single act of unprotected sexual intercourse. However, a formal control group with randomization is not available for comparison in any study (3–13, 15–19).

Several factors complicate the calculation of a failure rate for this method of emergency contraception. The day of ovulation for a particular menstrual cycle relative to the day of exposure can be determined only in retrospect when menses occur. Moreover, hormonal emergency contraception can modify the time of onset of menses.

Other confounding factors include dependence on the patient's history as to the time of the last menstrual period and day of exposure; the effect of regular versus irregular menstrual cycles on the calculation of midcycle exposure in a patient; the possibility that the patient is already pregnant at the time of treatment; the possibility that more than one act of unprotected coitus has occurred in this cycle and the timing of coitus prior to, within, or after the 72-hour window; whether both doses of medication were taken; whether they were taken at the prescribed times 12 hours apart; and the general fertility potential of the woman and her partner (28–30).

Some evidence exists that the contraceptive efficacy of standard combination oral-contraceptive pill regimens decreases if the patient is simultaneously taking hepatic enzyme-inducing drugs. No study has described a decrease in efficacy or lack of efficacy of the postcoital use of combination or progestin-only pills under these circumstances. Therefore, no data support the suggestion that the number of pills per dose in the combination method be increased from two to three in women on concomitant medications (31).

Also, most studies of contraceptive efficacy included patients who were lost to follow-up. There has been no consistent approach from one study to another as to including or excluding these patients from estimates of failure rates. It is not known which of these patients did not conceive or conceived and had a spontaneous abortion, underwent termination of pregnancy, or carried a pregnancy to term.

Therefore, a given method's ability to prevent an individual patient's chance of conceiving from a specific unprotected act of sexual intercourse can only be estimated. The failure rate of emergency contraception has been estimated using different approaches (30, 32), but the most frequently used method compares the probability of conception on each day of the cycle before and after the day of ovulation to the actual number of pregnancies conceived on those days (33).

A recent study has shown that conception can occur each of the 5 days before and on the day of ovulation (28). There is a 0.37 probability (95% confidence interval, 0.31–0.48) of conception when daily coitus occurs in an ovulatory cycle. However, with a single exposure, the daily estimated conception rate in this 6-day window varies from 0.10 to 0.33 (28).

Two reviews of the published literature concluded that the effectiveness rate of the combination method ranged between 55% and 94%, with a weighted average of 70–74% (30, 34). Because the observed number of pregnancies in these studies is likely to be overestimated and the expected number of pregnancies is likely to be underestimated, the true effectiveness rate is likely to be at least 75% (30).

It is important to communicate to patients that this 75% reduction in risk of pregnancy does not translate into a pregnancy rate of 25%. Rather, if 100 women have unprotected intercourse in the middle 2 weeks of their cycles, approximately 8 will become pregnant. Use of emergency contraceptive pills would reduce this number to 2 women (a 75% reduction). Thus, this method, although it reduces the risk of pregnancy substantially, is still less effective than consistent use of other contraceptive methods and is intended specifically for emergency use.

The progestin-only method appears to be more effective in preventing pregnancy than the combination-pill method. When compared in a randomized, double-blind trial, the proportion of pregnancies prevented with the progestin-only method was 85% compared with 57% for combination oral contraceptives. The crude relative risk of pregnancy between the two methods was 0.36, a significant difference (24).

▶ *Are there contraindications to the use of the oral emergency contraception method?*

Emergency oral contraception should not be used in a patient with a known or suspected pregnancy, hypersensitivity to any component of the product, or undiagnosed abnormal genital bleeding. Adverse events with this method of emergency contraception, such as those listed for the known contraindications to daily use of combination birth-control pills, have not been reported in published studies using evidence-based criteria. Although the daily dose of steroid hormones in the hormonal methods of emergency contraception is greater than that used for oral contraception, the duration of use is quite short (35). Some contraindications to the daily use of oral contraceptives are based on a presumption of long-term use (eg, among women older than 35 years who smoke) and are not likely to pertain to the short duration of use required for emergency contraception (35).

Despite the large number of women who have received emergency contraception, there have been no reports of major cardiovascular or neurologic side effects that show an identifiable relationship between the event and the ingestion of the hormones. Some studies, however, excluded women from participating if they had an absolute contraindication to taking oral contraceptives. Also, no studies have specifically investigated outcomes among patients with preexisting contraindications to oral contraceptives and compared them with women without contraindications. The World Health Organization has concluded that there are no contraindications to the Yuzpe method except pregnancy (36). Therefore, there is neither evidence of increased risk nor evidence of safety among women who have contraindications to the use of daily oral contraceptives. For a woman with a history of idiopathic thrombosis, the progestin-only regimen may be preferable (32).

▶ *Is there a time limit for initiating the treatment?*

In almost all studies, the first dose was administered within 72 hours after unprotected sexual intercourse. A small number of patients in two studies received the two doses between 72 hours and 120 hours after exposure. There was a low rate of conception (11, 16). Some authors have suggested emergency contraception can still have some benefit beyond 72 hours after unprotected intercourse (37, 38), but its use should be evaluated for each patient. Insertion of a copper intrauterine device represents an alternative that may still be used for 5–7 days after unprotected intercourse except in cases of rape or sexually transmitted disease (39).

There have been conflicting reports regarding the amount of elapsed time after exposure to treatment within the 72-hour time limit and its effect on the success rate of treatment. Two studies found significant differences in the raw pregnancy rate associated with the amount of time elapsed before beginning treatment (7, 8). An analysis of nine studies, however, found no difference in failure rates when treatment was started within 24, 48, or 72 hours (38).

A recent large, multicenter randomized controlled study found that efficacy was greater the sooner the first dose was taken after coitus. There was an inverse relationship between treatment success and time since unprotected coitus. This downward gradient between 24, 48, and 72 hours was true for both hormonal methods, and particularly so for the progestin-only method (24). Therefore, the first dose should be taken as early as possible.

▶ *Is there a benefit to making emergency contraception available to all patients of reproductive age at the time of a routine gynecologic visit?*

Two studies have evaluated the advance provision of emergency contraception at the time of a routine gynecologic visit to women of reproductive age as a means of increasing availability and use of the treatment. This approach makes the medication immediately available for use if unprotected intercourse or an acute contraception failure occurs. In one controlled trial of more than 1,000 subjects in Scotland, women given a hormonal emergency contraception method to keep at home for self-administration were compared with a control group of women who were simply educated about emergency contraception and how to obtain it (40). Women who had the method at home were more likely to use it than were those in the control group, and not more likely to use it more than once.

Another trial of women ages 16–24 years attending a publicly funded, family planning clinic in California compared women who were educated about the use of emergency contraception and provided with a single treatment dose of emergency contraception with women who received education alone (41). As in the other study, women given emergency contraception in advance were significantly more likely to use it than women in the control group. Because of the small sample size, the study did not evaluate the effect of advance provision of emergency contraception on pregnancy rates.

Both studies confirm that having emergency contraception on hand increases its use beyond that of patient education alone. The study designs and sample sizes have not been adequate to demonstrate a definitive impact on the rates of unintended pregnancies. However, it may be beneficial for physicians to offer reproductive-aged patients an advance prescription for emergency contraception at the time of a gynecologic visit to help reduce unwanted pregnancy; the patient should be advised to note the package expiration date of the prescription.

Summary

The following recommendations are based on good and consistent scientific evidence (Level A):

▶ Combination or progestin-only oral contraceptives for emergency contraception should be offered to women who have had unprotected sexual intercourse within 72 hours of intercourse.

▶ Because the progestin-only method produces less nausea and may be more effective than the combination oral-contraceptive method, this regimen should be strongly considered.

▶ To minimize nausea and vomiting with combination oral-contraceptive products, an antiemetic agent should be prescribed and the patient should take it 1 hour before the first oral contraceptive dose.

▶ During a routine gynecologic visit, physicians who wish to increase the availability and use of emergency contraception may offer patients an advance prescription for emergency contraception.

The following recommendations are based on limited or inconsistent scientific evidence (Level B):

▶ If possible, emergency contraception should be used within the first 24 hours after unprotected intercourse because efficacy may be greatest if used within 24 hours after exposure.

▶ Patients should be evaluated for pregnancy if menses have not begun within 21 days following emergency contraception treatment.

The following recommendations are based primarily on consensus and expert opinion (Level C):

▶ Counseling regarding effective contraceptive methods, sexually transmitted diseases, and safer sex practices should be undertaken, when feasible, at the time emergency contraception is prescribed.

▶ Data are insufficient to evaluate the effectiveness of emergency contraception treatment when initiated more than 72 hours and up to 120 hours after a single act of unprotected sexual intercourse. Therefore, the risk and benefits of treatment should be weighed on a case-by-case basis.

▶ No data specifically examine the risk of using hormonal methods of emergency contraception among women with contraindications to the use of conventional oral-contraceptive preparations; nevertheless, emergency contraception may be offered to such women.

▶ In a woman with a history of idiopathic thrombosis, the progestin-only regimen may be preferred.

References

1. Percival-Smith RK, Abercrombie B. Postcoital contraception: some characteristics of women who use this method. Contraception 1988;37:425–429 (Level II-3)

2. Rowlands S, Booth M, Guillebaud J. Behavioural patterns in women requesting postcoital contraception. J Biosoc Sci 1983;15:145–152 (Level III)

3. Bagshaw SN, Edwards D, Tucker AK. Ethinyl oestradiol and D-norgestrel is an effective emergency postcoital contraceptive: a report of its use in 1,200 patients in a family planning clinic. Aust N Z J Obstet Gynaecol 1988;28:137–140 (Level II-3)

4. Buttermore S, Nolan C. Six years of clinical experience using postcoital contraception in college women. J Am Coll Health 1993;42:61–63 (Level III)

5. Friedman EH, Rowley DE. Post-coital contraception—a two year evaluation of a service. Br J Fam Plann 1988;13:139–144 (Level II-3)

6. Glasier A, Thong KJ, Dewar M, Mackie M, Baird DT. Mifepristone (RU 486) compared with high-dose estrogen and progestogen for emergency postcoital contraception. N Engl J Med 1992;327:1041–1044 (Level I)

7. Ho PC, Kwan MS. A prospective randomized comparison of levonorgestrel with the Yuzpe regimen in post-coital contraception. Hum Reprod 1993;8:389–392 (Level I)

8. Kane LA, Sparrow MJ. Postcoital contraception: a family planning study. N Z Med J 1989;102:151–153 (Level II-3)

9. Luerti M, Tonta A, Ferla P, Molla R, Santini F. Post-coital contraception by estrogen/progestagen combination or IUD insertion. Contraception 1986;33:61–68 (Level II-3)

10. Percival-Smith RK, Abercrombie B. Postcoital contraception with dl-norgestrel/ethinyl estradiol combination: six years experience in a student medical clinic. Contraception 1987;36:287–293 (Level II-3)

11. Rowlands S, Guillebaud J, Bounds W, Booth M. Side effects of danazol compared with an ethinyloestradiol/norgestrel combination when used for postcoital contraception. Contraception 1983;27:39–49 (Level I)

12. Schilling LH. An alternative to the use of high-dose estrogens for postcoital contraception. J Am Coll Health Assoc 1979;27:247–249 (Level II-3)

13. Tully B. Post coital contraception—a study. Br J Fam Plann 1983;8:119–124 (Level II-3)

14. Van Santen MR, Haspels AA. Interception II: postcoital low-dose estrogens and norgestrel combination in 633 women. Contraception 1985;31:275–293 (Level II-3)

15. Webb AM, Russell J, Elstein M. Comparison of Yuzpe regimen, danazol, and mifepristone (RU486) in oral postcoital contraception. BMJ 1992;305:927–931 (Level I)

16. Yuzpe AA, Thurlow HJ, Ramzy I, Leyshon JI. Post coital contraception—a pilot study. J Reprod Med 1974;13:53–58 (Level II-3)

17. Yuzpe AA, Lancee WJ. Ethinylestradiol and dl-norgestrel as a postcoital contraceptive. Fertil Steril 1977;28:932–936 (Level II-3)

18. Yuzpe AA, Smith RP, Rademaker AW. A multicenter clinical investigation employing ethinyl estradiol combined with dl-norgestrel as a postcoital contraceptive agent. Fertil Steril 1982;37:508–513 (Level II-3)

19. Zuliani G, Colombo UF, Molla R. Hormonal postcoital contraception with an ethinylestradiol-norgestrel combination and two danazol regimens. Eur J Obstet Gynecol Reprod Biol 1990;37:253–260 (Level I)

20. Swahn ML, Westlund P, Johannisson E, Bygdeman M. Effect of post-coital contraceptive methods on the endometrium and the menstrual cycle. Acta Obstet Gynecol Scand 1996;75:738–744 (Level II-2)

21. Ling WY, Robichaud A, Zayid I, Wrixon W, MacLeod SC. Mode of action of dl-norgestrel and ethinylestradiol combination in postcoital contraception. Fertil Steril 1979;32:297–302 (Level II-3)

22. Ling WY, Wrixon W, Acorn T, Wilson E, Collins J. Mode of action of dl-norgestrel and ethinylestradiol combination in postcoital contraception. III. Effect of preovulatory administration following the luteinizing hormone surge on ovarian steroidogenesis. Fertil Steril 1983;40:631–636 (Level II-3)

23. Glasier A. Emergency postcoital contraception. N Engl J Med 1997;337:1058–1064 (Level III)

24. Task Force on Postovulatory Methods of Fertility Regulation. Randomised controlled trial of levonorgestrel versus the Yuzpe regimen of combined oral contraceptives for emergency contraception. Lancet 1998;352:428–433 (Level I)

25. Bracken MB. Oral contraception and congenital malformations in offspring: a review and meta-analysis of the prospective studies. Obstet Gynecol 1990;76:552–557 (Meta-analysis)

26. Trussell J, Ellertson C, Stewart F, Koenig J, Raymond EG. Emergency contraception: a cost-effective approach to reducing unintended pregnancy. Princeton, New Jersey: Office of Population Research, Princeton University, 1998 (Level III)

27. Raymond EG, Creinin MD, Barnhart KT, Lovvorn AE, Rountree RW, Trussell J. Meclizine for prevention of nausea associated with use of emergency contraceptive pills: a randomized trial. Obstet Gynecol 2000;95:271–277 (Level I)

28. Wilcox AJ, Weinberg CR, Baird DD. Timing of sexual intercourse in relation to ovulation. Effects on the probability of conception, survival of the pregnancy, and sex of the baby. N Engl J Med 1995;333:1517–1521 (Level II-3)

29. Yuzpe AA. Postcoital hormonal contraception: uses, risks, and abuses. Int J Gynaecol Obstet 1977;15:133–136 (Level III)

30. Trussell J, Ellertson C, Stewart F. The effectiveness of the Yuzpe regimen of emergency contraception. Fam Plann Perspect 1996;28:58–64, 87 (Meta-analysis)

31. Kubba A, Wilkinson C. Recommendations for clinical practice: emergency contraception. Prepared on behalf of the Faculty of Family Planning and Reproductive Health Care of the RCOG. London: Royal College of Obstetricians and Gynaecologists, 1998 (Level III)

32. Trussell J, Ellertson C. Efficacy of emergency contraception. Fertil Control Rev 1995;4:8–11 (Level III)

33. Dixon GW, Schlesselman JJ, Ory HW, Blye RP. Ethinyl estradiol and conjugated estrogens as postcoital contraceptives. JAMA 1980;244:1336–1339 (Level II-3)

34. Creinin MD. A reassessment of efficacy of the Yuzpe regimen of emergency contraception. Hum Reprod 1997; 12:496–498 (Level III)

35. Webb A. How safe is the Yuzpe method of emergency contraception? Fertil Control Rev 1995;4:16–18 (Level III)

36. World Health Organization. Family Planning and Population. Emergency contraception: a guide for service delivery. Geneva: WHO, 1998 (Level III)

37. Grou F, Rodrigues I. The morning-after pill—how long after? Am J Obstet Gynecol 1994;171:1529–1534 (Level III)

38. Trussell J, Ellertson C, Rodriquez G. The Yuzpe regimen of emergency contraception: how long after the morning after? Obstet Gynecol 1996;88:150–154 (Level III)

39. Fasoli M, Parazzini F, Cecchetti G, LaVecchia C. Postcoital contraception: an overview of published studies. Contraception 1989;39:459–468 (Level III)

40. Glasier A, Baird D. The effects of self-administering emergency contraception. N Engl J Med 1998;339:1–4 (Level II-1)

41. Raine T, Harper C, Leon K, Darney P. Emergency contraception: advance provision in a young, high-risk clinic population. Obstet Gynecol 2000;96:1–7 (Level II-1)

Additional Resources

Emergency Contraception Hotline:

1-888-NOT-2-LATE

World Wide Web Pages:

Emergency Contraception: http://ec.princeton.edu

Pastillas Anticonceptivas de Emergencia: http://www.en3dias.org.mx

PATH (Program for Appropriate Technology in Health): http://www.path.org/index.htm

American College of Obstetricians and Gynecologists http://www.acog.org

Publications:

Emergency contraception: resources for providers. Seattle, Washington: Program for Appropriate Technology in Health [PATH], 1997. To order, call 800-669-0156.

Emergency contraception: client materials for diverse audiences. Seattle, Washington: Program for Appropriate Technology in Health [PATH], 1998. To order, call 206-285-3500 or e-mail info@path.org

The MEDLINE database, the Cochrane Library, and ACOG's own internal resources and documents were used to conduct a literature search to locate relevant articles published between January 1985 and June 2000. The search was restricted to articles published in the English language. Priority was given to articles reporting results of original research, although review articles and commentaries also were consulted. Abstracts of research presented at symposia and scientific conferences were not considered adequate for inclusion in this document. Guidelines published by organizations or institutions such as the National Institutes of Health and the American College of Obstetricians and Gynecologists were reviewed, and additional studies were located by reviewing bibliographies of identified articles. When reliable research was not available, expert opinions from obstetrician–gynecologists were used.

Studies were reviewed and evaluated for quality according to the method outlined by the U.S. Preventive Services Task Force:

I   Evidence obtained from at least one properly designed randomized controlled trial.

II-1 Evidence obtained from well-designed controlled trials without randomization.

II-2 Evidence obtained from well-designed cohort or case–control analytic studies, preferably from more than one center or research group.

II-3 Evidence obtained from multiple time series with or without the intervention. Dramatic results in uncontrolled experiments also could be regarded as this type of evidence.

III   Opinions of respected authorities, based on clinical experience, descriptive studies, or reports of expert committees.

Based on the highest level of evidence found in the data, recommendations are provided and graded according to the following categories:

Level A—Recommendations are based on good and consistent scientific evidence.

Level B—Recommendations are based on limited or inconsistent scientific evidence.

Level C—Recommendations are based primarily on consensus and expert opinion.

ISSN 1099-3630

**The American College of
Obstetricians and Gynecologists
409 12th Street, SW
PO Box 96920
Washington, DC 20090-6920**

12345/54321

ACOG PRACTICE BULLETIN

CLINICAL MANAGEMENT GUIDELINES FOR
OBSTETRICIAN–GYNECOLOGISTS
NUMBER 13, FEBRUARY 2000

(Replaces Practice Pattern Number 4, July 1997)

This Practice Bulletin was developed by the ACOG Committee on Practice Bulletins—Obstetrics. The information is designed to aid practitioners in making decisions about appropriate obstetric and gynecologic care. These guidelines should not be construed as dictating an exclusive course of treatment or procedure. Variations in practice may be warranted based on the needs of the individual patient, resources, and limitations unique to the institution or type of practice.

External Cephalic Version

In the United States, there is a widespread belief that the overall cesarean delivery rate is higher than necessary. Efforts are being directed toward decreasing the number of these procedures, in part by encouraging physicians to make changes in their management practices. Because breech presentations are associated with a high rate of cesarean delivery, there is renewed interest in techniques such as external cephalic version (ECV) and vaginal breech delivery. The purpose of this document is to provide information about ECV by summarizing the relevant evidence presented in published studies and to make recommendations regarding its use in obstetric practice.

Background

Breech presentation occurs in 3–4% of term pregnancies. In 1997, 84.5% of all malpresentations, including breech presentation, resulted in cesarean deliveries (1). External cephalic version involves applying pressure to the mother's abdomen to turn the fetus in either a forward or backward somersault to achieve a vertex presentation. The goal of ECV is to increase the proportion of vertex presentations among fetuses that were formerly in the breech position near term. Once a vertex presentation is achieved, the chances for a vaginal delivery increase.

Clinical Considerations and Recommendations

▶ *Which patients are candidates for external cephalic version?*

Patients who have completed 36 weeks of gestation are preferred candidates for ECV for several reasons. First, if spontaneous version is going to occur, it is likely to have taken place by 36 completed weeks of gestation (2, 3). Second, risk of a spontaneous reversion is decreased after external cephalic version at term compared with earlier gestations. Preterm version attempts are associated with high initial success rates but also with higher reversion rates, necessitating additional procedures (4, 5). Third, if complications arise during an attempted version, emergency delivery of a term infant can be accomplished (6). Finally, most of the evidence pertaining to ECV comes from recent studies that selected patients near term.

There is scant information concerning ECV attempts among women who have a preexisting uterine scar or who undergo the procedure during the early stages of labor. For women with a previous cesarean delivery, compared with those who had not experienced cesarean delivery, results from one small randomized controlled trial indicate that they experience comparable success rates (7). Although no serious adverse events occurred in a small series (8), larger studies would be needed to establish the risk of uterine rupture. There are scattered reports of successful ECV performed during early labor; to date, however, no large study has been published (4, 5, 9, 10).

Contraindications to ECV are based on a common-sense approach designed to minimize the risks of an adverse outcome and to maximize the chances for success. Clearly any indication for a cesarean delivery in a patient, such as placenta previa, would be a contraindication to ECV (4, 9, 11–20), but there is insufficient evidence to construct a comprehensive list.

▶ *What are the benefits and risks of external cephalic version?*

The immediate benefit of successful version is an increased probability that the fetus will be in a vertex presentation for delivery. The ultimate goal is an uncomplicated vaginal delivery. Reports from published studies indicate there are fewer cesarean deliveries among women who have undergone successful version compared with women who have not undergone attempted version (4, 6, 18, 21–24). One randomized trial found no significant difference between the cesarean delivery rates of patients with an ECV attempt and controls who did not undergo ECV (25). In this study, however, the majority of patients undergoing ECV were between 33 and 36 weeks of gestation rather than closer to term as in the other reports. An additional randomized trial reported similar rates of cesarean delivery for women who underwent ECV and for those who did not, but the rate of breech vaginal deliveries was very high; approximately 80% of breech presentations in each group was delivered vaginally, resulting in an unusually low cesarean delivery rate (4).

Fetal heart rate changes during attempted versions are not uncommon but usually stabilize when the procedure is discontinued (4, 21, 23, 26, 27). Serious adverse effects associated with ECV do not occur often, but there have been a few reported cases of placental abruption and preterm labor. A report from Copenhagen described two cases of intrauterine death 2 and 5 weeks after version among 316 women and one instance of premature partial separation of the placenta 2 days following an unsuccessful version attempt, but the two deaths could not be causally linked to ECV with certainty (16). In the study including mothers at 36 weeks of gestation or less, two placental abruptions and one premature labor occurred shortly after version, resulting in one neonatal and two fetal deaths (25). Subsequently, there has been a follow-up study at the same institution, but changes in management practices and selection criteria had been made (18). Only term gestations were selected, and tocolytic agents as well as fetal monitoring were used during version attempts. There were no fetal deaths causally linked to ECV. The authors concluded that ECV can substantially decrease breech presentations and the cesarean delivery rate for these patients (18). A more recent study reported a placental abruption during an ECV attempt requiring emergency cesarean delivery of a viable but depressed infant (28). It was the only major complication attributed to ECV among 113 women. Although the incidence of serious complications associated with ECV is low, the potential is present, making it prudent to perform ECV in a facility that has ready access to cesarean delivery services.

▶ *What are the success rates for external cephalic version, and what factors are predictive of either success or failure?*

A review of 20 studies indicates that success rates for ECV range from 35% to 86%, with an average success rate of 58% (4, 6, 9, 12–14, 16–18, 21–25, 27, 29–31). Most authors report a positive association between parity and successful version (4, 6, 13, 21–25, 30, 31). A transverse or oblique lie is associated with higher immediate success rates (13, 29, 30). Opinion is divided about the predictiveness of other factors, including amniotic fluid volume, location of placenta, and maternal weight. Some reports indicate an association between normal or increased amounts of amniotic fluid and successful ECV (12, 13, 24, 32), whereas other reports do not (20). Two authors reported an association between successful ECV and placenta location (20, 24), whereas others failed to find an association (12, 13, 29). Two authors found obesity to be associated with a higher failure rate (23, 30), whereas others found maternal weight not to be a significant predictor of success (12, 13, 19, 20).

Although scoring systems have been developed to predict which candidates will have a successful version attempt, these have not been validated by multiple studies. One system considered parity, dilatation, estimated fetal weight, placenta location, and station. Nulliparity, advanced dilatation, fetal weight of less than 2,500 g, anterior placenta, and low station were less likely to be associated with success (20). Such variables may provide useful clinical information for obtaining informed consent from individuals for ECV; no single system, however, has been shown to have complete accuracy.

▶ *How does the use of tocolysis affect the success rate of external cephalic version?*

Two of six randomized controlled trials failed to find a significant advantage in using tocolytics during ECV attempts (19, 27). One third reported significantly greater success associated with hexoprenaline but not with ritodrine (33). An additional randomized study reported an initial advantage associated with the use of ritodrine, specifically among nulliparous women. However, as the physicians became proficient at the ECV technique, the advantage diminished (34). The largest randomized study using a ritodrine infusion found significant improvement only among nulliparous patients (35). Finally, a randomized study of terbutaline found the success rate of version associated with use of this tocolytic to be almost double the rate without its use (36). In the vast majority of published studies, a tocolytic agent was used routinely (6, 11–18, 20–23, 27–29, 37). Several studies used tocolytics selectively (5, 7, 9, 34), and some used no tocolytic agents (4, 25). Existing evidence may support the use of a tocolytic agent during ECV attempts, particularly in nulliparous patients.

▶ *Does successful version translate into lower cesarean delivery rates?*

Whether ECV results in a lower cesarean delivery rate for women with breech presentation who elect this procedure compared with those women who do not depends upon several factors. Obviously, the first factor is whether the version is successful. Clearly, women who have successful version have lower cesarean delivery rates than those who do not (6, 9, 12–14, 21–24, 26, 29, 30). Two randomized studies also have shown a significant decrease in cesarean delivery rates among patients assigned to version compared with those not assigned to version (18, 23). Factors that tend to lessen overall differences between version and nonversion groups include spontaneous conversion of presentation from breech to vertex or vice versa and the willingness of providers to perform vaginal breech deliveries. Clearly, cesarean delivery rates

for version and nonversion groups will be less when there is a greater willingness to attempt a vaginal breech delivery. The need to perform a cesarean delivery for other indications in women who have had a successful version also may lessen the overall impact of version on the cesarean delivery rate. One author has reported that women who have had successful ECV have higher cesarean delivery rates due to fetal distress and dystocia compared with matched controls who never required the procedure (31).

Although ECV may not lead to a substantial reduction in the national cesarean delivery rate, it is nonetheless a valuable management technique. In a properly selected population, this procedure poses little risk to either mother or fetus. If successful, ECV provides a clear benefit to the individual woman by allowing her an opportunity for a successful vertex vaginal delivery.

▶ *How does the use of anesthesia affect the success rate of external cephalic version?*

A randomized study found a significantly greater success rate associated with the use of epidural anesthesia, although the success rate was unusually low for the women who did not receive epidural anesthesia (32%) (38). Two studies reported results for women in whom ECV was performed while using epidural anesthesia (10, 15). In one study, use of epidural anesthesia was associated with a significantly greater success rate compared with no use of epidural anesthesia (15). However, the procedure was administered selectively to patients according to physician preference, raising the potential for selection bias. The other study merely noted that ECV was performed without difficulty on three women undergoing epidural anesthesia (10). It also has been suggested that epidural anesthesia be considered for women who failed a previous version attempt (39). Another randomized trial addressed the use of spinal anesthesia before the version attempt and found no significant difference between treatment groups (40). Currently, there is not enough consistent evidence to make a recommendation favoring spinal or epidural anesthesia during ECV attempts.

▶ *What is an example of a standard protocol for performing an external cephalic version attempt?*

Prior to attempting ECV, patients must provide informed consent and should undergo an ultrasound examination. The ultrasound examination is necessary to confirm the breech position of the fetus and rule out the presence of any anomalies that would complicate a vaginal delivery.

Fetal well-being should be assessed by a prior nonstress test or concurrent biophysical profile (see Fig. 1).

Because there is a chance that an expedient delivery may become necessary, patients should have ready access to a facility that is equipped to perform emergency cesarean deliveries. One version technique involves lifting the breech upward from the pelvis with one hand and providing pressure on the head with the other hand to produce a forward roll. If the forward roll fails, a backward somersault may be attempted. Version may be performed by one person or two. A version attempt will be abandoned if there is significant fetal bradycardia, if there is discomfort to the patient, or if the attempt cannot be completed easily or is unsuccessful after a brief period. Following the attempt, fetal evaluation is repeated and the patient is monitored until stable. Rh-negative patients may receive anti-D immune globulin. There is no support for routine practice of immediate induction of labor to minimize reversion.

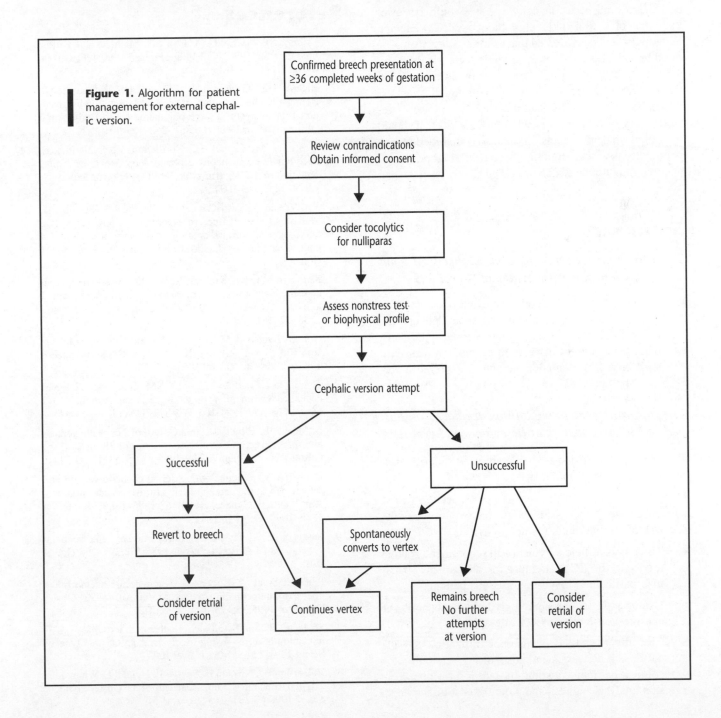

Figure 1. Algorithm for patient management for external cephalic version.

▶ *What are the cost implications of external cephalic version?*

A recent decision analysis measuring cost implications associated with four potential methods of managing term pregnancies with breech presentations predicted that use of ECV would result in fewer cesarean deliveries and lower costs than either scheduled cesarean delivery or trial of labor without an ECV attempt (41). Even if failed ECV attempts were followed by routine cesarean delivery, the overall cesarean delivery rate would be lower than that of a trial of labor without an ECV attempt. Sensitivity analysis revealed that as long as less than 52% of all breech presentations are eligible for a trial of labor, a policy of attempting ECV followed by either a trial of labor or routine cesarean delivery (for failed attempts) would be less expensive than a policy of routine cesarean delivery or trial of labor without ECV (41). It should be noted that the decision analysis included X-ray pelvimetry to assess eligibility for a trial of labor, a practice that may not be widely accepted.

Summary

The following recommendation is based on good and consistent scientific evidence (Level A):

▶ Because the risk of an adverse event occurring as a result of ECV is small and the cesarean delivery rate is significantly lower among women who have undergone successful version, all women near term with breech presentations should be offered a version attempt.

The following recommendations are based on limited or inconsistent scientific evidence (Level B):

▶ Patients should have completed 36 weeks of gestation before attempting ECV.

▶ Previous cesarean delivery is not associated with a lower rate of success; however, the magnitude of the risk of uterine rupture is not known.

▶ There is insufficient evidence to recommend routine tocolysis for ECV attempts for all patients, but it may particularly benefit nulliparous patients.

▶ Evidence is inconsistent regarding the benefits of anesthesia use during ECV attempts.

▶ Cost-effectiveness depends upon utilization of vaginal breech deliveries and costs of the version protocol at a particular institution, but at least one decision analysis suggests the policy is cost effective.

The following recommendations are based primarily on consensus and expert opinion (Level C):

▶ Fetal assessment before and after the procedure is recommended.

▶ External cephalic version should be attempted only in settings in which cesarean delivery services are readily available.

References

1. Ventura SJ, Martin JA, Curtin SC, Mathews TJ. Births: final data for 1997. Natl Vital Stat Rep 1999;47(18):1–96 (Level II-3)

2. Hickok DE, Gordon DC, Milberg JA, Williams MA, Daling JR. The frequency of breech presentation by gestational age at birth: a large population-based study. Am J Obstet Gynecol 1992;166:851–852 (Level II-2)

3. Westgren M, Edvall H, Nordstrom L, Svalenius E, Ranstam J. Spontaneous cephalic version of breech presentation in the last trimester. Br J Obstet Gynaecol 1985; 92:19–22 (Level II-3)

4. Van Veelen AJ, Van Cappellen AW, Flu PK, Straub MJ, Wallenburg HC. Effect of external cephalic version in late pregnancy on presentation at delivery: a randomized controlled trial. Br J Obstet Gynaecol 1989;96:916–921 (Level I)

5. Kornman MT, Kimball KT, Reeves KO. Preterm external cephalic version in an outpatient environment. Am J Obstet Gynecol 1995;172:1734–1738; discussion 1738–1741 (Level II-2)

6. Goh JT, Johnson CM, Gregora MG. External cephalic version at term. Aust N Z J Obstet Gynaecol 1993;33:364–366 (Level II-2)

7. Flamm BL, Fried MW, Lonky NM, Giles WS. External cephalic version after previous cesarean section. Am J Obstet Gynecol 1991;165;370–372 (Level I)

8. de Meeus JB, Ellia F, Magnin G. External cephalic version after previous cesarean section: a series of 38 cases. Eur J Obstet Gynecol Reprod Biol 1998;81:65–68 (Level III)

9. Cook HA. Experience with external cephalic version and selective vaginal breech delivery in private practice. Am J Obstet Gynecol 1993;168:1886–1889; discussion 1889–1890 (Level II-3)

10. Ferguson JE 2d, Dyson DC. Intrapartum external cephalic version. Am J Obstet Gynecol 1985;152:297–298 (Level II-3)

11. Lau TK, Stock A, Rogers M. Fetomaternal haemorrhage after external cephalic version at term. Aust N Z J Obstet Gynaecol 1995;35:173–174 (Level III)

12. Shalev E, Battino S, Giladi Y, Edelstein S. External cephalic version at term—using tocolysis. Acta Obstet Gynecol Scand 1993;72:455–457 (Level II-3)

13. Hellstrom AC, Nilsson B, Stange L, Nylund L. When does external cephalic version succeed? Acta Obstet Gynecol Scand 1990;69:281–285 (Level II-3)

14. Morrison JC, Myatt RE, Martin JN Jr, Meeks GR, Martin RW, Bucovaz ET, et al. External cephalic version of the breech presentation under tocolysis. Am J Obstet Gynecol 1986;154:900–903 (Level II-3)

15. Carlan SJ, Dent JM, Huckaby T, Whittington EC, Shaefer D. The effect of epidural anesthesia on safety and success of external cephalic version at term. Anesth Analg 1994;79:525–528 (Level II-3)

16. Thunedborg P, Fischer-Rasmussen W, Tollund L. The benefit of external cephalic version with tocolysis as a routine procedure in late pregnancy. Eur J Obstet Gynecol Reprod Biol 1991;42:23–27 (Level II-3)

17. Bewley S, Robson SC, Smith M, Glover A, Spencer JA. The introduction of external cephalic version at term into routine clinical practice. Eur J Obstet Gynecol Reprod Biol 1993;52:89–93 (Level II-3)

18. Mahomed K, Seeras R, Coulson R. External cephalic version at term. A randomized controlled trial using tocolysis. Br J Obstet Gynaecol 1991;98:8–13 (Level I)

19. Tan GW, Jen SW, Tan SL, Salmon YM. A prospective randomised controlled trial of external cephalic version comparing two methods of uterine tocolysis with a non-tocolysis group. Singapore Med J 1989;30:155–158 (Level I)

20. Newman RB, Peacock BS, VanDorsten JP, Hunt HH. Predicting success of external cephalic version. Am J Obstet Gynecol 1993;169:245–249; discussion 249–250 (Level II-3)

21. Dyson DC, Ferguson JE 2d, Hensleigh P. Antepartum external cephalic version under tocolysis. Obstet Gynecol 1986;67:63–68 (Level II-2)

22. Marchick R. Antepartum external cephalic version with tocolysis: a study of term singleton breech presentations. Am J Obstet Gynecol 1988;158:1339–1346 (Level II-2)

23. Brocks V, Philipsen T, Secher NJ. A randomized trial of external cephalic version with tocolysis in late pregnancy. Br J Obstet Gynaecol 1984;91:653–656 (Level II-1)

24. Hofmeyr GJ, Sadan O, Myer IG, Galal KC, Simko G. External cephalic version and spontaneous version rates: ethnic and other determinants. Br J Obstet Gynaecol 1986;93:13–16 (Level II-2)

25. Kasule J, Chimbira TH, Brown IM. Controlled trial of external cephalic version. Br J Obstet Gynaecol 1985;92:14–18 (Level I)

26. Stine LE, Phelan JP, Wallace R, Eglinton GS, Van Dorsten JP, Schifrin BS. Update on external cephalic version performed at term. Obstet Gynecol 1985;65:642–646 (Level II-3)

27. Robertson AW, Kopelman JN, Read JA, Duff P, Magelssen DJ, Dashow EE. External cephalic version at term: is a tocolytic necessary? Obstet Gynecol 1987;70:896–899 (Level I)

28. Calhoun BC, Edgeworth D, Brehm W. External cephalic version at a military teaching hospital: predictors of success. Aust N Z J Obstet Gynaecol 1995;35:277–279 (Level II-3)

29. Donald WL, Barton JJ. Ultrasonography and external cephalic version at term. Am J Obstet Gynecol 1990;162:1542–1545; discussion 1545–1547 (Level II-3)

30. Mauldin JG, Mauldin PD, Feng TI, Adams EK, Durkalski VL. Determining the clinical efficacy and cost savings of successful external cephalic version. Am J Obstet Gynecol 1996;175:1639–1644 (Level II-3)

31. Lau TK, Lo KW, Wan D, Rogers MS. Predictors of successful external cephalic version at term: a prospective study. Br J Obstet Gynaecol 1997;104:798–802 (Level II-3)

32. Healey M, Porter R, Galimberti A. Introducing external cephalic version at 36 weeks or more in a district general hospital: a review and an audit. Br J Obstet Gynaecol 1997;104:1073–1079 (Level II-3)

33. Stock A, Chung T, Rogers M, Ming WW. Randomized, double blind, placebo controlled comparison of ritodrine and hexoprenaline for tocolysis prior to external cephalic version at term. Aust N Z J Obstet Gynaecol 1993;33:265–268 (Level I)

34. Chung T, Neale E, Lau TK, Rogers M. A randomized, double blind, controlled trial of tocolysis to assist external cephalic version in late pregnancy. Acta Obstet Gynecol Scand 1996;75:720–724 (Level I)

35. Marquette GP, Boucher M, Theriault D, Rinfret D. Does the use of a tocolytic agent affect the success rate of external cephalic version? Am J Obstet Gynecol 1996;175:859–861 (Level I)

36. Fernandez CO, Bloom SL, Smulian JC, Ananth CV, Wendel GD Jr. A randomized placebo-controlled evaluation of terbutaline for external cephalic version. Obstet Gynecol 1997;90:775–779 (Level I)

37. Hanss JW Jr. The efficacy of external cephalic version and its impact on the breech experience. Am J Obstet Gynecol 1990;162:1459–1463; discussion 1463–1464 (Level II-3)

38. Schorr SJ, Speights SE, Ross EL, Bofill JA, Rust OA, Norman PF, et al. A randomized trial of epidural anesthesia to improve external cephalic version success. Am J Obstet Gynecol 1997;177:1133–1137 (Level I)

39. Neiger R, Hennessey MD, Patel M. Reattempting failed external cephalic version under epidural anesthesia. Am J Obstet Gynecol 1998;179:1136–1139 (Level III)

40. Dugoff L, Stamm CA, Jones OW 3rd, Mohling SI, Hawkins JL. The effect of spinal anesthesia on the success rate of external cephalic version: a randomized trial. Obstet Gynecol 1999;93:345–349 (Level I)

41. Gifford DS, Keeler E, Kahn KL. Reductions in cost and cesarean rate by routine use of external cephalic version: a decision analysis. Obstet Gynecol 1995;85:930–936 (Level III)

The MEDLINE database, the Cochrane Library, and ACOG's own internal resources and documents were used to conduct a literature search to locate relevant articles published between January 1981 and May 1999. The search was restricted to articles published in the English language. Priority was given to articles reporting results of original research, although review articles and commentaries also were consulted. Abstracts of research presented at symposia and scientific conferences were not considered adequate for inclusion in this document. Guidelines published by organizations or institutions such as the National Institutes of Health and the American College of Obstetricians and Gynecologists were reviewed, and additional studies were located by reviewing bibliographies of identified articles. When reliable research was not available, expert opinions from obstetrician–gynecologists were used.

Studies were reviewed and evaluated for quality according to the method outlined by the U.S. Preventive Services Task Force:

I   Evidence obtained from at least one properly designed randomized controlled trial.
II-1   Evidence obtained from well-designed controlled trials without randomization.
II-2   Evidence obtained from well-designed cohort or case–control analytic studies, preferably from more than one center or research group.
II-3   Evidence obtained from multiple time series with or without the intervention. Dramatic results in uncontrolled experiments could also be regarded as this type of evidence.
III   Opinions of respected authorities, based on clinical experience, descriptive studies, or reports of expert committees.

Based on the highest level of evidence found in the data, recommendations are provided and graded according to the following categories:

Level A—Recommendations are based on good and consistent scientific evidence.

Level B—Recommendations are based on limited or inconsistent scientific evidence.

Level C—Recommendations are based primarily on consensus and expert opinion.

ISSN 1099-3630

**The American College of
Obstetricians and Gynecologists
409 12th Street, SW
PO Box 96920
Washington, DC 20090-6920**

12345/43210

ACOG PRACTICE BULLETIN

CLINICAL MANAGEMENT GUIDELINES FOR
OBSTETRICIAN–GYNECOLOGISTS

NUMBER 22, NOVEMBER 2000

(Replaces Technical Bulletin Number 159, September 1991)

This Practice Bulletin was developed by the ACOG Committee on Practice Bulletins—Obstetrics with the assistance of William H. Barth, Jr, MD. The information is designed to aid practitioners in making decisions about appropriate obstetric and gynecologic care. These guidelines should not be construed as dictating an exclusive course of treatment or procedure. Variations in practice may be warranted based on the needs of the individual patient, resources, and limitations unique to the institution or type of practice.

Fetal Macrosomia

Suspected fetal macrosomia is a common obstetric condition. As birth weight increases, the likelihood of labor abnormalities, shoulder dystocia, birth trauma, and permanent injury to the neonate increases. The purpose of this document is to quantify those risks, address the accuracy and limitations of methods for estimating fetal weight, and suggest clinical management for the pregnancy with suspected fetal macrosomia.

Background

Definition

Two terms identify excessive fetal growth: *large for gestational age* and *macrosomia*. The term large for gestational age generally implies a birth weight equal to or greater than the 90th percentile for a given gestational age. For years, clinicians have relied on popular fetal growth curves to identify weight cutoffs for the 90th percentile for a given gestational age (1–3). A national reference for fetal growth is now available. A study using the 1991 U.S. Live Birth File of the National Center for Health Statistics reported data for fetal growth based on more than 3.8 million births (4). The 50th, 90th, and 95th percentiles for birth weight from 37 to 42 completed weeks of gestation are shown in Table 1.

The term *fetal macrosomia* implies growth beyond a specific weight, usually 4,000 g or 4,500 g, regardless of the gestational age. Although the risks of morbidity for infants and mothers when birth weight is between 4,000 g and 4,500 g are greater than those of the general obstetric population, these risks increase sharply beyond 4,500 g (5–10). Recent large cohort studies (11–14) further support the continued use of 4,500 g as an appropriate estimated weight beyond which the fetus should be considered macrosomic.

Rather than assigning a different minimum estimated fetal weight for macrosomia among infants of women with diabetes, understanding that maternal diabetes is an independent predictor of fetal morbidity will help avoid confusion. Regardless of their birth weight, infants of women with diabetes have

Table 1. Percentiles for Birth Weight for Gestational Age: U.S. 1991 Single Live Births to Resident Mothers 37–42 Completed Weeks

	Birth Weight (g)		
Gestational Age	50th Percentile	90th Percentile	95th Percentile
37	3,117	3,755	3,956
38	3,263	3,867	4,027
39	3,400	3,980	4,107
40	3,495	4,060	4,185
41	3,527	4,094	4,217
42	3,522	4,098	4,213

Modified from Alexander GR, Himes JH, Kaufman RB, Mor J, Kogan M. A United States national reference for fetal growth. Obstet Gynecol 1996;87:163–168

an increased risk of shoulder dystocia, clavicular fracture, and brachial plexus injury (14, 15–17).

Frequency of Occurrence

Information from the National Center for Health Statistics shows that 10% of all liveborn infants in the United States weigh more than 4,000 g (18). In contrast, only 1.5% weigh more than 4,500 g. The most serious complication of fetal macrosomia is shoulder dystocia. Fortunately, shoulder dystocia is rare, complicating only 1.4% of all vaginal deliveries (19). When birth weight exceeds 4,500 g, however, the risk of shoulder dystocia is increased, with rates reported from 9.2% to 24% (8, 11–14). In the presence of maternal diabetes, birth weights greater than 4,500 g have been associated with rates of shoulder dystocia from 19.9% to 50% (8, 12, 14). Figure 1 shows the relationship between birth weight, maternal diabetes status, spontaneous or assisted vaginal delivery, and the mean frequency of shoulder dystocia based on a study of more than 175,000 deliveries in California in 1992 (14).

Several issues complicate attempts to define precisely the incidence of shoulder dystocia among macrosomic infants. First, clinicians tend to underreport the occurrence of shoulder dystocia (20, 21). Second, the incidence of shoulder dystocia and the likelihood of subsequent fetal injury vary depending on the criteria used to render a diagnosis of dystocia (22). Studies requiring the use of auxiliary maneuvers other than gentle downward traction and episiotomy to effect delivery (16) report a lower overall incidence of shoulder dystocia—but greater proportional fetal morbidity—than those studies with less precise definitions (11). Finally, although macrosomia clearly increases risk, it is important to note that most instances of shoulder dystocia occur unpredictably among infants of normal birth weight (19, 23).

Risk Factors for Macrosomia

A number of factors predispose to newborn macrosomia. A large case–control study examined the relative contributions of proposed risk factors for macrosomia, excluding preexisting diabetes (24). In decreasing order of importance, these risk factors included a prior history of macrosomia, maternal prepregnancy weight, weight gain during pregnancy, multiparity, male fetus, gestational age greater than 40 weeks, ethnicity, maternal birth weight, maternal height, maternal age younger than 17 years, and a positive 50-g glucose screen with a negative result on the 3-hour glucose tolerance test. Although maternal smoking decreases the likelihood of newborn macrosomia (25), it should not be recommended as a protective measure for obvious reasons.

Both pregestational diabetes and gestational diabetes are associated with fetal macrosomia. Even in patients without diabetes, observational cohort studies and case–control studies demonstrate that graded increases in the level of maternal glycemia are associated with increases in newborn birth weight (26, 27). A study reported that 6% of mothers with untreated borderline gestational diabetes delivered infants exceeding 4,500 g, compared with only 2% of women with normal glucose tolerance (28). If gestational diabetes is unrecognized and untreated, the risk of macrosomia may be as high as 20% (29).

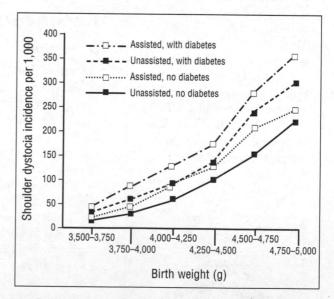

Figure 1. Frequency of shoulder dystocia for increasing birth weight by maternal diabetes status and method of vaginal delivery—spontaneous or assisted. (Nesbitt TS, Gilbert WM, Herrchen B. Shoulder dystocia and associated risk factors with macrosomic infants born in California. Am J Obstet Gynecol 1998;179:476–480)

Anthropometric studies suggest that the macrosomia produced by maternal glucose intolerance is different from that associated with other predisposing factors (30, 31). These macrosomic infants tend to have greater total body fat, greater shoulder and upper-extremity circumferences, greater upper-extremity skin-fold measurements, and smaller head-to-abdominal-circumference ratios than macrosomic infants of mothers without diabetes. Some have suggested that it is this altered fetal body shape that is responsible for the higher incidence of shoulder dystocia seen among infants of women with diabetes (31).

The relative contributions of maternal diabetes and obesity to fetal macrosomia remain controversial. One study reported that the risk for fetal macrosomia associated with unrecognized gestational diabetes persisted after controlling for both maternal body mass index and maternal weight gain (29). In a study among women with diet-controlled gestational diabetes, adjusting for maternal weight decreased the relative risk for large infants (greater than the 90th percentile) from 2.5 to 1.5 (32). Although both diabetes and maternal obesity increase the risk of fetal macrosomia, most agree that maternal obesity plays a greater role (7, 24, 33).

The interaction of maternal weight, weight gain during pregnancy, and newborn macrosomia is complex. There is little doubt that birth weight, in general, increases with maternal body mass index (34–36). Almost all authors report that obese women are more likely than women of normal weight to have large infants (35, 37). However, several issues confound this observation. First, obese women are more likely to have diabetes mellitus. One study demonstrated that morbidly obese women (>300 lb) are eight times more likely to deliver an infant exceeding 4,500 g (38). Second, high weight gain during pregnancy is itself a risk factor for excessive fetal growth (39). The risk of newborn macrosomia associated with excessive maternal weight gain is greater for obese women than for nonobese women (35, 37).

Understandably, gestational age influences birth weight and the risk of macrosomia. Among all races in the United States, the risk of macrosomia increases from 1.6% at term to 2.5% if gestational age exceeds 42 weeks (18). However, as Table 1 shows, there is little additional weight gain after 41 weeks of gestation.

A number of maternal historic factors and habits also influence infant birth weight. Women who have previously delivered an infant weighing more than 4,000 g are five to 10 times more likely to deliver an infant exceeding 4,500 g than women without such a history (5, 24, 40). To a degree, maternal birth weight may predict newborn weight. Women whose own birth weight exceeded 8 lb (approximately 3,600 g) are twice as likely to deliver infants greater than 4,000 g than are women whose birth weight was between 6 lb and 7.9 lb (approximately 2,700–3,500 g) (41). Finally, three cohort studies show that multiparity and grand-multiparity (≥ 5 deliveries) increase the risk of macrosomia (42–44).

Genetic, racial, and ethnic factors also influence birth weight and the risk of macrosomia. Male infants typically weigh more than female infants at any gestational age and, therefore, constitute a greater proportion of infants with birth weights exceeding 4,500 g (12, 45). The risk of macrosomia varies with race and ethnicity as well. Two reports, both of which controlled for diabetes, have demonstrated that Hispanic women have a higher risk of fetal macrosomia than do white, black, or Asian women (46, 47). Genetic factors such as parental height and race play a role in determining newborn birth weight, but these factors interact in a complex manner with environmental factors during pregnancy (48, 49). No combination of these risk factors predicts macrosomia well enough to be used clinically. Much of the variation in birth weights remains unexplained, and most infants greater than 4,500 g do not have identifiable risk factors (6).

Diagnosis

An accurate diagnosis of macrosomia can be made only by weighing the newborn after delivery. Unfortunately, the prenatal diagnosis of fetal macrosomia remains imprecise. Methods used to predict birth weight include assessment of maternal risk factors, clinical examination, and ultrasound measurement of the fetus. Although ultrasonography enables the direct measurement of various fetal body parts, its accuracy in predicting macrosomia has been unreliable (50–52). Furthermore, the superiority of ultrasound-derived estimates of fetal weight over clinical estimates has not been established (53–55). Indeed, parous women are able to predict the weight of their newborns as well as clinicians who use ultrasound measurements or Leopold's maneuvers (56).

Risks Associated with Macrosomia

Maternal Morbidity

The primary maternal risk associated with macrosomia is an increased risk of cesarean delivery. With birth weights greater than 4,500 g, cohort studies show that the risk of cesarean delivery for women attempting a vaginal delivery is at least double that of controls (5, 7, 13, 40). Almost all the increased risk is attributed to labor abnormalities

(5, 11). Not surprisingly, a study has demonstrated that the inaccurate ultrasonographic prediction of macrosomia predisposes to the diagnosis of labor abnormalities and cesarean delivery independent of actual birth weight (57). The risks of postpartum hemorrhage and significant vaginal lacerations also are elevated with macrosomia. A case–control study of risk factors for major obstetric hemorrhage (estimated blood loss >1 L) reported that a birth weight greater than 4,000 g doubled the odds of significant maternal blood loss (odds ratio [OR]: 1.9, 95% confidence interval [CI]: 1.38–2.6) (58). Although the risk of third- and fourth-degree lacerations is slightly increased with macrosomia (12), this is especially true if delivery is complicated by shoulder dystocia (59). Maternal infectious morbidity generally is limited to urinary tract infection in women undergoing elective cesarean delivery (60) and puerperal fever in women undergoing cesarean delivery after a trial of labor (12).

Fetal Morbidity and Mortality

The fetal injuries most commonly associated with macrosomia and shoulder dystocia are fracture of the clavicle and damage to the nerves of the brachial plexus, specifically C5 and C6, producing Erb-Duchenne paralysis. Fracture of the clavicle complicates 0.3–0.7% of all deliveries and usually resolves without permanent sequelae (61–63). For macrosomic infants, the risk of clavicular fracture is increased approximately 10-fold (63).

Brachial plexus injury is rare, with an incidence reported between 0.5 and 1.89 injuries per 1,000 vaginal deliveries (9, 15, 17, 63–65). Case–control studies demonstrate that the risk of brachial plexus injury among infants delivered vaginally is increased 18- to 21-fold when birth weight exceeds 4,500 g (9, 17, 63). Recent reports place the occurrence of brachial plexus injury for macrosomic infants delivered vaginally between 4% and 8% (12, 13, 65). Even though shoulder dystocia is underreported (20), the occurrence of brachial plexus injury in the absence of documented shoulder dystocia is well described (14, 21). Brachial plexus injury has been associated with cesarean delivery (66). As with clavicular fracture, most brachial plexus injuries resolve without permanent handicap. Among 59 confirmed brachial plexus injuries described in the Collaborative Perinatal Project, only 6 (12%) were still evident by age 4 months (64). By age 2 years, all but 4 (7%) had resolved. Other large case series confirm that 80–90% of brachial plexus injuries will resolve by age 1 year (23, 67). However, persistent injury may be more common with birth weights greater than 4,500 g (68). Nonetheless, as with shoulder dystocia, most brachial plexus injuries occur in nonmacrosomic infants (65).

Macrosomia is associated with a number of other risks to the newborn. These infants face an increased risk of depressed 5-minute Apgar scores and increased rates of admission to a neonatal intensive care unit (65). However, most of this risk likely is the result of complications of the birth process, because macrosomic infants do not have higher rates of fetal heart rate abnormalities in labor (5). Finally, overweight newborns are more likely to be overweight later in life than are normal-weight newborns (69).

Clinical Considerations and Recommendations

▶ *How accurate are clinical estimates of fetal weight?*

The two primary methods for clinical estimation of fetal weight are Leopold's maneuvers (abdominal palpation) and measurement of the height of the uterine fundus above the maternal symphysis pubis. In a prospective study of 602 term patients, clinical palpation alone predicted macrosomia as accurately as any reported ultrasonographic method (53). A study of more than 1,700 women concluded that although ultrasound-derived estimates are more accurate for newborns weighing between 2,500 g and 4,000 g, above this level, ultrasound measurement and clinical palpation have similar accuracy (70).

Measurement of the symphysis–fundal height alone is a poor predictor of fetal macrosomia. Although the average fundal height measurement is greater for fetuses exceeding 4,500 g (71), the utility of this measurement alone is questionable (72). To be useful, measurement of the uterine fundal height must be combined with clinical palpation or Leopold's maneuvers. Prospective studies designed to evaluate Leopold's maneuvers with fundal height measurement for the detection of macrosomia report sensitivities of 10–43%, specificities of 99.0–99.8%, and positive predictive values between 28% and 53% (55, 73). Ultrasound measurements of those women with suspected fetal macrosomia on the basis of clinical examination alone decreased sensitivity and positive predictive value without measurably affecting specificity (73). Prospective studies among women with diabetes also have shown that clinical estimates of macrosomia are as predictive as those derived with ultrasonography (54).

Finally, simply asking a parous woman her estimate of the fetal weight may provide an estimate as accurate as any other. In one study, a parous woman's ability to predict birth weight greater than 4,000 g was as accurate as that of clinicians using Leopold's maneuvers alone (56).

▶ *How accurate is ultrasound measurement in determining fetal weight?*

Ultrasound-derived estimates of fetal weight are obtained by entering the measurements of various fetal body parts, usually including the abdominal circumference, into one of several popular regression equations (74, 75). Most commercially available ultrasound units have one or more of these equations already programmed into the software of the system, allowing immediate calculation of estimated fetal weights. Unfortunately, most of the regression formulas currently in use are associated with significant errors when the fetus is macrosomic. For example, Hadlock's formula to predict fetal weight has a mean absolute percent error of 13% for infants greater than 4,500 g, compared with 8% for nonmacrosomic infants (76).

Ultrasound-derived diagnosis of an estimated fetal weight exceeding 4,500 g is not as accurate as many believe it to be. Among women without diabetes, ultrasound biometry used to detect macrosomia has a sensitivity of 22–44%, a specificity of 99%, a positive predictive value of 30–44%, and a negative predictive value of 97–99% (77, 78). Reports demonstrating greater accuracy generally rely on less stringent criteria for macrosomia, such as birth weight greater than 4,000 g or that exceeding the 90th percentile for a given gestational age. However, when birth weight exceeds 4,500 g, only 50% of fetuses weigh within 10% of the ultrasound-derived estimate (79). Using existing formulas, an estimated fetal weight would have to exceed 4,800 g for the fetus to have more than a 50% chance of being macrosomic (77, 80). These observations suggest that the usefulness of ultrasonography for obtaining estimated weights is limited, and these limitations are neither operator-dependent nor equipment-dependent (79).

As with clinical estimates of fetal weight, the true value of ultrasonography in the management of expected fetal macrosomia may be its ability to rule out the diagnosis, which may help avoid maternal morbidity. One study revealed that clinicians who suspected fetal macrosomia on the basis of an ultrasonogram were more likely to diagnose labor abnormalities and were more likely to perform cesarean deliveries despite normal birth weights (57).

▶ *Are interventions for treating suspected macrosomia available?*

For mothers without diabetes, no clinical interventions designed to treat or curb fetal growth when macrosomia is

suspected have been reported. For pregnancies that are complicated by diabetes mellitus, one clinical trial suggests that the addition of insulin to diet therapy may treat early macrosomia diagnosed between 29 and 33 weeks of gestation (81). This study randomized 98 women with a fetal abdominal circumference exceeding the 75th percentile for gestational age to either diet therapy alone or diet therapy with twice-daily insulin. The addition of insulin therapy decreased the likelihood of birth weight greater than the 90th percentile from 45% among those treated with diet only to 13% among those receiving insulin ($P < 0.01$) (81).

Three large cohort studies confirm that excessive weight gain during pregnancy is associated with fetal macrosomia, suggesting a possible role for caloric restriction (35, 37, 39). One of these studies demonstrated that for most women, excessive weight gain doubled the risk of delivering an infant weighing more than 4,500 g. Although this relationship held true for average, obese, and very obese women, the actual incidence of macrosomia was still low (between 2.7% and 5.6%). Although dietary regulation has long been a mainstay of therapy for gestational diabetes, a recent meta-analysis of four randomized clinical trials examining primary diet therapy for women with impaired glucose tolerance showed no significant reduction in the number of newborns weighing more than 4,000 g (OR: 0.73, 95% CI: 0.45–1.35) (82). Although maternal obesity and weight gain during pregnancy are two of the strongest birth weight predictors, no randomized clinical trials have investigated dietary intervention to prevent macrosomia among obese women without diabetes.

▶ *When is cesarean delivery appropriate for suspected macrosomia at a particular estimated fetal weight?*

Controversy surrounds the question of cesarean delivery for suspected fetal macrosomia. First, the risk of birth trauma associated with vaginal delivery increases with birth weight (9, 17, 63). Second, cesarean delivery reduces—but does not eliminate—the risk of birth trauma and brachial plexus injury associated with fetal macrosomia (7, 9, 17, 83). The protective effect of cesarean delivery is large. Using a multivariate analysis to investigate risk factors for brachial plexus injury, investigators reported an odds ratio for cesarean delivery of 0.01–0.20 (17). It thus seems logical that for each woman, there must be a fetal weight beyond which the risks of vaginal delivery to the fetus are high enough to warrant cesarean delivery.

Despite such reasoning, the clinical effectiveness of offering prophylactic cesarean delivery to women with any specific estimated fetal weight has not been established in randomized clinical trials. Currently, only one observational study has evaluated a policy of using ultrasound-derived fetal weight estimates to determine the route of delivery (84). The use of historic controls, the nonrandomized design of the study, the use of multiple interventions, and the small sample size severely limit the usefulness of conclusions from the study. In this study, 1,337 women with diabetes were offered elective cesarean delivery based on ultrasound-derived fetal weight estimates beyond 4,250 g and induction of labor if ultrasound measurements resulted in a prediction of a large-for-gestational-age infant with an estimated fetal weight less than 4,250 g (84). The study cohort was compared with a historic control group of 1,227 women with diabetes who were managed without intervention for accelerated fetal growth during the 3 years preceding implementation of the study protocol. Implementation of the study protocol was associated with a nonsignificant reduction in the risk of shoulder dystocia from 2.4% in controls to 1.1% in the intervention group. In addition, a significant increase in the institutional cesarean delivery rate from 21.7% in controls to 25.1% in the intervention group was reported. Although the sample size was insufficient for comparison, the risk of birth trauma was not eliminated (2 versus 1 brachial plexus injury, 12 versus 6 fractures).

Currently, no prospective studies have assessed the true risk of either shoulder dystocia or brachial plexus injury in conjunction with estimated fetal weight alone. Until well-designed randomized clinical trials of sufficient sample size are available, clinicians must rely on retrospective data to make clinical management decisions.

In addition, recent large cohort and case–control studies demonstrate the safety of allowing a trial of labor for estimated birth weights of more than 4,000 g (12, 13). Among the 2,924 infants previously identified with birth weights greater than 4,000 g in utero, only 48 injuries (1.6%) related to shoulder dystocia were noted. Among the 22 brachial plexus injuries with documented follow-up, only 5 (17%) were clinically evident at 6 months (68). A second study reported 27 episodes (11.4%) of shoulder dystocia and 3 instances (1.3%) of brachial plexus paralysis in a group of 236 neonates weighing at least 4,200 g (85). In an additional series of 87 infants with birth weights greater than 4,500 g who were delivered vaginally, investigators reported only 5 cases (5.7%) of Erb-Duchenne paralysis. By 3 months of age, all affected infants were without evidence of brachial plexus paralysis (13). A fourth study reported that of the 157 infants delivered vaginally with birth weights greater than

4,500 g, no permanent sequelae were identified by age 2 months (12). The risks of short-term morbidity associated with vaginal delivery in this group are low, and those of permanent injury are even lower.

In conjunction with published cost-effectiveness data, the sum of these reports does not support a policy of prophylactic cesarean delivery for suspected fetal macrosomia with estimated weights less than 5,000 g (86). Along with a description of the limitations of estimating fetal weight, the obstetrician should present accurate statistics for the short- and long-term risks of maternal and fetal morbidity for both vaginal and cesarean delivery as discussed previously.

Despite the poor predictive value of an estimated fetal weight beyond 5,000 g and a lack of evidence supporting cesarean delivery at any estimated fetal weight, most, but not all, authors agree that consideration should be given to cesarean delivery in this situation (7, 13, 65). Among infants with birth weights exceeding 5,000 g, there are reports of cesarean delivery rates of 35–60%, brachial paralysis rates of 7–11%, and a perinatal death rate as high as 2.4% (7). In contrast, despite reporting an OR of 45 (95% CI: 16–129) for brachial plexus injury among vaginally delivered infants exceeding 5,000 g, some investigators suggest that ultrasound-derived fetal weight estimates alone should not be used to determine the route of delivery (17, 52).

▶ *Is there a role for induction of labor in the management of term patients with suspected fetal macrosomia?*

Current evidence from cohort studies does not support a policy of early induction of labor in term patients with suspected fetal macrosomia. Three recent reports show that induction of labor at least doubles the risk of cesarean delivery without reducing shoulder dystocia or newborn morbidity (87–89). Although the increased risk of cesarean delivery with induction of labor is clear, on the basis of these reports, one cannot rule out the possibility of a small beneficial effect on fetal outcome. These studies, however, are affected by small sample size and possible bias introduced by their retrospective nature.

One randomized clinical trial of women without diabetes has addressed the role of induction of labor for suspected fetal macrosomia at term. A total of 273 women with ultrasound-derived estimated fetal weights between 4,000 g and 4,500 g were randomized to either planned induction of labor or expectant management (90). Inductions were performed with oxytocin or prostaglandins followed by oxytocin, depending on the condition of the cervix. The cesarean delivery rates were similar: 19.4% for the induction group and 21.6% for the expectant group. There were 11 cases of shoulder dystocia, 5 in the induction group and 6 in the expectant group. All were managed without brachial plexus injury or other trauma.

▶ *How many elective cesarean deliveries for suspected fetal macrosomia would have to be performed to prevent one case of brachial plexus injury?*

The cost-effectiveness of elective cesarean delivery for fetal macrosomia usually is expressed as the number of cesarean deliveries required to prevent one brachial plexus injury or the cost, in dollars, of each brachial plexus injury avoided. A case–control study of brachial plexus paralysis demonstrated that 51 cesarean deliveries would be needed to prevent one case of brachial plexus paralysis if the cutoff for cesarean delivery were 4,500 g among patients without diabetes (17). For a cutoff of 5,000 g, this number decreased to 19. Assuming persistent rates for brachial plexus impairment are between 5% and 22%, the authors suggested that to prevent a single permanent injury, the number of cesarean deliveries increases to between 233 and 1,026 for a birth weight cutoff of 4,500 g, and from 85 to 373 for a cutoff of 5,000 g. Another study using similar methods concluded that 155–588 cesarean deliveries are needed to prevent a single permanent injury using a cutoff of 4,500 g for infants of women without diabetes (65). However, because the authors did not consider the imperfect predictive values of ultrasonography for macrosomia, they underestimated the number of cesarean deliveries that would be needed to implement such a policy.

In two reports analyzing a policy of prophylactic cesarean delivery for macrosomia, which took into account the reported sensitivity and specificity of ultrasonography for the detection of macrosomia (4,500 g), it was calculated that 3,695 cesarean deliveries would be required to prevent one permanent injury at a cost of $8.7 million for each injury avoided (86, 91). For pregnancies complicated by diabetes, these figures were still high at 443 cesarean deliveries to prevent a single permanent injury. In summary, because of the lack of well-designed and well-executed randomized clinical trials, a policy of prophylactic cesarean delivery for suspected fetal macrosomia less than 5,000 g may not be effective for pregnancies without diabetes. Furthermore, even for pregnancies complicated by diabetes, the cost-effectiveness of such a policy is doubtful.

▶ *How should a diagnosis of suspected fetal macrosomia affect the management of labor and vaginal delivery?*

Perhaps the most important consideration for labor and delivery with suspected fetal macrosomia is the decision to conduct a midpelvic operative vaginal delivery. As depicted in Figure 1, the risk of shoulder dystocia is associated with assisted vaginal delivery. Case–control and cohort studies consistently demonstrate an increased risk of shoulder dystocia when the macrosomic fetus is delivered by forceps, especially midforceps for a prolonged second stage (8, 10, 14, 19, 92). Rates of shoulder dystocia with midforceps deliveries of infants greater than 4,500 g have been reported to be above 50%. Barring extreme emergencies, cesarean delivery should be performed for midpelvic arrest of the fetus with suspected macrosomia. If a decision is made to proceed with cesarean delivery in the presence of suspected macrosomia, the incision should be large enough to avoid a difficult abdominal delivery.

Suspected fetal macrosomia is not a contraindication to attempt vaginal birth after prior cesarean delivery. A cohort study compared maternal and fetal outcomes associated with a trial of labor for infants suspected to be macrosomic and with documented birth weights less than 4,000 g versus those greater than 4,000 g (93). The success rate for vaginal delivery was 58% for birth weights between 4,000 g and 4,499 g and 43% for birth weights of 4,500 g and higher. Maternal and newborn morbidities were equal. A case–control study examining risk factors for uterine rupture during a trial of labor found no association between rupture and birth weight greater than 4,000 g (94).

Summary

The following recommendation is based on good and consistent scientific evidence (Level A):

▶ The diagnosis of fetal macrosomia is imprecise. For suspected fetal macrosomia, the accuracy of estimated fetal weight using ultrasound biometry is no better than that obtained with clinical palpation (Leopold's maneuvers).

The following recommendations are based on limited or inconsistent scientific evidence (Level B):

▶ Suspected fetal macrosomia is not an indication for induction of labor, because induction does not improve maternal or fetal outcomes.

▶ Labor and vaginal delivery are not contraindicated for women with estimated fetal weights up to 5,000 g in the absence of maternal diabetes.

▶ With an estimated fetal weight greater than 4,500 g, a prolonged second stage of labor or arrest of descent in the second stage is an indication for cesarean delivery.

The following recommendations are based primarily on consensus and expert opinion (Level C):

▶ Although the diagnosis of fetal macrosomia is imprecise, prophylactic cesarean delivery may be considered for suspected fetal macrosomia with estimated fetal weights greater than 5,000 g in women without diabetes and greater than 4,500 g in women with diabetes.

▶ Suspected fetal macrosomia is not a contraindication to attempted vaginal birth after a previous cesarean delivery.

References

1. Lubchenco LO, Hansman C, Dressler M, Boyd E. Intrauterine growth as estimated from liveborn birth-weight data at 24 to 42 weeks of gestation. Pediatrics 1963;32:793–800 (Level III)

2. Williams RL. Intrauterine growth curves: intra- and international comparisons with different ethnic groups in California. Prev Med 1975;4:163–172 (Level III)

3. Brenner WE, Edelman DA, Hendricks CH. A standard of fetal growth in the United States of America. Am J Obstet Gynecol 1976;126:555–564 (Level III)

4. Alexander GR, Himes JH, Kaufman RB, Mor J, Kogan M. A United States national reference for fetal growth. Obstet Gynecol 1996;87:163–168 (Level III)

5. Modanlou HD, Dorchester WL, Thorosian A, Freeman RK. Macrosomia—maternal, fetal and neonatal implications. Obstet Gynecol 1980;55:420–424 (Level II-2)

6. Boyd ME, Usher RH, McLean FH. Fetal macrosomia: prediction, risks, proposed management. Obstet Gynecol 1983;61:715–722 (Level II-2)

7. Spellacy WN, Miller S, Winegar A, Peterson PQ. Macrosomia—maternal characteristics and infant complications. Obstet Gynecol 1985;66:158–161 (Level II-2)

8. Acker DB, Sachs BP, Friedman EA. Risk factors for shoulder dystocia. Obstet Gynecol 1985;66:762–768 (Level II-3)

9. McFarland LV, Raskin M, Daling JR, Benedetti TJ. Erb/Duchenne's palsy: a consequence of fetal macrosomia and method of delivery. Obstet Gynecol 1986;68:784–788 (Level II-2)

10. Gross TL, Sokol RJ, Williams T, Thompson K. Shoulder dystocia: a fetal-physician risk. Am J Obstet Gynecol 1987;156:1408–1418 (Level II-2)

11. Menticoglou SM, Manning FA, Morrison I, Harman CR. Must macrosomic fetuses be delivered by a cesarean section? A review of outcome for 786 babies ≥ 4,500 g. Aust N Z J Obstet Gynaecol 1992;32:100–103 (Level III)

12. Lipscomb KR, Gregory K, Shaw K. The outcome of macrosomic infants weighing at least 4500 grams: Los Angeles county + University of Southern California experience. Obstet Gynecol 1995;85:558–564 (Level II-3)

13. Bérard J, Dufour P, Vinatier D, Subtil D, Vanderstichèle S, Monnier JC, et al. Fetal macrosomia: risk factors and outcome. A study of the outcome concerning 100 cases >4500 g. Eur J Obstet Gynecol Reprod Biol 1998; 77:51–59 (Level II-3)

14. Nesbitt TS, Gilbert WM, Herrchen B. Shoulder dystocia and associated risk factors with macrosomic infants born in California. Am J Obstet Gynecol 1998;179:476–480 (Level II-3)

15. Acker DB, Gregory KD, Sachs BP, Friedman EA. Risk factors for Erb-Duchenne palsy. Obstet Gynecol 1988; 71:389–392 (Level II-3)

16. Bahar AM. Risk factors and fetal outcome in cases of shoulder dystocia compared with normal deliveries of a similar birth weight. Br J Obstet Gynaecol 1996;103: 68–872 (Level II-2)

17. Ecker JL, Greenberg JA, Norwitz ER, Nadel AS, Repke JT. Birth weight as a predictor of brachial plexus injury. Obstet Gynecol 1997;89:643–647 (Level II-2)

18. Ventura SJ, Martin JA, Curtin SC, Mathews TJ, Park MM. Births: final data for 1998. Natl Vital Stat Rep 2000;48: 1–100 (Level II-3)

19. Nocon JJ, McKenzie DK, Thomas LJ, Hansell RS. Shoulder dystocia: an analysis of risks and obstetric maneuvers. Am J Obstet Gynecol 1993;168:1732–1739 (Level II-2)

20. Gonik B, Hollyer L, Allen R. Shoulder dystocia recognition: differences in neonatal risks for injury. Am J Perinatol 1991;8:31–34 (Level II-3)

21. Jennett RJ, Tarby TJ, Kreinick CJ. Brachial plexus palsy: an old problem revisited. Am J Obstet Gynecol 1992;166: 1673–1677 (Level II-2)

22. Gross SJ, Shime J, Farine D. Shoulder dystocia: predictors and outcome. A five-year review. Am J Obstet Gynecol 1987;156:334–336 (Level II-3)

23. Morrison JC, Sanders JR, Magann EF, Wiser WL. The diagnosis and management of dystocia of the shoulder. Surg Gynecol Obstet 1992;175:515–522 (Level II-3)

24. Okun N, Verma A, Mitchell BF, Flowerdew G. Relative importance of maternal constitutional factors and glucose intolerance of pregnancy in the development of newborn macrosomia. J Matern Fetal Med 1997;6:285–290 (Level II-2)

25. Hellerstedt WL, Himes JH, Story M, Alton IR, Edwards LE. The effects of cigarette smoking and gestational weight change on birth outcomes in obese and normal-

weight women. Am J Public Health 1997;87:591–596 (Level II-2)

26. Sermer M, Naylor CD, Gare DJ, Kenshole AB, Ritchie JW, Farine D, et al. Impact of increasing carbohydrate intolerance on maternal-fetal outcomes in 3637 women without gestational diabetes. The Toronto Tri-Hospital Gestational Diabetes Project. Am J Obstet Gynecol 1995; 173:146–156 (Level II-2)

27. Verma A, Mitchell BF, Demianczuk N, Flowerdew G, Okun NB. Relationship between plasma glucose levels in glucose-intolerant women and newborn macrosomia. J Matern Fetal Med 1997;6:187–193 (Level II-2)

28. Naylor CD, Sermer M, Chen E, Sykora K. Cesarean delivery in relation to birth weight and gestational glucose tolerance: pathophysiology or practice style? Toronto Trihospital Gestational Diabetes Investigators. JAMA 1996;275:1165–1170 (Level II-2)

29. Adams KM, Li H, Nelson RL, Ogburn PL Jr, Danilenko-Dixon DR. Sequelae of unrecognized gestational diabetes. Am J Obstet Gynecol 1998;178:1321–1332 (Level II-2)

30. Nasrat H, Abalkhail B, Fageeh W, Shabat A, el Zahrany F. Anthropometric measurements of newborns of gestational diabetic mothers: does it indicate disproportionate fetal growth? J Matern Fetal Med 1997;6:291–295 (Level II-2)

31. McFarland MB, Trylovich CG, Langer O. Anthropometric differences in macrosomic infants of diabetic and nondiabetic mothers. J Matern Fetal Med 1998;7:292–295 (Level II-2)

32. Casey BM, Lucas MJ, McIntire DD, Leveno KJ. Pregnancy outcomes in women with gestational diabetes compared with the general obstetric population. Obstet Gynecol 1997;90:869–873 (Level II-2)

33. Lucas MJ, Lowe TW, Bowe L, McIntire DD. Class A1 gestational diabetes: a meaningful diagnosis? Obstet Gynecol 1993;82:260–265 (Level II-2)

34. Larsen CE, Serdula MK, Sullivan KM. Macrosomia: Influence of maternal overweight among a low-income population. Am J Obstet Gynecol 1990;162:490–494 (Level II-3)

35. Cogswell ME, Serdula MK, Hungerford DW, Yip R. Gestational weight gain among average-weight and overweight women—what is excessive? Am J Obstet Gynecol 1995;172:705–712 (Level II-2)

36. Ogunyemi D, Hullett S, Leeper J, Risk A. Prepregnancy body mass index, weight gain during pregnancy, and perinatal outcome in a rural black population. J Matern Fetal Med 1998;7:190–193 (Level II-3)

37. Bianco AT, Smilen SW, Davis Y, Lopez S, Lapinski R, Lockwood CJ. Pregnancy outcome and weight gain recommendations for the morbidly obese woman. Obstet Gynecol 1998;91:97–102 (Level II-2)

38. Perlow JH, Morgan MA, Montgomery D, Towers CV, Porto M. Perinatal outcome in pregnancy complicated by massive obesity. Am J Obstet Gynecol 1992;167:958–962 (Level II-2)

39. Parker JD, Abrams B. Prenatal weight gain advice: an examination of the recent prenatal weight gain recommendations of the Institute of Medicine. Obstet Gynecol 1992;79:664–669 (Level II-3)

40. Lazer S, Biale Y, Mazor M, Lewenthal H, Insler V. Complications associated with the macrosomic fetus. J Repro Med 1986;31:501–505 (Level II-2)

41. Klebanoff MA, Mills JL, Berendes HW. Mother's birth weight as a predictor of macrosomia. Am J Obstet Gynecol 1985;153:253–257 (Level II-2)

42. Toohey JS, Keegan KA Jr, Morgan MA, Francis J, Task S, deVeciana M. The "dangerous multipara": fact or fiction? Am J Obstet Gynecol 1995;172:683–686 (Level II-2)

43. Juntunen K, Kirkinen P, Kauppila A. The clinical outcome in pregnancies of grand grand multiparous women. Acta Obstet Gynecol Scand 1997;76:755–759 (Level II-3)

44. Babinszki A, Kerenyi T, Torok O, Grazi V, Lapinski RH, Berkowitz RL. Perinatal outcome in grand and great-grand multiparity: effects of parity on obstetric risk factors. Am J Obstet Gynecol 1999;181:669–674 (Level II-3)

45. Brunskill AJ, Rossing MA, Connel FA, Daling J. Antecedents of macrosomia. Paediatr Perinat Epidemiol 1991;5:392–401 (Level II-2)

46. Dooley SL, Metzger BE, Cho NH. Gestational diabetes mellitus. Influence of race on disease prevalence and perinatal outcome in a U.S. population. Diabetes 1991;40:25–29 (Level II-3)

47. Homko CJ, Sivan E, Nyirjesy P, Reece EA. The interrelationship between ethnicity and gestational diabetes in fetal macrosomia. Diabetes Care 1995;18:1442–1445 (Level II-3)

48. Little RE, Sing CF. Genetic and environmental influences on human birth weight. Am J Hum Genet 1987;40: 512–526 (Level III)

49. Wilcox MA, Newton CS, Johnson IR. Paternal influences on birth weight. Acta Obstet Gynecol Scand 1995;74: 15–18 (Level II-3)

50. Deter RL, Hadlock FP. Use of ultrasound in the detection of macrosomia: a review. J Clin Ultrasound 1985;13: 519–524 (Level III)

51. Rossavik IK, Joslin GL. Macrosomatia and ultrasonography: what is the problem? South Med J 1993; 86:1129–1132 (Level II-3)

52. Sandmire HF. Whither ultrasonic prediction of fetal macrosomia? Obstet Gynecol 1993;82:860–862 (Level III)

53. Chauhan SP, Cowan BD, Magann EF, Bradford TH, Roberts WE, Morrison JC. Intrapartum detection of a macrosomic fetus: clinical versus 8 sonographic models. Aust N Z J Obstet Gynaecol 1995;35:3:266–270 (Level II-2)

54. Johnstone FD, Prescott RJ, Steel JM, Mao JH, Chambers S, Muir N. Clinical and ultrasound prediction of macrosomia in diabetic pregnancy. Br J Obstet Gynaecol 1996; 103:747–754 (Level II-3)

55. Chauhan SP, Hendrix NW, Magann EF, Morrison JC, Kenney SP, Devoe LD. Limitations of clinical and sonographic estimates of birth weight: experience with 1034 parturients. Obstet Gynecol 1998;91:72–77 (Level II-2)

56. Chauhan SP, Sullivan CA, Lutton TD, Magann EF, Morrison JC. Parous patients' estimate of birth weight in postterm pregnancy. J Perinatol 1995;15:192–194 (Level II-2)

57. Levine AB, Lockwood CJ, Brown B, Lapinski R, Berkowitz RL. Sonographic diagnosis of the large for gestational age fetus at term: does it make a difference? Obstet Gynecol 1992;79:55–58 (Level II-2)

58. Stones RW, Paterson CM, Saunders NJ. Risk factors for major obstetric haemorrhage. Eur J Obstet Gynecol Reprod Biol 1993;48:15–18 (Level II-2)

59. el Madany AA, Jallad KB, Radi FA, el Hamdan H, O'deh HM. Shoulder dystocia: anticipation and outcome. Int J Gynaecol Obstet 1990;34:7–12 (Level II-2)

60. Irion O, Hirsbrunner Almagbaly P, Morabia A. Planned vaginal delivery versus elective caesarean section: a study of 705 singleton term breech presentations. Br J Obstet Gynaecol 1998;105:710–717 (Meta-analysis)

61. Oppenheim WL, Davis A, Growdon WA, Dorey FJ, Davlin LB. Clavicle fractures in the newborn. Clin Orthop 1990;250:176–180 (Level II-2)

62. Chez RA, Carlan S, Greenberg SL, Spellacy WN. Fractured clavicle is an unavoidable event. Am J Obstet Gynecol 1994;171:797–798 (Level II-2)

63. Perlow JH, Wigton T, Hart J, Strassner HT, Nageotte MP, Wolk BM. Birth trauma. A five-year review of incidence and associated perinatal factors. J Reprod Med 1996;41:754–760 (Level II-2)

64. Gordon M, Rich H, Deutschberger J, Green M. The immediate and long-term outcome of obstetric birth trauma. I. Brachial plexus paralysis. Am J Obstet Gynecol 1973;117:51–56 (Level II-2)

65. Bryant DR, Leonardi MR, Landwehr JB, Bottoms SF. Limited usefulness of fetal weight in predicting neonatal brachial plexus injury. Am J Obstet Gynecol 1998;179:686–689 (Level II-3)

66. Gherman RB, Goodwin TM, Ouzounian JG, Miller DA, Paul RH. Brachial plexus palsy associated with cesarean section: an in utero injury? Am J Obstet Gynecol 1997;177:1162–1164 (Level III)

67. Hardy AE. Birth injuries of the brachial plexus: incidence and prognosis. J Bone Joint Surg Br 1981;63-B:98–101 (Level III)

68. Kolderup LB, Laros RK Jr, Musci TJ. Incidence of persistent birth injury in macrosomic infants: association with mode of delivery. Am J Obstet Gynecol 1997;177:37–41 (Level II-2)

69. Seidman DS, Laor A, Stevenson DK, Sivan E, Gale R, Shemer J. Macrosomia does not predict overweight in late adolescence in infants of diabetic mothers. Acta Obstet Gynecol Scand 1998;77:58–62 (Level II-2)

70. Sherman DJ, Arieli S, Tovbin J, Siegel G, Caspi E, Bukovsky I. A comparison of clinical and ultrasonic estimation of fetal weight. Obstet Gynecol 1998;91:212–217 (Level II-3)

71. Wikstrom I, Bergstrom R, Bakketeig L, Jacobsen G, Lindmark G. Prediction of high birth weight from maternal characteristics, symphysis fundal height and ultrasound biometry. Gynecol Obstet Invest 1993;35:27–33 (Level II-2)

72. Neilson JP. Symphysis-fundal height measurement in pregnancy. Cochrane Database Syst Rev 2000; 2: CD000944. Review (Meta-analysis)

73. Gonen R, Spiegel D, Abend M. Is macrosomia predictable, and are shoulder dystocia and birth trauma preventable? Obstet Gynecol 1996;88:526–529 (Level II-3)

74. Shepard MJ, Richards VA, Berkowitz RL, Warsof SL, Hobbins JC. An evaluation of two equations for predicting fetal weight by ultrasound. Am J Obstet Gynecol 1982; 142: 47–54 (Level II-3)

75. Hadlock FP, Harrist RB, Carpenter RJ, Deter RL, Park SK. Sonographic estimation of fetal weight. The value of femur length in addition to head and abdomen measurements. Radiology 1984;150:535–540 (Level II-3)

76. Alsulyman OM, Ouzounian JG, Kjos SL. The accuracy of intrapartum ultrasonographic fetal weight estimation in diabetic pregnancies. Am J Obstet Gynecol 1997;177:503–506 (Level II-2)

77. Smith GC, Smith MF, McNay MB, Fleming JE. The relation between fetal abdominal circumference and birth weight: findings in 3512 pregnancies. Br J Obstet Gynaecol 1997;104:186–190 (Level II-3)

78. O'Reilly-Green CP, Divon MY. Receiver operating characteristic curves of sonographic estimated fetal weight for prediction of macrosomia in prolonged pregnancies. Ultrasound Obstet Gynecol 1997;9:403–408 (Level II-3)

79. Benacerraf BR, Gelman R, Frigoletto FD Jr. Sonographically estimated fetal weights: accuracy and limitation. Am J Obstet Gynecol 1988;159:1118–1121 (Level II-2)

80. McLaren RA, Puckett JL, Chauhan SP. Estimators of birth weight in pregnant women requiring insulin: a comparison of seven sonographic models. Obstet Gynecol 1995;85:565–569 (Level II-2)

81. Buchanan TA, Kjos SL, Montoro MN, Wu PY, Madrilejo NG, Gonzalez M, et al. Use of fetal ultrasound to select metabolic therapy for pregnancies complicated by mild gestational diabetes. Diabetes Care 1994;17:275–283 (Level II-1)

82. Walkinshaw SA. Dietary regulation for 'gestational diabetes.' Cochrane Database Syst Rev 2000;2:CD000070. Review (Meta-analysis)

83. Gregory KD, Henry OA, Ramicone E, Chan LS, Platt LD. Maternal and infant complications in high and normal weight infants by method of delivery. Obstet Gynecol 1998;92:507–513 (Level II-2)

84. Conway DL, Langer O. Elective delivery of infants with macrosomia in diabetic women: reduced shoulder dystocia versus increased cesarean deliveries. Am J Obstet Gynecol 1998;178:922–925 (Level II-2)

85. Blickstein I, Ben-Arie A, Hagay ZJ. Antepartum risks of shoulder dystocia and brachial plexus injury for infants weighing 4,200 g or more. Gynecol Obstet Invest 1998;45:77–80 (Level II-2)

86. Rouse DJ, Owen J, Goldenberg RL, Cliver SP. The effectiveness and costs of elective cesarean delivery for fetal macrosomia diagnosed by ultrasound. JAMA 1996;276: 1480–1486 (Level III)

87. Combs CA, Singh NB, Khoury JC. Elective induction versus spontaneous labor after sonographic diagnosis of fetal macrosomia. Obstet Gynecol 1993;81:492–496 (Level II-2)

88. Friesen CD, Miller AM, Rayburn WF. Influence of spontaneous or induced labor on delivering the macrosomic fetus. Am J Perinatol 1995;12:63–66 (Level II-2)

89. Leaphart WL, Meyer MC, Capeless EL. Labor induction with a prenatal diagnosis of fetal macrosomia. J Matern Fetal Med 1997;6:99–102 (Level II-2)

90. Gonen O, Rosen DJ, Dolfin Z, Tepper R, Markow S, Fejgin MD. Induction of labor versus expectant management in macrosomia: a randomized study. Obstet Gynecol 1997;89:913–917 (Level I)

91. Rouse DJ, Owen J. Prophylactic cesarean delivery for fetal macrosomia diagnosed by means of ultrasonography—a Faustian bargain? Am J Obstet Gynecol 1999;181: 332–338 (Level III)

92. Benedetti TJ, Gabbe SG. Shoulder dystocia. A complication of fetal macrosomia and prolonged second stage of labor with midpelvic delivery. Obstet Gynecol 1978;52: 526–529 (Level III)

93. Flamm BL, Goings JR. Vaginal birth after cesarean section: is suspected fetal macrosomia a contraindication? Obstet Gynecol 1989;74:694–697 (Level II-2)

94. Leung AS, Farmer RM, Leung EK, Medearis AL, Paul RH. Risk factors associated with uterine rupture during trial of labor after cesarean delivery: a case-control study. Am J Obstet Gynecol 1993;168:1358–1363 (Level II-2)

The MEDLINE database, the Cochrane Library, and ACOG's own internal resources and documents were used to conduct a literature search to locate relevant articles published between January 1985 and May 1999. The search was restricted to articles published in the English language. Priority was given to articles reporting results of original research, although review articles and commentaries also were consulted. Abstracts of research presented at symposia and scientific conferences were not considered adequate for inclusion in this document. Guidelines published by organizations or institutions such as the National Institutes of Health and the American College of Obstetricians and Gynecologists were reviewed, and additional studies were located by reviewing bibliographies of identified articles. When reliable research was not available, expert opinions from obstetrician–gynecologists were used.

Studies were reviewed and evaluated for quality according to the method outlined by the U.S. Preventive Services Task Force:

I   Evidence obtained from at least one properly designed randomized controlled trial.

II-1   Evidence obtained from well-designed controlled trials without randomization.

II-2   Evidence obtained from well-designed cohort or case–control analytic studies, preferably from more than one center or research group.

II-3   Evidence obtained from multiple time series with or without the intervention. Dramatic results in uncontrolled experiments also could be regarded as this type of evidence.

III   Opinions of respected authorities, based on clinical experience, descriptive studies, or reports of expert committees.

Based on the highest level of evidence found in the data, recommendations are provided and graded according to the following categories:

Level A—Recommendations are based on good and consistent scientific evidence.

Level B—Recommendations are based on limited or inconsistent scientific evidence.

Level C—Recommendations are based primarily on consensus and expert opinion.

ISSN 1099-3630

The American College of Obstetricians and Gynecologists
409 12th Street, SW, PO Box 96920
Washington, DC 20090-6920

12345/43210

ACOG PRACTICE BULLETIN

CLINICAL MANAGEMENT GUIDELINES FOR
OBSTETRICIAN–GYNECOLOGISTS

NUMBER 30, SEPTEMBER 2001

(Replaces Technical Bulletin Number 200, December 1994)

This Practice Bulletin was developed by the ACOG Committee on Practice Bulletins—Obstetrics with the assistance of Donald R. Coustan, MD. The information is designed to aid practitioners in making decisions about appropriate obstetric and gynecologic care. These guidelines should not be construed as dictating an exclusive course of treatment or procedure. Variations in practice may be warranted based on the needs of the individual patient, resources, and limitations unique to the institution or type of practice.

Gestational Diabetes

Gestational diabetes mellitus (GDM) is one of the most common clinical issues facing obstetricians and their patients. A lack of data from well-designed studies has contributed to the controversy surrounding the diagnosis and management of this condition. The purpose of this document is to provide a brief overview of our understanding of GDM and provide management guidelines that have been validated by appropriately conducted clinical research. When outcomes-based research is not available, expert opinion is provided to aid the practitioner.

Background

Definition and Prevalence

Diabetes is classified as type 1 or type 2 according to whether the patient requires insulin injections to avoid ketoacidosis. Gestational diabetes mellitus has been characterized as carbohydrate intolerance that begins or is first recognized during pregnancy. The prevalence of GDM varies in direct proportion to the prevalence of type-2 diabetes in a given population or ethnic group. Reported prevalence in the United States ranges from 1% to 14%, with 2–5% being the most common figure (1).

Maternal and Fetal Complications

Women with GDM are more likely to develop hypertensive disorders than women without GDM (2). Some of this additional risk may be related to the underlying risk factors for GDM (eg, increased maternal age and obesity). The diagnosis of GDM may prompt health care providers to intervene more readily for perceived problems (3). In women without GDM, there is a significant association between increasing carbohydrate intolerance and both preeclampsia and cesarean delivery (4). Women with GDM in Korea have a higher incidence of preeclampsia and primary cesarean delivery, yet only 10% of the women are obese (5). Whether the relationship with GDM is causal or not, clinicians should be aware of these risks. In addition, women with GDM have an increased risk of developing diabetes later in life.

The offspring of women with GDM are prone to such adverse events as macrosomia with its potential complications and hyperbilirubinemia. Infants of women with GDM are at increased risk for operative delivery, shoulder dystocia, and birth trauma. Because the risk factors for GDM (particularly obesity) are independent risk factors for fetal macrosomia, the role of maternal hyperglycemia has been widely debated. Although controlling for maternal obesity eliminated the apparent relationship between hyperglycemia and macrosomia in some studies (6, 7), these results may have been confounded because the women with GDM were treated. The relationship between GDM, fetal macrosomia, and other adverse outcomes has been confirmed in cohort studies in which maternal obesity and other potential confounders were controlled (8, 9), in a study of Korean women among whom only 10% were obese (5), and in another study of women whose abnormal glucose tolerance tests (GTTs) went clinically unrecognized (10). In women without GDM, there is an independent relationship between GTT levels and macrosomia (4, 11). When data were corrected for maternal weight, age, parity, and race, the 12% risk of macrosomia was independently attributable to GDM (9). A number of studies also have linked maternal hyperglycemia with long-term obesity and diabetes in the offspring (12–14). Nevertheless, considerable contro-versy remains regarding the exact relationship of these complications to maternal hyperglycemia.

Controversy of Current Screening Practices and Treatment Benefits

At one time, screening for GDM consisted of taking the patient's history. In 1973, O'Sullivan and Mahan proposed the 50-g, 1-hour laboratory screening test. This test has become widely used—94% of obstetric groups surveyed reported universal testing (15)—despite the absence of data to demonstrate a benefit to the population as a whole. However, as noted previously, maternal hyperglycemia is related to at least some of the adverse perinatal outcomes seen with GDM. Available evidence does not support the concept that women with GDM who do not have risk factors are of less concern than are those who do (16).

The use of traditional historic risk factors (family or personal history of diabetes, previous adverse pregnancy outcome, glycosuria, obesity) to identify GDM will miss approximately half of women with GDM (17, 18). If the risks of adverse outcomes are related to the presence or absence of confounding risk factors, rather than the GDM, then limited screening based on risk may be rea-

sonable. The U.S. Preventive Services Task Force has concluded that although there is insufficient evidence to recommend universal screening, screening high-risk women may be beneficial (19).

Despite the lack of population-derived data supporting the benefit of making the diagnosis of GDM, clinical recommendations often must be made without unassailable epidemiologic evidence. Older, admittedly flawed, studies suggested an increased perinatal mortality rate among undiagnosed or untreated women with GDM (20, 21). More recent studies that did not demonstrate an increase in perinatal mortality risk all included interventions of diet or insulin, antepartum testing, or merely making the diagnosis, which has been shown to be a powerful intervention in and of itself (3). If the perinatal mortality rate in undiagnosed and untreated GDM were double the background rate, as suggested in earlier studies, and GDM occurs in 2–5% of the population, any increase in overall perinatal loss attributable to discontinuing screening programs would likely go unnoticed.

Another important issue to consider is the possibility that some patients diagnosed with GDM may have preexisting type-2 diabetes, which can only be confirmed postpartum. One study found such patients to have a perinatal mortality rate 6 times higher than those with milder forms of GDM (22). Another study found mothers with GDM who had infants with birth defects were more likely to have high fasting glucose values, suggesting the presence of undiagnosed preexisting diabetes (23).

For the population to benefit from the diagnosis of GDM, there should be an effective treatment for the condition. Although a number of comparative studies of various treatments are available, there is little information regarding the effectiveness of treatment versus no treatment. In a pilot randomized trial comparing strict metabolic control with routine obstetric care in 300 women with GDM, there was no difference in the rate of macrosomia or other pregnancy outcomes (24). However, even the control subjects monitored their own glucose levels 1 day each week, and 10% were removed from the study and treated for hyperglycemia.

The first consideration in selecting a therapy for GDM is a determination of the treatment goals. Although the degree, if any, of excess perinatal mortal-ity associated with milder GDM has not been established, management plans typically include some type of fetal surveillance. A second goal of treatment may be the prevention of adverse pregnancy outcomes, such as macrosomia and its attendant consequences of operative delivery, shoulder dystocia, and birth trauma. Potential treatments toward this goal include diet, exercise, and insulin; oral agents also have been suggested. Safety, efficacy, and patient acceptance should be considered in choosing a treatment.

The goal of treatment is to lower the likelihood of macrosomia and its consequences; neonatal hypoglycemia also may be reduced (25). Although the quality of the information varies, evidence is available to confirm these benefits. However, there has been no demonstrated treatment benefit on long-term outcomes for the offspring such as obesity and the development of diabetes. It should be emphasized that although the evidence is inconclusive that treating GDM can prevent maternal and fetal complications, universal screening and treatment are widely practiced.

Clinical Considerations and Recommendations

▶ *How should screening for GDM be accomplished?*

All pregnant patients should be screened for GDM, whether by patient's history, clinical risk factors, or a laboratory screening test to determine blood glucose levels. The optimal method of screening is controversial, and there are insufficient data from which to draw firm conclusions.

A number of clinical risk factors have been demonstrated to be associated with an increased likelihood of GDM, including age, ethnicity, obesity, family history of diabetes, and past obstetric history (26). In one study, more than 3,000 pregnant women underwent both the 50-g, 1-hour screening test and the diagnostic oral GTT (27). Using a complex scoring system of weighted risk factors, the study found test thresholds for the 1-hour screening test varied depending on individual risk status. Sensitivity rates were similar to those of universal screening, and one third of the subjects avoided the glucose screening test. Thus, it appears it is possible to use historic risk factors to identify individuals who may have such a low risk for GDM that glucose challenge testing may not be worthwhile. Conversely, there may be groups of individuals at such high risk for GDM that it may be more convenient and cost-effective to proceed directly to the diagnostic GTT without obtaining the laboratory screening test.

Specific risk factors and the degree of their influence on GDM prevalence are difficult to quantify across populations. For example, in one Canadian study, African race was not associated with an increased risk of GDM (27), whereas in another large, observational study African race was found to be an independent predictor of the likelihood of GDM, even when investigators controlled for obesity (28). Because no single study can be generalized to the entire population, it seems reasonable

to base the definition of high and low risk for GDM on the prevalence of type-2 diabetes in each ethnic group. The relationship between obesity and GDM is most likely a continuum, so that the definition of the upper limit of normal weight suggested by the Institute of Medicine (ie, a body mass index ≤25) (29) should reasonably serve to identify individuals who are not obese. A low-risk individual meets all of the following criteria (30):

1. Age younger than 25 years
2. Not a member of an ethnic group with an increased risk for the development of type-2 diabetes (examples of high-risk ethnic groups include women of Hispanic, African, Native American, South or East Asian, or Pacific Islands ancestry)
3. Body mass index of 25 or less
4. No previous history of abnormal glucose tolerance
5. No previous history of adverse obstetric outcomes usually associated with GDM
6. No known diabetes in first degree relative

When the 1997 criteria, similar to those listed previously for low risk, were applied to data from more than 18,000 pregnancies in a predominantly Caucasian population, researchers determined that only 3% of women with GDM would not have been diagnosed (31). However, only 10% of the population would have been exempted from screening. For this reason, many physicians elect to screen all pregnant patients as a practical matter.

▶ *At what gestational age should laboratory screening be performed?*

A number of studies have demonstrated that the prevalence of GDM increases with advancing gestation (32–36). It has been customary to recommend the 50-g, 1-hour oral glucose challenge test be administered at 24–28 weeks of gestation. This arbitrary recommendation results from an attempt to balance two competing interests. Insulin resistance increases as pregnancy progresses, therefore, testing later in pregnancy will result in a higher yield of abnormal tests. However, the later the abnormality is diagnosed, the less time will be available for intervention. Although many practitioners choose to screen high-risk patients early in pregnancy, the benefit of early treatment of women with GDM identified early in pregnancy has not been demonstrated but rather has been accepted on a theoretical basis.

Patients who had GDM in a previous pregnancy have a 33–50% likelihood of recurrence in a subsequent pregnancy (37–39). If such patients were not tested between pregnancies, some of these recurrences may represent preexisting diabetes undetected between pregnancies. In such individuals there should still be a benefit to making the diagnosis of diabetes during the first half of pregnancy. Unlike typical patients with GDM, patients with abnormal glucose tolerance in the first half of pregnancy may manifest severe degrees of hyperglycemia.

▶ *How is laboratory screening accomplished?*

Although the use of random glucose measurements or fasting glucose measurements have been advocated to screen for GDM, inadequate data are available to evaluate the relative effectiveness of these approaches. Random glucose screening does not appear to be adequately sensitive (40). The screening test most commonly used in the United States is the 50-g, 1-hour glucose challenge, using a pure glucose load of 50 g in 150 mL of fluid. Glucose polymer solutions, which provide a lower osmotic load for a given glucose load, appear to be associated with fewer gastrointestinal symptoms and have been demonstrated to yield fair correlation with monomeric glucose solutions (41–43). The use of jelly beans instead of a pure glucose challenge has been shown to be better tolerated, but this method has poor sensitivity (40%) when compared with glucose polymer solutions (80–90%) (44).

Among subjects with GDM, for whom the function of the screening test is most critical, either higher (45) or similar (46) values were reported when the test was administered in the fasting state. Therefore, given the lack of evidence that fasting improves the accuracy of the screening test and the fact that fasting may pose significant logistic problems, the 50-g, 1-hour screening test may be administered without regard to the time elapsed since the last meal.

▶ *Should venous or capillary blood be used?*

The original description of the screening test used venous whole blood (17), but laboratories have switched from whole blood to plasma or serum samples. Studies of the screening test have generally used venous plasma. Convenient and relatively inexpensive meters for measuring glucose in capillary blood samples raise the possibility of performing the screening test in an office setting without expensive and complicated laboratory equipment. During fasting, capillary and venous blood have similar glucose concentrations, but after a meal or glucose challenge, capillary glucose is higher than venous glucose. Laboratory instruments are generally checked for quality against standard samples at regular intervals to ensure accuracy. Precision is an important factor. Two studies of various meters used in pregnancy demonstrated inadequate precision for all but one or two meter systems tested (47, 48). Therefore, if capillary blood samples are to be used for GDM screening, the precision of the meter should be known, and its correlation with

simultaneously obtained venous samples should be ascertained. Appropriate thresholds can then be derived. Office-based glucose testing is not recommended because of the difficulty in complying with required federal standards for testing. However, if used, it may be most practical to continue to use venous plasma samples and published thresholds for further testing.

▶ *Is there an appropriate threshold value for the laboratory screening test?*

The screening test threshold at which a diagnostic GTT is recommended will be arbitrary. The higher the threshold, the lower the sensitivity but the better the specific-ity and the lower the likelihood of a false-positive test result. The lower the threshold, the higher the sensitivity but the higher the likelihood of a false-positive test result and thus the performance of an unnecessary diagnostic GTT. O'Sullivan and Mahan (17) used venous whole blood samples and the Somogyi-Nelson method of glucose analysis. At the recommended threshold of 130 mg/dL, the screening test had a sensitivity of 79% and a specificity of 87%. When venous plasma and specific enzymatic methods of glucose analysis were used, 10% of women with GDM manifested screening test values between 130–139 mg/dL (18). Absolute sensitivity levels could not be determined because women with screening test values below 130 mg/dL did not undergo oral GTTs. When the threshold was lowered from 140 mg/dL to 130 mg/dL, the number of women requiring glucose tolerance testing increased from 14% to 23%, or approximately one quarter of patients.

Although a threshold of 140 mg/dL was recommended in the past, the most recent position statement of the American Diabetes Association ascribes a sensitivity of approximately 80% to this cutoff and 90% sensitivity with a threshold of 130 mg/dL and leaves the choice open (49). Because the precise cost-benefit ratio of diagnosing GDM remains unresolved, either threshold is acceptable.

▶ *How is GDM diagnosed?*

The diagnostic test specific for pregnancy and about which the greatest body of data exists is the 100-g, 3-hour oral GTT. Diagnostic criteria were originally derived by O'Sullivan and Mahan (50). Cutoff levels two standard deviations above the mean were found to be the best predictors for developing diabetes later in life. There are no well-designed studies that demonstrate whether these diagnostic criteria are optimal to identify pregnancies at risk for maternal or perinatal morbidity. The relationship between maternal glucose intolerance and adverse pregnancy outcomes appears to be more or less continuous with no absolute threshold (4). Two sets of criteria were adapted from the original O'Sullivan and Mahan values when laboratories switched to venous plasma or serum. These samples yield results approximately 14% higher than does whole blood. The National Diabetes Data Group published conversions derived by adding 15% to each of the four thresholds (51). Lower thresholds were subsequently derived by also correcting for the change to enzymatic methods of glucose analysis (52). Expert panels have supported both criteria, but there are no data from clinical trials to determine which is superior (Table 1) (53).

A positive diagnosis requires that two or more thresholds be met or exceeded. The test is administered in the morning after an overnight fast. Patients should not smoke before the test and should remain seated during the test. Patients should be instructed to follow an unrestricted diet, consuming at least 150 g of carbohydrate per day for at least 3 days prior to the test. This should avoid carbohydrate depletion, which could cause spuriously high values on the GTT.

Patients with only one abnormal value have been demonstrated to manifest increased risk for macrosomic infants and other morbidities (54, 55). However, because the relationship between carbohydrate metabolism, macrosomia, and other morbidity is a continuum (4, 56), and because not all of this morbidity arises from carbohydrate intolerance, it should be anticipated that no threshold will identify all patients at risk.

▶ *How should blood glucose be monitored in a woman with GDM?*

The optimal frequency of blood glucose testing in patients with GDM has not been established. Whether daily testing is essential for women with GDM has not been proven. One large, prospective trial compared seven-times-daily self-glucose monitoring using memory-based reflectance meters with weekly fasting and 2-hour laboratory glucose determinations supplemented by four-times-daily self-monitoring with only test strips and no meters (57). The more intensively monitored group had fewer primary cesarean deliveries and fewer macrosomic neonates, and their infants were less likely to experience shoulder dystocia and neonatal hypoglycemia than the more conventionally monitored group. Other centers have reported similar results with four-times-daily glucose monitoring (25, 58). Although daily self-glucose monitoring has not been demonstrated to reduce perinatal mortality in women with GDM, it appears to be useful in reducing potentially adverse outcomes such as macrosomia. However, evidence from well-designed, randomized trials that compare daily self-glucose monitoring with less frequent assessment in women with GDM is still needed.

Further uncertainty surrounds the timing of glucose determinations and the selection of appropriate thresholds for intervention. In nonpregnant individuals, diabetes is most often managed using preprandial glucose determinations. However, the fetus may be more sensitive to glucose excesses than to the nadirs of glucose values at various times of the day. In studies of preexisting diabetes, 1-hour postprandial glucose values were found to be more predictive of fetal macrosomia than were fasting values (59), and a 1-hour value of 130 mg/dL or more was found to be an appropriate threshold (60). A randomized trial compared preprandial with 1-hour postprandial glucose measurements in 66 women whose GDM was severe enough to require insulin treatment by 30 weeks of gestation (25). Macrosomia, neonatal hypoglycemia, and cesarean deliveries for shoulder dystocia were significantly lower among those who had postprandial monitoring, and their glycohemoglobin levels also decreased more markedly than did the levels of the subjects who used preprandial monitoring. No studies are available to compare the efficacy of 1-hour postprandial versus the more traditional 2-hour postprandial glucose determinations.

Table 1. Two Diagnostic Criteria for Gestational Diabetes Mellitus

Status	Plasma or Serum Glucose Level Carpenter/Coustan Conversion		Plasma Level National Diabetes Data Group Conversion	
	mg/dL	mmol/L	mg/dL	mmol/L
Fasting	95	5.3	105	5.8
One hour	180	10.0	190	10.6
Two hours	155	8.6	165	9.2
Three hours	140	7.8	145	8.0

Adapted from Expert Committee on the Diagnosis and Classification of Diabetes Mellitus. Report of the Expert Committee on the Diagnosis and Classification of Diabetes Mellitus. Diab Care 2000;23(suppl 1):S4–S19

Because these studies only included individuals with preexisting diabetes or those with GDM severe enough to require insulin treatment by 30 weeks of gestation, it remains to be established whether fasting or preprandial glucose measurements will suffice for individuals with milder forms of GDM. One study demonstrated a moderate correlation between fasting and 2-hour postprandial glucose values in GDM; if the fasting value was below 105 mg/dL, then only 17% of the 2-hour values exceeded 120 mg/dL (61). Given the available data, postprandial glucose values appear to be most effective at determining the likelihood of macrosomia and other adverse pregnancy outcomes in patients with GDM.

▶ *Is there a role for diet therapy in the treatment of GDM?*

Although there are no available data comparing medical nutrition therapy (diet) with no treatment in women with GDM, there is one such randomized trial of women who had abnormal glucose challenge test results but normal oral GTT results (62). Those on the prescribed diet delivered fewer macrosomic infants. Nutritional intervention in women with GDM should be designed to achieve normal glucose levels and avoid ketosis, while maintaining appropriate nutrition and weight gain. The American Diabetes Association recommends nutritional counseling, if possible by a registered dietitian, with individualization of the nutrition plan based on height and weight (49). The American Diabetes Association also recommends an average of 30 kcal/kg/d based on prepregnant body weight for nonobese individuals (49). The most appropriate diet for women with GDM has yet to be established.

The American Diabetes Association suggests that obese women (body mass index >30) may do well with moderate caloric restriction (30–33%) (49). Caloric restriction of 30% in obese women with GDM was associated with pregnancy outcomes (birth weight and macrosomia) similar to those of a group of matched controls who had normal values on the glucose challenge screening tests (63). One concern about caloric restriction is that, although glucose levels may decrease, there is the possibility that it may cause starvation ketosis (64). Levels of glucose, free fatty acids, and ketone bodies have been assessed during each trimester in long-term follow-up studies of infants of women with and without diabetes. These studies have reported an inverse association between maternal circulating levels of ketone acids in the second and third trimesters and psychomotor development and intelligence in the offspring at 3–5 years of age and through 9 years of age (65, 66). Even when investigators reevaluated their findings by taking into account socioeconomic status, race or ethnicity, and

the presence of gestational or preexisting diabetes, this association persisted. Although the correlation between IQ and ketone levels was weak (r = 0.2), it was statistically significant ($P = 0.02$); therefore, it would be prudent to avoid excessive ketonemia or ketonuria during pregnancy. When obese women with GDM were placed on moderate caloric restriction (25 kcal/kg of ideal nonpregnant weight per day), no ketonuria was detected during weekly clinic visits (67). Serum ketones were not reported. Available evidence does not support a recommendation for or against moderate caloric restriction in obese women with GDM. However, if caloric restriction is used, the diet should be restricted by no more than 33%, and ketonuria should be avoided.

Supplemental dietary fiber may improve glycemic control in women with type-2 diabetes. In a cohort study, increasing dietary fiber enrichment did not improve glucose control in patients with GDM (68). Available evidence does not support the prescription of fiber supplements for GDM.

▶ *Is there a role for insulin in the treatment of GDM?*

Some (69–71) but not all (72) prospective trials have demonstrated that insulin treatment of all women with GDM can reduce the likelihood of delivering a macrosomic baby. However, using such a paradigm would require that 100% of individuals be treated although less than half (between 9% and 40%) would benefit. It would be preferable to select the most appropriate patients for treatment.

One traditional approach has been to add insulin if medical nutrition therapy does not maintain fasting plasma glucose below 105 mg/dL or 2-hour values below 120 mg/dL or both. These thresholds have been extrapolated from recommendations for managing pregnancy in women with preexisting diabetes. A randomized trial demonstrated that using a 1-hour postmeal goal of 140 mg/dL was effective in preventing adverse outcomes in women with GDM severe enough to require insulin (25). It would be logical, although unproven, that similar thresholds should be used for initiating insulin treatment. A study of individuals with preexisting diabetes found the most appropriate target 1-hour postprandial glucose level for preventing macrosomia was 130 mg/dL (60). It may be reasonable to apply these data to women with GDM. Women with higher fasting glucose levels are more likely to require insulin therapy to achieve optimal glucose control than women with lower fasting glucose levels. Thirty-eight percent of women with GDM with an initial fasting plasma glucose level of 95 mg/dL or less required insulin to achieve "optimized control" (mean of seven daily values <100 mg/dL), whereas 70% required insulin when the initial fasting value was 95–104 mg/dL (73). Although each fasting glucose group delivered a similar, low proportion of babies with birth weights above the 90th percentile, large-for-gestational-age (LGA) babies were born to 29% of those treated with diet and 10% of those treated with insulin. All subjects with fasting values above 105 mg/dL were treated with insulin, and 14% had LGA offspring. These data suggest that insulin therapy should be considered for patients treated with medical nutrition therapy when 1-hour postprandial values exceed 130–140 mg/dL or 2-hour postprandial values exceed 120 mg/dL or fasting glucose exceeds 95 mg/dL.

Early third-trimester ultrasonography may help in identifying women with GDM who would benefit from insulin therapy despite relatively good metabolic control on diet. In a randomized trial of women with mild gestational diabetes, ultrasound abdominal circumference greater than the 75th percentile at 29–33 weeks of gestation was effective in selecting patients among whom the LGA rate was reduced to 13% with insulin therapy compared with 45% in those randomized to diet alone (74).

A frequent question is how long to attempt dietary management before adding insulin. One study suggested diet be tried for 2 weeks before adding insulin if the initial fasting plasma glucose was 95 mg/dL or less (75). In women with GDM with initial fasting values above 95 mg/dL, the results of diet therapy alone were less salutary. The available evidence does not support a clear recommendation as to the number of times glucose values should exceed targets before insulin is added or the dosage increased.

No particular insulin regimen or insulin dose has been demonstrated to be superior for GDM. Generally, it is easiest for the patient to start with the simplest regimen and work up to a more complex regimen as needed. Regardless of the starting dosage, subsequent dosage adjustments should be based on the blood glucose levels at particular times of day. Because free insulin apparently does not cross the placenta, all types of insulin have been used in patients with GDM. Insulin lispro (Humalog), an analog of human insulin with a single amino acid substitution, has a more rapid onset of action than regular insulin and may be useful in improving postprandial glucose concentrations. It has been used in GDM and has been demonstrated not to cross the placenta (76).

▶ *Is there a role for exercise in the treatment of GDM?*

Exercise often is recommended for individuals with diabetes, both as a way to achieve weight reduction and as a treatment to improve glucose metabolism. At least three randomized trials have explored exercise as an adjunct to, or substitute for, insulin in GDM. When women with GDM who needed intervention were randomly assigned to insulin or an exercise program, there was no difference in the likelihood of macrosomic infants, although glucose levels were not reported (77). A randomized trial of diet and exercise versus diet alone found improvement in both fasting plasma glucose and the response to a 50-g challenge in those who exercised (78) while a third study found improvement in cardiorespiratory fitness but no differences in glucose control with exercise (79). A regular exercise program has clear benefits for all women and may offer additional advantages for women with GDM. Women with GDM who lead an active lifestyle should be encouraged to continue a program of exercise approved for pregnancy.

▶ *Is there a role for oral antidiabetic agents in the treatment of GDM?*

Oral antidiabetic agents have been contraindicated in pregnancy. The early-generation sulfonylureas crossed the placenta and had the potential to stimulate the fetal pancreas, leading to fetal hyperinsulinemia. There also was concern about the potential for teratogenicity, although diabetes itself is teratogenic, and it is difficult to distinguish the effects of the treatment from those of the disease. Glyburide, a second-generation sulfonylurea, was compared with insulin in a randomized trial among patients with GDM who failed to achieve adequate glycemic control with diet alone (80). Glucose control was similar, and the glyburide group had pregnancy outcomes similar to those of the insulin group, including rates of cesarean delivery, preeclampsia, macrosomia (>4 kg), and neonatal hypoglycemia. Cord serum analyses showed no detectable glyburide in the infants. At this time, no other oral agent has been shown to be safe and effective in GDM, and this study has not been confirmed. Further study is recommended before the use of newer oral hypoglycemic agents can be supported for use in pregnancy.

▶ *Is fetal assessment indicated in pregnancies complicated by GDM?*

Antepartum fetal testing is recommended for patients with preexisting diabetes (81). If the increased risk of fetal demise in patients with preexisting diabetes is related to suboptimal metabolic control, it would be expected that patients with GDM who have poor metabolic control also would be at risk and thus merit antepartum fetal surveillance. Patients with well-controlled GDM are presumably at lower risk for fetal death than are those whose condition is not well controlled or who require insulin therapy, but there is no consensus regarding antepartum testing in women with well-controlled GDM. There are no data available from randomized trials of antepartum testing in patients with GDM. Most case series report good outcomes with a given testing protocol and conclude the protocol used is appropriate. Twice-weekly nonstress tests and amniotic fluid volume determinations were associated with no stillbirths and a 4.9% rate of cesarean delivery for nonreassuring fetal status in a cohort of women with GDM who had fasting glucose levels below 105 mg/dL (82).

Another cohort study of women with GDM who required only diet therapy and were monitored by daily fetal movement determinations beginning at 28 weeks of gestation and who underwent nonstress testing beginning at 40 weeks of gestation found no stillbirths or neonatal deaths (83). Patients requiring insulin or who had previous stillbirths, chronic hypertension, or pregnancy-induced hypertension underwent earlier fetal testing as did patients with preexisting diabetes. Because this latter study lacked sufficient power to evaluate perinatal mortality, it is not possible to make an unequivocal recommendation. Despite the lack of conclusive data, it would seem reasonable that women whose GDM is not well controlled, who require insulin, or have other risk factors such as hypertension or adverse obstetric history should be managed the same as individuals with preexisting diabetes. The particular antepartum test selected, whether nonstress test, contraction stress test, or biophysical profile, may be chosen according to local practice.

Ultrasonography has been used to estimate fetal weight, especially to predict macrosomia prior to delivery. However, the reliability of these measures has not been established (84–86). Regression formulas using combined fetal measures for weight estimates are associated with systematic errors. Using existing formulas, an estimated fetal weight would have to exceed 4,800 g for the fetus to have more than a 50% chance of being macrosomic (87, 88). In addition, the use of ultrasound-derived measures of fetal weight have not been shown to be superior to clinical measures.

▶ *When and how should delivery occur in pregnancies complicated by GDM?*

The timing of delivery in patients with GDM remains relatively open. When glucose control is good and no other complications supervene, there is no good evidence to support routine delivery before 40 weeks of gestation. In a study in which women with insulin-treated GDM and fetuses believed to be of appropriate weight for gestational age were randomized at 38 weeks of gestation to induction of labor within 1 week or expectant management, there was no difference in cesarean delivery rates

(89). However, the induction group delivered a smaller proportion of LGA babies. In a cohort multiple time series study, a policy of induction of labor at 38–39 weeks of gestation for women with insulin-treated GDM was compared with the results in expectantly managed historic controls (90). There was no significant difference in macrosomia or cesarean delivery rates, but shoulder dystocia was experienced by 10% of the expectant management group beyond 40 weeks of gestation versus 1.4% in the group induced at 38–39 weeks of gestation. Although significant, these data have not been confirmed by additional studies.

Available data do not address women with GDM not treated with insulin or those believed to have macrosomic fetuses. Individuals whose metabolic control does not meet the goals described earlier, or is undocumented, or those with risk factors such as hypertensive disorders or previous stillbirth should be managed the same as those with preexisting diabetes.

When GDM is well controlled and dates are well documented, respiratory distress syndrome at or beyond 39 weeks of gestation is rare enough that routine amniocentesis for pulmonary maturity is not necessary (91). At earlier gestational ages, or when control is poor or undocumented, pulmonary maturity should be assessed before induction. However, when early delivery is planned because of maternal or fetal compromise, the urgency of the indication should be considered in the decision to perform amniocentesis.

Cesarean delivery rates are higher in women with GDM compared with controls, and the difference is not entirely attributable to fetal macrosomia (3, 9). It may be that caregivers are more prone to perform cesarean deliveries in patients with GDM because of concern about the likelihood of shoulder dystocia. There are no data to support a policy of cesarean delivery purely on the basis of GDM. However, macrosomia is distinctly more common in women with GDM, and shoulder dystocia is more likely at a given birth weight in pregnancies complicated by diabetes than in nondiabetic pregnancies (92, 93). It may be reasonable, therefore, to recommend cesarean delivery without a trial of labor at some particular threshold of fetal weight.

One of the problems in trying to apply such a threshold is the poor accuracy of ultrasound prediction of birth weight. In particular, a study reported that when birth weight exceeds 4,500 g, only 50% of the fetuses weigh within 10% of the ultrasound-derived estimate (94). A decision analytic model was developed to estimate the potential effectiveness and costs of a policy of elective cesarean delivery for fetal macrosomia diagnosed by ultrasonography (95). Investigators factored in such considerations as the poor predictive accuracy of ultrasonography, the background cesarean delivery rates at various fetal weights, and the effect of maternal diabetes. The analysis predicted that in women with diabetes it would be necessary to perform 489 cesarean deliveries to prevent one permanent brachial plexus injury at a threshold of 4,000 g estimated fetal weight, or 443 cesarean deliveries at a threshold of 4,500 g estimated fetal weight. These figures are one fifth to one eighth of the figures developed for pregnancies of women without diabetes. The authors concluded such a policy may be tenable, although the merits are debatable. On the basis of available data, it is not possible to determine whether the potential benefits of cesarean delivery without labor at a given estimated fetal weight are similar for patients with GDM and those with preexisting diabetes. It would appear reasonable to recommend that patients with GDM be counseled regarding possible cesarean delivery without labor when the estimated fetal weight is 4,500 g or greater. When the estimated weight is 4,000–4,500 g, additional factors such as the patient's past delivery history, clinical pelvimetry, and the progress of labor may be helpful to consider in determining mode of delivery.

With an estimated fetal weight greater than 4,500 g, prolonged second stage of labor or arrest of descent in the second stage is an indication for cesarean delivery. Because of the higher likelihood of shoulder dystocia at a given birth weight in the pregnancies of women with diabetes, it may be best to apply the above recommendation to an estimated fetal weight greater than 4,000 g for GDM. Operative deliveries from the midpelvis should be avoided, if possible, in patients with GDM who have an estimated fetal weight of 4,000 g or more and a prolonged second stage of labor (92, 96).

▶ *Should women with a history of GDM be screened postpartum?*

Women with a history of GDM are at increased risk for developing diabetes (generally type-2 diabetes) later in life (97, 98). Diabetes will be diagnosed in some women soon after pregnancy, suggesting they had preexisting diabetes that was not diagnosed prior to pregnancy. Populations with a high prevalence of type-2 diabetes who do not have access to screening when not pregnant are at particularly high risk for this phenomenon (99). Current recommendations for the diagnosis and classification of diabetes in the nonpregnant state are based on the recommendations of an expert committee of the American Diabetes Association and are depicted in Table 2 (100). Diagnostic testing for diabetes may be performed after the immediate effects of pregnancy on glucose metabolism have dissipated and is most convenient at around the time of the postpartum checkup. However, there are no long-term follow-up studies that verify the benefit of postpartum diagnostic testing.

Although the American Diabetes Association advocates the use of a fasting plasma glucose determination as being less cumbersome than the oral GTT, the oral GTT will more accurately identify those women who had GDM and now have impaired glucose tolerance (101). Because the presence of such a condition may be important in counseling for future pregnancies, there may be advantages to performing the oral GTT as the initial diagnostic test after pregnancy complicated by GDM. If the results of both the fasting plasma glucose and the oral GTT are normal, subsequent follow-up tests may use the fasting plasma glucose.

The estimate of long-term risk for developing diabetes among women who had GDM depends on the diagnostic test used, the duration of follow-up, age, and other characteristics of the population studied; reported rates vary widely (102). In follow-up studies up to 28 years on the cohort of patients used to derive the O'Sullivan and Mahan criteria for GDM, diabetes was found in 50% of women who had GDM compared with 7% of controls (103). Factors identifiable during or shortly after pregnancy that increase the risk for subsequent diabetes

Table 2. Criteria for the Diagnosis of Diabetes Mellitus in the Nonpregnant State*

Normal Values	Impaired Fasting Glucose or Impaired Glucose Tolerance	Diabetes Mellitus
FPG <110 mg/dL	FPG 110–125 mg/dL	FPG ≥126 mg/dL
75-g, 2-h OGTT	75-g, 2-h OGTT	75-g, 2-h OGTT
2-h PG <140 mg/dL	2-h PG 140–199 mg/dL	2-h PG ≥200 mg/dL
		Symptoms of diabetes and PG (without regard to time since last meal) ≥ 200 mg/dL

*Abbreviations: FPG, fasting plasma glucose; OGTT, oral glucose tolerance test; PG, plasma glucose. The diagnosis of diabetes mellitus should be confirmed on a separate day by any of these three tests.

Data from Expert Committee on the Diagnosis and Classification of Diabetes Mellitus. Report of the Expert Committee on the Diagnosis and Classification of Diabetes Mellitus. Diab Care 2000;23(suppl 1):S4–S19

include the degree of abnormality of the diagnostic GTT, the presence or absence of obesity, the gestational age at diagnosis of GDM, and the degree of abnormality of the postpartum oral GTT (104, 105). Individuals at increased risk should be counseled regarding diet, exercise, and weight reduction or maintenance to forestall or prevent the onset of type-2 diabetes.

Summary of Recommendations

The following recommendations are based on limited or inconsistent scientific evidence (Level B):

▶ The laboratory screening test should consist of a 50-g, 1-hour oral glucose challenge at 24–28 weeks of gestation, which may be administered without regard to the time of the last meal.

▶ A screening test threshold of 140 mg/dL has 10% less sensitivity than a threshold of 130 mg/dL but fewer false-positive results; either threshold is acceptable.

▶ The screening test generally should be performed on venous plasma or serum samples using well-calibrated and well-maintained laboratory instruments.

▶ Available evidence does not support a recommendation for or against moderate caloric restriction in obese women with GDM. However, if caloric restriction is used, the diet should be restricted by no more than 33% of calories.

▶ For women with GDM and an estimated fetal weight of 4,500 g or more, cesarean delivery may be considered because it may reduce the likelihood of permanent brachial plexus injury in the infant.

▶ When medical nutritional therapy has not resulted in fasting glucose levels less than 95 mg/dL or 1-hour postprandial values less than 130–140 mg/dL or 2-hour postprandial values less than 120 mg/dL, insulin should be considered.

The following recommendations are based primarily on consensus and expert opinion (Level C):

▶ Although universal glucose challenge screening for GDM is the most sensitive approach, there may be pregnant women at low risk who are less likely to benefit from testing. Such low-risk women should have all of the following characteristics:

1. Age younger than 25 years
2. Not a member of a racial or ethnic group with high prevalence of diabetes (eg, Hispanic, African, Native American, South or East Asian, or Pacific Islands ancestry)
3. Body mass index of 25 or less
4. No history of abnormal glucose tolerance
5. No previous history of adverse pregnancy outcomes usually associated with GDM
6. No known diabetes in first degree relative

▶ There is insufficient evidence to determine the optimal antepartum testing regimen for women with GDM with relatively normal glucose levels on diet therapy and no other risk factors.

▶ Either the plasma or serum glucose level established by Carpenter and Coustan or the plasma level designated by the National Diabetes Data Group conversions are appropriate to use in the diagnosis of GDM.

References
1. Coustan DR. Gestational diabetes. In: National Institutes of Diabetes and Digestive and Kidney Diseases. Diabetes in America. 2nd ed. Bethesda, Maryland: NIDDK, 1995; NIH Publication No. 95-1468:703–717 (Level III)

2. Cousins L. Obstetric complications. In: EA Reece, DR Coustan, eds. Diabetes mellitus in pregnancy. 2nd ed. New York: Churchill Livingstone, 1995:287–302 (Level III)

3. Naylor CD, Sermer M, Chen E, Sykora K. Cesarean delivery in relation to birth weight and gestational glucose tolerance: pathophysiology or practice style? Toronto Trihospital Gestational Diabetes Investigators. JAMA 1996;275:1165–1170 (Level II-2)

4. Sermer M, Naylor CD, Gare DJ, Kenshole AB, Ritchie JW, Farine D, et al. Impact of increasing carbohydrate intolerance on maternal-fetal outcomes in 3637 women without gestational diabetes. The Toronto Tri-Hospital Gestational Diabetes Project. Am J Obstet Gynecol 1995;173:146–156 (Level II-3)

5. Jang HC, Cho NH, Min YK, Han IK, Jung KB, Metzger BE. Increased macrosomia and perinatal morbidity independent of maternal obesity and advanced age in Korean women with GDM. Diabetes Care 1997;20:1582–1588 (Level II-2)

6. Cundy T, Gamble G, Manuel A, Townend K, Roberts A. Determinants of birth-weight in women with established and gestational diabetes. Aust NZJ Obstet Gynaecol 1993;33:249–254 (Level II-2)

7. Dang K, Homko C, Reece EA. Factors associated with fetal macrosomia in offspring of gestational diabetic women. J Matern Fetal Med 2000;9:114–117 (Level II-2)

8. Langer O, Levy J, Brustman L, Anyaegbunam A, Merkatz R, Divon M. Glycemic control in gestational diabetes mellitus—how tight is tight enough: small for gestational age versus large for gestational age? Am J Obstet Gynecol 1989;161:646–653 (Level II-2)

9. Casey BM, Lucas MJ, McIntire DD, Leveno KJ. Pregnancy outcomes in women with gestational diabetes compared with the general obstetric population. Obstet Gynecol 1997;90:869–873 (Level II-2)

10. Adams KM, Li H, Nelson RL, Ogburn PL Jr, Danilenko-Dixon DR. Sequelae of unrecognized gestational diabetes. Am J Obstet Gynecol 1998;178:1321–1332 (Level II-2)

11. Tallarigo L, Giampietro O, Penno G, Miccoli R, Gregori G, Navalesi R. Relation of glucose tolerance to complications of pregnancy in nondiabetic women. N Engl J Med 1986;315:989–992 (Level II-3)

12. Pettitt DJ, Bennett PH, Saad MF, Charles MA, Nelson RG, Knowler WC. Abnormal glucose tolerance during pregnancy in Pima Indian women. Long-term effects on offspring. Diabetes 1991;40(suppl 2):126–130 (Level II-2)

13. Vohr BR, McGarvey ST, Tucker R. Effects of maternal gestational diabetes on offspring adiposity at 4–7 years of age. Diabetes Care 1999;22:1284–1291 (Level II-2)

14. Silverman BL, Metzger BE, Cho NH, Loeb CA. Impaired glucose tolerance in adolescent offspring of diabetic mothers. Relationship to fetal hyperinsulinism. Diabetes Care 1995;18:611–617 (Level II-2)

15. Wilkins-Haug L, Horton JA, Cruess DF, Frigoletto FD. Antepartum screening in the office-based practice: findings from the collaborative Ambulatory Research Network. Obstet Gynecol 1996;88:483–489 (Level III)

16. Weeks, JW, Major CA, de Veciana M, Morgan MA. Gestational diabetes: does the presence of risk factors influence perinatal outcome? Am J Obstet Gynecol 1994;171:1003–1007 (Level II-2)

17. O'Sullivan JB, Mahan CM, Charles D, Dandrow R. Screening criteria for high-risk gestational diabetic patients. Am J Obstet Gynecol 1973;116:895–900 (Level II-2)

18. Coustan DR, Nelson C, Carpenter MW, Carr SR, Rotondo L, Widness JA. Maternal age and screening for gestational diabetes: a population-based study. Obstet Gynecol 1989;73:557–561 (Level II-2)

19. Screening for diabetes mellitus. In: United States Preventive Services Task Force. Guide to clinical preventive services. 2nd ed. Baltimore: Williams & Wilkins, 1996:193–208 (Level III)

20. O'Sullivan JB, Charles D, Mahan CM, Dandrow RV. Gestational diabetes and perinatal mortality rate. Am J Obstet Gynecol 1973;116:901–904 (Level II-2)

21. Pettitt DJ, Knowler WC, Baird MR, Bennett PH. Gestational diabetes: infant and maternal complications of pregnancy in relation to third-trimester glucose tolerance in the Pima Indians. Diabetes Care 1980;3:458–464 (Level II-2)

22. Cundy T, Gamble G, Townend K, Henley PG, MacPherson P, Roberts AB. Perinatal mortality in type 2 diabetes. Diabet Med 2000;17:33–39 (Level II-2)

23. Schaefer-Graf UM, Buchanan TA, Xiang A, Songster G, Montoro M, Kjos SL. Patterns of congenital anomalies and relationship to initial maternal fasting glucose levels in pregnancies complicated by type 2 and gestational diabetes. Am J Obstet Gynecol 2000;182:313–320 (Level II-2)

24. Garner P, Okun N, Keely E, Wells G, Perkins S, Sylvain J, et al. A randomized controlled trial of strict glycemic control and tertiary level obstetric care versus routine obstetric care in the management of gestational diabetes: a pilot study. Am J Obstet Gynecol 1997;177:190–195 (Level I)

25. de Veciana M, Major CA, Morgan MA, Asrat T, Toohey JS, Lien JM, et al. Postprandial versus preprandial blood glucose monitoring in women with gestational diabetes mellitus requiring insulin therapy. N Engl J Med 1995;333:1237–1241 (Level I)

26. Solomon CG, Willett WC, Carey VJ, Rich-Edwards J, Hunter DJ, Colditz GA, et al. A prospective study of pregravid determinants of gestational diabetes mellitus. JAMA 1997;278:1078–1083 (Level II-3)

27. Naylor CD, Sermer M, Chen E, Farine D. Selective screening for gestational diabetes mellitus. Toronto Trihospital Gestational Diabetes Investigators. N Engl J Med 1997;337:1591–1596 (Level II-3)

28. Dooley SL, Metzger BE, Cho NH. Gestational diabetes mellitus. Influence of race on disease prevalence and perinatal outcome in a US population. Diabetes 1991;40(suppl 2):25–29 (Level III)

29. The nature and problem of obesity. In: Insitute of Medicine. Committee to Develop Criteria for Evaluating the Outcomes of Approaches to Prevent and Treat Obesity. Food and Nutrition Board. Weighing the options: criteria for evaluating weight-management programs. Washington, DC: National Academy Press, 1995:37–63 (Level III)

30. American Diabetes Association. Gestational diabetes mellitus. Diabetes Care 2001;24(suppl 1):S77–S79 (Level III)

31. Danilenko-Dixon DR, Van Winter JT, Nelson RL, Ogburn PL Jr. Universal versus selective gestational diabetes screening: application of 1997 American Diabetes Association recommendations. Am J Obstet Gynecol 1999;181:798–802 (Level II-2)

32. Jovanovic L, Peterson CM. Screening for gestational diabetes. Optimum timing and criteria for retesting. Diabetes 1985;34(suppl 2):21–23 (Level II-3)

33. Benjamin F, Wilson SJ, Deutsch S, Seltzer VL, Droesch K, Droesch J. Effect of advancing pregnancy on the glucose tolerance test and on the 50-g oral glucose load screening test for gestational diabetes. Obstet Gynecol 1986;68:362–365 (Level II-2)

34. Watson WJ. Serial changes in the 50-g oral glucose test in pregnancy: implications for screening. Obstet Gynecol 1989;74:40–43 (Level II–2)

35. Nahum GG, Huffaker, BJ. Correlation between first- and early third-trimester glucose screening test results. Obstet Gynecol 1990;76:709–713 (Level II-2)

36. Super DM, Edelberg SC, Philipson EH, Hertz RH, Kalhan SC. Diagnosis of gestational diabetes in early pregnancy. Diabetes Care 1991;14:288–294 (Level II-2)

37. Philipson EH, Super DM. Gestational diabetes mellitus: does it recur in subsequent pregnancy? Am J Obstet Gynecol 1989;160:1324–1331 (Level II-2)

38. Gaudier FL, Hauth JC, Poist M, Corbet D, Cliver SP. Recurrence of gestational diabetes mellitus. Obstet Gynecol 1992;80:755–758 (Level II-2)

39. Moses RG. The recurrence rate of gestational diabetes in subsequent pregnancies. Diabetes Care 1996;19:1348–1350 (Level II-2)

40. McElduff A, Goldring J, Gordon P, Wyndham L. A direct comparison of the measurement of a random plasma glucose and a post-50 g glucose load glucose, in the detection of gestational diabetes. Aust NZJ Obstet Gynecol 1994;34:28–30 (Level II-2)

41. Reece EA, Holford T, Tuck S, Bargar M, O'Connor T, Hobbins JC. Screening for gestational diabetes: one-hour carbohydrate tolerance test performed by a virtually tasteless polymer of glucose. Am J Obstet Gynecol 1987;156:132–134 (Level II-2)

42. Murphy NJ, Meyer BA, O'Kell RT, Hogard ME. Carbohydrate sources for gestational diabetes mellitus screening. A comparison. J Reprod Med 1994;39:977–981 (Level I)

43. Bergus GR, Murphy NJ. Screening for gestational diabetes mellitus: comparison of a glucose polymer and a glucose monomer test beverage. J Am Board Fam Pract 1992;5:241–247 (Level II-1)

44. Lamar ME, Kuehl TJ, Cooney AT, Gayle LJ, Holleman S, Allen SR. Jelly beans as an alternative to a fifty gram glucose beverage for gestational diabetes screening. Am J Obstet Gynecol 1999;181:1154–1157 (Level I)

45. Coustan DR, Widness JA, Carpenter MW, Rotondo L, Pratt DC, Oh W. Should the fifty-gram, one-hour plasma glucose screening test for gestational diabetes be administered in the fasting or fed state? Am J Obstet Gynecol 1986;154:1031–1035 (Level I)

46. Lewis GF, McNally C, Blackman JD, Polonsky KS, Barron WM. Prior feeding alters the response to the 50-g glucose challenge test in pregnancy. The Staub Traugott effect revisited. Diabetes Care 1993;16:1551–1556 (Level II-3)

47. Carr S, Coustan DR, Martelly P, Brosco F, Rotondo L. Precision of reflectance meters in screening for gestational diabetes. Obstet Gynecol 1989;73:727–731 (Level II-2)

48. Carr SR, Slocum J, Tefft L, Haydon B, Carpenter M. Precision of office-based blood glucose meters in screening for gestational diabetes. Am J Obstet Gynecol 1995;173:1267–1272 (Level II-2)

49. Nutritional management during pregnancy in preexisting diabetes. In: American Diabetes Association. Medical management of pregnancy complicated by diabetes. 3rd ed Alexandria, Virginia: ADA, 2000:70–86 (Level III)

50. O'Sullivan JB, Mahan CM. Criteria for the oral glucose tolerance test in pregnancy. Diabetes 1964;13:278–285 (Level II-3)

51. National Diabetes Data Group. Classification and diagnosis of diabetes mellitus and other categories of glucose intolerance. Diabetes 1979;28:1039–1057 (Level III)

52. Carpenter MW, Coustan DR. Criteria for screening tests for gestational diabetes. Am J Obstet Gynecol 1982;144:768–773 (Level II-3)

53. Expert Committee on the Diagnosis and Classification of Diabetes Mellitus. Report of the Expert Committee on the Diagnosis and Classification of Diabetes Mellitus. Diab Care 2000;23(suppl 1):S4–S19 (Level III)

54. Langer O, Brustman L, Anyaegbunam A, Mazze R. The significance of one abnormal glucose tolerance test value on adverse outcome in pregnancy. Am J Obstet Gynecol 1987;157:758–763 (Level II-2)

55. Lindsay MK, Graves W, Klein L. The relationship of one abnormal glucose tolerance test value and pregnancy complications. Obstet Gynecol 1989;73:103–106 (Level II-2)

56. Sacks DA, Greenspoon JS, Abu-Fadil S, Henry HM, Wolde-Tsadik G, Yao JF. Toward universal criteria for gestational diabetes: the 75-gram glucose tolerance test in pregnancy. Am J Obstet Gynecol 1995;172:607–614 (Level II-3)

57. Langer O, Rodriguez DA, Xenakis EM, McFarland MB, Berkus MD, Arrendondo F. Intensified versus conventional management of gestational diabetes. Am J Obstet Gynecol 1994;170:1036–1047 (Level II-1)

58. Goldberg JD, Franklin B, Lasser D, Jornsay DL, Hausknecht RU, Ginsberg-Fellner F, et al. Gestational diabetes: impact of home glucose monitoring on neonatal birth weight. Am J Obstet Gynecol 1986;154:546–550 (Level II-2)

59. Jovanovic-Peterson L, Peterson CM, Reed GF, Metzger BE, Mills JL, Knopp RH, et al. Maternal postprandial glucose levels and infant birth weight: the Diabetes in Early Pregnancy Study. The National Institute of Child Health and Human Development-Diabetes in Early Pregnancy Study. Am J Obstet Gynecol 1991;164: 103–111 (Level II-2)

60. Combs CA, Gunderson E, Kitzmiller JL, Gavin LA, Main EK. Relationship of fetal macrosomia to maternal postprandial glucose control during pregnancy. Diabetes Care 1992;15:1251–1257 (Level II-2)

61. Huddleston JF, Cramer MK, Vroon DH. A rationale for omitting two-hour postprandial glucose determinations in gestational diabetes. Am J Obstet Gynecol 1993;169:257–264 (Level II-2)

62. Bevier WC, Fischer R, Jovanovic L. Treatment of women with an abnormal glucose challenge test (but a normal oral glucose tolerance test) decreases the prevalence of macrosomia. Am J Perinatol 1999;16:269–275 (Level II-1)

63. Dornhorst A, Nicholls JSD, Probst F, Paterson CM, Hollier KL, Elkeles RS, et al. Calorie restriction for treatment of gestational diabetes. Diabetes 1991;40(suppl 2):161–164 (Level II-2)

64. Knopp RH, Magee MS, Raisys V, Benedetti T, Bonet B. Hypocaloric diets and ketogenesis in the management of obese gestational diabetic women. J Amer Coll Nutr 1991;10:649–667 (Level II-2)

65. Rizzo T, Metzger BE, Burns WJ, Burns K. Correlations between antepartum maternal metabolism and child intelligence. N Engl J Med 1991;325:911–916 (Level II-2)

66. Rizzo TA, Dooley SL, Metzger BE, Cho NH, Ogata ES, Silverman BL. Prenatal and perinatal influences on long-term psychomotor development in offspring of diabetic mothers. Am J Obstet Gynecol 1995;173:1753–1758 (Level II-2)

67. Algert S, Shragg P, Hollingsworth DR. Moderate caloric restriction in obese women with gestational diabetes. Obstet Gynecol 1985;65:487–491 (Level II-2)

68. Reece EA, Hagay Z, Caseria D, Gay LJ, DeGennaro N. Do fiber-enriched diabetic diets have glucose-lowering effects in pregnancy? Am J Perinatol 1993;10:272–274 (Level II-2)

69. O'Sullivan JB, Gellis SS, Dandrow RV, Tenney BO. The potential diabetic and her treatment in pregnancy. Obstet Gynecol 1966;27:683–689 (Level I)

70. Coustan DR, Lewis SB. Insulin therapy for gestational diabetes. Obstet Gynecol 1978;51:306–310 (Level I)

71. Thompson DJ, Porter KB, Gunnells DJ, Wagner PC, Spinnato JA. Prophylactic insulin in the management of gestational diabetes. Obstet Gynecol 1990;75:960–964 (Level I)

72. Persson B, Stangenberg M, Hansson U, Nordlander E. Gestational diabetes mellitus (GDM). Comparative evaluation of two treatment regimens, diet versus insulin and diet. Diabetes 1985;34(suppl 2):101–105 (Level I)

73. Langer O, Berkus M, Brustman L, Anyaegbunam A, Mazze R. Rationale for insulin management in gestational diabetes mellitus. Diabetes 1991;40(suppl 2):186–190 (Level II-3)

74. Buchanan TA, Kjos SL, Montoro MN, Wu PY, Madrilejo NG, Gonzalez M. Use of fetal ultrasound to select metabolic therapy for pregnancies complicated by mild gestational diabetes. Diabetes Care 1994;17:275–283 (Level II-1)

75. McFarland MB, Langer O, Conway DL, Berkus MD. Dietary therapy for gestational diabetes: how long is long enough? Obstet Gynecol 1999;93:978–982 (Level II-3)

76. Jovanovic L, Ilic S, Pettitt DJ, Hugo K, Gutierrez M, Bowsher RR, et al. Metabolic and immunologic effects of insulin lispro in gestational diabetes. Diabetes Care 1999;22:1422–1427 (Level I)

77. Bung P, Bung C, Artal R, Khodiguian N, Fallenstein F, Spätling L. Therapeutic exercise for insulin-requiring gestational diabetics: effects on the fetus—results of a randomized prospective longitudinal study. J Perinat Med 1993;21:125–137 (Level II-2)

78. Jovanovic-Peterson L, Durak EP, Peterson CM. Randomized trial of diet versus diet plus cardiovascular conditioning on glucose levels in gestational diabetes. Am J Obstet Gynecol 1989;161:415–419 (Level II-1)

79. Avery MD, Leon AS, Kopher RA. Effects of a partially home-based exercise program for women with gestational diabetes. Obstet Gynecol 1997;89:10–15 (Level I)

80. Langer O, Conway DL, Berkus MD, Xenakis EM, Gonzales O. A comparison of glyburide and insulin in women with gestational diabetes mellitus. New Engl J Med 2000;343:1134–1138 (Level I)

81. American College of Obstetricians and Gynecologists. Antepartum fetal surveillance. ACOG Practice Bulletin 9. Washington, DC: ACOG, 1999 (Level III)

82. Kjos SL, Leung A, Henry OA, Victor MR, Paul RH, Medearis AL. Antepartum surveillance in diabetic pregnancies: predictors of fetal distress in labor. Am J Obstet Gynecol 1995;173:1532–1539 (Level II-3)

83. Landon MB, Gabbe SG. Antepartum fetal surveillance in gestational diabetes mellitus. Diabetes 1985;34(suppl 2):50–54 (Level II-2)

84. Deter RL, Hadlock FP. Use of ultrasound in the detection of macrosomia: a review. J Clin Ultrasound 1985; 13:519–524 (Level III)

85. Rossavik IK, Joslin GL. Macrosomatia and ultrasonography: what is the problem? South Med J 1993;86: 1129–1132 (Level II-3)

86. Sandmire HF. Whither ultrasonic prediction of fetal macrosomia? Obstet Gynecol 1993;82:860–862 (Level III)

87. Smith GC, Smith MF, McNay MB, Fleming JE. The relation between fetal abdominal circumference and birthweight: findings in 3512 pregnancies. Br J Obstet Gynaecol 1997;104:186–190 (Level II-3)

88. McLaren RA, Puckett JL, Chauhan SP. Estimators of birth weight in pregnant women requiring insulin: a comparison of seven sonographic models. Obstet Gynecol 1995;85:565–569 (Level II-2)

89. Kjos SL, Henry OA, Montoro M, Buchanan TA, Mestman JH. Insulin-requiring diabetes in pregnancy: a randomized trial of active induction of labor and expectant management. Am J Obstet Gynecol 1993;169:611–615 (Level II-1)

90. Lurie S, Insler V, Hagay ZJ. Induction of labor at 38 to 39 weeks of gestation reduces the incidence of shoulder dystocia in gestational diabetic patients Class A2. Am J Perinatol 1996;13:293–296 (Level II-2)

91. Kjos SL, Walther FJ, Montoro M, Paul RH, Diaz F, Stabler M. Prevalence and etiology of respiratory distress in infants of diabetic mothers: predictive values of fetal lung maturation tests. Am J Obstet Gynecol 1990;163: 898–903 (Level II-3)

92. Acker DB, Sachs BP, Friedman EA. Risk factors for shoulder dystocia. Obstet Gynecol 1985;66:762–768 (Level II-2)

93. Langer O, Berkus MD, Huff RW, Samueloff A. Shoulder dystocia: should the fetus weighing greater than or equal to 4000 grams be delivered by cesarean section? Am J Obstet Gynecol 1991;165:831–837 (Level II-2)

94. Benacerraf BR, Gelman R, Frigoletto FD Jr. Sonographically estimated fetal weights: accuracy and limitation. Am J Obstet Gynecol 1988;159;1118–1121 (Level II-2)

95. Rouse DJ, Owen J, Goldenberg RL, Cliver SP. The effectiveness and costs of elective cesarean delivery for fetal macrosomia diagnosed by ultrasound. JAMA 1996;276: 1480–1486 (Level III)

96. Benedetti TJ, Gabbe SG. Shoulder dystocia. A complication of fetal macrosomia and prolonged second stage of labor with midpelvic delivery. Obstet Gynecol 1978; 52:526–529 (Level II-2)

97. Dornhorst A, Rossi M. Risk and prevention of type 2 diabetes in women with gestational diabetes. Diabetes Care 1998;21 suppl:B43–B49 (Level III)

98. Buchanan TA, Xiang A, Kjos SL, Lee WP, Trigo E, Nader I, et al. Gestational diabetes: antepartum characteristics that predict postpartum glucose intolerance and type 2 diabetes in Latino women. Diabetes 1998;47:1302–1310 (Level II-3)

99. Kjos SL, Buchanan TA, Greenspoon JS, Montoro M, Bernstein GS, Mestman JH. Gestational diabetes mellitus: the prevalence of glucose intolerance and diabetes mellitus in the first two months post partum. Am J Obstet Gynecol 1990;163:93–98 (Level II-2)

100. Report of the Expert Committee on the Diagnosis and Classification of Diabetes Mellitus. American Diabetes Association. Expert Committee on the Diagnosis and Classification of Diabetes Mellitus. Diabetes Care 2001;4(suppl 1):S5–S20 (Level III)

101. Conway DL, Langer O. Effects of the new criteria for type 2 diabetes on the rate of postpartum glucose intolerance in women with gestational diabetes. Am J Obstet Gynecol 1999;181:610–614 (Level II-2)

102. O'Sullivan JB. Diabetes mellitus after GDM. Diabetes 1991;29(suppl 2):131–135 (Level III)

103. O'Sullivan JB. Subsequent morbidity among gestational diabetic women. In: Sutherland HW, Stowers JM, eds. Carbohydrate metabolism in pregnancy and the newborn. New York: Churchill Livingstone, 1984:174–180 (Level I)

104. Coustan DR, Carpenter MW, O'Sullivan PS, Carr SR. Gestational diabetes: predictors of subsequent disordered glucose metabolism. Am J Obstet Gynecol 1993;168:1139–1145 (Level II-2)

105. Kjos SL, Peters RK, Xiang A, Henry OA, Montoro M, Buchanan TA. Predicting future diabetes in Latino women with gestational diabetes. Utility of early postpartum glucose testing. Diabetes 1995;44:586–591 (Level II-3)

The MEDLINE database, the Cochrane Library, and ACOG's own internal resources and documents were used to conduct a literature search to locate relevant articles published between January 1985 and June 2000. The search was restricted to articles published in the English language. Priority was given to articles reporting results of original research, although review articles and commentaries also were consulted. Abstracts of research presented at symposia and scientific conferences were not considered adequate for inclusion in this document. Guidelines published by organizations or institutions such as the National Institutes of Health and the American College of Obstetricians and Gynecologists were reviewed, and additional studies were located by reviewing bibliographies of identified articles. When reliable research was not available, expert opinions from obstetrician–gynecologists were used.

Studies were reviewed and evaluated for quality according to the method outlined by the U.S. Preventive Services Task Force:

I   Evidence obtained from at least one properly designed randomized controlled trial.

II-1   Evidence obtained from well-designed controlled trials without randomization.

II-2   Evidence obtained from well-designed cohort or case–control analytic studies, preferably from more than one center or research group.

II-3   Evidence obtained from multiple time series with or without the intervention. Dramatic results in uncontrolled experiments could also be regarded as this type of evidence.

III   Opinions of respected authorities, based on clinical experience, descriptive studies, or reports of expert committees.

Based on the highest level of evidence found in the data, recommendations are provided and graded according to the following categories:

Level A—Recommendations are based on good and consistent scientific evidence.

Level B—Recommendations are based on limited or inconsistent scientific evidence.

Level C—Recommendations are based primarily on consensus and expert opinion.

ISSN 1099-3630

The American College of Obstetricians and Gynecologists
409 12th Street, SW, PO Box 96920
Washington, DC 20090-6920

12345/54321

Gestational Diabetes. ACOG Practice Bulletin No. 30. American College of Obstetricians and Gynecologists. Obstet Gynecol 2001;98:525–538

ACOG PRACTICE BULLETIN

CLINICAL MANAGEMENT GUIDELINES FOR
OBSTETRICIAN–GYNECOLOGISTS

NUMBER 10, NOVEMBER 1999

(Replaces Technical Bulletin Number 217, December 1995)

This Practice Bulletin was developed by the ACOG Committee on Practice Bulletins—Obstetrics with the assistance of Susan M. Ramin, MD. The information is designed to aid practitioners in making decisions about appropriate obstetric and gynecologic care. These guidelines should not be construed as dictating an exclusive course of treatment or procedure. Variations in practice may be warranted based on the needs of the individual patient, resources, and limitations unique to the institution or type of practice.

Induction of Labor

The goal of induction of labor is to achieve vaginal delivery by stimulating uterine contractions before the spontaneous onset of labor. According to the National Center for Health Statistics, the overall rate of induction of labor in the United States has increased from 90 per 1,000 live births in 1989 to 184 per 1,000 live births in 1997 (1). Generally, induction of labor has merit as a therapeutic option when the benefits of expeditious delivery outweigh the risks of continuing the pregnancy. The benefits of labor induction must be weighed against the potential maternal or fetal risks associated with this procedure. The purpose of this bulletin is to review current methods for cervical ripening and induction of labor and to summarize the effectiveness of these approaches based on appropriately conducted outcomes-based research. These practice guidelines classify the indications for and contraindications to induction of labor, describe the various agents used for cervical ripening, cite methods used to induce labor, and outline the requirements for the safe clinical use of the various methods of inducing labor.

Background

In 1948, Theobald and associates described their use of the posterior pituitary extract, oxytocin, by intravenous drip for labor induction (2). Five years later, oxytocin was the first polypeptide hormone synthesized by du Vigneaud and associates (3). This synthetic polypeptide hormone has since been used to stimulate uterine contractions. Other methods used for induction of labor include membrane stripping, amniotomy, and administering prostaglandin E (PGE) analogues.

Cervical Ripening

If induction is indicated and the status of the cervix is unfavorable, agents for cervical ripening may be used. The status of the cervix can be determined by the Bishop pelvic scoring system (Table 1) (4). If the total score is more than 8,

Table 1. Bishop Scoring System

Score	Dilation (cm)	Effacement (%)	Station*	Cervical Consistency	Position of Cervix
0	Closed	0–30	–3	Firm	Posterior
1	1–2	40–50	–2	Medium	Midposition
2	3–4	60–70	–1, 0	Soft	Anterior
3	5–6	80	+1, +2	—	—

*Station reflects a –3 to +3 scale.

Modified from Bishop EH. Pelvic scoring for elective induction. Obstet Gynecol 1964;24:267

the probability of vaginal delivery after labor induction is similar to that after spontaneous labor.

Acceptable methods for cervical ripening include mechanical cervical dilators and administration of synthetic prostaglandin E_1 (PGE_1) and prostaglandin E_2 (PGE_2) (5-9). Mechanical dilation methods are effective in ripening the cervix and include hygroscopic dilators, osmotic dilators (*Laminaria japonicum*), the 24-French Foley balloon, and the double balloon device (Atad Ripener Device) (10-15). Laminaria ripen the cervix but may be associated with increased peripartum infections (6, 16).

Misoprostol, a synthetic PGE_1 analogue, can be administered intravaginally or orally and is used for both cervical ripening and induction. It currently is available as a 100-mcg or 200-mcg tablet, and can be broken to provide 25-mcg or 50-mcg doses. Misoprostol currently is approved by the U.S. Food and Drug Administration (FDA) for the prevention of peptic ulcers, but not for cervical ripening or induction of labor.

Two PGE_2 preparations are commercially available: a gel available in a 2.5-mL syringe containing 0.5 mg of dinoprostone and a vaginal insert containing 10 mg of dinoprostone. Both are approved by the FDA for cervical ripening in women at or near term. The vaginal insert releases prostaglandin (PG) at a slower rate (0.3 mg/h) than the gel. Both the gel and the vaginal insert have been reported to increase the probability of successful initial induction, shorten the interval from induction to delivery, and decrease the total and maximal doses of oxytocin needed to induce contractions (17).

Other pharmacologic methods for cervical ripening include continuous intravenous oxytocin drip, extraamniotic saline infusion, vaginal recombinant human relaxin, and intracervical purified porcine relaxin. The safety and efficacy of these latter methods are unclear.

Methods of Labor Induction

In addition to oxytocin and misoprostol, other agents can be used for induction of labor. The progesterone antagonist mifepristone (RU 486) is one such suitable and effective induction agent (18). Nonpharmacologic methods of labor induction include stripping the amniotic membranes, amniotomy, and nipple stimulation.

Oxytocin

Oxytocin, an octapeptide, is one of the most commonly used drugs in the United States. The physiology of oxytocin-stimulated labor is similar to that of spontaneous labor, although individual patients vary in sensitivity and response to oxytocin. Based on pharmacokinetic studies of synthetic oxytocin, uterine response ensues after 3–5 minutes of infusion, and a steady state of oxytocin is achieved in plasma by 40 minutes (19). The uterine response to oxytocin depends on the duration of the pregnancy; there is a gradual increase in response from 20 to 30 weeks of gestation, followed by a plateau from 34 weeks of gestation until term, when sensitivity increases (20). Cervical dilation, parity, and gestational age are predictors of the dose response to oxytocin for labor stimulation (21).

Membrane Stripping

Stripping the amniotic membranes is commonly practiced to induce labor. However, several studies have yielded conflicting results regarding the efficacy of membrane stripping (22–24). Significant increases in phospholipase A_2 activity and prostaglandin $F_{2\alpha}$ ($PGF_{2\alpha}$) levels occur from membrane stripping (25). Stripping membranes appears to be associated with a greater frequency of spontaneous labor and fewer inductions for postterm pregnancy. In a randomized trial of 195 normal pregnancies beyond 40 weeks of gestation, two thirds of the patients who underwent membrane stripping labored spontaneously within 72 hours, compared with one third of the patients who underwent examination only (26).

Amniotomy

Artificial rupture of the membranes may be used as a method of labor induction, especially if the condition of the cervix is favorable. Used alone for inducing labor, amniotomy can be associated with unpredictable and sometimes long intervals before the onset of contractions. However, in a trial of amniotomy combined with early oxytocin infusion compared with amniotomy alone, the induction-to-delivery interval was shorter with the amniotomy-plus-oxytocin method (27).

Clinical Considerations and Recommendations

▶ *What are the indications and contraindications to induction of labor?*

Indications for induction of labor are not absolute but should take into account maternal and fetal conditions, gestational age, cervical status, and other factors. Following are examples of maternal or fetal conditions that may be indications for induction of labor:

- Abruptio placentae
- Chorioamnionitis
- Fetal demise
- Pregnancy-induced hypertension
- Premature rupture of membranes
- Postterm pregnancy
- Maternal medical conditions (eg, diabetes mellitus, renal disease, chronic pulmonary disease, chronic hypertension)
- Fetal compromise (eg, severe fetal growth restriction, isoimmunization)
- Preeclampsia, eclampsia

Labor also may be induced for logistic reasons, for example, risk of rapid labor, distance from hospital, or psychosocial indications. In such circumstances, at least one of the criteria in the box should be met or fetal lung maturity should be established (28).

Generally, the contraindications to labor induction are the same as those for spontaneous labor and vaginal delivery. They include, but are not limited to, the following situations:

- Vasa previa or complete placenta previa
- Transverse fetal lie
- Umbilical cord prolapse
- Previous transfundal uterine surgery

Confirmation of Term Gestation

- Fetal heart tones have been documented for 20 weeks by nonelectronic fetoscope or for 30 weeks by Doppler.
- It has been 36 weeks since a positive serum or urine human chorionic gonadotropin pregnancy test was performed by a reliable laboratory.
- An ultrasound measurement of the crown–rump length, obtained at 6–12 weeks, supports a gestational age of at least 39 weeks.
- An ultrasound obtained at 13–20 weeks confirms the gestational age of at least 39 weeks determined by clinical history and physical examination.

However, the individual patient and clinical situation should be considered in determining when induction of labor is contraindicated. Several obstetric situations are not contraindications to the induction of labor but do necessitate special attention. These include, but are not limited to, the following:

- One or more previous low-transverse cesarean deliveries
- Breech presentation
- Maternal heart disease
- Multifetal pregnancy
- Polyhydramnios
- Presenting part above the pelvic inlet
- Severe hypertension
- Abnormal fetal heart rate patterns not necessitating emergent delivery

▶ *What criteria should be met before the cervix is ripened or labor is induced?*

Assessment of gestational age and consideration of any potential risks to the mother or fetus are of paramount importance for appropriate evaluation and counseling before initiating cervical ripening or labor induction. The patient should be counseled regarding the indications for induction, the agents and methods of labor stimulation, and the possible need for repeat induction or cesarean delivery.

Additional requirements for cervical ripening and induction of labor include cervical assessment, pelvic assessment, assessment of fetal size and presentation, and personnel familiar with the effects of uterine stimulants on the mother and fetus because uterine hyperstimulation may occur with induction of labor. Monitoring fetal heart rate and uterine contractions is recommended as for any high-risk patient in active labor. Although trained nursing personnel can monitor labor induction, a physician capable of performing a cesarean delivery should be readily available.

▶ *What is the relative effectiveness of available pharmacologic methods for cervical ripening?*

Intracervical or intravaginal PGE_2 (dinoprostone) commonly is used and is superior to placebo or no therapy in promoting cervical ripening (29). Several prospective randomized clinical trials and a meta-analysis have demonstrated that PGE_1 (misoprostol) is an effective method for cervical ripening (30-34). Misoprostol administered intravaginally has been reported to be either superior to or as efficacious as dinoprostone gel (9, 32, 34, 35). It is difficult, however, to compare the results of studies on misoprostol because of differences in endpoints, including Bishop score, duration of labor, total oxytocin use, successful induction, and cesarean delivery rate. The rates of operative vaginal delivery and cesarean delivery are inconsistent between trials. The cesarean delivery rate has been reported to be higher with dinoprostone compared with misoprostol (31); however, further studies are needed. The results of cesarean delivery rate with dinoprostone use are inconsistent; some have shown a reduction but most have not shown a significant decrease.

▶ *How should prostaglandin be administered?*

If there is inadequate cervical change with minimal uterine activity after one dose of intracervical PGE_2, a second dose may be given 6–12 hours later. The manufacturers recommend a maximum cumulative dose of 1.5 mg of dinoprostone (three doses or 7.5 mL of gel) within a 24-hour period. A minimum safe time interval between PG administration and initiation of oxytocin has not been determined. According to the manufacturers' guidelines, after use of 1.5 mg of dinoprostone in the cervix or 2.5 mg in the vagina, oxytocin induction should be delayed for 6–12 hours because the effect of PG may be heightened with oxytocin. After use of dinoprostone in sustained-release form, delaying oxytocin induction for 30–60 minutes after removal is sufficient. One quarter of one 100-mcg tablet (approximately 25-mcg) of misoprostol should be considered for cervical ripening and labor induction.

▶ *What are the potential complications with each method of cervical ripening, and how are they managed?*

Hyperstimulation may occur with the use of the PGE analogues. There is no uniform definition of uterine hyperstimulation. In some studies hyperstimulation is never defined. In others, uterine hyperstimulation has been defined as either a series of single contractions lasting 2 minutes or more or a contraction frequency of five or more in 10 minutes (36). Another definition of hyperstimulation is uterine contractions lasting 2 minutes or more or a contraction frequency of 5 or more in 10 minutes with evidence that the fetus is not tolerating this contraction pattern, as demonstrated by late deceleration, or fetal bradycardia (37). Fortunately, most women and their fetuses tolerate uterine hyperstimulation without adverse outcome.

The intracervical PGE_2 gel (0.5 mg) has a 1% rate of uterine hyperstimulation, while the intravaginal PGE_2 gel (2–5 mg) or vaginal insert is associated with a 5% rate (29, 36–38). Uterine hyperstimulation typically begins within 1 hour after the gel or insert is placed but may occur up to 9 1/2 hours after the vaginal insert has been placed (36–38).

Removing the PGE_2 vaginal insert usually will help reverse the effect of hyperstimulation. Irrigation of the cervix and vagina is not beneficial. Maternal side effects from low-dose PGE_2 (fever, vomiting, and diarrhea) are quite uncommon (17). Prophylactic antiemetics, antipyretics, and antidiarrheal agents usually are not needed. The manufacturers recommend that caution be exercised when using PGE_2 in patients with glaucoma, severe hepatic or renal dysfunction, or asthma. However, PGE_2 is a bronchodilator, and there are no reports of bronchoconstriction or significant blood pressure changes after the administration of the low-dose gel.

In several studies of misoprostol, the term tachysystole was used to define hyperstimulation without corresponding fetal heart rate abnormalities in order to distinguish this complication from hyperstimulation with fetal heart rate changes. Data indicate that both tachysystole (defined in some studies as six or more uterine contractions in 10 minutes in consecutive 10-minute intervals) and hyperstimulation (with and without fetal heart rate changes) are increased with a 50-mcg or greater dose of misoprostol (9, 30, 39, 40). There seems to be a trend toward lower rates of uterine hyperstimulation with fetal heart rate changes with lower dosages of misoprostol (25 mcg every 6 hours versus every 3 hours) (40). Although in studies of misoprostol there were no differences in perinatal outcome, the studies have been insufficient in size to exclude the possibility of uncommon serious adverse effects (40). The use of misoprostol in women with prior cesarean birth has been associated with an increase in uterine rupture (41). Misoprostol use for second-trimester pregnancy termination also has been associated with uterine rupture, especially when used with oxytocin infusion (40). An increase in meconium-stained amniotic fluid also has been reported with misoprostol use (34). Although misoprostol appears to be safe and effective in inducing labor in women with unfavorable cervices, further studies are needed to determine the optimal dosage, timing interval, and pharmacokinetics of misoprostol. Moreover, data are needed on the management of complications related to misoprostol and when it should be discontinued. If uterine hyperstimulation and a nonreassuring fetal heart rate pattern occur with misoprostol use and there is no response to routine corrective measures (maternal repositioning and supplemental oxygen administration), cesarean delivery should be considered. Subcutaneous terbutaline also can be used in an attempt to correct the nonreassuring fetal heart rate tracing or the abnormal contraction pattern or both.

Increased maternal and neonatal infection have been reported in connection with the use of laminaria and hygroscopic dilators when compared with the PGE_2 analogues (6, 12, 16).

▶ *What are the recommended guidelines for fetal surveillance for each type of prostaglandin preparation?*

The PG preparations should be administered at or near the labor and delivery suite, where uterine activity and fetal heart rate can be monitored continuously. The patient should remain recumbent for at least 30 minutes. The fetal heart rate and uterine activity should be monitored continuously for a period of 30 minutes to 2 hours after administration of the PGE_2 gel (42). The patient may be transferred elsewhere if there is no increase in uterine activity and the fetal heart rate is unchanged after this period of observation. Uterine contractions usually are evident in the first hour and exhibit peak activity in the first 4 hours (42, 43). Fetal heart rate monitoring should be continued if regular uterine contractions persist; maternal vital signs should be recorded as well.

Because uterine hyperstimulation can occur as late as 9 1/2 hours after placement of the PGE_2 vaginal insert, fetal heart rate and uterine activity should be monitored electronically from the time the device is placed until at least 15 minutes after it is removed (44). This controlled-release PGE_2 vaginal pessary should be removed at the onset of labor (37).

Patients treated with misoprostol should receive fetal heart rate and uterine activity monitoring in a hospital setting until further studies evaluate the safety of outpatient therapy.

▶ *Are cervical ripening methods restricted to inpatient use only?*

One small, randomized trial found that sequential outpatient administration of low-dose (2-mg) PGE_2 gel was no better than placebo in ripening the cervix in postterm patients (45). Larger controlled studies are needed to establish an effective and safe dose and vehicle for PGE_2 before application on an outpatient basis can be recommended. However, outpatient use may be appropriate in carefully selected patients.

▶ *What are the potential complications of various methods of induction?*

The side effects of oxytocin use are principally dose related; uterine hyperstimulation and subsequent fetal heart rate deceleration are the most common side effects. Hyperstimulation may result in abruptio placentae or uterine rupture. Fortunately, uterine rupture secondary to oxytocin use is rare even in parous women (46). Water intoxication can occur with high concentrations of oxytocin infused with large quantities of hypotonic solutions. The antidiuretic effect usually is observed only after prolonged administration with at least 40mU of oxytocin per minute (47).

Misoprostol appears to be safe and beneficial for inducing labor in a woman with an unfavorable cervix. Although the exact incidence of uterine tachysystole is unknown and the criteria used to define this complication are not always clear in the various reports, there are reports of uterine tachysystole occurring more frequently in women given misoprostol (30–32). There does not appear to be a significant increase in adverse fetal outcomes from tachysystole (31, 35); however, one also must consider the possibility of uterine rupture as a rare complication of induction of labor with misoprostol (40). The occurrence of complications does appear to be dose-dependent (9, 40). Oral misoprostol administration is associated with fewer abnormal fetal heart rate patterns and episodes of uterine hyperstimulation when compared with vaginal administration (48), but there are not yet enough data to support oral administration as an alternative method.

The potential risks associated with amniotomy include prolapse of the umbilical cord, chorioamnionitis, significant umbilical cord compression, and rupture of vasa previa. The physician should palpate for an umbili-

Table 2. Labor Stimulation with Oxytocin: Examples of Low- and High-Dose Oxytocin

Regimen	Starting Dose	Incremental Increase (mU/min)	Dosage Interval (min)
Low-Dose	0.5–1	1	30–40
	1–2	2	15
High-Dose	~6	~6	15
	6	6*, 3, 1	20–40

*The incremental increase is reduced to 3 mU/min in presence of hyperstimulation and reduced to 1 mU/min with recurrent hyperstimulation.

cal cord and avoid dislodging the fetal head. The fetal heart rate should be assessed before and immediately after amniotomy.

Stripping the amniotic membranes is associated with bleeding from undiagnosed placenta previa or low-lying placenta, and accidental amniotomy. Uterine hyperactivity and fetal heart rate decelerations have been reported in association with nipple stimulation (49).

▶ *When oxytocin is used for induction of labor, what dosage should be used and what precautions should be taken?*

Any of the low- or high-dose oxytocin regimens outlined in Table 2 are appropriate for labor induction (50–56). Most women attain normal progression of labor with 150–350 Montevideo units of uterine activity (50). Low-dose regimens and less frequent increases in dose are associated with decreased uterine hyperstimulation (52). High-dose regimens and more frequent dose increases are associated with shorter labor and less frequent cases of chorioamnionitis and cesarean delivery for dystocia, but increased rates of uterine hyperstimulation (52).

Each hospital's obstetrics and gynecology department should develop guidelines for the preparation and administration of oxytocin. Synthetic oxytocin generally is diluted 10 U in 1,000 mL of an isotonic solution for an oxytocin concentration of 10 mU/mL. Oxytocin should be administered by infusion using a pump that allows precise control of the flow rate and permits accurate minute-to-minute control. Bolus administration of oxytocin can be avoided by piggybacking the infusion into the main intravenous line near the venipuncture site. Oxytocin also can be administered by pulsatile infusion, which may better simulate spontaneous labor (53). The total amount of oxytocin given may be decreased by administering oxytocin in 10-minute pulse infusions (53, 57).

A numeric value for the maximum dose of oxytocin has not been established. The fetal heart rate and uterine contractions should be monitored closely. Oxytocin should be administered by trained personnel who are familiar with its effects.

▶ *How should complications associated with oxytocin use be managed?*

If hyperstimulation with a nonreassuring fetal heart rate occurs, intravenous infusion of oxytocin should be decreased or discontinued to correct the pattern. Additional measures may include turning the woman on her side and administering oxygen or more intravenous fluid. If hyperstimulation persists, use of terbutaline or other tocolytics may be considered.

Hypotension may occur following a rapid intravenous injection of oxytocin; therefore, it is imperative that a dilute oxytocin infusion be used even in the immediate puerperium. Although amniotic fluid embolism was once thought to be associated with oxytocin-induced labor, there is no causal relationship between oxytocin use or antecedent hyperstimulation and amniotic fluid embolism (58, 59).

▶ *Are the various methods of labor induction equally applicable to patients with intact or ruptured membranes?*

The same precautions should be exercised when prostaglandins are used for induction of labor with ruptured membranes as for intact membranes. Intravaginal PGE$_2$ for induction of labor in women with premature rupture of membranes appears to be safe and effective, although it has not been approved by the FDA for this indication (60). In a meta-analysis of labor induction in women with premature rupture of membranes at term, only one dose of intravaginal misoprostol was necessary for successful labor induction in 86% of the patients (61). There is no evidence that use of either of these prostaglandins increases the risk of infection in women with ruptured membranes (60, 61).

▶ *What methods can be used for induction of labor with intrauterine fetal demise in the late second or third trimester?*

Intravenous oxytocin usually is a safe and effective method of inducing labor for a fetal death near term but is less effective remote from term (62). Laminaria or hygroscopic cervical dilators may be beneficial before the use of oxytocin or PGE for induction (63, 64). High-dose PGE_2 vaginal suppositories and more concentrated intravenous oxytocin are effective for achieving delivery, particularly when the gestational age is 28 weeks or less (62, 65, 66). Reported side-effects associated with higher doses of PGE_2 include nausea, vomiting, and diarrhea, which may be ameliorated with pretreatment medications. Although PGE_2 vaginal suppositories have been used safely in the third trimester (67), the risk of uterine rupture is increased. Vaginal misoprostol, intramuscular or extraamniotic infusion of $PGF_{2\alpha}$, and mifepristone also have been used safely and effectively; however, studies are few. In one study, mifepristone (600 mg per day for 48 hours) was effective in achieving delivery within 72 hours after the initial dose in 63% of women (68). In another study using intravaginal misoprostol, the mean time from induction to delivery was 12.6 hours, and all women delivered by 48 hours (69).

▶ *What is the cost effectiveness of these agents?*

There is a significant cost difference for induction of labor between misoprostol and dinoprostone. The approximate cost of a 100-mcg tablet of misoprostol ranges from $0.36 to $1.20, whereas a dinoprostone gel kit ranges from $65 to $75, and the dinoprostone vaginal insert is $165 (34, 35, 39, 70). The cost would be increased further if oxytocin augmentation were needed. Moreover, dinoprostone is an unstable compound that requires refrigeration to maintain its potency, whereas misoprostol is stable at room temperature.

Summary

The following recommendations are based on good and consistent scientific evidence (Level A):

▶ Prostaglandin E analogues are effective in promoting cervical ripening and inducing labor.

▶ Women in whom induction of labor is indicated may be appropriately managed with either a low- or high-dose oxytocin regimen.

▶ Fetal heart rate and uterine activity should be continuously monitored from the time the PGE_2 vaginal insert is placed until at least 15 minutes after it is removed.

▶ High-dose PGE_2 vaginal suppositories may be used in the management of intrauterine fetal demise in the second trimester of pregnancy.

▶ Although the optimal dose and timing interval of misoprostol is unknown, lower doses (25 mcg every 3–6 hours) are effective for cervical ripening and induction of labor.

▶ With term premature rupture of membranes, labor may be induced with prostaglandins.

The following recommendations are based on evidence that may be limited or inconsistent (Level B):

▶ Misoprostol use in women with prior cesarean birth should be avoided because of the possibility of uterine rupture.

▶ The use of higher doses of misoprostol (50 mcg every 6 hours) to induce labor may be appropriate in some situations, although there are reports of increased risk of complications, including uterine hyperstimulation.

The following recommendations are based primarily on consensus and expert opinion (Level C):

▶ For women with third-trimester intrauterine fetal demise, intravaginal misoprostol can be used to induce labor.

▶ Fetal heart rate and uterine activity should be continuously monitored from 30 minutes to 2 hours after administration of PGE_2 gel.

References

1. Ventura SJ, Martin JA, Curtin SC, Mathews TJ. Births: Final data for 1997. National Center for Health Statistics, National Vital Statistics Reports, 1999;47(18):1–96 (Level II-3)

2. Theobald GW, Graham A, Campbell J, Gange PD, Driscoll WJ. The use of post-pituitary extract in physiological amounts in obstetrics. BMJ 1948;2:123–127 (Level III)

3. du Vigneaud V, Ressler C, Swan JM, Roberts CW, Katsoyannis PG, Gordon S. The synthesis of an octapeptide amide with the hormonal activity of oxytocin. J Am Chem Soc 1953;75:4879–4880 (Level III)

4. Bishop EH. Pelvic scoring for elective induction. Obstet Gynecol 1964;24:266–268 (Level III)

5. Cross WG, Pitkin RM. Laminaria as an adjunct in induction of labor. Obstet Gynecol 1978;51:606–608 (Level I)

6. Krammer J, Williams MC, Sawai SK, O'Brien WF. Preinduction cervical ripening: a randomized comparison of two methods. Obstet Gynecol 1995;85:614–618 (Level I)

7. Fletcher HM, Mitchell S, Simeon D, Frederick J, Brown D. Intravaginal misoprostol as a cervical ripening agent. Br J Obstet Gynaecol 1993;100:641–644 (Level I)

8. Porto M. The unfavorable cervix: methods of cervical priming. Clin Obstet Gynecol 1989;32:262–268 (Level III)

9. Wing DA, Rahall A, Jones MM, Goodwin TM, Paul RH. Misoprostol: an effective agent for cervical ripening and labor induction. Am J Obstet Gynecol 1995;172:1811–1816 (Level I)

10. Atad J, Hallak M, Ben-David Y, Auslender R, Abramovici H. Ripening and dilatation of the unfavourable cervix for induction of labour by a double balloon device: experience with 250 cases. Br J Obstet Gynaecol 1997;104:29–32 (Level III)

11. Blumenthal PD, Ramanauskas R. Randomized trial of Dilapan and Laminaria as cervical ripening agents before induction of labor. Obstet Gynecol 1990;75:365–368 (Level I)

12. Chua S, Arulkumaran S, Vanja K, Ratnam SS. Preinduction cervical ripening: prostaglandin E$_2$ gel vs. hygroscopic mechanical dilator. J Obstet Gynaecol Res 1997;23:171–177 (Level I)

13. Gilson GJ, Russell DJ, Izquierdo LA, Qualls CR, Curet LB. A prospective randomized evaluation of a hygroscopic cervical dilator, Dilapan, in the preinduction ripening of patients undergoing induction of labor. Am J Obstet Gynecol 1996;175:145–149 (Level I)

14. Lin A, Kupferminc M, Dooley SL. A randomized trial of extra-amniotic saline infusion versus laminaria for cervical ripening. Obstet Gynecol 1995;86:545–549 (Level I)

15. Lyndrup J, Nickelsen C, Weber T, Molnitz E, Guldbaek E. Induction of labour by balloon catheter with extra-amniotic saline infusion (BCEAS): a randomized comparison with PGE$_2$ vaginal pessaries. Eur J Obstet Gynecol Reprod Biol 1994;53:189–197 (Level I)

16. Kazzi GM, Bottoms SF, Rosen MG. Efficacy and safety of laminaria digitata for preinduction ripening of the cervix. Obstet Gynecol 1982;60:440–443 (Level II-2)

17. Brindley BA, Sokol RJ. Induction and augmentation of labor: basis and methods for current practice. Obstet Gynecol Surv 1988;43:730–743 (Level III)

18. Frydman R, Lelaidier C, Baton-Saint-Mleux C, Fernandez H, Vial, M, Bourget P. Labor induction in women at term with mifepristone (RU 486): a double-blind, randomized, placebo-controlled study. Obstet Gynecol 1992;80:972–975 (Level I)

19. Seitchik J, Amico J, Robinson AG, Castillo M. Oxytocin augmentation of dysfunctional labor. IV. Oxytocin pharmacokinetics. Am J Obstet Gynecol 1984;150:225–228 (Level III)

20. Caldeyro-Barcia R, Poseiro JJ. Physiology of the uterine contraction. Clin Obstet Gynecol 1960;3:386–408 (Level III)

21. Satin AJ, Leveno KJ, Sherman ML, McIntire DD. Factors affecting the dose response to oxytocin for labor stimulation. Am J Obstet Gynecol 1992;166:1260–1261 (Level II-3)

22. Crane J, Bennett K, Young D, Windrim R, Kravitz H. The effectiveness of sweeping membranes at term: a randomized trial. Obstet Gynecol 1997;89:586–590 (Level I)

23. Goldenberg M, Dulitzky M, Feldman B, Zolti M, Bider D. Stretching of the cervix and stripping of the membranes at term: a randomised controlled study. Eur J Obstet Gynecol Reprod Biol 1996;66:129–132 (Level I)

24. Wiriyasirivaj B, Vutyavanich T, Ruangsri RA. A randomized controlled trial of membrane stripping at term to promote labor. Obstet Gynecol 1996;87:767–770 (Level I)

25. McColgin SW, Bennett WA, Roach H, Cowan BD, Martin JN Jr, Morrison JC. Parturitional factors associated with membrane stripping. Am J Obstet Gynecol 1993;169:71–77 (Level I)

26. Allott HA, Palmer CR. Sweeping the membranes: a valid procedure in stimulating the onset of labour? Br J Obstet Gynaecol 1993;100:898–903 (Level I)

27. Moldin PG, Sundell G. Induction of labour: a randomised clinical trial of amniotomy versus amniotomy with oxytocin infusion. Br J Obstet Gynaecol 1996;103:306–312 (Level I)

28. American College of Obstetricians and Gynecologists. Assessment of fetal lung maturity. ACOG Educational Bulletin 230. Washington DC: ACOG, 1996 (Level III)

29. Rayburn WF. Prostaglandin E$_2$ gel for cervical ripening and induction of labor: a critical analysis. Am J Obstet Gynecol 1989;160:529–534 (Level III)

30. Buser D, Mora G, Arias F. A randomized comparison between misoprostol and dinoprostone for cervical ripening and labor induction in patients with unfavorable cervices. Obstet Gynecol 1997;89:581–585 (Level I)

31. Sanchez-Ramos L, Kaunitz AM, Wears RL, Delke I, Gaudier FL. Misoprostol for cervical ripening and labor induction: a meta-analysis. Obstet Gynecol 1997;89:633–642 (Meta-analysis)

32. Sanchez-Ramos L, Peterson DE, Delke I, Gaudier FL, Kaunitz AM. Labor induction with prostaglandin E$_1$ misoprostol compared with dinoprostone vaginal insert: a randomized trial. Obstet Gynecol 1998;91:401–405 (Level I)

33. Srisomboon J, Piyamongkol W, Aiewsakul P. Comparison of intracervical and intravaginal misoprostol for cervical ripening and labour induction in patients with an unfavorable cervix. J Med Assoc Thai 1997;80:189–194 (Level I)

34. Wing DA, Jones MM, Rahall A, Goodwin TM, Paul RH. A comparison of misoprostol and prostaglandin E$_2$ gel for preinduction cervical ripening and labor induction. Am J Obstet Gynecol 1995;172:1804–1810 (Level I)

35. Wing DA, Ortiz-Omphroy G, Paul RH. A comparison of intermittent vaginal administration of misoprostol with continuous dinoprostone for cervical ripening and labor induction. Am J Obstet Gynecol 1997;177:612–618 (Level I)

36. Rayburn WF, Wapner RJ, Barss VA, Spitzberg E, Molina RD, Mandsageer N, Yonekura ML. An intravaginal controlled-release prostaglandin E$_2$ pessary for cervical ripening and initiation of labor at term. Obstet Gynecol 1992;79:374–379 (Level I)

37. Witter FR, Rocco LE, Johnson TR. A randomized trial of prostaglandin E$_2$ in a controlled-release vaginal pessary for cervical ripening at term. Am J Obstet Gynecol 1992; 166:830–834 (Level I)

38. Witter FR, Mercer BM. Improved intravaginal controlled-release prostaglandin E$_2$ insert for cervical ripening at term. The Prostaglandin E$_2$ Insert Study Group. J Matern Fetal Med 1996;5:64–69 (Level I)

39. Magtibay PM, Ramin KD, Harris DY, Ramsey PS, Ogburn PL Jr. Misoprostol as a labor induction agent. J Matern Fetal Med 1998;7:15–18 (Level I)

40. Hofmeyr GJ. Vaginal misoprostol for cervical ripening and labour induction in late pregnancy. The Cochrane Library 1999; Issue 2:1–18 (Meta-analysis)

41. Wing DA, Lovett K, Paul RH. Disruption of prior uterine incision following misoprostol for labor induction in women with previous cesarean section. Obstet Gynecol 1998;91:828–830 (Level III)

42. Bernstein P. Prostaglandin E$_2$ gel for cervical ripening and labour induction: a multicentre placebo-controlled trial. CMAJ 1991;145:1249–1254 (Level I)

43. Miller AM, Rayburn WF, Smith CV. Patterns of uterine activity after intravaginal prostaglandin E$_2$ during preinduction cervical ripening. Am J Obstet Gynecol 1991; 165:1006–1009 (Level II-1)

44. American College of Obstetricians and Gynecologists. Monitoring during induction of labor with dinoprostone. ACOG Committee Opinion 209. Washington DC: ACOG, 1998 (Level III)

45. Sawai SK, Williams MC, O'Brien WF, Angel JL, Mastrogiannis DS, Johnson L. Sequential outpatient application of intravaginal prostaglandin E$_2$ gel in the management of postdates pregnancies. Obstet Gynecol 1991;78: 19–23 (Level I)

46. Flannelly GM, Turner MJ, Rassmussen MJ, Stronge JM. Rupture of the uterus in Dublin; An update. J Obstet Gynaecol 1993;13:440–443 (Level II-3)

47. Whalley PJ, Pritchard JA. Oxytocin and water intoxication. JAMA 1963:186;601–603

48. Toppozada MK, Anwar MY, Hassan HA, El-Gazaerly WS. Oral or vaginal misoprostol for induction of labor. Int J Gynaecol Obstet 1997;56:135–139 (Level I)

49. Schellpfeffer MA, Hoyle D, Johnson JWC. Antepartal uterine hypercontractility secondary to nipple stimulation. Obstet Gynecol 1985;65:588–591 (Level III)

50. Hauth JC, Hankins GD, Gilstrap LC III, Strickland DM, Vance P. Uterine contraction pressures with oxytocin induction/augmentation. Obstet Gynecol 1986;68: 305–309 (Level II-2)

51. Satin AJ, Leveno KJ, Sherman ML, Brewster DS, Cunningham FG. High- versus low-dose oxytocin for labor stimulation. Obstet Gynecol 1992;80:111–116 (Level II-1)

52. Crane JM, Young DC. Meta-analysis of low-dose versus high-dose oxytocin for labour induction. J Soc Obstet Gynaecol Can 1998;20:1215–1223 (Meta-analysis)

53. Cummiskey KC, Dawood MY. Induction of labor with pulsatile oxytocin. Am J Obstet Gynecol 1990;163: 1868–1874 (Level I)

54. Blakemore KJ, Qin NG, Petrie RH, Paine LL. A prospective comparison of hourly and quarter-hourly oxytocin dose increase intervals for the induction of labor at term. Obstet Gynecol 1990;75:757–761 (Level I)

55. Mercer B, Pilgrim P, Sibai B. Labor induction with continuous low-dose oxytocin infusion: a randomized trial. Obstet Gynecol 1991;77:659–663 (Level I)

56. Muller PR, Stubbs TM, Laurent SL. A prospective randomized clinical trial comparing two oxytocin induction protocols. Am J Obstet Gynecol 1992;167:373–380; discussion 380–381 (Level I)

57. Willcourt RJ, Pager D, Wendel J, Hale RW. Induction of labor with pulsatile oxytocin by a computer-controlled pump. Am J Obstet Gynecol 1994;170:603–608 (Level I)

58. Clark SL, Hankins GD, Dudley DA, Dildy GA, Porter TF. Amniotic fluid embolism: analysis of the national registry. Am J Obstet Gynecol 1995;172:1158–1169 (Level III)

59. Morgan M. Amniotic fluid embolism. Anaesthesia 1979; 34:20–32 (Level III)

60. Ray DA, Garite TJ. Prostaglandin E$_2$ for induction of labor in patients with premature rupture of membranes at term. Am J Obstet Gynecol 1992;166:836–843 (Level I)

61. Sanchez-Ramos L, Chen AH, Kaunitz AM, Gaudier FL, Delke I. Labor induction with intravaginal misoprostol in term premature rupture of the membranes: a randomized study. Obstet Gynecol 1997;89:909–912 (Level I)

62. Pitkin RM. Fetal death: diagnosis and management. Am J Obstet Gynecol 1987;157:583–589 (Level III)

63. Berkus MD, Laufe LE, Castillo M. Lamicel for induction of labor. J Reprod Med 1990;35:219–221 (Level II-2)

64. Sanchez-Ramos L, Kaunitz AM, Connor PM. Hygroscopic cervical dilators and prostaglandin E$_2$ gel for preinduction cervical ripening. A randomized, prospective comparison. J Reprod Med 1992;37:355–359 (Level I)

65. Kochenour NK. Management of fetal demise. Clin Obstet Gynecol 1987;30:322–330 (Level III)

66. American College of Obstetricians and Gynecologists. Diagnosis and management of fetal death. ACOG Technical Bulletin 176. Washington DC: ACOG, 1993 (Level III)

67. Kent DR, Goldstein AI, Linzey EM. Safety and efficacy of vaginal prostaglandin E$_2$ suppositories in the management of third-trimester fetal demise. J Reprod Med 1984;29: 101–102 (Level III)

68. Cabrol D, Dubois C, Cronje H, Gonnet JM, Guillot M, Maria B, et al. Induction of labor with mifepristone (RU 486) in intrauterine fetal death. Am J Obstet Gynecol 1990;163:540–542 (Level I)

69. Bugalho A, Bique C, Machungo F, Faaundes A. Induction of labor with intravaginal misoprostol in intrauterine fetal death. Am J Obstet Gynecol 1994;171:538–541 (Level III)

70. Chuck FJ, Huffaker BJ. Labor induction with intravaginal misoprostol versus intracervical prostaglandin E$_2$ gel (Prepidil gel): randomized comparison. Am J Obstet Gynecol 1995;173:1137–1142 (Level I)

The MEDLINE database, the Cochrane Library, and ACOG's own internal resources and documents were used to conduct a literature search to locate relevant articles published between January 1985 and February 1999. The search was restricted to articles published in the English language. Priority was given to articles reporting results of original research, although review articles and commentaries also were consulted. Abstracts of research presented at symposia and scientific conferences were not considered adequate for inclusion in this document. Guidelines published by organizations or institutions such as the National Institutes of Health and the American College of Obstetricians and Gynecologists were reviewed, and additional studies were located by reviewing bibliographies of identified articles. When reliable research was not available, expert opinions from obstetrician–gynecologists were used.

Studies were reviewed and evaluated for quality according to the method outlined by the U.S. Preventive Services Task Force:

I   Evidence obtained from at least one properly designed randomized controlled trial.

II-1   Evidence obtained from well-designed controlled trials without randomization.

II-2   Evidence obtained from well-designed cohort or case–control analytic studies, preferably from more than one center or research group.

II-3   Evidence obtained from multiple time series with or without the intervention. Dramatic results in uncontrolled experiments could also be regarded as this type of evidence.

III   Opinions of respected authorities, based on clinical experience, descriptive studies, or reports of expert committees.

Based on the highest level of evidence found in the data, recommendations are provided and graded according to the following categories:

Level A—Recommendations are based on good and consistent scientific evidence.

Level B—Recommendations are based on limited or inconsistent scientific evidence.

Level C—Recommendations are based primarily on consensus and expert opinion.

ISSN 1099-3630

**The American College of
Obstetricians and Gynecologists
409 12th Street, SW
PO Box 96920
Washington, DC 20090-6920**

12345/32109

ACOG PRACTICE BULLETIN

CLINICAL MANAGEMENT GUIDELINES FOR
OBSTETRICIAN–GYNECOLOGISTS
NUMBER 12, JANUARY 2000

This Practice Bulletin was developed by the ACOG Committee on Practice Bulletins—Obstetrics with the assistance of Susan M. Cox, MD. The information is designed to aid practitioners in making decisions about appropriate obstetric and gynecologic care. These guidelines should not be construed as dictating an exclusive course of treatment or procedure. Variations in practice may be warranted based on the needs of the individual patient, resources, and limitations unique to the institution or type of practice.

Intrauterine Growth Restriction

Intrauterine growth restriction (IUGR) is one of the most common and complex problems in modern obstetrics. Diagnosis and management are complicated by the use of ambiguous terminology and a lack of uniform diagnostic criteria. In addition, some authors do not make a clear distinction between suspected prenatal growth restriction and confirmed IUGR in the perinatal period. Furthermore, size alone is not an indication of a complication. As a result of this confusion, underintervention and overintervention can occur. This bulletin will focus on the etiology, diagnosis, and management of intrauterine growth restriction.

Background

Definitions

Several factors have contributed to the confusion in terminology associated with IUGR:

- By definition, 10% of infants in any population will have birth weights at or below the 10th percentile. Intrauterine growth restriction could be manifest at a weight above the population determined at the 10th percentile (eg, an undernourished infant born at the 15th percentile whose genetic make-up would have placed it at the 90th percentile). Distinctions between normal and pathologic growth often cannot reliably be made in clinical practice, especially prior to birth.

- Although defining a pathologic condition using a 10th percentile cutoff makes statistical sense, it may not be clinically relevant. One study suggests that adverse perinatal outcome generally is confined to those infants with birth weights below the 5th percentile, and in most cases below the 3rd percentile (1).

- Although specific ethnic- and geographic-based growth curves are increasingly used to evaluate birth weight, it remains unclear whether this is appropriate. These distinctions become even more difficult in ethnically heterogeneous and geographically mobile populations, such as those in the United States. Birth weight also is related to maternal height, parity, paternal height, and the fetus' sex.

The use of the terms "small for gestational age" (SGA) and "intrauterine growth restriction" has been confusing, and the terms often are used interchangeably. For the purpose of this document, SGA will be used only in reference to the infant and IUGR to the fetus.

Small for Gestational Age

Infants with a birth weight at the lower extreme of the normal birth weight distribution are termed SGA. In the United States, the most commonly used definition of SGA is a birth weight below the 10th percentile for gestational age (2, 3).

Intrauterine Growth Restriction

Intrauterine growth restriction is a term used to describe a fetus whose estimated weight appears to be less than expected, usually less than the 10th percentile, which is the convention this document will adopt. The term IUGR includes normal fetuses at the lower end of the growth spectrum, as well as those with specific clinical conditions in which the fetus fails to achieve its inherent growth potential as a consequence of either pathologic extrinsic influences (such as maternal smoking) or intrinsic genetic defects (such as aneuploidy).

Etiology

Several conditions have been found to be associated with IUGR (see the box). These antecedents can be divided into several broad categories: maternal, fetal, or placental. Maternal behavioral conditions include substance use (including smoking and alcohol use) (4–6), extremes of reproductive age (younger than 16 years and older than 35 years), little maternal weight gain (7), malnutrition, and low prepregnancy weight (7). In addition, low socioeconomic status is associated with IUGR (7).

Maternal Medical Conditions

Medical complications that affect the microcirculation causing fetal hypoxemia or vasoconstriction or a reduction in fetal perfusion also are significantly associated with IUGR (8). These include hypertension, both chronic and acute (as in preeclampsia) (9), and severe chronic diseases, such as renal insufficiency (10), systemic lupus

---

Risk Factors for Intrauterine Growth Restriction

- Maternal medical conditions
  - Hypertension
  - Renal disease
  - Restrictive lung disease
  - Diabetes (with microvascular disease)
  - Cyanotic heart disease
  - Antiphospholipid syndrome
  - Collagen-vascular disease
  - Hemoglobinopathies
- Smoking and substance use and abuse
- Severe malnutrition
- Primary placental disease
- Multiple gestation
- Infections (viral, protozoal)
- Genetic disorders
- Exposure to teratogens

---

erythematosus, antiphospholipid antibody syndrome, chronic anemia, and pregestational diabetes (especially White's classifications C, D, F, and R). Growth restriction may be preceded by defective maternal volume adaptation in early pregnancy (11, 12).

Placental association with IUGR is unique in that it can be the primary cause (eg, mosaicism) or merely involved in an adaptive process of a pregnancy complication. The placenta and impaired placental perfusion are the most common cause of SGA in nonanomalous infants (13), as seen in early-onset preeclampsia, which produces the most severe IUGR (14). Intrauterine growth restriction also is related to other placental abnormalities, including partial abruptions, previa, infarcts, and hematomas (15). In unexplained IUGR, placental mosaicism may be identified in up to 25% of patients (16). Factors not associated with IUGR include caffeine use in nonsmokers (6, 17) and passive smoking (18).

Substance Use and Abuse

Maternal alcohol abuse is associated with impaired fetal growth; virtually all neonates with fetal alcohol syndrome will exhibit significant growth restriction (6, 19). It is unknown whether a threshold effect exists for alcohol, but effects on the fetus are related to the amount consumed.

Women who smoke have a 3.5-fold increase of SGA infants, compared with nonsmokers (9). Newborns of smokers are smaller at every gestational age. Women who stop smoking before 16 weeks of gestation have infants with birth weights similar to those of babies of women who never smoked (20), and women who quit as late as the seventh month have mean birth weights higher than those who smoked during the entire pregnancy (21).

The incidence of IUGR is markedly increased in pregnant women who use illicit drugs, but it is difficult to differentiate the drug effect from the effects of other behaviors associated with drug use. The incidence of SGA infants in mothers with heroin addiction is as high as 50% (22) and is reported to be as high as 35% in patients managed with methadone (23). Cocaine abuse in pregnancy is associated with delivery of an SGA neonate in 30% or more of cases (24).

Malnutrition

There is a common belief that severe maternal malnutrition will result in fetal growth restriction. The data from studies of the Siege of Leningrad during World War II (25) and the Dutch famine of the same period (26) suggest that maternal intake must be reduced to below 1,500 kilocalories per day before a measurable effect on birth weight becomes evident. In these studies, it is not entirely clear, however, how much of the effect on birth weight was the result of IUGR and how much the result of preterm delivery.

Although low prepregnancy weight and low maternal weight gain have been positively associated with an increase in IUGR (7, 27, 28), and increased weight gain has been associated with decreased IUGR in some populations (29), there is as yet no demonstration that altering dietary recommendations or habits can affect birth weight in a positive manner. Rather, although there are associations between maternal prepregnancy weight, maternal weight gain, and birth weight, there has been no trial showing that any intervention to alter pregnancy weight gain has a beneficial effect on fetal weight gain.

Placental Disease

Primary placental disease (such as chorioangioma) is a rare but recognized cause of growth restriction (30). Placenta previa has been associated with an increase in growth restriction, presumably secondary to abnormal placental implantation. Confined placental mosaicism has been identified three times more frequently from placentas of SGA infants than in infants of normal growth (16).

Multiple Gestation

Intrauterine growth restriction is a common complication of multiple gestation. It is more pronounced in higher order multiple gestations when compared with twin gestations (31). Investigators have reported a greater likelihood of IUGR among surviving fetuses after multifetal reduction (32, 33). The growth restriction is a result of placental reserve inadequate to sustain the normal growth of more than one fetus. Growth restriction can occur in dizygotic twin gestations but is more common and severe in monozygotic twins. It is evident that equal sharing of functional placental mass is not the norm; rather, one twin is more likely to have a larger share of functional placental mass than the other (31).

Infections

Viral infections have been estimated to be etiologic in less than 5% of all growth-restricted fetuses (34). However, when evaluated in documented cases of in utero viral infection, the frequency of IUGR can be strikingly high. Fetal rubella infection is associated with growth restriction in up to 60% of cases (35). Cytomegalovirus also is a recognized cause of growth restriction (36). In one study, approximately 40% of fetuses with varicella syndrome exhibited growth restriction (37). Bacterial infections have not been shown to cause growth restriction. Some protozoal infections, such as *Toxoplasma gondii, Trypanosoma cruzi* (Chagas disease), and syphilis, are associated with growth restriction (38, 39).

Genetic Disorders

Chromosome anomalies are a major cause of IUGR (40, 41). Many fetal structural anomalies also are associated with an increased risk of growth restriction, with a relative risk ranging from as high as 24.7 with anencephaly to as low as 1.2 with pyloric stenosis (42).

Exposure to Teratogens

Maternal ingestion of certain medications is a recognized cause of growth restriction; the incidence and severity vary by substance, gestational age at exposure, duration of exposure, and dosage. Therapeutic agents known to be associated with growth restriction include anticonvulsants (eg, trimethadione, phenytoin) (43–45), folic acid antagonists (eg, methotrexate) (46), and warfarin (47, 48).

Morbidity and Mortality

Fetal Morbidity and Mortality

Perinatal morbidity and mortality is significantly increased in the presence of low birth weight for gestational age, especially with weights below the 3rd percentile for gestational age (1). One study found that 26% of all stillbirths were SGA (49). The risk of death in the presence of IUGR also is affected by gestational age and the primary etiology and may be further modified by the severity and progression of associated maternal etiologic factors (eg, hypertension) (50) (see Table 1).

Both intrapartum and neonatal complications are increased in the presence of IUGR. During labor, up to 50% of growth-restricted fetuses exhibit abnormal heart rate patterns, most often variable decelerations, and such fetuses have an increased cesarean delivery rate (51, 52). Oligohydramnios is a common finding in growth-restricted fetuses and may render the umbilical cord vulnerable to compression (53–55). Sustained antepartum cord compression in growth-restricted fetuses is a presumed cause of sudden fetal death (51, 55). Incidences of low Apgar scores and cord blood acidemia increase significantly in SGA neonates (56).

Neonatal Morbidity

Neonatal complications in the SGA infant include polycythemia, hyperbilirubinemia, hypoglycemia, hypothermia, and apneic episodes (57, 58), as well as low Apgar scores, umbilical artery pH less than 7.0, need for intubation in the delivery room, seizures, sepsis, and neonatal death (1). It is uncertain whether IUGR accelerates fetal pulmonary maturity. One study found a decreased incidence of both respiratory distress syndrome and intraventricular hemorrhage in infants with SGA compared with a control group of infants of appropriate size for their gestational age (59). In contrast, other studies failed to document a difference in lung profile in a matched series (60) and found no difference in the need for ventilatory support in newborns with SGA when compared with controls. The use of glucocorticoids in fetuses with IUGR has not been studied, but current recommendations are to give glucocorticoids to women with

Table 1. Corrected Perinatal Mortality Rates (Excluding Lethal Anomaly) Among Low-risk and High-risk (Screened/Unscreened) Pregnancies and Among SGA Fetuses (Screened/Unscreened), Manitoba Experience

Category	Number of Cases	Corrected Perinatal Mortality Rates (per 1,000 live births)
All cases	144,786	5.6
All low risk	101,350	3.8
All high risk	43,436	9.8
Screened high risk	31,740	2.2
All SGA (7% total population)	10,135	17.8
Unscreened SGA	7,460	21.3
Screened SGA*	2,675	8.4

* Serial fetal assessment management by fetal biophysical profile score.

Manning FA. Intrauterine growth retardation, etiology, pathophysiology, diagnosis, and treatment. In: Fetal medicine: principles and practice. Norwalk, Connecticut: Appleton & Lange, 1995:372

complicated pregnancies who are likely to deliver before 34 weeks of gestation (61).

Long-term development of infants born with SGA depends in part on the cause of the growth failure. In infants with karyotype abnormalities or viral infection, the etiology rather than the weight percentile ultimately will determine the outcome. There are conflicting data on whether infants catch up in growth. Most otherwise normal infants with SGA secondary to placental insufficiency will exhibit normal catch-up growth by the age of 2 years, although this pattern may not be seen universally in severely affected infants (58, 62–64) or in preterm growth-restricted infants (65). A comparison of 714 neonates of appropriate size for age with 347 SGA neonates, derived from several studies, indicated a twofold increase of major neurologic sequelae among SGA infants (54). There is no evidence to suggest that any specific management scheme or delivery route prevents neurologic injury in such fetuses. Long-term follow-up of infants with SGA shows that they are more prone to develop adult-onset hypertension and cardiovascular complications (66). It is important to note that IUGR and SGA both have a multitude of etiologies, and there is a danger in grouping them. There may be no consequences of low birth weight under some circumstances; under others, it may be devastating.

Antenatal Diagnosis of Intrauterine Growth Restriction

There are two essential steps involved in the antenatal recognition of growth restriction. The first step involves the elucidation of maternal risk factors associated with growth restriction and the clinical assessment of uterine size in relation to gestational age. The second step involves the ultrasonographic assessment of fetal size and growth, supplemented by invasive fetal testing for aneuploidy or viral infection in select cases.

Clinical Evaluation

The key physical finding in IUGR is a uterine size that is smaller than expected for gestational age. Several methods are available for clinical determination of uterine size, the most common of which is an objective measurement of fundal height. Such techniques, however, are prone to considerable inaccuracy and should be used for screening only, not as a sole guide to obstetric management in the presence of risk factors for or suspicions of IUGR. These inaccuracies are revealed in clinical studies suggesting that growth restriction is undetected in about one third of cases and is incorrectly diagnosed about 50% of the time (3, 67).

Prior to birth, the diagnosis of IUGR is not precise. Currently, the use of ultrasonographically estimated fetal weight, head- or femur-to-abdomen ratios, or serial observation of biometric growth patterns (growth velocity) are all acceptable and widely used methods to diagnose IUGR (68–72). This document does not address the concept of asymmetrical versus symmetrical IUGR, because it is unclear whether the distinction is important with respect to etiology or neonatal outcome.

Four standard fetal measurements generally are obtained as part of any complete obstetric ultrasound examination after the first trimester: 1) fetal abdominal circumference, 2) head circumference, 3) biparietal diameter, and 4) femur length (73). Fetal morphologic parameters can be converted to fetal weight estimates using published formulas and tables (74). An abdominal circumference within the normal range reliably excludes growth restriction with a false-negative rate of less than 10% (71). A small abdominal circumference or fetal weight estimate below the 10th percentile suggests the possibility of growth restriction, with the likelihood increasing as the percentile rank decreases (71). When IUGR is suspected, serial measurements of fetal biometric parameters provide an estimated growth rate. Such serial measurements are of considerable clinical value in confirming or excluding the diagnosis and assessing the progression and severity of growth restriction. Given the high incidence of genetic and structural defects associated with IUGR, a detailed ultrasound survey for the presence of fetal structural and functional defects may be indicated.

Amniotic fluid volume is an important diagnostic and prognostic parameter in fetuses with IUGR (75, 76). Oligohydramnios is highly suggestive of growth failure and indicates an increased risk of fetal death. Oligohydramnios is diagnosed ultrasonographically in approximately 77–83% of pregnancies with growth-restricted fetuses (75–77). In contrast, amniotic fluid volume often is normal even in a fetus with significant growth restriction; thus, the absence of oligohydramnios should not detract from the diagnosis of IUGR.

Although Doppler velocimetry of the umbilical arteries is not useful as a screening technique for IUGR (78, 79), it has been demonstrated to be useful once IUGR has been diagnosed. Not only are Doppler velocimetry findings normal in growth-restricted fetuses with chromosomal or other structural etiologies (80) but Doppler velocimetry has been shown to both reduce interventions and improve fetal outcome in pregnancies at risk for IUGR (81). Thus, once IUGR is suspected or diagnosed, Doppler velocimetry may be useful as a part of fetal evaluation. Fetuses with normal flow patterns seem less likely to benefit from consideration of early delivery than do their counterparts with abnormal studies.

Clinical Considerations and Recommendations

▶ *Which pregnancies should be screened for intrauterine growth restriction, and how is screening accomplished?*

Unfortunately, approximately one half of growth-restricted fetuses are not diagnosed until delivery. In essence, all pregnancies are screened for IUGR using serial fundal height measurements. A single measurement at 32–34 weeks of gestation is approximately 70–85% sensitive and 96% specific for detecting the growth-restricted fetus (82). A third-trimester ultrasound examination, with a single measurement of abdominal circumference, detects about 80% of IUGR fetuses (70). Even so, this does not justify ultrasonography as a screening tool, because fundal height measurement performs comparably (70). All pregnancies should be screened with serial fundal height assessments, reserving ultrasonography for those with risk factors, lagging growth, or no growth (69, 83, 84).

Women who have previously given birth to an SGA infant are at an increased risk for this condition in subsequent pregnancies (9). Physicians should consider an early ultrasound examination to confirm gestational age, as well as subsequent ultrasonography to evaluate sequential fetal growth, in women with significant risk factors.

▶ *What are the best ways to evaluate and monitor a pregnancy complicated by suspected intrauterine growth restriction?*

Once IUGR is suspected (ie, lagging fundal height), it should be confirmed using multiple ultrasonographic parameters, such as estimated weight percentile, amniotic fluid volume, elevated head circumference and abdominal circumference ratio, and possibly Doppler criteria (ie, elevated systolic–diastolic ratio or reversed or absent end-diastolic flow) (85). Identification of IUGR is improved by recording growth velocity or through two sets of examinations generally 2–4 weeks apart.

The diagnosis of IUGR as the fetus approaches term may be an indication for delivery (86). If pregnancy is remote from term or if delivery is not elected, the optimal mode of monitoring has not been established. Periodic fetal assessment (approximately weekly) using Doppler velocimetry, contraction stress test, traditional biophysical profile (BPP), modified BPP, or nonstress test (NST) are all accepted monitoring techniques. Randomized controlled trials have demonstrated that monitoring with Doppler velocimetry reduces the risk of perinatal morbidity (81). Comparable studies for the other methods have not been done.

Serial ultrasonograms to determine the rate of growth should be obtained approximately every 2–4 weeks. Measurements at shorter intervals (<2 weeks) may overlap with measurement errors. If any test result is abnormal (decreased amniotic fluid volume or low BPP scores), more frequent testing, possibly daily, may be indicated. An abnormal result from fetal heart rate testing (decreased variability) coupled with abnormal results from Doppler velocimetry suggests poor fetal well-being and a potential need for delivery, despite prematurity (72).

▶ *What interventions improve pregnancy outcome in cases of intrauterine growth restriction or suspected intrauterine growth restriction?*

Evidence from randomized controlled trials finds few interventions beneficial in preventing or treating IUGR. Avoidance of smoking during pregnancy has been shown to have a positive effect on birth weight (20). Treatment of infections such as malaria in endemic areas has been shown to be of some benefit (87, 88).

A number of interventions have been suggested for which there is insufficient evidence from randomized clinical trials to conclude either benefit or harm. Among them are bed rest, which demonstrated no benefit in one small study (89), and early delivery in the presence of pulsatile flow in waveforms from the umbilical vein, which remains to be assessed in a randomized control trial. Other interventions of questionable efficacy and safety include nutrient treatment or supplementation (90), zinc supplementation (91), calcium supplementation (92), plasma volume expansion (93), maternal oxygen therapy (94), heparin (47), and low-dose aspirin (95–99). Thus, such interventions should be used only in experimental protocols.

▶ *Is there any evidence that prenatal diagnosis or suspicion of intrauterine growth restriction with antenatal surveillance alters outcome?*

The nonanomalous fetus with IUGR should be monitored serially for risk of perinatal mortality and morbidity. Risk to the fetus can be determined by several methods: traditional or modified BPP, contraction stress test, NST, amniotic fluid volume, or Doppler velocimetry of fetal vessels. Unfortunately, these tests are performed to determine the optimal time for delivery and are not predictive of individual fetuses at greatest risk for a complicated neonatal course (100).

There are no randomized trials of interventions in a fetus with abnormal heart rate tracings. Thus, in the case of a very premature infant, delivery or expectant management are the usual courses of action at present. Overall experience with the NST confirms that with a reactive NST the fetus is not likely to die in utero immediately. In several studies, nonreactive or abnormal NSTs were found in fetuses with acidosis, hypoxemia, or both (101, 102). In four randomized clinical trials comparing BPP with conventional fetal monitoring in high-risk pregnancies (including those with IUGR), there was no obvious benefit for pregnancy outcome using BPP for surveillance (103), although different results might have been obtained in an IUGR-only population.

Doppler ultrasound has been shown to be useful in the assessment of the growth-restricted fetus (104). Absent or reversed end-diastolic flow velocities in the umbilical arteries have a poor positive predictive value but are associated with poor perinatal outcome and high perinatal mortality (105–107). In contrast, a normal systolic–diastolic ratio in a growth-restricted fetus has excellent negative predictive value and may be used as a rationale to delay delivery with some reassurance. Currently, there are not enough data to warrant cordocentesis in the management of IUGR.

With the exception of Manning's data, which includes IUGR among other high-risk conditions, there is no evidence that antenatal surveillance in fetuses with suspected IUGR alters perinatal outcome. Instead, it is used to predict which fetuses are at risk for in utero demise and thus may potentially benefit from preterm delivery. Currently, there are no intrauterine therapies available for affected fetuses; therefore, delivery is the optimal treatment in the mature fetus, but must be weighed against gestational age for the immature fetus.

▶ *How does knowledge of the etiology of intrauterine growth restriction alter management?*

If maternal medical conditions are thought to be the cause of IUGR, there is no evidence that changes in maternal medical management other than delivery alter outcome. For example, antihypertensive therapy has not been shown to have a benefit with respect to IUGR (108). However, it is still important to optimize maternal treatment.

Although the etiology and manifestations of IUGR are numerous, a concerted effort should be made to determine the underlying cause. If a lethal anomaly is identified, one would not usually undertake antepartum surveillance.

A detailed ultrasound survey should be performed to detect fetal structural defects. Fetal karyotype determinations are not routinely indicated in the assessment of growth-restricted fetuses, but should be considered when early or severe IUGR is detected or when the fetus has a recognized structural anomaly. It is estimated that about 10% of structurally abnormal fetuses with fetal growth restriction will have a karyotype anomaly.

Prenatal diagnosis of in utero infections also can be accomplished via amniotic fluid or fetal blood analyses. Viral infections associated with IUGR, such as rubella, cytomegalovirus, or varicella, can be diagnosed by polymerase chain reaction or by measuring viral-specific immunoglobulin M antibodies. There are, however, no in utero treatments for these infections. However, if toxoplasmosis is identified, medication taken by the mother may prevent the spread of maternal infection to the fetus (38).

▶ *When should a growth-restricted fetus be delivered?*

The fetus should be delivered if the risk of fetal death exceeds that of neonatal death, although in many cases these risks are difficult to assess. The timing of delivery in the growth-restricted fetus should be individualized. Early delivery may yield an infant with all the serious sequelae of prematurity, whereas delaying delivery may yield a hypoxic, acidotic infant with long-term neurologic sequelae. Gestational age and the findings of antenatal surveillance should be taken into account. The decision to deliver is based often on nonreassuring fetal assessment or a complete cessation of fetal growth assessed ultrasonographically over a 2–4-week interval. When extrauterine survival is likely despite significantly abnormal antenatal testing, delivery should be seriously considered.

Summary

The general approach to management of the fetus with ultrasonographically suspected IUGR involves risk factor modification when possible and the initiation of antepartum fetal surveillance, ultrasonography, and delivery when the risks of continued in utero development outweigh the benefits.

The risks to the growth-impaired fetus are well documented. Currently, although the incidence of IUGR has not changed appreciably, the prognosis for SGA infants has improved dramatically. It must be emphasized, however, that perinatal morbidity and mortality will continue to occur despite optimal management of the fetus with suspected IUGR. In those fetuses managed expectantly, antepartum injury or death may occur because current methods of fetal surveillance are less than perfect in the prediction of fetal outcome.

The following recommendations are based on good and consistent scientific evidence (Level A):

▶ The use of Doppler ultrasonography to measure umbilical artery waveforms in the management of IUGR is associated with a reduction in perinatal death, and may be considered a part of fetal evaluation once IUGR is suspected or diagnosed.

▶ Nutrient treatment or supplementation, zinc or calcium supplementation, plasma volume expansion, maternal oxygen therapy, antihypertensive therapy, heparin, and aspirin therapy have not been shown to be effective for prevention or treatment of IUGR.

The following recommendations are based primarily on consensus and expert opinion (Level C):

▶ Antepartum surveillance should be instituted once the possibility of extrauterine survival for the growth-restricted fetus has been determined. This may include Doppler velocimetry, contraction stress testing, NST with amniotic fluid volume assessment, and BPP.

▶ Routine screening for IUGR in low-risk patients should comprise classical clinical monitoring techniques. Ultrasound evaluation of the fetus is appropriate in patients determined to be at high risk.

References

1. McIntire DD, Bloom SL, Casey BM, Leveno KJ. Birth weight in relation to morbidity and mortality among newborn infants. N Engl J Med 1999;340:1234–1238 (Level II-2)

2. Battaglia FC, Lubchenco LO. A practical classification of newborn infants by weight and gestational age. J Pediatr 1967;71:159–163 (Level III)

3. Jahn A, Razum O, Berle P. Routine screening for intrauterine growth retardation in Germany: low sensitivity and questionable benefit for diagnosed cases. Acta Obstet Gynecol Scand 1998;77:643–648 (Level II-2)

4. Spinillo A, Capuzzo E, Nicola SE, Colonna L, Egbe TO, Zara C. Factors potentiating the smoking-related risk of fetal growth retardation. Br J Obstet Gynaecol 1994;101: 954–958 (Level II-2)

5. Lieberman E, Gremy I, Lang JM, Cohen AP. Low birth weight at term and the timing of fetal exposure to maternal smoking. Am J Public Health 1994;84:1127–1131 (Level II-2)

6. Shu XO, Hatch MC, Mills J, Clemens J, Susser M. Maternal smoking, alcohol drinking, caffeine consumption, and fetal growth: results from a prospective study. Epidemiology 1995;6:115–120 (Level II-3)

7. Nieto A, Matorras R, Serra M, Valenzuela P, Molero J. Multivariate analysis of determinants of fetal growth retardation. Eur J Obstet Gynecol Reprod Biol 1994;53:107–113 (Level II-2)

8. Rotmensch S, Liberati M, Luo JS, Kliman HJ, Gollin Y, Bellati U, et al. Color Doppler flow patterns and flow velocity waveforms of the intraplacental fetal circulation in growth-retarded fetuses. Am J Obstet Gynecol 1994; 171:1257–1264 (Level II-2)

9. Ounsted M, Moar VA, Scott A. Risk factors associated with small-for-dates and large-for-dates infants. Br J Obstet Gynaecol 1985;92:226–232 (Level II-2)

10. Cunningham FG, Cox SM, Harstad TW, Mason RA, Pritchard JA. Chronic renal disease and pregnancy outcome. Am J Obstet Gynecol 1990;163:453–459 (Level II-3)

11. Duvekot JJ, Cheriex EC, Pieters FA, Menheere PP, Schouten HJ, Peeters LL. Maternal volume homeostasis in early pregnancy in relation to fetal growth restriction. Obstet Gynecol 1995;85:361–367 (Level III)

12. Duvekot JJ, Cheriex EC, Pieters FA, Peeters LL. Severely impaired fetal growth is preceded by maternal hemodynamic maladaptation in very early pregnancy. Acta Obstet Gynecol Scand 1995;74:693–697 (Level III)

13. Salafia CM, Minior VK, Pezzullo JC, Popek EJ, Rosenkrantz TS, Vintzileos AM. Intrauterine growth restriction in infants of less than thirty-two weeks' gestation: associated placental pathologic features. Am J Obstet Gynecol 1995;173:1049–1057 (Level III)

14. Ounsted M, Moar V, Scott WA. Perinatal morbidity and mortality in small-for-dates babies: the relative importance of some maternal factors. Early Hum Dev 1981;5:367–375 (Level II-2)

15. Laurini R, Laurin J, Marsal K. Placental histology and fetal blood flow in intrauterine growth retardation. Acta Obstet Gynecol Scand 1994;73:529–534 (Level II-3)

16. Wilkins-Haug L, Roberts DJ, Morton CC. Confined placental mosaicism and intrauterine growth retardation: a case-control analysis of placentas at delivery. Am J Obstet Gynecol 1995;172:44–50 (Level II-2)

17. Cook DG, Peacock JL, Feyerabend C, Carey IM, Jarvis MJ, Anderson HR, et al. Relation of caffeine intake and blood caffeine concentrations during pregnancy to fetal growth: prospective population based study. BMJ 1996; 313:1358–1362 (Level II-3)

18. Fortier I, Marcoux S, Brisson J. Passive smoking during pregnancy and the risk of delivering a small-for-gesta-tion-al-age infant. Am J Epidemiol 1994;139:294–301 (Level II-3)

19. Virji SK. The relationship between alcohol consumption during pregnancy and infant birthweight. An epidemiologic study. Acta Obstet Gynecol Scand 1991;70:303–308 (Level II-3)

20. MacArthur C, Knox EG. Smoking in pregnancy: effects of stopping at different stages. Br J Obstet Gynaecol 1988; 95:551–555 (Level II-2)

21. Rush D, Cassano P. Relationship of cigarette smoking and social class to birth weight and perinatal mortality among all births in Britain, 5-11 April 1970. J Epidemiol Community Health 1983;37:249–255 (Level II-2)

22. Naeye RL, Blanc W, Leblanc W, Khatamee MA. Fetal complications of maternal heroin addiction: abnormal growth, infections and episodes of stress. J Pediatr 1973;83:1055–1061 (Level III)

23. Newman RG, Bashkow S, Calko D. Results of 313 consecutive live births of infants delivered to patients in the New York City Methadone Maintenance Treatment Program. Am J Obstet Gynecol 1975;121:233–237 (Level III)

24. Fulroth R, Phillips B, Durand DJ. Perinatal outcome of infants exposed to cocaine and/or heroin in utero. Am J Dis Child 1989;143:905–910 (Level II-3)

25. Anatov AN. Children born during the siege of Leningrad in 1942. J Pediatr 1947;30:250–259 (Level III)

26. Smith CA. Effect of maternal undernutrition upon the newborn infant in Holland (1944-1945). J Pediatr 1947; 30:229–243 (Level III)

27. Neggers YH, Goldenberg RL, Tamura T, Cliver SP, Hoffman HJ. The relationship between maternal dietary intake and infant birthweight. Acta Obstet Gynecol Scand 1997;165:71–75 (Level II-3)

28. Wen SW, Goldenberg RL, Cutter GR, Hoffman HJ, Cliver SP. Intrauterine growth retardation and preterm delivery: prenatal risk factors in an indigent population. Am J Obstet Gynecol 1990;162:213–218 (Level II-3)

29. Hickey CA, Cliver SP, Goldenberg RL, Kohatsu J, Hoffman HJ. Prenatal weight gain, term birth weight, and fetal growth retardation among high-risk multiparous black and white women. Obstet Gynecol 1993;81: 529–535 (Level II-2)

30. Pollack RN, Divon MY. Intrauterine growth retardation: definition, classification, and etiology. Clin Obstet Gynecol 1992;35:99–107 (Level III)

31. Sassoon DA, Castro LC, Davis JL, Hobel CJ. Perinatal outcome in triplet versus twin gestations. Obstet Gynecol 1990;75:817–820 (Level II-2)

32. Alexander JM, Hammond KR, Steinkampf MP. Multifetal reduction of high-order multiple pregnancy: comparison of obstetrical outcome with nonreduced twin gestations. Fertil Steril 1995;64:1201–1203 (Level II-2)

33. Silver RK, Helfand BT, Russell TL, Ragin A, Sholl JS, MacGregor SN. Multifetal reduction increases the risk of preterm delivery and fetal growth restriction in twins: a case-control study. Fertil Steril 1997;67:30–33 (Level II-2)

34. Klein JO, Remington JS. Current concepts of infections of the fetus and newborn infant. In: Remington JS, Klein JO, eds. Infectious diseases of the fetus & newborn infant. 4th ed. Philadelphia: W.B. Saunders, 1995:1–19 (Level III)

35. Peckham CS. Clinical and laboratory study of children exposed in utero to maternal rubella. Arch Dis Child 1972;47:571–577 (Level II-3)

36. Donner C, Liesnard C, Content J, Busine A, Aderca J, Rodesch F. Prenatal diagnosis of 52 pregnancies at risk for congenital cytomegalovirus infection. Obstet Gynecol 1993;82:481–486

37. Alkalay AL, Pomerance JJ, Rimoin DL. Fetal varicella syndrome. J Pediatr 1987;111:320–323 (Level III)

38. Daffos F, Forestier F, Capella-Pavlovsky M, Thulliez P, Aufrant C, Valenti D, et al. Prenatal management of 746 pregnancies at risk for congenital toxoplasmosis. N Engl J Med 1988;318:271–275 (Level III)

39. Ricci JM, Fojaco RM, O'Sullivan MJ. Congenital syphilis: The University of Miami/Jackson Memorial Medical Center experience, 1986-1988. Obstet Gynecol 1989;74:687–693 (Level II-2)

40. Nicolaides KH, Economides DL, Soothill PW. Blood gases, pH, and lactate in appropriate- and small-for-gestational-age fetuses. Am J Obstet Gynecol 1989;161: 996–1001 (Level II-3)

41. van Vugt JM, Karsdorp VH, van Zalen-Sprock RM, van Geijn HP. Fetal growth retardation and structural anomalies. Eur J Obstet Gynecol Reprod Biol 1991;42 Suppl: S79–S83 (Level III)

42. Khoury MJ, Erickson JD, Cordero JF, McCarthy BJ. Congenital malformations and intrauterine growth retardation: a population study. Pediatrics 1988;82:83–90 (Level II-3)

43. Battino D, Granata T, Binelli S, Caccamo ML, Canevini MP, Canger R, et al. Intrauterine growth in the offspring of epileptic mothers. Acta Neurol Scand 1992;86:555–557 (Level III)

44. Hiilesmaa VK, Teramo K, Granstrom ML, Bardy AH. Fetal head growth retardation associated with maternal antiepileptic drugs. Lancet 1981;2:165–167 (Level II-2)

45. Mastroiacovo P, Bertollini R, Licata D. Fetal growth in the offspring of epileptic women: results of an Italian multicentric cohort study. Acta Neurol Scand 1988;78:110–114 (Level II-2)

46. Aviles A, Diaz-Maqueo JC, Talavera A, Guzman R, Garcia EL. Growth and development of children of mothers treated with chemotherapy during pregnancy: current status of 43 children. Am J Hematol 1991;36:243–248 (Level III)

47. Hall JG, Pauli RM, Wilson KM. Maternal and fetal sequelae of anticoagulation during pregnancy. Am J Med 1980;68:122–140 (Level III)

48. Stevenson RE, Burton OM, Ferlauto GJ, Taylor HA. Hazards of oral anticogulants during pregnancy. JAMA 1980;243:1549–1551 (Level III)

49. Morrison I, Olsen J. Weight-specific stillbirths and associated causes of death: an analysis of 765 stillbirths. Am J Obstet Gynecol 1985;152:975–980 (Level III)

50. Piper JM, Langer O, Xenakis EM, McFarland M, Elliott BD, Berkus MD. Perinatal outcome in growth-restricted fetuses: do hypertensive and normotensive pregnancies differ? Obstet Gynecol 1996;88:194–199 (Level II-2)

51. Druzin ML, Gratacos J, Keegan KA, Paul RH. Antepartum fetal heart rate testing. VII. The significance of fetal bradycardia. Am J Obstet Gynecol 1981;139:194–198 (Level III)

52. Bekedam DJ, Visser GH. Effects of hypoxemic events on breathing, body movements, and heart rate variation: a study in growth-retarded human fetuses. Am J Obstet Gynecol 1985;153:52–56 (Level III)

53. Magann EF, Bass JD, Chauham SP, Young RA, Whitworth NS, Morrison JC. Amniotic fluid volume in normal singleton pregnancies. Obstet Gynecol 1997;90:524–528 (Level III)

54. Manning FA, Morrison I, Harman CR, Lange IR, Menticoglou S. Fetal assessment based on the fetal biophysical profile scoring: experience in 19,221 referred high-risk pregnancies. II. An analysis of false-negative fetal deaths. Am J Obstet Gynecol 1987;157:880–884 (Level III)

55. Peipert JF, Donnenfeld AE. Oligohydramnios: a review. Obstet Gynecol Surv 1991;46:325–339 (Level III)

56. Kramer MS, Olivier M, McLean FH, Willis DM, Usher RH. Impact of intrauterine growth retardation and body proportionality on fetal and neonatal outcome. Pediatrics 1990;86:707–713 (Level II-3)

57. Jones RA, Robertson NR. Problems of the small-for-dates baby. Clin Obstet Gynaecol 1984;11:499–524 (Level III)

58. Alkalay AL, Graham JM Jr, Pomerance JJ. Evaluation of neonates born with intrauterine growth retardation: review and practice guidelines. J Perinatol 1998;18:142–151 (Level III)

59. Procianoy RS, Garcia-Prats JA, Adams JM, Silvers A, Rudolph AJ. Hyaline membrane disease and intraventricular haemorrhage in small for gestational age infants. Arch Dis Child 1980;55:502–505 (Level II-2)

60. Piper JM, Langer O. Is lung maturation related to fetal growth in diabetic or hypertensive pregnancies? Eur J Obstet Gynecol Reprod Biol 1993;51:15–19 (Level II-3)

61. Effect of cortiscosteroids for fetal maturation on perinatal outcomes. NIH Consens Statement 1994;12:1–24 (Level III)

62. Fay RA, Ellwood DA. Categories of intrauterine growth retardation. Fetal Matern Med Rev 1993;5:203–212 (Level III)

63. Bergsjo P. Why are some children stunted at birth, and do they catch up with their peers in infancy? Acta Obstet Gynecol Scand Suppl 1997;165:1–2 (Level III)

64. Hadders-Algra M, Touwen BC. Body measurements, neurological and behavioural development in six-year-old children born preterm and/or small-for-gestational-age. Early Hum Dev 1990;22:1–13 (Level II-2)

65. Smedler C, Faxelius G, Bremme K, Lagerstrom M. Psychological development in children born with very low birth weight after severe intrauterine growth retardation: a 10-year follow-up study. Acta Paediatr 1992;81:197–203 (Level III)

66. Barker DJ, Osmond C, Golding J, Kuh D, Wadsworth ME. Growth in utero, blood pressure in childhood and adult life, and mortality from cardiovascular diseases. BMJ 1989;298:564–567 (Level II-3)

67. Kean LH, Liu DT. Antenatal care as a screening tool for the detection of small for gestational age babies in the low risk population. J Obstet Gynaecol 1996;16:77–82 (Level III)

68. Harding K, Evans S, Newnham J. Screening for the small fetus: a study of the relative efficacies of ultrasound biometry and symphysiofundal height. Aust N Z J Obstet Gynaecol 1995;35:160–164 (Level I)

69. Neilson JP, Munjanja SP, Whitfield CR. Screening for small for dates fetuses: a controlled trial. BMJ 1984; 289:1179–1182 (Level II-2)

70. Pearce JM, Campbell S. A comparison of symphysis-fundal height and ultrasound as screening tests for light-for-gestational age infants. Br J Obstet Gynaecol 1987;94: 100–104 (Level II-3)

71. Warsof SL, Cooper DJ, Little D, Campbell R. Routine ultrasound screen for antenatal detection of intrauterine growth restriction. Obstet Gynecol 1986;67:33–39 (Level II-2)

72. Weiner Z, Farmakides G, Schulman H, Lopresti S, Schneider E. Surveillance of growth-retarded fetuses with computerized fetal heart rate monitoring combined with Doppler velocimetry of the umbilical and uterine arteries. J Reprod Med 1996;41:112–118 (Level III)

73. Hadlock FP, Deter RL, Harrist RB, Park SK. Estimating fetal age: computer-assisted analysis of multiple fetal growth parameters. Radiology 1984;152:497–501 (Level II-3)

74. Shepard MJ, Richards VA, Berkowitz RL, Warsof SL, Hobbins JC. An evaluation of two equations for predicting fetal weight by ultrasound. Am J Obstet Gynecol 1982; 142:47–54 (Level III)

75. Chamberlain PF, Manning FA, Morrison I, Harman CR, Lange IR. Ultrasound evaluation of amniotic fluid volume. I. The relationship of marginal and decreased amniotic fluid volumes to perinatal outcome. Am J Obstet Gynecol 1984:150:245–249 (Level II-3)

76. Varma TR. Bateman S, Patel RH, Chamberlain GV, Pillai U. Ultrasound evaluation of amniotic fluid: outcome of pregnancies with severe oligohydramnios. Int J Gynaecol Obstet 1988;27:185–192 (Level II-2)

77. Philipson EH, Sokol RJ, Williams T. Oligohydraminios: clinical associations and predictive value for intrauterine growth retardation. Am J Obstet Gynecol 1983;146: 271–278 (Level II-2)

78. Davies JA, Gallivan S, Spencer JA. Randomised con- trolled trial of Doppler ultrasound screening of placental perfusion during pregnancy. Lancet 1992;340:1299–1303 (Level I)

79. Low JA. The current status of maternal and fetal blood flow velocimetry. Am J Obstet Gynecol 1991;164: 1049–1063 (Level III)

80. Wladimiroff JW, v.d.Wijngaard JA, Degani S, Noordam MJ, van Eyck J, Tonge HM. Cerebral and umbilical arterial blood flow velocity waveforms in normal and growth-retarded pregnancies. Obstet Gynecol 1987;69:705–709 (Level II-2)

81. Alfirevic Z, Neilson JP. Doppler ultrasonography in high-risk pregnancies: systemic review with meta-analysis. Am J Obstet Gynecol 1995;172:1379–1387 (Meta-analysis)

82. Leeson S, Aziz N. Customised fetal growth assessment. Br J Obstet Gynaecol 1997;104:648–651 (Level III)

83. Ewigman BG, Crane JP, Frigoletto FD, LeFevre ML, Bain RP, McNellis D. Effect of prenatal ultrasound screening on perinatal outcome. RADIUS Study Group. N Engl J Med 1993;329:821–827 (Level I)

84. Newnham JP, Evans SF, Michael CA, Stanley FJ, Landau LI. Effect of frequent ultrasound during pregnancy: a randomised conrolled trial. Lancet 1993;342:887–891 (Level I)

85. Doubilet PM, Benson CB. Sonographic evaluation of intrauterine growth retardation. AJR Am J Roentgenol 1995;164:709–717 (Level III)

86. Snijders R, Hyett J. Fetal testing in intra-uterine growth retardation. Curr Opin Obstet Gynecol 1997;9:91–95 (Level III)

87. Garner P, Brabin B. A review of randomized controlled trials of routine antimalarial drug prophylaxis during pregnancy in endemic malarious areas. Bull World Health Organ 1994;72:89–99 (Level III)

88. Taha Tel T, Gray RH, Mohamedani AA. Malaria and low birth weight in central Sudan. Am J Epidemiol 1993; 138:318–325 (Level II-2)

89. Laurin J, Persson PH. The effect of bedrest in hospital on fetal outcome in pregnancies complicated by intra-uterine growth retardation. Acta Obstet Gynecol Scand 1987; 66:407–411 (Level II-1)

90. Gulmezoglu AM, Hofmeyr GJ. Maternal nutrient supplementation for suspected impaired fetal growth (Cochrane Review). In: The Cochrane Library, Issue 2, 1999. Oxford: Update Software (Meta-analysis)

91. Mahomed K. Zinc supplementation in pregnancy (Cochrane Review). In: The Cochrane Library, Issue 2, 1999. Oxford: Update Software (Meta-analysis)

92. Carroli G, Duley L, Belizan JM, Villar J. Calcium supplementation during pregnancy: a systematic review of randomised controlled trials. Br J Obstet Gynaecol 1994; 101:753–758 (Meta-analysis)

93. Gulmezoglu AM, Hofmeyr GJ. Plasma volume expansion for suspected impaired fetal growth (Cochrane Review). In: The Cochrane Library, Issue 2, 1999. Oxford: Update Software (Level III)

94. Gulmezoglu AM, Hofmeyr GJ. Maternal oxygen administration for suspected impaired fetal growth. (Cochrane Review). In: The Cochrane Library, Issue 2, 1999. Oxford: Update Software (Level III)

95. Bar J, Hod M, Pardo J, Fisch B, Rabinerson D, Kaplan B, et al. Effect on fetal circulation of low-dose aspirin for prevention and treatment of pre-eclampsia and intrauterine growth restriction: Doppler flow study. Ultrasound Obstet Gynecol 1997;9:262–265

96. CLASP: a randomised trial of low-dose aspirin for the prevention and treatment of pre-eclampsia among 9364 pregnant women. CLASP (Collaborative Low-Dose Aspirin Study in Pregnancy) Collaborative Group. Lancet 1994; 343:619–629 (Level I)

97. Golding J. A randomised trial of low dose aspirin for primiparae in pregnancy. The Jamaica Low Dose Aspirin Study Group. Br J Obstet Gynaecol 1998;105:293–299 (Level I)

98. Leitich H, Egarter C, Husslein P, Kaider A, Schemper M. A meta-analysis of low dose aspirin for the prevention of intrauterine growth retardation. Br J Obstet Gynaecol 1997;104:450–459 (Meta-analysis)

99. Newnham JP, Godfrey M, Walters BJ, Phillips J, Evans SF. Low dose aspirin for the treatment of fetal growth restriction: a randomized controlled trial. Aust N Z J Obstet Gynaecol 1995;35:370–374 (Level I)

100. Craigo SD, Beach ML, Harvey-Wilkes KB, D'Alton ME. Ultrasound predictors of neonatal outcome in intrauterine growth restriction. Am J Perinatol 1996;13:465–471 (Level II-3)

101. Visser GH, Sandovsky G, Nicolaides KH. Antepartum fetal heart rate patterns in small-for-gestational-age third-trimester fetuses: correlations with blood gas values obtained at cordocentesis. Am J Obstet Gynecol 1990; 162:698–703 (Level II-2)

102. Donner C, Vermeylen D, Kirkpatrick C, de Maertelaer V, Rodesch F. Management of the growth-restricted fetus: the role of noninvasive tests and fetal blood sampling. Obstet Gynecol 1995;85:965–970 (Level II-3)

103. Alfirevic Z, Neilson JP. Biophysical profile for fetal assessment in high risk pregnancies (Cochrane review). In: The Cochrane Library, Issue 2, 1999. Oxford: Update Software (Meta-analysis)

104. Arduini D, Rizzo G. Doppler studies of deteriorating growth-retarded fetuses. Curr Opin Obstet Gynecol 1993;5:195–203 (Level III)

105. Kingdom JC, Burrell SJ, Kaufmann P. Pathology and clinical implications of abnormal umbilical artery Doppler waveforms. Ultrasound Obstet Gynecol 1997;9:271–286 (Level III)

106. Karsdorp VH, van Vugt JM, van Geijn HP, Kostense PJ, Arduini D, Montenegro N, et al. Clinical significance of absent or reversed end diastolic velocity waveforms in umbilical artery. Lancet 1994;344:1664–1668 (Level II-3)

107. Pardi G, Cetin I, Marconi AM, Lanfranchi A, Bozzetti P, Ferrazzi E, et al. Diagnostic value of blood sampling in fetuses with growth retardation. N Engl J Med 1993; 328:692–696 (Level III)

108. Redman CW. Fetal outcome in trial of antihypertensive treatment in pregnancy. Lancet 1976;2:753–756 (Level II-1)

The MEDLINE database, the Cochrane Library, and ACOG's own internal resources were used to conduct a literature search to locate relevant articles published between January 1985 and March 1999. The search was restricted to articles published in the English language. Priority was given to articles reporting results of original research, although review articles and commentaries also were consulted. Abstracts of research presented at symposia and scientific conferences were not considered adequate for inclusion in this document. Guidelines published by organizations or institutions such as the National Institutes of Health and the American College of Obstetricians and Gynecologists were reviewed, and additional studies were located by reviewing bibliographies of identified articles. When reliable research was not available, expert opinions from obstetrician–gynecologists were used.

Studies were reviewed and evaluated for quality according to the method outlined by the U.S. Preventive Services Task Force:

I Evidence obtained from at least one properly designed randomized controlled trial.

II-1 Evidence obtained from well-designed controlled trials without randomization.

II-2 Evidence obtained from well-designed cohort or case–control analytic studies, preferably from more than one center or research group.

II-3 Evidence obtained from multiple time series with or without the intervention. Dramatic results in uncontrolled experiments could also be regarded as this type of evidence.

III Opinions of respected authorities, based on clinical experience, descriptive studies, or reports of expert committees.

Based on the highest level of evidence found in the data, recommendations are provided and graded according to the following categories:

Level A—Recommendations are based on good and consistent scientific evidence.

Level B—Recommendations are based on limited or inconsistent scientific evidence.

Level C—Recommendations are based primarily on consensus and expert opinion.

ISSN 1099-3630

The American College of
Obstetricians and Gynecologists
409 12th Street, SW
PO Box 96920
Washington, DC 20090-6920

12345/43210

ACOG
PRACTICE BULLETIN

CLINICAL MANAGEMENT GUIDELINES FOR
OBSTETRICIAN–GYNECOLOGISTS
NUMBER 14, MARCH 2000

This Practice Bulletin was developed by the ACOG Committee on Practice Bulletins—Gynecology with the assistance of Dale Stovall, MD. The information is designed to aid practitioners in making decisions about appropriate obstetric and gynecologic care. These guidelines should not be construed as dictating an exclusive course of treatment or procedure. Variations in practice may be warranted based on the needs of the individual patient, resources, and limitations unique to the institution or type of practice.

Management of Anovulatory Bleeding

Anovulatory bleeding, the most common form of noncyclic uterine bleeding, is a condition for which women frequently seek gynecologic care and accounts for considerable patient anxiety and inconvenience. Over the past decade, significant advances have been made in the evaluation and management of women with anovulatory bleeding. The choice of treatment for anovulatory bleeding depends on several factors, including the woman's age, the severity of her bleeding, and her desire for future fertility. The purpose of this document is to provide management guidelines for the treatment of patients with menstrual irregularities associated with anovulation based on the best available evidence.

Background

Definition and Nomenclature

The terms menses, menstrual flow, and menstruation will be used in this document interchangeably, and each of these terms simply refer to the presence of menstrual effluent irrespective of whether the effluent is normal or abnormal. Anovulatory uterine bleeding is defined as noncyclic menstrual blood flow that may range from spotty to excessive, is derived from the uterine endometrium, and is due to anovulatory sex steroid production specifically excluding an anatomic lesion. Several terms have been used to describe anovulatory bleeding, including dysfunctional, irregular, and abnormal. In this bulletin, the term *anovulatory uterine bleeding* will be used as the standard terminology to describe menstrual bleeding arising from anovulation or oligo-ovulation.

Several descriptive terms also are used to describe menstrual bleeding patterns, including menorrhagia, metrorrhagia, polymenorrhea, and menometrorrhagia. Menorrhagia is defined as prolonged or excessive uterine bleeding that occurs at regular intervals, or more strictly, the loss of 80 mL or more of blood per menstrual cycle or bleeding that lasts for more than 7 days (1). Metrorrhagia is defined as irregular menstrual bleeding or bleeding between periods. Polymenorrhea is defined as frequent menstrual bleeding or, more strictly, menstrual bleeding that occurs every 21 days or less. Menometrorrhagia is defined as frequent menstrual bleeding that is excessive and irregular in amount and duration.

Ovulatory Cycle

During a normal ovulatory cycle—including follicular development, ovulation, corpus luteal function, and luteolysis—the endometrium is sequentially exposed to ovarian production of estrogen alone, followed by a combination of estrogen and progesterone; the cycle is culminated by estrogen and progesterone withdrawal. Ovulation is associated with a cyclic pattern of endometrial histology commencing with proliferation followed by secretion change, desquamation, and repair. Normal ovarian steroid production is important for nidation and pregnancy. From a clinical perspective, the result is cyclic, predictable, and relatively consistent menstrual blood loss (2).

Pathophysiology

With anovulation, a corpus luteum is not produced, and the ovary fails to secrete progesterone, although estrogen production continues. This condition results in continual endometrial proliferation without progesterone-induced desquamation and bleeding. The clinical result is bleeding that is noncyclic, unpredictable, and inconsistent in volume.

Continuous, unopposed estrogen stimulation of the endometrium results in unsustainable endometrial growth. The endometrium becomes excessively vascular without sufficient stromal support and becomes fragile, resulting in variable endometrial bleeding. Unlike the uniform, synchronized endometrial sloughing and bleeding that occurs with normal cyclic estrogen and progesterone stimulation, endometrial loss during continuous estrogen stimulation is irregular. As one area of bleeding begins to heal, another area begins to slough, resulting in irregular and prolonged menstrual flow.

Alterations in endometrial prostaglandin (PG) synthesis and release appear to occur in women with anovulatory uterine bleeding. In particular, lower concentrations of $PGF_{2\alpha}$ have been found in the endometrium of women with anovulatory bleeding as compared with women with ovulatory menstrual cycles (3). Furthermore, these investigators found a reverse correlation between the endometrial $PGF_{2\alpha}/PGE_2$ ratio and the amount of menstrual blood lost. Therefore, abnormal vasoconstriction produced by altered endometrial prostaglandins may enhance blood loss in women with chronic anovulation.

Establishing the Diagnosis

The diagnosis of anovulatory uterine bleeding is made after the exclusion of anatomic pathology. Diagnostic techniques to exclude anatomic pathology include physical examination supplemented by endometrial sampling, transvaginal ultrasonography, sonohysterography, hysterosalpingography, hysteroscopy, curettage, endometrial cultures, and timed tests for determining progesterone levels in serum. Recognized causes of anovulation are given in the box below and should be considered when evaluating the medical history and results of the physical examination. There are numerous other causes of noncyclic vaginal bleeding. The differential diagnosis of abnormal bleeding is listed in the box on the next page. In this document, recommendations are based on the assumption that the diagnosis of anovulatory bleeding has been firmly established.

The physical examination should include an assessment for obesity and hirsutism, because these findings are associated with chronic anovulation (4, 5). Thyroid disease may cause anovulation as well as hyperprolactinemia. Approximately one third of all women with hyperprolactinemia will have galactorrhea (6). In women of reproductive age with noncyclic uterine bleeding, pregnancy must be ruled out. If medical therapy fails to resolve bleeding thought to be the result of anovulation, an anatomic cause, including a malignant or premalignant lesion or a coagulopathy, should be reconsidered and the patient reevaluated.

Causes of Anovulation

Physiologic
- Adolescence
- Perimenopause
- Lactation
- Pregnancy

Pathologic
- Hyperandrogenic anovulation (eg, polycystic ovary syndrome, congenital adrenal hyperplasia, androgen-producing tumors)
- Hypothalamic dysfunction (eg, secondary to anorexia nervosa)
- Hyperprolactinemia
- Hypothyroidism
- Primary pituitary disease
- Premature ovarian failure
- Iatrogenic (eg, secondary to radiation or chemotherapy)

Differential Diagnosis of Noncyclic Uterine Bleeding

- Anovulation
- Uterine leiomyoma
- Endometrial polyp
- Endometrial hyperplasia or carcinoma
- Cervical or vaginal neoplasia
- Endometritis
- Adenomyosis
- Bleeding associated with pregnancy
  - threatened or incomplete abortion
  - trophoblastic disease
  - ectopic pregnancy
- Bleeding associated with the puerperium
  - retained products of conception
  - placental polyp
  - subinvolution of the uterus
- Coagulopathies (von Willebrand's disease, platelet abnormalities, thrombocytopenic purpura)
- Iatrogenic causes and medications
- Systemic diseases

Age Considerations of Anovulatory Bleeding

Adolescents (13–18 Years)

Anovulatory bleeding is a normal physiologic process in the perimenarchal years of the reproductive cycle. Ovulatory menstrual cycles may not be established until a year or more after menarche. This phenomenon is attributed to the immaturity of the hypothalamic–pituitary–gonadal axis. Anovulatory bleeding at this age can be excessive, resulting in anemia and requiring emergency care. Occasionally, adolescents with blood dyscrasias, including von Willebrand's disease and prothrombin deficiency, have heavy vaginal bleeding beginning at menarche. Disorders such as leukemia, idiopathic thrombocytopenic purpura, and hypersplenism can all produce platelet dysfunction and cause excessive bleeding. Studies have demonstrated a wide variation in the prevalence of blood dyscrasias ranging from 5% to 20% of hospitalized adolescents (7, 8). Because the prevalence of blood dyscrasias in the adolescent population is significant, routine screening for coagulation disorders is warranted in these patients, including a partial thromboplastin time, prothrombin time, and assessment of platelet function. Physical examination should include an assessment for petechiae or ecchymoses.

Women of Reproductive Age (19–39 Years)

Between 6% and 10% of women have hyperandrogenic chronic anovulation (eg, polycystic ovary syndrome), which includes noncyclic menstrual bleeding, hirsutism, and obesity (body mass index ≥ 25 kg/m^2). As many as 65% of hirsute, chronically anovulatory women are obese (4). Numerous underlying biochemical abnormalities exist, including noncyclic estrogen production, elevated serum testosterone levels, hypersecretion of luteinizing hormone, and hyperinsulinemia (9). A history of rapidly progressing hirsutism accompanied by virilization suggests a tumor. In most cases, tumors can be ruled out by testing testosterone and dehydroepiandrosterone sulfate levels in serum.

Although anovulation may be considered physiologic in adolescents, adult women of reproductive age who have menorrhagia, metrorrhagia, or amenorrhea require evaluation for a specific cause. The laboratory assessment of these women should include a pregnancy test, a fasting serum prolactin level, and determination of levels of thyroid-stimulating hormone (TSH). When the diagnosis of ovarian failure is suspected, levels of follicle-stimulating hormone (FSH) also should be determined. Anovulation was found to be the most common cause of amenorrhea in a series of 262 women who experienced adult-onset amenorrhea (10). Chronic anovulation that results from hypothalamic dysfunction, as diagnosed by a low FSH level, may be the result of excessive psychologic stress, exercise, or weight loss (10). Both hyperthyroidism and hypothyroidism can be excluded using the sensitive TSH assay. In patients with amenorrhea who have a negative pregnancy test result and normal FSH, TSH, and prolactin levels, the diagnosis of anovulation can be made.

Women of Later Reproductive Age (40 Years to Menopause)

The incidence of anovulatory uterine bleeding increases as women approach the end of their reproductive years. In this regard, perimenopausal women are not unlike their perimenarchal counterparts. In perimenopausal women, the onset of anovulatory cycles represents a continuation of declining ovarian function. These patients need to be educated regarding the specific health risks associated with menopause so that an early proactive approach toward the prevention of menopause-associated conditions, such as osteoporosis, can be initiated. In addition to the use of hormone replacement therapy for cycle control, important lifestyle changes include exercise, dietary modification, and smoking cessation.

Clinical Considerations and Recommendations

▶ *In women of each age group with anovulatory bleeding, when is endometrial evaluation indicated?*

Adolescents (13–18 Years). In 1995, the incidence of endometrial cancer in women between the ages of 15 and 19 years was 0.1 per 100,000 (11). In one report of endometrial carcinoma in adolescents, the patients experienced 2–3 years of anovulatory uterine bleeding (12). One patient experienced precocious puberty, which extended the number of years of unopposed estrogen exposure for someone of her age. All of the adolescents were obese. Because obesity is associated with conversion of androgens to estrogens and chronic anovulation, obese patients may be at an increased risk for developing endometrial hyperplasia and carcinoma. Therefore, one should consider endometrial assessment particularly for those adolescents who have a history of 2–3 years of untreated anovulatory bleeding and especially for those who are obese.

Women of Reproductive Age (19–39 Years). The incidence of endometrial carcinoma increases with age. However, the incidence of endometrial carcinoma is still very low in women between the ages of 19 and 39 years, reported as 9.5 per 100,000 in 1995 (11). However, there is a distinct increase in the incidence of endometrial carcinoma from ages 30–34 years (2.3/100,000 in 1995) to ages 35–39 years (6.1/100,000 in 1995) (11). Therefore, based on age alone, endometrial assessment to exclude cancer is indicated in any woman older than 35 years who is suspected of having anovulatory uterine bleeding.

Although endometrial carcinoma is rare in women younger than 35 years, patients between the ages of 19 and 35 years who do not respond to medical therapy or have prolonged periods of unopposed estrogen stimulation secondary to chronic anovulation are candidates for endometrial assessment.

Women of Later Reproductive Age (40 Years to Menopause). The incidence of endometrial carcinoma in women ages 40–49 years was 36.2 per 100,000 in 1995 (11). Therefore, all women older than 40 years who present with suspected anovulatory uterine bleeding should be evaluated with endometrial assessment (after pregnancy has been excluded).

▶ *What medical therapies are most appropriate for each age group?*

Because anovulatory uterine bleeding is by definition an endocrinologic abnormality, medical management is the preferred method of therapy. The goals of medical treatment for anovulatory bleeding are to alleviate acute bleeding, prevent future episodes of noncyclic bleeding, decrease the patient's risk of long-term complications from anovulation, and improve the patient's overall quality of life. To encourage compliance with medical therapy, it is important to counsel patients that treatment may cause initial heavy menstrual bleeding secondary to endometrial buildup, but will lighten over time (within three cycles).

Adolescents (13–18 Years). Most adolescents who experience anovulatory bleeding can be treated with medical therapy. Occasionally, adolescents may have acute, profuse menstrual bleeding. High-dose estrogen therapy is an appropriate treatment to control acute bleeding episodes because it promotes rapid endometrial growth to cover denuded endometrial surfaces. Patients with blood dyscrasias need to be treated for their specific disease, and leukemia needs to be ruled out in this population. Conjugated equine estrogens can be administered orally up to 10 mg/d in four divided doses or intravenously at 25 mg every 4 hours for up to 24 hours (13). In a retrospective study, most adolescent patients with acute bleeding (93%) responded to medical therapy (8). After acute bleeding has been treated, recurrent anovulatory bleeding should be prevented with either a cyclic progestogen or an oral contraceptive.

Women with chronic anovulation can be treated successfully using either a cyclic progestogen or an oral contraceptive. Oral contraceptives suppress both ovarian and adrenal androgen production and increase sex hormone binding globulin, further reducing bioavailable androgens (14, 15). They also may inhibit 5α-reductase activity in the skin of adults (16). Treatment with a low-dose combination oral contraceptive (≤35 µg ethinyl estradiol) is appropriate, and maintenance oral contraceptives are the treatment of choice in women with chronic anovulation, especially if they are hyperandrogenic and hirsute (17).

Women of Reproductive Age (19–39 Years). Adult women of reproductive age with anovulatory uterine bleeding can be treated safely with either a cyclic progestogen or oral contraceptives similar to those prescribed for adolescent patients. However, estrogen-containing oral contraceptives are relatively contraindicated in some women (eg, those with hypertension or diabetes). Estrogen-containing oral contraceptives are contraindicated for women older than 35 years who smoke or have a history of thromboembolic disease.

If pregnancy is desired, induction of ovulation with clomiphene citrate is the initial treatment of choice (18). Patients can have withdrawal bleeding induced with progestogen followed by initiation of therapy with clomiphene citrate, 50 mg/d for 5 days, beginning between days 3 and 5 of the menstrual cycle.

Women of Later Reproductive Age (40 Years to Menopause). Women who are older than 40 years and who have anovulatory uterine bleeding can be treated with cyclic progestogen, low-dose oral contraceptives, or cyclic hormone replacement therapy. Not unlike younger women, these patients usually have adequate estrogen production. However, women older than 40 years with oligomenorrhea may have reduced estrogen production. Women with hot flashes secondary to declining estrogen production can obtain symptomatic relief with estrogen replacement therapy in combination with continuous or cyclic progestogen. Up to 90% of perimenopausal women receiving continuous estrogen and cyclic progestogen therapy will respond with predictable progesterone withdrawal bleeding (19).

▶ *In patients who have completed childbearing, what is the benefit of treating anovulatory bleeding surgically rather than medically?*

Currently, there are few randomized trials comparing medical versus surgical therapy for anovulatory uterine bleeding. One randomized trial that compared endometrial resection with medical management for women with menorrhagia found that women who underwent medical therapy were less likely to be satisfied with their therapy (20). However, because of its reduced cost and risks, medical therapy should be offered before surgical intervention unless it is otherwise contraindicated. Surgical therapy is indicated for women with excessive anovulatory bleeding in whom medical management has failed and who have completed their childbearing. Avoidance of anemia, reduction of excessively heavy bleeding, and increased, though imperfect, predictability of bleeding are appropriate goals to attempt to achieve with medical therapy. Success and failure of medical therapy should be defined in partnership with the patient, to better achieve the therapeutic goal.

▶ *In women who have completed childbearing, what is the evidence of efficacy among surgical techniques?*

The surgical options include hysterectomy and endometrial ablation. Recent studies have reported morbidity rates of 7% (21) and 15% (22) for women undergoing hysterectomy for various indications. The overall mortality rate for hysterectomy is 12 deaths per 10,000 procedures, for all surgical indications (23). A surgical alternative to hysterectomy is endometrial ablation. Endometrial ablation can be performed with or without the assistance of hysteroscopy.

Hysteroscopic-assisted endometrial ablation can be performed with the resectoscope. Using the resectoscope, the endometrium can be removed or resected with an electrocautery loop or ablated with the rollerball. Endometrial ablation also can be accomplished with the YAG laser. An alternative to hysteroscopic-assisted endometrial ablation is thermal balloon ablation in which the endometrium is ablated by heating saline inside an intrauterine balloon to approximately 85°C. The most frequently reported complications of hysteroscopy are uterine perforation, which occurs in approximately 14 per 1,000 procedures (24) and fluid overload, which occurs in approximately 2 per 1,000 cases.

Studies evaluating the effectiveness of endometrial ablation have been performed in a group of women who were diagnosed with menorrhagia and who were not necessarily anovulatory. However, women with anovulatory uterine bleeding are candidates for endometrial ablation if they have failed medical therapy and have completed their childbearing. The proportion of women who are amenorrheic after undergoing an endometrial resection using the resectoscope or endometrial laser ablation is approximately 45%, and the percentage of women at 12 months postoperatively who are satisfied with their therapy approaches 90% (25, 26). This high degree of satisfaction indicates that reduction of flow is adequate symptom control for most women, and achievement of amenorrhea is not as important. Endometrial ablation with the thermal balloon yields an amenorrhea rate of approximately 15% and a 12-month postoperative satisfaction rate of approximately 90% (27, 28).

Patient satisfaction with hysterectomy and endometrial ablation performed for dysfunctional uterine bleeding has been compared. One study demonstrated a higher satisfaction rate in women who underwent hysterectomy as compared with women who underwent hysteroscopic-assisted endometrial ablation (29). Furthermore, the long-term satisfaction of women who have undergone endometrial ablation has been questioned. In a 3-year follow-up study, 8.5% of women who had undergone endometrial ablation later underwent repeat ablation, and an additional 8.5% had undergone hysterectomy (30). In a 5-year follow-up study, 34% of women who had undergone hysteroscopic ablation subsequently had a hysterectomy (31). Because women who undergo endometrial ablation can have residual active endometrium, these women should receive progestogen if they are prescribed estrogen replacement therapy.

Numerous studies have compared costs and surgical outcomes between endometrial resection or ablation and hysterectomy. The evidence suggests that hysteroscopic endometrial ablation results in less morbidity and shorter recovery periods and is more cost-effective than hysterectomy (32–37). However, if as many as one third of women who undergo endometrial ablation undergo hysterectomy within the following 5 years, that would have a significant impact on these cost analyses.

Evidence from randomized trials supports the use of either a gonadotropin-releasing hormone agonist or danazol prior to endometrial ablation or resection with regard to improved intrauterine operating environment and short-term postoperative outcome (38). The choice of agents should be based on cost, efficacy, and side effects. There are insufficient data to assess the value of progestogen therapy prior to endometrial ablation.

▶ *What is the role of high-dose estrogen in acute vaginal bleeding?*

Women who experience acute, profuse anovulatory bleeding are candidates for estrogen therapy. In approximately 90% of cases, acute bleeding does not require surgical intervention, but it can be treated with medical therapy (8). In a large series of 61 adolescents (mean age, 13.8 ± 2.1 years) with acute anovulatory uterine bleeding, only five (8.2%) failed medical therapy and required dilation and curettage to stop their bleeding. Conjugated equine estrogen therapy can be administered intravenously (25 mg every 4 hours for 24 hours). However, oral conjugated estrogen therapy at 10–20 mg per day in four divided doses can be substituted for intravenous estrogen administration. In a randomized trial of intravenous conjugated equine estrogen therapy versus placebo, conjugated estrogens were effective in stopping vaginal bleeding in a significantly greater proportion of women (72%) than those who received a placebo (38%)

(13). Although this study included women with biopsy-proven pathology, it is one of the few studies performed to assess the efficacy of intravenous estrogen therapy for the treatment of women with anovulatory uterine bleeding. Patients who do not respond to 1–2 doses of estrogen with a significant decline in blood loss or are not hemodynamically stable should undergo dilation and curettage. Furthermore, as high-dose estrogen therapy is commonly associated with nausea, concomitant medical therapy with antiemetics should be considered.

After the acute episode of bleeding has been controlled, amenorrhea should be maintained for several weeks to allow for resolution of anemia. The best method of therapy is a combination oral contraceptive. To extend the interval before the next menses, continuous oral contraceptives (without the use of placebo pills) can be given for several months; however, over time the patient will be susceptible again to breakthrough bleeding. Once the patient's anemia has resolved, cyclic oral contraceptives can be prescribed. All anemic patients should be given iron therapy.

Summary

The following recommendations are based on good and consistent scientific evidence (Level A):

▶ The treatment of choice for anovulatory uterine bleeding is medical therapy with oral contraceptives. Cyclic progestins also are effective.

▶ Women who have failed medical therapy and no longer desire future childbearing are candidates for endometrial ablation, which appears to be an efficient and cost-effective alternative treatment to hysterectomy for anovulatory uterine bleeding. However, endometrial ablation may not be definitive therapy.

The following recommendations are based primarily on consensus and expert opinion (Level C):

▶ An underlying coagulopathy, such as von Willebrand's disease, should be considered in all patients (particularly adolescents) with abnormal uterine bleeding, especially when bleeding is not otherwise easily explained or does not respond to medical therapy.

▶ Although there is limited evidence evaluating the efficacy of conjugated equine estrogen therapy in anovulatory bleeding, it is effective in controlling abnormal uterine bleeding.

References

1. Hallberg L, Hogdahl AM, Nilsson L, Rybo G. Menstrual blood loss—a population study. Variation at different ages and attempts to define normality. Acta Obstet Gynecol Scand 1966;45:320–351 (Level III)

2. Hallberg L, Nilsson L. Constancy of individual menstrual blood loss. Acta Obstet Gynecol Scand 1964;43:352–359 (Level III)

3. Smith SK, Abel MH, Kelly RW, Baird DT. The synthesis of prostaglandins from persistent proliferative endometrium. J Clin Endocrinol Metab 1982;55:284–289 (Level II-2)

4. Singh KB, Mahajan DK, Wortsman J. Effect of obesity on the clinical and hormonal characteristics of the polycystic ovary syndrome. J Reprod Med 1994;39:805–808 (Level II-2)

5. Falsetti L, Eleftheriou G. Hyperinsulinemia in the polycystic ovary syndrome: a clinical, endocrine and echographic study in 240 patients. Gynecol Endocrinol 1996;10:319–326 (Level II-2)

6. Schlechte J, Sherman B, Halmi N, VanGilder J, Chapler F, Dolan K, et al. Prolactin-secreting pituitary tumors in amenorrheic women: a comprehensive study. Endocr Rev 1980;1:295–308

7. Claessens EA, Cowell CL. Acute adolescent menorrhagia. Am J Obstet Gynecol 1981;139:277–280 (Level III)

8. Falcone T, Desjardins C, Bourque J, Granger L, Hemmings R, Quiros E. Dysfunctional uterine bleeding in adolescents. J Reprod Med 1994;39:761–764 (Level II-2)

9. Goudas VT, Dumesic DA. Polycystic ovary syndrome. Endocrinol Metab Clin North Am 1997;26:893–912 (Level III)

10. Reindollar RH, Novak M, Tho SP, McDonough PG. Adult-onset amenorrhea: a study of 262 patients. Am J Obstet Gynecol 1986;155:531–543 (Level III)

11. SEER cancer statistics review, 1973–1996 [serial online]. Available at <http://www-seer.ims.nci.nih.gov/Publications/CSR1973_1996>. Retrieved February 1, 2000 (Level II-3)

12. Stovall DW, Anderson RJ, De Leon FD. Endometrial adenocarcinoma in teenagers. Adolesc Pediatr Gynecol 1989; 2:157–159 (Level III)

13. DeVore GR, Owens O, Kase N. Use of intravenous Premarin in the treatment of dysfunctional uterine bleeding—a double-blind randomized controlled study. Obstet Gynecol 1982;59:285–291 (Level I)

14. Wild RA, Umstot ES, Andersen RN, Givens JR. Adrenal function in hirsutism. II. Effect of an oral contraceptive. J Clin Endocrinol Metab 1982;54:676–681 (Level III)

15. Wiebe RH, Morris CV. Effect of an oral contraceptive on adrenal and ovarian androgenic steroids. Obstet Gynecol 1984;63:12–14 (Level III)

16. Cassidenti DL, Paulson RJ, Serafini P, Stanczyk FZ, Lobo RA. Effects of sex steroids on skin 5 alpha-reductase activity in vitro. Obstet Gynecol 1991;78:103–107 (Level III)

17. Rittmaster RS. Clinical review 73: Medical treatment of androgen-dependent hirsutism. J Clin Endocrinol Mctab 1995;80:2559–2563 (Level III)

18. Hughes E, Collins J, Vandekerckhove P. Clomiphene citrate for unexplained subfertility in women (Cochrane review). In: The Cochrane Library, Issue 4, 1999. Oxford: Update Software. (Meta-analysis)

19. Strickland DM, Hammond TL. Postmenopausal estrogen replacement in a large gynecologic practice. Am J Gynecol Health 1988;2(1):26–31 (Level III)

20. Cooper KG, Parkin DE, Garratt AM, Grant AM. Two-year follow up of women randomised to medical management or transcervical resection of the endometrium for heavy menstrual loss: clinical and quality of life outcomes. Br J Obstet Gynaecol 1999;106:258–265 (Level I)

21. Carlson KJ, Miller BA, Fowler FJ Jr. The Maine Women's Health Study: I. Outcomes of hysterectomy. Obstet Gynecol 1994;83:556–565 (Level II-3)

22. Summitt RL Jr, Stovall TG, Steege JF, Lipscomb GH. A multicenter randomized comparison of laparoscopically assisted vaginal hysterectomy and abdominal hysterectomy in abdominal hysterectomy candidates. Obstet Gynecol 1998;92:321–326 (Level I)

23. Bachmann GA. Hysterectomy: A critical review. J Reprod Med 1990;35:839–862 (Level III)

24. Hulka JF, Peterson HA, Phillips JM, Surrey MW. Operative hysteroscopy: American Association of Gynecologic Laparoscopists' 1993 membership survey. J Am Assoc Gynecol Laparosc 1995;2:131–132 (Level II-3)

25. Bhattacharya S, Cameron IM, Parkin DE, Abramovich DR, Mollison J, Pinion SB, et al. A pragmatic randomised comparison of transcervical resection of the endometrium with endometrial laser ablation for the treatment of menorrhagia. Br J Obstet Gynaecol 1997;104:601–607 (Level I)

26. A randomized trial of endometrial ablation versus hysterectomy for the treatment of dysfunctional uterine bleeding: outcome at four years. Aberdeen Endometrial Ablation Trials Group. Br J Obstet Gynaecol 1999;106: 360–366 (Level I)

27. Amso NN, Stabinsky SA, McFaul P, Blanc B, Pendley L, Neuwirth R. Uterine thermal balloon therapy for the treatment of menorrhagia: the first 300 patients from a multicentre study. International Collaborative Uterine Thermal Balloon Working Group. Br J Obstet Gynaecol 1998;105: 517–523 (Level 1)

28. Meyer WR, Walsh BW, Grainger DA, Peacock LM, Loffer FD, Steege JF. Thermal balloon and rollerball ablation to treat menorrhagia: a multicenter comparison. Obstet Gynecol 1998;92:98–103 (Level I)

29. Pinion SB, Parkin DE, Abramovich DR, Naji A, Alexander DA, Russell IT, et al. Randomised trial of hysterectomy, endometrial laser ablation, and transcervical endometrial resection for dysfunctional uterine bleeding. BMJ 1994; 309:979–983 (Level I)

30. Chullapram T, Song JY, Fraser IS. Medium-term follow-up of women with menorrhagia treated by rollerball

endometrial ablation. Obstet Gynecol 1996;88:71–76 (Level II-3)

31. Unger JB, Meeks GR. Hysterectomy after endometrial ablation. Am J Obstet Gynecol 1996;175:1432–1436; discussions 1436–1437 (Level II-3)

32. Gannon MJ, Holt EM, Fairbank J, Fitzgerald M, Milne MA, Crystal AM, et al. A randomised trial comparing endometrial resection and abdominal hysterectomy for the treatment of menorrhagia. BMJ 1991;303:1362–1364 (Level I)

33. Brooks PG, Clouse J, Morris LS. Hysterectomy vs. resectoscopic endometrial ablation for the control of abnormal uterine bleeding. A cost-comparative study. J Reprod Med 1994;39:755–760 (Level II-2)

34. Goldenberg M, Sivan E, Bider D, Mashiach S, Seidman DS. Endometrial resection vs. abdominal hysterectomy for menorrhagia. Correlated sample analysis. J Reprod Med 1996;41:333–336 (Level II-2)

35. Cameron IM, Mollison J, Pinion SB, Atherton-Naji A, Buckingham K, Torgerson D. A cost comparison of hysterectomy and hysteroscopic surgery for the treatment of menorrhagia. Eur J Obstet Gynecol Reprod Biol 1996;70:87–92 (Level I)

36. Vilos GA, Pispidikis JT, Botz CK. Economic evaluation of hysteroscopic endometrial ablation versus vaginal hysterectomy for menorrhagia. Obstet Gynecol 1996;88:241–245 (Level II-2)

37. Brumsted JR, Blackman JA, Badger GJ, Riddick DH. Hysteroscopy versus hysterectomy for the treatment of abnormal uterine bleeding: a comparison of cost. Fertil Steril 1996;65:310–316 (Level II-2)

38. Fraser IS, Healy DL, Torode H, Song JY, Mamers P, Wilde F. Depot goserelin and danazol pre-treatment before rollerball endometrial ablation for menorrhagia. Obstet Gynecol 1996;87:544–550 (Level I)

The MEDLINE database, the Cochrane Library, and ACOG's own internal resources and documents were used to conduct a literature search to locate relevant articles published between January 1985 and May 1999. The search was restricted to articles published in the English language. Priority was given to articles reporting results of original research, although review articles and commentaries also were consulted. Abstracts of research presented at symposia and scientific conferences were not considered adequate for inclusion in this document. Guidelines published by organizations or institutions such as the National Institutes of Health and the American College of Obstetricians and Gynecologists were reviewed, and additional studies were located by reviewing bibliographies of identified articles. When reliable research was not available, expert opinions from obstetrician–gynecologists were used.

Studies were reviewed and evaluated for quality according to the method outlined by the U.S. Preventive Services Task Force:

I   Evidence obtained from at least one properly designed randomized controlled trial.

II-1   Evidence obtained from well-designed controlled trials without randomization.

II-2   Evidence obtained from well-designed cohort or case–control analytic studies, preferably from more than one center or research group.

II-3   Evidence obtained from multiple time series with or without the intervention. Dramatic results in uncontrolled experiments could also be regarded as this type of evidence.

III   Opinions of respected authorities, based on clinical experience, descriptive studies, or reports of expert committees.

Based on the highest level of evidence found in the data, recommendations are provided and graded according to the following categories:

Level A—Recommendations are based on good and consistent scientific evidence.

Level B—Recommendations are based on limited or inconsistent scientific evidence.

Level C—Recommendations are based primarily on consensus and expert opinion.

The American College of Obstetricians and Gynecologists
409 12th Street, SW
PO Box 96920
Washington, DC 20090-6920

12345/43210

ACOG PRACTICE BULLETIN

CLINICAL MANAGEMENT GUIDELINES FOR
OBSTETRICIAN–GYNECOLOGISTS

NUMBER 8, OCTOBER 1999

This Practice Bulletin was developed by the ACOG Committee on Practice Bulletins—Obstetrics with the assistance of David A. Baker, MD. The information is designed to aid practitioners in making decisions about appropriate obstetric and gynecologic care. These guidelines should not be construed as dictating an exclusive course of treatment or procedure. Variations in practice may be warranted based on the needs of the individual patient, resources, and limitations unique to the institution or type of practice.

Management of Herpes in Pregnancy

Genital herpes simplex virus (HSV) infection during pregnancy poses a significant risk to the developing fetus and newborn. In the United States, the incidence of this sexually transmitted disease (STD) has increased significantly since 1970 (1). Because many women of childbearing age are infected or are becoming infected, the risk of maternal transmission of this virus to the fetus or newborn is a major health concern. The purpose of this document is to define the stages of herpetic infection, outline the spectrum of maternal and neonatal infection, including rates of transmission and risks, and provide management guidelines that have been validated by appropriately conducted outcome-based research. Additional guidelines based on consensus and expert opinion also are presented to permit a review of most clinical aspects of HSV.

Background

Etiology

Two types of HSV, herpes simplex virus type 1 (HSV-1) and herpes simplex virus type 2 (HSV-2), can be identified on the basis of divergent biologic properties. They also can be differentiated by minor differences in antigenic composition and biochemical characteristics. Although they are distinct types, the degree of sharing of antigenic determinants between HSV-1 and HSV-2 results in cross-reacting antibodies capable of neutralizing the other virus type (2).

Initial contact with HSV usually occurs early in childhood and involves HSV-1. Less than 10% of primary infections with HSV-1 are clinically overt. Herpes simplex virus type 1 causes most nongenital herpetic lesions: eg, herpes labialis, gingivostomatitis, and keratoconjunctivitis. The female genital tract can be infected with HSV-1 or HSV-2. In the United States, most genital infection is from HSV-2.

Incidence

Herpes simplex virus infection of the genital tract is one of the most common viral STDs. Approximately 45 million adolescent and adult Americans have been infected with genital herpes based on positive serology test results for HSV-2 and estimates of genital HSV-1 infection (1). The greatest incidence of overt HSV-2 infection occurs in women in their late teens and early twenties. In one study, 5% of reproductive-aged women indicated a history of genital herpes virus infection (3). However, approximately 30% of the female population in the United States have antibodies to HSV-2 (1). Factors that influence the incidence of genital infection with HSV are age of the patient, duration of sexual activity, race, previous genital infections, family income, and number of sex partners (4). The number of initial visits to physicians' offices as a result of genital HSV infection increased from approximately 75,000 per year in 1978 to more than 150,000 per year in the early 1990s (1).

The last available data from the mid-1980s indicated that, in the United States, approximately 1,500–2,000 newborns contracted neonatal herpes each year (5). Most infections occur in the perinatal period from contact with infected maternal secretions. Most newborns acquire the virus from asymptomatic mothers without identified lesions (3, 6).

Presentation of Infection

There are three stages of HSV infection based on clinical presentation and serology (see the box). Primary infections are those in which no HSV-1 or HSV-2 antibodies are present. In nonprimary first-episode disease, HSV-1 antibodies are present in the woman who has HSV-2 infection or HSV-2 antibodies are present in the woman who has HSV-1 infection. In recurrent infections, homologous antibodies are present.

Clinical Designation of HSV Infection

Primary genital HSV: Antibodies to both HSV-1 and HSV-2 are absent at the time the patient acquires genital HSV due to HSV-1 or HSV-2.

Nonprimary first-episode genital HSV: Acquisition of genital HSV (due to HSV-1) with preexisting antibodies to HSV-2 or acquisition of genital HSV (due to HSV-2) with preexisting antibodies to HSV-1.

Recurrent genital HSV: Reactivation of genital HSV where the HSV type recovered from the lesion is the same type as the antibody in the sera.

Riley LE. Herpes simplex virus. Sem Perinatol 1998;22:284–292.

In the absence of systemic symptoms, the distinction between first-episode and recurrent herpetic infections is difficult. In one study, women with severe first-recognized clinical outbreaks of genital herpes in the second and third trimesters of pregnancy were evaluated serologically and virologically (7). Of these 23 women with clinical illnesses consistent with primary genital HSV infections, only one had serologically verified primary infection. This primary infection was caused by HSV-1. Three women had nonprimary HSV-2 infections, and 19 women had recurrent infections.

Primary Infection

Initial genital infection due to herpes may be either asymptomatic or associated with severe symptoms. With symptomatic primary infection, lesions may occur on the vulva, vagina, or cervix, or on all three between 2 and 14 days following exposure to infectious virus. These lesions are larger in number and size than those observed in patients with recurrent disease and patients who have had prior infection with HSV-1. The initial vesicles rupture and subsequently appear as shallow and eroded ulcers. Inguinal lymphadenopathy is demonstrated readily as the consequence of virus replication in the sites of lymphatic drainage (2).

When systemic symptoms (malaise, myalgia, and fever) occur, they are most commonly restricted to presumed primary herpetic infections. These symptoms reflect the viremia that occurs more likely with primary infection. Local symptoms of pain, dysuria, and soreness of the vulva and vagina are common in both primary and recurrent infections. The lesions of primary infection tends to resolve within 3 weeks without therapy. However, when secondary bacterial or mycotic infection is present and not treated, the lesions may persist up to 6 weeks.

Increased symptomatic and subclinical shedding from the lower genital tract of women occurs during the first 3 months after primary genital HSV-2 lesions have healed. Subclinical cervical and vulvar shedding occur at a rate of approximately 2.3% in women with HSV-2 infection and 0.65% in women with HSV-1 infection (8).

Nonprimary First Episode

Prior infection with HSV-1 does not fully protect a patient from initial infection with HSV-2 in the genital tract. It may be difficult for a physician to differentiate primary disease from nonprimary first-episode disease based only on clinical findings and patient symptoms (9); serologic confirmation would be required for definitive diagnosis.

A nonprimary first episode can be identified as a first clinically recognized genital HSV infection that does not behave clinically like a symptomatic primary infection. There are fewer systemic manifestations, less pain, a briefer duration of viral shedding, and a more rapid resolution of the clinical lesions in the nonprimary infection. These episodes usually are thought to be the result of an initial HSV-2 infection in the presence of partially protective HSV-1 antibodies.

Recurrent Infection

Recurrences of genital HSV infection can be symptomatic or subclinical, and there is significant variation from patient to patient in the frequency, severity, and duration of symptoms and amount of viral shedding (8, 10–12). Confinement of the ulcers to the genital area is more common in recurrent forms of the disease. The ulcers tend to be limited in size, number, and duration. Local symptoms predominate over systemic symptoms, with many patients indicating increased vaginal discharge or pain (13).

Shedding of the virus from the genital tract without symptoms or signs of clinical lesions (subclinical shedding) is episodic and lasts an average of 1.5 days (11). During this time, the virus quantity is lower than when a lesion is present; however, a susceptible partner can acquire the infection. Subclinical shedding makes this viral STD difficult to control and prevent.

Neonatal Herpes

Most neonatal HSV infection is the consequence of delivery of a neonate through an infected birth canal. There are three categories of neonatal disease: localized disease of the skin, eye, and mouth; central nervous system (CNS) disease with or without skin, eye, and mouth disease; or disseminated disease. Most infected neonates have localized skin, eye, and mouth disease, which generally is a mild illness. Localized disease may progress to encephalitis or disseminated disease. Subtle signs, such as poor feeding, listlessness, and irritability, may indicate CNS disease. One study of the predictors of mortality and morbidity of neonatal HSV showed no mortality with skin, eye, and mouth disease, 15% mortality with CNS disease, and 57% mortality with disseminated disease (14).

Transmission

Sexual and Direct Contact

Herpes simplex virus is transmitted via direct contact with an individual who is infected. Genital-to-genital contact or contact of the genital tract with an area that is infected with HSV, such as oral-to-genital contact, can result in transmission. One study showed that among sexual partners who were discordant for HSV infection, the annual risk of acquisition of genital HSV infection was 31.9% among women who were HSV-1-negative and HSV-2-negative versus 9.1% among women who were HSV-1-positive (4). Furthermore, most of the transmission between discordant couples occurs when there is no evidence of active lesions, which suggests that asymptomatic shedding is the source of more than half of all cases of transmission (15). In one study, about 10% of pregnant women were at risk of contracting primary HSV-2 infection from their HSV-2-seropositive husbands (16).

Maternal–Fetal Transmission

The vertical transmission of HSV appears to be related to gestational age and whether the disease is primary, nonprimary first episode, or recurrent. Investigators prospectively obtained HSV cultures on 15,923 women in early labor who were without signs or symptoms of genital HSV infection (17). Herpes simplex virus was isolated from 56 women (0.35%) with serum samples for HSV antibody testing available from 52 women. Eighteen women (35%) had serologic evidence of recently acquired, subclinical first-episode HSV, and 34 (65%) had asymptomatic recurrent disease. Herpes simplex virus infection developed in six (33%) of 18 neonates born to women with subclinical first-episode disease and in one (3%) of 34 infants born to women with recurrent HSV. This study also showed that preexisting antibody to HSV-2 but not to HSV-1 reduced the vertical transmission of HSV-2. In a more recent study, 8,538 women were prospectively evaluated during pregnancy and at delivery with HSV cultures. Investigators found that 94 (1.3%) of 7,046 women who were susceptible to either HSV-1 or HSV-2 seroconverted during pregnancy. Nine women acquired HSV at or near the time of delivery. Of these nine women, four delivered neonates who developed HSV (one died, and one had developmental delay). In this cohort, there were no cases of neonates with HSV-2 born to women with recurrent HSV (18). Vertical transmission rates at the time of vaginal delivery based on the type of maternal disease may be summarized as follows: primary HSV resulted in approximately 50% transmission; nonprimary first-episode HSV resulted in approximately 33% transmission; and recurrent HSV resulted in 0–3% transmission (17).

During Pregnancy

A threefold increase in the rate of spontaneous abortion following primary maternal genital infection with HSV early in pregnancy has been reported (17). However, this finding was not confirmed in a more recent study (18).

Primary infection in the second or third trimesters increases the risk for preterm delivery as well as the risk of HSV transmission to the newborn (17). Asymptomatic genital shedding of herpes from a subclinical primary genital infection may be associated with preterm delivery (18).

During pregnancy, primary maternal herpetic infection, in the absence of cross-protecting antibodies, theoretically may result in hematogenous dissemination of the virus to the fetus. Isolated case reports have associated in utero infection during the first 12–14 weeks of gestation with a variety of anomalies, such as microcephaly, microphthalmia, intracranial calcifications, and chorioretinitis (19–21).

Clinical Considerations and Recommendations

▶ *How can the diagnosis of HSV be confirmed?*

Herpes simplex virus infection may be documented in several ways. The standard and most sensitive test for detecting HSV from clinical specimens continues to be isolation of the virus by cell culture. Because HSV is a DNA virus, it produces cytopathic effects in cells indicative of virus replication. However, the sensitivity of this technique is affected by numerous factors related to sampling and transporting the specimen. Cytologic tests have a maximum sensitivity of 60–70% when dealing with overt clinical disease (22); thus, both the Papanicolaou and Tzanck tests are poor HSV screening procedures. Newer, more sensitive techniques are increasingly available, such as polymerase chain reaction and hybridization methods (23–25).

Early primary and nonprimary first-episode ulcers yield the virus in 80% of patients, whereas ulcers from recurrent infections are less likely to be culture-positive; only 40% of crusted lesions contain recoverable virus (26). When testing for HSV, overt lesions that are not in the ulcerated state should be unroofed and the fluid sampled.

Commercially available serologic tests designed to detect antibodies to genital herpes infection cannot reliably distinguish between HSV-1 and HSV-2. Serologic diagnosis of primary infection is possible by documenting seroconversion from a negative to a positive antibody titer. The usual time for obtaining a second specimen is 2–3 weeks after the onset of infection. The presence of an antibody titer in the initial specimen, obtained at the onset of disease, strongly suggests nonprimary first-episode or recurrent infection. Newer tests to differentiate between HSV-1 and HSV-2 antibodies are currently in development.

▶ *What is the optimal medical management of women with primary HSV infection during pregnancy?*

Antiviral therapy for primary infection is recommended for women with primary HSV infection during pregnancy to reduce viral shedding and enhance lesion healing. It is important to recognize that primary HSV cannot be distinguished from nonprimary first-episode disease unless serology is performed. Primary infection during pregnancy constitutes a higher risk for vertical transmission than does recurrent infection. The absence of episodes of symptomatic genital HSV infection throughout pregnancy does not eliminate the risk of asymptomatic shedding at delivery (27). Furthermore, suppressive therapy for the duration of the pregnancy needs to be considered to reduce the potential of continued viral shedding (8) and the likelihood of recurrent episodes (28).

Data are limited concerning prevention of disease in the fetus with maternal antiviral therapy. In one randomized study, 21 women received acyclovir and 25 did not to determine whether suppressive therapy started at 36 weeks of gestation could decrease viral shedding, prevent neonatal herpes, and reduce the need for cesarean delivery (29). Although the study did not differentiate between primary and nonprimary first episodes, it did show a significant reduction in cesarean delivery. There were no cases of neonatal herpes in either group, a finding that is compatible with a maximum 14% risk of infection with either therapy.

Significant benefits of acyclovir antiviral therapy using acyclovir have been shown in cases of pregnant women with disseminated HSV, herpes pneumonitis, herpes hepatitis, and herpes encephalitis (30–32).

▶ *What is the optimal medical management of women with recurrent HSV infection during pregnancy?*

A randomized trial of acyclovir given after 36 weeks of gestation in women with recurrent genital herpes infection demonstrated a significant decrease in clinical recurrences. The trial also showed a reduction in the number of cesarean deliveries performed for active infection, although this finding was not statistically significant (33).

▶ *What medications are available for treatment of HSV infection during pregnancy?*

Numerous compounds are available for the treatment of genital herpes (34), although none of these antiviral compounds has received approval for use in pregnancy by the U.S. Food and Drug Administration. These compounds are nucleoside analogues that selectively inhibit viral replication and produce minimal effect on the cell. Research in antiviral therapy has focused on improving bioavailability, which improves absorption and increases plasma levels of the compound while decreasing the number of daily doses of medication.

Acyclovir, a class-C medication, has selective activity against HSV-1 and HSV-2. In the treatment of primary genital herpes infections, oral acyclovir reduces viral shedding, reduces pain, and heals lesions faster when compared with a placebo (35). Acyclovir has been shown to be safe and has minimal side effects (36). However, only approximately 20% of each oral dose is absorbed.

The newer antiherpetic drugs valacyclovir and famciclovir are class-B medications. Their increased bioavailability means that they may require less frequent dosing to achieve the same therapeutic benefits as acyclovir. The U.S. Food and Drug Administration has approved both valacyclovir and famciclovir for the treatment of primary genital herpes, the treatment of episodes of recurrent disease, and the daily treatment for suppression of outbreaks of recurrent genital herpes.

Daily treatment with oral acyclovir significantly reduces symptomatic recurrences and suppresses subclinical viral shedding (28, 37). One study showed that 6 years of continuous daily acyclovir suppressive therapy did not produce the emergence of acyclovir-resistant isolates in immunocompetent patients (36). Valacyclovir therapy, 500 mg once daily, is effective in suppressing recurrent genital herpes (38). Suppressive famciclovir therapy requires a twice daily, 250 mg dosage (38). See Table 1.

Numerous studies have demonstrated the safety of acyclovir use during pregnancy (29, 32, 39). Neither medically indicated nor inadvertent use in the first trimester of pregnancy demonstrated any increased risk to the developing fetus. When acyclovir is given orally or intravenously, it crosses the placenta, concentrates in amniotic fluid and breast milk, and reaches therapeutic levels in the fetus (40). An acyclovir pregnancy registry has been maintained since 1984. In 1993, the Centers for Disease Control and Prevention published data showing no increase in fetal problems in women who received acyclovir during the first trimester of pregnancy (39).

▶ *Is there a role for universal screening during pregnancy or at delivery?*

Viral cultures are costly and imprecise. The correlation between asymptomatic viral shedding and ensuing neonatally acquired disease is poor. Negative cultures do not preclude the possibility of subsequent neonatal infection because the culture sensitivity is well below 100%, and infection may occur in the interim. Virologic monitoring is not recommended for pregnant women whose onset of disease antedated pregnancy or for those whose sexual partners have had herpetic lesions (27). Similarly, there are no data to support the value of culturing asymptomatic patients with a history of recurrent disease (11).

Table 1. Antiviral Treatment for Herpes Simplex Virus

Indication	Valacyclovir	Acyclovir	Famciclovir
First clinical episode	1,000 mg twice a day for 7–14 days	200 mg five times a day or 400 mg three times a day for 7–14 days	250 mg three times a day for 7–14 days
Recurrent episodes	500 mg twice a day for 5 days	200 mg five times a day or 400 mg three times a day for 5 days	125 mg twice a day for 5 days
Daily suppressive therapy	500 mg once a day (≤9 recurrences per year) or 1,000 mg once a day or 250 mg twice a day (>9 recurrences per year)	400 mg twice a day	250 mg twice a day

Baker DA. Antiviral therapy for genital herpes in nonpregnant and pregnant women. Int J Fertil 1998;43:243–248

▶ *In which situations should cesarean delivery be considered?*

Cesarean delivery is indicated in women with active genital lesions or symptoms of vulvar pain or burning, which may indicate an impending outbreak. The incidence of infection in infants whose mothers have recurrent infections is low, but cesarean delivery is warranted because of the potentially serious nature of the disease. The low incidence of neonatal HSV has raised concern that cesarean delivery is unwarranted for recurrent genital herpes (41). The extent to which maternal antibodies will protect a neonate from infection during a recurrence has not been determined with certainty. Cesarean delivery is not warranted in women with a history of HSV infection but with no active genital disease during labor (42).

▶ *Is cesarean delivery recommended for women with recurrent HSV lesions on areas distant from the vulva, vagina, or cervix (eg, thigh or buttock)?*

Among women with recurrent HSV and genital lesions at the time of labor, the risk of neonatal HSV infection associated with vaginal birth is low, estimated to be no more than 3% (17). In part, this low risk is probably attributable to preexisting maternal type-specific antibodies. When infection occurs among neonates of women with recurrent HSV, it is due either to shedding of the virus from the genital lesion itself or to shedding from the cervix. In patients with recurrent genital HSV and nongenital lesions at the time of labor, the only viral exposure faced by the infant during vaginal delivery is that of cervical shedding, which occurs in approximately 2% of such cases (43). Thus, the risk of neonatal HSV associated with vaginal delivery in a woman with recurrent HSV and nongenital lesions would appear to be very low. Cesarean delivery is not recommended for these women. Nongenital lesions should be covered with an occlusive dressing; the patient then can deliver vaginally.

▶ *In a patient with active HSV infection and ruptured membranes, is there any length of time at which vaginal delivery remains appropriate?*

In patients with active HSV infection and ruptured membranes at or near term, a cesarean delivery should be performed as soon as the necessary personnel and equipment can be readied. There is no evidence that there is a duration of premature rupture of membranes beyond which the fetus does not benefit from cesarean delivery (44).

▶ *How should a woman with active HSV and preterm premature rupture of membranes be managed?*

In the decision to deliver a patient with preterm premature rupture of membranes and active HSV, the risk of prematurity versus the potential risk of neonatal disease should be considered. In pregnancies remote from term, especially in women with recurrent disease, there is increasing support for continuing the pregnancy to gain benefit from time and glucocorticoids (45). If this expectant management plan is followed, treatment with an antiviral agent is indicated. Concern has been raised about the potential effects of glucocorticoids on patients with viral infection, but there is no conclusive evidence that this is a concern in this setting. The decision to perform a cesarean delivery depends on whether active lesions are present at the time of delivery.

The utility of suppressive antiviral therapy to prevent ascending infection has not been proven. The lack of evidence complicates the situation, because it is clear that premature neonates are at the greatest risk of infection. In such situations, it may be appropriate to consult personnel well versed in the management of such complicated cases.

▶ *Are invasive procedures contraindicated in women with HSV?*

In patients with recurrent HSV, invasive procedures, such as amniocentesis, percutaneous umbilical cord blood sampling, or transabdominal chorionic villus sampling may be performed; however, transcervical procedures should be delayed until lesions appear to have resolved. In a patient with primary HSV and systemic symptoms, it seems prudent to delay invasive procedures until symptoms appear to resolve.

Local neonatal infection may result from the use of fetal scalp electrode monitoring in patients with a history of herpes, even when lesions are not present (46–48). However, if there are indications for fetal scalp monitoring, it may be appropriate in a woman who has a history of recurrent HSV and no active lesions. If vesicular or vesiculopustular lesions develop at the site of the electrode, it is important to make a quick and accurate diagnosis and start systemic antiviral therapy.

▶ *Should women with active HSV breastfeed or handle their infants?*

Postnatally acquired disease can be as lethal as that acquired during delivery through an infected birth canal. Oropharyngeal or cutaneous lesions can be an effective source of virus. It is unlikely that breastfeeding will lead to neonatal infection; however, if the mother has an obvious lesion on the breast, breastfeeding is contraindicated. Because the herpes virus is transmitted through direct contact (eg, hand-to-mouth), neonatal infection may be acquired from family members other than the mother and from sites other than the genital tract (49, 50). Most strains of HSV responsible for nosocomial neonatal disease are HSV-1 rather than HSV-2. Mothers with active lesions should use caution when handling their babies.

Summary

The following recommendations are based on limited or inconsistent scientific evidence (Level B):

▶ Women with primary HSV during pregnancy should be treated with antiviral therapy.

▶ Cesarean delivery should be performed on women with first-episode HSV who have active genital lesions at delivery.

▶ For women at or beyond 36 weeks of gestation with a first episode of HSV occurring during the current pregnancy, antiviral therapy should be considered.

The following recommendations are based primarily on consensus and expert opinion (Level C):

▶ Cesarean delivery should be performed on women with recurrent HSV infection who have active genital lesions or prodromal symptoms at delivery.

▶ Expectant management of patients with preterm labor or preterm premature rupture of membranes and active HSV may be warranted.

▶ For women at or beyond 36 weeks of gestation who are at risk for recurrent HSV, antiviral therapy also may be considered, although such therapy may not reduce the likelihood of cesarean delivery.

▶ In women with no active lesions or prodromal symptoms during labor, cesarean delivery should not be performed on the basis of a history of recurrent disease.

References

1. Fleming DT, McQuillan GM, Johnson RE, Nahmias AJ, Aral SO, Lee FK. Herpes simplex virus type 2 in the United States, 1976 to 1994. N Engl J Med 1997;337: 1105–1111 (Level II-3)

2. Corey L, Spear PG. Infections with herpes simplex viruses. N Engl J Med 1986;314:686–691 (Level III)

3. Prober C, Corey L, Brown ZA, Hensleigh PA, Frenkel LM, Bryson YJ. The management of pregnancies complicated by genital infections with herpes simplex virus. Clin Infect Dis 1992;15:1031–1038 (Level III)

4. Mertz GL, Benedetti J, Ashley R, Selke SA, Corey L. Risk factors for the sexual transmission of genital herpes. Ann Intern Med 1992;116:197–202 (Level II-3)

5. Whitley RJ, Hutto C. Neonatal herpes simplex virus infections. Pediatr Rev 1985;7:119–126 (Level III)

6. Frenkel LM, Garratty EM, Shen JP, Wheeler N, Clark O, Bryson YJ. Clinical reactivation of herpes simplex virus type 2 infection in seropositive pregnant women with no history of genital herpes. Ann Intern Med 1993;118: 414–418 (Level II-3)

7. Hensleigh PA, Andrews WW, Brown Z, Greenspoon J, Yasukawa L, Prober CG. Genital herpes during pregnancy: inability to distinguish primary and recurrent infections clinically. Obstet Gynecol 1997;89:891–895 (Level III)

8. Koelle DM, Benedetti J, Langenberg A, Corey L. Asymptomatic reactivation of herpes simplex virus in women after the first episode of genital herpes. Ann Intern Med 1992;116:433–437 (Level II-3)

9. Mertz GL. Epidemiology of genital herpes infections. Infect Dis Clin North Am 1993;7:825–839 (Level III)

10. Brock BV, Selke S, Benedetti J, Douglas JM Jr, Corey L. Frequency of asymptomatic shedding of herpes simplex virus in women with genital herpes. JAMA 1990;263:418–420 (Level III)

11. Prober CG. Herpetic vaginitis in 1993. Clin Obstet Gynecol 1993;36:177–187 (Level III)

12. Wald A, Zeh J, Selke S, Ashley RL, Corey L. Virologic characteristics of subclinical and symptomatic genital herpes infections. N Engl J Med 1995;333:770–775 (Level II-3)

13. Hirsch MS. Herpes simplex virus. In: Mandell GL, Bennett JE, Dolin R, eds. Mandell, Douglas and Bennett's principles and practice of infectious diseases. 4th ed. New York: Churchill Livingstone, 1995:1336–1345 (Level III)

14. Whitley R, Arvin A, Prober C, Corey L, Burchett S, Plotkin S. Predictors of morbidity and mortality in neonates with herpes simplex infections. The National Institute of Allergy and infectious Diseases Collaborative Antiviral Study Group. N Engl J Med 1991;324:450–454 (Level III)

15. Mertz GJ, Schmidt O, Jourden JL, Guinan ME, Remington ML, Fahnlander A. Frequency of acquisition of first-episode genital infection with herpes simplex virus from symptomatic and asymptomatic source contacts. Sex Transm Dis 1985;12:33–39 (Level III)

16. Kulhanjian JA, Soroush V, Au DS, Bronzan RN, Yasukawa LL, Weylman LE. Identification of women at unsuspected risk of primary infection with herpes simplex virus type 2 during pregnancy. N Engl J Med 1992;326: 916–920 (Level II-3)

17. Brown ZA, Benedetti J, Ashley R, Burchett S, Selke S, Berry S. Neonatal herpes simplex virus infection in relation to asymptomatic maternal infection at the time of labor. N Engl J Med 1991;324:1247–1252 (Level II-3)

18. Brown ZA, Selke S, Zeh J, Kopelman J, Maslow A, Ashley RL. The acquisition of herpes simplex virus during pregnancy. N Engl J Med 1997;337:509–515 (Level II-3)

19. Altshuler G. Pathogenesis of congenital herpesvirus infection: case report including a description of the placenta. Am J Dis Child 1974;127:427–429 (Level III)

20. Chalhub EG, Baenziger J, Feigen RD, Middlekamp JN, Shackelford GD. Congenital herpes simplex type II infection with extensive hepatic calcification bone lesions and cataracts: complete postmortem examination. Dev Med Child Neurol 1977;19:527–534 (Level III)

21. Monif GR, Kellner KR, Donnelly WH Jr. Congenital herpes simplex type II infection. Am J Obstet Gynecol 1985;152:1000–1002 (Level III)

22. Woods GL. Update on laboratory diagnosis of sexually transmitted diseases. Clin Lab Med 1995;15:665–684 (Level III)

23. Hardy DA, Arvin AM, Yasukawa LL, Bronzan RN, Lewinsohn DM, Hensleigh PA. Use of polymerase chain reaction for successful identification of asymptomatic genital infection with herpes simplex virus in pregnant women at delivery. J Infect Dis 1990;162:1031–1035 (Level III)

24. Boggess KA, Watts DH, Hobson AC, Ashley RL, Brown ZA, Corey L. Herpes simplex type 2 detection by culture and polymerase chain reaction and relationship to genital symptoms and cervical antibody status during the third trimester of pregnancy. Am J Obstet Gynecol 1997;176: 443–451 (Level III)

25. Cone RW, Hobson AC, Palmer J, Remington M, Corey L. Extended duration of herpes simplex virus DNA in genital lesions detected by the polymerase chain reaction. J Infect Dis 1991;164:757–760 (Level III)

26. Mosely RC, Corey L, Benjamin D, Winter C, Remington ML. Comparison of viral isolation, direct immunofluorescence, and indirect immunoperoxidase techniques for detection of genital herpes simplex virus infection. J Clin Microbiol 1981;13:913–918 (Level II-2)

27. Arvin AM, Hensleigh PA, Prober CG, Au DS, Yasukawa LL, Wittek AE. Failure of antepartum maternal cultures to predict the infant's risk of exposure to herpes simplex virus at delivery. N Engl J Med 1986;315:796–800 (Level II-3)

28. Goldberg LK, Kaufman R, Kurtz TO, Conant MA, Eron LJ, Batenhorst RL. Long-term suppression of recurrent genital herpes with acyclovir. A 5-year benchmark. Acyclovir Study Group. Arch Dermatol 1993;129:582–587 (Level I)

29. Scott LL, Sanchez PJ, Jackson GL, Zeray F, Wendel GD Jr. Acyclovir suppression to prevent cesarean delivery after first-episode genital herpes. Obstet Gynecol 1996;87: 69–73 (Level I)

30. Grover L, Kane J, Kravitz J, Cruz A. Systemic acyclovir in pregnancy: a case report. Obstet Gynecol 1985;65:284–287 (Level III)

31. Lagrew DC Jr, Furlow TG, Hager WD, Yarrish RL. Disseminated herpes simplex virus infection in pregnancy. Successful treatment with acyclovir. JAMA 1984;252: 2058–2059 (Level III)

32. Brown ZA, Baker DA. Acyclovir therapy during pregnancy. Obstet Gynecol 1989;3:526–531 (Level III)

33. Brockelhurst P, Kinghorn G, Carney O, Helsen K, Ross E, Ellis E, et al. A randomised placebo controlled trial of suppressive acyclovir in late pregnancy in women with recurrent genital herpes infection. Br J Obstet Gynaecol 1998; 105:275–280 (Level I)

34. Lavoie SR, Kaplowitz LG. Management of genital herpes infection. Semin Dermatol 1994;13:248–255 (Level III)

35. Mertz GJ, Critchlow CW, Benedetti J, Reichman RC, Dolin R, Connor J. Double-blind placebo-controlled trial of oral acyclovir in first-episode genital herpes simplex virus infections. JAMA 1984;252:1147–1151 (Level I)

36. Fife KH, Crumpacker CS, Mertz GJ, Hill EL, Boone GS. Recurrence and resistance patterns of herpes simplex virus following cessation of > or = 6 years of chronic suppression with acyclovir. Acyclovir Study Group. J Infect Dis 1994;169:1338–1341 (Level II-3)

37. Wald A, Zeh J, Barnum G, Davis LG, Corey L. Suppression of subclinical shedding of herpes simplex virus type 2 with acyclovir. Ann Intern Med 1996;124: 8–15 (Level I)

38. Centers for Disease Control and Prevention. 1998 guidelines for treatment of sexually transmitted diseases. MMWR Morb Mortal Wkly Rep 1998;47(RR-1):20–24 (Level III)

39. Pregnancy outcomes following systemic acyclovir exposure. June 1, 1984–June 30, 1993. MMWR Morb Mortal Wkly Rep 1993;42:806–809 (Level III)

40. Frenkel LM, Brown ZA, Bryson YJ, Corey L, Unadkat JD, Hensleigh PA, et al. Pharmacokinetics of acyclovir in the term human pregnancy and neonate. Am J Obstet Gynecol 1991;164:569–576 (Level II-2)

41. Randolph AG, Washington E, Prober CG. Cesarean delivery for women presenting with genital herpes lesions. Efficacy, risks, and costs. JAMA 1993;270:77–82 (Decision Analysis)

42. Roberts SW, Cox SM, Dax J, Wendel GD Jr, Leveno KJ. Genital herpes during pregnancy: no lesions, no cesarean. Obstet Gynecol 1995;85:261–264 (Level II-2)

43. Wittek AE, Yeager AS, Au DS, Hensleigh PA. Asymptomatic shedding of herpes simplex virus from the cervix and lesion site during pregnancy. Correlation of antepartum shedding with shedding at delivery. Am J Dis Child 1984;138:439–442 (Level II-3)

44. Nahmias AJ, Josey WE, Naib ZM, Freeman MG, Fernandez RJ, Wheeler JH. Perinatal risk associated with maternal genital herpes simplex virus infection. Am J Obstet Gynecol 1971;110:825–837 (Level II-3)

45. National Institutes of Health. Consensus Development Conference Statement. Effect of corticoids for fetal maturation on perinatal outcomes, February 28–March 2, 1994. Am J Obstet Gynecol 1995;173:246–252 (Level III)

46. Amann ST, Fagnant RJ, Chartrand SA, Monif GR. Herpes simplex infection with short-term use of a fetal scalp electrode. A case report. J Reprod Med 1992;37:372–374 (Level III)

47. Golden SM, Merenstein GB, Todd WA, Hill JM. Disseminated herpes simplex neonatorum: a complication of fetal monitoring. Am J Obstet Gynecol 1977;129:917–918 (Level III)

48. Goldkrand JW. Intrapartum inoculation of herpes simplex virus by fetal scalp electrode. Obstet Gynecol 1982;59:263–265 (Level III)

49. Douglas J, Schmidt O, Corey L. Acquisition of neonatal HSV-1 infection from a paternal source contact. J Pediatr 1983;103:908–910 (Level III)

50. Hammerberg O, Watts J, Chernesky M, Luchsinger I, Rawls W. An outbreak of herpes simplex virus type 1 in an intensive care nursery. Pediatr Infect Dis J 1983;2:290–294 (Level III)

The MEDLINE database was used to conduct a literature search to locate relevant articles published between January 1985 and December 1998. The search was restricted to articles published in the English language. Priority was given to articles reporting results of original research, although review articles and commentaries also were consulted. Abstracts of research presented at symposia and scientific conferences were not considered adequate for inclusion in this document. Guidelines published by organizations or institutions such as the National Institutes of Health and the American College of Obstetricians and Gynecologists were reviewed, and additional studies were located by reviewing bibliographies of identified articles. When reliable research was not available, expert opinions from obstetrician–gynecologists were used.

Studies were reviewed and evaluated for quality according to the method outlined by the U.S. Preventive Services Task Force:

I   Evidence obtained from at least one properly designed randomized controlled trial.

II-1 Evidence obtained from well-designed controlled trials without randomization.

II-2 Evidence obtained from well-designed cohort or case–control analytic studies, preferably from more than one center or research group.

II-3 Evidence obtained from multiple time series with or without the intervention. Dramatic results in uncontrolled experiments also could be regarded as this type of evidence.

III   Opinions of respected authorities, based on clinical experience, descriptive studies, or reports of expert committees.

Based on the highest level of evidence found in the data, recommendations are provided and graded according to the following categories:

Level A—Recommendations are based on good and consistent scientific evidence.

Level B—Recommendations are based on limited or inconsistent scientific evidence.

Level C—Recommendations are based primarily on consensus and expert opinion.

ISSN 1099-3630

**The American College of
Obstetricians and Gynecologists
409 12th Street, SW
PO Box 96920
Washington, DC 20090-6920**

12345/32109

ACOG PRACTICE BULLETIN

CLINICAL MANAGEMENT GUIDELINES FOR
OBSTETRICIAN–GYNECOLOGISTS

NUMBER 24, FEBRUARY 2001

(Replaces Technical Bulletin Number 212, September 1995)

This Practice Bulletin was developed by the ACOG Committee on Practice Bulletins—Obstetrics with the assistance of Sandra A. Carson, MD, and D. Ware Branch, MD. The information is designed to aid practitioners in making decisions about appropriate obstetric and gynecologic care. These guidelines should not be construed as dictating an exclusive course of treatment or procedure. Variations in practice may be warranted based on the needs of the individual patient, resources, and limitations unique to the institution or type of practice.

Management of Recurrent Early Pregnancy Loss

Recurrent pregnancy loss is a common clinical problem in reproduction, occurring in approximately 1% of reproductive-aged women (1). A definite cause is established in no more than 50% of couples, and several alleged causes of recurrent pregnancy loss are controversial. Moreover, in the field of recurrent pregnancy loss, inappropriate emphasis often is given to unproven hypotheses and poorly designed clinical studies. Seeking a solution, some patients and physicians explore less-well-accepted etiologies and empirical or alternative treatments. This bulletin will provide the practitioner with a rational, modern approach to the management of recurrent pregnancy loss. New and controversial etiologies will be presented so that the practitioner can discuss them with couples who have a history of recurrent pregnancy loss.

Background

Broadly defined, pregnancy loss includes any type of loss of the conceptus from fertilized ovum to neonate. This bulletin covers the repetitive loss of recognized pregnancies in the first or early second trimester (<15 weeks of gestation). It usually is referred to as recurrent spontaneous abortion, miscarriage, or recurrent early pregnancy loss.

Recurrent abortion must be distinguished from sporadic spontaneous abortions that are nonconsecutive pregnancy losses occurring randomly during a woman's reproductive years. Sporadic pregnancy loss occurs in 10–15% of all clinically recognized pregnancies as first- or early second-trimester spontaneous abortions. Most of these pregnancy losses are clinically evident by the 12th week of gestation and are preembryonic or embryonic losses in which the demise of the conceptus precedes clinical features of pregnancy loss by one or more weeks.

Recurrent pregnancy loss typically is defined as two or three or more consecutive pregnancy losses. Most women with recurrent pregnancy loss have recurrent preembryonic or embryonic losses. Recurrent fetal loss is less common, and recurrent fetal loss at or beyond 14 weeks of gestation is infrequent.

Causes of Recurrent Pregnancy Loss

Genetic Abnormalities

Parental Structural Chromosome Abnormalities

In approximately 2–4% of couples with recurrent pregnancy loss, one partner will have a genetically balanced structural chromosome rearrangement. Balanced translocations account for the largest percentage of these karyotypic abnormalities. They can cause pregnancy loss because segregation during meiosis results in gametes with duplication or deficiency of chromosome segments. Other genetically balanced structural chromosome abnormalities, such as chromosome inversions, account for a small percentage of abnormal parental karyotypes among couples with recurrent pregnancy loss.

Molecular Genetic Abnormalities

In the past decade, the development of techniques for DNA analysis has resulted in identification of molecular genetic abnormalities as causes of various human diseases. One report indicated that highly skewed X-chromosome inactivation is associated with otherwise unexplained recurrent pregnancy loss (2). As yet, however, commercially available tests for this and other related molecular genetic abnormalities are not widely available.

Recurrent Preembryonic or Embryonic Aneuploidy

Analyses of karyotypes in consecutive abortions suggest that recurrent aneuploidy in the conceptus may be a cause of recurrent pregnancy loss. In one analysis of data, the karyotype of a second successive spontaneous abortion was abnormal in nearly 70% of cases when aneuploidy was found in the first abortus, but in only 20% of cases where the first abortus was chromosomally normal (3). However, these aneuploid losses may have been a result of the older age of the mothers, rather than a nonrandom event in predisposed couples (4). More recently, two groups of investigators using different techniques of analysis have shown that the next abortion in women with recurrent pregnancy loss was chromosomally abnor-

mal in 48% or more of cases (5, 6), raising the possibility of recurrent aneuploidy despite normal parental karyotypes. Supportive evidence comes from studies of preimplantation genetic studies of women with recurrent pregnancy loss in which more than 50% of embryos were found to have aneuploidy (7, 8).

Hormonal and Metabolic Disorders

Luteal Phase Defect

The luteal phase defect (LPD) has long been thought to be a cause of spontaneous abortion, but the evidence linking LPD to recurrent abortion is subject to criticism. Investigators initially hypothesized that with LPD, the corpus luteum failed to make enough progesterone to establish a mature endometrial lining suitable for placentation. This theory has evolved to implicate poor follicular-phase oocyte development, which results in disordered estrogen secretion and subsequent dysfunction of either the corpus luteum or progesterone effect. In turn, these effects could result from excess luteinizing hormone or hyperandrogenic states. Some investigators believe that LPD is a common cause of recurrent pregnancy loss, accounting for approximately 25–40% of cases. However, studies of this disorder have not included concurrently tested controls, a serious oversight given that normal women have endometrial histology suggestive of LPD in up to 50% of single menstrual cycles and 25% of sequential cycles (9). Thus, the association between LPD and recurrent pregnancy loss remains speculative.

Polycystic Ovary Syndrome

Investigators have found that 36–56% of women with recurrent pregnancy loss have polycystic ovary syndrome (PCOS) diagnosed by ultrasound examination of the ovaries (10–12). One group (11) demonstrated that more than half of women with ultrasonographic evidence of PCOS also had hypersecretion of luteinizing hormone. But ultrasonographic evidence of PCOS in women with recurrent pregnancy loss does not predict worse pregnancy outcome than in women with recurrent pregnancy loss without PCOS (10, 12, 13). However, it has been reported that women with PCOS who miscarry have higher levels of circulating androgens (10). There is no known therapy for reducing the risk of pregnancy loss in women with PCOS.

Other Metabolic Abnormalities

Maternal endocrinologic and metabolic disorders have been implicated as a cause of recurrent pregnancy loss. Women with poorly controlled type 1 (insulin-dependent) diabetes mellitus have an increased rate of abortion (14). However, there is no evidence that asymptomatic endocrinologic or metabolic disorders, such as mild thyroid disease or glucose intolerance, cause recurrent pregnancy loss.

Uterine Anatomic Abnormalities

Congenital uterine abnormalities have been associated most often with second-trimester pregnancy loss. However, 10–15% of women with recurrent early pregnancy loss have congenital uterine abnormalities. The most common malformations associated with pregnancy loss are variations of the double uterus (bicornuate, septate, or didelphic), with septate uterus predominating. The contribution of arcuate uterus to recurrent pregnancy loss is debated. A recent study using three-dimensional ultrasonography and hysteroscopy found that 15% of 61 women with recurrent pregnancy loss had an arcuate uterus, compared with only 3% of more than 1,000 women attending a gynecology clinic (15, 16). Other investigators doubt an association between an arcuate uterus and recurrent pregnancy loss (17, 18). Severe uterine synechiae (Asherman's syndrome) and uterine abnormalities associated with in utero exposure to diethylstilbestrol also may be associated with pregnancy loss. An association between submucosal leiomyoma and recurrent pregnancy loss is controversial.

Some investigators believe that poor vascularization of the uterine septum is a cause of spontaneous abortion, but studies provide mixed results. In one study of 12 pregnancies, all four successful pregnancies became implanted away from the uterine septum (19). However, the vascular density in uterine septa removed at the time of metroplasty is similar to that of the normal uterine wall (20).

Infectious Causes

Certain infectious agents, such as *Listeria monocytogenes,* are known to cause sporadic pregnancy loss, but no infectious agent has been proven to cause recurrent pregnancy loss. In addition, *Toxoplasma gondii* and some viruses (eg, rubella, herpes simplex, and measles viruses; cytomegalovirus; and coxsackieviruses) have been linked to sporadic abortion. However, none has been convincingly associated with recurrent pregnancy loss.

Environmental Factors, Occupational Factors, and Personal Habits

Although a common concern of patients, environmental factors rarely have been linked to sporadic pregnancy loss, and no associations between environmental factors and recurrent pregnancy loss have been established. Likewise, occupational exposures to certain products, such as certain organic solvents, rarely have been linked to sporadic pregnancy loss (21). However, no associations between occupational exposure or working itself and recurrent pregnancy loss have been established.

Study results are conflicting on the association of smoking, use of alcohol, and use of caffeine with sporadic pregnancy loss. They may act in a dose-dependent fashion or synergistically to increase the rate of sporadic pregnancy loss. However, none of these habits has been associated with recurrent pregnancy loss. Exercise does not appear to increase the rate of sporadic pregnancy loss, particularly in women in good physical condition, and there are no studies of exercise effects in women with recurrent pregnancy loss.

Thrombophilia

The most common inherited thrombophilic disorders are factor V Leiden and prothrombin G20210A mutation, found in approximately 8% and 3%, respectively, of Caucasian women in the United States. These mutations are associated with approximately 25% of isolated thrombotic events and approximately 50% of familial thrombosis. Other less common thrombophilias include deficiencies of the anticoagulants protein C, protein S, and antithrombin III. Some investigators have (22–25), and some have not (13, 26–29), found that one or more of these thrombophilic mutations are associated with recurrent pregnancy loss. In two studies (22, 30), however, these heritable thrombophilias were associated with second- or third-trimester fetal loss, not with first-trimester loss. Also, one group has found that next pregnancy outcomes among women with recurrent pregnancy losses are no different with or without factor V Leiden (13).

Despite the recent interest in this field, no treatment trials have been performed. Thus, which therapy, if any, is effective in promoting successful pregnancy among women with recurrent pregnancy loss and thrombophilia is uncertain.

Autoimmune Disorders

Antiphospholipid Antibodies

Antiphospholipid syndrome (APS) is an autoimmune disorder characterized by the presence of significant levels of antiphospholipid antibodies and one or more clinical features, among which are recurrent pregnancy loss, fetal death, and thrombosis (31). Antiphospholipid syndrome may occur as a primary condition in women with no other recognizable autoimmune disease, or as a secondary condition in patients with underlying autoimmune disease (eg, systemic lupus erythematosus). The diagnosis of APS is made by demonstrating lupus antico-agulant, anticardiolipin antibodies, or both.

Some investigators have found that a small percentage of women with recurrent pregnancy loss who test negative for anticardiolipin antibodies have antibodies to other phospholipids, such as phosphatidylserine or phosphatidylethanolamine (32). Others have found that no such relationship exists (33) or that testing for antibodies other than lupus anticoagulant and anticardiolipin antibodies does not increase the rate of diagnosis of APS (34). In addition, assays for phospholipid-binding antibodies other than anticardiolipin are not standardized. Finally, there is no proven treatment for women with recurrent pregnancy loss and phospholipid-binding antibodies other than lupus anticoagulant and anticardiolipin antibodies.

Thyroid Antibodies

Autoantibodies to thyroid antigens (thyroglobulin and thyroid peroxidase) are associated with an increased rate of pregnancy loss if identified in early pregnancy or immediately before pregnancy (35, 36). However, current evidence does not allow a definite conclusion regarding the association of antithyroid antibodies and recurrent pregnancy loss, and no treatment options have been proven beneficial.

Antinuclear Antibodies

A significant percentage (approximately 15%) of women with recurrent pregnancy loss have detectable antinuclear antibodies (ANA) (37, 38). Without treatment, subsequent pregnancy outcomes among women with a positive ANA test result are similar to those among women with a negative ANA test result. More important, a randomized treatment trial of women with recurrent pregnancy loss and a positive autoantibody result, including ANA, found no difference in pregnancy outcomes between women treated with prednisone and low-dose aspirin and women treated with placebo (39). Thus, currently available data do not support testing women with recurrent pregnancy loss for ANA.

Alloimmune Disorders

Alloimmune traits—immunologic differences between individuals—have been proposed as factors between reproductive partners that cause otherwise unexplained recurrent pregnancy loss. The tendency for 1) partners with recurrent loss to share human leukocyte antigens, 2) the female partner to fail to produce serum "blocking factor," and 3) the female partner to produce antileukocytotoxic antibodies against paternal leukocytes have been described. Others have refuted the significance of each of these factors. In addition, no test for these traits provides results that predict the next pregnancy outcome in patients treated or untreated for recurrent pregnancy loss (40, 41). More recently, some researchers have claimed that flow cytometric assays for maternal antibodies to paternal leukocytes are useful in evaluating couples with recurrent pregnancy loss. However, studies of these assays have lacked appropriate controls and are of unproven value in terms of indicating an efficacious treatment.

More recent investigations of the maternal–fetal immunologic relationship suggest that pregnancy losses may result from dysregulation of normal immune mechanisms, probably operating at the maternal–fetal interface. It has been proposed that a predominance of Th-2 lymphocytic cytokines is crucial for successful pregnancy and that Th-1 lymphocytic cytokines, such as interferon-γ and tumor necrosis factor-α, adversely affect embryo and trophoblast viability (42–44). The presence of natural killer (NK)-like cells secreting a transforming growth factor at the maternal–fetal interface may be necessary for successful pregnancy (45). Clinical studies have found decreased (45, 46) or increased (47) numbers of these cells in the luteal phase endometria of women with recurrent pregnancy loss. Pregnancy outcomes may be worse in women with recurrent pregnancy loss found to have increased numbers of NK-like cells in the luteal phase endometria (48), but further studies are necessary before valid conclusions can be drawn. One group has found that an embryotoxic factor, similar to interferon-γ, generated by patient leukocytes in vitro predicted pregnancy failure in the next pregnancy attempt (44), but others have not been able to reproduce these findings (49). Others have found that an increased percentage of circulating NK cells in women with recurrent pregnancy loss predicts a relatively poor next pregnancy outcome (50, 51). There is, however, no proven treatment for women with recurrent pregnancy loss found to have increased percentages of circulating NK cells.

Unexplained Recurrent Pregnancy Loss

In 50% or more of couples with recurrent pregnancy loss, an evaluation, including parental karyotypes, hysterosalpingography or hysteroscopy, and antiphospholipid antibody testing will be negative. Therefore, a majority (approximately 50–75%) of couples with recurrent pregnancy loss will have no certain diagnosis. Informative and sympathetic counseling appears to serve an important role in this situation. Live birth rates between 35% and 85% are commonly reported in couples with unexplained recurrent pregnancy loss who undertake an untreated or placebo-treated subsequent pregnancy (12, 52–55). Meta-analysis of randomized, prospective studies suggests that 60–70% of women with unexplained recurrent pregnancy loss will have a successful next pregnancy (56), figures that many couples will view as optimistic.

Clinical Considerations and Recommendations

▶ When is a diagnosis of recurrent pregnancy loss appropriate?

Traditionally, recurrent pregnancy loss has been defined as three consecutive spontaneous abortions. However, the risk of abortion after two successive abortions (30%) is clinically similar to the risk of recurrence among women with three or more consecutive abortions (33%) (37, 57–66). Thus, patients with two or more consecutive spontaneous abortions are candidates for an evaluation to determine the etiology, if any, for their pregnancy losses.

The number of previous pregnancy losses influences the likelihood of successful pregnancy. One study reported recurrent pregnancy loss rates of 29%, 27%, 44%, and 53% after 3, 4, 5, and 6 or more recurrent pregnancy losses, respectively (67). In addition, maternal age influences the recurrent pregnancy loss rate (67, 68), with a recurrent pregnancy loss rate of approximately 25% in women aged 30 years or younger and a recurrent pregnancy loss rate of 50–60% in those 40 years or older. Some investigators have found the prognosis for a successful pregnancy is increased by 10–20% in women with at least one previous live birth (58, 69), but others did not (67).

▶ Should all couples with recurrent pregnancy loss have chromosomal analysis performed?

Parents with recurrent pregnancy loss should be analyzed for balanced chromosome abnormalities because: 1) couples would like to know why they are experiencing repetitive pregnancy loss; 2) a couple in which one partner carries a balanced chromosome abnormality is at increased risk for having a fetus with an unbalanced chromosome abnormality and may benefit from prenatal genetic testing; and 3) the apparently normal offspring of a couple in which one partner carries a balanced chromosome abnormality is at risk for carrying the same balanced chromosome abnormality and, thus, is at risk for reproductive complications.

Balanced chromosome abnormalities occurring in one partner are relatively infrequent among couples with only recurrent pregnancy loss but no other adverse perinatal outcomes (eg, stillborns, anomalous infants). One study reported that of couples with recurrent loss, only 2.4% of female partners and 1.6% of male partners with a history of stillbirths or anomalous infants had a balanced chromosome abnormality, compared with 4.6% of female partners and 1.7% of male partners with a history of adverse perinatal outcomes (70). However, no historic factor unequivocally allows the clinician to determine which couples may benefit from karyotype analyses. In addition, phenotypically normal offspring do not exclude the possibility of a balanced chromosome abnormality in a couple with recurrent pregnancy loss.

Parental cytogenetic analysis should be offered to all couples with recurrent pregnancy loss. In addition, all couples in which one partner has been found to have a balanced translocation or inversion should be offered prenatal genetic diagnosis because of the increased risk of a karyotypic abnormality in the conceptus.

In addition, many experts obtain a karyotype of the abortus tissue when a couple with recurrent pregnancy loss experiences a subsequent spontaneous abortion. The rationale is that if the abortus is aneuploid, the physician and patient may conclude that a maternal cause of pregnancy loss is excluded. Also, an abnormal abortus karyotype is a legitimate explanation for the loss that may provide a source of comfort to the couple. However, no published evidence supports these hypotheses, and definite recommendations for routinely obtaining abortus karyotypes cannot be made.

▶ How should the uterine cavity be evaluated in a woman with recurrent pregnancy loss, and how should abnormal findings be treated?

Uterine anatomic abnormalities are diagnosed by hysterosalpingography, hysteroscopy, or sonohysteroscopy. Three-dimensional ultrasonography, although not routinely available in the United States, also has been shown to be useful in the diagnosis of uterine abnormalities. Suspicious or confusing cases can be evaluated further by magnetic resonance imaging. However, the relationship between uterine abnormalities and recurrent pregnancy loss is uncertain, and some authorities do not recommend routinely evaluating the uterine cavity by hysterosalpingography, hysteroscopy, or sonohysteroscopy (71).

No prospective, controlled trials have proved that the correction of uterine anatomic abnormalities benefits the next pregnancy outcome. Retrospectively analyzed case series suggest that 70–85% of women with recurrent pregnancy loss with bicornuate and septate uteri who undergo surgical correction will deliver viable live born infants in their next pregnancies (72), but these seemingly excellent results are subject to criticism because of the methods of patient selection and the lack of controls.

Hysteroscopic resection has been used successfully for treatment of the uterine septum, and subsequent pregnancy results are comparable to those for metroplasty (72). It is preferable to abdominal surgery because it is an outpatient procedure with low morbidity and allows for labor with expected vaginal delivery. Uterine synechiae also may be treated hysteroscopically.

▶ Should women with recurrent pregnancy loss be evaluated for luteal phase defect?

Although assessment of luteal phase progesterone production or effect is firmly entrenched in the traditional evaluation of women with recurrent pregnancy loss, the evidence supporting this practice is scant. The endometrium is considered out of phase when the histologic dating lags behind the menstrual dating by 2 days or more. However, interobserver variation in the interpretation of the biopsies is considerable (73), and modest intraobserver variation occurs (74). Because of 1) such variation, 2) the frequent finding of out-of-phase endometrial histology in normal women, and 3) the inconsistent expression of luteal phase defect in affected women, luteal phase defect is diagnosed only when two consecutive biopsies are out of phase. The measurement of luteal phase progesterone concentrations is not an adequate method for diagnosing or excluding luteal phase defect.

No properly designed studies have evaluated the role of progesterone treatment in women with recurrent pregnancy loss with luteal phase defect. Two meta-analyses of studies from the 1950s and 1960s reached conflicting conclusions regarding the efficacy of progesterone treatment in variously selected women with recurrent abortion (75, 76). The studies included in these meta-analyses are difficult to interpret because they 1) did not assess patients for luteal phase defect using currently accepted criteria, 2) employed 17-OH progesterone caproate or medroxyprogesterone as treatment, 3) used various inclusion criteria, and 4) entered patients after pregnancy had progressed to at least 8 weeks of gestation. Also, these studies totaled only 130 patients, and one of them (77) was not randomized. In addition, in a more recent randomized trial, a subgroup of women with PCOS and three or more miscarriages were randomized to treatment with either progesterone or placebo pessaries (78). There was no difference in the pregnancy outcomes.

Human chorionic gonadotropin has been used in an attempt to stimulate the corpus luteum support of pregnancy in women with recurrent abortion. One international multicentered trial randomized 75 women to receive either placebo or 10,000 IU of human chorionic gonadotropin at the first diagnosis of pregnancy and 5,000 IU weekly thereafter (79). No significant difference in the successful pregnancy rates (83% versus 79%) between the groups was found.

In summary, the relationship between the luteal phase defect and recurrent pregnancy loss remains a subject of controversy. It has not been shown conclusively that progesterone treatment or corpus luteum support influences pregnancy outcome in women with recurrent pregnancy loss.

▶ Should thyroid tests and tests for glucose intolerance be performed in women with recurrent pregnancy loss?

An association between recurrent pregnancy loss and asymptomatic endocrinologic or metabolic disorders such as mild thyroid disease or glucose intolerance has not been established. Thus, tests for thyroid dysfunction or glucose intolerance are not required in the evaluation of otherwise normal women with recurrent pregnancy loss.

An association between antithyroid antibodies and recurrent pregnancy loss has been reported by some investigators (31, 80–83). Very few patients identified in these studies are clinically hypothyroid, and less than 20% have abnormal thyroid-stimulating hormone test results (80). In addition, no treatments have proved to benefit next pregnancy outcome in women found to have antithyroid antibodies. Thus, tests for antithyroid antibodies are not required in the evaluation of women with recurrent pregnancy loss.

▶ Should women with recurrent pregnancy loss be evaluated for possible infectious causes, and should they be treated?

Endocervical *Chlamydia* and *Mycoplasma* have been implicated as causes of recurrent pregnancy loss, but study results are conflicting. Bacterial vaginosis may be associated with midtrimester pregnancy loss (84, 85), and one study found an increased rate of pregnancy loss in women with bacterial vaginosis undergoing in vitro fertilization (86). However, there is no direct evidence (confirmed by cultures) of *Chlamydia, Mycoplasma,* and organisms causing bacterial vaginosis in systematically analyzed recurrent abortus specimens. These infectious agents are very common. *Mycoplasma* may be recovered from the endocervix of one third of sexually active adults. One group of investigators found that women with recurrent pregnancy loss have a significantly higher rate of endometrial colonization with *Ureaplasma urealyticum* compared with controls, raising the speculation that endometrial (but not endocervical) colonization with

Mycoplasma may play a role in recurrent pregnancy loss. Existing nonrandomized studies of the effects of antibiotic treatment on subsequent pregnancy outcome in women with endocervical *Mycoplasma* colonization have yielded conflicting results.

Currently, routine serologic or endocervical cultures for *Chlamydia* or *Mycoplasma* and vaginal evaluation for bacterial vaginosis are not useful in evaluating otherwise healthy women presenting with recurrent abortion. In addition, empiric treatment with antibiotics in the absence of documented infection is not warranted.

▶ *Should women with recurrent pregnancy loss be evaluated for antiphospholipid syndrome?*

Antiphospholipid syndrome is associated with pregnancy loss in 3–15% of women with recurrent pregnancy loss (33, 87–90). Some investigators have emphasized the relationship between APS and second- or early third-trimester fetal death (91), whereas others have found that a small percentage of women with recurrent first-trimester pregnancy loss have antiphospholipid antibodies (90). Women with a previous fetal death (33, 92) and high levels of anticardiolipin immunoglobulin G (IgG) antibodies (92) are at the greatest risk of fetal loss in subsequent pregnancies. Therefore, women with recurrent pregnancy loss should be tested for antiphospholipid syndrome using standard assays for anticardiolipin antibodies and lupus anticoagulant.

Antiphospholipid syndrome is identified in a woman with recurrent pregnancy loss by the detection of lupus anticoagulant, β_2-glycoprotein I–dependent anticardiolipin antibodies, or both on two occasions at least 6 weeks apart (31). The IgG isotype of anticardiolipin is most relevant clinically, but tests repeatedly positive for IgM anticardiolipin may be used to make the diagnosis. In individuals demonstrating only anticardiolipin antibodies, definite APS is diagnosed when the antibody levels are repeatedly 20 units or greater. Repeatedly positive test results for anticardiolipin antibodies with levels of less than 20 units are of uncertain significance.

Women with APS benefit from treatment with heparin and low-dose aspirin during pregnancy. Two studies have shown that women with recurrent early pregnancy loss and positive test results for antiphospholipid antibodies benefit from treatment with low-dose aspirin and heparin. Successful pregnancy rates for these women are 70–75%, compared with less than 50% for the untreated patients (93, 94). These studies used heparin dosages in the range of 10,000–25,000 U/d, and neither study included women with a history of thrombosis or systemic lupus erythematosus.

▶ *Should women with recurrent pregnancy loss be evaluated for thrombophilias?*

The role of thrombophilia in recurrent pregnancy loss is a controversial subject of current research interest. Tests for factor V Leiden, the prothrombin G20210A mutation, or deficiencies of protein C, protein S, or antithrombin III should be considered in cases of otherwise unexplained fetal death in the second or third trimesters. However, the role of these heritable thrombophilias in recurrent early pregnancy loss is uncertain at present, and tests for these thrombophilias are not required as part of the evaluation. Whether antithrombotic treatment improves subsequent pregnancy outcomes in women with evidence of thrombophilia is uncertain.

▶ *Should women with recurrent pregnancy loss be evaluated for possible alloimmune causes?*

Results of tests for human leukocyte antigen types, maternal serum blocking factors, or maternal antileukocytic antibodies directed against the male partner's leukocytes have not been shown to predict subsequent pregnancy outcome. Therefore, testing is not recommended, and treatment is not warranted. Luteal phase biopsy to determine the status of NK-like cells is not recommended because of mixed results in the literature, the uncertainty of prognostic implications, and the lack of an effective treatment. Finally, in the absence of a proven effective treatment, tests for embryotoxic factor or determination of the percentage of circulating NK cells in women with recurrent pregnancy loss is not beneficial.

▶ *Is paternal lymphocyte immunization or intravenous immune globulin (IVIG) an effective treatment for recurrent pregnancy loss?*

The most widely used immunotherapeutic treatment regimen for women with unexplained recurrent loss involves immunizing the female partner with the male partner's leukocytes. Of several randomized, prospective studies (53, 54, 95), only one found a benefit to leukocyte immunization (96). The largest trial, and the only multicenter effort, found that women undergoing leukocyte immunization actually had a higher rate of pregnancy loss than placebo controls (55), suggesting that the treatment may be harmful. In addition, there is no consensus regarding patient selection or the dose, route, or timing of leukocyte immunization, and immunization using viable leukocytes carries risks similar to those of blood transfusion, including the transmission of viral diseases.

The second immunomodulatory therapy used as a treatment for recurrent pregnancy loss is IVIG (97). Initial interest in this therapy derives from the observation that IVIG contains antibodies that block antibody-mediated immune damage (98). Other known immunomodulating effects of IVIG include T cell receptor blockade, inhibition of NK-cell activity, inhibition of Th-1 cytokine secretion, Fc receptor blockade, complement inactivation, down-regulation of B cell responsiveness, and enhanced T cell suppressor cell function (99). However, only one of five randomized trials using IVIG treatment in women with recurrent pregnancy loss demonstrated a benefit (52); results of the others were negative (100–103). In addition, the results of two meta-analyses also were negative (104, 105).

Summary

The following recommendations are based on good and consistent scientific evidence (Level A):

▶ Women with recurrent pregnancy loss should be tested for lupus anticoagulant and anticardiolipin antibodies using standard assays. If test results are positive for the same antibody on two consecutive occasions 6–8 weeks apart, the patient should be treated with heparin and low-dose aspirin during her next pregnancy attempt.

▶ Mononuclear cell (leukocyte) immunization and IVIG are not effective in preventing recurrent pregnancy loss.

The following recommendations are based on limited or inconsistent scientific evidence (Level B):

▶ An association between the luteal phase defect and recurrent pregnancy loss is controversial. If a diagnosis of luteal phase defect is sought in a woman with recurrent pregnancy loss, it should be confirmed by endometrial biopsy.

▶ Luteal phase support with progesterone is of unproven efficacy.

The following recommendations are based primarily on consensus and expert opinion (Level C):

▶ Couples with recurrent pregnancy loss should be tested for parental balanced chromosome abnormalities.

▶ Women with recurrent pregnancy loss and a uterine septum should undergo hysteroscopic evaluation and resection.

▶ Cultures for bacteria or viruses and tests for glucose intolerance, thyroid abnormalities, antibodies to infectious agents, antinuclear antibodies, antithyroid antibodies, paternal human leukocyte antigen status, or maternal antipaternal antibodies are not beneficial and, therefore, are not recommended in the evaluation of otherwise normal women with recurrent pregnancy loss.

▶ Couples with otherwise unexplained recurrent pregnancy loss should be counseled regarding the potential for successful pregnancy without treatment.

References

1. Stirrat GM. Recurrent miscarriage. I: definition and epidemiology. Lancet 1990;336:673–675 (Level III)

2. Lanasa MC, Hogge WA, Kubic C, Blancato J, Hoffman EP. Highly skewed X-chromosome inactivation is associated with idiopathic recurrent spontaneous abortion. Am J Hum Genet 1999;65:252–254 (Level II-2)

3. Hassold TJ. A cytogenetic study of repeated spontaneous abortions. Am J Hum Genet 1980;32:723–730 (Level II-3)

4. Warburton D, Kline J, Stein Z, Hutzler M, Chin A, Hassold T. Does the karyotype of a spontaneous abortion predict the karyotype of a subsequent abortion? Evidence from 273 women with two karyotyped spontaneous abortions. Am J Hum Genet 1987;41:465–483 (Level II-3)

5. Stern JJ, Dorfmann AD, Gutierrez-Najar AJ, Cerrillo M, Coulam CB. Frequency of abnormal karyotypes among abortuses from women with and without a history of recurrent spontaneous abortion. Fertil Steril 1996;65:250–253 (Level II-2)

6. Daniely M, Aviram-Goldring A, Barkai G, Goldman B. Detection of chromosomal aberration in fetuses arising from recurrent spontaneous abortion by comparative genomic hybridization. Hum Reprod 1998;13:805–809 (Level II-3)

7. Vidal F, Gimenez C, Rubrio C, Simon C, Pellicer A, Santalo J, et al. FISH preimplantation diagnosis of chromosome aneuploidy in recurrent pregnancy wastage. J Assist Reprod Genet 1998;15:310–313 (Level III)

8. Simon C, Rubio C, Vidal F, Gimenez C, Moreno C, Parrilla JJ, et al. Increased chromosome abnormalities in human preimplantation embryos after in-vitro fertilization in patients with recurrent miscarriage. Reprod Fertil Dev 1998;10:87–92 (Level III)

9. Davis OK, Berkeley AS, Naus GJ, Cholst IN, Freedman KS. The incidence of luteal phase defect in normal, fertile women determined by serial endometrial biopsies. Fertil Steril 1989;51:582–586 (Level III)

10. Tulppala M, Stenman UH, Cacciatore B, Ylikorkala O. Polycystic ovaries and levels of gonadotropins and androgens in recurrent miscarriage: prospective study in 50 women. Br J Obstet Gynaecol 1993;100:348–352 (Level II-2)

11. Clifford K, Rai R, Watson H, Regan L. An informative protocol for the investigation of recurrent miscarriage: preliminary experience of 500 consecutive cases. Hum Reprod 1994;9:1328–1332 (Level III)

12. Liddell HS, Sowden K, Farquhar CM. Recurrent miscarriage: screening for polycystic ovaries and subsequent pregnancy outcome. Aust N Z J Obstet Gynaecol 1997; 37:402–406 (Level II-2)

13. Rai R, Backos M, Rushworth F, Regan L. Polycystic ovaries and recurrent miscarriage—a reappraisal. Hum Reprod 2000:15;612–615 (Level II-2)

14. Dorman JS, Burke JP, McCarthy BJ, Norris JM, Steenkiste AR, Aarons JH, et al. Temporal trends in spontaneous abortion associated with Type 1 diabetes. Diabetes Res Clin Pract 1999;43:41–47 (Level II-3)

15. Jurkovic D, Geipel A, Gruboeck K, Jauniaux E, Natucci M, Campbell S. Three-dimensional ultrasound for the assessment of uterine anatomy and detection of congenital anomalies: a comparison with hysterosalpingography and two-dimensional sonography. Ultrasound Obstet Gynecol 1995;5:233–237 (Level II-3)

16. Jurkovic D, Gruboeck K, Tailor A, Nicolaides KH. Ultrasound screening for congenital uterine anomalies. Br J Obstet Gynaecol 1997;104:1320–1321 (Level II-3)

17. Maneschi F, Zupi E, Marconi D, Valli E, Romanini C, Mancuso S. Hysteroscopically detected asymptomatic mullerian anomalies. Prevalence and reproductive implications. J Reprod Med 1995;40:684–688 (Level II-2)

18. Sorensen SS, Trauelsen AG. Obstetric implications of minor mullerian anomalies in oligomenorrheic women. Am J Obstet Gynecol 1987;156:1112–1118 (Level II-2)

19. Fedele L, Dorta M, Brioschi D, Guidici MN, Candiani GB. Pregnancies in septate uteri: outcome in relation to site of uterine implantation as determined by sonography. AJR Am J Roentgenol 1989;152:781–784 (Level III)

20. Dabirashrafi H, Bahadori M, Mohammad K, Alavi M, Moghadami-Tabrizi N, Zandinejad K, et al. Septate uterus: new idea on the histologic features of the septum in this abnormal uterus. Am J Obstet Gynecol 1995;172:105–107 (Level II-3)

21. Sharara FI, Seifer DB, Flaws JA. Environmental toxicants and female reproduction. Fertil Steril 1998;70:613–622 (Level III)

22. Rai R, Regan L, Hadley E, Dave M, Cohen H. Second-trimester pregnancy loss is associated with activated C resistance. Br J Haematol 1996;92:489–490 (Level II-2)

23. Brenner B, Mandel H, Lanir N, Younis J, Rothbart H, Ohel G, et al. Activated protein C resistance can be associated with recurrent fetal loss. Br J Haematol 1997;97:551–554 (Level II-2)

24. Ridker PM, Miletich JP, Buring JE, Ariyo AA, Prince DT, Manson JE, et al. Factor V Leiden mutation and risks of recurrent pregnancy loss. Ann Intern Med 1998;128: 1000–1003 (Level II-2)

25. Foka ZJ, Lambropoulos AF, Saravelos H, Karas GB, Karavida A, Agorastos T, et al. Factor V Leiden and pro-thrombin G20210A mutations, but not methylenetetrahy-drofolate reductase C677T, are associated with recurrent miscarriages. Hum Reprod 2000;15:459–462 (Level II-2)

26. Balasch J, Reverter JC, Fabregues F, Tassies D, Rafel M, Creus M, et al. First-trimester repeated abortion is not associated with activated protein C resistance. Hum Reprod 1997;12:1094–1097 (Level II-2)

27. Dizon-Townson DS, Meline L, Nelson LM, Varner M, Ward K. Fetal carriers of the factor V Leiden mutation are prone to miscarriage and placental infarction. Am J Obstet Gynecol 1997;177:402–405 (Level II-2)

28. Kutteh WH. Report from the Society for Gynecologic Investigation, Atlanta, Georgia, March 11-14, 1998. J Reprod Immunol 1998;40:175–182 (Level III)

29. Pauer HU, Neesen J, Hinney B. Factor V Leiden and its relevance in patients with recurrent abortions. Am J Obstet Gynecol 1998;178:629 (Level III)

30. Preston FE, Rosendaal FR, Walker ID, Briët E, Berntorp E, Conard J, et al. Increased fetal loss in women with heritable thrombophilia. Lancet 1996;348:913–916 (Level II-2)

31. Wilson R, Ling H, MacLean MA, Mooney J, Kinnane D, McKillop JH, et al. Thyroid antibody titer and avidity in patients with recurrent miscarriage. Fertil Steril 1999;71: 558–561 (Level II-3)

32. Yetman DL, Kutteh WH. Antiphospholipid antibody panels and recurrent pregnancy loss: prevalence of anticardiolipin antibodies compared with other antiphospholipid antibodies. Fertil Steril 1996;66:540–546 (Level II-2)

33. Branch DW, Silver R, Pierangeli S, van Leeuwen I, Harris EN. Antiphospholipid antibodies other than lupus anticoagulant and anticardiolipin antibodies in women with recurrent pregnancy loss, fertile controls, and antiphospholipid syndrome. Obstet Gynecol 1997;89:549–555 (Level II-2)

34. Bertolaccini ML, Roch B, Amengual O, Atsumi T, Khamashta MA, Hughes GR. Multiple antiphospholipid tests do not increase the diagnostic yield in antiphospholipid syndrome. Br J Rheumatol 1998;37:1229–1232 (Level II-2)

35. Stagnaro-Green A, Roman SH, Colin RH, el-Harazy E, Alvarez-Marfany M, Davies TF, et al. Detection of at-risk pregnancy by means of highly sensitive assays for thyroid autoantibodies. JAMA 1990;264:1422–1425 (Level II-2)

36. Lejeune B, Grun JP, de Nayer P, Servais G, Glinoer D. Antithyroid antibodies underlying thyroid abnormalities and miscarriage or pregnancy induced hypertension. Br J Obstet Gynaecol 1983;100:669–672 (Level II-2)

37. Harger JH, Archer DF, Marchese SG, Muracca-Clemens M, Garver KL. Etiology of recurrent pregnancy losses and outcome of subsequent pregnancies. Obstet Gynecol 1983;6:574–581 (Level II-3)

38. Ogasawara M, Kajiura S, Katano K, Aoyama T, Aoki K. Are serum progesterone levels predictive of recurrent miscarriage in future pregnancies? Fertil Steril 1997;68: 806–809 (Level II-3)

39. Laskin CA, Bombardier C, Hannah ME, Mandel FP, Ritchie JW, Farewell V, et al. Prednisone and aspirin in

women with autoantibodies and unexplained recurrent fetal loss. N Engl J Med 1997;337:148–153 (Level I)

40. Coulam CB. Immunologic tests in the evaluation of reproductive disorders: a critical review. Am J Obstet Gynecol 1992;167:1844–1851 (Level II-2)

41. Cowchock FS, Reece EA, Balaban D, Branch DW, Plouffe L. Repeated fetal losses associated with antiphospholipid antibodies: a collaborative randomized trial comparing prednisone with low-dose heparin treatment. Am J Obstet Gynecol 1992;166:1318–1323 (Level I)

42. Hill JA, Polgar K, Harlow BL, Anderson DJ. Evidence of embryo- and trophoblast-toxic cellular immune response(s) in women with recurrent spontaneous abortion. Am J Obstet Gynecol 1992;166:1044–1052 (Level II-2)

43. Hill JA, Polgar K, Anderson DJ. T-helper 1-type immunity to trophoblast in women with recurrent spontaneous abortion. JAMA 1995;273:1933–1936 (Level II-2)

44. Ecker JL, Laufer MR, Hill JA. Measurement of embryotoxic factors is predictive of pregnancy outcome in women with a history of recurrent spontaneous abortion. Obstet Gynecol 1993;81:84–87 (Level II-3)

45. Clark DA, Vince G, Flanders KC, Hirte H, Starkey P. CD56+ lymphoid cells in human first trimester pregnancy decidua as a source of novel transforming growth factor-beta 2-related immunosuppressive factors. Hum Reprod 1994;9:2270–2277 [erratum Hum Reprod 1994;9:2270–2277] (Level III)

46. Lachapelle MH, Miron P, Hemmings R, Roy DC. Endometrial T, B and NK cells in patients with recurrent spontaneous abortion: altered profile and pregnancy outcome. J Immunol 1996;256:4027–4034 (Level II-2)

47. Clifford K, Flanagan AM, Regan L. Endometrial CD56+ natural killer cells in women with recurrent miscarriage: a histomorphometric study. Hum Reprod 1999;14:2727–2730 (Level II-2)

48. Quenby S, Bates M, Doig T, Brewster J, Lewis-Jones DI, Johnson PM, et al. Pre-implantation endometrial leukocytes in women with recurrent miscarriage. Hum Reprod 1999;14:2386–2391 (Level II-2)

49. Hewitt MJ, Pratten MK, Regan L, Quenby SM, Baker PN. The use of whole rat embryo culture as a technique for investigating potential serum toxicity in recurrent miscarriage patients. Hum Reprod 2000;15:2200–2204 (Level II-2)

50. Coulam CB, Goodman C, Roussev RG, Thomason EJ, Beaman KD. Systemic CD56+ cells can predict pregnancy outcome. Am J Reprod Immunol 1995;33:40–46 (Level II-3)

51. Aoki K, Kajiura S, Metsumoto Y, Ogasawara M, Okada S, Yagami Y, et at. Preconceptual natural-killer-cell activity as a predictor of miscarriage. Lancet 1995;345:1340–1342 (Level II-2)

52. Coulam CB, Krysa L, Stern JJ, Bustillo M. Intravenous immunoglobulin for treatment of recurrent pregnancy loss. Am J Reprod Immunol 1995;34:333–337 (Level I)

53. Ho HN, Gill TJ 3rd, Hsieh HJ, Jiang JJ, Lee TY, Hsieh CY. Immunotherapy for recurrent spontaneous abortion in a Chinese population. Am J Reprod Immunol 1991;25:10–15 (Level I)

54. Cauchi MN, Lim D, Young DE, Kloss M, Pepperell RJ. Treatment of recurrent aborters by immunization with paternal cells—controlled trials. Am J Reprod Immunol 1991;25:16–17 (Level I)

55. Ober C, Karrison T, Odem RR, Barnes RB, Branch DW, Stephenson MD, et al. Mononuclear-cell immunisation in prevention of recurrent miscarriages: a randomised trial. Lancet 1999;354:365–369 (Level I)

56. Jeng GT, Scott JR, Burmeister LF. A comparison of meta-analytic results using literature vs. individual patient data. Paternal cell immunization for recurrent miscarriage. JAMA 1995;274:830–836 (Meta-analysis)

57. Stevenson AC, Dudgeon MY, McClure H. Observations on the results of pregnancies in women resident in Belfast. II. Abortions, hydatidiform moles and ectopic pregnancies. Ann Hum Genet 1959;23:395–414 (Level II-3)

58. Warburton D, Fraser FC. Spontaneous abortion risks in man: data from reproductive histories collected in a medical genetics unit. Am J Hum Genet 1964;16:1–25 (Level II-3)

59. Leridon H. Facts and artifacts in the study of intra uterine mortality: a reconsideration from pregnancy histories. Popul Stud 1976;30:319–335 (Level III)

60. Poland BJ, Miller JR, Jones DC, Trimble BK. Reproductive counseling in patients who have had a spontaneous abortion. Am J Obstet Gynecol 1977;127:685–691 (Level II-3)

61. Naylor AF, Warburton D. Sequential analysis of spontaneous abortion. II. Collaborative study data show that gravidity determines a very substantial increase in risk. Fertil Steril 1979;31:282–286 (Level II-3)

62. Shapiro S, Levine HS, Abramivicz M. Factors associated with early and late fetal loss. Adv Plan Parenthood 1970; VI:45–63 (Level III)

63. Awan AK. Some biologic correlates of pregnancy wastage. Am J Obstet Gynecol 1974;119:525–532 (Level III)

64. Boue J, Bou A, Lazer P. Retrospective and prospective epidemiological studies of 1,500 karyotyped spontaneous human abortions. Teratology 1975;12:11–26 (Level II-3)

65. FitzSimmons J, Jackson D, Wapner R, Jackson L. Subsequent reproductive outcome in couples with repeated pregnancy loss. Am J Med Genet 1983;16:583–587 (Level II-3)

66. Regan L. A prospective study of spontaneous abortion. In: Beard RW, Sharp F, eds. Early pregnancy loss: mechanisms and treatment. London: Springer–Verlag, 1988: 23–37 (Level II-2)

67. Clifford K, Rai R, Regan L. Future pregnancy outcome in unexplained recurrent first trimester miscarriage. Hum Reprod 1997;12:387–389 (Level II-2)

68. Quenby S, Farquharson RG. Human chorionic gonadotropin supplementation in recurrent pregnancy loss: a controlled trial. Fertil Steril 1994;62:708–710 (Level I)

69. Roman EA, Alberman E, Pharoah PO. Pregnancy order and fetal loss. Br Med J 1980;280(6215):715 (Level III)

70. Simpson JL, Martin AO. Prenatal diagnosis of cytogenetic disorders. Clin Obstet Gynecol 1976;19:841–853 (Level III)

71. Royal College of Obstetrians and Gynaecologists. The management of recurrent miscarriage. RCOG Guideline 17. London: RCOG, 1998 (Level III)

72. March CM, Israel R. Hysteroscopic management of recurrent abortion caused by septate uterus. Am J Obstet Gynecol 1987;156:834–842 (Level II-3)

73. Scott RT, Snyder RR, Strickland DM, Tyburski CC, Bagnall JA, Reed KR, et al. The effect of interobserver variation in dating endometrial histology on the diagnosis of luteal phase defects. Fertil Steril 1988;50:888–892 (Level II-3)

74. Daya S. Efficacy of progesterone support for pregnancy in women with recurrent miscarriage. A meta-analysis of controlled trials. Br J Obstet Gynaecol 1989;96:275–280 (Meta-analysis)

75. Scott RT, Snyder RR, Bagnall JW, Reed KD, Adair CF, Hensley SD. Evaluation of the impact of intraobserver variability on endometrial dating and the diagnosis of luteal phase defects. Fertil Steril 1993;60:652–657 (Level II-3)

76. Goldstein P, Berrier J, Rosen S, Sacks HS, Chalmers TC. A meta-analysis of randomized control trials of progestational agents in pregnancy. Br J Obstet Gynaecol 1989; 96:265–274 (Meta-analysis)

77. Clifford K, Rai R, Watson H, Franks S, Regan L. Does suppressing luteinising hormone secretion reduce the miscarriage rate? Results of a randomised controlled trial. BMJ 1996;312:1508–1511 (Level I)

78. Levine L. Habitual abortion. A controlled study of progestational therapy. West J Surg 1964;72:30–36 (Level II-1)

79. Harrison RF. Human chorionic gonadotropin (hCG) in the management of recurrent abortion; results of a multi-centre placebo-controlled study. Eur J Obstet Gynecol Reprod Biol 1992;47:175–179 (Level I)

80. Kutteh WH, Yetman DL, Carr AC, Beck LA, Scott RT Jr. Increased prevalence of antithyroid antibodies identified in women with recurrent pregnancy loss but not in women undergoing assisted reproduction. Fertil Steril 1999;71: 843–848 (Level II-3)

81. Pratt D, Novotny M, Kaberlein G, Dudkiewicz A, Gleicher N. Antithyroid antibodies and the association with nonspecific antibodies in recurrent pregnancy loss. Am J Obstet Gynecol 1993;168:837–841 (Level II-2)

82. Esplin MS, Branch DW, Silver R, Stagnaro-Green A. Thyroid autoantibodies are not associated with recurrent pregnancy loss. Am J Obstet Gynecol 1998;179: 1583–1586 (Level II-2)

83. Rushworth FH, Backos M, Rai R, Chilcott IT, Baxter N, Regan L. Prospective pregnancy outcome in untreated recurrent miscarriers with thyroid autoantibodies. Hum Reprod 2000;15:1637–1639 (Level II-3)

84. Kurki T, Sivonen A, Renkonen OV, Savia E, Ylikorkala O. Bacterial vaginosis in early pregnancy and pregnancy outcome. Obstet Gynecol 1992;80:173–177 (Level II-2)

85. Hay PE, Lamont RF, Taylor-Robinson D, Morgan DJ, Ison C, Pearson J. Abnormal bacterial colonisation of the genital tract and subsequent preterm delivery and late miscarriage. BMJ 1994;308:295–298 (Level II-2)

86. Ralph SG, Rutherford AJ, Wilson JD. Influence of bacterial vaginosis on conception and miscarriage in the first trimester: cohort study. BMJ 1999;319:220–223 (Level II-2)

87. Out HJ, Kooijman CD, Bruinse HW, Derksen RH. Histopathological findings in placentae from patients with intra-uterine fetal death and anti-phospholipid antibodies. Eur J Obstet Gynecol Reprod Biol 1991;41:179–186 (Level II-2)

88. Parazzini F, Acaia B, Faden D, Lovotti M, Marelli G, Cortelazzo S. Antiphospholipid antibodies and recurrent abortion. Obstet Gynecol 1991;77:854–858 (Level II-2)

89. Parke AL, Wilson D, Maier D. The prevalence of antiphospholipid antibodies in women with recurrent spontaneous abortion, women with successful pregnancies, and women who have never been pregnant. Arthritis Rheum 1991;34: 1231–1235 (Level II-2)

90. Rai RS, Regan L, Clifford K, Pickering W, Dave M, Mackie I, et al. Antiphospholipid antibodies and beta 2-glycoprotein-I in 500 women with recurrent miscarriage: results of a comprehensive screening approach. Hum Reprod 1995;10:2001–2005 (Level II-3)

91. Oshiro BT, Silver RM, Scott JR, Yu H, Branch DW. Antiphospholipid antibodies and fetal death. Obstet Gynecol 1996;87:489–493 (Level II-2)

92. Lockshin MD, Druzin ML, Goei S, Quamar T, Magid MS, Jovanovic L, et al. Antibody to cardiolipin as a predictor of fetal distress or death in pregnant patients with systemic lupus erythematosus. N Engl J Med 1985;313:152–156 (Level II-2)

93. Kutteh WH. Antiphospholipid antibody-associated recurrent pregnancy loss: treatment with heparin and low-dose aspirin is superior to low-dose aspirin alone. Am J Obstet Gynecol 1996;174:1584–1589 (Level I)

94. Rai R, Cohen H, Dave M, Regan L. Randomized controlled trial of aspirin and aspirin plus heparin in pregnant women with recurrent miscarriage associated with phospholipid antibodies (or antiphospholipid antibodies). BMJ 1997;314:253–257 (Level I)

95. Gatenby PA, Cameron K, Simes RJ, Adelstein S, Bennett MJ, Jansen RP, et al. Treatment of recurrent spontaneous abortion by immunization with paternal lymphocytes: results of a controlled trial. Am J Reprod Immunol 1993;29:88–94 (Meta-analysis)

96. Mowbray JF, Gibbings C, Liddell H, Reginald PW, Underwood JL, Beard RW. Controlled trial of treatment of recurrent spontaneous abortion by immunisation with paternal cells. Lancet 1985;1(8435):941–943 (Level I)

97. American Society for Reproductive Medicine. Intravenous immunoglobulin (IVIG) and recurrent spontaneous pregnancy loss. ASRM Practice Committee Report. Birmingham, Alabama: ASRM, 1998 (Level III)

98. Brand A, Witvliet M, Claas FH, Eernisse JG. Beneficial effect of intravenous gammaglobulin in a patient with complement-mediated autoimmune thrombocytopenia due to IgM-anti-platelet antibodies. Br J Haematol 1988;69: 507–511 (Level III)

99. Dwyer JM, Johnson C. The regulation of T cell responses by spontaneously active suppressor cells. Clin Exp Immunol 1982;50:406–415 (Level II-2)

100. Intravenous immunoglobulin in the prevention of recurrent miscarriage. The German RSA/IVIG Group. Br J Obstet Gynaecol 1994;101:1072–1077 (Level I)

101. Christiansen OB, Mathiesen O, Husth M, Rasmussen KL, Ingerslev HJ, Lauritsen JG, et al. Placebo-controlled trial of treatment of unexplained secondary recurrent spontaneous abortions and recurrent late spontaneous abortions with IVF immunoglobulin. Hum Reprod 1995;10: 2690–2695 (Level I)

102. Stephenson MD, Dreher K, Houlihan E, Wu V. Prevention of unexplained recurrent spontaneous abortion using intravenous immunoglobulin: a prospective, randomized, double-blinded, placebo-controlled trial. Am J Reprod Immunol 1998;39:82–88 (Level I)

103. Perino A, Vassiliadis A, Vucetich A, Colacurci N, Menato G, Cignitti M, et al. Short-term therapy for recurrent abortion using intravenous immunoglobulins: results of a double-blind placebo-controlled Italian study. Hum Reprod 1997;12:2388–2392 (Level I)

104. Daya S, Gunby J, Clark DA. Intravenous immunoglobulin therapy for recurrent spontaneous abortion: a meta-analysis. Am J Reprod Immunol 1998;39:69–76 (Meta-analysis)

105. Daya S, Gunby J, Porter F, Scott J, Clark DA. Critical analysis of intravenous immunoglobulin therapy for recurrent miscarriage. Hum Reprod Update 1999;5:475–482 (Meta-analysis)

The MEDLINE database, the Cochrane Library, and ACOG's own internal resources and documents were used to conduct a literature search to locate relevant articles published between January 1985 and October 2000. The search was restricted to articles published in the English language. Priority was given to articles reporting results of original research, although review articles and commentaries also were consulted. Abstracts of research presented at symposia and scientific conferences were not considered adequate for inclusion in this document. Guidelines published by organizations or institutions such as the National Institutes of Health and the American College of Obstetricians and Gynecologists were reviewed, and additional studies were located by reviewing bibliographies of identified articles. When reliable research was not available, expert opinions from obstetrician–gynecologists were used.

Studies were reviewed and evaluated for quality according to the method outlined by the U.S. Preventive Services Task Force:

I   Evidence obtained from at least one properly designed randomized controlled trial.

II-1 Evidence obtained from well-designed controlled trials without randomization.

II-2 Evidence obtained from well-designed cohort or case–control analytic studies, preferably from more than one center or research group.

II-3 Evidence obtained from multiple time series with or without the intervention. Dramatic results in uncontrolled experiments also could be regarded as this type of evidence.

III Opinions of respected authorities, based on clinical experience, descriptive studies, or reports of expert committees.

Based on the highest level of evidence found in the data, recommendations are provided and graded according to the following categories:

Level A—Recommendations are based on good and consistent scientific evidence.

Level B—Recommendations are based on limited or inconsistent scientific evidence.

Level C—Recommendations are based primarily on consensus and expert opinion.

ISSN 1099-3630

The American College of Obstetricians and Gynecologists
409 12th Street, SW, PO Box 96920
Washington, DC 20090-6920

12345/54321

ACOG PRACTICE BULLETIN

CLINICAL MANAGEMENT GUIDELINES FOR
OBSTETRICIAN–GYNECOLOGISTS

NUMBER 26, APRIL 2001

This Practice Bulletin was developed by the ACOG Committee on Practice Bulletins—Gynecology with the assistance of Mitchell D. Creinin, MD. The information is designed to aid practitioners in making decisions about appropriate obstetric and gynecologic care. These guidelines should not be construed as dictating an exclusive course of treatment or procedure. Variations in practice may be warranted based on the needs of the individual patient, resources, and limitations unique to the institution or type of practice.

Medical Management of Abortion

According to the U.S. Centers for Disease Control and Prevention, 1.18 million legal abortions were performed in the United States in 1997. Of these, 55.5% were performed at or before 56 days of gestation (calculated from the first day of the last menstrual period [LMP]) (1). Almost 98% of abortion procedures were performed by uterine curettage; all but 1% of these used suction curettage. There were 305 legal induced abortions per 1,000 live births, and the abortion rate was 20 per 1,000 women aged 15–44 years.

For the first time in 1997, medical abortions were counted and comprised 0.25% of all abortions; 0.45% of those procedures were performed up to 56 days of gestation. Because of the lack of availability of mifepristone, these procedures mostly represent the use of a combination of methotrexate and misoprostol. Over the past two decades, medical methods of abortion have developed throughout the world and are now used clinically in the United States. This document will present evidence of effectiveness, benefits, and risks of medical methods of abortion and provide a framework for the evaluation and counseling of women who are considering such medical methods.

Background

Although the idea of using medications to induce a late menses or cause abortion dates back centuries, medically proven regimens have arisen only in the past 50 years. In 1950, the folic acid antagonist 4-aminopteroylglutamic acid (aminopterin) was used orally to induce medically indicated abortions in women at less than 3 months of gestation (2). Almost 20 years passed before further medical abortion research was published that used natural prostaglandins such as prostaglandin E_2 and prostaglandin $F_{2\alpha}$, either vaginally or transcervically, to effect early abortion (3). However, regimens that were highly effective also caused intolerable nausea, vomiting, diarrhea, fever, and pain, necessitating pretreatment with analgesic, sedative, antiemetic, and antidiarrheal medications. With the development of prostaglandin analogues in the mid-1970s and newer analogues (ie, methyl-$PGF_{2\alpha}$) in the 1980s, gastrointestinal side effects were less frequent but were still considered, at that time, to occur at rates that were unacceptable clinically (4, 5).

In the early 1980s, scientists at Roussel-Uclaf, under the direction of Étienne-Émile Baulieu, were investigating compounds that would block glucocorticoid receptors. They noted that some of the compounds bound strongly to the similarly shaped progesterone receptor and blocked the action of progesterone. Further development led to the production of RU-486 (mifepristone), which began clinical testing in 1982. It was found that in gestations up to 49 days, complete abortion occurred in almost 80% of cases with dosages ranging from 50 mg to 400 mg daily in single or divided doses over 1–4 days (6–11). In 1985, investigators reported that adding small doses of prostaglandin analogue increased the efficacy of mifepristone as an abortifacient to nearly 100% (8, 9). These prostaglandin analogue doses were lower than those required when using the prostaglandin analogue alone. Consequently, complete abortion was achieved with fewer side effects.

In 1988, France became the first country to license mifepristone for use in combination with a prostaglandin analogue for early abortion. In the United States, laboratory and clinical researchers studied mifepristone until 1989. At that time, mifepristone was listed as a "dangerous drug" by the government, prohibiting its import into the United States for clinical use. As a result, U.S. investigators turned to low-dose methotrexate as a potential alternative. In 1993, researchers began using low-dose methotrexate and misoprostol for early abortion (12). Investigations have shown that the overall efficacy of methotrexate–misoprostol regimens is in the same range as mifepristone (13). However, these regimens generally take longer to effect abortion than those using mifepristone and a prostaglandin analogue. With mifepristone–misoprostol regimens used at or before 49 days of gestation, the abortion rate within 24 hours after administering a single dose of misoprostol is approximately 90% (14); however, with methotrexate–misoprostol, the rate is only 50–70% (15–18). No studies have directly compared the efficacies, side effects, and complication rates of mifepristone and methotrexate abortifacient regimens.

Recent investigations of misoprostol without mifepris-tone or methotrexate pretreatment indicate efficacy; however, as with other regimens using only a prostaglandin analogue, side effects occur more frequently (19–23).

Medications Currently Used in Medical Abortion

Mifepristone

Mifepristone, a derivative of norethindrone, binds to the progesterone receptor with an affinity equal to proges-

terone; however, it does not activate the receptor and, thus, acts as an antiprogestin (24). During early pregnancy, mifepristone alters the decidua, resulting in trophoblast separation. As a result, secretion of human chorionic gonadotropin (hCG) into the maternal circulation decreases, and bleeding ensues. This decidual action also increases prostaglandin release in vitro (25) and in vivo (26). Mifepristone has no direct effect on the trophoblast (27). In addition, mifepristone softens the cervix to allow expulsion of the pregnancy from the uterus.

Other potential medical applications of mifepristone include emergency contraception; cervical ripening and labor induction; and treatment of symptomatic leiomyoma uteri, endometriosis, Cushing's syndrome, breast cancer, and glaucoma (28). However, further studies are required before mifepristone can be considered for clinical use in these or additional circumstances.

Methotrexate

Methotrexate blocks dihydrofolate reductase, an enzyme involved in producing thymidine during DNA synthesis. Methotrexate has been used for more than 40 years to treat neoplastic diseases, rheumatoid arthritis, and psoriasis. Other medical applications include treatment of systemic lupus erythematosus, dermatomyositis, severe asthma, Crohn's disease, extrauterine pregnancy, and early abortion.

Methotrexate exerts its action primarily on the cytotrophoblast rather than the developing embryo. This explains methotrexate's efficacy in treating extrauterine gestations (29), most of which are anembryonic. Methotrexate inhibits syncytialization of the cytotrophoblast (30). Thus, methotrexate stops the process of implantation rather than weakening the implantation site directly. In contrast, the antiprogestin mifepristone has no direct effect on the trophoblast.

Serum levels in pregnant women receiving methotrexate (50 mg/m^2 intramuscularly) do not approach toxic levels and are undetectable within 48 hours after administration (31). Oral dosing results in serum levels approximately 15% lower than serum levels after parenteral treatment, and oral doses exceeding 30 mg/m^2 are absorbed to the same extent as doses of 30 mg/m^2 (32, 33).

Misoprostol

Misoprostol is a relatively inexpensive prostaglandin E$_1$ analogue in a tablet form, approved by the U.S. Food and Drug Administration (FDA) for oral administration, and is stable at room temperature. Misoprostol is used clinically 1) for preventing gastric ulcers in persons taking antiinflammatory drugs on a long-term basis, 2) in regimens for abortion, and 3) for cervical ripening for labor induction. Pharmacokinetic evaluation of oral and vaginal misoprostol demonstrates that oral misoprostol is absorbed more rapidly, resulting in a higher peak serum level (34).

Other Agents

Gemeprost was one of the initial prostaglandin analogues used with mifepristone in medical abortion regimens. Gemeprost, like misoprostol, is a prostaglandin E_1 analogue; however, it is available only as a vaginal suppository and requires refrigeration. Its lack of stability at room temperature is an important characteristic when considering use in developing countries. Gemeprost is still used in some parts of the world with mifepristone for early abortion and in regimens for second-trimester abortion.

Tamoxifen has been used in combination with misoprostol in some studies of early abortion. However, randomized trials have demonstrated no benefit of using tamoxifen over regimens for methotrexate–misoprostol (35) or misoprostol alone (23).

Treatment Regimens

Mifepristone Regimens

Mifepristone in combination with a prostaglandin analogue has been used for more than 10 years in France, Sweden, the United Kingdom, and China. The FDA-approved regimen includes mifepristone 600 mg, orally, followed approximately 48 hours later by misoprostol, 400 µg, orally. Efficacy with this regimen is approximately 96% for pregnancies up to 49 days of gestation (13). Complete abortion rates are higher with earlier gestations: approximately 96–98% when used up to 42 days of gestation (36, 37), 91–95% from 43 to 49 days of gestation (36, 37), and less than 85% beyond 49 days of gestation (36–38). Investigators have demonstrated that when abortion has not occurred within 3–4 hours after misoprostol administration, use of an additional dose does not improve efficacy (14, 36).

After receiving the prostaglandin analogue, the patient typically remains at the office or clinic for approximately 4 hours, during which time her activities are not restricted. If 4 hours pass without apparent expulsion of the pregnancy, the woman is examined before she leaves to determine whether abortion has occurred. A follow-up evaluation is scheduled 10–15 days later. If the woman had a confirmed abortion previously, a pelvic examination is done to ensure there are no complications. If clinical history and physical examination do not confirm expulsion, ultrasonography is performed. If complete abortion has not occurred, suction aspiration typically is performed.

Alternative regimens have been tested and shown to be equally effective. Regimens using lower doses of mifepristone (200 mg) have efficacy similar to those using 600 mg of mifepristone (39–42). Using 800 µg of misoprostol vaginally decreases the time to expulsion and results in fewer side effects (43). When using 800 µg of misoprostol vaginally, continuing pregnancy occurs in only 0.2–0.3% at or before 49 days of gestation, a rate lower than the 0.3–1.2% reported in studies using 600 mg of mifepristone followed by oral misoprostol (14, 36, 38). Although studies in the United States have demonstrated that a patient can safely and effectively self-administer the misoprostol (orally or vaginally) in her home (41, 42, 44), the FDA package labeling for mifepristone indicates the patient should return to her provider for the misoprostol.

Methotrexate Regimens

The combination of methotrexate and misoprostol is used for abortion in pregnancies of up to 49 days of gestation. Methotrexate is most commonly administered intramuscularly at a dose based on body surface area (50 mg/m^2), the same dose used for the management of ectopic pregnancy (29). Misoprostol (800 µg) vaginally is self-administered by the woman 3–7 days later at home using the same tablets that are used for oral dosing. A follow-up examination is performed at least 24 hours after misoprostol and is most commonly scheduled approximately 1 week after the methotrexate was administered. At this visit, a vaginal ultrasound examination should be performed to confirm passage of the gestational sac. If abortion has not occurred, the misoprostol dose is repeated. Further follow-up for women requiring a second dose of misoprostol is performed in 4 weeks except when embryonic cardiac activity was still visible on ultrasonography at the 1-week examination. These latter patients should return to the office in 1 week. If gestational cardiac activity is still present 2 weeks after initiating treatment or if expulsion has not occurred by the 4-week follow-up visit, suction aspiration is performed.

Complete abortion will occur in 92–96% of women receiving this regimen. Between 50 and 56 days of gestation, efficacy decreases to 82% (16). Although overall efficacy is equal to the standard regimen of mifepristone–misoprostol, approximately 15–20% of women taking regimens using methotrexate will need to wait up to 4 weeks after the misoprostol administration for abortion to occur (17, 45).

Regimens using 50 mg of methotrexate orally seem to be as effective as those using 50 mg/m^2 of methotrexate intramuscularly (17, 46, 47). Studies comparing 25-mg and 50-mg doses of methotrexate followed by vaginal misoprostol suggest that 25-mg regimens may be equally effective (17, 47). However, the only large study using 25 mg of methotrexate orally used a complex dosing regimen of misoprostol that also resulted in high rates of side effects (47).

A prospective randomized study demonstrated that, following methotrexate administration, the use of vaginally administered misoprostol moistened with water does not result in more rapid expulsion or greater overall efficacy than does dry misoprostol use in women of up to 49 days of gestation (45). It is possible that using moistened misoprostol improves efficacy between 50 and 56 days of gestation (47, 48).

Misoprostol Alone

Two independent investigators have demonstrated that 800 µg of misoprostol, vaginally, when moistened with water or saline, can result in complete abortion rates exceeding 90% in pregnancies up to 56 days of gestation (19–23). Studies with dry vaginal misoprostol demonstrate complete abortion rates of 50–67% (49–51). Studies showing that misoprostol alone is effective for abortion involve complex dosing regimens or require clinician application of the tablets. Additionally, this treatment results in significantly higher rates of side effects (nausea, vomiting, diarrhea, and fever and chills) than those using misoprostol after pretreatment with either mifepristone or methotrexate (19–23).

Counseling Patients

Medical Versus Surgical

Patient counseling must first stress early pregnancy options to be sure that a woman is certain about her decision to have an abortion. A medical abortion is not a means for easing the decision to have an abortion. If the patient is uncertain, then the decision about abortion technique must be delayed until she has reached a firm decision, even if the delay means that she will be unable to choose a medical option.

The general advantages and disadvantages of each approach (Table 1) should be explained early in the counseling process, because most women will have a clear preference (52, 53). Even for women who think they are unsure, most will have some preference after counseling (53).

Most women who choose medical abortion do so because of a desire to avoid surgery if at all possible (15, 52, 54–57). During a medical abortion, women must participate more actively and are more aware of bleeding and cramping than with surgical abortion. Additionally, the abortion process takes longer to complete than surgical abortion. Medical abortion may be available sooner in pregnancy than surgical abortion, because some facilities do not offer suction aspiration before 7 weeks of gestation. With medical abortion, expulsion of the pregnancy most likely will occur at home, but some women will still

Table 1. Features of Medical and Surgical Abortion

Medical Abortion	Surgical Abortion
Usually avoids invasive procedure	Involves invasive procedure
Usually avoids anesthesia	Allows use of sedation if desired
Requires two or more visits	Usually requires one visit
Days to weeks to complete	Complete in a predictable period
Available during early pregnancy	Available during early pregnancy
High success rate (~95%)	High success rate (99%)
Requires follow-up to ensure completion of abortion	Does not require follow-up in all cases
Requires patient participation throughout a multiple-step process	Requires participation in a single-step process

require surgical evacuation to complete the abortion. An early surgical abortion takes place most commonly in one visit and involves less waiting and less doubt about when the abortion occurs. In addition, the woman will not see any products of conception or blood clots during the procedure. Both medical and surgical methods have very low rates of complications.

Side Effects

Side effects from the various methods of medical abortion include bleeding and pain, nausea (12–47%), vomiting (9–45%), diarrhea (7–67%), warmth or chills (14–89%), headache (12–27%), dizziness (14–37%), and fatigue (Table 2) (16–18, 22, 23, 41, 44). Some side effects, such as bleeding and pain, are necessary for the medical abortion process to occur. Counseling should emphasize that the woman is likely to have bleeding that is much heavier than menses (and potentially with severe cramping) and is best described to patients as comparable to a miscarriage. The woman should understand how much bleeding is considered too much. The patient can be counseled that soaking of two pads per hour for 2 hours in a row (58) is not a point at which intervention is necessary, but is a time when it is good to check with the care provider. Whether it is imperative for the patient to seek emergency care at that point depends on how she is feeling, her baseline hemoglobin level, whether the bleeding seems to be slowing, and how far away she is from an emergency treatment provider.

Pain management, especially for the woman aborting at home, is important so that she feels in control of her situation. The woman should be sent home with appropriate instructions for analgesia with over-the-counter medications and prescriptions for oral narcotics to use when needed. The use of narcotic analgesics is more prevalent in the United States than in France. Using the standard mifepristone–misoprostol regimen, 81% of

Table 2. Side Effects in Selected U.S. Trials of Medical Abortion Regimens*

Side Effect	Percentage		
	Mifepristone	Methotrexate	Misoprostol
Nausea	36–45	19–47	12–43
Vomiting	13–14	9–12	8–45
Diarrhea	8–11	7–22	7–67
Headache	14–18	13–16	12–27
Dizziness	22–15	14	18–37
Thermoregulatory†	14–20	15–43	31–89

NR = not reported

*Studies are included only if the incidence of side effects were differentiated among the medications.

† Fever, warmth, hot flashes, or chills

Data from: Schaff EA, Stadalius LS, Eisinger SH, Franks P. Vaginal misoprostol administered at home after mifepristone (RU486) for abortion. J Fam Pract 1997;44:353–360; Schaff EA, Eisinger SH, Stadalius LS, Franks P, Gore BZ, Poppema S. Low-dose mifepristone 200 mg and vaginal misoprostol for abortion. Contraception 1999;59:1–6; Creinin MD, Vittinghoff E, Keder L, Darney PD, Tiller G. Methotrexate and misoprostol for early abortion: a multicenter trial. I. Safety and efficacy. Contraception 1996;53:321–327; Creinin MD, Vittinghoff E, Schaff E, Klaisle C, Darney PD, Dean C. Medical abortion with oral methotrexate and vaginal misoprostol. Obstet Gynecol 1997;90:611–616; Creinin MD. Medical abortion with methotrexate 75 mg intramuscularly and vaginal misoprostol. Contraception 1997;56:367–371; Jain JK, Meckstroth KR, Mishell DR Jr. Early pregnancy termination with intravaginally administered sodium chloride solution-moistened misoprostol tablets: historical comparison with mifepristone and oral misoprostol. Am J Obstet Gynecol 1999;181:1386–1391; and Jain JK, Meckstroth KR, Park M, Mishell DR Jr. A comparison of tamoxifen and misoprostol to misoprostol alone for early pregnancy termination. Contraception 2000;60:353–356

French women experienced cramping, and only 16% requested any pain medication, which consisted of a nonopiate analgesic (14). However, in the United States, 29% of women using the same regimen received a narcotic analgesic (38). Women in both of these trials were required to remain in the office for observation for 4 hours after taking misoprostol.

The incidence of each side effect will depend on the regimen (especially the prostaglandin analogue), the dose and route of administration of the prostaglandin analogue, and the gestational age. Gastrointestinal side effects are less common when dry misoprostol is administered vaginally than when oral misoprostol or moistened vaginal misoprostol is used. Oral ulcers resulting from use of methotrexate occur rarely in the reported literature.

Need for Follow-Up Dilation and Curettage

Complete abortion rates for methotrexate or mifepristone regimens generally range from 90% to 98% (13). A medical abortion "failure" occurs when a suction aspiration is performed for any reason, which includes when providers choose to intervene surgically, when women themselves request a surgical completion, and when true drug failures occur. With medical abortion, a true method failure has been defined as the presence of gestational cardiac activity on vaginal ultrasonography 2 weeks following either mifepristone or methotrexate administration. No studies have assessed the efficacy of additional doses of mifepristone, methotrexate, or misoprostol in these circumstances; however, given that the pregnancy would have advanced 2 weeks, it is unlikely that further medical treatment would be significantly effective. Continuing pregnancies are reported in less than 1% of women who begin treatment at or before 49 days of gestation regardless of regimen and should be terminated by surgical evacuation (12, 16, 17, 36, 38–40, 43, 44, 49, 59–62).

In most medical abortion research trials, the category of "incomplete abortion" includes women who have a persistent gestational sac on ultrasonography without evidence of embryonic cardiac activity or continuing development. Guidelines for intervention in this situation vary. Typically, protocols used in mifepristone studies consider a retained sac 2 weeks after the mifepristone is administered to be a reason for suction aspiration (36, 38, 40, 43, 63, 64). However, medical abortion studies using methotrexate and misoprostol demonstrate that intervention for a nonviable pregnancy is unnecessary and that expulsion will occur, on average, 22–29 days after the methotrexate is given (15–18, 49). Current recommendations with methotrexate regimens suggest waiting at least 29–45 days before recommending surgical evacuation (65) because 99% of expulsions occur by 36 days after the methotrexate is given (16). With this understanding, the most recent mifepristone studies performed in the United States allowed a period of approximately 36 days after mifepristone administration before recommending surgical intervention (41, 42)

Most commonly, women who have not aborted and are awaiting delayed expulsion will no longer feel pregnant or have medication-induced symptoms; the patient will be waiting for the onset of bleeding or cramping similar to anticipating the start of menses (16). Providers must differentiate this scenario from women who have incomplete expulsion of the pregnancy tissue, when symptoms can include prolonged and irregular bleeding episodes. Early trials of methotrexate and misoprostol use showed that serial evaluations of the beta subunit of human chorionic gonadotropin (β-hCG) did not aid in the diagnosis of incomplete abortion; all women with an incomplete abortion presented clinically and were not diagnosed by increasing or plateaued β-hCG levels (12, 49, 66).

When misoprostol is administered 2–5 days following methotrexate or mifepristone administration, β-hCG concentrations should decrease by at least 50% within a week of initiating the medication regimen. One study found that women who had a decrease in β-hCG concentrations of more than 50% between days 1 and 7 had a complete medical abortion (60). However, this study did not examine the predictive value of such testing. A retrospective analysis of women who participated in four separate methotrexate–misoprostol trials found that women with a complete abortion had an average decrease in β-hCG levels of 66% 24 hours after misoprostol was administered. All other subjects had an average decrease of 25% ($P = 0.0001$) (67). Thus, a patient whose serum β-hCG levels fail to decrease by a minimum of 50% over 24 hours is unlikely to have completely aborted.

Performing sensitive serum or urine hCG assays (detection threshold 25–50 mIU/mL) too soon after the termination of a pregnancy may result in an erroneous diagnosis of failed medical abortion. Two trials using methotrexate and misoprostol found that the average time for the disappearance of β-hCG was 33–34 days, but it can take as long as 90 days (49, 60). The utility of nonsensitive urine hCG assays in medical abortion follow-up warrants investigation.

Practitioners need to understand the difference between incomplete abortion and the normal course of medical abortion. Understanding this concept will require some clinicians to "retrain" themselves and change the way they have thought for years about the management of incomplete abortion. The sole purpose of ultrasound examination after misoprostol administration is to confirm that the gestational sac is no longer present. After expulsion, the uterus normally will contain sonographically hyperechoic tissue consisting of blood, blood clots, and decidua. Rarely does this finding during medical abortion indicate a need for intervention. In the absence of excessive bleeding, providers can follow such patients conservatively.

Very rarely do women who are having a medical abortion require an emergency dilation and curettage because of heavy bleeding. Overall, studies demonstrate that fewer than 1% of women will need emergent curettage because of appreciable bleeding (36, 40, 41, 64). Moreover, the risk of clinically significant bleeding and transfusion may be lower in women up to 49 days of gestation than those with more than 49 days (38); this relative risk will vary depending on the regimen used.

Nevertheless, physicians also must be able to provide surgical intervention in cases of incomplete abortion or severe bleeding, or have made plans to provide such care through others, and be able to assure patient access to medical facilities equipped to provide blood transfusions and resuscitation, if necessary (68). This is no different from requirements for patients who are primarily treated by surgical abortion. Clinicians other than obstetrician–gynecologists who wish to provide medical abortion services should work in conjunction with an obstetrician–gynecologist or be trained in surgical abortion in order to offer medical abortion treatment.

Postabortion Follow-Up

After initiating medical abortion treatment, follow-up is necessary to ensure complete abortion. Women as well as their practitioners often are unable to judge correctly if the women have aborted by evaluating symptomatology. In clinical trials with methotrexate and misoprostol, only about half of women who thought they had aborted actually had done so (16). Moreover, women may even experience symptom resolution consistent with a complete medical abortion and still have a persistent gestational sac (16) or even an ectopic pregnancy (41).

To date, clinical tracking of women choosing medical abortion has been diligent, primarily because these women have been participating in studies. To introduce these abortion methods into more widespread clinical practice requires continued emphasis on follow-up, because failure rates for medical abortion are higher than with surgical techniques, and both methotrexate and misoprostol are potentially teratogenic.

Clinical Considerations and Recommendations

▶ *Who are candidates for medical abortion?*

Women who are certain about their decision to have an abortion are candidates for medical abortion if they meet the gestational age criteria for the medications being used and if they have no medical or psychosocial contraindications to the medical abortion process. Medical contraindications to abortion with mifepristone regimens include confirmed or suspected ectopic pregnancy or undiagnosed adnexal mass, an intrauterine device in place, current long-term systemic corticosteroid therapy, chronic adrenal failure, severe anemia, known coagulopathy or anticoagulant therapy, and intolerance or allergy to mifepristone. Most clinical trials also excluded women with severe liver, renal, or respiratory disease; uncontrolled hypertension; cardiovascular disease (angina, valvular disease, arrhythmia, or cardiac failure); or severe anemia. A woman who has an intrauterine device in place and who wishes to have medical abortion must have the intrauterine device removed first.

Methotrexate regimens have not been tested in women with a hemoglobin level of less than 10 mg/dL, known coagulopathy, active liver disease (aspartate transaminase more than twice normal levels), active renal disease (creatinine level exceeding 1.5 mg/dL), acute inflammatory bowel disease, or an intolerance or allergy to methotrexate. Misoprostol should not be used in women who have an uncontrolled seizure disorder or an allergy or intolerance to misoprostol or other prostaglandins. Asthma is not a contraindication because misoprostol is a weak bronchodilator.

Although medical contraindications are infrequent, social or psychologic contraindications to medical abortion are more common. Women are not good candidates for medical abortion if they do not wish to take responsibility for their care, are anxious to have the abortion over quickly, cannot return for follow-up visits, or cannot understand the instructions because of language or comprehension barriers. Other nonmedical criteria to be considered are access to a phone in case of an emergency and distance from emergency medical treatment (such as suction curettage for hemorrhage).

▶ Which preoperative laboratory tests are needed?

Confirmation of pregnancy by ultrasonography or pregnancy testing is necessary before attempting abortion regardless of method. Preoperative assessment of hemoglobin or hematocrit levels and blood type is imperative. Tests of liver and kidney function are not indicated before the use of methotrexate unless the clinical history suggests abnormalities. Women who are Rh-negative are candidates for anti-D immune globulin administration, whether they opt for medical or surgical abortion.

▶ How does gestational age affect the choice of medical or surgical abortion?

The upper limit of gestational age at which a medical abortion regimen remains an option varies, depending on the types, dosages, and routes of administration of the medications. The complete abortion rate decreases with increasing gestational age; however, the relative efficacy of medical versus surgical abortion depends on these multiple medication factors.

Most women seeking early abortion will be eligible for both medical and surgical methods. Studies suggest that Scottish women were equally satisfied with medical abortion and surgical abortion at or before 49 days of gestation when the medical regimen was mifepristone and gemeprost (52). However, beyond 49 days of gestation, women were more satisfied with the surgical procedure. Among U.S. women at or before 49 days of gestation who indicated no preference, surgical abortion provided a better experience than medical abortion with methotrexate and misoprostol (53). The current applicability of the findings from both these studies is limited.

Acceptability is likely to be the driving force behind most patient decisions when all else is equal. The most common reason women choose medical abortion is a desire to avoid some aspect of a surgical procedure (15,

52, 54–57). As such, medical abortion acceptability studies will have positive results because the study participants were actively seeking an alternative to surgical abortion. Mifepristone regimens have been reported to be preferred for a next abortion in more than 70% of women who had a prior surgical abortion and by 80–96% of women overall (52, 54, 57, 69, 70). Experience with methotrexate regimens is virtually identical (15, 55, 60, 62, 71, 72).

▶ Does gestational age affect the choice and dosage of medications used for medical abortion?

Complete abortion rates with all medical abortion regimens are highest for earlier gestations and are clinically similar up to 49 days of gestation. After 49 days of gestation, certain regimens continue to provide high rates of complete abortion. Administration of vaginal misoprostol in regimens with mifepristone results in complete abortion in 96–97% of women (40–42), whereas regimens using oral misoprostol demonstrate significantly lower success rates at these later gestations. Similarly, misoprostol alone, when moistened and administered by a clinician using a speculum, results in complete abortion in approximately 90% of women through 56 days of gestation (22, 23). The same dose, with patient self-administration of dry tablets, results in complete abortion in only 50–58% (49, 73) of women. Two studies suggest that using moistened misoprostol tablets in regimens using methotrexate followed 3–7 days later by misoprostol 800 µg vaginally may improve efficacy between 50 and 56 days of gestation (47, 48). A prospective randomized trial demonstrated no improvement in immediate success or complete abortion rates when moistened misoprostol was used after administration of methotrexate in women up to 49 days of gestation (45).

▶ Should prophylactic antibiotics be used routinely in medical abortion?

Uterine infection is one of the most frequent complications reported after surgical abortion, noted in 0.1–4.7% of first-trimester procedures (74). However, endometritis is a rare complication of medical abortion because medical abortion usually involves no instrumentation of the cervix or uterine cavity. The majority of medical abortion studies report no infection, although a few mention isolated cases. In trials involving more than 500 participants, infection rates typically vary from 0.09% to 0.5% (38, 41, 42, 63, 75).

In a single study of 2,000 women in which 89% of participants returned for follow-up after abortion with mifepristone–misoprostol, researchers treated 5% of those who returned with antibiotics for presumed endometritis (40). Similarly, a recent nonconcurrent, comparative study of mifepristone (n=178) and surgical abortion (n=199) groups found an equivalent rate of antibiotic use for presumed postabortal endometritis (11% versus 12%, respectively) based mainly on the presence of lower abdominal pain (76).

Some authors recommend the universal use of prophylactic antibiotics for surgical abortion (77). However, no data exist to support such treatment with medical abortion.

▶ When is ultrasonography useful in the medical management of abortion?

During early pregnancy, transvaginal ultrasonography is the most accurate means of confirming intrauterine pregnancy and gestational age. A study of mifepristone abortion in China, Cuba, and India found that dating based on LMP closely correlated with estimates based on physical examination (70). However, two recently published studies report clinically significant discrepancies between gestational age based on LMP and that determined by ultrasonographic criteria in women receiving mifepristone and misoprostol for abortion (37, 78). The latter report included 222 women in Atlanta, of whom only 85% were able to predict gestational age within 2 weeks of the gestational age assigned by the clinician using ultrasound examination. Additionally, medical abortion studies in U.S. women using methotrexate and misoprostol show that the gestational age by LMP was confirmed for only 50–60% of study participants (79). Because efficacy for some regimens decreases significantly with increasing gestational age, the clinical relevance of erroneous gestational-age assignment will vary based on the regimen used.

Whereas all major U.S. trials of mifepristone or methotrexate have relied on transvaginal ultrasonography for dating and follow-up, the extensive French experience since 1989 used ultrasonography only about 30% of the time. In France, pregnancy termination services are offered only by authorized abortion clinics staffed by highly experienced providers. The clinicians use ultrasonography for preabortion screening when they find a discrepancy between uterine size and dating by LMP and when patients present with bleeding or symptoms suggestive of ectopic pregnancy. The high efficacy and safety results in the French trials suggest that this selective use of ultrasonography suffices when medical abortion is provided by experienced clinicians.

Transvaginal ultrasonography offers an efficient means of assessing outcome in medical abortion patients. Its primary objective is to determine whether the gestational sac is absent. Several alternatives to transvaginal ultrasonography exist for confirming termination of the pregnancy. If the protocol involves office administration of the misoprostol followed by an observation period, many patients will abort in the clinic setting. In this case, direct observation by inspection of the tissue suffices to confirm pregnancy expulsion. Other methods to verify abortion in other patients include checking for a history of bleeding combined with evidence of uterine involution on pelvic examination or hCG testing.

▶ Does analgesia affect the success rates for medical abortion?

Most studies using mifepristone and a prostaglandin analogue report the use of acetaminophen, paracetamol, or a narcotic for pain relief when indicated. However, cramping pain for nonabortion patients usually is treated with ibuprofen or other nonsteroidal antiinflammatory drugs (NSAIDs). Because these agents usually are thought to be "prostaglandin inhibitors," many researchers feel that their use would prevent the action of the prostaglandin analogue.

In fact, NSAIDs are prostaglandin synthetase inhibitors; thus, they do not block the action of prostaglandin but they do inhibit the synthesis of new prostaglandins. Therefore, such agents should not inhibit the action of a prostaglandin given for medical abortion. The only report to evaluate the effects of analgesics on abortion outcome was a retrospective analysis of NSAIDs and complete abortion in 416 women who received misoprostol after methotrexate administration for medical abortion up to 56 days of gestation (80). The complete abortion rate after a single dose of misoprostol was 54% in the women who used an NSAID for analgesia and 49% in those who used no medication or other medications ($P = 0.4$). The abortion rates after a repeat dose of misoprostol were 48% with an analgesic and 22% with no other medications ($P = 0.002$). Thus, the use of an NSAID correlated with a need for analgesia because the misoprostol was effecting abortion. It did not seem to interfere with the action of misoprostol to induce uterine contractions and pregnancy expulsion.

▶ How should a patient be counseled on potential teratogenicity if a medical method fails to lead to abortion? What further management should be recommended?

Teratogenicity of the medical abortifacients becomes an important issue if the pregnancy continues. There is no evidence to date of a teratogenic effect of mifepristone. Methotrexate, however, is an antimetabolite that can cause fetal anomalies when administered in the high doses used for chemotherapy or in doses exceeding conventional regimens (81, 82).

Evidence suggests that misoprostol can result in congenital anomalies when used during the first trimester, possibly due to mild uterine contractions resulting in decreased blood flow during organogenesis (83). Two types of anomalies associated with misoprostol have been described. Five cases of defects in the frontal or temporal bones were reported in infants born to women who had taken 400–600 μg of misoprostol orally or vaginally (84). More attention has been given to the association between misoprostol and limb abnormalities, both with and without Möbius' syndrome (masklike facies with bilateral sixth and seventh nerve palsy and frequently coincident micrognathia), in infants born to women who had taken 200–1,800 μg of misoprostol orally or vaginally between 4 and 12 weeks of gestation to attempt abortion (85). A case–control study from Brazil compared 96 infants with Möbius' syndrome matched with 96 infants with neural tube defects (86). Exposure to misoprostol during the first trimester occurred in 49% and 3%, respectively (odds ratio, 29.7; 95% confidence interval: 11.6–76.0). Of the women reporting misoprostol use, all but one used it to attempt abortion. One study reported six cases of limb reduction abnormalities in fetuses examined after failed abortion with methotrexate and misoprostol (62); most likely, these anomalies were similarly due to misoprostol. However, a recently published prospective analysis of 86 misoprostol-exposed infants and 86 unexposed infants found no significant difference in the rates of major or minor anomalies (87). The investigators did find a significantly increased risk of spontaneous abortion after misoprostol exposure (17% versus 6%, respectively; relative risk: 3.0, 95% confidence interval: 1.1–7.9). No conclusions regarding teratogenicity can be made from this analysis because of the extremely small sample size.

Because misoprostol is the common agent used with both mifepristone and methotrexate, the potential for teratogenicity is important for both types of medical abortion regimens. Providers must counsel women fully about the potential teratogenic effects of the drugs they will receive for medical abortion. In addition, patients must be informed of the need for a surgical abortion in the event of a continuing pregnancy.

▶ *When compared with surgical abortion, are there long-term risks to medical management of abortion? When compared with surgical abortion, does medical abortion affect future fertility?*

Long-term risks sometimes attributed to surgical abortion include potential effects on reproductive function, cancer incidence, and psychologic sequelae. However, the medical literature, when carefully evaluated, clearly demonstrates no significant negative impact on any of these factors with surgical abortion.

No studies have compared future fertility rates after medical and surgical abortion. Future fertility with medical abortion has only been evaluated within a 1-year period after medical abortion in a group of 93 women who received methotrexate and misoprostol for abortion (88). Although none of the women were actively attempting to achieve pregnancy, 25% became pregnant, a rate higher than the rate expected for this group of women using contraception. By comparison, another study reported a pregnancy rate of 13% within 1 year after a first surgical abortion (89).

▶ *Is medical abortion likely to be less expensive than surgical abortion?*

In general, the cost of an abortion will vary depending on location, patient demand, and the number of providers. For example, surgical abortion on the West coast is less expensive than on the East coast. However, cost in a private physician's office tends to be greater than in a clinic. The cost of a medical abortion will depend on the medications used, the personnel involved within an office, and the local laws regarding who can provide abortion services.

▶ *Are there adverse effects associated with repeated use of medical terminations of pregnancy?*

No well-designed prospective studies address the issue of repeat medical abortion. However, expert opinion suggests there currently is no pathophysiologic basis to believe that repeat medical abortion would have an untoward effect on fertility.

Summary

The following recommendations are based on good and consistent scientific evidence (Level A):

▶ Medical abortion should be considered an appropriate alternative to surgical abortion in selected, carefully counseled, and informed patients up to 49 days of gestation (as calculated from the first day of the LMP).

▶ Gestational age should be confirmed before abortion is undertaken; either clinical evaluation or ultrasonography may be used.

The following recommendations are based on limited or inconsistent scientific evidence (Level B):

▶ Women who do not abort after receiving mifepristone plus misoprostol, methotrexate plus misoprostol, or misoprostol alone to induce abortion should be prepared to have a surgical abortion because of the risks of teratogenicity with both methotrexate and misoprostol.

▶ For women who desire termination of pregnancy in the first trimester but after 49 days of gestation, the surgical method currently is the preferred treatment.

The following recommendations are based primarily on consensus and expert opinion (Level C):

▶ Patients should demonstrate the willingness and ability to comply with all steps in the medical abortion process.

▶ Emergency services including curettage should be available for management of excessive vaginal bleeding or other problems, even though fewer than 1% of women having a medical abortion will need emergent curettage.

References

1. Abortion surveillance—United States, 1997. MMWR Morb Mortal Wkly Rep CDC Surveill Summ 2000;49 (SS-11):1–44 (Level III)

2. Thiersch JB. Therapeutic abortions with a folic acid antagonist, 4-aminopteroylglutamic acid (4-amino P.G.A.) administered by the oral route. Am J Obstet Gynecol 1952;63:1298–1304 (Level III)

3. Karim SM. Once a month vaginal administration of prostaglandins E_2 and $F_{2\alpha}$ for fertility control. Contraception 1971,3:173–183 (Level II-3)

4. Bygdeman M, Bremme K, Christensen N, Lundström V, Gréen K. A comparison of two stable prostaglandin E analogues for termination of early pregnancy and for cervical dilatation. Contraception 1980;22:471–483 (Level II-3)

5. Smith SK, Baird DT. The use of 16,16-dimethyl-*trans*-Δ^2-PGE_1 methyl ester (ONO 802) vaginal suppositories for the termination of early pregnancy. A comparative study. Br J Obstet Gynaecol 1980;87:712–717 (Level II-1)

6. Kovacs L, Sas M, Resch BA, Ugocsai G, Swahn ML, Bygdeman M, et al. Termination of very early pregnancy by RU 486—an antiprogestational compound. Contraception 1984;29:399–410 (Level II-1)

7. Birgerson L, Odlind V, Johansson E. Clinical effects of RU 486 administered for seven days in early pregnancy. In: Baulieu EE, Segal SJ, eds. The antiprogestin steroid RU 486 and human fertility control. New York: Plenum, 1985:235–241 (Level II-3)

8. Swahn ML, Cekan S, Wang G, Lundstrom V, Bygdeman M. Pharmacokinetic and clinical studies of RU 486 for fertility regulation. In: Baulieu EE, Segal SJ, eds. The antiprogestin steroid RU 486 and human fertility control. New York: Plenum, 1985:249–258 (Level II-3)

9. Bygdeman M, Swahn ML. Progesterone receptor blockage. Effect on uterine contractility and early pregnancy. Contraception 1985;32:45–51 (Level II-3)

10. Shoupe D, Mishell DR Jr, Brenner PF, Spitz IM. Pregnancy termination with a high and medium dosage regimen of RU-486. Contraception 1986;33:455–461 (Level II-1)

11. Birgerson L, Odlind V. Early pregnancy termination with antiprogestins: a comparative clinical study of RU 486 given in two dose regimens and Epostane. Fertil Steril 1987;48:565–570 (Level II-1)

12. Creinin MD, Darney PD. Methotrexate and misoprostol for early abortion. Contraception 1993;48:339–348 (Level II-3)

13. Kahn JG, Becker BJ, MacIssa L, Amory JK, Neuhaus J, Olkin I, et al. The efficacy of medical abortion: a meta-analysis. Contraception 2000;61:29–40 (Meta-analysis)

14. Peyron R, Aubény E, Targosz V, Silvestre L, Renault M, Elkik F, et al. Early termination of pregnancy with mifepristone (RU 486) and the orally active prostaglandin misoprostol. N Engl J Med 1993;328:1509–1513 (Level II-3)

15. Creinin MD, Vittinghoff E, Galbraith S, Klaisle C. A randomized controlled trial comparing misoprostol three and seven days after methotrexate for early abortion. Am J Obstet Gynecol 1995;173:1578–1584 (Level I)

16. Creinin MD, Vittinghoff E, Keder L, Darney PD, Tiller G. Methotrexate and misoprostol for early abortion: a multicenter trial. I. Safety and efficacy. Contraception 1996; 53:321–327 (Level II-3)

17. Creinin MD, Vittinghoff E, Schaff E, Klaisle C, Darney PD, Dean C. Medical abortion with oral methotrexate and vaginal misoprostol. Obstet Gynecol 1997;90:611–616 (Level II-3)

18. Creinin MD. Medical abortion with methotrexate 75 mg intramuscularly and vaginal misoprostol. Contraception 1997;56:367–371 (Level II-3)

19. Carbonell JL, Varela L, Velazco A, Fernandez C. The use of misoprostol for termination of early pregnancy. Contraception 1997;55:165–168 (Level II-3)

20. Carbonell JL, Varela L, Velazco A, Fernandez C, Sanchez C. The use of misoprostol for abortion at ≤9 weeks' gestation. Eur J Contracept Reprod Health Care 1997;2: 181–185 (Level II-3)

21. Esteve JL, Varela L, Velazco A, Tanda R, Cabezas E, Sanchez C. Early abortion with 800 µg of misoprostol by the vaginal route. Contraception 1999;59:219–225 (Level II-3)

22. Jain JK, Meckstroth KR, Mishell DR Jr. Early pregnancy termination with intravaginally administered sodium chloride solution-moistened misoprostol tablets: historical comparison with mifepristone and oral misoprostol. Am J Obstet Gynecol 1999;181:1386–1391 (Level II-2)

23. Jain JK, Meckstroth KR, Park M, Mishell DR Jr. A comparison of tamoxifen and misoprostol to misoprostol alone for early pregnancy termination. Contraception 2000;60: 353–356 (Level I)

24. Gravanis A, Schaison G, George M, deBrux J, Satyaswaroop PG, Baulieu EE, et al. Endometrial and pituitary responses to the steroidal anti-progestin RU 486 in postmenopausal women. J Clin Endocrinol Metab 1985; 60:156–163 (Level II-3)

25. Kelly RW, Healy DL, Cameron MJ, Cameron IT, Baird DT. RU 486 stimulation of PGF_2–alpha production in isolated endometrial cells in short term culture. In: Baulieu EE, Segal SJ, eds. The antiprogestin steroid RU 486 and human fertility control. New York: Plenum, 1985:259–262 (Level II-2)

26. Herrmann WL, Schindler AM, Wyss R, Bischof P. Effects of the antiprogesterone RU 486 in early pregnancy and during the menstrual cycle. In: Baulieu EE, Segal SJ, eds. The antiprogestin steroid RU 486 and human fertility control. New York: Plenum, 1985:179–198 (Level III)

27. Schindler AM, Zanon P, Obradovic D, Wyss R, Graff P, Herrmann WL. Early ultrastructural changes in RU-486-exposed decidua. Gynecol Obstet Invest 1985;20:62–67 (Level II-3)

28. Baulieu EE. RU 486 (mifepristone). A short overview of its mechanisms of action and clinical uses at the end of 1996. Ann N Y Acad Sci 1997;828:47–58 (Level III)

29. Lipscomb GH, Bran D, McCord ML, Portera JC, Ling FW. Analysis of three hundred fifteen ectopic pregnancies treated with single-dose methotrexate. Am J Obstet Gynecol 1998;178:1354–1358 (Level II-3)

30. DeLoia JA, Stewart-Akers AM, Creinin MD. Effects of methotrexate on trophoblast proliferation and local immune responses. Hum Reprod 1998;13:1063–1069 (Level II-3)

31. Creinin MD, Krohn MA. Methotrexate pharmacokinetics and effects in women receiving methotrexate 50 mg and 60 mg per square meter for early abortion. Am J Obstet Gynecol 1997;177:1444–1449 (Level I)

32. Henderson ES, Adamson RH, Oliverio VT. The metabolic fate of tritiated methotrexate. II. Absorption and excretion in man. Cancer Res 1965;25:1018–1024 (Level II-3)

33. Jundt JW, Browne BA, Fiocco GP, Steele AD, Mock D. A comparison of low dose methotrexate bioavailability: oral solution, oral tablet, subcutaneous and intramuscular dosing. J Rheumatol 1993;20:1845–1849 (Level II-3)

34. Zieman M, Fong SK, Benowitz NL, Bankster D, Darney PD. Absorption kinetics of misoprostol with oral or vaginal administration. Obstet Gynecol 1997;90:88–92 (Level II-1)

35. Wiebe ER. Tamoxifen compared to methotrexate when used with misoprostol for abortion. Contraception 1999; 59:265–270 (Level II-1)

36. Aubeny E, Peyron R, Turpin CL, Renault M, Targosz V, Silvestre L, et al. Termination of early pregnancy (up to 63 days of amenorrhea) with mifepristone and increasing doses of misoprostol. Int J Fertil Menopausal Stud 1995; 40(suppl 2):85–91 (Level II-3)

37. Creinin MD, Spitz IM. Use of various ultrasound criteria to evaluate the efficacy of mifepristone and misoprostol for medical abortion. Am J Obstet Gynecol 1999;181: 1419–1424 (Level II-3)

38. Spitz IM, Bardin CW, Benton L, Robbins A. Early pregnancy termination with mifepristone and misoprostol in the United States. N Engl J Med 1998;338:1241–1247 (Level II-3)

39. McKinley C, Thong KJ, Baird DT. The effect of dose of mifepristone and gestation on the efficacy of medical abortion with mifepristone and misoprostol. Hum Reprod 1993;8:1502–1505 (Level II-1)

40. Ashok PW, Penney GC, Flett GM, Templeton A. An effective regimen for early medical abortion: a report of 2000 consecutive cases. Hum Reprod 1998;13:2962–2965 (Level II-3)

41. Schaff EA, Eisinger SH, Stadalius LS, Franks P, Gore BZ, Poppema S. Low-dose mifepristone 200 mg and vaginal misoprostol for abortion. Contraception 1999;59:1–6 (Level II-3)

42. Schaff EA, Fielding SL, Eisinger SH, Stadalius LS, Fuller L. Low-dose mifepristone followed by vaginal misoprostol at 48 hours for abortion up to 63 days. Contraception 2000;61:41–46 (Level II-3)

43. el-Refaey H, Rajasekar D, Abdalla M, Calder L, Templeton A. Induction of abortion with mifepristone (RU 486) and oral or vaginal misoprostol. N Engl J Med 1995;332:983–987 (Level I)

44. Schaff EA, Stadalius LS, Eisinger SH, Franks P. Vaginal misoprostol administered at home after mifepristone (RU486) for abortion. J Fam Pract 1997;44:353–360 (Level II-3)

45. Creinin MD, Carbonell JL, Schwartz JL, Varela L, Tanda R. A randomized trial of the effect of moistening misoprostol before vaginal administration when used with methotrexate for abortion. Contraception 1999;59:11–16 (Level I)

46. Creinin MD. Oral methotrexate and vaginal misoprostol for early abortion. Contraception 1996;54:15–18 (Level I)

47. Carbonell JL, Varela L, Velazco A, Cabezas E, Fernandez C, Sanchez C. Oral methotrexate and vaginal misoprostol for early abortion. Contraception 1998;57:83–88 (Level I)

48. Carbonell Esteve JL, Varela L, Velazco A, Tanda R, Sanchez C. 25 mg or 50 mg of oral methotrexate followed by vaginal misoprostol 7 days after for early abortion: a randomized trial. Gynecol Obstet Invest 1999;47:182–187 (Level I)

49. Creinin MD, Vittinghoff E. Methotrexate and misoprostol versus misoprostol alone for early abortion. A randomized controlled trial. JAMA 1994;272:1190–1195 (Level I)

50. Bugalho A, Faundes A, Jamisse L, Usfa M, Maria E, Bique C. Evaluation of the effectiveness of vaginal misoprostol to induce first trimester abortion. Contraception 1996;53: 244–246 (Level II-1)

51. Koopersmith TB, Mishell DR Jr. The use of misoprostol for termination of early pregnancy. Contraception 1996; 53:238–242 (Level I)

52. Henshaw RC, Naji SA, Russell IT, Templeton AA. Comparison of medical abortion with surgical vacuum aspiration: women's preferences and acceptability of treatment. BMJ 1993;307:714–717 (Level II-1)

53. Creinin MD. Randomized comparison of efficacy, acceptability and cost of medical versus surgical abortion. Contraception 2000;63:117–124 (Level I)

54. Tang GW, Lau OW, Yip P. Further acceptability evaluation of RU 486 and ONO 802 as abortifacient agents in a

Chinese population. Contraception 1993;48:267–276 (Level III)

55. Creinin MD, Burke AE. Methotrexate and misoprostol for early abortion: a multicenter trial. Acceptability. Contraception 1996;54:19–22 (Level III)

56. Cameron ST, Glasier AF, Logan J, Benton L, Baird DT. Impact of the introduction of new medical methods on therapeutic abortions at the Royal Infirmary of Edinburgh. Br J Obstet Gynaecol 1996;103:1222–1229 (Level II-2)

57. Winikoff B, Ellertson C, Elul B, Sivin I. Acceptability and feasibility of early pregnancy termination by mifepristone-misoprostol. Results of a large multicenter trial in the United States. Mifepristone Clinical Trial Group. Arch Fam Med 1998;7:360–366 (Level II-3)

58. Creinin MD, Aubeny E. Medical abortion in early pregnancy. In: Paul M, Lichtenberg ES, Borgatta L, Grimes DA, Stubblefield PG, eds. A clinician's guide to medical and surgical abortion. New York: Churchill Livingstone, 1999:91–106 (Level III)

59. Thong KJ, Baird DT. Induction of abortion with mifepristone and misoprostol in early pregnancy. Br J Obstet Gynaecol 1992;99:1004–1007 (Level II-3)

60. Schaff EA, Eisinger SH, Franks P, Kim SS. Combined methotrexate and misoprostol for early induced abortion. Arch Fam Med 1995;4:774–779 (Level II-3)

61. Hausknecht RU. Methotrexate and misoprostol to terminate early pregnancy. N Engl J Med 1995;333:537–540 (Level II-3)

62. Wiebe ER. Abortion induced with methotrexate and misoprostol: a comparison of various protocols. Contraception 1997;55:159–163 (Level II-1)

63. Ulmann A, Silvestre L, Chemama L, Rezvani Y, Renault M, Aguillaume CJ, et al. Medical termination of early pregnancy with mifepristone (RU 486) followed by a prostaglandin analogue. Study in 16,369 women. Acta Obstet Gynecol Scand 1992;71:278–283 (Level II-3)

64. Winikoff B, Sivin I, Coyaji KJ, Cabezas E, Xiao B, Gu S, et al. Safety, efficacy, and acceptability of medical abortion in China, Cuba, and India: a comparative trial of mifepristone-misoprostol versus surgical abortion. Am J Obstet Gynecol 1997;176:431–437 (Level II-1)

65. National Abortion Federation. Recommendations for use of methotrexate and misoprostol in early abortion. National Abortion Federation Protocol. Washington, DC: NAF, 2000 (Level III)

66. Creinin MD. Methotrexate for abortion at ≤42 days gestation. Contraception 1993;48:519–525 (Level II-3)

67. Creinin MD. Change in serum β-human chorionic gonadotropin after abortion with methotrexate and misoprostol. Am J Obstet Gynecol 1996;174:776–778 (Level II-3)

68. Use of approved drugs for unlabeled indications. FDA Drug Bull 1982;12:4–5 (Level III)

69. Winikoff B, Sivin I, Coyaji KJ, Cabezas E, Xiao B, Gu S, et al. The acceptability of medical abortion in China, Cuba and India. Int Fam Plann Perspect 1997;23:73–78, 89 (Level II-1)

70. Ellertson C, Elul B, Winikoff B. Can women use medical abortion without medical supervision? Reprod Health Matters 1997;9:149–161 (Level III)

71. Schaff EA, Eisinger SH, Franks P, Kim SS. Methotrexate and misoprostol for early abortion. Fam Med 1996;28:198–203 (Level II-1)

72. Wiebe ER. Abortion induced with methotrexate and misoprostol. CMAJ 1996;154:165–170 (Level II-3)

73. Ozeren M, Bilekli C, Aydemir V, Bozkaya H. Methotrexate and misoprostol used alone or in combination for early abortion. Contraception 1999;59:389–394 (Level I)

74. Lichtenberg ES, Grimes DA, Paul M. Abortion complications: prevention and management. In: Paul M, Lichtenberg ES, Borgatta L, Grimes DA, Stubblefield PG, eds. A clinician's guide to medical and surgical abortion. New York: Churchill Livingstone, 1999:197–216 (Level III)

75. Silvestre L, Dubois C, Renault M, Rezvani Y, Baulieu EE, Ulmann A. Voluntary interruption of pregnancy with mifepristone (RU 486) and a prostaglandin analogue. A large-scale French experience. N Engl J Med 1990;322:645–648 (Level II-1)

76. Jensen JT, Astley SJ, Morgan E, Nichols MD. Outcomes of suction curettage and mifepristone abortion in the United States: a prospective comparison study. Contraception 1999;59:153–159 (Level II-2)

77. Sawaya GF, Grady D, Kerlikowske K, Grimes DA. Antibiotics at the time of induced abortion: the case for universal prophylaxis based on a meta-analysis. Obstet Gynecol 1996;87:884–890 (Meta-analysis)

78. Ellertson C, Elul B, Ambardekar S, Wood L, Carroll J, Coyaji K. Accuracy of assessment of pregnancy duration by women seeking early abortions. Lancet 2000;355:877–881 (Level III)

79. Creinin MD, Jerald H. Success rates and estimation of gestational age for medical abortion vary with transvaginal ultrasonographic criteria. Am J Obstet Gynecol 1999;180:35–41 (Level II-3)

80. Creinin MD, Shulman T. Effect of nonsteroidal anti-inflammatory drugs on the action of misoprostol in a regimen for early abortion. Contraception 1997;56:165–168 (Level II-2)

81. Darab DJ, Minkoff R, Sciote J, Sulik KK. Pathogenesis of median facial clefts in mice treated with methotrexate. Teratology 1987;36:77–86 (Level II-3) (animal)

82. Kozlowski RD, Steinbrunner JV, MacKenzie AH, Clough JD, Wilke WS, Segal AM, et al. Outcome of first-trimester exposure to low-dose methotrexate in eight patients with rheumatic disease. Am J Med 1990;88:589–592 (Level II-3)

83. Yip SK, Tse AO, Haines CJ, Chung TK. Misoprostol's effect on uterine arterial blood flow and fetal heart rate in early pregnancy. Obstet Gynecol 2000;95:232–235 (Level II-3)

84. Fonseca W, Alencar AJ, Mota FS, Coelho HL. Misoprostol and congenital malformations. Lancet 1991;338:56 (Level III)

85. Gonzalez CH, Vargas FR, Perez AB, Kim CA, Brunoni D, Marques-Dias MJ, et al. Limb deficiency with or without Möbius sequence in seven Brazilian children associated with misoprostol use in the first trimester of pregnancy. Am J Med Genet 1993;47:59–64 (Level III)

86. Pastuszak AL, Schuler L, Speck-Martins CE, Coelho KE, Cordello SM, Vargas F, et al. Use of misoprostol during

pregnancy and Mobius' syndrome in infants. N Engl J Med 1998;338:1881–1885 (Level II-2)

87. Schuler L, Pastuszak A, Sanseverino TV, Orioli IM, Brunoni D, Ashton-Prolla P, et al. Pregnancy outcome after exposure to misoprostol in Brazil: a prospective, controlled study. Reprod Toxicol 1999;13:147–151 (Level II-2)

88. Creinin MD. Conception rates after abortion with methotrexate and misoprostol. Int J Gynaecol Obstet 1999;65:183–188 (Level II-2)

89. Steinhoff PG, Smith RG, Palmore JA, Diamond M, Chung CS. Women who obtain repeat abortions: a study based on record linkage. Fam Plann Perspect 1979;11:30–38 (Level III)

The MEDLINE database, the Cochrane Library, and ACOG's own internal resources and documents were used to conduct a literature search to locate relevant articles published between January 1985 and March 2000. The search was restricted to articles published in the English language. Priority was given to articles reporting results of original research, although review articles and commentaries also were consulted. Abstracts of research presented at symposia and scientific conferences were not considered adequate for inclusion in this document. Guidelines published by organizations or institutions such as the National Institutes of Health and the American College of Obstetricians and Gynecologists were reviewed, and additional studies were located by reviewing bibliographies of identified articles. When reliable research was not available, expert opinions from obstetrician–gynecologists were used.

Studies were reviewed and evaluated for quality according to the method outlined by the U.S. Preventive Services Task Force:

I   Evidence obtained from at least one properly designed randomized controlled trial.

II-1 Evidence obtained from well-designed controlled trials without randomization.

II-2 Evidence obtained from well-designed cohort or case–control analytic studies, preferably from more than one center or research group.

II-3 Evidence obtained from multiple time series with or without the intervention. Dramatic results in uncontrolled experiments also could be regarded as this type of evidence.

III   Opinions of respected authorities, based on clinical experience, descriptive studies, or reports of expert committees.

Based on the highest level of evidence found in the data, recommendations are provided and graded according to the following categories:

Level A—Recommendations are based on good and consistent scientific evidence.

Level B—Recommendations are based on limited or inconsistent scientific evidence.

Level C—Recommendations are based primarily on consensus and expert opinion.

ISSN 1099-3630

The American College of Obstetricians and Gynecologists
409 12th Street, SW, PO Box 96920
Washington, DC 20090-6920

12345/54321

ACOG PRACTICE BULLETIN

CLINICAL MANAGEMENT GUIDELINES FOR
OBSTETRICIAN–GYNECOLOGISTS

NUMBER 11, DECEMBER 1999

(Replaces Technical Bulletin Number 184, September 1993)

This Practice Bulletin was developed by the ACOG Committee on Practice Bulletins—Gynecology with the assistance of Kamran S. Moghissi, MD and Craig A. Winkel, MD. The information is designed to aid practitioners in making decisions about appropriate obstetric and gynecologic care. These guidelines should not be construed as dictating an exclusive course of treatment or procedure. Variations in practice may be warranted based on the needs of the individual patient, resources, and limitations unique to the institution or type of practice.

Medical Management of Endometriosis

Endometriosis represents a significant health problem for women of reproductive age. Defined as the presence of endometrial-like glands and stroma in any extrauterine site, endometriosis continues to defy our complete understanding regarding etiology, the relationship between extent of disease and the degree of symptoms, its relationship to fertility, and the most appropriate means of therapy. The purpose of this document is to present the evidence, including risks and benefits, for the effectiveness of medical therapy for women who experience symptoms and problems believed to be secondary to endometriosis.

Background

Incidence

Endometriosis is a gynecologic condition that occurs in 7–10% of women in the general population and up to 50% of premenopausal women (1), with a prevalence of 38% (range, 20–50%) (2–4) in infertile women, and in 71–87% of women with chronic pelvic pain (5–7). Contrary to much speculation, there are no data to support the view that the incidence of endometriosis is increasing, although improved recognition of endometriosis lesions (8) may have led to an increase in the rate of detection. There also appears to be no particular racial predisposition to endometriosis.

A familial association of endometriosis has been documented (9), and patients with an affected first-degree relative have nearly a 10-fold increased risk of developing endometriosis. The proposed inheritance is characteristic of a polygenic-multifactorial mechanism.

Etiology

Although the pathogenesis of endometriosis remains unclear, leading theories include retrograde menstruation, hematogenous or lymphatogenous transport, and coelomic metaplasia. It has been suggested that virtually all women are potentially vulnerable to the development of the lesions of endometriosis, but appropriate immunocompetency in most eradicates such lesions in a timely fashion, preventing clinical sequelae (10). Menstrual flow that produces a greater volume of retrograde menstruation may increase the risk of developing endometriosis. Cervical or vaginal atresia with outflow obstruction also is linked with the development of endometriosis (11). Early menarche, regular cycles (especially without intervening pregnancy-induced amenorrhea), and a longer and heavier than normal flow are associated with this disease (12). Because endometriosis is an estrogen-dependent disease, factors that reduce estrogen levels, such as exercise-induced menstrual disorders, decreased body-fat content, and tobacco smoking, are associated with reduced risk of developing endometriosis (12).

Clinical Manifestations

The clinical manifestations of endometriosis are variable and unpredictable in both presentation and course. Dysmenorrhea, chronic pelvic pain, dyspareunia, uterosacral ligament nodularity, and adnexal mass (either symptomatic or asymptomatic) are among the most well-recognized manifestations (13–16). A significant number of women with endometriosis remain asymptomatic.

The association between endometriosis and infertility remains the subject of considerable debate. It is clear that endometriosis may induce infertility as a result of anatomic distortion secondary to invasive endometriosis and related adhesions. Although it was previously believed that patients with minimal and mild endometriosis displayed reduced monthly fecundity rates (17), a cause-and-effect relationship has not been proven, and more recent prospective controlled trials suggest that minimal to mild endometriosis is not associated with reduced fecundity (18) and may not be a direct cause of infertility (19).

Pelvic pain that is typical of endometriosis is characteristically described as secondary dysmenorrhea (with pain frequently commencing prior to the onset of menses), deep dyspareunia (exaggerated during menses), or sacral backache with menses. Endometriosis that involves specific organs may result in pain or physiologic dysfunction of those organs, such as perimenstrual tenesmus or diarrhea in cases of bowel involvement or dysuria and hematuria in cases of bladder involvement.

The pain associated with endometriosis has little relationship to the type or location of the lesions that are visible at laparoscopy (20). Surgical assessment is complicated by the varying, and subtle appearances of endometriosis (21, 22), and may be demonstrated histologically in a normal-appearing peritoneum (23, 24). It has been shown that the depth of infiltration of endometriosis lesions correlates best with pain severity (6, 25, 26). Systematic analysis of the source of pain in awake patients undergoing laparoscopy (sometimes referred to as "pain mapping") demonstrates that pain arises from stimulation of adjacent normal peritoneal surfaces that extend well beyond the visible lesions of endometriosis. This suggests that painful lesions are those involving peritoneal surfaces innervated by peripheral spinal nerves, rather than those innervated by the autonomic nervous system (20).

Diagnosis

Direct visualization confirmed by histologic examination, especially of lesions with nonclassical appearance (21, 22, 27), remains the standard for diagnosing endometriosis. The presence of two or more of the following histologic features is used as the threshold criteria for the diagnosis by a pathologist (28):

- Endometrial epithelium
- Endometrial glands
- Endometrial stroma
- Hemosiderin-laden macrophages

Visual inspection as the sole means for making the diagnosis of endometriosis requires an experienced surgeon who is familiar with the protean appearances of endometriosis. Experience is associated with increased diagnostic accuracy (8, 21, 22), but the correlation between visual inspection and histologic confirmation of the presence of endometriosis in biopsy specimens is imperfect (22). The finding of microscopic endometriosis in normal-appearing peritoneum (23, 24) exemplifies the inaccuracy of diagnosis by visualization alone. Peritoneal biopsy may be used for diagnosing questionable peritoneal lesions (22).

Because tissue confirmation of the diagnosis of endometriosis requires a surgical procedure, investigators have searched for a noninvasive alternative. The correlation between the presence of moderate and severe endometriosis and an increased concentration of CA 125 in serum has been known for more than 10 years (29). Although the specificity of CA 125 measurements had been reported to be greater than 85%, with sensitivities between 20% and 50% (30–33), the clinical utility of measuring CA 125 as a diagnostic marker for endometriosis appears to be limited. Determining the level of CA 125 in serum appears to be useful in detecting women with severe endometriosis but is of questionable value in detecting women with minimal or mild disease (34, 35).

Measurement of peritoneal fluid levels, however, appears to be better for detecting minimal and moderate disease (34).

Concentrations of CA 125 in serum also have been studied as a marker to determine the response to medical therapy for endometriosis. Although CA 125 levels may decrease during treatment when compared with pretreatment values (36–38), posttreatment values that are normal do not confirm the absence of endometriosis (36, 38), nor are they useful for predicting disease recurrence (37).

Imaging studies, such as ultrasonography, magnetic resonance imaging, and computed tomography, appear to be useful only in the presence of a pelvic or adnexal mass. Ovarian endometriomas, visualized ultrasonographically, typically appear as cysts that contain low-level, homogeneous internal echoes consistent with old blood. Imaging studies alone appear to have greater predictive accuracy in differentiating ovarian endometriomas from other adnexal masses than when used in combination with measurement of CA 125 levels in plasma (39). Magnetic resonance imaging may detect deeply infiltrating endometriosis that involves the uterosacral ligaments and the cul-de-sac, but lacks sensitivity in detecting rectal involvement (40).

**American Society for Reproductive Medicine
Revised Classification of Endometriosis**

Patient's name _____ Date _____

Stage I (minimal) — 1–5
Stage II (mild) — 6–15
Stage III (moderate) — 16–40
Stage IV (severe) — >40

Laparoscopy_____ Laparotomy _____ Photography_____
Recommended treatment _____

Total _____

Prognosis _____

Peritoneum	Endometriosis	<1 cm	1–3 cm	>3 cm
	Superficial	1	2	4
	Deep	2	4	6
Ovary	R Superficial	1	2	4
	Deep	4	16	20
	L Superficial	1	2	4
	Deep	4	16	20

		Partial	Complete
	Posterior cul-de-sac obliteration	4	40

	Adhesions	<1/3 Enclosure	1/3–2/3 Enclosure	>2/3 Enclosure
Ovary	R Filmy	1	2	4
	Dense	4	8	16
	L Filmy	1	2	4
	Dense	4	8	16
Tube	R Filmy	1	2	4
	Dense	4*	8*	16
	L Filmy	1	2	4
	Dense	4*	8*	16

*If the fimbriated end of the fallopian tube is completely enclosed, change the point assignment to 16. Denote appearance of superficial implant types as red [(R), red, red-pink, flamelike, vesicular blobs, clear vesicles], white [(W), opacifications, peritoneal defects, yellow-brown], or black [(B), black, hemosiderin deposits, blue]. Denote percent of total described as R___%, W___%, and B___%. Total should equal 100%.

Figure 1. Modified from the revised American Fertility Society classification of endometriosis. (Reprinted with permission from the American Society for Reproductive Medicine. Fertility and Sterility 1996;67(5):819–820)

Classification

Numerous classification schemas have been proposed to describe endometriosis by anatomic location and severity of disease. The American Society for Reproductive Medicine (ASRM [formerly the American Fertility Society]) classification, which is the most commonly used system, was revised for the third time in 1996 (41) (see Figure 1) but still has limitations and inherent defects. The system is not a good predictor of pregnancy following treatment despite adjustments to the point scores and cut-points for disease stage. The ASRM system does not correlate well with the symptoms of pain and dyspareunia (6). The true value of the ASRM 1996 revised system is in uniform recording of operative findings and perhaps for comparing the results of various therapies.

Clinical Considerations and Recommendations

▶ *In women with endometriosis-related pain who desire future fertility, how does medical therapy compare with no therapy for the treatment of pain and long-term preservation of fertility potential?*

Deeply infiltrating endometriosis, rather than surface noninfiltrating endometriosis, is commonly associated with pelvic pain (6). At present, evidence suggests that pain associated with endometriosis can be reduced with the use of a variety of medications (progestins, danazol, oral contraceptives, nonsteroidal antiinflammatory drugs, and gonadotropin-releasing hormone [GnRH] agonists) (42–47). There is also evidence that such medical therapies are likely to reduce the size of endometriosis lesions and, thus, the stage of disease (42, 48, 49). There are no data, however, showing that medical therapy eradicates the lesions. Although medical treatment may eliminate the symptoms associated with endometriosis, there is no evidence that such treatment has an impact on the future fertility of women with endometriosis. Because early-stage endometriosis is more likely to be associated with pain symptoms without associated alterations in fecundity, it is unlikely that such data will be forthcoming. Furthermore, whereas infiltrating lesions of endometriosis are associated with pain, studies are lacking that suggest the absence of treatment is associated with a progressive or future decline in fertility.

In a woman with normal or minor gynecologic findings suggesting mild disease (pelvic tenderness, uterosacral

nodularity), ovarian suppression with a combination oral contraceptive may be effective in reducing pain (50). The efficacy of continuous administration of oral contraceptives compared with cyclic administration has not been tested in a prospective fashion. Oral contraceptives probably should not be used for more than 3 months if the patient experiences no relief of symptoms. Furthermore, there is no reason to suspect that one oral contraceptive is better than another for suppression of pain symptoms. If recurrent symptoms do not respond to oral contraceptives, then therapy with medroxyprogesterone acetate (MPA), danazol, or a GnRH agonist may be appropriate.

Danazol, when used in doses of 600–800 mg per day appears to as effective as GnRH agonists for pain relief in most patients, but is associated with a significantly greater incidence of side effects (51). The cost of treatment with danazol is about one third less than treatment with a GnRH agonist but nearly twice as costly as treatment with oral contraceptives and oral or depot MPA.

▶ *In women with endometriosis-related pain who desire future fertility, how does medical therapy compare with surgical therapy alone for the management of pain and long-term preservation of fertility potential?*

The debate regarding medical treatment versus surgical treatment for the management of pain related to endometriosis continues despite of the lack of substantive data on either side of the argument. Surgical therapy for women with endometriosis is associated with a significant reduction in pain symptoms during the first 6 months following surgery (52). With continued follow-up, however, a substantial portion (44%) of women experience recurrence of symptoms within 1 year postoperatively (53). The cumulative recurrence rate of pain symptoms during the initial 5 years following discontinuation of therapy with a GnRH agonist is 53% (54). No evidence exists regarding the effectiveness of adjunctive treatment with danazol, oral contraceptives, or progestins in comparison with surgical treatment alone in the management of endometriosis-related pelvic pain. A major issue in considering comparisons of surgical treatment with medical treatment is the experience and expertise of the surgeon.

Likewise, debate continues over the best means of surgical therapy. One opinion considers vaporization or cautery of peritoneal implants adequate, whereas the other recommends surgical excision as necessary for adequate treatment (55). Currently, there are limited data to show that one method is better than the other. Moreover, there are no data regarding whether surgical therapy influences long-term fertility. Also, no data exist to indicate whether medical or surgical treatments result in the best fertility outcomes.

▶ *Following surgical diagnosis of endometriosis, what is the role of surgical destruction of lesions, or medical therapy in conjunction with surgery, for long-term pain relief in patients with minimal to moderate endometriosis that has been completely resected?*

It is probably impossible to completely resect all endometriosis lesions, if for no other reason than in up to 25% of biopsies of normal-appearing peritoneum one will find histologic evidence of endometriosis (23, 24). In addition, even when experienced surgeons attempt to resect completely a deeply infiltrating lesion, histologic study often reveals that the lesion is incompletely resected (26).

Operative laparoscopy for surgical treatment of pelvic pain related to endometriosis appears to have numerous advantages over laparotomy. These include more rapid recovery, the potential to decrease postoperative adhesion formation (56), and complication rates of 10% with laparoscopy (57). Although technical difficulties can be overcome partially through skill and experience, the efficacy of surgical therapy still depends heavily on the surgeon. Regardless of the technique employed—excision, endocoagulation, electrocautery, or laser vaporization—no study demonstrates the superiority of any one method, and recurrence rates average 19% (58). For successful surgical treatment, considering the varied appearances of endometriosis, the challenge lies in the surgeon's ability to recognize all visible lesions.

The only prospective, double-blind, randomized, controlled trial designed to evaluate the effectiveness of laparoscopic surgery for women with pelvic pain was reported in 1994 (52). Of the women who underwent laser ablation of endometriosis and laser uterosacral nerve ablation, 62% experienced pain relief 6 months after surgery, compared with 22% who underwent laparoscopic visualization only (52). If one considers the results of this study and a number of retrospective analyses, it appears that surgical treatment alone will confer pain relief in approximately two thirds of women for up to 1 year.

Postoperative medical treatment could be useful when residual disease is expected, when pain is not relieved, or to extend the pain-free interval following surgery. Although not demonstrated on the basis of clinical studies available at present, postoperative treatment should minimize the risk of recurrence. Two studies support the use of postoperative

GnRH agonists to extend the period of pain relief. In a randomized, controlled trial of an intranasal GnRH agonist, 31% of women who received the GnRH agonist following laparoscopy needed additional medical treatment 18 months following surgery, whereas 57% of the women who received placebo required additional medical suppression (59).

The efficacy of other hormonal therapy in conjunction with surgery for treating women with endometriosis remains unclear. Oral MPA has been shown to induce regression of endometriosis lesions. One study has demonstrated that depot MPA is safe and effective in reducing pain associated with endometriosis (45). Importantly, depot MPA confers contraception during therapy while the use of low-dose danazol (200–400 mg) to reduce the dose-related side effects may not prevent conception and thus exposes the patient to the potential for teratogenesis. A combination of low-dose danazol and oral contraceptives appears to offer a similar degree of efficacy while providing effective contraception (45).

Few reports have examined the use of danazol as an adjunct to surgical therapy. It appears that danazol treatment for 3 months following laparoscopic surgery for women with Stage III and Stage IV endometriosis offers no advantage over expectant management with regard to pain recurrence (60).

▶ *Following surgical diagnosis of endometriosis, what is the role of surgical destruction of lesions, or medical therapy in conjunction with surgery, for long-term pain relief in patients with severe endometriosis with residual disease present?*

The recurrence rates for endometriosis appear to correlate with severity of disease (54), with a recurrence rate over a 7-year period following medical treatment of 37% for women with mild disease and 74% for women with severe disease. Although one might conclude that postoperative medical treatment would make sense for the woman with severe endometriosis with residual disease, there are no data documenting the efficacy of this therapy. In most cases, studies of the efficacy of postoperative medical treatment specifically address those patients with minimal to moderate disease, excluding those with severe endometriosis. Treatment with a GnRH agonist prior to laparoscopic surgery was associated with a higher fecundity rate within the first year following surgery than with preoperative danazol or gestrinone (61). However, such therapy was not associated with a reduction in operating time or any decrease in recurrence rate 1 year after surgery for ovarian endometriomata (62). For women with severe endometriosis, with or without suspected residual disease, the efficacy of either preoperative or postoperative medical therapy has yet to be established.

▶ *In women receiving a 3–6-month regimen of GnRH analog therapy for treatment of endometriosis-related pelvic pain, what are the advantages and disadvantages of an "add-back" regimen?*

Gonadotropin-releasing hormone agonists have been shown to be efficacious and safe for treating women with endometriosis-related pelvic pain (47, 49, 63–66). However, because these agents create a state of relative estrogen deficiency, their use has been limited generally to a 6-month course of therapy, particularly because of the potential effects on bone density, as well as the side effects, most notably vasomotor symptoms.

To minimize both the loss of bone and side effects, add-back regimens (using either sex-steroid hormones or other specific bone-sparing agents) have been advocated for use in women undergoing long-term therapy (ie, >6 months). Such treatment strategies have included progestins alone (67–69), progestins and organic bisphosphonates (70), low-dose progestins and estrogens (71,72), pulsatile parathyroid hormone (73), and nasal calcitonin (74). Although there are no published studies specifically designed to compare the various add-back regimens, virtually all add-back regimens (except nasal calcitonin) have considerable efficacy in reducing the loss of bone mineral density associated with GnRH agonist treatment. Some regimens appear to reduce vasomotor symptoms better than others; parathyroid hormone therapy has little effect on such symptoms.

The potential advantages of add-back therapy for women undergoing short-term (3–6 months) GnRH agonist therapy are twofold. First, while it has been shown that the bone loss after 3 months of treatment with a GnRH agonist is less than that after 6 months of treatment (69, 70, 72), add-back therapy does reduce the bone loss observed after only 3 months of GnRH agonist therapy (72). Add-back treatment does not diminish the efficacy of pain relief observed during 3 months or 6 months of GnRH agonist therapy. Second, add-back regimens that employ progestins alone (67–72) or in combination with estrogens (71, 72, 75) reduce significantly the vasomotor symptoms associated with GnRH agonist treatment. There appear to be no disadvantages to the use of an add-back regimen in combination with a GnRH agonist other than the incremental cost associated with the additional medication.

▶ *In women who have had a good response to GnRH therapy and who may benefit from an extended duration of therapy with add-back therapy (>6 months), what is the safety and efficacy of such long-term treatment?*

There are few data available on the use of GnRH agonists for more than 6 months. The major concern with prolonged use of GnRH agonists is the loss of bone mineral density that is observed during 6 months of therapy with these drugs (76). The mean loss of bone mineral density during a 6-month course of therapy with GnRH agonists ranges from 5.9% to 15% and may depend on the dose, route, and particular agonist being used (77). Marked individual differences in susceptibility to bone loss have been noted. Bone loss during a 6-month course of intranasal GnRH agonist was less than that observed with the intramuscular form (3% versus 5%) (78). Gonadotropin-releasing hormone agonists do not have adverse effects on triglyceride or cholesterol metabolism (79), as may be seen with danazol (80) or MPA (81).

A 12-month course of GnRH agonist therapy was associated with approximately a 6% decrease in bone density. The addition of norethindrone acetate alone or in combination with conjugated equine estrogens had no adverse impact on pain relief but did prevent bone mineral loss (44); there was also an associated increase in low-density lipoprotein cholesterol, a decrease in high-density lipoprotein cholesterol, and an increase in triglycerides. The clinical significance of these latter changes is unclear. Currently, there are no data regarding extended treatment with GnRH agonists beyond 1 year. Patients receiving this treatment should be monitored regularly for physical findings, bone density, and serum lipid parameters.

If the woman has previously undergone therapy with a GnRH agonist, it appears safe to retreat with a GnRH agonist alone provided there has been suitable time for recovery of bone mineral density since the previous course of treatment (82). If bone mineral density has not recovered fully, or if bone density has not been evaluated, the use of either a potent progestin or danazol is recommended. No studies have been reported to evaluate bone density after progestin administration following initial GnRH agonist therapy. Finally, a GnRH agonist in combination with add-back treatment may be considered, especially if the add-back regimen is commenced coincidentally with the reinitiation of therapy with the GnRH agonist. The long-term effects of multiple courses of treatment with a GnRH agonist have yet to be assessed.

▶ *In a woman with symptoms consistent with endometriosis, is empiric medical therapy (without definitive surgical diagnosis) an efficacious and cost-effective approach to pain relief?*

The need for laparoscopy (or any other surgical procedure) for diagnosis or treatment of pelvic pain secondary to suspected endometriosis has been the subject of debate (83). Arguments against the requirement to perform surgery to definitively diagnose endometriosis include the imprecision of surgical diagnosis as well as the inherent risks of surgery. "Empiric" therapy is used commonly in clinical gynecology when the signs and symptoms support the particular diagnosis being entertained and the consequences of an inaccurate diagnosis are likely to be minimal (eg, mild cystitis, suspected pelvic infection, and bacterial vaginosis).

In a woman with pelvic pain, diagnostic evaluation should include a thorough history and physical examination to rule out other gynecologic causes of pain, such as chronic pelvic inflammatory disease, leiomyomata uteri, and ovarian cysts. Nongynecologic causes of pain, such as gastrointestinal and urinary tract problems, may be ruled out by appropriate testing. Consideration also should be given to pelvic ultrasonography, complete blood count, urinalysis, and endocervical sampling for gonococcal and chlamydial infection if signs and symptoms warrant.

Based on a well-designed, prospective, randomized, controlled, double-blind clinical trial, the following statement can be made (7). After an appropriate pretreatment evaluation (to exclude other conditions) and failure of initial treatment with oral contraceptives and nonsteroidal antiinflammatory drugs, empiric therapy with a 3-month course of a GnRH agonist is appropriate. This approach is associated with clinically and statistically significant improvement in dysmenorrhea, pelvic pain, and pelvic tenderness. Furthermore, if the diagnostic algorithm described is employed prior to the initiation of empiric GnRH therapy, the likelihood of endometriosis being present on posttreatment laparoscopy is 78–87%. Thus, it appears that empiric treatment with a GnRH agonist (ie, without surgical diagnosis) is efficacious.

Comparing costs of empiric medical management versus definitive surgical diagnosis is more difficult to address. Although there are a lack of well-designed studies that compare the actual costs between the two approaches, it has been estimated that the cost of 3 months of empiric therapy is less than that of a laparoscopic procedure. No trials comparing primary medical and surgical

therapies have been reported, nor have data been reported regarding the percentage of women who will still require surgical therapy following satisfactory empiric treatment.

▶ *In asymptomatic women in whom endometriosis is discovered incidentally, how does medical therapy compare with no intervention for long-term pain relief and preservation of fertility?*

The pathophysiology of endometriosis remains poorly understood. Largely because of failure to identify a suitable animal model, there is little systematic research regarding either the progression of the disease or the prediction of clinical outcomes. The presence of endometriosis among asymptomatic infertility patients varies between 20% and 50%, suggesting that it may not always be pathologic. In biopsies of apparently normal peritoneum, one can demonstrate the presence of endometrial glands and stroma in 25%, thus confirming the presence of endometriosis (23). In 50% of cases, endometriosis regresses spontaneously or remains constant (84). There are a number of obstacles, therefore, to predicting what the presence of endometriosis holds for a given woman. There are no data available regarding medical therapy for prevention of disease progression or for prevention of future pain.

Although preliminary data suggest that the destruction of all apparent lesions is associated with improved fecundity during the next 36 months (85), there are no data available on which to make a recommendation regarding medical therapy to prevent progression of disease or to prevent pain symptoms.

Endometriosis frequently is associated with infertility, although a cause-and-effect relationship between the two remains controversial. Essential steps in the development of endometriosis require a series of complex interactions between peritoneal leukocytes and endometrial cells, but the exact etiologic factor(s) remains unknown. In addition, both specific and nonspecific immunologic alterations are likely required. Whether these are the result or the cause of the disease also remains unclear. Although the pathophysiology of infertility arising from endometriosis that results in distortion of normal anatomy is relatively easy to understand, the mechanisms by which nonadhesive disease leads to infertility are still not clear.

There are no data to support the suggestion that medical treatment to prevent the progression of the disease will result in successful fertility in the future. It is not even clear whether fertility can be predicted based on the presence of endometriosis unless there is gross distortion of tubal and ovarian anatomy.

▶ *In women with endometriosis-related pain who have completed childbearing, how does medical management compare with no therapy for long-term pain relief?*

The rates for recurrence of pain symptoms following medical or surgical treatment for endometriosis do not differ greatly. Following surgical therapy, about two thirds of patients experience recurrence of pain symptoms within 2 years of surgery (52, 56). However, the recurrence of pain symptoms may be delayed by the addition of 3 months of treatment with a GnRH agonist (59).

Medical therapy alone is likely to result in a significant pain-free interval following treatment with a GnRH agonist (54, 86) in the absence of surgical treatment. In addition, treatment with either oral contraceptives, danazol, or progestins has been shown to reduce, at least in the short term, pain symptoms associated with endometriosis (43, 45, 46). Currently, there are no follow-up data beyond 7 years after medical treatment. The long-term impact of medical therapy on pain recurrence beyond this period remains unclear.

▶ *In a woman with pelvic pain arising from known endometriosis, does the presence of an ovarian endometrioma on ultrasound influence the efficacy or safety of employing medical therapy for pain relief?*

The reliability of ultrasonography for diagnosing endometriosis depends on the nature of the lesions. The endovaginal ultrasonographic approach appears to be superior to the transvesical approach for the evaluation of an ovarian mass. For the diagnosis of ovarian endometriomas, ultrasonography is reliable, with sensitivity up to 83% and specificity of 98% (87). Scattered internal echoes that tend to appear homogeneous are characteristic of endometriomas.

Gonadotropin-releasing hormone agonist treatment resulted in a greater than 25% reduction in the diameter of endometriomas for more than 80% of the women observed, compared with 30% of those treated with danazol (61). These authors did not report on the reduction in pain symptoms. Although it is theorized that preoperative medical treatment of the woman with an ovarian endometrioma might facilitate surgery by reducing inflammation and vascularity, there are no studies that address this practice. A 3-month preoperative course of a GnRH agonist has been reported to produce decreased cyst wall thickness and inflammation (88), but was not associated with either reduced operating time or reduced incidence of recurrence

1 year later (62). There is only anecdotal information regarding responses of suspected ovarian endometriomas to therapy with oral contraceptives or MPA. When medical treatment is used in a woman with an ovarian mass that is assumed to be an endometrioma, the potential for missed diagnosis or delay in diagnosis of a more serious condition (such as a malignant or borderline tumor) must always be kept in mind.

Because it is likely that the pain associated with endometriosis is most closely related to deeply infiltrating peritoneal disease rather than the ovarian endometrioma, medical therapy aimed at suppressing ovarian function is likely to result in a similar reduction in pain symptoms, whether or not there is a coincident ovarian endometrioma. There are no studies, however, of the efficacy of medical therapy for pain in the presence or absence of an endometrioma.

▶ *In patients with pain or bleeding arising from known endometriosis affecting nonreproductive organs, what is the evidence for the efficacy of medical therapy for these symptoms?*

Extrapelvic endometriosis has been reported in a variety of sites, including the upper abdomen, the diaphragm, the abdominal wall (particularly the umbilicus), the perineum (episiotomy scar), and the thorax (89, 90). In addition, endometriosis may invade the full thickness of the rectum, large and small bowel, ureters, or bladder. The symptoms that are associated with endometriosis at these sites vary depending on location and depths of infiltration, including women who experience cyclic episodes of gross hematuria, hematochezia, and hemoptysis. Although a number of therapeutic approaches have been employed for women with presumed extrapelvic endometriosis (91), the efficacy of ovarian suppression with a GnRH agonist appears to support it as the first line of therapy (92, 93). Based on current available evidence, medical treatment appears to be efficacious for women with signs and symptoms of extrapelvic endometriosis provided other, potentially serious diseases have been excluded.

▶ *In a woman who has undergone a total abdominal hysterectomy for definitive therapy for endometriosis, what is the risk of symptomatic recurrence with estrogen replacement therapy, and is there a role for suppressive therapy after total abdominal hysterectomy with bilateral salpingo-oophorectomy if there is residual disease?*

The rates of recurrence of endometriosis after initial conservative surgery tend to vary based on stage or extent of disease at the time of surgery. It is particularly difficult, however, to distinguish between recurrence and persistence of endometriosis. Recurrence rates range between 20% and 40% within 5 years after surgery for endometriosis (52, 53, 55, 94).

Hysterectomy, with or without bilateral oophorectomy, is often regarded as "definitive" therapy for the treatment of endometriosis associated with intractable pelvic pain, adnexal masses, or multiple previous conservative surgical procedures. Based on the results of a recently published retrospective analysis of women monitored for a mean duration of 58 months after hysterectomy, ovarian conservation was associated with a 62% likelihood of recurrent symptoms and a 31% chance of requiring additional surgical treatment (95). In women who underwent bilateral adnexectomy, there was a 10% chance of recurrence of symptoms with only a 4% likelihood of additional surgery (95). The relative risk for pain recurrence after total abdominal hysterectomy was found to be 6.1 (95% confidence interval: 2.5–14.6) with ovarian preservation when compared with women who have their ovaries removed. The relative risk of additional surgery was 8.1 (95% confidence interval: 2.1–31.3) with ovarian conservation (95).

Symptoms may recur in women even after hysterectomy and oophorectomy. Endometriosis may recur in up to 15% of women whether or not the patients are treated with estrogen replacement therapy following bilateral oophorectomy (96). Although the true rate of recurrence is unknown, among those patients in whom recurrent symptoms result in an additional surgical procedure, endometriosis lesions may be demonstrated. The most common site of recurrent lesions is the large and small bowel. It is not clear whether such lesions were present at the time of the oophorectomy and were overlooked or were not visualized because they were present only as microscopic disease in normal-appearing peritoneum.

After total abdominal hysterectomy with bilateral salpingo-oophorectomy, delayed initiation of estrogen replacement therapy has been thought to decrease the risk of recurrent symptoms. Furthermore, the possibility does exist that estrogen replacement therapy may support infiltration of endometriosis lesions and result in continued progression of the disease (97). Currently, there are limited data on which to base a recommendation. It appears there is no advantage, in terms of recurrence rate, in delaying introduction of estrogen treatment following surgery (96, 98). There is also a concern about the possibility of estrogen induced malignant transformation in residual endometriosis implants (99),

which has led some to recommend the routine addition of a progestin to the estrogen therapy, although there are no outcomes-based evidence to support this recommendation.

Although limited data indicate hormone replacement therapy may stimulate the growth of residual ovarian or endometrial tissue after total abdominal hysterectomy, the overall benefits of hormone replacement (cardiovascular benefits, reduced risk of osteoporosis, relief of vasomotor symptoms) may outweigh these risks, and the decision should be individualized.

Summary

The following recommendations are based on good and consistent scientific evidence (Level A):

▶ For pain relief, treatment with a GnRH agonist for at least 3 months or with danazol for at least 6 months appears to be equally effective in most patients.

▶ When relief of pain from treatment with a GnRH agonist supports continued therapy, the addition of add-back therapy reduces or eliminates GnRH-induced bone mineral loss without reducing the efficacy of pain relief.

The following recommendations are based on limited or inconsistent scientific evidence (Level B):

▶ Therapy with a GnRH agonist is an appropriate approach to the management of the woman with chronic pelvic pain, even in the absence of surgical confirmation of endometriosis, provided that a detailed initial evaluation fails to demonstrate some other cause of pelvic pain.

▶ For pain relief, oral contraceptives and oral or depot MPA are effective in comparison with placebo and may be equivalent to other more costly regimens.

▶ Hormone replacement therapy with estrogen is not contraindicated following hysterectomy and bilateral salpingo-oophorectomy for endometriosis.

The following recommendations are based primarily on consensus and expert opinion (Level C):

▶ For severe endometriosis, medical treatment alone may not be sufficient.

▶ Because endometriosis often is unpredictable and may regress, expectant management may be appropriate in asymptomatic patients.

References

1. Wheeler JM. Epidemiology of endometriosis-associated infertility. J Reprod Med 1989;34:41–46 (Level III)

2. Rawson JM. Prevalence of endometriosis in asymptomatic women. J Reprod Med 1991;36:513–515 (Level III)

3. Strathy JH, Molgaard CA, Coulam CB, Melton LJ 3d. Endometriosis and infertility: a laparoscopic study of endometriosis among fertile and infertile women. Fertil Steril 1982;38:667–672 (Level II-2)

4. Verkauf BS. Incidence, symptoms, and signs of endometriosis in fertile and infertile women. J Fla Med Assoc 1987;74:671–675 (Level II-2)

5. Carter JE. Combined hysteroscopic and laparoscopic findings in patients with chronic pelvic pain. J Am Assoc Gynecol Laparosc 1994;2:43–47 (Level III)

6. Koninckx PR, Meuleman C, Demeyere S, Lesaffre E, Cornillie FJ. Suggestive evidence that pelvic endometriosis is a progressive disease, whereas deeply infiltrating endometriosis is associated with pelvic pain. Fertil Steril 1991;55:759–765 (Level III)

7. Ling FW. Randomized controlled trial of depot leuprolide in patients with chronic pelvic pain and clinically suspected endometriosis. Pelvic Pain Study Group. Obstet Gynecol 1999;93:51–58 (Level I)

8. Ripps BA, Martin DC. Endometriosis and chronic pelvic pain. Obstet Gynecol Clin North Am 1993;20:709–717 (Level III)

9. Cramer DW. Epidemiology of endometriosis. In: Wilson EA, ed. Endometriosis. New York: Alan R. Liss Inc, 1987:5–22 (Level III)

10. Vigano P, Vercellini P, Di Blasio AM, Colombo A, Candiani GB, Vignali M. Deficient antiendometrium lymphocyte-mediated cytotoxicity in patients with endometriosis. Fertil Steril 1991;56:894–899 (Level II-2)

11. Keltz MD, Berger SB, Comite F, Olive DL. Duplicated cervix and vagina associated with infertility, endometriosis, and chronic pelvic pain. Obstet Gynecol 1994;84:701–703 (Level III)

12. Cramer DW, Wilson E, Stillman RJ, Berger MJ, Belisle S, Schiff I, et al. The relation of endometriosis to menstrual characteristics, smoking and exercise. JAMA 1986;255:1904–1908 (Level II-2)

13. Adamson GD. Diagnosis and clinical presentation of endometriosis. Am J Obstet Gynecol 1990;162:568–569 (Level III)

14. Management of endometriosis in the presence of pelvic pain. The American Fertility Society. Fertil Steril 1993;60:952–955 (Level III)

15. Luciano AA, Pitkin RM. Endometriosis: approaches to diagnosis and treatment. Surg Annu 1984;16:297–312 (Level III)

16. Muse K. Clinical manifestations and classification of endometriosis. Clin Obstet Gynecol 1988;31:813–822 (Level III)

17. Candiani GB, Vercellini P, Fedele L, Colombo A, Candiani M. Mild endometriosis and infertility: a critical review of epidemiologic data, diagnostic pitfalls, and classification limits. Obstet Gynecol Surv 1991;46:374–382 (Level III)

18. Berube S, Marcoux S, Langevin M, Maheux R. Fecundity of infertile women with minimal or mild endometriosis and women with unexplained infertility. Canadian Collaborative Group on Endometriosis. Fertil Steril 1998;69:1034–1041 (Level II-2)

19. Ronnberg L. Endometriosis and infertility. Ann Med 1990;22:91–96 (Level III)

20. Demco L. Mapping the source and character of pain due to endometriosis by patient-assisted laparoscopy. J Am Assoc Gynecol Laparosc 1998;5:241–245 (Level III)

21. Martin DC, Hubert GD, Vander Zwaag R, el-Zeky FA. Laparoscopic appearances of peritoneal endometriosis. Fertil Steril 1989;51:63–67 (Level III)

22. Stripling MC, Martin DC, Chatman DL, Zwaag RV, Poston WM. Subtle appearance of pelvic endometriosis. Fertil Steril 1988;49:427–431 (Level III)

23. Murphy AA, Green WR, Bobbie D, dela Cruz ZC, Rock JA. Unsuspected endometriosis documented by scanning electron microscopy in visually normal peritoneum. Fertil Steril 1986;46:522–524 (Level III)

24. Redwine DB, Yocum LB. A serial section study of visually normal pelvic peritoneum in patients with endometriosis. Fertil Steril 1990;54:648–651 (Level III)

25. Koninckx PR, Martin DC. Deep endometriosis: a consequence of infiltration or retraction or possibly adenomyosis externa? Fertil Steril 1992;58:924–928 (Level III)

26. Koninckx PR, Oosterlynck D, D'Hooghe T, Meuleman C. Deeply infiltrating endometriosis is a disease whereas mild endometriosis could be considered a non-disease. Ann NY Acad Sci 1994;734:333–341 (Level III)

27. Jansen RP, Russell P. Nonpigmented endometriosis: clinical, laparoscopic, and pathologic definition. Am J Obstet Gynecol 1986;155:1154–1159 (Level III)

28. Pittaway DE. CA-125 in women with endometriosis. Obstet Gynecol Clin North Am 1989;16:237–252 (Level II-1)

29. Barbieri RL, Niloff JM, Bast RC Jr, Scaetzl E, Kistner RW, Knapp RC. Elevated serum concentrations of CA-125 in patients with advanced endometriosis. Fertil Steril 1986;45:630–634 (Level II-2)

30. Barbati A, Cosmi EV, Spaziani R, Ventura R, Montanino G. Serum and peritoneal fluid CA-125 in patients with endometriosis. Fertil Steril 1994;61:438–442 (Level II-2)

31. Franchi M, Beretta P, Zanaboni F, Donadello N, Ghezzi F. Use of serum CA125 measurement in patients with endometriosis. Ital J Gynaecol Obstet 1993;5:149–152 (Level III)

32. Moretuzzo RW, DiLauro S, Jenison E, Chen SL, Reindollar RH, McDonough PG. Serum and peritoneal lavage fluid CA-125 levels in endometriosis. Fertil Steril 1988;50:430–433 (Level II-2)

33. Pittaway DE, Fayez JA. The use of CA-125 in the diagnosis and management of endometriosis. Fertil Steril 1986; 46:790–795 (Level II-2)

34. Colacurci N, Fortunato N, DeFranciscis P, Fratta M, Cioffi M, Zarcone R, et al. A. Serum and peritoneal CA-125 levels as diagnostic test for endometriosis. Eur J Obstet Gynecol Reprod Biol 1996;66:41–43 (Level III)

35. Mol BW, Bayram N, Lijmer JG, Wiegerinck MA, Bongers MY, van der Veen F, Bossuyt PM. The performance of CA-125 measurement in the detection of endometriosis: a meta-analysis. Fertil Steril 1998;70:1101–1108 (Meta-analysis)

36. Chen FP, Soong YK, Lee N, Lo SK. The use of serum CA-125 as a marker for endometriosis in patients with dysmenorrhea for monitoring therapy and for recurrence of endometriosis. Acta Obstet Gynecol Scand 1998;77: 665–670 (Level III)

37. Ozaksit G, Caglar T, Cicek N, Kuscu E, Batioglu S, Gokmen O. Serum CA 125 levels before, during and after treatment for endometriosis. Int J Gynaecol Obstet 1995; 50:269–273 (Level III)

38. Takahashi K, Kijima S, Yoshino K, Shibukawa T, Kitao M. Serum CA 125 as a marker for patients with external endometriosis. Int J Fertil 1989;34:143–148 (Level II-2)

39. Guerriero S, Mais V, Ajossa S, Paoletti AM, Angiolucci M, Melis GB. Transvaginal ultrasonography combined with CA-125 plasma levels in the diagnosis of endometrioma. Fertil Steril 1996;65:293–298 (Level II-2)

40. Kinkel K, Chapron C, Balleyguier C, Fritel X, Dubuisson JB, Moreau JF. Magnetic resonance imaging characteristics of deep endometriosis. Hum Reprod 1999;14: 1080–1086 (Level III)

41. Revised American Society for Reproductive Medicine classification of endometriosis: 1996. Fertil Steril 1997; 67:817–821 (Level III)

42. Bergqvist A, Bergh T, Hogstrom L, Mattson S, Nordenskjold F, Rasmussen C. Effects of triptorelin versus placebo on the symptoms of endometriosis. Fertil Steril 1998;69:702–708 (Level I)

43. Bulletti C, Flamigni C, Polli V, Giacomucci E, Albonetti A, Negrini V, et al. The efficacy of drugs in the management of endometriosis. J Am Assoc Gynecol Laprosc 1996;3:495–501 (Level II-2)

44. Hornstein MD, Surrey ES, Weisberg GW, Casino LA. Leuprolide acetate depot and hormonal add-back in endometriosis: a 12-month study. Lupron Add-Back Study Group Obstet Gynecol 1998;91:16–24 (Level I)

45. Vercellini P, De Giorgi O, Oldani S, Cortesi I, Panazza S, Crosignani PG. Depot medroxyprogesterone acetate versus an oral contraceptive combined with very-low-dose danazol for long-term treatment of pelvic pain associated with endometriosis. Am J Obstet Gynecol 1996;175: 396–401 (Level I)

46. Vercellini P, Cortesi I, Crosignani PG. Progestins for symptomatic endometriosis: a critical analysis of the evidence. Fertil Steril 1997;68:393–401 (Critical Analysis)

47. Rock JA, Truglia JA, Caplan RJ. Zoladex (goserelin acetate implant) in the treatment of endometriosis: a randomized comparison with danazol. The Zoladex Endometriosis Study Group Obstet Gynecol 1993;82: 198–205 (Level I)

48. Wheeler JM, Knittle JD, Miller JD. Depot leuprolide acetate versus danazol in the treatment of women with symptomatic endometriosis: a multicenter, double-blind, randomized clinical trial. II. Assessment of safety. The Lupron Endometriosis Study Group. Am J Obstet Gynecol 1993;169:26–33 (Level I)

49. Zorn JR, Mathieson J, Risquez F, Comaru-Schally AM, Schally AV. Treatment of endometriosis with delayed release preparation of the agonist D-Trp6-luteinizing hormone-releasing hormone: long-term follow-up in a series of 50 patients. Fertil Steril 1990;53:401–406 (Level II-3)

50. Vercellini P, Trespidi L, Colombo A, Vendola N, Marchini M, Crosignani PG. A gonadotropin-releasing hormone agonist versus a low-dose oral contraceptive for pelvic pain associated with endometriosis. Fertil Steril 1993; 60:75–79 (Level I)

51. Telimaa S, Puolakka J, Ronnberg L, Kauppila A. Placebo-controlled comparison of danazol and high-dose medroxyprogesterone acetate in the treatment of endometriosis. Gynecol Endocrinol 1987;1:13–23 (Level I)

52. Sutton CJ, Ewen SP, Whitelaw N, Haines P. Prospective, randomized, double-blind, controlled trial of laser laparoscopy in the treatment of pelvic pain associated with minimal, mild, and moderate endometriosis. Fertil Steril 1994;62:696–700 (Level I)

53. Sutton CJ, Pooley AS, Ewen SP, Haines P. Follow-up report on a randomized controlled trial of laser laparoscopy in the treatment of pelvic pain associated with minimal to moderate endometriosis. Fertil Steril 1997; 68:1070–1074 (Level I)

54. Waller KG, Shaw RW. Gonadotropin-releasing hormone analogues for the treatment of endometriosis: long-term follow-up. Fertil Steril 1993;59:511–515 (Level I)

55. Redwine DB. Conservative laparoscopic excision of endometriosis by sharp dissection: life table analysis of reoperation and persistent or recurrent disease. Fertil Steril 1991;56:628–634 (Level II-3)

56. Cook AS, Rock JA. The role of laparoscopy in the treatment of endometriosis. Fertil Steril 1991;55:663–680 (Level III)

57. Saidi MH, Vancaillie TG, White AJ, Sadler RK, Akright BD, Farhardt SA. Complications of major operative laparoscopy. A review of 452 cases. J Reprod Med 1996; 41:471–476 (Level III)

58. Revelli A, Modottii M, Ansaldi C, Massobrio M. Recurrent endometriosis: a review of biological and clinical aspects. Obstet Gynecol Surv 1995;50:747–754 (Level III)

59. Hornstein MD, Hemmings J, Yuzpe AA, Heinrichs WL. Use of nafarelin versus placebo after reductive laparoscopic surgery for endometriosis. Fertil Steril 1997;68: 860–864 (Level I)

60. Bianchi S, Busacca M, Agnoli B, Candiani M, Calia C, Vignali M. Effects of 3 month therapy with danazol after laparoscopic surgery for stage III/IV endometriosis: a randomized study. Hum Reprod 1999;14:1335–1337 (Level I)

61. Donnez J, Nisolle M, Clerckx F. Evaluation of preoperative use of danazol, gestrinone, lynestrenol, buserelin spray and buserelin implant, in the treatment of endometriosis associated infertility. In: Chadha DR, Buttram VC Jr eds. Current concepts in endometriosis. New York: Alan R. Liss, Inc, 1990:427–442 (Level II-2)

62. Muzii L, Marana R, Caruana P, Mancuso S. The impact of preoperative gonadotropin-releasing hormone agonist treatment in laparoscopic excision of ovarian endometriotic cysts. Fertil Steril 1996;65:1235–1237 (Level II-1)

63. Dlugi AM, Miller JD, Knittle J, Lupron Depot (leuprolide acetate for depot suspension) in the treatment of endometriosis: A randomized, placebo-controlled, double-blind study. Lupron Study Group. Fertil Steril 1990; 54:419–427 (Level I)

64. Henzl MR, Corson SL, Moghissi K, Buttram VC, Berqvist C, Jacobson J. Administration of nasal nafarelin as compared with oral danazol for endometriosis. A multicenter double-blind comparative clinical trial. N Engl J Med 1988;318:485–489 (Level I)

65. Hornstein MD, Yuzpe AA, Burry KA, Heinrichs LR, Buttram VC Jr, Orwoll ES. Prospective randomized double-blind trial of 3 versus 6 months of nafarelin therapy for endometriosis associated with pelvic pain. Fertil Steril 1995;63:955–962 (Level I)

66. Tummon IS, Pepping ME, Binor Z, Radwanska E, Dmowski WP. A randomized, prospective comparison of endocrine changes induced with intranasal leuprolide or danazol for treatment of endometriosis. Fertil Steril 1989;51:390–394 (Level I)

67. Cedars MI, Lu JK, Meldrum DR, Judd HL. Treatment of endometriosis with a long-acting gonadotropin-releasing hormone agonist plus medroxyprogesterone acetate. Obstet Gynecol 1990;75:641–645 (Level III)

68. Makarainen L, Ronnberg L, Kauppila A. Medroxyprogesterone acetate supplementation diminishes the hypoestrogenic side effects of gonadotropin-releasing hormone agonist without changing its efficacy in endometriosis. Fertil Steril 1996;65:29–34 (Level I)

69. Surrey ES, Judd HL. Reduction of vasomotor symptoms and bone mineral density loss with combined norethindrone and long-acting gonadotropin-releasing hormone agonist therapy of symptomatic endometriosis: a prospective randomized trial. J Clin Endocrinol Metab 1992; 75:558–563 (Level I)

70. Surrey ES, Fournet N, Voigt B, Judd HL. Effects of sodium etidronate in combination with low-dose norethindrone in patients administered a long-acting GnRH agonist. a preliminary report. Obstet Gynecol 1993;81: 581–586 (Level I)

71. Kiilholma P, Tuimala R, Kivinen S, Korhonen M, Hagman E. Comparison of the gonadotropin-releasing hormone agonist goserelin acetate alone versus goserelin combined with estrogen progestin add-back therapy in the treatment of endometriosis. Fertil Steril 1995;64:903–908 (Level I)

72. Moghissi KS, Schlaff WD, Olive DL, Skinner MA, Yin H. Goserelin acetate (Zoladex) with or without hormone replacement therapy for the treatment of endometriosis. Fertil Steril 1998;69:1056–1062 (Level I)

73. Finkelstein JS, Klibanski A, Schaefer EH, Hornstein MD, Schiff I, Neer RM. Parathyroid hormone for the prevention of bone loss induced by estrogen deficiency. N Engl J Med 1994;331:1618–1623 (Level I)

74. Roux C, Pelissier C, Listrat V, Kolta S, Simonetta C, Guignard M, et al. Bone loss during gonadotropin releasing hormone agonist treatment and use of nasal calcitonin. Osteoporos Int 1995;5:185–190 (Level I)

75. Howell R, Edmonds DK, Dowsett M, Crook D, Lees B, Stevenson JC. Gonadotropin-releasing hormone analogue (goserelin) plus hormone replacement therapy for the treatment of endometriosis: a randomized controlled trial. Fertil Steril 1995;64:474–481 (Level I)

76. Fogelman I. Gonadotropin-releasing hormone agonists and the skeleton. Fertil Steril 1992;57:715–724 (Level III)

77. Dawood MY. Hormonal therapies for endometriosis: implications for bone metabolism. Acta Obstet Gynecol Scand 1994;159:22–34 (Level III)

78. Agarwal SK, Harmrang C, Henzl MR, Judd HL. Nafarelin vs. leuprolide acetate depot for endometriosis. Changes in bone mineral density and vasomotor symptoms. Nafarelin Study Group. J Reprod Med 1997;42:413–423 (Level I)

79. Lemay A, Brideau NA, Forest JC, Dodin S, Maheux R. Cholesterol fractions and apolipoproteins during endometriosis treatment by a gonadotrophin releasing hormone (GnRH) agonist implant or by danazol. Clin Endocrinol (Oxf)1991;35:305–310 (Level II-3)

80. Fahraeus L, Larsson-Cohn U, Ljungberg S, Wallentin L. Profound alterations of the lipoprotein metabolism during danazol treatment in premenopausal women. Fertil Steril 1984;42:52–57 (Level III)

81. Fahraeus L, Sydsjo A, Wallentin L. Lipoprotein changes during treatment of pelvic endometriosis with medroxyprogesterone acetate. Fertil Steril 1986;45:503–506 (Level III)

82. Hornstein MD, Yuzpe AA, Burry K, Buttram VC Jr, Heinrichs LR, Soderstrom RM, et al. Retreatment with nafarelin for recurrent endometriosis symptoms: efficacy, safety and bone mineral density. Fertil Steril 1997; 67:1013–1018 (Level III)

83. Howard FM. The role of laparoscopy in chronic pelvic pain: promises and pitfalls. Obstet Gynecol Surv 1993; 48:357–387 (Level III)

84. Wardle PG, Hull MG. Is endometriosis a disease? Baillieres Clin Obstet Gynaecol 1993;7:673–685 (Level III)

85. Marcoux S, Maheux R, Berube S. Laparoscopic surgery in infertile women with minimal or mild endometriosis. Canadian Collaborative Group on Endometriosis. N Engl J Med 1997;337:217–222 (Level I)

86. Canadian Consensus Conference on Endometriosis Chapter 2 Consensus Statements. J SOGC 1999;21: 471–473 (Level III)

87. Guerriero S, Mais V, Ajossa S, Paoletti AM, Angiolucci M, Labate F, et al. The role of endovaginal ultrasound in differentiating endometriomas from other ovarian cysts. Clin Exp Obstet Gynecol 1995;22:20–22 (Level III)

88. Donnez J, Nisolle M, Clerckx F, Casanas-Roux F, Saussoy P, Gillerot S. Advanced endoscopic techniques used in dysfunctional bleeding, fibroids and endometriosis, and the role of gonadotropin-releasing hormone agonist treatment. Br J Gynaecol 1994;101(Suppl 10):2–9 (Level III)

89. Shimizu I, Nakanishi R, Yoshino I, Yasumoto K. An endometrial nodule in the lung without pelvic endometriosis. J Cardiovasc Surg (Torino) 1998;39:867–868 (Level III)

90. Hughes ML, Bartholomew D, Paluzzi M. Abdominal wall endometriosis after amniocentesis. A case report. J Reprod Med 1997;42:597–599 (Level III)

91. Shek Y, De Lia JE, Pattillo RA. Endometriosis with a pleural effusion and ascites. Report of a case treated with nafarelin acetate. J Reprod Med 1995;40:540–542 (Level III)

92. Espaulella J, Armengol J, Bella F, Lain JM, Calaf J. Pulmonary endometriosis: conservative treatment with GnRH agonists. Obstet Gynecol 1991;78:535-537 (Level III)

93. Johnson WM 3d, Tyndal CM. Pulmonary endometriosis: treatment with danazol. Obstet Gynecol 1987;69:506–507 (Level III)

94. Wheeler JH, Malinak LR. Recurrent endometriosis: incidence, management, and prognosis. Am J Obstet Gynecol 1983;146:247–253 (Level III)

95. Namnoun AB, Hickman TN, Goodman SB, Gehlbach DL, Rock JA. Incidence of symptom recurrence after hysterectomy for endometriosis. Fertil Steril 1995;64:898–902 (Level III)

96. Redwine DB. Endometriosis persisting after castration: clinical characteristics and results of surgical management. Obstet Gynecol 1994;83:405–413 (Level III)

97. Lam AM, French M, Charnock FM. Bilateral ureteric obstruction due to recurrent endometriosis associated with hormone replacement therapy. Aust N Z J Obstet Gynaecol 1992;32:83–84 (Level III)

98. Hickman TN, Namnoun AB, Hinton EL, Zacur HA, Rock JA Timing of estrogen replacement therapy following hysterectomy with oophorectomy for endometriosis. Obstet Gynecol 1998;91:673–677 (Level II-3)

99. Gucer F, Pieber D, Arikan MG. Malignancy arising in extraovarian endometriosis during estrogen stimulation. Eur J Gynaecol Oncol 1998;19:39–41 (Level III)

The MEDLINE database, the Cochrane Library, and ACOG's own internal resources were used to conduct a literature search to locate relevant articles published between January 1985 and May 1999. The search was restricted to articles published in the English language. Priority was given to articles reporting results of original research, although review articles and commentaries also were consulted. Abstracts of research presented at symposia and scientific conferences were not considered adequate for inclusion in this document. Guidelines published by organizations or institutions such as the National Institutes of Health and the American College of Obstetricians and Gynecologists were reviewed, and additional studies were located by reviewing bibliographies of identified articles. When reliable research was not available, expert opinions from obstetrician–gynecologists were used.

Studies were reviewed and evaluated for quality according to the method outlined by the U.S. Preventive Services Task Force:

I   Evidence obtained from at least one properly designed randomized controlled trial.

II-1   Evidence obtained from well-designed controlled trials without randomization.

II-2   Evidence obtained from well-designed cohort or case–control analytic studies, preferably from more than one center or research group.

II-3   Evidence obtained from multiple time series with or without the intervention. Dramatic results in uncontrolled experiments could also be regarded as this type of evidence.

III   Opinions of respected authorities, based on clinical experience, descriptive studies, or reports of expert committees.

Based on the highest level of evidence found in the data, recommendations are provided and graded according to the following categories:

Level A—Recommendations are based on good and consistent scientific evidence.

Level B—Recommendations are based on limited or inconsistent scientific evidence.

Level C—Recommendations are based primarily on consensus and expert opinion.

ISSN 1099-3630

**The American College of
Obstetricians and Gynecologists
409 12th Street, SW
PO Box 96920
Washington, DC 20090-6920**

12345/32109

ACOG PRACTICE BULLETIN

CLINICAL MANAGEMENT GUIDELINES FOR
OBSTETRICIAN–GYNECOLOGISTS

NUMBER 3, December 1998

(Replaces Technical Bulletin Number 150, December 1990)

This Practice Bulletin was developed by the ACOG Committee on Practice Bulletins— Gynecology with the assistance of Steven J. Ory, MD. The information is designed to aid practitioners in making decisions about appropriate obstetric and gynecologic care. These guidelines should not be construed as dictating an exclusive course of treatment or procedure. Variations in practice may be warranted based on the needs of the individual patient, resources, and limitations unique to the institution or type of practice.

Medical Management of Tubal Pregnancy

Ectopic pregnancy is a major health problem for women of reproductive age and, in the United States, is the leading cause of pregnancy-related death during the first trimester. Diagnosis and treatment of tubal pregnancy before tubal rupture occurs decreases the risk of death. Early detection may make it possible for some patients to receive medical therapy instead of surgery. Methotrexate, a folinic acid antagonist, has been used to treat patients with small unruptured tubal pregnancies. The purpose of this document is to present evidence, including risks and benefits, about methotrexate as an alternative treatment for selected ectopic pregnancies.

Background

Incidence

The incidence of ectopic pregnancy has increased in the United States since 1970, the year the Centers for Disease Control (CDC; now the Centers for Disease Control and Prevention) first began collecting data, when the rate was 4.5 per 1,000 reported pregnancies. In 1992, there were an estimated 108,800 ectopic pregnancies, accounting for about 20 per 1,000 pregnancies and about 9% of all pregnancy-related deaths (1). Current data do not include conditions diagnosed and treated in physicians' offices; therefore, the true incidence of ectopic pregnancy is probably underestimated.

Etiology

Prior pelvic inflammatory disease, especially that caused by *Chlamydia trachomatis*, is the most important risk factor for ectopic pregnancy; observed odds ratios range from 2.0 to 7.5 (2). Other factors that appear to be associated with an increased risk of ectopic pregnancy include prior ectopic pregnancy, cigarette smoking, prior tubal surgery (especially for distal tubal disease), diethylstilbestrol exposure, and increasing age.

A history of infertility, independent of tubal disease, and ovulation induction also appear to be risk factors for ectopic pregnancy. Ectopic pregnancy is more likely to be diagnosed early in patients being treated for infertility. Such patients may be good candidates for medical therapy.

Effects of Therapy

Methotrexate is a folinic acid antagonist that inhibits dihydrofolic acid reductase, interfering with DNA synthesis, repair, and cellular replication. Actively proliferating tissue such as malignant cells, bone marrow, fetal cells, buccal and intestinal mucosa, and cells of the urinary bladder generally are more sensitive to these effects of methotrexate. Methotrexate has the potential for serious toxicity. Toxic effects usually are related to the amount and duration of therapy, but toxicity has been seen even with low doses. When methotrexate is used as a treatment for ectopic pregnancy, most reported side effects have been mild and self-limiting (3–12). This is probably a reflection of the lower dosage and shortened duration of treatment compared with dosages used in treating malignancies.

Diagnosis

Serial quantitative levels of the beta subunit of human chorionic gonadotropin (β-hCG) can be used in combination with transvaginal ultrasonography and, in some cases, suction curettage and serum progesterone measurements to differentiate failed intrauterine pregnancy, threatened abortion, and intrauterine or ectopic pregnancies. A presumptive diagnosis of unruptured tubal ectopic pregnancy is required before medical management can be considered.

Beta Subunit of Human Chorionic Gonadotropin

The mean plasma concentration of human chorionic gonadotropin (hCG) is significantly lower for an ectopic pregnancy than for a viable intrauterine pregnancy, but there is no definitive laboratory level permitting distinction between the two. A consistently declining hCG level indicates a nonviable pregnancy.

Conventionally, serial hCG testing to diagnose suspected ectopic pregnancy is performed at 48-hour intervals; a 66% or greater increase should be observed in a normal pregnancy. Approximately 15% of normal intrauterine pregnancies are associated with less than a 66% increase in hCG, and 17% of ectopic pregnancies have normal doubling times (13). Limitations of serial hCG testing include its inability to distinguish a failing intrauterine pregnancy from an ectopic pregnancy and the inherent 48-hour delay. A prospective study of asymptomatic patients described a 36% sensitivity and a 63–71% specificity (14). However, most reports and clinicians have found serial hCG testing useful in the early diagnosis of ectopic pregnancy. The rate of hCG doubling decreases from every 1.4–1.5 days in early pregnancy to every 3.3–3.5 days at 6–7 weeks of gestation, at which point the reliability of serial testing may be diminished.

The elimination of hCG after treatment of ectopic pregnancy follows a two-phase distribution. The major elimination has a half-life of 5–9 hours and a second, longer phase has a half-life of 22–32 hours.

The quantitation of hCG has been complicated by the existence of three different reference standards for hCG assays, the existence of multiple antibodies in commercial assays, and confusing nomenclature. These complicating factors can cause varying and inconsistent results, both from one laboratory to another and within the same laboratory, and affect interpretation of the results and clinical management.

Ultrasonography

Transvaginal ultrasonography often can detect intrauterine pregnancy within 5 weeks of the last menstrual period. The concept of the discriminatory hCG zone, originally applied to transabdominal ultrasonography, is the range of serum hCG concentration above which a normal intrauterine gestation can be visualized consistently. When the hCG level exceeds the discriminatory zone, the absence of an intrauterine gestational sac is suggestive of ectopic pregnancy, but this also can occur with multiple gestation or failed intrauterine pregnancy. The specific discriminatory zone varies with the hCG assay chosen, the reference standard with which it is calibrated, and the available ultrasound resolution. Findings also may be compromised by obesity, fibroids, and the axis of the uterus. An intrauterine gestational sac in a normal uterus usually can be seen with transvaginal ultrasonography when the hCG level is between 1,000 to 2,000 mIU/mL (1st and 2nd International Reference Preparation or IRP) (15, 16). If the precise gestational age is known, as in the case of patients receiving hCG for ovulation induction or oocyte retrieval, the failure to detect a gestational sac 24 days or later after conception is presumptive evidence of an abnormal pregnancy (13).

Historically, detection of an intrauterine sac has led to the presumptive exclusion of ectopic pregnancy, based on the estimate of the incidence of heterotopic pregnancy of 1 in 30,000. This figure was calculated almost 50 years ago by multiplying the incidence of ectopic pregnancy by that of dizygotic twinning, thus producing a hypothetical estimate. The incidence of heterotopic pregnancy appears to have increased with the use of assisted reproductive techniques. It has been reported to be as high as 1% in some series (17), although the overall incidence of heterotopic pregnancy is probably much lower.

The identification of an ectopic gestational sac is diagnostic of ectopic pregnancy, but it is not seen in all cases. Sensitivity and specificity of transvaginal ultrasonography to identify ectopic pregnancy vary according to criteria used for diagnosis. Reported sensitivity of transvaginal ultrasonography ranges from 20.1% to 84% and specificity from 98.9% to 100%, depending on the criteria applied (18). Color flow Doppler may aid in the diagnosis of ectopic pregnancy; however, it requires considerably greater technical expertise (19, 20).

Serum Progesterone

Some clinicians maintain that measurement of serum progesterone levels may be useful for distinguishing viable intrauterine pregnancies from spontaneous abortions and ectopic pregnancies, but serum progesterone levels cannot distinguish ectopic pregnancy from spontaneous abortion (21). There is no single progesterone value that will definitively confirm the viability or nonviability of an intrauterine pregnancy or the presence of an ectopic pregnancy. Serum progesterone levels increase during pregnancy (22). If the duration of the pregnancy is unknown, interpretation of the test results is less reliable. The use of ovulation-induction agents is associated with higher serum progesterone levels in intrauterine and ectopic pregnancies.

Of pregnant patients with serum progesterone values of less than 5 ng/mL, 85% have spontaneous abortions, 0.16% have viable intrauterine pregnancies, and 14% have ectopic pregnancies (23). Pregnant patients with serum progesterone levels between 20.0 and 24.9 ng/mL have ectopic pregnancies in 4% of cases; 2% of ectopic pregnancies occur with serum progesterone levels greater than 25 ng/mL. Most ectopic pregnancies (52%) are associated with serum progesterone levels between 10 and 20 ng/mL, thus limiting the clinical utility of this assessment (24).

The absence of products of conception on curettage in the presence of an elevated β-hCG level is evidence of a presumptive diagnosis of ectopic pregnancy. More rarely, gestational trophoblastic disease, nongestational choriocarcinoma, or an embryonal cell tumor may be the cause.

Success Rates

Success is defined as resolution of the ectopic pregnancy without surgical intervention. Reported success rates range from 67% to 100%, with a median of 84% for the single-dose methotrexate regimen (3–12). The largest study involved 120 women and had an overall success rate of 94.1% (10). Variation in success rates may be affected by the selection criteria and differences in management. Of those cases with successful outcome, as many as 25% required more than one dose of methotrexate (3, 6, 8, 25).

Clinical Considerations and Recommendations

▶ *Who are candidates for medical management?*

General factors to consider in determining candidates for medical therapy include the size of the ectopic mass, whether it has ruptured, and the desire for future fertility. Patients should be hemodynamically stable without active bleeding or signs of hemoperitoneum. Furthermore, they should be willing and able to return for follow-up care.

Criteria for Receiving Methotrexate

Absolute indications

   Hemodynamically stable without active bleeding or signs of hemoperitoneum

   Nonlaparoscopic diagnosis

   Patient desires future fertility

   General anesthesia poses a significant risk

   Patient is able to return for follow-up care

   Patient has no contraindications to methotrexate

Relative indications

   Unruptured mass ≤3.5 cm at its greatest dimension

   No fetal cardiac motion detected

   Patients whose β-hCG level does not exceed a predetermined value (6,000–15,000 mIU/mL)

Contraindications to Medical Therapy

Absolute contraindications

   Breastfeeding

   Overt or laboratory evidence of immunodeficiency

   Alcoholism, alcoholic liver disease, or other chronic liver disease

   Preexisting blood dyscrasias, such as bone marrow hypoplasia, leukopenia, thrombocytopenia, or significant anemia

   Known sensitivity to methotrexate

   Active pulmonary disease

   Peptic ulcer disease

   Hepatic, renal, or hematologic dysfunction

Relative contraindications

   Gestational sac ≥3.5 cm

   Embryonic cardiac motion

Absolute and relative indications and contraindications to medical therapy are shown in the boxes.

▶ *How is methotrexate used in the medical management of tubal ectopic pregnancy?*

Because injected methotrexate is a relatively new treatment for ectopic pregnancy, a standardized protocol has yet to be defined. There are small variations among the published protocols, but all share a basic strategy. The differences are in the amount of methotrexate given, the frequency of follow-up visits, and the types of tests and procedures routinely used to monitor treatment response.

Before methotrexate is injected, blood is drawn to determine baseline laboratory values for renal, liver, and bone marrow function, as well as to measure the β-hCG level. Progesterone also may be measured. Blood type, Rh factor, and the presence of antibodies should be determined. Patients who are Rh negative receive Rh immune globulin. The methotrexate dose usually is calculated according to estimated body surface area (50 mg/m^2) and is given in one dose. Treatment with a standard 75 mg dose (11) and multiple serial doses with a folinic acid rescue on alternate days (four doses of methotrexate [1.0 mg/kg] on days 0, 2, 4, and 6 and four doses of leucovorin [0.1 mg/kg] on days 1, 3, 5, and 7) (26, 27) also have been successful. Methotrexate is given either in divided doses, half into each buttock, or in one intramuscular injection (3–12).

Follow-up care continues until β-hCG levels are nondetectable. Time to resolution is variable and can be protracted, taking a month or longer (3, 5, 6, 9, 10, 12). With the single-dose regimen, levels of β-hCG usually increase during the first several days following methotrexate injection and peak 4 days after injection. If a treatment response is observed, hCG levels should decline by 7 days after injection (4, 10, 11). If the β-hCG level does not decline by at least 15% from day 4 to day 7, the patient may require either surgery (4), or a second dose of methotrexate if no contraindications exist (3, 5, 10–12). If there is an adequate treatment response, hCG determinations are reduced to once a week. An additional dose of methotrexate may be given if β-hCG levels plateau or increase in 7 days (6–10). Surgical intervention may be required for patients who do not respond to medical therapy. Ultrasound examination may be repeated to evaluate significant changes in clinical status, such as increased pelvic pain, bleeding, or inadequate declines of β-hCG levels (5, 6, 9, 10).

▶ *What are the potential problems associated with medical management of ectopic pregnancy?*

Potential problems can be divided into three categories: 1) drug-related side effects, 2) treatment-related compli-

---

Side Effects Associated with Methotrexate Treatment

Drug side effects

Nausea

Vomiting

Stomatitis

Diarrhea

Gastric distress

Dizziness

Severe neutropenia (rare)

Reversible alopecia (rare)

Pneumonitis

Treatment effects

Increase in abdominal pain (occurs in up to two thirds of patients)

Increase in β-hCG levels during first 1–3 days of treatment

Vaginal bleeding or spotting

Signs of treatment failure and tubal rupture

Significantly worsening abdominal pain, regardless of change in β-hCG levels

Hemodynamic instability

Levels of β-hCG that do not decline by at least 15% between day 4 and day 7 postinjection

Increasing or plateauing β-hCG levels after the first week of treatment

---

cations, and 3) treatment failure (see the box). If medical therapy fails, additional treatment is required; in case of tubal rupture, rapid surgical intervention is necessary. It is important, therefore, to monitor patients for signs and symptoms of tubal rupture and treatment failure.

During treatment, patients should be counseled to discontinue folinic acid supplements, including prenatal vitamins. Because of its potential toxicity, patients receiving methotrexate should be monitored carefully. Physicians using this drug should be aware of potential side effects and signs of toxicity and be advised to avoid the use of nonsteroidal antiinflammatory drugs.

An initial increase in β-hCG levels often occurs by the third day and is not a cause for alarm (4, 10, 11). Most patients experience at least one episode of increased abdominal pain sometime during treatment (5, 6, 9–11). Because abdominal pain also is suggestive of tubal rupture, care should be taken to evaluate any significant change in discomfort. The pain associated with resolution of tubal pregnancy usually can be distinguished from tubal rupture. It generally is milder, of limited duration (24–48 hours), and not associated with signs of an acute abdomen or hemodynamic instability.

Medical treatment has failed when β-hCG levels either increase or plateau by day 7 postinjection, indicating a continuing ectopic pregnancy, or when the tube ruptures. Tubal rupture may occur despite declining β-hCG levels (6, 9, 10).

▶ *How should patients be counseled about immediate and long-term effects of medical therapy?*

Patients should receive information about the types of side effects they may experience and about activity restrictions during treatment. They should be informed of the ongoing risk of tubal rupture during treatment; it is important to educate patients about symptoms of tubal rupture and emphasize the need to seek immediate medical attention if these symptoms occur (see the box).

It is difficult to assess the impact of methotrexate treatment for ectopic pregnancy on a woman's ability to conceive. Published evidence regarding conception rates following methotrexate administration is limited. One study reported a 20% conception rate among 15 women, with a mean follow-up time of 11.8 months (5). Another study reported a significantly greater conception rate of 79.6%, with a mean time to conception of 3.2 months (10); 12.8% of the conceptions were recurrent ectopic pregnancies. The impact of methotrexate on future fertility requires further study.

▶ *How cost-effective is methotrexate treatment?*

There is evidence that methotrexate therapy is a cost-effective treatment for small unruptured ectopic pregnancies when compared with laparoscopic salpingostomy. The direct cost advantages are due to elimination of oper-

ating room use, anesthesia services, and surgical fees. Indirect costs decrease as a result of quicker recovery times; however, the amount of savings depends on the proportion of patients eligible to receive medical therapy and the overall success rate. A study comparing direct costs of methotrexate with laparoscopic salpingostomy found there are significant savings if methotrexate is used as the primary therapy (28). An additional study looked retrospectively at patients treated for ectopic pregnancy and also found methotrexate was cost-effective (29).

▶ *Is there ever a role for expectant management?*

Distinguishing patients who are experiencing spontaneous resolution of their ectopic pregnancies from patients who have proliferating ectopic pregnancies and require active intervention is a clinical dilemma. In patients who are suspected to be undergoing spontaneous clinical resolution, expectant management is an option that has been used in the hope of avoiding therapy that might otherwise be unnecessary. Candidates for successful expectant management must be willing to accept the potential risks of tubal rupture and hemorrhage; they should be asymptomatic and have objective evidence of resolution (generally manifested by declining hCG levels). In general, patients with early, small tubal gestations with lower hCG levels are the best candidates for observant management. Approximately 20–30% of ectopic pregnancies are associated with declining hCG levels at the time of presentation (30). If the initial hCG level is less than 200 mIU/mL, 88% of patients experience spontaneous resolution. Lower success rates can be anticipated with higher hCG levels (31). Reasons for abandoning expectant management include intractable or significant increase in pain, failure of hCG levels to decrease, and tubal rupture with hemoperitoneum.

Summary

The following recommendations are based on limited or inconsistent scientific evidence (Level B):

▶ Intramuscular methotrexate is an appropriate method for treating selected patients with small, unruptured tubal pregnancies.*

▶ Successful treatment with methotrexate may require more than one dose of methotrexate.*

▶ Failure of β-hCG levels to decrease by at least 15% from day 4 to day 7 after methotrexate administration indicates the need for an additional dose of methotrexate or surgery.*

---

* Evidence is limited but consistent.

Counseling Patients

Patients should be instructed on the following points:

To expect to experience one or more side effects, including abdominal pain, vaginal bleeding or spotting, or medication side effects

To contact the physician in the presence of sudden onset of severe abdominal pain; substantial increase in abdominal pain; heavy vaginal bleeding; or dizziness, syncope, or tachycardia

To avoid alcoholic beverages, vitamins containing folic acid, nonsteroidal antiinflammatory drugs, and sexual intercourse until advised otherwise

The following recommendation is based primarily on consensus and expert opinion (Level C):

▶ There may be a role for expectant management of hemodynamically stable patients with presumptive ectopic pregnancy in whom β-hCG levels are low (<200 mIU/mL) and declining.

References

1. Centers for Disease Control and Prevention. Ectopic pregnancy—United States, 1990–1992. MMWR Morb Mortal Wkly Rep 1995;44:46–48 (Level II-3)

2. Chow WH, Daling JR, Cates W Jr, Greenberg RS. Epidemiology of ectopic pregnancy. Epidemiol Rev 1987;9: 70–94 (Level III)

3. Corsan GH, Karacan M, Qasim S, Bohrer MK, Ransom MX, Kemmann E. Identification of hormonal parameters for successful systemic single-dose methotrexate therapy in ectopic pregnancy. Hum Reprod 1995;10:2719–2722 (Level II-3)

4. Fernandez H, Bourget P, Ville Y, Lelaidier C, Frydman R. Treatment of unruptured tubal pregnancy with methotrexate: pharmacokinetic analysis of local versus intramuscular administration. Fertil Steril 1994;62:943–947 (Level I)

5. Glock JL, Johnson JV, Brumsted JR. Efficacy and safety of single-dose systemic methotrexate in the treatment of ectopic pregnancy. Fertil Steril 1994;62:716–721 (Level II-3)

6. Gross Z, Rodriguez JJ, Stalnaker BL. Ectopic pregnancy: nonsurgical, outpatient evaluation and single-dose methotrexate treatment. J Reprod Med 1995;40:371–374 (Level III)

7. Henry MA, Gentry WL. Single injection of methotrexate for treatment of ectopic pregnancies. Am J Obstet Gynecol 1994;171:1584–1587 (Level II-3)

8. Ransom MX, Garcia AJ, Bohrer M, Corsan GH, Kemmann E. Serum progesterone as a predictor of methotrexate success in the treatment of ectopic pregnancy. Obstet Gynecol 1994;83:1033–1037 (Level II-3)

9. Stika CS, Anderson L, Frederiksen MC. Single-dose methotrexate for the treatment of ectopic pregnancy: Northwestern Memorial Hospital three-year experience. Am J Obstet Gynecol 1996;174:1840–1846; discussion 1846–1848 (Level II-3)

10. Stovall TG, Ling FW. Single-dose methotrexate: an expanded clinical trial. Am J Obstet Gynecol 1993;168: 1759–1765 (Level II-3)

11. Wolf GC, Nickisch SA, George KE, Teicher JR, Simms TD. Completely nonsurgical management of ectopic pregnancies. Gynecol Obstet Invest 1994;37:232–235 (Level II-3)

12. Yao M, Tulandi T, Falcone T. Treatment of ectopic pregnancy by systemic methotrexate, transvaginal methotrexate, and operative laparoscopy. Int J Fertil 1996;41:470–475 (Level II-3)

13. Kadar N, Caldwell BV, Romero R. A method of screening for ectopic pregnancy and its indications. Obstet Gynecol 1981;58:162–166 (Level II-2)

14. Shepherd RW, Patton PE, Novy MJ, Burry KA. Serial beta-hCG measurements in the early detection of ectopic pregnancy. Obstet Gynecol 1990;75:417–420 (Level III)

15. Fossum GT, Davajan V, Kletzky OA. Early detection of pregnancy with transvaginal ultrasound. Fertil Steril 1988;49:788–791 (Level II-3)

16. Goldstein SR, Snyder JR, Watson C, Danon M. Very early pregnancy detection with endovaginal ultrasound. Obstet Gynecol 1988;72:200–204 (Level II-3)

17. Svare J, Norup P, Grove Thomsen S, Hornnes P, Maigaard S, Helm P, et al. Heterotopic pregnancies after in-vitro fertilization and embryo transfer—a Danish survey. Hum Reprod 1993;8:116–118 (Level III)

18. Brown DL, Doubilet PM. Transvaginal sonography for diagnosing ectopic pregnancy: positivity criteria and performance characteristics. J Ultrasound Med 1994;13:259–266 (Level III)

19. Kirchler HC, Seebacher S, Alge AA, Muller-Holzner E, Fessler S, Kolle D. Early diagnosis of tubal pregnancy: changes in tubal blood flow evaluated by endovaginal color Doppler sonography. Obstet Gynecol 1993;82:561– 565 (Level II-2)

20. Pellerito JS, Troiano RN, Quedens-Case C, Taylor KJ. Common pitfalls of endovaginal color Doppler flow imaging. Radiographics 1995;15:37–47 (Level III)

21. Stovall TG, Ling FW, Carson SA, Buster JE. Serum progesterone and uterine curettage in differential diagnosis of ectopic pregnancy. Fertil Steril 1992;57:456–457 (Level III)

22. Stern JJ, Voss F, Coulam CB. Early diagnosis of ectopic pregnancy using receiver-operator characteristic curves of serum progesterone concentrations. Hum Reprod 1993;8: 775–779 (Level III)

23. McCord ML, Muram D, Buster JE, Arheart KL, Stovall TG, Carson SA. Single serum progesterone as a screen for ectopic pregnancy: exchanging specificity and sensitivity to obtain optimal test performance. Fertil Steril 1996; 66:513–516 (Level II-3)

24. Gelder MS, Boots LR, Younger JB. Use of a single random serum progesterone value as a diagnostic aid for ectopic pregnancy. Fertil Steril 1991;55:497–500 (Level II-2)

25. Lipscomb GH, Bran D, McCord ML, Portera JC, Ling FW. Analysis of three hundred fifteen ectopic pregnancies treated with single-dose methotrexate. Am J Obstet Gynecol 1998;178:1354–1358 (Level II-3)

26. Hajenius PJ, Engelsbel S, Mol BW, Van der Veen F, Ankum WM, Bossuyt PM, et al. Randomised trial of systemic methotrexate versus laparoscopic salpingostomy in tubal pregnancy. Lancet 1997;350:774–779 (Level I)

27. Stovall TG, Ling FW, Gray LA, Carson SA, Buster JE. Methotrexate treatment of unruptured ectopic pregnancy: a report of 100 cases. Obstet Gynecol 1991;77:749–753 (Level II-3)

28. Alexander JM, Rouse DJ, Varner E, Austin JM Jr. Treatment of the small unruptured ectopic pregnancy: a

cost analysis of methotrexate versus laparoscopy. Obstet Gynecol 1996;88:123–127 (Level III)

29. Creinin MD, Washington AE. Cost of ectopic pregnancy management: surgery versus methotrexate. Fertil Steril 1993;60:963–969 (Level II-2)

30. Shalev E, Peleg D, Tsabari A, Romano S, Bustan M. Spontaneous resolution of ectopic tubal pregnancy: natural history. Fertil Steril 1995;63:15–19 (Level II-3)

31. Korhonen J, Stenman UH, Ylöstalo P. Serum human chorionic gonadotropin dynamics during spontaneous resolution of ectopic pregnancy. Fertil Steril 1994;61:632–636 (Level III)

The MEDLINE database, the Cochrane Library, and ACOG's own internal resources and documents were used to conduct a literature search to locate relevant articles published between January 1985 and June 1998. The search was restricted to articles published in the English language. Priority was given to articles reporting results of original research, although review articles and commentaries also were consulted. Abstracts of research presented at symposia and scientific conferences were not considered adequate for inclusion in this document. Guidelines published by organizations or institutions such as the National Institutes of Health and the American College of Obstetricians and Gynecologists were reviewed, and additional studies were located by reviewing bibliographies of identified articles. When reliable research was not available, expert opinions from obstetrician–gynecologists were used.

Studies were reviewed and evaluated for quality according to the method outlined by the U.S. Preventive Services Task Force:

I   Evidence obtained from at least one properly designed randomized controlled trial

II-1 Evidence obtained from well-designed controlled trials without randomization

II-2 Evidence obtained from well-designed cohort or case–control analytic studies, preferably from more than one center or research group

II-3 Evidence obtained from multiple time series with or without the intervention. Dramatic results in uncontrolled experiments could also be regarded as this type of evidence.

III Opinions of respected authorities, based on clinical experience, descriptive studies, or reports of expert committees

Based on the highest level of evidence found in the data, recommendations are provided and graded according to the following categories:

Level A—Recommendations are based on good and consistent scientific evidence.

Level B—Recommendations are based on limited or inconsistent scientific evidence.

Level C—Recommendations are based primarily on consensus and expert opinion.

ISSN 1099-3630   12345/21098

**The American College of
Obstetricians and Gynecologists
409 12th Street, SW
PO Box 96920
Washington, DC 20090-6920**

ACOG PRACTICE BULLETIN

CLINICAL MANAGEMENT GUIDELINES FOR
OBSTETRICIAN–GYNECOLOGISTS

NUMBER 17, JUNE 2000

(Replaces Technical Bulletin Number 196, August 1994)

This Practice Bulletin was developed by the ACOG Committee on Practice Bulletins—Obstetrics with the assistance of Michael Belfort, MD. The information is designed to aid practitioners in making decisions about appropriate obstetric and gynecologic care. These guidelines should not be construed as dictating an exclusive course of treatment or procedure. Variations in practice may be warranted based on the needs of the individual patient, resources, and limitations unique to the institution or type of practice.

Operative Vaginal Delivery

The incidence of operative vaginal delivery in the United States is estimated to be 10–15% (1), and although these procedures are safe in appropriate circumstances, controversy about them persists. Recent reports have highlighted the potential for maternal and neonatal complications associated with operative vaginal delivery, although the risks associated with alternative procedures also must be considered. This document will address specific controversial issues about the use of forceps and vacuum extractors for operative vaginal delivery and present the available information on which to base decisions concerning their use. The technical aspects of the use of forceps and vacuum extractors are beyond the scope of this publication.

Background

Clinical studies performed before the 1970s suggested that the risk of fetal morbidity and mortality was higher when the second stage of labor exceeded 2 hours. Currently, more intensive intrapartum surveillance provides the ability to identify the fetus that may not be tolerating labor well. Thus, the length of the second stage of labor is not in itself an absolute or even strong indication for operative termination of labor. When other obstetric factors prevail, however, there is a place for forceps or vacuum-assisted operations.

Operative vaginal deliveries are accomplished by applying direct traction on the fetal skull with forceps, or by applying traction to the fetal scalp by means of a vacuum extractor. The indications for operative vaginal delivery performed with either the vacuum extractor or forceps are the same (see the box, "Indications for Operative Vaginal Delivery").

The rate of cesarean deliveries in the United States has declined from 22.8% in 1987 to 20.8% in 1997 (2). During the same period, the percentage of births delivered by forceps or vacuum extraction increased slightly, from 9.0% to 9.4% (2). Of this number, the percentage of forceps deliveries has decreased

---

Indications for Operative Vaginal Delivery

No indication for operative vaginal delivery is absolute. The following indications apply when the fetal head is engaged and the cervix is fully dilated.

- Prolonged second stage:

  —Nulliparous women: lack of continuing progress for 3 hours with regional anesthesia, or 2 hours without regional anesthesia

  —Multiparous women: lack of continuing progress for 2 hours with regional anesthesia, or 1 hour without regional anesthesia

- Suspicion of immediate or potential fetal compromise.

- Shortening of the second stage for maternal benefit.

---

and the percentage of vacuum extraction deliveries has increased. Although some authors have suggested that operative vaginal deliveries have been replaced by cesarean deliveries, the relationship remains unclear. Geographic differences in operative delivery rates have been reported, with the lowest rate in the northeast United States and the highest rate in the South.

In 1988, ACOG redefined the classification of station and types of forceps deliveries. The revised classification uses the level of the leading bony point of the fetal head in centimeters at or below the level of the maternal ischial spines to define station (0–5 cm), instead of the previously used method of describing the birth canal in terms of thirds (0–3+).

The definitions of types of forceps deliveries also were refined to avoid the inclusion of either trivial or extremely difficult deliveries under the category of midforceps (see the box, "Criteria for Types of Forceps Deliveries"). Before this reclassification, a rotational delivery from occiput posterior at 0 station was classified the same as a delivery from left occiput anterior on the perineum. In a validation of ACOG's reclassification, investigators demonstrated that the lower the fetal head and the less rotation required, the less the risk of injury to the mother and the child (3). Assessment of clinical pelvimetry and fetal position is important in predelivery evaluation (see the box, "Predelivery Considerations").

Clinical Issues

Complications of Operative Vaginal Delivery

General statements about the applicability of operative vaginal delivery and the procedures for implementation in a particular situation are difficult. Selection of the appropriate instrument and decisions about the potential maternal and fetal consequences should be based on clinical findings at the time of delivery. Research into the complications of operative vaginal delivery is hampered by a number of potential biases, including the level of experience of the operators, the small numbers of patients studied under similar circumstances, changes in practice and definition, and the inability to achieve statistical power to answer relevant questions. The following discussion is based on currently available evidence and attempts to address maternal and fetal complications associated with operative vaginal delivery.

In a randomized trial comparing elective low-forceps delivery with spontaneous vaginal delivery in 50 term patients, there were no significant immediate differences in maternal or neonatal outcome variables. The researchers did show that in the forceps group, the mean time to delivery was shorter (10.2 minutes versus 18 minutes) and the cord arterial pH was higher (7.27 versus 7.23) (4). However, a larger randomized study comparing outlet forceps delivery with spontaneous vaginal delivery in 333 women at term showed that, although the use of forceps had no immediate adverse effects on the neonate, there was no significant shortening of the second stage of labor. However, the incidence of maternal perineal trauma increased in primiparous women (5).

Criteria for Types of Forceps Deliveries

Outlet forceps

1. Scalp is visible at the introitus without separating labia.
2. Fetal skull has reached pelvic floor.
3. Sagittal suture is in anteroposterior diameter or right or left occiput anterior or posterior position.
4. Fetal head is at or on perineum.
5. Rotation does not exceed 45°.

Low forceps

Leading point of fetal skull is at station ≥ +2 cm and not on the pelvic floor.

Rotation is 45° or less (left or right occiput anterior to occiput anterior, or left or right occiput posterior to occiput posterior).

Rotation is greater than 45°.

Midforceps

Station is above +2 cm but head is engaged.

High forceps

Not included in classification.

Predelivery Considerations

Position: the relationship of the fetal presenting part to the maternal pelvis. In a cephalic presentation the designated point is the occiput, while in a breech presentation it is the sacrum. The position always is described in relation to the maternal left and right sides of the pelvis.

Presentation: the relationship between the leading fetal part and the maternal pelvic inlet. The fetus may have a cephalic, breech, or shoulder presentation.

Lie: the relationship between the fetal and maternal longitudinal axes, which may be longitudinal, oblique, or transverse.

Engagement: the relationship that is present when the widest diameter of the fetal presenting part (biparietal diameter in a cephalic presentation, and bitrochanteric diameter in a breech presentation) has passed beyond the plane of the maternal pelvic brim. In a cephalic presentation the head usually is engaged when the leading point of the skull is at or below the maternal ischial spines.

Asynclitism: the relationship between the anterior and posterior parietal bones and the sagittal suture with the maternal pelvis. When neither of the parietal bones precedes the sagittal suture, the head is synclitic; if the anterior parietal bone precedes the sagittal suture, there is anterior asynclitism; and when the posterior parietal bone precedes the sagittal suture, there is posterior asynclitism.

Clinical Pelvimetry: assessment of the maternal pelvis before performing midpelvic delivery.

A meta-analysis comparing vacuum extraction to forceps delivery showed that vacuum extraction was associated with significantly less maternal trauma and less need for general and regional anesthesia. Overall, fewer cesarean deliveries were carried out in the vacuum extractor group (6). Other studies comparing vacuum extraction to forceps delivery indicate that more maternal morbidity (soft tissue injury, discomfort) occurs with forceps delivery (7, 8).

Both forceps delivery and vacuum extraction have been associated with the development of maternal hematomas, (9) and possibly linked to pelvic floor injury. However, other factors associated with pelvic floor injury include normal spontaneous vaginal delivery, episiotomy, prolonged second stage of labor, and increased fetal size (10).

To evaluate the risk of operative vaginal delivery with suspected fetal macrosomia, one study compared 2,924 macrosomic infants (birth weight >4,000 g) to those with a birth weight between 3,000 g and 3,999 g. Macrosomic

infants delivered by forceps had a sixfold higher rate of significant injury (relative risk = 6.7; confidence interval, 6.5–6.9). Forceps delivery in this situation also was associated with a fourfold risk of clinically persistent neurologic abnormalities when compared with spontaneous vaginal delivery or cesarean delivery. The overall incidence of persistent injury was low (0.3%), and the authors calculated that as many as 258 elective cesarean deliveries would have to be performed for macrosomia to prevent a single case of persistent injury (11). In addition, a randomized study of forceps and vacuum-assisted vaginal delivery identified three factors associated with the development of shoulder dystocia: use of vacuum device ($P = 0.04$), time required for delivery ($P = 0.03$), and birth weight ($P = 0.0001$) (12). Therefore, a trial of labor and judicious use of operative vaginal delivery techniques for macrosomic infants are not contraindicated, although caution should be used given the possibility of shoulder dystocia.

Potential Newborn Complications of Vacuum-Assisted Deliveries

With forceps, almost unlimited compression and traction can be applied to the fetal head and cervical spine. Vacuum extractors are designed to limit the amount of traction on the fetal skull because detachment can occur. Nevertheless, traction achieved with vacuum extraction is substantial (up to 50 lb) (13) and can result in significant fetal injury if misused. The vacuum cup can cause scalp lacerations if torsion is excessive. In addition, separation of the scalp from the underlying structures can lead to cephalohematoma, which is more common in infants delivered by vacuum extractor (14–16%) than in those delivered with forceps (2%) (6, 7). The incidence of subgaleal hematomas (collections of blood occurring in the potential space between the cranial periosteum and the epicranial aponeurosis) following vacuum deliveries is estimated to range from 26 to 45 per 1,000 vacuum deliveries (14, 15).

Other potential neonatal complications associated with vacuum deliveries include intracranial hemorrhage, hyperbilirubinemia, and retinal hemorrhage. The higher rates of neonatal jaundice associated with vacuum delivery may be related to the higher rate of cephalohematoma (16). There is a higher rate of retinal hemorrhages (38%) with vacuum delivery than with forceps delivery (17%) (6, 7, 17, 18). However, corneal abrasions and external ocular trauma are more common with forceps delivery than with normal spontaneous delivery and are rare with vacuum extraction unless the cup is inadvertently placed over the eye. Long-term sequelae are extremely rare, and ophthalmologic screening should be reserved for specific cases (18). Overall, the incidence of serious complications with vacuum extraction is approximately 5% (19). Given the maternal and neonatal risks associated with operative vaginal delivery, it is important that the patient be made aware of the potential complications of the proposed procedure.

In 1998, the U.S. Food and Drug Administration (FDA) released a Public Health Advisory to alert individuals that vacuum extractors may cause serious or fatal complications, including subgaleal (subaponeurotic) hematoma and intracranial hemorrhage (20). The FDA indicated that between 1994 and 1998, 12 deaths and nine serious injuries were reported among neonates on whom vacuum-assisted devices had been used. This rate was greater than five times the rate for the preceding 11 years. According to the advisory, data collected from 1989 to 1995 showed that use of the vacuum cup had increased from 3.5% to 5.9% of all deliveries. Among the FDA recommendations for use of the vacuum device, two are particularly useful:

1. Rocking movements or torque should not be applied to the device; only steady traction in the line of the birth canal should be used.

2. Clinicians caring for the neonate should be alerted that a vacuum device has been used so that they can adequately monitor the neonate for the signs and symptoms of device-related injuries.

A recent study evaluating the incidence of severe birth trauma following operative deliveries assessed the outcome of 83,340 singleton infants born to nulliparous women between 1992 and 1994 in California (21). A database was created linking birth and death certificates with hospital discharge records of maternal and neonatal outcomes. The lowest risk of fetal injury was found in infants delivered spontaneously. An intermediate risk was observed for those infants delivered by forceps or vacuum alone or by cesarean delivery during labor. The highest risk of fetal injury was reported for those infants who were delivered with combined forceps and vacuum extraction or who were delivered by cesarean following failed operative vaginal delivery. There was no difference in outcome between vacuum and forceps delivery versus cesarean delivery during labor (Table 1). The morbidity that previously had been thought to be due to operative vaginal delivery actually may have resulted from the process of abnormal labor that led to the need for intervention. The study population was large, but data were collected retrospectively from medical records and hospital discharge reports. Therefore, detailed information on the operative vaginal delivery, frequency of congenital anom-

Table 1. Effect of Delivery on Neonatal Injury

Delivery Method	Death	Intracranial Hemorrhage	Other*
Spontaneous vaginal delivery	1/5,000	1/1,900	1/216
Cesarean delivery during labor	1/1,250	1/952	1/71
Cesarean delivery after vacuum/forceps	N/R	1/333	1/38
Cesarean delivery with no labor	1/1,250	1/2,040	1/105
Vacuum alone	1/3,333	1/860	1/122
Forceps alone	1/2,000	1/664	1/76
Vacuum and forceps	1/1,666	1/280	1/58

Abbreviation: N/R indicates not reported.

*Facial nerve/brachial plexus injury, convulsions, central nervous system depression, mechanical ventilation

Data from Towner D, Castro MA, Eby-Wilkens E, Gilbert WM. Effect of mode of delivery in nulliparous women on neonatal intracranial injury. N Engl J Med 1999;341:1709–1714

alies, or number of infants readmitted following the initial discharge was not available. Despite its limitations, this study confirms that injury can occur before operative delivery as a result of abnormal labor forces and that not all neonatal injuries are the result of poor operative technique.

Long-Term Infant Consequences

One randomized comparison of vacuum versus forceps delivery that evaluated children at 9 months of age found no statistically significant differences between the two groups regarding head circumference, weight, head-circumference-to-weight ratio, hearing, or vision (22). The study did note that infants delivered with the vacuum device were more likely to have been readmitted with jaundice than were those delivered with forceps.

In another study, the effects of forceps delivery on cognitive development were examined in a cohort of 3,413 children. No significant differences were seen in the 1,192 children delivered with forceps (114 were midforceps), compared with the 1,499 delivered spontaneously (23). A 10-year matched follow-up evaluation of 295 children delivered by vacuum extractor and 302 control patients who had been delivered spontaneously at the same hospital revealed no differences between the two groups in terms of scholastic performance, speech, ability of self-care, or neurologic abnormality (24).

Clinical Considerations and Recommendations

▶ *What are contraindications to operative vaginal delivery?*

Under certain circumstances, operative vaginal delivery should be avoided or, at the least, carefully considered in terms of relative maternal and fetal risk. Most authorities consider vacuum extraction inappropriate in pregnancies before 34 weeks of gestation because of the risk of fetal intraventricular hemorrhage. Operative delivery also is contraindicated if a live fetus is known to have a bone demineralization condition (eg, osteogenesis imperfecta), a bleeding disorder (eg, alloimmune thrombocytopenia, hemophilia, or von Willebrand's disease) is present, the fetal head is unengaged, or the position of the fetal head is unknown.

Operative vaginal delivery should be performed only by individuals with privileges for such procedures and in settings in which personnel are readily available to perform a cesarean delivery in the event the operative vaginal delivery is unsuccessful. One study showed that in cases in which the vacuum extractor was used to deliver fetuses with nonreassuring fetal heart rate patterns, blood gas parameters did not differ from those in cases with normal spontaneous deliveries. The authors concluded that the use of vacuum extraction is not contraindicated in cases of nonreassuring fetal heart rate patterns (25).

▶ *Is there a role for a trial of operative vaginal delivery?*

Few studies address the issue of maternal and neonatal outcome after an unsuccessful attempt at operative delivery. Earlier published reports were small retrospective studies that suggested outcome was no worse after failed operative delivery (26, 27). In a recent report of 102 cases of failed instrument delivery, almost half (43%) of cases where a trial of operative vaginal delivery was attempted resulted in the need for cesarean delivery. Of those where success was expected, only 3% went on to cesarean delivery (28). In addition, the California study previously discussed demonstrated significantly higher incidences of intracranial hemorrhage and other birth trauma following a failed operative vaginal delivery (21). Unless the preoperative assessment is highly suggestive of a successful outcome, trial of operative vaginal delivery is best avoided.

▶ *Is there a role for the use of alternative instruments after a failed attempt?*

Persistent efforts to obtain a vaginal delivery using different instruments may increase the potential for maternal and fetal injury and often indicates cephalopelvic disproportion. Although studies are limited, the weight of available evidence appears to be against attempting multiple efforts at operative vaginal delivery with different instruments, unless there is a compelling and justifiable reason (28). The California study reported that the incidence of intracranial hemorrhage was highest in infants delivered by combined vacuum and forceps compared with other reported methods of delivery (21). The incidences of other injuries also were increased with combined methods of operative vaginal delivery.

▶ *What special equipment and techniques should be considered with the use of a vacuum extractor?*

Vacuum extractors differ substantially from the original metal cup and currently vary by material, cup size and shape, and the method of vacuum application to the fetal scalp (manual or automatic). The proliferation and increased use of these instruments have resulted in the development of a number of different techniques. Randomized trials comparing soft vacuum cups to the original metal cup indicate that the pliable cup is associated with decreased fetal scalp trauma but increased rates of detachment from the fetal head (29–32). However, there are no differences between Apgar scores, cord pH, neurologic outcome, retinal hemorrhage, maternal trauma, and blood loss (32). These findings support those of another study, which found a 22% incidence of significant fetal scalp trauma with the soft cup, as opposed to a 37% incidence with the metal cup. This study also concluded the soft cup was more likely to fail than the metal cup when excessive caput was present (29).

Data show that the use of rapid vacuum application leads to a reduction in time to delivery (33, 34). No differences in detachment from the fetal scalp or in maternal or neonatal morbidity between the two techniques have been noted (33, 34). Specifically, one randomized study of 94 women comparing a one-step rapid application of vacuum with conventional stepwise application of vacuum found a significant reduction in the time from application to delivery (6 minutes) in the rapid application group without any differences in maternal or neonatal morbidity (33).

Cephalohematoma has been shown to be more likely to develop as the duration of vacuum application increases. One study demonstrated that 28% of neonates in whom the application-to-delivery time exceeded 5 minutes developed cephalohematoma (35). A further technical issue that has raised questions is whether the vacuum should be reduced between contractions to prevent fetal scalp injury. A randomized controlled trial involving 322 patients at 34 weeks or more of gestation highlighted factors involved in the development of fetal cephalohematoma from vacuum extraction using the M-cup (a semirigid plastic cup, modeled after the Malmstrom cup). To prevent fetal loss of station, 164 patients had continuous vacuum application (600 mm Hg) during and between contractions as well as during active efforts at delivery. In the comparison group, 158 patients had intermittent suction (reduction of vacuum application to 100 mm Hg between contractions) and no effort to prevent loss of station between contractions. Time to delivery, method failure, maternal lacerations, episiotomy extension, incidence of cephalohematoma, and neonatal outcome were similar between the two groups. Overall, the efficacy of the vacuum cup was 93.5%, and the cephalohematoma rate was 11.5%. The authors concluded that there are no differences in maternal or fetal outcome with intermittent reduction in vacuum or attempts to prevent loss of station. They also concluded that the results obtained with the M-cup are comparable to those reported with the stainless-steel Malmstrom cup (36).

▶ *Is there a role for midforceps rotational deliveries in current practice?*

The decrease in experienced teachers and the increase in medical–legal concerns have reduced the number of current practitioners skilled in the art of midcavity rotational delivery. Studies comparing midforceps and cesarean deliveries indicate that midforceps delivery is not associated with worse neonatal outcome (Apgar score, cord blood gas, neonatal intensive care admissions, birth trauma) than is cesarean delivery (37, 38). In addition, outcome appeared no worse for those infants in whom Kielland's forceps rotation was attempted but was unsuccessful (38). One retrospective analysis compared 358 midforceps deliveries with 486 cesarean deliveries and found maternal morbidity (intraoperative and postoperative complications, blood loss, and length of stay) to be higher in the cesarean delivery group (37). Another study reported similar findings in a 5-year retrospective study involving 253 patients (38).

A retrospective study compared 552 deliveries with Kielland's forceps rotation, 95 cases using Scanzoni maneuver with a different type of forceps, and 160 cases using manual rotation and forceps. Investigators found no significant differences in maternal or neonatal outcomes between the groups regardless of whether the indication was relative dystocia or nonreassuring fetal status (39). An earlier study found that Kielland's forceps rotation was associated with a higher incidence of neonatal trauma, although the analysis did not specify the indications for operative delivery (40).

There are no randomized controlled studies of long-term follow-up from which to draw conclusions. However, retrospective case–control analyses seem to indicate no differences in outcome between midforceps delivery and cesarean delivery or vacuum extraction (41, 42). A matched-pairs analysis of patients 2 years after a midforceps delivery compared with a group delivered via cesarean delivery (matched for the immediate indication for operative delivery, birth weight, gestational age, sex, and race) found no difference in abnormal outcomes between the groups (41). An 18-year follow-up study of males delivered by midcavity Kielland's forceps rotation did not show any late adverse effects when subjects were compared with males delivered by vacuum extractor (42). Thus, there appears to be a role for midforceps rotational deliveries in current practice. However, given the potential complications, this procedure is only for practitioners skilled in midforceps delivery and for cases where maternal and fetal assessment prior to the operation suggest a high chance of success.

Summary

The following recommendations are based on good and consistent scientific evidence (Level A):

▶ Both forceps and vacuum extractors are acceptable and safe instruments for operative vaginal delivery. Operator experience should determine which instrument should be used in a particular situation.

▶ The vacuum extractor is associated with an increased incidence of neonatal cephalohematomata, retinal hemorrhages, and jaundice when compared with forceps delivery.

The following recommendations are based on limited or inconsistent scientific evidence (Level B):

▶ Operators should attempt to minimize the duration of vacuum application, because cephalohematoma is more likely to occur as the interval increases.

▶ Midforceps operations should be considered an appropriate procedure to teach and to use under the correct circumstances by an adequately trained individual.

▶ The incidence of intracranial hemorrhage is highest among infants delivered by cesarean following a failed vacuum or forceps delivery. The combination of vacuum and forceps has a similar incidence of intracranial hemorrhage. Therefore, an operative vaginal delivery should not be attempted when the probability of success is very low.

The following recommendations are based primarily on consensus and expert opinion (Level C):

▶ Operative vaginal delivery is not contraindicated in cases of suspected macrosomia or prolonged labor; however, caution should be used because the risk of shoulder dystocia increases with these conditions.

▶ Neonatal care providers should be made aware of the mode of delivery in order to observe for potential complications associated with operative vaginal delivery.

References

1. Bofill JA, Rust OA, Perry KG, Roberts WE, Martin RW, Morrison JC. Operative vaginal delivery: a survey of fellows of ACOG. Obstet Gynecol 1996;88:1007–1010 (Level III)

2. Ventura SJ, Martin JA, Curtin SC, Mathews TJ. Births: final data for 1997. Natl Vital Stat Rep 1999;47(18):1–96 (Level II-3)

3. Hagadorn-Freathy AS, Yeomans ER, Hankins GD. Validation of the 1988 ACOG forceps classification system. Obstet Gynecol 1991;77:356–360 (Level II-2)

4. Carmona F, Martinez-Roman S, Manau D, Cararach V, Iglesias X. Immediate maternal and neonatal effects of low-forceps delivery according to the new criteria of The American College of Obstetricians and Gynecologists compared with spontaneous vaginal delivery in term pregnancies. Am J Obstet Gynecol 1995;173:55–59 (Level I)

5. Yancey MK, Herpolsheimer A, Jordan GD, Benson WL, Brady K. Maternal and neonatal effects of outlet forceps delivery compared with spontaneous vaginal delivery in term pregnancies. Obstet Gynecol 1991;78:646–650 (Level I)

6. Johanson RB, Menon BKV. Vacuum extraction versus forceps for assisted vaginal delivery (Cochrane Review). In: The Cochrane Library, Issue 4, 1999. Oxford: Update Software (Meta-analysis)

7. Dell DL, Sightler SE, Plauche WC. Soft cup vacuum extraction: a comparison of outlet delivery. Obstet Gynecol 1985;66:624–628 (Level I)

8. Johanson R, Pusey J, Livera N, Jones P. North Staffordshire/Wigan assisted delivery trial. Br J Obstet Gynaecol 1989;96:537–544 (Level I)

9. Gei AF, Belfort MA. Forceps-assisted vaginal delivery. Obstet Gynecol Clin North Am 1999;26:345–370 (Level III)

10. Handa VL, Harris TA, Ostergard DR. Protecting the pelvic floor: obstetric management to prevent incontinence and pelvic organ prolapse. Obstet Gynecol 1996;88:470–478 (Level III)

11. Kolderup LB, Laros RK Jr, Musci TJ. Incidence of persistent birth injury in macrosomic infants: association with mode of delivery. Am J Obstet Gynecol 1997;177:37–41 (Level II-2)

12. Bofill JA, Rust OA, Devidas M, Roberts WE, Morrison JC, Martin JN Jr. Shoulder dystocia and operative vaginal delivery. J Matern Fetal Med 1997;6:220–224 (Level I)

13. Moolgaoker AS, Ahamed SOS, Payne PR. A comparison of different methods of instrumental delivery based on electronic measurements of compression and traction. Obstet Gynecol 1979;54:299–309 (Level II-3)

14. Boo NY. Subaponeurotic haemorrhage in Malaysian neonates. Singapore Med J 1990;31:207–210 (Level II-3)

15. Govaert P, Defoort P, Wigglesworth JS. Cranial haemorrhage in the term newborn infant. Clin Dev Med 1993;129:1–223 (Level III)

16. Vacca A, Grant A, Wyatt G, Chalmers I. Portsmouth operative delivery trial: a comparison of vacuum extraction and forceps delivery. Br J Obstet Gynaecol 1983;90:1107–1112 (Level I)

17. Williams MC, Knuppel RA, O'Brien WF, Weiss A, Kanarek KS. A randomized comparison of assisted vaginal delivery by obstetric forceps and polyethylene vacuum cup. Obstet Gynecol 1991;78:789–794 (Level I)

18. Holden R, Morsman DG, Davidek GM, O'Connor GM, Coles EC, Dawson AJ. External ocular trauma in instrumental and normal deliveries. Br J Obstet Gynaecol 1992;99:132–134 (Level II-2)

19. Robertson PA, Laros RK Jr, Zhao RL. Neonatal and maternal outcome in low-pelvic and midpelvic operative deliveries. Am J Obstet Gynecol 1990;162:1436–1442; discussion 1442–1444 (Level II-2)

20. Center for Devices and Radiological Health. FDA Public Health Advisory: need for caution when using vacuum assisted delivery devices. May 21, 1998. Available at http://www.fda.gov/cdrh/fetal598.html. Retrieved December 31, 1999 (Level III)

21. Towner D, Castro MA, Eby-Wilkens E, Gilbert WM. Effect of mode of delivery in nulliparous women on neonatal intracranial injury. N Engl J Med 1999; 341:1709–1714 (Level II-2)

22. Carmody F, Grant A, Mutch L, Vacca A, Chalmers I. Follow up of babies delivered in a randomized controlled comparison of vacuum extraction and forceps delivery. Acta Obstet Gynecol Scand 1986;65:763–766 (Level I)

23. Wesley BD, van den Berg BJ, Reece EA. The effect of forceps delivery on cognitive development. Am J Obstet Gynecol 1993;169:1091–1095 (Level II-2)

24. Ngan HY, Miu P, Ko L, Ma HK. Long-term neurological sequelae following vacuum extractor delivery. Aust N Z J Obstet Gynaecol 1990;30:111–114 (Level II-2)

25. Vintzileos AM, Nochimson DJ, Antsaklis A, Varvarigos I, Guzman ER, Knuppel RA. Effect of vacuum extraction on umbilical cord blood acid-base measurements. J Matern Fetal Med 1996;5:11–17 (Level II-2)

26. Revah A, Ezra Y, Farine D, Ritchie K. Failed trial of vacuum or forceps—maternal and fetal outcome. Am J Obstet Gynecol 1997;176:200–204 (Level II-3)

27. Boyd ME, Usher RH, McLean FH, Norman BE. Failed forceps. Obstet Gynecol 1986;68:779–783 (Level II-3)

28. Edozien LC, Williams JL, Chattopadhyay I, Hirsch PJ. Failed instrumental delivery: how safe is the use of a second instrument? J Obstet Gynaecol 1999;19:460–462 (Level III)

29. Chenoy R, Johanson R. A randomized prospective study comparing delivery with metal and silicone rubber vacuum extractor cups. Br J Obstet Gynaecol 1992;99:360–363 (Level I)

30. Cohn M, Barclay C, Fraser R, Zaklama M, Johanson R, Anderson D, et al. A mulitcentre randomized trial comparing delivery with a silicone rubber cup and rigid metal vacuum extractor cups. Br J Obstet Gynaecol 1989;96:545–551 (Level I)

31. Hofmeyr GJ, Gobetz L, Sonnendecker EW, Turner MJ. New design rigid and soft vacuum extractor cups: a preliminary comparison of traction forces. Br J Obstet Gynaecol 1990;97:681–685 (Level I)

32. Kuit JA, Eppinga HG, Wallenburg HC, Huikeshoven FJ. A randomized comparison of vacuum extraction delivery with a rigid and a pliable cup. Obstet Gynecol 1993;82:280–284 (Level I)

33. Lim FT, Holm JP, Schuitemaker NW, Jansen FH, Hermans J. Stepwise compared with rapid application of vacuum in ventouse extraction procedures. Br J Obstet Gynaecol 1997;104:33–36 (Level I)

34. Svenningsen L. Birth progression and traction forces developed under vacuum extraction after slow or rapid application of suction. Eur J Obstet Gynecol Reprod Biol 1987;26:105–112 (Level II-2)

35. Bofill JA, Rust OA, Devidas M, Roberts WE, Morrison JC, Martin JN Jr. Neonatal cephalohematoma from vacuum extraction. J Reprod Med 1997;42:565–569 (Level I)

36. Bofill JA, Rust OA, Schorr SJ, Brown RC, Roberts WE, Morrison JC. A randomized trial of two vacuum extraction techniques. Obstet Gynecol 1997;89:758–762 (Level I)

37. Bashore RA, Phillips WH Jr, Brinkman CR 3rd. A comparison of the morbidity of midforceps and cesarean delivery. Am J Obstet Gynecol 1990;162:1428–1434; discussion 1434–1435 (Level II-2)

38. Traub AI, Morrow RJ, Ritchie JW, Dornan KJ. A continuing use for Kielland's forceps? Br J Obstet Gynaecol 1984;91:894–898 (Level II-2)

39. Healy DL, Quinn MA, Pepperell RJ. Rotational delivery of the fetus: Kielland's forceps and two other methods compared. Br J Obstet Gynaecol 1982;89:501–506 (Level II-2)

40. Chiswick ML, James DK. Kielland's forceps: association with neonatal morbidity and mortality. Br Med J 1979;1:7–9 (Level II-3).

41. Dierker LJ Jr, Rosen MG, Thompson K, Lynn P. Midforceps deliveries: long-term outcome of infants. Am J Obstet Gynecol 1986;154:764–768 (Level II-2)

42. Nilsen ST. Boys born by forceps and vacuum extraction examined at 18 years of age. Acta Obstet Gynecol Scand 1984;63:549–554 (Level II-2)

The MEDLINE database, the Cochrane Library, and ACOG's own internal resources and documents were used to conduct a literature search to locate relevant articles published between January 1985 and November 1999. The search was restricted to articles published in the English language. Priority was given to articles reporting results of original research, although review articles and commentaries also were consulted. Abstracts of research presented at symposia and scientific conferences were not considered adequate for inclusion in this document. Guidelines published by organizations or institutions such as the National Institutes of Health and the American College of Obstetricians and Gynecologists were reviewed, and additional studies were located by reviewing bibliographies of identified articles. When reliable research was not available, expert opinions from obstetrician–gynecologists were used.

Studies were reviewed and evaluated for quality according to the method outlined by the U.S. Preventive Services Task Force:

I   Evidence obtained from at least one properly designed randomized controlled trial.

II-1   Evidence obtained from well-designed controlled trials without randomization.

II-2   Evidence obtained from well-designed cohort or case–control analytic studies, preferably from more than one center or research group.

II-3   Evidence obtained from multiple time series with or without the intervention. Dramatic results in uncontrolled experiments also could be regarded as this type of evidence.

III   Opinions of respected authorities, based on clinical experience, descriptive studies, or reports of expert committees.

Based on the highest level of evidence found in the data, recommendations are provided and graded according to the following categories:

Level A—Recommendations are based on good and consistent scientific evidence.

Level B—Recommendations are based on limited or inconsistent scientific evidence.

Level C—Recommendations are based primarily on consensus and expert opinion.

ISSN 1099-3630

The American College of Obstetricians and Gynecologists
409 12th Street, SW
PO Box 96920
Washington, DC 20090-6920

12345/43210

ACOG PRACTICE BULLETIN

CLINICAL MANAGEMENT GUIDELINES FOR
OBSTETRICIAN–GYNECOLOGISTS

NUMBER 20, SEPTEMBER 2000

(Replaces Educational Bulletin Number 177, February 1993)

This Practice Bulletin was developed by the ACOG Committee on Practice Bulletins—Obstetrics with the assistance of Kim Boggess, MD. The information is designed to aid practitioners in making decisions about appropriate obstetric and gynecologic care. These guidelines should not be construed as dictating an exclusive course of treatment or procedure. Variations in practice may be warranted based on the needs of the individual patient, resources, and limitations unique to the institution or type of practice.

Perinatal Viral and Parasitic Infections

Many viral and parasitic infections are associated with significant maternal and fetal consequences if acquired during pregnancy. In the United States, some of the most commonly encountered infections with subsequent perinatal effects include cytomegalovirus (CMV), parvovirus B19, varicella zoster virus (VZV), and toxoplasmosis. The purpose of this document is to describe these infections, their modes of transmission, and their maternal and fetal effects, and to offer guidelines for counseling about and management of these infections during pregnancy.

Background

In general, perinatal infections have more severe fetal consequences when they occur early in gestation, because first-trimester infections may disrupt organogenesis. Second- and third-trimester infections can cause neurologic impairment or growth disturbances. In utero infection may be associated with certain ultrasound findings, including intrauterine growth restriction, echogenic bowel, intracranial or intrahepatic calcifications, hydrocephalus, microcephaly, isolated ascites, pericardial or pleural effusions, or nonimmune hydrops, although congenital infections also can be asymptomatic.

Cytomegalovirus

Cytomegalovirus is a double-stranded DNA herpesvirus that is transmitted by contact with infected blood, saliva, or urine, or by sexual contact. The incubation period of CMV is 28–60 days, with a mean of 40 days. Infection induces an immunoglobulin M (IgM) antibody response that disappears within 30–60 days. Viremia can be detected 2–3 weeks following primary infection. Primary CMV infection in adults generally is asymptomatic. Occasionally, patients experience a mononucleosislike syndrome, with leukocytosis, lymphocytosis, abnormal liver function tests, fever, malaise, myalgias, and chills (1). After the initial infection, CMV remains latent in host cells; recurrent infection can occur following reactivation of latent virus. In rare cases, recurrent CMV infection can occur by infection with a new strain of virus.

Prevalence of both primary and recurrent infection in pregnant women varies regionally from 0.7% to 4% for primary infection and up to 13.5% for recurrent infection (2). Vertical transmission of CMV may occur as a result of transplacental infection after primary or recurrent CMV infection, exposure to contaminated genital tract secretions at parturition, or breastfeeding. Most infants with congenital CMV are asymptomatic at birth. Clinical findings of symptomatic congenital CMV infection include jaundice, petechiae, thrombocytopenia, hepatospleno-megaly, growth restriction, and nonimmune hydrops (3, 4). The annual cost of treating the complications of CMV infections in the United States is estimated to be approximately $2 billion (2), which reflects the 50–80% seropositivity rate of pregnant women.

Cytomegalovirus is the most common congenital infection, occurring in 0.2–2.2% of all neonates (5), and is the leading cause of congenital hearing loss. Vertical transmission may occur at any stage of pregnancy, with the overall risk of infection greatest when the infection occurs during the third trimester. However, more serious fetal sequelae occur after maternal CMV infection during the first trimester. With primary maternal CMV infection, the risk of transmission to the fetus is 30–40% (6). Of those infected in utero following a primary infection, 10% will have signs and symptoms of CMV infection at birth and develop sequelae (7). Approximately 30% of severely infected infants die, and 80% of survivors have severe neurologic morbidity (5, 8). The incidence of severe fetal infection is much lower after recurrent maternal infection than after primary infection. Vertical transmission after a recurrent infection is 0.15–2% (8, 9). Infants infected after maternal CMV reactivation generally are asymptomatic at birth. Congenital hearing loss is typically the most severe sequela of secondary infection, and congenital infection following recurrent infection is unlikely to produce multiple sequelae (9). Cytomegalovirus infection acquired as a result of exposure to infected cervical secretions or breast milk is typically asymptomatic and is not associated with severe neonatal sequelae.

Parvovirus B19

Parvovirus B19 is a single-stranded DNA virus that causes the childhood exanthem erythema infectiosum, also known as fifth disease. In immunocompetent adults, the most common symptoms of parvovirus B19 infection are a reticular rash on the trunk and peripheral arthropathy, although approximately 33% of infections are asymptomatic (10). Another manifestation of parvovirus B19 infection is transient aplastic crisis, which is more common in those with an underlying hemoglobinopathy. Most infections are mild; most individuals recover completely from parvovirus B19 infection and require only supportive care.

Transmission of parvovirus B19 most commonly occurs through respiratory secretions and hand-to-mouth contact. The infected person generally is infectious 5–10 days after exposure prior to the onset of the rash or other symptoms and is no longer infectious with the onset of the rash (11). Both IgM and IgG are produced in response to infection. The IgM response, which persists for 1 to several months, is indicative of a recent infection. IgG antibodies persist indefinitely and, in the absence of IgM, indicate prior infection and immunity. Prevalence of seropositivity to parvovirus B19 increases with age and is greater than 60% in adolescents and adults (11). The risk of maternal infection of parvovirus B19 varies with level of exposure to the infected individual. Exposure to a household member infected with parvovirus B19 is associated with an approximate 50% risk of seroconversion (12–15). The risk of transmission in a child care setting or classroom is lower, ranging from approximately 20% to 50% (15–17).

Recent maternal infection with parvovirus B19 constitutes a low risk for fetal morbidity (18), although some cases have been associated with adverse fetal effects. Transplacental transmission has been reported to be as high as 33% (19), and fetal infection with parvovirus B19 has been associated with spontaneous abortion, hydrops fetalis, and stillbirth. The rate of fetal loss among women with serologically proven parvovirus B19 infection ranges from 2% to 9% (20–22). In utero, parvovirus B19 infection is responsible for up to 18% of cases of nonimmune hydrops fetalis in some series (23, 24). Hydrops fetalis results from aplastic anemia, myocarditis, or chronic fetal hepatitis. Severe effects are seen most frequently among fetuses when maternal parvovirus B19 infection occurs at less than 20 weeks of gestation (20). Stillbirth resulting from maternal infection has occurred from 1 to 11 weeks after maternal infection. However, hydrops is unlikely to develop if it has not occurred by 8 weeks after maternal infection (23). Long-term development appears to be normal in fetuses with congenital parvovirus B19 infection that do not succumb to the disease (25, 26).

Varicella Zoster Virus

Varicella zoster virus is a DNA herpesvirus that is highly contagious and is transmitted by respiratory droplets or close contact. The attack rate among susceptible contacts is 60–90% after exposure. The incubation period after infection is 10–20 days, with a mean of 14 days (27). The period of infectivity begins 48 hours before the rash appears and lasts until the vesicles crust over. The primary infection causes chickenpox, which is characterized by fever, malaise, and a maculopapular pruritic rash that becomes vesicular. After the primary infection, VZV remains dormant in sensory ganglia and can be reactivated to cause a vesicular erythematous skin rash known as herpes zoster. The antibody to VZV develops within a few days after the onset of infection, and prior infection with VZV confers lifelong immunity.

Varicella infection is uncommon in pregnancy (occurring in 0.4–0.7 per 1,000 patients), because of the high prevalence of natural immunity (28). Pregnancy complicated by maternal varicella infection is associated with untoward maternal, fetal, and neonatal effects. The disease usually is a benign and self-limited illness in children; however, varicella national mortality data indicate that although less than 5% of varicella cases occur among adults 20 years of age or older, that group contributes to 55% of varicella-related deaths (29). Severe complications, such as encephalitis and pneumonia, are more common in adults than in children; VZV pneumonia in pregnancy is a risk factor for maternal mortality (30, 31).

In pregnancy, varicella may be transmitted across the placenta, resulting in congenital or neonatal chickenpox. The risk of congenital varicella syndrome is limited to exposure during the first 20 weeks of gestation, occurs uncommonly (up to 2%), and is characterized by skin scarring, limb hypoplasia, chorioretinitis, and microcephaly (32–34). Neonatal VZV infection is associated with a high neonatal death rate when maternal disease develops from 5 days before delivery up to 48 hours postpartum as a result of the relative immaturity of the neonatal immune system and the lack of protective maternal antibody (35, 36).

Toxoplasmosis

Toxoplasmosis is caused by the intracellular parasite *Toxoplasma gondii*. *T gondii* exists in several forms: a trophozoite, which is the invasive form, and a cyst or an oocyst, which are latent forms. Human infection is acquired by consuming cysts in undercooked meat of infected animals, by insect contamination of food, by contact with oocysts from the feces of infected cats (the only definitive hosts), or by contact with infected materials or insects in soil. Infection with *T gondii* usually is asymptomatic, although after an incubation of 5–18 days, some nonspecific symptoms may occur. Most often, toxoplasmosis presents as asymptomatic cervical lym-

phadenopathy, with symptoms occurring in only 10–20% of adult cases. Other symptoms include fever, malaise, night sweats, myalgias, and hepatosplenomegaly. Parasitemia can occur after infection, which, in pregnant women, can seed the placenta and cause subsequent fetal infection. Congenital transmission of *T gondii* from an infected woman was the first form of transmission to be recognized, and transmission depends on the time of acquisition of maternal infection. The later in gestation that the infection occurs, the more likely transmission is to occur. The rate of vertical transmission increases from 10% to 15% in the first trimester, to 25% in the second trimester, and to more than 60% in the third trimester (37, 38). The severity of infection depends on gestational age at the time of transmission. The earlier the fetus is infected, the more severe the disease. Most infected infants do not have clinical signs of infection at birth, but 55–85% will develop sequelae, including chorioretinitis (leading to severe impairment of vision), hearing loss, or mental retardation (39–41). Other clinical manifestations of congenital toxoplasmosis include rash, hepatosplenomegaly, ascites, fever, periventricular calcifications, ventriculomegaly, and seizures (42–44).

After an acute infection, IgM antibodies appear early and reach maximum levels in 1 month. IgG antibodies appear after IgM antibodies, are detectable within a few weeks after infection, and confer immunity. High titers of both IgG and IgM may persist for years. In the immunocompetent adult, the clinical course is benign and self-limited.

Clinical Considerations and Recommendations

Cytomegalovirus

▶ *How is maternal CMV infection diagnosed?*

The majority of adult CMV infections are asymptomatic, which makes diagnosis of primary infection difficult. Cytomegalovirus may be detected by culture or polymerase chain reaction (PCR) of infected blood, urine, saliva, cervical secretions, or breast milk, although diagnosis of CMV infection in adults usually is confirmed by serologic testing. Serum samples collected 3–4 weeks apart, tested in parallel for anti-CMV IgG, are essential for the diagnosis of primary infection. Seroconversion from negative to positive or a significant increase (greater than fourfold, eg, from 1:4 to 1:16) in anti-CMV IgG titers is evidence of infection. The presence of CMV-specific IgM is a useful but not completely reliable indication of a primary infection. IgM titers may not be positive during an acute infection, or they may persist for months after the primary infection (45). A small proportion of women with recurrent infection will demonstrate anti-CMV IgM (7). The reported sensitivity of CMV IgM serologic assays ranges from 50% to 90% (45).

▶ *How is fetal CMV infection diagnosed?*

Congenital CMV may be suspected prenatally after a documented maternal primary infection or, more typically, after detection of ultrasound findings suggestive of infection (46). These include abdominal and liver calcifications, calcification of the lateral border of the lateral ventricles, hydrops, echogenic bowel, ascites, hepatosplenomegaly, and ventriculomegaly (46–53). Fetuses that demonstrate abnormalities, particularly if they involve the central nervous system, generally have a much poorer prognosis (46, 54).

Cytomegalovirus has been diagnosed prenatally by detection of anti-CMV IgM in fetal blood (55–57), although this test has a high false-positive rate (58). In addition, IgM is not detectable in the first half of pregnancy, presumably because of the immaturity of the fetal immune system, limiting the usefulness of fetal serologic testing. Testing for fetal thrombocytopenia or abnormal liver function has been suggested as a method to diagnose congenital CMV. However, these tests are not specific for CMV, and normal results do not preclude severe infection.

Cytomegalovirus can be detected in the amniotic fluid of infected fetuses by either culture or PCR. The sensitivity of CMV culture ranges from 50% to 69%, compared with a sensitivity of 77–100% for PCR. Negative and positive predictive values are comparable between amniotic fluid culture and PCR (55–57, 59–64). The sensitivity of amniotic fluid testing for prenatal diagnosis of congenital CMV infection is markedly lower if performed before 21 weeks of gestation (65), and the time interval between maternal infection and testing may influence the reliability (62). Although these tests are promising, neither amniotic fluid culture nor PCR can detect all cases of congenital CMV infection. In addition, the detection of CMV in amniotic fluid does not predict the severity of congenital CMV infection. A combination of amniotic fluid culture and PCR has been suggested to have a sensitivity of 80–100% in identifying infected fetuses (56). Fetal blood sampling is less sensitive than amniotic fluid testing (64). Specific ultrasonographic findings may further assist in the accurate diagnosis of a congenitally infected infant with a poor prognosis.

▶ *How are maternal, fetal, and congenital neonatal infections with cytomegalovirus treated?*

Currently, no therapies are available for the treatment of maternal or fetal CMV infection. Antiviral treatment with ganciclovir or foscarnet is approved only for treatment of CMV retinitis in patients with acquired immunodeficiency syndrome (AIDS). However, ganciclovir has been shown in vitro to cross the placenta by simple diffusion (66), and there are reports of its postnatal use for the treatment of congenital CMV (67–69). Ganciclovir and CMV hyperimmune gamma globulin have shown promise for the treatment of neonates with congenital CMV infection (70–72). The effectiveness of treatment in the prevention of long-term neurologic sequelae has not been proven.

A live attenuated vaccine using the Towne 125 strain has been developed, and appears to be safe, somewhat protective (73–76), and economically beneficial (77). There is reluctance to embrace vaccination because of concerns about the ability of the vaccine strain to reactivate and potentially infect the host, the potential for viral shedding from the cervix or breast milk, and the possible oncogenic potential of vaccine virus (78). However, the science in this area is advancing rapidly, and new treatment options may become available.

▶ *How should women at high risk be counseled about prevention of CMV?*

Factors associated with an increased risk of CMV infection include history of abnormal cervical cytology, lower socioeconomic status, birth outside North America, first pregnancy at younger than 15 years, and infection with other sexually transmitted diseases. The greatest impact obstetrician–gynecologists can have on reducing CMV disease is by educating patients about preventive measures. Counseling should cover careful handling of potentially infected articles, such as diapers, and thorough hand-washing when around young children or immunocompromised individuals, explaining that careful attention to hygiene is effective in helping to prevent transmission (3, 12, 79). In addition, women should be counseled, when appropriate, about the avoidance of high-risk behaviors, such as intravenous drug use and sharing of needles. Condom use should be encouraged as a method of contraception.

▶ *Should women at high risk be screened before or during pregnancy?*

Currently, routine serologic testing for CMV during pregnancy is not recommended (4, 7, 80, 81). Maternal IgM antibody screening is limited for differentiating primary from recurrent infection, which makes it difficult to use such results in counseling patients about fetal risk. In addition, maternal immunity does not eliminate the possibility of fetal infection.

Although the virus is not highly contagious, some groups of women are at higher risk for the acquisition of CMV infection. Eleven percent of seronegative child care workers demonstrate seroconversion within 10 months of hire (82), and 53% of families of young children have one or more family members seroconvert within a year (83, 84). In two cross-sectional studies, increasing parity had an independent effect on increasing CMV seroprevalence, demonstrating the possibility of child-to-mother transmission (85). Therefore, women with young children or those who work with young children should be advised that the risk of infection can be reduced significantly by safe-handling techniques, such as the use of latex gloves and rigorous hand-washing after handling diapers or after exposure to respiratory secretions (3, 12, 86).

Parvovirus B19

▶ Which methods are available to diagnose maternal parvovirus B19 infection?

Maternal serology is the most commonly used test to diagnose acute infection with parvovirus B19. Enzyme-linked immunosorbent assay (ELISA), radioimmunoassay, and Western blot tests can measure the antibody to parvovirus B19 (20). The sensitivity of IgM and IgG assays is generally 79% (10, 87). Identification of parvovirus-specific IgM in maternal serum is diagnostic of a primary infection, although a laboratory with experience should measure titers, because false-positive results can occur. Previous exposure and infection with parvovirus B19 is indicated by the presence of antiparvovirus B19 IgG in the absence of IgM and has not been associated with adverse perinatal outcome.

Parvovirus B19 can be identified by direct visualization of viral particles in infected tissues or serum by electron microscopy or by identification of characteristic intranuclear inclusions within erythroblasts (88).

▶ What methods are available for diagnosing fetal parvovirus B19 infection?

Diagnosis of fetal parvovirus B19 infection can be accomplished by isolation of viral particles in abortuses or placental specimens (89, 90). Polymerase chain reaction also has been used to detect parvovirus B19 in fetal specimens, including autopsy tissue, serum, amniotic fluid, and placenta (91–95).

Sensitivity of PCR for detection of parvovirus may be as high as 100%, although data are limited by small sample sizes (94, 96). Reliable serologic tests for specific IgM antibodies in the fetus are not available. As with other intrauterine infections, IgM antibodies appear in the fetal circulation after 22 weeks of gestation, limiting the usefulness of such tests.

Ultrasonography has been the mainstay for diagnosing fetal parvovirus infection. Severely infected fetuses typically have evidence of hydrops fetalis. Serial ultrasound examinations for up to 10 weeks after maternal infection are indicated. If the fetus shows no signs of hydrops fetalis, additional tests are unnecessary.

▶ How are maternal, fetal, and congenital neonatal infections with parvovirus B19 managed?

After documented exposure to parvovirus B19, the woman should have serologic testing to determine if she is immune with evidence of antiparvovirus IgG. If non-immune, the test should be repeated in 3–4 weeks and paired samples tested to document whether the woman is seropositive for parvovirus. If seroconversion does not occur, the fetus is not at risk for in utero infection. If seroconversion does occur, the fetus should be monitored for 10 weeks by serial ultrasound examination to evaluate for presence of hydrops fetalis, placentomegaly, and growth disturbances (9).

In a series of 618 pregnant women exposed to parvovirus, only 311 (50.3%) were susceptible to infection. Of those susceptible, only 52 contracted parvovirus. None of the 52 infants exposed to maternal parvovirus developed hydrops fetalis (14). However, if hydrops fetalis develops, percutaneous umbilical blood sampling should be performed to determine the fetal hematocrit, leukocyte and platelet count, and viral DNA in preparation for supportive care using transfusion (97, 98). Intrauterine transfusion should be considered if anemia is present (21, 99).

▶ Should seronegative women with work-related exposure be taken out of work?

When outbreaks of parvovirus B19 infection occur in situations in which prolonged, close-contact exposure occurs, as in schools, homes, or child care centers, options for prevention of transmission are limited (20). Exposure cannot be eliminated by identifying and excluding persons with acute parvovirus B19 infection; up to 20% are asymptomatic, and those with infection are infectious before they develop symptoms. Exclusion of pregnant women from the workplace during endemic periods is controversial, and a policy to routinely exclude members of high-risk groups from work during an outbreak of parvovirus B19 is not recommended (14, 20).

Varicella Zoster Virus

▶ *How is maternal VZV infection diagnosed?*

Usually, this diagnosis is based on clinical findings, and laboratory testing is not needed, especially if a rash occurs after known exposure. If laboratory diagnosis is required, the VZV antigen can be demonstrated within skin lesions or vesicular fluid by immunofluorescence. Varicella infection also can be documented by the detection of the fluorescence antibody to the membrane antigen or of the VZV antibody by ELISA (28).

▶ *How is fetal VZV infection diagnosed?*

Although two small studies estimate the rate of congenital varicella syndrome after maternal infection with VZV to be 1–2% (32, 34), these studies were subject to bias, and these rates may be overestimated. The risk of congenital varicella syndrome is small; however, the outcome for the affected infant is serious enough that a reliable method of prenatal diagnosis would be valuable.

Fetal varicella can be suspected by the presence of ultrasonographic abnormalities. Ultrasound findings suggestive of congenital varicella include hydrops, hyperechogenic foci in the liver and bowel, cardiac malformations, limb deformities, microcephaly, and intrauterine growth restriction. In one series, five fetuses with congenital VZV demonstrated some ultrasound findings that suggested infection, and all the infants died by 4 months of age (100). However, not all fetuses with congenital VZV that have ultrasound abnormalities do poorly (101). Although the sensitivity of ultrasonography is unknown, it is the preferred method of diagnosis of congenital VZV.

Invasive prenatal diagnosis in women who acquire VZV in the first half of pregnancy may serve to provide reassurance if test results are negative (102). However, if the virus is present, identifying it by culture or viral DNA by PCR in chorionic villi, amniotic fluid or fetal blood, or the viral-specific antibody does not accurately predict the severity of fetal infection (101, 103).

▶ *What therapies are available and effective for maternal, fetal, and congenital neonatal infections with varicella?*

Oral acyclovir, if instituted within 24 hours of the rash, has been shown to reduce the duration of new lesion formation and the total number of new lesions and to improve constitutional symptoms in children, adolescents, and adults (104–106). Oral acyclovir appears to be safe and can be prescribed for pregnant women if lesions develop (107). Maternal varicella complicated by pneumonia should be treated with intravenous acyclovir, because intravenous acyclovir may reduce maternal morbidity and mortality associated with varicella pneumonia (31, 108).

Maternal treatment with acyclovir has not been shown to ameliorate or prevent the fetal effects of congenital varicella syndrome (109). Varicella-zoster immune globulin (VZIG) should be given to infants born to women who develop varicella between 5 days before and 2 days after delivery, although this does not universally prevent neonatal varicella (110). Infants who develop varicella within the first 2 weeks of life should be treated with intravenous acyclovir (107, 111).

▶ *What preventive strategies are effective for varicella?*

Nonpregnant women of childbearing age should be questioned about previous infection with varicella preconceptionally and offered vaccination if no report of chickenpox is elicited. Varicella vaccine has been available since March 1995 and is approved for use in healthy susceptible persons 12 months or older (112). Conception should be delayed until 1 month after the second vaccination dose is given.

Among women who do not recall a history of varicella, 70–90% have detectable antibodies (112). Antenatal VZV screening of all pregnant women with negative or indeterminate varicella histories is not believed to be cost-effective by some (113). However, others argue that from a cost-effectiveness/cost-benefit standpoint, management based on immune testing is preferable to universal VZIG administration when caring for pregnant women exposed to VZV with a negative or indeterminate infection history (114). Patients known to be nonimmune to VZV should be counseled to avoid contact with individuals who have chickenpox. If exposure does occur, prophylactic intervention with VZIG early in the incubation period can prevent or attenuate the disease manifestations of VZV in susceptible contacts at high risk from this infection (106). Expeditious determination of the VZV membrane antigen or equivalent anti-VZV antibody status in pregnant women exposed to VZV appears to be a rapid, satisfactory method for determining who should promptly receive VZIG passive immunization (115). Although VZIG is effective in reducing the severity of maternal varicella when administered up to 72 hours after exposure, it should be given as soon as possible (116, 117). Maternal administration of VZIG does not ameliorate or prevent fetal infection.

Toxoplasmosis

▶ *How is maternal toxoplasmosis infection diagnosed?*

Isolation of *T gondii* from blood or body fluids establishes that the infection is acute; however, serologic testing for the detection of the specific antibody to *T gondii* is the primary method of diagnosis. Numerous antibody assays are available. The Sabin-Feldman dye test is the IgG test with which all others are compared, but it is performed at only a few reference laboratories. Indirect fluorescent antibody, indirect hemagglutination and agglutination tests, and ELISA also are available to detect the antitoxoplasma antibody. However, serologic assays for toxoplasmosis are not well standardized and have a high false-positive rate. IgM titers may persist at high levels (eg, ≥1:512) for years in healthy individuals (118). Both IgG and IgM testing should be used for the initial evaluation of patients suspected to have toxoplasmosis. Testing of serial specimens 3 weeks apart in parallel gives the most accurate assessment if the initial test results are equivocal. In cases in which clinical suspicion is high, specimens should be saved for repeat testing because of the wide variation between laboratories. Repeat testing in a well-recognized reference laboratory should be performed if there is evidence of a primary infection.

▶ *Which methods are available for diagnosing and monitoring fetal infection?*

Ultrasonography can demonstrate severe congenital toxoplasmosis; suggestive findings include ventriculomegaly, intracranial calcifications, microcephaly, ascites, hepatosplenomegaly, and intrauterine growth restriction. Testing fetal blood samples after 20 weeks of gestation for the presence of specific IgM is the most sensitive test in diagnosing congenital toxoplasmosis (119). Using fetal blood for antibody testing or mouse inoculation, amniotic fluid for PCR, or fetal ultrasonography to detect ventriculomegaly, 77–93% of infected infants were identified prenatally, although no single test was very sensitive (43, 120). Successful identification of *T gondii* intrauterine infection with PCR testing of amniotic fluid allows for earlier testing than fetal blood sampling, with high sensitivity (37, 121–124), although false-positive and false-negative findings do occur (125).

▶ *How are maternal, fetal, and congenital neonatal infections with toxoplasmosis treated?*

Treatment of the pregnant woman with acute toxoplasmosis reduces but does not eliminate the risk of congenital infection (42, 43). Identification of acute maternal infection necessitates immediate institution of treatment until results of fetal testing are known. Spiramycin, which concentrates in the placenta, may reduce the risk of fetal transmission by 60% (126), but as a single agent, it does not treat established fetal infection. Spiramycin is available only through the U.S. Food and Drug Administration after serologic confirmation at a reference laboratory; it is recommended for pregnant women at risk unless fetal infection is documented. If fetal infection is established, pyrimethamine, sulfonamides, and folinic acid are added to the regimen because they more effectively eradicate parasites in the placenta and in the fetus than spiramycin alone (127). With treatment, even early fetal infection with toxoplasmosis can result in successful pregnancy outcomes (128).

Treatment of infants with symptomatic congenital toxoplasmosis consists of pyrimethamine and sulfadiazine, alternating monthly with spiramycin, for 1 year (127). Treatment will diminish or resolve intracranial calcifications if present, suggesting improved neurologic function (129).

▶ *Should women be screened for toxoplasmosis during pregnancy?*

A multicenter study in the United States found that approximately 38% of pregnant women have evidence of prior toxoplasmosis infection (130). Evidence of previous infection signifies that the future mother is not at risk of giving birth to a child with congenital toxoplasmosis. Serologic screening as a way to prevent congenital toxoplasmosis would have the most impact in countries with a high frequency of seropositivity, and routine prenatal screening is performed in France and Austria (39). However, in the United States, routine screening during pregnancy currently is not recommended, except in women infected with human immunodeficiency virus (HIV). Serologic screening during pregnancy may yield equivocal results, because IgM antibodies can persist for long periods (131). Exceptional circumstances may justify toxoplasmosis titer screening for pregnant women who are cat owners. One study in Belgium demonstrated a 63% reduction in the rate of maternal toxoplasmosis infection after institution of an educational program that recommended avoiding eating undercooked or raw meat, wearing gloves when working with soil, and avoiding caring for cats unless they are strictly "indoor cats" whose food is rigidly controlled (131).

Summary

The following recommendations are based on limited and inconsistent scientific data (Level B):

▶ Pregnant women who are seronegative for VZV and exposed to chickenpox should receive VZIG.

▶ Pregnant women who develop chickenpox should be treated with oral acyclovir to minimize maternal symptoms; if pneumonia develops, they should be treated with intravenous acyclovir.

▶ Pregnant women who have acute parvovirus B19 infection during pregnancy should be monitored with serial ultrasound examinations for at least 10 weeks following infection for the presence of hydrops fetalis.

▶ Fetuses with evidence of hydrops should undergo fetal blood sampling and transfusion as needed.

▶ Pregnant women who acquire toxoplasmosis should be treated with spiramycin. When diagnosed, fetal toxoplasmosis should be treated with a combination of pyrimethamine, sulfadiazine, and folinic acid, alternating with spiramycin.

The following recommendations are based primarily on consensus and expert opinion (Level C):

▶ Routine serologic screening of all pregnant women for CMV and toxoplasmosis is not recommended.

▶ Nonpregnant women of reproductive age who have no history of varicella infection should be offered varicella vaccine.

▶ The diagnosis of toxoplasmosis should be confirmed by a reliable reference laboratory.

▶ Pregnant women exposed to parvovirus B19 should have serologic screening performed to determine if they are at risk for seroconversion.

▶ Pregnant women should be counseled about methods to prevent acquisition of CMV or toxoplasmosis during pregnancy.

References

1. Klemola E, Kaariainen L. Cytomegalovirus as a possible cause of a disease resembling infectious mononucleosis. Br Med J 1965;5470:1099–1102 (Level III)

2. Fowler KB, Stagno S, Pass RF. Maternal age and congenital cytomegalovirus infection: screening of two diverse newborn populations, 1980–1990. J Infect Dis 1993;168:552–556 (Level II-3)

3. Adler SP, Finney JW, Manganello AM, Best AM. Prevention of child-to-mother transmission of cytomegalovirus by changing behaviors: a randomized controlled trial. Pediatr Infect Dis J 1996;15:240–246 (Level II-1)

4. Daniel Y, Gull I, Peyser MR, Lessing JB. Congenital cytomegalovirus infection. Eur J Obstet Gynecol Reprod Biol 1995;63:7–16 (Level III)

5. Stagno S, Pass RF, Dworsky ME, Alford CA Jr. Maternal cytomegalovirus infection and perinatal transmission. Clin Obstet Gynecol 1982;25:563–576 (Level III)

6. Stagno S, Pass RF, Cloud G, Britt WJ, Henderson RE, Walton PD, et al. Primary cytomegalovirus infection in pregnancy. Incidence, transmission to fetus, and clinical outcome. JAMA 1986;256:1904–1908 (Level II-2)

7. Hagay ZJ, Biran G, Ornoy A, Reece EA. Congenital cytomegalovirus infection: a long-standing problem still seeking a solution. Am J Obstet Gynecol 1996;174:241–245 (Level III)

8. Stagno S, Whitley RJ. Herpesvirus infections of pregnancy. Part 1: Cytomegalovirus and Epstein-Barr virus infections. N Engl J Med 1985;313:1270–1274 (Level II-3)

9. Fowler KB, Stagno S, Pass RF, Britt WJ, Boll TJ, Alford CA. The outcome of congenital cytomegalovirus infection in relation to maternal antibody status. N Engl J Med 1992;326:663–667 (Level II-2)

10. Chorba T, Coccia P, Holman RC, Tattersall P, Anderson LJ, Sudman J, et al. The role of parvovirus B19 in aplastic crisis and erythema infectiosum (fifth disease). J Infect Dis 1986;154:383–393 (Level II-2)

11. Thurn J. Human parvovirus B19: historical and clinical review. Rev Infect Dis 1988;10:1005–1011 (Level III)

12. Cytomegalovirus (CMV) infection and prevention. Atlanta, Georgia: Centers for Disease Control and Prevention, 1998 (Level III)

13. Rice PS, Cohen BJ. A school outbreak of parvovirus B19 infection investigated using salivary antibody assays. Epidemiol Infect 1996;116:331–338 (Level II-3)

14. Harger JH, Adler SP, Koch WC, Harger GF. Prospective evaluation of 618 pregnant women exposed to parvovirus B19: risks and symptoms. Obstet Gynecol 1998;91:413–420 (Level II-3)

15. Valeur-Jensen AK, Pedersen CB, Westergaard T, Jensen IP, Lebech M, Andersen PK, et al. Risk factors for parvovirus B19 infection in pregnancy. JAMA 1999; 281:1099–1105 (Level II-2)

16. Gillespie SM, Cartter ML, Asch S, Rokos JB, Gary GW, Tsou CJ, et al. Occupational risk of human parvovirus B19 infection for school and day-care personnel during an outbreak of erythema infectiosum. JAMA 1990;263: 2061–2065 (Level II-3)

17. Cartter ML, Farley TA, Rosengren S, Quinn DL, Gillespie SM, Gary GW, et al. Occupational risk factors for infection with parvovirus B19 among pregnant women. J Infect Dis 1991;163:282–285 (Level II-2)

18. Guidozzi F, Ballot D, Rothberg AD. Human B19 parvovirus infection in an obstetric population. A prospective study determining fetal outcome. J Reprod Med 1994;39:36–38 (Level III)

19. Public Health Laboratory Service Working Party on Fifth Disease. Prospective study of human parvovirus (B19) infection in pregnancy. BMJ 1990;300:1166–1170 (Level II-3)

20. Risks associated with human parvovirus B19 infection. MMWR Morbid Mortal Wkly Rep 1989;38:81–88, 93–97 (Level III)

21. Rodis JF, Quinn DL, Gary GW Jr, Anderson LJ, Rosengren S, Cartter ML, et al. Management and outcomes of pregnancies complicated by human B19 parvovirus infection: a prospective study. Am J Obstet Gynecol 1990;163:1168–1171 (Level III)

22. Gratacos E, Torres PJ, Vidal J, Antolin E, Costa J, Jimenez de Anta MT, et al. The incidence of human parvovirus B19 infection during pregnancy and its impact on perinatal outcome. J Infect Dis 1995;171:1360–1363 (Level II-2)

23. Yaegashi N, Okamura K, Yajima A, Murai C, Sugamura K. The frequency of human parvovirus B19 infection in nonimmune hydrops fetalis. J Perinat Med 1994;22: 159–163 (Level III)

24. Jordan JA. Identification of human parvovirus B19 infection in idiopathic nonimmune hydrops fetalis. Am J Obstet Gynecol 1996;174:37–42 (Level II-3)

25. Miller E, Fairley CK, Cohen BJ, Seng C. Immediate and long term outcome of human parvovirus B19 infection in pregnancy. Br J Obstet Gynaecol 1998;105:174–178 (Level II-3)

26. Rodis JF, Rodner C, Hansen AA, Borgida AF, Deoliveira I, Shulman Rosengren S, et al. Long-term outcome of children following maternal human parvovirus B19 infection. Obstet Gynecol 1998;91:125–128 (Level II-2)

27. Preblud SR, Orenstein WA, Bart KJ. Varicella: clinical manifestations, epidemiology and health impact in children. Pediatr Infect Dis 1984;3:505–509 (Level III)

28. Enders G. Serodiagnosis of Varicella-Zoster virus infection in pregnancy and standardization of the ELISA IgG and IgM antibody tests. Dev Biol Stand 1982;52: 221–236 (Level III)

29. Varicella-related deaths among adults—United States, 1997. MMWR Morb Mortal Wkly Rep 1997;46: 409–412 (Level III)

30. Paryani SG, Arvin AM. Intrauterine infection with varicella-zoster virus after maternal varicella. N Engl J Med 1986;314:1542–1546 (Level II-3)

31. Smego RA Jr, Asperilla MO. Use of acyclovir for varicella pneumonia during pregnancy. Obstet Gynecol 1991;78:1112–1116 (Level III)

32. Enders G, Miller E, Cradock-Watson J, Bolley I, Ridehalgh M. Consequences of varicella and herpes zoster in pregnancy: prospective study of 1739 cases. Lancet 1994;343:1548–1551 (Level II-2)

33. Jones KL, Johnson KA, Chambers CD. Offspring of women infected with varicella during pregnancy: a prospective study. Teratology 1994;49:29–32 (Level II-2)

34. Pastuszak AL, Levy M, Schick B, Zuber C, Feldkamp M, Gladstone J, et al. Outcome after maternal varicella infection in the first 20 weeks of pregnancy. N Engl J Med 1994;330:901–905 (Level II-2)

35. Brunell PA. Placental transfer of varicella-zoster antibody. Pediatrics 1966;38:1034–1038 (Level III)

36. Brunell PA. Fetal and neonatal varicella-zoster infections. Semin Perinatol 1983;7:47–56 (Level III)

37. Hohlfeld P, Daffos F, Costa JM, Thulliez P, Forestier F, Vidaud M. Prenatal diagnosis of congenital toxoplasmosis with a polymerase-chain-reaction test on amniotic fluid. N Engl J Med 1994;331:695–699 (Level II-2)

38. Foulon W, Villena I, Stray-Pedersen B, Decoster A, Lappalainen M, Pinon JM, et al. Treatment of toxoplasmosis during pregnancy: a multicenter study of impact on fetal transmission and children's sequelae at age 1 year. Am J Obstet Gynecol 1999;180:410–415 (Level II-3)

39. Stray-Pedersen B. Toxoplasmosis in pregnancy. Baillieres Clin Obstet Gynaecol 1993;7:107–137 (Level III)

40. Wilson CB, Remington JS, Stagno S, Reynolds DW. Development of adverse sequelae in children born with subclinical congenital Toxoplasma infection. Pediatrics 1980;66:767–774 (Level II-3)

41. de Roever-Bonnet H, Koppe JG, Loewer-Seger DH. Follow-up of children with congenital toxoplasma infection and children who became serologically negative after 1 year of age, all born in 1964–1965. In: Thalhammer O, Baumgarten K, Pollak A, eds. Perinatal medicine: Sixth European Congress, Vienna. Littleton, Massachusetts: PSG Publishing Company, 1979:61–75 (Level III)

42. Desmonts G, Couvreur J. Congenital toxoplasmosis. A prospective study of 378 pregnancies. N Engl J Med 1974;290:1110–1116 (Level II-3)

43. Daffos F, Forestier F, Capella-Pavlovsky M, Thulliez P, Aufrant C, Valenti D, et al. Prenatal management of 746 pregnancies at risk for congenital toxoplasmosis. N Engl J Med 1988;318:271–275 (Level II-3)

44. Remington JS, McLeod R, Desmonts G. Toxoplasmosis. In: Remington JS, Klein JO, eds. Infectious disease of the fetus and newborn infant. 4th ed. Philadelphia: WB Saunders, 1995:140–267 (Level III)

45. Stagno S, Tinker MK, Elrod C, Fuccillo DA, Cloud G, O'Beirne AJ. Immunoglobulin M antibodies detected by enzyme-linked immunosorbent assay and radioimmunoassay in the diagnosis of cytomegalovirus infections in pregnant women and newborn infants. J Clin Microbiol 1985;21:930–935 (Level II-3)

46. Drose JA, Dennis MA, Thickman D. Infection in utero: US findings in 19 cases. Radiology 1991;178:369–374 (Level III)

47. Stein B, Bromley B, Michlewitz H, Miller WA, Benacerraf BR. Fetal liver calcifications: sonographic appearance and postnatal outcome. Radiology 1995; 197:489–492 (Level III)

48. Ghidini A, Sirtori M, Vergani P, Mariani S, Tucci E, Scola GC. Fetal intracranial calcifications. Am J Obstet Gynecol 1989;160:86–87 (Level III)

49. Yamashita Y, Iwanaga R, Goto A, Kaneko S, Yamashita F, Wasedna N, et al. Congenital cytomegalovirus infection associated with fetal ascites and intrahepatic calcifications. Acta Paediatr Scand 1989;78:965–967 (Level III)

50. Forouzan I. Fetal abdominal echogenic mass: an early sign of intrauterine cytomegalovirus infection. Obstet Gynecol 1992;80:535–537 (Level III)

51. Twickler DM, Perlman J, Maberry MC. Congenital cytomegalovirus infection presenting as cerebral ventriculomegaly on antenatal sonography. Am J Perinatol 1993;10:404–406 (Level III)

52. Weiner Z. Congenital cytomegalovirus infection with oligohydramnios and echogenic bowel at 14 weeks' gestation. J Ultrasound Med 1995;14:617–618 (Level III)

53. Yaron Y, Hassan S, Geva E, Kupferminc MJ, Yavetz H, Evans MI, et al. Evaluation of fetal echogenic bowel in the second trimester. Fetal Diagn Ther 1999;14:176–180 (Level II-3)

54. Bale JF Jr, Blackman JA, Sato Y. Outcome in children with symptomatic congenital cytomegalovirus infection. J Child Neurol 1990;5:131–136 (Level III)

55. Lynch L, Daffos F, Emanuel D, Giovangrandi Y, Meisel R, Forestier F, et al. Prenatal diagnosis of fetal cytomegalovirus infection. Am J Obstet Gynecol 1991;165: 714–718 (Level III)

56. Donner C, Liesnard C, Content J, Busine A, Aderca J, Rodesch F. Prenatal diagnosis of 52 pregnancies at risk for congenital cytomegalovirus infection. Obstet Gynecol 1993;82:481–486 (Level III)

57. Nicolini U, Kustermann A, Tassis B, Fogliani R, Galimberti A, Percivalle E, et al. Prenatal diagnosis of congenital human cytomegalovirus infection. Prenat Diagn 1994;14:903–906 (Level III)

58. Stango S. Cytomegalovirus. In: Remington JS, Klein JO, eds. Infectious disease of the fetus and newborn infant. 4th ed. Philadelphia: WB Saunders, 1995:312–353 (Level III)

59. Hohlfeld P, Vial Y, Maillard-Brignon C, Vaudaux B, Fawer CL. Cytomegalovirus fetal infection: prenatal diagnosis. Obstet Gynecol 1991;78:615–618 (Level III)

60. Lamy ME, Mulongo KN, Gadisseux JF, Lyon G, Gaudy V, Van Lierde M. Prenatal diagnosis of fetal cytomegalovirus infection. Am J Obstet Gynecol 1992;166:91–94 (Level III)

61. Hogge WA, Buffone GJ, Hogge JS. Prenatal diagnosis of cytomegalovirus (CMV) infection: a preliminary report. Prenat Diagn 1993;13:131–136 (Level III)

62. Revello MG, Baldanti F, Furione M, Sarasini A, Percivalle E, Zavattoni M, et al. Polymerase chain reaction for prenatal diagnosis of congenital human cytomegalovirus infection. J Med Virol 1995;47:462–466 (Level II-3)

63. Lipitz S, Yagel S, Shalev E, Achiron R, Mashiach S, Schiff E. Prenatal diagnosis of fetal primary cytomegalovirus infection. Obstet Gynecol 1997;89: 763–767 (Level II-3)

64. Lazzarotto T, Guerra B, Spezzacatena P, Varani S, Gabrielli L, Pradelli P, et al. Prenatal diagnosis of congenital cytomegalovirus infection. J Clin Microbiol 1998;36:3540–3544 (Level II-3)

65. Donner C, Liesnard C, Brancart F, Rodesch F. Accuracy of amniotic fluid testing before 21 weeks' gestation in prenatal diagnosis of congenital cytomegalovirus infection. Prenat Diagn 1994;14:1055–1059 (Level II-3)

66. Gilstrap LC, Bawdon RE, Roberts SW, Sobhi S. The transfer of the nucleoside analog ganciclovir across the perfused human placenta. Am J Obstet Gynecol 1994;170:967–972; discussion 972–973 (Level III)

67. Attard-Montalto SP, English MC, Stimmler L, Snodgrass GJ. Ganciclovir treatment of congenital cytomegalovirus infection: a report of two cases. Scand J Infect Dis 1993;25:385–388 (Level III)

68. Fukuda S, Miyachi M, Sugimoto S, Goshima A, Futamura M, Morishima T. A female infant successfully treated by ganciclovir for congenital cytomegalovirus infection. Acta Paediatr Jpn 1995;37:206–210 (Level III)

69. Stronati M, Revello MG, Cerbo RM, Furione M, Rondini G, Gerna G. Ganciclovir therapy of congenital human cytomegalovirus hepatitis. Acta Paediatr 1995;84: 340–341 (Level III)

70. Nigro G, Scholz H, Bartmann U. Ganciclovir therapy for symptomatic congenital cytomegalovirus infection in infants: a two-regimen experience. J Pediatr 1994;124: 318–322 (Level II-3)

71. Barbi M, Binda S, Primache V, Novelli C. Cytomegalovirus in peripheral blood leukocytes of infants with congenital or postnatal infection. Pediatr Infect Dis J 1996;15:898–903 (Level II-3)

72. Whitley RJ, Cloud G, Gruber W, Storch GA, Demmler GJ, Jacobs RF, et al. Ganciclovir treatment of symptomatic congenital cytomegalovirus infection: results of a phase II study. National Institute of Allergy and Infectious Diseases Collaborative Antiviral Study Group. J Infect Dis 1997;175:1080–1086 (Level II-3)

73. Plotkin SA, Starr SE, Friedman HM, Gonczol E, Brayman K. Vaccines for the prevention of human cytomegalovirus infection. Rev Infect Dis 1990;12 (Suppl 7):S827–S838 (Level III)

74. Plotkin SA, Starr SE, Friedman HM, Brayman K, Harris S, Jackson S, et al. Effect of Towne live virus vaccine on cytomegalovirus disease after renal transplant. A controlled trial. Ann Intern Med 1991;114:525–531 (Level I)

75. Plotkin SA, Higgins R, Kurtz JB, Morris PJ, Campbell DA Jr, Shope TC, et al. Multicenter trial of Towne strain attenuated virus vaccine in seronegative renal transplant recipients. Transplantation 1994;58:1176–1178 (Level I)

76. Adler SP, Hempfling SH, Starr SE, Plotkin SA, Riddell S. Safety and immunogenicity of the Towne strain cytomegalovirus vaccine. Pediatr Infect Dis J 1998; 17:200–206 (Level II-3)

77. Porath A, McNutt RA, Smiley LM, Weigle KA. Effectiveness and cost benefit of a proposed live cytomegalovirus vaccine in the prevention of congenital disease. Rev Infect Dis 1990;12:31–40 (Level III)

78. Scott LL, Hollier LM, Dias K. Perinatal herpesvirus infections. Herpes simplex, varicella, and cytomegalovirus. Infect Dis Clin North Am 1997;11:27–53 (Level III)

79. Raynor BD. Cytomegalovirus infection in pregnancy. Semin Perinatol 1993;17:394–402 (Level III)

80. Adler SP. Cytomegalovirus and pregnancy. Curr Opin Obstet Gynecol 1992;4:670–675 (Level III)

81. Grangeot-Keros L, Simon B, Audibert F, Vial M. Should we routinely screen for cytomegalovirus antibody during pregnancy? Intervirology 1998;41:158–162 (Level III)

82. Pass RF, August AM, Dworsky M, Reynolds DW. Cytomegalovirus infection in day-care center. N Engl J Med 1982;307:477–479 (Level II-2)

83. Olson LC, Ketusinha R, Mansuwan P, Snitbhan R. Respiratory tract excretion of cytomegalovirus in Thai children. J Pediatr 1970;77:499–504 (Level II-3)

84. Yeager AS. Transmission of cytomegalovirus to mothers by infected infants: another reason to prevent transfusion-acquired infections. Pediatr Infect Dis 1983;2: 295–297 (Level III)

85. Tookey PA, Ades AE, Peckham CS. Cytomegalovirus prevalence in pregnant women: the influence of parity. Arch Dis Child 1992;67:779–783 (Level II-3)

86. Biomedical Research Institute. CMV: diagnosis, prevention, and treatment. 2nd ed. St. Paul, Minnesota: Children's Hospital of St. Paul & Children's Biomedical Research Institute, 1989 (Level III)

87. Anderson LJ, Tsou C, Parker RA, Chorba TL, Wulff H, Tattersall P, et al. Detection of antibodies and antigens of human parvovirus B19 by enzyme-linked immunosorbent assay. J Clin Microbiol 1986;24:522–526 (Level II-2)

88. Schwarz TF, Nerlich A, Hottentrager B, Jager G, Wiest I, Kantimm S, et al. Parvovirus B19 infection of the fetus. Histology and in situ hybridization. Am J Clin Pathol 1991;96:121–126 (Level III)

89. Schwarz TF, Nerlich A, Hillemanns P. Detection of parvovirus B19 in fetal autopsies. Arch Gynecol Obstet 1993;253:207–213 (Level III)

90. Sifakis S, Ergazaki M, Sourvinos G, Koffa M, Koumantakis E, Spandidos DA. Evaluation of Parvo B19, CMV and HPV viruses in human aborted materi-

al using the polymerase chain reaction technique. Eur J Obstet Gynecol Reprod Biol 1998;76:169–173 (Level II-3)

91. Clewley JP. Polymerase chain reaction assay of parvovirus B19 DNA in clinical specimens. J Clin Microbiol 1989;27:2647–2651 (Level II-3)

92. Salimans MM, van de Rijke FM, Raap AK, van Elsacker-Niele AM. Detection of parvovirus B19 DNA in fetal tissues by in situ hybridisation and polymerase chain reaction. J Clin Pathol 1989;42:525–530 (Level III)

93. Kovacs BW, Carlson DE, Shahbahrami B, Platt LD. Prenatal diagnosis of human parvovirus B19 in nonimmune hydrops fetalis by polymerase chain reaction. Am J Obstet Gynecol 1992;167:461–466 (Level III)

94. Torok TJ, Wang QY, Gary GW Jr, Yang CF, Finch TM, Anderson LJ, et al. Prenatal diagnosis of intrauterine infection with parvovirus B19 by the polymerase chain reaction technique. Clin Infect Dis 1992;14:149–155 (Level III)

95. Rogers BB, Mak SK, Dailey JV, Saller DN Jr, Buffone GJ. Detection of parvovirus B19 DNA in amniotic fluid by PCR DNA amplification. Biotechniques 1993;15: 406–408, 410 (Level III)

96. Torok TJ. Human parvovirus B19. In: Remington JS, Klein JO, eds. Infectious disease of the fetus and newborn infant. 4th ed. Philadelphia: WB Saunders, 1995:668–702 (Level III)

97. Peters MT, Nicolaides KH. Cordocentesis for the diagnosis and treatment of human fetal parvovirus infection. Obstet Gynecol 1990;75:501–504 (Level III)

98. Levy R, Weissman A, Blomberg G, Hagay ZJ. Infection by parvovirus B 19 during pregnancy: a review. Obstet Gynecol Surv 1997;52:254–259 (Level III)

99. Fairley CK, Smoleniec JS, Caul OE, Miller E. Observational study of effect of intrauterine transfusions on outcome of fetal hydrops after parvovirus B19 infection. Lancet 1995;346:1335–1337 (Level II-3)

100. Pretorius DH, Hayward I, Jones KL, Stamm E. Sonographic evaluation of pregnancies with maternal varicella infection. J Ultrasound Med 1992;11:459–463 (Level III)

101. Lecuru F, Taurelle R, Bernard JP, Parrat S, Lafay-pillet MC, Rozenberg F, et al. Varicella zoster virus infection during pregnancy: the limits of prenatal diagnosis. Eur J Obstet Gynecol Reprod Biol 1994;56:67–68 (Level III)

102. Kustermann A, Zoppini C, Tassis B, Della Morte M, Colucci G, Nicolini U. Prenatal diagnosis of congenital varicella infection. Prenat Diagn 1996;16:71–74 (Level III)

103. Isada NB, Paar DP, Johnson MP, Evans MI, Holzgreve W, Qureshi F, et al. In utero diagnosis of congenital varicella zoster virus infection by chorionic villus sampling and polymerase chain reaction. Am J Obstet Gynecol 1991;165:1727–1730 (Level III)

104. Balfour HH Jr, Rotbart HA, Feldman S, Dunkle LM, Feder HM Jr, Prober CG, et al. Acyclovir treatment of varicella in otherwise healthy adolescents. The Collaborative Acyclovir Varicella Study Group. J Pediatr 1992;120:627–633 (Level I)

105. Wallace MR, Bowler WA, Murray NB, Brodine SK, Oldfield EC 3d. Treatment of adult varicella with oral acyclovir. A randomized, placebo-controlled trial. Ann Intern Med 1992;117:358–363 (Level I)

106. Ogilvie MM. Antiviral prophylaxis and treatment in chickenpox. A review prepared for the UK Advisory Group on Chickenpox on behalf of the British Society for the Study of Infection. J Infect 1998;36(Suppl 1): 31–38 (Level III)

107. Kesson AM, Grimwood K, Burgess MA, Ferson MJ, Gilbert GL, Hogg G, et al. Acyclovir for the prevention and treatment of varicella zoster in children, adolescents and pregnancy. J Paediatr Child Health 1996;32:211–217 (Level III)

108. Cox SM, Cunningham FG, Luby J. Management of varicella pneumonia complicating pregnancy. Am J Perinatol 1990;7:300–301 (Level III)

109. American Academy of Pediatrics Committee on Infectious Diseases: the use of oral acyclovir in otherwise healthy children with varicella. Pediatrics 1993; 91:674–676 (Level III) [erratum Pediatrics 1993;91:858]

110. Miller E, Cradock-Watson JE, Ridehalgh MK. Outcome in newborn babies given anti-varicella-zoster immunoglobulin after perinatal maternal infection with varicella-zoster virus. Lancet 1989;8659:371–373 (Level II-3)

111. Williams H, Latif A, Morgan J, Ansari BM. Acyclovir in the treatment of neonatal varicella. J Infect 1987;15: 65–67 (Level III)

112. Centers for Disease Control and Prevention. Prevention of varicella: recommendations of the Advisory Committee on Immunization Practices (ACIP). MMWR Morb Mortal Wkly Rep 1996;45(RR-11):1–36 (Level III)

113. Glantz JC, Mushlin AI. Cost-effectiveness of routine antenatal varicella screening. Obstet Gynecol 1998;91: 519–528 (Level III)

114. Rouse DJ, Gardner M, Allen SJ, Goldenberg RL. Management of the presumed susceptible varicella (chickenpox)-exposed gravida: a cost-effectiveness/cost-benefit analysis. Obstet Gynecol 1996;87:932–936 (Level III)

115. McGregor JA, Mark S, Crawford GP, Levin MJ. Varicella zoster antibody testing in the care of pregnant women exposed to varicella. Am J Obstet Gynecol 1987; 157:281–284 (Level II-3)

116. Brunell PA, Ross A, Miller LH, Kuo B. Prevention of varicella by zoster immune globulin. N Engl J Med 1969;280:1191–1194 (Level II-1)

117. Varicella-zoster immune globulin for the prevention of chickenpox. Recommendations of the Immunization Practices Advisory Committee, Centers for Disease Control. Ann Intern Med 1984;100:859–865 (Level III)

118. Montoya JG, Remington JS. Toxoplasma gondii. In: Mandell GL, Bennett JE, Dolin R, eds. Principles and practices in infectious disease. 5th ed. New York: Churchill Livingstone, 2000:2858–2888 (Level III)

119. Fricker-Hidalgo H, Pelloux H, Racinet C, Grefenstette I, Bost-Bru C, Goullier-Fleuret A, et al. Detection of Toxoplasma gondii in 94 placentae from infected women by polymerase chain reaction, in vivo, and in vitro cultures. Placenta 1998;19:545–549 (Level II-3)

120. Hezard N, Marx-Chemla C, Foudrinier F, Villena I, Quereux C, Leroux B, et al. Prenatal diagnosis of congenital toxoplasmosis in 261 pregnancies. Prenat Diagn 1997;17:1047–1054 (Level II-3)

121. Grover CM, Thulliez P, Remington JS, Boothroyd JC. Rapid prenatal diagnosis of congenital Toxoplasma infection by using polymerase chain reaction and amniotic fluid. J Clin Microbiol 1990;28:2297–2301 (Level II-2)

122. van de Ven E, Melchers W, Galama J, Camps W, Meuwissen J. Identification of Toxoplasma gondii infections by BI gene amplification. J Clin Microbiol 1991;29:2120–2124 (Level III)

123. Cazenave J, Forestier F, Bessieres MH, Broussin B, Begueret J. Contribution of a new PCR assay to the prenatal diagnosis of congenital toxoplasmosis. Prenat Diagn 1992;12:119–127 (Level II-2)

124. Jenum PA, Holberg-Petersen M, Melby KK, Stray-Pedersen B. Diagnosis of congenital Toxoplasma gondii infection by polymerase chain reaction (PCR) on amniotic fluid samples. The Norwegian experience. APMIS 1998;106:680–686 (Level II-3)

125. Guy EC, Pelloux H, Lappalainen M, Aspock H, Hassl A, Melby KK, et al. Interlaboratory comparison of polymerase chain reaction for the detection of Toxoplasma gondii DNA added to samples of amniotic fluid. Eur J Clin Microbiol Infect Dis 1996;15:836–839 (Level III)

126. Mombro M, Perathoner C, Leone A, Nicocia M, Moiraghi Ruggenini A, et al. Congenital toxoplasmosis: 10-year follow up. Eur J Pediatr 1995;154:635–639 (Level II-3)

127. Stray-Pedersen B. Treatment of toxoplasmosis in the pregnant mother and newborn child. Scand J Infect Dis Suppl 1992;84:23–31 (Level III)

128. Berrebi A, Kobuch WE, Bessieres MH, Bloom MC, Rolland M, Sarramon MF, et al. Termination of pregnancy for maternal toxoplasmosis. Lancet 1994;344:36–39 (Level II-3)

129. Patel DV, Holfels EM, Vogel NP, Boyer KM, Mets MB, Swisher CN, et al. Resolution of intracranial calcifications in infants with treated congenital toxoplasmosis. Radiology 1996;199:433–440 (Level II-3)

130. Sever JL, Ellenberg JH, Ley AC, Madden DL, Fuccillo DA, Tzan NR, et al. Toxoplasmosis: maternal and pediatric findings in 23,000 pregnancies. Pediatrics 1988; 82:181–192 (Level II-3)

131. Foulon W. Congenital toxoplasmosis: is screening desirable? Scand J Infect Dis Suppl 1992;84:11–17 (Level II-3)

The MEDLINE database, the Cochrane Library, and ACOG's own internal resources and documents were used to conduct a literature search to locate relevant articles published between January 1985 and January 2000. The search was restricted to articles published in the English language. Priority was given to articles reporting results of original research, although review articles and commentaries also were consulted. Abstracts of research presented at symposia and scientific conferences were not considered adequate for inclusion in this document. Guidelines published by organizations or institutions such as the National Institutes of Health and the American College of Obstetricians and Gynecologists were reviewed, and additional studies were located by reviewing bibliographies of identified articles. When reliable research was not available, expert opinions from obstetrician–gynecologists were used.

Studies were reviewed and evaluated for quality according to the method outlined by the U.S. Preventive Services Task Force:

I   Evidence obtained from at least one properly designed randomized controlled trial.

II-1   Evidence obtained from well-designed controlled trials without randomization.

II-2   Evidence obtained from well-designed cohort or case–control analytic studies, preferably from more than one center or research group.

II-3   Evidence obtained from multiple time series with or without the intervention. Dramatic results in uncontrolled experiments also could be regarded as this type of evidence.

III   Opinions of respected authorities, based on clinical experience, descriptive studies, or reports of expert committees.

Based on the highest level of evidence found in the data, recommendations are provided and graded according to the following categories:

Level A—Recommendations are based on good and consistent scientific evidence.

Level B—Recommendations are based on limited or inconsistent scientific evidence.

Level C—Recommendations are based primarily on consensus and expert opinion.

ISSN 1099-3630

The American College of
Obstetricians and Gynecologists
409 12th Street, SW
PO Box 96920
Washington, DC 20090-6920   12345/43210

ACOG PRACTICE BULLETIN

CLINICAL MANAGEMENT GUIDELINES FOR
OBSTETRICIAN–GYNECOLOGISTS

NUMBER 1, JUNE 1998

This Practice Bulletin was developed by the ACOG Committees on Practice Bulletins—Obstetrics and Gynecology with the assistance of Brian M. Mercer, MD. The information is designed to aid practitioners in making decisions about appropriate obstetric and gynecologic care. These guidelines should not be construed as dictating an exclusive course of treatment or procedure. Variations in practice may be warranted based on the needs of the individual patient, resources, and limitations unique to the institution or type of practice.

Premature Rupture of Membranes

Preterm delivery occurs in approximately 11% of all births in the United States and is a major factor contributing to perinatal morbidity and mortality. Despite extensive research in this area, the rate of preterm birth has increased by 17% over the past 15 years (1). Premature rupture of membranes (PROM) is a complication in one quarter to one third of preterm births. In both term and preterm births, numerous controversies exist regarding optimal methods of clinical assessment and treatment of PROM. Management hinges on evaluation of the relative risks of infection, cord accident, operative delivery, and of the gestational age in patients not in labor. The purpose of this document is to review the current understanding of this condition and to provide management guidelines that have been validated by appropriately conducted outcome-based research. Additional guidelines based on consensus and expert opinion also are presented to permit a review of most clinical aspects of PROM.

Background

The definition of PROM is rupture of membranes before the onset of labor. When membrane rupture occurs before 37 weeks of gestation, it is referred to as preterm PROM. Premature rupture of membranes can result from a wide array of pathologic mechanisms acting individually or in concert (2). The gestational age at membrane rupture has significant implications regarding the etiology and consequences of PROM. Management may be dictated by the presence of overt intrauterine infection, advanced labor, or fetal compromise. When such factors are not present, especially with preterm PROM, other interventions may have a significant impact on maternal and infant morbidity. An accurate assessment of gestational age and knowledge of the maternal, fetal, and neonatal risks are essential to appropriate evaluation, counseling, and management of patients with PROM.

Etiology

Membrane rupture may occur for a variety of reasons. At term, weakening of the membranes may result from physiologic changes combined with shearing forces created by uterine contractions (2, 3). Intrauterine infection has been shown to play an important role in preterm PROM, especially at earlier gestational ages (4). Factors associated with an increase in PROM include lower socioeconomic status, sexually transmissible infections, prior preterm delivery (especially due to PROM), vaginal bleeding, cervical conization, and cigarette smoking during pregnancy (2, 5–7). Uterine distention (hydramnios, twins), emergency cervical cerclage, prior antepartum antibiotic treatment, and preterm labor also may be associated with PROM (2, 6, 8). In many cases, however, PROM may occur in the absence of recognized risk factors.

Term Premature Rupture of Membranes

At term, PROM complicates approximately 8% of pregnancies and is generally followed by the onset of labor and delivery. In a large randomized trial, half of women with PROM who were managed expectantly delivered within 5 hours, and 95% delivered within 28 hours of membrane rupture (9). Other studies have reported similar rates (10).

The most significant maternal risk of term PROM is intrauterine infection, a risk that increases with the duration of membrane rupture (6, 9–12). Fetal risks associated with PROM include umbilical cord compression and ascending infection.

Preterm Premature Rupture of Membranes

Regardless of management or clinical presentation, birth within 1 week is the most likely outcome of any patient with PROM prior to term. A review of 13 randomized trials reported that approximately 75% of patients with preterm PROM who were managed expectantly delivered within 1 week (13). The earlier in gestation that PROM occurs, the greater the potential for pregnancy prolongation. With expectant management, 2.8–13% of women can anticipate cessation of fluid leakage (12, 14).

Of women with preterm PROM, clinically evident intraamniotic infection occurs in 13–60% and postpartum infection occurs in 2–13% (14–18). The incidence of infection increases with decreasing gestational age at membrane rupture (19, 20) and increases with digital vaginal examination (21). With appropriate management, however, serious maternal sequelae are uncommon (13, 16). Fetal malpresentation is increased with preterm PROM. Abruptio placentae affects 4–12% of pregnancies with preterm PROM (22, 23).

The most significant risks to the fetus after preterm PROM are complications of prematurity. At all gestational ages prior to term, respiratory distress has been reported to be the most common complication (15, 24). Other serious forms of morbidity, including necrotizing enterocolitis and intraventricular hemorrhage, also are associated with prematurity but are less common nearer to term. The presence of maternal infection poses the additional risk of neonatal infection. Infection, cord accident, and other factors contribute to the 1–2% risk of antenatal fetal demise after preterm PROM (13).

Midtrimester Premature Rupture of Membranes

Premature rupture of membranes occurring before and around the time of neonatal viability often is referred to as midtrimester PROM. Premature rupture of membranes at 16–26 weeks of gestation complicates almost 1% of pregnancies (7, 25). Before the 1970s, delivery in the second trimester was generally associated with neonatal death resulting from complications of prematurity. Primarily because of advances in neonatal intensive care over the past two decades, neonates are surviving at increasingly younger gestational ages. Currently, overall infant survival after delivery at 24–26 weeks of gestation is reported to be between 50% and 75% (24, 26, 27). Survival rates in pregnancies complicated by PROM are comparable (28–30) but decreased in the presence of infection or deformations.

A small number of patients with midtrimester PROM will have an extended latency period. In a review of 12 studies evaluating patients with midtrimester PROM, the mean latency period ranged from 10.6 to 21.5 days (25). Although delivery occurred within 1 week of membrane rupture in 57% of patients, in 22% of patients pregnancy continued for 1 month. Most studies of midtrimester PROM have been retrospective and include only those patients amenable to expectant management. Patients usually are excluded from analysis in the presence of labor, infection, prolapsed membranes, and fetal demise, thus potentially exaggerating the latency period to delivery and deceptively decreasing the apparent maternal and infant morbidity.

Reported maternal complications of midtrimester PROM include intraamniotic infection, endometritis, abruptio placentae, retained placentae, and postpartum hemorrhage. Maternal sepsis is a rare but serious complication reported to affect approximately 1% of cases (25, 29).

The incidence of stillbirth subsequent to PROM at 16–25 weeks of gestation ranges from 3.8% to 21.7% (7, 15, 31) compared with 0–2% with PROM at 30–36 weeks of gestation (32, 33). This increased rate of death may be explained by increased susceptibility of the umbilical cord to compression or of the fetus to hypoxia and intrauterine infection. Alternatively, this finding may reflect the lack of intervention for fetal compromise prior to neonatal viability. The fetal survival rate subsequent to PROM at less than 24 weeks of gestation has been reported to be about 30%, compared with a 57% survival rate with rupture at 24–26 weeks of gestation (25).

Several trials have described outcomes of survivors after PROM at 16–26 weeks of gestation (7, 29–31, 34, 35). Although up to 69% of these neonates were reported as having normal neurologic development, these results may be biased by a lack of follow-up. Generalized developmental delay, delayed motor development, and other less frequent complications, including cerebral palsy, chronic lung disease, blindness, hydrocephalus, and mental retardation, also were reported to occur.

A variety of conditions that are associated with fetal lung compression or oligohydramnios or both can result in pulmonary hypoplasia. Reported risks of pulmonary hypoplasia after PROM at 16–26 weeks of gestation vary from less than 1% to 27% (18, 29). Pulmonary hypoplasia rarely occurs with membrane rupture subsequent to 26 weeks of gestation, presumably because alveolar growth adequate to support postnatal development already has occurred (36, 37). Prolonged oligohydramnios also is associated with in utero deformation including abnormal facies (ie, low-set ears and epicanthal folds) and limb positioning abnormalities.

When leakage of amniotic fluid occurs after amniocentesis, the outcome is better than after spontaneous preterm PROM. In one study of 603 women who had second-trimester amniocentesis for prenatal diagnosis of genetic disorders, seven women (1.2%) experienced PROM, and leakage stopped in all with conservative management (8).

Clinical Considerations and Recommendations

▶ *How is premature rupture of membranes diagnosed?*

An accurate diagnosis is crucial to the management of suspected membrane rupture. Most cases can be diagnosed on the basis of the history and physical examination (38). Other causes of discharge include urinary leakage, excess vaginal discharge with advanced dilatation or membrane prolapse, cervicitis, bloody show, semen, and vaginal douches. Symptoms suggestive of PROM should be confirmed. Delay in evaluation may result in a missed opportunity for intervention.

Examination should be performed in a manner that minimizes the risk of introducing infection, particularly prior to term. Digital cervical examinations increase the risk of infection and add little information to that available with speculum examination (21, 39). Thus, digital examinations should be avoided unless prompt labor and delivery are anticipated. Sterile speculum examination can confirm the diagnosis of PROM as well as provide an opportunity to inspect for cervicitis or umbilical cord or fetal prolapse, assess cervical dilatation and effacement, and obtain cultures as appropriate (40).

The diagnosis of membrane rupture is confirmed by the visualization of amniotic fluid in the posterior vaginal fornix or clear fluid passing from the cervical canal. If the diagnosis remains in question, the pH of the vaginal sidewalls or fluid pool can be assessed.

The pH of the vaginal secretions is generally 4.5–6.0 whereas amniotic fluid usually has a pH of 7.1–7.3. Nitrazine paper will turn blue with a pH above 6.0–6.5. False-positive results may occur in the presence of blood or semen contamination, alkaline antiseptics, or bacterial vaginosis. Alternatively, false-negative results may occur with prolonged leakage and minimal residual fluid. More information can be obtained by swabbing the posterior fornix (avoiding cervical mucus) and allowing the vaginal fluid to dry on a microscope slide. The presence of arborization (ferning) under microscopic visualization further suggests membrane rupture.

When the clinical history or physical examination is unclear, ultrasound examination may be useful to document oligohydramnios, which in the absence of fetal urinary tract malformations or significant growth restriction is suggestive of membrane rupture. Membrane rupture can be diagnosed unequivocally with ultrasonographically guided transabdominal instillation of indigo carmine dye (1 mL in 9 mL sterile normal saline), followed by observation for passage of blue fluid from the vagina within 30 minutes of amniocentesis.

▶ *What is the optimal method of initial management for a patient with PROM at term?*

Fetal heart rate monitoring may be used to assess fetal status. Dating criteria should be reviewed to assign gestational age because virtually all aspects of subsequent care will hinge on that information. Group B streptococcal status and the need for intrapartum prophylaxis should be determined (41).

▶ *When should labor be induced in patients with term PROM?*

Fetal presentation, gestational age, and status should be established before determining whether labor should be induced. The decision to induce labor involves an assessment of the relative risks of infection or fetal compromise (which may increase with the duration of PROM) versus the risks of failed induction and operative vaginal delivery (which may increase with induced as opposed to spontaneous labor).

If the condition of the cervix is unfavorable, there is little difference in outcome when comparing induction to expectant management. Options evaluated ranged from immediate induction to observation for up to 24–72 hours prior to induction (9, 42–45). While time from admission to delivery is shortened with induction, time in labor is longer, and the need for operative vaginal delivery seems to be higher (44, 46).

Risk of cesarean delivery and risk of neonatal infectious complications do not appear to depend on the mode of management (expectant versus induction), although the risks of maternal infection may increase with expectant management (9, 43, 45). Thus, it is reasonable for consideration of the patient's wishes and hospitalization costs to influence management.

▶ *What does the initial evaluation involve once PROM has been confirmed?*

Fetal presentation, gestational age, and status should be determined. The gravida with evident intrauterine infection, abruptio placentae, or evidence of fetal compromise is best cared for by expeditious delivery. In the absence of an indication for immediate delivery, swabs for diagnosis of *Chlamydia trachomatis* and *Neisseria gonorrhoeae* may be obtained from the cervix if appropriate. The need for group B streptococcal intrapartum prophylaxis should be determined (41).

▶ *When should one elect delivery for the fetus near term in the presence of premature rupture of membranes?*

After initial assessment, relative maternal and fetal risks with expectant management, neonatal risks with early delivery, and the potential neonatal benefit from expectant management can then be determined. Because serious neonatal morbidity is uncommon with demonstrated pulmonary maturity and delivery after 32–36 weeks of gestation (33), amniotic fluid may be collected from the vaginal pool or by amniocentesis for assessment of fetal pulmonary maturity.

If pulmonary maturity has been documented after PROM at 32–36 weeks of gestation, labor induction may be considered. Available clinical trial data concerning expectant management versus immediate induction at 30–34 weeks of gestation (32) and at 32–36 weeks of gestation

(33) show increased risks of chorioamnionitis and prolonged hospitalization with expectant management but equal risks of respiratory distress syndrome, intraventricular hemorrhage, necrotizing enterocolitis, and neonatal death. It is noteworthy that in the studies cited (32, 33), which were conducted in major centers with neonatal intensive care units, antibiotics (32, 33) or antenatal corticosteroids (32) were not utilized. Although it is uncertain whether the use of prophylactic antibiotics and antenatal corticosteroids will improve the outcome of expectant management at these gestational ages, it is clear that delivery of a preterm infant should take place in a facility with experience in the management of such infants.

The gravida who experiences PROM before 30–32 weeks of gestation and whose condition is stable is generally best served by expectant management. The prophylactic use of antibiotics and antenatal corticosteroids can help reduce the risks of gestational age-dependent neonatal morbidity.

▶ *What general approaches are utilized in patients with preterm PROM managed expectantly?*

Expectant management of preterm PROM generally consists of modified bed rest to potentially enhance amniotic fluid reaccumulation and complete pelvic rest to avoid infection. Patients should be assessed periodically for evidence of infection or labor. In a patient with preterm PROM, a temperature exceeding 38.0°C (100.4°F) may be indicative of infection, although some investigators have suggested that fever, with additional factors such as uterine tenderness and maternal or fetal tachycardia, is a more accurate indicator of maternal infection (15, 47). Leukocyte counts are nonspecific in the absence of clinical evidence of infection, especially if antenatal corticosteroids have been administered.

If the presence of intraamniotic infection is suspected and additional diagnostic confirmation is required, amniocentesis may be considered (48). The diagnosis of intraamniotic infection may be suggested by an amniotic fluid glucose concentration of less than 20 mg/dL, by a positive Gram stain, or a positive amniotic fluid culture (49–51). The presence of amniotic fluid leukocytes alone is not diagnostic of infection. In a case-control study comparing amniotic fluid tests used to predict infection, investigators concluded interleukin-6 was the only test that had significant clinical value in predicting neonatal complications (51). Other investigators have rejected amniocentesis because of a low success rate and the need for repeat procedures (52).

▶ *Should tocolytics be considered in patients with preterm PROM in labor?*

Prophylactic tocolysis after preterm PROM has been shown to prolong latency in the short term (53–55), while therapeutic tocolysis (ie, instituting tocolysis only after contractions have ensued) has not been shown to prolong latency (56). No study to date has demonstrated that tocolytics benefit neonatal outcome, but none has utilized antibiotics or antenatal corticosteroids. As detailed below, use of both antibiotics and antenatal corticosteroids improves outcome in patients with preterm PROM who are not having contractions. The effect of tocolysis to permit antibiotic and antenatal corticosteroid administration in the patient with preterm PROM who is having contractions has yet to be investigated.

▶ *Should antenatal corticosteroids be administered to patients with preterm PROM?*

Two meta-analyses have evaluated the impact of corticosteroid use after preterm PROM on respiratory distress syndrome. These studies produced somewhat conflicting results. While both found significant reduction in respiratory distress syndrome with antenatal corticosteroid administration, one found the opposite result after deleting the study with the lowest quality score after having accepted it based on predetermined criteria (57). The other meta-analysis demonstrated a significant benefit with corticosteroids (58), including reduced rates of neonatal periventricular hemorrhage, necrotizing enterocolitis, and death.

A more recent trial of corticosteroid use after preterm PROM demonstrated a significant reduction in respiratory distress syndrome with corticosteroid administration (18% versus 44%) (59). All patients in this study also received prophylactic antibiotics. Further, multivariate analysis of prospective observational trials also has suggested a benefit of antenatal corticosteroid use regardless of membrane rupture (60).

The National Institutes of Health Consensus Development Panel recommends corticosteroid use for women with PROM prior to 30–32 weeks of gestation in the absence of intraamniotic infection (61). The available data indicate that the benefit of antenatal corticosteroids may outweigh the risk in these patients between 24 and 32 weeks of gestation. Should the pregnancy extend beyond the week that antenatal corticosteroids have known benefit, it is unclear if repeat therapy is efficacious.

Because of the possible adverse fetal effects and possible effects on maternal immune status of repeated weekly courses of antenatal corticosteroids, it would seem reasonable to adopt a rescue approach to therapy in the treatment of perterm labor rather than a routine readministration regimen. Following the initial course of antenatal corticosteroids, repeated doses should only be given on an as-needed basis (ie, if the woman is retreated for threatened preterm birth).

▶ *Should antibiotics be administered to patients with preterm PROM in an effort to prolong the latency period?*

A large number of randomized prospective clinical trials assessing the utility of adjunctive antibiotic therapy during expectant management of preterm PROM have been published over the past 10 years and are summarized in two meta-analyses. One meta-analysis demonstrated significant prolongation of pregnancy and reduced chorioamnionitis, postpartum endometritis, neonatal sepsis, pneumonia, and intraventricular hemorrhage with antibiotic treatment compared with expectant management alone (13). The other meta-analysis indicated significant reduction in neonatal sepsis and intraventricular hemorrhage (62). An additional large, multicenter trial utilizing antibiotics but no antenatal corticosteroids or tocolytics demonstrated a significant reduction in perinatal morbidity, including respiratory distress syndrome and necrotizing enterocolitis (47). In that same study, patients negative for group B streptococci also experienced longer pregnancies and less neonatal sepsis and pneumonia. A recent prospective, double-blinded trial that did utilize antenatal corticosteroids for all patients found similar perinatal benefits associated with the use of antibiotics (63).

A number of regimens appear to be effective in prolonging the latency period. Investigators in the National Institute of Child Health and Human Development trial (47) demonstrated significant perinatal benefit with a combination of ampicillin and erythromycin administered intravenously for the first 48 hours, followed by oral amoxicillin and erythromycin for an additional 5 days if delivery did not occur. The other clinical trial utilized intravenous ampicillin followed by oral amoxicillin or intravenous ampicillin/sulbactam followed by oral amoxicillin/clavulanate (63). The available clinical data provide no basis for selecting one of the prophylactic regimens over the other. The administration of antibiotics to prolong the latency period must be distinguished from well-established protocols directed at prevention of group B streptococcal infection in term and preterm patients (41). Either of the prophylactic antibiotic regimens utilized by the aforementioned clinical trials would appropriately treat group B streptococcal infections. Once labor begins, however, the need for group B streptococcal prophylaxis needs to be determined.

▶ Can women with preterm PROM be managed at home?

Generally, hospitalization for bed rest and pelvic rest is indicated after preterm PROM. Recognizing that latency is frequently brief, that intrauterine and fetal infection may occur suddenly, and that the fetus is at risk for umbilical cord compression, ongoing surveillance of both mother and fetus is necessary.

One clinical trial of discharge after preterm PROM suggested that gravidas can be discharged before delivery to reduce health care costs (64). Those with preterm PROM and no evidence of intrauterine infection, labor, or fetal compromise were evaluated in hospital for 72 hours. Those with negative cervical cultures and no evident labor, intrauterine infection, or fetal compromise were then randomly assigned to either continued inpatient management or discharge. Only 67 of 349 women (18%) were eligible for discharge after 72 hours. There were no identifiable differences in latency, or in the incidences of intraamniotic infection, variable decelerations, or cesarean delivery. Infant outcomes also were similar.

While the potential for a reduction in health care costs with antepartum discharge is enticing, it is important to ensure that such management will not be associated with increased risks and costs related to perinatal morbidity and mortality. Any cost savings from antenatal discharge may be rapidly lost with a small increase in neonatal intensive care unit stay. Further study regarding the risks and benefits of home care after preterm PROM is warranted.

▶ What is the optimal form of antepartum fetal surveillance for patients with preterm PROM managed expectantly?

Fetal testing offers the opportunity to identify occult umbilical cord compression. One study demonstrated a 32% incidence of variable decelerations after preterm PROM (38). In addition, nonreactive nonstress tests have been associated with perinatal infection. With daily fetal evaluation, one study demonstrated the last test before delivery to be nonreactive in 78% of patients who subsequently developed infection (versus 14% for those with a reactive test) (65). Biophysical profile test scores of 6 or less within 24 hours of delivery also have been demonstrated to correlate with positive amniotic fluid cultures and perinatal infection. At least eight studies have confirmed this association (66). Most of these studies have included daily fetal assessment after preterm PROM. An abnormal test should lead to reassessment of the clinical circumstances and may lead to a decision to proceed to delivery.

However, no evidence exists that any specific form or frequency of fetal surveillance directly improves perinatal outcome.

▶ What is the optimal management for a patient with preterm PROM and a cervical cerclage?

A retrospective comparative study demonstrated prolongation of pregnancy but increased maternal and perinatal morbidity and perinatal mortality when the cerclage was left in place following PROM (67). Two additional studies found no significant increase in maternal or perinatal morbidity in patients with cerclage removal when compared with patients with PROM and no cerclage (68, 69).

There are limited data to suggest removal of cerclage after PROM, but management with antibiotics or antenatal corticosteroids has not been addressed. The optimal management of preterm PROM in the presence of a cerclage is yet to be determined.

▶ How does management differ in patients with second-trimester PROM?

Initial management of gravidas with midtrimester PROM should reflect the potential for neonatal survival. Those presenting at 24–26 weeks of gestation may be considered viable (24, 70) and treated with expectant management. Given the lack of clinical trial data regarding optimal management of these patients, the recommendations reflect general clinical practice.

Women presenting with PROM before presumed viability should be counseled regarding the impact of immediate delivery and the potential risks and benefits of expectant management. Counseling should include a realistic appraisal of neonatal outcomes, including the availability of obstetric monitoring and neonatal intensive care facilities. Because of advances in perinatal care, morbidity and mortality rates continue to improve rapidly (24). An attempt should be made to provide parents with the most up-to-date information possible.

Although no evidence or consensus exists regarding the benefit of an initial period of inpatient observation in these patients, evaluation for the confirmation of PROM, evidence of infection, and the presence of associated fetal anomalies is essential if expectant management is to be considered. In addition to clinical follow-up, it may be useful to instruct patients to abstain from intercourse, limit their activities, and monitor their temperatures. Hospitalization for the duration of amniotic fluid leakage also may be appropriate.

Summary

Reports of patient care and outcome use ranges of gestational age. These ranges may be arbitrary. The recommendations that follow are based on available published data supplemented by consensus and expert opinion, with the recognition that the recommendations may not apply uniformly to patients at the extremes of gestational age.

The following recommendations are based on good and consistent scientific evidence (Level A):

▶ With term PROM, labor may be induced at the time of presentation or patients may be observed for up to 24–72 hours for the onset of spontaneous labor.

▶ Antibiotics prolong the latency period and improve perinatal outcome in patients with preterm PROM and should be administered according to one of several published protocols if expectant management is to be pursued prior to 35 weeks of gestation.

▶ Antenatal corticosteroids should be administered to gravidas with PROM before 32 weeks of gestation to reduce the risks of respiratory distress syndrome, neonatal intraventricular hemorrhage, necrotizing enterocolitis, and neonatal death.

▶ Digital cervical examinations should not be performed in patients with PROM who are not in labor and in whom immediate induction of labor is not planned.

▶ Patients with PROM prior to 30–32 weeks of gestation should be managed conservatively if no maternal or fetal contraindications exist.

The following recommendations are based primarily on consensus and expert opinion (Level C):

▶ Tocolysis may be utilized in patients with preterm PROM to permit administration of antenatal corticosteroids and antibiotics.

▶ Antenatal corticosteroids may be administered to gravidas with PROM up to 34 weeks of gestation.

References

1. Ventura SJ, Martin JA, Curtin SC, Mathews TJ. Report of final natality statistics, 1995. Monthly vital statistics report; vol 45, no. 11, supp. Hyattsville, Maryland: National Center for Health Statistics, 1997 (Level III)

2. French JI, McGregor JA. The pathobiology of premature rupture of membranes. Semin Perinatol 1996;20:344–368 (Level III)

3. Lavery JP, Miller CE, Knight RD. The effect of labor on the rheologic response of chorioamniotic membranes. Obstet Gynecol 1982;60:87–92 (Level II-3)

4. McGregor JA, French JI. Evidence-based prevention of preterm birth and rupture of membranes: infection and inflammation. J SOGC 1997;19:835–852 (Level III)

5. Harger JH, Hsing AW, Tuomala RE, Gibbs RS, Mead PB, Eschenbach DA, et al. Risk factors for preterm premature rupture of fetal membranes: a multicenter case-control study. Am J Obstet Gynecol 1990;163:130–137 (Level II-2)

6. Novak-Antolic Z, Pajntar M, Verdenik I. Rupture of the membranes and postpartum infection. Eur J Obstet Gynecol Reprod Biol 1997;71:141–146 (Level II-3)

7. Taylor J, Garite TJ. Premature rupture of the membranes before fetal viability. Obstet Gynecol 1984;64:615–620 (Level II-3)

8. Gold RB, Goyert GL, Schwartz DB, Evans MI, Seabolt LA. Conservative management of second trimester postamniocentesis fluid leakage. Obstet Gynecol 1989;74:745–747 (Level III)

9. Hannah ME, Ohlsson A, Farine D, Hewson SA, Hodnett ED, Myhr TL, et al. Induction of labor compared with expectant management for prelabor rupture of the membranes at term. N Engl J Med 1996;334:1005–1010 (Level I)

10. Wagner MV, Chin VP, Peters CJ, Drexler B, Newman LA. A comparison of early and delayed induction of labor with spontaneous rupture of membranes at term. Obstet Gynecol 1989;74:93–97 (Level II-1)

11. Guise JM, Duff P, Christian JS. Management of term patients with premature rupture of membranes and an unfavorable cervix. Am J Perinatol 1992;9:56–60 (Level II-2)

12. Johnson JWC, Egerman RS, Moorhead J. Cases with ruptured membranes that "reseal." Am J Obstet Gynecol 1990;163:1024–1032 (Level II-2)

13. Mercer BM, Arheart KL. Antimicrobial therapy in expectant management of preterm premature rupture of the membranes. Lancet 1995;346:1271–1279 (Meta-analysis)

14. Mercer BM. Management of premature rupture of membranes before 26 weeks' gestation. Obstet Gynecol Clin North Am 1992;19:339–351 (Level III)

15. Beydoun SN, Yasin SY. Premature rupture of the membranes before 28 weeks: conservative management. Am J Obstet Gynecol 1986;155:471–479 (Level II-3)

16. Garite TJ, Freeman RK. Chorioamnionitis in the preterm gestation. Obstet Gynecol 1982;59:539–545 (Level II-3)

17. Simpson GF, Harbert GM Jr. Use of β-methasone in management of preterm gestation with premature rupture of membranes. Obstet Gynecol 1985;66:168–175 (Level II-2)

18. Vergani P, Ghidini A, Locatelli A, Cavallone M, Ciarla I, Cappellini A, et al. Risk factors for pulmonary hypoplasia in second-trimester premature rupture of membranes. Am J Obstet Gynecol 1994;170:1359–1364 (Level II-3)

19. Hillier SL, Martius J, Krohn M, Kiviat N, Holmes KK, Eschenbach DA. A case-control study of chorioamnionic infection and histologic chorioamnionitis in prematurity. N Engl J Med 1988;319:972–978 (Level II-3)

20. Morales WJ. The effect of chorioamnionitis on the developmental outcome of preterm infants at one year. Obstet Gynecol 1987;70:183–186 (Level II-3)

21. Schutte MF, Treffers PE, Kloosterman GJ, Soepatmi S. Management of premature rupture of membranes: the risk of vaginal examination to the infant. Am J Obstet Gynecol 1983;146:395–400 (Level II-3)

22. Ananth CV, Savitz DA, Williams MA. Placental abruption and its association with hypertension and prolonged rupture of membranes: a methodologic review and meta-analysis. Obstet Gynecol 1996;88:309–318 (Meta-analysis)

23. Gonen R, Hannah ME, Milligan JE. Does prolonged preterm premature rupture of the membranes predispose to abruptio placentae? Obstet Gynecol 1989;74:347–350 (Level II-2)

24. Fanaroff AA, Wright LL, Stevenson DK, Shankaran S, Donovan EF, Ehrenkranz RA, et al. Very-low-birth-weight outcomes of the National Institute of Child Health and Human Development Neonatal Research Network, May 1991 through December 1992. Am J Obstet Gynecol 1995; 173:1423–1431 (Level II-3)

25. Schucker JL, Mercer BM. Midtrimester premature rupture of the membranes. Semin Perinatol 1996;20:389–400 (Level III)

26. Hack M, Taylor HG, Klein N, Eiben R, Schatschneider C, Mercuri-Minich N. School-age outcomes in children with birth weights under 750 g. N Engl J Med 1994;331:753–759 (Level II-2)

27. Kilpatrick SJ, Schlueter MA, Piecuch R, Leonard CH, Rogido M, Sola A. Outcome of infants born at 24-26 weeks' gestation: I. Survival and cost. Obstet Gynecol 1997;90:803–808 (Level II-3)

28. Bottoms SF, Paul RH, Iams JD, Mercer BM, Thom EA, Roberts JM, et al. Obstetric determinants of neonatal survival: influence of willingness to perform cesarean delivery on survival of extremely low-birth-weight infants. Am J Obstet Gynecol 1997;176:960–966 (Level II-3)

29. Moretti M, Sibai BM. Maternal and perinatal outcome of expectant management of premature rupture of the membranes in midtrimester. Am J Obstet Gynecol 1988;159: 390–396 (Level II-3)

30. Rib DM, Sherer DM, Woods JR Jr. Maternal and neonatal outcome associated with prolonged premature rupture of membranes below 26 weeks' gestation. Am J Perinatol 1993;10:369–373 (Level II-3)

31. Bengtson JM, VanMarter LJ, Barss VA, Greene MF, Tuomala RE, Epstein MF. Pregnancy outcome after premature rupture of the membranes at or before 26 weeks' gestation. Obstet Gynecol 1989;73:921–926 (Level II-3)

32. Cox SM, Leveno KJ. Intentional delivery versus expectant management with preterm ruptured membranes at 30–34 weeks' gestation. Obstet Gynecol 1995;86:875–879 (Level I)

33. Mercer BM, Crocker LG, Boe NM, Sibai BM. Induction versus expectant management in premature rupture of the membranes with mature amniotic fluid at 32 to 36 weeks: a randomized trial. Am J Obstet Gynecol 1993;169:775–782 (Level I)

34. Major CA, Kitzmiller JL. Perinatal survival with expectant management of midtrimester rupture of membranes. Am J Obstet Gynecol 1990;163:838–844 (Level II-3)

35. Morales WJ, Talley T. Premature rupture of membranes at <25 weeks: a management dilemma. Am J Obstet Gynecol 1993;168:503–507 (Level II-3)

36. Rotschild A, Ling EW, Puterman ML, Farquharson D. Neonatal outcome after prolonged preterm rupture of the membranes. Am J Obstet Gynecol 1990;162:46–52 (Level II-3)

37. van Eyck J, van der Mooren K, Wladimiroff JW. Ductus arteriosus flow velocity modulation by fetal breathing movements as a measure of fetal lung development. Am J Obstet Gynecol 1990;163:558–566 (Level II-3)

38. Smith CV, Greenspoon J, Phelan JP, Platt LD. Clinical utility of the nonstress test in the conservative management of women with preterm spontaneous premature rupture of the membranes. J Reprod Med 1987;32:1–4 (Level II-3)

39. Lenihan JP Jr. Relationship of antepartum pelvic examinations to premature rupture of the membranes. Obstet Gynecol 1984;83:33–37 (Level II-1)

40. Munson LA, Graham A, Koos BJ, Valenzuela GJ. Is there a need for digital examination in patients with spontaneous rupture of the membranes? Am J Obstet Gynecol 1985; 153:562–563 (Level II-3)

41. American College of Obstetricians and Gynecologists. Prevention of early-onset group B streptococcal disease in newborns. ACOG Committee Opinion 173. Washington, DC: ACOG, 1996 (Level III)

42. Ingemarsson I. Controversies: premature rupture of membranes at term—no advantage of delaying induction >24 hours. J Perinat Med 1996;24:573–579 (Level III)

43. Mozurkewich EL, Wolf FM. Premature rupture of membranes at term: a meta-analysis of three management schemes. Obstet Gynecol 1997;89:1035–1043 (Meta-analysis)

44. Ottervanger HP, Keirse MJ, Smit W, Holm JP. Controlled comparison of induction versus expectant care for prelabor rupture of the membranes at term. J Perinatol Med 1996;24: 237–242 (Level I-1)

45. Sanchez-Ramos L, Chen AH, Kaunitz AM, Gaudier FL, Delke I. Labor induction with intravaginal misoprostol in term premature rupture of membranes: a randomized study. Obstet Gynecol 1997;89:909–912 (Level I)

46. Alcalay M, Hourvitz A, Reichman B, Luski A, Quint J, Barkai G, et al. Prelabour rupture of membranes at term: early induction of labour versus expectant management. Eur J Obstet Gynecol Reprod Biol 1996;70:129–133 (Level I)

47. Mercer BM, Miodovnik M, Thurnau GR, Goldenberg RL, Das AF, Ramsey RD, et al. Antibiotic therapy for reduction of infant morbidity after preterm premature rupture of the membranes: a randomized controlled trial. JAMA 1997;278: 989–995 (Level I)

48. Gomez R, Romero R, Edwin SS, David C. Pathogenesis of preterm labor and preterm premature rupture of membranes associated with intraamniotic infection. Infect Dis Clin North Am 1997;11:135–176 (Level III)

49. Belady PH, Farkouh LJ, Gibbs RS. Intra-amniotic infection and premature rupture of the membranes. Clin Perinatol 1997;24:43–57 (Level III)

50. Broekhuizen FF, Gilman M, Hamilton PR. Amniocentesis for gram stain and culture in preterm premature rupture of the membranes. Obstet Gynecol 1985;66:316–321 (Level II-3)

51. Romero R, Yoon BH, Mazor M, Gomez R, Gonzalez R, Diamond MP, et al. A comparative study of the diagnostic performance of amniotic fluid glucose, white blood cell count, interleukin-6, and Gram stain in the detection of microbial invasion in patients with preterm premature rupture of membranes. Am J Obstet Gynecol 1993;169:839–851 (Level II-2)

52. Ohlsson A, Wang E. An analysis of antenatal tests to detect infection in preterm premature rupture of the membranes. Am J Obstet Gynecol 1990;162:809–818 (Level III)

53. Christensen KK, Ingemarsson I, Leideman T, Solum H, Svenningsen N. Effect of ritodrine on labor after premature rupture of the membranes. Obstet Gynecol 1980;55:187–190 (Level I)

54. Levy DL, Warsof SL. Oral ritodrine and preterm premature rupture of membranes. Obstet Gynecol 1985;66:621–623 (Level II-1)

55. Weiner CP, Renk K, Klugman M. The therapeutic efficacy and cost-effectiveness of aggressive tocolysis for premature labor associated with premature rupture of the membranes. Am J Obstet Gynecol 1988;159:216–222 (Level I)

56. Garite TJ, Keegan KA, Freeman RK, Nageotte MP. A randomized trial of ritodrine tocolysis versus expectant management in patients with premature rupture of membranes at 25 to 30 weeks of gestation. Am J Obstet Gynecol 1987;157:388–393 (Level II-1)

57. Ohlsson A. Treatments of preterm premature rupture of the membranes: a meta-analysis. Am J Obstet Gynecol 1989;160:890–906 (Meta-analysis)

58. Crowley PA. Antenatal corticosteroid therapy: a meta-analysis of the randomized trials, 1972 to 1994. Am J Obstet Gynecol 1995;173:322–335 (Meta-analysis)

59. Lewis DF, Brody K, Edwards MS, Brouillette RM, Burlison S, London SN. Preterm premature ruptured membranes: a randomized trial of steroids after treatment with antibiotics. Obstet Gynecol 1996;88:801–805 (Level I)

60. Wright LL, Verter J, Younes N, Stevenson D, Fanaroff AA, Shankaran S, et al. Antenatal corticosteroid administration and neonatal outcome in very low birth weight infants: the NICHD Neonatal Research Network. Am J Obstet Gynecol 1995;173:269–274 (Level II-3)

61. National Institutes of Health. National Institutes of Health Consensus Development Conference Statement: Effect of corticosteroids for fetal maturation on perinatal outcomes, February 28–March 2, 1994. Am J Obstet Gynecol 1995;173:246–252 (Level III)

62. Egarter C, Leitich H, Karas H, Wieser F, Husslein P, Kaider A, et al. Antibiotic treatment in preterm premature rupture of membranes and neonatal morbidity: a meta-analysis. Am J Obstet Gynecol 1996;174:589–597 (Meta-analysis)

63. Lovett SM, Weiss JD, Diogo MJ, Williams PT, Garite TJ. A prospective double-blind, randomized, controlled clinical trial of ampicillin-sulbactam for preterm premature rupture of membranes in women receiving antenatal corticosteroid therapy. Am J Obstet Gynecol 1997;176:1030–1038 (Level I)

64. Carlan SJ, O'Brien WF, Parsons MT, Lense JJ. Preterm premature rupture of membranes: a randomized study of home versus hospital management. Obstet Gynecol 1993;81:61–64 (Level I)

65. Vintzileos AM, Campbell WA, Nochimson DJ, Weinbaum PJ. The use of the nonstress test in patients with premature rupture of the membranes. Am J Obstet Gynecol 1986;155:149–153 (Level II-3)

66. Hanley ML, Vintzileos AM. Biophysical testing in premature rupture of the membranes. Semin Perinatol 1996;20:418–425 (Level III)

67. Ludmir J, Bader T, Chen L, Lindenbaum C, Wong G. Poor perinatal outcome associated with retained cerclage in patients with premature rupture of membranes. Obstet Gynecol 1994;84:823–826 (Level II-2)

68. Yeast JD, Garite TR. The role of cervical cerclage in the management of preterm premature rupture of the membranes. Am J Obstet Gynecol 1988;158:106–110 (Level II-2)

69. Blickstein I, Katz Z, Lancet M, Molgilner BM. The outcome of pregnancies complicated by preterm rupture of the membranes with and without cerclage. Int J Gynecol Obstet 1989;28:237–242 (Level II-2)

70. American College of Obstetricians and Gynecologists. Perinatal care at the threshold of viability. ACOG Committee Opinion 163. Washington, DC: ACOG, 1995 (Level III)

The MEDLINE database, the Cochrane Library, and ACOG's own internal resources and documents were used to conduct a literature search to locate relevant articles published between 1980 and August 1997. The search was restricted to articles published in the English language. Priority was given to articles reporting results of original research although review articles and commentaries also were consulted. Abstracts of research presented at symposiums and scientific conferences were not considered adequate for inclusion in this document. Guidelines published by organizations or institutions such as the National Institutes of Health and ACOG were reviewed, and additional studies were located by reviewing bibliographies of identified articles. When reliable research was not available, expert opinions from obstetrician–gynecologists were used. Studies were reviewed and evaluated for quality according to the method outlined by the U.S. Preventive Services Task Force.

I Evidence obtained from at least one properly designed randomized controlled trial.

II-1 Evidence obtained from well-designed controlled trials without randomization.

II-2 Evidence obtained from well-designed cohort or case-control analytic studies, preferably from more than one center or research group.

II-3 Evidence obtained from multiple time series with or without the intervention. Dramatic results in uncontrolled experiments also could be regarded as this type of evidence.

III Opinions of respected authorities, based on clinical experience, descriptive studies, or reports of expert committees.

Based on the highest level of evidence found in the data, the recommendations are graded according to the following categories:

A The recommendation is based on good and consistent scientific evidence

B The recommendation is based on limited or inconsistent scientific evidence

C The recommendation is based primarily on consensus and expert opinion

ISSN 1099-3630   12345/21098

ACOG *PRACTICE BULLETIN*

CLINICAL MANAGEMENT GUIDELINES FOR
OBSTETRICIAN–GYNECOLOGISTS
NUMBER 15, APRIL 2000

This Practice Bulletin was developed by the ACOG Committee on Practice Bulletins— Gynecology with the assistance of Ann J. Davis, MD and Susan R. Johnson, MD, MS. The information is designed to aid practitioners in making decisions about appropriate obstetric and gynecologic care. These guidelines should not be construed as dictating an exclusive course of treatment or procedure. Variations in practice may be warranted based on the needs of the individual patient, resources, and limitations unique to the institution or type of practice.

Premenstrual Syndrome

Premenstrual syndrome (PMS) is a common problem for many women. Determining the appropriate clinical management of this condition often creates frustration for both physicians and patients. Until recently, the difficulty in managing PMS was largely attributed to imprecise diagnostic criteria, poorly designed clinical trials, and the promotion of treatment options for which there was no scientific support. In the mid-1980s, however, rigorous criteria for the diagnosis of PMS were defined. Since then, most studies of pathophysiology and treatment have met recognized standards of scientific design. This document will examine the evidence for commonly used approaches in the treatment of PMS and identify those that are effective.

Background

Premenstrual syndrome has been defined as "the cyclic occurrence of symptoms that are of sufficient severity to interfere with some aspects of life and that appear with consistent and predictable relationship to the menses" (1). Although the symptoms themselves are not unique, the restriction of the symptoms to the luteal phase of the menstrual cycle is pathognomonic of PMS (2).

Epidemiology

Premenstrual symptoms are common and are considered a normal aspect of ovulatory cycles. Most surveys have found that as many as 85% of menstruating women report one or more premenstrual symptoms. Severe symptoms that meet the criteria for PMS, however, are much less common, with only 5–10% of women reporting significant impairment in their lifestyles because of PMS (3, 4).

Risk Factors

Advancing age often is cited as a risk factor for PMS, based on surveys that find women are most likely to seek treatment after age 30 years. However, this syndrome can occur in menstruating women of any age. Genetics appears to play a role in PMS; the concordance rate of PMS is twice as high among monozygotic twins as among dizygotic twins (5, 6). Although women with PMS have a high rate of affective disorders, a causal relationship has not yet been demonstrated (7, 8).

There are no significant personality profile differences between women with PMS and asymptomatic women (9). Furthermore, PMS is not more likely to be diagnosed in women with higher levels of stress (10). However, women who have PMS may not tolerate stress as well as women who do not have PMS. Premenstrual symptoms seem to affect women irrespective of culture or socioeconomic status, although specific symptoms may vary in frequency by culture (11–13).

Etiology

The etiology of PMS is incompletely understood, but considerable progress has been made in the past decade in understanding some facets of the pathophysiology. Circulating sex steroid levels (progesterone, estrogen, and testosterone) are normal, although there may be an underlying neurobiologic vulnerability to normal fluctuations of one or more of these hormones (14, 15). Most likely, the biochemical changes involve central-nervous-system–mediated neurotransmitter interactions with sex steroids. Serotoninergic dysregulation is currently the most plausible theory. Among the several studies supporting this theory is a well-designed study in which women with severe PMS responded better to selective serotonin reuptake inhibitors (SSRIs) than to noradrenergic antidepressants such as maprotiline (16). Because not all women with PMS respond to SSRIs, other etiologic factors probably are involved.

Clinical Considerations and Recommendations

Establishing evidenced-based recommendations for PMS is difficult for many reasons. Definitions and inclusion criteria for PMS vary significantly among studies. In addition, the PMS patient populations studied in rigorous trials also may be different from the patient population of a given practitioner. For example, many recent PMS trials have properly included only women with the full-blown syndrome, including mood-related symptoms, whereas many women seek care from their practitioners for a less severe condition, with primarily somatic symptoms.

▶ ***How is the diagnosis of PMS established?***

The key elements of the diagnosis are a) symptoms consistent with PMS; b) restriction of these symptoms to the luteal phase of the menstrual cycle assessed prospectively; c) impairment of some facet of the woman's life; and d) exclusion of other diagnoses that may better explain the symptoms.

The National Institute of Mental Health criteria for diagnosis are 1) a marked change of about 30% in the intensity of symptoms measured instrumentally, from cycle days 5 to 10 (as compared with those premenstrually), within the 6-day interval prior to menses and 2) documentation of these changes for at least two consecutive cycles (17). Another definition of PMS developed for research purposes by the University of California at San Diego is based on women's prospective self-reports. Their definition requires that patients have the cyclic manifestation of at least 1 of 6 behavioral symptoms and 1 of 4 somatic symptoms (see the box). Dysfunction in social or economic performance is included in this definition. Finally, the *Diagnostic and Statistical Manual of Mental Disorders*, fourth edition, includes similar criteria for the diagnosis of premenstrual dysphoric disorder, which identifies women with PMS who have more severe emotional symptoms (18).

The diagnosis of PMS should be based on prospective symptom diaries, because as many as half of the

---

Diagnostic Criteria for Premenstrual Syndrome

Premenstrual syndrome can be diagnosed if the patient reports at least one of the following affective and somatic symptoms during the 5 days before menses in each of the three prior menstrual cycles*:

Affective

> Depression
>
> Angry outbursts
>
> Irritability
>
> Anxiety
>
> Confusion
>
> Social withdrawal

Somatic

> Breast tenderness
>
> Abdominal bloating
>
> Headache
>
> Swelling of extremities

*These symptoms are relieved within 4 days of the onset of menses, without recurrence until at least cycle day 13. The symptoms are present in the absence of any pharmacologic therapy, hormone ingestion, or drug or alcohol use. The symptoms occur reproducibly during two cycles of prospective recording. The patient suffers from identifiable dysfunction in social or economic performance.

Adapted from Mortola JF, Girton L, Yen SC. Depressive episodes in premenstrual syndrome. Am J Obstet Gynecol 1989;161:1682–1687

women reporting a luteal phase pattern will be found to have some other pattern when such diaries are examined. Because some women experience cycle-to-cycle variability in symptoms, reviewing 2–3 months of prospective charting is preferable to reviewing a single cycle (19).

In the clinical setting, a simple system in which the woman records the dates of her menstrual periods and notes her symptoms on a daily basis is usually sufficient (20). However, a variety of standardized instruments and diaries developed for research purposes are also available. The most commonly used are the Calendar of Premenstrual Experiences (COPE) (21) and the Prospective Record of the Impact and Severity of Menstruation (PRISM) (22). Another type of instrument, the Visual Analogue Scales (VAS), may be especially appropriate in non-English-reading populations (23).

A careful medical and psychologic history and physical examination in conjunction with the prospective symptom diary usually will direct the clinician toward the correct diagnosis. Laboratory testing should be restricted to the identification of other disorders suggested by the evaluation, such as measuring levels of thyroid-stimulating hormone when hypothyroidism is suspected. Routine measurement of steroid hormones or gonadotropins is not useful.

▶ *How is PMS objectively differentiated from similar conditions?*

Only a small portion of women presenting for evaluation and treatment of PMS are likely to have PMS. For example, in a sample of women who responded to a newspaper recruitment for a PMS study, the most common symptoms reported were consistent with PMS: irritability, depression, mood swings, anxiety, mastalgia, abdominal bloating, weight gain, fatigue, aggression, headache, tension, muscle aches, food cravings, and breast swelling (24). However, individuals who respond to such recruitment may not be representative of the general population. In this study, after a complete evaluation, 60% of the women also were found to have psychiatric disorders.

The phenomenon of *menstrual magnification* (sometimes called premenstrual or perimenstrual exacerbation) helps explain this situation. Many medical and psychiatric conditions are exacerbated in the late luteal or menstrual phase of the cycle, leading a woman to believe that she must be experiencing PMS. The underlying mechanism of this increase in symptoms is not understood.

The differential diagnosis of PMS therefore includes any medical and psychiatric condition that either has some of the many symptoms associated with PMS or is subject to menstrual magnification. Depressive disorders, which share a similar set of symptoms, are the most common consideration (25). Depressive disorders also are subject to the magnification effect, making the distinction from PMS even more difficult. A key feature of depressive disorders, however, is that symptoms are almost always present every day of the cycle. Other psychiatric conditions that may be magnified are panic disorder and generalized anxiety disorder.

The most common medical disorders subject to menstrual magnification are migraines, seizure disorders, irritable bowel syndrome, asthma, chronic fatigue syndrome, and allergies. Endocrine abnormalities such as thyroid and adrenal disorders also should be considered. The diagnosis of these conditions usually is straightforward because the key symptoms are not part of the typical PMS symptom set, and emotional symptoms are not prominent, as they are in PMS.

Finally, women in the period of transition to menopause may have symptoms typical of PMS, especially mood disturbance, fatigue, and hot flashes. Because menstrual periods often are less predictable, these women may be less aware of the relationship of the symptoms to the menstrual cycle. The correct diagnosis usually can be made by considering the patient's age, a history of recent menstrual cycle changes, and a symptom diary showing sporadic or daily occurrence of symptoms.

▶ *Which patients require therapeutic intervention for PMS?*

Premenstrual syndrome, by definition, is associated with symptoms that interfere with some part of the patient's normal life, but there are usually no medical sequelae if the disorder is not treated. Therefore, the decision to treat the disorder should be based on the patient's desire for an improvement in her symptoms. Furthermore, because there is a wide range of symptom severity, the treatment approach should match the patient's needs.

▶ *What is the evidence supporting the effectiveness of the following common treatments for PMS?*

A wide variety of supportive, lifestyle, and dietary supplementation approaches to PMS have been recommended over the years, and a few of these have been demonstrated to have real benefit. Therefore, these strategies can be recommended to women with mild to moderate symptoms as a primary therapy and to women with severe symptoms as adjunctive therapy.

Women with severe symptoms or with symptoms resistant to nonmedical approaches should be considered for drug therapy. Although no drugs currently are specifically approved by the U.S. Food and Drug Administration for the treatment of PMS, several available drugs have been found to be effective for PMS and can be prescribed.

Supportive Therapy. Supportive therapy has been employed as a central component in PMS management, although it has not been studied rigorously. Reassurance and informational counseling may relieve many anxieties and increase the patient's sense of control. Women anecdotally report relief when they are informed that PMS is a common medical problem with a physiologic basis. Supportive therapy may contribute in part to the high response rate to placebos for virtually every form of treatment used for PMS.

The value of more formal psychologic interventions has not been conclusively demonstrated. The best evidence is for relaxation therapy. In one small comparative study, relaxation therapy had its greatest effects in women with the most severe symptoms (26). In a study of cognitive behavior therapy, the comparison group who received information about PMS, relaxation training, and lifestyle and nutrition guidelines fared nearly as well as the study group who received cognitive restructuring training (27).

Aerobic Exercise. Aerobic exercise has been found in epidemiologic studies to be associated with fewer reported PMS symptoms, and exercise has been found to reduce symptoms among people with depressive disorders. Limited evidence supports a similar role for this intervention in PMS. In a 3-month randomized trial of 23 women with prospectively diagnosed PMS, the group taking regular moderate aerobic exercise reported more improvement than the control group who did nonaerobic exercise (28). In another small prospective but not randomized study, two groups of women who exercised aerobically reported fewer PMS symptoms at the end of a 6-month trial than did a nonexercising comparison group (29). Although the evidence base is modest at this time, aerobic exercise can be recommended to all women with PMS because of its numerous other health benefits.

Dietary Supplementation. Calcium and magnesium have each been shown to be effective in the treatment of PMS. However, most of these trials have tested small numbers of patients and must be validated in larger trials before strong evidence-based recommendations can be made. One large well-designed multicenter trial of 466 women with PMS reported that 1,200 mg/d of calcium carbonate was efficacious in reducing total symptom scores (30). Two small trials have found that 200–400 mg of magnesium may be somewhat effective (31, 32).

Minimal data are available on the effectiveness of vitamin E and the treatment of premenstrual syndrome. Vitamin E has been recommended as a treatment for mastalgia. In one randomized, double-blind, controlled study comparing vitamin E 400 IU/d during the luteal phase with placebo, vitamin E was found to improve significantly affective and somatic symptoms in PMS patients (33). Although effectiveness probably is minimal, no serious side effects are reported with vitamin E 400 IU/d, and as an antioxidant it has other beneficial effects.

In one study, mood symptomatology and carbohydrate food cravings were shown to be improved by carbohydrate-rich beverages (34). This small, well-designed study should be repeated with larger numbers of subjects before evidence-based recommendations can be made. One hypothesis to explain these benefits is that diets rich in carbohydrates increase levels of tryptophan, the precursor to serotonin.

Well-designed scientific studies have not demonstrated that primrose oil is effective in the treatment of PMS. However, it may be useful in treating breast tenderness (35).

On the basis of a recent systematic review of several weak clinical studies, vitamin B_6 is considered to be of limited clinical benefit in the treatment of PMS (36). Dosages in excess of 100 mg/d may cause medical harm, including peripheral neuropathy (36).

Selective Serotonin Reuptake Inhibitors. The SSRIs are the initial drugs of choice for severe PMS. Fluoxetine is the most studied drug of this group. Its use has been studied in almost 1,000 women in rigorous trials. The largest, a 6-month, multicenter trial, evaluated 313 women with PMS who were prescribed dosages of 20–60 mg/d (37). Investigators observed 44% dropouts at dosages of 60 mg/d and 11% at dosages of 20 mg/d. This study, along with several smaller, shorter-duration placebo-controlled trials, have consistently reported the efficacy of fluoxetine. The dosage in these trials generally was 20 mg/d throughout the menstrual cycle administered as a single morning dose to avoid insomnia. One study reported efficacy in 64 women with PMS over a mean treatment time of 18 months (38). In this 18-month study, symptoms recurred in most of the women not taking fluoxetine and resolved when treatment was restarted.

Other SSRI drugs that have had a beneficial effect similar to that of fluoxetine are sertraline, paroxetine, clomipramine, fluvoxamine, and nefazodone. In the largest study of sertraline, in which there were 233 subjects, dosages ranged from 50 to 150 mg/d (39).

Intermittent therapy, with an SSRI given only during the symptomatic phase, also has been efficacious in several small, randomized, double-blind, placebo-controlled trials (40–42). This method of administration has many advantages: it is less expensive, reduces the overall rate of side effects, and is more acceptable to many women. The drug is started between 7 and 14 days before the next menstrual period, with the start day individualized to begin the medication at or just before the expected onset of symptoms.

Side effects associated with fluoxetine include headaches, nausea, and jitteriness. Insomnia often can be avoided by early-morning dosing or, if appropriate, by lowering the dosage. Decreased libido also is problematic in some patients. In cases in which improvement of libido is not seen after dosage changes, alternative therapies may be considered (4).

Other Pharmacologic Approaches. Some placebo-controlled trials have shown alprazolam, an anxiolytic medication, to be effective as a treatment for PMS (43–45), and some have not (46). There is a potential for dependency and development of tolerance with this medication, especially if dosing is not limited to the luteal phase. Sedation also can be a bothersome side effect in some patients, and withdrawals can be problematic. Alprazolam may potentially be useful for PMS patients who are not relieved by other interventions. It may be especially useful if agitation and anxiety are the primary symptoms.

Because complaints of fluid retention are common in the luteal phase, diuretic therapy has been advocated. No evidence exists that thiazide diuretics are of benefit. Spironolactone, an aldosterone antagonist with antiandrogenic properties, is the only diuretic that has been shown to be of benefit in PMS. Several randomized, double-blind, placebo-controlled trials have shown a significant reduction in somatic and affective complaints (47–51). Usual dosage in most studies is 100 mg/d in the morning during the 14-day luteal phase. However, not all reports evaluating spironolactone for PMS have shown benefit.

Historically, natural progesterone has been one of the most commonly employed therapies in women with PMS, but careful scientific scrutiny has not supported an overall benefit of this hormone when compared with placebo, whether administered as a vaginal suppository (52) or as oral micronized progesterone (45). Progesterone may be helpful for specific symptoms, such as breast tenderness and bloating, or specific psychologic symptoms, such as worrying (53).

▶ *What is the role of hormonal suppression in the treatment of PMS?*

Oral Contraceptives. Although oral contraceptives are widely prescribed for the treatment of PMS, few data support their effectiveness. In one randomized trial, a triphasic formulation reduced physical symptoms but not mood alterations (54). In another study comparing triphasic and monophasic regimens, the monophasic formulation was less likely to cause mood alterations (55). Many patients experience breast tenderness, nausea, mood alterations, and other side effects the first few months of oral contraceptive use. The evidence suggests that oral contraceptives should be considered if symptoms are primarily physical, but may not be effective if mood symptoms are more prevalent.

Gonadotropin-Releasing Hormone Agonists. Improvement in PMS symptoms with gonadotropin-releasing hormone (GnRH) agonists has been reported in the majority of well-designed studies (56–57) but not in all of them (58). The hypoestrogenic side effects and cost of GnRH agonists limit the usefulness of this method except in severe cases of PMS unresponsive to other treatment.

If this therapy is to be used for more than a few months, bone loss becomes a concern. The most commonly used approach is add-back estrogen therapy (with progestin if indicated). Add-back therapy also may result in a return of symptoms, although studies are limited and sometimes confusing. In a double-blind, placebo-controlled study of 10 women, both estrogen add-back therapy alone and progesterone therapy alone were associated with a significant recurrence of symptoms (15). Another small rigorous study evaluated eight women with PMS. Administration of the GnRH agonist resulted in an improvement of approximately 75% in luteal phase symptom scores. The addition of estrogen as well as progesterone was associated with worsening symptoms, but a similar worsening also was seen with placebo (59). If hormone therapy results in a return of symptoms, alendronate should be considered for osteoporosis prevention.

Bilateral Salpingo-Oophorectomy. Surgery for PMS is controversial because it is irreversible, it is associated with morbidity and mortality, and the resulting hypoestrogenemia must be addressed to prevent long-term complications. If employed, this approach should be reserved for those severely affected patients who meet strict diagnostic criteria and who do not respond to any potentially effective therapy other than GnRH agonists (60). These limitations are critical, because a major cause of therapeutic failure with any of the described treatments is an incorrect diagnosis of PMS. It is advisable to perform a diagnostic trial with an agonist for a minimum of 3 months to determine if oophorectomy will be effective. An additional advantage to an extended trial with an agonist is the opportunity to assess the woman's tolerance for estrogen replacement therapy.

Summary

The following recommendations are based on good and consistent scientific evidence (Level A):

▶ Women in whom PMS has been diagnosed should meet standard diagnostic criteria and should have the timing of their symptoms confirmed using a prospective symptom calendar.

▶ Risk factors such as increased imposed stress and specific personality profiles are not helpful in differentiating women with PMS from those without PMS.

The SSRIs, particularly fluoxetine and sertraline, have been shown to be effective in treating PMS.

The bulk of scientific evidence does not support the usefulness of natural progesterone or primrose oil in the treatment of PMS.

The following recommendations are based on limited or inconsistent scientific evidence (Level B):

▶ The use of GnRH agonists and surgical oophorectomy have been shown to be effective in PMS. However, the side effects of GnRH agonists and oophorectomy limit their usefulness in most patients.

▶ Treatment with the anxiolytic alprazolam is effective in some patients. Its side effects limit its use as a first-line approach.

▶ Carbohydrate-rich foods and beverages may improve mood symptoms and food cravings in women with PMS and are a reasonable first-line approach in many patients.

▶ Calcium supplements have been shown to be effective in the treatment of PMS.

▶ Magnesium, vitamin B_6, and vitamin E may have minimal effectiveness in the treatment of PMS.

Oral contraceptives may improve physical symptoms of PMS.

The following recommendations are based primarily on consensus and expert opinion (Level C):

▶ Supportive therapy is central to the management of all PMS patients.

▶ Aerobic exercise can be recommended to PMS patients.

▶ As an overall clinical approach, treatments should be employed in increasing orders of complexity. Using this principle, in most cases, the therapies should be used in the following order:

▶ **Step 1.** Supportive therapy, complex carbohydrate diet, aerobic exercise, nutritional supplements (calcium, magnesium, vitamin E), spironolactone

▶ **Step 2.** The SSRIs (fluoxetine or sertraline as the initial choice); for women who do not respond, consider an anxiolytic for specific symptoms

▶ **Step 3.** Hormonal ovulation suppression (oral contraceptives or GnRH agonists)

References

1. Gise LH, Kase NG, Berkowitz RL, eds. Contemporary issues in obstetrics and gynecology. Vol 2. The premenstrual syndromes. New York: Churchill Livingstone, 1988 (Level III)

2. Mortola JF. Issues in the diagnosis and research of premenstrual syndrome. Clin Obstet Gynecol 1992;35: 587–598 (Level III)

3. Stout AL, Steege JF. Psychosocial assessment of women seeking treatment for premenstrual syndrome. J Psychosom Res 1985;29:621–629 (Level III)

4. Steiner M. Premenstrual syndromes. Annu Rev Med 1997;48:447–455 (Level III)

5. Kendler KS, Silberg JL, Neale MC, Kessler RC, Heath AC, Eaves LJ. Genetic and environmental factors in the aetiology of menstrual, premenstrual and neurotic symptoms: a population-based twin study. Psychol Med 1992;22: 85–100 (Level II-3)

6. Condon JT. The premenstrual syndrome: a twin study. Br J Psychiatry 1993;162:481–486 (Level II-3)

7. Halbreich U, Endicott J. Relationship of dysphoric premenstrual changes to depressive disorders. Acta Psychiatr Scand 1985;71:331–338 (Level III)

8. DeJong R, Rubinow DR, Roy-Byrne P, Hoban MC, Grover GN, Post RM. Premenstrual mood disorder and psychiatric illness. Am J Psychiatry 1985:142:1359–1361 (Level III)

9. Trunnell EP, Turner CW, Keye WR. A comparison of the psychological and hormonal factors in women with and without premenstrual syndrome. J Abnorm Psychol 1988;97:429–436 (Level II-2)

10. Beck LE, Girvertz R, Mortola JF. The predictive role of psychosocial stress on symptom severity in premenstrual syndrome. Psychosom Med 1990;52:536–543 (Level III)

11. Adenaike OC, Abidoye RO. A study of the incidence of premenstrual syndrome in a group of Nigerian women. Public Health 1987;101:49–58 (Level III)

12. Hasin M, Dennerstein L, Gotts G. Menstrual cycle related complaints: a cross-cultural study. J Psychosom Obstet Gynaecol 1988;9:35–42 (Level II-3)

13. Stout AL, Grady TA, Steege JF, Blazer DG, George LK, Melville ML. Premenstrual symptoms in black and white community samples. Am J Psychiatry 1986;143; 1436–1439 (Level III)

14. Freeman EW. Premenstrual syndrome: current perspectives on treatment and etiology. Curr Opin Obstet Gynecol 1997;9:147–153 (Level III)

15. Schmidt PJ, Nieman LK, Danaceau MA, Adams LF, Rubinow DR. Differential behavioral effects of gonadal

steroids in women with and in those without premenstrual syndrome. N Engl J Med 1998;338:209–216 (Level I)

16. Eriksson E, Hedberg MA, Andersch B, Sundblad C. The serotonin reuptake inhibitor paroxetin is superior to the noradrenaline reuptake inhibitor maprotiline in the treatment of premenstrual syndrome. Neuropsychopharmacology 1995;12:167–176 (Level II-2)

17. Hamilton JA, Parry BL, Alagna S, Blumenthal S, Herz E. Premenstrual mood changes: a guide to evaluation and treatment. Psychiatr Ann 1984;14:426-435 (Level III)

18. American Psychiatric Association. Diagnostic and statistical manual of mental disorders: DSM-IV. 4th ed. Washington, DC: APA, 1994:714–718 (Level III)

19. Hart WG, Coleman GJ, Russell JW. Assessment of premenstrual symptomatology: a re-evaluation of the predictive validity of self-report. J Psychosom Res 1987;31:185–190 (Level III)

20. Johnson SR. Clinician's approach to the diagnosis and management of premenstrual syndrome. Clin Obstet Gynecol 1992;35:637–657 (Level III)

21. Mortola JF, Girton L, Beck L, Yen SS. Diagnosis of premenstrual syndrome by a simple, prospective, and reliable instrument: the calendar of premenstrual experiences. Obstet Gynecol 1990;76:302–307 (Level II-2)

22. Reid RL. Premenstrual syndrome. Curr Probl Obstet Gynecol Fertil 1985;8(2):1–57 (Level III)

23. McCormack HM, Horne DJ, Sheather S. Clinical applications of visual analogue scales: a critical review. Psychol Med 1988;18:1007–1019 (Level I)

24. Corney RH, Stanton R. A survey of 658 women who report symptoms of premenstrual syndrome. J Psychosom Res 1991;35:471–482 (Level III)

25. Plouffe L Jr, Stewart KS, Craft KS, Maddox MS, Rausch JL. Diagnostic and treatment results from a southeastern academic center-based premenstrual syndrome clinic: the first year. Am J Obstet Gynecol 1993;169:295–303; discussion 303–307 (Level III)

26. Goodale IL, Domar AD, Benson H. Alleviation of premenstrual syndrome symptoms with the relaxation response. Obstet Gynecol 1990;75:649–655 (Level I)

27. Christensen AP, Oei TP. The efficacy of cognitive behaviour therapy in treating premenstrual dysphoric changes. J Affect Disord 1995;33:57–63 (Level II-3)

28. Steege JF, Blumenthal JA. The effects of aerobic exercise on premenstrual symptoms in middle-aged women: a preliminary study. J Psychosom Res 1993;37:127–133 (Level II-1)

29. Prior JC, Vigna Y, Sciarretta D, Alojado N, Schulzer M. Conditioning exercise decreases premenstrual symptoms: a prospective, controlled 6-month trial. Fertil Steril 1987;47:402–408 (Level II-2)

30. Thys-Jacobs, Starkey P, Bernstein D, Tian J. Calcium carbonate and the premenstrual syndrome: effects on premenstrual and menstrual symptoms. Premenstrual Syndrome Study Group. Am J Obstet Gynecol 1998;179:444–452 (Level I)

31. Facchinetti F, Borella P, Sances G, Fioroni L, Nappi RE, Genazzani AR. Oral magnesium successfully relieves premenstrual mood changes. Obstet Gynecol 1991;78:177–181 (Level I)

32. Walker AF, De Souza MC, Vickers MF, Abeyasekera S, Collins ML, Trinca LA. Magnesium supplementation alleviates premenstrual symptoms of fluid retention. J Womens Health 1998;7:1157–1165 (Level I)

33. London RS, Murphy L, Kitlowski KE, Reynolds MA. Efficacy of alpha-tocopherol in the treatment of the premenstrual syndrome. J Reprod Med 1987;32:400–404 (Level I)

34. Sayegh R, Schiff I, Wurtman J, Spiers P, McDermott J, Wurtman R. The effect of a carbohydrate-rich beverage on mood, appetite, and cognitive function in women with premenstrual syndrome. Obstet Gynecol 1995,86:520–528 (Level II-2)

35. Budeiri D, Li Wan Po A, Dorman JC. Is evening primrose oil of value in the treatment of premenstrual syndrome? Control Clin Trials 1996;17:60–68 (Level III)

36. Wyatt KM, Dimmock PW, Jones PW, Shaughn O'Brien PM. Efficacy of vitamin B-6 in the treatment of premenstrual syndrome: systematic review. BMJ. 1999;318:1375–1381 (Level III)

37. Steiner M, Steinberg S, Stewart D, Carter D, Berger C, Reid R, et al. Fluoxetine in the treatment of premenstrual dysphoria. Canadian Fluoxetine/Premenstrual Dysphoria Collaborative Study Group. N Engl J Med 1995;332:1529–1534 (Level I)

38. Pearlstein TB, Stone AB. Long-term fluoxetine treatment of late luteal phase dysphoric disorder. J Clin Psychiatry 1994;55:332–335 (Level II-2)

39. Yonkers KA, Halbreich U, Freeman E, Brown C, Endicott J, Frank E, et al. Symptomatic improvement of premenstrual dysphoric disorder with sertraline treatment. A randomized controlled trial. Sertraline Premenstrual Dysphoric Collaborative Study Group. JAMA 1997;278:983–988 (Level I)

40. Steiner M, Korzekwa M, Lamont J, Wilkins A. Intermittent fluoxetine dosing in the treatment of women with premenstrual dysphoria. Psychopharmacol Bull 1997;33:771–774 (Level II-3)

41. Young SA, Hurt PH, Benedek DM, Howard RS. Treatment of premenstrual dysphoric disorder with sertraline during the luteal phase: a randomized, double-blind, placebo-controlled crossover trial. J Clin Psychiatry 1998;59:76–80 (Level II-1)

42. Wikander I, Sundblad C, Andersch B, Dagnell I, Zylberstein D, Bengtsson F, et al. Citalopram in premenstrual dysphoria: is intermittent treatment during luteal phases more effective than continuous medication throughout the menstrual cycle? J Clin Psychopharmacol 1998;18:390–398 (Level I)

43. Harrison WM, Endicott J, Nee J. Treatment of premenstrual dysphoria with alprazolam. A controlled study. Arch Gen Psychiatry 1990;47:270–275 (Level I)

44. Smith S, Rinehart JS, Ruddock VE, Schiff I. Treatment of premenstrual syndrome with alprazolam: results of a dou-

ble-blind, placebo-controlled, randomized crossover clinical trial. Obstet Gynecol 1987;70:37–43 (Level I)

45. Freeman EW, Rickels K, Sondheimer SJ, Polansky M. A double-blind trial of oral progesterone, alprazolam, and placebo in treatment of severe premenstrual syndrome. JAMA 1995;274:51–57 (Level I)

46. Schmidt PJ, Grover GN, Rubinow DR. Alprazolam in the treatment of premenstrual syndrome: a double-blind, placebo-controlled trial. Arch Gen Psychiatry 1993;50: 467–473 (Level I)

47. O'Brien PM, Craven D, Selby C, Symonds EM. Treatment of premenstrual syndrome by spironolactone. Br J Obstet Gynaecol 1979;86:142–147 (Level I)

48. Vellacott ID, Shroff NE, Pearce MY, Stratford ME, Akbar FA. A double-blind, placebo-controlled evaluation of spironolactone in the premenstrual syndrome. Curr Med Res Opin 1987;10:450–456 (Level I)

49. Wang M, Hammarback S, Lindhe BA, Backstrom T. Treatment of premenstrual syndrome by spironolactone: a double-blind, placebo controlled study. Acta Obstet Gynecol Scand 1995;74:803–808 (Level I)

50. Burnet RB, Radden HS, Easterbrook EG, McKinnon RA. Premenstrual syndrome and spironolactone. Aust N Z J Obstet Gynaecol 1991;31:366–368 (Level I)

51. Hellberg D, Claesson B, Nilsson S. Premenstrual tension: a placebo-controlled efficacy study with spironolactone and medroxyprogesterone acetate. Int J Gynaecol Obstet 1991;34:243–248 (Level II-1)

52. Freeman E, Rickels K, Sondheimer SJ, Polansky M. Ineffectiveness of progesterone suppository treatment for premenstrual syndrome. JAMA 1990;264:349–353 (Level I)

53. Baker ER, Best RG, Manfredi RL, Demers LM, Wolf GC. Efficacy of progesterone vaginal suppositories in alleviation of nervous symptoms in patients with premenstrual syndrome. J Assist Reprod Genet 1995;12:205–209 (Level II-1)

54. Graham CA. Sherwin BB. A prospective treatment study of premenstrual symptoms using a triphasic oral contraceptive. Psychosom Res 1992;36:257–266 (Level II-2)

55. Backstrom T, Hansson-Malmstrom Y, Lindhe BA, Cavilli-Bjorkman B, Nordenstrom S. Oral contraceptives in premenstrual syndrome: a randomized comparison of triphasic and monophasic preparations. Contraception 1992;46:253–268 (Level II-1)

56. Johnson SR. Premenstrual syndrome therapy. Clin Obstet Gynecol 1998;41:405–421 (Level III)

57. Freeman EW, Sondheimer SJ, Rickels K. Gonadotropin-releasing hormone agonist in treatment of premenstrual symptoms with and without ongoing dysphoria: a controlled study. Psychopharmacol Bull 1997;33:303–309 (Level I)

58. West CP, Hillier H. Ovarian suppression with the gonadotrophin-releasing hormone agonist goserelin (Zoladex) in management of the premenstrual tension syndrome. Hum Reprod 1994;9:1058–1063 (Level I)

59. Mortola JF, Girton L, Fischer U. Successful treatment of severe premenstrual syndrome by combined use of gonadotropin-releasing hormone agonist and estrogen/progestin. J Clin Endocrinol Metab 1991;72:252A–252F (Level III)

60. Casson P, Hahn PM, Van Vugt DA, Reid RL. Lasting response to ovariectomy in severe intractable premenstrual syndrome. Am J Obstet Gynecol 1990;162:99–105 (Level II-3)

The MEDLINE database, the Cochrane Library, and ACOG's own internal resources and documents were used to conduct a literature search to locate relevant articles published between January 1985 and May 1999. The search was restricted to articles published in the English language. Priority was given to articles reporting results of original research, although review articles and commentaries also were consulted. Abstracts of research presented at symposia and scientific conferences were not considered adequate for inclusion in this document. Guidelines published by organizations or institutions such as the National Institutes of Health and the American College of Obstetricians and Gynecologists were reviewed, and additional studies were located by reviewing bibliographies of identified articles. When reliable research was not available, expert opinions from obstetrician–gynecologists were used.

Studies were reviewed and evaluated for quality according to the method outlined by the U.S. Preventive Services Task Force:

I   Evidence obtained from at least one properly designed randomized controlled trial.

II-1 Evidence obtained from well-designed controlled trials without randomization.

II-2 Evidence obtained from well-designed cohort or case–control analytic studies, preferably from more than one center or research group.

II-3 Evidence obtained from multiple time series with or without the intervention. Dramatic results in uncontrolled experiments also could be regarded as this type of evidence.

III   Opinions of respected authorities, based on clinical experience, descriptive studies, or reports of expert committees.

Based on the highest level of evidence found in the data, recommendations are provided and graded according to the following categories:

Level A—Recommendations are based on good and consistent scientific evidence.

Level B—Recommendations are based on limited or inconsistent scientific evidence.

Level C—Recommendations are based primarily on consensus and expert opinion.

ISSN 1099-3630

**The American College of
Obstetricians and Gynecologists
409 12th Street, SW
PO Box 96920
Washington, DC 20090-6920**

12345/43210

ACOG PRACTICE BULLETIN

CLINICAL MANAGEMENT GUIDELINES FOR
OBSTETRICIAN–GYNECOLOGISTS

NUMBER 27, MAY 2001

*(Replaces Educational Bulletin Number 228, September 1996,
and Committee Opinion Number 160, October 1995)*

This Practice Bulletin was developed by the ACOG Committee on Practice Bulletins— Obstetrics with the assistance of Katharine Wenstrom, MD. The information is designed to aid practitioners in making decisions about appropriate obstetric and gynecologic care. These guidelines should not be construed as dictating an exclusive course of treatment or procedure. Variations in practice may be warranted based on the needs of the individual patient, resources, and limitations unique to the institution or type of practice.

Prenatal Diagnosis of Fetal Chromosomal Abnormalities

The prevalence of chromosomal abnormalities in clinically recognized early pregnancy loss is approximately 50% (1). Aneuploid fetuses account for 6–11% of all stillbirths and neonatal deaths (2). Chromosome defects compatible with life but causing significant morbidity occur in 0.65% of newborns, and another 0.2% have structural chromosomal rearrangements that will eventually affect reproduction (3). Although it is not possible to identify all aneuploidies antenatally, screening and diagnostic programs to detect the most common autosomal trisomy in liveborn infants, Down syndrome, are well established. This document will provide clinical management guidelines for the prenatal detection of these aneuploidies.

Background

Down syndrome and other autosomal trisomies primarily occur as the result of meiotic nondisjunction, which increases with maternal age. Genetic amniocentesis has been offered to women who will be age 35 years and older at delivery because at this age the incidence of trisomy starts to increase rapidly and because the midtrimester risk of Down syndrome roughly equals the most often quoted risk of procedure-related pregnancy loss (1/200) (Table 1). However, only 12.9% of all children are born to women age 35 years and older (4). Therefore, even if all women older than 35 years requested amniocenteses, only a minority of Down syndrome pregnancies would be identified. Because younger women have the majority of pregnancies, younger women give birth to the majority of children with Down syndrome (5).

Table 1. Midtrimester and Term Risk of Down Syndrome or Any Aneuploidy

Maternal Age	Midtrimester		Term Liveborn	
	DS	All Aneuploidies	DS	All Aneuploidies
33	1/417	1/208	1/625	1/345
34	1/333	1/152	1/500	1/278
35	1/250	1/132	1/384	1/204
36	1/192	1/105	1/303	1/167
37	1/149	1/83	1/227	1/130
38	1/115	1/65	1/175	1/103
39	1/89	1/53	1/137	1/81
40	1/69	1/40	1/106	1/63
41	1/53	1/31	1/81	1/50
42	1/41	1/25	1/64	1/39
43	1/31	1/19	1/50	1/30
44	1/25	1/15	1/38	1/24
45	1/19	1/12	1/30	1/19

Abbreviation: DS, Down syndrome.

Adapted from Hook EB, Cross PK, Schreinemachers DM. Chromosomal abnormality rates at amniocentesis and in live-born infants. JAMA 1983;249:2034–2038. Copyrighted 1983, American Medical Association.

Screening and Testing for Genetic Abnormalities

Of Down syndrome pregnancies, 97% occur in families with no previous history of the syndrome (6). Screening tests are used to identify those women who are not known to be at high risk but are nevertheless carrying a fetus with Down syndrome. Screening tests have a high false-positive rate because the threshold for declaring a screening test result positive is set to capture most individuals who truly have the condition at the expense of including some who do not. Women with positive screening test results should be offered a definitive diagnostic test such as amniocentesis or chorionic villus sampling (CVS).

Second-Trimester Screening

Maternal Serum Screening

Until the mid-1980s, there was no way to identify younger women at risk of having children with Down syndrome. Down syndrome screening for younger women was initiated when researchers discovered that the mean level of maternal serum alpha fetoprotein (AFP) in pregnancies complicated by fetal Down syndrome is 0.7 multiples of the (normal) median (MoM) (7–9).

It was soon discovered that human chorionic gonadotropin (hCG) levels are higher (2.04 MoM) and unconjugated estriol levels are lower (0.79 MoM) in Down syndrome pregnancies (10–13). The relative risks derived from maternal serum levels of these three analytes are used to modify the maternal age-related risk. This protocol has been validated extensively and has become the preferred Down syndrome screening test for women younger than 35 years (13–16). At a cutoff chosen to produce a 5% or greater screen-positive rate, the multiple-marker screening test identifies approximately 60% of all Down syndrome pregnancies in women younger than 35 years. In women 35 years and older, it detects 75% or more of all Down syndrome cases and certain other aneuploidies. The screen-positive rate increases with maternal age (Table 2) (17). Some laboratories use the midtrimester Down syndrome risk of a 35-year-old woman as the screen-positive cutoff. Other laboratories select a screen-positive cutoff that will result in an acceptable balance between a high detection rate and a low screen-positive rate (usually 1:190 or 1:200). The basis of these screening protocol calculations of risk is the maternal age-related risk of Down syndrome, a risk based on previously lower rates of birth to women older than 35 years, which may now be obsolete. Screening protocols may benefit from revision using current data on maternal age.

Maternal blood sampling can be performed between 15 and 20 weeks of gestation but is most accurate when performed between 16 and 18 weeks of gestation. Accurate pregnancy dating is essential. If the estimated date of delivery is changed after the test results have returned, it is important to recalculate the results or provide the laboratory with a new blood sample if the original specimen was drawn at less than 15 weeks of gestation.

Table 2. Multiple-Marker Down Syndrome Screening Test Detection and Screen-Positive Rates, According to Maternal Age

Maternal Age	Screen-Positive Rate (%)	Detection Rate (%) (with Estriol)
20	2.4	41
25	2.9	44
30	5.0	52
35	14.0	71
40	40.0	91

Modified with permission from Haddow JE, Palomaki GE, Knight GJ, Cunningham GC, Lustig LS, Boyd PA. Reducing the need for amniocentesis in women 35 years of age or older with serum markers for screening. N Engl J Med 1994;330:1114–1118. Copyright ©1994 Massachusetts Medical Society. All rights reserved.

The multiple-marker screening test also can detect approximately 60–75% of fetuses with trisomy 18 when a separate analysis is performed that uses low levels of all three analytes with or without consideration of maternal age (18, 19). Although serum screening does not detect other aneuploidies with great frequency, the aneuploidies likely to be missed by serum screening usually are ultimately lethal (eg, trisomy 13) or are sex-chromosome abnormalities not associated with profound mental retardation or other severe physical or developmental limitations.

The contribution of estriol measurement is a subject of debate, with some centers offering AFP plus hCG alone. Some investigators consider free beta subunits of hCG (β-hCG) to be superior to the intact hCG molecule, but neither has been definitively proven to be superior. New analytes also are constantly being tested. Dimeric inhibin A is the most promising new second-trimester analyte and is now used by some commercial laboratories in combination with the three traditional analytes. With a screen-positive rate of 5% or less, this new four-analyte combination appears to detect 67–76% of Down syndrome cases in women younger than 35 years (20, 21).

Ultrasound Screening

Aneuploid fetuses may have major anatomic malformations, often discovered by chance during an ultrasound examination performed for another indication. All abnormalities involving a major organ or structure, with a few notable exceptions, or the finding of two or more minor structural abnormalities in the same fetus, indicate high risk for fetal aneuploidy (22–24) (Table 3). Structural anomalies can have many etiologies; if an aneuploidy is suspected, only a karyotype analysis of fetal cells can provide a definitive diagnosis.

Table 3. Aneuploid Risk of Major Anomalies

Structural Defect	Population Incidence	Aneuploidy Risk	Most Common Aneuploidy
Cystic hygroma	1/120 EU–1/6,000 B	60–75%	45X (80%); 21,18,13,XXY
Hydrops	1/1,500–4,000 B	30–80%*	13,21,18,45X
Hydrocephalus	3–8/10,000 LB	3–8%	13,18, triploidy
Hydranencephaly	2/1,000 IA	Minimal	
Holoprosencephaly	1/16,000 LB	40–60%	13,18,18p-
Cardiac defects	7–9/1,000 LB	5–30%	21,18,13,22,8,9
Complete atrioventricular canal		40–70%	21
Diaphragmatic hernia	1/3,500–4,000 LB	20–25%	13,18,21,45X
Omphalocele	1/5,800 LB	30–40%	13,18
Gastroschisis	1/10,000–15,000 LB	Minimal	
Duodenal atresia	1/10,000 LB	20–30%	21
Bowel obstruction	1/2,500–5,000 LB	Minimal	
Bladder outlet obstruction	1–2/1,000 LB	20–25%	13,18
Prune belly syndrome	1/35,000–50,000 LB	Low	18,13,45X
Facial cleft	1/700 LB	1%	13,18, Deletions
Limb reduction	4–6/10,000 LB	8%	18
Club foot	1.2/1,000 LB	6%	18,13,4p-,18q-
Single umbilical artery	1%	Minimal	

Abbreviations: EU, early ultrasonography; B, birth; LB, livebirth; IA, infant autopsy.

*30% if diagnosed ≥24 weeks; 80% if diagnosed ≤17 weeks

Data from Shipp TD, Benacerraf BR. The significance of prenatally identified isolated clubfoot: is amniocentesis indicated? Am J Obstet Gynecol 1998;178:600–602; and Nyberg DA, Crane JP. Chromosome abnormalities. In: Nyberg DA, Mahony BS, Pretorius DH. Diagnostic ultrasound of fetal anomalies: text and atlas. Chicago: Year Book Medical, 1990:676–724

First-Trimester Screening

Maternal Serum Analytes

Many maternal serum analytes have been evaluated for possible use for first-trimester Down syndrome screening, although preliminary data remain controversial and testing is not yet standard of care. The most discriminatory analytes at this gestational age appear to be β-hCG and pregnancy-associated plasma protein A (PAPP-A) (25, 26). The median free β-hCG in affected Down syndrome pregnancies is approximately 1.79 MoM, whereas the median PAPP-A is approximately 0.43 MoM. Because of the low correlation between these two analytes, each contributes unique biologic information to the screening test. The combination of free β-hCG, PAPP-A, and maternal age appears to yield detection and false-positive rates comparable to second-trimester serum screening (63% and 5.5%, respectively) (27). Unfortunately, free β-hCG may not be higher in Down syndrome pregnancies until 12 weeks of gestation, and PAPP-A seems to lose its discrimination value after 13 weeks of gestation, making accurate assessment of gestational age and careful timing of the screening test essential (28).

Nuchal Lucency Measurement

Nuchal lucency measurement has been suggested as another screening test for Down syndrome in the first trimester. The ultrasound finding of an increase in the size of the normal, clear area behind the fetal neck early in pregnancy is associated with an increased incidence of Down syndrome, congenital heart disease, and other congenital anomalies. Although the precise etiology and significance of the nuchal lucency are unknown, the finding may reflect accumulation of lymph fluid related to delayed development of the lymphatic ducts. An increased nuchal lucency measurement in combination with maternal age has been reported to identify 27–89% of Down syndrome pregnancies, with a screen-positive rate of 2.8–9.3% (28). Some of this wide variation may result from differences in techniques for measuring and criteria for defining an increase. Other factors include differences in study population, ultrasonographic technique, sonographer training, definition of screen positivity, and the quality of both pregnancy and pediatric follow-up. Much of the early work was derived from women at high risk (eg, prior to scheduled CVS or amniocentesis in women age 35 years or older), and results of trials in unselected low-risk women have produced conflicting results (29–31). Variability in Down syndrome detection rates is likely to be caused by the existence of significant methodologic limitations for many of the studies. Many

of the reports provide minimal information on the extent of pregnancy or pediatric follow-up; therefore, under-ascertainment of cases of Down syndrome is likely.

Clinical Considerations and Recommendations

▶ *Who is at high risk and should be offered prenatal diagnosis for fetal aneuploidy?*

Women with singleton pregnancies who will be age 35 years or older at delivery should be offered prenatal diagnosis. The midtrimester risk that a pregnant 35-year-old woman is carrying a fetus with Down syndrome is 1/250 (32); the risk of any aneuploidy is 1/132 (Table 1). These numbers are higher than the term risks because a large proportion of aneuploid pregnancies are spontaneously aborted before term delivery. The risks at term are 1/384 for Down syndrome and 1/204 for all aneuploidies.

In addition to women age 35 years and older, patients with a risk of fetal aneuploidy high enough to justify an invasive diagnostic procedure include the following:

- *Women who have previously had pregnancies complicated by autosomal trisomy.* The chance that such a woman could have another pregnancy with the same or a different autosomal trisomy is approximately 1% until her age-related risk exceeds 1%; then it is assumed to equal her age-related risk.

- *A fetus with a major structural defect identified by ultrasonography.* The discovery of one major or two or more minor fetal structural abnormalities increases the likelihood of aneuploidy sufficiently to warrant fetal genetic testing (22–24). However, detection of a fetal defect known not to be associated with aneuploidy (eg, fetal cleft lip discovered during an ultrasound examination ordered because the mother has a cleft lip) or an isolated malformation not usually associated with aneuploidy may not require further testing (Table 3).

- *Women who have previously had a pregnancy complicated by a sex chromosome aneuploidy.* If the previous child had an extra X chromosome, the chromosome may be maternal or paternal in origin. If it is maternal, it is age related. As with autosomal trisomies, the recurrence risk is 1% until the maternal age-related risk exceeds 1%. A woman whose previous child was karyotype 47,XYY is not at high risk of recurrence, because the extra chromosome in this situation is paternal in origin. The karyotype 45,X has a very low recurrence risk. Parents of children with 47,XYY or 45,X karyotypes may still request prenatal diagnosis in future pregnancies for reassurance.

- *Men or women with a chromosome translocation.* Women or men carrying balanced translocations, although phenotypically normal themselves, are at risk of producing unbalanced gametes, resulting in abnormal offspring. For most translocations, the observed risk of abnormal liveborn children is less than the theoretic risk, because a portion of these gametes result in nonviable conceptions. In general, carriers of chromosome translocations identified after the birth of an abnormal child have a 5–30% risk of having unbalanced offspring in the future, while those identified for other reasons (eg, during an infertility work-up) have a 0–5% risk (1). Genetic counseling may be helpful in such situations.

- *Men or women who are carriers of chromosome inversions.* An inversion occurs when two breaks occur in the same chromosome, and the intervening genetic material is inverted before the breaks are repaired. Although no genetic material is lost or duplicated, the rearrangement may alter gene function. Each carrier's risk is related to the method of ascertainment, the chromosome involved, and the size of the inversion and, thus, should be determined individually. The observed risk is approximately 5–10% if the inversion is identified after the birth of an abnormal child and 1–3% if ascertainment occurs by some other means (1). One exception is a pericentric inversion of chromosome 9, which is a population variant of no clinical consequence.

- *Parental aneuploidy.* Women with trisomy 21 or 47,XXX and men with 47,XYY usually are fertile and have a 30% risk of having trisomic offspring. In men with a normal karyotype who have oligospermia and undergo intracytoplasmic sperm injection to conceive, there is an increased incidence of abnormal karyotype in the sperm. However, this has not been reflected in an increase in karyotypically abnormal offspring in these pregnancies.

▶ *How is fetal aneuploidy diagnosed?*

Amniocentesis. Traditional genetic amniocentesis usually is offered between 15 and 20 weeks of gestation. Many large, multicenter studies have confirmed the safety of genetic amniocentesis, as well as its cytogenetic diagnostic accuracy (greater than 99%) (33). The fetal loss rate is approximately 0.5% (34), and minor complications occur infrequently. These include transient vaginal spotting or amniotic fluid leakage in approximately 1–2% of all cases and chorioamnionitis in less than one in 1,000 cases. Needle injuries to the fetus have been reported but are very rare when amniocentesis is performed under continuous ultrasound guidance. Amniotic fluid cell culture failure is uncommon.

Safe performance of genetic amniocentesis requires specialized training and ongoing experience. Several studies have confirmed that the incidence of pregnancy loss, blood-contaminated specimens, leaking of amniotic fluid, and the need for more than one needle puncture are related to the experience of the operator, the use of a small-gauge needle, and ultrasound guidance (35–37).

Early amniocentesis, performed from 11 weeks to 13 weeks of gestation, has been widely studied, and the technique is similar to traditional amniocentesis (38–40). However, early amniocentesis results in significantly higher pregnancy loss and complication rates than traditional amniocentesis. In a recent multicenter randomized trial, the spontaneous pregnancy loss rate following early amniocentesis was 2.5%, compared with 0.7% with traditional amniocentesis (41). The overall incidence of talipes was 1.4% after the early procedure, compared with 0.1% (the same as the background rate) after traditional amniocentesis, and membrane rupture was more likely after the early procedure. Finally, significantly more amniotic fluid culture failures occurred after the early procedure, necessitating an additional invasive procedure for diagnosis. For these reasons, many centers no longer offer early amniocentesis.

Chorionic Villus Sampling. Indications for CVS are similar to those for amniocentesis, except for a few rare genetic conditions that require chorionic villi for diagnosis. Chorionic villus sampling generally is performed at 10–12 weeks of gestation. The primary advantage of CVS over amniocentesis is that results are available much earlier in pregnancy, which provides reassurance for parents when results are normal and, when results are abnormal, allows earlier and safer methods of pregnancy termination.

Placental villi may be obtained through transcervical or transabdominal access to the placenta. Skill in ultrasound-guided procedures and extensive specialized training are required before attempting CVS, and maintenance of skills with regularly scheduled procedures is essential. Some active cervical infections (such as chlamydia or herpes) are a contraindication to transcervical CVS. Relative contraindications to CVS include vaginal infection, vaginal bleeding or spotting, extreme anteversion or retroversion of the uterus, and patient body habitus precluding easy access to the uterus or clear visualization of intrauterine structures with ultrasonography (42–44).

Several major collaborative trials report success rates of more than 99% with cytogenetic analysis and total pregnancy loss rates of 0.6–0.8% for CVS in excess of traditional amniocentesis (33, 45–48, 49). As with early amniocentesis, the reported excess loss rate may result from the CVS procedure itself, but it also may incorporate the expected spontaneous loss rate between 9 and 16 weeks of gestation. Patients considering CVS should be counseled that there may be a slightly higher risk of pregnancy loss associated with CVS than with traditional amniocentesis (34).

Although there have been reports of an association between CVS and limb reduction and oromandibular defects, the risk for these anomalies is unclear (50). In an analysis by the World Health Organization, an incidence of limb reduction defects of 6 per 10,000 was reported, which is not significantly different from the incidence in the general population (49). However, a workshop on CVS and limb reduction defects sponsored by the U.S. National Center for Environmental Health and the Centers for Disease Control and Prevention concluded that oromandibular–limb hypogenesis appeared to be more common after CVS. It found the risk is highest when CVS is performed before 9 menstrual weeks (51). In addition, a panel convened by the National Institute of Child Health and Development and the American College of Obstetricians and Gynecologists concluded that oromandibular–limb hypogenesis appeared to be more common among CVS-exposed infants and appeared to correlate, but may not be limited to, CVS performed earlier than 7 weeks (50). Women considering CVS who are concerned about the possible association of CVS with limb defects can be reassured that when the procedure is performed after 9 menstrual weeks, the risk is low and probably not higher than the general population risk.

Cordocentesis. Cordocentesis, also known as percutaneous umbilical blood sampling (PUBS), involves puncturing the umbilical vein under direct ultrasound guidance. Karyotype analysis of fetal blood usually can be accomplished within 24–48 hours. The procedure-related pregnancy loss rate, including all indications for the procedure, has been reported to be less than 2% (34, 52).

▶ *Is there a role for chromosomal analysis when a fetal ultrasound marker of aneuploidy is identified during an ultrasound examination undertaken for an unrelated indication?*

A variety of second-trimester ultrasound findings have been associated with Down syndrome. Although identification of a major anomaly indicates the need for diagnostic follow-up, ultrasound markers are less strongly associated with aneuploidy. Many of these ultrasound markers have not been well studied in unselected, low-risk women. It is, therefore, unclear how to interpret many of these findings in a given patient particularly in

conjunction with age and serum screening results. Some ultrasound markers associated with Down syndrome include nuchal fold thickness, shortened femur or humerus, pyelectasis, and hyperechogenic bowel. Although some ultrasound markers have been confirmed by multiple investigators to be associated with Down syndrome, others have been described in only one series or have been found to have contradictory associations with Down syndrome across studies (53, 54). The lack of uniformity in the definition of an abnormal finding (eg, how to define a shortened femur) and the lack of consensus on which markers are most significant make this screening approach complex.

Several series have attempted to determine which of these ultrasound markers are most predictive of fetal Down syndrome; short femur and humerus (alone or in combination) and nuchal fold thickening appear to be most promising (55, 56). Most series have found that a combination of two or more positive findings substantially increases risk and warrants further counseling regarding invasive testing. The degree to which an individual patient's risk is increased over age-related and serum analyte calculated risk is unclear. These ultrasound markers have been associated with aneuploidy only if identified in the second trimester.

▶ *Is ultrasonographic screening useful in pregnant women identified to be at high-risk for fetal aneuploidy?*

For the woman at high risk for fetal Down syndrome, usually by virtue of age or multiple-marker screening test results, an ultrasound examination may support the need for prenatal diagnosis. This is particularly true if one of the ultrasound markers for Down syndrome is present or if a gross fetal abnormality is seen. Much more commonly, the ultrasound examination is normal. It has been suggested that the absence of any ultrasound evidence for Down syndrome may decrease the risk sufficiently in high-risk women to avoid amniocentesis. Most invasive testing for Down syndrome occurs in women with a risk just above established cutoffs. Therefore, even a small decrease in the risk of Down syndrome, as determined by normal ultrasound results, may put such women in a lower risk category and avoid the need for invasive testing. This decrease in risk could have a significant impact on the overall number of invasive diagnostic tests performed.

Some studies suggest that the risk for Down syndrome may be reduced by 45–80% over the risk cited before the normal ultrasound examination with knowledgeable interpretation of these markers (57–59). These rates are based on ultrasound examinations performed by experienced operators. Several small studies have been published describing rates of Down syndrome detection between 68% and 93% using various scoring indexes combining maternal age and ultrasound markers. These studies report false-positive rates between 17% and 27% (58, 60, 61).

Risk adjustment is possible only if the ultrasound abnormalities are rigidly defined and the portion of Down syndrome fetuses with them is known. Many investigators have suggested that these measures are laboratory specific, and data may not apply in other centers (62). In addition, ultrasound markers often include anatomic abnormalities as well as biometric measures. The reproducibility of significant ultrasound findings and the magnitude of the decrease in risk for aneuploidy are not yet firmly established. The use of ultrasonographic screening for Down syndrome in high-risk women to avoid invasive testing (eg, women age 35 years and older) is, therefore, controversial and should be limited to specialized centers (55, 57, 63).

▶ How should a finding of an isolated choroid plexus cyst be further evaluated?

Choroid plexus cysts arise in the choroid plexus of the lateral ventricle and are typically recognized by ultrasonography in the early to middle second trimester. Choroid plexus cysts may be associated with trisomy 18 (64, 65), which has prompted consideration of the need for invasive testing of the fetus if detected. A meta-analysis reported that the risk of trisomy 18 associated with isolated choroid plexus cysts in all women (all ages combined) is 1/374 (64). Another analysis evaluated published data from more than 200,000 ultrasound examinations and determined that only in women age 32 and older, the presence of an isolated choroid plexus cyst increases the midtrimester risk of trisomy 18 enough to justify genetic testing of the fetus (65). Two recent studies found that with an isolated choroid plexus cyst, testing was justified only if serum screening results were abnormal or the patient was older than 35 years (66, 67). However, in these studies, cysts were commonly noted at the time of genetic amniocentesis; thus, the mother's age at diagnosis also may affect incidence. Therefore, with detection of an isolated choroid plexus cyst, further testing is necessary only if serum screening results are abnormal or the patient is older than 32 years at delivery.

▶ Is there a role for serum screening in women who will be age 35 years and older at delivery?

Because the maternal age-related risk of Down syndrome is the basis of the serum screening protocol, both the Down syndrome detection rate and the screen positive rate increase with maternal age (Table 2) (13). The screen-positive rate for all women age 35 years and older is approximately 25%; for women age 40 years, it is 40%; and by age 44, it is approximately 70% (17, 68).

Counseling should include discussion of age-specific multiple-marker screening detection rates and screen-positive rates, the detection rate of aneuploidies other than Down syndrome the identity and prognosis of the aneuploidies likely to be missed by serum screening, and the risks and benefits of replacing a diagnostic test with a screening test. Counseling should be provided by a practitioner familiar with these components.

▶ How does prenatal diagnosis differ in multiple gestations?

Diagnostic options are more limited in multiple gestations (69). In women with twins, the risk of trisomy 21 should be calculated by considering the maternal age-related risk of Down syndrome and the probability that either or both fetuses could be affected. Counseling in this situation should include a discussion of options for pregnancy management if only one fetus is found to be affected. These options include terminating the entire pregnancy, selective second-trimester termination of the affected fetus, and continuing the pregnancy. It has been estimated that the midtrimester risk of fetal Down syndrome in a twin pregnancy in women age 33 years is approximately the same as the risk for that of a singleton pregnancy in women age 35 years, thus justifying counseling for amniocentesis (70, 71).

Scant data exist concerning fetal loss with twin gestation and amniocentesis or CVS. According to some small series, the fetal loss rate with amniocentesis in multiple gestations is approximately 3.5%; this was not higher than the background loss rate for twins in the second trimester in one series with a control group (52, 72, 73). Similar information for twin gestations from small, nonrandomized series exists for CVS (73–75).

A complex counseling issue arises in the presence of a monochorionic twin gestation, in which case the likelihood of discordance in the karyotype is low, and patients may opt for having a karyotype analysis performed on a single fetus. However, in order to offer this option to a patient, the diagnosis of monochorionic twin gestation must have been made with a high degree of confidence. There are no data concerning loss rates following amniocentesis in higher-order multiple gestations.

▶ Can women who are younger than 35 years (at delivery) elect to have genetic amniocentesis?

Because of the inherent risk of fetal aneuploidy (Table 1), women younger than 35 years may request genetic amniocentesis. Each patient should weigh the risk of amniocentesis against her desire to determine whether the fetus has an abnormal karyotype, in the context of her own values and beliefs. Consequently, some patients younger than 35 years may request genetic amniocentesis primarily rather than only after abnormal maternal serum or ultrasound screening.

▶ *Should Down syndrome screening be performed in the patient who would decline pregnancy termination?*

Prenatal diagnosis is not performed solely for the purposes of pregnancy termination; it can provide useful information for the physician and the patient. If it is determined that the fetus has an aneuploidy, management of pregnancy, labor, and delivery can be optimized (76).

Summary of Recommendations

The following recommendation is based on good and consistent scientific evidence (Level A):

▶ Early amniocentesis (<13 weeks) is not recommended because of the higher risk of pregnancy loss and complications compared with traditional amniocentesis (15–17 weeks).

The following recommendations are based primarily on consensus and expert opinion (Level C):

▶ Women with singleton pregnancies who will be age 35 years or older at delivery should be offered prenatal diagnosis for fetal aneuploidy.

▶ Patients with a risk of fetal aneuploidy high enough to justify an invasive diagnostic procedure include women with a previous pregnancy complicated by an autosomal trisomy or sex chromosome aneuploidy, a major fetal structural defect identified by ultrasonography, either parent with a chromosome translocation, and carriers of a pericentric chromosome inversion or parental aneuploidy.

▶ A combination of one major or two or more minor ultrasound markers of Down syndrome substantially increases risk and warrants further counseling regarding invasive testing.

▶ The use of ultrasonographic screening for Down syndrome in high-risk women (eg, women age 35 years and older) to avoid invasive testing should be limited to specialized centers.

▶ With an isolated choroid plexus cyst, testing is indicated only if serum screening results are abnormal or the patient will be older than 32 years at delivery.

▶ Cervical infections with chlamydia or herpes are contraindications to transcervical CVS.

▶ Counseling for amniocentesis in a twin pregnancy in women age 33 years is indicated because the midtrimester risk of fetal Down syndrome is approximately the same as for that of a singleton pregnancy at age 35 years.

▶ Nondirective counseling before genetic amniocentesis does not require a patient to commit to pregnancy termination if the result is abnormal.

References

1. Gardner RJM, Sutherland GR. Pregnancy loss and infertility. In: Chromosome abnormalities and genetic counseling. 2nd ed. New York: Oxford University Press, 1996: 311–321. Oxford Monographs on Medical Genetics No. 29 (Level III)

2. Alberman ED, Creasy MR. Frequency of chromosomal abnormalities in miscarriages and perinatal deaths. J Med Genet 1977;14:313–315 (Level III)

3. Milunsky A, Milunsky J. Genetic counseling: preconception, prenatal, and perinatal. In: Milunsky A, ed. Genetic disorders and the fetus: diagnosis, prevention, and treatment. 4th ed. Baltimore: The Johns Hopkins University Press, 1998:1–52 (Level III)

4. Ventura SJ, Martin JA, Curtin SC, Mathews TJ, Park MM. Births: final data for 1998. Natl Vital Stat Rep 2000; 48(3):1–100 (Level III)

5. Shah YG, Eckl CJ, Stinson SK, Woods JR Jr. Biparietal diameter/femur length ratio, cephalic index, and femur length measurements: not reliable screening techniques for Down syndrome. Obstet Gynecol 1990;75:186–188 (Level II-2)

6. Adams MM, Erickson JD, Layde PM, Oakley GP. Down's syndrome. Recent trends in the United States. JAMA 1981;246:758–760 (Level III)

7. Cuckle HS, Wald NJ, Lindenbaum RH. Maternal serum alpha-fetoprotein measurement: a screening test for Down syndrome. Lancet 1984;1(8383):926–929 (Level II-2)

8. Cuckle HS, Wald NJ, Thompson SG. Estimating a woman's risk of having a pregnancy associated with Down's syndrome using her age and serum alpha-fetoprotein level. Br J Obstet Gynaecol 1987;94:387–402 (Level II-2)

9. Combining maternal serum α-fetoprotein measurements and age to screen for Down syndrome in pregnant women under age 35. New England Regional Genetics Group Prenatal Collaborative Study of Down Syndrome Screening. Am J Obstet Gynecol 1989;160:575–581 (Level II-3)

10. Bogart MH, Pandian MR, Jones OW. Abnormal maternal serum chorionic gonadotropin levels in pregnancies with

fetal chromosome abnormalities. Prenat Diagn 1987;7: 623–630 (Level II-2)

11. Wald NJ, Cuckle HS, Densem JW, Nanchahal K, Canick JA, Haddow JE, et al. Maternal serum unconjugated oestriol as an antenatal screening test for Down's syndrome. Br J Obstet Gynaecol 1988;95:334–341 (Level II-2)

12. Wald NJ, Cuckle HS, Densem JW, Nanchahal K, Royston P, Chard T, et al. Maternal serum screening for Down's syndrome in early pregnancy. BMJ 1988;297:883–887 (Level II-2)

13. Haddow JE, Palomaki GE, Knight GJ, Williams J, Pulkkinen A, Canick JA, et al. Prenatal screening for Down's syndrome with use of maternal serum markers. N Engl J Med 1992;327:588–593 (Level II-3)

14. Cheng EY, Luthy DA, Zebelman AM, Williams MA, Lieppman RE, Hickok DE. A prospective evaluation of a second-trimester screening test for fetal Down syndrome using maternal serum alpha-fetoprotein, hCG, and unconjugated estriol. Obstet Gynecol 1993;81:72–77 (Level II-2)

15. Burton BK, Prins GS, Verp MS. A prospective trial of prenatal screening for Down syndrome by means of maternal serum α-fetoprotein, human chorionic gonadotropin, and unconjugated estriol. Am J Obstet Gynecol 1993;169: 526–530 (Level II-3)

16. Wenstrom KD, Williamson RA, Grant SS, Hudson JD, Getchell JP. Evaluation of multiple-marker screening for Down syndrome in a statewide population. Am J Obstet Gynecol 1993;169:793–797 (Level II-2)

17. Haddow JE, Palomaki GE, Knight GJ, Cunningham GC, Lustig LS, Boyd PA. Reducing the need for amniocentesis in women 35 years of age or older with serum markers for screening. N Engl J Med 1994;330:1114–1118 (Level II-2)

18. Canick JA, Palomaki GE, Osathanondh R. Prenatal screening for trisomy 18 in the second trimester. Prenat Diagn 1990;10:546–548 (Level III)

19. Palomaki GE, Haddow JE, Knight GJ, Wald NJ, Kennard A, Canick JA, et al. Risk-based prenatal screening for trisomy 18 using alpha-fetoprotein, unconjugated oestriol and human chorionic gonadotropin. Prenat Diagn 1995;15:713–723 (Level II-3)

20. Wald NJ, Densem JW, George L, Muttukrishna S, Knight PG. Prenatal screening for Down's syndrome using inhibin-A as a serum marker. Prenat Diagn 1996;16: 143–153 (Level II-2)

21. Wenstrom KD, Owen J, Chu DC, Boots L. Prospective evaluation of free beta-subunit of human chorionic gonadotropin and dimeric inhibin A for aneuploidy detection. Am J Obstet Gynecol 1999;181:887–892 (Level II-2)

22. Marchese CA, Carozzi F, Mosso R, Savin E, Campogrande M, Viora E, et al. Fetal karyotype in malformations detected by ultrasound [abstract]. Am J Hum Genet 1985;37:A223 (Abstract)

23. Williamson RA, Weiner CP, Patil S, Benda J, Varner MW, Abu-Yousef MM. Abnormal pregnancy sonogram: selective indication for fetal karyotype. Obstet Gynecol 1987;69:15–20 (Level III)

24. Wladimiroff JW, Sachs ES, Reuss A, Stewart PA, Pijpers L, Niermeijer MF. Prenatal diagnosis of chromosome abnormalities in the presence of fetal structural defects. Am J Med Genet 1988;29:289–291 (Level II-3)

25. Wald NJ, George L, Smith D, Densem JW, Petterson K. Serum screening for Down's syndrome between 8 and 14 weeks of pregnancy. International Prenatal Screening Research Group. Br J Obstet Gynaecol 1996;103:407–412 (Level III)

26. Haddow JE, Palomaki GE, Knight GJ, Williams J, Miller WA, Johnson A. Screening of maternal serum for fetal Down's syndrome in the first trimester. N Engl J Med 1998;338:955–961 (Level II-3)

27. Canick JA, Kellner LH, Saller DN Jr, Palomaki GE, Walker RP, Osathanondh R. Second-trimester levels of maternal urinary gonatropin peptide in Down syndrome pregnancy. Prenat Diagn 1995;15:739–744 (Level II-2)

28. Wald NJ, Kennard A, Hackshaw A, McGuire A. Antenatal screening for Down's syndrome. Health Technol Assess 1998;2:i–iv, 1–112 (Level III)

29. Pajkrt E, de Graaf IM, Mol BW, van Lith JM, Bleker OP, Bilardo CM. Weekly nuchal translucency measurements in normal fetuses. Obstet Gynecol 1998;91:208–211 (Level III)

30. Kornman LH, Morssink LP, Beekhuis JR, DeWolf BT, Heringa MP, Mantingh A. Nuchal translucency cannot be used as a screening test for chromosomal abnormalities in the first trimester of pregnancy in a routine ultrasound practice. Prenat Diagn 1996;16:797–805 (Level II-3)

31. Hafner E, Schuchter K, Leibhart E, Philipp K. Results of routine fetal nuchal translucency measurement at weeks 10–13 in 4233 unselected pregnant women. Prenat Diagn 1998;18:29–34 (Level II-3)

32. Hook EB, Cross PK, Schreinmachers DM. Chromosomal abnormality rates at amniocentesis and in live born infants. JAMA 1983;249(15):2034–2038 (Level II-3)

33. Jackson LG, Zachary JM, Fowler SE, Desnick RJ, Golbus MS, Ledbetter DH, et al. A randomized comparison of transcervical and transabdominal chorionic-villus sampling. The U.S. National Institute of Child Health and Human Development Chorionic-Villus Sampling and Amniocentesis Study Group. N Engl J Med 1992;327: 594–598 (Level I)

34. Gardner RJM, Sutherland GR. Prenatal diagnostic procedures. In: Chromosome abnormalities and genetic counseling. 2nd ed. New York: Oxford University Press, 1996:336–344. Oxford Monographs on Medical Genetics No. 29 (Level III)

35. Mennuti MT, DiGaetano A, McDonnell A, Cohen AW, Liston RM. Fetal-maternal bleeding associated with genetic amniocentesis: real-time versus static ultrasound. Obstet Gynecol 1983;62:26–30 (Level II-2)

36. Romero R, Jeanty P, Reece EA, Grannum P, Bracken M, Berkowitz R, et al. Sonographically monitored amniocen-

tesis to decrease intraoperative complications. Obstet Gynecol 1985;65:426–430 (Level II-2)

37. Leschot NJ, Verjaal M, Treffers PE. Risks of midtrimester amniocentesis; assessment in 3000 pregnancies. Br J Obstet Gynaecol 1985;92:804–807 (Level II-3)

38. Nicolaides K, Brizot M de L, Patel F, Snijders R. Comparison of chorionic villus sampling and amniocentesis for fetal karyotyping at 10–13 weeks' gestation. Lancet 1994;344:435–439 (Level II-1)

39. Johnson JM, Wilson RD, Winsor EJ, Singer J, Dansereau J, Kalousek DK. The early amniocentesis study: a randomized clinical trial of early amniocentesis versus midtrimester amniocentesis. Fetal Diagn Ther 1996;11: 85–93 (Level I)

40. Sundberg K, Bang J, Smidt-Jensen S, Brocks V, Lundsteen C, Parner J, et al. Randomised study of risk of fetal loss related to early amniocentesis versus chorionic villus sampling. Lancet 1997;350:697–703 (Level I)

41. Randomised trial to assess safety and fetal outcome of early and midtrimester amniocentesis. The Canadian Early and Mid-trimester Amniocentesis Trial (CEMAT) Group. Lancet 1998;351:242–247 (Level I)

42. Infection and chorionic villus sampling [letter]. Lancet 1985;2:609–610 (Level III)

43. Brambati B, Oldrini A, Ferrazzi E, Lanzani A. Chorionic villus sampling: an analysis of the obstetric experience of 1,000 cases. Prenat Diagn 1987;7:157–169 (Level II-3)

44. Brambati B, Lanzani A, Oldrini A. Transabdominal chorionic villus sampling. Clinical experience of 1159 cases. Prenat Diagn 1988;8:609–617 (Level III)

45. Multicentre randomised clinical trial of chorion villus sampling and amniocentesis. First report. Canadian Collaborative CVS-Amniocentesis Clinical Trial Group. Lancet 1989;1(8628):1–6 (Level I)

46. Rhoads GG, Jackson LG, Schlesselman SE, de la Cruz FF, Desnick RJ, Golbus MS, et al. The safety and efficacy of chorionic villus sampling for early prenatal diagnosis of cytogenetic abnormalities. N Engl J Med 1989;320: 609–617 (Level I)

47. Ledbetter DH, Martin AO, Verlinsky Y, Pergament E, Jackson L, Yang-Feng T, et al. Cytogenetic results of chorionic villus sampling: high success rate and diagnostic accuracy in the United States collaborative study. Am J Obstet Gynecol 1990;162:495–501 (Level II-2)

48. Medical Research Council European trial of chorion villus sampling. MRC working party on the evaluation of chorion villus sampling. Lancet 1991;337:1491–1499 (Level I)

49. Kuliev A, Jackson L, Froster U, Brambati B, Simpson JL, Verlinsky Y, et al. Chorionic villus sampling safety. Report of World Health Organization/EURO meeting in association with the Seventh International Conference on Early Prenatal Diagnosis of Genetic Diseases, Tel-Aviv, Israel, May 21, 1994. Am J Obstet Gynecol 1996;174:807–811 (Level III)

50. Holmes LB. Report of National Institute of Child Health and Human Development Workshop on Chorionic Villus Sampling and Limb and Other Defects, October 20, 1992. Teratology 1993;48:7–13 (Level III)

51. Botto LD, Olney RS, Mastroiacovo P, Khoury MJ, Moore CA, Alo CJ, et al. Chorionic villus sampling and transverse digital deficiencies: evidence for anatomic and gestational-age specificity of the digital deficiencies in two studies. Am J Med Genet 1996;62:173–178 (Level II-2)

52. Ghidini A, Sepulveda W, Lockwood CJ, Romero R. Complications of fetal blood sampling. Am J Obstet Gynecol 1993;168:1339–1344 (Level III)

53. Bromley B, Lieberman E, Laboda L, Benacerraf BR. Echogenic intracardiac focus: a sonographic sign for fetal Down syndrome. Obstet Gynecol 1995;86:998–1001 (Level II-3)

54. Petrikovsky BM, Challenger M, Wyse LJ. Natural history of echogenic foci within ventricles of fetal heart. Ultrasound Obstet Gynecol 1995;5:92–94 (Level III)

55. Vintzileos AM, Egan JF. Adjusting the risk for trisomy 21 on the basis of second-trimester ultrasonography. Am J Obstet Gynecol 1995;172:837–844 (Level II-3)

56. Bahado-Sing RO, Deren O, Tan A, D'Ancona RL, Hunter D, Copel JA, et al. Ultrasonographically adjusted midtrimester risk of trisomy 21 and significant chromosomal defects in advanced maternal age. Am J Obstet Gynecol 1996;175:1563–1568 (Level II-3)

57. Nyberg DA, Luthy DA, Cheng EY, Sheley RC, Resta RG, Williams MA. Role of prenatal ultrasonography in women with positive screen for Down syndrome on the basis of maternal serum markers. Am J Obstet Gynecol 1995;173: 1030–1035 (Level II-3)

58. Sohl BD, Scioscia AL, Budorick NE, Moore TR. Utility of minor ultrasonographic markers in the prediction of abnormal fetal karyotype at a prenatal diagnostic center. Am J Obstet Gynecol 1999;181:898–903 (Level II-3)

59. Vintzileos AM, Guzman ER, Smulian JC, Day-Salvatore DL, Knuppel RA. Indication-specific accuracy of second-trimester genetic ultrasonography for the detection of trisomy 21. Am J Obstet Gynecol 1999;181(5 Pt 1): 1045–1048 (Level II-3)

60. Bromley B, Lieberman E, Benacerraf BR. The incorporation of maternal age into the sonographic scoring index for the detection at 14–20 weeks of fetuses with Down's syndrome. Ultrasound Obstet Gynecol 1997;10:321–324 (Level II-2)

61. Bromley B, Shipp T, Benacerraf BR. Genetic sonogram scoring index: accuracy and clinical utility. J Ultrasound Med 1999;18:523–528; quiz 529–530 [erratum J Ultrasound Med 1999;18:594] (Level II-3)

62. Landwehr JB Jr, Johnson MP, Hume RF, Yaron Y, Sokol RJ, Evans MI. Abnormal nuchal findings on screening ultrasonography: aneuploidy stratification on the basis of ultrasonographic anomaly and gestational age at detection. Am J Obstet Gynecol 1996;175:995–999 (Level II-3)

63. Bahado-Singh R, Oz U, Kovanci E, Cermik D, Copel J, Mahoney MJ, et al. A high-sensitivity alternative to "routine" genetic amniocentesis: multiple urinary analytes, nuchal thickness, and age. Am J Obstet Gynecol 1999; 180(1 Pt 1):169–173 (Level II-3)

64. Gross SJ, Shulman LP, Tolley EA, Emerson DS, Felker RE, Simpson JL, et al. Isolated fetal choroid plexus cysts

and trisomy 18: a review and meta-analysis. Am J Obstet Gynecol 1995;172:83–87 (Meta-analysis)

65. Gupta JK, Khan KS, Thornton JG, Lilford RJ. Management of fetal choroid plexus cysts. Br J Obstet Gynaecol 1997;104:881–886 (Level III)

66. Brown T, Kliewer MA, Hertzberg BS, Ruiz C, Stamper TH, Rosnes J, et al. A role for maternal serum screening in detecting chromosomal abnormalities in fetuses with isolated choroid plexus cysts: a prospective multicentre study. Prenat Diagn 1999;19:405–410 (Level II-2)

67. Sullivan A, Giudice T, Vavelidis F, Thiagarajah S. Choroid plexus cysts: Is biochemical testing a valuable adjunct to targeted ultrasonography? Am J Obstet Gynecol 1999;181: 260–265 (Level II-2)

68. Wenstrom KD, Desai R, Owen J, DuBard MB, Boots L. Comparison of multiple-marker screening with amniocentesis for detection of fetal aneuploidy in women equal to or greater than 35. Am J Obstet Gynecol 1995;173: 1287–1292 (Level II-2)

69. Jenkins TM, Wapner RJ. The challenge of prenatal diagnosis in twin pregnancies. Curr Opin Obstet Gynecol 2000;12:87–92 (Level III)

70. Meyers C, Adam R, Dungan J, Prenger V. Aneuploidy in twin gestations: when is maternal age advanced? Obstet Gynecol 1997;89:248–251 (Level II-3)

71. Rodis JF, Egan JF, Craffey A, Ciarleglio L, Greenstein RM, Scorza WE. Calculated risk of chromosomal abnormalities in twin gestations. Obstet Gynecol 1990;76: 1037–1041 (Level III)

72. Librach CL, Doran TA, Benzie RJ, Jones JM. Genetic amniocentesis in seventy twin pregnancies. Am J Obstet Gynecol 1984;148:585–591 (Level II-3)

73. Wapner RJ, Johnson A, Davis G, Urban A, Morgan P, Jackson L. Prenatal diagnosis in twin gestations: a comparison between second-trimester amniocentesis and first-trimester chorionic villus sampling. Obstet Gynecol 1993;82:49–56 (Level II-2)

74. De Catte L, Liebaers I, Foulon W, Bonduelle M, Van Assche E. First trimester chorionic villus sampling in twin gestations. Am J Perinatol 1996;13:413–417 (Level II-2)

75. van den Berg C, Braat AP, Van Opstal D, Halley DJ, Kleijer WJ, den Hollander NS, et al. Amniocentesis or chorionic villus sampling in multiple gestations? Experience with 500 cases. Prenat Diagn 1999;19: 234–244 (Level II-3)

76. Clark SL, DeVore GR. Prenatal diagnosis for couples who would not consider abortion. Obstet Gynecol 1989;73: 1035–1037 (Level III)

The MEDLINE database, the Cochrane Library, and ACOG's own internal resources and documents were used to conduct a literature search to locate relevant articles published between January 1985 and April 2000. The search was restricted to articles published in the English language. Priority was given to articles reporting results of original research, although review articles and commentaries also were consulted. Abstracts of research presented at symposia and scientific conferences were not considered adequate for inclusion in this document. Guidelines published by organizations or institutions such as the National Institutes of Health and the American College of Obstetricians and Gynecologists were reviewed, and additional studies were located by reviewing bibliographies of identified articles. When reliable research was not available, expert opinions from obstetrician–gynecologists were used.

Studies were reviewed and evaluated for quality according to the method outlined by the U.S. Preventive Services Task Force:

I   Evidence obtained from at least one properly designed randomized controlled trial.

II-1 Evidence obtained from well-designed controlled trials without randomization.

II-2 Evidence obtained from well-designed cohort or case–control analytic studies, preferably from more than one center or research group.

II-3 Evidence obtained from multiple time series with or without the intervention. Dramatic results in uncontrolled experiments also could be regarded as this type of evidence.

III   Opinions of respected authorities, based on clinical experience, descriptive studies, or reports of expert committees.

Based on the highest level of evidence found in the data, recommendations are provided and graded according to the following categories:

Level A—Recommendations are based on good and consistent scientific evidence.

Level B—Recommendations are based on limited or inconsistent scientific evidence.

Level C—Recommendations are based primarily on consensus and expert opinion.

ISSN 1099-3630

**The American College of
Obstetricians and Gynecologists
409 12th Street, SW
PO Box 96920
Washington, DC 20090-6920**

12345/54321

ACOG PRACTICE BULLETIN

CLINICAL MANAGEMENT GUIDELINES FOR
OBSTETRICIAN–GYNECOLOGISTS
NUMBER 21, OCTOBER 2000

This Practice Bulletin was developed by the ACOG Committee on Practice Bulletins—Gynecology with the assistance of Linda A. Barbour, MD and Kathryn L. Hassell, MD. The information is designed to aid practitioners in making decisions about appropriate obstetric and gynecologic care. These guidelines should not be construed as dictating an exclusive course of treatment or procedure. Variations in practice may be warranted based on the needs of the individual patient, resources, and limitations unique to the institution or type of practice.

Prevention of Deep Vein Thrombosis and Pulmonary Embolism

In the United States, venous thromboembolism remains a leading cause of death and morbidity among hospitalized patients. Overall, approximately 60,000 deaths per year are attributed to venous thromboembolism and the subsequent complications, including postthrombotic syndrome, venous insufficiency, pulmonary hypertension, and pulmonary dysfunction (1). Venous thromboembolism often has no symptoms, and pulmonary embolism is not suspected clinically in 70–80% of patients in whom it is detected postmortem. Most patients who die from pulmonary embolism do so within 30 minutes of the event, reinforcing the need for rapid and accurate diagnosis. Fatal pulmonary embolism is a common preventable cause of death in hospitalized patients. Venous thromboembolism also predisposes patients to long-term morbidity from postthrombotic syndrome. The purpose of this document is to review the current literature on the prevention of thromboembolism in gynecologic patients, discuss the rationale behind sometimes conflicting guidelines, and offer evidence-based recommendations to address the most clinically relevant issues in the management of these patients.

Background

Detection of Deep Vein Thrombosis

Detection of deep vein thrombosis (DVT) is difficult, especially when patients are asymptomatic. Thus, the occurrence of venous thromboembolism in surgical patients varies from one study to another. Most trials examining the efficacy of DVT prophylaxis in general surgical and gynecologic patients have used the fibrinogen I-125 uptake test to diagnose DVT. This technique is sensitive for detecting DVT only distally (calf) and is poor at detecting DVT in the upper thigh (2, 3). Because of concerns about the transmission of blood-borne diseases, the fibrinogen I-125 uptake test is no longer commercially available in the United States or in many European countries. Equally inhibiting is the limited sensitivity and predictive value of duplex compression ultrasonography and impedance plethysmography to detect asymptomatic proximal vein thrombosis (4–8). Compression ultrasound examination of the femoral and popliteal veins and calf trifurcation has been found to be a highly sensitive (>90%) and specific (>99%) method of detecting proximal vein DVT, but less reliable (50%) for detecting calf vein DVT (6, 8).

Diagnosis of pelvic vein thrombosis and internal iliac thrombosis is exceedingly difficult even with magnetic resonance imaging, which is considered the imaging modality of choice (9). Fatal pulmonary emboli have been reported at postmortem examination to be from internal iliac or pelvic veins, for which there is no highly sensitive diagnostic imaging technique. Because diagnosis is difficult, perioperative prophylaxis has become the mainstay of management.

Prophylaxis in Gynecologic Surgery

The prevalence of venous thromboembolism after surgery varies and depends on multiple risk factors. Most events occur within 7 days postoperatively in gynecologic surgical patients; however, patients continue to be at risk for the first 3 weeks after discharge, probably secondary to decreased ambulation. Patients undergoing surgery for cancer or orthopedic surgery are at the highest risk for later complications from venous thromboembolism; the risk of pulmonary embolism continues for 30 days after surgery (10). Postoperative venous thromboembolism, as diagnosed by the fibrinogen I-125 uptake test, ranges from 7% to 29% in general gynecologic surgery and up to 45% in patients with malignant disease (11–13). Pulmonary embolism occurs in 0.1–5% of cases depending on the level of risk. Unfortunately, pulmonary embolism occurs without clinical evidence of DVT in 50–80% of cases and is fatal in approximately 10–20% of cases (14).

In a univariate analysis of all characteristics identified to be statistically significantly related to venous thromboembolism, significant variables included recurrent malignant disease, a prior history of DVT, duration of anesthesia greater than 5 hours, prior pelvic radiation, venous stasis changes or venous varicosities, and age older than 45 years (11). The same analysis concluded that the type of surgery, specifically radical vulvectomy

with inguinal lymphadenopathy or pelvic exenteration (ie, surgeries that result in extensive periods of immobilization), was a significant variable in determining risk.

Hypercoagulable States

It is now estimated that nearly half of patients with thrombosis have an identifiable thrombotic disorder (15, 16) as a result of the discovery of the factor V Leiden mutation (resistance to activated protein C) and the prothrombin gene mutation G20210A. The most commonly identified hypercoagulable states are listed in Table 1. It has been observed that approximately 50–60% of patients with a hereditary form of thrombosis will not experience a thrombotic event until an environmental risk factor such as oral contraceptive use, pregnancy, orthopedic trauma, immobilization, or surgery is present (17, 18). Currently, the coexistence of multiple inherited risk factors has been acknowledged, which markedly increases the risk of thrombosis (16). Antiphospholipid antibody syndrome is an acquired hypercoagulable state that often manifests as venous or arterial thrombosis, thrombocytopenia, recurrent fetal loss, intrauterine growth restriction, or early preeclampsia (19, 20). Hyperhomocystinemia may be acquired or inherited and is associated with an increased risk of venous thromboembolism and early atherosclerotic disease with arterial thrombosis.

Preoperative patients should be classified according to levels of risk of thrombosis to determine the benefits and risks of pharmacologic and physical methods of preventing venous thromboembolism. Table 2 summarizes the classification of risk level based on published data.

Prophylaxis Alternatives

Graduated Compression Stockings

The use of graduated compression stockings, which reduce stasis, is by far the simplest of the prophylactic approaches and has the advantages of being inexpensive, easy to use, and free of side effects if properly fitted (21). Graduated compression stockings reduce the prevalence of DVT (especially calf) in medium-risk patients when compared with placebo according to a meta-analysis of all randomized controlled trials (21), including one study of gynecologic surgery (22). However, patients with malignant disease and other high-risk conditions have not been evaluated in sufficient numbers to reach conclusions about the use of graduated compression stockings in these settings (23).

Pneumatic Compression

If used at induction of anesthesia and continued until patients are fully ambulatory, pneumatic compression

Table 1. Common Hypercoagulable States

Abnormality	Prevalence in Patients with Thrombosis	Testing Methods	Can patients be tested during pregnancy?	Is the test reliable during acute thrombosis?	Is the test reliable while on anti-coagulation?
Factor V Leiden	40–70%*	APC resistance assay	No	Yes	Yes
		DNA analysis	Yes	Yes	Yes
Prothrombin gene mutation G20210A	8–30%[†]	DNA analysis	Yes	Yes	Yes
Antiphospholipid antibody	10–15%[‡]	Functional assay (eg, dilute Russell viper venom time)	Yes	Yes	Yes
		Anticardiolipin antibodies	Yes	Yes	Yes
		β_2-Glycoprotein-1 antibodies	Yes	Yes	Yes
Protein C deficiency	—	Protein C activity	Yes	No	No
Protein S deficiency	10–15%[§]	Protein S total and free antigen	Yes	No	No
AT-III deficiency	—	AT-III activity	Yes	No	No
Hyperhomocystinemia	8–25%	Fasting plasma homocystine	Yes	Unclear	Yes

* Bokarewa MI, Bremme K, Blombäck M. Arg[506]-Gln mutation in factor V and risk of thrombosis during pregnancy. Br J Haematol 1996;92:473–478; Hellgren M, Svensson PJ, Dahlbäck B. Resistance to activated protein C as a basis for venous thromboembolism associated with pregnancy and oral contraceptives. Am J Obstet Gynecol 1995;173:210–213; Faioni EM, Razzari C, Martinelli I, Panzeri D, Franchi F, Mannucci PM. Resistance to activated protein C in unselected patients with arterial and venous thrombosis. Am J Hematol 1997;55:59–64

[†] Grandone E, Margaglione M, Colaizzo D, D'Andrea G, Cappucci G, Brancaccio V, et al. Genetic susceptibility to pregnancy-related venous thromboembolism: roles of factor V Leiden, prothrombin G20210A, and methylenetetrahydrofolate reductase C677T mutations. Am J Obstet Gynecol 1998;179:1324–1328; Martinelli I, Taioli E, Bucciarelli P, Akhavan S, Mannucci PM. Interaction between the G20210A mutation of the prothrombin gene and oral contraceptive use in deep vein thrombosis. Arterioscler Thromb Vasc Biol 1999;19:700–703; Salomon O, Steinberg DM, Zivelin A, Gitel S, Dardik R, Rosenberg N, et al. Single and combined prothrombotic factors in patients with idiopathic venous thromboembolism: prevalence and risk assessment. Arterioscler Thromb Vasc Biol 1999;19:511–518

[‡] Ginsberg JS, Wells PS, Brill-Edwards P, Donovan D, Moffat K, Johnston M, et al. Antiphospholipid antibodies and venous thromboembolism. Blood 1995;86:3685–3691

[§] Aiach M, Borgel D, Gaussem P, Emmerich J, Alhenc-Gelas M, Gandrille S. Protein C and protein S deficiencies. Semin Hematol 1997;34:205–216; De Stefano V, Leone G, Mastrangelo S, Tripodi A, Rodeghiero F, Castaman G, et al. Clinical manifestations and management of inherited thrombophilia: retrospective analysis and follow-up after diagnosis of 238 patients with congenital deficiency of antithrombin III, protein C, protein S. Thromb Haemost 1994;72:352–358; Pabinger I, Schneider B. Thrombotic risk in hereditary antithrombin III, protein C, or protein S deficiency. A cooperative, retrospective study. Gesellschaft fur Thrombose- und Hamostaseforschung (GTH) Study Group on Natural Inhibitors. Arterioscler Thromb Vasc Biol 1996;16:742–748

appears to be effective in reducing DVT in medium-risk and high-risk patients (21, 23–25). Pneumatic compression may be useful in reducing leg DVT in high-risk patients with malignant disease; however, its efficacy in preventing pulmonary embolism is unknown because of limited sample sizes (26). Patient compliance is essential for the effectiveness of pneumatic compression.

Low-Dose Heparin

Low-dose unfractionated heparin has been shown to be effective as prophylaxis for DVT and pulmonary embolism in moderate-risk patients without underlying malignancy or other clinical risk factors. A review of ran-

domized trials published before 1988, which included gynecologic patients, showed that low-dose heparin decreased DVT by nearly 70% and pulmonary embolism by 40–50% (27). Unfractionated heparin, 5,000 U administered every 8 hours postoperatively, does appear to be effective prophylaxis for DVT in patients undergoing gynecologic oncologic surgery, as demonstrated in a randomized unblinded trial (28). Although the efficacy in reducing postoperative venous thrombosis was similar between low-dose heparin and intermittent pneumatic calf compression, patients receiving low-dose heparin required significantly more postoperative transfusions (25). In a randomized, multicenter, double-blinded trial

Table 2. Classification of Risk Levels for Venous Thromboembolism Among Gynecologic Surgery Patients

Classification	Definition
Low risk (<3% risk of DVT*)	Age ≤40 y and Surgery lasting <30 min
Moderate risk (10–40% risk of DVT)	Age >40 y and Surgery of any duration No other clinical risk factors
High risk (40–70% risk of DVT; 1–5% risk of pulmonary embolism)	Age >40 y plus risk factors: • Prior DVT or pulmonary embolism • Varicose veins • Infection • Malignancy • Estrogen therapy • Obesity • Prolonged surgery

*DVT indicates deep vein thrombosis.

Data from NIH Consensus Conference. Prevention of venous thrombosis and pulmonary embolism. JAMA 1986;256:744–749

of 631 patients with evaluable venograms who were undergoing abdominal or pelvic surgery for cancer, low-dose heparin, 5,000 U every 8 hours, was as good as low-molecular-weight heparin (LMWH) (enoxaparin, 40 mg once a day) in the prevention of DVT (29). A trial of patients undergoing gynecologic surgery, in which 84% of the patients had underlying malignancy, used two different preoperative regimens of unfractionated heparin and compared them with no perioperative prophylaxis. The findings of this study suggest that two to nine doses of heparin preoperatively were not statistically better in preventing DVT than only one preoperative dose of 5,000 U administered 2 hours before the surgery (28). Both regimens used heparin every 8 hours postoperatively until discharge.

Low-Molecular-Weight Heparin

Low-molecular-weight heparin has been used in numerous trials for prophylaxis in abdominal surgery with at least the same efficacy as unfractionated heparin in preventing DVT. This finding has been substantiated in a meta-analysis of 36 double-blinded randomized controlled trials, 25 of which were in the general surgery population (30, 31). Some data suggest there is a lower bleeding risk with LMWH compared with unfractionated heparin (30). Once-daily administration and a lower rate of heparin-induced thrombocytopenia are additional advantages of LMWH over unfractionated heparin (23). A randomized, double-blinded multicenter trial that used

the fibrinogen I-125 uptake test compared two different doses of dalteparin (2,500 antifactor-Xa U versus 5,000 antifactor-Xa U) in the general surgery population in which 66% of patients had malignant disease (32). It found the efficacy overall was better in the high-dose LMWH group than in the low-dose LMWH group (6.6% DVT and 12.7% DVT, respectively) in preventing DVT, but bleeding complications were higher in the high-dose group (4.7% versus 2.7%). However, in the subgroup with malignant disease, efficacy remained better in the high-dose group than the low-dose group (8.5% DVT versus 14.9% DVT) but bleeding complications were no different (4.6% versus 3.6%). In a randomized study of 80 patients undergoing pelvic or abdominal surgery for malignancy that used the fibrinogen I-125 uptake test, dalteparin (5,000 antifactor-Xa U) was equally effective as unfractionated heparin, 5,000 U administered every 8 hours. Seventy-five percent of the patients had gynecologic cancers, and there was no difference in blood loss between the groups (33).

Anesthesia Concerns

The use of major conduction anesthesia (spinal or epidural) in patients receiving heparin or LMWH thromboembolic prophylaxis is controversial (34). Intraoperative or postoperative anticoagulation after regional anesthesia is thought to be safe; however, the safety of LMWH, unfractionated heparin, or oral anticoagulants administered before the procedure is unclear. In a retrospective review of 61 reported cases of spinal hematoma associated with epidural or spinal anesthesia, 42 (61%) were associated with a hemostatic abnormality (35). At least 25 patients received heparin intravenously or subcutaneously, and in 15 of 32 patients with indwelling catheters, the spinal hematomas occurred immediately after the removal of the epidural catheter. Unfractionated low-dose heparin appeared not to pose a significant risk for spinal hematoma in over 5,000 patients who received it in combination with a single-dose spinal or epidural anesthesia, nor did antiplatelet prophylaxis (36). Low-molecular-weight heparin, however, may pose a risk if it is used preoperatively, intraoperatively, or within 3 hours postoperatively in patients receiving continuous epidural analgesia. In 1997, the U.S. Food and Drug Administration issued a public health advisory regarding reported cases of epidural or spinal hematomas with concurrent use of enoxaparin and spinal or epidural anesthesia or spinal puncture (37). Many of the epidural or spinal hematomas caused neurologic injury, including long-term or permanent paralysis, and approximately 75% of the patients were elderly women undergoing orthopedic surgery.

Clinical Considerations and Recommendations

▶ *Who are candidates for perioperative DVT thromboprophylaxis?*

Candidates for surgical prophylaxis include patients who are found to have deficiencies of protein C, protein S, or antithrombin III (AT-III), who have the factor V Leiden or prothrombin gene mutation G20210A without a personal history of thrombosis, or who experience orthopedic trauma (15, 18, 38–40), especially if they have a strong family history of thrombosis.

In addition, Table 2 outlines a risk stratification adopted from the 1986 National Institutes of Health Consensus Conference (41). Most of the evidence for determining risk status was obtained from the control arms of more than 100 trials conducted primarily among patients older than 40 years who were undergoing general surgery.

▶ *Which prophylactic methods should be considered for low-, medium-, and high-risk patients undergoing gynecologic surgery?*

Patients in the low-risk category (as defined in Table 2) who are undergoing gynecologic surgery probably do not need any thromboprophylactic agent as long as they are quickly mobilized.

Patients in the moderate-risk category would likely benefit from prophylaxis with either graduated compression stockings, pneumatic compression, low-dose unfractionated heparin (5,000 U every 8 hours) in which the first dose is given before surgery, or low-dose LMWH (dalteparin, 2,500 U once a day, or enoxaparin, 40 mg once a day). However, the need for prophylaxis should include consideration of the length and complexity of surgery, the patient's age, and the evaluation of other risk factors. In the United States, dalteparin and enoxaparin are considerably more expensive alternatives to standard heparin and have not been shown to be significantly more efficacious or associated with less bleeding risks in comparison with low-dose unfractionated heparin in moderate-risk patients. Prophylaxis with thigh-high graduated compression stockings has not been as extensively studied for moderate-risk patients compared with standard heparin.

High-risk patients should be offered standard heparin, 5,000 U every 8 hours (28). A more expensive alternative for high-risk patients is LMWH given as either dalteparin, 5,000 antifactor-Xa U once a day, or enoxa-parin, 40 mg once a day (the first dose given the evening before surgery). However, it is not clear that the latter approach offers any advantage or is significantly more efficacious (29, 32). Pneumatic compression appears to be as effective (23) but has not been as well studied as heparin and LMWH.

Adding graduated compression stockings or pneumatic compression to anticoagulant therapy may be a good alternative for high-risk patients, especially those undergoing radical vulvectomy with inguinal lymphadenectomy or pelvic exenteration for malignancy (23, 25), although no clinical trials have confirmed this approach.

▶ *Should patients discontinue oral contraceptives or hormone replacement therapy before surgery?*

There are no studies to confirm the clinical benefit of stopping oral contraceptives preoperatively (42). The hypercoagulable changes induced by oral contraceptives do not return to normal for 4–6 weeks after discontinuation of therapy (43). The risk of postoperative thromboembolism has been reported to be 0.96% for oral contraceptive users and 0.5% for nonusers (44). However, the risk of stopping oral contraceptives 4–6 weeks before major surgery must be balanced against the risks of pregnancy (which carries a much higher risk of DVT and pulmonary embolism than does oral contraceptive use), the effects of surgery and anesthesia on pregnancy, and the possibility of subsequent termination of pregnancy with its associated physical and psychologic risks.

Discontinuation of hormone replacement therapy (HRT) before major gynecologic surgery to prevent deep vein thrombosis or pulmonary embolism has not been evaluated in randomized clinical trials. However, three retrospective case-control studies have evaluated the risk of hospital admission for deep vein thrombosis in HRT users (45–47). These studies reported that the current users of HRT had an increased risk of VTE (odds ratio 2.1 to 3.6) when compared with matched HRT nonusers, and that past use did not affect this risk. However, the absolute risk for both users and nonusers of HRT was low. One analysis of nearly 350,000 women aged 50–79 years reported that of these, 292 women were admitted to the hospital with DVT or pulmonary embolism, which represents only a modest increase in morbidity (risk of 1.3 per 10,000 per year for nonusers; risk of less than 2 additional cases per 10,000 women per year in HRT users) (47). For women with other risk factors who are undergoing gynecologic surgery, the benefit of stopping HRT has not yet been established.

▶ *Which patients should be tested for clotting abnormalities, and which tests should be ordered?*

Because of its high prevalence in the Caucasian population, all patients who are not Hispanic, Asian, or African American who have a history of DVT may be tested for the factor V Leiden mutation (16, 48–54). In non-Caucasian patients, the decision to test should be individualized. Patients with histories of extensive or recurrent thrombosis or family histories of thrombosis may have the factor V Leiden mutation in combination with another congenital or acquired disorder (55). Patients with a strong family history of thrombosis who are negative for the factor V Leiden mutation may benefit from testing for the prothrombin gene mutation G20210A and deficiencies in the natural inhibitors, including protein C, protein S, and AT-III. Patients with a history of thrombosis, recurrent fetal loss, early or severe preeclampsia, severe unexplained intrauterine growth restriction, or unexplained thrombocytopenia may be tested for antiphospholipid antibodies. Fasting plasma homocystine levels may be assessed, especially in women of childbearing age who have had venous or arterial thrombosis, because elevated levels can be treated with vitamins (folic acid, vitamin B_{12}, and vitamin B_6). The specific tests and optimal timing for testing are described in Table 1.

▶ *Should women on prolonged heparin be evaluated for heparin-induced osteoporosis or heparin-induced thrombocytopenia?*

Heparin-induced osteoporosis appears to occur predominantly in patients taking heparin for 7 weeks or longer (56, 57) and is not an issue for those taking prophylactic or short-term doses.

Heparin-induced thrombocytopenia is uncommon with the use of porcine heparin (1–3%) and is less common with LMWH (<1%), but immune-related thrombocytopenia can have severe thrombotic consequences (58). Platelet counts should be monitored at the initiation of standard heparin therapy and periodically up to 15 days after starting heparin (59). If the platelet count is unchanged at that time, further platelet counts are not needed because the vast majority of immune, heparin-induced thrombocytopenia occurs within 15 days of starting standard heparin therapy. If confirmed, heparin therapy should be stopped immediately. A low-molecular-weight heparinoid (danaparoid sodium) is available in the United States and was shown to be efficacious in

93% of 88 patients with heparin-induced thrombocytopenia and thrombosis not related to pregnancy (60). Lepirudin (recombinant hirudin), a direct thrombin inhibitor, also is available for intravenous use in patients with heparin-induced thrombocytopenia (59).

▶ *What special considerations should be given when using low-molecular-weight heparin in patients undergoing regional anesthesia?*

Low-molecular-weight heparin has a longer half-life than standard heparin, and its anticoagulant activity cannot be measured using an activated partial thromboplastin time. If used in low doses as a once-a-day regimen, at least 12 hours should lapse after administration before offering central neural blockade. No regional anesthesia should be employed within 12 hours of an injection of LMWH, and LMWH should be withheld for at least 2 hours after removal of an epidural catheter (35, 36, 61). The safety of a twice-daily dose of LMWH in patients receiving epidural anesthesia has not been studied sufficiently, and it is not known whether 24 hours is an adequate amount of time to wait after the last injection. In institutions in which an antifactor-Xa level can be obtained in a timely manner, it may be reasonable to offer spinal or epidural anesthesia as long as the antifactor-Xa levels are not above the prophylactic range. However, the safety of this practice has not been evaluated prospectively.

▶ *Which prophylactic methods are considered cost-effective?*

It is estimated that half of patients with proximal DVT and one third of patients with distal DVT develop a postthrombotic syndrome characterized by pain, swelling, and occasional ulceration of the skin and legs (62). Prophylaxis with either graduated compression stockings, pneumatic compression, low-dose standard heparin, or LMWH is less expensive than no prophylaxis in patients undergoing general abdominal surgery (63, 64). Routine surveillance is the most expensive strategy because of the lack of sensitivity of noninvasive tests to diagnose DVT (63). Although a cost analysis in Europe determined LMWH to be more cost-effective than unfractionated heparin (63), LMWH is substantially more expensive in the United States than in Europe. A cost-analysis in the United States determined that pneumatic compression was more cost-effective than either LMWH or unfractionated heparin (65).

Summary

The following recommendations are based on good and consistent scientific evidence (Level A):

▶ Alternatives for thromboprophylaxis for moderate-risk patients undergoing gynecologic surgery include the following:

1. Thigh-high graduated compression stockings placed intraoperatively and continued until the patient is fully ambulatory

2. Pneumatic compression placed intraoperatively and continued until the patient is fully ambulatory

3. Unfractionated heparin (5,000 U) administered 2 hours before surgery and continued postoperatively every 8 hours until discharge

4. Low-molecular-weight heparin (dalteparin, 2,500 antifactor-Xa U, or enoxaparin, 40 mg) administered 12 hours before surgery and once a day postoperatively until discharge

▶ Alternatives for prophylaxis for high-risk patients undergoing gynecologic surgery, especially for malignancy, include:

1. Pneumatic compression placed intraoperatively and continued until the patient is fully ambulatory

2. Unfractionated heparin (5,000 U) administered 8 hours before surgery and continued postoperatively until discharge

3. Dalteparin (5,000 antifactor-Xa U) administered 12 hours before surgery and then once a day thereafter

4. Enoxaparin (40 mg) administered 12 hours before surgery and then once a day thereafter

The following recommendations are based primarily on consensus and expert opinion (Level C):

▶ Low-risk patients who are undergoing gynecologic surgery do not require specific prophylaxis other than early ambulation.

▶ Postoperative prophylaxis should be continued for 7 days or until discharge.

References

1. Hirsh J, Hoak J. Management of deep vein thrombosis and pulmonary embolism. A statement for healthcare professionals. Council on Thrombosis (in consultation with the Council on Cardiovascular Radiology), American Heart Association. Circulation 1996;93:2212–2245 (Level III)

2. Lensing AW, Hirsh J. 125I-fibrinogen leg scanning: reassessment of its role for the diagnosis of venous thrombosis in post-operative patients. Thromb Haemost 1993;69:2–7 (Level III)

3. Weinmann EE, Salzman EW. Deep vein thrombosis. N Engl J Med 1994;331:1630–1641 (Level III)

4. Agnelli G, Cosmi B, Ranucci V, Renga C, Mosca S, Lupattelli L, et al. Impedance plethysmography in the diagnosis of asymptomatic deep vein thrombosis in hip surgery. A venography-controlled study. Arch Intern Med 1991;151:2167–2171 (Level II-2)

5. Borris LC, Christiansen HM, Lassen MR, Olsen AD, Schøtt P. Comparison of real-time B-mode ultrasonography and bilateral ascending phlebography for detection of postoperative deep vein thrombosis following elective hip surgery. The Venous Thrombosis Group. Thromb Haemost 1989;61:363–365 (Level II-2)

6. Jongbloets LM, Lensing AW, Koopman MM, Büller HR, ten Cate JW. Limitations of compression ultrasound for the detection of symptomless postoperative deep vein thrombosis. Lancet 1994;343:1142–1144 (Level II-2)

7. Lensing AW, Doris CI, McGrath FP, Cogo A, Sabine MJ, Ginsberg J, et al. A comparison of compression ultrasound with color Doppler ultrasound for the diagnosis of symptomless postoperative deep vein thrombosis. Arch Intern Med 1997;157:765–768 (Level II-2)

8. Wells PS, Lensing AW, Davidson BL, Prins MH, Hirsh J. Accuracy of ultrasound for the diagnosis of deep venous thrombosis in asymptomatic patients after orthopedic surgery. A meta-analysis. Ann Intern Med 1995;122:47–53 (Meta-analysis)

9. Spritzer CE, Evans AC, Kay HH. Magnetic resonance imaging of deep venous thrombosis in pregnant women with lower extremity edema. Obstet Gynecol 1995; 85:603–607 (Level III)

10. Bergqvist D. Prolonged prophylaxis against postoperative venous thromboembolism. Haemostasis 1996;26(suppl 4):379–387 (Level III)

11. Clarke-Pearson DL, DeLong ER, Synan IS, Coleman RE, Creasman WT. Variables associated with postoperative deep venous thrombosis: a prospective study of 411 gynecology patients and creation of a prognostic model. Obstet Gynecol 1987;69:146–150 (Level III)

12. Clarke-Pearson DL, Jelovsek FR, Creasman WT. Thromboembolism complicating surgery for cervical and uterine malignancy: incidence, risk factors, and prophylaxis. Obstet Gynecol 1983;61:87–94 (Level II-2)

13. Crandon AJ, Koutts J. Incidence of post-operative deep vein thrombosis in gynaecological oncology. Aust NZ J Obstet Gynaecol 1983;23:216–219 (Level III)

14. Farquharson DI, Orr JW Jr. Prophylaxis against thromboembolism in gynecologic patients. J Reprod Med 1984;29:845–862 (Level III)

15. Bauer KA. Management of patients with hereditary defects predisposing to thrombosis including pregnant women. Thromb Haemost 1995;74:94–100 (Level III)

16. Florell SR, Rodgers GM. Inherited thrombotic disorders: an update. Am J Hematol 1997;54:53–60 (Level III)

17. De Stefano V, Leone G, Mastrangelo S, Tripodi A, Rodeghiero F, Castaman G, et al. Clinical manifestations and management of inherited thrombophilia: retrospective analysis and follow-up after diagnosis of 238 patients with congenital deficiency of antithrombin III, protein C, protein S. Thromb Haemost 1994;72:352–358 (Level III)

18. Middledorp S, Henkens CM, Koopman MM, van Pampus EC, Hamulyák K, van der Meer J, et al. The incidence of venous thromboembolism in family members of patients with factor V Leiden mutation and venous thrombosis. Ann Intern Med 1998;128:15–20 (Level II-2)

19. Petri M. Pathogenesis and treatment of the antiphospholipid antibody syndrome. Med Clin North Am 1997; 81:151–177 (Level III)

20. Shapiro GA. Antiphospholipid syndrome in obstetrics and gynecology. Semin Thromb Hemost 1994;20:64–70 (Level III)

21. Wells PS, Lensing AW, Hirsh J. Graduated compression stockings in the prevention of postoperative venous thromboembolism. A meta-analysis. Arch Intern Med 1994; 154:67–72 (Meta-analysis)

22. Turner GM, Cole SE, Brooks JH. The efficacy of graduated compression stockings in the prevention of deep vein thrombosis after major gynaecological surgery. Br J Obstet Gynaecol 1984;91:588–591 (Level I)

23. Clagett GP, Anderson FA Jr, Heit J, Levine MN, Wheeler HB. Prevention of venous thromboembolism. Chest 1995;108 (suppl 4):312S–334S (Level III)

24. Clarke-Pearson DL, Synan IS, Hinshaw WM, Coleman RE, Creasman WT. Prevention of postoperative venous thromboembolism by external pneumatic calf compression in patients with gynecologic malignancy. Obstet Gynecol 1984;63:92–98 (Level I)

25. Clarke-Pearson DL, Synan IS, Dodge R, Soper JT, Berchuck A, Coleman RE. A randomized trial of low-dose heparin and intermittent pneumatic calf compression for the prevention of deep venous thrombosis after gynecologic oncology surgery. Am J Obstet Gynecol 1993; 168:1146–1153; discussion 1153–1154 (Level I)

26. Clagett GP, Reisch JS. Prevention of venous thromboembolism in general surgical patients. Results of meta-analysis. Ann Surg 1988;208:227–240 (Meta-analysis)

27. Collins R, Scrimgeour A, Yusuf S, Peto R. Reduction in fatal pulmonary embolism and venous thrombosis by perioperative administration of subcutaneous heparin. Overview of results of randomized trials in general orthopedic and urologic surgery. N Engl J Med 1988;318: 1162–1173 (Level III)

28. Clarke-Pearson DL, DeLong E, Synan IS, Soper JT, Creasman WT, Coleman RE. A controlled trial of two low-dose-heparin regimens for the prevention of postoperative deep vein thrombosis. Obstet Gynecol 1990;75:684–689 (Level I)

29. Enoxacan Study Group. Efficacy and safety of enoxaparin versus unfractionated heparin for prevention of deep vein thrombosis in elective cancer surgery: a double-blind randomized multicentre trial with venographic assessment. Br J Surg 1997;84:1099–1103 (Level I)

30. Kakkar VV, Boeckl O, Boneu B, Bordenave L, Brehm OA, Brücke P, et al. Efficacy and safety of a low-molecular-weight heparin and standard unfractionated heparin for prophylaxis of postoperative venous thromboembolism: European multicenter trial. World J Surg 1997;21:2–8; discussion 8–9 (Level I)

31. Koch A, Bouges S, Ziegler S, Dinkel H, Daures JP, Victor N. Low molecular weight heparin and unfractionated heparin in thrombosis prophylaxis after major surgical intervention: update of previous meta-analyses. Br J Surg 1997;84:750–759 (Meta-analysis)

32. Bergqvist D, Burmark US, Flordal PA, Frisell J, Hallböök T, Hedberg M, et al. Low molecular weight heparin started before surgery as prophylaxis against deep vein thrombosis: 2500 versus 5000 XaI units in 2070 patients. Br J Surg 1995;82:496–501 (Level I)

33. Fricker JP, Vergnes Y, Schach R, Heitz A, Eber M, Grunebaum L, et al. Low dose heparin versus low molecular weight heparin (Kabi 2165, Fragmin) in the prophylaxis of thromboembolic complications of abdominal oncological surgery. Eur J Clin Invest 1988;18:561–567 (Level I)

34. Haljamäe H. Thromboprophylaxis, coagulation disorders, and regional anesthesia. Acta Anaesthesiol Scand 1996; 40:1024–1040 (Level III)

35. Vandermeulen EP, Van Aken H, Vermylen J. Anticoagulants and spinal-epidural anesthesia. Anesth Analg 1994; 79:1165–1177 (Level III)

36. Horlocker TT. Regional anesthesia and analgesia in the patient receiving thromboprophylaxis. Reg Anesth 1996;21:503–507 (Level III)

37. U.S. Department of Health and Human Services. FDA Public Health Advisory. Subject: Reports of epidural or spinal hematomas with the concurrent use of low molecular weight heparin and spinal/epidural anesthesia or spinal puncture. Rockville, Maryland: Food and Drug Administration, December 1997 (Level III)

38. Friederich PW, Sanson BJ, Simioni P, Zanardi S, Huisman MV, Kindt I, et al. Frequency of pregnancy-related venous thromboembolism in anticoagulant factor-deficient

women: implications for prophylaxis. Ann Intern Med 1996;125:955–960 (Level III)

39. Pabinger I, Schneider B. Thrombotic risk in hereditary antithrombin III, protein C, or protein S deficiency. A cooperative, retrospective study. Gesellschaft fur Thrombose- und Hamostaseforschung (GTH) Study Group on Natural Inhibitors. Arterioscler Thromb Vasc Biol 1996;16:742–748 (Level III)

40. Thomas DP, Roberts HR. Hypercoagulability in venous and arterial thrombosis. Ann Intern Med 1997;126:638–644 (Level III)

41. Prevention of venous thrombosis and pulmonary embolism. NIH Consensus Development. JAMA 1986;256:744–749 (Level III)

42. Hutchison GL. Oral contraception and post-operative thromboembolism: an epidemiological review. Scott Med J 1989;34:547–549 (Level III)

43. Robinson GE, Burren T, Mackie IJ, Bounds W, Walshe K, Faint R, et al. Changes in hemostasis after stopping the combined contraceptive pill: implications for major surgery. BMJ 1991;302:269–271 (Level III)

44. Vessey M, Mant D, Smith A, Yeates D. Oral contraceptives and venous thromboembolism: findings in a large prospective study. Br Med J (Clin Res Ed) 1986;292:526 (Level II-2)

45. Daly E, Vessey MP, Hawkins MM, Carson JL, Gough P, Marsh S. Risk of venous thromboembolism in users of hormone replacement therapy. Lancet 1996;348:977–980 (Level II-2)

46. Jick H, Derby LE, Myers MW, Vasilakis C, Newton KM. Risk of hospital admission for idiopathic venous thromboembolism among users of postmenopausal oestrogens. Lancet 1996;348:981–983 (Level II-2)

47. Perez Gutthann S, Garcia Rodríguez LA, Castellsague J, Duque Oliart A. Hormone replacement therapy and risk of venous thromboembolism: population based case-control study. BMJ 1997;314:796–800 (Level II-2)

48. Bokarewa MI, Bremme K, Blombäck M. Arg506-Gln mutation in factor V and risk of thrombosis during pregnancy. Br J Haematol 1996;92:473–478 (Level II-3)

49. Dahlbäck B. Resistance to activated protein C as risk factor for thrombosis: molecular mechanisms, laboratory investigation, and clinical management. Semin Hematol 1997;34:217–234 (Level III)

50. Dizon-Townson DS, Nelson LM, Jang H, Varner MW, Ward K. The incidence of the factor V Leiden mutation in an obstetric population and its relationship to deep vein thrombosis. Am J Obstet Gynecol 1997;176:883–886 (Level III)

51. Faioni EM, Razzari C, Martinelli I, Panzeri D, Franchi F, Mannucci PM. Resistance to activated protein C in unselected patients with arterial and venous thrombosis. Am J Haematol 1997;55:59–64 (Level II-2)

52. Hellgren M, Svensson PJ, Dahlbäck B. Resistance to activated protein C as a basis for venous thromboembolism associated with pregnancy and oral contraceptives. Am J Obstet Gynecol 1995;173:210–213 (Level II-2)

53. Rintelen C, Mannhalter C, Ireland H, Lane DA, Knöbl P, Lechner K, et al. Oral contraceptives enhance the risk of clinical manifestation of venous thrombosis at a young age in females homozygous for factor V Leiden. Br J Haematol 1996;93:487–490 (Level III)

54. Vandenbroucke JP, Koster T, Briët E, Reitsma PH, Bertina RM, Rosendaal FR. Increased risk of venous thrombosis in oral-contraceptive users who are carriers of factor V Leiden mutation. Lancet 1994;344:1453–1457 (Level II-2)

55. Rosendaal FR. Thrombosis in the young: epidemiology and risk factors. A focus on venous thrombosis. Thromb Haemost 1997;78:1–6 (Level III)

56. Barbour LA. Current concepts of anticoagulant therapy in pregnancy. Obstet Gynecol Clin North Am 1997;24:499–521 (Level III)

57. Dahlman TC. Osteoporotic fractures and the recurrence of thromboembolism during pregnancy and the puerperium in 184 women undergoing thromboprophylaxis with heparin. Am J Obstet Gynecol 1993;168:1265–1270 (Level III)

58. Warkentin TE, Levine MN, Hirsh J, Horsewood P, Roberts RS, Gent M, et al. Heparin-induced thrombocytopenia in patients treated with low-molecular weight heparin or unfractionated heparin. N Engl J Med 1995;332:1330–1335 (Level II-2)

59. Hirsh J, Warkentin TE, Raschke R, Granger C, Ohman EM, Dalen JE. Heparin and low-molecular-weight heparin: mechanism of action, pharmacokinetics, dosing considerations, monitoring, efficacy and safety. Chest 1998;114 (suppl 5):489S–510S (Level III)

60. Magnani HN. Heparin-induced thrombocytopenia (HIT): an overview of 230 patients treated with Orgaran (Org 10172). Thromb Haemost 1993;70:554–561 (Level II-3)

61. Hynson JM, Katz JA, Bueff HU. Epidural hematoma associated with enoxaparin. Anesth Analg 1996;82:1072–1075 (Level III)

62. Prandoni P, Lensing AW, Cogo A, Cuppini S, Villalta S, Carta M. The long-term clinical course of acute deep venous thrombosis. Ann Intern Med 1996;125:1–7 (Level III)

63. Bergqvist D, Lindgren B, Mätzsch T. Comparison of the cost of preventing postoperative deep vein thrombosis with either unfractionated or low molecular weight heparin. Br J Surg 1996;83:1548–1152 (Level II-2)

64. Bergqvist D, Jendteg S, Johansen L, Persson U, Ödegaard K. Cost of long-term complications of deep venous thrombosis of the lower extremities: an analysis of a defined patient population in Sweden. Ann Intern Med 1997;126:454–457 (Level II-2)

65. Maxwell GL, Myers ER, Clarke-Pearson DL. Cost-effectiveness of deep venous thrombosis prophylaxis in gynecologic oncology surgery. Obstet Gynecol 2000;95:206–214 (Level III)

The MEDLINE database, the Cochrane Library, and ACOG's own internal resources and documents were used to conduct a literature search to locate relevant articles published between January 1985 and April 2000. The search was restricted to articles published in the English language. Priority was given to articles reporting results of original research, although review articles and commentaries also were consulted. Abstracts of research presented at symposia and scientific conferences were not considered adequate for inclusion in this document. Guidelines published by organizations or institutions such as the National Institutes of Health and the American College of Obstetricians and Gynecologists were reviewed, and additional studies were located by reviewing bibliographies of identified articles. When reliable research was not available, expert opinions from obstetrician–gynecologists were used.

Studies were reviewed and evaluated for quality according to the method outlined by the U.S. Preventive Services Task Force:

I   Evidence obtained from at least one properly designed randomized controlled trial.

II-1 Evidence obtained from well-designed controlled trials without randomization.

II-2 Evidence obtained from well-designed cohort or case–control analytic studies, preferably from more than one center or research group.

II-3 Evidence obtained from multiple time series with or without the intervention. Dramatic results in uncontrolled experiments also could be regarded as this type of evidence.

III   Opinions of respected authorities, based on clinical experience, descriptive studies, or reports of expert committees.

Based on the highest level of evidence found in the data, recommendations are provided and graded according to the following categories:

Level A—Recommendations are based on good and consistent scientific evidence.

Level B—Recommendations are based on limited or inconsistent scientific evidence.

Level C—Recommendations are based primarily on consensus and expert opinion.

ISSN 1099-3630

The American College of
Obstetricians and Gynecologists
409 12th Street, SW
PO Box 96920
Washington, DC 20090-6920   12345/43210

ACOG PRACTICE BULLETIN

CLINICAL MANAGEMENT GUIDELINES FOR
OBSTETRICIAN–GYNECOLOGISTS

NUMBER 4, MAY 1999

(Replaces Educational Bulletin Number 147, October 1990)

This Practice Bulletin was developed by the ACOG Committee on Practice Bulletins—Obstetrics with the assistance of Michael L. Socol, MD, and T. Flint Porter, MD, MPH. The information is designed to aid practitioners in making decisions about appropriate obstetric and gynecologic care. These guidelines should not be construed as dictating an exclusive course of treatment or procedure. Variations in practice may be warranted based on the needs of the individual patient, resources, and limitations unique to the institution or type of practice.

Prevention of Rh D Alloimmunization

Before the introduction of anti-D immune globulin (formerly referred to as Rho[D] immune globulin), hemolytic disease of the fetus and newborn affected 9–10% of pregnancies and was a major cause of perinatal morbidity and mortality (1, 2). Among Rh D-alloimmunized pregnancies, mild-to-moderate hemolytic anemia and hyperbilirubinemia occur in 25–30% of fetuses/neonates, and hydrops fetalis occurs in another 25% of such cases (3). The administration of anti-D immune globulin is successful in reducing the rate of developing antibodies to the D antigen. Protocols for the antenatal and postpartum administration of anti-D immune globulin have been responsible for the dramatic decrease in alloimmunization and subsequent hemolytic disease in the past two decades. However, Rh D alloimmunization remains a clinical concern, with many cases due to failure to follow established protocols. Finally, there is concern that overuse of anti-D immune globulin may lead to a worldwide shortage. The purpose of this document is to provide direction for the appropriate and efficient management of patients at risk in order to further decrease the frequency of Rh D alloimmunization.

Background

Nomenclature

Nomenclature of blood group systems, including the Rh system, may appear confusing to the clinician. According to the *American Medical Association Manual of Style*, erythrocyte antigen and phenotype terminology should use single letters or dual letters depending on the antigen in question (eg, O, AB, Le, Rh) (4). A second designation should be used for specific subtypes (eg, Rh D, Rh C). This publication uses the designation Rh D to signify the erythrocyte antigen.

Women who carry the Rh D antigen are identified as Rh D positive, and those who do not carry the Rh D antigen are identified as Rh D negative. The use of immune globulin to counter the Rh D antigen is referred to as anti-D immune globulin.

Causes of Rh D Alloimmunization

One study indicates that 17% of Rh D-negative women who do not receive anti-D immune globulin prophylaxis during pregnancy will become alloimmunized (5). Nearly 90% of these cases result from fetomaternal hemorrhage at delivery. Approximately 10% of cases result from spontaneous antenatal fetomaternal hemorrhage, and most of these cases occur in the third trimester. The amount of Rh D-positive blood required to cause alloimmunization is small. Most women who become alloimmunized do so as a result of fetomaternal hemorrhage of less than 0.1 mL (6).

Several first- and second-trimester clinical events may cause Rh D alloimmunization. Therapeutic and spontaneous abortions are associated respectively with a 4–5% and a 1.5–2% risk of alloimmunization in susceptible (nonalloimmunized) women (6–8). Ectopic pregnancy also is associated with alloimmunization in susceptible women. Threatened abortion infrequently causes alloimmunization, although approximately 10% of women with threatened abortion have evidence of fetomaternal hemorrhage (9).

Clinical procedures, which may breach the integrity of the choriodecidual space, also may cause Rh D alloimmunization. Chorionic villus sampling is associated with a 14% risk of fetomaternal hemorrhage (10) of more than 0.6 mL (11), and amniocentesis is associated with a 7–15% risk of fetomaternal hemorrhage, even if the placenta is not traversed (5, 12). Likewise, cordocentesis and other percutaneous fetal procedures pose a risk for fetomaternal hemorrhage, although the actual risk of alloimmunization has not been quantified (13, 14). External cephalic version, whether or not it is successful, results in fetomaternal hemorrhage in 2–6% of cases (15, 16).

Anti-D Immune Globulin to Prevent Alloimmunization

The correct administration of anti-D immune globulin dramatically reduces the rate of alloimmunization. Initial studies proved that the postpartum administration of a single dose of anti-D immune globulin to susceptible Rh D-negative women within 72 hours of delivery reduced the alloimmunization rate by 90% (17). It was subsequently recognized that third-trimester antenatal alloimmunization posed a lingering and significant problem; later it was shown that the routine antenatal administration of anti-D immune globulin to Rh D-negative women at 28–29 weeks

of gestation reduced the rate of third-trimester alloimmunization from nearly 2% to 0.1% (6). With the effectiveness of anti-D immune globulin clearly demonstrated, authorities recommended its administration to Rh D-negative women who were undergoing clinical events or procedures associated with potential fetomaternal hemorrhage.

In the United States, recommendations for the administration of anti-D immune globulin were introduced in the 1970s. The current antenatal immunoprophylaxis regimen of a single dose of 300 μg at 28 weeks of gestation was based on recommendations from the 1977 McMaster Conference, and is associated with a low failure rate (18). The efficacy of the single antenatal dose of 300 μg at 28 weeks of gestation is comparable to the same dose given at both 28 weeks and 34 weeks of gestation (6). In one study of antenatal prophylaxis, three women who delivered more than 12 weeks after their antenatal dose was administered became alloimmunized. Based on these limited data, some authorities recommend that if delivery has not occurred within 12 weeks of the injection, at 28 weeks of gestation, a second 300 μg dose of anti-D immune globulin should be given (5).

In the United Kingdom, recommendations (19, 20) differ somewhat from those in the United States in that antenatal prophylaxis is given at both 28 weeks and 34 weeks of gestation, and the dose for each antenatal administration, as well as the dose given after delivery, is 100 μg. These recommendations are based on two studies (21, 22) that demonstrated the superiority of a regimen of 100 μg of anti-D immune globulin at 28 weeks and 34 weeks of gestation and postpartum compared with a regimen of only postpartum administration. The British regimen uses less anti-D immune globulin (300 μg versus 600 μg) to achieve similarly low rates of alloimmunization (7, 20), but requires a third injection at 34 weeks of gestation.

Anti-D immune globulin is extracted by cold alcohol fractionation from plasma donated by individuals with high-titer D immune globulin G antibodies. It has been shown experimentally that one prophylactic dose of 300 μg of anti-D immune globulin can prevent Rh D alloimmunization after an exposure to up to 30 mL of Rh D-positive blood or 15 mL of fetal cells (23). For exposure to larger volumes of Rh D-positive blood, more anti-D immune globulin is required. Accordingly, the American Association of Blood Banks and the National Blood Transfusion Service of the United Kingdom recommend that Rh D-negative mothers delivering Rh D-positive infants undergo a test to screen for fetomaternal hemorrhage in excess of the amount covered by the standard dose of anti-D immune globulin. This test will determine if additional anti-D immune globulin is necessary (24, 25). In the past, the American College of Obstetricians and Gynecologists recommended that only women with certain high-risk conditions, such as those experiencing abruptio placenta or manual removal of the placenta, be screened for excess fetomaternal hemorrhage. However, this policy has been shown to miss 50% of cases requiring more than the standard postpartum dose of anti-D immune globulin (26).

The risk of transmission of viral infections (human immunodeficiency virus [HIV] and hepatitis B and hepatitis C viruses) through anti-D immune globulin is minimal to absent (27). All plasma lots used for the production of anti-D immune globulin have been tested for viral infection since 1985. Moreover, the fractionation process used to prepare anti-D immune globulin effectively removes any viral particles that may be present.

Failure to Prevent Rh D Alloimmunization

In spite of recommendations for immunoprophylaxis, 0.1–0.2% of susceptible Rh D-negative women still become alloimmunized (21). There are two primary reasons for the continuing problem.

One reason women become alloimmunized is failure to implement recommended immunoprophylaxis protocols, resulting in preventable Rh D alloimmunizations. Two recent studies from the United Kingdom emphasize the scope of the problem. One study of more than 900 Rh D-negative women reported that only 59% received recommended treatment with anti-D immune globulin after potentially alloimmunizing clinical events (8). Another study showed that 16% of 63 cases of Rh D alloimmunization occurred because of failure to follow recommendations for administration of anti-D immune globulin (28). Preventable Rh D alloimmunization occurs in susceptible Rh D-negative women for the following three reasons:

1. Failure to administer an antenatal dose of anti-D immune globulin at 28–29 weeks of gestation

2. Failure to recognize clinical events that place patients at risk for alloimmunization and failure to administer anti-D immune globulin appropriately

3. Failure to administer or failure to administer timely anti-D immune globulin postnatally to women who have given birth to an Rh D-positive or untyped fetus

The second reason for the continuing problem of Rh D alloimmunization is the small rate (0.1–0.2%) of spontaneous immunization despite the recommended prophylaxis protocol. These cases most often occur in pregnancies during which there have been no prior overt sensitizing events. This problem may become the largest single cause of new Rh D alloimmunization, because alloimmunization from other causes has decreased proportionally (28).

Potential Shortage of Anti-D Immune Globulin

Anti-D immune globulin is collected by apheresis from volunteer donors who have high titers of circulating anti-Rh D antibodies. The donated plasma is pooled and fractionated by commercial manufacturers, and anti-D immune globulin is prepared in varying doses. The number of potential donors may be dwindling worldwide, raising concern about future supplies of anti-D immune globulin (29, 30). Experts in the United Kingdom estimate that supplies of anti-D immune globulin are inadequate for immunoprophylaxis of all susceptible Rh D-negative women, both primigravidas and multiparas, if standard recommendations are followed (19). In Australia, a shortage prompted importation of anti-D immune globulin. Subsequently, some physicians proposed strictly limiting the dose given for first-trimester indications and discontinuing administration of anti-D immune globulin after external cephalic version (unless fetomaternal hemorrhage is documented), ectopic pregnancy, or threatened miscarriage (31). Others disagreed, considering it unethical to withhold anti-D immune globulin in any situation. Estimates regarding future needs compared with potential supply in the United States have not been published; however, limiting doses for first-trimester indications and using lower doses of Rh D immune globulin for antenatal prophylaxis may be necessary.

Cost-Effectiveness of Rh D Prophylaxis Programs

The cost-effectiveness of preventing perinatal mortality and morbidity secondary to Rh D hemolytic disease of the newborn is an important consideration. Economic analysis of anti-D immune globulin prophylaxis is based on the cost of anti-D immune globulin and the number of alloimmunizations that would be prevented. In 1977, the McMaster Conference concluded that routine postnatal prophylaxis was cost-effective but that routine antenatal treatment should be undertaken only if supplies of anti-D immune globulin were adequate and if cases of hemolytic disease of the newborns occurred that might have been prevented by antenatal treatment (7). Some experts concluded that antenatal prophylaxis is effective only in primigravidas (32), and the debate regarding the cost-effectiveness of antenatal prophylaxis of all pregnant women remains unsettled (20, 32–37). The Scottish National Blood Transfusion Service has concluded that the administration of 100 µg of anti-D immune globulin at 28 weeks and 34 weeks of gestation is cost-effective only in primigravidas (38). Others estimate that the most cost-effective antenatal regimen is a single dose of 250 µg of anti-D immune globulin at 28 weeks of gestation (39).

The use of anti-D prophylaxis in the case of certain clinical events is even more controversial. For example, the risk of Rh D alloimmunization from threatened abortion in the first trimester is uncertain, though probably very small. The cost-effectiveness of anti-D immune globulin for threatened abortion, which has never been studied, is questionable (19).

In summary, the cost-effectiveness of antenatal Rh D immune globulin to all Rh D-negative pregnant women and in all circumstances wherein fetomaternal hemorrhage might occur has not been proved. Available data support that third-trimester antenatal prophylaxis is cost-effective in primigravidas. As long as the supply of anti-D immune globulin is adequate and data do not exist to support other recommendations, most experts believe that it is unethical to withhold anti-D immune globulin from any patient at risk of Rh D alloimmunization (19). Recommendations for the use of anti-D immune globulin in this document will be made accordingly.

Clinical Considerations and Recommendations

▶ *Should anti-D immune globulin ever be withheld from a woman undergoing sterilization?*

The use of anti-D immune globulin following postpartum and postabortal sterilization should be guided by the patient's desire for protection against any chance of alloimmunization. Proponents of its use maintain that anti-D immune globulin administration will preserve the future option of transfusing Rh D-positive blood in times of emergency (40). Opponents of this view cite the low probability of sensitization with the previous pregnancy and the improbability of receiving Rh D-incompatible blood (41).

▶ *How should one deal with the issue of paternity?*

If the father is known to be Rh D negative, antenatal prophylaxis is unnecessary. If there is doubt about the father's identity or his blood type, anti-D immune globulin prophylaxis should be given.

▶ *Is it necessary to repeat antibody screening in patients at 28 weeks of gestation prior to the administration of anti-D immune globulin?*

The American Association of Blood Banks recommends that the physician should consider a repeat antibody screen prior to the administration of antenatal anti-D immune globulin if the patient was screened for antibodies prior to 28 weeks of gestation (24). The primary rationale for repeating the antibody screen is to identify women who have become alloimmunized before 28 weeks of gestation in order to manage their pregnancies properly. However, the incidence of Rh D alloimmunization occurring prior to 28 weeks of gestation is reported to be as low as 0.18% (18), and the cost-effectiveness of routinely repeating the antibody test has not been studied. The consequences of antenatal Rh D alloimmunization can be severe, but the decision to obtain a repeat antibody screen should be dictated by individual circumstances and left to the judgment of the physician.

▶ *Is anti-D immune globulin indicated in a sensitized pregnancy?*

If Rh D antibodies are present, anti-D immune globulin is not beneficial, and management should proceed in accordance with protocols for Rh D-alloimmunized pregnancies.

▶ *How should a D^u blood type be interpreted, and what management should be undertaken?*

In the past, a woman whose blood was typed as D^u was thought to have blood cells positive for a variant of the Rh D antigen. Nomenclature and practice have changed in recent years, and currently the D^u designation has been changed to "weak D positive" (24). Patients with this designation are considered Rh D positive and should not receive anti-D immune globulin. In some centers, the D^u antigen is not assessed, and women may unnecessarily receive anti-D immune globulin. In the rare circumstance of delivery by a woman whose antenatal Rh status is negative or unknown and whose postpartum screen reveals a D^u-positive or weak D-positive result, anti-D immune globulin should be given, and the possibility of fetomaternal hemorrhage should be investigated (24).

▶ *Is threatened abortion an indication for anti-D immune globulin prophylaxis?*

Whether to administer anti-D immune globulin to a patient with threatened abortion and a live embryo or fetus at or before 12 weeks of gestation is controversial, and no evidence-based recommendation can be made. The Rh D antigen has been reported on fetal erythrocytes as early as 38 days of gestation (42), and fetomaternal hemorrhage has been documented in women with threatened abortion from 7 to 13 weeks of gestation (9). However, Rh D alloimmunization apparently attributable to threatened abortion is exceedingly rare. Experts have compared the overall benefit with the cost of the widespread use of anti-D immune globulin for a condition as common as threatened abortion (19, 43), and, thus, many physicians do not routinely administer anti-D immune globulin to women with threatened abortion and a live embryo or fetus up to 12 weeks of gestation.

▶ *How much anti-D immune globulin should be given for first-trimester events and procedures?*

Because the red cell mass of the first-trimester fetus is small, the dose of anti-D immune globulin necessary for first-trimester events is 50 μg to protect against sensitization by 2.5 mL of red blood cells (5, 44). If therapeutic or spontaneous abortion occurs after the first trimester, the standard 300 μg dose is recommended (5).

▶ *Should anti-D immune globulin be given in cases of molar pregnancy?*

Although reported (45), the risk of Rh D alloimmunization in cases of hydatidiform mole is unknown. In theory, Rh D alloimmunization would not occur in cases of classic complete molar pregnancy because organogenesis does not occur, and Rh D antigens are probably not present on trophoblast cells, although this theory has been disputed (46–48). In partial and transitional molar pregnancies, however, the embryo may not die until after erythrocyte production has begun, making maternal exposure to the Rh D antigen possible (49). Given that the diagnosis of partial versus complete molar pregnancy depends on pathologic and cytogenetic evaluations, it seems reasonable to administer anti-D immune globulin to Rh D-negative women who are suspected of molar pregnancy and who undergo uterine evacuation.

▶ *Should anti-D immune globulin be given in cases of intrauterine fetal death occurring in the second or third trimester?*

Fetal death is due to fetomaternal hemorrhage in 11–13% of cases in which no obvious other cause (eg, maternal hypertensive disease, fetal anomalies) is found (50, 51). Rh D alloimmunization has been reported in cases of fetal death from massive fetomaternal hemorrhage (52), although the influence of this cause on the overall problem of Rh D alloimmunization is unknown. The efficacy of anti-D immune globulin in this clinical situation has not been tested in properly designed trials. However, authorities agree that anti-D immune globulin should be administered to Rh D-negative women who experience fetal death in the second or third trimester. All such cases should be screened for excessive fetomaternal hemorrhage to determine if additional anti-D immune globulin is required (25, 53).

▶ *Is second- or third-trimester antenatal hemorrhage an indication for anti-D immune globulin prophylaxis?*

In patients with second- or third-trimester antenatal hemorrhage, the risk of Rh D alloimmunization is uncertain. Although the efficacy of anti-D immune globulin in this clinical situation has not been tested in properly designed trials, authorities agree that anti-D immune globulin should be administered to Rh D-negative women with second- or

third-trimester hemorrhage (25, 53). Man-agement of the patient with persistent or intermittent antenatal bleeding is complex. Though unproven, one commonly used strategy is to monitor the Rh D-negative patient with continuing antenatal hemorrhage with serial indirect Coombs testing approximately every 3 weeks. If the result is positive, indicating the persistence of anti-D immune globulin, no additional treatment is necessary. If the Coombs test is negative, excessive fetomaternal hemorrhage may have occurred, and a Kleihauer-Betke test should be performed in order to determine the amount of additional anti-D immune globulin necessary.

▶ *Is anti-D immune globulin prophylaxis indicated after abdominal trauma in susceptible pregnant women?*

Although the exact risk of Rh D alloimmunization is unknown, abdominal trauma may be associated with fetomaternal hemorrhage, which may lead to alloimmunization (54–57). The efficacy of anti-D immune globulin in this clinical situation has not been tested in properly designed trials. However, authorities agree that anti-D immune globulin should be administered to Rh D-negative women who have experienced abdominal trauma (25, 53). Also, all of these patients should be screened for excessive fetomaternal hemorrhage.

▶ *What should be done if an Rh D-negative patient is discharged without receiving anti-D immune globulin after a potentially sensitizing event?*

Volunteers have been shown to receive partial protection if anti-D immune globulin was given as late as 13 days after exposure (58). The longer prophylaxis is delayed the less likely it is that the patient will be protected, but it has been recommended that a patient may still receive some benefit from anti-D immune globulin as late as 28 days postpartum (5).

▶ *How long does the effect of anti-D immune globulin last?*

The half-life of anti-D immune globulin is 24 days, although titers decrease over time. If delivery occurs within 3 weeks of the standard antenatal anti-D immune globulin administration, the postnatal dose may be withheld in the absence of excessive fetomaternal hemorrhage (53). The same is true when anti-D immune globulin is given for antenatal procedures, such as external cephalic version or amniocentesis, or for third-trimester bleeding. An excessive amount of fetal erythrocytes not covered by anti-D immune globulin administration can be assumed to have entered maternal blood if either the results of the Kleihauer-Betke test are positive or the results of the indirect Coombs test are negative.

▶ *Should administration of anti-D immune globulin be repeated in patients with a postdate pregnancy?*

One study found that three patients became alloimmunized to the Rh D antigen when delivery occurred more than 12 weeks after the standard prophylaxis at 28 weeks of gestation (5). Based on these limited data, some experts have recommended that if delivery has not occurred within 12 weeks after injection at 28 weeks of gestation, a second antenatal dose should be given (5). Because this recommendation is based on so few cases, the final decision whether to administer a second dose should be left to the physician's judgment.

▶ *Should all Rh D-negative women be screened for excessive fetomaternal hemorrhage after delivery of an Rh D-positive infant?*

The risk of excessive fetomaternal hemorrhage exceeding 30 mL (the amount covered by the standard 300 µg dose of anti-D immune globulin) at the time of delivery is approximately 1 in 1,250 (5). Previous American College of Obstetricians and Gynecologists documents have recommended that only pregnancies designated as high risk be screened for excessive fetomaternal hemorrhage, including cases of abdominal trauma, abruptio placentae, placenta previa, intrauterine manipulation, multiple gestation, or manual removal of the placenta. However, such a screening program has been reported to detect only 50% of patients who required additional anti-D immune globulin (26). Based on this finding, the American Association of Blood Banks has recommended that all Rh D-negative women who deliver Rh D-positive infants be screened using the Kleihauer-Betke or rosette test (24).

Summary

The reduction in the incidence of Rh D alloimmunization is a prototype for the effectiveness of preventive medicine. Some controversies remain, however, such as the use of anti-D immune globulin in patients with either threatened abortion or antenatal hemorrhage. Similarly, it may not be cost-effective either to screen all Rh D-negative patients with an indirect Coombs test at 24–28 weeks of gestation or to screen all postpartum patients for excessive fetomaternal hemorrhage.

The following recommendations are based on good and consistent scientific evidence (Level A):

The Rh D-negative woman who is not Rh D-alloimmunized should receive anti-D immune globulin:

▶ At approximately 28 weeks of gestation, unless the father of the baby is also known to be Rh D negative

▶ Within 72 hours after the delivery of an Rh D-positive infant

▶ After a first-trimester pregnancy loss

▶ After invasive procedures, such as chorionic villus sampling, amniocentesis, or fetal blood sampling

The following recommendations are based primarily on consensus and expert opinion (Level C):

Anti-D immune globulin prophylaxis should be considered if the patient has experienced:

▶ Threatened abortion

▶ Second- or third-trimester antenatal bleeding

▶ External cephalic version

▶ Abdominal trauma

References

1. Mollison PL, Engelfreit CP, Contreras M. Haemolytic disease of the newborn in blood. In: Transfusion in clinical medicine. 8th ed. Oxford: Blackwell Scientific Publications, 1987:637–687 (Level III)

2. Huchcroft S, Gunton P, Bowen T. Compliance with postpartum Rh isoimmunization prophylaxis in Alberta. Can Med Assoc J 1985;133:871–875 (Level II-3)

3. Tannirandorn Y, Rodeck CH. New approaches in the treatment of haemolytic disease of the fetus. Baillieres Clin Haematol 1990;3:289–320 (Level III)

4. Iverson C, Flanagin A, Fontanarosa PB, Glass RM, Glitman P, Lantz JC, et al. American Medical Association manual of style. 9th ed. Baltimore: Williams and Wilkins, 1998 (Level III)

5. Bowman JM. Controversies in Rh prophylaxis. Who needs Rh immune globulin and when should it be given? Am J Obstet Gynecol 1985;151:289–294 (Level III)

6. Bowman JM. The prevention of Rh immunization. Transfus Med Rev 1988;2:129–150 (Level III)

7. McMaster conference on prevention of Rh immunization. 28–30 September, 1977. Vox Sang 1979;36:50–64 (Level III)

8. Howard HL, Martlew VJ, McFadyen IR, Clarke CA. Preventing Rhesus D haemolytic disease of the newborn by giving anti-D immunoglobulin: are the guidelines being adequately followed? Br J Obstet Gynaecol 1997;104:37–41 (Level II-3)

9. Von Stein GA, Munsick RA, Stiver K, Ryder K. Fetomaternal hemorrhage in threatened abortion. Obstet Gynecol 1992;79:383–386 (Level II-2)

10. Brambati B, Guercilena S, Bonnachi I, Oldrini A, Lanzani A, Piceni L. Feto-maternal transfusion after chorionic villus sampling: clinical implications. Hum Reprod 1986;1:37–40 (Level II-3)

11. Blakemore KJ, Baumgarten A, Schoenfeld-Dimaio M, Hobbins JC, Mason EA, Mahoney MJ. Rise in maternal

serum alpha-fetoprotein concentration after chorionic villus sampling and the possibility of isoimmunization. Am J Obstet Gynecol 1986;155:988–993 (Level III)

12. Blajchman MA, Maudsley RF, Uchida I, Zipursky A. Letter: Diagnostic amniocentesis and fetal-maternal bleeding. Lancet 1974;1:993–994 (Level III)

13. Daffos F, Capella-Pavlovsky M, Forestier F. Fetal blood sampling during pregnancy with use of a needle guided by ultrasound: a study of 606 consecutive cases. Am J Obstet Gynecol 1985;153:655–660 (Level II-3)

14. Pielet BW, Socol ML, MacGregor SN, Ney JA, Dooley SL. Cordocentesis: an appraisal of risks. Am J Obstet Gynecol 1988;159:1497–1500 (Level III)

15. Lau TK, Stock A, Rogers M. Fetomaternal hemorrhage after external cephalic version at term. Aust N Z J Obstet Gynaecol 1995;35:173–174 (Level II-3)

16. Marcus RG, Crewe-Brown H, Krawitz S, Katz J. Fetomaternal haemorrhage following successful and unsuccessful attempts at external cephalic version. Br J Obstet Gynaecol 1975;82:578–580 (Level III)

17. Freda VJ, Gorman JG, Pollack W, Bowe E. Prevention of Rh hemolytic disease—ten years' clinical experience with Rh immune globulin. N Engl J Med 1975;292:1014–1016 (Level III)

18. Bowman JM, Chown B, Lewis M, Pollock JM. Rh isoimmunization during pregnancy: antenatal prophylaxis. Can Med Assoc J 1978;118:623–627 (Level III)

19. Robson SC, Lee D, Urbaniak S. Anti-D immunoglobulin in RhD prophylaxis. Br J Obstet Gynaecol 1998;105:129–134 (Level III)

20. Statement from the consensus conference on anti-D prophylaxis. 7 and 8 April 1997. The Royal College of Physicians of Edinburgh. The Royal College of Obstetricians and Gynaecologists, UK. Vox Sang 1998;74:127–128 (Level III)

21. Tovey LA, Townley A, Stevenson BJ, Taverner J. The Yorkshire antenatal anti-D immunoglobulin trial in primigravidae. Lancet 1983;2:244–246 (Level II-2)

22. Huchet J, Dallemagne S, Huchet C, Brossard Y, Larsen M, Parnet-Mathieu F. Antepartum administration of preventive treatment of Rh-D immunization in rhesus-negative women. Parallel evaluation of transplacental passage of fetal blood cells. Results of a multicenter study carried out in the Paris region. J Gynecol Obstet Biol Reprod (Paris) 1987;16:101–111 (Level II-2)

23. Pollack W, Ascari WQ, Kochesky RJ, O'Connor RR, Ho TY, Tripodi D. Studies on Rh prophylaxis. 1. Relationship between doses of anti-Rh and size of antigenic stimulus. Transfusion 1971;11:333–339 (Level II-1)

24. Snyder EL. Prevention of hemolytic disease of the newborn due to anti-D. Prenatal/perinatal testing and Rh immune globulin administration. American Association of Blood Banks Association Bulletin 1998;98(2):1–6 (Level III)

25. National Blood Transfusion Service Immunoglobulin Working Party. Recommendations for the use of anti-D immunoglobulin. 1991;137–145 (Level III)

26. Ness PM, Baldwin ML, Niebyl JR. Clinical high-risk designation does not predict excess fetal-maternal hemorrhage. Am J Obstet Gynecol 1987;156:154–158 (Level II-3)

27. Centers for Disease Control and Prevention. Lack of transmission of human immunodeficiency virus through Rho (D) immune globulin (human). MMWR 1987;36:728–729 (Level II-3)

28. Hughes RG, Craig JI, Murphy WG, Greer IA. Causes and clinical consequences of Rhesus (D) haemolytic disease of the newborn: a study of a Scottish population, 1985–1990. Br J Obstet Gynaecol 1994;101:297–300 (Level III)

29. Beveridge HE. Dwindling supplies of anti-D. Med J Aust 1997;167:509–510 (Level III)

30. Nelson M, Popp HJ, Kronenberg H. Dwindling supplies of anti-D. Med J Aust 1998;168:311 (Level III)

31. de Crespigny L, Davison G. Anti-D administration in early pregnancy—time for a new protocol. Aust N Z J Obstet Gynaecol 1995;35:385–387 (Level III)

32. Tovey LA, Taverner JM. A case for the antenatal administration of anti-D immunoglobulin to primigravidae. Lancet 1981;1:878–881 (Level III)

33. Clarke C, Whitfield AG. Rhesus immunization during pregnancy: the cause for antenatal anti-D. BMJ 1980;280:903–904 (Level III)

34. Tovey GH. Should anti-D immunoglobulin be given antenatally? Lancet 1980;2:466–468 (Level II-3)

35. Bowman JM, Friesen AD, Pollack JM, Taylor WE. WinRho: Rh immune globulin prepared by ion exchange for intravenous use. Can Med Assoc J 1980;123:1121–1127 (Level II-3)

36. Bowman JM, Pollock JM. Failures of intravenous Rh immune globulin prophylaxis: an analysis of the reasons for such failures. Transfus Med Rev 1987;1:101–112 (Level III)

37. Torrance GW, Zipursky A. Cost-effectiveness of antepartum prevention of Rh immunization. Clin Perinatol 1984;11:267–281 (Level III)

38. Cairns JA. Economics of antenatal prophylaxis. Br J Obstet Gynaecol 1998;105(suppl 18):19–22 (Level III)

39. Vick S, Cairns J, Urbaniak S, Whitfield C, Raafat A. Cost-effectiveness of antenatal anti-D prophylaxis. Health Econ 1996;5:319–328 (Cost-effectiveness analysis)

40. Gorman JG, Freda VJ. Rh immune globulin is indicated for Rh-negative mothers undergoing sterilization. Am J Obstet Gynecol 1972;112:868–869 (Level III)

41. Scott JR, Guy LR. Is Rh immunoglobulin indicated in patients having puerperal sterilization? Obstet Gynecol 1975;46:178–180 (Level II-3)

42. Bergstrom H, Nillson L, Ryttinger L. Demonstration of Rh antigens in a 38-day old fetus. Am J Obstet Gynecol 1967;1:130–133 (Level III)

43. Haines P. An overview from a panel member. Br J Obstet Gynaecol 1998;105(suppl 18):5–6 (Level III)

44. Stewart FH, Burnhill MS, Bozorgi N. Reduced dose of Rh immunoglobulin following first trimester pregnancy termination. Obstet Gynecol 1978;51:318–322 (Level II-1)

45. Price JR. RH sensitization by hydatiform mole. N Engl J Med 1968;278:1021 (Level III)

46. Fischer HE, Lichtiger B, Cox I. Expression of Rh0(D) antigen in choriocarcinoma of the uterus in an Rh0(D)-negative patient: report of a case. Hum Pathol 1985;16: 1165–1167 (Level III)

47. van't Veer MB, Overbeeke MA, Geertzen HG, van der Lans SM. The expression of Rh-D factor in human trophoblast. Am J Obstet Gynecol 1984;150:1008–1010 (Level III)

48. Goto S, Nishi H, Tomoda Y. Blood group Rh-D factor in human trophoblast determined by immunofluorescent method. Am J Obstet Gynecol 1980;137:707–712 (Level III)

49. Morrow CP, Curtin JP. Tumors of the placental trophoblast. In: Synopsis of gynecologic oncology. 5th ed. New York: Churchill Livingstone, 1998:315–351 (Level III)

50. Laube DW, Schauberger CW. Fetomaternal bleeding as a cause for "unexplained" fetal death. Obstet Gynecol 1982;60:649–651 (Level III)

51. Owen J, Stedman CM, Tucker TL. Comparison of predelivery versus postdelivery Kleihauer-Betke stains in cases of fetal death. Am J Obstet Gynecol 1989;161:663–666 (Level III)

52. Stedman CM, Quinlan RW, Huddleston JF, Cruz AC, Kellner KR. Rh sensitization after third-trimester fetal death. Obstet Gynecol 1988;71:461–463 (Level III)

53. American Association of Blood Banks. Technical Manual. 12th ed. Bethesda, Maryland: American Association of Blood Banks, 1996 (Level III)

54. Rose PG, Strohm PL, Zuspan FP. Fetomaternal hemorrhage following trauma. Am J Obstet Gynecol 1985;153:844–847 (Level II-2)

55. Chhibber G, Zacher M, Cohen AW, Kline AJ. Rh isoimmunization following abdominal trauma: a case report. Am J Obstet Gynecol 1984;149:692 (Level III)

56. Kettel LM, Branch DW, Scott JR. Occult placental abruption after maternal trauma. Obstet Gynecol 1988;71: 449–453 (Level III)

57. Dahmus MA, Sibai BM. Blunt abdominal trauma: are there any predictive factors for abruptio placentae or maternal-fetal distress? Am J Obstet Gynecol 1993; 169:1054–1059 (Level III)

58. Samson D, Mollison PL. Effect on primary Rh immunization of delayed administration of anti-Rh. Immunology 1975;28:349–357 (Level II-1)

The MEDLINE database, the Cochrane Library, and ACOG's own internal resources and documents were used to conduct a literature search to locate relevant articles published between January 1980 and December 1998. The search was restricted to articles published in the English language. Priority was given to articles reporting results of original research, although review articles and commentaries also were consulted. Abstracts of research presented at symposia and scientific conferences were not considered adequate for inclusion in this document. Guidelines published by organizations or institutions such as the National Institutes of Health and the American College of Obstetricians and Gynecologists were reviewed, and additional studies were located by reviewing bibliographies of identified articles. When reliable research was not available, expert opinions from obstetrician–gynecologists were used.

Studies were reviewed and evaluated for quality according to the method outlined by the U.S. Preventive Services Task Force:

I   Evidence obtained from at least one properly designed randomized controlled trial.

II-1 Evidence obtained from well-designed controlled trials without randomization.

II-2 Evidence obtained from well-designed cohort or case–control analytic studies, preferably from more than one center or research group.

II-3 Evidence obtained from multiple time series with or without the intervention. Dramatic results in uncontrolled experiments could also be regarded as this type of evidence.

III Opinions of respected authorities, based on clinical experience, descriptive studies, or reports of expert committees.

Based on the highest level of evidence found in the data, recommendations are provided and graded according to the following categories:

Level A—Recommendations are based on good and consistent scientific evidence.

Level B—Recommendations are based on limited or inconsistent scientific evidence.

Level C—Recommendations are based primarily on consensus and expert opinion.

ISSN 1099-3630   12345/32109

The American College of Obstetricians and Gynecologists
409 12th Street, SW
PO Box 96920
Washington, DC 20090-6920

ACOG PRACTICE BULLETIN

CLINICAL MANAGEMENT GUIDELINES FOR
OBSTETRICIAN–GYNECOLOGISTS

NUMBER 7, SEPTEMBER 1999

(Replaces Technical Bulletin Number 111, December 1987)

This Practice Bulletin was developed by the ACOG Committee on Practice Bulletins—Gynecology with the assistance of Douglas W. Laube, MD. The information is designed to aid practitioners in making decisions about appropriate obstetric and gynecologic care. These guidelines should not be construed as an exclusive course of treatment or procedure. Variations in practice may be warranted based on the needs of the individual patient, resources, and limitations unique to the institution or type of practice.

Prophylactic Oophorectomy

In the United States, approximately 600,000 hysterectomies are performed each year, one half of which involve oophorectomy (1). Historically, the putative benefits of prophylactic oophorectomy have included the alleviation of symptoms related to retained ovaries and the prevention of cancer. These benefits are countered by arguments favoring the retention of ovaries, which allows continued hormone production in both premenopausal and postmenopausal women. This document will weigh the risks and benefits of prophylactic oophorectomy and provide a framework for the evaluation and counseling of patients who would be candidates for this procedure.

Background

Prophylactic oophorectomy is the removal of the ovaries for the potential benefit of preventing long-term morbidity and mortality. The term *prophylactic* implies that the ovaries are normal at the time of removal. Oophorectomy can be performed either alone as a planned surgical procedure or in conjunction with other planned surgical procedures such as hysterectomy or colectomy. *Incidental oophorectomy* is a term commonly used when the ovaries are removed at the time of another indicated surgery, and this term should not be used interchangeably with *prophylactic oophorectomy*. The term *incidental* implies that the surgery occurs by chance or without consequence. There are obvious consequences associated with oophorectomy; therefore, when oophorectomy is performed for future benefit, the surgery should be termed *prophylactic*.

Ovarian Physiology

The ovary is a complex metabolic organ consisting of follicular and stromal compartments. Follicles produce both androgens and estrogen, and stromal tissue synthesizes androgens. With the loss of all follicles around menopause, both androgen and estrogen levels decrease, but the ovary remains a source of androgens that are peripherally converted to estrogen. The role of endogenous androgens and the consequences of their removal may be significant but have not yet been clarified.

The positive effects of estrogen production on lipid metabolism and bone remodeling remain the primary argument for retention of the ovaries in premenopausal women. The benefits of estrogen are well documented (2–4), but any benefits of ovarian androgen production remain to be documented.

Cancer Prevention

In the United States, one in 70 women will develop ovarian cancer in her lifetime. Between 4% and 14% of these women will have had antecedent hysterectomies in which the ovaries were retained (5). Current screening techniques for ovarian cancer, including the use of ultrasonography and tumor markers, are neither sensitive nor specific enough to detect early cancer as part of a screening program for the general population. A high proportion of ovarian cancer is detected when it is in advanced stages. Prevention of ovarian cancer is the primary reason for prophylactic oophorectomy. Although oophorectomy does not eliminate the risk of cancer (patients still can develop peritoneal carcinoma, which acts like ovarian cancer), reported cases are rare (6).

The literature has recorded elective oophorectomy rates of between 50% and 66% in women 40–64 years of age undergoing hysterectomy (7, 8). Data from the Centers for Disease Control and Prevention collected between 1988 and 1993 concur that ovarian retention occurs in approximately 40–50% of patients undergoing hysterectomy at 40 years of age or older (1). It has been suggested that, in the United States, approximately 1,000 cases of ovarian cancer can be prevented if prophylactic oophorectomy is practiced in all women older than 40 years of age who undergo hysterectomy. This assumes an annual incidence of 24,000 new ovarian cancer cases and does not take into account the incidence of peritoneal carcinoma. The dilemma for the patient and the clinician is whether the estimated number of cancer cases prevented (1,000) is worth the number of oophorectomies performed (approximately 300,000) (9). The benefit of prophylactic oophorectomy may be offset by the consequence of estrogen loss early in life.

Factors to Consider for Prophylactic Oophorectomy

The potential risks and benefits of this procedure need to be considered within the context of the potential risks and benefits of extended hormone production or prescribed hormone replacement. The potential for alleviation of symptoms related to ovarian function should be considered, especially in patients with documented premenstrual syndrome. New developments in genetic testing, early diagnosis, refinements in diagnostic imaging, knowledge of hormone interactions with the cardiovascular and central nervous systems, and refined surgical techniques must all be considered with the individual patient.

Risk Factors for Ovarian Cancer

There is no consensus regarding the benefits of oophorectomy performed at the time of hysterectomy. Patients at greater risk for developing ovarian cancer are those with low parity, decreased fertility, and delayed childbearing if they did not use oral contraceptives (6, 10–12).

Women who have used oral contraceptives have a lower risk for invasive epithelial ovarian cancer than nonusers do. Both hospital and population studies revealed that, among those who have used oral contraceptives, the risk continues to decrease as years of use increase, although there is little additional protection conferred by oral contraceptives beyond 6 years of use. The protective benefits of higher parity, as well as longer duration of breastfeeding, also have been reported. Use of fertility drugs may be associated with a higher risk of ovarian cancer, as is a history of longer premenopausal sexual activity without contraception. There are no consistent data linking age at menarche, age at menopause, or duration of estrogen replacement therapy with development of epithelial ovarian cancer (10).

Operative Risk at the Time of Hysterectomy

There are no studies evaluating increased operative risk or morbidity at the time of abdominal hysterectomy when prophylactic oophorectomy is included. Retrospective studies looking at prophylactic oophorectomy at the time of vaginal hysterectomy have shown that the ovaries can be removed successfully in 65–97% of patients (13, 14). One study found no significant increase in operating time, estimated blood loss, length of hospital stay, or postoperative morbidity between patients who had their ovaries removed and those who did not (13). Another study found that oophorectomy added 23.4 minutes to the total operating time compared with vaginal hysterectomy alone (14).

Genetic Factors

The emergence of data suggesting the close link of ovarian cancer with familial breast–ovarian cancer syndromes has contributed to arguments favoring oophorectomy in subsets of patients identified with genetic risk factors.

The role of *BRCA1* mutations in ovarian cancer indicates that these tumors have unique biologic clinical and pathologic features (15). Recent evidence identifies the significant contribution of *BRCA1* mutations to the development of ovarian cancer, revealing that this mutation occurs in approximately 5% of women in whom cancer is diagnosed before 70 years of age (16). Although screening for *BRCA1* mutations has been suggested, it is difficult to define those women at risk based only on the number of family members affected. Because of the relatively small number (5%) of all ovarian cancers related to inherited mutations in the *BRCA1* gene, the optimal strategy for decreasing cancer mortality in these patients has yet to be determined.

BRCA2 mutations increase the risk of ovarian cancer but to a lesser degree than *BRCA1* mutations (17). The risk of ovarian cancer in families with Lynch syndrome II is reported to be 3.5 times higher than expected, with the estimated cumulative risk by 70 years of age still less than 10% (18). The mean age at diagnosis for ovarian cancer in women with Lynch syndrome II is approximately 45 years of age, roughly 20 years earlier than in the general population (19).

Clinical Considerations and Recommendations

▶ *Who are candidates for prophylactic oophorectomy?*

In determining candidates who would benefit from prophylactic oophorectomy, the advantages and disadvantages of prophylactic oophorectomy need to be evaluated (11, 20). The decision to perform prophylactic oophorectomy should be based not only on the patient's age but also on other factors that weigh individual risk for developing ovarian cancer against loss of ovarian function (see the box).

▶ *With ovary retention, what is the risk of needing a future oophorectomy for benign disease?*

The retention of ovaries following prior hysterectomy has been reported to contribute to reoperation in up to 5% of patients (21, 22), with pain in the retained ovary or ovaries the most commonly cited reason. In a retrospective study of more than 1,200 women who had at least one ovary retained after undergoing hysterectomy for benign indications, there was an approximate 4% reoperation rate (23). The author noted that the risk of having pathology in retained ovaries after hysterectomy was sig-

---

Patient Factors to Consider in Prophylactic Oophorectomy

Age

Parity

Previous abdominal surgery

Risk of ovarian cancer

Menopausal status

Family and personal history

Desire and willingness to use hormone replacement therapy

Risk for osteoporosis

Risk for coronary heart disease

Effect on self-image

---

nificantly higher in women who had only one ovary retained, compared with those who had both ovaries retained. In addition, the mean age at the time of hysterectomy was significantly lower in women who developed ovarian disorders following hysterectomy than in those who did not develop subsequent ovarian disorders. These findings suggest that the removal of one ovary at the time of hysterectomy in premenopausal women indicates the suspicion of clinical disease. The likelihood of future pathology in the retained ovary is therefore greater. Also, the younger the woman is at the time of hysterectomy, the more years there are for her to develop nonmalignant ovarian disorders that will require oophorectomy. In another study that followed a group of 84 premenopausal women undergoing radical hysterectomy, 27% experienced early loss of hormonal function or required subsequent oophorectomy (24).

▶ *Is prophylactic oophorectomy associated with increased morbidity?*

The morbidity associated with prophylactic oophorectomy is primarily related to the loss of estrogen. It is unclear whether exogenous estrogen fully compensates for the lost function of the ovaries, but it appears that estrogen replacement therapy is adequate compensation. However, there may be underlying advantages of ovarian function that have not yet been identified, particularly postmenopausal androgen production. Also, patients who do not take hormone replacement therapy will experience symptoms of early menopause, such as vasomotor hot flashes and vaginal atrophy (25), and are at a higher risk for osteoporosis (3, 26).

▶ *Should hormone replacement therapy be recommended for women undergoing prophylactic oophorectomy?*

Hormone replacement therapy should be recommended for women undergoing prophylactic oophorectomy just as it is for women undergoing natural menopause. The benefit of estrogen replacement therapy appears to be the same in natural or surgical menopause (3, 27), and the same risks and benefits should be discussed with the patient. If the patient is premenopausal, her need for estrogen replacement may be even greater because of her age and potential life span.

The favorable effects of estrogen replacement on bone metabolism have been well documented since the first reports of randomized trials. Additionally, in an evaluation of 27 premenopausal women undergoing oophorectomy, levels of lipoprotein A and cholesterol, along with other hemostatic factors, were found to be lower or not statistically different from preoperative levels, when estrogen replacement therapy was given (28). These observations are consistent with the beneficial effects of estrogen on cardiovascular hemodynamics and cardiovascular disease.

Despite the potentially favorable effects of estrogen replacement and the development of a number of promising synthetic hormone replacement medications, current estrogen replacement usage rates in postmenopausal women are low, and compliance with hormone replacement therapy is poor (29). Therefore, an unwillingness to accept hormone replacement therapy represents a potentially serious health problem, making the decision for elective oophorectomy more difficult.

▶ *What is the risk–benefit relationship associated with oophorectomy?*

The risk–benefit relationship for an individual woman is difficult to calculate. Compliance with estrogen replacement therapy and the risks of coronary artery disease and osteoporosis versus the risk of reoperation or ovarian cancer must be considered. Speroff and colleagues used Markov cohort modeling to evaluate prophylactic oophorectomy considering the influence of estrogen on coronary heart disease, breast cancer, and osteoporotic fractures (30). When compliance with estrogen replacement therapy was perfect, oophorectomy yielded longer life expectancy. When actual drug-taking behavior is considered, retaining the ovaries resulted in longer survival. While only a theoretical model, this analysis emphasizes the need to consider patient compliance with estrogen replacement therapy in decision making.

▶ *When is prophylactic oophorectomy indicated as adjunctive treatment for premenopausal women with breast cancer?*

Prophylactic oophorectomy as adjunctive treatment in the management of premenopausal breast cancer has been practiced for more than 40 years. The efficacy of this procedure has been assumed as part of an accepted endocrine management strategy for breast cancer. Today, with the use of multiagent chemotherapy, tamoxifen, and GnRH agonists, the role for oophorectomy is unclear. Large, prospective trials are currently underway to evaluate the efficacy of oophorectomy for node-positive, estrogen-sensitive breast tumors in premenopausal women.

▶ *Are there genetic risks that should be considered in the decision to perform prophylactic oophorectomy?*

Women with *BRCA1* have a 45% lifetime risk of ovarian cancer, and *BRCA2* conveys a 25% risk (12). Although large-scale prospective data are lacking, most clinicians agree that prophylactic oophorectomy in select women at high risk of inherited ovarian cancer *(BRCA1 and BRCA2)* should be considered (11, 31, 32). Multicenter studies are currently ongoing to assess the assumed benefit of prophylactic oophorectomy in this subset of patients. Because the average age of ovarian cancer in women with these genetic mutations is mid 40s, prophylactic oophorectomy should be performed at completion of childbearing or at 35 years of age.

Contemporary recommendations for women with Lynch syndrome II include at least an annual physical examination with bimanual rectovaginal examination, determinations of CA 125 levels, and transvaginal ultrasonography, with consideration of laparoscopic prophylactic bilateral oophorectomy upon completion of childbirth or by 35 years of age (11). The role of oophorectomy at the time of surgery for primary nonhereditary (sporadic) colorectal cancer is not clear. Some contemporary literature suggests that removing ovaries in this group of women decreases the likelihood of metastatic disease to the ovary (18). Prior to surgical intervention, a familial syndrome should be established by a full pedigree analysis, and the patient should be counseled as to the ethical and medical implications of this testing.

▶ *Are there other considerations in assessing the risks and benefits of prophylactic oophorectomy?*

The decision to perform prophylactic oophorectomy should be individual to the patient. Ovarian retention or removal in some patients may have a distinct bearing on their self-image. In addition to the ovarian contribution to the hormonal milieu, questions regarding the patient's self-image, reproductive function, and sexuality should be considered. Intact reproductive organs may be linked to self-perception of sexuality. Body image also may be related to the occurrence of posthysterectomy depression, although other factors, including preoperative depression, prior psychiatric disturbances, age younger than 35 years, nulliparity, and fewer than 12 years of formal education, also may serve as risk factors (33).

Summary

The following recommendations are based primarily on consensus and expert opinion (Level C):

▶ The decision to perform prophylactic oophorectomy should not be based only on age; it should be a highly individualized decision that takes into account several patient factors and choices.

▶ Removal of one ovary at the time of hysterectomy in premenopausal women may indicate the suspicion of clinical disease. The likelihood of future pathology in the retained ovary is therefore greater. The patient should be counseled before surgery that if ovarian pathology is found, bilateral oophorectomy may be indicated.

▶ Hormone replacement therapy should be considered for women undergoing prophylactic oophorectomy, and patients should be counseled about the risks and benefits of hormone replacement therapy prior to undergoing surgery.

▶ Compliance with hormone replacement therapy is important in women undergoing prophylactic oophorectomy to reduce the risk of future morbidity.

▶ Prophylactic oophorectomy should be considered for select women at high risk of inherited ovarian cancer.

▶ In addition to health risks and benefits, patient counseling should include consideration of how oophorectomy may relate to the individual patient's body image, perceptions concerning sexuality, and personal feelings.

References

1. Lepine LA, Hillis SD, Marchbanks PA, Koonin LM, Morrow B, Kieke BA, et al. Hysterectomy surveillance—United States 1980–1993. MMWR Morb Mortal Wkly Rep 1997;46:1–15 (Level II-3)

2. Bush TL, Barrett-Connor E, Cowan LD, Criqui MH, Wallace RB, Suchindran CM, et al. Cardiovascular mortality and noncontraceptive use of estrogen in women: results from the Lipid Research Clinics Program Follow-up Study. Circulation 1987;75;1102–1109 (Level II-2)

3. Ettinger B, Genant HK, Cann CE. Postmenopausal bone loss is prevented by treatment with low-dosage estrogen with calcium. Ann Intern Med 1987;106:40–45 (Level II-1)

4. Effects of estrogen or estrogen/progestin regimens on heart disease risk factors in postmenopausal women: The Postmenopausal Estrogen/Progestin Interventions (PEPI) Trial. The Writing Group of the PEPI Trial. JAMA 1995;273:199–208 (Level I)

5. Sightler SE, Boike GM, Estape RE, Averette HE. Ovarian cancer in women with prior hysterectomy: a 14-year experience at the University of Miami. Obstet Gynecol 1991;78:681–684 (Level II-3)

6. Piver MS, Jishi MF, Tsukada Y, Nava G. Primary peritoneal carcinoma after prophylactic oophorectomy in women with a family history of ovarian cancer. Cancer 1993;71:2751–2755 (Level III)

7. Dicker RC, Scally MJ, Greenspan JR, Layde PM, Ory HW, Maze JM, et al. Hysterectomy among women of reproductive age. JAMA 1982;248:323–327 (Level II-3)

8. Pokras R, Hufnagel VG. Hysterectomy in the United States, 1965–84. Am J Public Health 1988;78:852–853 (Level II-3)

9. Averette HE, Nguyen HN. The role of prophylactic oophorectomy in cancer prevention. Gynecol Oncol 1994;55:S38–S41 (Level III)

10. Whittemore AS, Harris R, Itnyre J. Characteristics relating to ovarian cancer risk: collaborative analysis of 12 US case-control studies. II. Invasive epithelial ovarian cancers in white women. Collaborative Ovarian Cancer Group. Am J Epidemiol 1992;136:1184–1203 (Level II-2)

11. NIH consensus conference. Ovarian cancer: screening, treatment, and follow-up. NIH Consensus Development Panel on Ovarian Cancer. JAMA 1995;273:491–497 (Level III)

12. Narod SA, Risch H, Moslehi R, Dorum A, Neuhausen S, Olsson H, et al. Oral contraceptives and the risk of hereditary ovarian cancer. Hereditary Ovarian Cancer Clinical Study Group. N Engl J Med 1998;339:424–428 (Level II-2)

13. Ballard LA, Walters MD. Transvaginal mobilization and removal of ovaries and fallopian tubes after vaginal hysterectomy. Obstet Gynecol 1996;87:35–39 (Level II-2)

14. Davies A, O'Connor H, Magos AL. A prospective study to evaluate oophorectomy at the time of vaginal hysterectomy. Br J Obstet Gynaecol 1996;103:915–920 (Level II-2)

15. Rubin SC, Benjamin I, Behbakht K, Takahashi H, Morgan MA, LiVolsi VA, et al. Clinical and pathological features of ovarian cancer in women with germ-line mutations of *BRCA1*. N Engl J Med 1996;335:1413–1416 (Level II-2)

16. Stratton JF, Gayther SA, Russell P, Dearden J, Gore M, Blake P, et al. Contribution of *BRCA1* mutations to ovarian cancer. N Engl J Med 1997;336:1125–1130 (Level II-3)

17. Ford D, Easton DF. The genetics of breast and ovarian cancer. Br J Cancer 1995;72:805–812 (Level III)

18. Burke W, Petersen G, Lynch P, Botkin J, Daly M, Garber J, et al. Recommendations for follow-up care of individuals with an inherited predisposition to cancer. I. Hereditary nonpolyposis colon cancer. JAMA 1997;277:915–919 (Level III)

19. Watson P, Lynch HT. Extracolonic cancer in hereditary nonpolyposis colorectal cancer. Cancer 1993;71:677–685 (Level II-3)

20. Irwin KL, Weiss NS, Lee NC, Peterson HB. Tubal sterilization, hysterectomy, and the subsequent occurrence of epithelial ovarian cancer. Am J Epidemiol 1991;134: 362–369 (Level II-2)

21. Christ JE, Lotze EC. The residual ovary syndrome. Obstet Gynecol 1975;46:551–556 (Level II-3)

22. Grogan RH, Duncan CJ. Ovarian salvage in routine abdominal hysterectomy. Am J Obstet Gynecol 1955;70: 1277–1283 (Level III)

23. Plockinger B, Kolbl H. Development of ovarian pathology after hysterectomy without oophorectomy. J Am Coll Surg 1994;178:581–585 (Level II-2)

24. Parker M, Bosscher J, Barnhill D, Park R. Ovarian management during radical hysterectomy in the premenopausal patient. Obstet Gynecol 1993;82:187–190 (Level II-3)

25. American College of Obstetricians and Gynecologists. Hormone replacement therapy. ACOG Educational Bulletin 247. Washington, DC: ACOG, 1998 (Level III)

26. Lindsay R, Tohme JF. Estrogen treatment of patients with established postmenopausal osteoporosis. Obstet Gynecol 1990;76:290–295 (Level II-1)

27. Lindsay R. Estrogen/progestogen therapy: prevention and treatment of postmenopausal osteoporosis. Proc Soc Exp Biol Med 1989;191:275–277 (Level III)

28. Lip GY, Blann AD, Jones AF, Beevers DG. Effects of hormone-replacement therapy on hemostatic factors, lipid factors, and endothelial function in women undergoing surgical menopause: implications for prevention of atherosclerosis. Am Heart J 1997;134:764–771 (Level II-3)

29. Ravnikar VA. Compliance with hormone therapy. Am J Obstet Gynecol 1987;156:1332–1334 (Level III)

30. Speroff T, Dawson NV, Speroff L, Haber RJ. A risk-benefit-analysis of elective bilateral oophorectomy: effect of changes in compliance with estrogen therapy on outcome. Am J Obstet Gynecol 1991;164:165–174 (Level III)

31. Struewing JP, Watson P, Easton DF, Ponder BA, Lynch HT, Tucker MA. Prophylactic oophorectomy in inherited breast/ovarian cancer families. J Natl Cancer Inst Monogr 1995;17:33–35 (Level II-2)

32. Burke W, Daly M, Garber J, Botkin J, Kahn MJ, Lynch P, et al. Recommendations for follow-up care of individuals with an inherited predisposition to cancer. II. BRCA1 and BRCA2. JAMA 1997;277:997–1003 (Level III)

33. Moore JT, Tolley DH: Depression following hysterectomy. Psychosomatics 1976;17:86–89 (Level II-3)

The MEDLINE database, the Cochrane Library, and ACOG's own internal resources were used to conduct a literature search to locate relevant articles published between January 1985 and January 1999. The search was restricted to articles published in the English language. Priority was given to articles reporting results of original research, although review articles and commentaries also were consulted. Abstracts of research presented at symposiums and scientific conferences were not considered adequate for inclusion in this document. Guidelines published by organizations or institutions such as the National Institutes of Health and ACOG were reviewed, and additional studies were located by reviewing bibliographies of identified articles. When reliable research was not available, expert opinions from obstetrician–gynecologists were used.

Studies were reviewed and evaluated for quality according to the method outlined by the U.S. Preventive Services Task Force:

I   Evidence obtained from at least one properly designed randomized controlled trial.

II-1   Evidence obtained from well-designed controlled trials without randomization.

II-2   Evidence obtained from well-designed cohort or case–control analytic studies, preferably from more than one center or research group.

II-3   Evidence obtained from multiple time series with or without the intervention. Dramatic results in uncontrolled experiments also could be regarded as this type of evidence.

III   Opinions of respected authorities, based on clinical experience, descriptive studies, or reports of expert committees.

Based on the highest level of evidence found in the data, recommendations are provided and graded according to the following categories:

Level A—Recommendations are based on good and consistent scientific evidence.

Level B—Recommendations are based on limited or inconsistent scientific evidence.

Level C—Recommendations are based primarily on consensus and expert opinion.

ISSN 1099-3630

The American College of Obstetricians and Gynecologists
409 12th Street, SW
PO Box 96920
Washington, DC 20090-6920

12345/32109

ACOG *PRACTICE BULLETIN*

CLINICAL MANAGEMENT GUIDELINES FOR
OBSTETRICIAN–GYNECOLOGISTS

NUMBER 16, MAY 2000

(Replaces Educational Bulletin Number 192, May 1994)

This Practice Bulletin was developed by the ACOG Committee on Practice Bulletins— Gynecology with the assistance of Elizabeth A. Stewart, MD. The information is designed to aid practitioners in making decisions about appropriate obstetric and gynecologic care. These guidelines should not be construed as dictating an exclusive course of treatment or procedure. Variations in practice may be warranted based on the needs of the individual patient, resources, and limitations unique to the institution or type of practice.

Surgical Alternatives to Hysterectomy in the Management of Leiomyomas

Uterine leiomyomas (also called fibroids) are the most common solid pelvic tumors in women and the leading indication for hysterectomy. Although most women with uterine leiomyomas are asymptomatic and can be followed without treatment, some will require more active measures. Hysterectomy remains the most common treatment for leiomyomas because it is the only treatment that provides a cure and eliminates the possibility of recurrence. Many women seek an alternative to hysterectomy because they desire future childbearing or wish to retain their uteri even if they have completed childbearing. As alternatives to hysterectomy become increasingly available, the efficacies of these treatments and the risk of potential problems are important to delineate. The purpose of this bulletin is to review the literature about surgical alternatives to hysterectomy and to offer treatment recommendations.

Background

As benign neoplasms, uterine leiomyomas usually require treatment only when they cause symptoms. The two most common symptoms for which women seek treatment are abnormal uterine bleeding and pelvic pressure or pain. However, not all bleeding is caused by leiomyomas; therefore, other causes of abnormal bleeding should be ruled out. The most common kind of abnormal uterine bleeding associated with leiomyomas is menorrhagia. Often, menses last 7 days or more, frequently resulting in iron deficiency anemia. This heavy flow also may require frequent changes of sanitary protection, causing significant interruptions in a woman's work or social schedule.

Uterine leiomyomas are clinically apparent in 25–50% of women (1), although studies in which careful pathologic examination of the uterus is carried out suggest the prevalence may be as high as 80% (2). The lack of a simple, inexpensive, and safe long-term medical treatment means that most symptomatic leiomyomas are still managed surgically.

Leiomyomas range greatly in size. Both size and location can play a role in symptoms and potential treatments. Leiomyomas may be subserosal, submucosal, or intramural; however, some types may be combined, for example, largely intramural with a submucosal extension.

The pelvic and abdominal discomfort that women experience with leiomyomas often is referred to as pressure and often is analogous to the discomforts women experience during pregnancy due to the enlarging of the uterus. In addition to pelvic pressure, the leiomyomas may press on adjacent structures, leading to difficulty with urination or defecation or dyspareunia.

Surgical Alternatives to Hysterectomy

In choosing a surgical alternative to hysterectomy, both safety and efficacy need to be established for each procedure. It must be recognized that all surgical alternatives to hysterectomy allow the possibility for new leiomyomas to form, and preexisting leiomyomas that were too small to be detected or were intentionally not removed may exhibit significant growth, necessitating another procedure. Complications of other surgical procedures may lead to an unanticipated hysterectomy.

Myomectomy

For women who desire future childbearing or who prefer to retain their uteri, myomectomy may be an option. Myomectomy removes only the visible and accessible leiomyomas, and the uterus is reconstructed. Most myomectomies traditionally have been performed by laparotomy.

Laparoscopic Myomectomy

Endoscopic myomectomy is now a treatment option for many women. Laparoscopic myomectomy minimizes the size of the abdominal incision, although it usually requires a minimum of three small incisions. Because the laparoscope usually is inserted at the umbilicus, the uterus must be small enough to be well-visualized with this approach; thus, this technique would not be appropriate for large uteri.

Hysteroscopic Procedures

Hysteroscopic procedures are primarily efficacious for the control of leiomyoma-related bleeding and do not significantly reduce uterine size. Only if a leiomyoma is submucosal or has a submucosal component can it be removed through the vagina (ie, hysteroscopic myomectomy).

For women with primarily intramural leiomyomas or women who have simultaneous hysteroscopic myomectomies, destruction of the endometrium by endometrial ablation can decrease bleeding. Endometrial ablation can be performed for a variety of indications, and it also can be useful in the control of leiomyoma-related menorrhagia. Endometrial ablation can utilize a variety of techniques, including laser ablation, thermal ablation, physical resection, or chemical destruction. Theoretically, even if leiomyomas remain, menstrual bleeding cannot occur because there is no endometrium. These procedures require hysteroscopic expertise.

Procedures Under Development

Several innovative options are being studied as possible alternative treatments for leiomyomas. Although all of these procedures may prove to be effective treatments for leiomyomas compared with current options, the number of patients treated have been small, the follow-up periods have been relatively short, and the safety of the procedures in women desiring pregnancy has not been demonstrated.

Uterine artery embolization is a radiologic alternative to surgery that involves partial blockage of the uterine arteries and, thus, decreased blood flow to the leiomyomatous uterus. Several case series of embolizations have been reported, with 8–53 patients monitored for intervals of 3–20 months (3–5). These reports suggest that most patients have a significant decrease in bleeding symptoms, as well as a reduction in uterine size. However, uterine artery embolization may have serious consequences including infection, massive uterine bleeding, and uterine necrosis, requiring emergency surgery (6). Patients can experience significant uterine pain, ischemia, and hypoxic changes following embolization of the myoma. Therefore, uterine artery embolization is regarded as investigational. Myolysis involves delivering electric current with needles or the use of lasers to coagulate myomas at the time of laparoscopy. A large series of cases have been reported from a single center (7).

As the biology of leiomyomas is better understood, new medical treatment options may become available. Both the progesterone antagonist mifepristone (RU 486) and gonadotropin-releasing hormone (GnRH) antagonists have been shown in small studies to produce equivalent levels of uterine shrinkage and rates of amenorrhea to GnRH agonists (8–10), with the attendant advantages of normal follicular levels of estradiol (mifepristone) and rapidity of action (antagonists). Understanding the derangements of growth factors and genes that lead to leiomyoma formation and growth also may lead to new medical therapies aimed at these underlying mechanisms (11).

Clinical Considerations and Recommendations

▶ *In symptomatic women with leiomyomas and an indication for surgery, does hysterectomy produce a better outcome than myomectomy in relation to long-term morbidity (eg, pain, bleeding, recurrence, operative complications, and patient satisfaction)?*

Randomized studies are difficult to perform on this subject for which patient preference often is strong. However, reports of retrospective series have provided some information on this topic.

Abdominal Myomectomy. Although early studies suggested the morbidity associated with myomectomy was increased compared with hysterectomy, more recent studies suggest that the risks of the two procedures are similar (12–14). However, women choosing myomectomy face the additional risks of recurrence of leiomyomas and the possibility of having to proceed with hysterectomy because of intraoperative complications.

There is less outcomes research available for myomectomy than there is for hysterectomy (15). However, clinical experience and pooled results of numerous small studies suggest that there is excellent resolution of menorrhagia symptoms (overall 81% resolution; range, 40–93%) with similar results for resolution of pelvic pressure with abdominal myomectomy (1).

In the long term, however, the risk of formation of new leiomyomas limits the efficacy of myomectomy. There are a number of studies that have examined the use of ultrasonography to assess the recurrence risk of leiomyomas after abdominal myomectomy (16–19). Clearly, an estimate depends on the detection power of the measuring instrument. Thus, later studies using transvaginal ultrasonography tend to give higher estimates of recurrence (51% at 5 years) compared with earlier transabdominal ultrasound studies (27% at 10 years) but, presumably, are more accurate (16, 17). Studies have indicated that women who experience childbirth after a myomectomy appear to have a decreased recurrence risk

(16, 17). There have been conflicting reports over whether the preoperative use of GnRH agonists affects recurrence risk (18, 19).

The clinically relevant endpoint is whether a second surgical procedure is needed after conservative surgery. A summary of a small case series conducted since the 1920s suggests the risk of follow-up treatment (in this instance, defined as hysterectomy, second myomectomy, or radiation therapy) varied from 3% to 32%, with a mean risk of 15%, although no information on the length of follow-up was given (1). In a relatively large series (125 patients followed at least 5 years and up to 23 years), there was evidence that recurrence depended on the number of leiomyomas present, with a recurrence risk of 11% for a single myoma and a recurrence risk of 26% with multiple myomas (20). A more recent study of 80 patients found a similar reoperation rate of 18% after 10 years (21).

The risk of undergoing an unexpected hysterectomy at the time of myomectomy appears to be low with skilled surgical technique (<1%), even when uterine size is substantial (14, 22–24). There may, however, be higher rates of hysterectomy for surgeons inexperienced in the procedure. Blood loss and the risk of transfusion may be increased in women with larger uteri (14, 25).

Laparoscopic Myomectomy. There are a number of case series of laparoscopic myomectomies, the largest of them reporting on more than 200 patients covering a period in excess of 5 years (26–28). The two major concerns with laparoscopic myomectomy versus hysterectomy are the removal of large myomas through small abdominal incisions and the repair of the uterus. The introduction of more efficient morcellators has made the removal easier, although skilled operative technique is necessary because injury to other organs is possible. Although there are multiple techniques available for laparoscopic suturing, there is controversy as to whether the closure techniques available are equal to those achieved at laparotomy. This is most relevant to women contemplating a future pregnancy.

Recommendations differ regarding cases amenable to a laparoscopic approach; most recommend a laparotomy or a laparoscopically assisted approach with leiomyomas in excess of 5–8 cm, multiple leiomyomas, or the presence of deep intramural leiomyomas (26–28). In addition to routine surgical complications, reported complications include a 2–8% conversion rate to a more open procedure, the formation of uteroperitoneal fistulas, and the possibility of uterine rupture during a subsequent pregnancy (26–28). It appears that the risk of recurrent leiomyomas may be higher after a laparoscopic myomectomy than after a traditional myomectomy, with a 33% recurrence risk at 27 months (29).

Hysteroscopic Myomectomy. Several series of between 100 and 200 patients undergoing hysteroscopic myomectomies with good results have been published. In a series in which almost all patients were treated for menorrhagia, 16% of the submucosal resection group ultimately underwent a second surgery after a mean follow-up of 9 years (30). In the same series, women undergoing ablation with or without submucosal myomectomy had an 8% chance of undergoing a second surgery after a mean of 6 years of follow-up (30). In a series of 167 patients who were followed for 3 years after hysteroscopic myomectomy plus myolysis, approximately 5% underwent a second surgery (31). For women desiring pregnancy, fertility rates appear good: 59% of patients with submucosal leiomyomas conceived after hysteroscopic myomectomy (32).

Endometrial Ablation. Endometrial ablation appears to be an effective therapy for the control of menstrual bleeding in women with abnormal bleeding only. For leiomyomas, one study suggested endometrial ablation had a failure rate of 40%, compared with a failure rate of 5% in women with a normal uterus (33). Thus, ablation for women with clinically significant leiomyomas may prove to be a less desirable course of action than for women with idiopathic menorrhagia. Currently, there is no evidence to support the use of this procedure for women with leiomyomas; however, new techniques are being explored.

Complications with all techniques involving operative hysteroscopy include the risk of injury to intraabdominal structures either by uterine perforation or secondary to electrical or thermal injury (34). In addition, there can be significant complications as a consequence of the distending medium used. The uterine vasculature can rapidly absorb the substance distending the uterus. Fatal events have been reported with air embolism using an Nd-YAG laser with saline as the distending medium, as well as with hyponatremic encephalopathy with sorbitol as the distending medium (35, 36). Many newer technologies have been designed to minimize this risk, including systems that accurately measure inflow and outflow of hysteroscopic fluids and devices that use physiologic saline as the uterine distending medium.

▶ *In women with leiomyomas who are candidates for surgery, does the use of adjunctive medical treatment result in better outcomes?*

Preoperative Adjuvants. Gonadotropin-releasing hormone agonists have been used widely for preoperative treatment of uterine leiomyomas, both for myomectomy and hysterectomy. These medications are very effective in inducing amenorrhea and causing uterine shrinkage in a large proportion of women who take them. However, they are expensive and have significant side effects for most women in the short term and significant effects on bone density if taken over longer periods.

Currently, GnRH agonists are the only drugs available that result in clinically significant uterine shrinkage and amenorrhea. When a significant reduction in uterine volume is necessary to achieve surgical goals (eg, when the patient prefers a low-transverse incision instead of a vertical incision or an endoscopic procedure), GnRH agonists may be useful.

By inducing amenorrhea, GnRH agonists have been shown to improve hematologic parameters, shorten hospital stay, and decrease blood loss, operating time, and postoperative pain when given for 2–3 months preoperatively (37–39). However, because no study has shown a significant decrease in transfusion risk or improvement in quality of life, and the cost of these medications is substantial, the decision to use GnRH agonists preoperatively remains complex. It also is worth noting that in a study that achieved hematologic improvement with GnRH agonist treatment in 74% of women, there was a 46% improvement rate in the placebo group with iron supplementation alone (38). One surgical disadvantage to preoperative GnRH agonist therapy is that it may make the leiomyomas softer and the surgical planes less distinct. Although many studies find the operative time equivalent for laparotomies, one study of laparoscopic myomectomies found that overall operating time decreased after GnRH agonist treatment. However, in the subgroup in which the largest leiomyoma was hypoechoic, operative time was longer because of the difficulty in dissection (39).

Intraoperative Adjuvants. Several studies suggest that the infiltration of vasopressin into the myometrium decreases blood loss at the time of myomectomy. A study of 20 patients demonstrated that vasopressin significantly decreased blood loss compared with saline injection in a randomized myomectomy study (40). Two studies compared the use of physical vascular compression, primarily a tourniquet around the lower uterine segment, with pharmacologic vasoconstriction (vasopressin administration). In one study using a Penrose drain tourniquet and vascular clamps, there was no significant difference between the two techniques (25). A more recent study using a Foley catheter as a tourniquet found blood loss to be significantly greater in the tourniquet group (41). There are no studies comparing tourniquet with placebo. Additionally, one study demonstrated that injection of vasopressin into the cervix at the time of operative hysteroscopy decreased blood loss, fluid intravasation, and operative time (42).

▶ *In pregnant women who have undergone a myomectomy, does a planned cesarean delivery versus a trial of labor help prevent uterine rupture?*

No study directly addresses the issue of cesarean delivery versus a trial of labor after myomectomy. The widely quoted clinical dictum is that if the endometrial cavity is entered at the time of myomectomy, then cesarean delivery is recommended. This appears to arise from a 3-year collaborative trial of data reporting a rate of uterine rupture of approximately 0.1% (43). Most of these ruptures had cesarean deliveries as antecedents, and because myomectomy also can produce a transmural incision in the uterus, it appears to have been treated in an analogous way. However, in the original study, the incidence of uterine rupture after myomectomy was only 0.002% (43). There are rare case reports of rupture remote from term after traditional abdominal myomectomy (44, 45). Uterine rupture can carry significant consequences for both mother and fetus.

However, several case reports have demonstrated uterine rupture at 33–34 weeks of gestation following laparoscopic myomectomy (46–48) and myolysis (49, 50). Although most of the case reports detail ruptures with intramural leiomyomas, one describes a case in which the 5-cm leiomyoma was subserosal; however, in this case no suturing was performed (48). Clearly long-term follow-up is necessary to determine the safety of innovative approaches to leiomyomas in women attempting pregnancy, and patients should be counseled preoperatively regarding these issues.

▶ *In women with leiomyomas who desire to become pregnant, does removal of leiomyomas versus expectant management increase the pregnancy rate?*

It is difficult to assess the contributions of leiomyomas to infertility for several reasons. First, there is a high prevalence of leiomyomas in the population, and the incidence of leiomyomas increases with age, as does infertility. Because not all leiomyomas are symptomatic, many women may conceive without even knowing that they have them. Finally, studies to date have been case series; randomized trials have not been conducted.

It appears that distortion of the uterine cavity may cause infertility and lead to pregnancy complications (51, 52). One study examining women attempting in vitro fertilization showed a decreased implantation rate in women with distortion of the cavity (53). When myomectomies have been performed on infertile patients with no other

infertility factor, pregnancy rates have been reported in the range of 40–60% after 1–2 years (54–56). However, the use of additional fertility treatments in these studies was not excluded and may have contributed to the increase as well.

Two recent studies have examined the effect of leiomyomas on the outcome of assisted reproduction when there is no distortion of the uterine cavity. Using age-matched patients with similar embryo characteristics, the first study found significant decreases in both clinical pregnancies (53% versus 37%) and delivery rates (48% versus 33%) in patients with leiomyomas (57). The second study showed both significantly decreased pregnancy rates and implantation rates with both intramural and submucosal leiomyomas but not with subserosal leiomyomas (58). Although a general problem with the myomatous uterus or other associated factors may play a role in this process, indications for myomectomy in women undergoing assisted reproductive techniques remain to be clarified.

Some surgeons feel that a prophylactic myomectomy for women with large fibroids who want to preserve future fertility may be appropriate in some circumstances. The evidence that the complication rate is low in skilled surgical hands, even with substantial uterine size, suggests myomectomy may be indicated (14, 22–24); however, the risk of recurrent myomas is high, which may make myomectomy a less effective treatment (16, 17). Consideration of multiple factors is important, including size and location of myomas, previous fertility, and the woman's age.

▶ *In menopausal women with leiomyomas, what is the effect of hormone replacement therapy on leiomyoma growth, bleeding, and pain?*

For many years, health care providers have counseled patients that leiomyomas are a self-limiting problem that will resolve when a woman completes the transition to menopause. Because leiomyomas are responsive to estrogen, the hypoestrogenism of menopause most women experience results in uterine shrinkage, and all women have cessation of physiologic menses. However, as more women elect hormone replacement therapy, there is the possibility that problems with leiomyomas may persist into menopause.

There is some evidence that women with leiomyomas who take hormone replacement therapy are more likely to have abnormal bleeding. In a study using hysteroscopy to evaluate women with abnormal bleeding who were taking hormone replacement therapy (using women with no abnormal bleeding as controls), women with structural abnormalities of the cavity, including endometrial polyps and submucosal leiomyomas, had an increased likelihood of abnormal bleeding (59).

A small pilot study examined whether hormone replacement therapy during menopause caused an increase in size of asymptomatic leiomyomas (60). This study showed a significant increase in leiomyoma dimension after 1 year of transdermal hormone replacement therapy but no increase with oral conjugated estrogens. Because the clinical magnitude of the increase associated with the transdermal route is small (14.3–19.7 mm) and the follow-up time short, it is not clear whether this will result in clinically significant changes.

▶ *In asymptomatic women with leiomyomas, does expectant management produce a better outcome than surgical treatment in relation to long-term morbidity?*

Expectant management in an asymptomatic patient should be the norm; however, in some instances an asymptomatic leiomyomatous uterus might require treatment. If there is concern that the mass is not a leiomyoma but instead a sarcoma, further evaluation is warranted. Traditionally, the major clinical sign used to make this distinction was rapid growth in uterine size. However, in a study of 1,332 hysterectomy specimens for which the preoperative diagnosis was uterine leiomyomas, sarcomas were not only rare (2–3 per 1,000) but no more common in the subgroup of women who had experienced rapidly enlarging uterine size (61). If a comparison is made between the prevalence of leiomyosarcomas discovered incidentally (1:2,000) and the mortality rate for hysterectomy for benign disease (1.0–1.6 per 1,000 for premenopausal women), the decision to proceed to hysterectomy to find potential sarcomas should be made cautiously (62). Other risk factors for sarcomas, including increasing age or a history of prior pelvic radiation, may influence this decision. Alternatively, both endometrial biopsy and magnetic resonance imaging appear to be useful in diagnosing sarcomas and differentiating them from other intrauterine lesions (63, 64).

In rare circumstances, the uterus will cause significant compression of the ureters that can lead to the compromise of renal function, which requires further evaluation. Finally, in a woman contemplating pregnancy or experiencing recurrent miscarriage, significant distortion of the uterine cavity may require intervention in an asymptomatic patient (51, 52). Proximity of the leiomyoma to the placental implantation site and large size of the leiomyoma appear to increase obstetric risk, including placental abruption and premature labor. However, no consensus exists for when myomectomy should be rec-

ommended in women desiring pregnancy but with no history of infertility (52).

Historically, it has been argued that uterine size alone should be an indication for hysterectomy. The argument has usually been twofold. The first issue was that a large leiomyomatous uterus made assessment of the ovaries and early surveillance for ovarian cancer impossible. However, the National Institutes of Health and National Cancer Institute Consensus Conference acknowledge the futility of routine pelvic examinations in the identification of early ovarian cancer. Second, the argument is made that because of increased morbidity during surgery for a large uterus, surgery is a safer option when the uterus is smaller. Although some studies have shown increased morbidity, others show no differences in perioperative complications (13, 14, 62). This currently does not appear to be a cogent argument for intervention.

▶ *In women with leiomyomas planning future pregnancies who are candidates for surgery, what is the impact on future fertility (pregnancy rate) of surgery versus expectant management?*

As with any woman with leiomyomas, asymptomatic women with leiomyomas who desire future fertility should be managed expectantly because they have no indication for surgery. For mildly symptomatic women, given the risk of recurrence, intervening as close to the desired pregnancy as practical is desirable. The consequences of postoperative adhesions after myomectomy are unclear and should be avoided, despite the availability of assisted reproductive technology. Finally, although the risk of hysterectomy appears low for most surgical alternatives to hysterectomy, it is never eliminated. This risk should be considered in determining the appropriate treatment for women planning future pregnancies.

Summary

The following recommendations are based on good and consistent scientific evidence (Level A):

▶ In women with symptomatic leiomyomas, hysterectomy provides a definitive cure.

▶ In women with symptomatic leiomyomas, abdominal myomectomy is a safe and effective option for women who wish to retain their uterus. If this option is selected, women should be counseled preoperatively about the relatively high risk of reoperation.

▶ Use of GnRH agonists preoperatively is beneficial, especially when improvement of hematologic status and uterine shrinkage are important goals. Benefits of the use of GnRH agonists should be weighed against their cost and side effects for individual patients.

▶ The use of vasopressin at the time of myomectomy appears to limit blood loss.

The following recommendation is based on limited or inconsistent scientific evidence (Level B):

▶ The clinical diagnosis of rapidly growing leiomyomas has not been shown to predict uterine sarcoma and thus should not be used as the sole indication for myomectomy or hysterectomy.

The following recommendations are based primarily on consensus and expert opinion (Level C):

▶ Laparoscopic myomectomy appears to be a safe and effective option for women with a small number of moderately sized uterine leiomyomas who do not desire future fertility. Further studies are necessary to evaluate the safety of this procedure for women planning pregnancy.

▶ Hysteroscopic myomectomy is an effective option for controlling menorrhagia in women with submucosal leiomyomas.

▶ Although endometrial ablation appears to be an effective option in controlling menorrhagia in women without leiomyomas, further studies are needed in women who have clinically significant leiomyomas.

▶ Because leiomyomas may be a factor in infertility for some patients, the issues are complex, and myomectomy should not be performed without first completing a comprehensive fertility evaluation.

▶ Although postmenopausal women with leiomyomas may have more bleeding problems and some increase in leiomyoma size while taking hormone replacement therapy, there appears to be no reason to withhold this treatment option from women who desire or need such therapy.

References

1. Buttram VC Jr, Reiter RC. Uterine leiomyomata: etiology, symptomatology, and management. Fertil Steril 1981;36:433–445 (Level III)

2. Cramer SF, Patel A. The frequency of uterine leiomyomas. Am J Clin Pathol 1990;94:435–438 (Level II-3)

3. Bradley EA, Reidy JF, Forman RG, Jarosz J, Braude PR. Transcatheter uterine artery embolisation to treat large uterine fibroids. Br J Obstet Gynaecol 1998;105:235–240 (Level III)

4. Goodwin SC, Vedantham S, McLucas B, Forno AE, Perrella R. Preliminary experience with uterine artery embolization for uterine fibroids. J Vasc Interv Radiol 1997;8:517–526 (Level III)

5. Ravina JH, Herbreteau D, Ciraru-Vigneron N, Bouret JM, Houdart E, Aymard A, et al. Arterial embolisation to treat uterine myomata. Lancet 1995;346:671–672 (Level III)

6. Barbieri RL. Ambulatory management of uterine leiomyomata. Clin Obstet Gynecol 1999;42:196–205 (Level III)

7. Goldfarb HA. Bipolar laparoscopic needles for myoma coagulation. J Am Assoc Gynecol Laparosc 1995;2:175–179 (Level II-2)

8. Kettel LM, Murphy AA, Morales AJ, Rivier J, Vale W, Yen SS. Rapid regression of uterine leiomyomas in response to daily administration of gonadotropin-releasing hormone antagonist. Fertil Steril 1993;60:642–646 (Level III)

9. Murphy AA, Kettel LM, Morales AJ, Roberts VJ, Yen SS. Regression of uterine leiomyomata in response to the antiprogesterone RU 486. J Clin Endocrinol Metab 1993;76:513–517 (Level III)

10. Murphy AA, Morales AJ, Kettel LM, Yen SS. Regression of uterine leiomyomata to the antiprogesterone RU486: dose-response effect. Fertil Steril 1995;64:187–190 (Level III)

11. Stewart EA, Nowak RA. Leiomyoma-related bleeding: a classic hypothesis updated for the molecular era. Hum Reprod Update 1996;2:295–306 (Level III)

12. Hillis SD, Marchbanks PA, Peterson HB. Uterine size and risk of complications among women undergoing abdominal hysterectomy for leiomyomas. Obstet Gynecol 1996;87:539–543 (Level II-2)

13. Iverson RE Jr, Chelmow D, Strohbehn K, Waldman L, Evantash EG. Relative morbidity of abdominal hysterectomy and myomectomy for management of uterine leiomyomas. Obstet Gynecol 1996;88:415–419 (Level II-2)

14. Ecker JL, Foster JT, Friedman AJ. Abdominal hysterectomy or abdominal myomectomy for symptomatic leiomyoma: a comparison of preoperative demography and postoperative morbidity. J Gynecol Surg 1995;11:11–18 (Level II-2)

15. Carlson KJ, Miller BA, Fowler FJ Jr. The Maine Women's Health Study: I. Outcomes of hysterectomy. Obstet Gynecol 1994;83:556–565 (Level II-3)

16. Candiani GB, Fedele L, Parazzini F, Villa L. Risk of recurrence after myomectomy. Br J Obstet Gynaecol 1991;98:385–389 (Level II-3)

17. Fedele L, Parazzini F, Luchini L, Mezzopane R, Tozzi L, Villa L. Recurrence of fibroids after myomectomy: a transvaginal ultrasonographic study. Hum Reprod 1995;10:1795–1796 (Level II-3)

18. Fedele L, Vercellini P, Bianchi S, Brioschi D, Dorta M. Treatment with GnRH agonists before myomectomy and

the risk of short-term myoma recurrence. Br J Obstet Gynaecol 1990;97:393–396 (Level I)

19. Friedman AJ, Daly M, Juneau-Norcross M, Fine C, Rein MS. Recurrence of myomas after myomectomy in women pretreated with leuprolide acetate depot or placebo. Fertil Steril 1992;58:205–208 (Level I)

20. Malone LJ. Myomectomy: recurrence after removal of solitary and multiple myomas. Obstet Gynecol 1969;34:200–203 (Level II-3)

21. Acien P, Quereda F. Abdominal myomectomy: results of a simple operative technique. Fertil Steril 1996;65:41–51 (Level II-3)

22. Smith DC, Uhlir JK. Myomectomy as a reproductive procedure. Am J Obstet Gynecol 1990;162:1476–1479; discussion 1479–1482 (Level III)

23. Chong RK, Thong PH, Tan SL, Thong PW, Salmon YM. Myomectomy: indications, results of surgery and relation to fertility. Singapore Med J 1988;29:35–37 (Level III)

24. LaMorte AI, Lalwani S, Diamond MP. Morbidity associated with abdominal myomectomy. Obstet Gynecol 1993; 82:897–900 (Level III)

25. Ginsburg ES, Benson CB, Garfield JM, Gleason RE, Friedman AJ. The effect of operative technique and uterine size on blood loss during myomectomy: a prospective randomized study. Fertil Steril 1993;60:956–962 (Level I)

26. Dubuisson JB, Chapron C, Levy L. Difficulties and complications of laparoscopic myomectomy. J Gynecol Surg 1996;12:159–165 (Level II-3)

27. Nezhat C, Nezhat F, Silfen SL, Schaffer N, Evans D. Laparoscopic myomectomy. Int J Fertil 1991;36:275–280 (Level II-3)

28. Seinera P, Arisio R, Decko A, Farina C, Crana F. Laparoscopic myomectomy: indications, surgical technique and complications. Hum Reprod 1997;12:1927–1930 (Level II-3)

29. Nezhat FR, Roemisch M, Nezhat CH, Seidman DS, Nezhat CR. Recurrence rate after laparoscopic myomectomy. J Am Assoc Gynecol Laparosc 1998;5:237–240 (Level III)

30. Derman SG, Rehnstrom J, Neuwirth RS. The long-term effectiveness of hysteroscopic treatment of menorrhagia and leiomyomas. Obstet Gynecol 1991;77:591–594 (Level II-3)

31. Phillips DR, Milim SJ, Nathanson HG, Haselkorn JS. Experience with laparoscopic leiomyoma coagulation and concomitant operative hysteroscopy. J Am Assoc Gynecol Laparosc 1997;4:425–433 (Level II-3)

32. Ubaldi F, Tournaye H, Camus M, Van der Pas H, Gepts E, Devroey P. Fertility after hysteroscopic myomectomy. Hum Reprod Update 1995;1:81–90 (Level III)

33. Yin CS, Wei RY, Chao TC, Chan CC. Hysteroscopic endometrial ablation without endometrial preparation. Int J Gynaecol Obstet 1998;62:167–172 (Level II-3)

34. Kivnick S, Kanter MH. Bowel injury from rollerball ablation of the endometrium. Obstet Gynecol 1992;79: 833–835 (Level III)

35. Arieff AI, Ayus JC. Endometrial ablation complicated by fatal hyponatremic encephalopathy. JAMA 1993;270: 1230–1232 (Level III)

36. Challener RC, Kaufman B. Fatal venous air embolism following sequential unsheathed (bare) and sheathed quartz fiber Nd:YAG laser endometrial ablation. Anesthesiology 1990;73:548–551 (Level III)

37. Gerris J, Degueldre M, Peters AA, Romao F, Stjernquist M, al-Taher H. The place of Zoladex in deferred surgery for uterine fibroids. Zoladex Myoma Study Group. Horm Res 1996;45:279–284 (Level I)

38. Stovall TG, Muneyyirci-Delale O, Summitt RL Jr, Scialli AR. GnRH agonist and iron versus placebo and iron in the anemic patient before surgery for leiomyomas: a randomized controlled trial. Leuprolide Acetate Study Group. Obstet Gynecol 1995;86:65–71 (Level I)

39. Zullo F, Pellicano M, De Stefano R, Zupi E, Mastrantonio P. A prospective randomized study to evaluate leuprolide acetate treatment before laparoscopic myomectomy: efficacy and ultrasonographic predictors. Am J Obstet Gynecol 1998;178:108–112 (Level I)

40. Frederick J, Fletcher H, Simeon D, Mullings A, Hardie M. Intramyometrial vasopressin as a haemostatic agent during myomectomy. Br J Obstet Gynaecol 1994;101:435–437 (Level I)

41. Fletcher H, Frederick J, Hardie M, Simeon D. A randomized comparison of vasopressin and tourniquet as hemostatic agents during myomectomy. Obstet Gynecol 1996;87:1014–1018 (Level I)

42. Phillips DR, Nathanson HG, Milim SJ, Haselkorn JS, Khapra A, Ross PL. The effect of dilute vasopressin solution on blood loss during operative hysteroscopy: a randomized controlled trial. Obstet Gynecol 1996;88:761–766 (Level I)

43. Garnet JD. Uterine rupture during pregnancy: an analysis of 133 patients. Obstet Gynecol 1964;23:898–905 (Level II-3)

44. Golan D, Aharoni A, Gonen R, Boss Y, Sharf M. Early spontaneous rupture of the post myomectomy gravid uterus. Int J Gynaecol Obstet 1990;31:167–170 (Level III)

45. Ozeren M, Ulusoy M, Uyanik E. First-trimester spontaneous uterine rupture after traditional myomectomy: case report. Isr J Med Sci 1997;33:752–753 (Level III)

46. Dubuisson JB, Chavet X, Chapron C, Gregorakis SS, Morice P. Uterine rupture during pregnancy after laparoscopic myomectomy. Hum Reprod 1995;10:1475–1477 (Level III)

47. Harris WJ. Uterine dehiscence following laparoscopic myomectomy. Obstet Gynecol 1992;80:545–546 (Level III)

48. Pelosi MA 3rd, Pelosi MA. Spontaneous uterine rupture at thirty-three weeks subsequent to previous superficial laparoscopic myomectomy. Am J Obstet Gynecol 1997; 177:1547–1549 (Level III)

49. Arcangeli S, Pasquarette MM. Gravid uterine rupture after myolysis. Obstet Gynecol 1997;89:857 (Level III)

50. Vilos GA, Pispidikis JT, Botz CK. Economic evaluation of hysteroscopic endometrial ablation versus vaginal hys-

terectomy for menorrhagia. Obstet Gynecol 1996;88:
241–245 (Level II-2)

51. Garcia CR, Tureck RW. Submucosal leiomyomas and
infertility. Fertil Steril 1984;42:16–19 (Level III)

52. Rice JP, Kay HH, Mahony BS. The clinical significance of
uterine leiomyomas in pregnancy. Am J Obstet Gynecol
1989;160:1212–1216 (Level II-2)

53. Farhi J, Ashkenazi J, Feldberg D, Dicker D, Orvieto R,
Ben Rafael Z. Effect of uterine leiomyomata on the results
of in-vitro fertilization treatment. Hum Reprod 1995;10:
2576–2578 (Level II-2)

54. Babaknia A, Rock JA, Jones HW Jr. Pregnancy success
following abdominal myomectomy for infertility. Fertil
Steril 1978;30:644–647 (Level III)

55. Gehlbach DL, Sousa RC, Carpenter SE, Rock JA.
Abdominal myomectomy in the treatment of infertility. Int
J Gynaecol Obstet 1993;40:45–50 (Level III)

56. Sudik R, Husch K, Steller J, Daume E. Fertility and pregnancy outcome after myomectomy in sterility patients. Eur J
Obstet Gynecol Reprod Biol 1996;65:209–214 (Level II-2)

57. Stovall DW, Parrish SB, Van Voorhis BJ, Hahn SJ, Sparks
AE, Syrop CH. Uterine leiomyomas reduce the efficacy of
assisted reproduction cycles: results of a matched follow-
up study. Hum Reprod 1998;13:192–197 (Level II-2)

58. Eldar-Geva T, Meagher S, Healy DL, MacLachlan V,
Breheny S, Wood C. Effect of intramural, subserosal, and
submucosal uterine fibroids on the outcome of assisted
reproductive technology treatment. Fertil Steril 1998;70:
687–691 (Level II-2)

59. Akkad AA, Habiba MA, Ismail N, Abrams K, al-Azzawi
F. Abnormal uterine bleeding on hormone replacement:
the importance of intrauterine structural abnormalities.
Obstet Gynecol 1995;86:330–334 (Level II-2)

60. Sener AB, Seckin NC, Ozmen S, Gokmen O, Dogu N,
Ekici E. The effects of hormone replacement therapy on
uterine fibroids in postmenopausal women. Fertil Steril
1996;65:354–357 (Level II-1)

61. Parker WH, Fu YS, Berek JS. Uterine sarcoma in patients
operated on for presumed leiomyoma and rapidly growing
leiomyoma. Obstet Gynecol 1994;83:414–418 (Level II-3)

62. Reiter RC, Wagner PL, Gambone JC. Routine hysterectomy for large asymptomatic uterine leiomyomata: a reappraisal. Obstet Gynecol 1992;79:481–484 (Level II-3)

63. Schwartz LB, Diamond MP, Schwartz PE. Leiomyosarcomas: clinical presentation. Am J Obstet Gynecol
1993;168:180–183 (Level II-3)

64. Schwartz LB, Zawin M, Carcangiu ML, Lange R,
McCarthy S. Does pelvic magnetic resonance imaging differentiate among the histologic subtypes of uterine
leiomyomata? Fertil Steril 1998;70:580–587 (Level II-3)

The MEDLINE database, the Cochrane Library, and ACOG's own internal resources and documents were used to conduct a literature search to locate relevant articles published between January 1985 and May 1999. The search was restricted to articles published in the English language. Priority was given to articles reporting results of original research, although review articles and commentaries also were consulted. Abstracts of research presented at symposia and scientific conferences were not considered adequate for inclusion in this document. Guidelines published by organizations or institutions such as the National Institutes of Health and the American College of Obstetricians and Gynecologists were reviewed, and additional studies were located by reviewing bibliographies of identified articles. When reliable research was not available, expert opinions from obstetrician–gynecologists were used.

Studies were reviewed and evaluated for quality according to the method outlined by the U.S. Preventive Services Task Force:

I   Evidence obtained from at least one properly designed randomized controlled trial.

II-1   Evidence obtained from well-designed controlled trials without randomization.

II-2   Evidence obtained from well-designed cohort or case–control analytic studies, preferably from more than one center or research group.

II-3   Evidence obtained from multiple time series with or without the intervention. Dramatic results in uncontrolled experiments also could be regarded as this type of evidence.

III   Opinions of respected authorities, based on clinical experience, descriptive studies, or reports of expert committees.

Based on the highest level of evidence found in the data, recommendations are provided and graded according to the following categories:

Level A—Recommendations are based on good and consistent scientific evidence.

Level B—Recommendations are based on limited or inconsistent scientific evidence.

Level C—Recommendations are based primarily on consensus and expert opinion.

ISSN 1099-3630

The American College of
Obstetricians and Gynecologists
409 12th Street, SW
PO Box 96920
Washington, DC 20090-6920

12345/43210

ACOG PRACTICE BULLETIN

CLINICAL MANAGEMENT GUIDELINES FOR
OBSTETRICIAN–GYNECOLOGISTS

NUMBER 18, JULY 2000

This Practice Bulletin was developed by the ACOG Committee on Practice Bulletins— Gynecology with the assistance of Andrew M. Kaunitz, MD. The information is designed to aid practitioners in making decisions about appropriate obstetric and gynecologic care. These guidelines should not be construed as dictating an exclusive course of treatment or procedure. Variations in practice may be warranted based on the needs of the individual patient, resources, and limitations unique to the institution or type of practice.

The Use of Hormonal Contraception in Women with Coexisting Medical Conditions

Although numerous studies have addressed the safety and effectiveness of hormonal contraceptive use in healthy women, data are far less complete for women with underlying medical problems or other special circumstances. Because recommendations vary widely, substantial confusion exists with respect to contraceptive guidelines for women with coexisting medical conditions or other concerns. Using available scientific evidence, this Practice Bulletin will provide information to facilitate contraceptive counseling and selection for women with coexisting medical conditions.

Background

Decisions regarding contraception for women with coexisting medical problems may be complicated. In some cases, medications taken for certain chronic conditions may alter the effectiveness of hormonal contraception, and pregnancy in these cases may pose substantial risks to the mother as well as her fetus. Package labeling approved by the U.S. Food and Drug Administration for progestin-only oral contraceptives (OCs) is occasionally the same as that for combined estrogen-progestin preparations. For instance, current labeling for norethindrone progestin-only OCs no longer lists a history of thromboembolism as a contraindication (1). Such a history, however, remains listed as a contraindication in package labeling for norgestrel progestin-only pills and for depot medroxyprogesterone acetate (DMPA) injections.

Sometimes, simultaneous use of two contraceptive methods is appropriate. For instance, although hormonal contraception provides effective birth control for women at risk for human immunodeficiency virus or other sexually transmitted diseases (or those currently infected), such patients also should be encouraged to use male or female condoms correctly and consistently to prevent disease. For women concomitantly using major teratogens, such as isotretinoin or thalidomide, simultaneous use of two methods of contraception (eg, OCs and condoms) also may be appropriate.

This Practice Bulletin will focus on selection of hormonal contraceptives for women with coexisting medical problems. However, practitioners should recognize that the use of other nonhormonal forms of contraception, such as intrauterine devices, represent a safe, effective choice for many women.

Clinical Considerations and Recommendations

This document will address the use of combination OCs in women who have the following conditions and risk factors:

- Older than 35 years
- Smoke tobacco products
- Hypertension
- Diabetes
- Migraine headaches
- Fibrocystic breast changes, fibroadenoma, or family history of breast cancer
- Uterine fibroids
- Lipid disorders
- Breastfeeding/postpartum
- Take concomitant medication
- Anticipate surgery
- Venous thromboembolism (VTE)
- Systemic lupus erythematosus (SLE)
- Sickle cell disease

In addition, the document will review clinical settings in which the use of progestin-only contraceptives represent safe alternatives for women with contraindications to combination OCs (see the box). The effect of DMPA use on bone mineral density (BMD) will be reviewed, particularly with respect to adolescent candidates. Practitioners should be aware that patients who have any of the previously mentioned conditions or risk factors and use OCs require close monitoring and follow-up evaluation.

Indications for Contraception Methods Other Than Oral Contraceptives

In women with the following conditions, use of progestin-only oral contraceptives, depot medroxyprogesterone acetate,* or implants may be safer than combination oral contraceptives. An intrauterine device also represents an appropriate contraceptive choice for women with these conditions.

- Migraine headaches
- Older than 35 years and smoke cigarettes
- History of thromboembolic disease
- Coronary artery disease
- Congestive heart failure
- Cerebrovascular disease
- Less than 2 weeks postpartum[†]
- Hypertension with vascular disease or older than 35 years
- Diabetes with vascular disease or older than 35 years
- Systemic lupus erythematosus with vascular disease, nephritis, or antiphospholipid antibodies
- Hypertriglyceridemia

* Because of its long duration of action and potential for hypoestrogenic effects, depot medroxyprogesterone acetate may be less appropriate than other progestin-only contraceptives for some women with these listed conditions.

[†]Use of an intrauterine device may not be an appropriate contraceptive choice.

▶ *Is combination OC use safe for women older than 35 years?*

Use of combination OCs is safe in healthy, nonsmoking women older than 35 years. Recent large U.S. population-based case–control studies found no increased risk of myocardial infarction (2) or stroke (3) among healthy, nonsmoking women older than 35 years who use OCs formulated with less than 50 µg of estrogen.

Perimenopausal women benefit from the more regular menses and positive effect on BMD (4, 5) offered by combination OCs. In addition, use of combination OCs may reduce vasomotor symptoms in perimenopausal women (6). Furthermore, the reduced risk of endometrial and ovarian cancers associated with OC use is of particular importance to older women of reproductive age.

As increasing numbers of women in their late 40s and early 50s use combination OCs, the question of when women no longer need contraception and can consider transitioning to hormone replacement therapy will arise more frequently. Assessment of follicle-stimulating hormone levels to determine when older OC users have become menopausal and thus no longer need contraception is expensive and may be misleading (7–10). Until a well-validated tool to confirm menopause is available, an alternative approach is for healthy, nonsmoking women doing well on combination OCs to discontinue OCs routinely between the ages of 50 and 55 years. By age 55, the likelihood that a woman has reached menopausal status is at least 85% (11, 12).

▶ *Is combination OC use safe for women who smoke cigarettes?*

Smoking represents the single most important preventable cause of death and disability in U.S. women (13). At every opportunity, women should be encouraged to quit smoking, regardless of hormonal contraception use.

Numerous epidemiologic studies conducted from the 1960s through the 1980s observed high relative risks of myocardial infarction among women who used OCs formulated with 50 μg or more of estrogen and smoked cigarettes, compared with women who neither smoked nor used OCs (14). The absolute rates of myocardial infarction in this study increased substantially among OC users who smoked and were in their mid-30s or older. Accordingly, package labeling for combination OCs was modified to warn clinicians and OC users of the risks associated with smoking among OC users in general and particularly among those aged 35 years and older.

Data are sparse on U.S. women older than 35 years who smoke and use OCs. Recently, epidemiologic studies assessing the risk of arterial events among U.S. women using contemporary OCs formulated with less than 50 μg of estrogen have been published. These large case–control studies found no evidence that use of these lower-dose contemporary formulations increased risks of myocardial infarction (2) or stroke (3) in nonsmokers or in women who smoked, regardless of their age. Reflecting current U.S. clinical practice, these studies included few OC users who were older than 35 years or who smoked. Therefore, unless other studies confirm the safety of contemporary combination OCs in older women who smoke, practitioners should prescribe combination OCs to such women with caution, if at all. Nonetheless, the recent U.S. studies provide evidence that combination OCs should not be denied to women younger than 30 years who smoke cigarettes (15). When considering OCs for women who are between the ages of 30 and 35 years and are smokers, the number of cigarettes smoked and the competing risk of pregnancy should be taken into account. In women who are older than 35 years and are smokers, the risk of using OCs is likely to exceed the risk of pregnancy.

▶ *Is combination OC use safe for women with chronic hypertension?*

Hypertension is a common condition associated with increased maternal and fetal risks should pregnancy occur, which emphasizes the importance of effective contraception for women with chronic hypertension.

Use of OCs appears to increase blood pressure, even with contemporary OC preparations. A small clinical trial found that an OC containing 30 μg of ethinyl estradiol and 150 μg of progestin increased the ambulatory blood pressure of normotensive women (approximately 8 mm Hg systolic and 6 mm Hg diastolic) (16). A small cross-sectional study of Italian women with mild hypertension found that those using combination OCs (most with 30 μg of estrogen) had ambulatory systolic blood pressures approximately 7 mm Hg higher than those not using OCs (17).

It is unclear if the use of contemporary OCs in women with hypertension increases the risk of vascular events. A large Danish case–control study of women with cerebral thromboembolism found that the risk of stroke was increased threefold in hypertensive women whether or not they used OCs (18). A large World Health Organization study conducted in developing and European countries observed that combination OC users with a history of hypertension had an increased risk of myocardial infarction and stroke (19). A pooled analysis of two U.S. population-based, case–control studies on OC use and myocardial infarction (2) and stroke (3) suggests that current OC use may not substantially increase the risk of stroke or myocardial infarction in women with hypertension. However, the studies included too few women who were hypertensive or older than 35 years to draw firm conclusions.

In healthy women of reproductive age, the incidence of myocardial infarction or stroke with use of low-dose OCs is extremely low. Although the relative risk of these conditions is increased in women with hypertension, the absolute risk remains low. In view of the increased risk of myocardial infarction and stroke associated with hypertension and uncertainty regarding additional risks of OCs, the decision to use OCs in these patients should be weighed against the risk of pregnancy associated with hypertension, and the noncontraceptive benefits of OCs should be taken into account. Women with well-controlled and monitored hypertension who are aged 35 years or younger are appropriate candidates for a trial of combination OCs formulated with 35 μg or less of estrogen, provided they are otherwise healthy, show no evidence of end-organ vascular disease, and do not smoke cigarettes. If blood pressure remains well-controlled with careful monitoring several months after initiating OCs, use can be continued.

Although coronary artery disease, congestive heart failure, and cerebrovascular disease are uncommon in women of reproductive age, the risk of pregnancy and delivery in these women can be substantial, making effective contraception important. Inadequate data are available to address the use of OCs in women with these conditions; therefore, given the increased risk of venous thromboembolism with combined OCs, their use is contraindicated. However, progestin-only contraceptives such as DMPA, progestin-only OCs, or levonorgestrel implants may be appropriate.

▶ Is combination OC use safe for women with diabetes?

Pregnancy in women with diabetes is associated with an array of serious maternal and perinatal complications, which emphasizes the importance of effective contraception in this patient population. In theory, the steroids in combination OCs might impair carbohydrate metabolism and accelerate the occurrence of vascular disease in diabetic women. Fortunately, current combination OCs do not appear to have this effect. In a cross-sectional U.S. study, 43 women with type 1 (formerly insulin-dependent) diabetes who used combination OCs for 1–7 years (mean duration, 3.4 years) were compared with a similar number of women with type 1 diabetes who were not using OCs. The overall mean age and duration of diabetes was 23 and 14 years, respectively, in this study group. Hemoglobin A_{lc} values were similar in the OC users and nonusers, which suggests that OC use did not affect control of diabetes. Likewise, the degree of nephropathy and retinopathy was similar in both groups, which suggests that OC use did not accelerate the development of diabetic vascular disease (20).

Although studies of OC use in women with type 2 (formerly non–insulin-dependent) diabetes have not been reported, two recent papers offer reassurance that combination OC use does not precipitate this disease. A prospective cohort study, which followed more than 98,000 U.S. women nurses, found that use of combination OCs did not significantly increase the risk of developing type 2 diabetes over a 4-year follow-up period; likewise, past use did not appear to increase risk (21). In a California population of Hispanic women with gestational diabetes followed for up to 7 years postpartum, use of combination OCs did not accelerate the development of type 2 diabetes. The use of progestin-only pills by the relatively small subgroup of women who nursed their infants was associated with a significantly increased risk of developing type 2 diabetes (22), an unexpected finding that is difficult to interpret.

Although the above data support the use of combination OCs in women with diabetes, based on theoretical concerns, such use should be limited to nonsmoking, otherwise healthy women with diabetes who are younger than 35 years and show no evidence of hypertension, nephropathy, retinopathy, or other vascular disease. Practitioners who provide contraception to women with diabetes should coordinate care with the physician treating the diabetes and follow such patients closely. Appropriate follow-up includes monitoring blood pressure, weight, and lipid status. Regardless of hormonal contraception use, women with the following risk factors should undergo blood glucose screening every 3 years: history of gestational diabetes, family history of diabetes in parents or siblings, obesity (body weight greater than 120% of ideal) or hypertension, and member of high-risk ethnic groups (African American, Hispanic, Native American).

▶ Is combination OC use safe for women with migraine headaches?

Headaches are a frequent occurrence in women of reproductive age. Most of these headaches are tension headaches, not migraines (23). Some women with migraines experience improvement in their symptoms with the use of OCs, while some women's symptoms worsen. However, in women using OCs, most migraines occur during the hormone-free interval. Because the presence of true migraine headaches affects the decision to use OCs, careful consideration of the diagnosis is important.

A large hospital-based case–control study performed at five European centers found that women with classic migraines (with aura) had a statistically significant fourfold increased risk of ischemic stroke; women with simple migraine (without aura) had a threefold increased risk that was not statistically significant (24). Women with a history of migraines using OCs (<50 µg of estrogen) had a greater than sixfold increased risk of ischemic stroke (not statistically significant [OR 6.6; 95% CI, 0.8–55]) when compared with women who were not using OCs and who had no migraine headaches. Compared with women who did not smoke, did not use OCs, and had no history of migraines, women who smoked, were using OCs, and had a history of migraines had a 34-fold increased risk of ischemic stroke (OR 34.4; 95% CI, 3.3–361).

A pooled analysis of two large, U.S. population-based case–control studies also observed a statistically significant twofold elevated risk of ischemic stroke, as well as hemorrhagic stroke (not statistically significant) among current users of OCs who reported migraine headaches compared with women with migraines who did not use OCs (3). A large Danish population-based case–control study found that among women with a history of migraine headaches, the risk of stroke was elevated approximately threefold (*P*< 0.01) (18). Neither study categorized migraines by type. The additional risk of thrombotic stroke attributable to women with migraines using OCs has been estimated as 8 per 100,000 women at age 20 years, and 80 per 100,000 women at age 40 years (25).

Although cerebrovascular events rarely occur among women with migraines who use combination OCs, the impact of a stroke on a woman of reproductive age is so devastating that clinicians should consider the use of progestin-only, intrauterine, or barrier contraceptives in this setting. Concerns remain that all women with migraines are at increased risk of stroke. However, because absolute risk remains low, the use of combination OCs may be considered for women with migraine headaches if they do not have focal neurologic signs, do not smoke, are otherwise healthy, and are younger than 35 years.

▶ *Does the use of combination OCs increase the risk of breast cancer in women with fibrocystic breast changes, fibroadenoma, or a family history of breast cancer?*

Women with fibroadenoma, benign breast disease with epithelial hyperplasia with or without atypia, or a family history of breast cancer have an increased risk of breast cancer (26). A recently published massive reanalysis of 54 studies assessing the association of OC use and breast cancer risk, however, provides reassurance to these women and to their clinicians regarding OC use. Overall, this reanalysis found that 10 years or more after discontinuing OC use, the risk of breast cancer was identical among these former OC users and those who never used OCs. Small but significantly increased relative risks (RR) were observed in current OC users (RR, 1.24) and those who had used OCs in the previous 1–4 years (RR, 1.16) or 5–9 years earlier (RR, 1.07). The increase in risk was restricted to women with localized disease; there was an associated reduced risk of metastatic disease, which suggests that much if not all of the risk can be attributed to early diagnosis of existing disease (27).

A positive family history of breast cancer in a mother or sister, or both, or a history of benign breast disease should not be regarded as contraindications to OC use. Use of OCs has an identical effect on the risk of breast cancer for women with and without each of these two risk categories (27).

▶ *What are the effects of combination OC use in women with uterine leiomyomata?*

Use of combination OCs reduces menstrual blood loss in women with normal menses as well as in those with men-

orrhagia (28). A Swedish study conducted in the 1960s using high-dose oral contraceptives, which are not currently used, noted OC use significantly reduced bleeding in women with menorrhagia associated with uterine fibroids (29). Oral contraceptive use also reduces dysmenorrhea (28). Some practitioners routinely employ the use of combination OCs as first-line medical management in women with menorrhagia or dysmenorrhea associated with uterine leiomyomata. Several large epidemiologic studies have observed that OC use does not induce the growth of uterine fibroids and may decrease bleeding disorders in these women (30–32).

▶ *Is combination OC use safe for women with lipid disorders?*

The term "dyslipidemia" includes disorders of lipoprotein metabolism that lead to atherosclerosis. These abnormalities arise from genetic and secondary factors and are caused by excessive entry of lipoproteins into the bloodstream, an impairment in their removal, or both.

The estrogen component of combination OCs enhances removal of low-density lipoprotein (LDL) and increases levels of high-density lipoprotein (HDL) cholesterol. Both of these actions can have a favorable effect on a woman's risk of coronary artery disease. Oral estrogen also increases triglyceride levels; however, in the setting of concomitantly increased HDL and decreased LDL levels, the moderate triglyceride elevations caused by oral estrogen use do not appear to increase the risk of atherogenesis. Numerous epidemiologic studies of past use of OCs find no increased risk of cardiovascular disease, arguing against any adverse long-term effect of OCs on the risk of atherogenesis (33). The progestin component of combination OCs antagonizes these estrogen-induced lipid changes, which increases LDL levels and decreases HDL and triglyceride levels. Accordingly, among women taking combination OCs with an identical dose of estrogen, the choice (and dose) of the progestin component affects net lipid changes. It is not known whether the differential lipid effects of distinct OC formulations have any clinical significance in women with normal baseline lipid levels or those with lipid disorders.

Using guidelines from the National Cholesterol Education Program (34), experts have recommended that most women with controlled dyslipidemia can use combination OCs formulated with 35 µg or less of estrogen. In contrast, in women with uncontrolled LDL cholesterol greater than 160 mg/dL or multiple additional risk factors for coronary artery disease (including smoking, diabetes, obesity, hypertension, family history of premature coronary artery disease, HDL level <35 mg/dL, or triglyceride level >250 mg/dL), use of alternative contraceptives should be considered (35). Fasting serum lipid levels should be monitored as frequently as each month after initiating combination OC use in dyslipidemic women; less frequent monitoring is appropriate once stabilization of lipid parameters has been observed.

Ongoing communication with the patient's primary care physician (or internist) is appropriate, and the importance of a low-fat diet, daily exercise, and the achievement of ideal body weight should be emphasized (22). Concomitant hormonal contraception and lipid-lowering therapy may be appropriate in some women.

▶ *What hormonal contraceptive options are available for postpartum and lactating women?*

Postpartum women remain in a hypercoagulable state for weeks after childbirth. Product labeling for combination OCs advises deferring use until 4 weeks postpartum in nonbreastfeeding women. Because first ovulation after delivery can occur in as little as 25 days (36), some practitioners initiate the use of combination OCs in non-breastfeeding women as early as 2 weeks after childbirth, although no data support or refute the safety of this approach. Because progestin-only OCs, DMPA, and implants do not contain estrogen, these methods may be safely initiated immediately postpartum (37).

Combination OCs are not recommended as the first choice for breastfeeding mothers because of the negative effect of contraceptive doses of estrogen on lactation. The estrogenic component of combination OCs can reduce the volume of milk production and the caloric and mineral content of breast milk in lactating women (38). However, use of combination OCs by well-nourished breastfeeding women does not appear to result in infant development problems (38). Their use can be considered once milk flow is well established.

Progestin-only contraceptives do not impair lactation and, in fact, may increase the quality and duration of lactation (39). In nursing women using progestin-only OCs, very small amounts of progestin are passed into the breast milk, and no adverse effects on infant growth have been observed (40). Product labeling for progestin-only pills may suggest that fully breastfeeding women begin tablets 6 weeks postpartum and advise partially breastfeeding women to begin at 3 weeks.

Like other progestin-only methods, DMPA use does not adversely affect breastfeeding (38). Product labeling for DMPA advises initiation of use within the first 5 days postpartum if not breastfeeding and, if exclusively breast-feeding, at 6 weeks postpartum. When initiated immediately postpartum, however, use of DMPA does not adversely affect lactation (38) or infant development (41).

Product labeling for progestin subdermal implants indicates that insertion should be deferred until 6 weeks postpartum in lactating women. Studies of the effects of implant use on lactation and infant development investigated outcomes of insertion at least 30 days postpartum (42, 43). Although the results of these studies have been reassuring, data assessing immediate postpartum implant insertion in breastfeeding women are needed. Given the lack of procoagulation effect and the apparent safety in nursing mothers with DMPA and implants, their immediate postpartum use in both lactating and nonlactating women appears reasonable.

▶ *What hormonal contraceptive options are available for women taking concomitant medications?*

For women with seizure disorders, the frequency of seizures may increase during pregnancy (44). In addition, the risk of birth defects is intrinsically increased in these women (44). Finally, many anticonvulsants are teratogens (44). Each of these observations emphasizes the importance of providing effective contraception for women with seizure disorders.

Anticonvulsants that induce hepatic enzymes can decrease serum concentrations of the estrogen or progestin component of OCs, or both (45) (see the box, "Interaction of Anticonvulsants and Combination Oral Contraceptives"). This effect has been observed with phenobarbital (46), phenytoin, carbamazepine (47), felbamate (48), and topiramate (49). Therapeutic doses of vigabatrin do not induce hepatic enzymes. Nonetheless, a small clinical trial found ethinyl estradiol levels lower than during placebo use in two of 13 volunteers taking this anticonvulsant (50). Although each of these studies demonstrated reduced serum levels of OC steroids during anticonvulsant use, and many of them demonstrated associated breakthrough bleeding, investigators did not observe ovulation or accidental pregnancy during anticonvulsant use. Although some clinicians prescribe OCs containing 50 μg of ethinyl estradiol to women taking these anticonvulsants, no published data support the enhanced contraceptive efficacy of this practice. Use of condoms in conjunction with OCs or use of DMPA or an intrauterine device may be considered for such women (see the box).

In contrast to the above anticonvulsants, use of valproic acid (51), gabapentin (52), and tiagabine (53) does not appear to decrease serum levels of contraceptive steroids in women using combination OCs. Practitioners should be aware, however, that studies of the latter agents were performed using anticonvulsant doses lower than those used in clinical practice (54).

Interaction of Anticonvulsants and Combination Oral Contraceptives

Anticonvulsants that decrease steroid levels in women taking combination oral contraceptives

    Barbiturates (including phenobarbital and primidone)

    Phenytoin

    Carbamazepine

    Felbamate

    Topiramate

    Vigabatrin

Anticonvulsants that do not decrease steroid levels in women taking combination oral contraceptives

    Valproic acid

    Gabapentin*

    Lamotrigine*

    Tiagabine*

*Pharmacokinetic study used anticonvulsant dose lower than that usedin clinical practice.

Although there have been many anecdotal reports of OC failure in women taking concomitant antibiotics, pharmacokinetic evidence of lower serum steroid levels exists only for rifampin (55) and griseofulvin (56) (see the box, "Interaction of Antiinfective Agents and Combination Oral Contraceptives"). Because OC steroids are strikingly reduced in women concomitantly taking rifampin, such women should not rely on combination OCs, progestin-only OCs, or implants for contraceptive protection. Pharmacokinetic studies have not demonstrated lowered

---

Interaction of Antiinfective Agents and Combination Oral Contraceptives

Antiinfective agents that decrease steroid levels in women taking combination oral contraceptives

    Rifampin

    Griseofulvin

Antiinfective agents that do not decrease steroid levels in women taking combination oral contraceptives

    Tetracycline

    Doxycycline

    Ampicillin

    Metronidazole

    Quinolone antibiotics

OC steroid levels with concomitant use of tetracycline (57), doxycycline (58), ampicillin or metronidazole (59), or quinolone antibiotics (60–62).

Serum progestin levels during use of progestin-only OCs and implants are lower than during combined OC use. Accordingly, these low-dose progestin-only contraceptives are not appropriate choices for women using concomitant liver enzyme inducers (40, 63). The contraceptive efficacy of DMPA in women taking hepatic enzyme inducers has not been explicitly studied. A potential advantage of using DMPA in women with seizure disorders is DMPA's intrinsic anticonvulsant effect (23).

▶ *Is hormonal contraceptive use safe for women with a history of thromboembolism?*

The estrogenic component of combination OCs, which increases hepatic production of serum globulins involved in coagulation (including factor VII, factor X, and fibrinogen), increases the risk of VTE in users. Beginning in 1995, European studies clarified that, compared with nonusers, current users of OCs formulated with 35 μg or less of estrogen experience a threefold to fourfold increased risk of VTE. This risk, in absolute terms, remains lower than the increased risk of VTE during pregnancy.

The goal of screening OC candidates with respect to VTE risk is to identify those women for whom the VTE risk associated with OC use outweighs OC benefits. In addition to current use of exogenous estrogens, risk factors for VTE include pregnancy and the puerperium, personal or family history of VTE, obesity, surgery, and certain familial coagulation disorders. Although cigarette smoking, hypertension, and diabetes represent risk factors for arterial disease, including myocardial infarction and stroke, they do not increase VTE risk (64). Likewise, the presence of superficial varicose veins does not increase VTE risk (64). Health risks (including VTE) associated with pregnancy, noncontraceptive OC benefits, and the potential for effective use of contraceptives that do not increase VTE risk (eg, progestin-only OCs and intrauterine and barrier methods) should all be factored into risk–benefit considerations. Practitioners should be aware that package labeling for DMPA and for certain brands of progestin-only OCs inappropriately indicates that a history of VTE contraindicates the use of these progestin-only methods.

Women with a documented history of unexplained VTE or VTE associated with pregnancy or exogenous estrogen use should not use combination OCs unless they are currently taking anticoagulants. An OC candidate who had experienced a single episode of VTE years earlier associated with a nonrecurring risk factor (eg, VTE occurring after immobilization following a motor vehicle accident) may not currently be at increased risk for VTE. Accordingly, the decision to initiate combination OCs in such a candidate can be individualized.

▶ *Should women awaiting surgery discontinue combination OC use?*

Venous thromboembolism with pulmonary embolism remains a major cause of fatalities associated with surgical (including gynecologic) procedures. Findings of a large British prospective cohort study suggested that the risk of postoperative VTE was approximately twice as high ($P>0.05$) in OC users as in nonusers (65). A prospective study found that, among women taking OCs formulated with 30 μg of estrogen, OC-induced procoagulant changes did not substantially resolve until 6 or more weeks after OC discontinuation (66). Accordingly, the risks associated with stopping OCs 1 month or more before major surgery should be balanced against the risks of an unintended pregnancy (67). In current OC users having major surgical procedures, heparin prophylaxis should be considered (67). Because of the low perioperative risk of VTE, it currently is not considered necessary to discontinue combination OCs before laparoscopic tubal sterilization or other brief surgical procedures.

▶ *Is OC use safe in women with hypercoagulable states?*

Women with factor V Leiden mutation who use OCs experience a risk of VTE 30 times higher than non-OC users who are not carriers of the mutation (68). A clotting assay can determine activated protein C resistance, and a polymerase chain reaction test can identify the presence of factor V Leiden mutation. Such screening would identify approximately 5% of U.S. OC candidates as having factor V Leiden mutation; however, the great majority of these women will never experience VTE, even if they use combination OCs (69). Given the rarity of fatal VTE, one group of investigators concluded that screening more than 1 million combination OC candidates for thrombophilic markers would, at best, prevent two OC-associated deaths (70). Some practitioners may choose to test for factor V Leiden mutation in women with a positive family history of VTE who are considering OC use or pregnancy. In this setting, the clinician should weigh factors including age of onset of thrombosis in affected family members, the clinical setting, and severity of thrombotic episodes. The risks, benefits, and financial implications of such selective testing, however, are unknown.

Women using warfarin for chronic anticoagulation may experience menorrhagia and, rarely, hemoperitoneum following rupture of ovarian cysts. In addition, warfarin is a teratogen. Because use of combination OCs can reduce menstrual blood loss (28) and does not increase the risk of recurrent thrombosis in well-anticoagulated women (69, 71), some authorities recommend their use in such patients. Because intramuscular injection of DMPA consistently suppresses ovulation (72), DMPA represents another potential contraceptive choice in anticoagulated women.

▶ *Does the use of emergency contraception increase the risk of VTE?*

Use of postcoital (emergency) contraception may increase in the United States with the recent availability of a dedicated product. A recent retrospective cohort analysis from Britain found no cases of thromboembolism in more than 100,000 episodes of postcoital contraception use with the Yuzpe regimen (73).

▶ *Are hormonal contraceptives safe for women with SLE?*

Because the risks of maternal and perinatal morbidity as well as mortality can be high in pregnancies complicated by SLE, effective contraception is an important component of the care of such women. Particular concerns about hormonal contraception use in women with SLE relate to the increased risk of venous and arterial thrombosis in women with this disease. A small retrospective cohort study noted that while combination OC use was associated with flareups in SLE patients with renal disease, progestin-only OC use was not associated with increased disease activity (74). One retrospective cohort study of 85 women with SLE noted that among 31 patients using combination OCs, increased disease activity was not precipitated by OC use. However, deep vein thrombosis was diagnosed in two OC users; both of these women had antiphospholipid antibodies (75). A small prospective cohort study found that use of progestin-only OCs or contraceptive injections was not associated with increased SLE activity (76).

Existing data from observational studies suggest that combination OC use should be avoided in SLE patients with a history of vascular disease, nephritis, or antiphospholipid antibodies, although progestin-only methods are safe alternatives. Data are insufficient to address the use of combination OCs among women with stable or inactive disease who have no history of thrombosis, nephropathy, or antiphospholipid antibodies (77). If such women do not wish to use progestin-only methods, use of combination OCs with close monitoring can be considered in selected cases.

▶ Is hormonal contraceptive use safe for women with sickle cell disease?

In persons with sickle cell disease, abnormal hemoglobin precipitates and becomes rigid when subjected to oxygen deprivation. Vasooclusive episodes in those with sickle cell disease, however, differ from intravascular thrombosis (78). Pregnancy in women with sickle cell disease carries increased risks of maternal complications and is associated with elevated rates of spontaneous abortion, intrauterine growth restriction, and neonatal mortality.

No well-controlled study has assessed whether VTE risk in OC users with sickle cell disease is higher than in other combination OC users. Accordingly, recommendations regarding use of combination OCs in this patient population vary widely. On the basis of studies of pregnant women with sickle cell disease, small observational studies of women with sickle cell disease who use combination OCs, and theoretical considerations, the consensus is that pregnancy carries a greater risk than combination OC use.

Two controlled studies have assessed the use of DMPA in women with sickle cell disease (79, 80). Both of these found that use of DMPA reduced the incidence of painful crises. Accordingly, DMPA may be a particularly appropriate contraceptive for women with sickle cell disease.

▶ What are the effects of DMPA on bone density?

Use of DMPA in contraceptive doses suppresses ovarian production of estradiol. Thus, there has been concern that women using DMPA for contraception might develop osteopenia. A New Zealand study of women who used DMPA for at least 5 years found significantly reduced bone density in the lumbar spine and femoral neck compared with premenopausal controls (81). A subsequent study performed by the same investigator noted that among women who had used DMPA for at least 3 years, deficits in BMD of the lumbar spine were reversible following DMPA discontinuation (82). Five recent cross-sectional studies suggest that DMPA use decreases BMD of the spine (83–87). In the largest of these studies, the median duration of DMPA use was 12 years. In this study, initiation of DMPA use before age 21 years and use for more than 15 years were identified as risk factors for osteopenia (84). None of these cross-sectional studies found evidence of osteoporosis or fractures in DMPA users.

Information on the effects of DMPA use on BMD during adolescence is limited. However, a small study compared BMD of the lumbar spine in females aged 12–21 years. In this prospective cohort study, BMD in those using no hormones was compared with those using DMPA, OCs, or implants. After 1 year of use, bone density in DMPA users decreased 1.5%, whereas it increased 1.5% in OC users, 2.5% in levonorgestrel implant users, and 2.9% in those using no hormones. None of those who initially selected an OC continued after 2 years. However, followup BMD measurements at 2 years showed a total decrease of 3.1% in DMPA users and total increases of 9.5% in nonhormone users and 9.3% in implant users (88).

The rate-of-loss trends in BMD seen with DMPA seem to be similar to those noted during lactation (89, 90) in that no long-term decrease occurs. Two recent cross-sectional studies of menopausal women found no long-term BMD declines in former DMPA users. In these reports, BMD in former DMPA users was not significantly different from never-users (91, 92). Estrogen supplementation (eg, conjugated estrogen, 1.25 mg daily, or equivalent doses of other estrogens) can be considered for long-term users of DMPA, including adolescents. However, no data address the effect of such an add-back regimen on BMD in women using DMPA. Caution should be exercised in prescribing DMPA for adolescents, women known to be at high risk for low BMD, and perimenopausal women.

Summary

The following recommendations are based on good and consistent scientific evidence (Level A):

▶ Women with fibroadenoma, benign breast disease with epithelial hyperplasia with or without atypia, or a family history of breast cancer are at little or no additional risk of breast cancer because of OC use. Therefore, OCs can be prescribed for such women if they are otherwise appropriate candidates.

▶ Progestin-only preparations are safe and preferable forms of hormonal contraception for lactating women. Combination OCs are not recommended as the first choice for breastfeeding mothers because of the negative impact of contraceptive doses of estrogen on lactation. However, use of combination OCs by well-nourished breastfeeding women does not appear to result in infant development problems; therefore, their use can be considered once milk flow is well established.

▶ Hormonal contraceptive effectiveness is compromised by the use of the antibiotics rifampin and griseofulvin; thus, women taking these antibiotics should use nonhormonal contraceptives.

▶ Progestin-only preparations are appropriate for women at increased risk for VTE. Combination OCs are not recommended for women with a documented history of unexplained VTE or VTE associated with pregnancy or exogenous estrogen use, unless they are taking anticoagulants.

▶ Combination OCs should be prescribed with caution, if ever, to women who are older than 35 years and are smokers. Women younger than 30 years who smoke and are otherwise healthy generally can be prescribed combination OCs.

▶ If desired, healthy, nonsmoking women doing well on combination OCs may continue their use until menopause.

The following recommendations are based on limited or inconsistent scientific evidence (Level B):

▶ Women with well-controlled and monitored hypertension aged 35 years and younger are appropriate candidates for a trial of combination OCs formulated with 35 µg or less of estrogen, provided they are otherwise healthy with no evidence of end-organ vascular disease and do not smoke cigarettes. If blood pressure remains well-controlled several months after initiating OCs, use can be continued.

▶ The use of combination OCs by women with diabetes should be limited to such women who do not smoke, are younger than 35 years, and are otherwise healthy with no evidence of hypertension, nephropathy, retinopathy, or other vascular disease.

▶ Women with migraine headaches who have focal neurologic signs are not appropriate candidates for OC use. Combination OCs can be used by women with simple migraine headaches (ie, no focal neurologic signs) if they do not smoke, are younger than 35 years, and are otherwise healthy. If such women experience increased frequency or severity of headaches or develop headaches with focal neurologic signs or symptoms, they should discontinue OC use.

▶ Combination OCs may be beneficial in treating dysmenorrhea and menorrhagia in women with uterine fibroids.

▶ The risks associated with stopping OCs 1 month or more before major surgery should be balanced against the risks of an unintended pregnancy. In current OC users undergoing major surgical procedures, heparin prophylaxis should be considered. Because of the low perioperative risk of VTE, it generally is considered unnecessary to discontinue combination OCs before laparoscopic tubal sterilization or other brief surgical procedures.

▶ Progestin-only OCs and contraceptive injections appear to be the hormonal contraception methods of choice for women with SLE. Use of combination OCs in women with SLE can be considered if the women have stable or inactive disease and no history of thrombosis, nephropathy, or antiphospholipid antibodies.

The following recommendations are based primarily on consensus and expert opinion (Level C):

▶ Most women with controlled dyslipidemia can use combination OCs formulated with 35 µg or less of estrogen. In women with uncontrolled LDL cholesterol greater than 160 mg/dL, a triglyceride level greater than 250 mg/dL, or multiple additional risk factors for coronary artery disease, alternative contraceptives should be considered.

▶ DMPA has noncontraceptive benefits and is the contraceptive method of choice for many women with sickle cell disease.

▶ Progestin-only contraceptives may be appropriate for women with coronary artery disease, congestive heart failure, or cerebrovascular disease. However, combination oral contraceptives are contraindicated in these women.

References

1. Corfman P. Labeling guidance text for progestin-only oral contraceptives. Contraception 1995;52:71–76 (Level III)

2. Sidney S, Siscovick DS, Petitti DB, Schwartz SM, Quesenberry CP, Psaty BM, et al. Myocardial infarction and use of low-dose oral contraceptives: a pooled analysis of 2 US studies. Circulation 1998;98:1058–1063 (Level II-2)

3. Schwartz SM, Petitti DB, Siscovick DS, Longstreth WT Jr, Sidney S, Raghunathan TE, et al. Stroke and use of low-dose oral contraceptives in young women: a pooled analysis of two US studies. Stroke 1998;29:2277–2284 (Level II-2)

4. Gambacciani M, Spinetti A, Taponeco F, Cappagli B, Piaggesi L, Fioretti P. Longitudinal evaluation of perimenopausal vertebral bone loss: effects of a low-dose oral contraceptive preparation on bone mineral density and metabolism. Obstet Gynecol 1994;83:392–396 (Level I)

5. Sulak PJ. Oral contraceptives: therapeutic uses and quality-of-life benefits—case presentations. Contraception 1999;59(suppl):35S–38S (Level III)

6. Casper RF, Dodin S, Reid RL. The effect of 20 µg ethinyl estradiol/1 mg norethindrone acetate (Minestrin), a low-dose oral contraceptive, on vaginal bleeding patterns, hot flashes, and quality of life in symptomatic perimenopausal women. Menopause 1997;4:139–147 (Level I)

7. Gebbie AE, Glasier A, Sweeting V. Incidence of ovulation in perimenopausal women before and during hormone replacement therapy. Contraception 1995;52:221–222 (Level II-3)

8. Burger HG. Diagnostic role of follicle-stimulating hormone (FSH) measurements during the menopausal transition—an analysis of FSH, oestradiol and inhibin. Eur J Endocrinol 1994;130:38–42 (Level III)

9. Castracane VD, Gimpel T, Goldzieher JW. When is it safe to switch from oral contraceptives to hormonal replacement therapy? Contraception 1995;52:371–376 (Level II-2)

10. Creinin MD. Laboratory criteria for menopause in women using oral contraceptives. Fertil Steril 1996;66:101–104 (Level II-3)

11. Stanford JL, Hartge P, Brinton LA, Hoover RN, Brookmeyer R. Factors influencing the age at natural menopause. J Chronic Dis 1987;40:995–1002 (Level II-3)

12. McKinlay SM, Bifano NL, McKinlay JB. Smoking and age at menopause in women. Ann Intern Med 1985;103: 350–356 (Level II)

13. American College of Obstetricians and Gynecologists. Smoking and women's health. ACOG Educational Bulletin 240. Washington, DC: ACOG, 1997 (Level III)

14. Croft P, Hannaford PC. Risk factors for acute myocardial infarction in women: evidence from the Royal College of General Practitioners' oral contraception study. BMJ 1989;298:165–168 (Level II-2)

15. Schwingl PJ, Ory HW, Visness CM. Estimates of the risk of cardiovascular death attributable to low-dose oral contraceptives in the United States. Am J Obstet Gynecol 1999;180:241–249 (Level III)

16. Cardoso F, Polonia J, Santos A, Silva-Carvalho J, Ferreira-de-Almeida J. Low-dose oral contraceptives and 24-hour ambulatory blood pressure. Int J Gynaecol Obstet 1997;59:237–243 (Level II-3)

17. Narkiewicz K, Graniero GR, D'Este D, Mattarei M, Zonzin P, Palatini P. Ambulatory blood pressure in mild hypertensive women taking oral contraceptives. A case-control study. Am J Hyperten 1995;8:249–253 (Level II-2)

18. Lidegaard O. Oral contraceptives, pregnancy and the risk of cerebral thromboembolism: the influence of diabetes, hypertension, migraine and previous thrombotic disease. Br J Obstet Gynaecol 1996;102:153–159 (Level II-2)

19. WHO Collaborative Study of Cardiovascular Disease and Steroid Hormone Contraception. Ischemic stroke and combined oral contraceptives: results of an international, multicentre, case-control study. Lancet 1996;348:498–505 (Level II-2)

20. Garg SK, Chase HP, Marshall G, Hoops SL, Holmes DL, Jackson WE. Oral contraceptives and renal and retinal complications in young women with insulin-dependent diabetes mellitus. JAMA 1994;271:1099–1102 (Level II-2)

21. Chasan-Taber L, Willett WC, Stampfer MJ, Hunter DJ, Colditz GA, Spiegelman D, et al. A prospective study of oral contraceptives and NIDDM among U.S. women. Diabetes Care 1997;20:330–335 (Level II-2)

22. Kjos SL, Peters RK, Xiang A, Thomas D, Schaefer U, Buchanan T. Contraception and the risk of type 2 diabetes mellitus in Latina women with prior gestational diabetes mellitus. JAMA 1998;28:533–538 (Level II-3)

23. Mattson RH, Rebar RW. Contraceptive methods for women with neurologic disorders. Am J Obstet Gynecol 1993;168(6 Pt 2):2027–2032 (Level II-3)

24. Chang CL, Donaghy M, Poulter N. Migraine and stroke in young women: case control study. The World Health Organisation Collaborative Study of Cardiovascular Disease and Steroid Hormone Contraception. BMJ 1999;318:13–18 (Level II-2)

25. MacGregor EA, Guillebaud J. Combined oral contraceptives, migraine and ischaemic stroke. Clinical and Scientific Committee of the Faculty of Family Planning and Reproductive Health Care and the Family Planning Association. Br J Fam Plann 1998;24:53–60 (Level III)

26. Dupont WD, Page DL. Risk factors for breast cancer in women with proliferative breast disease. N Engl J Med 1985;312:146–151 (Level II-2)

27. Collaborative Group on Hormonal Factors in Breast Cancer. Breast cancer and hormonal contraceptives: collaborative reanalysis of individual data on 53,297 women with breast cancer and 100,239 women without breast cancer from 54 epidimiological studies. Lancet 1996;347: 1713–1727 (Level III)

28. Larsson G, Milsom I, Lindstedt G, Rybo G. The influence of a low-dose combined oral contraceptive on menstrual blood loss and iron status. Contraception 1992;46: 327–334 (Level III)

29. Nilsson L, Rybo G. Treatment of menorrhagia. Am J Obstet Gynecol 1971;110:713–720 (Level II-2)

30. Ross RK, Pike MC, Vessey MP, Bull D, Yeates D, Casagrande JT. Risk factors for uterine fibroids: reduced risk associated with oral contraceptives. BMJ (Clin Res Ed) 1986;293:359–362 (Level II-2)

31. Marshall LM, Spiegelman D, Goldman MB, Manson JE, Colditz GA, Barbieri RL, et al. A prospective study of reproductive factors and oral contraceptive use in relation to the risk of uterine leiomyomata. Fertil Steril 1998;70: 432–439 (Level II-2)

32. Parazzini F, Negri E, LaVecchia C, Fedele L, Rabaiotti M, Luchini L. Oral contraceptive use and risk of uterine fibroids. Obstet Gynecol 1992;79:430–433 (Level II-2)

33. Chasen-Taber L, Stampfer MJ. Epidemiology of oral contraceptives and cardiovascular disease. Ann Intern Med 1998;128:467–477 (Level III)

34. National Cholesterol Education Program Expert Panel on Detection, Evaluation, and Treatment of High Blood Cholesterol in Adults. Report of the National Cholesterol Education Program Expert Panel on Detection, Evaluation, and Treatment of High Blood Cholesterol in Adults. Arch Intern Med 1988;148:36–69 (Level III)

35. Knopp RH, LaRosa JC, Burkman RT Jr. Contraception and dyslipidemia. Am J Obstet Gynecol 1993;168: 1994–2005 (Level III)

36. Campbell OM, Gray RH. Characteristics and determinants of postpartum ovarian function in women in the United States. Am J Obstet Gynecol 1993;169:55–60 (Level II-2)

37. American College of Obstetricians and Gynecologists. Hormonal contraception. ACOG Technical Bulletin 198. Washington, DC: ACOG, 1994 (Level III)

38. World Health Organization (WHO) Task Force on Oral Contraceptives. Effects of hormonal contraceptives on breast milk composition and infant growth. Stud Fam Plann 1988;19(6 Pt 1):361–369 (Level II-2)

39. Koetsawang S. The effects of contraceptive methods on the quality and quantity of breast milk. Int J Gynaecol Obstet 1987;25(suppl):115–127 (Level III)

40. McCann MF, Potter LS. Progestin-only oral contraception: a comprehensive review. Contraception 1994;50(suppl 1): S1–S195 (Level III)

41. Karim M, Ammar R, el-Mahgoub S, el-Ganzoury B, Fikri F, Abdou I. Injected progestogen and lactation. BMJ 1971;1:200–203 (Level II-2)

42. Shaaban MM, Salem HT, Abdullah KA. Influence of levonorgestrel contraceptive implants, Norplant, initiated early postpartum upon lactation and infant growth. Contraception 1985;32:623–635 (Level II-2)

43. Abdulla KA, Elwan SI, Salem HS, Shaaban MM. Effect of early postpartum use of the contraceptive implants, NORPLANT, on the serum levels of immunoglobulins of the mothers and their breastfed infants. Contraception 1985;32:261–266 (Level II-2)

44. O'Brien MD, Gilmour-White S. Epilepsy and pregnancy. BMJ 1993;307:492–495 (Level III)

45. Back DJ, Orme ML. Pharmacokinetic drug interactions with oral contraceptives. Clin Pharmacokinet 1990;18: 472–484 (Level III)

46. Back DJ, Bates M, Bowden A, Breckenridge AM, Hall MJ, Jones H, et al. The interaction of phenobarbital and other anticonvulsants with oral contraceptive steroid therapy. Contraception 1980;22:495–503 (Level II-3)

47. Crawford P, Chadwick DJ, Martin C, Tjia J, Back DJ, Orme M. The interaction of phenytoin and carbamazepine with combined oral contraceptive steroids. Br J Clin Pharmacol 1990;30:892–896 (Level II-3)

48. Saano V, Glue P, Banfield CR, Reidenberg P, Colucci RD, Meehan JW, et al. Effects of felbamate on the pharmacokinetics of a low-dose combination oral contraceptive. Clin Pharmacol Ther 1995;58:523–531 (Level I)

49. Rosenfeld WE, Doose DR, Walker SA, Nayak RK. Effect of topiramate on the pharmacokinetics of an oral contraceptive containing norethindrone and ethinyl estradiol in patients with epilepsy. Epilepsia 1997;38:317–323 (Level II-3)

50. Bartoli A, Gatti G, Cipolla G, Barzaghi N, Veliz G, Fattore C, et al. A double-blind, placebo-controlled study on the effect of vigabatrin on in vivo parameters of hepatic microsomal enzyme induction and on the kinetics of steroid oral contraceptives in healthy female volunteers. Epilepsia 1997;38:702–707 (Level I)

51. Crawford P, Chadwick D, Cleland P, Tjia J, Cowie A, Back DJ, et al. The lack of effect of sodium valproate on the pharmacokinetics of oral contraceptive steroids. Contraception 1986;33:23–29 (Level II-3)

52. Eldon MA, Underwood BA, Randinitis EJ, Sedman AJ. Gabapentin does not interact with a contraceptive regimen of norethindrone acetate and ethinyl estradiol. Neurology 1998;50:1146–1148 (Level II-3)

53. Mengel HB, Houston A, Back DJ. An evaluation of the interaction between tiagabine and oral contraceptives in female volunteers. J Pharm Med 1994;4:141–150 (Level II-3)

54. Natsch S, Hekster YA, Keyser A, Deckers CL, Meinardi H, Renier WO. Newer anticonvulsant drugs: role of pharmacology, drug interactions and adverse reactions in drug choice. Drug Saf 1997;17:228–240 (Level III)

55. Back DJ, Breckenridge AM, Crawford F, MacIver M, Orme ML, Park BK, et al. The effect of rifampicin on norethisterone pharmacokinetics. Euro J Clin Pharmacol 1979;15:193–197 (Level III)

56. Geurts TB, Goorissen EM, Sitsen JM. Summary of drug interactions with oral contraceptives. Pearl River, New York: Parthenon Publishing, 1993:27–124 (Level III)

57. Murphy AA, Zacur HA, Charache P, Burkman RT. The effect of tetracycline on levels of oral contraceptives. Am J Obstet Gynecol 1991;164(1 Pt 1):28–33 (Level II-3)

58. Neely JL, Abate M, Swinker M, D'Angio R. The effect of doxycycline on serum levels of ethinyl estradiol, norethindrone, and endogenous progesterone. Obstet Gynecol 1991;77:416–420 (Level II-2)

59. Joshi JV, Joshi UM, Sankholi GM, Krishna U, Mandlekar A, Chowdhury V, et al. A study of interaction of low-dose combination oral contraceptive with ampicillin and metronidazole. Contraception 1980;22:643–652 (Level II-2)

60. Maggiolo F, Puricelli G, Dottorini M, Caprioli S, Bianchi W, Suter F. The effect of ciprofloxacin on oral contraceptive steroid treatments. Drugs Exp Clin Res 1991;17: 451–454 (Level II-1)

61. Back DJ, Tjia J, Martin C, Millar E, Mant T, Morrison P, et al. The lack of interaction between temafloxacin and combined oral contraceptive steroids. Contraception 1991;43:317–323 (Level II-2)

62. Csemiczky G, Alvendal C, Landgren BM. Risk for ovulation in women taking a low-dose oral contraceptive (Microgynon) when receiving antibacterial treatment with a fluoroquinolone (ofloxacin). Adv Contracep 1996;12: 101–109 (Level II-1)

63. Haukkamaa M. Contraception by Norplant subdermal capsules is not reliable in epileptic patients on anticonvulsant treatment. Contraception 1986;33:559–565 (Level II-3)

64. World Health Organization. Cardiovascular disease and steroid hormone contraception. Report of a WHO Scientific Group. World Health Organ Tech Rep Ser 1998;877:i-vii,1–89 (Level III)

65. Vessey M, Mant D, Smith A, Yeates D. Oral contraceptives and venous thromboembolism: findings in a large prospective study. BMJ (Clin Res Ed) 1986;292:526 (Level II-2)

66. Robinson GE, Burren T, Mackie IJ, Bounds W, Walshe K, Faint R, et al. Changes in haemostasis after stopping the combined contraceptive pill: implications for major surgery. BMJ 1991;302:269–271 (Level II-3)

67. Bonnar J. Can more be done in obstetric and gynecologic practice to reduce morbidity and mortality associated with venous thromboembolism? Am J Obstet Gynecol 1999; 180:784–791(Level III)

68. Vandenbroucke JP, Koster T, Briet E, Reitsma PH, Bertina RM, Rosendaal FR. Increased risk of venous thrombosis in oral-contraceptive users who are carriers of factor V Leiden mutation. Lancet 1994;344:1453–1457 (Level II-2)

69. Comp PC. Thrombophilic mechanisms of OCs. Int J Fertil Womens Med 1997;42 (suppl 1):170–176 (Level III)

70. Price DT, Ridker PM. Factor V Leiden mutation and the risks for thromboembolic disease: a clinical perspective. Ann Intern Med 1997;127:895–903 (Level III)

71. Comp PC, Zacur HA. Contraceptive choices in women with coagulation disorders. Am J Obtset Gynecol 1993;168:1990–1993 (Level III)

72. Mishell DR Jr. Pharmacokinetics of depot medroxyprogesterone acetate contraception. J Reprod Med 1996; 41(suppl):381–390 (Level III)

73. Vasilakis C, Jick SS, Jick H. The risk of venous thromboembolism in users of postcoital contraceptive pills. Contraception 1999;59:79–83 (Level II-2)

74. Jungers P, Dougados M, Pelissier C, Kuttenn F, Tron F, Lesavre P, et al. Influence of oral contraceptive therapy on the activity of systemic lupus erythematosus. Arthritis Rheum 1982:25:618–623 (Level III)

75. Julkunen HA. Oral contraceptives in systemic lupus erythematosus: side-effects and influence on the activity of SLE. Scand J Rheumatol 1991;20:427–433 (Level III)

76. Mintz G, Gutierrez G, Deleze M, Rodriguez E. Contraception with progestagens in systemic lupus erythematosus. Contraception 1984;30:29–58 (Level II-2)

77. Petri M, Robinson C. Oral contraceptives and systemic lupus erythematosus. Arthritis Rheum 1997;40:797–803 (Level III)

78. Charache S, Niebyl JR. Pregnancy in sickle cell disease. Clin Haematol 1985;14:729–746 (Level III)

79. De Ceulaer K, Gruber C, Hayes R, Serjeant GR. Medroxyprogesterone acetate and homozygous sickle-cell disease. Lancet 1982;2:229–231 (Level II-2)

80. de Abood M, de Castillo Z, Guerrero F, Espino M, Austin KL. Effect of Depo-Provera or Microgynon on the painful crises of sickle cell anemia patients. Contraception 1997;56:313–316 (Level I)

81. Cundy T, Evans M, Roberts H, Wattie D, Ames R, Reid IR. Bone density in women receiving depot medroxyprogesterone acetate for contraception. BMJ 1991;303:13–16 (Level II-2)

82. Cundy T, Cornish J, Evans M, Roberts H, Reid IR. Recovery of bone density in women who stop using medroxyprogesterone acetate. BMJ 1994;308:247–248 (Level II-2)

83. Gbolade B, Ellis S, Murby B, Randall S, Kirkman R. Bone density in the long term users of depot medroxyprogesterone acetate. Br J Obstet Gynaecol 1998;105:790–794 (Level II-3)

84. Cundy T, Cornish J, Roberts H, Elder H, Reid IR. Spinal bone density in women using depot medroxyprogesterone contraception. Obstet Gynecol 1998;92:569–573 (Level II-2)

85. Paiva LC, Pinto-Neto AM, Faundes A. Bone density among long-term users of medroxyprogesterone acetate as a contraceptive. Contraception 1998;58:351–355 (Level II-2)

86. Scholes D, Lacroix AZ, Ott SM, Ichikawa LE, Barlow WE. Bone mineral density in women using depot medroxyprogesterone acetate for contraception. Obstet Gynecol 1999;93:233–238 (Level II-2)

87. Tang OS, Tang G, Yip P, Li B, Fan S. Long-term depot-medroxyprogesterone acetate and bone mineral density. Contraception 1999;59:25–29 (Level II-2)

88. Cromer BA, Blair JM, Mahan JD, Zibners L, Naumovski Z. A prospective comparison of bone density in adolescent girls receiving depot medroxyprogesterone acetate (Depo-Provera), levonorgestrel (Norplant), or oral contraceptives. J Pediatr 1996;129:671–676 (Level II-2)

89. Kolthoff N, Eiken P, Kristensen B, Nielsen SP. Bone mineral changes during pregnancy and lactation: a longitudinal cohort study. Clin Sci (Colch) 1998;94:405–412 (Level II-3)

90. Kalkwarf HJ, Specker BL, Bianchi DC, Ranz J, Ho M. The effect of calcium supplementation on bone density during lactation and after weaning. N Engl J Med 1997;337:523–528 (Level I)

91. Orr-Walker BJ, Evans MC, Ames RW, Clearwater JM, Cundy TR, Reid IR. The effect of past use of the injectable contraceptive depot medroxyprogesterone acetate on bone mineral density in normal post-menopausal women. Clin Endocrinol (Oxf) 1998;49:615–618 (Level II-3)

92. Petitti DB, Piaggio G, Mehta S, Cravioto MC, Meirik O. Steroid hormone contraception and bone mineral density: a cross sectional study in an international population. Obstet Gynecol 2000;95:736–744 (Level II-3)

The MEDLINE database, the Cochrane Library, and ACOG's own internal resources and documents were used to conduct a literature search to locate relevant articles published between January 1985 and March 1998. The search was restricted to articles published in the English language. Priority was given to articles reporting results of original research, although review articles and commentaries also were consulted. Abstracts of research presented at symposia and scientific conferences were not considered adequate for inclusion in this document. Guidelines published by organizations or institutions such as the National Institutes of Health and the American College of Obstetricians and Gynecologists were reviewed, and additional studies were located by reviewing bibliographies of identified articles. When reliable research was not available, expert opinions from obstetrician–gynecologists were used.

Studies were reviewed and evaluated for quality according to the method outlined by the U.S. Preventive Services Task Force:

I   Evidence obtained from at least one properly designed randomized controlled trial.

II-1 Evidence obtained from well-designed controlled trials without randomization.

II-2 Evidence obtained from well-designed cohort or case–control analytic studies, preferably from more than one center or research group.

II-3 Evidence obtained from multiple time series with or without the intervention. Dramatic results in uncontrolled experiments also could be regarded as this type of evidence.

III   Opinions of respected authorities, based on clinical experience, descriptive studies, or reports of expert committees.

Based on the highest level of evidence found in the data, recommendations are provided and graded according to the following categories:

Level A—Recommendations are based on good and consistent scientific evidence.

Level B—Recommendations are based on limited or inconsistent scientific evidence.

Level C—Recommendations are based primarily on consensus and expert opinion.

ISSN 1099-3630

The American College of Obstetricians and Gynecologists
409 12th Street, SW
PO Box 96920
Washington, DC 20090-6920

12345/32109

ACOG PRACTICE BULLETIN

CLINICAL MANAGEMENT GUIDELINES FOR
OBSTETRICIAN–GYNECOLOGISTS
NUMBER 6, SEPTEMBER 1999

This Practice Bulletin was developed by the ACOG Committee on Practice Bulletins— Obstetrics with the assistance of Robert M. Silver, MD, Richard L. Berkowitz, MD, and James Bussel, MD. The information is designed to aid practitioners in making decisions about appropriate obstetric and gynecologic care. These guidelines should not be construed as dictating an exclusive course of treatment or procedure. Variations in practice may be warranted based on the needs of the individual patient, resources, and limitations unique to the institution or type of practice.

Thrombocytopenia in Pregnancy

Thrombocytopenia in pregnant women is diagnosed frequently by obstetricians because platelet counts are now included with automated complete blood cell counts (CBCs) obtained during routine prenatal screening (1). The condition is common, occurring in 7–8% of pregnancies (2). Thrombocytopenia can result from a variety of physiologic or pathologic conditions, several of which are unique to pregnancy. Some causes of thrombocytopenia are serious medical disorders that have the potential for profound maternal and fetal morbidity. In contrast, other conditions, such as gestational thrombocytopenia, are benign and pose no maternal or fetal risks. Because of the increased recognition of maternal and fetal thrombocytopenia, there are numerous controversies regarding obstetric management. Clinicians must weigh the risks of maternal and fetal bleeding complications against the costs and morbidity of diagnostic tests and invasive interventions.

Background

Platelet Function

Unlike other bleeding disorders in which bruising often is the initial clinical manifestation, platelet disorders, such as thrombocytopenia, usually result in bleeding into mucous membranes. Although bruising can occur, the most common manifestations of thrombocytopenia are petechiae, ecchymoses, epistaxis, gingival bleeding, and menometrorrhagia. In contrast to hemophilia, bleeding into joints usually does not occur; life-threatening bleeding is less common but can occur, resulting in hematuria, gastrointestinal bleeding, and, although rare, intracranial hemorrhage.

Definition of Thrombocytopenia

The normal range of the platelet count in nonpregnant individuals is 150,000–400,000/μL. In this population, thrombocytopenia is defined as any platelet value less than 150,000/μL, with counts of 100,000–150,000/μL indicative of mild thrombocytopenia, 50,000–100,000/μL indicative of moderate thrombocytopenia, and less than 50,000/μL indicative of severe thrombocytopenia. The definition of thrombocytopenia is somewhat arbitrary and not necessarily clinically relevant. Clinically significant bleeding usually is limited to patients with platelet counts less than 10,000/μL. Serious bleeding complications are rare, even in those with severe thrombocytopenia (3). Excessive bleeding associated with trauma or surgery is uncommon unless the patient's platelet count is less than 50,000/μL. The mean platelet count in pregnant women is lower than in nonpregnant individuals (4, 5).

Differential Diagnosis of Thrombocytopenia

Thrombocytopenia is due to either increased platelet destruction or decreased platelet production. In pregnancy, the former is responsible for most cases (2). Increased platelet destruction can be caused by an immunologic destruction, abnormal platelet activation, or platelet consumption resulting from excessive bleeding or exposure to abnormal vessels. Decreased platelet production is less common, and usually is associated with either leukemia, aplastic anemia, or folate deficiency (6, 7).

The most common cause of thrombocytopenia during pregnancy is gestational thrombocytopenia, which accounts for about two thirds of cases (2) (see the box).

Gestational Thrombocytopenia

Gestational thrombocytopenia, also termed essential thrombocytopenia or benign or incidental thrombocytopenia of pregnancy, is by far the most common cause of mild thrombocytopenia during pregnancy, affecting up to 8% of gestations (2). There are several characteristics of this condition (2). First, the thrombocytopenia is relatively mild with platelet counts usually remaining greater than 70,000/μL. However, a lower threshold for gestational thrombocytopenia has never been established. Second, women are asymptomatic with no history of bleeding. The thrombocytopenia usually is detected as part of routine prenatal screening. Third, women have no history of thrombocytopenia prior to pregnancy (except in previous pregnancies). Although gestational thrombocytopenia may recur in subsequent pregnancies (8), the recurrence risk is unknown. Fourth, platelet counts usually return to normal within 2–12 weeks following delivery.

Causes of Thrombocytopenia in Pregnancy

Gestational thrombocytopenia

Pregnancy-induced hypertension

HELLP syndrome

Pseudothrombocytopenia (laboratory artifact)

Human immunodeficiency virus (HIV) infection

Immune thrombocytopenic purpura

Systemic lupus erythematosus

Antiphospholipid syndrome

Hypersplenism

Disseminated intravascular coagulation

Thrombotic thrombocytopenic purpura

Hemolytic uremic syndrome

Congenital thrombocytopenias

Medications (heparin, quinine, quinidine, zidovudine, sulfonamides)

Finally, there is an extremely low risk of fetal or neonatal thrombocytopenia. In a large, prospectively evaluated cohort study of 756 women with gestational thrombocytopenia, only one woman's infant had a platelet count of less than 50,000/μL (9). However, this infant had thrombocytopenia due to congenital bone marrow dysfunction. Another study confirmed the extremely low risk of fetal thrombocytopenia in women with gestational thrombocytopenia (10). Thus, women with gestational thrombocytopenia are not at risk for maternal or fetal hemorrhage or bleeding complications.

Although its cause is uncertain, gestational thrombocytopenia may be due to accelerated platelet consumption (4). Antiplatelet antibodies often are detectable in women with gestational thrombocytopenia, but neither their presence nor their absence can be used to diagnose the disorder or differentiate it from immune thrombocytopenic purpura (ITP) (11). Indeed, there are no specific diagnostic tests to definitively distinguish gestational thrombocytopenia from mild ITP (1). The primary means of differentiation is to monitor platelet counts closely, to look for levels that decrease below the 50,000–70,000/μL range, and to document a normal neonatal platelet count and a restoration of normal maternal platelet values after delivery.

Thrombocytopenia with an Immunologic Basis

Thrombocytopenia with an immunologic basis during pregnancy can be broadly classified as two disorders: neonatal alloimmune thrombocytopenia and ITP, an autoimmune condition. Neonatal alloimmune thrombocytopenia has no effect on the mother but probably is responsible for more intracranial hemorrhage due to thrombocytopenia than all the other primary thrombocytopenic conditions combined. In contrast, ITP may affect both mothers and fetuses, but with appropriate management the outcome for both is excellent.

Neonatal Alloimmune Thrombocytopenia

Neonatal alloimmune thrombocytopenia is the platelet equivalent of hemolytic (Rh) disease of the newborn, developing as a result of maternal alloimmunization to fetal platelet antigens. It affects one in 1,000–2,000 live births and can be a serious and potentially life-threatening condition (12, 13). Unlike Rh disease, neonatal alloimmune thrombocytopenia can occur during a first pregnancy. Almost half of the clinically evident cases of neonatal alloimmune thrombocytopenia are discovered in the first live-born infant (14).

In typical cases of unanticipated neonatal alloimmune thrombocytopenia, the mother is healthy and has a normal platelet count, and her pregnancy, labor, and delivery are indistinguishable from those of other low-risk obstetric patients. The neonates, however, are either born with evidence of profound thrombocytopenia or develop symptomatic thrombocytopenia within hours after birth. Affected infants often manifest generalized petechiae or ecchymoses over the presenting fetal part. Hemorrhage into viscera and bleeding following circumcision or venipuncture also may ensue. The most serious complication of neonatal alloimmune thrombocytopenia is intracranial hemorrhage, which occurs in 10–20% of infants (14, 15). Fetal intracranial hemorrhage due to neonatal alloimmune thrombocytopenia can occur in utero, and 25–50% of fetal intracranial hemorrhage in untreated mothers may be detected by ultrasonography before the onset of labor (16). Ultrasonographic findings may include intracranial hemorrhage, porencephalic cysts, and obstructive hydrocephalus. These observations are in contrast to neonatal intracranial hemorrhage due to ITP, which is exceedingly rare and usually occurs during the neonatal period.

Several polymorphic, diallelic antigen systems residing on platelet membrane glycoproteins are responsible for neonatal alloimmune thrombocytopenia. Many of these antigen systems have several names because they were identified in different parts of the world concurrently. Recently, a uniform nomenclature has been adopted that describes these antigens as human platelet antigens (HPA-1 and HPA-2), with alleles designated as "a" or "b" (17). Although there are at least 10 officially recognized platelet-specific antigens at this time, more than 50% of

the reported cases in Caucasians and most of the severe cases have occurred as a result of sensitization against HPA-1a, also known as Pl[A1] and Zw[a].

Fetal thrombocytopenia due to HPA-1a sensitization tends to be severe and can occur early in gestation. In a cohort study of 107 fetuses with neonatal alloimmune thrombocytopenia (97 with HPA-1a incompatibility) studied in utero before receiving any therapy, 50% had initial platelet counts of less than 20,000/μL (13). This percentage included 21 of 46 fetuses tested before 24 weeks of gestation. Furthermore, this series documented that the fetal platelet count decreases at a rate of more than 15,000/μL per week in the absence of therapy.

The recurrence risk of neonatal alloimmune thrombocytopenia is extremely high and approaches 100% in cases involving HPA-1a if the subsequent sibling carries the pertinent antigen (13). Thus, the recurrence risk is related to the zygosity of the father. As with red cell alloimmunization, the disease tends to be equally severe or progressively worse in subsequent pregnancies.

Immune Thrombocytopenic Purpura

Acute ITP is a self-limited disorder that usually occurs in childhood. It may follow a viral infection and rarely persists. Chronic ITP typically occurs in the second or third decade of life and has a female to male ratio of 3:1 (18). Estimates of the frequency of ITP during pregnancy vary widely, affecting one in 1,000–10,000 pregnancies (19).

Immune thrombocytopenic purpura is characterized by immunologically mediated platelet destruction. The patient produces IgG antiplatelet antibodies that recognize platelet membrane glycoproteins. This process leads to increased platelet destruction by cells of the reticuloendothelial system (18). The rate of destruction exceeds the compensatory ability of the bone marrow to produce new platelets, which leads to thrombocytopenia. Most of the platelet destruction occurs in the spleen, although other sites also are involved.

There are no pathognomonic signs, symptoms, or diagnostic tests for ITP; it is a diagnosis of exclusion. However, four findings have been traditionally associated with the condition: 1) persistent thrombocytopenia (platelet count <100,000/μL with or without accompanying megathrombocytes on the peripheral smear), 2) normal or increased numbers of megakaryocytes determined from bone marrow, 3) exclusion of other systemic disorders or drugs that are known to be associated with thrombocytopenia, and 4) absence of splenomegaly.

Most women with ITP have a history of bruising easily and petechiae, or of possible epistaxis and gingival bleeding, which precedes their pregnancy, but some women are completely asymptomatic. Important hemorrhagic symptoms rarely occur unless the platelet count is less than 20,000/µL. It is believed that the course of ITP usually is not affected by pregnancy, although there have been anecdotal reports of patients' conditions worsening during pregnancy and improving postpartum (20, 21). Pregnancy may be adversely affected by severe thrombocytopenia, and the primary risk to the mother is hemorrhage during the peripartum period.

Maternal IgG antiplatelet antibodies can cross the placenta, placing the fetus and neonate at risk for the development of thrombocytopenia. Retrospective case series of ITP in pregnancy indicate that 12–15% of infants born to mothers with ITP will develop platelet counts less than 50,000/µL (22, 23). Sometimes, this results in minor clinical bleeding such as purpura, ecchymoses, or melena. On rare occasions, fetal thrombocytopenia associated with ITP leads to intracranial hemorrhage unrelated to the mode of delivery. When it occurs, intracranial hemorrhage can result in severe neurologic impairment and even death. Serious bleeding complications are estimated to occur in 3% of infants born to women with ITP, and the rate of intracranial hemorrhage is less than 1% (22, 23). These data may overestimate the risk, as a result of publication bias. In a prospective, population-based study of almost 16,000 pregnancies delivered at a single center, no infant born to a mother with ITP suffered intracranial hemorrhage (9). The only three infants with intracranial hemorrhage had neonatal alloimmune thrombocytopenia, not ITP. The platelet count of the affected newborn usually will decrease after delivery, and the nadir may not be reached for several days (20).

Pregnancy-Induced Hypertension

Pregnancy-induced hypertension (PIH) is reported to be the cause of 21% of cases of maternal thrombocytopenia (9). The thrombocytopenia usually is moderate, and platelet counts rarely decrease below 20,000/µL. Clinical hemorrhage is uncommon unless the patient develops disseminated intravascular coagulopathy, but a decreasing maternal platelet count generally is considered a sign of worsening disease and is an indication for delivery.

In some cases, microangiopathic hemolytic anemia and elevated liver function tests are associated with thrombocytopenia in individuals with PIH. Such individuals are considered to have HELLP syndrome.

The cause of thrombocytopenia in women with severe PIH is unknown. The disease is associated with a state of accelerated platelet destruction, platelet activation, increased platelet volume, and increased megakaryocyte activity (21). Increased levels of platelet-associated IgG have been detected in patients with PIH (24). However, this finding is nonspecific and does not necessarily imply an immunologic basis for the thrombocytopenia. Platelet function also may be impaired in women with PIH, even if their platelet count is normal. It is noteworthy that the platelet count may decrease before the other clinical manifestations of PIH are apparent (25).

The neonates of mothers with PIH are at increased risk of neonatal thrombocytopenia (2). However, this is true only for infants born prematurely, and especially those with growth restriction. Term infants of mothers with PIH are no more likely to have thrombocytopenia than are controls. In a study of 1,414 mothers with hypertension, neonatal thrombocytopenia associated with PIH rarely decreased below 20,000/µL and caused no fetal bleeding complications (9).

Clinical Considerations and Recommendations

▶ *What is the appropriate workup for maternal thrombocytopenia?*

When thrombocytopenia is diagnosed in a pregnant woman, it is important that the diagnosis be as precise as possible. The differential diagnosis of thrombocytopenia in pregnancy includes gestational thrombocytopenia, pseudothrombocytopenia, HIV infection, drug-induced thrombocytopenia, PIH, HELLP syndrome, thrombotic thrombocytopenic purpura, hemolytic uremic syndrome, disseminated intravascular coagulation, systemic lupus erythematosus, antiphospholipid syndrome, and congenital thrombocytopenias. These disorders usually can be determined on the basis of a detailed medical and family history and a physical examination, with attention to blood pressure, splenomegaly, HIV serology, and adjunctive laboratory studies as appropriate.

A CBC and examination of the peripheral blood smear generally are indicated in the evaluation of maternal thrombocytopenia. A CBC is helpful to exclude pancytopenia. Evaluation of the peripheral smear serves to rule out platelet clumping that may be associated with pseudothrombocytopenia. Bone marrow biopsy rarely is needed to distinguish between inadequate platelet production and increased platelet turnover. Numerous assays have been developed for both platelet-associated (direct) antibodies and circulating (indirect) antiplatelet antibodies. Although many individuals with ITP will have elevated levels of platelet-associated antibodies and sometimes circulating antiplatelet antibodies, these assays are not recommended for the routine evaluation of maternal thrombocytopenia (26). Tests for antiplatelet antibodies are nonspecific, poorly standardized, and subject to a large degree of interlaboratory variation (1). Also, gestational thrombocytopenia and ITP cannot be differentiated on the basis of antiplatelet antibody testing (11).

If drugs and other medical disorders are excluded, the primary differential diagnosis in the first and second trimesters will be either gestational thrombocytopenia or ITP. It should be noted that although gestational thrombocytopenia can occur in the first trimester, it typically becomes manifest later in pregnancy. In general, in a woman with no history of thrombocytopenia or the milder the thrombocytopenia, the more likely she is to have gestational thrombocytopenia. If the platelet count is less than 70,000/μL, ITP is more likely to be present, and if the platelet count is less than 50,000/μL, ITP is almost certainly present. During the third trimester or postpartum period, the sudden onset of significant maternal thrombocytopenia should lead to consideration of PIH, thrombotic thrombocytopenic purpura, hemolytic uremic syndrome, acute fatty liver, or disseminated intravascular coagulation, although ITP can present this way as well.

▶ **When should women with ITP receive medical therapy?**

The goal of medical therapy during pregnancy in women with ITP is to minimize the risk of bleeding complications associated with severe thrombocytopenia. Because the platelet function of these patients usually is normal, it is not necessary to maintain their counts in the normal range. There is general agreement that asymptomatic pregnant women with platelet counts greater than 50,000/μL do not require treatment. Also, most authorities recommend treatment in the presence of a platelet count significantly less than 50,000/μL or in the presence of bleeding. However, the degree of thrombocytopenia in asymptomatic pregnant women that requires treatment is somewhat controversial, and consultation from a physician experienced in these matters should be considered. Higher counts (eg, >50,000/μL) are desirable for invasive procedures and delivery, which may be associated with hemorrhage, the need for surgery, or the desire to use regional anesthesia. Bleeding times are not useful in assessing platelet function in patients with ITP.

▶ **What therapy should be used to treat ITP during pregnancy?**

The first line of treatment for ITP is prednisone, usually initiated in a dosage of 1–2 mg/kg/d. A response to antenatal corticosteroids usually occurs within 3–7 days and reaches a maximum within 2–3 weeks. Once platelet counts reach acceptable levels, the dosage can be tapered by 10–20% per week until the lowest dosage required to maintain a platelet count greater than 50,000/μL is reached. An increase in the platelet count occurs in about 70% of patients, and up to 25% will achieve complete remission (27).

Intravenous immune globulin (IVIG) is appropriate therapy for cases refractory to steroids as well as in circumstances such as platelet counts less than 10,000/μL in the third trimester, or platelet counts less than 30,000/μL associated with bleeding or with preoperative or predelivery status. A response to therapy can be expected in as few as 6 hours or in as many as 72 hours. In 70% of cases, the platelet count will return to pretreatment levels within 30 days after treatment (26, 28). Intravenous immune globulin is costly and of limited availability. When considering use of IVIG, it is prudent to seek consultation from a physician experienced in such cases.

Splenectomy is associated with complete remission in approximately 66% of patients with ITP (18); however, it often is not successful in patients who do not respond to intravenous immunoglobulin (29). The procedure usually is avoided during pregnancy because of fetal risks and technical difficulties late in gestation. However, splenectomy can be accomplished safely during pregnancy, ideally in the second trimester. It is appropriate for severe cases (platelet counts of less than 10,000/μL) that have failed treatment with antenatal corticosteroids and IVIG (26).

Platelet transfusions should be used only as a temporary measure to control life-threatening hemorrhage or to prepare a patient for surgery. The usual increase in platelets of approximately 10,000/μL per unit of platelets transfused is not achieved in patients with ITP because of the decreased survival of donor platelets. Thus, 6–10 U of platelet concentrate should be transfused. Other drugs used to treat ITP such as colchicine, azathioprine, vinca alkaloids, cyclophosphamide, and danazol have potential adverse fetal effects.

▶ **What additional specialized care should women with ITP receive?**

Other than serial assessment of the maternal platelet count (every trimester in asymptomatic women in remission and more frequently in thrombocytopenic individuals), little specialized care is required. Pregnant women with ITP should be instructed to avoid nonsteroidal anti-inflammatory agents, salicylates, and trauma. Individuals with splenectomies should be immunized against pneumococcus, *Hemophilus influenzae,* and meningococcus. If the diagnosis of ITP is made, consultation and ongoing evaluation with a physician experienced in such matters is appropriate.

▶ *Can fetal or neonatal intracranial hemorrhage be prevented in pregnancies complicated by ITP?*

It is logical to assume that therapies known to increase the maternal platelet count in patients with ITP also would improve the fetal platelet count. However, medical therapies such as IVIG (30) and steroids (22, 30–32) do not reliably prevent fetal thrombocytopenia or improve fetal outcome. Because some of these therapies (eg, IVIG) have not been adequately tested in appropriate trials, there are insufficient data to recommend maternal medical therapy for fetal indications.

Some investigators have recommended cesarean delivery to decrease the risk of intracranial hemorrhage by avoiding the potential trauma associated with vaginal birth (33). This strategy was based on anecdotal reports of intracranial hemorrhage associated with vaginal delivery (34) as well as the biologic plausibility of the hypothesis. Others have proposed that cesarean delivery be reserved for fetuses with platelet counts less than 50,000/μL (35, 36). This tactic was prompted by the observation that the risk of fetal bleeding is inversely proportional to the platelet count, and bleeding problems are extremely rare in fetuses with platelet counts more than 50,000/μL (31, 37).

Cesarean delivery has never been proven to prevent intracranial hemorrhage reliably. Several reports indicate that hemorrhagic complications in infants with thrombocytopenia are unrelated to the mode of delivery (22, 31, 37, 38). In a review of 474 neonates born to mothers with ITP, 29% of infants born vaginally with thrombocytopenia had a bleeding complication, compared with 30% delivered by cesarean birth (31). In this study, the rate of intracranial hemorrhage also was similar for both modes of delivery: 4% after vaginal delivery and 3% after cesarean delivery. In addition, it is unclear that intracranial hemorrhage is an intrapartum phenomenon. The neonatal platelet count often dramatically decreases after delivery. Thus, intracranial hemorrhage during the neonatal period could be mistakenly attributed to intrapartum events. No case of intracranial hemorrhage has been proven definitively to have occurred during labor (22, 23). Because cesarean delivery does not clearly prevent intraventricular hemorrhage, many obstetricians choose the mode of delivery in ITP based on obstetric considerations alone.

▶ *What tests or characteristics can be used to predict fetal thrombocytopenia in pregnancies complicated by ITP?*

No maternal test or characteristic can reliably predict the severity of thrombocytopenia in all cases of infants born to mothers with ITP. Maternal characteristics and serology, including prior splenectomy, platelet count, and the presence of platelet-associated antibodies, all correlate poorly with neonatal thrombocytopenia (39, 40). Fetal thrombocytopenia is rare in the absence of circulating antiplatelet antibodies (10), but exceptional cases have been reported (41). Also, these assays are difficult to perform and have a low positive predictive value (10).

▶ *Is there any role for fetal platelet count determination in ITP?*

At this time, most obstetricians do not obtain fetal platelet counts (42). Scalp sampling is fraught with inaccuracies and technical difficulties, and cordocentesis carries a 1–2% risk of necessitating an emergent cesarean delivery for fetal indications (43). The low incidence of intracranial hemorrhage and the lack of demonstrated difference in neonatal outcome between vaginal and cesarean deliveries also supports the opinion that the determination of fetal platelet count is unwarranted for ITP (22, 23, 31, 37, 44). A substantial minority of perinatologists (42) feel that the 5% risk of fetal thrombocytopenia of less than 20,000/μL and the attendant theoretically increased risk of an intracranial hemorrhage warrant informing patients of the availability of cordocentesis or scalp sampling during labor when choosing mode of delivery (45–47).

▶ *What is the appropriate neonatal care for infants born of pregnancies complicated by ITP?*

Regardless of the mode, delivery should be accomplished in a setting where an available clinician familiar with the disorder can treat any neonatal complications and have access to the medications needed for treatment.

▶ *Can a patient with thrombocytopenia be given regional anesthesia?*

The literature offers only limited and retrospective data to address this issue. However, two studies (48, 49) reported on a total of 184 patients with platelet counts less than 150,000/μL. Of these, 113 patients received epidural anesthesia without neurologic complication or sequelae. In all of these patients, the diagnosis was gestational thrombocytopenia. Another study of patients with platelet counts less than 100,000/μL due to preeclampsia, ITP, or infection also received epidural anesthesia without complication (50). Although the complication of greatest concern is that of epidural hematoma, there are only two cases in the literature of parturients who developed an epidural hematoma after regional anesthesia. One patient had preeclampsia and a lupus anticoagulant (51) and the other had an ependymoma (52). Cases reported in nonparturients have almost always been associated with anticoagulant therapy.

Although limited, data support the safety of epidural anesthesia in patients with platelet counts greater than 100,000/µL. In women with gestational thrombocytopenia with platelet counts less than 99,000/µL but greater than 50,000/µL, epidural anesthesia also may be safe, but its use in such patients will require a consensus among the obstetrician, anesthesiologist, and patient. When platelet counts are less than 50,000/µL, epidural anesthesia should not be given.

▶ **When should an evaluation for possible neonatal alloimmune thrombocytopenia be initiated, and what tests are useful in making the diagnosis?**

The most appropriate screening program incorporates evaluation of patients with a history of infants with otherwise unexplained bleeding or thrombocytopenia. Neonatal alloimmune thrombocytopenia should be suspected in cases of otherwise unexplained fetal or neonatal thrombocytopenia, porencephaly, or intracranial hemorrhage (either in utero or after birth). The laboratory diagnosis includes determination of platelet type and zygosity of both parents and the confirmation of maternal antiplatelet antibodies with specificity for paternal (or fetal–neonatal) platelets and the incompatible antigen. Platelet typing may be determined serologically or by genotyping because the genes and polymorphisms responsible for most cases of neonatal alloimmune thrombocytopenia have been identified. This is helpful when the father is heterozygous for the pertinent antigen because fetal platelet antigen typing can be performed using amniocytes (53). Chorionic villus sampling should not be performed because of its potential increased sensitization to antiplatelet antibodies. The laboratory evaluation of neonatal alloimmune thrombocytopenia can be complex, results may be ambiguous, and an antigen incompatibility cannot always be identified. Accordingly, testing for this disorder should be performed in an experienced regional laboratory that has special interest and expertise in neonatal alloimmune thrombocytopenia.

There is a theoretical benefit from population-based screening for platelet antigen incompatibility. However, such a program has not been shown to be clinically useful or cost-effective and is not currently recommended. Another area of controversy is the patient whose sister has had a pregnancy complicated by neonatal alloimmune thrombocytopenia. It may be worthwhile to evaluate these patients for platelet antigen incompatibility or human leukocyte antigen phenotype. However, the theoretical advantages of testing these women must be weighed against the potential for anxiety, cost, and morbidity without proven benefit.

▶ **How can one determine the fetal platelet count in pregnancies complicated by neonatal alloimmune thrombocytopenia?**

Unfortunately, as with ITP, there are no good indirect methods to determine the fetal platelet count. Maternal antiplatelet antibody titers correlate poorly with the severity of the disease. Also, characteristics such as the outcome of previously affected siblings (eg, birth platelet count or intracranial hemorrhage recognized after delivery) do not reliably predict the severity of fetal thrombocytopenia (13). Currently, the only accurate means of estimating the fetal platelet count is to sample the fetal blood directly, although this may increase the risk of fetal exsanguination.

▶ **What is the appropriate obstetric management of neonatal alloimmune thrombocytopenia?**

The primary goal of the obstetric management of pregnancies complicated by neonatal alloimmune thrombocytopenia is to prevent intracranial hemorrhage and its associated complications. In contrast to ITP, however, the higher frequency of intracranial hemorrhage associated with neonatal alloimmune thrombocytopenia justifies more aggressive interventions. Also, strategies intended to avoid intracranial hemorrhage must be initiated antenatally because of the risk of in utero intracranial hemorrhage.

The optimal management of fetuses at risk for neonatal alloimmune thrombocytopenia (those testing positive for the incompatible antigen or those whose fathers are homozygous for the antigen) remains controversial. The management decisions for these cases should be individualized and are best made after consultation with obstetric and pediatric specialists familiar with the disorder as soon as the diagnosis is made. Several therapies have been used in an attempt to increase the fetal platelet count and to avoid intracranial hemorrhage, including maternal treatment with IVIG, with or without steroids (15, 54–60), and fetal platelet transfusions (59, 61, 62). Intravenous immune globulin administered to the mother appears to be the most consistently effective antepartum therapy for neonatal alloimmune thrombocytopenia (15). However, none of these therapies is effective in all cases. Direct fetal administration of IVIG does not reliably improve the fetal platelet count, although only a few cases have been reported. Platelet transfusions with maternal platelets are consistently effective in raising the fetal platelet count. However, the short half-life of transfused platelets requires weekly procedures and may worsen the alloimmunization.

It is unknown whether it is necessary to determine the fetal platelet count before initiating therapy. The risks of cordocentesis in the setting of neonatal alloimmune thrombocytopenia must be weighed against the ability to determine the need for and the effectiveness of therapy. Although unproven, the benefit of transfusing maternal platelets at the time of cordocentesis may reduce the risk of bleeding complications from the procedure (63). The optimal time during gestation to first assess the fetal platelet count also is controversial. When fetal blood sampling is indicated, performance at 22–24 weeks of gestation may optimize medical therapy.

Most investigators recommend determination of the fetal platelet count once fetal pulmonary maturity is achieved, but before the onset of labor (eg, 37 weeks of gestation). A trial of labor is permitted for fetuses with platelet counts greater than 50,000/μL, while those with severe thrombocytopenia are delivered by cesarean birth. Although this strategy is of unproven efficacy, the high rate of intracranial hemorrhage in neonatal alloimmune thrombocytopenia is considered to warrant these interventions. Delivery should be accomplished in a setting equipped to handle a neonate with severe thrombocytopenia.

▶ *What is appropriate obstetric management for gestational thrombocytopenia?*

Pregnancies with gestational thrombocytopenia are not at risk for maternal bleeding complications or fetal thrombocytopenia (4, 9). Thus, such interventions as the determination of the fetal platelet count or cesarean delivery are not indicated in patients with this condition. Women with gestational thrombocytopenia do not require any additional testing or specialized care, except follow-up platelet counts.

▶ *Is it necessary to treat thrombocytopenia associated with PIH?*

The primary treatment of maternal thrombocytopenia in the setting of PIH or HELLP syndrome is delivery. Although antepartum reversal of thrombocytopenia has been reported with medical therapy (64), this course of treatment is not usual (65, 66). More importantly, the underlying pathophysiology of PIH will only resolve following birth. Thus, other than to allow for medical stabilization, the effect of betamethasone on fetal pulmonary maturity, or in special cases at preterm gestations, severe thrombocytopenia due to PIH is an indication for delivery (66).

Major hemorrhage is infrequent in patients with PIH but minor bleeding such as operative site oozing during cesarean delivery is common. Platelet transfusions occasionally are needed to improve hemostasis in patients with severe thrombocytopenia or DIC. However, transfusions are less effective in these women because of accelerated platelet destruction. Therefore, platelet transfusions are best reserved for patients with severe thrombocytopenia and active bleeding. An exception is the patient undergoing cesarean delivery. Although of uncertain benefit, many authorities recommend platelet transfusions to increase the platelet count to more than 50,000/μL before cesarean delivery (66).

Platelet counts often decrease for 24–48 hours after birth, followed by a rapid recovery (67–69). Most patients will achieve normal platelet counts within a few days to a week postpartum (67, 69). However, although rare, thrombocytopenia may continue for a prolonged period, which often is associated with persistent multisystem dysfunction (68). Plasma exchange has been reported to improve the platelet count in women with HELLP syndrome (70), but the efficacy remains unproven. Although thrombocytopenia associated with PIH or HELLP syndrome may improve after treatment with steroids or uterine curettage (71, 72), the clinical benefit of these therapies also is uncertain.

Summary

The following recommendation is based on good and consistent scientific evidence (Level A):

▶ Neonatal alloimmune thrombocytopenia should be treated with IVIG as the initial approach when fetal thrombocytopenia is documented.

The following recommendations are based on limited or inconsistent scientific evidence (Level B):

▶ The mode of delivery in pregnancies complicated by ITP should be chosen based on obstetric considerations alone. Prophylactic cesarean delivery does not appear to reduce the risk of fetal or neonatal hemorrhage.

▶ Epidural anesthesia is safe in patients with platelet counts greater than 100,000/μL.

▶ Mild maternal thrombocytopenia ($\geq 70,000$/μL) in asymptomatic pregnant women with no history of bleeding problems is usually benign gestational thrombocytopenia. These women should receive routine prenatal care with periodic repeat platelet counts (monthly to bimonthly).

The following recommendations are based primarily on consensus and expert opinion (Level C):

▶ Platelet counts of at least 50,000/µL rarely require treatment.

▶ Neonatal alloimmune thrombocytopenia should be suspected in cases of otherwise unexplained fetal or neonatal thrombocytopenia, hemorrhage, or porencephaly.

▶ Prior to initiating any plan of treatment for a woman based on thrombocytopenia in her fetus, consultation should be sought from a physician with experience dealing with that problem.

▶ Laboratory testing for neonatal alloimmune thrombocytopenia should be performed in a regional laboratory with special interest and expertise in dealing with the problem.

References

1. Rouse DJ, Owen J, Goldenberg RL. Routine maternal platelet count: an assessment of technologically driven practice. Am J Obstet Gynecol 1998;179:573–576 (Level III)

2. Burrows RF, Kelton JG. Thrombocytopenia at delivery: a prospective survey of 6,715 deliveries. Am J Obstet Gynecol 1990;162:731–734 (Level II-3)

3. Lacey JV, Penner JA. Management of idiopathic thrombocytopenic purpura in the adult. Semin Thromb Hemost 1977;3:160–174 (Level III)

4. Burrows RF, Kelton JG. Incidentally detected thrombocytopenia in healthy mothers and their infants. N Engl J Med 1988;319:142–145 (Level II-3)

5. Nagey DA, Alger LS, Edelman BB, Heyman MR, Pupkin MJ, Crenshaw C Jr. Reacting appropriately to thrombocytopenia in pregnancy. South Med J 1986;79:1385–1388 (Level III)

6. Jih DM, Werth VP. Thrombocytopenia after a single dose of methotrexate. J Am Acad Dermatol 1998;39:349–351 (Level III)

7. Mant MJ, Connolly T, Gordon PA, King EG. Severe thrombocytopenia probably due to acute folic acid deficiency. Crit Care Med 1979;7:297–300 (Level III)

8. Ruggeri M, Schiavotto C, Castaman G, Tosetto A, Rodeghiero F. Gestational thrombocytopenia: a prospective study. Haematologica 1997;82:341–342 (Level II-3)

9. Burrows RF, Kelton JG. Fetal thrombocytopenia and its relation to maternal thrombocytopenia. N Engl J Med 1993;329:1463–1466 (Level II-3)

10. Samuels P, Bussel JB, Braitman LE, Tomaski A, Druzin ML, Mennuti MT, et al. Estimation of the risk of thrombocytopenia in the offspring of pregnant women with presumed immune thrombocytopenic purpura. N Engl J Med 1990;323:229–235 (Level II-3)

11. Lescale KB, Eddleman KA, Cines DB, Samuels P, Lesser ML, McFarland JG, et al. Antiplatelet antibody testing in thrombocytopenic pregnant women. Am J Obstet Gynecol 1996;174:1014–1018 (Level II-2)

12. Blanchette VS, Chen L, de Friedberg ZS, Hogan VA, Trudel E, Decary F. Alloimmunization to the Pl^{A1} platelet antigen: results of a prospective study. Br J Haematol 1990;74:209–215 (Level II-3)

13. Bussel JB, Zabusky MR, Berkowitz RL, McFarland JG. Fetal alloimmune thrombocytopenia. N Engl J Med 1997;337:22–26 (Level II-2)

14. Mueller-Eckhardt C, Kiefel V, Grubert A, Kroll H, Weisheit M, Schmidt S, et al. 348 cases of suspected neonatal alloimmune thrombocytopenia. Lancet 1989;1:363–366 (Level II-3)

15. Bussel JB, Berkowitz RL, Lynch L, Lesser ML, Paidas MJ, Huang CL, et al. Antenatal management of alloimmune thrombocytopenia with intravenous gamma-globulin: a randomized trial of the addition of low-dose steroid to intravenous gamma-globulin. Am J Obstet Gynecol 1996;174:1414–1423 (Level I)

16. Herman JH, Jumbelic MI, Ancona RJ, Kickler TS. In utero cerebral hemorrhage in alloimmune thrombocytopenia. Am J Pediatr Hematol Oncol 1986;8:312–317 (Level III)

17. von dem Borne AE, Decary F. Nomenclature of platelet-specific antigens. Transfusion 1990;30:477 (Level III)

18. George JN, el-Harake MA, Raskob GE. Chronic idiopathic thrombocytopenic purpura. N Engl J Med 1994;331:1207–1211 (Level III)

19. Sainio S, Joutsi L, Jarvenpaa AL, Kekomaki R, Koistinen E, Riikonen S, et al. Idiopathic thrombocytopenic purpura in pregnancy. Acta Obstet Gynecol Scand 1998; 77:272–277 (Level III)

20. Kelton JG, Inwood MJ, Barr RM, Effer SB, Hunter D, Wilson WE, et al. The prenatal prediction of thrombocytopenia in infants of mothers with clinically diagnosed immune thrombocytopenia. Am J Obstet Gynecol 1982;144:449–454 (Level II-3)

21. McCrae KR, Samuels P, Schreiber AD. Pregnancy-associated thrombocytopenia: pathogenesis and management. Blood 1992;80:2697–2714 (Level III)

22. Payne SD, Resnik R, Moore TR, Hedriana HL, Kelly TF. Maternal characteristics and risk of severe neonatal thrombocytopenia and intracranial hemorrhage in pregnancies complicated by autoimmune thrombocytopenia. Am J Obstet Gynecol 1997;177:149–155 (Level II-3)

23. Silver RM, Branch DW, Scott JR. Maternal thrombocytopenia in pregnancy: time for a reassessment. Am J Obstet Gynecol 1995;173:479–482 (Level III)

24. Burrows RF, Hunter DJ, Andrew M, Kelton JG. A prospective study investigating the mechanism of thrombocytopenia in preeclampsia. Obstet Gynecol 1987;70:334–338 (Level II-2)

25. Redman CW, Bonnar J, Beilin L. Early platelet consumption in pre-eclampsia. BMJ 1978;1:467–469 (Level II-2)

26. George JN, Woolf SH, Raskob GE, Wasser JS, Aledort LM, Ballem PJ, et al. Idiopathic thrombocytopenic purpura: a practice guideline developed by explicit methods for the American Society of Hematology. Blood 1996;88:3–40 (Level III)

27. Karpatkin S. Autoimmune thrombocytopenic purpura. Am J Med Sci 1971;261:127–138 (Level III)

28. Bussel JB, Pham LC. Intravenous treatment with gamma globulin in adults with immune thrombocytopenic purpu-

ra: review of the literature. Vox Sang 1987;52:206–211 (Level III)

29. Law C, Marcaccio M, Tam P, Heddle N, Kelton JG. High-dose intravenous immune globulin and the response to splenectomy in patients with idiopathic thrombocytopenic purpura. N Engl J Med 1997;336:1494–1498 (Level III)

30. Kaplan C, Daffos F, Forestier F, Tertian G, Catherine N, Pous JC, et al. Fetal platelet counts in thrombocytopenic pregnancy. Lancet 1990;336:979–982 (Level II-3)

31. Cook RL, Miller RC, Katz VL, Cefalo RC. Immune thrombocytopenic purpura in pregnancy: a reappraisal of management. Obstet Gynecol 1991;78:578–583 (Level II-3)

32. Christiaens GC, Nieuwenhuis HK, von dem Borne AE, Ouwehand WH, Helmerhorst FM, Van Dalen CM, et al. Idiopathic thrombocytopenic purpura in pregnancy: a randomized trial on the effect of antenatal low dose corticosteroids on neonatal platelet count. Br J Obstet Gynaecol 1990;97:893–898 (Level I)

33. Carloss HW, McMillan R, Crosby WH. Management of pregnancy in women with immune thrombocytopenic purpura. JAMA 1980;224:2756–2758 (Level III)

34. Jones RW, Asher MI, Rutherford CJ, Munro HM. Autoimmune (idiopathic) thrombocytopenic purpura in pregnancy and the newborn. Br J Obstet Gynaecol 1977;84:679–683 (Level III)

35. Ayromlooi J. A new approach to the management of immunologic thrombocytopenic purpura in pregnancy. Am J Obstet Gynecol 1978;130:235–236 (Level III)

36. Scott JR, Cruikshank DP, Kochenour NK, Pitkin RM, Warenski JC. Fetal platelet counts in the obstetric management of immunologic thrombocytopenic purpura. Am J Obstet Gynecol 1980;136:495–499 (Level III)

37. Burrows RF, Kelton JG. Pregnancy in patients with idiopathic thrombocytopenic purpura: assessing the risks for the infant at delivery. Obstet Gynecol Surv 1993;48:781–788 (Level III)

38. Laros RK Jr, Kagan R. Route of delivery for patients with immune thrombocytopenic purpura. Am J Obstet Gynecol 1984;148:901–908 (Level III)

39. Scott JR, Rote NS, Cruikshank DP. Antiplatelet antibodies and platelet counts in pregnancies complicated by autoimmune thrombocytopenic purpura. Am J Obstet Gynecol 1983;145:932–939 (Level II-3)

40. Burrows RF, Kelton JG. Low fetal risks in pregnancies associated with idiopathic thrombocytopenic purpura. Am J Obstet Gynecol 1990;163:1147–1150 (Level II-3)

41. Risk of thrombocytopenia in offspring of mothers with presumed immune thrombocytopenic purpura. N Engl J Med 1990;323:1841–1843 (Level III)

42. Peleg D, Hunter SK. Perinatal management of women with immune thrombocytopenic purpura: survey of United States perinatologists. Am J Obstet Gynecol 1999;180:645–649 (Level II-3)

43. Ghidini A, Sepulveda W, Lockwood CJ, Romero R. Complications of fetal blood sampling. Am J Obstet Gynecol 1993;168:1339–1344 (Level III)

44. Berry SM, Leonardi MR, Wolfe HM, Dombrowski MP, Lanouette JM, Cotton DB. Maternal thrombocytopenia.

Predicting neonatal thrombocytopenia with cordocentesis. J Reprod Med 1997;42:276–280 (Level III)

45. Garmel SH, Craigo SD, Morin LM, Crowley JM, D'Alton ME. The role of percutaneous umbilical blood sampling in the management of immune thrombocytopenic purpura. Prenat Diagn 1995;15:439–445 (Level III)

46. De Carolis S, Noia G, DeSantis M, Trivellini C, Mastromarino C, De Carolis MP, et al. Immune thrombocytopenic purpura and percutaneous umbilical blood sampling: an open question. Fetal Diagn Ther 1993;8:154–160 (Level II-2)

47. Scioscia AL, Grannum PA, Copel JA, Hobbins JC. The use of percutaneous umbilical blood sampling in immune thrombocytopenic purpura. Am J Obstet Gynecol 1988;159:1066–1068 (Level II-3)

48. Beilin Y, Zahn J, Comerford M. Safe epidural analgesia in thirty parturients with platelet counts between 69,000 and 98,000 mm-3. Anesth Analg 1997;85:385–388 (Level III)

49. Rolbin SH, Abbott D, Musclow E, Papsin F, Lie LM, Freedman J. Epidural anesthesia in pregnant patients with low platelet counts. Obstet Gynecol 1988;71:918–920 (Level III)

50. Rasmus KT, Rottman RL, Kotelko DM, Wright WC, Stone JJ, Rosenblatt RM. Unrecognized thrombocytopenia and regional anesthesia in parturients: a retrospective review. Obstet Gynecol 1989;73:943–946 (Level III)

51. Lao TT, Halpern SH, MacDonald D, Huh C. Spinal subdural haematoma in a parturient after attempted epidural anaesthesia. Can J Anaesth 1993;40:340–345 (Level III)

52. Roscoe MWA, Barrington TW. Acute spinal subdural hematoma. A case report and review of literature. Spine 1984;9:672–675 (Level III)

53. McFarland JG, Aster RH, Bussel JB, Gianopoulos JG, Derbes RS, Newman PJ. Prenatal diagnosis of neonatal alloimmune thrombocytopenia using allele-specific oligonucleotide probes. Blood 1991;78:2276–2282 (Level III)

54. Bussel JB, Berkowitz RL, McFarland JG, Lynch L, Chitkara U. Antenatal treatment of neonatal alloimmune thrombocytopenia. N Engl J Med 1988:319:1374–1378 (Level II-2)

55. Lynch L, Bussel JB, McFarland JG, Chitkara U, Berkowitz RL. Antenatal treatment of alloimmune thrombocytopenia. Obstet Gynecol 1992;80:67–71 (Level II-2)

56. Marzusch K, Schnaidt M, Dietl J, Weist E, Hofstaetter C, Golz R. High-dose immunoglobulin in the antenatal treatment of neonatal alloimmune thrombocytopenia: case report and review. Br J Obstet Gynaecol 1992;99:260–262 (Level III)

57. Mir N, Samson D, House MJ, Kovar IZ. Failure of antenatal high-dose immunoglobulin to improve fetal platelet count in neonatal alloimmune thrombocytopenia. Vox Sang 1988;55:188–189 (Level III)

58. Bowman J, Harman C, Mentigolou S, Pollack J. Intravenous fetal transfusion of immunoglobulin for alloimmune thrombocytopenia. Lancet 1992;340:1034–1035 (Level III)

59. Nicolini U, Tannirandorn Y, Gonzalez P, Fisk NM, Beacham J, Letsky EA, et al. Continuing controversy in

alloimmune thrombocytopenia: fetal hyperimmunoglobulinemia fails to prevent thrombocytopenia. Am J Obstet Gynecol 1990;163:1144–1146 (Level III)

60. Zimmermann R, Huch A. In-utero fetal therapy with immunoglobulin for alloimmune thrombocytopenia. Lancet 1992;340:606 (Level III)

61. Kaplan C, Daffos F, Forestier F, Cox WL, Lyon-Caen D, Dupuy-Montbrun MC, et al. Management of alloimmune thrombocytopenia: antenatal diagnosis and in utero transfusion of maternal platelets. Blood 1988;72:340–343 (Level III)

62. Murphy MF, Pullon HW, Metcalfe P, Chapman JF, Jenkins E, Waters AH, et al. Management of fetal alloimmune thrombocytopenia by weekly in utero platelet transfusions. Vox Sang 1990;58:45–49 (Level III)

63. Paidas MJ, Berkowitz RL, Lynch L, Lockwood CJ, Lapinski R, McFarland JG, et al. Alloimmune thrombocytopenia: fetal and neonatal losses related to cordocentesis. Am J Obstet Gynecol 1995;172:475–479 (Level II-2)

64. Clark SL, Phelan JR, Allen SH, Golde SR. Antepartum reversal of hematologic abnormalities associated with the HELLP syndrome. A report of three cases. J Reprod Med 1986;31:70–72 (Level III)

65. Weinstein L. Syndrome of hemolysis, elevated liver enzymes, and low platelet count: a severe consequence of hypertension in pregnancy. Am J Obstet Gynecol 1982;142:159–167 (Level III)

66. Sibai BM. The HELLP syndrome (hemolysis, elevated liver enzymes, and low platelets): much ado about nothing? Am J Obstet Gynecol 1990;162:311–316 (Level III)

67. Katz VL, Thorp JM Jr, Rozas L, Bowes WA Jr. The natural history of thrombocytopenia associated with preeclampsia. Am J Obstet Gynecol 1990;163:1142–1143 (Level II-3)

68. Martin JN Jr, Blake PG, Lowry SL, Perry KG Jr, Files JC, Morrison JC. Pregnancy complicated by preeclampsia-eclampsia with the syndrome of hemolysis, elevated liver enzymes, and low platelet count: how rapid is postpartum recovery? Obstet Gynecol 1990;76:737–741 (Level II-3)

69. Neiger R, Contag SA, Coustan DR. The resolution of preeclampsia-related thrombocytopenia. Obstet Gynecol 1991;77:692–695 (Level II-3)

70. Martin JN Jr, Files JC, Blake PG, Norman PH, Martin RW, Hess LW, et al. Plasma exchange for preeclampsia. I. Postpartum use for persistently severe preeclampsia-eclampsia with HELLP syndrome. Am J Obstet Gynecol 1990;162:126–137 (Level III)

71. Magann EF, Martin JN Jr, Isaacs JD, Perry KG Jr, Martin RW, Meydrech EF. Immediate postpartum curettage: accelerated recovery from severe preeclampsia. Obstet Gynecol 1993;81:502–506 (Level I)

72. Magann EF, Bass D, Chauhan SP, Sullivan DL, Martin RW, Martin JN Jr. Antepartum corticosteroids: disease stabilization in patients with the syndrome of hemolysis, elevated liver enzymes, and low platelets (HELLP). Am J Obstet Gynecol 1994;171:1148–1153 (Level I)

The MEDLINE database, the Cochrane Library, and ACOG's own internal resources were used to conduct a literature search to locate relevant articles published between January 1985 and January 1999. The search was restricted to articles published in the English language. Priority was given to articles reporting results of original research, although review articles and commentaries also were consulted. Abstracts of research presented at symposiums and scientific conferences were not considered adequate for inclusion in this document. Guidelines published by organizations or institutions such as the National Institutes of Health and ACOG were reviewed, and additional studies were located by reviewing bibliographies of identified articles. When reliable research was not available, expert opinions from obstetrician–gynecologists were used.

Studies were reviewed and evaluated for quality according to the method outlined by the U.S. Preventive Services Task Force:

I   Evidence obtained from at least one properly designed randomized controlled trial.

II-1   Evidence obtained from well-designed controlled trials without randomization.

II-2   Evidence obtained from well-designed cohort or case–control analytic studies, preferably from more than one center or research group.

II-3   Evidence obtained from multiple time series with or without the intervention. Dramatic results in uncontrolled experiments also could be regarded as this type of evidence.

III   Opinions of respected authorities, based on clinical experience, descriptive studies, or reports of expert committees.

Based on the highest level of evidence found in the data, recommendations are provided and graded according to the following categories:

Level A—Recommendations are based on good and consistent scientific evidence.

Level B—Recommendations are based on limited or inconsistent scientific evidence.

Level C—Recommendations are based primarily on consensus and expert opinion.

ISSN 1099-3630

**The American College of
Obstetricians and Gynecologists
409 12th Street, SW
PO Box 96920
Washington, DC 20090-6920**   12345/32109

ACOG PRACTICE BULLETIN

CLINICAL MANAGEMENT GUIDELINES FOR
OBSTETRICIAN–GYNECOLOGISTS
NUMBER 19, AUGUST 2000

(Replaces Educational Bulletin Number 234, March 1997)

This Practice Bulletin was developed by the ACOG Committee on Practice Bulletins— Obstetrics with the assistance of Linda A. Barbour, MD, MSPH. The information is designed to aid practitioners in making decisions about appropriate obstetric and gynecologic care. These guidelines should not be construed as dictating an exclusive course of treatment or procedure. Variations in practice may be warranted based on the needs of the individual patient, resources, and limitations unique to the institution or type of practice.

Thromboembolism in Pregnancy

During pregnancy, women have a fivefold increased risk of venous thromboembolism (VTE), compared with nonpregnant women. The absolute risk of symptomatic venous thrombosis during pregnancy is between 0.5 and 3.0 per 1,000 women based on studies using radiographic documentation (1–3). Pulmonary embolism (PE) is a leading cause of maternal death in the United States (4). The prevalence and severity of this condition warrant consideration of anticoagulant therapy in pregnancy for women at risk for VTE. Such therapy includes the treatment of acute thrombotic events, prophylaxis for patients with a history of thrombotic events or identified acquired or congenital thrombophilias, and prevention and treatment of systemic embolization in women with valvular heart disease. The purpose of this document is to review the current literature on the prevention and management of thromboembolism in obstetric patients, discuss the data behind sometimes conflicting guidelines from expert panels, and offer evidence-based recommendations to address the most clinically relevant issues in the management of these patients.

Background

Numerous changes in the coagulation system account for the hypercoagulable state associated with pregnancy (see the box). Recently, it has been recognized that up to half of women who have thrombotic events during pregnancy possess an underlying congenital or acquired thrombophilia (5). The most common thrombophilias in the Caucasian population are the factor V Leiden mutation, which has a prevalence of 5% in this population, and the prothrombin gene mutation G20210A, which has a prevalence of 2% in this population (5, 6). In approximately 50% of patients with a hereditary thrombophilia, the initial thrombotic event occurs in the presence of an additional risk factor such as pregnancy, oral contraceptive use, orthopedic trauma, immobilization, or surgery (7, 8).

Pregnancy-Associated Changes in Coagulation

Increases in clotting factors (I, VII, VIII, IX, X)

Decreases in protein S

Decreases in fibrinolytic activity

Increased venous stasis

Vascular injury associated with delivery

Increased activation of platelets

Resistance to activated protein C

Risk of Thromboembolism During Pregnancy

Traditionally, it was believed that the risk of venous thrombosis was greatest in the third trimester and immediately postpartum. More recent studies using objective criteria for diagnosis have found that antepartum deep vein thrombosis (DVT) is at least as common as postpartum thrombosis and occurs with equal frequency in all three trimesters (1). However, PE is more common postpartum.

Women with a history of thromboembolism have an increased risk of recurrence when they become pregnant; however, the estimates of recurrence are based primarily on two retrospective studies and range from 7.5% to 12% (9, 10). No studies differentiated the risk of recurrence based on underlying factors such as acquired or congenital thrombophilias, use of oral contraceptives, pregnancy, orthopedic trauma, recent surgery, or the occurrence of the event in the antepartum versus postpartum period. Most of the estimates of recurrence are based on women who had their initial event during oral contraceptive use or pregnancy. Risk factors for thromboembolic disorders are noted in the box.

Anticoagulation Medications in Pregnancy

Although many terms have been used to classify anticoagulant regimens, the following terminology will be used in this document:

- Low-dose prophylaxis—a fixed dose of anticoagulant given 1–2 times per day without use of routine monitoring to verify a therapeutic prolongation of the activated partial thromboplastin time (APTT).

- Adjusted-dose prophylaxis—anticoagulant administered for prophylaxis to achieve traditional therapeutic effects, given 2–3 times per day with frequent laboratory testing to verify adequate APTT prolongation of at least 1.5 to 2.5.

Heparin

There is considerable clinical experience with heparin use in pregnancy (11). Heparin requirements appear to increase during pregnancy because of increases in heparin-binding proteins, plasma volume, renal clearance, and heparin degradation by the placenta, which reduces the bioavailability of heparin (12). There are no prospective trials that have determined adequate prophylactic doses in pregnancy. The major concerns with heparin use during pregnancy are not fetal but maternal and include heparin-induced osteoporosis and heparin-induced thrombocytopenia (HIT).

Two prospective trials of pregnant women exposed to heparin confirmed a mean bone loss of 5% (13, 14), with approximately one third sustaining a 10% or greater decrease in bone density (13). The complete reversibility of this process has not been clearly established, nor does there appear to be a clear dose-response relationship (15). In selected patients, such as those who have a strong family history of osteoporosis or are smokers, postpartum evaluation of bone density may have prognostic and therapeutic implications (13, 14).

There are two types of heparin-induced thrombocytopenia. The more common type is the benign, reversible nonimmune form, which occurs in patients within the first few days of therapy and typically resolves by 5 days. This

Risk Factors for Deep Vein Thrombosis and Thromboembolic Disorders

Hereditary Thrombophilia (prevalence in general population)

Factor V Leiden mutation (5–9%)*

AT-III deficiency (0.02–0.2%)

Protein C deficiency (0.2–0.5%)

Protein S deficiency (0.08%)

Hyperhomocystinemia (1–11%)

Prothrombin gene mutation (2–4%)

Prior history of deep vein thrombosis

Mechanical heart valve

Atrial fibrillation

Trauma/prolonged immobilization/major surgery

Other familial hypercoagulable states

Antiphospholipid syndrome

*For African Americans, about 1%; for Caucasians, 6–11%.

Data from Lockwood CJ. Heritable coagulopathies in pregnancy. Obstet Gynecol Surv 1999;54:754–765

condition does not require cessation of heparin therapy. The less common but more severe type is the immune form of HIT, which occurs within 5–14 days of full-dose heparin therapy in as many as 3% of patients (16) and may result in widespread thrombosis (17, 18). The occurrence of autoimmune thrombocytopenia from prophylactic doses of heparin has been reported, but is rare. Deep vein thrombosis and PE are the most frequent clinical presentations of the immune form of HIT. It has been recommended, therefore, that platelet counts be checked on day 5 and then periodically for the first 2 weeks of heparin therapy. If the HIT is severe, heparin therapy must be stopped and alternative anticoagulation therapy initiated; low-molecular-weight heparin (LMWH) may not be a safe alternative because it has a low cross reactivity with heparin. In such situations, consultation with someone with expertise in the field may be needed (17, 18).

Low-Molecular-Weight Heparin

Low-molecular-weight heparin may reduce three of the complications caused by standard heparin: bleeding, osteoporosis, and thrombocytopenia (16, 18, 19). However, virtually all data on LMWH come from nonpregnant patients. It has been conclusively demonstrated that LMWH does not cross the placenta into the fetal circulation (20, 21). Although the bioavailability of LMWH should be improved over standard heparin because of the reduction of heparin binding, the increases in renal clearance and volume of distribution of the drug may necessitate dosage increases in pregnancy (22, 23). Another advantage of LMWH is that dosing can be limited to once or twice daily (22, 24). If laboratory monitoring is used, monitoring peak antifactor Xa levels every 4–6 weeks should be utilized particularly when twice daily dosing is given. The APTT does not correlate well with the anticoagulant effect of LMWH.

Warfarin

Warfarin derivatives cross the placenta and in most cases are relatively contraindicated in pregnancy; therefore, they primarily are used postpartum or in patients with certain types of mechanical heart valves (25–29). Warfarin use should be restricted to the second or early third trimester in selected patients in whom prolonged high-dose heparin therapy is relatively contraindicated. A skeletal embryopathy resulting in stippled epiphyses and nasal and limb hypoplasia can occur when warfarin is given between 6 and 12 weeks of gestation (30). Midtrimester exposure may result in optic atrophy, microcephaly, and developmental delay. Bleeding can occur in the fetus at any time, resulting in a high fetal loss rate (30).

Clinical Considerations and Recommendations

▶ *Who are candidates for thromboprophylaxis in pregnancy?*

Thromboprophylaxis is defined as administration of anticoagulants because of an increased risk of VTE during pregnancy rather than treatment for an acute event. Often this can be accomplished using relatively low doses, which have a minimal effect on laboratory measures of coagulation. Such low-dose prophylaxis carries fewer risks than full therapeutic anticoagulation. There are certain high-risk conditions that require dosage adjustments to achieve higher therapeutic levels of anticoagulation (adjusted-dose heparin prophylaxis). Each patient's regimen should be individualized once the risks of heparin therapy are weighed against the benefits (31).

Patients with the following conditions are at highest risk and should have adjusted-dose heparin prophylaxis (12):

- Artificial heart valves (some investigators recommend warfarin therapy after the first trimester in certain circumstances) (26–29)

- Antithrombin-III (AT-III) deficiency (with or without a history of thrombosis; also referred to as "antithrombin deficiency") (32, 33)

- Antiphospholipid syndrome (some investigators recommend low-dose prophylaxis for this condition if there is no history of DVT) (34, 35)

- History of rheumatic heart disease with current atrial fibrillation (36)

- Homozygous factor V Leiden mutation, homozygous prothrombin G20210A mutation

- Patients receiving chronic anticoagulation for recurrent thromboembolism

Patients who are identified carriers of other inherited thrombophilias who do not have a history of thrombosis but have a strong family history of thrombosis (36) and noncarriers with a history of thromboembolic events before the current pregnancy (34) appear to be at lower risk and may be candidates for low-dose prophylaxis. However, no data exist to support or refute this approach.

It is not clear whether patients with a history of thrombosis identified with a protein C or protein S deficiency should receive low-dose or adjusted-dose heparin prophylaxis during pregnancy. It is also not known whether asymptomatic women who have been identified as carriers of inherited thrombophilia (except AT-III or homozygosity to the factor V Leiden or prothrombin G20210A mutation) and who are without a personal or family history of thromboembolism should receive heparin prophylaxis because there is marked variation in the penetrance of the thrombotic trait.

Patients with a history of idiopathic thrombosis, extensive or life-threatening thrombosis, recurrent thrombosis, thrombosis related to a high estrogen state, or who have an underlying thrombophilia or postthrombotic syndrome are likely to be at a higher risk of recurrence in pregnancy than patients with a definite transient provocation (orthopedic trauma or surgery) without any of these risk factors. The former group should consider antepartum thromboprophylaxis beginning in the first trimester and continuing until 6 weeks postpartum. It is unclear whether patients who have sustained VTE from a transient and highly thrombogenic provocation (eg, orthopedic trauma) and who have no other risk factors may benefit from antepartum prophylaxis. Their risk of recurrence is likely higher than the baseline population, and an increasing number of thrombophilic states are being identified in patients who sustain thromboses in the setting of recognized transient provocations (37). Although data are limited, some experts recommend that, at minimum, such patients be given postpartum prophylaxis with warfarin.

▶ *How should a prophylactic heparin regimen be administered during pregnancy?*

Because of the absence of adequate prospective trials, a number of different prophylactic regimens have been offered by varying consensus panels, often based on nonpregnant patient studies (34, 38, 39) (see the box).

One study determined that during pregnancy, a doubling of the dose of heparin was required to achieve the same anticoagulant response of a nonpregnant patient taking 5,000 U of heparin twice daily for low-dose prophylaxis (12). Some patients who are AT-III deficient will not respond to heparin and may require AT-III factor therapy (40).

Pregnant patients who require adjusted-dose heparin for anticoagulation for long-term prophylaxis may theoretically benefit from the higher bioavailability and more consistent therapeutic anticoagulation with LMWH (41, 42).

▶ *Who should be tested for inherited or acquired thrombophilias?*

Women who have a history of thrombosis should be offered testing, especially if such testing would affect management. It is controversial whether to test women who do not have a history of thrombosis but have a fami-

---

Prophylactic Heparin Regimens in Pregnancy

Unfractionated Heparin

Low–dose prophylaxis:

1. 5,000–7,500 U every 12 hours during the first trimester
   7,500–10,000 U every 12 hours during the second trimester
   10,000 U every 12 hours during the third trimester unless the APTT* is elevated. The APTT may be checked near term and the heparin dose reduced if prolonged

OR

2. 5,000–10,000 U every 12 hours throughout pregnancy

Adjusted-dose prophylaxis:

≥10,000 U twice a day to three times a day to achieve APTT of 1.5–2.5

Low-Molecular-Weight Heparin

Low-dose prophylaxis:

Dalteparin, 5,000 U once or twice daily, or enoxaparin, 40 mg once or twice daily

Adjusted-dose prophylaxis:

Dalteparin, 5,000–10,000 U every 12 hours, or enoxaparin, 30–80 mg every 12 hours

*APTT indicates activated partial thromboplastin time.

Data from Colvin BT, Barrowcliffe TW. The British Society for Haematology guidelines on the use and monitoring of heparin 1992: second revision. J Clin Pathol 1993;46:97–103. Ginsberg JS, Hirsh J. Use of antithrombotic agents during pregnancy. Chest 1998;114: 524S–530S. Maternal and Neonatal Haemostasis Working Party of the Haemostasis and Thrombosis Task. Guidelines on the presentation, investigation and management of thrombosis associated with pregnancy. J Clin Pathol 1993;46:489–496

---

ly history of thrombosis. Women who have a first-degree relative with an AT-III deficiency or homozygous factor V Leiden or prothrombin G20210A mutation may benefit from testing. Individuals with a strong family history of thrombophilias may be more likely to have multiple inherited risk factors with an increased risk of thrombosis (4–40%) during pregnancy (32, 43, 44). The coexistence of multiple inherited risk factors has been demonstrated. In one study, 15% of patients with protein C deficiency and 39% with protein S deficiency also were positive for factor V Leiden mutations, which markedly increased the risk of thrombosis for the patient (45).

Patients with a history of thrombosis, recurrent fetal loss, early or severe preeclampsia, or severe unexplained intrauterine growth restriction may be tested for antiphospholipid antibodies. Prophylactic anticoagulation for patients with antiphospholipid syndrome has been shown to improve pregnancy outcome (35, 46).

Deficiencies in protein C, protein S, and AT-III and mutations, including factor V Leiden, prothrombin G20210A, and C677T in the methylenetetrahydrofolate reductase (MTHFR) gene associated with hyperhomocystinemia, also have been associated with severe early preeclampsia, unexplained fetal loss or stillbirth, and placental abruption (47–49). However, there are no randomized clinical trials supporting the efficacy of anticoagulation therapy in preventing these conditions. It is important to discuss with the patient the implications of a positive test result for one of these thrombophilias and to determine whether patient management would be altered during the pregnancy or in the future if the test results are positive.

▶ Which tests should be ordered?

The following tests may be ordered to evaluate the risk for thromboembolic events in women with a history of thrombosis, a family history of thrombosis, or a first-degree relative with a specific mutation:

- Lupus anticoagulant (for women with a personal history of VTE)
- Anticardiolipin antibodies (for women with a personal history of VTE)
- Factor V Leiden mutation
- Prothrombin G20210A mutation
- AT-III antigen activity levels
- Fasting homocysteine levels or the MTHFR mutation
- Protein C antigen activity levels
- Protein S antigen activity levels (free and total)

Given the low prevalence of AT-III and the variable pathogenicity of protein C and protein S, consideration should be given to testing only when all other studies have yielded negative results. It is important to note that physiologic changes in normal pregnancy result in marked alterations in protein S and activated protein C resistance, which is associated with the factor V Leiden mutation; therefore, deferral of testing until after pregnancy may be warranted. For example, protein S levels decline by 40% in pregnancy (50, 51). Also, testing for AT-III, protein C, and protein S in the setting of extensive clotting, warfarin use, or heparin administration may result in falsely low values (33, 52, 53). DNA testing for the factor V Leiden,

prothrombin G20210A mutation, and the MTHFR mutation are reliable in pregnancy.

▶ How is deep vein thrombosis detected in pregnancy?

A high index of suspicion is required for the diagnosis of DVT in pregnancy because some of the symptoms of DVT are similar to the common symptoms of pregnancy. Noninvasive testing for DVT includes compression ultrasound (CUS), which uses firm compression with the ultrasound transducer probe to detect an intraluminal filling defect and impedance plethysmography (IPG), which measures impedance flow with pneumatic cuff inflation around the thigh. In the symptomatic nonpregnant patient, IPG has a sensitivity of 83% and specificity of 92% of detecting proximal DVT. Compression ultrasound has a sensitivity of 95% for proximal DVT (73% for distal DVT) and specificity of 96% for detecting all DVT (54), with a negative predictive value of 98% and a positive predictive value of 97% in the nonpregnant symptomatic patient. It has been shown that if serial (3 or more follow-up tests over 7–14 days) IPGs have normal results in a symptomatic pregnant patient with a suspected DVT, it appears safe to withhold anticoagulation (55).

If the clinical suspicion is high and noninvasive test results are negative, limited venography with abdominal shielding that results in fetal exposure less than 0.05 rads should be considered (56). If iliac or pelvic thrombosis is suspected, full venography can be performed (bilateral venography without shielding results in fetal exposure <1.0 rads) (56). Diagnosis of pelvic vein thrombosis and internal iliac thrombosis is difficult. Although the use of venography is widespread, MRI may become the imaging modality of choice in these circumstances, but its role still is not well defined in the pregnant patient (57).

▶ How is the diagnosis of pulmonary embolism made if suspected clinically?

The diagnosis of PE has traditionally been evaluated initially with ventilation–perfusion scanning (V/Q). A V/Q scan results in minimal radiation exposure to the fetus (<0.1 rads). However, any outcome other than high probability or normal requires further testing because of insufficient accuracy to rule out PE in patients for which there is a high clinical suspicion (58). Unfortunately, about 40–60% of V/Q scans are nondiagnostic in the nonpregnant population (neither high probability nor normal), and further evaluation becomes necessary. If noninvasive testing (IPG, CUS) reveals a proximal DVT, then anticoagulation therapy can be initiated. If the results of these tests are negative, but clinical suspicion is high, then pulmonary angiography should be considered (54).

Spiral computed tomography (CT) may be useful for diagnosing PE; however, there is still difficulty reliably identifying emboli below the segmental level (59). Both sensitivity and specificity of spiral CT in nonpregnant patients for central pulmonary artery embolus are approximately 94%. It also may detect abnormalities other than PE responsible for symptoms (pleural effusions, consolidation, emphysema, pulmonary masses) and may be more specific in patients with underlying cardiopulmonary disease (60–62). Magnetic resonance angiography also may be promising, but current technology limits adequate visualization of subsegmental defects (63, 64). Both techniques are unstudied in pregnancy.

▶ How should heparin be administered to women with acute thrombosis or embolism during pregnancy?

Acute thromboembolism associated with pregnancy requires an intravenous heparin bolus of 5,000 U (80 IU/kg) followed by continuous infusion of at least 30,000 IU for 24 hours titrated to achieve full anticoagulation (3, 65). Intravenous anticoagulation should be maintained for at least 5–7 days. The patient can then be changed to subcutaneous adjusted-dose heparin therapy. Subcutaneous injections should be given to pregnant patients every 8 hours to prolong the APTT at least 1.5–2.5 times control throughout the dosing interval, similar to patients who are not pregnant (58, 66). The APTT cannot gauge the adequacy of anticoagulation with therapeutic heparin in patients with antiphospholipid syndrome for which small amounts of heparin may markedly increase the APTT. Levels of antifactor Xa may be used instead.

Therapeutic heparinization with subcutaneous dosing every 8–12 hours should be continued for at least 3 months after the acute event. After 3 months of therapeutic heparinization, experts differ as to what should be done for the remainder of the pregnancy. Some recommend using a lower dose of subcutaneous heparin. Others recommend continuing therapeutic anticoagulation for the remainder of the pregnancy (34).

Low-molecular-weight heparin may be an alternative treatment for acute thromboembolism. Although the actual dosing is unclear in pregnancy, dosage should be adjusted based on maternal weight. Although laboratory testing appears not to be essential in the nonpregnant patient, the role of monitoring antifactor Xa levels is not clear in the pregnant patient. The effectiveness of LMWH is less affected by changes in maternal physiology than is heparin, but there are still changes as pregnancy progresses. Therefore, it may be warranted to periodically reevalu-

ate antifactor Xa levels during pregnancy in a woman on adjusted-dose or full anticoagulation. Ideally, dosing should be enough to achieve a peak antifactor Xa level of 0.5–1.2 U/mL (22, 34). Some experts also check trough levels to ensure that they remain in the lower limits of the anticoagulation range. Pending further informative data, the clinician may either use peak or trough levels, or both, to assess anticoagulation.

▶ How is anticoagulation managed in the intrapartum and postpartum period?

Intrapartum care is complicated, and treatment approaches vary. In such situations, it may be helpful to consult with personnel who have expertise in the intrapartum management of such patients. Patients requiring therapeutic adjusted-dose heparin during pregnancy, including those with recent thromboembolism, and patients with mechanical heart valves may be switched to intravenous heparin at the time of labor and delivery to take advantage of its short half-life (1½ hours). Patients can then be switched to warfarin postpartum. Heparin and warfarin therapy should be overlapped for the first 5–7 days postpartum until an international normalized ratio (INR) of approximately 2.0–3.0 has been achieved (67).

Patients receiving prophylactic anticoagulation with heparin should be instructed to withhold their injections at the onset of labor. Patients requiring adjusted-dose, prophylactic anticoagulation for high-risk conditions can resume their heparin injections 4–8 hours after an uncomplicated delivery, and warfarin can be administered the following morning. Postpartum dosing for women on low-dose prophylactic heparin varies widely, although all concur that the postpartum period is one of high risk. There are no definitive studies to guide one's approach in such situations.

▶ Can regional anesthesia be administered to patients receiving anticoagulants?

The use of major conduction anesthesia (spinal or epidural) in patients receiving thromboembolic prophylaxis is controversial (68, 69). Intraoperative or postoperative anticoagulation after regional anesthesia is thought to be safe; however, the safety of LMWH, unfractionated heparin, or oral anticoagulants administered before the procedure is unclear. Because there are no studies addressing anticoagulation in pregnancy relative to the use of conduction anesthesia, data from nonpregnant patients must be used.

Unfractionated low-dose heparin (≤5,000 IU twice daily) appeared not to pose a significant risk for spinal hematoma in over 5,000 nonpregnant patients who received it in combination with spinal or epidural anesthesia (70).

Although extensive clinical testing in Europe during the past decade suggested that there was no increased risk in patients receiving perioperative LMWH thromboprophylaxis, the U.S. Food and Drug Administration reported cases of epidural or spinal hematomas in nonpregnant patients with concurrent use of enoxaparin (a low-molecular-weight heparin) and spinal or epidural anesthesia or spinal puncture (71). Many of the epidural or spinal hematomas caused neurologic injury, including long-term or permanent paralysis. The discrepancy in the incidence of epidural or spinal hematomas in the European versus the United States literature may be related to higher dosing and preference in the United States of continuous epidurals rather than single shot spinals (70, 72). In one British study of pregnant women, there were no spinal hematomas in the 43 women receiving LMWH thromboprophylaxis who also received epidural analgesia (22). However, the doses given were lower than are currently employed and usually administered once a day.

The American Society of Regional Anesthesia has recommended that patients receiving higher doses of LMWH (specifically enoxaparin, 1 mg/kg twice daily) should not receive neuraxial blocks for 24 hours from the last dose (73). Also, obtaining an antifactor Xa level before placing the block was not recommended because it was believed not to be adequately predictive of the risk of bleeding. Needle placement in patients receiving low-dose, once daily LMWH should occur at least 10–12 hours after the LMWH dose. No specific recommendations were made for patients using an intermediate dose of 30–40 mg of enoxaparin twice daily. However, given that twice daily dosing may maintain antifactor Xa levels between 0.1 and 0.2 IU/mL 12 hours after injection, it would seem prudent to delay epidural anesthesia for 24 hours after the last injection. Alternatively, patients could be switched to standard heparin at term because a normal APTT usually is sufficient to ensure the safety of epidural anesthesia in a heparin anticoagulated patient as long as the platelet count also is normal.

Summary

The following recommendations are based primarily on consensus and expert opinion (Level C):

▶ Pregnant patients with a history of isolated venous thrombosis directly related to a transient, highly thrombogenic event (orthopedic trauma, complicated surgery) in whom an underlying thrombophilia has been excluded may be offered heparin prophylaxis or no prophylaxis during the antepartum period. However, they should be counseled that their risk of thromboembolism is likely to be higher than the normal population. Prophylactic warfarin should be offered for 6 weeks postpartum.

▶ Pregnant patients with a history of idiopathic thrombosis, thrombosis related to pregnancy or oral contraceptive use, or a history of thrombosis accompanied by an underlying thrombophilia other than homozygous for the factor V Leiden mutation, heterozygous for both the factor V Leiden and the prothrombin G20210A mutation, or AT-III deficiency should be offered antepartum and postpartum low-dose heparin prophylaxis.

▶ Patients without a history of thrombosis but who have an underlying thrombophilia and have a strong family history of thrombosis also are candidates for antepartum and postpartum prophylaxis. At the minimum, postpartum prophylaxis should be offered.

▶ Pregnant patients with a history of life-threatening thrombosis, with recent thrombosis, with recurrent thrombosis, receiving chronic anticoagulation, or patients with thrombosis found to be AT-III deficient, homozygous for the factor V Leiden mutation or prothrombin G20210A mutation, heterozygous for both the factor V Leiden and the prothrombin G20210A mutation should be given adjusted-dose heparin every 8 hours to maintain the APTT at least 1.5 times control throughout the dosing interval. Low-molecular-weight heparin administered twice daily also is an alternative.

▶ Patients at risk for thrombosis should receive warfarin postpartum for 6 weeks to achieve an INR of approximately 2.0–3.0. Heparin should be given immediately postpartum with warfarin for at least 5 days until the INR is therapeutic.

▶ Patients with antiphospholipid syndrome and a history of thrombosis require adjusted-dose prophylactic anticoagulation.

▶ Patients who are candidates for either prophylactic or therapeutic heparin may be given enoxaparin or dalteparin during pregnancy. However, because of the lack of data regarding adequate dosing during pregnancy, antifactor Xa levels may be monitored.

▶ The safety of epidural anesthesia with twice-daily dosing of LMWH is of concern and should be withheld until 24 hours after the last injection.

▶ Epidural anesthesia appears to be safe in women taking unfractionated low-dose heparin if the APTT is normal.

References

1. Gherman RB, Goodwin TM, Leung B, Byrne JD, Hethumumi R, Montoro M. Incidence, clinical characteristics, and timing of objectively diagnosed venous thromboembolism during pregnancy. Obstet Gynecol 1999;94:730–734 (Level II-3)

2. Lindqvist P, Dahlback B, Marsal K. Thrombotic risk during pregnancy: a population study. Obstet Gynecol 1999;94:595–599 (Level II-2)

3. Toglia MR, Weg JG. Venous thromboembolism during pregnancy. N Engl J Med 1996;335:108–114 (Level III)

4. Berg CJ, Atrash HK, Koonin LM, Tucker M. Pregnancy-related mortality in the United States, 1987–1990. Obstet Gynecol 1996;88:161–167 (Level II-3)

5. Grandone E, Margaglione M, Colaizzo D, D'Andrea G, Cappucci G, Brancaccio V, et al. Genetic susceptibility to pregnancy-related venous thromboembolism: roles of factor V Leiden, prothrombin G20210A, and methylenetetrahydrofolate reductase C677T mutations. Am J Obstet Gynecol 1998;179:1324–1328 (Level II-2)

6. Dizon-Townson DS, Nelson LM, Jang H, Varner MW, Ward K. The incidence of the factor V Leiden mutation in an obstetric population and its relationship to deep vein thrombosis. Am J Obstet Gynecol 1997;176:883–886 (Level III)

7. De Stefano V, Leone G, Mastrangelo S, Tripodi A, Rodeghiero F, Castaman G, et al. Clinical manifestations and management of inherited thrombophilia: retrospective analysis and follow-up after diagnosis of 238 patients with congenital deficiency of antithrombin III, protein C, protein S. Thromb Haemost 1994;72:352–358 (Level III)

8. Middledorp S, Henkens CM, Koopman MM, van Pampus EC, Hamulyák K, van der Meer J, et al. The incidence of venous thromboembolism in family members of patients with factor V Leiden mutation and venous thrombosis. Ann Intern Med 1998;128:15–20 (Level II-2)

9. Badaracco MA, Vessey MP. Recurrence of venous thromboembolic disease and use of oral contraceptives. Br Med J 1974;1:215–217 (Level II-2)

10. Tengborn L, Bergqvist D, Mätzsch T, Bergqvist A, Hedner U. Recurrent thromboembolism in pregnancy and puerperium. Is there a need for thromboprophylaxis? Am J Obstet Gynecol 1989:160(1);90–94 (Level II-2)

11. Ginsberg JS, Kowalchuk G, Hirsh J, Brill-Edwards P, Burrows R. Heparin therapy during pregnancy. Risks to the fetus and mother. Arch Intern Med 1989;149:2233–2236 (Level II-3)

12. Barbour LA, Smith JM, Marlar RA. Heparin levels to guide thromboembolism prophylaxis during pregnancy. Am J Obstet Gynecol 1995;173:1869–1873 (Level III)

13. Barbour LA, Kick SD, Steiner JF, LoVerde ME, Heddleston LN, Lear JL, et al. A prospective study of heparin-induced osteoporosis in pregnancy using bone densitometry. Am J Obstet Gynecol 1994;170:862–869 (Level II-2)

14. Dahlman TC, Sjöberg HE, Ringertz H. Bone mineral density during long-term prophylaxis with heparin in pregnancy. Am J Obstet Gynecol 1994;170:1315–1320 (Level II-2)

15. Dahlman TC. Osteoporotic fractures and the recurrence of thromboembolism during pregnancy and the puerperium in 184 women undergoing thromboprophylaxis with heparin. Am J Obstet Gynecol 1993;168:1265–1270 (Level III)

16. Warkentin TE, Levine MN, Hirsh J, Horsewood P, Roberts RS, Gent M, et al. Heparin-induced thrombocytopenia in patients treated with low-molecular-weight heparin or unfractionated heparin. N Engl J Med 1995;332:1330–1335 (Level II-2)

17. Kelton JG. The clinical management of heparin-induced thrombocytopenia. Semin Hematol 1999;36(suppl 1):17–21 (Level III)

18. Hirsh J, Warkentin TE, Raschke R, Granger C, Ohman EM, Dalen JE. Heparin and low-molecular-weight heparin: mechanisms of action, pharmacokinetics, dosing considerations, monitoring, efficacy, and safety. Chest 1998;114:489S–510S (Level III)

19. Bergqvist D. Low molecular weight heparins. J Intern Med 1996:240;63–72 (Level III)

20. Forestier F, Solé Y, Aiach M, Alhenc Gelás M, Daffos F. Absence of transplacental fragmin (Kabi) during second and third trimesters of pregnancy. Thromb Haemost 1992;67:180–181 (Level III)

21. Omri A, Delaloye JF, Andersen H, Bachmann F. Low molecular weight heparin Novo (LHN-1) does not cross the placenta during the second trimester of pregnancy. Thromb Haemost 1989;61:55–56 (Level II-2)

22. Nelson-Piercy C, Letsky EA, de Swiet M. Low-molecular-weight heparin for obstetric thromboprophylaxis: experience of sixty-nine pregnancies in sixty-one women at risk. Am J Obstet Gynecol 1997;176:1062–1068 (Level III)

23. Dulitzki M, Pauzner R, Langevitz P, Pras M, Many A, Schiff E. Low-molecular-weight heparin during pregnancy and delivery: preliminary experience with 41 pregnancies. Obstet Gynecol 1996;87:380–383 (Level III)

24. Rasmussen C, Wadt B, Jacobsen B. Thromboembolic prophylaxis with low molecular weight heparin during pregnancy. Int J Gynaecol Obstet 1994;47:121–125 (Level III)

25. Orme ML, Lewis PJ, de Swiet M, Serlin MJ, Sibeon R, Baty JD, et al. May mothers given warfarin breast-feed their infants? BMJ 1977;1(6076):1564–1565 (Level III)

26. Chan WS, Anand S, Ginsberg JS. Anticoagulation of pregnant women with mechanical heart valves. Arch Intern Med 2000;160:191–196 (Level III)

27. Iturbe-Alessio I, Fonseca M, Mutchinik O, Santos MA, Zajarías A, Salazar E. Risks of anticoagulant therapy in pregnant women with artificial heart valves. N Engl J Med 1986;315:1390–1393 (Level II-2)

28. Born D, Martinez EE, Almeida PAM, Santos DV, Carvalho AC, Moron AF, et al. Pregnancy in patients with prosthetic heart valves: the effects of anticoagulation on mother, fetus, and neonate. Am Heart J 1992;124:413–417 (Level II-2)

29. Salazar E, Izaguirre R, Verdejo J, Mutchinick O. Failure of adjusted doses of subcutaneous heparin to prevent thromboembolic phenomena in pregnant patients with mechanical cardiac valve prostheses. J Am Coll Cardiol 1996;27: 1698–1703 (Level III)

30. Hall JG, Pauli RM, Wilson KM. Maternal and fetal sequelae of anticoagulation during pregnancy. Am J Med 1980;68:122–140 (Level III)

31. McColl MD, Ramsay JE, Tait RC, Walker ID, McCall F, Conkie JA, et al. Risk factors for pregnancy associated venous thromboembolism. Thromb Haemost 1997;78: 1183–1188 (Level III)

32. Conard J, Horellou MH, Van Dredan P, Lecompte T, Samama M. Thrombosis and pregnancy in congenital deficiencies in AT III, protein C or protein S: study of 78 women. Thromb Haemost 1990;63:319–320 (Level III)

33. Van Boven HH, Lane DA. Antithrombin and its inherited deficiency states. Semin Hematol 1997;34:188–204 (Level III)

34. Ginsberg JS, Hirsh J. Use of antithrombotic agents during pregnancy. Chest 1998;114:524S–530S (Level III)

35. Branch DW, Silver RM, Blackwell JL, Reading JC, Scott JR. Outcome of treated pregnancies in women with antiphospholipid syndrome: an update of the Utah experience. Obstet Gynecol 1992;80:614–620 (Level II-2)

36. Barbour LA, Pickard J. Controversies in thromboembolic disease during pregnancy: a critical review. Obstet Gynecol 1995;86:621–633 (Level III)

37. Gerhardt A, Scharf RE, Beckmann MW, Struve S, Bender HG, Pillny M, et al. Prothrombin and factor V mutations in women with a history of thrombosis during pregnancy and the puerperium. N Engl J Med 2000;342:374–380 (Level II-2)

38. Colvin BT, Barrowcliffe TW. The British Society for Haematology Guidelines on the use and monitoring of heparin 1992: second revision. BCSH Haemostasis and Thrombosis Task Force. J Clin Pathol 1993;46:97–103 (Level III)

39. Maternal and Neonatal Haemostasis Working Party of the Haemostasis and Thrombosis Task. Guidelines on the prevention, investigation and management of thrombosis associated with pregnancy. J Clin Pathol 1993;46:489–496 (Level III)

40. Lechner K, Kyrle PA. Antithrombin III concentrates—are they clinically useful? Thromb Haemost 1995;73:340–348 (Level III)

41. Barbour LA. Current concepts of anticoagulant therapy in pregnancy. Obstet Gynecol Clin North Am 1997;24: 499–521 (Level III)

42. Weitz JI. Drug therapy: low molecular weight heparin. N Engl J Med 1997;337:688–698 (Level III)

43. Miletich JP. Thrombophilia as a multigenic disorder. Semin Thromb Hemost 1998;24(suppl 1):13–20 (Level III)

44. Friederich PW, Sanson BJ, Simioni P, Zanardi S, Huisman MV, Kindt I, et al. Frequency of pregnancy-related venous thromboembolism in anticoagulant factor-deficient women: implications for prophylaxis. Ann Intern Med 1996;125:955–960 (Level III)

45. Florell SR, Rodgers GM. Inherited thrombotic disorders: an update. Am J Hematol 1997;54:53–60 (Level III)

46. Rai R, Cohen H, Dave M, Regan L. Randomised controlled trial of aspirin and aspirin plus heparin in pregnant women with recurrent miscarriage associated with phospholipid antibodies (or antiphospholipid antibodies). BMJ 1997;314:253–257 (Level I)

47. Brenner B, Mandel H, Lanir N, Younis J, Rothbart H, Ohel G, et al. Activated protein C resistance can be associated with recurrent fetal loss. Br J Haematol 1997;97:551–554 (Level II-2)

48. Dizon-Townson D, Meline L, Nelson LM, Varner M, Ward K. Fetal carriers of the factor V Leiden mutation are prone to miscarriage or placental infarction. Am J Obstet Gynecol 1997;177:402–405 (Level II-2)

49. Kupferminc MJ, Eldor A, Steinman N, Many A, Bar-Am A, Jaffa A, et al. Increased frequency of genetic thrombophilia in women with complications of pregnancy. N Engl J Med 1999;340:9–13 (Level II-2)

50. Faught W, Garner P, Jones C, Ivey B. Changes in protein C and protein S levels in normal pregnancy. Am J Obstet Gynecol 1995;172:147–150 (Level II-3)

51. Lefkowitz JB, Clarke SH, Barbour LA. Comparison of protein S functional and antigenic assays in normal pregnancy. Am J Obstet Gynecol 1996;175:657–650 (Level II-3)

52. Rao AK, Kaplan R, Sheth S. Inherited thrombophilic states. Semin Thromb Hemost 1998;24(suppl 1):3–12 (Level III)

53. Reiter W, Ehrensberger H, Steinbrückner B, Keller F. Parameters of haemostasis during acute venous thrombosis. Thromb Haemost 1995;74:596–601 (Level III)

54. Douketis JD, Ginsberg JS. Diagnostic problems with venous thromboembolic disease in pregnancy. Haemostasis 1995;25:58–71 (Level III)

55. Hull RD, Raskob GE, Carter CJ. Serial impedance plethysmography in pregnant patients with clinically suspected deep-vein thrombosis. Clinical validity of negative findings. Ann Intern Med 1990;112:663–667 (Level II-3)

56. Ginsberg JS, Hirsh J, Rainbow AJ, Coates G. Risks to the fetus of radiologic procedures used in the diagnosis of maternal venous thromboembolic disease. Thromb Haemost 1989;61:189–196 (Level III)

57. Spritzer CE, Evans AC, Kay HH. Magnetic resonance imaging of deep venous thrombosis in pregnant women with lower extremity edema. Obstet Gynecol 1995;85: 603–607 (Level III)

58. Ginsberg JS. Management of venous thromboembolism. N Engl J Med 1996;335(24):1816–1828 (Level III)

59. Hansell DM. Spiral computed tomography and pulmonary embolism: current state. Clin Radiol 1997;52:575–581 (Level III)

60. Cross JJ, Kemp PM, Walsh CG, Flower CD, Dixon AK. A randomized trial of spiral CT and ventilation perfusion

scintigraphy for the diagnosis of pulmonary embolism. Clin Radiol 1998;53:177–182 (Level I)

61. Lipchik RJ, Goodman LR. Spiral computed tomography in the evaluation of pulmonary embolism. Clin Chest Med 1999;20:731–738 (Level III)

62. Kim KI, Muller NL, Mayo JR. Clinically suspected pulmonary embolism: utility of spiral CT. Radiology 1999;210:693–697 (Level III)

63. Meaney JF, Weg JG, Chenevert TL, Stafford-Johnson D, Hamilton BH, Prince MR. Diagnosis of pulmonary embolism with magnetic resonance angiography. N Engl J Med 1997;336:1422–1427 (Level II-2)

64. Woodard PK, Yusen RD. Diagnosis of pulmonary embolism with spiral computed tomography and magnetic resonance angiography. Curr Opin Cardiol 1999;14: 442–447 (Level III)

65. Bates SM, Ginsberg JS. Thrombosis in pregnancy. Curr Opin Hematol 1997;4:335–343 (Level III)

66. Ramin SM, Ramin KD, Gilstrap LC. Anticoagulants and thrombolytics during pregnancy. Semin Perinatol 1997;21: 149–153 (Level III)

67. Hyers TM, Agnelli G, Hull RD, Weg JG, Morris TA, Samama M, et al. Antithrombotic therapy for venous thromboembolic disease. Chest 1998;114:561S–578S (Level III)

68. Haljamäe H. Thromboprophylaxis, coagulation disorders, and regional anesthesia. Acta Anaesthesiol Scand 1996;40:1024–1040 (Level III)

69. Hynson JM, Katz JA, Bueff HU. Epidural hematoma associated with enoxaparin. Anesth Analg 1996;82:1072–1075 (Level III)

70. Horlocker TT, Wedel DJ. Neuraxial block and low-molecular-weight heparin: balancing perioperative analgesia and thromboprophylaxis. Reg Anesth Pain Med 1998;23(6 Suppl 2);164–177 (Level III)

71. U.S. Department of Health and Human Services. FDA Public Health Advisory, Subject: reports of epidural or spinal hematomas with the concurrent use of low molecular weight heparin and spinal/epidural anesthesia or spinal puuncture. Rockville, Maryland: Food and Drug Administration, December 1997 (Level III)

72. Tryba M. European practice guidelines: thromboembolism prophylaxis and regional anesthesia. Reg Anesth Pain Med 1998;23(6 Suppl 2):178–182 (Level III)

73. American Society of Regional Anesthesia (ASRA). Recommendations for neuraxial anesthesia and anticoagulation. Richmond, VA: ASRA, 1998 (Level III

The MEDLINE database, the Cochrane Library, and ACOG's own internal resources and documents were used to conduct a literature search to locate relevant articles published between January 1985 and March 1998. The search was restricted to articles published in the English language. Priority was given to articles reporting results of original research, although review articles and commentaries also were consulted. Abstracts of research presented at symposia and scientific conferences were not considered adequate for inclusion in this document. Guidelines published by organizations or institutions such as the National Institutes of Health and the American College of Obstetricians and Gynecologists were reviewed, and additional studies were located by reviewing bibliographies of identified articles. When reliable research was not available, expert opinions from obstetrician–gynecologists were used.

Studies were reviewed and evaluated for quality according to the method outlined by the U.S. Preventive Services Task Force:

I   Evidence obtained from at least one properly designed randomized controlled trial.

II-1   Evidence obtained from well-designed controlled trials without randomization.

II-2   Evidence obtained from well-designed cohort or case–control analytic studies, preferably from more than one center or research group.

II-3   Evidence obtained from multiple time series with or without the intervention. Dramatic results in uncontrolled experiments could also be regarded as this type of evidence.

III   Opinions of respected authorities, based on clinical experience, descriptive studies, or reports of expert committees.

Based on the highest level of evidence found in the data, recommendations are provided and graded according to the following categories:

Level A—Recommendations are based on good and consistent scientific evidence.

Level B—Recommendations are based on limited or inconsistent scientific evidence.

Level C—Recommendations are based primarily on consensus and expert opinion.

ISSN 1099-3630

The American College of
Obstetricians and Gynecologists
409 12th Street, SW
PO Box 96920
Washington, DC 20090-6920   12345/43210

ACOG PRACTICE BULLETIN

CLINICAL MANAGEMENT GUIDELINES FOR
OBSTETRICIAN–GYNECOLOGISTS

NUMBER 32, NOVEMBER 2001

*(Replaces Technical Bulletin Number 181, June 1993, and
Committee Opinion Number 241, September 2000)*

This Practice Bulletin was developed by the ACOG Committee on Practice Bulletins—Obstetrics with the assistance of Sarah Kilpatrick, MD, PhD. The information is designed to aid practitioners in making decisions about appropriate obstetric and gynecologic care. These guidelines should not be construed as dictating an exclusive course of treatment or procedure. Variations in practice may be warranted based on the needs of the individual patient, resources, and limitations unique to the institution or type of practice.

Thyroid Disease in Pregnancy

Because thyroid disease is the second most common endocrine disease affecting women of reproductive age, obstetricians often care for patients who have been previously diagnosed with alterations in thyroid gland function. In addition, both hyperthyroidism and hypothyroidism may initially manifest during pregnancy. Obstetric conditions, such as gestational trophoblastic disease or hyperemesis gravidarum, may themselves affect thyroid gland function. This document will review the thyroid-related pathophysiologic changes created by pregnancy and the maternal–fetal impact of thyroid disease.

Background

Definitions

Thyrotoxicosis is the clinical and biochemical state that results from an excess production of and exposure to thyroid hormone from any etiology. In contrast, hyperthyroidism is thyrotoxicosis caused by hyperfunctioning of the thyroid gland (1). Graves' disease is an autoimmune disease characterized by production of thyroid-stimulating immunoglobulin (TSI) and thyroid-stimulating hormone-binding inhibitory immunoglobulin (TBII) that act on the thyroid-stimulating hormone (TSH) receptor to mediate thyroid stimulation or inhibition, respectively. Thyroid storm is characterized by a severe, acute exacerbation of the signs and symptoms of hyperthyroidism.

Hypothyroidism is caused by inadequate thyroid hormone production. Postpartum thyroiditis is an autoimmune inflammation of the thyroid gland that presents as new-onset, painless hypothyroidism, transient thyrotoxicosis, or thyrotoxicosis followed by hypothyroidism within 1 year postpartum.

Physiologic Changes in Thyroid Function During Pregnancy

Table 1 depicts how thyroid function test (TFT) results change in normal pregnancy and in hyperthyroid and hypothyroid states. The concentration of thyroid binding globulin (TBG) increases in pregnancy because of reduced hepatic clearance and estrogenic stimulation of TBG synthesis (2). The test results that change significantly in pregnancy are those that are influenced by serum TBG concentration. These tests include total thyroxine (TT_4), total triiodothyronine (TT_3), and resin triiodothyronine uptake (RT_3U). Although there may be a transient increase in free thyroxine (FT_4) and free thyroxine index (FTI) in the first trimester (possibly related to human chorionic gonadotropin [hCG] stimulation), this increase does not result in elevations beyond the normal nonpregnant range (3).

Plasma iodide levels decrease during pregnancy because of fetal use of iodide and increased maternal renal clearance of iodide (2). This alteration is associated with a noticeable increase in thyroid gland size in approximately 15% of women (2, 4). In two longitudinal studies of more than 600 women without thyroid disease, thyroid volume, measured by ultrasonography, significantly increased in pregnancy (with a mean increase in size of 18% that was noticeable in most women) and returned to normal in the postpartum period (4, 5). None of these women had abnormal TFT results despite their enlarged thyroid glands.

Thyroid Function and the Fetus

The fetal thyroid begins concentrating iodine at 10–12 weeks of gestation and is controlled by pituitary TSH by approximately 20 weeks of gestation. Fetal serum levels of TSH, TBG, FT_4, and free triiodothyronine (FT_3) increase throughout gestation, reaching mean adult levels at approximately 36 weeks of gestation (6). Thyroid-stimulating hormone does not cross the placenta, and only small amounts of thyroxine (T_4) and triiodothyronine (T_3) cross the placenta. In neonates with congenital hypothyroidism, enough maternal thyroid hormone crosses the placenta to prevent the overt stigmata of hypothyroidism at birth and maintain cord blood thyroid hormone levels at 25–50% of normal (7). However, thyrotropin-releasing hormone (TRH), iodine, and TSH receptor immunoglobulins do cross the placenta, as do the thioamides propylthiouracil (PTU) and methimazole.

Hyperthyroidism

Signs and Symptoms

Hyperthyroidism is seen in 0.2% of pregnancies; Graves' disease accounts for 95% of these cases (8). The signs and symptoms of hyperthyroidism include nervousness, tremors, tachycardia, frequent stools, excessive sweating, heat intolerance, weight loss, goiter, insomnia, palpitations, and hypertension. Distinctive symptoms of Graves' disease are ophthalmopathy (signs including lid lag and lid retraction) and dermopathy (signs include localized or pretibial myxedema). Although some symptoms of hyperthyroidism are similar to symptoms of pregnancy or nonthyroid disease, serum TFTs differentiate thyroid disease from nonthyroid disease.

Inadequately treated maternal thyrotoxicosis is associated with a greater risk of preterm delivery, severe preeclampsia, and heart failure than treated, controlled maternal thyrotoxicosis (9, 10). Although untreated hyperthyroidism has been associated with miscarriage (8, 11), it is difficult to find concrete data to support this claim.

Fetal and Neonatal Effects

Inadequately treated hyperthyroidism also is associated with an increase in medically indicated preterm deliveries, low birth weight (LBW), and possibly fetal loss (9, 10). In one study, all of seven fetal losses occurred in persistently hyperthyroid women (9).

Fetal and neonatal risks associated with Graves' disease are related either to the disease itself or to thioamide treatment of the disease. The possibility of fetal thyro-

Table 1. Changes in Thyroid Function Test Results in Normal Pregnancy and in Thyroid Disease

Maternal Status	TSH	FT_4	FTI	TT_4	TT_3	RT_3U
Pregnancy	No change	No change	No change	Increase	Increase	Decrease
Hyperthyroidism	Decrease	Increase	Increase	Increase	Increase or no change	Decrease
Hypothyroidism	Increase	Decrease	Decrease	Decrease	Decrease or no change	Increase

Abbreviations: TSH, thyroid-stimulating hormone; FT_4, free thyroxine; FTI, free thyroxine index; TT_4, total thyroxine; TT_3, total triiodothyronine; RT_3U, resin T3 uptake.

toxicosis should be considered in all women with a history of Graves' disease (8). If fetal thyrotoxicosis is diagnosed, consultation with a clinician with expertise in such conditions is warranted.

Because a large proportion of thyroid dysfunction in women is mediated by antibodies that cross the placenta (Graves' disease and chronic autoimmune thyroiditis), there is a legitimate concern for risk of immune-mediated hypothyroidism and hyperthyroidism to develop in the neonate. Women with Graves' disease have TSI and TBII that can stimulate or inhibit the fetal thyroid. The latter (TBII) may cause transient hypothyroidism in neonates of women with Graves' disease (12, 13). One to five percent of these neonates have hyperthyroidism or neonatal Graves' disease due to the transplacental passage of maternal TSI (11). The incidence is low because of the balance of stimulatory and inhibitory antibodies with thioamide treatment (14). Maternal antibodies are cleared less rapidly than thioamides in the neonate, resulting in a sometimes delayed presentation of neonatal Graves' disease (14). The incidence of neonatal Graves' disease is unrelated to maternal thyroid function. The neonates of women who have been treated surgically or with radioactive iodine 131 (I-131) prior to pregnancy and require no thioamide treatment are at higher risk for neonatal Graves' disease because they lack suppressive thioamide (14).

Etiology and Differential Diagnosis

The most common cause of hyperthyroidism is Graves' disease. The other clinical characteristics of Graves' disease also are immune-mediated but they are less understood. The diagnosis of Graves' disease is generally made by documenting elevated levels of FT_4 or an elevated FTI, with suppressed TSH in the absence of a nodular goiter or thyroid mass. Although most patients with Graves' disease have TSH receptor, antimicrosomal, or antithyroid peroxidase antibodies, measurement of these is neither required nor recommended for the diagnosis (11). Other etiologies of thyrotoxicosis are excess production of TSH, gestational trophoblastic neoplasia, hyperfunctioning thyroid adenoma, toxic multinodular goiter, subacute thyroiditis, and extrathyroid source of thyroid hormone.

Hypothyroidism

It is well accepted that having one autoimmune disease increases the likelihood of developing another; autoimmune thyroid dysfunction is no exception. For example, there is a 5–8% incidence of hypothyroid disease in patients with type 1 (insulin-dependent) diabetes (15). Women with type 1 diabetes also have a 25% risk of developing postpartum thyroid dysfunction (15).

Signs and Symptoms

The classic signs and symptoms of hypothyroidism are fatigue, constipation, intolerance to cold, muscle cramps, hair loss, dry skin, prolonged relaxation phase of deep tendon reflexes, and carpal tunnel syndrome. These are initially indolent and nonspecific but may progress to weight gain, intellectual slowness, voice changes, and insomnia. If left untreated, hypothyroidism will progress to myxedema and myxedema coma. It is unusual for advanced hypothyroidism to present in pregnancy. Subclinical hypothyroidism is defined as elevated TSH with normal FTI in an asymptomatic patient. Untreated hypothyroidism is associated with an increased risk of preeclampsia, but it is not clear from the available data whether subclinical hypothyroidism carries a similar risk (16, 17).

Fetal and Neonatal Effects

In retrospective studies, a high incidence of LBW in neonates was associated with inadequately treated hypothyroidism (16, 17). The etiology of LBW in these studies was preterm delivery (medically indicated), preeclampsia, or placental abruption. One study reported two stillbirths, both of which were associated with placental abruption and preeclampsia (17). It is not clear whether hypothyroidism is associated with intrauterine growth restriction independent of other complications. Women with iodine-deficient hypothyroidism are at significant risk of having babies with congenital cretinism (growth failure, mental retardation, and other neuropsychologic deficits). In an iodine-deficient population, treatment with iodine in the first and second trimesters of pregnancy significantly reduces the incidence of the neurologic abnormalities of cretinism (18).

Untreated congenital hypothyroidism also results in cretinism. The incidence of congenital hypothyroidism is 1 per 4,000 newborns, and only 5% of neonates are identified by clinical symptoms at birth, likely due to the ameliorative effects of maternal thyroid hormone (2). All 50 states and the District of Columbia offer screening of newborns for congenital hypothyroidism. If identified and treated within the first few weeks of life, near-normal growth and intelligence can be expected (19).

Etiology and Differential Diagnosis

Most cases of hypothyroidism are the result of a primary thyroid abnormality; a small number of cases are caused by hypothalamic dysfunction. The most common etiologies of hypothyroidism in pregnant or postpartum women are Hashimoto's disease (chronic thyroiditis or chronic autoimmune thyroiditis) (1), subacute thyroiditis, thyroidectomy, radioactive iodine treatment, and iodine deficiency. In developed countries, Hashimoto's disease is the most common etiology (20) and is characterized by the production of antithyroid antibodies, including thyroid antimicrosomal and antithyroglobulin antibodies. Both Hashimoto's disease and iodine deficiency are associated with goiter (a sign of compensatory TSH production), while subacute thyroiditis is not associated with goiter.

Worldwide, the most common cause of hypothyroidism is iodine deficiency (8). Although iodine deficiency is rare in the United States, some populations may benefit from consideration of this etiology of hypothyroidism, including certain immigrant populations and those with poor nutrition.

Clinical Considerations and Recommendations

▶ *What laboratory tests are used to diagnose and manage thyroid disease during pregnancy?*

The mainstay of thyroid function evaluation is TSH testing; such testing is now performed using monoclonal antibodies, making it more sensitive than the original radioimmunoassay. The American Association of Clinical Endocrinologists (21) and the American Thyroid Association (22) recommend TSH testing as the initial test for the screening and evaluation of symptomatic disease for all men and women. The free component is the biologically active portion and is not subject to change in conditions that alter TBG, such as pregnancy. In a pregnant patient suspected of being hyperthyroid or hypothyroid, TSH and FT_4 or FTI should be measured. Free thyroxine assessment by either direct immunoradiometric or chemiluminescent methods is generally available and preferred over the equilibrium dialysis method. However, FTI can be calculated as the product of TT_4 and RT_3U if FT_4 is not available. Measurement of FT_3 usually is only pursued in thyrotoxic patients with suppressed TSH but normal FT_4 measurements. Elevated FT_3 indicates T_3 toxicosis, which may occur before excessive FT_4 production develops (11, 23).

Another test of thyroid function is the TRH stimulation test, which evaluates the secretory ability of the pituitary. The various antibody tests include TSH receptor antibodies, which can be either stimulatory (TSI) or inhibitory (TBII), and antimicrosomal antibodies. The usefulness of these various antibodies in pregnancy is complex and will be discussed as follows.

Although the incidence of neonatal Graves' disease is associated with extremely high levels of maternal TSI, the clinical usefulness of evaluating these levels is not clear. In general, perinatal experts suggest there is no practical use for measuring TSI routinely (8), while endocrinologists suggest that measuring TSI in the third trimester is useful (11, 14, 24, 25). Routine evaluation of maternal TSI levels is not recommended, but such evaluation may be helpful in some circumstances.

▶ *What medications can be used to treat hyperthyroidism and hypothyroidism in pregnancy, and how should they be administered and adjusted during pregnancy?*

Hyperthyroidism in pregnancy is treated with thioamides, specifically PTU and methimazole, which decrease thyroid hormone synthesis by blocking the organification of iodide. Propylthiouracil also reduces the peripheral conversion of T4 to T3 and, thus, may have a quicker suppressant effect than methimazole. Traditionally, PTU has been preferred in pregnant patients because it was believed that PTU crossed the placenta less well than methimazole and because methimazole was associated with fetal aplasia cutis, a congenital skin defect of the scalp (26). However, recent data have refuted both of these arguments. One study comparing FT4 and TSH in newborn cord blood samples of women treated with PTU with those of women treated with methimazole found no significant difference in mean FT4 or TSH levels. Furthermore, there was no relationship between maternal dosage of thioamide and cord blood levels of TSH or FT4 (27). A retrospective study that compared 99 women treated with PTU with 36 women treated with methimazole reported no cases of aplasia cutis and similar rates of fetal anomalies (3%) (28). Finally, there was no significant difference in the incidence of aplasia cutis between control women without thyroid disease and women with hyperthyroidism who were treated with methimazole (26).

Thioamide treatment of Graves' disease can suppress fetal and neonatal thyroid function. However, it usually is transient and rarely requires therapy. Fetal goiter also has been associated with thioamide treatment for Graves' disease, presumably due to drug-induced fetal hypothyroidism (29). Fetal thyrotoxicosis secondary to maternal antibodies is rare, but all fetuses of women with Graves' disease should be monitored for appropriate growth and normal heart rate. However, in the absence of these findings, routine screening for fetal goiter by ultrasonography is unnecessary. All neonates of women with thyroid disease are at risk for neonatal thyroid dysfunction, and the neonate's pediatrician should be aware of the maternal diagnosis.

Women taking PTU may breastfeed because only small amounts of the medication cross into breast milk. Studies have demonstrated that TFT results were normal in neonates after 1–8 months of breastfeeding from women taking PTU (30, 31). Methimazole also is considered safe for breastfeeding; however, it is present in a higher ratio in breast milk (30).

The goal of management of hyperthyroidism in pregnancy is to maintain the FT_4 or FTI in the high normal range using the lowest possible dose of thioamides to minimize fetal exposure to thioamides. Thus, once treatment has started, it may be helpful to measure FT_4 or FTI every 2–4 weeks and titrate the thioamide until FT_4 or FTI are consistently in the high normal range (8). In more than 90% of patients, improvement will be seen within 2–4 weeks after thioamide treatment begins (11).

One side effect of thioamides is agranulocytosis. The incidence of agranulocytosis is 0.1–0.4%; it usually presents with a fever and sore throat. If a patient on thioamides develops these symptoms, a complete blood cell count should be drawn and the medication should be discontinued. Treatment with the other thioamide carries a significant risk of cross reaction. Other major side effects of thioamides, including thrombocytopenia, hepatitis, and vasculitis, occur in less than 1% of patients; minor side effects, including rash, nausea, arthritis, anorexia, fever, and loss of taste or smell, occur in 5% of patients (11).

Beta-blockers may be used during pregnancy to ameliorate the symptoms of thyrotoxicosis until thioamides decrease thyroid hormone levels. Propranolol is the most common beta-blocker used for this indication. Thyroidectomy should be reserved for women in whom thioamide treatment is unsuccessful.

Iodine 131 is contraindicated in pregnant women because of the risk of fetal thyroid ablation; therefore, women should avoid pregnancy for 4 months after I-131 treatment (23). Unfortunately, our understanding of fetal thyroid ablation and the consequent risk of fetal hypothyroidism from exposure to maternal I-131 comes from the inadvertent treatment of pregnant women (32, 33). Counseling of women exposed to I-131 in pregnancy should focus on the gestational age at exposure. If the woman was at less than 10 weeks of gestation when exposed to I-131, it is unlikely the fetal thyroid was ablated. If exposure occurred at 10 weeks of gestation or later, the woman must consider the risks of induced congenital hypothyroidism and consider whether to continue the pregnancy. Breastfeeding should be avoided for at least 120 days after treatment with I-131 (34).

Treatment of hypothyroidism in pregnant women is the same as for nonpregnant women and involves administering levothyroxine at sufficient doses to normalize TSH levels. It takes approximately 4 weeks for the thyroxine therapy to alter the TSH level. Therefore, levothyroxine therapy should be adjusted at 4-week intervals until TSH levels are stable. Data indicate pregnancy increases maternal thyroid hormone requirements in women with hypothyroidism diagnosed before pregnancy (2, 35). In these studies, TSH levels increased while FTI decreased during pregnancy in these women, necessitating an increase in mean thyroxine dose from 0.1 mg/day before pregnancy to 0.148 mg/day during pregnancy (35). In stable patients, it is prudent to check TSH levels every trimester in pregnant women with hypothyroidism (21).

▶ *What changes in thyroid function occur with hyperemesis gravidarum, and should TFTs be performed routinely in women with hyperemesis?*

Nausea and vomiting of pregnancy have been attributed to the high hCG levels in the first trimester, and women with hyperemesis gravidarum have been assumed to have particularly high hCG levels and to be at risk for hyperthyroidism. In a prospective study of 67 women with singleton pregnancies and hyperemesis, 66% were found to have biochemical hyperthyroidism with an undetectable level of TSH or elevated FTI or both (36). The biochemical hyperthyroidism resolved in all of the women without treatment by 18 weeks of gestation (36). Further, the women with the most severe hyperemesis had significantly higher FTIs than those with mild or moderate disease.

Complete resolution of biochemical and clinical hyperthyroidism also has been reported in other studies (37, 38). These studies have reported that some women with hyperemesis gravidarum required a short course of thioamides; however, most of these women had resolution of their signs and symptoms without treatment (38, 39). Women who required treatment throughout the remainder of their pregnancies had other symptoms of thyroid disease, including thyroid enlargement, persistent tachycardia despite fluid replacement, and abnormal response to TRH stimulation (39). In a study comparing pregnant women with hyperemesis and those without hyperemesis, there was no difference in mean TSH or FT_3 levels (40). Levels of FT_4 and hCG were significantly higher in the women with hyperemesis, but hCG levels correlated significantly and positively with FT_4 levels and negatively with TSH levels only in the hyperemesis group. Other studies have replicated these results and shown suppression of TSH when compared with controls (37). Hyperemesis gravidarum is associated with biochemical hyperthyroidism but rarely with clinical hyperthyroidism and is largely transitory, requiring no treatment. Routine measurements of thyroid function are not recommended in patients with hyperemesis gravidarum unless other overt signs of hyperthyroidism are evident.

▶ *How is thyroid storm diagnosed and treated in pregnancy?*

Thyroid storm is a medical emergency characterized by an extreme hypermetabolic state. It is rare—occurring in 1% of hyperthyroid pregnant patients—but has a high risk of maternal heart failure (9). Older literature described a maternal mortality of up to 25% but this has not been substantiated by more recent data (9, 41). Thyroid storm is diagnosed by a combination of the following signs and symptoms: fever; tachycardia out of proportion to the fever; changed mental status, including restlessness, nervousness, confusion, and seizures; vomiting; diarrhea; and cardiac arrhythmia (42). Often there is an identified inciting event such as infection, surgery, labor, or delivery. However, the diagnosis can be difficult to make and requires expedient treatment to avoid the severe consequences of untreated thyroid storm, which include shock, stupor, and coma. If thyroid storm is suspected, serum FT_4, FT_3, and TSH levels should be evaluated to help confirm the diagnosis, but therapy should not be withheld pending the results.

Therapy for thyroid storm consists of a standard series of drugs (see box) (8, 42). Each drug has a specific role in the suppression of thyroid function. Propylthiouracil or methimazole blocks additional synthesis of thyroid hormone, and PTU also inhibits peripheral conversion of T_4 to T_3. Saturated solution of potassium iodide and sodium iodide block the release of thyroid hormone from the gland. Dexamethasone decreases thyroid hormone release and peripheral conversion of T_4 to T_3, and propranolol inhibits the adrenergic effects of excessive thyroid hormone. Finally, phenobarbital can be used to reduce extreme agitation or restlessness and may increase the catabolism of thyroid hormone (42). In addition to pharmacologic management, general supportive measures should be undertaken, including administration of oxygen, maintenance of intravascular volume and electrolytes, use of antipyretics, use of a cooling blanket, and appropriate maternal and fetal monitoring; invasive central monitoring and continuous maternal cardiac monitoring in an intensive care setting may be indicated. Coincident with treating the thyroid storm, the perceived underlying cause of the storm should be treated. As with other acute maternal illnesses, fetal well-being should be appropriately evaluated with

Treatment of Thyroid Storm in Pregnant Women

1. Propylthiouracil (PTU), 600–800 mg orally, stat, then 150–200 mg orally every 4–6 hours. If oral administration is not possible, use methimazole rectal suppositories.

2. Starting 1–2 hours after PTU administration, saturated solution of potassium iodide (SSKI), 2–5 drops orally every 8 hours, *or*

   sodium iodide, 0.5–1.0 g intravenously every 8 hours, *or*

   Lugol's' solution, 8 drops every 6 hours, *or*

   lithium carbonate, 300 mg orally every 6 hours.

3. Dexamethasone, 2 mg intravenously or intramuscularly every 6 hours for four doses.

4. Propranolol, 20–80 mg orally every 4–6 hours, *or* propranolol, 1–2 mg intravenously every 5 minutes for a total of 6 mg, then 1–10 mg intravenously every 4 hours.

   If the patient has a history of severe broncho-spasm:

   Reserpine, 1–5 mg intramuscularly every 4–6 hours

   Guanethidine, 1mg/kg orally every 12 hours

   Diltiazem, 60 mg orally every 6–8 hours

5. Phenobarbital, 30–60 mg orally every 6–8 hours as needed for extreme restlessness.

Data from Ecker JL, Musci TJ. Thyroid function and disease in pregnancy. Curr Probl Obstet Gynecol Fertil 2000;23:109–122; and Molitch ME. Endocrine emergencies in pregnancy. Bailliere's Clin Endocrinol Metab 1992;6:167–191

ultrasonography, biophysical profile, or nonstress test depending on the gestational age of the fetus. In general, it is prudent to avoid delivery in the presence of thyroid storm unless fetal indications for delivery outweigh the risks to the woman.

▶ *How should a thyroid nodule or thyroid cancer during pregnancy be assessed?*

The incidence of thyroid cancer in pregnancy is 1 per 1,000 (43). Any thyroid nodule discovered during pregnancy should be diagnostically evaluated, because malignancy will be found in up to 40% of these nodules (34, 44). Pregnancy itself does not appear to alter the course of thyroid cancer (43, 45). Whether pregnancy increases the risk of recurrence of thyroid cancer or the risk that a thyroid nodule becomes cancerous is less clear (34). In a cohort study comparing thyroid cancer in pregnant or postpartum women with nonpregnant women, there were no differences in the presenting physical findings, tumor type, tumor size, presence of metastases, time between diagnosis and treatment, recurrence rates, or death rates (43). Women in this study were monitored for a median of 20 years. These data strongly suggest that pregnancy does not affect the outcome of thyroid cancer. In addition, except for the time between diagnosis and surgery, there was no difference in outcome between those women who had thyroidectomy during pregnancy and those who had the procedure after pregnancy. Significantly more pregnant women presented with no symptoms, emphasizing the importance of the physical examination during pregnancy.

Another study compared pregnancy outcomes among women with thyroid cancer who fell into one of three categories: 1) before treatment, 2) after thyroidectomy but before I-131 treatment, and 3) after treatment with both thyroidectomy and I-131 (46). The study found no differences in stillbirths, LBW, or malformations among the three groups. The incidence of spontaneous abortion was significantly higher in women who had any treatment for thyroid cancer but was not different between those women who had surgery only and those who had surgery and I-131 treatment.

If a diagnosis of cancer is made, a multidisciplinary treatment plan should be determined. The options are pregnancy termination, treatment during pregnancy, and preterm or term delivery with treatment after pregnancy. This decision will be affected by the gestational age at diagnosis and the tumor characteristics. Definitive treatment for thyroid cancer is thyroidectomy and radiation. Thyroidectomy can be performed during pregnancy, preferably in the second trimester, but radiation should be deferred until after pregnancy. Breastfeeding should be avoided for at least 120 days after I-131 treatment (34).

▶ *How is postpartum thyroiditis diagnosed and treated?*

Postpartum thyroiditis occurs in 5% of women who do not have a history of thyroid disease (47). Studies have found that approximately 44% of women with postpartum thyroiditis have hypothyroidism, while the remaining women are evenly split between thyrotoxicosis and thyrotoxicosis followed by hypothyroidism (47, 48). In one study, goiter was present in 51% of women with postpartum thyroiditis (48). Postpartum thyroiditis also may occur after pregnancy loss and has a 70% risk of recurrence (49, 50).

The diagnosis of postpartum thyroiditis is made by documenting new-onset abnormal levels of TSH or FT_4 or both. If the diagnosis is in doubt, measuring antimicrosomal or thyroperoxidase antithyroid peroxidase antibodies may be useful to confirm the diagnosis.

The need for treatment in women with postpartum thyroiditis is less clear. In a prospective study of 605 asymptomatic pregnant and postpartum women, only five women, or 11% of the women diagnosed with postpartum thyroiditis, developed permanent hypothyroidism (48). Furthermore, none of the women with thyrotoxicosis required treatment, and only 40% of those with hypothyroidism required treatment (48). Those who were treated received T_4 for extremely high levels of TSH with suppressed T_4 or increasing goiter size. Because of the low incidence of postpartum thyroiditis and the low likelihood of requiring treatment, screening with TFTs and antimicrosomal antibodies in asymptomatic women is not warranted (47, 51).

Women who develop a goiter in pregnancy or postpartum or who develop postpartum hypothyroid or hyperthyroid symptoms (including excessive fatigue, weight gain, dry skin, dry hair, cold intolerance, persistent amenorrhea, difficulty concentrating, depression, nervousness, or palpitations) should have their TSH and FT_4 levels evaluated (47, 48, 51). As noted previously, thyroid antimicrosomal or antithyroid peroxidase antibodies also may be useful. Because some of these symptoms are common in the postpartum state, clinicians must use their judgment to determine whether the symptoms warrant evaluation. If the patient has hypothyroidism, the decision to treat depends on the severity of abnormality and symptoms. Women with the highest levels of TSH and antithyroid peroxidase antibodies have the highest risk for developing permanent hypothyroidism (48).

▶ *Which pregnant patients should be screened for thyroid dysfunction?*

It is appropriate to perform indicated testing of thyroid function in women with a personal history of thyroid disease or symptoms of thyroid disease. The performance of TFTs in asymptomatic pregnant women who have a mildly enlarged thyroid is not warranted. Development of a significant goiter or distinct nodules should be evaluated as in any patient.

An observational study has drawn considerable attention to the subject of maternal subclinical hypothyroidism and resulted in calls from some professional organizations for universal screening for maternal hypothyroidism (20). Investigators screened maternal serum samples—obtained in the second trimester for purposes of maternal serum alphafetoprotein screening for neural tube defects—for elevated TSH levels (20). Out of 25,216 samples, only 75 women had TSH levels above the 99.7th percentile. The investigators then compared the results of neuropsychologic testing for 62 children of hypothyroid women with those of 124 children of matched women with normal thyroid glands when the children were approximately 8 years of age. They found no significant difference in mean IQ scores between the children of hypothyroid women and controls ($P = 0.06$). There was a significant difference in mean IQ scores when the children of untreated hypothyroid women were compared with controls but not between children of untreated and treated hypothyroid women. Among the children of the untreated women, 19% had full-scale IQ scores of 85 or lower, compared with only 5% of the children of women with normal thyroid glands.

It is important to acknowledge the limitations of the current understanding of this issue. The data available are observational. There have been no intervention trials to demonstrate the efficacy of screening and treatment to improve neuropsychologic performance in the offspring of hypothyroid women. The available data are consistent with the possibility that maternal hypothyroidism is associated with a decrement in some neuropsychologic testing. However, the association needs further testing to document its validity and, if confirmed, evidence that treatment ameliorates the effect. For all of these reasons, it would be premature to recommend universal screening for hypothyroidism during pregnancy.

Summary of Recommendations

The following recommendation is based on good and consistent scientific evidence (Level A):

▶ Levels of TSH or FT_4/FTI should be monitored to manage thyroid disease in pregnancy.

The following recommendations are based on limited or inconsistent scientific evidence (Level B):

▶ Either PTU or methimazole can be used to treat pregnant women with hyperthyroidism.

▶ Thyroid function tests are not indicated in asymptomatic pregnant women with slightly enlarged thyroid glands.

The following recommendations are based primarily on consensus and expert opinion (Level C):

▶ There is no need to measure TFTs routinely in women with hyperemesis.

▶ There are insufficient data to warrant routine screening of asymptomatic pregnant women for hypothyroidism.

▶ Indicated testing of thyroid function may be performed in women with a personal history of thyroid disease or symptoms of thyroid disease.

▶ The presence of maternal thyroid disease is important information for the pediatrician to have at the time of delivery.

▶ Thyroid nodules should be investigated to rule out malignancy.

References

1. Jameson JL, Weetman AP. Disorders of the thyroid gland. In: Braunwald E, Fauci AS, Hauser SL, Kasper DL, Longo DL, Jameson JL, eds. Harrison's principles of internal medicine. 15th ed. New York: McGraw-Hill, 2001: 2060–2084 (Level III)

2. Burrow GN, Fisher DA, Larsen PR. Maternal and fetal thyroid function. N Engl J Med 1994;331:1072–1078 (Level III)

3. Ecker JL, Musci TJ. Treatment of thyroid disease in pregnancy. Obstet Gynecol Clin North Am 1997;24:575–589 (Level III)

4. Glinoer D, de Nayer P, Bourdoux P, Lemone M, Robyn C, van Steirteghem A, et al. Regulation of maternal thyroid during pregnancy. J Clin Endocrinol Metab 1990;71: 276–287 (Level II-2)

5. Rasmussen NG, Hornnes PJ, Hegedus L. Ultrasonographically determined thyroid size in pregnancy and post partum: the goitrogenic effect of pregnancy. Am J Obstet Gynecol 1989;160:1216–1220 (Level II-2)

6. Thorpe-Beeston JG, Nicolaides KH, Felton CV, Butler J, McGregor AM. Maturation of the secretion of thyroid hormone and thyroid-stimulating hormone in the fetus. N Eng J Med 1991;324:532–536 (Level II-3)

7. Utiger RD. Maternal hypothyroidism and fetal development [letter]. N Engl J Med 1999;341:601–602 (Level III)

8. Ecker JL, Musci TJ. Thyroid function and disease in pregnancy. Curr Probl Obstet Gynecol Fertil 2000;23:109–122 (Level III)

9. Davis LE, Lucas MJ, Hankins GD, Roark ML, Cunningham FG. Thyrotoxicosis complicating pregnancy. Am J Obstet Gynecol 1989;160:63–70 (Level II-2)

10. Millar LK, Wing DA, Leung AS, Koonings PP, Montoro MN, Mestman JH. Low birth weight and preeclampsia in pregnancies complicated by hyperthyroidism. Obstet Gynecol 1994;84:946–949 (Level II-2)

11. Weetman AP. Graves' disease. N Engl J Med 2000;343: 1236–1248 (Level III)

12. Matsuura N, Harada S, Ohyama Y, Shibayama K, Fukushi M, Ishikawa N, et al. The mechanisms of transient hypothyroxinemia in infants born to mothers with Graves' disease. Pediatr Res 1997;42:214–218 (Level II-2)

13. McKenzie JM, Zakarija M. Fetal and neonatal hyperthyroidism and hypothyroidism due to maternal TSH receptor antibodies. Thyroid 1992;2:155–163 (Level III)

14. Laurberg P, Nygaard B, Glinoer D, Grusssendorf M, Orgiazzi J. Guidelines for TSH-receptor antibody measurements in pregnancy: results of an evidence-based symposium organized by the European Thyroid Association. Eur J Endocrinol 1998;139:584–586 (Level III)

15. Alvarez-Marfany M, Roman SH, Drexler AJ, Robertson C, Stagnaro-Green A. Long-term prospective study of postpartum thyroid dysfunction in women with insulin dependent diabetes mellitus. J Clin Endocrinol Metab 1994;79:10–16 (Level II-2)

16. Leung AS, Millar LK, Koonings PP, Montoro M, Mestman JH. Perinatal outcome in hypothyroid pregnancies. Obstet Gynecol 1993;81:349–353 (Level II-2)

17. Davis LE, Leveno KJ, Cunningham FG. Hypothyroidism complicating pregnancy. Obstet Gynecol 1988;72:108–112 (Level II-2)

18. Cao XY, Jiang XM, Dou ZH, Rakeman MA, Zhang ML, O'Donnell K, et al. Timing of vulnerability of the brain to iodine deficiency in endemic cretinism. N Engl J Med 1994;331:1739–1744 (Level II-1)

19. Screening for congenital hypothyroidism. In: U.S. Preventive Services Task Force. Guide to clinical preventive services. 2nd ed. Baltimore: Williams & Wilkins, 1996:503–507 (Level III)

20. Haddow JE, Palomaki GE, Allan WC, Williams JR, Knight GJ, Gagnon J, et al. Maternal thyroid deficiency during pregnancy and subsequent neuropsychological development of the child. N Engl J Med 1999;341:549–555 (Level II-2)

21. American Association of Clinical Endocrinologists. AACE clinical practice guidelines for evaluation and treatment of hyperthyroidism and hypothyroidism. Jacksonville, Florida: AACE, 1996 (Level III)

22. Ladenson PW, Singer PA, Ain KB, Bagchi N, Bigos ST, Levy EG, et al. American Thyroid Association guidelines for detection of thyroid dysfunction. Arch Intern Med 2000;160:1573–1575 [erratum Arch Intern Med 2001;161: 284] (Level III)

23. Gittoes NJ, Franklyn JA. Hyperthyroidism. Current treatment guidelines. Drugs 1998;55:543–553 (Level III)

24. Davies TF, Roti E, Braverman LE, Degroot LJ. Thyroid controversy—stimulating antibodies. J Clin Endocrinol Metab 1998;83:3777–3785 (Level III)

25. Wallace C, Couch R, Ginsberg J. Fetal thyrotoxicosis: a case report and recommendations for prediction, diagnosis, and treatment. Thyroid 1995;5:125–128 (Level III)

26. Van Dijke CP, Heydendael RJ, De Kleine MJ. Methimazole, carbimazole and congenital skin defects. Ann Intern Med 1987;106:60–61 (Level II-3)

27. Momotani N, Noh JY, Ishikawa N, Ito K. Effects of propl-thiouracil and methimazole on fetal thyroid status in mothers with Graves' hyperthyroidism. J Clin Endocrinol Metab 1997;82:3633–3636 (Level II-1)

28. Wing DA, Millar LK, Koonings PP, Montoro MN, Mestman JH. A comparison of propylthiouracil versus methimazole in the treatment of hyperthyroidism in pregnancy. Am J Obstet Gyencol 1994;170:90–95 (Level II-1)

29. Davidson KM, Richards DS, Schatz DA, Fisher DA. Successful in utero treatment of fetal goiter and hypothyroidism. N Engl J Med 1991;324:543–546 (Level III)

30. Briggs GG, Freeman RK, Yaffe SJ. Drugs in pregnancy and lactation: a reference guide to fetal and neonatal risk. Baltimore: Williams & Wilkins, 1998 (Level II-2)

31. Momotani N, Yamashita R, Yoshimoto M, Noh J, Ishikawa N, Ito K. Recovery from foetal hypothyroidism: evidence for the safety of breast-feeding while taking propyl-thiouracil. Clin Endocrinol (Oxf) 1989;31:591–595 (Level II-3)

32. Berg GE, Nystrom EH, Jacobsson L, Lindberg S, Lindstedt RG, Mattsson S, et al. Radioiodine treatment of hyperthyroidism in a pregnant women. J Nucl Med 1998;39(2):357–361 (Level III)

33. Evans PM, Webster J, Evans WD, Bevan JS, Scanlon MF. Radioiodine treatment in unsuspected pregnancy. Clin Endocrinol (Oxf) 1998;48:281–283 (Level III)

34. McClellan DR, Francis GL. Thyroid cancer in children, pregnant women, and patients with Graves' disease. Endocrinol Metab Clin North Am 1996;25:27–48 (Level III)

35. Mandel SJ, Larsen PR, Seely EW, Brent GA. Increased need for thyroxine during pregnancy in women with primary hypothyroidism. N Engl J Med 1990;323:91–96 (Level II-3)

36. Goodwin TM, Montoro M, Mestman JH. Transient hyperthyroidism and hyperemesis gravidarum: clinical aspects. Am J Obstet Gynecol 1992;167:648–652 (Level II-2)

37. Kimura M, Amino N, Tamaki H, Ito E, Mitsuda N, Miyai K, et al. Gestational thyrotoxicosis and hyperemesis gravidarum: possible role of hCG with higher stimulating activity. Clin Endocrinol (Oxf) 1993;38:345–350 (Level II-2)

38. Lao TT, Chin RK, Chang AM. The outcome of hyperemetic pregnancies complicated by transient hyperthyroidism. Aust N Z J Obstet Gynaecol 1987;27:99–101 (Level II-3)

39. Shulman A, Shapiro MS, Bahary C, Shenkman L. Abnormal thyroid function in hyperemesis gravidarum. Acta Obstet Gynecol Scand 1989;68:533–536 (Level II-2)

40. Leylek OA, Cetin A, Toyaksi M, Erselcan T. Hyperthyroidism in hyperemesis gravidarum. Int J Gynaecol Obstet 1996;55:33–37 (Level II-2)

41. Burrow GN. The management of thyrotoxicosis in pregnancy. N Engl J Med 1985;313:562–565 (Level II-3)

42. Molitch ME. Endocrine emergencies in pregnancy. Baillieres Clin Endocrinol Metab 1992;6:167–191 (Level III)

43. Moosa M, Mazzaferri EL. Outcome of differentiated thyroid cancer diagnosed in pregnant women. J Clin Endocrinol Metab 1997;82:2862–2866 (Level II-2)

44. Mazzaferri EL. Management of a solitary thyroid nodule. N Engl J Med 1993;328:553–559 (Level III)

45. Vini L, Hyer S, Pratt B, Harmer C. Management of differentiated thyroid cancer diagnosed during pregnancy. Eur J Endocrinol 1999;140:404–406 (Level III)

46. Schlumberger M, De Vathaire F, Ceccarelli C, Delisle MJ, Francese C, Couette JE, et al. Exposure to radioactive

iodine-131 for scintigraphy or therapy does not preclude pregnancy in thyroid cancer patients. J Nucl Med 1996;37:606–612 (Level II-2)

47. Gerstein HC. How common is postpartum thyroiditis? A methodology overview of the literature. Arch Intern Med 1990;150:1397–1400 (Level II-2)

48. Lucas A, Pizarro E, Granada ML, Salinas I, Foz M, Sanmarti A. Postpartum thyroiditis: epidemiology and clinical evolution in a nonselected population. Thyroid 2000;10:71–77 (Level II-2)

49. Lazarus JH, Ammari F, Oretti R, Parkes AB, Richards CJ, Harris B. Clinical aspects of recurrent postpartum thyroiditis. Br J Gen Pract 1997;47:305–308 (Level II-3)

50. Marqusee E, Hill JA, Mandel SJ. Thyroiditis after pregnancy loss. J Clin Endocrinol Metab 1997;82:2455–2457 (Level II-3)

51. Screening for thyroid disease. In: U.S. Preventive Services Task Force. Guide to clinical preventive services. 2nd ed. Baltimore: Williams & Wilkins, 1996:209–218 (Level III)

The MEDLINE database, the Cochrane Library, and ACOG's own internal resources and documents were used to conduct a literature search to locate relevant articles published between January 1985 and August 2000. The search was restricted to articles published in the English language. Priority was given to articles reporting results of original research, although review articles and commentaries also were consulted. Abstracts of research presented at symposia and scientific conferences were not considered adequate for inclusion in this document. Guidelines published by organizations or institutions such as the National Institutes of Health and the American College of Obstetricians and Gynecologists were reviewed, and additional studies were located by reviewing bibliographies of identified articles. When reliable research was not available, expert opinions from obstetrician–gynecologists were used.

Studies were reviewed and evaluated for quality according to the method outlined by the U.S. Preventive Services Task Force:

I   Evidence obtained from at least one properly designed randomized controlled trial.

II-1   Evidence obtained from well-designed controlled trials without randomization.

II-2   Evidence obtained from well-designed cohort or case–control analytic studies, preferably from more than one center or research group.

II-3   Evidence obtained from multiple time series with or without the intervention. Dramatic results in uncontrolled experiments could also be regarded as this type of evidence.

III   Opinions of respected authorities, based on clinical experience, descriptive studies, or reports of expert committees.

Based on the highest level of evidence found in the data, recommendations are provided and graded according to the following categories:

Level A—Recommendations are based on good and consistent scientific evidence.

Level B—Recommendations are based on limited or inconsistent scientific evidence.

Level C—Recommendations are based primarily on consensus and expert opinion.

ISSN 1099-3630

The American College of Obstetricians and Gynecologists
409 12th Street, SW, PO Box 96920
Washington, DC 20090-6920

12345/54321

Thyroid disease in pregnancy. ACOG Practice Bulletin No. 32. American College of Obstetricians and Gynecologists. Obstet Gynecol 2001;98:883–892

ACOG PRACTICE BULLETIN

CLINICAL MANAGEMENT GUIDELINES FOR
OBSTETRICIAN–GYNECOLOGISTS

NUMBER 28, JUNE 2001

This Practice Bulletin was developed by the ACOG Committee on Practice Bulletins— Gynecology with the assistance of Maida Taylor, MD. The information is designed to aid practitioners in making decisions about appropriate obstetric and gynecologic care. These guidelines should not be construed as dictating an exclusive course of treatment or procedure. Variations in practice may be warranted based on the needs of the individual patient, resources, and limitations unique to the institution or type of practice.

Use of Botanicals for Management of Menopausal Symptoms

Lack of confidence in the espoused benefits of hormone replacement therapy (HRT) coupled with a significant array of side effects of HRT, results in fewer than 1 in 3 women choosing to take HRT. The use of alternatives to conventional HRT has become more accessible and acceptable to many women. As more women choose these alternatives, physicians are confronted with the challenges of how to advise patients about alternative medicine and how to determine which therapies may be safe and effective. This document will examine available scientific information on alternative therapies for treatment of menopausal symptoms and provide recommendations on efficacy and potential adverse consequences.

Background

Discontent with Current Pharmaceutical Regimens

Hormone replacement therapy is associated with various side effects and complications; 30–40% of patients experience some degree of abnormal bleeding in the first year of hormone use, which often results in discontinuation of use (1). Initiating HRT also is viewed by some women as treating menopause as a medical disorder, which is seen by a large segment of the population as a natural, normal part of the aging process. In addition, many women believe that estrogen therapy may increase the risk of breast cancer, and the fear of breast cancer is most often cited as the reason for lack of initiation (2).

Complementary and Alternative Medicine

Complementary medicine can be defined as those systems, practices, interventions, modalities, professions, therapies, applications, theories, or claims that are currently not an integral part of the conventional medical system (3). Alternatively, conventional medicine refers to medicine as it is generally practiced and widely taught by medical doctors, doctors of osteopathy, and their allied health professionals (4). Alternative medicine encompasses a number of systematic medical practices based on physical assessments that differ from physiology as it is taught in Western medical institutions. The most recognizable and widely employed alternatives are biologic-based therapies such as botanical medicines, dietary supplements, vitamins, minerals, and orthomolecular medicine. In a 1998 survey, alternative medicine visits exceeded visits to conventional primary care providers, and 70% of such encounters were never discussed with the patient's regular personal physician (5). In addition, a national survey reported the highest rates of use in the groups aged 35–49 years (42%) and 50–64 years (44%) (6). Three theories were proposed by the investigator as tentative predictors of use of alternatives therapies: 1) dissatisfaction with conventional medicine; 2) viewing alternatives as more empowering because of their over-the-counter status; and 3) perceiving alternatives as more compatible with personal values or ethical or religious belief systems. Predictors of alternative care use were reported to include higher educational level, poorer health status, holistic orientation to health, having had a transformational experience changing one's world view, and several chronic health conditions such as anxiety, back problems, chronic pain, and urinary tract problems. Only 4.4% of respondents relied primarily on alternative therapies.

In 1997, out-of-pocket expenditures for alternative therapies were estimated at $27 billion, which was more than the out-of-pocket expenditures for all physician services that year (7). Recently, third-party carriers have started providing coverage for alternative therapies, sometimes assessing an extra premium for such expanded benefits.

Complementary and Alternative Medicines Used in Menopause

The symptoms associated with perimenopause and menopause stimulate a healthy concern about wellness and motivate women to undertake appropriate interventions to lower health risks associated with menopause. Interest in alternative medicine can be viewed simply as a natural extension of interest in nutrition, exercise, and other behavioral, nonpharmacologic interventions directed at maintaining well-being. Unfortunately, many of the alternatives promoted and touted as substitutes for HRT do not offer any substantiated health benefits.

According to the North American Menopause Society, nonhormonal interventions commonly used for menopause include a healthy diet, exercise, vitamins, and calcium supplements. The North American Menopause Society also indicates that more than 30% of women use acupuncture, natural estrogen, herbal supplements, or so-called plant estrogens (8). Alternative therapies to conventional HRT include botanical products, vitamins and minerals, unconventional hormones and steroids sold over-the-counter as nutritional supplements or as cosmetics, and nonproprietary single and combination estrogen and progestin preparations custom blended by compounding pharmacies.

Most studies of menopausal interventions, including phase-III clinical trials of estrogenic drugs, show a 20–30% response rate in placebo groups. Unconventional interventions need to be studied in well-controlled trials before their use can be supported. Documentation of efficacy is essential because these products should yield effective results of a magnitude large enough to warrant their costs, which are substantial.

Botanical Medicine

Up to one half of drugs commonly used today are either plant products or phytochemicals that were initially isolated from botanical material but are now synthesized by chemical processing techniques. Outside of pharmaceutical preparations, plants are used therapeutically in the form of herbs, oils, pills, teas, or tinctures (see box). In

---

Therapeutic Forms of Botanical Preparations

Bulk herbs are raw or dried plants used in toto, as pulvers or powders, or to make teas and tinctures. The powders also can be put into capsules or compounded into tablet form.

Oils are concentrates of fat-soluble chemicals from herbs, often highly concentrated, and usually used externally. Many are highly toxic if ingested.

Tablets or capsules can be compounded for ease of use and often with the intent of providing a fixed metered dose.

Teas may be used to extract solubles in herbs by adding hot water, and the "potency" is determined by the steeping time. Teas are traditionally brewed 1–2 minutes, infusions for 20–30 minutes, while preparation of a decoction requires boiling the plant material in water for 10–20 minutes.

Tinctures are alcohol-extracted concentrates usually added to water or placed directly into the mouth or under the tongue.

addition, currently used products include highly concentrated extracts of phytochemicals, synthetic derivatives, and even steroids like dehydroepiandrosterone (DHEA) and androstenedione, which are classified as food supplements because they are produced from plant precursor sterols.

Dietary Plant Estrogen/Phytoestrogens

Plants do not make estrogens in the classic sense of the term. Plants make sterol molecules, many of which exert weak estrogenic activity in animals although their effects increase when large quantities are ingested. These compounds, phytoestrogens, often possess structural similarities to more active human and animal estrogens. Plant sterols are used as the precursors for the biosynthetic production of mass-manufactured therapeutic pharmaceutical-grade steroids. A number of plants used to treat symptoms of menopause have been identified in botanical medicine texts as having estrogenic activity, but research has contradicted these traditional assumptions (9).

Phytoestrogens are classified into three groups (10):

1. Isoflavones, particularly, genistein and daidzein, are plant sterol molecules found in soy and garbanzo beans and other legumes, which are most often consumed in products like tempeh, soy, miso, and tofu. Generally, 1 g of soy protein yields 1.2–1.7 mg of isoflavones, depending on the type of soybean used as the source of the protein.

2. Lignins are a constituent of the cell wall of plants and are bioavailable as a result of the effect of intestinal bacteria on grains. The highest amounts are found in the husk of seeds used to produce oils, especially flaxseed. The whole seed added to salad or cereal, or flaxseed meal or flour can be used as a food additive.

3. Coumestans have steroidlike activity but are not a significant source of phytoestrogens for most individuals. High concentrations are found in red clover, sunflower seeds, and bean sprouts and are known to have estrogenic effects when ingested by animals.

Asian diets are typically high in soy foods and contain an average of 40–80 mg of active forms of isoflavones per day, while American diets average less than 3 mg per day. American and European diets tend to elevate plasma levels of sex hormones and decrease sex-hormone-binding-globulin concentrations, thus increasing the exposure of peripheral tissues to the effects of circulating estrogens. High-soy diets act through several mechanisms to lower effective circulating and tissue levels of steroids. High isoflavone intake may depress luteinizing hormone (LH) levels and secondarily depresses estrogen production (11, 12).

The plant lignan and isoflavonoid glycosides become hormonelike compounds with weak estrogenic and antioxidative activity through the action of intestinal flora. Red clover is a rich source of isoflavones, as well as coumestans, and is used commercially to make isoflavone supplements. These compounds exert detectable effects on circulating gonadotropins and sex steroids, suggesting that they have biological activity (12). They also can act on intracellular enzymes, protein synthesis, growth factors, cellular proliferation, differentiation, and angiogenesis. Limited observational studies on isolated populations in cross-cultural comparison suggest that the incidence of cancer and atherosclerotic disease decreases with increasing intake of bioflavonoids and that diphenolic isoflavonoids and lignans are cancer-protective compounds (13). These protective effects have accrued in populations over a lifetime. It is unclear that changing one's intake of isoflavones or soy protein at age 50 years will significantly lower the lifetime risk of these diseases. A directive advising lifelong adherence to a diet rich in a variety of fruits and vegetables while limiting the intake of animal protein and fat should apply to men and women of all ages, not just those experiencing their menopausal transition. Moreover, no single synthetic or chemical derived from soy is thought to match the benefits derived from ingesting soy foods. The effects—either beneficial or detrimental—of prolonged intake of supra-dietary levels of soy or isoflavone are unknown.

Bean products are rich sources of diphenols, which are thought to lower cancer risk by modifying hormone metabolism and production and limiting cancer cell growth. Bean foods also provide large amounts of fiber, and fiber modifies the level of sex hormones by increasing gastrointestinal motility. Fiber alters bile acid metabolism and partially interrupts the enterohepatic circulation causing increased estrogen excretion by decreasing the rate of estrogen reuptake in the enterohepatic system (14).

Manufacturing and Regulating Botanicals

The federal Dietary Supplement Health and Education Act of 1994 (DSHEA) defined dietary supplements and limited the claims that can be made on supplement labels and in supporting literature. Manufacturers are responsible for ensuring the safety of their supplement products. Supplements are neither foods nor drugs, so manufacturers do not have to provide any evidence to support purported benefits before marketing their products. The Food and Drug Administration (FDA) oversees the industry, but the Federal Trade Commission is responsible for identifying inappropriate or unsubstantiated claims and enforcing DSHEA regulations.

In 1997, the FDA proposed a new dietary supplement rule allowing supplements to make structural or functional claims, but not disease claims. Such language as "supports well-being" or "helps promote heart health" would be allowed, while statements like "lowers cholesterol" would not be permitted. Supplements that "…expressly or implicitly claim to diagnose, treat, prevent, or cure a disease…[would be] …regarded as drugs and have to meet the safety and effectiveness standards for drugs…" (15). The American Botanical Council objects to the FDA attempting to redefine the DSHEA, while the American Medical Association supports the refined definitions.

Botanicals are subject to a high degree of variation in production. Plants grown in the field may have different amounts of active constituents due to growing conditions. Products coming out of production facilities may vary greatly in the amount of active ingredients.

The botanical industry has set up voluntary guidelines, and some manufacturers have signed agreements in kind affirming that they will produce products set to an industry-defined standard. However, without mandatory oversight, problems of adulteration, contamination, and dose standardization will continue. Consequently, buyers and their physicians need to beware.

Uses for Botanicals in Menopausal Women

A brief description of several commonly used botanicals follows. Also included are their suggested and advertised uses.

Vasomotor Symptoms

Soy Products. The effects of soy protein found in whole foods, soy protein isolates, and those of isoflavone isolates made into powders or pills may not all be the same. Even soy foods are not necessarily reliable sources of biologically active isoflavones. The alcohol processing often used in the manufacture of tofu and soy milk removes the biologically active forms, the aglyconic isoflavones. Producers of soy foods recognize that the public is interested in isoflavone supplements, and many indicate in their product labeling the amounts and forms of isoflavones found in the foodstuff. Although the mechanisms of action of soy and dietary isoflavones are not fully understood, they appear to involve binding to the estrogen receptor. For this reason, one should not assume these dietary supplements are safe for women with estrogen-dependent cancers, most importantly breast cancer.

Black Cohosh. Black cohosh was the principle ingredient in Lydia Pinkham's Vegetable Compound, an ethanolic extract sold over-the-counter in the United States and in Europe. A black cohosh extract is one of the leading botanicals sold in Germany and is the country's top selling menopausal herbal remedy. The German Commission E Monographs state that black cohosh has estrogen-like action, suppresses LH, binds to estrogen receptors, has no contraindications to its use, and that the only side effect is occasional gastric discomfort (16).

Black cohosh has been found to reduce LH levels in rats that had ovariectomies and to reduce LH levels in postmenopausal women after 8 weeks of use (17). Despite these LH effects, other studies in humans and animals indicate that black cohosh has no estrogenic effects on sex-steroid-dependent tissues. In one unpublished double-blind, randomized study, black cohosh did not affect follicle-stimulating hormone, LH, estradiol, estrone, prolactin, sex-hormone-binding globulin, endometrial thickness, or vaginal maturation index (18). No claims are made regarding cardiac or bone effects, and black cohosh is suggested only for treatment of menopausal symptoms such as hot flashes, sleep disorders, anxiety, and depression and for nonmenopausal conditions like dysmenorrhea and premenstrual syndrome.

Evening Primrose. The evening primrose plant (also called evening star) produces seeds rich in gamma linolenic acid (GLA) and also contains several anticoagulant substances. Commercial preparations made from fixed oil sources are generally 72% linolenic acid (LA) and 14% GLA. Thus, each 500-mg capsule will contain 45 mg of GLA and 365 mg of LA plus lesser amounts of oleic, palmitic, and stearic acid. Because GLA is elaborated by the placenta, and because high concentrations are found in breast milk, it is suggested that GLA is the nutritionally perfect fatty acid for humans. With respect to the gynecologic uses of GLA, evening primrose is commonly recommended for mastalgia and mastodynia, premenstrual syndrome, menopausal symptoms, and bladder symptoms.

Dong Quai. Dong Quai (also seen as Dang Gui and Tang Kuei), a type of angelica, is the most commonly prescribed Chinese herbal medicine for "female problems" (19). Dong Quai supposedly regulates and balances the menstrual cycle and is said to strengthen the uterus. Dong Quai is used in traditional Chinese medicine to nourish and "tonify" blood. It also is said to exert estrogenic activity. Most herbal practitioners seem to agree it is contraindicated during pregnancy and lactation.

Mood Disturbances

St. John's Wort. Extracts of the flower *hypericum perforatum,* known as St. John's wort, have been used for centuries to treat mild to moderate depression. The constituents include hypericin, pseudohypericin, and flavonoids. Several unconfirmed mechanisms of action for the psychotropic effects of St. John's wort have been proposed, including monamine oxidase inhibition, suppression of corticotropin-releasing hormone, and serotonin receptor blockade. Hypericin does not appear to be a monamine oxidase inhibitor (20).

Commercial preparations often contain generally recommended doses; one capsule three times a day provides a cumulative dose equivalent to the upper limit of doses found in the literature to date. Side effects are similar to, but far less than, those of standard antidepressant medications, including dry mouth, dizziness, and constipation.

Valerian Root. Valerian root, the common valerian or garden heliotrope, has been used traditionally as a tranquilizer and soporific. The active constituent has never been identified but is thought to be a gamma aminobutyric acid (GABA) derivative. Note that a similar GABA-like compound has been found in chamomile, which is also proffered as an herbal sleep aid. Before the advent of benzodiazepines and barbiturates, many psychiatric disorders were treated with valerian. Although it has no demonstrable toxicity and degrades rapidly, there have been reports of dystonic reactions and visual disturbances, perhaps mediated by other drugs used concomitantly. Little is known about the actions, effects, or potential interactions of valerian with other drugs. After L-tryptophan was taken off the market, valerian use became popular again. Most botanical texts advise against its use during pregnancy and lactation.

Loss of Libido/Vaginal Dryness/Dyspareunia

Chasteberry. Chasteberry or vitex also is known as Chaste tree, Monk's pepper, agnus castus, Indian spice, sage tree hemp, and tree wild pepper. It has been recommended by some for vaginal dryness at menopause and also for depression. Vitex contains hormonelike substances, which competitively bind receptors and produce antiandrogenic effects; it is often recommended to reduce libido in males because of its proposed value as an anti-aphrodisiac. Antithetically, vitex also is recommended by some to enhance libido in menopausal women.

In vitro and animal studies have suggested that vitex inhibits prolactin, and perhaps explains the purported benefit of recommending vitex for mastalgia and premenstrual syndrome. A placebo-controlled, double-blind clinical trial of 20 male subjects used 120-, 240-, and 480-mg extracts of vitex, which did not demonstrate any effect on prolactin (21). Another single-armed study in 56 women with mastodynia showed a reduction in prolactin in the treatment group compared with controls (22). Studies, the quality of which cannot be assessed, claim that vitex corrects inadequate luteal phase, and that it restores LH activity.

Ginseng. There are many types of ginseng (*Panax ginseng*)—Siberian, Korean, American, White, and Red. All are promoted as "adaptogens," which help one cope with stress and supposedly boost immunity. Ginseng also is reputed to be an aphrodisiac, a claim that is unsubstantiated by medical evidence. It also is promoted as a means of improving athletic performance and inducing weight loss without the need for diet or exercise. There is evidence that ginseng does not improve athletic performance, despite claims made (23). Reports of antioxidant effects and reduced rates of disease, particularly cancer rates, are suspect because the products in general use have been found to contain little or no active ingredients (24).

Menstrual Disorders/Menorrhagia

Wild Yam. Yam extracts, tablets, and creams claim to be progesterone substitutes and also are touted as a natural source of DHEA. Sterol structures from the plant are used as precursors in the biosynthesis of progesterone, DHEA, and other steroids, but do not have inherent biological activity. Claims are made that the plant sterol dioscorea is converted into progesterone in the body and alleviates "estrogen dominance." There is no human biochemical pathway for bioconversion of dioscorea to progesterone or DHEA in vivo. Mexican yam extract more accurately is estrogenic, containing considerable diosgenin, an estrogenlike substance found in plants. Some estrogenic effects might be expected from eating these species of yams, but only if large quantities of raw yams are consumed (25). Yams from the grocery store generally are not the varieties known to contain significant amounts of dioscorea or diosgenin. Yam extracts also are purported to be effective for uterine cramps.

Clinical Considerations and Recommendations

A limited body of scientific information about botanicals is available in English. A few publications from Europe and Asia are available in full text. Most of the literature includes in vitro effects, animal models, and open, often single-armed or nonrandomized studies. The amount and sophistication of studies of most alternative therapies do not meet the current standards for evidence-based recommendations.

▶ *Are there useful nonpharmaceutical supplements or botanicals for treatment of vasomotor symptoms, including hot flashes, flushes, and night sweats?*

Soy/Isoflavone Isolates. In one study, women given a soy protein supplement with 40 mg of protein and 76 mg of isoflavones had a 45% reduction in vasomotor symptoms compared with a 30% reduction in controls who received a placebo (26). Other research demonstrated a 40% reduction in vasomotor symptoms when diet was supplemented with soy flour, but the vaginal maturation index did not improve (27). Based on these limited studies, the use of soy may have benefits.

Black Cohosh. Although a dozen studies of women taking black cohosh extracts show an apparent reduction in symptomatology, the studies are largely unblinded, use unvalidated tools to measure outcomes, and contain small numbers of patients. Based on this limited evidence, there appears to be a positive effect on sleep disorders, mood disturbance, and hot flashes (28). There have been no reports of black cohosh toxicity. No clinical studies have reported efficacy or safety of black cohosh beyond 6 months of use. Black cohosh should not be confused with blue cohosh, *Caulophyllum thalictroides,* which has weak nicotine activity and toxic potential.

Evening Primrose. A meta-analysis of clinical trials of evening primrose oil used to treat premenstrual syndrome concluded that of the seven controlled trials, only five were properly randomized (29). In the only one of the five trials that was blinded, evening primrose was ineffective in treating premenstrual syndrome. To date, there is only one randomized, double-blind, placebo-controlled study of the use of GLA in the treatment of vasomotor symptoms during menopause (30). Although the women taking GLA had "significant improvement... in the maximum number of night time flushes," GLA provided no benefits beyond those seen with placebo.

Dong Quai. Kaiser Permanente conducted a double-blind controlled clinical trial using a daily dose of 4.5 g of dong quai (9). Dong quai and placebo both reported a 25% reduction in hot flashes. Critics of the study have noted that the dose of dong quai was lower than that often used in traditional Chinese medicine, and that dong quai is never employed as an isolated intervention. The argument is made that the botanicals must be taken together in a balanced formula and that the therapeutic outcome requires that proper synergy take place between the components. However, its benefit cannot be substantiated based on available evidence.

Dong quai is potentially toxic. It contains numerous coumarinlike derivatives and may cause excessive bleeding or interactions with other anticoagulants (31). Dong quai also contains psoralens and is potentially photosensitizing, which has led to concern about an increased risk of sun-exposure-related skin cancers (32).

Ginseng. Ginsana, the largest manufacturer of ginseng, funded a study of 384 women to investigate the effects of ginseng in menopausal women. No differences were found between treatment subjects and placebo controls in vasomotor symptoms, but significant improvements were reported in quality of life measures, particularly depression, general health, and well-being scores (33).

▶ *Are there alternative, nonpharmaceutical supplements or botanicals that have demonstrated usefulness in the treatment of sleep, mood and affective, cognitive, and other behavioral disorders associated with menopause syndrome?*

St. John's Wort. A meta-analysis of 15 controlled trials encompassing 1,757 cases found that St. John's wort hypericin in doses less than 1.2 mg per day produced a 61% improvement in mild to moderate depression, while doses up to 2.7 mg per day produced a 75% improvement (34). Its efficacy in the treatment of severe depression is not documented. Some have suggested that St. John's wort is helpful in treating seasonal affective disorder. No clinical studies have reported results or safety parameters beyond 2 years of use.

St. John's wort is also potentially photosensitizing (24), and concern has been raised about an increased rate of cataracts. The issue of possible interactions between St. John's wort and selective serotonin reuptake inhibitors or monamine oxidase inhibitors has been raised. Some consultants advise against using St. John's wort for weeks to months after stopping these drugs. Interaction with anesthetic agents has also been reported (35).

Valerian Root. In 1998, the U.S. Pharmacopeia (USP) stated in its monograph on valerian: "Studies supporting this use are not good enough to prove that it is effective. Therefore, USP advisory panels do not support its use" (36). There is a case report of high-output congestive heart failure, tachycardia, and delirium attributed to acute withdrawal from valerian (37). Based on available data, valerian appears not to be useful, and may be harmful.

▶ *Are there alternative, nonpharmaceutical supplements or botanicals that have been shown to be useful for treatment of decreased libido, vaginal dryness, or dyspareunia?*

Soy/Isoflavones. Findings regarding the effects of soy supplements on vaginal maturation index are inconsistent with some showing improvements (11) and others showing no change (12). Different isoflavones may have a differential impact on estrogen-sensitive tissues, so that various types of dietary soy may affect the lower genital tract with a significant degree of variability (12, 27). Therefore, some soy products may be useful in the treatment of vaginal dryness and dyspareunia, although sources of isoflavones and beneficial amounts have yet to be clarified.

Chasteberry or Vitex. Although vitex's supposed anti-hormonal activity serves as the basis for advising its use in treating mastalgia, all claims of efficacy in women are poorly documented. Although studies of vitex use in menopause are limited, a recent randomized trial assessed the effects of vitex in women with premenstrual syndrome, which may apply to women with similar complaints in menopause. After three cycles of vitex, significant improvements in mood alteration, anger, headache, and breast fullness were reported on a self assessment screening tool. However, other menstrual symptoms, like bloating, remained unchanged. Physician ratings of patients' conditions also indicated better effects than with placebo (38).

Ginseng. No published studies have documented that ginseng has an effect on libido in menopausal women. Moreover, 54 ginseng products examined by the American Botanical Council proved to have little ginseng (60%) or no ginseng (25%), and many were heavily adulterated with caffeine (24). Other analyses have found significant variation in the active ingredient, ginsenosides, as well as high levels of pesticides or lead. Ginseng may hold some promise in the treatment of fatigue, depression, immunosuppression, and other health problems, but it cannot be recommended as a treatment for menopause. For its other indications, caution is advised given the poor production standards and lack of quality evidence for the claims made.

▶ *Are there alternative, nonpharmaceutical supplements or botanicals that are useful for the treatment of menstrual disorders during perimenopause and menopause?*

Wild and Mexican Yam. Based on the lack of bioavailability, the hormones in wild and Mexican yam would not be expected to have any efficacy. Wild yam extracts are neither estrogenic nor progestational, and although many yam extract products contain no yam, some are laced with progesterone. Perhaps some may even contain medroxyprogesterone. Oral ingestion does not produce serum levels. There are no published reports demonstrating the efficacy of wild yam cream. A 1-month supply costs more than $25, while a month of commercially produced vaginal estrogen cream costs less than $20 (39).

▶ *Are there useful alternative, nonpharmaceutical supplements or botanicals for the prevention of coronary heart disease and osteoporosis?*

Soy/Isoflavone Isolates. There is some evidence to indicate that high isoflavone intake may favorably affect lipid profile and is, by extension, thought to reduce cardiac disease risk. However, study results are conflicting. A study in Finland found an inverse relationship between isoflavone intake and coronary heart disease in both women and men (40), but similar benefits have not been demonstrated in the United States (41). A meta-analysis showed higher soy intake is associated with significant improvement in lipid profiles (42). Soy protein intake of approximately 47 g per day correlated with a statistically significant 9.3% reduction in serum cholesterol, a 12.9% reduction in serum low-density lipoprotein cholesterol, a 10.5% reduction in serum triglycerides, and an insignificant 2.4% increase in high-density lipoproteins. Isoflavone isolates containing 40 mg of isoflavone isolates have been shown to induce a 23% increase in arterial compliance after 1 year of use, an increase equal to that seen in women receiving conjugated equine estrogens (43).

Dietary soy or isolated isoflavone supplements may have a salutary effect on bone mass. Ipriflavone, a synthetic version of genistein, slows bone reabsorption and stimulates collagen synthesis in bone. Pharmaceutical quality ipriflavone is approved in Europe and Japan for treatment of osteoporosis using 600 mg per day. Ipriflavone with supplemental calcium has been found to decrease bone loss in natural menopause in some studies (44, 45), but not others (46), to decrease bone loss after surgically induced menopause (47), and in women with gonadotropin-agonist-induced bone loss (48).

▶ *Does the use of alternative therapies require any special medical monitoring?*

No published studies have investigated the role of clinical monitoring in patients using alternative medicine therapies. However, alternative steroid products may pose a risk for consequences of excessive steroid ingestion. Androgens are associated with abnormal liver functions as well as potential hyperandrogenicity. Estrogens compounded by an alternative therapy pharmacy may produce varying serum estradiol levels in women or increased estrogen bioactivity without detectable changes in circulating estradiol. Risks of excessive levels include hepatic effects and increased risk of deep vein thrombosis.

Although most botanicals appear to be harmless, products may be adulterated or contaminated. In addi-

Counseling Patients About Complementary and Alternative Medicine

- All patients should be asked about their use of herbal therapies and dietary supplements. Use of these products should be documented in the patient's chart.

- "Natural" is not an assurance of safety or efficacy.

- Potentially dangerous drug–herb interactions occur.*

- Lack of standardization of botanicals may result in variability of content and efficacy from batch to batch, from a single manufacturer, or between manufacturers.

- Lack of quality control and regulation may result in contamination, adulteration, or potential misidentification of plant products.

- Errors in compounding may result in toxic or lethal outcomes in custom-blended herbal preparations.

- Botanicals should not be used by women planning to become pregnant in the near future or during pregnancy or lactation without professional advice.

- Botanicals should not be taken in larger than recommended doses or for longer than recommended duration.

- Several botanicals have known adverse effects and toxicities.

- Infants, children, and the elderly should not use botanicals without professional advice.

- Patients should be counseled in a rational, judicious, and balanced manner about the relative risks and benefits of conventional therapies and alternative interventions.

- Adverse events and outcomes should be documented in the chart, therapy discontinued, and reported to the U.S. Food and Drug Administration.

- Because the expected placebo response for menopausal treatment ranges from 10% to 30%, a small positive response to any treatment, conventional or alternative, may not necessarily represent a pharmacologic effect. Anecdotal experience is not a substitute for well-constructed clinical trials. Nonetheless, the effect of support, counseling, and empathetic care should not be discounted or dismissed.

*For a complete listing of potentially dangerous drug–herb interactions see Newall CA, Anderson LA, Phillipson JD. Herbal medicines: a guide for health-care professionals. London: Pharmaceutical Press, 1996.

Modified from Cirigliano M, Sun A. Advising patients about herbal therapies [letter]. JAMA 1998;280:1565–1566. Copyright 1998, American Medical Association.

tion, all menopausal women taking any pharmaceutical or alternative preparation should have blood pressure readings, mammograms, and Pap tests at recommended intervals. Women using estrogen supplements who are relying on unconventional estrogenic or progestational therapies such as transdermal progesterone cosmetic creams should be monitored according to standard guidelines for women taking unopposed estrogen—that is, endometrial surveillance should be considered. In counseling patients, the risk of adverse effects from these therapies must be weighed against the costs associated with any routine testing. Further guidelines for counseling patients regarding the use of complementary and alternative medicine are shown in the box. Also, it is important for clinicians to be aware of issues surrounding referral to alternative care providers (3).

Summary of Recommendations

Given the general lack of standardization of products, the relatively short duration of therapy and follow-up in the available data, and the difficulty of interpreting the available clinical data, few recommendations can be made with confidence. The following conclusions can be drawn in reference to short-term (≤ 2 years) use of botanical and alternative medicine for the management of menopause.

The following recommendations are based primarily on consensus and expert opinion (Level C):

► Soy and isoflavones may be helpful in the short-term (≤ 2 years) treatment of vasomotor symptoms. Given the possibility that these compounds may interact with estrogen, these agents should not be considered free of potential harm in women with estrogen-dependent cancers.

► St. John's wort may be helpful in the short-term (≤ 2 years) treatment of mild to moderate depression in women.

► Black cohosh may be helpful in the short-term (≤ 6 months) treatment of women with vasomotor symptoms.

► Soy and isoflavone intake over prolonged periods may improve lipoprotein profiles and protect against osteoporosis. Soy in foodstuffs may differ in biological activity from soy and isoflavones in supplements.

References

1. Ettinger B, Pressman A, Bradley C. Comparison of continuation of postmenopausal hormone replacement therapy: transdermal versus oral estrogen. Menopause 1998;5: 152–156 (Level II-3)

2. Creasman WT. Is there an association between hormone replacement therapy and breast cancer? J Womens Health 1998;7:1231–1246 (Level III)

3. American College of Obstetricians and Gynecologists. Complementary and alternative medicine. ACOG Committee Opinion 227. Washington, DC: ACOG, 1999 (Level III)

4. National Center for Complementary and Alternative Medicine. Expanding horizons of healthcare. Bethesda, Maryland: NCCAM, 2000, NCCAM Clearinghouse publication no. X-38 (Level III)

5. Eisenberg DM, Davis RB, Ettner SL, Appel S, Wilkey S, Van Rompay M, et al. Trends in alternative medicine use in the United Sates, 1990–1997: results of a follow-up national survey. JAMA 1998;280:1569–1575 (Level III)

6. Astin JA. Why patients use alternative medicine: results of a national study. JAMA 1998;279:1548–1553 (Level III)

7. Eisenberg DM. Advising patients who seek alternative medical therapies. Ann Intern Med 1997;127:61–69 (Level III)

8. Kaufert P, Boggs PP, Ettinger B, Woods NF, Utian WH. Women and menopause: beliefs, attitudes, and behaviors. The North American Menopause Society 1997 Menopause Survey. Menopause 1998;5:197–202 (Level III)

9. Hirata JD, Swiersz LM, Zell B, Small R, Ettinger B. Does dong quai have estrogenic effects in postmenopausal women? A double-blind, placebo-controlled trial. Fertil Steril 1997;68:981–986 (Level I)

10. Kurzer MS, Xu X. Dietary phytoestrogens. Annu Rev Nutr 1997;17:353–381 (Level III)

11. Wilcox G, Wahlqvist ML, Burger HG, Medley G. Oestrogenic effects of plant foods in postmenopausal women. BMJ 1990;301:905–906 (Level II-3)

12. Baird DD, Umbach DM, Lansdell L, Hughes CL, Setchell KD, Weinberg CR, et al. Dietary intervention study to assess estrogenicity of dietary soy among postmenopausal women. J Clin Endocrinol Metab 1995;80:1685–1690 (Level I)

13. Tham DM, Gardner CD, Haskell WL. Clinical review 97: Potential health benefits of dietary phytoestrogens: a review of the clinical, epidemiological, and mechanistic evidence. J Clin Endocrinol Metab 1998;83:2223–2235 (Level III)

14. Rose DP, Lubin M, Connolly JM. Effects of diet supplementation with wheat bran on serum estrogen levels in the follicular and luteal phases of the menstrual cycle. Nutrition 1997;13:535–539 (Level II-3)

15. Mitka M. FDA never promised an herb garden—but sellers and buyers eager to see one grow [news]. JAMA 1998;280:1554–1556 (Level III)

16. Blumenthal M, ed. The complete German Commission E monographs: therapeutic guide to herbal medicines. Austin, Texas: American Botanical Council, 1998 (Level III)

17. Duker EM, Kopanski L, Jarry H, Wuttke W. Effects of extracts from Cimicifuga racemosa on gonadotropin release in menopausal women and ovariectomized rats. Planta Med 1991;57:420–424 (Level II-3)

18. Liske E, Wustenberg P. Therapy of climacteric complaints with cimicifuga racemosa: herbal medicine with clinically proven evidence [abstract]. Menopause 1998;5:250 (Level III)

19. Beinfield H, Korngold E. Between heaven and earth: a guide to Chinese medicine. New York: Ballantine Books, 1991 (Level III)

20. Bennett DA Jr, Phun L, Polk JF, Voglino SA, Zlotnik V, Raffa RB. Neuropharmacology of St. John's Wort (Hypericum). Ann Pharmacother 1998;32:1201–1208 (Level III)

21. Merz PG, Schrodter A, Rietbrock S, Gorkow Ch, Loew D. Prolktinsekretion und Vertraglichkeit unter der Behandlung mit einem Agnus-castus-Spezialextrakt (B1095E1). Erste Ergebnisse zum Einflub auf die Prolaktinsekretion. In: Loew D, Rietbrock N, eds. Phytopharmaka in Forschung und klinischer Anwendung. Darmstadt: Steinkopff, 1995:93–97 (German)

22. Wuttke W, Gorkow Ch, Jarry J. Dompainergic compounds in Vitex agtnus castus. In: Loew D, Rietbrock N, eds. Phytopharmaka in Forschung und kinischer Anwendug. Darmstadt: Steinkopff, 1995:81–91 (German)

23. Allen JD, McLung J, Nelson AG, Welsch M. Ginseng supplementation does not enhance healthy young adults' peak aerobic exercise performance. J Am Coll Nutr 1998; 17:462–466 (Level II-1)

24. O'Hara M, Kiefer D, Farrell K, Kemper K. A review of 12 commonly used medicinal herbs. Arch Fam Med 1998; 7:523–536 (Level III)

25. Mirkin G. Estrogen in yams. JAMA 1991;265:912 (Level III)

26. Albertazzi P, Pansini F, Bonaccorsi G, Zanotti L, Forini E, De Aloysio D. The effect of dietary soy supplementation on hot flushes. Obstet Gynecol 1998;91:6–11 (Level II-1)

27. Murkies AL, Lombard C, Strauss BJ, Wilcox G, Burger HG, Morton MS. Dietary flour supplementation decreases post-menopausal hot flushes: effect of soy and wheat. Maturitas 1995;21:189–195 (Level I)

28. Warnecke G. Influence of a phytopharmaceutical on climacteric complaints. Die Medizinische Welt 1985; 36:871–874 (German)

29. Budeiri D, Li Wan Po A, Dornan JC. Is evening primrose oil of value in the treatment of premenstrual syndrome? Control Clin Trials 1996;17:60–68 (Level III)

30. Chenoy R, Hussain S, Tayob Y, O'Brien PM, Moss MY, Morse PF. Effect of oral gamolenic acid from evening primrose oil on menopausal flushing. BMJ 1994; 308:501–503 (Level I)

31. Fugh-Berman A. Herb-drug interactions. Lancet 2000; 355:134–138 [erratum Lancet 2000;355:1020] (Level III)

32. Tyler VE. The honest herbal: a sensible guide to the use of herbs and related remedies. 3rd ed. Binghamton, New York: Pharmaceutical Products Press, 1993 (Level III)

33. Wiklund IK, Mattsson LA, Lindgren R, Limoni C. Effects of a standardized ginseng extract on quality of life and physiological parameters in symptomatic postmenopausal women: a double-blind, placebo-controlled trial. Swedish Alternative Medicine Group. Int J Clin Pharmacol Res 1999;19:89–99 (Level I)

34. Linde K, Ramirez G, Mulrow CD, Pauls A, Weidenhammer W, Melchart D. St. John's wort for depression—an overview and meta-analysis of randomised clinical trials. BMJ 1996;313:253–258 (Meta-analysis)

35. Koupparis LS. Harmless herbs: a cause for concern [letter]? Anaesthesia 2000;55:101–102 (Level III)

36. U.S. Pharmacopeia Botanical monograph series: information for the health care professional and consumer. Rockville, Maryland: US Pharmacopeial Convention, Inc., 1998 (Level III)

37. Garges HP, Varia I, Doraiswany PM. Cardiac complications and delirium associated with valerian root withdrawal [letter]. JAMA 1998;280:1566–1567 (Level III)

38. Schellenberg R. Treatment for the premenstrual syndrome with agnus castus fruit extract: prospective, randomised, placebo controlled study. BMJ 2001;322:134–137 (Level I)

39. Gorski T. Wild yam cream threatens women's health. Nutr Forum 1997;14:23–24 (Level III)

40. Knekt P, Jarvinen R, Reunanen A, Maatela J. Flavonoid intake and coronary mortality in Finland: a cohort study. BMJ 1996;312:478–481 (Level II-3)

41. Rimm EB, Katan MB, Ascherio A, Stampfer MJ, Willett WC. Relation between intake of flavonoids and risk for coronary heart disease in male health professionals. Ann Intern Med 1996;125:384–389 (Level II-3)

42. Anderson JW, Johnstone BM, Cook-Newell ME. Meta-analysis of the effects of soy protein intake on serum lipids. N Engl J Med 1995;333:276–282 (Meta-analysis)

43. Nestel PJ, Pomeroy S, Kay S, Komesaroff, Behrsing J, Cameron JD, et al. Isoflavones from red clover improve systemic arterial compliance but not plasma lipids in menopausal women. J Clin Endocrinol Metab 1999;84: 895–898 [erratum J Clin Endocrinol Metab 1999;84:3647] (Level II-3)

44. Valente M, Bufalino L, Castiglione GN, D'Angelo R, Mancuso A, Galoppi P, et al. Effects of 1-year treatment with ipriflavone on bone in postmenopausal women with low bone mass. Calcif Tissue Int 1994;54:377–380 (Level I)

45. Gambacciani M, Ciaponi M, Cappagli B, Piaggesi L, Genazzani AR. Effects of combined low dose of the isoflavone derivative ipriflavone and estrogen replacement on bone mineral density and metabolism in postmenopausal women. Maturitas 1997;28:75–81 (Level I)

46. Alexandersen P, Toussaint A, Christiansen C, Devogelaer JP, Roux C, Fechtenbaum J, et al. Ipriflavone in the treatment of postmenopausal osteoporosis: a randomized controlled trial. JAMA 2001;285:1482–1488 (Level I)

47. Gambacciani M, Spinetti A, Cappagli B, Taponeco F, Felipetto R, Parrini D, et al. Effects of ipriflavone administration on bone mass and metabolism in ovariectomized women. J Endocrinol Invest 1993;16:333–337 (Level I)

48. Gambacciani M, Spinetti A, Piaggesi L, Cappagli B, Taponeco F, Manetti P, et al. Ipriflavone prevents the bone mass reduction in premenopausal women treated with gonadotropin hormone-releasing hormone agonists. Bone Miner 1994;26:19–26 (Level I)

Web Resources

The National Library of Medicine
(http://www.nlm.nih.gov/)

The National Center for Complementary and Alternative Medicine (http://nccam.nih.gov)

The NIH Office of Dietary Supplements
(http://dietary-supplements.info.nih.gov)

The Richard and Hinda Rosenthal Center for Complementary & Alternative Medicine (http://cpmcnet.columbia.edu/dept/rosenthal/)

The American Botanical Council
(http://www.herbalgram.org)

Health World Online (http://www.healthy.net)

Quackwatch (http://www.quackwatch.com)

ConsumerLab (http://www.consumerlab.com)

The MEDLINE database, the Cochrane Library, and ACOG's own internal resources and documents were used to conduct a literature search to locate relevant articles published between January 1985 and January 2001. Priority was given to articles reporting results of original research, although review articles and commentaries also were consulted. Abstracts of research presented at symposia and scientific conferences were not considered adequate for inclusion in this document. Guidelines published by organizations or institutions such as the National Institutes of Health and the American College of Obstetricians and Gynecologists were reviewed, and additional studies were located by reviewing bibliographies of identified articles. When reliable research was not available, expert opinions from obstetrician–gynecologists were used.

Studies were reviewed and evaluated for quality according to the method outlined by the U.S. Preventive Services Task Force:

I   Evidence obtained from at least one properly designed randomized controlled trial.

II-1 Evidence obtained from well-designed controlled trials without randomization.

II-2 Evidence obtained from well-designed cohort or case–control analytic studies, preferably from more than one center or research group.

II-3 Evidence obtained from multiple time series with or without the intervention. Dramatic results in uncontrolled experiments could also be regarded as this type of evidence.

III   Opinions of respected authorities, based on clinical experience, descriptive studies, or reports of expert committees.

Based on the highest level of evidence found in the data, recommendations are provided and graded according to the following categories:

Level A—Recommendations are based on good and consistent scientific evidence.

Level B—Recommendations are based on limited or inconsistent scientific evidence.

Level C—Recommendations are based primarily on consensus and expert opinion.

ISSN 1099-3630

**The American College of
Obstetricians and Gynecologists
409 12th Street, SW
PO Box 96920
Washington, DC 20090-6920**

12345/54321

ACOG PRACTICE BULLETIN

CLINICAL MANAGEMENT GUIDELINES FOR
OBSTETRICIAN–GYNECOLOGISTS

NUMBER 5, JULY 1999

(Replaces Practice Bulletin Number 2, October 1998)

This Practice Bulletin was developed by the ACOG Committee on Practice Bulletins— Obstetrics with the assistance of James R. Scott, MD. The information is designed to aid practitioners in making decisions about appropriate obstetric and gynecologic care. These guidelines should not be construed as dictating an exclusive course of treatment or procedure. Variations in practice may be warranted based on the needs of the individual patient, resources, and limitations unique to the institution or type of practice.

Vaginal Birth After Previous Cesarean Delivery

A trial of labor after previous cesarean delivery has been accepted as a way to lower the overall cesarean delivery rate. In 1995, 27.5% of women who had a previous cesarean delivery attempted vaginal birth; some clinicians believe that an even higher percentage is possible (1). Although there is a strong consensus that trial of labor is appropriate for most women who have had a previous low-transverse cesarean delivery, increased experience with vaginal birth after cesarean delivery (VBAC) indicates there are several potential problems. This document will review the current risks and benefits of VBAC in various situations and provide practical management guidelines.

Background

Beginning in the 1970s, the marked reduction in the maternal death rate focused obstetricians' attention on fetal morbidity and mortality. Physicians in the United States, facing increased medical–legal pressures, performed fewer vaginal breech deliveries and fewer midpelvic forceps deliveries. In addition, non-reassuring fetal status was diagnosed more frequently because of wide variations in the interpretation of continuous electronic fetal monitoring. Finally, dystocia, as an indication for cesarean delivery, was diagnosed more frequently. Consequently, the cesarean delivery rate in the United States increased from 5% to 20.8% between 1970 and 1995 (1) and reached 24.7% in 1988 (2, 3).

With few exceptions, major improvements in newborn outcome from the increased cesarean delivery rate are yet to be proven (4). It generally is agreed that the current rate is high. The overall number of cesarean deliveries can be reduced safely and effectively when the indications for primary cesarean birth are reviewed and audited (5–7). However, most efforts have focused on decreasing the number of elective repeat cesarean births because they account for one third of all cesarean deliveries.

Changing Concepts

The dictum "once a cesarean, always a cesarean" dominated obstetric practice in the United States for nearly 70 years (8). This concept began changing gradually about 30 years ago as improvements in obstetric care made trial of labor safer for both mother and infant. In 1981, when the VBAC rate was only 3%, the National Institutes of Health began to encourage trial of labor. The American College of Obstetricians and Gynecologists also was a leader in this effort (9), and a number of reports have documented the relative safety of trial of labor (10–14). Some third-party payers and managed care organizations have mandated that all women who had previous cesarean deliveries must undergo trial of labor. Consequently, physicians may find themselves pressured to attempt trial of labor either in situations that they consider to be unsuitable or with patients who do not desire the procedure.

Recent Issues

Despite more than 800 citations in the literature, there are no randomized trials to prove that maternal and neonatal outcomes are better with VBAC than with repeat cesarean delivery. Published evidence suggests that the benefits of VBAC outweigh the risks in most women with a prior low-transverse cesarean delivery. Nevertheless, most studies of VBAC have been conducted in university or tertiary-level centers with in-house staff coverage and anesthesia. The safety of trial of labor is less well documented in smaller community hospitals or facilities where resources may be more limited (15–18). It has become apparent that VBAC is associated with a small but significant risk of uterine rupture with poor outcome for both mother and infant (19–22). Reports indicate that maternal and infant complications also are associated with an unsuccessful trial of labor. Increasingly, these adverse events during trial of labor have led to malpractice suits (22–24). These developments, which have led to a more circumspect approach to trial of labor by even the most ardent supporters of VBAC, illustrate the need to reevaluate VBAC recommendations (23, 25).

Clinical Considerations and Recommendations

▶ *Who are candidates for a trial of labor?*

Most patients who have had a low-transverse uterine incision from a previous cesarean delivery and who have no contraindications for vaginal birth are candidates for a trial of labor. Women who have had two previous low-transverse cesarean deliveries also may be considered for

a trial of labor, but the risk of uterine rupture increases with the number of previous uterine incisions (13). Following are selection criteria useful in identifying candidates for VBAC:

- One or two prior low-transverse cesarean deliveries
- Clinically adequate pelvis
- No other uterine scars or previous rupture
- Physician immediately available throughout active labor capable of monitoring labor and performing an emergency cesarean delivery
- Availability of anesthesia and personnel for emergency cesarean delivery

There has been a tendency to expand the list of obstetric circumstances under which VBAC may be appropriate. These include multiple previous cesarean deliveries (26, 27), unknown uterine scar (13, 28), breech presentation (29, 30), twin gestation (31, 32), postterm pregnancy (33), and suspected macrosomia (34, 35). Whether trial of labor should be encouraged for patients with these obstetric circumstances and a low-vertical uterine incision is controversial (18, 36, 37). Although success has been reported in some series, continuing analysis of the risk of adverse outcome is necessary before VBAC is routinely adopted in these circumstances.

▶ *What is the success rate for trials of labor?*

Most published series indicate that approximately 60–80% of trials of labor after a previous cesarean delivery result in successful vaginal births (14, 38, 39). However, these success rates often apply to a selected population. Patients thought to be inappropriate candidates for a trial of labor usually have been excluded, and the exact percentage of women undergoing trial of labor is not consistently stated.

Although a number of scoring systems have been used, there is no completely reliable way to predict whether a trial of labor will be successful in an individual patient (40–44). The success rates of VBAC in women whose first cesarean delivery was performed for a nonrecurring indication are similar to those of patients who have not undergone previous cesarean delivery (45). A woman who has undergone vaginal delivery at least once before or after her previous cesarean birth also is more likely to have a successful trial of labor than the woman who has not undergone vaginal delivery (45, 46).

Many patients with a previous diagnosis of dystocia successfully deliver vaginally, but the percentage is consistently lower (50–70%) than for those with nonrecurring indications (12, 14, 47, 48). The lower rate is most likely related to the accuracy of the original diagnosis of dystocia.

▶ *What are the risks and benefits associated with VBAC?*

Neither repeat cesarean delivery nor trial of labor is risk free. When VBAC is successful, it is associated with less morbidity than repeat cesarean delivery. The advantages include fewer blood transfusions, fewer postpartum infections, and shorter hospital stays, usually with no increased perinatal morbidity (11, 12, 14).

It often is stated that the cost of VBAC is less than that of repeat cesarean delivery. However, for a true analysis of all the costs one has to include the costs to the hospital, the method of reimbursement (ie, per diem diagnosis-related group or capitation), and medical malpractice payments. Higher costs may be incurred by a hospital if a woman has a prolonged labor or has significant complications, or if the newborn is admitted to a neonatal intensive care unit. Furthermore, 20–40% of women will fail the trial of labor, which will incur surgical costs. Increased time or attendance for a woman undergoing a trial of labor results in increased cost to the physician. The difficulty in assessing the cost-benefit of VBAC is that the costs are not all incurred by one entity.

Those patients who fail a trial of labor are at increased risk for infection and morbidity (49–52). Infants born by repeat cesarean delivery after a failed trial of labor also have increased rates of infection (53). In contrast to previous reports, the most recent series showed that major maternal complications such as uterine rupture, hysterectomy, and operative injury were more likely for women who underwent a trial of labor than for those who elected repeat cesarean delivery (50).

Rupture of the uterine scar can be life-threatening for both mother and infant (19–22). When catastrophic uterine rupture occurs, some patients will require hysterectomy and some infants will die or will be neurologically impaired (22, 50). In most cases, the cause of uterine rupture in a patient who has undergone VBAC is unknown, but poor outcomes can result even in appropriate candidates.

The occurrence of uterine rupture is dependent on the type and location of the previous incision. Estimated occurrence based on the literature is as follows (18, 39):

• Classical uterine scar (4–9%)

• T-shaped incision (4–9%)

• Low-vertical incision (1–7%)

• Low-transverse incision (0.2–1.5%)

The most common sign of uterine rupture is a non-reassuring fetal heart rate pattern with variable decelerations that may evolve into late decelerations, bradycardia, and undetectable fetal heart rate. Other findings are more variable and include uterine or abdominal pain, loss of station of the presenting part, vaginal bleeding, and hypovolemia.

▶ *What are contraindications for VBAC?*

A trial of labor is not recommended in patients at high risk for uterine rupture. Circumstances under which a trial of labor should not be attempted are as follows:

• Prior classical or T-shaped incision or other transfundal uterine surgery (54)

• Contracted pelvis (18)

• Medical or obstetric complication that precludes vaginal delivery

• Inability to perform emergency cesarean delivery because of unavailable surgeon, anesthesia, sufficient staff, or facility

A combination of factors, which singly may not be compelling for cesarean delivery in a patient without a uterine scar, may influence the decision to forego VBAC and recommend repeat cesarean delivery.

▶ *How should patients be counseled?*

The enthusiasm for VBAC varies greatly among patients and physicians. It is reasonable for women to undergo a trial of labor in a safe setting, but the potential complications should be discussed thoroughly and documented (55). If the type of previous incision is in doubt, attempts should be made to obtain medical records. After thorough counseling that weighs the individual benefits and risks of VBAC, the ultimate decision to attempt this procedure or undergo a repeat cesarean delivery should be made by the patient and her physician (see Fig. 1). Global mandates for a trial of labor after a previous cesarean delivery are inappropriate because individual risk factors are not considered. It should be recognized that there are repeat elective cesarean deliveries that are clinically indicated (56). The informed consent process and the plan of management should be documented in the prenatal record.

▶ *How does management of labor differ for patients undergoing VBAC?*

Despite extensive data on VBAC, there is relatively little information on how labor should be conducted. Management of labor varies in different situations.

External Cephalic Version. Limited data suggest that external cephalic version for breech presentation may be as successful for VBAC candidates as for women who have not undergone previous cesarean delivery (57).

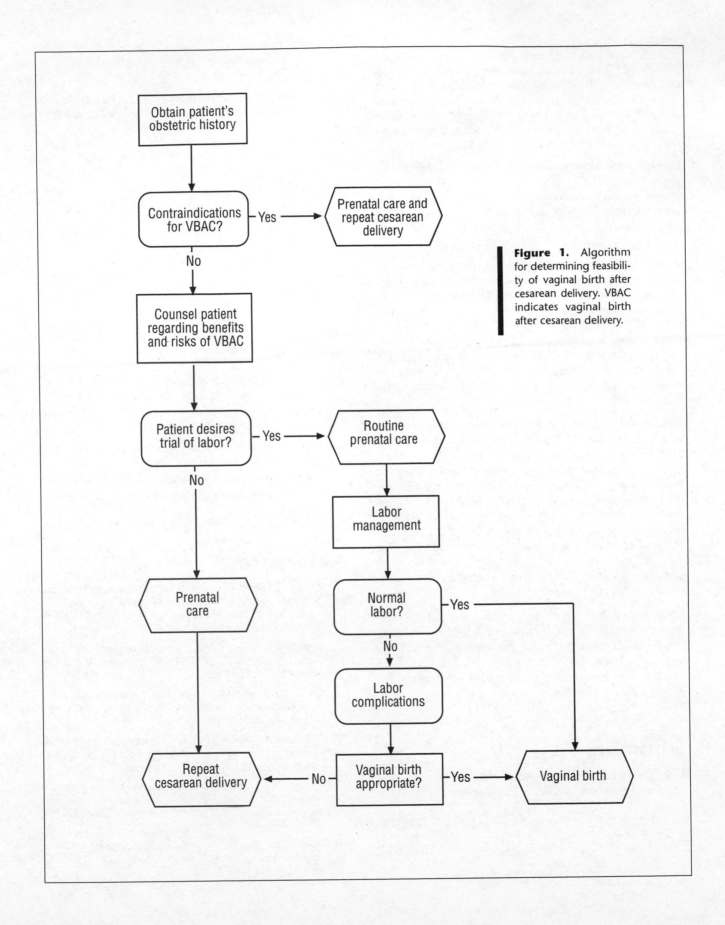

Figure 1. Algorithm for determining feasibility of vaginal birth after cesarean delivery. VBAC indicates vaginal birth after cesarean delivery.

Analgesia. Vaginal birth after cesarean delivery is not a contraindication to epidural anesthesia, and adequate pain relief may encourage more women to choose a trial of labor (58, 59). Success rates for VBAC are similar in women who do and those who do not receive epidural analgesia, as well as in those women who receive other types of pain relief (60–62). Epidural analgesia rarely masks the signs and symptoms of uterine rupture.

Intrapartum Management. Once labor has begun, the patient should be evaluated promptly. Most authorities recommend continuous electronic monitoring. Personnel who are familiar with the potential complications of VBAC should be present to watch for nonreassuring fetal heart rate patterns and inadequate progress in labor.

Induction. Induction or augmentation with oxytocin has been suspected as a factor responsible for uterine rupture. A meta-analysis found no relationship between the use of oxytocin and rupture of the uterine scar (14). However, other studies indicate that high infusion rates of oxytocin place women at greater risk (63, 64). Although there are studies that suggest that prostaglandin gel applied to the cervix or vagina appears to be safe (65–67), there are occasional reports of uterine rupture with prostaglandin preparations (68, 69).

Delivery. There is nothing unique about delivery of the infant after a trial of labor. The need to explore the uterus after successful vaginal delivery is controversial. Most asymptomatic scar dehiscences heal well, and there are no data to suggest that future pregnancy outcome is better if the dehiscence is surgically repaired. Excessive vaginal bleeding or signs of hypovolemia at delivery require prompt and complete assessment of the previous scar and the entire genital tract.

▶ *How should future pregnancies be managed after uterine rupture?*

If the site of the ruptured scar is confined to the lower segment, the rate of repeat rupture or dehiscence in labor is 6% (70). If the scar includes the upper segment of the uterus, the repeat rupture rate is 32% (70, 71). Therefore, women who have had a prior uterine rupture should undergo repeat cesarean delivery as soon as the fetus is mature.

Summary

The following recommendations are based on good and consistent scientific evidence (Level A):

▶ Most women with one previous cesarean delivery with a low-transverse incision are candidates for VBAC and should be counseled about VBAC and offered a trial of labor.

▶ Epidural anesthesia may be used for VBAC.

▶ A previous uterine incision extending into the fundus is a contraindication for VBAC.

The following recommendations are based on limited or inconsistent scientific evidence (Level B):

▶ Women with two previous low-transverse cesarean deliveries and no contraindications who wish to attempt VBAC may be allowed a trial of labor. They should be advised that the risk of uterine rupture increases as the number of cesarean deliveries increases.

▶ Use of oxytocin or prostaglandin gel for VBAC requires close patient monitoring.

▶ Women with a vertical incision within the lower uterine segment that does not extend into the fundus are candidates for VBAC.

The following recommendations are based primarily on consensus and expert opinion (Level C):

▶ Because uterine rupture may be catastrophic, VBAC should be attempted in institutions equipped to respond to emergencies with physicians immediately available to provide emergency care.

▶ After thorough counseling that weighs the individual benefits and risks of VBAC, the ultimate decision to attempt this procedure or undergo a repeat cesarean delivery should be made by the patient and her physician.

References

1. Curtin SC. Rates of cesarean birth and vaginal birth after previous cesarean, 1991–95. Monthly vital statistics report; vol 45, no. 11 (suppl 3). Hyattsville, Maryland: National Center for Health Statistics, 1997 (Level II-3)

2. Centers for Disease Control. Rates of cesarean delivery— United States, 1991. MMWR Morb Mortal Wkly Rep 1993;42:285–289 (Level II-3)

3. Stafford RS. Alternative strategies for controlling rising cesarean section rates. JAMA 1990; 263:683–687 (Level III)

4. Scheller JM, Nelson KB. Does cesarean delivery prevent cerebral palsy or other neurologic problems of childhood? Obstet Gynecol 1994;83:624–630 (Level III)

5. Lagrew DC Jr, Morgan MA. Decreasing the cesarean section rate in a private hospital: success without mandated clinical changes. Am J Obstet Gynecol 1996;174:184–191 (Level II-3)

6. Myers SA, Gleicher N. A successful program to lower cesarean-section rates. N Engl J Med 1988;319:1511–1516 (Level II-3)

7. Robson MS, Scudamore IW, Walsh SM. Using the medical audit cycle to reduce cesarean section rates. Am J Obstet Gynecol 1996;174:199–205 (Level II-2)

8. Cragin EB. Conservatism in obstetrics. N Y Med J 1916; 104:1–3 (Level III)

9. American College of Obstetricians and Gynecologists. Vaginal delivery after previous cesarean birth. ACOG Practice Patterns 1. Washington, DC: ACOG, 1995 (Level III)

10. Cowan RK, Kinch RA, Ellis B, Anderson R. Trial of labor following cesarean delivery. Obstet Gynecol 1994;83:933–936 (Level II-3)

11. Flamm BL, Newman LA, Thomas SJ, Fallon D, Yoshida MM. Vaginal birth after cesarean delivery: results of a 5-year multicenter collaborative study. Obstet Gynecol 1990;76:750–754 (Level II-3)

12. Flamm BL, Goings JR, Liu Y, Wolde-Tsadik G. Elective repeat cesarean delivery versus trial of labor: a prospective multicenter study. Obstet Gynecol 1994;83:927–932 (Level II-2)

13. Miller DA, Diaz FG, Paul RH. Vaginal birth after cesarean: a 10-year experience. Obstet Gynecol 1994;84:255–258 (Level III)

14. Rosen MG, Dickinson JC, Westhoff CL. Vaginal birth after cesarean: a meta-analysis of morbidity and mortality. Obstet Gynecol 1991;77:465–470 (Meta-analysis)

15. Hawkins JL, Gibbs CP, Orleans M, Martin-Salvaj G, Beaty B. Obstetric anesthesia work force survey, 1981 versus 1992. Anesthesiology 1997;87:135–143 (Level II-3)

16. Holland JG, Dupre AR, Blake PG, Martin RW, Martin JN Jr. Trial of labor after cesarean delivery: experience in the non-university level II regional hospital setting. Obstet Gynecol 1992;79:936–939 (Level II-3)

17. Raynor BD. The experience with vaginal birth after cesarean delivery in a small rural community practice. Am J Obstet Gynecol 1993;168:60–62 (Level III)

18. Scott JR. Avoiding labor problems during vaginal birth after cesarean delivery. Clin Obstet Gynecol 1997;40:533–541 (Level III)

19. Farmer RM, Kirschbaum T, Potter D, Strong TH, Medearis AL. Uterine rupture during trial of labor after previous cesarean section. Am J Obstet Gynecol 1991;165:996–1001 (Level II-2)

20. Jones RO, Nagashima AW, Hartnett-Goodman MM, Goodlin RC. Rupture of low transverse cesarean scars during trial of labor. Obstet Gynecol 1991;77:815–817 (Level III)

21. Leung AS, Farmer RM, Leung EK, Medearis AL, Paul RH. Risk factors associated with uterine rupture during trial of labor after cesarean delivery: a case-control study. Am J Obstet Gynecol 1993;168:1358–1363 (Level II-2)

22. Scott JR. Mandatory trial of labor after cesarean delivery: an alternative viewpoint. Obstet Gynecol 1991;77:811–814 (Level III)

23. Phelan JP. VBAC: time to reconsider? OBG Manage 1996:62–68 (Level III)

24. Stalnaker BL, Maher JE, Kleinman GE, Macksey JM, Fishman LA, Bernard JM. Characteristics of successful claims for payment by the Florida Neurologic Injury Compensation Association Fund. Am J Obstet Gynecol 1997;177:268–271 (Level III)

25. Flamm BL. Once a cesarean, always a controversy. Obstet Gynecol 1997;90:312–315 (Level III)

26. Granovsky-Grisaru S, Shaya M, Diamant YZ. The management of labor in women with more than one uterine scar: is a repeat cesarean section really the only "safe" option? J Perinat Med 1994;22:13–17 (Level II-2)

27. Pruett KM, Kirshon B, Cotton DB, Poindexter AN 3rd. Is vaginal birth after two or more cesarean sections safe? Obstet Gynecol 1988;72:163–165 (Level III)

28. Beall M, Eglinton GS, Clark SL, Phelan JP. Vaginal delivery after cesarean section in women with unknown types of uterine scar. J Reprod Med 1984;29:31–35 (Level II-2)

29. Ophir E, Oettinger M, Yagoda A, Markovits Y, Rojansky N, Shapiro H. Breech presentation after cesarean section: always a section? Am J Obstet Gynecol 1989;161:25–28 (Level III)

30. Sarno AP Jr, Phelan JP, Ahn MO, Strong TH Jr. Vaginal birth after cesarean delivery. Trial of labor in women with breech presentation. J Reprod Med 1989;34:831–833 (Level III)

31. Miller DA, Mullin P, Hou D, Paul RH. Vaginal birth after cesarean section in twin gestation. Am J Obstet Gynecol 1996;175:194–198 (Level II-2)

32. Strong TH Jr, Phelan JP, Ahn MO, Sarno AP Jr. Vaginal birth after cesarean delivery in the twin gestation. Am J Obstet Gynecol 1989;161:29–32 (Level III)

33. Yeh S, Huang X, Phelan JP. Postterm pregnancy after previous cesarean section. J Reprod Med 1984;29:41–44 (Level II-2)

34. Flamm BL, Goings JR. Vaginal birth after cesarean section: is suspected fetal macrosomia a contraindication? Obstet Gynecol 1989;74:694–697 (Level II-2)

35. Phelan JP, Eglinton GS, Horenstein JM, Clark SL, Yeh S. Previous cesarean birth. Trial of labor in women with macrosomic infants. J Reprod Med 1984;29:36–40 (Level II-2)

36. Martin JN Jr, Perry KG Jr, Roberts WE, Meydrech EF. The case for trial of labor in the patient with a prior low-segment vertical cesarean incision. Am J Obstet Gynecol 1997;177:144–148 (Level III)

37. Naef RW 3rd, Ray MA, Chauhan SP, Roach H, Blake PG, Martin JN Jr. Trial of labor after cesarean delivery with a lower-segment, vertical uterine incision: is it safe? Am J Obstet Gynecol 1995;172:1666–1673; discussion 1673–1674 (Level II-2)

38. Flamm BL. Vaginal birth after cesarean section. In: Flamm BL, Quilligan EJ, eds. Cesarean section: guidelines for appropriate utilization. New York: Springer-Verlag, 1995:51–64 (Level III)

39. Pridjian G. Labor after prior cesarean section. Clin Obstet Gynecol 1992;35:445–456 (Level III)

40. Abitbol MM, Taylor UB, Castillo I, Rochelson BL. The cephalopelvic disproportion index. Combined fetal sonography and x-ray pelvimetry for early detection of cephalopelvic disproportion. J Reprod Med 1991;36:369–373 (Level II-3)

41. Krishnamurthy S, Fairlie F, Cameron AD, Walker JJ, Mackenzie JR. The role of postnatal x-ray pelvimetry after caesarean section in the management of subsequent delivery. Br J Obstet Gynaecol 1991;98:716–718 (Level III)

42. Pickhardt MG, Martin JN Jr, Meydrech EF, Blake PG, Martin RW, Perry KG Jr, et al. Vaginal birth after cesarean delivery: are there useful and valid predictors of success or failure? Am J Obstet Gynecol 1992;166:1811–1815; discussion 1815–1819 (Level II-3)

43. Thurnau GR, Scates DH, Morgan MA. The fetal–pelvic index: a method of identifying fetal–pelvic disproportion in women attempting vaginal birth after previous cesarean delivery. Am J Obstet Gynecol 1991;165:353–358 (Level II-2)

44. Troyer LR, Parisi VM. Obstetric parameters affecting success in a trial of labor: designation of a scoring system. Am J Obstet Gynecol 1992;167:1099–1104 (Level II-3)

45. Bedoya C, Bartha JL, Rodriguez I, Fontan I, Bedoya JM, Sanchez-Ramos J. A trial of labor after cesarean section in patients with or without a prior vaginal delivery. Int J Gynecol Obstet 1992;39:285–289 (Level II-2)

46. Eglinton GS. Effect of previous indications for cesarean on subsequent outcome. In: Phelan JP, Clark SL, eds. Cesarean delivery. New York: Elsevier, 1988:476–483 (Level III)

47. Demianczuk NN, Hunter DJ, Taylor DW. Trial of labor after previous cesarean section: prognostic indicators of outcome. Am J Obstet Gynecol 1982;142:640–642 (Level II-3)

48. Hoskins IA, Gomez JL. Correlation between maximum cervical dilatation at cesarean delivery and subsequent vaginal birth after cesarean delivery. Obstet Gynecol 1997;89:591–593 (Level II-2)

49. Hadley CB, Mennuti MT, Gabbe SG. An evaluation of the relative risks of a trial of labor versus elective repeat cesarean section. Am J Perinatol 1986;3:107–114 (Level II-2)

50. McMahon MJ, Luther ER, Bowes WA Jr, Olshan AF. Comparison of a trial of labor with an elective second cesarean section. N Engl J Med 1996;335:689–695 (Level II-2)

51. Mootabar H, Dwyer JF, Surur F, Dillon TF. Vaginal delivery following previous cesarean section in 1983. Int J Gynaecol Obstet 1984;22:155–160 (Level II-2)

52. Yetman TJ, Nolan TE. Vaginal birth after cesarean section: a reappraisal of risk. Am J Obstet Gynecol 1989;161:1119–1123 (Level II-3)

53. Hook B, Kiwi R, Amini SB, Fanaroff A, Hack M. Neonatal morbidity after elective repeat cesarean section and trial of labor. Pediatrics 1997;100:348–353 (Level II-2)

54. Pelosi MA 3rd, Pelosi MA. Spontaneous uterine rupture at thirty-three weeks subsequent to previous superficial laparo-scopic myomectomy. Am J Obstet Gynecol 1997;177:1547–1549 (Level III)

55. American College of Obstetricians and Gynecologists. Informed consent. ACOG Assistant 4. Washington, DC: ACOG, 1998 (Level III)

56. Gregory KD, Henry OA, Gellens AJ, Hobel CJ, Platt LD. Repeat cesareans: how many are elective? Obstet Gynecol 1994;84:574–578 (Level II-3)

57. Flamm BL, Fried MW, Lonky NM, Giles WS. External cephalic version after previous cesarean section. Am J Obstet Gynecol 1991;165:370–372 (Level II-2)

58. Johnson C, Oriol N. The role of epidural anesthesia in trial of labor. Reg Anesth 1990;15:304–308 (Level III)

59. Sakala EP, Kaye S, Murray RD, Munson LJ. Epidural analgesia. Effect on the likelihood of a successful trial of labor after cesarean section. J Reprod Med 1990;35:886–890 (Level II-2)

60. Flamm BL, Lim OW, Jones C, Fallon D, Newman LA, Mantis JK. Vaginal birth after cesarean section: results of a multicenter study. Am J Obstet Gynecol 1988;158:1079–1084 (Level II-2)

61. Meehan FP, Burke G, Kehoe JT. Update on delivery following prior cesarean section: a 15-year review 1972– 1987. Int J Gynaecol Obstet 1989;30:205–212 (Level III)

62. Stovall TG, Shaver DC, Solomon SK, Anderson GD. Trial of labor in previous cesarean section patients, excluding classical cesarean sections. Obstet Gynecol 1987;70:713–717 (Level II-3)

63. Grubb DK, Kjos SL, Paul RH. Latent labor with an unknown uterine scar. Obstet Gynecol 1996;88:351–355 (Level I)

64. Johnson C, Oriol N, Flood K. Trial of labor: a study of 110 patients. J Clin Anesth 1991;3:216–218 (Level III)

65. Stone JL, Lockwood CJ, Berkowitz G, Alvarez M, Lapinski R, Valcamonico A, et al. Use of cervical prostaglandin E_2 gel in patients with previous cesarean section. Am J Perinatol 1994;11:309–312 (Level II-2)

66. Blanco JD, Collins M, Willis D, Prien S. Prostaglandin E_2 gel induction of patients with a prior low transverse cesarean section. Am J Perinatol 1992;9:80–83 (Level II-2)

67. Norman M, Ekman G. Preinductive cervical ripening with prostaglandin E_2 in women with one previous cesarean section. Acta Obstet Gynecol Scand 1992;71:351–355 (Level II-2)

68. Bennett BB. Uterine rupture during induction of labor at term with intravaginal misoprostol. Obstet Gynecol 1997;89:832–833 (Level III)

69. Wing DA, Lovett K, Paul RH. Disruption of uterine incision following misoprostol for labor induction in women with previous cesarean delivery. Obstet Gynecol 1998;91:828–830 (Level III)

70. Ritchie EH. Pregnancy after rupture of the pregnant uterus. A report of 36 pregnancies and a study of cases reported since 1932. J Obstet Gynaecol Br Commonw 1971;78:642–648 (Level III)

71. Reyes-Ceja L, Cabrera R, Insfran E, Herrera-Lasso F. Pregnancy following previous uterine rupture. Study of 19 patients. Obstet Gynecol 1969;34:387–389 (Level III)

The MEDLINE database, the Cochrane Library, and ACOG's own internal resources and documents were used to conduct a literature search to locate relevant articles published between January 1985 and March 1998. The search was restricted to articles published in the English language. Priority was given to articles reporting results of original research, although review articles and commentaries also were consulted. Abstracts of research presented at symposiums and scientific conferences were not considered adequate for inclusion in this document. Guidelines published by organizations or institutions such as the National Institutes of Health and ACOG were reviewed, and additional studies were located by reviewing bibliographies of identified articles. When reliable research was not available, expert opinions from obstetrician–gynecologists were used.

Studies were reviewed and evaluated for quality according to the method outlined by the U.S. Preventive Services Task Force:

I   Evidence obtained from at least one properly designed randomized controlled trial.

II-1   Evidence obtained from well-designed controlled trials without randomization.

II-2   Evidence obtained from well-designed cohort or case–control analytic studies, preferably from more than one center or research group.

II-3   Evidence obtained from multiple time series with or without the intervention. Dramatic results in uncontrolled experiments also could be regarded as this type of evidence.

III   Opinions of respected authorities, based on clinical experience, descriptive studies, or reports of expert committees.

Based on the highest level of evidence found in the data, the recommendations are graded according to the following categories:

Level A—The recommendation is based on good and consistent scientific evidence.

Level B—The recommendation is based on limited or inconsistent scientific evidence.

Level C—The recommendation is based primarily on consensus and expert opinion.

ISSN 1099-3630

**The American College of
Obstetricians and Gynecologists
409 12th Street, SW
PO Box 96920
Washington, DC 20090-6920**

12345/32109

Practice Patterns

Practice Patterns

Number 6, October 1997

ACOG Practice Patterns

Evidence-Based Guidelines for Clinical Issues in Obstetrics and Gynecology

Management of Postterm Pregnancy

Purpose

Postterm pregnancy is one of the more common high-risk problems confronting many obstetricians. In the 1950s, attention in the United States became focused on prolonged pregnancy when it was recognized that some postterm infants exhibited dysmaturity that led to significant morbidity and mortality (1).

Postterm pregnancy, by definition, is a gestation of 42 weeks or more (294 days or more from the first day of the last menstrual period). The reported frequency is 3–12%. About 80% of all pregnancies last 38–42 weeks, 10% are delivered preterm, and the remaining 10% extend beyond the start of the 43rd week and are considered postterm. Although many apparent cases of postterm pregnancy are the result of an inability to define the date of conception, some cases clearly progress to excessively long gestations. Accurate assessment of gestational age and diagnosis of postterm gestation, as well as recognition and management of risk factors, can reduce the risk of adverse sequelae in most of these cases.

Antenatal surveillance and induction of labor are two widely used strategies that theoretically diminish fetal risk of an adverse outcome. The purpose of this document is to examine the evidence and make recommendations about these two management strategies.

Objectives

These practice guidelines will enable physicians to

- Determine whether there is an optimal time to begin antenatal surveillance in postterm pregnancies
- Determine which strategy—induction or surveillance—is appropriate for patients experiencing postterm pregnancies
- Determine whether prostaglandin gel can be used for induction of labor in patients with postterm pregnancy

Methods

The MEDLINE database was used to conduct a literature search to locate relevant articles published between 1985 and 1995 specifically comparing expectant monitoring to induction of labor in postterm pregnancies. The search was restricted to articles published in the English language. Articles reporting results of original research were given priority, although review articles, meta-analyses, and commentaries were also consulted. Abstracts of research presented at symposia and scientific conferences were not considered adequate for inclusion in this document.

Studies were reviewed and evaluated for quality according to the method outlined by the U.S. Preventive Services Task Force:

I Evidence obtained from at least one properly designed randomized controlled trial

II-1 Evidence obtained from well-designed controlled trials without randomization

II-2 Evidence obtained from well-designed cohort or case-control analytic studies, preferably from more than one center or research group

II-3 Evidence obtained from multiple time series with or without the intervention. Dramatic results in uncontrolled experiments could also be regarded as this type of evidence.

III Opinions of respected authorities, based on clinical expertise, descriptive studies, or reports of expert committees

Background

Etiologic Factors

The most frequent cause of apparently prolonged gestation is error in determining the time of ovulation and conception according to the time of the last menstrual period (1). Frequently encountered problems are the patient's failure to recall accurately the last menstrual dates and the variable length of the proliferative phase of the cycle, which allows the ovulation date to vary by days to weeks. When postterm pregnancy actually exists, the cause is usually unknown. In rare instances, postterm pregnancy is associated with fetal conditions such as anencephaly and placental sulfatase deficiency.

Assessment of Gestational Age

The accurate determination of the time of conception is extremely important in reducing the false diagnosis of postterm pregnancy and in ascertaining precisely the point at which the pregnancy becomes high risk. The estimated date of delivery (EDD) is most reliably and accurately determined early in pregnancy. Consistency between historical and physical data is important in establishing the reliability of dating. Regularity and length of menstrual cycles and the first day of the last spontaneous menses should be recorded. An EDD can be calculated by subtracting 3 months from the first day of the last menses and adding 7 days (Naegele's rule). Other clinical data should be consistent with the EDD:

• The mother usually feels the fetus move (quickening) at about 16–20 weeks.
• The fetal heart can be heard with a nonelectronic fetal stethoscope by 18–20 weeks in most patients.
• The size of the uterus at early examination (in the first trimester) should be consistent with dates.
• At 20 weeks, the fundal height should be about 20 cm above the symphysis pubis, which usually corresponds with the umbilicus.

Inconsistencies or concern about the accuracy of the dating requires further assessment with ultrasonography. Useful measurements include the crown–rump length of the fetus during the first trimester and the biparietal diameter or head circumference and the femur length during the second trimester. Because of the normal variationsin size of infants in the third trimester, dating the pregnancy at that time is unreliable (±3 weeks) (1).

Results

When should antenatal monitoring of a postterm pregnancy begin?

It is generally accepted that all postterm patients receive some form of antenatal monitoring, despite a lack of evidence that it improves the outcome. The literature search failed to locate any studies involving postterm patients who were not monitored. Due to ethical and medicolegal concerns, it is highly unlikely that any subsequent studies will include a no-monitoring group. Conversely, for the same reasons previously stated, there is no evidence that antenatal monitoring adversely affects patients experiencing postterm pregnancies. Therefore, even though evidence of either a positive or negative effect is lacking, antenatal surveillance has become a standard practice on the basis of universal acceptance.

Patients who have passed their EDD but who have not yet completed 42 weeks of gestation constitute another group for whom antenatal surveillance has been proposed. Some studies report a greater complication rate among women giving birth during the latter week of this 2-week period (Level II-2: 2, 3). However, no randomized controlled trial has demonstrated a benefit attributable to earlier testing (Level II-2: 4). Although complications may occur more frequently, there is no evidence that antenatal monitoring, commencing at the completion of 40 weeks of gestation, improves fetal outcome.

In most studies of postterm pregnancies, women are recruited and monitoring begins prior to 42 completed weeks of gestation (Level I: 5–10), further complicating matters. As with postterm patients, there is no demonstrable evidence that any form of antenatal testing is beneficial for patients between 40 and 42 completed weeks; however, monitoring is often performed during this time frame. From a scientific viewpoint, it is unknown whether routine antenatal surveillance of patients between 40 and 42 completed weeks of gestation improves the outcome of delivery.

What form of antenatal surveillance should be performed, and how frequently should a postterm patient be reevaluated?

There is no consistency in the literature regarding either the form or frequency of antenatal surveillance among postterm patients (Level I: 5–14) (Level II-2: 15) (Level II-3: 16). Generally, patients receive some combination of ultrasonography, cervical examination, and nonstress testing, but there are wide variations of practice. Frequency of testing varies; often, individual tests are administered according to different schedules. No recommendation based on published research can be made regarding the indicated form or frequency of antenatal surveillance among postterm patients.

Postterm patient with a favorable cervix: Induction or expectant management?

Among postterm patients who are otherwise at low risk for complications, labor is usually induced if the cervix is favorable. Recent studies of postterm pregnancies comparing outcomes of labor induction with those of expectant management excluded women with favorable cervices (Level I: 5–7, 9, 11, 12) (Level II-3: 16). Often, when women allocated to expectant management experienced a change in cervical status, expectant management ceased and an induction of labor was initiated (Level I: 5, 7, 9, 11, 14). In studies where women with favorable cervices were managed expectantly, there was no indication that expectant management had a deleterious effect on the outcome, but results were not stratified according to the condition of the cervix (Level I: 8, 10, 13) (Level II-2: 15). Thus, for women who are experiencing postterm pregnancies and who have favorable cervices, there is not enough information to determine whether either labor induction or expectant management results in the best outcome. According to current obstetric practice, labor is induced in most of these women.

Postterm patient with an unfavorable cervix: Induction or expectant management?

Among women with otherwise low-risk pregnancies who are postterm and have unfavorable cervices, studies confirm that either expectant management or immediate induction is associated with a very low complication rate and good outcomes (Level I: 5–7, 11, 12). One recent study was stopped because the primary measurements, perinatal mortality and morbidity, were so rare that recruiting enough women to calculate a statistical difference in management strategies was deemed impractical (Level I: 5).

The largest study to date, the Canadian Post-Term Pregnancy Trial, reported a significant increase in the cesarean birth rate for fetal distress among women managed expectantly (Level I: 6). However, the authors could not identify a particular cause related to postterm status. Smaller studies report mixed results regarding cesarean birth rates (increased: Level I: 9, 13) (no statistically significant difference: Level I: 5, 7, 10–12, 14). Two studies reported an increase in cesarean delivery rates only among certain subgroups of patients (Level I: 8) (Level II-2: 15). The evidence is inconsistent regarding how the selection of one strategy over another affects the cesarean birth rate.

What is the role of prostaglandin gel (PGE$_2$) in managing a postterm pregnancy?

Most studies conclude that PGE$_2$ gel is a valuable tool for improving cervical ripeness and inducing labor. A double-blind, placebo-controlled trial reported significant changes in Bishop scores, shorter durations of labor, lower maximum doses of oxytocin, and a reduced incidence of cesarean deliveries among postterm patients who received PGE$_2$ gel (Level I: 17). Another study, using outpatient-administered PGE$_2$ gel, confirmed these findings (Level I: 18). Compared with oxytocin for induction, PGE$_2$ gel has been associated with a lower failure rate and, consequently, a reduced cesarean delivery rate (Level I: 19). In contrast, the National Institute of Child Health and Human Development study reported no reduction in the cesarean delivery rate or the induction-to-delivery interval among postterm patients who were induced with PGE$_2$, although the gel was more effective than placebo in initiating persistent contractions in nulliparous women (Level I: 5).

Many studies used PGE$_2$ gel to induce labor, but there does not appear to be a standardized dose (5, 6, 9, 10, 15, 20). Postapplication monitoring was carried out in all studies to ensure fetal well-being; the medication was well tolerated, with few reported side effects.

Which method is more cost-effective?

A formal cost analysis based on results from the Canadian study concluded that expectant management costs slightly more than routine induction, assuming a slightly higher rate of cesarean delivery and more antenatal testing in the expectant group (Level III: 21). Expectant management cost $193 (in 1992 Canadian dollars) more than routine induction at 41 weeks. In contrast, a study reported higher costs associated with immediate induction, based on longer hospitalizations for patients undergoing inductions compared with patients managed expectantly (Level I: 14).

Summary and Recommendations

Based on the highest level of evidence found in the data, the following recommendations are provided and graded according to the following categories:

A There is good evidence to support the recommendation.

B There is fair evidence to support the recommendation.

C There is insufficient evidence to support the recommendation; however, the recommendation may be made on other grounds.

Evaluation of a Postterm Patient

- Antenatal surveillance of postterm pregnancies should be initiated by 42 weeks of gestation despite a lack of evidence that monitoring improves outcomes (C: III).
- There is insufficient evidence that initiating antenatal surveillance between 40–42 completed weeks of gestation improves outcomes.
- No single antenatal surveillance protocol for monitoring fetal well-being in a postterm pregnancy appears superior to another.

Managing a Postterm Pregnancy

- It is unknown whether induction or expectant management is preferable to manage an otherwise uncomplicated postterm patient with a favorable cervix (A:I).
- There is good evidence that either induction or expectant management will result in good outcomes among postterm patients with unfavorable cervices and without additional complications (A: I).

Prostaglandin Gel

Prostaglandin gel can be used safely in postterm pregnancies to promote cervical changes and induce labor (A: I).

Cost-Effectiveness

There is mixed evidence regarding which strategy is more cost-effective. No recommendation can be made.

References

1. American College of Obstetricians and Gynecologists. Ultrasonography in pregnancy. ACOG Technical Bulletin 187. Washington, DC: ACOG, 1993

2. Bochner CJ, Williams J, Castro L, Medearis A, Hobel CJ, Wade M. The efficacy of starting post-term antenatal testing at 41 weeks as compared with 42 weeks of gestational age. Am J Obstet Gynecol 1988;159:550–554

3. Guidetti DA, Divon MY, Langer O. Postdate fetal surveillance: is 41 weeks too early? Am J Obstet Gynecol 1989;161:91–93

4. Usher RH, Boyd ME, McLean FH, Kramer MS. Assessment of fetal risk in postdate pregnancies. Am J Obstet Gynecol 1988;158:259–264

5. A clinical trial of induction of labor versus expectant management in post-term pregnancy. The National Institute of Child Health and Human Development Network of Maternal–Fetal Medicine Units. Am J Obstet Gynecol 1994;170:716–723

6. Hannah ME, Hannah WJ, Hellmann J, Hewson S, Milner R, Willan A. Induction of labor as compared with serial antenatal monitoring in post-term pregnancy. A randomized controlled trial. The Canadian Multicenter Post-Term Pregnancy Trial Group. N Engl J Med 1992;326:1587–1592

7. Martin JN Jr, Sessums JK, Howard P, Martin RW, Morrision JC. Alternative approaches to the management of gravidas with prolonged-postterm-postdate pregnancies. J Miss State Med Assoc 1989; 30:105–111

8. Augensen K, Bergsjø, Eikeland T, Askvik K, Carlsen J. Randomised comparison of early versus late induction of labour in post-term pregnancy. Br Med J 1987;294:1192–1195

9. Dyson DC, Miller PD, Armstrong MA. Management of prolonged pregnancy: induction of labor versus antepartum fetal testing. Am J Obstet Gynecol 1987;156:928–934

10. Cardozo L, Fysh J, Pearce JM. Prolonged pregnancy: the management debate. Br Med J 1986;293:1059–1063

11. Herabutya Y, Prasertsawat PO, Tongyai T, Isarangura NA, Ayudthya N. Prolonged pregnancy: the management dilemma. Int J Gynecol Obstet 1992;37:253–258

12. Hedèn L, Ingemarsson I, Ahlström H, Solum T. Induction of labor versus conservative management in prolonged pregnancy: controlled study. Int J Feto-Maternal Med 1991;4:231–236

13. Bergsjø P, Huang GD, Yu SQ, Gao ZZ, Bakketeig LS. Comparison of induced versus non-induced labor in post-term pregnancy. A randomized prospective study. Acta Obstet Gynecol Scand 1989;68:683–687

14. Witter FR, Weitz CM. A randomized trial of induction at 42 weeks gestation versus expectant management for postdates pregnancies. Am J Perinat 1987;4:206–211

15. Almström H, Granström L, Ekman G. Serial antenatal monitoring compared with labor induction in post-term pregnancies. Acta Obstet Gynecol Scand 1995;74:599–603

16. Shaw KJ, Medearis AL, Horenstein J, Walla CA, Paul RH. Selective labor induction in postterm patients: observations and outcomes. J Reprod Med 1992;37:157–161

17. Rayburn W, Gosen R, Ramadei C, Woods R, Scott J Jr. Outpatient cervical ripening with prostaglandin E₂ gel in uncomplicated postdate pregnancies. Am J Obstet Gynecol 1988;158:1417–1423

18. Sawai SK, O'Brien WF, Mastrogiannis DS, Krammer J, Mastry MG, Porter GW. Patient-administered outpatient intravaginal prostaglandin E₂ suppositories in post-date pregnancies: a double-blind, randomized, placebo-controlled study. Obstet Gynecol 1994;84:807–810

19. Papageorgiou I, Tsionou C, Minaretzis D, Michalas S, Aravantinos D. Labor characteristics of uncomplicated prolonged pregnancies after induction with intracervical prostaglandin E2 gel versus intravenous oxytocin. Gynecol Obstet Invest 1992;34:92–96

20. Egarter C, Kofler E, Fitz R, Husslein P. Is induction of labor indicated in prolonged pregnancy? Gynecol Obstet Invest 1989:27:6–9

21. Goeree R, Hannah M, Hewson S. Cost-effectiveness of induction of labour versus serial antenatal monitoring in the Canadian Multicentre Postterm Pregnancy Trial. Can Med Assoc J 1995;152:1445–1450

12345/10987

Number 5, August 1997

ACOGPractice Patterns

Evidence-Based Guidelines for Clinical Issues in Obstetrics and Gynecology

Routine Ultrasound in Low-Risk Pregnancy

Purpose

The accepted indications for ultrasound during pregnancy are numerous (1). Approximately 60% to 70% of pregnant women in the United States undergo ultrasound at various times in gestation (1, 2). The purpose of this document is to present evidence regarding benefit or lack of benefit of routine ultrasound in women with low-risk pregnancy who do not already have an indication for ultrasound use.

Objectives

These practice guidelines will enable physicians to:

- Estimate the sensitivity and specificity of ultrasound in detecting fetal anomalies in low-risk pregnancy
- Describe the potential benefit, if any, from routine ultrasound in low-risk pregnancies, specifically for
  — improving the survival rates of anomalous fetuses
  — improving overall perinatal morbidity and mortality
  — reducing the rate of unnecessary interventions

Methods

The MEDLINE database was used to conduct a literature search, which was restricted to articles published in the English language. Only studies conducted since 1985 were included because of implicit limitations in ultrasound technology prior to that time. For the purpose of assessing benefit of routine ultrasound in low-risk pregnancy, the evidence was limited to randomized clinical trials with a priori hypotheses appropriate to the stated purposes of this document. For the purpose of estimating the sensitivity of ultrasound in detecting fetal anomalies, evidence of any level was considered as long as the following were provided: a description of the study population, the rate of anomalies detected in infants at birth, and the numbers of fetuses representing true positives, true negatives, false positives, and false negatives. Studies that reported data by numbers of anomalies rather than fetuses were not considered because of overestimation of sensitivity.

Studies were reviewed and evaluated for quality according to the method outlined by the U.S. Preventive Services Task Force:

I Evidence obtained from at least one properly designed randomized controlled trial
II-1 Evidence obtained from well-designed controlled trials without randomization
II-2 Evidence obtained from well-designed cohort or case–control analytic studies, preferably from more than one center or research group

II-3 Evidence obtained from multiple time series with or without the intervention. Dramatic results in uncontrolled experiments could also be regarded as this type of evidence.

III Opinions of respected authorities, based on clinical experience, descriptive studies, or reports of expert committees

Results

What is the proportion of correctly identified fetal anomalies (sensitivity) and the proportion of correctly identified fetuses without anomalies (specificity) detected by ultrasound in low-risk pregnancy?

Estimates of the sensitivity of a fetal anatomic survey to detect fetal anomalies are shown in Table 1 (Level I: 3) (Level II-3: 4–6). Estimated sensitivity varies widely from 17% to 74%.

Some of the variation in reported sensitivity across studies may be accounted for by biases. For the two studies reporting the highest sensitivity (Level II-3: 4, 6), the overall rate of anomalies detected at birth was substantially below the reported rate of 3%, suggesting underdetection of anomalies at birth (7). The bias would tend to result in an overestimation of sensitivity. The lowest sensitivity is reported by the only study (Level I: 3) in which patient recruitment was practice based, rather than hospital based. A community-based population is the least likely to have an inadvertent selection bias. Although practice-based recruitment is not as optimal as that which is community based, the utilization of a large number of general obstetric practices in that study likely improved the chance that the study population was representative of low-risk women. Another potential bias is variation in the skill of individuals performing the ultrasound examination. In the Helsinki study, which included patient populations from two hospitals, sensitivity was more than twofold higher in the university hospital (77%) than in the city hospital (36%) (Level I: 8). A similar order of advantage was seen in the Routine Antenatal Diagnostic Imaging with Ultrasound (RADIUS) study, which reported a relative detection rate of 2.7 (confidence interval [CI] 1.3–5.8) in tertiary versus nontertiary ultrasound units (Level I: 3).

Thus, there is insufficient evidence to indicate a single estimate of the sensitivity of routine ultrasound screening for fetal anomalies. Instead, it should be acknowledged that there is a range of sensitivity, depending on the clinical setting and skill of those performing the examinations. Evidence does indicate that specificity

TABLE 1. Estimated Sensitivity of Second-Trimester Ultrasound to Detect Anomalies

Study	Study Design	Patient Source	Study (n)	Gestational Age at Ultrasound	Anomalies Detected at Birth	Anomalies Detected by Ultrasound	Sensitivity
Chitty et al 1991[4]	1988–89 series (retrospective)	Hospital based	8,342	<24 weeks	1.5%	93/125	74%
Crane et al 1994[3]	Randomized clinical trial	Practice based	7,575*	18–20 weeks 31–33 weeks	2.3%	31/187	17%
Levi et al 1995[5]	1990–92 series (prospective)	Hospital based	9,601	<23 weeks	2.4%	120/235	51%
Shirley et al 1992[6]	1989–90 series (prospective)	Hospital based	6,183	<22 weeks	1.4%	51/84	61%

*Number of women having ultrasound in the routine-ultrasound arm of the trial.

of a fetal anatomic survey exceeds 99% (Level I: 3) (Level II-3: 4–6). This suggests that, in low-risk populations, ultrasound may be helpful in ruling out anomalies, but it is not particularly reliable in detecting them.

The evidence for the following results was assessed from publications of three trials: the Helsinki study (Level I: 8), the Stockholm study (Level I: 9), and the RADIUS study (Level I: 2, 3, 10). For these trials, the timing of routine ultrasound was early to midsecond trimester; for the RADIUS study, an additional ultrasound was performed in the early third trimester. One additional trial was used to judge evidence for potential benefit unrelated to the ascertainment of fetal anomalies because this study used routine first-trimester ultrasound (Level I: 11). Indicated ultrasound examinations were permitted in the usual-care arm of each study.

Does routine ultrasound improve the survival rates of anomalous infants?

A potential benefit of the antenatal detection of anomalies, particularly life-threatening ones, is the delivery of these infants in tertiary centers capable of providing immediate, risk-appropriate care. Only one randomized clinical trial specifically addressed this question (Level I: 3). In a subgroup analysis of infants with life-threatening anomalies, 75% (21/28) in the routinely screened group survived versus 52% (11/21) in the routine-care group. This difference did not reach statistical significance (relative survival rate 1.4 [CI 0.9–2.3]), although this may in part be attributed to the relatively small sample size. Thus, there is insufficient evidence to support or refute benefit of routine ultrasound in reducing the mortality of infants with life-threatening anomalies.

Does routine ultrasound improve overall perinatal morbidity and mortality?

A benefit of routine diagnostic ultrasound in reducing perinatal morbidity and mortality might be anticipated by ameliorating the perinatal risk associated with inaccurate gestational age and undiagnosed conditions (eg, multiple gestation). In two of the trials, the perinatal mortality rate was similar between the routine-ultrasound and usual-care groups (Level I: 2, 9). In one trial, the perinatal mortality rate was significantly improved (4.2/1,000 versus 8.4/1,000; P <0.05) (Level I: 8). The improvement was largely attributable to pregnancy termination of anomalous fetuses.

Perinatal morbidity as measured by admission to a neonatal unit was no different between the study groups in two trials (Level I: 8, 9). In the RADIUS study, rates of both moderate morbidity (eg, presumed neonatal sepsis, grade I or II intraventricular hemorrhage, stay of >5 days in the neonatal unit) and severe morbidity (eg, mechanical ventilation for >48 hours, stay of >30 days in the neonatal unit) were similar between the routine-ultrasound and usual-care groups (Level I: 2).

In one trial, there were fewer births of less than 2,500 g in the routine-ultrasound group (2.5% versus 4.0%; P = 0.005) (Level I: 9). In addition, for those women who reported smoking, the mean birth weight was greater in the routine-ultrasound group than in the usual-care group (3,413 g versus 3,354 g; P = 0.047). For infants of nonsmoking women, mean birth weight was also higher in the routine-ultrasound group compared with those of nonsmokers in the usual-care group, although this was not significantly different between groups. The investigators speculated that this improvement in birth weight of reported smokers receiving routine ultrasound may be attributed to healthier maternal behaviors after these women saw their fetuses on ultrasound. A similar birth weight distribution among all women was reported between the routine-ultrasound and usual-care groups in two other trials (Level I: 2, 8).

There is evidence from all trials to indicate that more twin gestations are diagnosed earlier with routine ultrasound. Subgroup analyses of twins, although showing no difference in perinatal mortality with routine ultrasound versus usual care, do not permit definitive conclusions because of limited power. In the RADIUS study, subgroup analyses also were performed for small-for-gestational-age infants and those born at 42 weeks or more. The data from this trial do not support an improvement in overall outcome for these conditions with routine ultrasound (Level I: 2).

In summary, evidence indicates that routine ultrasound does not significantly alter perinatal outcome, except for lowering perinatal mortality as the result of induced abortions following the detection of abnormalities.

Does routine ultrasound reduce the rate of obstetric interventions?

The evidence does not support any benefit from routine ultrasound in reducing the number of maternal hospital days or the cesarean delivery rate (Level I: 8–10). The evidence also does not demonstrate an overall reduction in the rate of induction of labor; these rates were similar between the routine-ultrasound and usual-care groups in all four trials (Level I: 8–11). The rate of induction specifically for postterm pregnancy was reduced in two trials (Level I: 9, 10) but not in the other two (Level I: 8, 11). However, for the trial finding the greatest reduction in induction for postterm pregnancy (3.7% to 1.7%, $P < 0.0001$), the study protocol did not permit correction of gestational age by indicated ultrasound in the usual-care arm (Level I: 9).

Only one trial examined the rate of induction for suspected small-for-gestational-age fetuses (Level I: 10). There was an increased rate of induction for this indication: 0.74% with routine ultrasound versus 0.28% in the usual-care arm. However, a similar proportion of induced pregnancies in each group resulted in infant birth weights at less than the 10th percentile (39% routine ultrasound, 43% usual care).

Only one trial examined other interventions (eg, tests for fetal well-being, performance of amniocentesis, recommendation for bed rest, version). It found no difference except for a decrease in the overall use of tocolysis (3.4% versus 4.2%, $P = 0.01$) (Level I: 10).

Cost Considerations

No cost–benefit analysis of routine versus selective ultrasound has been performed. Because the evidence supports neither an improvement in perinatal morbidity or mortality nor an overall reduction in unnecessary interventions with routine ultrasound, the cost of obstetric care would likely be increased in proportion to the excess number of ultrasound examinations in women having routine use versus selective (indicated) use. In one study, it was estimated that routine ultrasound added, on average, 1.6 scans per pregnancy. If more than 4 million pregnant women were screened annually in the United States at $200 per scan, costs would increase by more than $1 billion (2). However, this estimate includes a percentage of women who would have undergone ultrasound examination for medical indications as well. If estimates were confined to women who would not have had ultrasound examinations, the incremental cost has been calculated to be below $350 million (Level III: 12). If interventions were to be developed that improve outcome in obstetric complications such as twin gestation, or if a larger proportion of women ascertained to have fetuses with major anomalies chose pregnancy termination, then a cost advantage of routine ultrasound in low-risk pregnancy is plausible.

Summary and Recommendations

Based on the highest level of evidence found in the data, the following recommendations are provided and graded according to the following categories:

A There is good evidence to support the recommendation.
B There is fair evidence to support the recommendation.
C There is insufficient evidence to support the recommendation; however, the recommendation may be made on other grounds.

- The specificity of a fetal anatomic survey in detecting fetal anomalies can be anticipated to exceed 99% (A: I; II-3).
- The sensitivity of a fetal anatomic survey in detecting fetal anomalies cannot be estimated with precision; rather, it should be acknowledged that sensitivity may vary in different clinical settings and with different levels of skill of professionals performing the examination (A: I; II-3).
- It is uncertain whether an improvement in the survival of fetuses with life-threatening anomalies can be expected from routine ultrasound in low-risk pregnancy (C: I).
- In a population of women with low-risk pregnancy, neither a reduction in perinatal morbidity and mortality nor a lower rate of unnecessary interventions can be expected from routine diagnostic ultrasound. Thus ultrasound should be performed for specific indications in low-risk pregnancy (A: I).

References

1. American College of Obstetricians and Gynecologists. Ultrasonography in pregnancy. ACOG Technical Bulletin 187. Washington, DC: ACOG, 1993

2. Ewigman BG, Crane JP, Frigoletto FD, LeFevre ML, Bain RP, McNellis D. Effect of prenatal ultrasound screening on perinatal outcome. RADIUS Study Group. N Engl J Med 1993;329:821–827

3. Crane JP, LeFevre ML, Winborn RC, Evans JK, Ewigman BG, Bain RP, et al. A randomized trial of prenatal ultrasonographic screening: impact on the detection, management, and outcome of anomalous fetuses. The RADIUS Study Group. Am J Obstet Gynecol 1994;171:392–399

4. Chitty LS, Hunt GH, Moore J, Lobb MO. Effectiveness of routine ultrasonography in detecting fetal structural abnormalities in a low risk population. BMJ 1991;303:1165–1169

5. Levi S, Schaaps JP, De Havay P, Coulon R, Defoort P. End-result of routine ultrasound screening for congenital anomalies: the Belgium Multicentric Study 1984–92. Ultrasound Obstet Gynecol 1995; 5:366–371

6. Shirley IM, Bottomley F, Robinson VP. Routine radiographer screening for fetal abnormalities by ultrasound in an unselected low risk population. Br J Radiol 1992;65:564–569

7. Watkins ML, Edmonds L, McClearn A, Mullins L, Mulinare J, Khoury M. The surveillance of birth defects: the usefulness of the revised US standard birth certificate. Am J Public Health 1996;86:731–734

8. Saari-Kemppainen A, Karjalainen O, Ylostalo P, Heinonen OP. Ultrasound screening and perinatal mortality: controlled trial systematic one-stage screening in pregnancy. The Helsinki Ultrasound Trial. Lancet 1990;336:387–391

9. Waldenstrom U, Axelsson O, Nilsson S, Eklund G, Fall O, Lindeberg S, et al. Effects of routine one-stage ultrasound screening in pregnancy: a randomised controlled trial. Lancet 1988;2:585–588

10. LeFevre ML, Bain RP, Ewigman BG, Frigoletto FD, Crane JP, McNellis D. A randomized trial of prenatal ultrasonographic screening: impact on maternal management and outcome. RADIUS (Routine Antenatal Diagnostic Imaging with Ultrasound) Study Group. Am J Obstet Gynecol 1993; 169:483–489

11. Ewigman B, LeFevre M, Hesser J. A randomized trial of routine prenatal ultrasound. Obstet Gynecol 1990;76:189–194

12. Copel JA, Platt LD, Campbell S. Prenatal ultrasound screening and perinatal outcome [letter]. N J Med 1994;330:571–572

Practice Patterns are clinical practice guidelines developed by The American College of Obstetricians and Gynecologists (ACOG) to assist practitioners and patients in making decisions about appropriate obstetric and gynecologic care. Each Practice Pattern focuses on a clinical issue and is based on a review and analysis of the scientific literature. The information and recommendations reflect scientific and clinical knowledge current as of the publication date and are subject to change as advances in diagnostic techniques and treatments emerge. In addition, variations of practice, taking into account the needs of the individual patient, resources, and limitations unique to the institution or type of practice, may warrant alternative treatment or procedures to the recommendations outlined in this document. Therefore, these guidelines should not be construed as dictating an exclusive course of treatment or procedure.

ISSN 1083-3331

12345/10987

Number 7, October 1997

ACOGPractice Patterns

Evidence-Based Guidelines for Clinical Issues in Obstetrics and Gynecology

Shoulder Dystocia

Purpose

Shoulder dystocia is an obstetric emergency. Failure of the shoulders to deliver spontaneously immediately places both the pregnant woman and fetus at risk for injury. Reported incidence ranges from less than 1% to slightly more than 4% among vaginal cephalic deliveries. Differences in reported rates are partly due to clinical variation in describing shoulder dystocia. The diagnosis of shoulder dystocia has a subjective component. Although severe cases are readily apparent, milder forms may be over- or underestimated. As a result, researchers differ in their approaches to defining shoulder dystocia. Some accept a clinician's judgment, noted in the chart, that shoulder dystocia occurred. Others require documentation of specific release maneuvers or other procedures to substantiate a diagnosis of shoulder dystocia. As a result, incidence figures vary. Over time, several maneuvers to release impacted shoulders have been developed, but the rarity and urgency of this event makes prospective studies to compare them impractical. Prevention is largely confined to planned cesarean delivery for pregnancies considered to be most at risk for shoulder dystocia.

The purpose of this document is to provide information based on published studies regarding the prediction, prevention, and management of deliveries complicated by shoulder dystocia to assist obstetrician–gynecologists in providing care to their patients.

Objectives

These practice guidelines will enable physicians to:

- Determine whether shoulder dystocia can be predicted
- Identify strategies to manage shoulder dystocia
- Determine whether elective cesarean delivery is an effective strategy to prevent shoulder dystocia

Methods

The MEDLINE database was used to conduct a literature search to locate relevant articles published between 1985 and 1997. The search was restricted to articles published in the English language. Articles reporting results of original research were given priority, although review articles and commentaries were consulted as well. Abstracts of research presented at symposia and scientific conferences were not considered adequate for inclusion in this document. Guidelines published by organizations or institutions such as the National Institutes of Health and the American College of Obstetricians and Gynecologists were reviewed, and additional studies were located by reviewing bibliographies of articles located via MEDLINE. Studies were collected and grouped according to topic. In most cases, studies involving fewer than 50 subjects were not evaluated. When reliable research was not available, expert opinions from obstetrician–gynecologists were used.

Studies were reviewed and evaluated for quality according to the method outlined by the U.S. Preventive Services Task Force:

I Evidence obtained from at least one properly designed randomized controlled trial

II-1 Evidence obtained from well-designed controlled trials without randomization

II-2 Evidence obtained from well-designed cohort or case-control analytic studies, preferably from more than one center or research group

II-3 Evidence obtained from multiple time series with or without the intervention. Dramatic results in uncontrolled experiments could also be regarded as this type of evidence

III Opinions of respected authorities, based on clinical experience, descriptive studies, or reports of expert committees

Results

Can shoulder dystocia be accurately predicted and prevented?

The ideal management strategy for shoulder dystocia is prevention. Theoretically, most cases of shoulder dystocia could be avoided if fetuses at risk were identified before labor and selected for elective cesarean delivery. However, this strategy relies on several underlying assumptions that, in reality, are not true. These erroneous assumptions are

- Risk factors for shoulder dystocia can always be identified prior to labor.
- The presence of risk factors is highly predictive of shoulder dystocia.
- Risks associated with shoulder dystocia are greater than risks associated with planned cesarean deliveries to avoid shoulder dystocia.
- Costs associated with planned cesarean deliveries to avoid shoulder dystocia are less than the costs associated with shoulder dystocia-related injuries.

Predictors of shoulder dystocia

There have been many efforts to identify risk factors. Macrosomia and maternal diabetes consistently appear across many studies as the two risk factors most strongly associated with shoulder dystocia (Level II-2: 1–5) (Level II-3: 6). Pregnant women who have diabetes are two to six times more likely to experience shoulder dystocia than women who do not have diabetes (Level II-2: 1, 3, 5). The incidence of shoulder dystocia increases in direct proportion to infant birth weight whether or not the woman has diabetes, although women who have diabetes experience significantly greater rates of shoulder dystocia in each weight group (Level II-2: 2, 4, 5, 7–9) (see Tables 1 and 2).

TABLE 1. Risk of Shoulder Dystocia According to Diabetic Status

Author	Increase in Risk Associated with Diabetic Status
Acker et al 1985[1]	Rate ratio 5.2
Bahar 1996[3]	Odds ratio 4.3; 95% CI 2.2–8.3
Langer et al 1991[5]	Relative risk <4,000 g 2.6; 95% CI 1.29–5.34
	Relative risk >4,000 g 3.6; 95% CI 2.37–4.76
Sandmire et al 1988[4]	Relative risk 6.5; 95% CI 1.5–27.1

TABLE 2. Rate of Shoulder Dystocia Related to Birth Weight and Diabetic Status

Birth Weight (g)	Women Without Diabetes (%)	Women with Diabetes (%)
<4,000	0.1–1.1	0.6–3.7
4,000–4,449	1.1–10.0	4.9–23.1
≥4,500	4.1–22.6	20.0–50.0

Sources: Acker DB, Sachs BP, Friedman EA. Risk factors for shoulder dystocia. Obstet Gynecol 1985;66:762–768; al-Najashi S, al-Suleiman SA, el-Yahia A, Rahman MS, Rahman J. Shoulder dystocia: a clinical study of 56 cases. Aust N Z J Obstet Gynaecol 1989;29:129–132; Langer O, Berkus MD, Huff RW, Samueloff A. Shoulder dystocia: should the fetus weighing ≥4,000 grams be delivered by cesarean section? Am J Obstet Gynecol 1991;165:831–837.

Although risk increases with birth weight and diabetic status, a substantial proportion of cases occur among women who do not have diabetes and among infants with birth weights of less than 4,000 g. Predicting which patients are likely to experience shoulder dystocia based on the presence of risk factors has been unsuccessful. Acker et al reported a low sensitivity when diabetes mellitus and macrosomia were used to predict cases of shoulder dystocia; the presence of these risk factors accurately predicted only 55% of cases (Level II-2: 1). Additional studies failed to find any combination of risk factors that could predict which pregnancies would be complicated by shoulder dystocia (Level II-2: 3, 4, 7, 8, 10). In each case, risk factors could be identified, but their predictive value was not high enough to be useful in a clinical setting.

Planned cesarean delivery

Because identification of antenatal risk factors has not proved useful in preventing shoulder dystocia, a broad policy of planned cesarean delivery for macrosomic fetuses has been suggested. This strategy seeks to prevent shoulder dystocia by identifying a subgroup with a known risk factor, macrosomia, and selecting those fetuses for cesarean delivery. To be successful, several elements must exist. There must be a high correlation between macrosomia and shoulder dystocia, as well as a reliable method for identifying fetal macrosomia. In addition, the risks associated with shoulder dystocia must be greater than the risks associated with the additional cesarean deliveries resulting from the policy.

For women who do not have diabetes, the policy is unfeasible. Although there is a greater incidence of shoulder dystocia among macrosomic infants, most do not experience this complication. Consequently, if all fetuses suspected of being macrosomic underwent cesarean delivery, there would be a disproportionate impact on the increased cesarean rate compared with the reduction in rate of shoulder dystocia (Level II-2: 5, 8) (Level II-3: 11). For example, Gross et al projected a 27% increase in the total cesarean rate (rising from 15.1% to 19.1%) if cesarean deliveries were performed for all patients with fetuses that weighed 4,000 g or more; unfortunately, the number of shoulder dystocia cases would be reduced by only 42% (Level II-2: 8). Delpapa et al reported similar results among fetuses with estimated birth weights of 4,000 g or more; in their study, an additional 76 cesarean deliveries would have prevented only five cases of shoulder dystocia, none of which resulted in permanent injury (Level II-3: 11). A recently published decision analysis estimated an additional 2,345 cesarean deliveries would be required, at a cost of $4.9 million annually, to prevent one permanent injury resulting from shoulder dystocia if all fetuses suspected of weighing 4,000 g or more underwent cesarean delivery (Level III: 12).

Even if the weight threshold were increased to 4,500 g, the policy remains questionable. Opinion is divided over whether the benefits outweigh the risks. More cases of shoulder dystocia would be prevented, but the impact on the cesarean delivery rate would also be greater. Depending on the distribution of shoulder dystocia cases within a given population, planned cesarean delivery may provide more benefits than risks. Two investigators reported more than 50% of their cases occurred among infants weighing 4,500 g or more, but this finding was unusual (Level II-3: 6, 13). Others report that 20% or less of shoulder dystocia cases could be prevented by cesarean delivery for infants with birth weights of 4,500 g or more (Level II-2: 1, 5, 7) (Level II-3:14).

Gross et al argued that despite preventing fewer cases overall, infants weighing 4,500 g or more could benefit from planned cesarean delivery without adversely affecting the cesarean delivery rate; within the population studied, 20 cases of shoulder dystocia would have been prevented among 42 spontaneous vaginal deliveries with birth weights of 4,500 g or greater, and the cesarean delivery rate would only have increased from 15.1% to 15.7% (Level II-2: 8). Another investigator supporting routine cesarean delivery for birth weights greater than 4,500 g calculated the policy would reduce the incidence of shoulder dystocia by more than 50% while increasing the cesarean rate by only 1.7% (Level II-3: 6). At the other end of the spectrum, Baskett et al projected that implementing the policy within their study population would have resulted in an additional 817 cesarean deliveries while preventing only 69 cases of shoulder dystocia and 15 cases of brachial plexus palsy (Level II-2: 7). A separate study of 590 vaginal deliveries of infants weighing 4,500 g or more found only 54 cases of shoulder dystocia, with five brachial palsies, three fractured clavicles, and no permanent injuries (Level II-3: 15). According to a decision analysis, the national impact of this policy would be $8.7 million annually, with an additional 3,695 cesarean deliveries required to prevent one permanent injury (Level III: 12). The cesarean delivery rate would be projected to rise from 19.1% to 27.6% (Level III: 12). According to the evidence, the costs associated with routine cesarean delivery for estimated fetal weights of 4,500 g or more would be costly without commensurate benefits.

Among women with diabetes, shoulder dystocia cases are more concentrated within the heavier birth weight classes (Level II-2: 1, 2, 5). Approximately 70% of cases among women with diabetes occur at infant birth weights of 4,000 g or more, compared with 50% among those of women without diabetes. Therefore, a policy of planned cesarean delivery is more likely to prevent shoulder dystocia cases among pregnant women with diabetes. The evidence confirms this finding. Acker et al reported that almost 55% of shoulder dystocia among women with diabetes could be prevented if fetuses that weighed 4,000 g or more underwent cesarean delivery (Level II-2: 1). Langer et al found that 76% of shoulder dystocia cases among pregnant women with diabetes could be prevented if fetuses weighing 4,250 g or more underwent cesarean delivery (Level II-2: 5). In contrast, Keller et al found no justification for a 4,000-g threshold among women with gestational diabetes because more than half the cases occurred in infants weighing less than 4,000 g and the ultrasound estimates of fetal weight were inaccurate (Level II-2: 9). A decision analysis projected that a 4,500-g threshold for fetuses of women with diabetes would require an additional 443 procedures to prevent one permanent brachial plexus injury, at a cost of $930,000 (Level III: 12). The studies indicate that for pregnant women with diabetes who are suspected of carrying macrosomic fetuses, a planned cesarean delivery may be a reasonable course of action, depending on the incidence of shoulder dystocia, the accuracy of predicting macrosomia, and the cesarean delivery rate within a specific population.

The policy of planned cesarean delivery relies also on accurate estimates of fetal weight. Fetal weights are calculated from measurements taken during ultrasound examinations. Ultrasonography is an inaccurate predictor of macrosomia. Among the general population, ultrasonography could correctly identify macrosomia only about 60% of the time, according to a pooled estimate of 13 studies (Level III: 12). Within the diabetic population, ultrasonography has provided mixed results. There is evidence of accelerated fetal growth, most notably in the abdominal circumference and chest-to-head ratio (Level II-2: 16–18). However, the clinical usefulness of this information has been limited. One study correctly predicted 88.8% of macrosomia cases among pregnant women with diabetes, based on measurements of abdominal circumference and estimated fetal weight (Level II-2: 17). However, there are no studies documenting the usefulness of identifying macrosomic fetuses for planned cesarean delivery among women with diabetes.

How often does shoulder dystocia result in an injury to the newborn?

Brachial plexus injuries and fractures of the clavicle and humerus are associated with shoulder dystocia. The most potentially serious, brachial plexus injuries, can be caused by extreme amounts of traction and flexion exerted on the infant's neck. These injuries may result in permanent disability. The reported incidence of brachial plexus injuries following a delivery complicated by shoulder dystocia varies widely from 4% to 40% (1, 2, 6–9, 13, 14, 19–22). Fortunately, most cases resolve without permanent disability. Reports indicate between 9% and 25% of brachial plexus injuries persist (2, 7, 9, 14). Placed in perspective, fewer than 10% of all shoulder dystocia cases result in a persistent brachial plexus injury (2, 7, 9, 14). Moreover, brachial plexus injuries can occur without shoulder dystocia and at birth weights of less than 4,000 g (23).

Are any of the maneuvers used to release impacted shoulders either more likely to cause injuries or more likely to be successful?

Because of the rarity and urgency of shoulder dystocia, only a limited amount of data exists comparing management techniques. Two separate studies confirm that the combination of traction and fundal pressure is associated with brachial plexus injuries as well as with fractures of the humerus and clavicle (Level II-2: 7) (Level II-3: 20). There is no indication, however, that any particular management technique is superior to another once shoulder dystocia occurs.

There is evidence that injuries might and do occur despite application of appropriate obstetric maneuvers (Level II-3: 24). During a series of deliveries, the obstetrician wore a tactile-sensing device that recorded the peak and duration of forces applied to the head and neck of the fetus. During the study, two cases of shoulder dystocia occurred to infants with similar birth weights and obstetric protocols. One infant sustained a shoulder dystocia-related injury and the other did not (Level II-3: 24).

The McRoberts maneuver relies on maternal manipulation and is reported to be effective (Level II-2: 7, 19) (Level II-3: 25). Successful use of the McRoberts maneuver is documented in the scientific literature. The maneuver involves sharply flexing the patient's legs against her abdomen. Results from a laboratory study using models of the maternal pelvis, fetal head, and fetal shoulders demonstrated that less force was required to deliver fetuses using the McRoberts maneuver compared with the standard lithotomy position (26).

Summary and Recommendations

Based on this highest level of evidence found in the data, the following recommendations are provided and graded according to the following categories:

A There is good evidence to support the recommendation.
B There is fair evidence to support the recommendation.
C There is insufficient evidence to support the recommendation; however, the recommendation may be made on other grounds.

Prediction and prevention of shoulder dystocia

- Most cases of shoulder dystocia cannot be predicted or prevented because accurate methods for identifying which fetuses will experience this complication do not exist, and performing cesarean deliveries for all women suspected of carrying a macrosomic fetus is not appropriate (B: II-2).
- Ultrasonographic measurements to estimate macrosomia have limited accuracy (B: II-2).
- Planned cesarean delivery on the basis of suspected macrosomia in the general population is not a reasonable strategy because the number and cost of additional cesarean deliveries required to prevent one permanent injury is excessive (B: II-2).
- Planned cesarean delivery may be a reasonable strategy for diabetic pregnant women with estimated fetal weights exceeding 4,250–4,500 g (B: II-2).

Shoulder dystocia as a cause of injury to newborns

- Injuries are a common outcome associated with shoulder dystocia and may occur despite use of appropriate standard obstetric maneuvers (B: II-3). Brachial plexus injuries, fractures of the humerus, and fractures of the clavicle are the most commonly reported injuries associated with shoulder dystocia (A: II-2).
- Fewer than 10% of all deliveries complicated by shoulder dystocia will result in a persistent brachial plexus injury (A:II-2).

Release techniques

- There is no evidence that any one maneuver is superior to another in releasing an impacted shoulder or reducing the chance of injury. However, the McRoberts maneuver is easily facilitated and has a high success rate without an associated increase in risk of injury to the newborn (B: II-2).
- Traction combined with fundal pressure has been associated with a high rate of brachial plexus injuries and fractures (B: II-2).

References

1. Acker DB, Sachs BP, Friedman EA. Risk factors for shoulder dystocia. Obstet Gynecol 1985;66:762–768

2. al-Najashi S, al-Suleiman SA, el-Yahia A, Rahman MS, Rahman J. Shoulder dystocia: a clinical study of 56 cases. Aust N Z J Obstet Gynaecol 1989;29:129–132

3. Bahar AM. Risk factors and fetal outcome in cases of shoulder dystocia compared with normal deliveries of a similar birthweight. Br J Obstet Gynaecol 1996;103:868–872

4. Sandmire HF, O'Halloin TJ. Shoulder dystocia: its incidence and associated risk factors. Int J Gynaecol Obstet 1988;26:65–73

5. Langer O, Berkus MD, Huff RW, Samueloff A. Shoulder dystocia: should the fetus weighing ≥ 4000 grams be delivered by cesarean section? Am J Obstet Gynecol 1991; 165:831–837

6. el Madany AA, Jallad KB, Radi FA, el Hamdan H, O'deh HM. Shoulder dystocia: anticipation and outcome. Int J Gynecol Obstet 1990;34:7–12

7. Baskett TF, Allen AC. Perinatal implications of shoulder dystocia. Obstet Gynecol 1995;86:14–17

8. Gross TL, Sokol RJ, Williams T, Thompson K. Shoulder dystocia: a fetal–physician risk. Am J Obstet Gynecol 1987;156:1408–1418

9. Keller JD, Lopez-Zeno JA, Dooley SL, Socol ML. Shoulder dystocia and birth trauma in gestational diabetes: a five-year experience. Am J Obstet Gynecol 1991;165:928–930

10. Nocon JJ, McKenzie DK, Thomas LJ, Hansell RS. Shoulder dystocia: an analysis of risks and obstetric maneuvers. Am J Obstet Gynecol 1993;168:1732–1739

11. Delpapa EH, Mueller-Heubach E. Pregnancy outcome following ultrasound diagnosis of macrosomia. Obstet Gynecol 1991;78:340–343

12. Rouse DJ, Owen J, Goldenberg RL, Cliver SP. The effectiveness and costs of elective cesarean delivery for fetal macrosomia diagnosed by ultrasound. JAMA 1996;276:1480–1486

13. Hassan AA. Shoulder dystocia: risk factors and prevention. Aust N Z J Obstet Gynaecol 1988;28:107–109

14. Morrison JC, Sanders JR, Magann EF, Wiser WL. The diagnosis and management of dystocia of the shoulder. Surg Gynecol Obstet 1992;175:515–522

15. Menticoglou SM, Manning FA, Morrison I, Harman CR. Must macrosomic fetuses be delivered by a cesarean section? A review of outcome for 786 babies greater than or equal to 4,500 g. Aust N Z J Obstet Gynaecol 1992;32:100–103

16. Bracero LA, Baxi LV, Rey HR, Yeh MN. Use of ultrasound in antenatal diagnosis of large-for-gestational age infants in diabetic gravid patients. Am J Obstet Gynecol 1985;152:43–47

17. Tamura RK, Sabbagha RE, Depp R, Dooley SL, Socol ML. Diabetic macrosomia: accuracy of third trimester ultrasound. Obstet Gynecol 1986;67:828–832

18. Modanlou HD, Komatsu G, Dorchester W, Freeman RK, Bosu SK. Large-for-gestational-age neonates: anthropometric reasons for shoulder dystocia. Obstet Gynecol 1982;60:417–423

19. Gonik B, Hollyer L, Allen R. Shoulder dystocia recognition: differences in neonatal risks for injury. Am J Perinatol 1991;8:31–34

20. Gross SJ, Shime J, Farine D. Shoulder dystocia: predictors and outcome. A five-year review. Am J Obstet Gynecol 1987;156:334–336

21. Hopwood HG Jr. Shoulder dystocia: fifteen years' experience in a community hospital. Am J Obstet Gynecol 1982;144:162–166

22. Lurie S, Insler V, Hagay ZJ. Induction of labor at 38 to 39 weeks of gestation reduces the incidence of shoulder dystocia in gestational diabetic patients class A2. Am J Perinatol 1996;13:293–296

23. Graham EM, Forouzan I, Morgan MA. A retrospective analysis of Erb's palsy cases and their relation to birth weight and trauma at delivery. J Matern Fetal Med 1997;6:1–5

24. Allen R, Sorab J, Gonik B. Risk factors for shoulder dystocia: an engineering study of clinician-applied forces. Obstet Gynecol 1991;77:352–355

25. Smeltzer JS. Prevention and management of shoulder dystocia. Clin Obstet Gynecol 1986;29:299–308

26. Gonik B, Allen R, Sorab J. Objective evaluation of the shoulder dystocia phenomenon: effect of maternal pelvic orientation on force reduction. Obstet Gynecol 1989;74:44–48

Practice Patterns are clinical practice guidelines developed by The American College of Obstetricians and Gynecologists (ACOG) to assist practitioners and patients in making decisions about appropriate obstetric and gynecologic care. Each Practice Pattern focuses on a clinical issue and is based on a review and analysis of the scientific literature. The information and recommendations reflect scientific and clinical knowledge current as of the publication date and are subject to change as advances in diagnostic techniques and treatments emerge. In addition, variations of practice, taking into account the needs of the individual patient, resources, and limitations unique to the institution or type of practice, may warrant alternative treatment or procedures to the recommendations outlined in this document. Therefore, these guidelines should not be construed as dictating an exclusive course of treatment or procedure.

ISSN 1083-3331

12345/10987

Policy Statements

Policy Statements

ACOG *Statement of Policy*
As issued by the ACOG Executive Board

This document was developed by a joint task force of the American Academy of Family Physicians and the American College of Obstetricians and Gynecologists.

AAFP--ACOG JOINT STATEMENT ON COOPERATIVE PRACTICE AND HOSPITAL PRIVILEGES

Access to maternity care is an important public health concern in the United States. Providing comprehensive perinatal services to a diverse population requires a cooperative relationship among a variety of health professionals, including social workers, health educators, nurses and physicians. Prenatal care, labor and delivery, and postpartum care have historically been provided by midwives, family physicians and obstetricians. All three remain the major caregivers today. A cooperative and collaborative relationship among obstetricians, family physicians and nurse midwives is essential for provision of consistent, high-quality care to pregnant women.

Regardless of specialty, there should be shared common standards of perinatal care. This requires a cooperative working environment and shared decision making. Clear guidelines for consultation and referral for complications should be developed jointly. When appropriate, early and ongoing consultation regarding a woman's care is necessary for the best possible outcome and is an important part of risk management and prevention of professional liability problems. All family physicians and obstetricians on the medical staff of the obstetric unit should agree to such guidelines and be willing to work together for the best care of patients. This includes a willingness on the part of obstetricians to provide consultation and back-up for family physicians who provide maternity care. The family physician should have knowledge, skills and judgment to determine when timely consultation and/or referral may be appropriate.

The most important objective of the physician must be the provision of the highest standards of care, regardless of specialty. Quality patient care requires that all providers should practice within their degree of ability as determined by training, experience and current competence. A joint practice committee with obstetricians and family physicians should be established in health care organizations to determine and monitor standards of care and to determine proctoring guidelines. A collegial working relationship between family physicians and obstetricians is essential if we are to provide access to quality care for pregnant women in this country.

The American College of Obstetricians and Gynecologists
409 12th Street, SW, PO Box 96920 • Washington, DC 20090-6920 Telephone 202 638 5577

AAFP--ACOG JOINT STATEMENT ON COOPERATIVE PRACTICE AND HOSPITAL PRIVILEGES
Page 2

A. Practice privileges

The assignment of hospital privileges is a local responsibility and privileges should be granted on the basis of training, experience and demonstrated current competence. All physicians should be held to thesame standards for granting of privileges, regardless of specialty, in order to assure the provision of high-quality patient care. Prearranged, collaborative relationships should be established to ensure ongoing consultations, as well as consultations needed for emergencies.

The standard of training should allow any physician who receives training in a cognitive or surgical skill to meet the criteria for privileges in that area of practice. Provisional privileges in primary care, obstetric care and cesarean delivery should be granted regardless of specialty as long as training criteria and experience are documented. All physicians should be subject to a proctorship period to allow demonstration of ability and current competence. These principles should apply to all health care systems.

B. Interdepartmental relationships

Privileges recommended by the department of family practice shall be the responsibility of the department of family practice. Similarly, privileges recommended by the department of obstetrics-gynecology shall be the responsibility of the department of obstetrics-gynecology. When privileges are recommended jointly by the departments of family practice and obstetrics-gynecology, they shall be the joint responsibility of the two departments.

Published July 1980
Reformatted July 1988
Revised and Retitled March 1998

ACOG *Statement of Policy*

As issued by the ACOG Executive Board

ABORTION POLICY

The following statement is the American College of Obstetricians and Gynecologists' (ACOG) general policy related to abortion, with specific reference to the procedure referred to as "intact dilatation and extraction" (intact D & X).

1. The abortion debate in this country is marked by serious moral pluralism. Different positions in the debate represent different but important values. The diversity of beliefs should be respected.

2. ACOG recognizes that the issue of support of or opposition to abortion is a matter of profound moral conviction to its members. ACOG, therefore, respects the need and responsibility of its members to determine their individual positions based on personal values or beliefs.

3. Termination of pregnancy before viability is a medical matter between the patient and physician, subject to the physician's clinical judgment, the patient's informed consent and the availability of appropriate facilities.

4. The need for abortions, other than those indicated by serious fetal anomalies or conditions which threaten maternal welfare, represents failures in the social environment and the educational system.

The most effective way to reduce the number of abortions is to prevent unwanted and unintended pregnancies. This can be accomplished by open and honest education, beginning in the home, religious institutions and the primary schools. This education should stress the biology of reproduction and the responsibilities involved by boys, girls, men and women in creating life and the desirability of delaying pregnancies until circumstances are appropriate and pregnancies are planned.

In addition, everyone should be made aware of the dangers of sexually transmitted diseases and the means of protecting each other from their transmission. To accomplish these aims, support of the community and the school system is essential.

The medical curriculum should be expanded to include a focus on the components of reproductive biology which pertain to conception control. Physicians should be encouraged to apply these principles in their own practices and to support them at the community level.

Society also has a responsibility to support research leading to improved methods of contraception for men and women.

The American College of Obstetricians and Gynecologists
409 12th Street, SW, PO Box 96920 • Washington, DC 20090-6920 Telephone 202 638 5577

ABORTION POLICY
Page 2

5. Informed consent is an expression of respect for the patient as a person; it particularly respects a patient's moral right to bodily integrity, to self-determination regarding sexuality and reproductive capacities, and to the support of the patient's freedom within caring relationships.

A pregnant woman should be fully informed in a balanced manner about all options, including raising the child herself, placing the child for adoption, and abortion. The information conveyed should be appropriate to the duration of the pregnancy. The professional should make every effort to avoid introducing personal bias.

6. ACOG supports access to care for all individuals, irrespective of financial status, and supports the availability of all reproductive options. ACOG opposes unnecessary regulations that limit or delay access to care.

7. If abortion is to be performed, it should be performed safely and as early as possible.

8. ACOG opposes the harassment of abortion providers and patients.

9. ACOG strongly supports those activities which prevent unintended pregnancy.

The College continues to affirm the legal right of a woman to obtain an abortion prior to fetal viability. ACOG is opposed to abortion of the healthy fetus that has attained viability in a healthy woman. Viability is the capacity of the fetus to survive outside the mother's uterus. Whether or not this capacity exists is a medical determination, may vary with each pregnancy and is a matter for the judgment of the responsible attending physician.

Intact Dilatation and Extraction

The debate regarding legislation to prohibit a method of abortion, such as the legislation banning "partial birth abortion," and "brain sucking abortions," has prompted questions regarding these procedures. It is difficult to respond to these questions because the descriptions are vague and do not delineate a specific procedure recognized in the medical literature. Moreover, the definitions could be interpreted to include elements of many recognized abortion and operative obstetric techniques.

ACOG believes the intent of such legislative proposals is to prohibit a procedure referred to as "intact dilatation and extraction" (Intact D & X). This procedure has been described as containing all of the following four elements:

1. deliberate dilatation of the cervix, usually over a sequence of days;
2. instrumental conversion of the fetus to a footling breech;
3. breech extraction of the body excepting the head; and
4. partial evacuation of the intracranial contents of a living fetus to effect vaginal delivery of a dead but otherwise intact fetus.

Because these elements are part of established obstetric techniques, it must be emphasized that unless all four elements are present in sequence, the procedure is not an intact D & X. Abortion intends to terminate a pregnancy while preserving the life and health of the mother. When abortion is performed after 16 weeks, intact D & X is one method of terminating a pregnancy.

ABORTION POLICY
Page 3

The physician, in consultation with the patient, must choose the most appropriate method based upon the patient's individual circumstances.

According to the Centers for Disease Control and Prevention (CDC), only 5.3% of abortions performed in the United States in 1993, the most recent data available, were performed after the 16th week of pregnancy. A preliminary figure published by the CDC for 1994 is 5.6%. The CDC does not collect data on the specific method of abortion, so it is unknown how many of these were performed using intact D & X. Other data show that second trimester transvaginal instrumental abortion is a safe procedure.

Terminating a pregnancy is performed in some circumstances to save the life or preserve the health of the mother.

Intact D & X is one of the methods available in some of these situations. A select panel convened by ACOG could identify no circumstances under which this procedure, as defined above, would be the only option to save the life or preserve the health of the woman. An intact D & X, however, may be the best or most appropriate procedure in a particular circumstance to save the life or preserve the health of a woman, and only the doctor, in consultation with the patient, based upon the woman's particular circumstances can make this decision. The potential exists that legislation prohibiting specific medical practices, such as intact D & X, may outlaw techniques that are critical to the lives and health of American women. **The intervention of legislative bodies into medical decision making is inappropriate, ill advised, and dangerous.**

Approval by the Executive Board
General policy: January 1993
Reaffirmed: September 2000
Intact D & X statement: January 1997
Combined: September 2000

ACOG *Statement of Policy*

As issued by the ACOG Executive Board

ACCESS TO WOMEN'S HEALTH CARE

Excellence in women's health care is an essential element of the long-term physical, intellectual, social and economic well-being of any society. It is a basic determinant of the health of future generations.

The American College of Obstetricians and Gynecologists is the representative organization of physicians who are qualified specialists in providing health services unique to women. ACOG calls for quality health care appropriate to every woman's needs throughout her life and for assuring that a full array of clinical services be available to women without costly delays or the imposition of geographic, financial, attitudinal or legal barriers.

The College and its membership are committed to facilitating both access to and quality of women's health care. Fellows should exercise their responsibility to improve the health status of women and their offspring both in the traditional patient-physician relationships and by working within their community and at the state and national levels to assure access to high-quality programs meeting the health needs of all women.

In addition, it is critical that all Americans be provided with adequate and affordable health coverage. Despite economic prosperity and substantial job creation during the 1990s, there remains a considerable and increasing portion of the American population that does not have health insurance coverage. As a result, those individuals often defer obtaining preventive and medical services, jeopardizing the health and well being of themselves and their families. The College supports universal coverage that is designed to improve the individual and collective health of society. Expanding health coverage to all Americans must become a high priority.

Approved by the Executive Board July 1988
Amended September 1999

The American College of Obstetricians and Gynecologists
409 12th Street, SW, PO Box 96920 • Washington, DC 20090-6920 Telephone 202 638 5577

ACOG *Statement of Policy*

As issued by the ACOG Executive Board

HOME DELIVERY

Labor and delivery, while a physiologic process, clearly presents potential hazards to both mother and fetus before and after birth. These hazards require standards of safety which are provided in the hospital setting and cannot be matched in the home situation.

We support those actions that improve the experience of the family while continuing to provide the mother and her infant with accepted standards of safety available only in hospitals which conform to standards as outlined by the American Academy of Pediatrics and the American College of Obstetricians and Gynecologists.

Approved by the Executive Board May 1975
Amended March 1979
Reaffirmed September 1999

The American College of Obstetricians and Gynecologists
409 12th Street, SW, PO Box 96920 • Washington, DC 20090-6920 Telephone 202 638 5577

ACOG *Statement of Policy*

As issued by the ACOG Executive Board

This document was developed jointly by the American Academy of Pediatrics and the American College of Obstetricians and Gynecologists.

JOINT STATEMENT ON HUMAN IMMUNODEFICIENCY VIRUS SCREENING

The problem of perinatal transmission of HIV infection was first appreciated in 1982. In 1991, the Institute of Medicine (IOM) recommended a policy of routine counseling and offering testing (with specific informed consent) for HIV infection to all pregnant women. Since 1991, there have been major advances in the treatment of HIV infection, including demonstration in 1994 of the efficacy of zidovudine to reduce perinatal transmission. The U.S. Public Health Service subsequently issued guidelines for use of zidovudine to reduce perinatal transmission and for counseling and voluntary testing for pregnant women. Dramatic declines in reported pediatric AIDS cases have been observed as a consequence of implementation of these guidelines. However, for a variety of reasons, screening pregnant women in the United States has been far from universal and infected babies continue to be born to undiagnosed infected women. Further reduction in the rate of perinatal HIV infection will require wider application of both screening to identify infected women, and treatments, which have demonstrated efficacy in reducing vertical transmission.

The IOM recently completed a study of interventions that would be helpful to further HIV infection in the United States (Reducing the Odds). They have recommended that "the United States should adopt a national policy of universal HIV testing, with patient notification, as a routine component of prenatal care". Early diagnosis of HIV infection in pregnant women allows them to institute effective antiretroviral therapy for their own health and to reduce the risk of HIV transmission to their infants. The use of "patient notification" provides women the opportunity to decline to be tested but eliminates the obligation to provide extensive pretest counseling, which has been a barrier to testing in many settings. Care providers would be charged with responsibility for the details of how the notification would take place. The IOM has recommended universal testing for two reasons. First, attempts to identify those "at risk" for infection inevitably fail to identify some infected individuals. Second, universal testing of all pregnant women avoids stereotyping and stigmatizing any social or ethnic group. The IOM recognizes in its report that many states now have laws requiring a formal, and in many cases written informed consent process prior to testing. They recommend that the Federal government adopt policies that will encourage these states to change their laws.

The American College of Obstetricians and Gynecologists

409 12th Street, SW, PO Box 96920 • Washington, DC 20090-6920 Telephone 202 638 5577

JOINT STATEMENT ON HUMAN IMMUNODEFICIENCY VIRUS SCREENING
Page 2

The AAP and the ACOG strongly support efforts to further reduce the rate of perinatal transmission of HIV in the United States. We therefore support the recommendation of the IOM for universal HIV testing with patient notification as a routine component of prenatal care. If a patient declines testing, this should be noted in the medical record. We recognize that current laws in some states may prevent implementation of this recommendation at this time. We encourage our members and Fellows to include counseling as a routine part of care, but not as a prerequisite for, and barrier to, prenatal HIV testing.

Approved by the ACOG Executive Board
Approved by the AAP Executive Board
May 1999

ACOG *Statement of Policy*

As issued by the ACOG Executive Board

JOINT STATEMENT OF PRACTICE RELATIONSHIPS BETWEEN OBSTETRICIAN-GYNECOLOGISTS AND CERTIFIED NURSE-MIDWIVES/CERTIFIED MIDWIVES*

It is critical that obstetrician-gynecologists and certified nurse-midwives/certified midwives have a clear understanding of their individual, collaborative and interdependent responsibilities. As agreed upon by the American College of Nurse-Midwives and the American College of Obstetricians and Gynecologists, the maternity care team must include either an obstetrician-gynecologist with hospital privileges or other physician with hospital privileges to provide complete obstetric care. The American College of Obstetricians and Gynecologists and the American College of Nurse-Midwives believe that the appropriate practice of the certified nurse-midwife/certified midwife includes the participation and involvement of the obstetrician-gynecologist as mutually agreed upon in written medical guidelines/protocols. The American College of Obstetricians and Gynecologists and the American College of Nurse-Midwives also believe that the obstetrician-gynecologist should be responsive to the desire of certified nurse-midwives/ certified midwives for the participation and involvement of the obstetrician-gynecologist. The following principles represent a joint statement of the American College of Obstetricians and Gynecologists and the American College of Nurse-Midwives and are recommended for consideration in all practice relationships and agreements.

1. Clinical practice relationship between the obstetrician-gynecologist and the certified nurse-midwife/certified midwife should provide for:

a. mutually agreed upon written medical guidelines/protocols for clinical practice which define the individual and shared responsibilities of the certified nurse-midwife/certified midwife and the obstetrician-gynecologist in the delivery of health care services;

b. mutually agreed upon written medical guidelines/protocols for ongoing communication which provide for and define appropriate consultation between the obstetrician-gynecologist and certified nurse-midwife/certified midwife; and other health care providers in the services offered (ACNM, 1997);

c. informed consent about the involvement of the obstetrician-gynecologist, certified nurse-midwife/certified midwife, and other health care providers in the services offered;

d. periodic and joint evaluation of services rendered, e.g., chart review, case review, patient evaluation, review of outcome statistics; and

e. periodic and joint review and updating of the written medical guidelines/protocols.

The American College of Obstetricians and Gynecologists
409 12th Street, SW, PO Box 96920 • Washington, DC 20090-6920 Telephone 202 638 5577

JOINT STATEMENT OF PRACTICE RELATIONSHIPS BETWEEN OBSTETRICIAN-GYNECOLOGISTS AND CERTIFIED NURSE-MIDWIVES/CERTIFIED MIDWIDWIVES*
Page 2

2. Quality of care is enhanced by the interdependent practice of the obstetrician-gynecologist and the certified nurse-midwife/ certified midwife working in a relationship of mutual respect, trust and professional responsibility. This does not necessarily imply the physical presence of the physician when care is being given by the certified nurse-midwife/ certified midwife nor statutory language requiring supervision of certified nurse-midwife/ certified midwife.

3. Administrative relationships, including employment agreements, reimbursement mechanisms, and corporate structures, should be mutually agreed upon by the participating parties.

4. Access to practice within the hospital setting for the obstetrician-gynecologist and the certified nurse-midwife/certified midwife who have a practice relationship in concurrence with these principles is strongly urged by the respective professional organizations.

The American College of Obstetricians and Gynecologists and the American College of Nurse-Midwives strongly urge the implementation of these principles in all practice relationships between obstetrician-gynecologists and certified nurse-midwives/certified midwives.

* Midwifery as used throughout this document refers to the education and practice of certified nurse-midwives (CNMs) and certified midwives (CMs) who have been certified by the American College of Nurse-Midwives (ACNM) or ACNM Certification Council, Inc. (ACC).

Resources:

American College of Nurse-Midwives. Collaborative management in midwifery practice for medical gynecological and obstetrical conditions. Washington, DC: ACNM, 1997

American College of Obstetricians and Gynecologists. Guidelines for implementing collaborative practice. Washington, DC: ACOG, 1995

American College of Nurse-Midwives
American College of Obstetricians and Gynecologists
September 1, 2001

ACOG *Statement of Policy*

As issued by the ACOG Executive Board

PREGNANCY DISABILITY

Pregnancy is a physiologic process. All pregnant patients, however, have a variable degree of disability, on an individual basis, as indicated below, during which time they are unable to perform their usual activities.

1. In an uncomplicated pregnancy, disability occurs near the termination of pregnancy, during labor, delivery and the puerperium. The process of labor and puerperium is disabling in itself. The usual duration of such disability is approximately six to eight weeks.

2. Complications of pregnancy may occur which give rise to other disability. Examples of such complications include toxemia, infection, hemorrhage, ectopic pregnancy and abortion.

3. A woman with pre-existing disease, which in itself is not disabling, may become disabled with the addition of pregnancy. Certain patients with heart disease, diabetes, hypertensive cardiovascular disease, renal disease and other systemic conditions may become disabled during their pregnancy because of the adverse effect pregnancy has upon these conditions.

The onset, termination and cause of the disability as related to pregnancy can only be determined by a physician.

Approved by the Executive Committee March 1974
Reaffirmed September 1999

The American College of Obstetricians and Gynecologists
409 12th Street, SW, PO Box 96920 • Washington, DC 20090-6920 Telephone 202 638 5577

ACOG *Statement of Policy*
As issued by the ACOG Executive Board

TOBACCO ADVERTISING AIMED AT WOMEN

The American College of Obstetricians and Gynecologists opposes the unconscionable targeting of women by the tobacco industry.

The health risks of tobacco use to women are well documented. It also is well known that smoking by a pregnant woman may be harmful to her fetus. It is unnecessary to catalogue all of these risks here. Because of these well known dangers, it is irresponsible for tobacco companies to single out women, especially educationally or otherwise disadvantaged women, and encourage them to smoke.

Tobacco companies must stop encouraging young women to smoke cigarettes. The health of women and of our future generations demand at least that much consideration.

Approved by the Executive Board July 1990
Reaffirmed July 2000

The American College of Obstetricians and Gynecologists
409 12th Street, SW, PO Box 96920 • Washington, DC 20090-6920 Telephone 202 638 5577

Lists of Titles

Lists of Titles

ACOG Committee Opinions

List of Titles

December 2001

Committee Opinions are intended to provide timely information on controversial issues, ethical concerns, and emerging approaches to clinical management. They represent the considered views of the sponsoring committee based on interpretation of published data in peer-reviewed journals. Committee Opinions are reviewed periodically for continued relevance or needed update. *Note:* Because individual Committee Opinions are withdrawn from and added to the series on a continuing basis, the titles listed in this index may not be identical to those contained in complete sets. A list of withdrawn and replaced titles appears at the end.

Number	Title	Publication Date	Reaffirmed Date	Page
Committee on Coding and Nomenclature				
205	Tubal Ligation with Cesarean Delivery (Obstet Gynecol Vol. 92, No. 2)	August 1998		110
*249	Coding Responsibility (Obstet Gynecol Vol. 97, No. 1)	January 2001		11
*250	Inappropriate Reimbursement Practices by Third-Party Payers (Obstet Gynecol Vol. 97, No. 1)	January 2001		36
Committee on Genetics (to be published as a separate volume)				
161	Fragile X Syndrome	October 1995	2000	
162	Screening for Tay–Sachs Disease	November 1995	2000	
183	Routine Storage of Umbilical Cord Blood for Potential Future Transplantation (*Joint with Committee on Obstetric Practice*)	April 1997	2000	97
189	Advanced Paternal Age: Risks to the Fetus	October 1997	2000	
192	Genetic Screening of Gamete Donors	October 1997	2001	
212	Screening for Canavan Disease (Obstet Gynecol Vol. 92, No. 5)	November 1998	2000	
223	First-Trimester Screening for Fetal Anomalies with Nuchal Translucency (Obstet Gynecol Vol. 94, No. 4)	October 1999	2001	
230	Maternal Phenylketonuria (Obstet Gynecol Vol. 95, No. 1)	January 2000		
238	Genetic Screening for Hemoglobinopathies (Obstet Gynecol Vol. 96, No. 1)	July 2000		
239	Breast–Ovarian Cancer Screening (Obstet Gynecol Vol. 96, No. 2)	August 2000		
*257	Genetic Evaluation of Stillbirths and Neonatal Deaths (Obstet Gynecol Vol. 97, No. 5)	May 2001		
Committee on Gynecologic Practice				
152	Recommendations on Frequency of Pap Test Screening	March 1995	1998	82
164	Incidental Appendectomy	December 1995	2000	42
186	Role of the Obstetrician–Gynecologist in the Diagnosis and Treatment of Breast Disease	September 1997	2000	90
191	Length of Hospital Stay for Gynecologic Procedures	October 1997	2000	48
195	Role of Loop Electrosurgical Excision Procedure in the Evaluation of Abnormal Pap Test Results	November 1997	2000	88
203	Hepatitis Virus Infections in Obstetrician–Gynecologists (Obstet Gynecol Vol. 92, No. 1)	July 1998	2001	27
224	Tamoxifen and the Prevention of Breast Cancer in High-Risk Women (Obstet Gynecol Vol. 94, No. 4)	October 1999	2001	107
226	Hormone Replacement Therapy in Women with Previously Treated Breast Cancer (Obstet Gynecol Vol. 94, No. 5)	November 1999	2001	31
232	Tamoxifen and Endometrial Cancer (Obstet Gynecol Vol. 95 No. 4)	April 2000	2001	104
235	Hormone Replacement Therapy in Women Treated for Endometrial Cancer (Obstet Gynecol Vol. 95, No. 5)	May 2000	2001	29

*Title issued since publication of 2001 Compendium of Selected Publications

Number	Title	Publication Date	Reaffirmed Date	Page
Committee on Gynecologic Practice (continued)				
240	Statement on Surgical Assistants (Obstet Gynecol Vol. 96, No. 2) *(Joint with Committee on Obstetric Practice)*	August 2000		103
242	Concurrent Chemoradiation in the Treatment of Cervical Cancer (Obstet Gynecol Vol. 96, No. 4)	October 2000		15
243	Performance and Interpretation of Imaging Studies by Obstetrician–Gynecologists (Obstet Gynecol Vol. 96, No. 5)	November 2000		60
244	Androgen Treatment of Decreased Libido (Obstet Gynecol Vol. 96, No. 5)	November 2000		5
245	Mifepristone for Medical Pregnancy Termination (Obstet Gynecol Vol. 96, No. 6)	December 2000		49
246	Primary and Preventive Care: Periodic Assessments (Obstet Gynecol Vol. 96, No. 6)	December 2000		75
247	Routine Cancer Screening (Obstet Gynecol Vol. 96, No. 6)	December 2000		92
*253	Nongynecologic Procedures (Obstet Gynecol Vol. 97, No. 3)	March 2001		55
*262	Risk of Breast Cancer with Estrogen–Progestin Replacement Therapy (Obstet Gynecol 2001;98:1181–1183)	December 2001		85
*263	Von Willebrand's Disease in Gynecologic Practice (Obstet Gynecol 2001;98:1185–1186)	December 2001		116
Committee on Obstetric Practice				
125	Placental Pathology	July 1993	2000	66
138	Utility of Umbilical Cord Blood Acid–Base Assessment	April 1994	2000	114
158	Guidelines for Diagnostic Imaging During Pregnancy	September 1995	2000	23
163	Perinatal Care at the Threshold of Viability *(Joint with AAP Committee on Fetus and Newborn)*	November 1995	1997	62
173	Prevention of Early-Onset Group B Streptococcal Disease in Newborns	June 1996	1999	67
174	Use and Abuse of the Apgar Score *(Joint with AAP Committee on Fetus and Newborn)*	July 1996	1999	111
180	New Ultrasound Output Display Standard	November 1996	2000	53
183	Routine Storage of Umbilical Cord Blood for Potential Future Transplantation *(Joint with Committee on Genetics)*	April 1997	2000	97
197	Inappropriate Use of the Terms Fetal Distress and Birth Asphyxia	February 1998	2001	40
210	Antenatal Corticosteroid Therapy for Fetal Maturation (Obstet Gynecol Vol. 92, No. 4)	October 1998		7
228	Induction of Labor with Misoprostol (Obstet Gynecol Vol. 94, No. 5)	November 1999	2001	44
231	Pain Relief During Labor *(Joint with American Society of Anesthesiologists)* (Obstet Gynecol Vol. 95, No. 2)	February 2000	2001	59
234	Scheduled Cesarean Delivery and the Prevention of Vertical Transmission of HIV Infection (Obstet Gynecol Vol. 95, No. 5)	May 2000	2001	100
240	Statement on Surgical Assistants *(Joint with Committee on Gynecologic Practice)* (Obstet Gynecol Vol. 96, No. 2)	August 2000		103
248	Response to Searle's Drug Warning on Misoprostol (Obstet Gynecol Vol. 96, No. 6)	December 2000		83
*252	Fetal Surgery for Open Neural Tube Defects (Obstet Gynecol Vol. 97, No. 3)	March 2001		21
*256	Optimal Goals for Anesthesia Care in Obstetrics *(Joint with American Society of Anesthesiologists)* (Obstet Gynecol Vol. 97, No. 5)	May 2001		56
*258	Fetal Pulse Oximetry (Obstet Gynecol 2001;98:523–524)	September 2001		19
*260	Circumcision (Obstet Gynecol 2001;98:707–708)	October 2001		9
*264	Air Travel During Pregnancy (Obstet Gynecol 2001;98:1187–1188)	December 2001		3
*265	Mode of Term Singleton Breech Delivery (Obstet Gynecol 2001;98:1189–1190)	December 2001		51
Committee on Primary Care				
227	Complementary and Alternative Medicine (Obstet Gynecol Vol. 94, No. 5)	November 1999	2001	12
Committee on Professional Liability				
236	Coping with the Stress of Malpractice Litigation (Obstet Gynecol Vol. 95, No. 6)	June 2000		17
237	Informed Refusal (Obstet Gynecol Vol. 95, No. 6)	June 2000		46

*Title issued since publication of 2001 Compendium of Selected Publications

The following Committee Opinions will be replaced by *Ethics in Obstetrics and Gynecology:*
46 Endorsement of Institutional Ethics Committees
108 Ethical Dimensions of Informed Consent
136 Preembryo Research: History, Scientific Background, and Ethical Considerations
144 Sexual Misconduct in the Practice of Obstetrics and Gynecology: Ethical Considerations
156 End-of-Life Decision Making: Understanding the Goals of Care
159 Ethical Guidance for Patient Testing
170 Physician Responsibility Under Managed Care: Patient Advocacy in a Changing Health Care Environment
177 Sex Selection
181 Ethical Issues in Obstetric–Gynecologic Education
194 Obstetrician–Gynecologists' Ethical Responsibilities, Concerns, and Risks Pertaining to Adoption
204 Institutional Responsibility to Provide Legal Representation
214 Patient Choice and the Maternal–Fetal Relationship
215 Nonselective Embryo Reduction: Ethical Guidance for the Obstetrician–Gynecologist
216 Sterilization of Women, Including Those with Mental Disabilities
217 Ethical Issues Related to Expert Testimony by Obstetricians and Gynecologists
225 Responsibilities of Physicians Regarding Surrogate Motherhood
233 Ethical Dimensions of Seeking and Giving Consultation
254 Commercial Enterprises in Medical Practice: Selling and Promoting Products
255 Human Immunodeficiency Virus: Ethical Guidelines for Obstetricians and Gynecologists
259 Guidelines for Relationships with Industry
261 Medical Futility

The following Committee Opinions will be replaced by *Adolescent Health:*
139 Adolescents' Right to Refuse Long-Term Contraceptives
154 Condom Availability for Adolescents
190 Prevention of Adolescent Suicide

The following Committee Opinions will be replaced by *Special Issues in Women's Health:*
200 Mandatory Reporting of Domestic Violence
201 Cultural Competency in Health Care
202 Access to Health Care for Women with Physical Disabilities

The following Committee Opinions have been withdrawn from circulation:
87 Deception
101 Current Status of Cystic Fibrosis Carrier Screening
104 Anesthesia for Emergency Deliveries
105 Postpartum Tubal Sterilization
121 Obstetric Management of Patients with Spinal Cord Injury
129 Commercial Ventures in Medicine: Concerns About the Patenting of Procedures
133 Colposcopy Training and Practice
149 Financial Influences on Mode of Delivery
151 Female Genital Mutilation
153 Absence of Endocervical Cells on a Pap Test
167 Perinatal and Infant Mortality Statistics
171 Cost Containment in Medical Care
172 Home Uterine Activity Monitoring (replaced by Practice Bulletin No. 31)
175 Scope of Services for Uncomplicated Obstetric Care
179 Rate of Vaginal Births After Cesarean Delivery
184 Hepatitis B Immunization for Adolescents
187 Fetal Fibronectin Preterm Labor Risk Test (replaced by Practice Bulletin No. 31)
196 Vitamin A Supplementation During Pregnancy
207 Liability Implications of Recording Procedures or Treatments
213 Ethical Considerations in Research Involving Pregnant Women
221 Telecommunication in Medicine
222 Quality of Laboratory and Imaging Services: Physician Responsibility in the Age of Managed Care
241 Screening for Hypothyroidism (replaced by Practice Bulletin No. 32)
251 SalEst as a Predictor of Risk for Preterm Labor (replaced by Practice Bulletin No. 31)

Current Committee Opinions
125 138 152 158 161 162 163 164 173 174 180 183 186
189 191 192 195 197 203 205 210 212 223 224 226 227
228 230 231 232 234 235 236 237 238 239 240 242 243
244 245 246 247 248 249 250 252 253 256 257 258 260
262 263 264 265

ACOG EDUCATIONAL and PRACTICE BULLETINS

LIST OF TITLES — DECEMBER 2001

Educational and Practice Bulletins provide obstetricians and gynecologists with current information on established techniques and clinical management guidelines. ACOG continuously surveys the field for advances to be incorporated in these series and monitors existing bulletins to ensure they are current. Individual bulletins are withdrawn from and added to these series on a continuing basis. Also listed are current Practice Patterns, which provide evidence-based guidelines. A list of withdrawn and replaced titles appears at the end.

Current Bulletins

▶ 1 ▶ 3 ▶ 4 ▶ 5 ▶ 6 ▶ 7 ▶ 8
▶ 9 ▶ 10 ▶ 11 ▶ 12 ▶ 13 ▶ 14 ▶ 15
▶ 16 ▶ 17 ▶ 18 ▶ 19 ▶ 20 ▶ 21 ▶ 22
▶ 23 ▶ 24 ▶ 25 ▶ 26 ▶ 27 ▶ 28 ▶ 29
▶ 30 ▶ 31 ▶ 32 207 210 218 222
227 230 236 244 246 247 248
251 253 255 258 260

       (February 2001, Obstet Gynecol Vol. 97, No. 2)   372

▶ *27 Prenatal Diagnosis of Fetal Chromosomal Abnormalities
       (May 2001, Obstet Gynecol Vol. 97, No. 5)   457

▶ *29 Chronic Hypertension in Pregnancy (Obstet Gynecol 2001;98:177–185)   285

▶ *30 Gestational Diabetes (Obstet Gynecol 2001;98:525–538)   320

▶ *31 Assessment of Risk Factors for Preterm Birth (Obstet Gynecol 2001;98:709–716)   277

▶ *32 Thyroid Disease in Pregnancy (Obstet Gynecol 2001;98:879–888)   537

    207 Fetal Heart Rate Patterns: Monitoring, Interpretation and Management (July 1995) 161

    218 Dystocia and the Augmentation of Labor (December 1995)   154

    227 Management of Isoimmunization in Pregnancy (August 1996)   188

    230 Assessment of Fetal Lung Maturity (November 1996)   131

    236 Teratology (April 1997)

    244 Antiphospholipid Syndrome (February 1998)   121

    248 Viral Hepatitis in Pregnancy (July 1998, Obstet Gynecol Vol. 92, No. 1)   240

    251 Obstetric Aspects of Trauma Management (September 1998, Obstet Gynecol Vol. 92, No. 3) 195

    253 Special Problems of Multiple Gestation (November 1998, Obstet Gynecol Vol. 92, No. 5)   222

    260 Smoking Cessation During Pregnancy (September 2000, Obstet Gynecol Vol. 96, No. 3)   218

Gynecology

▶   7 Prophylactic Oophorectomy (September 1999, Obstet Gynecol Vol. 94, No. 3)   487

▶   11 Medical Management of Endometriosis (December 1999, Obstet Gynecol Vol. 94, No. 6)   397

▶   14 Management of Anovulatory Bleeding (March 2000, Obstet Gynecol Vol. 95, No. 3)   355

▶   15 Premenstrual Syndrome (April 2000, Obstet Gynecol Vol. 95, No. 4)   448

▶   16 Surgical Alternatives to Hysterectomy in the Management
        of Leiomyomas (May 2000, Obstet Gynecol Vol. 95, No. 5)   493

▶   18 The Use of Hormonal Contraception in Women with Coexisting Medical Conditions
        (July 2000, Obstet Gynecol Vol. 96, No. 1)   502

▶   21 Prevention of Deep Vein Thrombosis and Pulmonary Embolism
        (October 2000, Obstet Gynecol Vol. 96, No. 4)   469

▶ *23 Antibiotic Prophylaxis for Gynecologic Procedures (January 2001, Obstet Gynecol Vol. 97, No. 1) 268

▶ *25 Emergency Oral Contraception (March 2001, Obstet Gynecol Vol. 97, No. 3)   294

▶ *26 Medical Management of Abortion (April 2001, Obstet Gynecol Vol. 97, No. 4)   384

▶ *28 Use of Botanicals for Management of Menopausal Symptoms
        (June 2001, Obstet Gynecol Vol. 97, No. 6)   547

    210 Health Maintenance for Perimenopausal Women (August 1995)   169

    222 Sterilization (April 1996)   233

Reproductive Endocrinology and Fertility

Practice Patterns

     6 Management of Postterm Pregnancy (October 1997)   569

     7 Shoulder Dystocia (October 1997)   581

*Title issued since publication of 2001 Compendium of Selected Publications
▶ Practice Bulletin

The following Educational and Technical Bulletins will be replaced by *Ethics in Obstetrics and Gynecology*:
- 136   Ethical Decision-Making in Obstetrics and Gynecology

The following Educational and Technical Bulletins will be replaced by *Adolescent Health*:
- 249   Confidentiality in Adolescent Health Care
- 254   Primary and Preventive Health Care for Female Adolescents
- 256   Oral Contraceptives for Adolescents: Benefits and Safety

The following Educational and Technical Bulletins will be replaced by *Special Issues in Women's Health*:
- 194   Substance Abuse
- 201   Pediatric Gynecologic Disorders
- 240   Smoking and Women's Health
- 242   Sexual Assault
- 252   Adolescent Victims of Sexual Assault
- 257   Domestic Violence
- 259   Adult Manifestations of Childhood Sexual Abuse

The following Educational and Technical Bulletins have been withdrawn from circulation:
- 109   Methods of Midtrimester Abortion
- 125   Infertility
- 128   Amenorrhea
- 156   Nonmalignant Conditions of the Breast
- 160   Immunization During Pregnancy
- 162   Carcinoma of the Endometrium
- 163   Fetal and Neonatal Neurologic Injury
- 164   The Intrauterine Device
- 171   Rubella and Pregnancy
- 173   Women and Exercise
- 175   Invasive Hemodynamic Monitoring in Obstetrics and Gynecology
- 176   Diagnosis and Management of Fetal Death
- 178   Management of Gestational Trophoblastic Disease
- 181   Thyroid Disease in Pregnancy (replaced by Practice Bulletin No. 32)
- 182   Depression in Women
- 183   Cervical Cytology: Evaluation and Management of Abnormalities
- 186   Vulvar Cancer
- 187   Ultrasonography in Pregnancy
- 189   Exercise During Pregnancy and the Postpartum Period
- 191   Hysteroscopy
- 193   Genital Human Papillomavirus Infections
- 195   Substance Abuse in Pregnancy
- 197   Managing the Anovulatory State: Medical Induction of Ovulation
- 198   Hormonal Contraception
- 199   Blood Component Therapy
- 200   Diabetes and Pregnancy (replaced by Practice Bulletin No. 30)
- 202   Hyperandrogenic Chronic Anovulation
- 203   Evaluation and Treatment of Hirsute Women
- 204   Septic Shock
- 205   Preconceptional Care
- 206   Preterm Labor (replaced by Practice Bulletin No. 31)
- 208   Genetic Technologies
- 211   Sexual Dysfunction
- 213   Urinary Incontinence
- 214   Pelvic Organ Prolapse
- 215   Gynecologic Ultrasonography
- 216   Umbilical Artery Blood Acid–Base Analysis
- 223   Chronic Pelvic Pain
- 224   Pulmonary Disease in Pregnancy
- 225   Obstetric Analgesia and Anesthesia
- 226   Vaginitis
- 229   Nutrition and Women
- 231   Seizure Disorders in Pregnancy
- 235   Hemorrhagic Shock
- 238   Lower Urinary Tract Operative Injuries
- 239   Operative Laparoscopy
- 241   Vulvar Nonneoplastic Epithelial Disorders
- 243   Postpartum Hemorrhage
- 245   Antimicrobial Therapy for Obstetric Patients
- 250   Ovarian Cancer

Index

Index

Index

Note: Italicized letters *f* and *t* following page numbers indicate figures and tables, respectively.